THE
INDO-ARYAN
LANGUAGES

ROUTLEDGE LANGUAGE FAMILY SERIES

Each volume in this series contains an in-depth account of the members of some of the world's most important language families. Written by experts in each language, these accessible accounts provide detailed linguistic analysis and description. The contents are carefully structured to cover the natural system of classification: phonology, morphology, syntax, lexis, semantics, dialectology, and sociolinguistics.

Every volume contains extensive bibliographies for each language, a detailed index and tables, and maps and examples from the languages to demonstrate the linguistic features being described. The consistent format allows comparative study, not only between the languages in each volume, but also across all the volumes in the series.

The Austronesian Languages of Asia
and Madagascar
*Edited by Nikolaus Himmelmann
& Sander Adelaar*

The Bantu Languages
*Edited by Derek Nurse
& Gérard Philippson*

The languages of the Caucasus
Edited by Alice Harris

The Celtic Languages
Martin J. Ball & James Fife

The Dravidian Languages
Edited by Sanford B. Steever

The Germanic Languages
*Edited by Ekkehard Konig
& Johan van der Auwera*

The Indo-Aryan Languages
*Edited by George Cardona
& Dhanesh K. Jain*

The Indo-European Languages
*Edited by Paolo Ramat
& Anna Giacalone Ramat*

The Iranian Languages
Edited by Gernot Windfuhr

The Khoesan languages
Edited by Raïner Vossen

The Mongolic Languages
Edited by Juha Janhunan

The Oceanic Languages
*Edited by John Lynch, Malcolm Ross
& Terry Crowley*

The Romance Languages
*Edited by Martin Harris
& Nigel Vincent*

The Semitic Languages
Edited by Robert Hetzron

The Sino-Tibetan Languages
*Edited by Graham Thurgood
& Randy J. Lapolla*

The Slavonic Languages
*Bernard Comrie &
Greville G. Corbett*

The Turkic Languages
*Edited by Eva Csato
& Lars Johanson*

The Uralic Languages
Edited by Daniel Abondolo

THE

INDO-ARYAN

LANGUAGES

Edited by
George Cardona and Dhanesh Jain

Routledge
Taylor & Francis Group

LONDON AND NEW YORK

First published 2003 by Routledge
2 Park Square, Milton Park, Abingdon, Oxon OX14 4RN

Simultaneously published in the USA and Canada
by Routledge
711 Third Avenue, New York, NY 10017, USA

Routledge is an imprint of the Taylor & Francis Group, an informa business

First published in paperback 2007
© 2003, 2007 George Cardona and Dhanesh Jain, selection and editorial matter;
the contributors, their own chapters

Typeset in Times by Laserscript Ltd, Mitcham, Surrey

British Library Cataloguing in Publication Data
A catalogue record for this book is available from the British Library

Library of Congress Cataloging in Publication Data
A catalog record for this book has been requested

ISBN HB: 978–0–7007–1130–7
ISBN PB: 978–0–415–77294–5

CONTENTS

PREFACE

In November 1996, Jonathan Price of Curzon Press approached George Cardona with a request to edit a volume on the Indo-Aryan languages as one of a series of what he called 'language-family descriptive books'. This would be an apt characterization of Sir George Abraham Grierson's *Linguistic Survey of India*, the final volume of which appeared in 1928. Despite the undisputed and well deserved high standing of Grierson's survey, it is inevitably out of date. Jules Bloch's *L'Indo-aryen du veda aux temps modernes*, translated into English by Alfred Master, is a magnificent overview of historical changes in Indo-Aryan and of course involves summary characterizations of its different stages, but this was not intended to supply descriptions of even the major languages. Colin P. Masica's more recent work, *The Indo-Aryan Languages* (Cambridge: Cambridge University Press, 1991), though of a very high quality, makes no pretence at giving full descriptive statements about the languages. Moreover, new data have been and continue to be made available, especially for Dardic. In view of all this, the time appeared propitious for such a new enterprise. It seemed difficult, however, for a single person to carry out the editorial work, especially since many of the contributions would appropriately be by scholars in India. Dhanesh Jain agreed to serve as coeditor, and we undertook the work.

It was decided that *The Indo-Aryan Languages* should include descriptions not only of the major modern Indo-Aryan languages but also of Old Indo-Aryan and Middle Indo-Aryan as well as a general introduction, thus ensuring a historical as well as a synchronic perspective. In addition, chapters on the writing systems used for Indo-Aryan languages and on aspects of the sociolinguistics of these languages were deemed desirable. Originally, we envisioned also chapters on the typological characteristics and subgroupings of modern Indo-Aryan languages. The scholar who was the obvious first choice to write on these topics, however, declined our invitation and the second scholar who was invited also declined, pleading that the data available and the research done to date would make a contribution of his largely redundant in view of the fairly recent contributions on this topic by Masica and Ramanujan. In addition, considerable work remains to be done before a detailed picture of subgroups of modern Indo-Aryan languages is arrived at which could possibly command consensus. Accordingly, we have had to do without the chapters originally planned for and have made do by referring to recent work in this area (see sections 1.3.2 and 1.4 of the general introduction in this volume).

As can be seen from the table of contents, the modern languages included in this volume have been arranged as follows. Beginning with the major national languages – Hindi, Urdu, Bangla – we proceed to languages reflecting broad typological divisions, from east to west and southwest, ending with the isolate Sinhala and with Dardic, devoting a separate chapter to Kashmiri. One feature which was imposed on us by circumstance is that Indo-Aryan languages in the diaspora outside the subcontinent area have not been dealt with separately, although we originally envisioned including a chapter on Indo-Aryan languages in migration.

The task of selecting and inviting contributors, although for the most part fairly straightforward, was made difficult by one circumstance. Sad to say, it is hard to find scholars to compose acceptable contemporary descriptions of certain languages, especially relatively minor ones such as the languages of Rajasthan and Pahāḍī languages. This is all the more regrettable because the study of such languages could yield important insights into questions of language migration and transitional areas.

Invitations were sent to select scholars in late August of 1997, and contributions were to be in the hands of the editors by the end of 1998. Some of those we approached, however, had to decline our invitation due to prior commitments or considerations of age and health, two others withdrew after agreeing to contribute, and one contributor withdrew because he could not agree to modify a script found unacceptable. Unfortunately, after these developments we could not find any one to compose a chapter on Marwari or other languages of Rajasthan. On the other hand, Vit Bubenik and Lachman Khubchandani graciously stepped in to supply chapters on later Prakrits and Sindhi respectively, and Professor G. C. Goswami kindly agreed to serve as coauthor of the chapter on Asamiya. After such matters were settled, the chapters and contributors shown in the table of contents were made final. In addition, maps were drawn up. We express our thanks to Elena Bashir for composing the map of Dardic and Nuristani.

We are grateful to all the scholars who have contributed to this volume not only for the care with which they prepared their chapters but also for their spirit of cooperation in considering suggestions made by the editors. As editors, however, we felt we could not impose on individual scholars our judgements of data with which they might not agree. Nor could we require that they deal with their subjects all in the same manner, except for a general style sheet which was agreed upon beforehand. Consequently, the reader will notice considerable variation both in the scope of treatment – for example, with only phonology and morphology treated in one chapter – and in the manner of treating and presenting data.

The original intention was that this volume should appear late in the year 2000, and most contributors were extremely cooperative, with the greater part of chapters in the hands of the editors by the end of 1998. Due to the complications noted earlier, however, some contributions could not reach us until mid-June of 2000. These delays, nevertheless, served a purpose, in that original contributors could modify their chapters so as to make later editorial work easier. The complete edited set of contributions was submitted to the publisher on 30 June 2000.

Contributors have made every effort possible to make their work up to date, including renewed fieldwork. Nevertheless, in view of the time at which contributions were composed and submitted, authors could not take into consideration the recognition of three new states: Jharkhand, Chhattisgarh, and Uttaranchal. Obviously, materials published after final submissions could not be included, so that this book will immediately be out of date in some respects. This is especially true with respect to the ongoing efforts and discussions concerning the Indus Valley materials and the question of the Indo-Aryan homeland (see general introduction, section 3). For example, recent work on the Indus script (Natwar Jha and N. S. Rajaram, *The Deciphered Indus Script: Methodology, Readings, Interpretations*, Delhi: Aditya Prakashan, 2000) and on evidence in the *Ṛgveda* concerning the history of Indo-Aryans (Shrikant Talageri, *Rigveda: A Historical Analysis*, Delhi: Aditya Prakashan, 2000), as well as Michael Witzel's even more recent article 'Autochthonous Aryans? The evidence from Old Indian and Iranian texts' (*Electronic Journal of Vedic Studies* 7.3 [May 25, 2001) appeared too late to be taken into consideration in the general introduction. Nor has it been possible to discuss the import of chariots with spoked wheels, already well known in the *Rgveda*, a subject which recently has given rise to extended discussions in the electronic discussion group Indology. Suffice it to say that, in our opinion, M. Sparreboom's *Chariots in the Veda* (Memoirs of the Kern Institute No. 3, Leiden: E. J. Brill, 1985) represents the most complete and judicious treatment of the available literary evidence. Despite such inevitable omissions, we have reason to hope the present volume will give readers a fair and well founded picture of the Indo-Aryan languages and their background.

George Cardona, University of Pennsylvania, Philadelphia
Dhanesh Jain, Delhi

Postscript

We wish to thank the editorial staff of Ratna Sagar, Delhi, for their help in producing the indexes.

PREFACE TO THE PAPERBACK EDITION

We are happy to know that a paperback edition of *The Indo-Aryan Languages* is in order. Errors, predominantly typographical, that came to the attention of authors have been corrected in the text of this edition. In order to maintain the accuracy of the index, it was not possible also to incorporate additions that would have entailed changes in pagination. Therefore, as part of this preface, we include bibliographic additions. The new bibliographic entries, which should be consulted also for references in the body of the new edition's text, are listed here according to the order of the chapters of the work. Limitations of space precluded our discussing any of the new materials listed.

George Cardona, Philadelphia
Dhanesh Jain, Delhi

ADDITIONAL BIBLIOGRAPHY

General introduction

Bryant, Edwin Francis (2001) *The Quest for the Origins of Vedic Culture: The Indo-Aryan Migration Debate*, Oxford and New York: Oxford University Press. [Published version of Bryant (1997)]
—— and Patton, Laurie L. (eds.) (2005) *The Indo-Aryan Controversy: Evidence and Inference in Indian History*, London and New York: Routledge.
Cardona, George (2004) 'Pāṇinian sūtras of the type अन्येभ्योऽपि दृश्यते', in Dhaky, M. A. and Shah, J. B. (eds.) *Jambūjyoti (Munivara Jambūvijaya Festschrift)*, Ahmedabad: Shreshti Kasturbhai Lalbhai Smarak Nidhi, Sharadaben Chimanbhai Educational Research Centre, pp. 91–107. [= Cardona (in press a)]
—— (2005) 'From Vedic to modern Indic languages', in Booij, Gert, Lehmann, Christian, Mugdan, Joachim, and Skopeteas, Stavros (eds.), *Morphologie/Morphology: Ein internationales Handbuch zur Flexion und Wortbildung/An International Handbook on Inflection and Word-Formation*, Berlin/New York: Walter de Gruyter, pp. 1712–29.
Francfort, Henri-Paul (2005) 'La civilisation de l'Oxus et les Indo-Iraniens et Indo-Aryens/ *Oxus Civilization or BMAC, Indo-Iranians and Indo-Aryans*', in Fussman et al. (2005), pp. 253–328.
Fussman, Gérard (2005) 'Entre fantasmes, science et politique: l'entrée des Āryas en Inde/ *Fantasms, science and politics: Āryans on their way to India*', in Fussman et al. (2005), pp. 197–232.
—— Kellens, Jean, Francfort, Henri-Paul, and Tremblay, Xavier (eds.) (2005) *Ārya, Aryens et Iraniens en Asie Centrale* (Collège de France, Publications de l'Institut de Civilisation Indienne, Fascicule 72), Paris: De Boccard.
von Hinüber, Oskar (2001) *Das ältere Mittelindisch im Überblick*, Wien: Verlag der Österreichishcen Akademie der Wissenschaften (Second, revised edition).

Jamison, Stephanie (2006) Review of Bryant, Edwin Francis and Patton, Laurie L. (2005) *Journal of Indo-European Studies* 34: 255–61.
Matras, Yaron (2002) *Romani: a linguistic introduction*, Cambridge/New York: Cambridge University Press.
Southworth, Franklin C. (2005) *Linguistic Archaeology of South Asia*, London/New York: Routledge Curzon.
Witzel, Michael (in press) *The Aryan Question, Pro and Contra*, Gurgaon: Three Essays.

Writing systems of the Indo-Aryan languages

Lenz, Timothy (2003) *A New Version of the Gāndhārī Dharmapada and a Collection of Previous-Birth Stories, British Library Kharoṣṭhī Fragments 16 + 25* (Gandhāran Buddhist Texts 3), Seattle: University of Washington Press.
Salomon, Richard (2006) 'Kharoṣṭhī syllables used as location markers in Gandhāran stūpa architecture', in Callieri, Pierfrancesco (ed.), *Architetti, capomastri, artigiani: l'organizzazione dei cantieri e della produzione artistica nell'Asia ellenistica, Studi offerti a Domenico Faccenna nel suo ottantesimo compleanno* (Serie Orientale Roma Volume 100), Roma: Istituto Italiano per l'Africa e l'Oriente, pp. 181–224.

Sanskrit

Cardona, George (2007) 'Sanskrit morphology', in Kaye, Alan S. (ed.), *Morphologies of Asia and Africa*, Winona Lake, Indiana: Eisenbrauns, pp. 771–820.
Jamison, Stephanie (2004) 'Sanskrit', in Woodard, Roger G. (ed.), *Encyclopedia of the World's Ancient Languages*. Cambridge: Cambridge University Press, pp. 673–99.

Urdu

Bashir, Elena (to appear, 2006) 'Change in progress: Negation in Hindi and Urdu', pp. 3–29 in Singh, Rajendra (ed.), *Yearbook of South Asian Languages and Linguistics*, Berlin: Mouton de Gruyter.
Butt, Miriam (1993a) 'Object Specificity and Agreement in Hindi/Urdu', *Chicago Linguistic Society* 29: 89–103.
—— (1993b) 'A Reanalysis of Long Distance Agreement in Urdu', *Berkeley Linguistic Society* 19: 52–63.
Butt, Miriam and King, T. H. (1991) 'Semantic Case in Urdu', *Chicago Linguistic Society* 27: 31–45.
Hussain, Sarmad (1997) *Phonetic correlates of lexical stress in Urdu*, Ph.D. dissertation, Northwestern University. AAT 9814230.
Lampp, Claire M. (2006) *Negation in modern Hindi-Urdu: The development of nahII*. M.A. thesis, The University of North Carolina at Chapel Hill. AAT 1435050.
Naim, C. M. (2000) *Introductory Urdu* (2 vols.), Chicago: University of Chicago South Asia Language and Area Center; also: New Delhi: Government of India, Ministry of Human Resource Development, National Council for Promotion of Urdu.

Maithili

Jha, Govind (1999) *Kalyāṇī Kośa: A Maithili-English Dictionary*, Darbhanga: Mahārājādhirāja Kāmeśvara Siṃha Kalyāṇī Foundation.
Jha, Sunil K. (2001) *Maithili: Some Aspects of its Phonetics and Phonology*, Delhi: Motilal Banarsidass. [Published version of Jha, Sunil K. (1984)]
Yadav, Ramawatar (2004) 'On diachronic origins of converbs in Maithili', *Contributions to Nepalese Studies* 31, 2: 215–41.

Sinhala

Fritz, Sonja (2002) *The Dhivehi Language: A Descriptive and Historical Grammar of Maldivian and its Dialects* (2 vols.) (Beiträge zur Südasienforschung, Südasien-Institut, Universität Heidelberg, Band 191), Würzburg: Ergon Verlag.

Dardic

Baart, Joan L. G. (2003) 'Tonal Features in Languages of Northern Pakistan', in Baart, Joan L. G. and Sindhi, Ghulam Hyder (eds.), *Pakistani Languages and Society: Problems and Prospects*, Islamabad: National Institute of Pakistan Studies, Quaid-i-Azam University and Summer Institute of Linguistics, pp.132–44.
—— (2004) 'Contrastive Tone in Kalam Kohistani', *Linguistic Discovery* 2(2): 1–20.
—— and Baart-Bremer, Esther L. (2001) *Bibliography of Languages of Northern Pakistan.* (NIPS – SIL Working Paper Series, 1), Islamabad: National Institute of Pakistan Studies, Quaid-i-Azam University and Summer Institute of Linguistics.
Bashir, Elena (in press) 'Contact-induced change in Khowar', in Saeed, Shafqat (ed.), *New Perspectives on Pakistan: Contexts, Realities and Visions of the Future*, Karachi: Oxford University Press, pp. 205–38.
—— Baig, Rahmat Karim, and Nigah, Maula (in progress) 'A Digital Khowar-English Dictionary with Audio: 1000 words', Digital Dictionaries of South Asia, Digital South Asia Library, University of Chicago, http://dsal.uchicago.edu.
Heegaard, Jan (1998) 'Variational Patterns in Vowel Length in Kalashamon', in Niemi, Jussi, Odlin, Terence and Heikkinen, Janni (eds.), *Language Contact, Variation, and Change (Studies in Language* 32), Joensuu: University of Joensuu, Faculty of Humanities, pp. 125–35.
Heegård, Jan (2002) 'Linguistic and Political Aspects of Alphabet-Making for a Threatened Language', in Lindberg. Carl-Erik and Nordahl Lund, Steffen (eds.), *17th Scandinavian Conference of Linguistics II* (*Odense Working Papers in Language and Communication 19*), Odense: University of Southern Denmark, Institute of Language and Communication, pp. 161–76.
—— and Mørch, Ida E. (2004) 'Retroflex Vowels and Other Peculiarities in Kalasha', in Saxena, Anju (ed.), *Himalayan Languages. Past and Present*, Berlin: Mouton de Gruyter, pp. 57–76.
Inam Ullah (in progress) 'A Digital Torwali-English Dictionary with Audio', http://dsal.uchicago.edu/dictionaries/torwali/about/about.html.
—— (2004) 'Lexical Database of the Torwali Dictionary', paper presented at the Asia Lexicography Conference, Chiangmai, Thailand, 24–26 May, 2004, http://dsal.uchicago.edu/dictionaries/torwali/about/about.html.
Kohistani, Razwal (1999) *Basic Shina-Urdu dictionary: A Dictionary of the Palas Dialect*, Rawalpindi: Shina Research Forum-Karakorum.
Lunsford, Wayne A. (2001) 'An Overview of Linguistic Structures in Torwali: A Language of Northern Pakistan', M.A. thesis, University of Texas at Arlington, http://www.flionline.org/papers.html.
Petersen, Jan Heegård (2006) *Local Case Marking in Kalasha*, Ph.D. thesis, University of Copenhagen.
Schmidt, Ruth Laila (2000) 'Typology of Shina Pronouns', *Berliner Indologische Studien* 13/14: 201–13.
—— (2001) 'Compound Tenses in the Shina of Indus Kohistan', in Lönne, Dirk W. (ed.), *Tohfa-e-Dil, Festschrift Helmut Nespital*, Reinbek: Dr. Inge Wezler Verlag für Orientalistische Fachpublikationen, pp. 433–52.
—— (2003) 'Converbs in a Kohistani Shina Narrative', *Acta Orientalia* 64: 137–52.
—— (2004a) 'Compound Verbs in the Shina of Kohistan', *Acta Orientalia* 65: 19–31.
—— (2004b) 'A Grammatical Comparison of Shina Dialects', in Saxena, Anju (ed.) *Himalayan Languages Past and Present*, Berlin: Mouton de Gruyter, pp. 33–55.

—— and Kohistani, Razwal (2001) 'Nominal Inflections in the Shina of Indus Kohistan', *Acta Orientalia* 62: 107–43.

Strand, Richard F. (2000) 'Açarêtâ Lexicon', on Strand 2001–2006.

—— (2001) 'The Tongues of Peristân', in Cacopardo, Alberto M. and Cacopardo, Augusto S. *Gates of Peristan: History, Religion and Society in the Hindu Kush*, Rome: Istituto Italiano per l'Africa e l'Oriente, pp. 251–59.

—— (2001–2006) *Nuristan. Hidden Land of the Hindu-Kush*, http://users.sedona.net/~strand/index.html. (This site contains uniquely available and continually updated material on Pashai, Khowar, Atshareta (Palula), and Dameli, as well as on issues of classification).

—— (in progress) 'The Sound System of Açarêtâ', on Strand 2001–2006.

Trail, Ronald L. and Cooper, Gregory R. (1999) *Kalasha Dictionary: With English and Urdu* (Studies in Languages of Northern Pakistan 7), Islamabad: National Institute of Pakistan Studies and Summer Institute of Linguistics.

Zoller, Claus Peter (2005) *A Grammar and Dictionary of Indus Kohistani, Volume I: Dictionary* (Trends in Linguistics, Documentation 21–1), Berlin: Mouton de Gruyter.

—— (in progress) *A Grammar and Dictionary of Indus Kohistani, Volume II: Grammar*.

Kashmiri

Hook, Peter Edwin and Koul, Omkar N. (2004) 'Case as Agreement: Non-nominative subjects in Shina and Kashmiri', in Bhaskarrao, Peri and Subbarao, K. V. (eds.) *Non-nominative Subjects*, Amsterdam: Benjamin, vol. 2, pp. 101–14.

—— (2006) 'Valency sets in Kashmiri', in Tsunoda, Tasaku and Kageyama, Taro (eds.) *Voice and Grammatical Relations:* Papers in honor of Masayoshi Shibatani, Amsterdam: Benjamin, pp. 43–84.

Koul, Omkar N. (2005) *Studies in Kashmiri Linguistics*, Delhi: Indian Institute of Language Studies.

Koul, Omkar N. and Wali, Kashi (eds.) (2002) *Topics in Kashmiri Linguistics*, Delhi: Creative Books.

—— (2006) *Modern Kashmiri Grammar*, Springfield: Dunwoody Press.

GENERAL ABBREVIATIONS

Abbreviations are listed in upper case characters. They are used also in various formats: all caps, small caps, lower case, for different purposes. These are clear from the contexts in which authors have used the abbreviations, and it was thought unnecessary and unwise to impose a single format for the entire volume.

1P	first person
1PROX	first proximal
2P	second person
2PI	second person intimate
2PN	second person neutral
2PROX	second proximal
3P	third person
Ø	nominative/deleted noun phrase – Marathi
A	actual
ABL	ablative
ACC	accusative
ACT	active
ADC	anaphoric deictic category
ADJ	adjective
ADV	adverb
ADV PTCPL	adverbial participle
AG	agent
AGN	agentive
AGR	agreement
AMC	assertion marker clitic
ANIM	animate
AOR	aorist
APH	anaphoric deictic category
ASP	aspirated
AUG	augment
AUX	auxiliary
C	consonant
CAUS	causative
CL	classifier
CLT	clitic
COLL	collective
COMIT	comitative
COMP	complement

COMPR	comparison
COMPV	comparative
COMPRV PTCLE	comparative particle
COMPZ	complementizer
CON	continuous
CONC	concessive
COND/CONDIT	conditional
CONJ	conjunction
CONJT	conjunctive
CONT	contingent
CONV	converb
COR	correlative
COR EQ	correlative equative
CP	conjunctive participle
COR MAR	correlative marker
CV	compound verb
DAT	dative
DDC	distal deictic category
DEF	definite
DEM	demonstrative
DIR	direct (case)
DIST	distal
DO	direct object
DU	dual
EMPHR	emphasizer
EMPH(T)	emphatic
EQ	equative
ERG	ergative
EXCL	exclusive
EXH	exhortative
F	feminine
F	future (in the abbreviation P/F)
FAM	familiar
FOC	focusing (clefting) form of verb
FOR	formal
FUT	future
G	gender
GEN	genitive
GER	gerund
GERC	gerciple
GERDV	gerundive
HAB	habitual
HI	high
HON	honorific

HORT	hortative
HUM	human
I	intimate only in 2PI – Dardic
IMP	imperative
IMPERF	imperfect
IMPV/IMPFCTV	imperfective
INANIM	inanimate
INCL	inclusive
INCRV	increment vowel
IND	indicative
INDEF	indefinite
INDEFPL	indefinite plural
INDIR	indirect
INDIV	individuative
INF	infinitive
INFER	inferential
INJ	injunctive
INSTR	instrumental
INTENS	intensifier
INTER	interrogative
INTI	intimate
INTR	intransitive
INVOL	involitive verb form
INVOLOPT	involitive optative
IO	indirect object
IRR	irrealis
KN	known
LIT	literally
LO	low
LOC	locative
M	masculine
MAR	marker
MID-HON	mid-honorific
MID	middle
MOD	modifier
N	noun
N	neutral only in 2PN – Bangla
NA	not attested
NEG	negative
NOM	nominative
NON-HON	non-honorific
NP	noun phrase

NS	non-specific
NT	neuter
NUM	numeral
O	object
OBJ	objective
OBL	oblique
OBLIG	obligative
OPT	optative
ORD	ordinal
OZC	overt versus zero case
P	person, plural
P	present (in the abbreviation P/F)
P(C)P	perfect (conjunctive) participle
PASS	passive
PAST PTCPL	past participle
PERF	perfect
P/F	present/future
PFTV/PFV	perfective
PL	plural
POL	polite
POSS	possessive
POT	potential
PP	postposition
PPC	positive polarity copula
PPP	past perfective participle
PR	pronoun
PRC	participial relative clause
PRED	predicate
PRES	present
PRES FUT	present-future
PRES PTCPL	present participle
PRESUMP	presumptive
PROG	progressive
PROH	prohibitive
PROX	proximate
PS	pronominal suffix
PSFX	pronomial suffix
PST	past tense
PST PTCPL	past participle
PTCLE	particle
PTCPL	participle
Q	quantifier
QUES	question, question particle
QUES PTCLE	question particle
QUOT	quotative

RC	relative clause
REDU	reduplicated item
REDUP	reduplication
REFL	reflexive
REL	relative, relative affix
REL EQ	relative equative
REL PTCPL	relative participle
RELTVZ	relativizing form; 'participial' relative
REM	remote
REP CLT	reportative clitic
REPORT	reportative particle
RSO	reported speech operator
S	subject
SEG	segmental
SFX	suffix
SG	singular
SIMP	simple
SOV	subject-object-verb
SPEC	specific
SRC	sentential relative clause
STAT	stative
SUBJ	subjunctive
SUG	suggestive
SURP	surprise verbal form
TCCM	topicalized complement clause marker
TOP	topic
TR	transitive
UHON	ultra-honorific pronoun
UNASP	unaspirated
UNKN	unknown
V	vowel
VB	verb
VBN	verbal noun
VD	voiced
VL	voiceless
VOC	vocative
VOLOPT	volitive optative
VP	verb phrase

Languages

AG	language of the Ādi Granth
Ar	Arabic
Aś Pkt	Aśokan Prākrit
Ash	Aṣkũ (Ashkun)
Av	Avestan

BHS	Buddhist Hybrid Sanskrit
E	English
Gr	Greek
Gu	Gujarati
H	Hindi
H/U, HU	Hindi/Urdu, Hindi-Urdu
IA	Indo-Aryan
K	Kashmiri
Kt	Kati
Mar	Marathi
MIA	Middle Indo-Aryan
MSH	Modern Standard Hindi
MSP	Modern Standard Panjabi
NIA	New Indo-Aryan
NM	Nagpuri Marathi
NWIA	Northwest Indo-Aryan
OIA	Old Indo-Aryan
OP	Old Persian
P	Persian
Pā	Pāli
PHU	Panjabi-affected Hindi-Urdu
PIA	Proto-Indo-Aryan
PIE	Proto-Indo-European
PIIr	Proto-Indo-Iranian
Pkt	Prakrit
Pr	Prasun
R	Rajasthani
Sd	Sindhi
Skt	Sanskrit
SM	Standard Marathi
Tr	Tregāmī
U	Urdu
Wg	Waigalī

LIST OF MAPS

LIST OF FIGURES

LIST OF CONTRIBUTORS

Professor George Cardona, Department of Linguistics, 619 Williams Hall, University of Pennsylvania, Philadelphia, PA 19104-6305 USA

Dr. Dhanesh Jain, Ratna Sagar P. Ltd., Virat Bhavan, Mukherjee Nagar Commercial Complex, Delhi – 110009 India

Professor Richard Salomon, Department of Asian Languages and Literature, University of Washington, Box 353521, Seattle, WA 98195-3521 USA

Professor Thomas Oberlies, Seminar für Indologie und Buddhismuskunde, Universität Göttingen, Hainbundstraße 21, D-37085, Göttingen

Professor Vit Bubenik, Department of Linguistics, Memorial University of Newfoundland, St John's, Canada A1B 3X9

Professor Michael C. Shapiro, Department of Asian Languages and Literature, University of Washington, Box 353521 Seattle, WA 98195-3521 USA

Professor emeritus Ruth Laila Schmidt, Department of Cultural Studies and Oriental Languages, University of Oslo, P.O. Box 1010, Blindern NO-0315 Oslo, Norway

Dr. Probal Dasgupta, Linguistic Research Unit, Indian Statistical Institute, 203 B.T. Road, Kolkata 700108 India

Professor G. C. Goswami, 'Goswami Bhavan', Ambikagiri Nagar, Guwahati – 781024 India

Dr. Jyotiprakash Tamuli, Department of Linguistics, Gauhati University, Guwahati – 781014 India

Dr. Tapas S. Ray, Central Institute of English and Foreign Languages Hyderabad – 500007 India

Professor Ramawatar Yadav, Novel Academy, P.O. Box 38, Mahendrapool, Pokhara, Nepal

Dr. Sheela Verma (Lecturer Emerita), Department of South Asian Studies, University of Wisconsin 1232, Van Hise Hall, 1220 Linden Drive, Madison, WI 53706 USA

Professor Manindra K. Verma (Emeritus), Department of Linguistics, University of Wisconsin 1232, Van Hise Hall, 1220 Linden Drive, Madison, WI 53706 USA

Professor Theodore Riccardi, Department of Middle East and Asian Languages and Cultures, Kent Hall, Columbia University, New York, NY 10027 USA

Professor Christopher Shackle, Department of South Asia, School of Oriental and African Studies, Thornhaugh Street, Russell Square, London WC1H OXG, England

Professor Lachman M. Khubchandani, Centre for Communication Studies, 270 Sindh Society, Aundh, Pune – 411007 India

Dr. Babu Suthar, Department of South Asia Regional Studies, Williams Hall, University of Pennsylvania, Philadelphia, PA 19104-6305 USA

Professor Rajeshwari Pandharipande, Department of Linguistics, 4088 Foreign Languages Building, 707 South Mathews Ave., Urbana, IL 61801 USA

Professor Rocky V. Miranda, 7-18 Madhuvana Layout, Srirampura 2nd stage, Mysore – 570023 India

Professor James W. Gair (Emeritus), Department of Linguistics, Cornell University, 49 South Street, Trumansburg, NY 14866 USA

Dr. Elena Bashir, Department of South Asian Languages and Civilizations, The University of Chicago, 1130 East 59th Street, Chicago, IL 60637 USA

Professor Omkar N. Koul (Former Director, Central Institute of Indian Languages), C-13, Greenview Apartments, Plot No. 33, Sector 9, Rohini, Delhi – 110085 India

CHAPTER ONE

GENERAL INTRODUCTION

George Cardona and Dhanesh Jain

CONTENTS

LIST OF TABLES

LIST OF FIGURES

LIST OF MAPS

1 THE INDO-ARYAN LANGUAGES

1.1 General

Indo-Aryan languages are spoken mainly in the Indian subcontinent, also referred to as South Asia. The countries represented by this area include India, Pakistan, Bangladesh, Nepal, Bhutan and the islands of Sri Lanka and the Maldives. Also known as the SAARC (South Asian Association for Regional Co-operation) countries, these seven states together form the heartland of the Indo-Aryan speaking area.

This speaking area covers over 4.5 million square kilometres and includes a population of more than 1.06 billion. In 1991 there were close to 875 million speakers of Indo-Aryan languages. In the year 2001 this figure is projected to cross the 1 billion mark (Breton 1999: 200). Figure 1.1 gives the numbers of mother tongue speakers of the Indo-Aryan languages in South Asia and their projection for the year 2001. English remains the dominant language for official work and higher education as well as for communication within and outside the countries concerned.

We should understand the geolinguistic position of the Indo-Aryan languages speaking area. This geographical area is bounded by the Himalayan mountain range in the north and in the east, thus being separated with regard to easy access and communicability from the rest of the Asian subcontinent. The southern part extends into

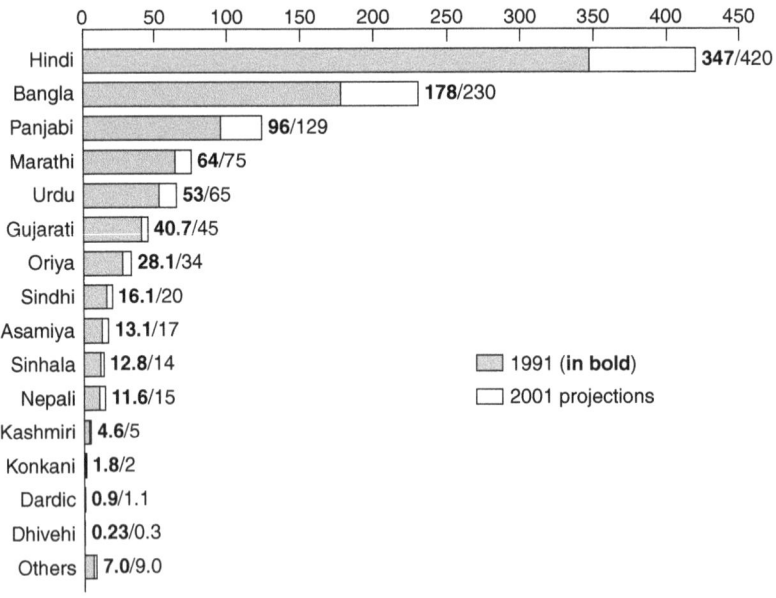

FIGURE 1.1: INDO-ARYAN MOTHER TONGUE SPEAKERS IN SOUTH ASIA (IN MILLIONS)

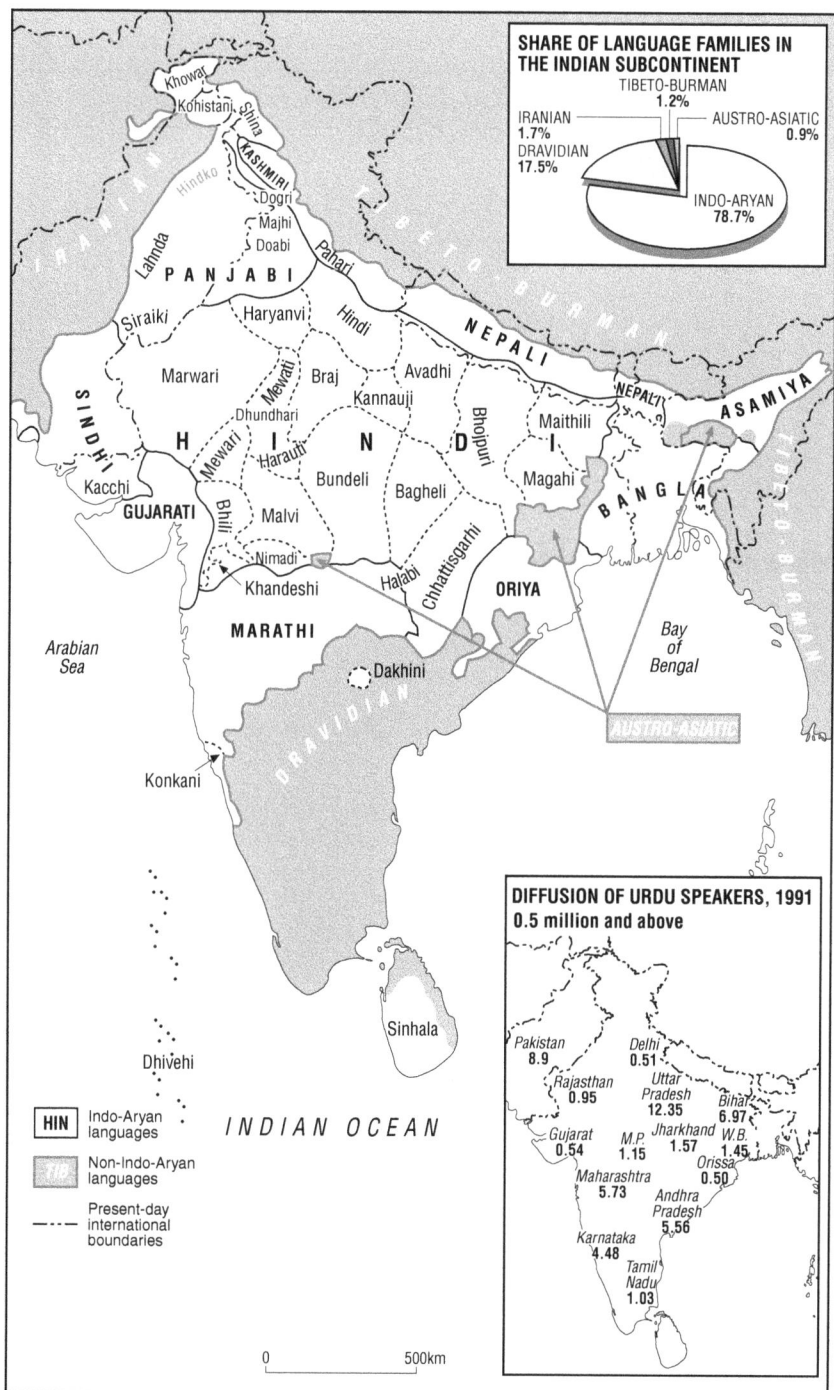

MAP 1.1: INDO-ARYAN LANGUAGES IN THE SOUTH ASIAN SUBCONTINENT

The subdivision in the Hindi area, shown in broken lines, is based on Breton (1999: 46), 1961 data. The states of Uttaranchal, Jharkhand and Chhattisgarh were carved out of Uttar Pradesh, Bihar, and Madhya Pradesh, respectively, in 2000. The inset map of Urdu speakers gives estimated figures for these states for 1991.

TABLE 1.1: MOTHER TONGUE SPEAKERS OF INDO-ARYAN AND OTHER LANGUAGE FAMILIES IN SOUTH ASIA

India 1991 Population 838,583,988

Indo-Aryan			Dravidian			Austro-Asiatic			Tibeto-Burman			Iranian		
Hindi	337,272,114	(39.85%)	Telugu	66,017,615	(7.80%)	Santhali	5,216,325	(.62%)	Meithei	1,310,000	(.16%)	Pashto	11,080,000	(13.15%)
Bangla	69,595,738	(8.22%)	Tamil	53,006,368	(6.26%)	Ho	949,216	(.11%)	Bodo	1,221,881	(.15%)	Baluchi	2,600,000	(3.09%)
Marathi	62,481,681	(7.38%)	Kannada	32,753,676	(3.87%)	Khasi	912,283	(.11%)	Tripuri	694,440	(.08%)			
Urdu	43,406,932	(5.13%)	Malayalam	30,377,176	(3.59%)	Mundari	(861,378	(.10%)	Garo	675,642	(.08%)			
Gujarati	40,673,814	(4.81%)	Others	6,790,291	(.81%)	Others	1,550	(.18%)	Mizo	538,842	(.06%)			
Oriya	28,061,313	(3.32%)							Miri	390,583	(.05%)			
Panjabi	23,378,744	(2.76%)							Mikir	366,229	(.04%)			
Asamiya	13,079,696	(1.55%)							Others	2,895,323	(.35%)			
Kashmiri*	4,045,000	(.48%)												
Sindhi	2,122,848	(.25%)												
Nepali	2,076,645	(.25%)												
Konkani	1,760,607	(.21%)												
Dardic* (excluding Kashmiri)	25,000	(.003%)												
Others	3,293,059	(.39%)												
TOTAL	631,273,191	(75.28%)	TOTAL	188,945,126	(22.53%)	TOTAL	9,490,157	(1.13%)	TOTAL	8,092,940	(0.97%)	TOTAL	13,700,000	(16.26%)

Pakistan 1981 Population 84,253,644

Indo-Aryan			Dravidian		
Panjabi	50,900,000	(60.44%)	Brahui	1,020,000	(1.21%)
Sindhi	9,920,000	(11.77%)			
Urdu	6,400,000	(7.6%)			
Dardic, Kashmiri*	42,000	(0.05%)			
TOTAL	67,242,000	(79.81%)	TOTAL	1,020,000	(1.21%)

Indo-Aryan		Dravidian		Austro-Asiatic		Tibeto-Burman		Iranian
Bangladesh 1991 Population 109,876,977								
Bangla	108,600,000 (98.84%)	Oraon*		Santhali*	110,000 (0.1%)	Araknese, Garo and others*	500,000	
Urdu*	275,000 (.25%)							
Others*	225,000 (.21%)							
TOTAL	109,100,000 (99.3%)				110,000 (0.1%)		500,000 (.5%)	
Nepal 1991 Population 18,491,097								
Nepali	9,303,000 (50.3%)					Tamang, Newari and others	3,200,000	
Hindi & Others	5,997,000 (32.4%)							
TOTAL	15,300,000 (82.7%)						3,200,000 (17.3%)	
Bhutan* 1991 Population 700,000								
Nepali	200,000					Dzongkha and others	500,000	
TOTAL	200,000 (28.6%)						500,000 (71.4%)	
Sri Lanka 1981 Population 14,846,750								
Sinhala	11,035,000 (74.3%)	Tamil	3,652,000					
TOTAL	11,035,000 (74.3%)		3,652,000 (24.6%)					
Maldives* 1991 Population 223,000 (1990 213,215)								
Dhivehi	223,000							

* Estimated figures for 1991, based on the last held census in Kashmir (India) 1981, Pakistan 1981, Bangladesh 1974 (language percentages), Sri Lanka 1981 (ethnic groups), Maldives 1990. Some figures may vary in absence of precise census data for languages; Breton (1999) is most reliable. Population of Bangladesh is variously given as 109,876,977 or 111,445,185 or 119.9 million. Figures for India are taken from the Census of India 1991 (1997: 11–20). The percentage of speakers of each language has been worked out on the total population of India including the projected population for Jammu and Kashmir where the 1991 Census was not held. The population figures, percentages or totals may not equal the sum of mother tongue speakers because of languages not shown here, or rounding off of figures.

the Indian Ocean, dividing it into the Arabian Sea and the Bay of Bengal. The southernmost point of the area is the island of Sri Lanka, where Dravidian separates Sinhala from mainland Indo-Aryan by a thousand kilometres. In the southwest are the Maldives, where Dhivehi is spoken. In the west, the mountains separate the subcontinent from Iranian-speaking Western Asia, allowing traffic mostly through the passes.

Table 1.1 gives a composite picture of the major Indo-Aryan languages of the region, listing the Indo-Aryan languages spoken in each country; it also gives the language families Indo-Aryan comes in contact with and the numbers of their speakers.

The numbers for Kashmiri and other Dardic language speakers in India are estimated, since no census took place in Kashmir in 1991. Similarly, 1991 language figures for Bangladesh, Nepal, Bhutan, and the Maldives are calculated on the basis of the previously held census. In the case of India, non-scheduled languages like Bhili, Halabi and Khandeshi are included under 'others'.

The Indo-Aryan language diaspora includes Romany and languages spoken in Fiji, Mauritius, Guyana, Trinidad and South Africa, as well as among immigrants in Britain, Canada, and the United States.

1.2 Multilingualism across language families

There are five language families spread over the South Asian area: Indo-Aryan, Iranian, Dravidian, Austro-Asiatic or Munda and Tibeto-Burman. Table 1.2 gives the numbers of speakers of these five language families in the subcontinent, of which Indo-Aryan accounts for 78.7% of the population (Breton 1999: 183).

The Indo-Aryan language area is surrounded by other language families: Iranian languages in the west, Dravidian in the south, and Tibeto-Burman in the north and east. Figure 1.2 shows the relative geographical position of peripheral Indo-Aryan and the neighbouring non-Indo-Aryan language families. Indo-Aryan speaking people living in contiguous areas have traditionally spoken another language or sometimes two languages belonging to different language families, and the contiguity of Indo-Aryan with other language families has had significant consequences on these languages, an outcome of long-standing multilingualism. Thus, for example, Asamiya has no retroflexes; Sinhala in Sri Lanka has no aspirated stops.

1.3 Stages of Indo-Aryan

1.3.1 Introduction

Indo-Aryan languages have a long history of transmission, not only in the form of literary works and treatises dealing with logical, philosophical, and ritual matters but

TABLE 1.2: MOTHER TONGUE SPEAKERS OF FIVE LANGUAGE FAMILIES IN SOUTH ASIA, 1991

	in millions	%
Indo-Aryan	877	78.7
Dravidian	195	17.5
Iranian	19	1.7
Tibeto-Burman	13	1.2
Austro-Asiatic	10	0.9

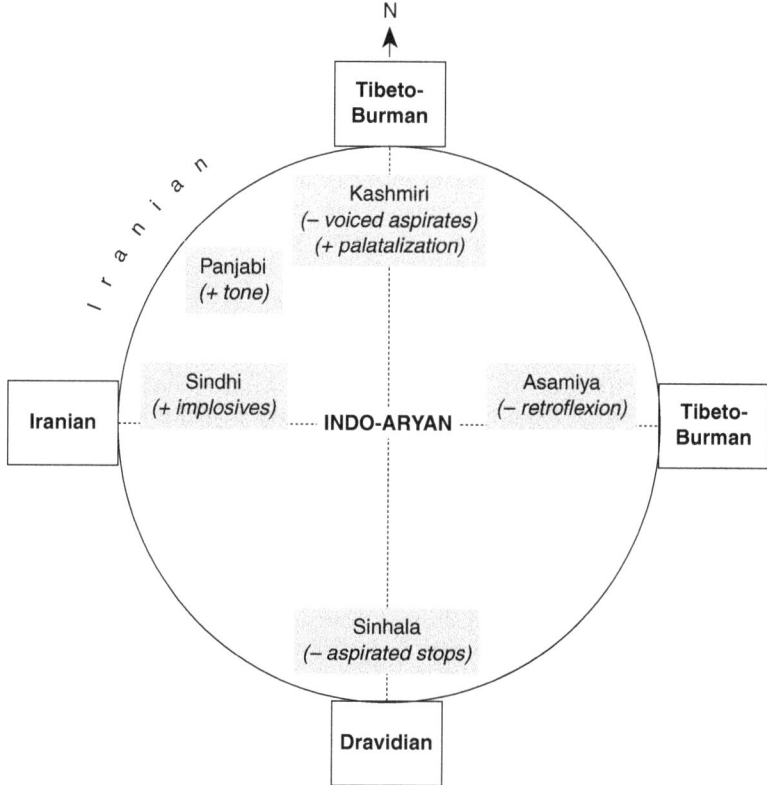

FIGURE 1.2: THE SURROUNDING LANGUAGE FAMILIES OF INDO-ARYAN AND THE
DEVELOPMENT OF FEATURES IN INDO-ARYAN LANGUAGES

also in phonetic, phonological and grammatical descriptions. The languages are
divisible into three major stages: Old-, Middle- and New- (or Modern-) Indo-Aryan.

The first is represented by an enormously rich literature stretching over millennia,
including Vedic texts and later literary works of various genres. In addition, we are
privileged to have knowledge of the details of Old Indo-Aryan of different eras and
areas through extraordinarily perceptive descriptions of phonetics and phonology
relative to traditions of Vedic recitation in prātiśākhya works and Pāṇini's *Aṣṭādhyāyī*,
the brilliant set of rules describing the language current at around the fifth century BC,
with important dialectal observations and contrasts drawn between the then current
speech and earlier Vedic usage. Moreover, observations by Yāska (possibly antedating
Pāṇini) and Patañjali (second century BC) inform us about some dialect features of Old
Indo-Aryan in early times (see section 1.4). Inscriptional Middle Indo-Aryan also gives
us, in the inscriptions of Aśoka, a good, albeit rough, idea of the dialect features of
Middle Indo-Aryan in the mid third century BC (see section 1.4). In addition to
inscriptional materials, later Middle Indo-Aryan too supplies an extraordinarily rich
legacy of literature in different genres, from the Theravāda Buddhist texts in Pāli,
through literary works in different Prākrits – both as incorporated in Sanskrit dramas

and as independent works of drama, poetry and prose – to grammars of Pāli composed in this language. There is no consensus concerning the earliest work definitively ascribable to a particular modern Indo-Aryan language, but evidence of the modern stage certainly takes us back at least to the twelfth century (Chatterji 1953: 1).

It is important to keep in mind that the divisions in question are not chronologically layered in sequences that can always be dated precisely or which should be considered absolutely discrete, although scholars do indeed treat them in this manner (e.g. Masica 1991: 51, Meenakshi 1995: 73). It is certainly true that there are distinct stages. Vedic saṃhitās clearly ceased to be composed at a time before Pāṇini, and there is definite evidence of language change between the time that Pāṇini composed his grammar (*śabdānuśāsana*) and Kātyāyana formulated his vārttikas. On the other hand, it has long been recognized (see, e.g., Grierson 1927: 121 note 2, Bloomfield and Edgerton 1932: 20–5) that from earliest times Old Indo-Aryan speech was subject to the influence of Middle Indo-Aryan. Thus, a form like *vikaṭe* (voc. sg. f.) 'deformed' is best explained on the assumption that at the time that the R̥gveda was compiled there were already Indo-Aryan dialects with some Middle Indo-Aryan features: *vikaṭa-* < *vikr̥ta-*, with Middle Indo-Aryan *-aṭ-* instead of Old Indo-Aryan *-r̥t-*. Similarly, although Pāṇini composed his grammar in the environment of native Sanskrit speakers who controlled what Pāṇinīyas characterize as correct speech forms (*śabda, sādhuśabda*) in opposition to incorrect speech forms (*apaśabda*), which could be – and were, at least in some quarters – considered corruptions (*apabhraṃśa*) of correct terms, the language he describes had assimilated forms which must have originated in dialects with Middle Indo-Aryan characteristics. For example, in Pāṇini's speech a word for 'jackal' shows various stem forms (*Aṣṭādhyāyī* 7.1.95–7: *tr̥jvat kroṣṭuḥ, striyāṃ ca, vibhāṣā tr̥tīyādiṣv aci*): *kroṣṭr̥-* in the nominative as well as the accusative singular and dual (*kroṣṭā kroṣṭārau kroṣṭāraḥ* [nom. sg., du., pl.], *kroṣṭāram kroṣṭārau* [acc. sg., du.]) and as the base for the feminine derivate *kroṣṭrī-*; *kroṣṭu-* in the accusative plural (*kroṣṭūn*) and before consonant-initial endings (*kroṣṭubhyām* [instr.-dat.-abl. du.], *kroṣṭubhiḥ* [instr. pl.], *kroṣṭuṣu* [loc. pl.]); both *kroṣṭu-* and *kroṣṭr̥-* before vowel-initial endings starting with the instrumental (e.g. *kroṣṭrā/kroṣṭunā* [instr. sg.], *kroṣṭre/kroṣṭave* [dat. sg.]). It is generally accepted that *kroṣṭu-* represents a Middle Indo-Aryan development, with *-r̥-* replaced by *-u-*, resulting in a mixed paradigm typical of Middle Indic, as in Pāli (e.g. instr. sg. *pitunā, pitarā* 'father'). Similarly, Pāṇini's speech had a derivative *maireya-* (A 6.2.70: *aṅgāni maireye*) denoting an intoxicating drink; the underlying nominal base of this is *maira-*, which, it is generally accepted, represents a Middle Indic development of OIA *madira-* 'intoxicating' (*madirā-* 'liquor'). Again, as is clear from what Kātyāyana and Patañjali say in their discussions of A 1.3.1: *bhūvādayo dhātavaḥ*, in the fourth to second centuries BC, polished Old Indo-Aryan speech coexisted with dialects in which one used forms like *āṇavayati* 'commands', *vaṭṭati* 'occurs, is', and *vaḍḍhati* 'grows' instead of *ājñāpayati, vartate,* and *vardhate* (see Sanskrit section 1.2). The items in question show not only phonological developments characteristic of Middle Indo-Aryan but also a Middle Indic grammatical feature: the active ending *-ti* instead of the middle *-te*. Moreover, there is evidence from about the same era of interaction in syntax between polished Sanskrit and speech of a Middle Indo-Aryan type. In his commentary on JS 1.3.8.29 (*ekadeśatvāc ca vibhaktivyatyaye syāt*), Śabara (ŚBh. 1.3.8.29, Abhyankar and Joshi 1976: I:228: *ata eva hi vibhaktivyatyaye'pi pratyayo bhavati: asmakair āgacchāmīty asmakaikadeśa upalabdhe asmakebhya ity eva śabdaḥ smaryate. tato'smakebhya ity eṣo'rtha upalabhyate*) gives the examples

(1) (a) *aśmakair   āgacchāmi*   (b) *aśmakebhya āgacchāmi*
   instr. pl.   1sg.pres.   abl.pl.
   Aśmaka   come
       'I am coming from Aśmaka.'

A speaker uses (1a), with the instrumental plural *aśmakaiḥ*, intending to say that he is coming from Aśmaka. In polished Sanskrit, however, (1b), with the corresponding ablative *aśmakebhyaḥ*, is appropriate for expressing this meaning. An interlocutor who commands Sanskrit understands the meaning intended by recalling the appropriate form. That is, there were speakers who made mistakes in using Sanskrit. It happens that the usage illustrated by (1a) reflects Middle Indo-Aryan syntax; see below, section 1.3.2.2(4). Moreover, although (1a) is cited by Śabara, dating from approximately the fourth century AD, this illustrates a principle stated by Jaimini, who dates from about the second century BC, namely that Sanskrit speakers can recall appropriate forms on the basis of partial agreement even where there is a difference in a case affix.

In sum, the available evidence is best accounted for under the view that at the same time that a more polished speech (Sanskrit) was in use in particular contexts and situations, more vernacular dialects (Prākrits) were also being used. The situation at any given time is never simple: changes which tended to be generalized – such as the gradual lenition and deocclusion of intervocalic stops and assimilation in clusters – are seen to take place at different rates in different areas, although the overarching treatment in terms of syllable structure is at the basis of all such developments (cf. Ghatage 1962: 130). Moreover, the history of Indo-Aryan literary transmission shows a recurring promotion of dialects of a given era to the status of literary media coexisting with later vernaculars – elevated Prākrits at the time that Apabhraṁśa dialects had less status, Apabhraṁśa literary norms at a time when early New Indo-Aryan languages were coming into their own – as well as the coexistence of such literary standards with more vernacular varieties, not only, as noted, at the time when Sanskrit was the polished elite language but also later – with Apabhraṁśa forms showing up in Prākrit works – and Sanskrit persisting throughout as the source of elegant and learned diction.

There are, of course, also some fairly definite dates available for compositions in Old Indo-Aryan and others, as can be seen from the discussions on individual languages in this volume.

1.3.2 Major characteristics of different stages

It will be useful to give a brief overview of major developments which resulted in differences that characterize stages of Indo-Aryan and led ultimately to the state of affairs one sees in the modern Indo-Aryan languages. In particular, it is worth noting that many of the developments in question are already foreshadowed in earlier stages. The principal facts for major modern languages are dealt with in the chapters concerning these languages, and in a brief introductory chapter, it is not possible to deal even summarily with the complex nets of phonological and grammatical features which link the modern languages. Masica (1991: 212–419, chapters 8–10) supplies a good conspectus of major aspects of nominal and verbal morphology as well as syntax for the modern languages, and an excellent survey of the phonological features of South Asian languages is given by Ramanujan and Masica (1969). For additional details concerning the earlier stages and historical developments, the reader is referred to the chapters in this volume on Sanskrit, Aśokan Prākrit and Pāli, and Prākrits and Apabhraṁśa, as well as to Masica's chapter on historical phonology (1991: 154–211), and to the magisterial treatment of the overall history of Indo-Aryan by Jules Bloch (Bloch 1934, Bloch-Master 1965).

1.3.2.1 Old Indo-Aryan

The vowel system of Old Indo-Aryan is innovative in that Proto-Indo-Iranian short diphthongs *ai au* were monophthongized to *e o* and the corresponding long diphthongs *āi āu* developed to *ai au*. The historical origins of *e, o, ai* and *au* are reflected in several phonological alternations: *ay av āy āv* occur before vowels instead of *e o ai au*; *e ai o au* respectively occur instead of sequences *ă + ĭ ă + ŭ ă + e ă + -o*; one has *-ā3i* and *-ā3v* (with trimoric *ā3*) instead of *-e* and *-o* – as in *agnā3i* (voc. sg.) 'Agni', *vāyā3v* 'Vāyu' – in vocative forms where elongation of a vowel is called for.

The consonantal system of Old Indo-Aryan is conservative with respect to Iranian in retaining voiced aspirated stops (see section 2.1.1). Accordingly, the effects of what is called Bartholomae's Law are regularly in effect insofar as sequences consisting of voiced aspirates followed by voiceless dental stops develop to voiced unaspirated stops followed by voiced aspirates, so that one has *-gdh-, -ddh-, -bdh-* as in *snigdha-* 'moist, affectionate' and the past participles *dugdha-* 'milked', *kruddha-* 'angered', *labdha-* 'obtained', all with the affix *-ta-*. Due to analogic developments, forms of the reduplicated stem of *dhā* 'put, make' are exempted: present forms *dhat-thaḥ* (2du. act.), *dhat-taḥ* (3du. act.), *dhat-tha* (2pl. act.) instead of **daddhaḥ* and so on. Originally, Bartholomae's Law affected also *s*, so that earliest Indo-Aryan had **-gzh-, -dzh-, -bzh-*, whence, by a subsequent sound change, *-kṣ-, -ts-, -ps-*. This is reflected in Vedic archaisms of the type *adukṣat* (3sg. aor. act.) 'milked', *bapsati* (3pl. pres.) 'devour'. *bapsati* is from a reduplicated stem of the base *bhas* (e.g. Vedic *bhasati* [3sg. subj.]), and it shows the effects of Grassmann's Law, whereby an aspirate is deaspirated in a syllable immediately preceding a syllable with an aspirate. The same rule accounts for *bi-bhar-ti* 'bears' as opposed to the Vedic intensive *bhari-bhar-ti*, with *bhari-* since the immediately following syllable does not have an aspirate. In earliest Indo-Aryan, the bases of *dugdha-* 'milked', *buddha-* 'awakened' also had initial aspirates, reflected in forms such as *dhokṣyati* (3sg. fut. act.), *bhotsyate* (3sg. fut. mid.). However, as a result of phonological and analogic developments, such bases came to be treated synchronically as having unaspirated initials. In conjunction with this, moreover, early Indo-Aryan developed a process of 'aspiration throw-back', whereby an unaspirated stop was aspirated in particular contexts. Thus, for example, the desiderative of *grah* 'seize, grab' has a stem *jighṛkṣa-*, with *-gh-*, although the base has no other forms with *gh*, and *-kṣ-* instead of the etymologically expected *-ps-*. In accordance with this process, speakers created forms of the type *adhukṣat*, with base-initial aspirates. The result was a system in which, as described by Pāṇini, aspiration and voicing apply to affix-initial *t-* and *th-* preceded by voiced aspirates, deaspiration applies to aspirates in reduplicated syllables, historically diaspirate bases like *dhugh, bhudh* synchronically have unaspirated initials (*duh, budh*), and aspiration throwback applies. In this system, Grassmann's Law no longer is a strictly phonological rule that can take effect across morpheme boundaries. The deaspiration in question applies in reduplicated syllables (*abhyāsa: Aṣṭādhyāyī* 8.4.54: *abhyāse car ca*) – without requiring that the immediately following syllable begin with an aspirate – and the imperative *jahi* 'smite, kill' represents a relic that requires a special rule (*Aṣṭādhyāyī* 6.4.36: *hanter jaḥ* [*hau* 35]). On the procedures in question and their dialectal distribution, see Wackernagel 1896: 126–32 (§§106–12), Sag 1974, 1976, Schindler 1976, Cardona 1991.

Another characteristic of Old Indo-Aryan phonology also is a complex system of alternations determined by the contexts of sounds pronounced without intervening pauses: sandhi alternations. There are also clear indications that processes which were originally strictly phonological came to be limited by grammatical properties, as in the case of deaspiration noted earlier. Comparably, word boundaries came to inhibit the application of certain processes; e.g. *-iṣ ṭ-*, with retroflexion of *-s* after *-i-* and of *ṭ-* after *-ṣ*, but later *-is t-* due to the word boundary.

The phonotactics of Old Indo-Aryan generally disallow vowel sequences except at word boundaries, where hiatus sequences like *-a ā-* are allowed, but permit both clusters of different consonants and geminates. Indeed, one of the noteworthy features of Old Indo-Aryan is the doubling of consonants, as in *tattra* (*tatra*) 'there', to give a syllable transition. As has been noted (e.g. Kuiper 1991: 51–4), however, geminates in underlying forms of lexical items are rare in early Indo-Aryan.

Old Indo-Aryan is conservative in its suprasegmental system in that it generally retains an accentual system with three underlying pitches: high (*udātta*), low (*anudātta*) and high-low (*svarita*). This system is in full force in the current spoken language Pāṇini describes. In at least one respect, the tripartite tone system represents historical changes: a svarita syllable can result from an earlier sequence of two syllables, one with high and the other with low tone, e.g. *nadyàḥ* (nom. pl. f.) 'rivers' < *nadíyaḥ*. A more drastic change took place, however, in that svarita syllables were eliminated in some dialects, resulting in systems with only high- and low-pitched syllables (see Cardona 1993).

The verb morphology of Old Indo-Aryan exhibits from early on tendencies to reduce contrasts. To begin with, there are merely traces of an earlier aspectual system (see Sanskrit, section 3.1.1) in conjunction with tense distinctions, superseded by an essentially tense system in which past, present and future were distinguished. Within this tense system, moreover, a three-way contrast in the preterite was reduced to two, with the elimination of the contrast between formal perfects and imperfects, e.g. *uvāca* (3sg. perf. act.) and *abravīt* (3sg. imperf. act.), both meaning 'said'. The modal system of Old Indo-Aryan also underwent simplification, the subjunctive and injunctive being gradually eliminated. Moreover, the imperative and optative came to be linked closely with present-imperfect stems. Thus, though in Vedic one had both root-aorist imperatives like *pāhi* (2sg.) 'drink', *śrudhi* (2sg.) 'hear' and present imperatives like *piba* 'drink', *śṛnudhi* 'hear', in the current language Pāṇini describes the regular imperatives were *piba* and *śṛṇu* only.

Conversely, present-imperfect passives, which in earliest Indo-Aryan could have merely passive endings with a verb base (e.g. *stave* 'is praised'), came to have *-ya-* obligatorily (*stūyate* 'is praised'), although the third singular passive aorist type *akāri* 'has been made' still has only a base followed by a passive affix, and other aorist forms as well as the future lack an affix linked obligatorily with passive function.

The Old Indo-Aryan verb system stayed quite rich despite simplifications. The dual remained a distinct category, and active affixes were opposed to medio-passive affixes. The system of vowel alternation was vigorous, with minor exceptions. The verb base or root (*dhātu*) remained the unit on which other forms were based. For example, *gam* 'go': pres. *gaccha-* (*gacchati* etc.), aor. *agama-* (*agamat* etc., Vedic also root aorist *agan* etc.), fut. *gamiṣya-* (*gamiṣyati* etc.); *śru* 'hear, listen': pres. *śṛṇo-/śṛṇu-* (*śṛṇoti śṛṇutaḥ śṛṇvanti* etc.), aor. *aśrauṣ-/aśroṣ-* (act. *aśrauṣīt* etc., mid. *aśroṣṭa* etc.), fut. *śroṣya-* (*śroṣyati* etc.).

The Old Indo-Aryan nominal system also remained complex. Here too, the dual remained a distinct category, and vowel alternation played a major role. Moreover, in the pronominal system, allomorphy took the form of different bases, although one can already see a tendency to extend the domains of particular allomorphs. For example, the third person proximate pronoun has not only *i-* (e.g., nom. sg. m. *ayam*), *ana-* (e.g. instr. sg. m. *anena*), and *a-* (e.g. instr.-dat-.abl. du. *ābhyām*) but also a stem *ima-* and a corresponding feminine *imā-* in forms such as *ime* (nom. pl. m.), *imam* (acc. sg. m.), *imām* (acc. sg. f.). The tendency to extend *ima-* is already noticeable in Vedic: the genitive singular *imasya* for the regular *asya* is used in the Ṛgveda; the derivate *ịmathā́* 'in a way similar to that of the present (worshippers)' with the suffix *thā* after *ima-*, is formed in the same way as are *prạtnathā́* 'in a way similar to that of the ancients', *pūrvathā́* 'in a way similar to that of the ones who preceded us', *viśvathā́* 'in a way similar to that of all (worshippers)', with which it is conjoined in a Ṛgvedic passage (RV 5.44.1, repeated elsewhere); and in the current language Pāṇini describes *ima-* is obligatory in the derivate *imaka-* 'this so and so'.

1.3.2.2 Middle Indo-Aryan

There are developments the results of which make Middle Indo-Aryan, from its very earliest stages, fundamentally different from Old Indo-Aryan with respect to phonology and grammar. In turn, Middle Indo-Aryan is divisible into several stages, distinguished by phonological and grammatical characteristics that are summarized in subsequent chapters: early Middle Indo-Aryan represented by Aśoka's inscriptions and Pāli, later stages represented in various Prākrits – with Māhārāṣṭrī traditionally granted highest status – and the latest stage, Apabhraṁśa.

The phonological systems of Old and Middle Indo-Aryan differ both with respect to constituents and their distribution. As a result of monophthongization, *ai* and *au* are replaced by *e* and *o*, merging with old *e* and *o*, but due to the disallowance of superheavy syllables, Middle Indo-Aryan developed *ĕ* and *ŏ*, which Old Indo-Aryan did not have except in particular contexts of Vedic recitation. *ṛ*-vowels also were eliminated in Middle Indo-Aryan, replaced by *a*, *i*, and *u* according to contexts and dialects. All word-final consonants were dropped except *-m*, which developed to the nasal segment *ṁ* (called *niggahīta* in the Pāli grammatical tradition and generally pronounced *ŋ*), and initial consonant clusters were simplified. Further, medial clusters of dissimilar consonants were gradually eliminated through anaptyxis or assimilation, so that Middle Indo-Aryan has an abundance of bases with underlying geminates.

The direction of assimilation depends in general on the types of consonants in question; cf. Bloch-Master 1965: 82–9, Ghatage 1962: 111–30, von Hinüber 1986: 112–27. It is anticipatory ($C_1C_2 > C_2C_2$) if both consonants are non-nasal stops – e.g. Pāli *mutta-* (OIA *mukta-*) 'released', *satta-* (*saptan-*) 'seven' – but perseverative ($C_1C_2 > C_1C_1$) if the first consonant stands higher than the second in a sonority hierarchy: non-nasal stops, nasal stops, liquids and glides. Each successive type assimilates to any preceding type on the scale; e.g. Pāli *aggi-* (*agni-*) 'fire', *attan-* (*ātman-*) 'self', *cakka-* (*cakra-*) 'wheel', *sagga-* (*svarga-*) 'heaven', *sappa-* (*sarpa-*) 'snake'. In addition, clusters of stops and *-y-* develop to palatal geminates in some areas, as in Pāli *ajja* (*adya*) 'today', *añña-* (*anya-*) 'other', *majjha-* (*madhya-*) 'middle', and *-jñ-* develops to *-ññ-*: Pāli *yañña-* (*yajña-*) 'rite'. Contrary to the norm, however, *-ry-* develops to *-yy-*, as in Pāli *ayya-*, Pkt. *ajja-* (*ārya-*) 'noble, sir', *kayya-* 'to be done, job' (*kārya-*). Similarly, *-rv-* develops to *-vv-* (Pāli *-bb-*), as in *savva-* 'all, whole' (Pāli *sabba-*, Skt. *sarva-*). This doubtless is to be explained on the basis of a systematic prohibition that from earliest Indo-Aryan times disallowed a sequence *-rr-* (see Sanskrit section 2.5.2.9).

As shown in section 1.3.1, some of these developments have parallels in earlier Indo-Aryan. Already in earliest Indo-Aryan, one sees word boundaries coming into play in such a manner that phonological adjustments are made less conditioned by purely phonological factors. In earliest Middle Indo-Aryan, word boundaries gain ascendancy to the point that, except in extremely closely bound sequences, there are no general sandhi adjustments dictated by purely phonological factors. For example, Pāli has sequences such as *yo ca* 'and one who ...', *ko imaṁ paṭhaviṁ vijessati* 'who will be victorious over this earth?' in contrast to Skt. *yaś ca, ka imām pṛthivīṁ vijeṣyati*. Moreover, the sandhi rules there are differ radically from those prevalent in Old Indo-Aryan. For example, vowel lengthening applies before quotative *ti* and vowel deletion applies in sequences of vowels: Pāli *sukhāyā ti* 'for happiness', *neva* 'not' (*na eva*).

Middle Indo-Aryan also differs essentially from Old Indo-Aryan with respect to the possible weight of syllables. Old Indo-Aryan allowed not only light and heavy syllables (e.g. Skt. *ta-dā* 'then', *tat-tra* 'there') but also superheavy syllables, as in Skt. *mātrā-* 'measure, mora', *āpnoti* 'reaches, obtains', although there is evidence in early Vedic texts of strategies to avoid such syllables (see Wackernagel 1896: 315, Hoenigswald 1989). Middle Indo-Aryan, however, generally disallows superheavy syllables, which are eliminated either through epenthesis (e.g. *sūriya-* 'sun', Skt. *sūrya-*) or by shortening a vowel, as in Pāli *pappoti* 'reaches' (Skt. *prāpnoti*). Now, there are indications of such a tendency already in Old Indo-Aryan. As Pāṇini notes (see Sanskrit, section 2.5.2.15), although doubling applies optionally in most dialects to a consonant preceded by a vowel and followed by a consonant, as in *tat-tra* alternating with *ta-tra/tat-ra*, in certain dialects this is disallowed if the vowel is long – as in *dātra* 'sickle' – and in at least one dialect no doubling is allowed at all.

From earliest Middle Indo-Aryan, certain grammatical categories are eliminated except for relic traces. Singular and plural alone regularly contrast. In the verb system, medio-passive endings are gradually eliminated, though they still occur in Aśokan inscriptions and Pāli; and early Middle Indo-Aryan has a single preterite category, regularly reflecting aorists, although some traces of perfects and the imperfect remain. In addition, vowel alternations characterizing different subgroups within single classes of forms are on their way out from earliest Middle Indo-Aryan. For example, in contrast to Skt. *śaknoti* 'is able', *śaknuvanti* 'are able', Pāli has *sakkoti, sakkonti*.

One of the most fundamental changes affecting the Middle Indo-Aryan verb system is the adoption of the present stem as the basis for other tense forms. In this connection, Middle Indo-Aryan developed types which were impermissible in Sanskrit. Thus, for example, although Pāli still has aorist forms like *agamā* and *agami* (3sg.), derived from the base *gam* 'go', it also has *agacchi*, based on the present stem *gaccha-*. Some formations related to passives can serve to bring the same point home. Aśokan (JRE 1) *pānasatasahasāni ālabhiyisu* 'a hundred thousand animals were killed' has the preterite *ālabhiyisu*, but in Sanskrit only *ālapsata* (3pl. aor. pass.) is appropriate, with the sigmatic affix following the base *labh*. Similarly,

(1) *tasmiṁ kho brāhmaṇa yaññe neva gāvo haññiṁsu na ajeḷakā haññiṁsu na kukkuṭasūkarā haññiṁsu na vividhā pāṇā saṁghātaṁ āpajjiṁsu na rukkhā chijjiṁsu yūpatthāya na dabbhā lūyiṁsu barihisatthāya* (DN, *Kūṭadantasutta* 23) 'At that ritual, o brāhmaṇa, cattle were not killed (*na haññiṁsu*), nor were goats or rams killed, nor fowl or pigs killed, nor did various kinds of living beings undergo (*āpajjiṁsu*) destruction; trees were not cut down (*chijjiṁsu*) for sacrificial poles (*yūpatthāya*), nor were bunches of darbha grass cut (*lūyiṁsu*) for a barhis (*barihisatthāya*).'

contains a series of third plural aorists formed to passive stems: *haññiṁsu* 'were killed' (pres. *haññanti*), *āpajjiṁsu* 'underwent' (pres. *āpajjanti*), *chijjiṁsu* 'were cut down' (pres. *chijjanti*), *lūyiṁsu* 'were cut' (pres. *lūyanti*). The corresponding Sanskrit forms would be *ahasata, āpatsata, achitsata, alaviṣata*: aorists in which the sigmatic affix -*s-/-iṣ-* follows the verb bases *han* (→ *ha*), *pad* (*ā pad*), *chid*, and *lū* (→ *lav-*), not the passive stems. In a comparable manner, future forms such as Aśokan *ālabhiyisaṁti* 'will be killed' and Pāli *chijjissati* 'will be cut off', *paṭihaññissati* 'will be destroyed' are impermissible in Sanskrit – which has *ālapsyante, chetsyate, haniṣyate* or *ghāniṣyate* instead – and infinitives of the type JM *dijjiuṁ* 'to be given' are also impermissible in Sanskrit.

Such formations of Middle Indo-Aryan also illustrate a reanalysis that took place in the formation of some passives. In Old Indo-Aryan, the combination of medio-passive endings and the stem affix -*ya-* followed zero-grade bases, as illustrated. In the MIA system reflected in Pāli, on the other hand, the alternation in question is consonantal for consonant-final bases that appear with final geminates due to the assimilation of their final consonants and the original -*y-* of the affix in the passive: *haññ* : *han, chijj* : *chid*, *sakk* (*sakkaï* [OIA *śakyate*] 'can be ...') : *sak*. Vararuci captures this nicely for Prākrits when he says (PrPr. 6.8–9: *yaka iaijjau, nāntyadvitve*) that the Sanskrit suffix *yak* (*ya* with a marker *k*) is replaced in Prākrit by *ia* and *ijja* (e.g. *gā-ia-i, gā-ijja-i* 'is sung'), but not (*na*) if there is doubling of the final consonant (*antyadvitve*) when the object of an act or the act itself is signified.

The nominal systems of Middle Indo-Aryan also are characterized by a lesser degree of allomorphy than obtains in Old Indo-Aryan and a reduction of syntactically distinct forms. Thus, from earliest Middle Indo-Aryan, the number of thematized nominals was extended, as in Pāli *gacchanto* 'going', *mahanto* (nom. sg. m.); *ima-* 'this' has a larger domain than in Old Indo-Aryan (e.g. Pāli m. sg. abl. *imasmā*, dat-gen. *imassa*, loc. *imasmiṁ*, with comparable plural forms and feminine forms from a stem *imā-*); and the line between nominal and pronominal inflexion became less sharp, so that locative singular forms reflecting OIA -*smi* occur in categories where this ending was not allowed earlier (e.g. Aś. *vijitamhi, vijitasi* 'in the empire' alongside *vijite*).

General syntactic patterns prevalent in Old Indo-Aryan – including the usual subject-object-verb word order, relative *ja-* (Aśokan and Pāli *ya-*) and interrogative *ka-* – are found also in Middle Indo-Aryan, but the case system involved is progressively reduced. Except in purpose clauses (e.g. *yūpatthāya, barhisatthāya* in (1) above), dative and genitive merge in a single case, historically the genitive. Similarly, historically instrumental forms served in roles played earlier by distinct ablative forms, as in

(2) Pāli:

pathavyā	*ekarajjena*	*saggassa*	*gamanena*	*vā* |
gen. sg. f.	instr. sg. nt.	gen. sg. nt.	instr. sg. nt.	ptcle.
earth	being one king	heaven	going	or

sabbalokādhipaccena	*sotāpattiphalaṁ*	*varaṁ*
instr. sg. nt.	nom.sg. nt.	nom.sg. nt.
being lord of all worlds	reaching the stream	better

'The fruit of entering onto the noble path is better than being the sole ruler of the earth, attaining heaven, having suzerainty over all the worlds.' (DhP 178)

Aśoka's inscriptions too exhibit the use of originally instrumental forms where Sanskrit would use an ablative; e.g.

(3) *mama*   *puttā ca*   *pottā*   *ca*   *param ca*   *tena*   *y[am]*
    my   sons and   son's sons and   after   that which
    me apaccam   *āva*   *samvattakappā* (GRE 5)
    me descendant up to   end of the world
    'my sons and grandsons and whatever descendants thereafter up to the end of the world'

(4) JM: *jharei*   *romakūvehim* *seo*   *durabhigandhao*
         3sg. pres. instr. pl.   nom. sg. m. nom. sg. m.
         flows   pores   sweat   foul smelling
    'Foul smelling sweat flows from the pores.' (Erz. 4.23)

In (2), *varam* 'better' is construed with a series of instrumental singular forms. (3) has *param* construed with the instrumental singular *tena*; Dhauli, Shāhbhāzgaṛhī and Mānsehrā have the same construction, while Kālsī has *palam ca tehi*, with the plural *tehi*. In (4), *jharei* (3sg. pres.) 'flows' is construed with the instrumental plural *romakūvehim* referring to a point of departure. Although the use of an instrumental in such constructions is not the norm in the standard current language Pāṇini describes and would be considered to reflect colloquial usage (see section 1.3.1 (1a,b)), nevertheless, the use of the instrumental where an ablative would be in order according to the standard Sanskrit is known also from Old Indo-Aryan, as in

(5) *rakṣasā*   *apahṛtā*   *bhāryā*   *prāṇaiḥ*   *priyatarā* *tava*
    instr.sg.nt. nom.sg.f.   nom.sg.f. instr.pl.m. nom.sg.f.   gen.sg.
    demon   taken away wife   breath   dearer   you
    'The wife dearer to you than your life breaths was carried off by the demon.' (Rām. 6.70.40cd)

Moreover, even in the standard current language there were already constructions in which ablatives and instrumentals alternated; thus, *pṛthak* 'separately', *vinā* 'without', *nānā* 'separately, distinctly' are construed with both.

An even greater reduction of contrastive cases is found in Apabhraṃśa, where a historical instrumental can be used in the role of a locative, as in

(6) *tahŏ*   *dāhiṇabhāem̐* *bharahu thakku*
    gen.sg.   instr.sg.   nom.sg. nom.sg.
    it   southern part Bharat located
    'Bharat stands in its southern section.' (PC 1.11.8ab)

Such usage is already foreshadowed in earlier Prākrits, in Buddhist Hybrid Sanskrit – as noted by Edgerton (1953: 44 [section 7.30]), who refers to the Apabhraṃśa merger – and in the Pāli use of formal instrumental plurals in locative function (Lüders 1954: 152–6, Oberlies 1997: 2).

Together with the extensive use of postpositions, the late Middle Indo-Aryan developments approach the Modern Indo-Aryan contrast of direct and oblique forms, with postpositions. Postpositions themselves were in use from earliest Indo-Aryan, indeed from Indo-Iranian times. Some also could be used redundantly, but following upon a case form that of itself served to signal a syntactic role (see Sanskrit, section 3.3(1), (3)). Even the Prākrit use of *-to* in complex case forms of the type *-ehimto* has parallels in earlier Indo-Aryan, where the *Ṛgveda* already has *patsutaḥ* 'under foot', with the suffix *-tas* – which serves as an alternative to ablative endings – following the locative plural *patsu*, and *patsutaś-śīḥ* 'lying at the feet'.

From earliest Indo-Aryan also, finite preterital verb forms could alternate with participial forms, which were paired with related finite forms. Thus, in

(7) *na   tvāvāṁ   indra   kaścana   na   jāto*
    neg.   nom.sg.m.   voc.sg.   indef.nom.sg.m.   neg.   nom.sg.m.
    not   like you   Indra   any one   not   born

    na   jàniṣayte
    neg.   3sg.fut.mid.
    not   will be born   (ṚV 1.81.5cd)
    'There is no one the likes of you, Indra: neither has he been born nor will he be born.'

the future form *janiṣyate* is paired with the participial form *jātaḥ* (there is a finite aorist *ajaniṣṭa* 'has been born, was born'). Moreover, like the corresponding aorist, the participle in *-ta* could be used with reference to an act accomplished at some time in the past including the day on which one speaks, in contrast with the imperfect and perfect. The aorist was the sole finite preterite regularly used in early Middle Indo-Aryan, where it also alternated with a participle, as in

(8) Pāli: *mayaṁ tumhākaṁ anāgamabhāvena aññesaṁ adamhā 'ti āhaṁsu. mayaṁ ājīvikaṁ paṭipucchitvā nakkhattaṁ na sobhanaṁ ti nāgatā detha no dārikaṁ ti. amhehi tumhākaṁ anāgamanabhāvena aññesaṁ dinnā. idāni dinnadārikaṁ kathaṁ puna ānessāma* (Jātaka I.258) '(The country folk) said (*āhaṁsu* [3pl. pret.]), "because of your (*tumhākaṁ* [gen. pl.]) not coming (*anāgamabhāvena*), we (*mayaṁ*) gave (*adamha* [1pl. pret.]) (the girl) to others (*aññesaṁ* [gen.-dat. pl.])." (The city folk said,) "we did not (*na*) come (*āgatā* [nom.pl.m.]) because we learned from asking (*paṭipucchitvā* 'after asking') the Ājīvika that the star configuration (*nakkattaṁ* [nom. sg. nt.]) was not (*na*) auspicious (*sobhanaṁ*); give (*detha* [2pl. imper.]) us (*no*) the girl (*dārikaṁ* [acc. sg. f.])." (The country folk said,) "Because of your (*tumhākaṁ* [gen. pl.]) not coming (*anāgamabhāvena*), we (*amhehi* [instr. pl.]) gave (*dinnā* [nom. sg. f.]) (her) to others (*aññesaṁ*). How (*kathaṁ*) will we now (*idāni*) bring (*ānessāma* [1pl. fut.]) back the girl who has already been given (*dinnadārikaṁ*)?"'

where the finite active construction *mayaṁ* (*dārikaṁ*) *adamha* 'we gave the girl' and its equivalent passive participial construction *amhehi* (*dārikā*) *dinnā* are used (see Hendriksen 1944: 50–81 for a study of the preterital past participle in Pāli).

What sets most of later Middle Indo-Aryan apart, however, is that – aside from a reduced aorist system in Ardhamāgadhī – finite preterite forms were eliminated, leaving only the type *amhehi dinnā* illustrated in (8). Also typical of this syntax are examples such as the following, which illustrate verb agreement in gender and number for both intransitives and transitives:

(9) *samāgao   bāhirāo Varadhaṇū*
    past ptcpl.-nom.sg.m.   abl.sg.   nom.sg.
    come   outside   Varadhanu
    'Varadhanu came from outside the city.' (Erz. 12.8)

(10) *samāgayā   rayaṇī*
     past ptcpl.-nom.sg.f.   nom.sg.f.
     come   night
     'Night fell.' (Erz. 12.12)

(11) *vaḍakoṭṭarāo   niggantūṇa   ḍakko   bhuyaṅgameṇa   ego*
    abl.sg.   absol.   past ptcpl.-nom.sg.m.   instr.sg.   nom.sg.m.
    tree hollow come down bitten   snake   one
    dārago
    boy
    'A snake came down from a hollow in the tree and bit one of the boys.' (Erz.
    1.10–11)

(12) *kosalāhiveṇa   amhāṇa   gavesaṇanimittaṁ   pesiyā   paccyaïyapurisā*
    instr.sg.   gen.pl. acc.sg.nt.   nom.pl.m. past ptcpl.-nom.pl.m.
    king of Kosala of us to search   sent   trusted men
    'The king of Kosala has sent some trusted men to search for us.' (Erz. 12.9–10)

(13) *bhaṇiyaṁ   ca   tīe   jā   sā   tume*
    past ptcpl.-nom.sg.nt. ptcl. instr.sg.f. rel.pr.nom.sg.f. nom.sg.f. instr.sg.
    said   and her   who   she   you
    diṭṭhā   mahāsaratīre   tīe   pesiyam   imaṁ
    past ptcpl.-nom.sg.f. loc.sg.nt.   instr.sg.f. nom.sg.nt. nom.sg.nt.
    seen   shore of the great lake her   sent   this
    'And she said, "The one you saw by the shore of the great lake sent this".' (Erz.
    9.6–7)

(14) *tattha   diṭṭhāo   do   pavarakannāo*
    there   seen-nom.pl.f. two excellent girls-nom.pl.f.
    'There (he) saw two excellent girls.' (Erz. 14.5–6)

(15) *taṁ   pavisamāṇena   ya   diṭṭhaṁ ...   dhavalaharaṁ*
    acc.sg.nt. pres. ptcpl.-instr.sg. ptcle past ptcpl.-nom.sg.nt. nom.sg.nt.
    it   entering   and seen   palace
    'And as he entered it (the city), he saw ... a palace.' (Erz. 14.4–5)

The neuter singular is used neutrally, as in the common phrases *teṇa bhaṇiyaṁ*, *teṇa vuttaṁ* 'he said', *tīe bhaṇiyaṁ* 'she said'.

Clearly, the stage is set for the final step of developing ergative syntax. Nevertheless, this step was not yet taken, even in late Prākrits. For example, one says *sā tume diṭṭhā* 'you saw her' (cf. (13)), but one does not say **taṁ tume diṭṭhā*, with an accusative feminine. The latter would be the equivalent of the ergative construction in a language like Gujarati, where the object nominal in such an instance would show the object marker *ne*. The general use of passives in the ability sense is also absent. Consider also the following examples from Apabhraṁśa:

(16) *pahilaü   kalasu   laïu   amarindeṁ   vīyaü*
    nom.sg.m. nom.sg.m. past ptcpl.-nom.sg.m. instr.sg.   nom.sg.m
    first   pot   taken   lord of the gods second
    huavaheṇa
    instr.sg.
    Agni
    'The lord of the gods took the first water pot, Agni the second.' (PC 2.5.1)

(17) *navamaü   sambhāviü   dharaṇindeṁ   dasamaü kalasu   laïjaï   candeṁ*
    ninth   honoured   by Dharaṇindra   tenth   pot   is taken by Candra
    'Dharaṇindra honoured the ninth, the tenth water pot is taken by Candra.' (PC 2.5.5)

(18) *aṇṇa*   *kalasa*   *uccāïa*   *aṇṇehiṁ*
     other-nom.pl.m.   pot-nom.pl.m.   lifted-nom.pl.m.   other-instr.pl.m.
     'Other pots were taken up by others.' (PC 2.5.6)

In (17), the overt passive *laïjaï* is used, so that it is reasonable to conclude that the syntax involving past participles of the type *laïu*, *uccāïa* is still a passive syntax in a system where finite preterite forms had been superseded by participial forms.

1.4 Subgroups of Indo-Aryan languages

That modern Indo-Aryan languages are divisible into affiliated subgroups is beyond doubt. Thus, it is reasonable to say that there are eastern, northwestern, southwestern, and midlands groups. On the other hand, the precise manner in which a family tree is to be drawn up as well as the exact affiliation of particular languages – such as Maithili, Magahi and Bhojpuri – are issues which have not been fully settled since the pioneering work of Beames, Hoernle and Grierson. For summaries of various subgroupings envisioned by different scholars, see Shapiro and Schiffman 1981: 70–87, Masica 1991: 446–63. Major points contributing to the general difficulties of establishing definitive subgroupings are: reaching consensus on sufficiently large groups of innovations carried out in common by various languages, such that they can be subgrouped on the basis of these common innovations; agreeing on what features are indeed to be treated as innovations and which represent retentions. Basic to all such decisions is the absence of a well documented detailed knowledge of the earliest history of the modern languages to be subgrouped. An example will serve to illustrate. Grierson (1917–20a,b, 1927) divided Indo-Aryan into what he termed outer, mediate and inner sub-branches, the first subdivided into northwestern, eastern group, and southern groups and the inner sub-branch subdivided into central and Pahāṛī subgroups. A major criterion for recognizing an outer sub-branch was the occurrence of -*l*- in past participle forms, portrayed in a map (Grierson 1927: 140). Thus, Grierson notes (1927: 140–1 [cf. 1917–20b: 84]), 'Gujarātī is an Inner language, but, as we shall see, it has been superimposed on another language of the Outer sub-branch, of which traces can still be observed. One of these traces is the existence of this very l-participle, which is used much as in Sindhī, as in *māryō* or *mārē-l*, struck.' Grierson did not, however, establish how the formation in question could be a common innovation of all the languages concerned, and S. K. Chatterji (1926: 167) was without doubt justified when he denied that an -*l*-past was a valid criterion for an establishing outer group, noting that it functioned as a past marker only in Eastern languages and Marathi and that it was an inherited adjectival (participial) suffix, with this function in Gujarati and elsewhere. Moreover, no historical evidence is cited to demonstrate how the use of such participial forms developed in late Prākrit or the earlier stages of languages like Gujarati, for which we have early sources. Southworth (forthcoming) also puts considerable emphasis on this criterion (section 5.1), along with which he considers (section 5.2) additional evidence: gerundives in -*(i)tavya* and future forms derived therefrom, the developments of OIA *$\dot{r}$*, word accent, the change of *l* to *n*, the deletion of non-initial post-consonantal *h*, and lexical evidence. On the basis of these isoglosses and the loss of contrast between short and long high vowels, Southworth (forthcoming section 5.3) arrives at a subgrouping which is compatible with Grierson's. He envisions a group that '... might be called "South/ Eastern Indo-Aryan", as opposed to the remaining languages, which could be characterized as "North-Central Indo-Aryan".' In addition, he concludes that, '...

Eastern Hindi seems to be an intermediate or transitional zone, as Grierson suggested . . .' Although Southworth goes on, in his chapter six, to consider historical correlates of the conclusions he reaches on the basis of modern Indo-Aryan, I think it fair to say that these conclusions are not sufficiently backed up by detailed facts about the chronology of changes to merit their being accepted as established.

Despite such difficulties and indeterminacies, it is clear that from very early times the Indo-Aryan territory had subdivisions which match in general the ones I have given above. Speakers of Sanskrit were aware from early on not only of differences between their current language and Vedic but also of areal differences at a given time. Well known examples stem from Yāska and Patañjali, who speak of usages proper to the Kamboja, Saurāṣṭra, the east and midlands, as well as of Ārya speakers (see Sanskrit section 1.2). It is noteworthy that *śav* is said to occur in Kamboja, a northwestern people whom in his commentary on Nirukta 2.2 Durga refers to as Mleccha (Bhadkamkar 1918: 166.5–6: *gatyartho dhātuḥ kambojeṣv eva bhāṣyate mlecchesu prakṛtyā prayujyata ākhyātapadabhāvena*): *śyav, śav, śiyav* 'go' are used in Avestan and Old Persian (e.g. OP 3sg. imperf. *aśiyava* 'went'); see also section 2.2.

Patañjali refers to the use of *hamm* 'go' in Saurāṣṭra. Another feature of the speech of this area is noted in the metrical version of the Pāṇinīyaśikṣā, which says that nasalized vowels as in *arā̃m* (acc. pl. m.) 'spokes' of ṚV 8.77.3b (*khe ạrā̃m ịvạ khedàyā* '(. . . pushed . . . down) like spokes in the wheel navel with an instrument for pressing together') are pronounced in the manner that a woman from Saurāṣṭra pronounces *takram* 'buttermilk': *takrã̃m*, with a fully nasalized final vowel (PŚ 26: *yathā saurāṣṭrikā nārī takrã̃m ity abhibhāṣate | evaṁ raṅgāḥ prayoktavyā khe arā̃m iva khedayā*).

Patañjali is well aware of the *r/l* alternation in particular lexical items. He notes (Bh. on 8.2.18 [III.398.18–23]) that -*l*- optionally becomes -*r*- in certain terms, such as *vāla*- 'hair,' and that -*r*- optionally becomes -*l*- in others. Among the latter is *kalman*- for *karman*-, a term mentioned in a ślokavārttika cited by Patañjali (Bh. on 1.4.51 [I.336.6–10]), who explains that this refers to a contrary direct object (*viparītaṁ karma*), an incomplete object in the sense that not all operations pertaining to the expression of action participants classed as karman apply with respect to one named by the term *kalman*-. It is fair to say that the -*l*-form is considered less polished than the corresponding -*r*-form.

Old Indo-Aryan was of course dialectally differentiated (see Emeneau 1966). The earliest distribution of dialect areas would have to stem from Vedic times, and the texts, right back to the Ṛgveda, show evidence of dialect differences, reflected, for example, in the use of forms of the type *dakṣi* and *dhakṣi* (2sg. imper.) 'burn' (Cardona 1991). Witzel (1989, 1991) has done extensive work on delineating Vedic dialects and the features which characterize them. Where possible, he has also rightly associated the areas with later Middle Indic dialect areas, as in the distribution of intervocalic -*l*- from -*ḍ*- (Witzel 1989: 211). Without wishing to diminish the value of Witzel's major contribution, I have nevertheless to say that some of the conclusions and claims made are subject to doubt. One claim Witzel makes concerns an important development in the Indo-Aryan verb system: the contrast among aorist, imperfect and perfect forms (see Sanskrit, section 3.1.3.2.1). Witzel says (1989: 139):

> While the origin and the spread of the gen. in -*ai* is a good example of the influence of a centrally located innovative area, the following case, that of the spread of the narrative perfect, is a late phenomenon that began in the East and

subsequently moved westwards very haltingly, so that it did not reach Pāṇini at all, but still affected, in late Vedic, the Western Kaṭha and Maitr. texts.

Since Whitney's investigation into the use of the imperfect and perfect in the Saṁhitās and the Brāhmaṇas, we know that the older texts, i.e., the Yajurveda Saṁhitās and some of the Brāhmaṇas, use the imperfect to tell stories, legends, etc., a feature corresponding to Pāṇini's rules (3.2.110 sqq.). However, the younger Brāhmaṇas, especially the ŚB, tell such stories in the perfect tense.

The use of the perfect in reporting events not witnessed by a speaker is known to Pāṇini, for his current language (*Aṣṭādhyāyī* 3.2.115: *parokṣe liṭ* [Cardona 1997: 149–50]), so that it is not precise to say 'the spread of the narrative perfect ... did not reach Pāṇini at all'.

There is a large variety of Prākrits, traditionally named after regions and their inhabitants: Māhārāṣṭrī, Śaurasenī and so on. Thus, Bharata mentions (NŚ 17.48: *māgadhy avantijā prācyā śauraseny ardhamāgadhī | bāhlīkā dākṣiṇatyā ca sapta bhāṣāḥ prakīrtitā*) seven languages as being well known: Māgadhī, the language of Avanti, the language of the east, Śaurasenī, Ardhamāgadhī, Bāhlīkā, and the language of the south. Theoreticians of poetics and grammarians of Prākrits also enumerate and characterize different Prākrits, among which Māhārāṣṭrī is given the highest status (see Acharya 1968: 56–123, Prākrits sections 1–2). The closest thing we have comparable to a dialect map of Middle Indo-Aryan is represented by Aśoka's inscriptions of the third century BC. As has been recognized (see Bloch 1950: 43–5, Aśokan/Pāli section 1.2), the major rock edicts show that east, northwest and west constitute three major dialect areas. There are, nevertheless, both gaps and problems of detail. For example, the occurrence of forms like *phara* 'fruit', *maṁgara* 'ceremony for auspicious result' – with -r- instead of -l- (*phala-*, *maṁgala*) – in fragments from Sopārā in the southwest have been explained as hyper-Pālisms (Alsdorf 1960: 251) or, without further explanation, as due to Iranian influence (Caillat 1989b: 419).

2 OTHER RELATIONS

2.1 Relations with Indo-European languages

2.1.1 Indo-Iranian

The most definitively established and accepted subgroup within Indo-European is Indo-Iranian, a subgroup adjacent to Slavic – with which it shares the retraction of *s* after *i u r* (including IIr. *ṛ*) and velars – characterized by certain retentions and innovations. A noteworthy innovation carried out in Indo-Iranian is the centralization of non-high vowels, so that IIr. *ă* correspond to *ĕ ŏ ă* of other Indo-European languages; e.g. Skt. *as* 'be' (3sg. pres. ind. *asti*), *aṣṭán-* 'eight' (nom.-acc. pl. *aṣṭau*), *mánas-* 'mind', *aj* 'lead, drive' (3sg. pres. ind. *ajàti*), *dhā* 'put, make' (3sg. pres. indic. act. *dadhàti*), *jñā* 'know' (3sg. pres. ind. act. *jánāti*), *bhrā́tṛ-* 'brother' (nom. sg. *bhrātā̀*); Av. *asti* 'is,' *ašta-* 'eight', *manah-* 'mind, spirit', *azaᶦti* 'leads', *dā* 'make' (3sg. pres. ind.act. *dadā̀ᶦtī, daδāᶦti*), *znā* 'know' (3pl. pres. ind. *-zānənti*), *brātar-* 'brother'; Gr. *estì* 'is', *óktō* 'eight', *ménos* 'ardor, force', *ágei* 'leads', *thḕ* 'put, make' (1sg. pres. ind. act. *títhēmi*), *gnō* 'know' (1sg. aor. act. *égnōn*), *phrā́tēr* 'member of a brotherhood'. This merger took place in Indo-Iranian after the palatalization of velars before *e*, so that palatals alternate with velars, as in Skt. *cakārà* (3sg. perf. act.), Av. *cāxrarᵊ* (3pl. perf. act.) 'made, did' versus Skt. *kṛṇoti̯*, Av. *kərənao͟iti* (3sg. pres. ind. act.). There are also grammatical innovations particular to Indo-Iranian. For example, after stems ending in *-a*, an *n* generally occurs with the genitive plural ending *-ām*, reflecting an innovation modelled on stems in *-n*; e.g. Skt. *martyā́nām* 'of mortals, men', Av. *mašiiāṇǝm*, OP *martiyānām*. The intimate relation between Avestan and Sanskrit has on several occasions been illustrated by showing that a passage from the Avesta is literally translatable into Sanskrit by simply applying phonological correspondence rules. Jackson (1892: xxxi– xxxii) made this point using Yašt 10.6, an illustration repeated by Mayrhofer (1997: 102, see Renou 1957: 45 (note 7) for additional references).

In addition to several other similarities in their grammatical systems, Indo-Aryan and Iranian have significant vocabulary items in common; e.g. ritual terms such as Skt. *yajñá-* 'rite of worship, sacrificial rite', Av. *yasna-* 'worship, act of worship, sacrifice', Skt. *hótr̥-*, Av. *zaotar-* 'a certain ritual officiant', and Skt. *sóma-* and Av. *haoma-*, which refer to a ritually important plant and the juice pressed from it, as well as names of divinities and mythological beings, such as Skt. *mitrá-* 'Mitra', Av. *miθra-* 'Mithra'. In addition, speakers of both language subgroups used comparable terms to refer to themselves as a people: Skt. *ā́rya-*, Av. *airiia-*, OP *ariya-* 'Ārya, Aryan'. Now, *ārya* has various meanings centering about the notion of noble, venerable, honorable, but this term was also explicitly used with reference to a particular group of people, characterized by the way they spoke. In the *Mahābhāṣya* passage alluded to above in section 1.4 Patañjali (Bh. I.9.25–10.1) uses the locative plurals *kambojeṣu, surāṣṭreṣu, prācyamadhyeṣu* and *udīcyeṣu* to refer to Kamboja, Surāṣṭra, the east and midlands and the north as areas where *śav* is used (*bhāṣito bhavati* 'is found spoken') as a verb meaning 'go' and so on. In the same context, he uses the phrases *āryā bhāṣante* 'Āryas say' and *āryāḥ prayuñjate* 'Āryas use'. In the comparable passage of his *Nirukta*, Yāska (Nir. 2.2 [161.11–13]) says *śavatir gatikarmā kambojeṣv eva bhāṣyate ... vikāram asyāryeṣu bhāṣante śava iti* '*śav* meaning "go" is used only in Kamboja ... in the Ārya community one uses a derivate (*vikāram* [acc. sg.] 'modification') *śava* ("corpse").' Here, Yāska uses the locative plural *āryeṣu* parallel to *kambojeṣu*, both terms referring to communities in which particular usages prevail. The terms comparable to *ārya* are similarly used in Iranian. Thus, Achemenid rulers speak of themselves as *ariya-ciṣṣa* (nom. sg. m.) 'of Arya lineage' (see Kent 1953: 170a), and Darius once says of one of his inscriptions, 'moreover, it was in Ariya' (DB 4.89: *patišam ariyā āha*).

Although Indo-Iranian must be recognized as a distinct subgroup, Indo-Aryan and Iranian also diverged and are distinguished from each other by characteristic retentions and innovations. One major Iranian innovation is the deaspiration of voiced aspirates, retained in Indo-Aryan: Skt. *bhrā́tr̥-, dhā́, gharma-* 'heat': Av. *brātar-, dā, garəma-* 'hot, heat'. In connection with this, the voicing and aspiration known as Bartholomae's Law remains a regular process in Old Indo-Aryan (section 1.3.2.1) but is eliminated in Iranian. Thus, early Avestan *aogədā* (3sg. inj. mid.) 'speaks, says' shows *-g-da* from **-gh-ta*, with voicing, aspiration by Bartholomae's Law, and subsequent deaspiration of *dh* to *d*; but due to deaspiration, later the base is *aog-*, so that the regular third singular imperfect in younger Avestan is *aoxta* 'said'. This also illustrates another innovation that distinguishes Iranian from Indo-Aryan: the former developed spirants that are lacking in the latter. Additional examples are Av. *fra* (preverb) 'forth', *puθra-* 'son', *θβąm* 'you' (2sg. pr. acc.): Skt. *pra, putra-, tvā́m*. Further, IIr. *s* changed to *h* in Iranian except before non-nasal stops and *n*, as in Av. *hapta* 'seven', *hiiāt̰* (3sg. opt.) 'be', *barahi* (2sg. pres. ind.) 'you carry', *ahmi* (1sg. pres. ind.) 'am' versus Skt. *saptan-, bharasi, syāt, asmi* (on the Iranian counterparts of Old Indo-Aryan *ś* and so on see section 2.1.2). Moreover, although Indo-Iranian shows vocalization to *i* of a Proto-Indo-European laryngeal – as in Skt., Av., OP *pitā* (nom. sg.) 'father' – a laryngeal in an interior syllable of a polysyllabic term is lost in Iranian but retained in Indo-Aryan: Skt. *bravīti* (3sg. pres. ind.) 'says', *vṛṇīte* (3sg. pres. ind. mid.) 'chooses' versus Av. *mraoˡti* 'says', *vər°ṇtē* 'wishes'. On the other hand, the contrast between *xš* and *š* in examples such as Av. *vāxš* (nom. sg. fem.) 'speech', *šaēˡti* (3sg. pres. ind.) 'dwells' as opposed to *kṣ* in Skt. *vākṣu* (loc. pl.), *kṣeti* illustrates an Indo-Aryan innovation.

In grammar also, both Indo-Aryan and Iranian show retentions and innovations which distinguish them. Thus, Iranian has a demonstrative pronoun *di* (Av. *dim*, OP *-dim*) absent from Indo-Aryan. On the other hand, Indo-Aryan shows a thematized present *vindati* 'finds' while the athematic infixed present still exists in Iranian (Av. *vinastī*, *vinasti* [3sg. pres. ind. act.]). Further, Iranian has some inchoatives that Indo-Aryan lacks; thus, Av. *tafsaṯ* (3sg. imperf.) 'got hot', OP *xšnāsātiy* (3sg. subj.) '(lest one) should learn'.

2.1.2 Nuristani

[Following the conventions of specialists in the area, in this section *č*, *ǰ* and *ǰh* designate palatal stops with affricated release, *ċ* and *j* and have the values [ts] and [dz] in citations from Iranian and Nuristani.]

There is a small group of languages – Ashkun (Aṣkū), Kati (Katī), Prasun (Pṛasū, Pṛasun), Waigali (Wāigalī), and Tregami (Tregāmī) – formerly referred to as Kafiri (Kāfirī) and now referred to as Nuristani (Nūristānī) languages – spoken in the Hindu Kush, the affiliation of which has been disputed for some time. For recent surveys of the field, see Strand 1998, 1999, Degener 1998: 4–9.

Most scholars competent to judge hold that Nuristani represents either a distinct subgroup of an Indo-Iranian-Nuristani group or a special area within Indo-Aryan that remained isolated after the main group of Indo-Aryans moved south into the Panjab. Morgenstierne (1974: 9) gives a 'simplified model' envisaging two possible lines of descent such that: "ur-Kafirs" 'separated from Indian in pre-Vedic times' or 'branched off already before the final separation of Indian from Iranian'. It has been shown, however, that Nuristani is definitely separate from Dardic, which is a subgroup of Indo-Aryan (see Morgenstierne 1965: 139).

A group of phonological characteristics sets Nuristani languages apart. To begin with, they do not have aspirated stops; e.g. Kt. *kur* 'donkey', Ash. *lota* 'found' in contrast to Skt. *khara-*, Av. *xara-* and Skt. *labh* 'gain, obtain' (past ptcpl. *labdha-*). Given that Nuristani lacks spirants *f*, *θ*, and *x* typical of Iranian, which deaspirated voiced aspirates (section 2.1.1), it is reasonable to conclude that the deaspiration took place independently in Iranian and Nuristani (Buddruss 1977: 24, cf. Morgenstierne 1926: 53). As Buddruss has also noted (1977: 24), this accords with the fact that Nuristani does not show *h* for PIIr. *s* or another characteristic of Iranian: *-st-* for *-tt-* (cf. Morgenstierne 1926: 60). In addition, unlike Iranian, Nuristani does not show evidence that interior laryngeals were dropped (Morgenstierne 1926: 61). All this speaks against strong Iranian affiliation or admixture of Iranian through borrowings in Nuristani, although Nuristani shows, as does Iranian, different reflexes corresponding to Indo-Aryan *kṣ* (Morgenstierne 1974: 7).

Major differences between Indo-Aryan and Nuristani concern the developments of PIE *$\hat{k}$*, *$\hat{g}$*, *$\hat{g}h$*, *k^w*, *g^w*, *g^wh*. The reflexes of these in Indo-Aryan and Iranian are well known, as shown in table 1.3.

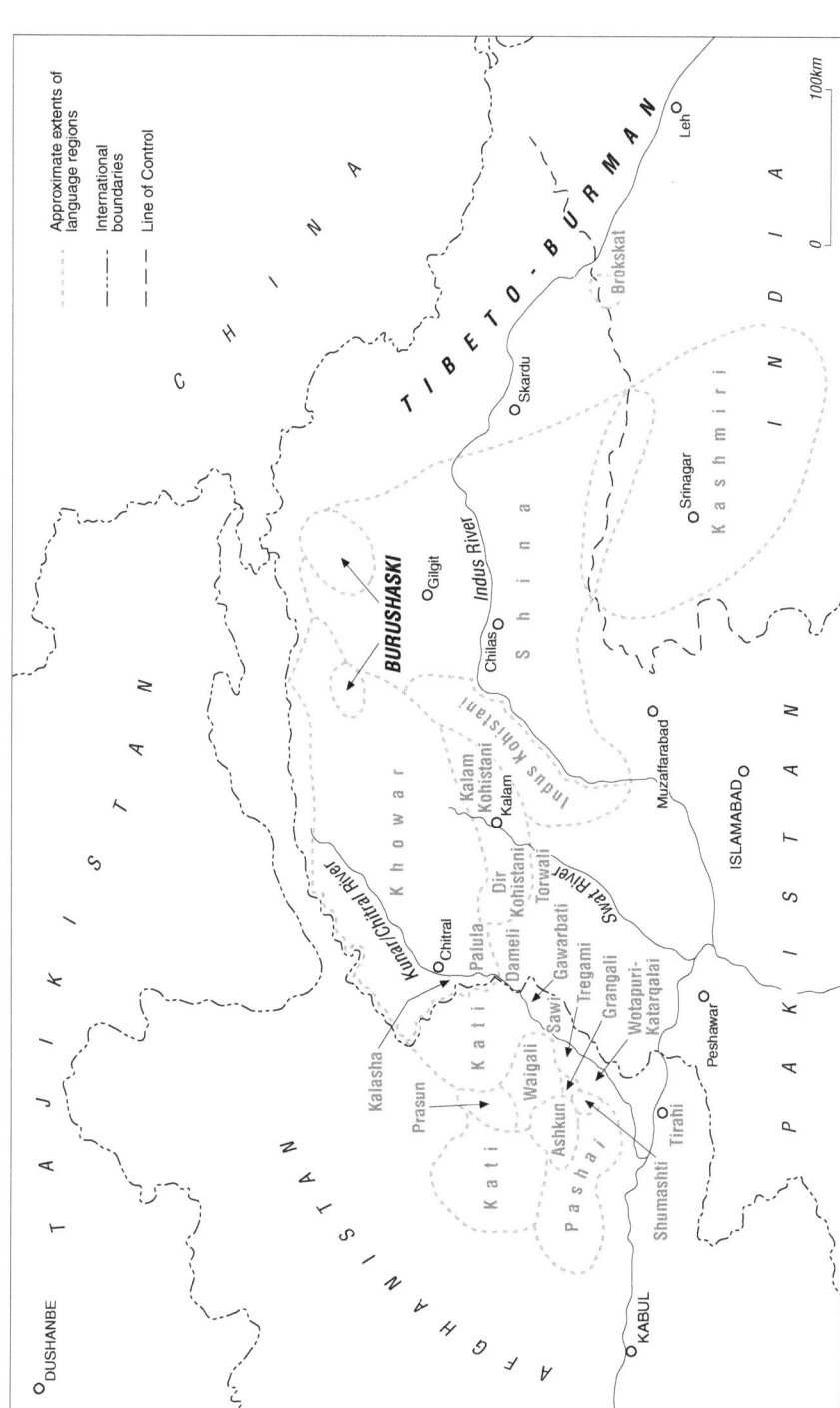

MAP 1.2: DARDIC AND NURISTANI

TABLE 1.3: REFLEXES OF PIE *k̂, ĝ, ĝh, kʷ, gʷ, gʷh IN INDO-ARYAN, IRANIAN AND NURISTANI

PIE	Indo-Iranian	Sanskrit	Avestan	Old Persian	Nuristani
A.					
*k̂	*ć	ś	s	θ	ć [ts]/š
*ĝ	*ǰ	j [ǰ]	z	d	j [dz]/z
*ĝh	*ǰh	h	z	d	j [dz]/z
*gʷ	*g	g	g	g	g
*gʷh	*gh	gh	g	g	g
B. Before original front vowels					
*kʷ	č	c [č]	č	č	č
*gʷ	*ǰ	j [ǰ]	ǰ	ǰ	ǰ/ž
*gʷh	*ǰh	h	ǰ	ǰ	ǰ/ž
		(< jh [ǰh])			

Nuristani appears to go more with Iranian than Indo-Aryan. For example (Morgenstierne 1926: 52–3, 1929: 195–200, 1945: 228–30, 1974: 7, Buddruss 1977: 23, 28–30):

Skt. *śvan-/śun-* : Av. *span-/-sŭn-* : Wg., Tr. *ćũ* 'dog'
Skt. *jānu-* : Av. *zānu-* : Kt. *jõ*, Ash., Wg. *zã̄* 'knee'
Skt. *hṛd-* : Av. *zərᵊd-* : Kt. *jire*, Pr. *zir* 'heart'
Skt. *ka-* : Av. *ka-* : Ash. *kō* (obl.), Kt. Wg. *kĩ̄* interrogative pronoun (Turner 1966: 127a [2574])
Skt. *go-, gava-*: Av. *go-* 'cow, ox': Ash. *ga* 'cow' (Turner 1966: 222a [4147])
Skt. *ghana-* 'firm, dense': Wg. *ganala-štä* 'heavy' (Turner 1966: 238b [4424])
Skt. *jyā-* : Av. *ǰyā-* : Ash., Kt., Pr., Wg. *ǰī̄/žī̄* 'bow string'
Skt. *han* (3sg. pres. ind. *hanti*) : Av. *ǰan* (*ǰaⁱṇti*): Kt. *ǰäř*, Wg. *žäř* 'kill'

Mayrhofer (1997: 107) emphasizes this point: 'Les langues du Nouristan se comportent comme les langues iraniennes *dans cette évolution phonétique certainement très ancienne*, non comme les langues indo-aryennes'. [emphasis in original]

Mayrhofer also assumes (1997: 108) not only that the Iranian reflexes *s/θ* and *z/d* represent common Iranian *ts* and *dz*, with different outcomes in eastern and southwestern Iranian, but also that Iranian appears to coincide here with Nuristani: 'c'est là une évolution qui semble coïncider avec celle du Nouristani: indo-iranien *ć*, *ǰ(h)* > nour. *ts, dz* (*contre* véd. *ś, j/h*).'

Mayrhofer immediately goes on (1997: 108) to say he presents this only with extreme reserve, and in this I consider he is right. The evidence does not require that the changes in question have been carried out in common, thereby establishing Iranian affiliation for Nuristani. To begin with, a change of palatal to dental affricates could have taken place in Nuristani languages independently of Iranian, just as in certain northwestern languages such as Kashmiri one finds *ts* (*ć*) and *tsh* (*ćh*) from Indo-Aryan *c* and *ch*; e.g. K *tsōr* (*ćōr*) 'four', *pãtsh* (*pã̄ćh*, with word-final aspiration), *tshapun* (*ćhapun*) 'to be hidden', *pritshun* (*prićhun*) 'to ask'. In addition, the Nuristani developments are complex. As has been pointed out (see Buddruss 1977: 29), Ashkun and Waigali frequently show *š* where Kati and Prasun have a dental affricate, as in Kt. *duć*, Pr. *lez(e)* versus Wg. *dōš* 'ten'. These and other complications make it plausible to consider that the dental affricate reflexes corresponding to OIA *ś, j, h* represent the outcome of developments independent of Iranian contact or affiliation. This accords well with the fact that Nuristani lacks other typically Iranian features and also (Buddruss 1977: 24) shows some archaic morphological features which also speak for Indic affiliation. Further, some details concerning Grassmann's Law have to be considered. Av. *xumba-* 'pot' as opposed to Skt. *kumbha-* can be considered evidence to show that deaspiration as formulated under Grassmann's Law did not apply yet in Proto-Indo-Iranian (Schindler 1976: 626). In this light, consider Skt. *jahi* (2sg. imp.) 'strike, kill'. This is an isolated relic in Old Indo-Aryan that presupposes **jhadhi*, to which Grassmann's Law applied. Moreover, the palatal of this form should be explained as an analogic extension from the full-grade forms of the present: **jhanti* (> *hanti*) and so on. For an inherited imperative would have *-a-* from a preform **g^wh̥n-dhi*, so that palatalization is not expected. If, then, deaspiration by Grassmann's Law did not operate in Proto-Indo-Iranian, the ancestor of *jahi* must have had an initial aspirate in Proto-Indo-Aryan. Consequently, the Old Indo-Aryan : Nuristani correspondence in B of table 1.3 is actually *jh* : *ǰ*. Since, moreover, the Nuristani deaspiration of aspirates is to be considered to have taken effect independently of the Iranian deaspiration of voiced aspirates, one can operate with PIA **jh* as a proto-phoneme ancestral to OIA **jh* (> *h*) and Nuristani *ǰ/ž*. Thus, the apparently great differences in the treatment of PIE **k̂* and so on cannot serve to demonstrate that Nuristani languages are definitely to be considered a branch separate from Indo-Aryan.

In sum, it is reasonable to conclude (Bloch-Master 1965: 54, Buddruss 1977: 33, cf. Fussmann 1977: 24–5, 69) that Nuristani represents a group of dialects which remained cut off from the main Indo-Aryan group that migrated into the Panjab area of the subcontinent, so that it retained some old features of phonology and grammar, and that it and the main of Indo-Aryan body later underwent separate developments. Under this scenario, then, one has to do with Indo-Iranian consisting of only Indo-Aryan and Iranian. Under an alternative thesis, on the other hand, an Indo-Iranian-Nuristani subgroup of Indo-European is posited. Even this has, nevertheless, to concede that Nuristani and Indo-Aryan are more closely related to each other than either is to Iranian. Research is still being carried out in this area and David Nelson, who earlier (1986) contributed a study of Nuristani historical linguistics, informs me that he will soon publish a monograph concerning principally cultural-religious aspects of pre-Islamic society Nuristani from which he concludes that this should be considered a group distinct from Indo-Aryan.

2.1.3 Bangani

Bangani (Baṅgāṇī) is spoken in Bangan, on the westernmost tip of Garhwal (Uttaranchal). According to the work of Zoller (1988, 1989, 1993), this language shows certain archaisms and, surprisingly, phonological outcomes characteristic of centum languages; for example: *kɔpɔ* 'hoof', *dɔkɔ* 'ten', *dɔkru* 'tear', *gɔmbɔ/gumbhɔ* 'molar', *gimɔ* 'winter' (Abbi 1997 [1998]: 3, 6, 7, 9, 11) as opposed to Skt. *śapha-*, *daśa-*, *aśru-*, *jambha-*, *hima-* ('snow'). Zoller's evidence and methodology were disputed by van Driem and Sharma (1996, 1997). Zoller responded (1997) in turn, saying that van Driem and Sharma themselves were guilty of both misrepresentation and not knowing the area they were investigating; indeed, he says they never actually set foot in Bangan. Abbi revisited the area and reported (1997 [1998]) that her fieldwork reconfirms much of Zoller's evidence. The issue remains contentious and open, with more data needed.

2.2 Relations to non-Indo-European languages

2.2.1 General

The Indian subcontinent has long been home to speakers of languages belonging to different language families, principally Indo-European (Indo-Aryan), Dravidian, and Austro-Asiatic (Munda). It is to be expected that speakers of these languages who were in contact with each other should have been subject to possible influence of other languages on their own. Scholars have long been aware of and remarked on the changes which the language reflected in earliest Vedic underwent over time, gradually becoming more and more "Indianized", so that one can speak of an Indian linguistic area (Emeneau 1956, 1971, 1974, 1980, Kuiper 1967a). Scholars have also differed concerning the degree of influence exerted by Munda or Dravidian languages on Indo-Aryan at different stages and the manner in which such influence was made felt.

It is proper to emphasize from the outset that Old Indo-Aryan should be viewed as encompassing a variety of regional and social dialects spoken natively, developing historically in the way any living language does, and whose speakers interacted in a society where diglossia and polyglossia were the norm. Sanskrit speakers show an awareness of these facts. Thus, it is not only historically true that early Vedic root aorists of the type *akar, agan* were gradually replaced by forms of the types *akārṣīt, agamat* (see Sanskrit section 3.1.7) but also that Yāska and Patañjali were aware of such changes and brought the fact out in their paraphrases; see Mehendale 1968: 15–33. Pāṇini accounted for major features of Vedic which differed from his current language, and he was aware of this language being in a state of flux, a living changing language (see Cardona 2004). In addition, such early native speakers of Sanskrit give us evidence of attitudes towards different varieties of speech which should be taken into consideration.

2.2.2 Speech varieties as viewed in Sanskrit sources

Passages in the *Mahābhāṣya* indicate that as far as Patañjali was concerned one could have usage that was acceptable (*iṣṭa* 'desired, desirable') though apparently not in conformity with the standard language as accounted for in the *Aṣṭādhyāyī*, which therefore required additions or extended interpretation. One famous example is the dialogue in the Bhāṣya on 2.4.56: *ajer vy aghañapoḥ*. According to this rule, *vī* should occur with ārdhadhātuka affixes instead of *aj* 'drive', except with the suffixes **ghañ** and **ap** (a with different markers); e.g. *ud-āja-* 'driving up' (**ghañ**), *ud-aja-* (**ap**) 'driving (cattle) up' but *pra-vāy-aka-* 'one who drives', *pra-vay-anīya-* 'to be driven'. In the Bhāṣya on 2.4.56 (I.488.17–22) an interpretation is suggested which allows for *aj* to occur in derivates such as *prājitṛ-* 'driver'. To emphasize that this is a desired form, Patañjali recounts the dialogue: A certain grammarian (*kaścid vaiyākaraṇaḥ*) says to a chariot driver, *ko 'sya rathasya pravetā* 'Who is the driver of this car?' The driver answers, *āyuṣmann ahaṁ prājitā* 'Sir, I am the driver', upon which the grammarian accuses him of using an incorrect speech form (*apaśabdaḥ*). The driver retorts that the grammarian knows what should obtain by rule (*prāptijñaḥ*) but not what is desired (*iṣṭijñaḥ*): this term is desirable (*iṣyata etad rūpam*). Patañjali doubtless reflects a historical change in the language between Pāṇini's time and area and his. At the same time, he is clearly willing to countenance that usage could include terms which a strict grammarian might consider improper. And he puts this in terms of a contrast between a grammarian and a charioteer.

Another famous *Mahābhāṣya* passage (see Cardona 1997: 550 [**834**]) concerns sages (*ṛṣi-*) who were characterized by the way they pronounced the phrases *yad vā naḥ* and *tad vā naḥ: yar vā ṇaḥ, tar vā ṇaḥ.* Although these sages spoke with such vernacular features, they did not do so during ritual acts. Consequently, they did not incur demerit on account of such usage. That is, the strict canons of correct usage applied most stringently with respect to ritual, where incorrect usage involved incurring demerit and having to perform expiatory acts. In everyday usage, no such demerit resulted. On the contrary, both accepted forms and those considered incorrect served equally to convey meanings, and what distinguished correct speech was that one gained merit from such usage accompanied by a knowledge of its grammatical formation.

One must recognize also that the standard speech could include elements which originally were not part of the Sanskrit norm (see section 1.3.1). Moreover, Śabara remarks (on JS 1.3.5.10 [II.151]) that although authority (*pramāṇam*) is granted to a learned elite (*śiṣṭāḥ* [nom. pl.]) whose behaviour is authoritative with respect to what cannot be known directly (*yat tu śiṣṭācāraḥ pramāṇam iti tat pratyakṣānavagate 'rthe*) and who are the experts (*abhiyuktāḥ*) as concerns the meanings of terms, nevertheless Mlecchas are more expert as concerns the care and binding of birds (*yat tv abhiyuktāḥ śabdārtheṣu śiṣṭā iti tatrocyate : abhiyuktatarāḥ pakṣiṇāṁ poṣaṇe bandhane ca mlecchāḥ*). Consequently, when it comes to terms like *pika-* 'cuckoo', which Āryas do not use in any meaning but which Mlecchas do (ŚBh. 1.3.5.10 [II.149]: *atha yāñ chabdān āryā na kasmiṁścid artha ācaranti mlecchās tu kasmiṁścit prayuñjate yathā pika . . .*), authority is granted to Mleccha usage.

Now, among the northern Mleccha people listed in the *Bhīṣmaparvan* of the *Mahābhārata* (Mbh. 6.10.63cd–64ab: *uttarāś cāpare mlecchā janā bharatasattama | yavanāś ca sakāmbojā dāruṇā mlecchajātayaḥ*) are the Yavanas and the Kambojas. As noted earlier (section 1.4), Yāska and Patañjali recognize the use of *śav* as a verbal base in Kamboja, and neither stigmatizes it. This is noteworthy, along with an additional point illustrated by Patañjali in another famous passage, the *Mahābhāṣya* on 2.4.10: *śūdrāṇām aniravasitānām* (see Cardona 1976: 265–6). Patañjali here considers the possibility that *aniravasitānām* 'not excluded' has to do with exclusion from Āryāvartta and rejects this interpretation on the grounds that the rule will then not allow for treating as singular a compound such as *śakayavana-* 'Śaka and Yavana'. This requires that Patañjali have considered the Śaka and Yavana, who dwelt outside the limits of Āryāvartta, to be part of the accepted social system, a conclusion which D. R. Bhandarkar reached in 1934. For otherwise he could not have considered them śūdras, a requirement for the compound in question to come within the purview of *Aṣṭādhyāyī* 2.4.10.

There is thus evidence to show that before the second century BC and possibly before Pāṇini's time Mlecchas who inhabited areas outside the bounds of Āryāvartta (on this see Kane 1968–77: II.11–18) could be absorbed into the prevalent social system and that terms from speech areas such as that of the Kambojas could be treated as Indo-Aryan. This does not, of course, mean that the Āryas treated Mlecchas and their language in a favourable light. On the contrary. Clearly, they were relegated to the lower social strata, and it is well known (cf. Kane 1968–77: I.100, 121, 290) that strictures were in force concerning Mlecchas and their languages. Thus, for example, the *Gautamadharmasūtra* (1.9.17: *na mlecchāśucyadhārmikaiḥ saha sambhāṣeta*) prohibits cooperative discourse with Mlecchas as well as with Āryas who are impure by virtue of not performing the acts expected of them and with Brahmins who have fallen from their status. Yet the very same text recognizes that one must at times carry on such discourse.

For Gautama goes on to say (GDhS 1.9.18: *sambhāṣya puṇyakṛto manasā dhyāyet*) that if one does engage in such discourse, one should meditate on meritorious persons. The *Mitākṣarā* not only specifies that the meritorious people in question are those such as Vasiṣṭha, it also makes an interesting remark commenting on GDhS 1.9.17. The formulation of the sūtra – not only using *sambhāṣeta* 'speak with' but also *saha* 'with' – is such that it implies not just speaking with the persons in question but being engaged in a joint venture (*ekakāryo bhūtvā*) with them, so that there is no fault in speaking to them incidentally, as when one asks the way somewhere (*tena mārgapraśnādau na doṣaḥ*). Whether or not one accepts Haradatta's interpretation, the text itself leaves no doubt concerning two points: Ārya brāhmaṇas normally were not supposed to engage in discourse with Mlecchas, but they had to do so on occasion.

In brief, the picture is that of a society in which an Ārya group considered itself the carrier of a higher culture and strived to keep this culture and the language associated with it but at the same time had necessarily to interact with groups like Mlecchas, whose language and customs were considered lesser. The result of such interaction, both with other Indo-Aryans who spoke dialects with Middle Indo-Aryan features and with non-Indo-Aryans, was that Sanskrit was effected through adoption of lexical terms and grammatical features. As linguists have learned and earlier Indian scholars recognized (see Cardona 1999: 102–3), such change takes place over generations: what speakers of one generation may consider deviant their children perceive as normal and propagate. There is no cogent reason to consider that such changes due to contact had not been carried out gradually over generations for a long time before.

2.2.3 Modern views

Although scholars generally agree that Old Indo-Aryan was indeed affected by "autochthonous" languages and that there is indeed a South Asia linguistic area (see, e.g., Emeneau 1956, 1980, Kuiper 1967a, Masica 1976), there are disagreements concerning the possible degree to which such effects should be seen in early Vedic and whether the features at issue could reflect also developments from Indo-European sources. In addition to the extent and sources of lexical borrowings, the main points of contention concern four features commonly considered characteristic of a South Asian linguistic area (see Kuiper 1991: 9, Hock 1996: 18–19): (1) a contrast between retroflex and dental consonants, (2) the use of a quotative particle (Skt. *iti*), (3) the use of absolutives (Skt. *-tvā, -ya*), (4) the general unmarked word order subject-object-verb; see Sanskrit sections 2.3.1, 2.3.3, 3.2.4.1, 3.3.

2.2.3.1 Retroflex and dental consonants

Early sources recognize for Vedic a contrast between retroflex and dental consonants. For example, the *Taittirīyaprātiśākhya*, which gives detailed descriptions of pronunciation, says that retroflex stops are produced by curling the tongue back and having the apex make contact behind the alveolar ridge, dental stops *t* and so on by having the apex make contact at the roots of the upper teeth (see Sanskrit section 2.3.1). It also states (TPr. 2.44–45: *sparśasthāneṣūṣmāṇa ānupūrvyeṇa, karaṇamadhyaṁ tu vivṛtam*) that spirants are produced at the same places as stops, differing from them in that the middle of the active articulator is now distanced from the place of production. Modern scholars too generally have accepted that the contrast between retroflex and dental consonants was characteristic of earliest Indo-Aryan.

One scholar, however, has claimed that the Indo-Aryan of the original *Ṛgveda* did not have retroflex consonants: 'However, to the speech of the Ṛgvedic poets, retroflexion was most probably still a foreign habit' (Deshpande 1979: 298). Deshpande (1979: 247) sees support for this position in something said in *Aitareyāraṇyaka* 3.2.6:

> How far are the retroflexes in the existing *Ṛgveda* historically authentic? In my view, they are authentic only in that they represent the sounds in the text as it was preserved in the Śākala school at the time of the formation of this particular recension. Beyond this point we are entering the field of reconstruction. If we know that at a certain point there had been doubts and differences concerning Ṛgvedic retroflexion, then we should be less categorical about ascribing retroflexion existing in the present text to the original. Such an indication is to be found in the *Aitareya-Āraṇyaka* ...

The basic issue is brought out in part of this text (AiĀr. 3.2.6: *sa yadi cikitset saṇakāram bravāṇīm̐3 aṇakārām̐3 iti saṇakāram eva brūyāt saṣakāram bravāṇīm̐3 aṣakārām̐3 iti saṣakāram eva brūyāt*) where, according to Sāyaṇa's interpretation, a student considers whether to pronounce the continuously recited Vedic text with or without *ṇ* and *ṣ*, and is told that he should pronounce it with these sounds. It is not possible to consider here differences among modern scholars concerning details of interpretation, but I think it appropriate to emphasize the general context of the passage in question. The third chapter of the *Aitareya-Āraṇyaka* concerns the secret knowledge associated with meditating on what constitutes saṁhitā (AiĀr. 3.2.1: *athātaḥ saṁhitāyā upaniṣat*). In speech, a saṁhitā is the close junction of two successive units A and B, with no pause between the two. The text considers the conjunction of various entities A and B (earth and heaven, speech and mind, etc.) and what joins them (the ether and so on), along with different viewpoints of various teachers. Such mystical equations are of course linked to the close junction of speech units, as the text explicitly brings out (AiĀr. 3.1.5) when it says that the prior element and following elements (*pūrvarūpam, uttarararūpam*) are successive syllables (*pūrvam akṣaram, uttaram [akṣaram]*). Moreover, the text speaks also of nirbhuja and pratṛṇṇa, that is, of the continuously recited text (*saṁhitāpāṭha*) and the text split into word-constituents (*padapāṭha*). In accordance with the context of Aitareya-Āraṇyaka 3.2.6, then, this is properly understood to concern *ṇ* and *ṣ* which occur where such successive units are involved, that is, where the final and initial segments of words come into conjunction. Thus, the deliberation in question concerns whether one should pronounce *ṇ, ṣ* or *n, s* in such situations. To this extent, I can agree with Deshpande. On the other hand, I think it is inappropriate to blend the instances that involve word boundaries with those which do not, merely saying (Deshpande 1979: 248) that saṁhitā 'is frequently used for "whole" texts' and, 'However, whether internal or external, the sounds *ṇ* and *ṣ* in the present *Ṛgveda* passage *mo ṣu ṇaḥ* and in words like *viṣṇave* or *vidatheṣu* are produced by the same basic historical rules which cover both the internal and external *ṣ* and *ṇ*.' This, as well as the speculative development Deshpande (1979: 249) subsequently presents concerning the isolated (Bloomfield and Edgerton 1932: 87) *paṇyāt paṇyatarā* and *panyāt panyatarā* in Kṛṣṇayajurveda texts – only to disclaim it – omits a well known phenomenon: the gradual effect of word boundaries on phonological rules (see above, section 1.3.2.1, Sanskrit section 2.5.2.10, Hock 1979, 1996: 51 note 24). Note, for example, Pāṇini's well formulated rules (8.4.27–8: *naś ca dhātusthoruṣubhyaḥ, upasargād bahulam*) accounting for retroflex *ṇ-* in Vedic for *n-* of the clitic pronominal form *nas* after a verb with a consonant that conditions retroflexion (e.g. *agnḗ rakṣā̀ ṇaḥ* [ṚV 7.15.13 and elsewhere] 'Agni, protect us'), after *uru*, and after *ṣu*, but only optional retroflexion after a preverb. In sum, I think one must agree that the *Aitareyāraṇyaka* affords no cogent reason to doubt that retroflex consonants constituted a separate set of phonemes in earliest Indo-Aryan (Kuiper 1991: 13–14).

It is universally accepted that retroflex consonants appear in Sanskrit items of unquestioned Indo-European pedigree, such as *nīḍa-* 'resting place, nest', *mīḍha-* 'reward' (Av. *mižda-*), *līḍha-* (past ptcpl.) 'licked' (PIE **liĝh-to-*), *ūḍha-* 'transported' (**uĝh-to-*), *viṭ* (nom. sg.) 'settlement' (see Kuiper 1967b: 115–21), *ṣaṭ* (nom.-acc. pl.) 'six', *viḍ-bhiḥ* (instr. pl.). It is also beyond question that from earliest Vedic texts one has examples which show such that retroflex consonants contrast phonemically with dentals; cf. *dīdivi-* 'shining', *īdhe* (3sg. perf. mid.) 'kindled', *adīdhet* (3sg. imperf.) 'appeared', *ūdhar* (nom.-acc. sg.) 'udder', *-vit* (nom. sg., e.g. *aśvavit* 'one who gets horses', *govit* 'one who gets cattle'), *-kṣid-bhyaḥ* (dat. pl. *bandhukṣid-bhyaḥ* 'dwelling in kinship'), all attested in the *R̥gveda*.

The question how such a contrast developed has engaged scholars over a long time; for presentations of views and evidence, see Bloch 1924: 4–5, 1930: 732–3, Emeneau 1954 (1980: 89), 1956 (1980: 110–11), Kuiper 1967a: 82–91, Tikkanen 1987: 284–96, Talageri 1993: 147–55, Hamp 1996, Hock 1996: 49–53. Now, if one operates with a change of the type PIE **liĝh-to-* > *līḍha-* – generally portrayed as taking place through a series of intermediate stages (**ližḍha-* > **ližḍha-* > **liẓḍha-*, see Kuiper 1967b: 119, Hamp 1996: 722–3, Hock 1996: 49) – and presupposes that the change type *-Vžḍh-* > *-V̄ḍh-* by way of *-Vẓḍh-* took place in pre-Vedic Indo-Aryan, then the phonemic contrast between dental and retroflex stops is established for this period. It is also not crucial that the retraction in question have originally resulted in true retroflex consonants known from earliest phonetic descriptions. For even if the changes which affected sequences of the type **-Vžḍh-* led to merely retracted – say alveolar – stops, once the loss of the spirant, with compensatory lengthening, took place, the result was a contrast between dental and retracted consonants. I doubt that any one would wish to maintain that at some time in Indo-Aryan after these changes there was no contrast between the type *līḍha-*, *ūḍha-* and *īdhe*, *ūdhar*. Moreover, other developments led to additional instances of contrastive retroflexion. Thus, the nominative singular of the base *sah* 'one who prevails over' is *ṣāṭ*, with *ṣ-*, which is also found in the word for 'six' (*ṣaṣ-*: nom.-acc. pl. *ṣaṭ*, instr. pl. *ṣaḍbhiḥ*).

After these contrasts were established, of course, Indo-Aryan speakers could borrow lexical items from languages which had contrastive retroflexion, without adaptive replacement of retroflexes by dentals. If these Indo-Aryan speakers already had true retroflexes, they could adopt lexical items as such, and speakers of other languages in contact with them could be not only the source of borrowings with such retroflexes but also borrowers of terms with dentals that were retained in the borrowings. In addition, from very early on there were dialects of Indo-Aryan in which a development typical of Middle Indic took place, whereby *-r̥-* was replaced by a different vowel and a following dental was retracted and clusters *-rt(h)-*, *-rd(h)-* developed to *-ṭṭh-* and *-ḍḍh-*. Such items also could be borrowed in standard Old Indo-Aryan without replacement. Moreover, one has to accept that there are numerous instances of what has been called spontaneous retroflexion, such that a retroflex consonant occurs instead of a dental from Vedic times on without any of the conditions noted (see Wackernagel 1896: 172–3, Burrow 1971); e.g. *dī* : *ḍī* 'fly', *at* : *aṭ* 'go about, wander'.

If, on the other hand, Indo-Aryan speakers had only the sort of retracted consonants noted, the influence of the lending language(s) could be presumed greater, though still only phonetic and not phonemic: borrowings would now be considered the sources for changing earlier retracted consonants to true retroflexes. A generation of bilingual speakers would take the Indo-Aryan terms with retracted stops, convert them to items with true retroflexes and pass this system on to the next generation. In either case, I think it most plausible to operate with a scenario such that Indo-Aryan speakers interacting with speakers of non-Indo-Aryan in a situation of bilingualism and diglossia that did not involve cultural, technical or military domination of either group (Southworth 1979: 191), borrowed from and lent to the languages of these speakers (cf. Hock 1996). This accounts for the steady increase in non-Indo-European terms with retroflexes.

As to what non-Indo-Aryan languages are concerned, obvious candidates are Dravidian and Munda languages. The number of such borrowings into early Indo-Aryan has been the topic of ongoing debate. Some scholars (e.g. Das 1995) have objected to the efforts of colleagues in tracing non-Indo-Aryan borrowing due to language contact. In my opinion, one of the scholars in question has himself (Kuiper 1995) effectively answered the objections. Moreover, even some who object to Dravidian or Munda origins for particular terms finally admit a substantial number of borrowings (e.g. Oberlies 1994). In the most recent contribution to this topic, Witzel (1999a) has made the interesting observation that the earliest parts of the *R̥gveda*, what he calls level I (1999a: §0.3), has no Dravidian loanwords and that such borrowings start to appear in the middle and late *R̥gveda* (1999a: §§1.1, 1.6). 'Instead', he says (1999a: §1.1), 'we find ... some three hundred words from one or more unknown language(s), especially one working with prefixes.' In view of this structural property, Witzel refers to the substrate in question as Para-Munda. I am not competent to judge details concerning Munda or "Para-Munda" materials, but one should note that Witzel himself (1999a: §1.2) says, 'It must be stressed that neither the commonly found Drav. nor Munda etymologies are up to the present standard of linguistic analysis, where both the root and all affixes are explained. This is why most of the subsequent etymologies have to be regarded as preliminary.' In addition, although Witzel gives a long list of Vedic terms in which he sees Para-Munda prefixes, he does not, so far as I can see, give examples of entire words demonstrably borrowed from Munda and which could have served as a basis for abstracting prefixes. Moreover, while asking rhetorically, 'Is the Indus language therefore a kind of Proto-Munda?' Witzel (1999a: §1.3) admits, 'Against this may speak first of all, as Kuiper states (1991), that the RV substrate does not have infixes like Munda.'

2.2.3.2 Other features

It is also worth noting that Witzel's major claim concerns loanwords. For there are also grammatical features of Old Indo-Aryan, not so limited in their early R̥gvedic occurrence, which scholars have seen as due to borrowing from Dravidian. One of these is the use of absolutives instead of participial subordinate clauses, a construction that is not limited to the later strata of the *R̥gveda*.

This construction has been the object of a great many studies, a good survey of which appears in the work of Tikkanen (1987: 37–75), who also (1987: 265–77) discusses Indo-European parallels. As has been recognized, the affixes in question reflect Indo-European materials, but the syntax in question is undoubtedly an Indo-Aryan innovation in the sense that it is here that this construction became obligatory, finally disallowing a subordinate participial construction (cf. Kuiper 1991: 10). Similarly, *iti*, used as a quotative particle, has an Indo-European pedigree, but in contrast even with Iranian, Skt. *iti* regularly follows the cited utterance (see Kuiper 1967a: 91–5, 98–102).

2.2.3.3 Conclusions

Whatever else one might think, the evidence in question is best explained as reflecting the influence on Indo-Aryan of non-Indo-Aryan languages. It is stretching things to say that, because contrastive retroflex consonants can be accounted for in part on the basis of regular historical developments from Indo-European, and because early Indo-Aryan shows traces of a participial subordinate construction, and because *iti* has an Indo-European etymology, the pertinent features characteristic of Indo-Aryan developed independently of any extraneous influences. The types of interaction evident in the earliest Indo-Aryan sources, moreover, make it plausible to conjecture that initially there was bilingualism and that subsequently Indo-Aryan gained a cultural ascendancy in particular spheres such that non-Indo-Aryan speakers – in particular Dravidians – adopted Indo-Aryan speech, which they influenced (cf. Krishnamurti 1969: 324).

On the other hand, it is also a fact that one cannot explain all the factors in question, especially a great many lexical items (cf. Masica 1979), purely on the basis of known Dravidian and Austro-Asiatic languages. Scholars have therefore also accepted the probability of there being substrate(s) of other kinds (recently, Tikkanen 1987: 322, 1988).

3 THE HOMELAND QUESTION

For some time it was believed that the Indo-Aryans invaded the subcontinent, subduing original inhabitants – in particular that Indo-Aryans destroyed fortifications of the Indus Valley civilization – and some Vedic passages were invoked in support of this view. Later research showed this to be incorrect, that the Indus Valley civilization did not collapse suddenly and that it was not overrun by invading Indo-Aryans (Dyson 1993: 572–7). Instead, scholars have come to accept that the Indo-Aryans either migrated into the subcontinent gradually, without any invasion or physical overthrow of an earlier civilization, or were there as original inhabitants. Under the second hypothesis, scholars have also accepted that the Indus Valley civilization (referred to as the Indus-Sarasvati civilization) was Indo-Aryan. As a consequence, they maintain also that the earliest Old Indo-Aryan corpus, the *Ṛgveda*, is much older than the date commonly assigned to it – around 1500 BC.

Under the first hypothesis, the following represents what many if not all modern scholars would accept as a reasonable position:

> The original location of the Indo-Iranian group was probably to the north of modern Afghanistan, east of the Caspian sea, in the area which is now Turkmenistan, Uzbekistan, and Tajikistan, where Iranian languages are still spoken. From there, some Iranians migrated to the south and west, the Indo-Aryans to the south and east. From geographical references in the earliest Indo-Aryan literary document, the *Ṛgveda*, it is clear that the earliest settlement of Indo-Aryans was in the northwest of the Indian subcontinent. Migration did not take place at once. It is now generally accepted that there was doubtless a series of migrations, although the view that an Indo-Aryan invasion took place was once seriously entertained. The date of entry of the Indo-Aryans into the Indian

subcontinent cannot be determined precisely, though the beginning of the second millennium BC is plausible and generally accepted. (Cardona in press b, cf. 1974: 439)

A variation on this general view – accounting for the presence of Indo-Aryans in the Middle East in the middle of the second millennium BC (see Mayrhofer 1966) – has an early group of Indo-Aryans, representing a southern group of Proto-Indo-Iranian, occupying a broad stretch of territory:

> At this time the north-western part of the Indian subcontinent was only a part of the territory occupied by the southern half of the Aryans, and from here it stretched into eastern Iran and across the northern part of central and western Iran to within striking distance of the Near East. To the north, in Central Asia, lay the Iranians, who, beginning about 1400 BC, moved south and by degrees took over the territory previously occupied by the Proto-Indoaryans. (Burrow 1973: 140)

The contending views have given rise to protracted debates, ably surveyed by Bryant (1997, 1999, 2001), and a large number of monographs arguing against the immigration thesis has appeared in recent years: Talageri 1993, Feuerstein, Kak and Frawley 1995, Rajaram 1995, Rajaram and Frawley 1997, and Elst 1999 are representative, as are most of the papers in Deo and Kamath 1993 (with the exception of Mehendale 1993 and Mukerjee 1993). The most recent works known to me representing the thesis that Indo-Aryans migrated into the subcontinent are Kochar 1999, Sharma 1999 and Witzel (in press).

As has been generally recognized, the chronology usually accepted for the Ṛgveda is not assured by definitive textual evidence. Indeed, earlier scholars without any possible connection with questions about an Indus Valley or Indus-Sarasvatī civilization had concluded that the Ṛgveda had to be dated much earlier than was usually accepted (e.g. Jacobi 1893, 1894, 1895, 1896); arguments based on information concerning the positions of asterisms according to Vedic texts have very recently come to the fore once more (Narahari Achar 1999, Witzel 1999b). It has also to be admitted that the archaeological evidence available does not serve to confirm Indo-Aryan migrations into the subcontinent.

Moreover, there is no textual evidence in the early literary traditions unambiguously showing a trace of such migration. To be sure, one passage has been invoked as definite evidence. In view of the importance given to this passage, it is worth considering with care:

> *sāyuṁ cāmāvasuṁ ca janayāṁ cakāra. sā hovāca : imau bibhṛtemau sarvam āyur eṣyata iti. prāṅ āyuḥ pravavrāja. tasyaite kurupañcālāḥ kāśividehā iti. etad āyavaṁ pravrājam. pratyaṅ amāvasuḥ. tasyaite gāndhāraya sparśavo 'rāṭṭā iti. etad āmāvasavam* (BŚS 18.44 [Caland 1904–13: 397.8–12]) 'She (Urvaśī) gave birth to Āyu and Amāvasu. And she said: take care of these two; they will reach their full life span. Āyu went eastward. Of him there are these: the Kuru-Pañcālas, the Kāśi-Videhas. This is the going forth of Āyu. Amāvasu (went) westward. Of him there are these: the Gāndhāris, the Sparśa, and the Arāṭṭas. This is the (going forth) of Amāvasu.'

The passage concerns the legend of Purūravas and Urvaśī, specifically her allowing two offspring to live after doing away with previous children who had been borne to her. The syntax of this passage is straightforward but calls for a few comments in light of the manner in which it has been interpreted. *pravavrāja* (3sg. act. perf.) 'went forth, wandered' is used explicitly in *prāṅ āyuḥ pravavrāja*, which specifies not only an agent but also a place: the nominative singular *prāṅ* 'facing east' indicates the direction in which Āyu went forth. Obviously, he must have gone forth from the place where he originated. As a parallel, note the repeated use of *sa ha tata eva ... pra vavrāja* 'From there he (Bhṛgu, son of Varuṇa) went ...' – with *tataḥ* 'thence' and *prāṅ* 'directed to the east', *dakṣiṇā* 'south', *pratyaṅ* 'directed to the west', *udaṅ* 'directed to the north' – in the *Śatapathabrāhmaṇa* (SBr. 11.6.1.3–6). *pratyaṅ amāvasuḥ* does not have an overt verb form, but according to normal rules of syntax *pravavrāja* is to be understood from the preceding context. Compare, for example, SBr. 7.4.1.35: *paścād agneḥ prāṅ āsīnothottarato dakṣiṇātha puraṣtāt pratyaṅ ... (ājyena juhoti 34)* 'Seated to the west of the fire, facing east, (the yajamāna offers ghee to the image of a man), then (seated) to the north (of the fire, facing) south, then (seated) to the east, facing west ...'), where *ājyena juhoti* 'offers ghee', *agneḥ* 'of the fire', and the participle *āsīnaḥ* (nom. sg. m.) 'seated' are understood in subsequent instructions. Accordingly, *pratyaṅ amāvasuḥ* is to be understood as saying that Amāvasu went west, the direction opposite to that which Āyu took. The text thus speaks of two wanderings, and syntax requires one to supply in *etad āmāvasavam* the term *pravrājam* 'going forth', from the earlier phrase *etad āyavaṃ pravrājam*.

Witzel, however, has interpreted this passage differently. According to him, this says that Amāvasu, whose name is to be understood etymologically (*amā-vasu-* 'stay-at-home'), remained in the west while Āyu (etymologically 'who goes') migrated east:

> In the case of ancient N. India, we do not know anything about the immigration of various tribes and clans, except for a few elusive remarks in the RV, ŚB or BŚS. This text retains at 18.44: 397.9 sqq. the most pregnant memory, perhaps, of an immigration of the Indo-Aryans into Northern India and of their split into two groups: *prāṅ Ayuḥ* [sic] *pravavrāja. tasyaite Kuru-Pañcālāḥ Kāśī-Videhā ity. etad Āyavam. Pratyaṅ amāvasus tasyaite Gāndhārayas *Parśavo 'raṭṭā* [sic] *ity. etad Āmāvasavam.* 'Ayu went eastwards. His (people) are the Kuru-Pañcāla and the Kāśī-Videha. This is the Āyava migration. (His other people) stayed at home in the West. His people are the Gāndhārī, Parśu and Aratta. This is the Amāvasava (group)'. (Witzel 1989: 235)
>
> Taking a look at the data relating to the immigration of Indo-Aryans into South Asia, one is struck by the number of vague reminiscences of foreign localities and tribes in the Ṛgveda, in spite of repeated assertions to the contrary in the secondary literature. Then, there is the following direct statement contained in the (admittedly late) BŚS, 18.44: 397.9 sqq which has once again been overlooked, not having been translated yet: 'Ayu went eastwards. His (people) are the Kuru-Pañcāla and the Kāśī-Videha. This is the Āyava (migration). (His other people) stayed at home in the West. His people are the Gāndhārī, Parśu and Aratta. This is the Amāvasava (group)'. (Witzel 1995b: 320–1).

Later, Witzel (1995b: 328–29) comes back to the same point:

> The Pūru appear to be a broad conglomerate of tribes, to which at one time the Bharatas also belonged. They could boast, even in the Ṛgveda, of a long royal genealogy (see below) with a possible side branch. Both they and the Bharatas seem to belong to the Āyu, whom the BŚS (quoted above) described as the ancestors of the Āyava tribes: i.e. the ones (Kuru-Pañcāla, Kosala-Videha) who 'moved forward' [from the northwest of South Asia into the heartland], instead of

'staying behind' as the Āmāvāsya [sic] tribes (Gandhāri, Araṭa [sic], Parśu) did. As I have just related, they (along with the Bharatas) occupy centre-stage in much of the Ṛgveda, succeeding earlier groups of migrants such as the Turvaśa and the Yadu.

It is beyond dispute that the interpretation Witzel gives to this passage does not accord with its syntax. This was pointed out, though without considering details, by Elst (1998, similarly 1999: 164–5). In an e-mail message kindly conveyed to me by S. Kalyanaraman (11 April 1999), Witzel reacted to Elst's objection and amended his rendition, referring to a passage from a forthcoming paper, where he translates, 'Āyu went (ay/i : pra-vraj) eastwards. His (people) are the Kuru-Pañcāla and the Kāśī-Videha. This is the Āyava (group). Amāvasu (stayed at home, amā vas) in the West. His (people) are the Gāndhārī, Parśu and Araṭṭa. This is the Āmāvasyava [sic] (group).' Even this, however, fails to meet the requirements of syntax. Although at least one scholar has accepted Witzel's interpretation of the Baudhāyanaśrautasūtra passage (Sharma 1999: 87–9), then, one must conclude that, without resort to unwarranted liberty of interpretation, this text cannot serve to document an Indo-Aryan migration into the main part of the subcontinent. Witzel also notes (1995b: 338–9) that the Yadu-Turvaśa and the Anu-Druhyu had been established in the Panjab by the time the Ṛgveda was composed and that, 'They retain only the dimmest recollection of their move into South Asia ...'

If there is no clear textual evidence showing early Indo-Aryan remembrance of a migration, it is also the case that major arguments put forth by those who maintain that the Indo-Aryans were indigenous to the subcontinent are not cogent. As noted, many of these authors either maintain or strongly suspect that the Indus-Sarasvatī civilization was Indo-Aryan, and it has been argued that the Brāhmī script developed from the script of this civilization, a thesis which had been advanced earlier also (see Salomon 1998: 20–1). Thus, for example, concluding the "Aryan invasion model" to be antiquated, because of recent archaeological findings, Feuerstein, Kak and Frawley say (1995: 135):

> With the retirement of that model due to the new archaeological evidence and the reinterpretation of the Vedic scriptures, the world of scholarship must now confront the revolutionary fact that the language on the seals and other artifacts is very probably Indo-European after all.

They go on (1995: 136–8) to argue that the Brāhmī script should be considered to derive from the Indus-Sarasvati writing and, without citing samples of evidence, assert (1995: 138), 'Furthermore, a structural analysis of the inscriptions indicates that the texts on the steatite seals follow grammatical rules like that [sic] of Sanskrit', although they immediately go on to say, 'Nevertheless, one cannot claim that the script has been deciphered.' The principal thesis is advanced with a combination of caution and daring (Feuerstein, Kak and Frawley 1995: 138):

> Of course, the demonstration that Brahmi is derived from the Indus-Sarasvati script does not, by itself, establish that the urbanites from Mohenjo-Daro and Harappa were Indo-Aryan. Yet, the structural similarities in the Indus-Sarasvati and the Brahmi texts do point to that conclusion. This, in turn, reinforces the other continuities between the Indus-Sarasvati culture and the Vedic peoples that the archaeological discoveries of the past few decades have revealed.

They also admit (1995: 138) 'the possibility that some of the Harappan inscriptions may be in a non-Indo-European language'.

Now, to say that 'a structural analysis' of seals indicates that these texts reflect grammatical rules like those of Sanskrit is to make a major claim that is difficult to reconcile with saying, 'one cannot claim that the script has been deciphered'. Moreover, Feuerstein, Kak and Frawley neither give any sample to demonstrate how the texts on the steatite seals follows rules like those of Sanskrit nor refer to any work in which such a demonstration has been carried out. In the absence of such demonstration, we are faced with an unsupported assertion. In another context, Feuerstein, Kak and Frawley (1995: 109) argue that '... the Vedic peoples did not come as conquerors and destroyers from outside India, but lived in and even built the cities in the Land of the Seven Rivers', in support of which they say, 'God Agni (associated with fire) is invoked to protect the Aryans with a hundred cities.' They do not cite any text explicitly but refer (1995: 293 notes 10, 11) to four Ṛgvedic passages where forms of *pur* are used and to a passage (pp. 327–30) from a book by D. Frawley (unfortunately not accessible to me) where Vedic cities are discussed. In view of the importance this claim has for the type of civilization envisioned, it would have been proper to discuss and refute Rau's use of Vedic sources (1976, 1983: 35–8, 1997), in particular his conclusion (1976: 52) that *pur* does not refer to the cities of the Indus Valley civilization.

Accepting the thesis that Indo-Aryans were indigenous to the subcontinent also entails accepting that Indo-Aryan originated here. In turn, as Hock notes (1999: 1), this can be reconciled with the relation of Indo-Aryan to other Indo-European languages under either of two views: (a) the other Indo-European languages derive from Proto-Indo-Aryan, or (b) Proto-Indo-European, from which Proto-Indo-Aryan and other Indo-European groups descend, was originally spoken in the Indian subcontinent. S. S. Misra (1992) has argued for (a), maintaining that Vedic should be considered to represent the Proto-Indo-European system. Hock (1999) has rebutted Misra's arguments. In particular, it is very difficult to see how the Vedic vowel system could account for the alternation of velars and palatals as in *kṛ* : *cakārà* (see section 2.1.1), a point concerning which Elst (1999: 124) too finds it best to accept that Indo-Iranian has innovated. Thesis (b) is most explicitly stated by Talageri (1993: 144): 'The most logical interpretation of the evidence and the facts, is that the original homeland of the Indo-European language lay in India.' Hock (1999: 11–17), who alludes to Feuerstein, Kak and Frawley 1995: 155, takes up this possibility and presents (1999: 16–17) what I consider the chief difficulty involved:

> What would have to be assumed is that the various Indo-European languages moved out of India in such a manner that they maintained their relative position to each other during and after the migration. However, given the bottle-neck nature of the route(s) out of India, it would be immensely difficult to do so.

In the present state of knowledge, it is fair to say that the strongest arguments for assuming Indo-Aryans to have migrated into the subcontinent is linguistic. For the archaeological evidence available to date has not sufficed to establish either of the competing theses. The point may be illustrated with the role played in the discussion by evidence concerning the horse denoted by the Sanskrit term *áśva-* (PIE **eḱwe/o-*). It is known from the earliest texts that Vedic Indo-Aryans both used horses yoked (*yuj* 'join, yoke') to chariots (*ratha-*) and rode them. For example, Ṛ V 2.34.8 (*yad yuñjate marutò ... aśvān rathèṣu*) speaks of when the Maruts yoke (*yuñjate* [3pl. mid. pres.]) their horses (*aśvān* [acc. pl.]) to their chariots (*rathèṣu* [loc. pl.]) and in another Ṛgvedic passage (6.16.43: *agnè yukṣvā hi ye tavā́śvāso deva sadhavàḥ*) Agni is asked to yoke (*yukṣva* [2sg. aor. imper. mid.]) his horses (*ye tavā́śvāsaḥ* 'your horses' [nom. pl.]), which are capable of carrying out what is to be done (*sādhavaḥ*). A hymn to the Maruts speaks not only of a saddle (*sadas*) on the back (*pṛṣṭhe*) of their horses, a restraining rope (*yamaḥ*) through their nostrils (*nasoḥ*: RV 5.61.2c: *pṛṣṭhe sadò nasor yamàḥ*), and a whip (*codaḥ*) at their hind quarters (*jaghane*, RV 5.61.3a: *jaghane codà eṣā́m*), but also pictures the Maruts (*naraḥ* 'powerful men' [nom. pl.]) as having spread (*vi ... yamuḥ* [3pl. aor.]) their thighs (*sakthā́ni*) as women (*janayaḥ*) spread their thighs in producing a child (*putrakṛthe*, RV 5.61.3bc: *vi sakthā́ni naro yamuḥ | putrakṛthe na janàyaḥ*). Those who maintain that the Indo-Aryan migrated into the subcontinent point to the absence of evidence of the horse in the Indus Valley/Sarasvatī-Sindhu materials. Thus, Parpola (1988: 196) says, 'A major reason against assuming that the Harappans spoke an Indo-European language is that the horse is not represented among the many realistically depicted animals of the Harappan seals and figurines' and refers (1988: 196 note 12) to the absence of 'clear osteological evidence of the horse (*Equus caballus*) in the Indian subcontinent prior to *c.* 2000 BC'. On the other hand, a recognized expert in the field claimed to have established the existence of such evidence (Bökönyi 1997). Other authoritative experts, however, have presented arguments for doubting Bökönyi's claim (see Meadow and Patel 1997 with references).

To be sure, one may dismiss the method of comparative linguistics as 'a failed paradigm' (Rajaram 1995: 144–5) without further ado. Then further discussion is without purpose. Yet there is linguistic evidence which should not be ruled out of court. Moreover, to have Indo-Aryans come into the subcontinent and give rise therein to a magnificent culture of enormous achievement does no disservice to them or their past.

Fortunately for those contributing to this volume, our task begins with Old Indo-Aryan in full bloom with early Vedic, and we can go on from there to view a long and rewarding history and present state of a major group of languages.

ACKNOWLEDGEMENTS

Sections 1.1–1.2 of this chapter were originally written by Dhanesh Jain, who also produced tables 1.1 and 1.2 and figures 1.1 and 1.2; George Cardona composed the remaining sections. Both authors, however, are responsible for the final form of the chapter. We thank Elena Bashir, Henry Hoenigswald, Hans Hock and Bhadriraju Krishnamurti for their careful reading of and comments on drafts of this chapter, as well as Franklin C. Southworth for sending Cardona a copy of chapters 5 and 6 of his forthcoming work, in which he treats subgrouping. Since Southworth's book has yet to be published, we thought it inappropriate to enter into details concerning his arguments. See now Southworth 2005.

REFERENCES

[Works not available to the authors at the time of writing are marked with an asterisk.]

AiĀr	*Aitareyāraṇyaka* (Apte)
Aś	Aśokan
Aśokan/Pāli	'Aśokan Prakrit and Pāli' in this volume
Aṣṭādhyāyī	References to chapter, quarter-chapter and rule according to the text in Cardona 1997: 607–731
Bh.	*Mahābhāṣya* (Abhyankar)

BŚS	*Baudhāyanaśrautasūtra*: (Caland)
DB	Darius, Bagistan (Behistun) (Kent)
DhP	*Dhammapada* (Hinüber and Norman)
DN	*Dīghanikāya*
Erz.	Erzählungen (Jacobi)
G	Girnār (Bloch 1950)
GDhS	*Gautamadharmasūtra* (Kale)
J	Jaugaḍa (Bloch 1950)
Jātaka	Fausbøll
JM	Jainamāhārāstrī (Jacobi)
JS	*Jaiminisūtra* (Abhyankar and Joshi)
Mbh.	*Mahābhārata* (Sukthankar et al.)
Nir.	*Nirukta*: (Bhadkambkar)
NŚ	*Nāṭyasāstra* (Joshi)
PC	*Paümacariu* (Bhayani)
Prākrits	'Prākrits and Apabhraṁśa' in this volume
PrPr.	*Prākṛtaprakāśa* (Upādhyāya)
PŚ	*Pāṇinīyaśikṣā* (Giri)
Rām.	*Rāmāyaṇa* (Bhatt et al.)
RE	Aśokan Rock edict (Bloch 1950)
ṚV	*Ṛgveda*: (Sontakke et al.)
Sanskrit	'Sanskrit' in this volume
ŚBh.	*Śābarabhāṣya*: (Abhyankar and Joshi)
ŚBr.	*Śatapathabrāhmaṇa*
TPr.	*Taittirīyaprātiśākhya* (Sham Sastri and Rangacarya)

Abbi, Anvita (1997 [1998]) 'Debate on archaism of some select Bangani words', *Indian Linguistics* 58: 1–14.

Abhyankar, Kashinath Vasudev (1962–72) *The Vyākaraṇa-mahābhāṣya of Patañjali, edited by Franz Kielhorn, third edition* ... (3 vols.), Poona: Bhandarkar Oriental Research Institute.

Abhyankar, Kashinath Vasudev and Joshi, Ganesh Ambadas (1976) *Śrījaiminipraṇītaṁ Mīmāṁsādarśanam* ... (7 vols.) (Ānandāśrama Sanskrit Series 97), Pune: Ānandāśrama.

Acharya, Krishna Chandra (1968) *Mārkaṇḍeya's Prākṛta-Sarvasya ... Critically edited with Introduction, Variant Readings and useful Indices etc.* (Prakrit Text Society Series XI, Prakrit Grammar Series I), Ahmedabad: Prakrit Text Society.

Alsdorf, Ludwig (1960) 'Contributions to the study of Aśoka's inscriptions', in *Sushil Kumar De Felicitation Volume* (*Bulletin of the Deccan College Research Institute* 20), Poona: Deccan College, pp. 249–75. (Reprinted (1974) in Wezler, Albrecht (ed.), *Ludwig Alsdorf: Kleine Schriften* (Glasenap-Stiftung Band 10), Wiesbaden: Steiner, pp. 428–54.)

Anonymous a (nd) 'India at a glance: languages spoken', http://www.censusindia.net/language. html.

Anonymous b (nd) 'Census data online, table 26: three main languages in every state, 1991', http://www.censusindia.net/cendat/languagemenu.html.

Anthony, David (1997) 'Current thoughts on the domestication of the horse in Asia', *South Asian Studies* 13: 315–16.

Apte, Hari Narayana (1898) *Aitareyāraṇyakam* (Ānandāśrama Sanskrit Series 38), Poona: Ānandāśrama.

Bhadkamkar, H. M. (1918) *The Nirukta of Yāska* (*with Nighaṇṭu*) *edited with Durga's Commentary*, by ... assisted by R. G. Bhadkamkar, volume I (Reprinted (1985) Poona: Bhandarkar Oriental Research Institute).

Bhatt, G. H. et al. (1960–72) *The Vālmīki-Rāmāyaṇa Critically Edited for the First Time* (7 vols.), Baroda: Oriental Institute.

Bhayani, H. C. (1953–60) *Svayambhūdeva's Paümacariu* (3 vols., Singhi Jain Series 34, 35, 36), Bombay: Bharatiya Vidya Bhavan.

Bloch, Jules (1924) 'Sanskrit et Dravidien', *Bulletin de la Société Linguistique de Paris* 25: 1–21 (Reprinted in Caillat (1985), pp. 81–101).

—— (1930) 'Some problems of Indo-Aryan philology: Forlong Lectures for 1929', *Bulletin of the School of Oriental Studies* 5: 719–56 (Reprinted in Caillat (1985), pp. 183–220).

—— (1934) *L'Indo-aryen du veda aux temps modernes*, Paris: Adrien-Maisonneuve.

—— (1950) *Les inscription d'Aśoka traduites et commentées* (Collection Emile Senart 8), Paris: «Société d'Édition Les Belles Lettres».

Bloch-Master: see Master, Alfred (1965).

Bloomfield, Maurice and Edgerton, Franklin (1932) *Vedic Variants: A Study of the Variant Readings in the Repeated Mantras of the Veda*, Volume II: *Phonetics*, Philadelphia: University of Pennsylvania.

Bökönyi, Sándor (1997) 'Horse remains from the prehistoric site of Surkotada, Kutch, late 3rd millennium BC', *South Asian Studies* 13: 297–307.

Breton, Roland J.-L. (1999) *Atlas of the Languages and Ethnic Communities of South Asia*, New Delhi: Sage.

Bronkhorst, Johannes and Deshpande, Madhav M. (eds.) (1999) *Aryan and Non-Aryan in South Asia: Evidence, Interpretation and Ideology* (Harvard Oriental Series Opera Minora volume 3), Cambridge, MA: Department of Sanskrit and Indian Studies, Harvard University.

Bryant, Edwin Francis (1997) The Indigenous Aryan Debate, Columbia University doctoral dissertation.

—— (1999) 'Linguistic substrata and the indigenous Aryan debate', in Bronkhorst and Deshpande (eds.), pp. 59–84.

Buddruss, Georg (1977) 'Nochmals zur Stellung der Nuristan-Sprachen des afghanistanischen Hindukusch', *Münchener Studien zur Sprachwissenschaft* 36: 19–38.

Burrow, T. (1971) 'Spontaneous cerebrals in Sanskrit', *Bulletin of the School of Oriental Studies* 34: 538–59.

—— (1973) 'The Proto-Indoaryans', *Journal of the Royal Asiatic Sociey* 1973: 123–40.

Caillat, Colette (ed.) (1985) *Recueil d'articles de Jules Bloch, 1906–1955* (Publications de l'Institut de Civilisation Indienne, Série in–8°, fascicule 52), Paris: Collège de France, Institut de Civilisation Indienne.

—— (ed.) (1989a) *Dialectes dans les littératures indo-aryennes, Actes du colloque international organisé par l'UA 1058 sous les auspices du C.N.R.S. . . .* (Publications de l'Institut de Civilisation Indienne, série in–8°, fascicule 55), Paris: Collège de France, Institut de Civilisation Indienne.

—— (1989b) 'Sur l'authenticité linguistique des édits d'Asoka', in Caillat (ed.) 1989a, pp. 413–32.

Caland, W. (1904–13) *The Baudhāyana Śrauta Sūtra belonging to the Taittirīya Saṃhitā*, Calcutta: Asiatic Society (Reprinted (1982) in two volumes with a new appendix, Delhi: Munshiram Manoharlal).

Cardona, George (1974) 'Indo-Iranian languages', in *Encyclopædia Britannica* fifteenth edition, Chicago: University of Chicago, volume 9, pp. 438–9.

—— (1976) *Pāṇini, A Survey of Research* (Trends in Linguistics, State of the Art Reports), The Hague and Paris: Mouton (Indian edition (1980): Delhi: Motilal Banarsidass, reprinted 1997).

—— (1991) 'On the dialect status of Vedic forms of the types *dakṣ-* / *dhakṣ-*, in Lakshmi Bai, B. and Ramakrishna Reddy, B. (eds.) *Studies in Dravidian and General Linguistics, A Festschrift for Bh. Krishnamurti* (Osmania University Publications in Linguistics 6), pp. 263–73.

—— (1993) 'The bhāṣika accentuation system', *Studien zur Indologie und Iranistik* 18: 1–40.

—— (1997) *Pāṇini: His Work and its Traditions, Part I: General Introduction and Background* (second edition, revised and enlarged), Delhi: Motilal Banarsidass.

—— (1999) 'Approaching the Vākyapadīya', *Journal of the American Oriental Society* 119: 88–125.

—— (in press a) 'Pāṇinian sūtras of the type *anyebhyo 'pi dṛśyate*', Jambuvijaya felicitation volume. [See now Cardona (2004)]

—— (in press b) 'Indo-Iranian languages', in *Encyclopædia Britannica*. [Revised version of Cardona (1974).]

Census of India (1991). Language, Series 1 – India, Paper 1 of 1997, New Delhi: Registrar General of India.

Chatterji, Suniti Kumar (1926) *The Origin and Development of the Bengali Language* (2 vols.), Calcutta: Calcutta University Press (Reprinted (1970) (3 vols.), London: Allen & Unwin, (1975), (3 vols.), Calcutta: Rupa & Co.). [The original work was in two volumes, continuously paginated. With the 1970 reprint, a third volume was added, containing supplementary additions and corrections. In the 1975 reprint, the additions and corrections originally included in volume II were incorporated in the supplementary volume, along with further additions and corrections as of 1971 and an index of Bengali words in Bangla script.]

—— (1953) 'A study of the New Indo-Aryan speech treated in the "Ukti-vyakti-prakaraṇa"', in Acharya Jina Vijaya Muni (ed.) *Ukti-vyakti-prakaraṇa of Pandita Damodara* [*An elementary handbook of Sanskrit composition with parallel illustrations in Old Kosali of the twelfth century*] (Singhi Jain Series 39), Bombay: Bharatiya Vidya Bhavan.

Das, Rahul Peter (1995) 'The hunt for foreign words in the Ṛgveda', *Indo-Iranian Journal* 38: 207–38.

Degener, Almuth (1998) *Die Sprache von Nisheygram im afghanischen Hindukusch* (Neuindische Studien 14), Wiesbaden: Harrassowitz.

Deo, S. D. and Kamath, Suryanath (eds.) (1993) *The Aryan Problem* [*Papers presented at the Seminar on the Aryan Problem held at Bangalore in July 1999*], Pune: Bharatiya Itihasa Sankalana Samiti.

Deshpande, Madhav M. (1979) 'Genesis of Ṛgvedic retroflexion: a historical and socio-linguistic investigation', in Deshpande and Hook (eds.), pp. 235–315 (Revised version in Deshpande, Madhav M. (1993) *Sanskrit & Prakrit Sociolinguistic Issues* [MLBD Series in Linguistics VI], Delhi: Motilal Banarsidass, pp. 129–211).

—— (1993) See 1979.

Deshpande, Madhav M. and Hook, Peter Edwin (1979) *Aryan and non-Aryan in India* (Michigan Papers on South and Southeast Asia 14), Ann Arbor: Center for South and Southeast Asian Studies, The University of Michigan.

Dil, Anwar S. (1980) *Language and Linguistic Area: Essays by Murray B. Emeneau, Selected and Introduced* ..., Stanford: Stanford University Press.

van Driem, George and Sharma, Suhnu R. (1996) 'In search of kentum Indo-Europeans in the Himalayas', *Indogermanische Forschungen* 101: 107–46.

—— (1997) 'Some grammatical observations on Bangani', *Indogermanische Forschungen* 102: 179–98.

Dyson, Robert H., Jr. (1993) 'Paradigm changes in the study of the Indus civilization', in Possehl (1993), pp. 571–81.

Edgerton, Franklin (1953) *Buddhist Hybrid Sanskrit Grammar and Dictionary, Volume I: Grammar*, New Haven: Yale University Press (Reprinted (1970), Delhi: Motilal Banarsidass).

Elst, Koenraad (1998) 'The Vedic corpus provides no evidence for the so-called Aryan invasion of India', http://members.xoom.com/_XMCM/KoenraadElst/articles/vedicevidence.html (22 October 1998).

—— (1999) *Update on the Aryan Invasion Debate*, New Delhi: Aditya Prakashan.

Emeneau, Murray B. (1954) 'Linguistic prehistory of India', *Proceedings of the American Philosophical Society* 98: 282–92 (Reprinted in Dil (1980), pp. 85–104 [reference to the reprint]).

—— (1956) 'India as a linguistic area', *Language* 32: 3–16 (Reprinted in Hymes, Dell (ed.), *Language in Culture and Society*, New York: Harper and Row, pp. 642–51, Dil (1980), pp. 105–25 [reference to the last reprint]).

—— (1962) 'Bilingualism and structural borrowing', *Proceedings of the American Philosophical Society* 106: 430–42 (Reprinted in Dil (1980), pp. 38–65 [reference to the reprint]).

—— (1966) 'The Dialects of Old Indo-Aryan', in Birnbaum, Henrik and Puhvel, Jaan (eds.), *Ancient Indo-European Dialects*, Los Angeles: University of California Press, pp. 123–38.

—— (1971) 'Dravidian and Indo-Aryan: the Indian linguistic area', in Sjoberg, Andrée F. (ed.) *Symposium on Dravidian Civilization*, Austin and New York: Jenkins Publishing Company and Pemberton Press, pp. 33–68 (Reprinted in Dil (1980), pp. 167–96 [reference to the reprint]).

—— (1974) 'The Indian linguistic area revisited', *International Journal of Dravidian Linguistics* 3: 92–134 (Reprinted in Dil (1980), pp. 92–134 [reference to the reprint]).

—— (1980) 'Linguistic area: introduction and continuation', in Dil (1980), pp. 1–18.

Erdosy, George (ed.) (1995) *The Indo-Aryans of Ancient South Asia, Language, Material Culture and Ethnicity*, Berlin: de Gruyter (Reprinted (1997), Delhi: Munshiram Manoharlal).

Fausbøll, V. (1962–4) *The Jātaka together with its Commentary, being Tales of the Anterior Births of Gotama Buddha, for the first time edited in the original Pāli* (6 vols.), London: Messrs Luzak & Company for the Pali Text Society.

Feuerstein, Georg, Kak, Subhash and Frawley, David (1995) *In Search of the Cradle of Civilization: New Light on Ancient India*, Wheaton, IL: Theosophical Publishers (Reprinted (1999), Delhi: Motilal Banarsidass).

Fussman, Gérard (1977) 'Pour une problématique nouvelle des religions indiennes anciennes', *Journal Asiatique* 265: 21–70.

Ghatage, A. M. (1962) *Historical Linguistics and Indo-Aryan Languages* (University of Bombay, Wilson Philological Lectures for the year 1957–58), Bombay: University of Bombay.

Giri, Goswami Prasad (1987) *Pāṇinīyaśikṣā of Pāṇini, Edited with 'Pradip' Sanskrit Commentary, Svaravaidic Panktivivarana, Notes of Pt. Rudraprasad Avasthi and 'Prahlad' Hindi Commentary* (Haridas Sanskrit Series 59), Varanasi: Chowkhamba Sanskrit Series Office.

Grierson, Sir George Abraham (1903–28) *Linguistic Survey of India* (11 vols. in 19), Calcutta: Office of the Superintendent of Government Printing. (Reprinted (1967–73), Delhi: Motilal Banarsidass). [The following are the contents directly related to Indo-Aryan: vol. I, pt. I (1927): Introductory, pt. II (1928): Comparative Vocabulary; vol. V, Indo-Aryan family, Eastern group: pt. I (1903): Specimens of the Bengali and Assamese languages, pt. II (1903): Specimens of the Bihārī and Oriyā languages; vol. VI (1904), Indo-Aryan family, Mediate group: Specimens of the eastern Hindi language; vol. VII (1905), Indo-Aryan family, Southern group: Specimens of the Marāṭhī language; vol. VIII (1919), Indo-Aryan family, Northwestern group: pt. I: Specimens of Sindhī and Lahndā; pt. II: Specimens of the Dardic or Piśācha languages (including Kāshmiri); vol. IX, Indo-Aryan family. Central group: pt. I (1916): Specimens of western Hindi and Pañjābī; pt. II (1908): Specimens of Rājasthāni and Gujarāti; pt. III (1907): The Bhīl languages, including Khāndēśi, Banjari or Labhānī, Bahrūpia, etc.; pt. IV (1916): Specimens of the Pahārī languages and Gujurī; vol. XI (1922): Gypsy languages.]

—— (1917–20a) 'Indo-Aryan vernaculars', *Bulletin of the School of Oriental Studies* 1.2: 47–81.

—— (1917–20b) 'Indo-Aryan vernaculars', *Bulletin of the School of Oriental Studies* 1.3: 51–85. [Continuation of (1917–20a).]

—— (1927) *Linguistic Survey of India, Volume I, Part I: Introductory*, Calcutta: Office of the Superintendent of Government Printing. (Reprinted (1973), Delhi: Motilal Banarsidass.)

Hamp, Eric P. (1996) 'On the Indo-European origins of the retroflexes in Sanskrit', *Journal of the American Oriental Society* 116: 719–23.

Hendriksen, Hans (1944) *Syntax of the Infinite Verb-forms of Pāli*, Copenhagen: Einar Munksgaard.

von Hinüber, Oskar (1986) *Das ältere Mittelindisch im Überblick* (Österreichische Akademie der Wissenschaften, Philosophisch-historische Klasse, Sitzungsberichte, 467. Band), Wien: Verlag der Österreichischen Akademie der Wissenschaften.

von Hinüber, Oskar and Norman, K. R. (1994) *Dhammapada, edited by ... with complete word index compiled by Shoko Tabata and Tetsuya Tabata*, Oxford: Pali Text Society.

Hock, Hans Henrich (1979) 'Retroflexion rules in Sanskrit', *South Asian Languages Analysis* 1: 47–62.

—— (1996) 'Pre-ṛgvedic convergence between Indo-Aryan and Dravidian? A survey of issues and controversies', in Houben, Jan E. M. (ed.), *Ideology & Status of Sanskrit: Contributions to the History of the Sanskrit Language*, Leiden: E. J. Brill, pp. 17–58.

—— (1999) 'Out of India? The linguistic evidence', in Bronkhorst and Deshpande (eds.), pp. 1–18.

—— (2000) 'Wem gehört die Vergangenheit? Früh- und Vorgeschichte und indische Selbst-wahrnehmung', in Bergunder, Michael and Dass, Rahul Peter (eds.) *"Arier" und "Draviden": Konstruktionen der Vergangenheit als Grundlage für Selbst- und Fremdwahrnehmungen* (Neue Hallesche Berichte, Bd. 2), Halle: Verlag der Franckeschen Stiftungen zu Halle, pp. 232–50.

Hoenigswald, Henry M. (1989) 'Overlong syllables in Ṛgvedic cadences', *Journal of the American Oriental Society* 109: 559–63.

Jackson, A. V. Williams (1892) *An Avesta Grammar in Comparison with Sanskrit, Part I: Phonology, Inflection, Word-formation, with an Introduction on the Avesta*, Stuttgart: W. Kohlhammer Verlag (Reprinted (1968), Darmstadt: Wissenschaftliche Buchgesellschaft).

Jacobi, Hermann (1886) *Ausgewählte Erzählungen in Mâhârâshṭrî: zur Einführung in das Studium des Prâkṛit*, Leipzig: Hirzel (Reprinted (1967), Darmstadt: Wissenschaftliche Buchgesellschaft).

—— (1893) 'Über das Alter des Rig-Veda', in *Festgruß an Rudolf von Roth*, pp. 68–74 (Reprinted in Kölver (1970), pp. 258–64).

—— (1894) 'On the date of the Rig-Veda', *Indian Antiquary* 23: 154–9.

—— (1895) 'Der vedische Kalender und das Alter des Veda', *Zeitschrift der Deutschen Morgenländischen Gesellschaft* 49: 218–30 (Reprinted in Kölver (1970), pp. 265–77).

—— (1896) 'Nochmals über das Alter des Veda', *Zeitschrift der Deutschen Morgenländischen Gesellschaft* 50: 69–83 (Reprinted in Kölver (1970), pp. 278–92).

Joshi, K. L. (1984) *Nāṭyaśāstra of Bharatamuni with the Commentary Abhinavabhāratī by Abhinavaguptacharya*, vol. II: *Chapters 8–18* (Parimal Sanskrit Series 4), Delhi: Parimal Publications.

Kale, Gangadhar Rao (1966) *Gautamapraṇītadharmasūtrāṇi* (Ānandāśrama Sanskrit Series 61), Pune: Ānandāśrama.

Kane, Pandurang Vaman (1968–77) *History of Dharmaśāstra (Ancient and Mediæval Religious and Civil Law in India)* (2nd ed., 5 vols.), Poona: Bhandarkar Oriental Research Institute.

Kent, Roland G. (1953) *Old Persian: Grammar, Texts, Lexicon*, second edition, revised (American Oriental Series 33), New Haven: American Oriental Society (Reprinted 1989).

*Kochar, Rajesh (1999) *The Vedic People, Their History and Geography*, Delhi: Orient Longman.

Kölver, Bernhard (1970) *Hermann Jacobi: Kleine Schriften* (2 vols., Glasenapp-Stiftung Band 4,1–4,2), Wiesbaden: Franz Steiner Verlag.

Krishnamurti, Bhadriraju (1969) 'Comparative Dravidian studies', in Sebeok, Thomas A. (ed.), *Current Trends in Linguistics, Volume 5: Linguistics in South Asia*. The Hague and Paris: Mouton, pp. 309–33.

—— (1991) 'The emergence of the syllable types of stems (C)VCC(V) and (C)V̄C(V) in Indo-Aryan and Dravidian: conspiracy or convergence?', in Boltz, William G. and Shapiro, Michael C (eds.) *Historical Phonology of Asian Languages*, Amsterdam, Philadelphia: John Benjamins, pp. 160–75.

Kuiper, F. B. J. (1967a) 'The genesis of a linguistic area', *Indo-Iranian Journal* 10: 81–102 (Reprinted in Lubotsky et al. (eds.), pp. 78–99).
—— (1967b) 'The Sanskrit nom. sg. *víṭ*', *Indo-Iranian Journal* 10: 103–25 (Reprinted in Lubotsky et al. (eds.), pp. 383–405).
—— (1991) *Aryans in the Rigveda* (Leiden Studies in Indo-European 1), Amsterdam-Atlanta, GA: Rodopi.
—— (1995) 'On a hunt for "possible" objections', *Indo-Iranian Journal* 38: 239–47.
Lubotsky, A., Oort, M. S. and Witzel, M. (eds.) (1997) *F. B. J. Kuiper: Selected Writings on Indian Linguistics and Philology*, Amsterdam-Atlanta, GA: Rodopi.
Lüders, Heinrich (1954) *Beobachtungen über die Sprache des buddhistischen Urkanons, aus dem Nachlass herausgegeben von Ernst Waldschmidt* (Abhandlungen der Deutschen Akademie der Wissenschaften zu Berlin, Klasse für Sprache, Literatur und Kunst, Jahrgang 1952 Nr. 10), Berlin: Akademie Verlag.
Masica, Colin P. (1976) *Defining a Linguistic Area*: South Asia, Chicago: University of Chicago Press.
—— (1979) 'Aryan and non-Aryan elements in North Indian agriculture', in Deshpande and Hook (eds.), pp. 55–151.
—— (1991) *The Indo-Aryan Languages*, Cambridge: Cambridge University Press.
Master, Alfred (1965) *Jules Bloch Indo-Aryan from the Vedas to Modern Times, English edition Largely Revised by the Author and Translated . . .*, Paris: Adrien-Maisonneuve.
Mayrhofer, Manfred (1966) *Die Indo-Arier im alten Vorderasien mit einer analytischen Bibliographie*, Wiesbaden: Harrassowitz.
—— (1983) 'Lassen sich Vorstufen der Uriranischen nachweisen?', Anzeiger, Akademie Wien 120: 249–55.
—— (1997) 'L'indo-iranien', in Bader, Françoise (ed.), *Langues indo-européennes*, Paris: CNRS, pp. 101–22.
Meadow, Richard H. and Patel, Ajita (1997) 'A comment on "Horse remains from Surkotada" by Sándor Bököknyi', *South Asian Studies* 13: 308–15.
Meenakshi, K. (1995) 'Linguistics and the study of early Indian history', in Thapar, Romila (ed.) *Recent Perspectives in Early Indian History*, Bombay: Popular Prakashan, pp. 53–79.
Mehendale, M. A. (1968) *Some Aspects of Indo-Aryan Linguistics*, Bombay: University of Bombay.
—— (1993) 'The Indo-Aryans, the Indo-Iranians and the Indo-Europeans', in Deo and Kamath (eds.), pp. 43–50.
Misra, Satya Swarup (1992) *The Aryan Problem: A Linguistic Approach*, Delhi: Munshiram Manoharlal.
Morgenstierne, G. (1926) *Report on a Linguistic Mission to Afghanistan* (Instituttet for Sammenlignende Kulturforskning Series C 1–2), Oslo: H. Aschenhough & Co. (W. Nygaard).
—— (1929) 'The language of the Ashkun Kafirs', *Norsk Tidsskrift for Sprogvidenskap* 2: 192–289.
—— (1945) 'Indo-European *k̂* in Kafiri', *Norsk Tidsskrift for Sprogvidenskap* 13: 225–38.
—— (1965) 'Dardic and Kāfir languages', in Lewis, B., Pellat, Ch. and Schacht, J. (eds.) *The Encyclopedia of Islam . . . volume II* (2nd reprint, 1983), Leiden: Brill, pp. 138–9.
—— (1973) 'Die Stellung der Kafirsprachen', *Irano-Dardica* (*Beiträge zur Iranistik*, Band 5), Wiesbaden: Dr. Ludwig Reichert Verlag, pp. 327–43.
—— (1974) 'Languages of Nuristan and surrounding regions', in Jettmar, Karl in collaboration with Lennart Edelberg *Cultures of the Hindukush: Selected Papers from the Hindu-Kush Cultural Conference held at Moesgård*, 1970 (Beiträge zur Südasienforschung, Südasien-Institut, Universität Heidelberg, Band 1), Wiesbaden: Franz Steiner Verlag, pp. 1–10.
Mukerjee, B. N. (1993) 'The Indo-European question in Central Asia', in Deo and Kamath (eds.), pp. 58–69.
Narahari Achar, B. N. (1999) 'On exploring the Vedic sky with modern computer software', *Electronic Journal of Vedic Studies* 5.2.

*Nelson, D. N. (1986) *The Historical Development of the Nuristani Languages*, Univ. of Minnesota doctoral dissertation.

Oberlies, Thomas (1994) Review-article of Kuiper (1991), *Indo-Iranian Journal* 37: 333–49.

—— (1997) 'Pali, Pāṇini and "popular" Sanskrit', *Journal of the Pali Text Society* 23: 1–26.

Parpola, Asko (1988) 'The coming of the Aryans to Iran and India and the cultural and ethnic identity of the Dāsas', *Studia Orientalia* 64: 195–302.

—— (2002) 'From the dialects of Old-Indo-Aryan to Proto-Indo-Aryan and Proto-Iranian', in Sims-Williams, Nicholas (ed.) *Indo-Iranian Languages and Peoples* (Proceedings of the British Academy 116). London: Oxford University Press for the British Academy, pp. 43–102.

Possehl, Gregory L. (ed.) (1993) *Harappan Civilization: A Recent Perspective* (second revised edition), New Delhi-Bombay-Calcutta: American Institute of Indian Studies and Oxford & IBH Publishing Co.

Rajaram, Navaratna S. (1995) *The Politics of History: Aryan Invasion Theory and Subversion of History*, New Delhi: Voice of India.

Rajaram, Navaratna S. and Frawley, David (1997) *Vedic Aryans and the Origins of Civilization: A Literary and Scientific Perspective* (2nd edition), New Delhi: Voice of India.

Ramanujan, A. K. and Masica, Colin (1969) 'Toward a phonological typology of the Indian linguistic area', in Sebeok, Thomas (ed.) *Current Trends in Linguistics, Volume V: Linguistics in South Asia*, The Hague and Paris: Mouton, pp. 543–77.

Rau, Wilhelm (1976) *The Meaning of pur in Vedic Literature* (Abhandlungen der Marburger Gelehrten Gesellschaft Jahrgang 1973, Nr. 1), München: Fink.

—— (1983) *Zur vedischen Altertumskunde* (Akademie der Wissenschaften un der Literatur, Mainz, Abhandlungen der Geistes- und Sozialwissenschaftlichen Klasse Jahrgang 1983, Nr. 1), Wiesbaden: Steiner.

—— (1997) 'The earliest literary evidence for permanent Vedic settlements', in Witzel, M. (ed.) *Inside the Texts, Beyond the Texts: New Approaches to the Study of the Vedas* (Harvard Oriental Series Opera Minora 2), Cambridge, MA: Department of Sanskrit and Indian Studies, Harvard University, pp. 203–6.

Renou, Louis (1957) *Introduction générale*: see Wackernagel.

Sag, Ivan (1974) 'The Grassmann's Law ordering pseudoparadox', *Linguistic Inquiry* 5: 591–606

—— (1976) 'Pseudosolutions to the pseudoparadox', *Linguistic Inquiry* 7: 609–22.

Salomon, Richard (1998) *Indian Epigraphy: A Guide to the Study of Inscriptions in Sanskrit, Prakrit, and other Indo-Aryan Languages*, New York, Oxford: Oxford University Press.

Schindler, Jochem (1976) 'Diachronic and synchronic remarks on Bartholomae's and Grassmann's Laws', *Linguistic Inquiry* 7: 622–37.

Shama Sastri, R. and Rangacarya, K. (1906) *The Taittirīya-Prātiśākhya with the Commentaries: Tribhāṣyaratna and Vaidikābharaṇa* (Reprinted (1985) Delhi: Motilal Banarsidass).

Shapiro, Michael C. and Schiffman, Harold F. (1981) *Language and Society in South Asia* (MLBD Series in Linguistics 1), Delhi: Motilal Banarsidass.

Sharma, Ram Sharan (1999) *Advent of the Aryans in India*, Delhi: Manohar.

Sontakke, N. S. et al. (1933–51) *Ṛgveda-Samhitā with the commentary of Sayaṇāchārya* (5 vols.), Poona: Vaidic Samshodhan Mandal.

Southworth, Franklin C. (1979) 'Lexical evidence for early contacts between Indo-Aryan and Dravidian', in Deshpande and Hook (eds.), pp. 191–233.

—— (forthcoming) *Linguistic Archaeology of the South Asian Subcontinent*. [Chapter 5: The Grierson hypothesis revisited: subgroups of Indo-Aryan, chapter 6: Historical implications of the inner-outer hypothesis.]

Strand, Richard F. (1998) 'Peoples and languages of Nuristān', on web page *Nuristân, Hidden land of the Hindu-Kush* (http://users.sedona.net/~ strand).

—— (1999) 'A bibliography of the languages and cultures of Nuristān and environs', on web page *Nuristân, Hidden land of the Hindu-Kush* (http://users.sedona.net/~ strand).

Sukthankar, Vishnu S. et al. (1933–71) *The Mahābhārata for the First Time Critically Edited*

... (21 vols.), Poona: Bhandarkar Oriental Research Institute.

Talageri, Shrikant G. (1993) *The Aryan Invasion Theory: A Reappraisal*, New Delhi: Aditya Prakashan.

Tikkanen, Bertil (1987) *The Sanskrit Gerund: A Synchronic, Diachronic and Typological Analysis* (*Studia Orientalia* 62), Helsinki: Finnish Oriental Society.

—— (1988) 'On Burushaski and other ancient substrata in northwestern South Asia', *Studia Orientalia* 64: 303–25.

Turner, R. L. (1966) *A Comparative Dictionary of the Indo-Aryan Languages*, London: Oxford University Press (Second impression, 1973, reprinted (1999), Delhi: Motilal Banarsidass).

Upādhyāya, Baladeva (1972) *Prākṛtaprakāsa of Vararuci with the Sañjīvanī, Subodhinī, Manoramā and Prākṛtamañjarī Commentaries and Hindi Translation* (Sarasvatībhavana-Granthamālā 102), Varanasi: Varanaseya Sanskrit Vishvavidyalaya.

Wackernagel, Jakob (1896) *Altindische Grammatik, Band I: Lautlehre*, Göttingen: Vandenhoek & Ruprecht (Reprinted (1957) with *Introduction générale* by Louis Renou and *Nachträge* by Albert Debrunner, Göttingen: Vandenhoek & Ruprecht).

Witzel, Michael (1989) 'Tracing the Vedic dialects', in Caillat (ed.) 1989a, pp. 97–265.

—— (1991) 'Notes on Vedic dialects (1)', *Zinbun* 1990: 31–70.

—— (1995a) 'Early Indian history: linguistic and textual parameters', in Erdosy (ed.) 1995, pp. 85–125.

—— (1995b) 'Rgvedic history: poets, chieftains and polities', in Erdosy (ed.) 1995, pp. 307–52.

—— (1999a) 'Substrate languages in Old Indo-Aryan (Rgvedic, middle and late Vedic)', *Electronic Journal of Vedic Studies* 5.1.

—— (1999b) 'The Pleiades and the bears viewed from inside the Vedic texts', *Electronic Journal of Vedic Studies* 5.2.

Zoller, Claus Peter (1988) 'Bericht über besondere Archaismen im Bangani, einer Western Pahari-Sprache', *Münchener Studien zur Sprachwissenschaft* 49: 173–200.

—— (1989) 'Bericht über grammatische Archaismen im Bangani', *Münchener Studien zur Sprachwissenschaft* 50: 159–218.

—— (1993) 'A note on Bangani', *Indian Linguistics* 54: 112–14.

—— (1997) 'The van Driem enigma or: In search of instant facts', Bangani web page 4 Mar 1997 15:34:06 +0100 (CET).

CHAPTER TWO

SOCIOLINGUISTICS OF THE INDO-ARYAN LANGUAGES

Dhanesh Jain

CONTENTS

LIST OF TABLES

LIST OF FIGURES

1 INTRODUCTION

कोस कोस पे पानी बदले, चार कोस पे बानी ।
kos kos pe pani bədle, car kos pe bani.
Water changeth every *kos* (= 2 miles),
speech at every fourth.

This old Hindi saying is a pointer to the spatial variation in speech – how in the Hindi-speaking region speech changes as one moves from one place to another. By this reckoning, the area is a veritable kaleidoscope of languages. Here Indo-Aryan languages interact with one another and on their peripheries with those of other language families namely, Iranian, Dravidian, Austro-Asiatic and Tibeto-Burman.

One speech form merges imperceptibly into another, and acquires a new name. In the Middle Indo-Aryan times, some languages were named after the region and its inhabitants, e.g. Mahārāṣṭrī and Śaursenī (Cardona, General Introduction 1.4, this volume). The practice continues in modern times in language names such as Panjabi, Sindhi, Kashmiri, Gujarati, Asamiya, Konkani and several others.

There is no agreement on the number of languages or dialects spoken in the subcontinent. The Census of India recorded 845 languages spoken in 1951, 1652 in 1961, 105 in 1971, 105 in 1981 and 114 in 1991. It is interesting to see how the census arrived at this number in 1991. The respondent was given the freedom to name his mother tongue which the census enumerator recorded faithfully. The number of raw returns of mother tongue came to 10,400. This number was subjected to linguistic scrutiny which resulted in 1576 rationalized mother tongues and 1796 names which were treated as 'unclassified' and relegated to 'other' mother tongues category. Linguistic methodology was further applied to the 1576 mother tongues to arrive at the number 114 (Census of India 1991, Language: 8). This number, however, does not include the languages spoken by less than ten thousand speakers, a practice which the census operation has followed since 1971 (see also section 8).

1.1 Linguistic diversity

The publication in 1960 of 'Linguistic Diversity in South Asia', edited by Charles Ferguson and John Gumperz, marked the formal announcement of the beginning of the field of sociolinguistics. This special volume of the *International Journal of American Linguistics*, containing field data on Indo-Aryan and Dravidian languages, carried a comprehensive subtitle: 'Studies in regional, social and functional variation'. Drawing material from Indo-Aryan Hindi and Bengali, and Dravidian Tamil and Kannada, the study opened up the field of sociolinguistic research. It included works by Ferguson, Gumperz, Bright, Pillai, Dimock, Chowdhury, McCormack and Naim. Some of these scholars contributed significantly to our understanding of the sociolinguistics of the Indo-Aryan languages in the decades to come.

The word 'diversity' aptly sums up the linguistic situation in South Asia. Shapiro and Schiffman (1981) have made an extensive and in-depth study of the nature of this diversity.

On the basis of the shared features of languages, Emeneau (1956) called the region 'India as a linguistic area'. Pandit (1972) narrowed it down to 'India as a sociolinguistic area', which was enlarged to 'South Asia as a sociolinguistic area' by Ferguson (1991). Ferguson has identified eight aspects of language use which characterize South Asia: multilingualism, ancient literacy, diverse scripts, dialect variation, register variation, kinship terms, forms of address and politeness formulas (Ferguson 1991: 27), almost all of which involve a selection from among the multiple choices available in language use.

2 THE STUDY OF LANGUAGE USE

2.1 Language use in Old Indo-Aryan

The study of language in general, and of grammar in particular, received attention from the ancient Indo-Aryans. Cardona (1997: 547–8) discusses how the study of grammar was viewed as a means of achieving the ultimate. He quotes Patañjali: 'Grammar should be studied in order that we have (i.e. attain) union with the great god' (p. 548). Pāṇini's grammar of Sanskrit (*c.* 500 BC), which came to be called *Aṣṭādhyāyī* later on, remains an unexcelled work of grammar of any language. Pāṇini makes a distinction between the language of sacred texts (*chandas*) and the usual language of communication (*bhāṣā*) (Cardona 1974: 616). Multiplicity of codes is a feature of Old Indo-Aryan (OIA) and Middle Indo-Aryan (MIA) languages, which flourished into multilingualism by the New Indo-Aryan (NIA) times. Other aspects of language, such as language use, choice of codes and observance of linguistic norms also received due attention from the *ācāryas* (the learned ones).

Within Indo-Aryan, Sanskrit enjoyed a higher status than its later stages, Prākrit and Apabhraṁśa. Grammarians of Sanskrit held their language in high regard; Daṇḍin in his *Kāvyādarśa* (2.33) calls it *daivī vāk*, 'speech of the gods'. Its use was reserved for the highest in the social hierarchy. Deshpande (1979, 1993) has done pioneering work in the field of historical sociolinguistics of South Asia and much insight into the subject can be gained from his various works.

In Sanskrit dramaturgy, the rules of language use are clearly laid out. It prescribes the code to be used by dramatis personae, when, by whom, and so on. The choice was governed by specified rules between the speaker and the addressee. In Sanskrit plays, for example, the king spoke in Sanskrit whereas MIA speech forms were used by queens, maid-servants and so on. Bharata (second century BC–fourth century AD?) in his treatise on drama *Nāṭyaśāstra* (Kavi 1956) says that Māgadhī is to be used by those employed in the king's harems and Ardhamāgadhī by servants, children of the king and guild heads. Bhāsa (*c.* 300) and Aśvaghoṣa (*c.* 100) make use of Śaursenī, Māgadhī and Ardhamāgadhī (Keith 1923: 74). Various Prākrits were spoken which were understood by the king and his servants, both in drama and in real life. The king's wives were proficient in both Sanskrit and in Prākrit, speaking in Sanskrit to the king and in Prākrit to the maids. Meenakshi (1999: 3) gives an interesting example of the use of appropriate terms of address for the king.

In Kalidasa's *Abhijñānaśākuntalam* (AD 500) the heroine Śakuntalā addresses Duṣyanta, the king hero, alternately as *paurava* 'son of Puru' or *āryaputra* 'son of *ārya/* father-in-law', depending on their perceived relationship at the time of address. First, she calls him *paurava* before their *gāndharva vivāha* 'marriage by consent'. Later, due to a curse Duṣyanta fails to recognize her. Oblivious of the curse, she addresses him as *āryaputra*, but when he fails to recognize her she switches back to *paurava*. Towards the end, when he recognizes her, she again addresses him as *āryaputra*. In one speech event, she switches her term of address three times. Interestingly, in ancient India, husband and wife did not address each other by their (first) names, just as in modern times a wife does not say the name of her husband (Jain 1973, chapter 5).

Sanskrit drama depicts a multilingual speech community in which people understood more than two codes in use. These codes were assigned different roles according to the prestige enjoyed or prescribed for them. In drama, all characters had a passive and, at times, active control of the codes being used in a speech situation. This reflects a multilingual society which simultaneously used temporal and spatial dialects of Indo-Aryan in addition to neighbourhood languages belonging to Dravidian, Tibeto-Burman and Austro-Asiatic families. (For a similar situation in modern times, see section 4.1.)

2.2 Language use in Middle Indo-Aryan

OIA split into several MIA dialects, one of which was Māgadhī. In a detailed study of Māgadhī, Bhattacharya (1993) gives its history, phonology and morphology, based on data from Aśokan inscriptions and Sanskrit drama. Of particular interest is the introduction, where Bhattacharya (1993: 1–54) presents the views of grammarians on language and its actual usage in Sanskrit drama, spanning two millennia.

For a long period of time, Māgadhī was relegated to a low position by Sanskrit rhetoricians, especially in dramaturgy.

Bhattacharya (1993: 27–54) discusses the use of Māgadhī in various Sanskrit plays, a summary of which is given in table 2.1. Māgadhī was the spoken language of eastern India, which was inhabited by a large number of fishermen. In plays its use was sparse and was used by fishermen and, among others, by Jain monks and the king's brother-in-law (in *Mrcchakaṭika*). Bhattacharya (1993: 29) surmises that 'Māgadhī has some strong phonetic similarities which scholars think are due to its coming in close contact with Non-Aryan languages. And, for this reason, it is sometimes assumed that in Sanskrit plays it is spoken by the lower classes.'

TABLE 2.1: THE USE OF MĀGADHĪ IN SANSKRIT DRAMA (AFTER BHATTACHARYA 1993: 27–54)

Playwright	Period	Title of work	Character(s) who speak Māgadhī
Spoken language(s): MIA			
Śūdraka	*c.* AD 200	*Mrcchakaṭika*	servants, two *cāṇḍālas* 'butchers', king's brother-in-law
Kālidāsa	*c.* AD 400–500	*Abhijñānaśākuntalam*	fisherman, constable
Viśākhadatta	*c.* AD 900	*Mudrārākṣasa*	the servant, Jain monks, *cāṇḍāla*, the messenger
Spoken language(s): NIA			
Kṛṣṇa Miśra	*c.* AD 1100	*Prabodhacandrodaya*	the messenger, Jain (digambara) monk
Somadeva	*c.* AD 1200	*Lalitavigraha Rājanāṭaka*	bards, spy
Jyotīśvara Kaviśekhara	*c.* AD 1400	*Dhūrtasamāgama*	barber
Uddaṇḍin	*c.* AD 1700	*Mallikāmāruta*	elephant drivers

Varieties of MIA were the chosen languages of Buddhism and Jainism since about 500 BC. To reach the masses, the two religious faiths opted to use the spoken language. Buddha used his own Prākrit dialect to spread his doctrine. He rejected the plea of his Brahmin monks, who preferred Sanskrit to Prākrit, and ordained that 'everyone should use his own particular dialect in reciting the sacred texts' (Deshpande 1993: 7). The Buddhist literature is mostly in Pāli. Mahavira in the Jain tradition preached in Ardhamāgadhī.

In the history of IA, some languages have come to be associated with certain religions and their canonical literature (table 2.2). Initially, these religions were preached and practised in the spoken language of the period which continued to be the vehicle of their literature even after it had ceased to be a spoken language.

This raises a question that needs to be investigated: how are monks and the king's brother-in-law (in *Mṛcchakaṭika*) assigned to speak in a code which was otherwise prescribed for 'low status people'? Is this because of the social tension that prevailed between the two communities – the Brahminical and the non-Brahminical? Or, does it reflect the use of the spoken language, namely Prākrit?

To answer this, we need to distinguish between the norm and actual usage. This, in fact, is a difficulty of sociolinguistic reconstruction – distinguishing the norm from actual usage as well as relating the two. The norm in the case of Sanskrit drama prescribed the use of Prākrits by characters of low status. Prākrit, however, was the spoken language and was also adopted for liturgical use by Buddhists and Jains. The use of Prākrit, Māgadhī by the Jain monks, reflects actual and not normative usage. Dramaturgy did not prescribe the use of Māgadhī for monks. In Sanskrit drama, their speech reflects the spoken language and not the norm.

We have access to the rules of language use as prescribed by Sanskrit *ācāryas* and their discussion on language use has been a subject of study by Deshpande (see Deshpande 1979, 1993; Deshpande and Hook 1979). We enter into a new and difficult area of sociolinguistic reconstruction when we want to relate these norms to actual usage in those times. A study of normative usage alone will not give us a complete picture of language use – neither of contemporary usage nor in reconstruction. The reconstruction of actual usage in OIA and its relationship with norms is a new area. So far, scholars of Sanskrit have broken new ground (see, for example, Deshpande 1993, Houben 1996). It remains to be seen how sociolinguists, who are used to working with contemporary data, deal with reconstructed data or with reconstruction itself.

3 THE ROLE AND USE OF SCRIPT

There has been a growing concern among sociolinguists regarding the study of the written language and the implications of the interaction between spoken and written language. This concern is reflected in the studies of diglossia in languages such as

TABLE 2.2: RELIGIONS AND IA LANGUAGES USUALLY ASSOCIATED WITH THEIR CANONICAL LITERATURE

Brahminical	Sanskrit	OIA
Theravāda Buddhism	Pāli	MIA
Jain-Śvetāmbara	Ardhamāgadhī	MIA
Jain-Digambara	Śaursenī	MIA
Sikhism	Panjabi (in Gurmukhi)	NIA

Arabic and Tamil, and Indo-Aryan languages such as Bangla (Ferguson 1959) and Sinhala. The affinity and cleavage between the written and the spoken language has implications for sociolinguists, including language planners, among others.

A detailed account of the writing system and its development in Indo-Aryan is given in Masica (1991: 133–53) and Salomon (1998: 7–17). The use of the written word – or its absence – has had an interesting history in OIA. Old Indo-Aryans attached great importance to the correctness of the spoken word. The emphasis historically was on the correct recitation of religious texts and the spoken word carried sanctity in the Vedic tradition.

The use of metrical and *sūtra* forms was well suited to oral transmission. The Vedas were composed in metres which were easier to memorize than words in prose. A massive amount of literature was thus transferred from one generation to the next in the long tradition of oral transmission.

In the history of Indo-Aryan, writing was a later development and its adoption has been slow even in modern times (see below). The first written word comes to us through Aśokan inscriptions dating back to the third century BC. Originally, Brāhmī was used to write Prākrit (MIA); for Sanskrit (OIA) it was used only four centuries later (Masica 1991: 135). The MIA traditions of Buddhist and Jain texts show a greater regard for the written word than the OIA Brahminical tradition, though writing was available to Old Indo-Aryans. In modern times, even printing took off in India quite late and was slow to pick up. Printing appeared in Europe in 1439, but in 1556 in India. Europe had printed twenty million copies of various publications by the end of the fifteenth century, as against only thousands in the early nineteenth century in India (*The Wealth of India*, Vol. VII, 1971: 76).

This oral-rich tradition has served communicative needs in India. The recitation of mantras from old texts continues till modern times as part of religious and social rituals. The medieval *bhakti* poetry, sung in several NIA languages, can be seen as a continuation of that oral tradition. *Jātrās* (travelling *bhajan* and drama troupes) combined mythology with events in neighbouring towns to keep the villagers informed about the outside world. Compositions were spread beyond the regional dialect area through religious establishments, migrant preachers, ascetics and performers belonging to that group (Gumperz and Naim 1960: 96).

Singing, which was an integral part of folk and cultural life in India, has now been taken over by films and the electronic media. Indian classical music – Hindustani and Carnatic – is passed down from generation to generation, without recourse to written notations. Basic notes were fixed while singing was improvised. The writing of musical notation started in the twentieth century. Historically, in comparison to oral transmission of knowledge, adoption of writing has been slow.

By the time we reach NIA, the role of script has reached the other extreme. As against a disregard for writing in the OIA Brahminical tradition, many NIA languages have developed their own scripts contributing their share to the (linguistic) diversity of the area. To the speakers of a language, the existence of a writing system and subsequently of written literature elevates the language to a 'literary' status. The use of writing leads to the folk belief that the written language is the 'real' language (Ferguson 1968: 30). This becomes clear by examining the role of Nagari, Arabic and Gurmukhi for the NIA languages.

Among the NIA languages, Nagari is used to write Hindi, Marathi and Nepali, besides Sanskrit and several other languages. Derivatives of Brahmi, in addition to Nagari – which itself is a derivate of Brahmi among others – are used for Bangla (and Asamiya), Oriya, Gujarati, Sinhala and Gurmukhi, as well as for the Dravidian Telugu, Tamil, Malayalam and Kannada. Arabic is used to write Urdu, Sindhi, Kashmiri and

Panjabi. Dhivehi, in the Maldives, has adapted nine consonantal characters from the Arabic numerals 1–9 (Gair and Cain 1996: 565).

Scripts are often named after the language for which they are used. Language names such as English, Hindi, Urdu and Panjabi are used to refer to Roman, Nagari, Arabic and Gurmukhi, respectively. Scripts, like languages, become identity-markers. As a result, some languages are written in more than one script, often depending on which social group writes them. The choice of Arabic, Nagari or Gurmukhi is sometimes made not by linguistic or communicative needs of the speech community, but on religious and political grounds.

3.1 One script, many languages

Arabic can be called the 'national' script of Pakistan. It is written in two mutually readable styles, *Naskh* and *Nastaliq*, which are adapted to the individual phonological requirements of the language concerned. The Arabic script has been quite flexible as it has been adapted to the phonological structure of other languages (Kaye 1996: 745), while Nagari has rarely invented new symbols (Masica 1991: 146). *Nastaliq* is used to write Urdu, Panjabi, Baluchi and Brahui, whereas *Naskh* is used for Sindhi and Pashto with some overlapping between the two styles. With the adoption of the Arabic script for Urdu, Panjabi, Sindhi (IA), Pashto and Baluchi (Iranian), and Brahui (Dravidian), the question of the script in which a language is written often becomes redundant. A billboard like *Khan Cloth House* or a street name like *Sadar Bazar* written in Arabic would be variously read as written in the language one identifies with. However, in a place like Peshawar where *Naskh* and *Nastaliq* are used, the choice of script-style is an index of language preference (Ruth Schmidt, personal communication); a Pashto speaker would write *Sadar Bazar* in *Naskh* whereas an Urdu speaker would write it in *Nastaliq*, which would be interpreted as written in Pashto and Urdu, respectively. Similarly, in Sindh most people would differentiate a sign written in *Nastaliq* Urdu from one written in *Naskh* Sindhi (Elena Bashir, personal communication). (For Panjabi, see below.) Among competing languages, one script is differentially named, depending on the dominant language the reader speaks (see table 2.3).

The fact remains that the multiplicity of scripts for Indo-Aryan languages in India was resolved largely in Pakistan by the adoption of a single script for languages belonging to three families. This homogeneity, though brought in by state and religious patronage, was broken by the adoption of Bangla and its script in Bangladesh, formerly East Pakistan.

Lahore, in Pakistan, is predominantly a Panjabi-speaking town. There is an unequal distribution in the roles of Urdu and Panjabi as written and spoken languages in Lahore. The written language is Urdu, the national language of Pakistan, taught in schools and used on billboards and for street names, along with English. Panjabi in written form is limited to literary journals and private letters. Urdu in Lahore plays the role of a prestige language as dictated by the *ahle-zabān* 'speakers of the (proper/polished) language', whereas Panjabi is the language exclusively used by people without education (Shackle 1970: 247). Since Urdu carries prestige and government patronage, the written word is read as being in Urdu and *not* Panjabi.

A comparison of Lahore with Delhi is in order. Street names in Delhi were in English and Hindi, i.e. in Roman and Nagari. On demands with populist overtones, they were also written in Urdu and Panjabi, i.e. in *Nastaliq* and Gurmukhi. In the Panjabi-speaking Lahore, street names are written in English and Urdu. The demand for Panjabi did not arise since the script used for Panjabi is the same as the one used for Urdu, namely *Nastaliq*. Thus, Delhi uses four scripts to write four languages for street names; Lahore economizes by using two scripts – Roman and Arabic – to write three languages – English, Urdu and Panjabi – (or maybe more). Panjabi in Delhi is ambiguous for the language or the script; in Lahore the reference is to the language alone.

3.2 Many scripts, one language

Panjabi is written in three scripts: Arabic, Gurmukhi and Nagari, popularly identified with Muslims, Sikhs and Hindus, respectively. Table 2.3 shows the association of script with religion.

Lahore's neighbouring town Amritsar, in India, has a mixed population of Sikhs and Hindus – predominantly Sikhs. The sacred book of the Sikhs, *Guru Granth Sahab*, is in Gurmukhi, which is also the official script of the state, Panjab. Besides Gurmukhi, Roman and Nagari are used for writing purposes in Amritsar. Gurmukhi, compulsorily taught in schools and used on billboards, is the official script of the official language and has a high visibility. This is not the case with Panjabi when written in Arabic and Nagari in Lahore and Jammu. In Jammu, the extent of written Panjabi (Dogri) is as low as it is in Lahore, though scripts and dominant religions differ. In fact, in Lahore and Jammu, there is an imbalance in the roles of Panjabi as a spoken and written language; in both towns it is largely a spoken language. Arabic or Nagari hardly serve the predominantly spoken language of the two towns.

Table 2.3 shows a one-to-one relationship between two constituents, such as a Panjabi dialect and the religion it is associated with, but conceals the load of such a relationship. It does not convey that Gurmukhi in Amritsar outweighs Arabic and Nagari in Lahore and Jammu in the functional load it carries. As such, table 2.3 should not be read with the precision expected of a numerical table. Nor is it suggested here that the identification of religion with script is absolute or exclusive; it is either the folk perception or imposition by language planners. Sindhi, Siraiki and Kashmiri, besides Urdu, have traditionally been written in Arabic by non-Muslims as well and are, in fact, written thus even now, just as Gurmukhi is written by non-Sikhs and Nagari by non-Hindus also (see 5.1.).

Leaving aside for a moment the liturgical needs fulfilled by Gurmukhi or Panjabi, the need for writing Panjabi has a parallel with OIA. Like OIA, Panjabi has a rich oral tradition of passing down poetry from one generation to the next without any quibblings about Gurmukhi, Arabic or Nagari as the vehicle of such transmission. This oral tradition has been quite strong in the three Panjabi regions – Amritsar, Lahore and Jammu. Bulleshah (1680–1758), a popular folk poet of Panjabi, is fondly sung by Panjabi speakers of all regions and faiths.

TABLE 2.3: SCRIPTS USED FOR WRITING PANJABI AND THEIR USUAL RELIGIOUS ASSOCIATION

Place	Dialect	Script	Religion
Amritsar	Majhi	Gurmukhi	Sikhism
Lahore	Panjabi	Arabic	Islam
Jammu	Dogri	Nagari	Hinduism

4 MULTILINGUALISM

4.1 Multilingualism across language families

Speakers of four language families – Indo-Aryan, Dravidian, Austro-Asiatic and Tibeto-Burman – share the district town of Jalpaiguri in West Bengal. They have been living side-by-side with each other for a long time (figure 2.1). In Koraput and Ranchi, the three language families, – IA, Dravidian and Austro-Asiatic – are numerically better represented. There are several examples of speakers of three language families living together in significant numbers such as Ganjam (Orissa), Sundergarh (Orissa) and Santhal Pargana (Bihar).

Table 2.4 shows the extent of multilingualism within and across language families in the three district towns of Koraput, Ranchi and Jalpaiguri in the states of Oriya-speaking Orissa, Hindi-speaking Bihar and Bengali-speaking West Bengal, respectively – all largely Indo-Aryan speaking areas.

At least nine languages are spoken in Koraput and seven each in Ranchi and Jalpaiguri, by a population of two to three million people each. Our understanding is that they represent a stable population. Not everyone speaks all the seven to nine languages but, importantly, they are multilinguals – not just bilinguals – and are able to communicate with each other in their day-to-day living. They learn these languages by default as they grow up and not through formal schooling. Schools do not teach more than three languages, one of which is English.

These cases are important to understand the changes induced by multilingualism across language families just as what influence one language may have on the other within the same family. The choice available is likely to lead to assigning of differing roles to languages. How the communicative needs of a community are fulfilled is yet another question which, with many others, makes these and similar districts worth field investigation.

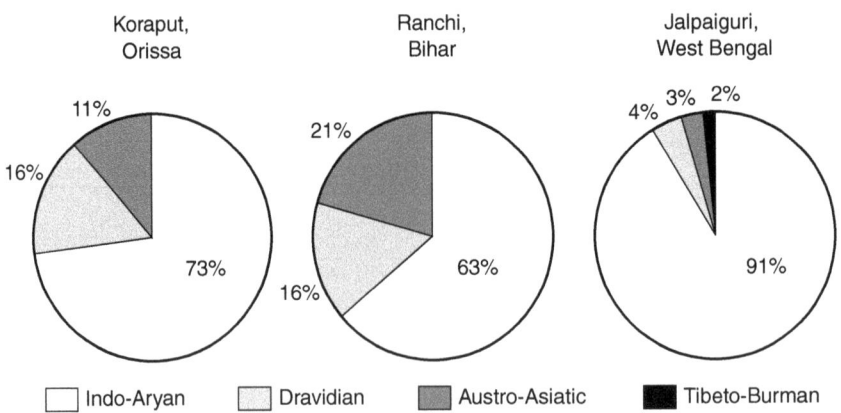

FIGURE 2.1: MULTILINGUALISM ACROSS LANGUAGE FAMILIES IN THREE DISTRICTS OF INDIA

TABLE 2.4: MULTILINGUALISM WITHIN AND ACROSS LANGUAGE FAMILIES IN THREE DISTRICTS OF INDIA. CENSUS OF INDIA 1981

Indo-Aryan		Dravidian		Austro-Asiatic		Tibeto-Burman	
Koraput, Orissa							
Population: 2,444,922, Area 26,961 sq. km, Density 91 persons per sq. km							
Oriya	1,571,783	Khond	169,195	Kui	187,209		
Bangla	99,434	Telugu	158,541	Savara	60,022		
Hindi	33,719	Gondi	40,453	Gadaba	16,239		
TOTAL	1,704,936		368,189		263,470		
	(73%)		(16%)		(11%)		
Ranchi, Bihar							
Population: 3,029,214, Area 18,331.0 sq. km, Density 165 persons per sq. km							
Hindi	1,662,062	Oraon	468,430	Mundari	470,489		
Urdu	179,818			Santhali	54,340		
Bangla	55,709			Kharia	97,326		
TOTAL	1,897,589		468,430		622,155		
	(63%)		(16%)		(21%)		
Jalpaiguri, West Bengal							
Population: 2,201,794, Area 6227.0 sq. km, Density 354 persons per sq. km							
Bangla	1,517,424	Kurukh	89,008	Santhali	37,718	Bodo	21,924
Hindi	337,353			Munda	27,652		
Nepali	135,860						
TOTAL	1,990,637		89,008		65,370		21,924
	(91%)		(4%)		(3%)		(1%)

Since languages spoken by less than 10,000 people are not shown here, there is a difference between population and the sum of language speakers. Oraon and Kurukh refer to the same language.

4.2 Trilingualism and bilingualism

For the first time in 1991, the Indian census recorded figures for speakers of the mother tongue and 'two other languages known' and introduced the term 'trilingualism', denoting the knowledge of a third language. Seven per cent reported speaking competence in three languages as against nineteen per cent for two languages. The percentage of bilinguals has been steadily going up: 1961: 9.70%, 1971: 13.04%, 1981: 13.34% and 1991: 19.44%. In thirty years (from 1961 to 1991), the number and percentage of bilinguals (or its reporting) has doubled.

Figure 2.2 gives the percentage of trilinguals and bilinguals in 1991 (Census of India, 1991, *Bilingualism and Trilingualism*). Konkani, Sindhi and Urdu, which are spoken in diaspora, have the largest incidence of bilingualism and, to an extent, of trilingualism. On the other hand, it needs investigation as to why mother tongue speakers of Bangla, Hindi and Tamil have shown the least inclination to learn another language. These are the three most prestigious languages and are socio-politically distinct from others. Bengalis are known for the love of their language, for Tamils it is a politically sensitive issue, and Hindi is the national language of the country. Geographically, the outside contact of these languages is significantly less than that of other languages.

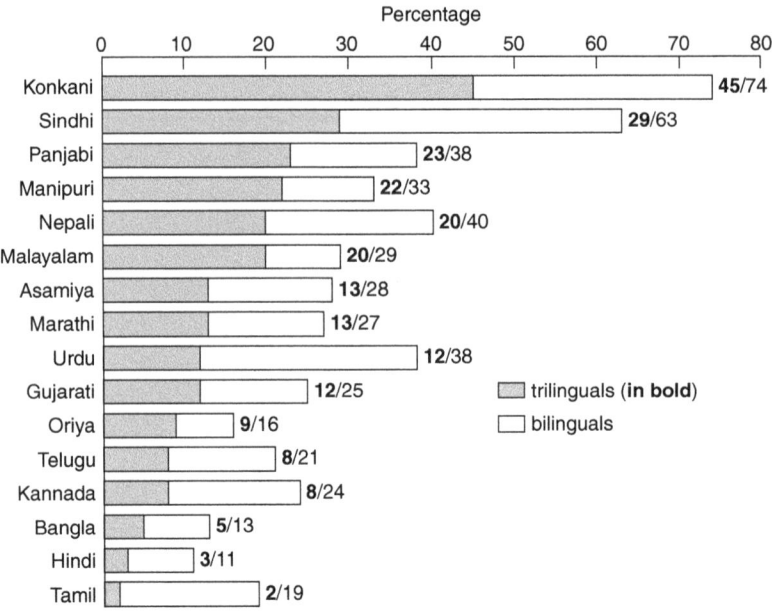

FIGURE 2.2: MULTILINGUALISM IN INDIA (PERCENTAGE OF TRILINGUALS AND BILINGUALS IN 1991)

Source: Census of India 1991, *Bilingualism and Trilingualism*

4.3 Language maintenance and language shift

Mukherjee's study (1996) of language maintenance and language shift among the Panjabis and Bengalis of Delhi is based on interviews with one hundred households of Delhi in 1978. Both categories of her subjects represent post-1947 immigrants to Delhi. Among the Panjabis, she selected for her study Panjabi Hindus, who account for 48% of Panjabi speakers, 52% being Sikhs. Her findings are of great interest for studies of language shift and maintenance in a multilingual setting.

The 1971 Census gave the following data on mother tongue speakers in Delhi: Hindi 75.3%, Panjabi 13.4%, Urdu 5.7%, Bengali 1.1%, Others 4.5%. Both Panjabis and Bengalis shared an immigrant status but differed in their linguistic responses to a new setting. Panjabi Hindus were quick to identify themselves with Hindi as they associated Panjabi with Sikhism and Urdu with Islam. Panjabis, in general, suffered from signs of self-hatred as far as their speech habits were concerned, in contrast to self-pride displayed by Bengali speakers. 'For the Hindus, it appeared that Panjabi was increasingly becoming a rough, crude and vulgar language most appropriately used only when abusing or fighting' (p. 37). Mukherjee quotes a Panjabi informant, 'Why should I send my children to Panjabi schools? They will forget all their manners and speak rudely like the Sardars, saying *tu, te* rather than *ap*' (p. 75).

This can be compared with a similar attitude towards Panjabi in the Panjabi-speaking town of Lahore. The generally accepted value scheme ranks the three languages in the order of English, Urdu and Panjabi. The educated people have an attitude of 'affectionate contempt' towards Panjabi, whose literature is dismissed 'as a collection of rustic crudity, suitable only for Sikhs' (Shackle 1970: 247–8). Or 'Most Panjabis exhibited various degrees of culture shame about their language' (Rahman 1996: 77).

In general, both communities in Delhi use their mother tongue at home, but not at school or office. Bengali shows greater retention among the younger generation whereas Panjabi is getting lost among second-generation Panjabi speakers. The younger generation can understand Panjabi but is not able to speak it (Mukherjee 1996: 91). This conforms to the attitude of self-hatred for Panjabi and self-love for Bengali. Panjabi ranks lower than the other two competing languages, English and Hindi.

Mukherjee (1996: 173) concludes that linguistic assimilation is combined with language shift among the Panjabis and with stable bilingualism among the Bengalis. Panjabi Hindus faced socio-economic insecurity in Delhi and political domination of the Sikhs in Panjab and, therefore, had to readjust their linguistic alignment. The Bengalis, on the other hand, did not face any social or political threat and were able to maintain their pattern of linguistic behaviour.

5 HINDI AND URDU

Hindi and Urdu share a common structure and morphology but are written in different scripts – Nagari and Arabic. The two are national languages of India and Pakistan, respectively, and have often been identified with Hindus and Muslims. Such identification started at the beginning of the nineteenth century (Beg 1996: 43, Das Gupta 1970: 52–3). Chatterji (1960: 107) predates it to the seventeenth–eighteenth centuries. Hindi and Urdu have been a subject of controversy which is extensively discussed by Rai (1984). We shall briefly examine the linguistic basis of the identification of Urdu with Muslims.

5.1 Urdu and Muslims

In 1991, the percentage of Muslims who reported Urdu as their mother tongue was 43% in India, 7.6% in Pakistan and less than 1% in Bangladesh. Within India, in four states – Assam, Jammu and Kashmir, Kerala and West Bengal – less than 1% out of a Muslim population of 33 million reported Urdu as their mother tongue. This figure for the Hindi belt is 69% and in the Dravidian-speaking areas: 94% in Andhra Pradesh, 86% in Karnataka, 39% in Tamil Nadu, but a meagre 0.3% among the 3 million Muslims in Kerala. Religion merges with language in Delhi, where in 1961 the number of Muslims equals the number of Urdu mother tongue speakers. Elsewhere, they report the dominant language of the area as their mother tongue – Bengali, Malayalam, Bhojpuri, Magahi or Maithili. In terms of language loyalty, the local language supersedes Urdu. Gradually, fewer Muslims are reporting Urdu as their mother tongue. The all-India percentage of Urdu mother tongue speakers among Muslims has gone down from 49% in 1961 to 47% in 1971 and 1981, to 43% in 1991. In a parallel development among the younger generation of Muslims, Nagari seems to be replacing Arabic, the most identifiable visual tag which separates Urdu from Hindi. Beg (1996: 80) cites a notice for a prayer meeting at a mosque, in a predominantly Muslim locality of Aligarh, given in Nagari:

यहाँ ईद की नमाज़ सुबह 7 बजे है।

yəhã id ki nəmaz subəh 7 bəje hæ.

'The Id prayer here is (will be held) at 7 in the morning.'

The younger generation has almost crossed over to Hindi and other regional languages and Urdu has become the language of oral communication (Beg 1996: 12). In a random survey in Bhopal, in nine out of eleven mosques we found short notices written in Hindi along with Urdu. We understand that most mosques in Ludhiana, Panjab, carry such notices in Gurmukhi. It requires field investigation to measure the extent of this ongoing replacement.

The criterion for declaring Urdu as the national language of Pakistan in the mid-twentieth century was not the numerical strength – only 4% of the population spoke Urdu – but the religious association of Urdu with Islam or its perception as such. Fifty years later, at the turn of the century, such an association or its perception seems to be weakening. To understand ground realities it will be necessary to separate political considerations from actual usage.

6 LANGUAGE USE IN DELHI COURTS

The use of codes in the courts of Delhi is a subject fit for an independent study to assess how a multilingual speech community uses its repertoire of a variety of codes and mixes them without causing any break in communication. The availability of two or more codes is not perceived as an obstruction or handicap; on the contrary, it allows the speaker to choose the appropriate code or a mixture of two or more suitable in a given social context, thus assigning differing roles to codes for effective communication.

Delhi courts present an interesting picture of how English, Hindi and Urdu are used in spoken and written forms in a multilingual setting. Delhi seats the highest court of the country, the Supreme Court down to the district-level courts. English is used to an almost exclusive level in the highest court, but increasingly mixed with Hindi and/or Urdu in the lower courts. In the district-level court, for example, English and Hindi are freely intermixed by the judges, counsels and persons appearing in the court. Evidence given in Hindi or Urdu is immediately translated and recorded in English by the judge or stenographer. The courtroom vocabulary is drawn from Persian which was the language of administration and court during the Mughal period but was replaced by Urdu in the British times. In the last fifty years, courts have retained Urdu though gradually Nagari has replaced *Nastaliq*.

The word *court* itself is an interesting example to show how this word and its equivalents are used in Delhi courts. Hindi has four words for *court*, all from different sources. Their broad semantic areas are given in table 2.5 as found in written and spoken Hindi. At times, their usage overlaps and they compete with one another in encroaching upon each others' semantic area.

Among the major sources of Hindi vocabulary, we might add *tatsama* and *tadbhava* words of which *tatsama*, broadly speaking, are borrowings from Sanskrit. Words which have undergone phonetic changes in the course of Indo-Aryan development and are not directly borrowed from Sanskrit are called *tadbhava*. Such doublets are a common feature of NIA. Thus *vivah* 'marriage' (*tatsama*) is used alongside *byah* (*tadbhava*). Together they compete with borrowings from English *marriage, wedding*, Persian *šadi* and Arabic *nikah*. They all share a defined socio-semantic distribution like the words for *court* discussed here.

Going back to the court usage, the English *court* appears unmarked while the other three are marked in their semantic distribution. The Sanskrit *nyayalǝy* has the lowest functional load of the four. The Arabic *ǝdalǝt* has frozen expressions like *xuda ki ǝdalǝt* 'God's court' but is also being commonly used in new coinages like *lok ǝdalǝt*

TABLE 2.5: THE USE OF THE WORD *COURT* AND ITS EQUIVALENTS IN DELHI'S COURTS

Words	*court*	*nyayalɔy*	*ədalət*	*kɔcæhri*
Source	English	Sanskrit	Arabic	*tadbhava*
Usage	written, spoken	mostly written	written, spoken	mostly spoken
Formal or not	yes as in *supreme court*	yes as in *ucc* *nyayalɔy* 'high court'	sometimes	no
Reference to the place, building, as in *I have a date in court= aj meri tarikh hæ*	yes	no	no	yes
Reference to the institution as in *The court passed a judgement*	yes	yes	yes	no

(Sanskrit–Arabic) 'people's court', or *tælifon ədalət* (English–Arabic) 'telephone court'. Not included in the table are words like *ijləs* (Persian) 'courtroom' which have restricted usage, or compounds like *kort–kɔcæhri* (English–*tadbhava*) 'court–court'. Hindi sometimes forms compounds in which two words from different sources are put together to heighten the emphasis: *dhən–dɔlət* (Sanskrit–Persian) 'wealth–wealth', *kort–kɔcæhri*, cited above, (English–*tadbhava*), *phəl–frut* (Hindi–English) 'fruit–fruit'. These borrowings are so well adopted in Hindi that their varying sources do not bother the speaker or the hearer (see also section 7.1.).

6.1 Vocabulary

The working language of the courts has retained its vocabulary of Perso-Arabic roots. Urdu *dava* 'case', *jəvab* 'reply', *jəvabdava* 'written statement, reply', *təlbana* 'process fee' are some commonly used words in the lower courts. Some Urdu words like *jənab* and *vəkil* compete with the English *sir, your honour* and *advocate, lawyer*. Arguments take place in English and Hindi–Urdu. In the upper courts – High Court and Supreme Court – English is the exclusive language of spoken and written transactions.

At times, a different register of English is marked for different courts: *your honour* of the lower courts becomes *your lordship* in the higher courts. A reversal of usage marks *your lordship* for flattery in lower courts, and *your honour* as demeaning in higher courts; genuine slips become embarrassing. Sanskritic vocabulary is yet to enter the courts of Delhi.

7 LANGUAGE PLANNING

7.1 New coinages in Hindi

New coinages, especially where accepted English borrowings were available, brought in with them the question of acceptance. Their acceptance relates closely to the previous linguistic experience of Hindi speakers: phonetically, uncommon consonant clusters raise their 'difficulty' or acceptance level and semantically, whether the components of the new coinage are within the range of the lexical repertoire, oral or written, of the user or not. Let us take for example, three technology-related words – *telephone, television* and *computer*. The new Hindi words for *telephone* and *television* are compounds *dūr-bhaš* and *dūr-dəršən*, contrasting with the newly-coined *əbhi-kəlitr* (Sanskrit *əbhi-* Sanskrit *kəlitr*) for *computer*. *dūr, bhaš* and *dəršən*, though all from Sanskrit are commonly used in Hindi in one form or the other. Their acceptance has been greater than that of *əbhikəlitr*, both of whose elements were not within the range of the previous linguistic experience of an average Hindi speaker.

The Indian Institute of Technology in Delhi has a Computer Centre and a Hindi Officer. The task of the Hindi Officer, as in government establishments, is to oversee the use of Hindi, especially written Hindi, in the establishment. The laboratory known as the *Computer Centre* has a billboard in Hindi, in 18-inch high lettering, which reads *əbhikəlitr kendr*. The only time it is heard on the campus is during the ragging of new students, as a mock check of their knowledge of Hindi. On its use on the campus, however, *abhikəlitr* has been a born loser when competing with the English *computer*. Those working on the campus know of and refer to the laboratory as the *Computer Centre*, seldom by the Hindi term.

This is not to suggest that jocular usages do not promote a new word. Many new coinages were objects of jokes but were accepted slowly even though competing with English loans. However, as mentioned above, they owed their acceptance largely to the user's previous linguistic experience. In addition to this, continued use helps in the gradual acceptance of words, as in the cases of *dūrbhāš* and *dūrdəršən* cited above. What is true of these three coinages applies to the bulk of new coinages in Hindi. In a written questionnaire, Mukherjee (1992: 76) found that only 9 out of 52 understood Sanskritized Hindi. For the language planner, it is essential to keep the multiplicity of codes in mind when coining new words. High Hindi borrowings from Sanskrit of the *nyayaləy* type do not correspond with ground realities, as we find borrowings from other languages such as English, Arabic and Persian, or the current NIA words carrying a greater functional load than new coinages based on Sanskritic roots. The new coinage *əbhikəlitr* for *computer* is a non-starter in spoken and written language and competes poorly with the English *computer*. This is but one example of the failure of language planners for the national language of India, Hindi. New coinages, for lack of field evaluation, remain confined to the bulky tomes prepared by the language commissions. This reflects a missing step in language planning in India. Many loanwords, on the other hand, whether they came from Persian or from Arabic through Persian, are so well assimilated that it is not generally known where they came from. *Inquilab* 'revolution' and *zindabad* 'long live' were the two most popular words during India's freedom movement. *Inquilab* is Arabic while *zindabad* is Persian (Abbas 1969: 30).

8 CENSUS AS A LANGUAGE DATABASE

The Census of India, the single largest linguistic database on languages and the number of their speakers, has regularly been publishing valuable language data every ten years since 1881. In its language data, it has followed the geneological classification of languages as laid out by Grierson's *Linguistic Survey of India* since its availability. In a few cases, languages were reclassified on the basis of later findings.

In Pakistan, Bangladesh and Sri Lanka, this decadal rhythm has been occasionally interrupted and language enumeration often given up. In Bhutan, census operations have yet to start (Breton 1999: 20).

Without undermining its contribution, it can be said that the Indian census data at times has its limitations and needs to be evaluated with caution. Sometimes it is incomplete. No census, for example, was held in Jammu and Kashmir in 1951 and 1981 due to 'disturbed conditions'. Census records for Tamil Nadu were lost in the floods in 1981. In cases of infants and deaf-mutes, the language spoken by the mother is treated as the mother tongue. Out of a population of one billion in India at the turn of the century, on 11 May 2000 precisely, thirty million *cannot* speak as such but are recorded as mother tongue speakers of the language 'usually spoken by the mother'.

District-wise data of the language/dialect spoken were last recorded in 1961. Thereafter, Bhojpuri, Maithili, Magahi and many others were clubbed together under Hindi. District-wise dialect information is not available since then. Similarly, reporting of languages spoken by less than 10,000 people was stopped. Vital information regarding endangered languages is thus being missed. Singh and Manoharan (1993: 14) plead for their inclusion: '(This) policy needs to be revised, not only because such small languages are remnants of the historical tradition of their speakers but also because these languages are intrinsic to the identity of their speakers, even though they are surrounded by speakers of more dominant languages.'

9 AN ETHNOGRAPHY OF SPEAKING

9.1 Pronominal usage

Brown and Gilman's study (1960) of pronouns of several languages of Europe gave a thrust to such studies among languages of the world. They distributed usage of second person pronouns, such as *tu* and *vous* of French, abbreviated T and V, on two dimensions of power and solidarity. Among Indo-Aryan and Dravidian languages too, pronominal usage has been a subject of study by various scholars. Schmidt and Kharel (1972) discuss the pronouns of Nepali, Das (1968) describes the pronouns of Bengali and shows how the use of pronouns is related to other terms of address. Chandrasekhar (1970) points out how pronouns are tied to low and high castes in Malayalam and that plural pronouns are also pronouns of respect. Bean's studies (1970) review literature on the subject and discuss pronouns of Kannada. Pillai (1971) discusses pronominal usage in Tamil in relation to other aspects of the spoken language. In Jaffna, Tamil pronouns can indicate both respect and disrespect (Suseendrarajah 1970). Misra's (1977) discussion of Hindi second person pronouns is based on data drawn from four novels of Premchand: *Godan, Gaban, Nirmala* and *Seva Sadan*. Jain (1999) drew his data on Hindi pronouns largely from questionnaires given to 200 subjects of Sagar in Madhya Pradesh and briefly gives the pronominal usage in old and middle English. Mehrotra's (1985) data on the use of secret (code) language between buyer and seller came from tape recordings made in Benaras. His study includes address forms, modes of greeting and the use of names and nick-names in Hindi.

A crucial aspect of pronominal usage is the agreement of pronoun with the verb. In Hindi, second person pronouns are not free from their co-occurrence restrictions of verbal endings (Jain 1973: 91–103). Hindi has three second person pronouns and three verbal endings to agree with them as illustrated here with the verb stem *a* 'come':

tu	*a*	'you come' (singular singular)
tum	*ao*	'you come' (plural plural)
ap	*aiye*	'you come' (plural plural)

Historically V*o* (V = verb stem) has belonged to *tum*, and V*iye* to *ap*, so that we had sentences like *tum ao* and *ap aiye*. By a semantic split in V*o*, we also have a sentence like *ap ao* which carries greater respect than *tum ao*, though lesser than *ap aiye*. If A is a pronoun and X a verbal form, we have a sentence AX. Similarly, if B is a pronoun more respectful than A and Y a verbal form more respectful than X, we have another sentence BY, more respectful than AX. Presumably, in an effort to find a sentence between AX and BY in terms of respect or social distance, we got a sentence BX:

A	X	*tum*	*ao*
B	Y	*ap*	*aiye*
B	X	*ap*	*ao*

None of the forms is lost, we have only added a new one. It could be asked why BX and why not AY? If we can get *ap ao*, then why can't we have **tum aiye*?

Ap-o seems to fulfil a social need. It is a new point in the continuum of social distance which had the high respect of *ap* yet was less distant than *ap aiye*. It is used in relationships where *ap aiye* would be used otherwise. The change is from more respectful to less respectful, so we get *ap ao* but not **tum aiye*.

The pronoun it seems is more dominant in the speaker's mind than the verb, even though the verb assumes the pronoun. In their choice of forms, people seem more conscious of pronouns than of verb forms; respect is associated more with pronouns than with verbs. This is indicated by the fact that the pronoun has been learned without learning the corresponding verb. Pronominal rather than verbal meanings are uppermost in the speaker's mind. Social contents were considered more important to learn than grammatical rules. They internalized the social rule but not the grammatical rule, as is clear from the fact that *ap-o* is considered a grammatical violation but not a social one.

In the final analysis, we are left with three pronouns occurring with four verbal forms which form the basis of their social distribution: *tu a*, *tum ao*, *ap ao* and *ap aiye*. This raises a theoretical as well as practical question. Is it possible to discuss pronominal usage without working on their co-occurrence with their verbal forms? Most modern day Hindi grammars and descriptions of Hindi miss out on *ap ao*.

9.2 A plea for *ap-o*

A study of pronominal usage necessarily requires a study of their agreement with co-occurring verbal forms. It will have implications for the semantics of pronouns involved as well as their historical development. It is not adequate to say that Hindi has three second person pronouns, as do most grammatical descriptions of Hindi, but when studied with verbal forms we shall posit four pronominal distinctions for Hindi. Kellogg (1876: 433) called *ap-o* 'incorrect' and warned against such 'laxity of usage' but acknowledged its presence. Ironically, more than a hundred years later when there is no stigma attached to the form and is used more frequently than before, it should be missing entirely from descriptions of Hindi. Kellogg (1876) and Guru (1920) draw all their data and examples from written works, whereas other grammars are either 'intuition-based' or based on incomplete data. Prescriptivists like Kellogg acknowledged the use of *ap-o*; but the descriptivists of today do not even acknowledge its existence.

Even those describing second person pronominal usage miss the point. By not considering verbal agreement to be a part of pronominal usage, they miss out a pronoun, leaving their description incomplete. In many Indo-Aryan and Dravidian languages, pronouns take a certain verbal form which is an essential part of their description.

Ferguson (1991: 183) called it a 'mismatch phenomena in politeness agreement with second person pronouns' and complains of their exclusion from grammatical theories:

> Agreement phenomena, by which one grammatical element matches another in terms of some categorial feature, present a challenge to contemporary theories of grammar. Agreement in features of politeness has, however, received very little attention, often not being noted in lists of possible agreement features.

In addition to this, a study of verbal endings will explain some of the changes taking place. Table 2.6 gives the distributional change of the respect feature. Two of the forms *aiyo* and *ao* are shown to have suffered a partial loss in distribution and merged with zero (Jain 1975: 93). This reassignment of features has also resulted in semantic change. The co-occurrence of *tum* with *aiyo* and *tu* with *ao* is lost in the later stage: *aiyo* has dropped its [+respect] feature whereas *ao* has lost its [−respect] feature. By excluding agreement the aspect of historical development is missed. A case of 'mismatch' phenomenon in Ferguson's terms, *ap ao* is a historical development. Its exclusion has resulted in an incomplete grammatical description of Hindi pronouns and of politeness behaviour.

TABLE 2.6: A CHANGE IN THE DISTRIBUTION OF FEATURES OF HINDI *AIYO* AND *AO*

	Singular	Plural
Old stage (early nineteenth century)	*aiyo, ao*	*aiyo, ao*
Later stage (1970+)	*aiyo*	*ao*

10 CONCLUSION

Language use in IA has involved a multiplicity of alternates to choose from: codes, scripts, lexicon, and so on. Twenty-five hundred years ago Buddha chose to communicate his message in the language of the masses. The Sufi and Sant poets of medieval times followed the Buddha path of colloquial speech (Rai 1984: 275) and the tradition has been kept alive by Hindi films in modern times. They have all received popular acceptance. The Buddha model of speech can be a model for language planners of the subcontinent. Across time and space in a multiple-choice situation in matters of script – whether Sanskrit written in Brāhmī, Nagari or Grantha and Panjabi in Arabic, Nagari or Gurmukhi – the choice of script seems to be a matter of regional preference.

In the history of language use in IA, we often find parallels between old and modern times. Ancient India was probably not so different from later India in its linguistic make-up and complexity (George Cardona, personal communication). This continuity is worth exploring. If we understand the present we can better reconstruct the past and the interaction of language and society in old India. Then, may be we can explain how speech changes every few miles and water every *kos*.

REFERENCES

Abbas, Khwaja Ahmad (1969) 'A link language for the common man', in *Language and Society in India*, Simla: Indian Institute of Advanced Study.

Bean, Susan S. (1970) 'Two's company, three's a crowd', *American Anthropologist*, 72: 562–4.

Beg, M. K. A. (1996) *Sociolinguistic Perspective of Hindi and Urdu in India*, New Delhi: Bahri Publications.

Bhattacharya, Jagat Ram (1993) *Origin and Development of Māgadhī*, University of Calcutta Ph.D. thesis (unpublished).

Breton, Roland J. L. (1999 updated edition) *Atlas of the Languages and Ethnic Communities of South Asia*, New Delhi: Sage Publications.

Brown, Roger W. and Gilman, A. (1960) 'The pronouns of power and solidarity', in Thomas A. Sebeok (ed.) *Style in Language*, Cambridge, Mass.: MIT Press.

Cardona, George (1974) 'Indo-Iranian Languages', *Encyclopaedia Britannica*, Chicago: University of Chicago. (Fifteenth edition (1991) Vol. 22: 612–24.)

—— (1997, second edition, revised and enlarged) *Pāṇini: His Work and its Traditions*, Delhi: Motilal Banarsidass.

Census of India (1981) *Population by Languages / Mother Tongue*, Series 1–India, Part IV B (i), Table C–7, New Delhi: Registrar General of India.

Census of India (1991) *Bilingualism and Trilingualism*, Series 1–India, Part IV B (i) (b)-C Series, New Delhi: Registrar General of India.

—— *Language*, Series 1–India, paper 1 of 1997, New Delhi: Registrar General of India.

Chandrasekhar, A. (1970) 'Personal pronouns and pronominal forms in Malayalam', *Anthropological Linguistics*, 12 (7): 246–55.

Chatterji, Suniti Kumar (1960) *Indo-Aryan and Hindi*, Calcutta: K. L. Mukhopadhyay.

Das, Sisir Kumar (1968) 'Forms of address and terms of reference in Bengali', *Anthropological Linguistics*, 10 (4): 19–31.

Das Gupta, Jyotirindra (1970) *Language Conflict and National Development*, Bombay: Oxford University Press.

Deshpande, Madhav M. (1979) *Sociolinguistic Attitudes in India: A Historical Reconstruction*, Ann Arbor: Karoma Publishers, Inc.

—— (1993) *Sanskrit and Prākrit: Sociolinguistic Issues*, Delhi: Motilal Banarsidass.

Deshpande, Madhav M. and Hook, Peter Edwin (eds.) (1979) *Aryan and Indo-Aryan in India*, Ann Arbor: University of Michigan.

Emeneau, M. B. (1956) 'India as a linguistic area', *Language*, 32: 3–16.

Ferguson, Charles A. (1959) 'Diglossia', *Word*, 15: 325–40. (Reprinted in Thom Huebner (ed.) (1996) *Sociolinguistic Perspectives*, Charles A. Ferguson, New York: Oxford University Press, pp. 25–39.)

—— (1968) 'Language development', in J. A. Fishman, C. A. Ferguson and J. Das Gupta (eds.), *Language Problems of Developing Nations*, New York: John Wiley and Sons.

—— (1991) 'South Asia as a sociolinguistic area', in E. Dimock, B. Kachru and Bh. Krishnamurti (eds.), *Dimensions of South Asia as a Sociolinguistic Area: Papers in Memory of Gerald Kelly*, New Delhi: Oxford and IBH, pp. 25–36. (Reprinted in Thom Huebner (ed.) (1996) *Sociolinguistic Perspectives*, Charles A. Ferguson, New York: Oxford University Press.)

Ferguson, Charles A. and Gumperz, John J. (eds.) (1960) 'Linguistic diversity in South Asia: Studies in regional, social and functional variation', *International Journal of American Linguistics*, 26: 3, Part 2.

Gair, James W. and Cain, Bruce C. (1996) 'Sinhala', in Peter T. Daniels and William Bright (eds.), *The World's Writing Systems*, New York and Oxford: Oxford University Press, pp. 564–8.

Grierson, George Abraham (1903–28) *Linguistic Survey of India*, 11 Vols. (Reprinted (1967) Delhi: Motilal Banarsidass.)

Gumperz, John J. (1964) 'Linguistic and social interaction in two communities', *American Anthropologist, The Ethnography of Communication*, edited by Gumperz, J. J. and Hymes, Dell 66: 6, part 2, pp. 137–53. (Reprinted in J. J. Gumperz (1971) *Language in Social Groups*, Stanford: Stanford University Press, pp. 151–76.)

Gumperz, John J. and Naim, C. M. (1960) 'Formal and informal standards in the Hindi regional language area', in Charles A. Ferguson and John J. Gumperz (1960) 'Linguistic diversity in South Asia: Studies in regional, social and functional variation', *International Journal of American Linguistics*, 26: 3, Part 2, pp. 92–118.

Guru, Kamta Prasad (1920) *Hindi Vyakaran* (in Hindi), Varanasi: Kashi Nagari Pracharini Sabha.

Houben, Jan E. M. (ed.) (1996) *Ideology and Status of Sanskrit: Contributions to the History of the Sanskrit Language*. New York: E. J. Brill.

Jain, Dhanesh K. (1973) *Pronominal Usage in Hindi: A Sociolinguistic Study*, University of Pennsylvania Ph.D. thesis (unpublished).

—— (1975) 'The semantic basis of some Hindi imperatives', *Indian Linguistics*, 36.2: 173–84.

Jain, Vinay (1999) *Sociolinguistics: A Study of Pronominal Usage in English and Hindi*, New Delhi: Commonwealth.

Kavi, Rama Krishna M. (ed.) (1956 second edition) *Nāṭyaśāstra of Bharatamuni* (Gaekwad's Oriental Series 36), Baroda: Oriental Institute, M.S. University of Baroda.

Kaye, Alan S. (1996) 'Adaptation of Arabic script', in Peter T. Daniels and William Bright (eds.), *The World's Writing Systems*, New York and Oxford: Oxford University Press, pp. 743–62.

Keith, Berriedale A. (1923) *The Sanskrit Drama in its Origin, Development, Theory and Practice*, Oxford: Oxford University Press. (Reprinted (1998) Delhi: Motilal Banarsidass.)

Kellogg, S. H. (1876) *A Grammar of the Hindi Language*, London: Kegan Paul. (Reprinted (1972) New Delhi: Oriental Books Reprint Corporation.)

Masica, Colin P. (1991) *The Indo-Aryan Languages*, Cambridge: Cambridge University Press.

Meenakshi, K. (1999) 'Why not Aryaputri?', *Dravidian Linguistic Association News*, Vol. 23, No. 11, Thiruvananthapuram.

Mehrotra, Raja Ram (1985) *Sociolinguistics in Hindi Contexts*, Berlin: Mouton de Gruyter.

Misra, K. S. (1977) *Terms of Address and Second Person Pronominal Usage in Hindi: A Sociolinguistic Study*, New Delhi: Bahri Publications.

Mukherjee, Aditi (1992) 'Planning Hindi for mass communication', *The Administrator*, Vol. XXXVII, Oct.–Dec.: 73–80.

—— (1996) *Language Maintenance and Language Shift: Punjabis and Bengalis in Delhi*, New Delhi: Bahri Publications.

Pandit, Prabodh B. (1972) *India as a Sociolinguistic Area*, Poona: University of Poona.

Pillai, M. Shanmugam (1971) 'Address terms and the social hierarchy of the Tamils', in *Proceedings of the First All-India Conference of Dravidian Linguists*, Trivandrum, pp. 424–32.

Rahman, Tariq (1996) 'The Punjabi Movement in Pakistan', *International Journal of Sociology of Language*, 122: 73–88.

Rai, Amrit (1984) *A House Divided: The Origin and Development of Hindi/Hindavi*, Delhi: Oxford University Press.

Salomon, Richard (1998) *Indian Epigraphy*, New York: Oxford University Press.

Schmidt, Ruth and Kharel, N. R. (1972) 'Honorific registers in the multi-ethnic society of Nepal', Paper prepared for Association for Asian Studies Annual Conference, New York (March 1972).

Shackle, C. (1970) 'Punjabi in Lahore', *Modern Asian Studies*, London, 4 (3): 239–67.

Shapiro, Michael and Schiffman, Harold (1981) *Language and Society in South Asia*, Delhi: Motilal Banarsidass.

Singh, K. S. and Manoharan, S. (1993) *Languages and Scripts: People of India*, National Series, Vol. IX, Delhi: Anthropological Survey of India and Oxford University Press.

Suseendrarajah, S. (1970) 'Reflections of certain social differences in Jaffna Tamil', *Anthropological Linguistics*, 12 (7): 239–45.

The Wealth of India, Vol. VII (1971) New Delhi: Publications and Information Directorate, Council of Scientific and Industrial Research.

FURTHER READING

Breton, Roland J. L. (1999 updated edition) *Atlas of the Languages and Ethnic Communities of South Asia*, New Delhi: Sage Publications.

Deshpande, Madhav M. (1979) *Sociolinguistic Attitudes in India: A Historical Reconstruction*, Ann Arbor: Karoma Publishers, Inc.

Ferguson, Charles (1996) *Sociolinguistic Perspectives*, New York: Oxford University Press.

Gair, James W. (1998) *Studies in South Asian Linguistics: Sinhala and Other South Asian Languages*, selected and edited by Barbara C. Lust. New York: Oxford University Press.

Gumperz, John J. (1971) *Language in Social Groups*, Stanford: Stanford University Press.

Houben, Jan E. M. (ed.) (1996) *Ideology and Status of Sanskrit: Contributions to the History of the Sanskrit Language*, New York: E. J. Brill.

Ishtiaq, M. (1999) *Language Shifts among the Scheduled Tribes in India: A Geographical Study*, Delhi: Motilal Banarsidass.

Kansakar, Tej R. (1996) 'Multilingualism and the language situation in Nepal', *Linguistics of the Tibeto-Burman Area*, 19.2: 17–30.

Khubchandani, Lachman M. (1983) *Plural Languages, Plural Cultures: Communication, Identity and Sociopolitical Change in Contemporary India*, Honolulu: University of Hawaii Press.

Rai, Alok (2001) *Hindi Nationalism*, Delhi: Orient Longman.

Rai, Amrit (1984) *A House Divided: The Origin and Development of Hindi/Hindavi*, Delhi: Oxford University Press.

Rahman, Tariq (1998) *Language and Politics in Pakistan*, Karachi: Oxford University Press.

Salomon, Richard (1998) *Indian Epigraphy*, New York: Oxford University Press.

Shapiro, Michael and Schiffman, Harold (1981) *Language and Society in South Asia*, Delhi: Motilal Banarsidass.

CHAPTER THREE

WRITING SYSTEMS OF THE INDO-ARYAN LANGUAGES

Richard Salomon

CONTENTS

LIST OF TABLES

LIST OF FIGURES

1 GENERAL OVERVIEW: SCRIPTS USED FOR THE INDO-ARYAN LANGUAGES

The history of the written forms of the IA languages mainly concerns the ancient Brāhmī script and its numerous varieties and derivatives over more than two millennia. From the time of the earliest surviving documents and down to the present day, most of the IA languages have used one or more of these scripts. There are, however, some important exceptions. In ancient times, Gāndhārī, the IA language of the northwestern fringe of the South Asian cultural area, was written in the Kharoṣṭhī script (see 3.2), which is not directly related to Brāhmī. Since medieval times, several of the NIA languages, most notably Urdu, have been written in adapted forms of the Perso-Arabic script (5.1), and in modern times these scripts are the principal ones used for the various IA languages of Pakistan as well as for some IA languages in India. In recent centuries the Roman script (5.2) has also sporadically been used in connection with some IA languages. Despite these important exceptions, on the whole the history of the writing systems used to write the IA languages is intimately linked with the Brāhmī script family.

1.1 Scripts of the NIA languages

The principal Indian-derived scripts currently in wide use for IA languages are: Nagari (or Devanagari), used for Hindi and affiliated languages including various dialects of Bihar, Madhya Pradesh and Rajasthan, for Marathi, for Nepali (in Nepal), and frequently but not exclusively for Sanskrit; Gurmukhi, used for Panjabi; Gujarati, used for Gujarati and Kacchi; Bangla, used for Bangla and, with slight alterations, for

Asamiya; Oriya, used for Oriya; and Sinhala, used for Sinhala (in Sri Lanka). These scripts are conveniently presented in comparative charts in Ojhā 1918: plates 77–9 (Sinhala not included), Renou and Filliozat 1953: 693–5, and Masica 1991: 138–42. Up-to-date descriptions from a linguistic point of view are given in the relevant sections of part VI, 'South Asian Writing Systems' in Daniels and Bright 1996: 371–441. Lambert 1953 provides detailed descriptions for Nagari, Gujarati and Bangla.

In addition to these major scripts which are associated with official languages of India and neighbouring countries and which are widely used for printed literature, there also are, or at least were until the relatively recent past, a vast variety of local scripts, many used for handwritten documents only. The most important of these local scripts were Śāradā, used for Kashmiri (nowadays written in a Perso-Arabic script); Ṭākrī, with several sub-varieties such as Ḍogrī and Camĕālī, used for local dialects in and around the Panjab; Laṇḍā and its varieties, used for dialects of the Sind and Panjab; Maithilī and Kaithī, used for local dialects in Bihar; Moḍī, used for Marathi; and Chakma (a variant of Burmese script) used for the Chittagong hills dialect of Bangla (Grierson 1903–27: vol. 5.1: 321–3). Specimens of some of these local scripts are provided in Ojhā 1918: plates 77–9 and in Renou and Filliozat (ibid.), and more abundant examples appear among the specimens of languages reproduced in handwriting in Grierson 1903–27, especially in volumes 5 (Indo-Aryan Languages, Eastern Group), 8 (Northwestern group) and 9 (Central group). Leitner 1883 is a rare example of detailed documentation of the local scripts of a particular area, namely the west and northwest. In general, however, these local scripts are not well documented, and little published information is available about their current status. Many of them have fallen out of use within the last century, largely due to the standardizing effect of printing technology and of the language policy of the republic of India since independence, which has favoured the propagation of the official languages of the individual states, and along with each of them, a standard script (Masica 1991: 143–4).

For practical purposes, the Brāhmī-derived scripts used for the NIA languages can be divided into four geographical groups, based on their genealogical relationships and the consequent visual similarities of their characters:

(a)   The western–northwestern group, including Gurmukhi, Śāradā, Ṭākrī, Laṇḍā and their many subvarieties.
(b)   The northern–central group, comprising Nagari, Gujarati, and their varieties.
(c)   The eastern group, composed of Bangla and its Asamiya variant, Oriya, and Maithilī, Kaithī and the other scripts of Bihar.
(d)   The southern group, comprising (among IA languages) only Sinhala, although Oriya has some features resembling this group.

Overall, however, the scripts used for IA languages do not constitute a natural grouping, since they are only a subset of the Brāhmī-derived script family as a whole. This family has developed mainly along geographic patterns rather than according to language families, and this is why Sinhala and, to a lesser extent Oriya, are formally more like the south Indian scripts used for Dravidian languages. To speak of 'IA scripts', in other words, is to set up an artificial category, since a more natural division of the Brāhmī-derived scripts as a whole would be into north Indian, south Indian, Southeast Asian and Central Asian groups.

1.2 Scripts of the OIA and MIA languages

Whereas among the NIA languages there is a general (though by no means complete) pattern of one-to-one correspondence between language or dialect and script or script variety, the situation is entirely different with regard to the OIA and MIA languages, particularly Sanskrit. Although in modern usage Sanskrit is most commonly written or printed in Nagari, in theory it can be represented by virtually any of the main Brāhmī-based scripts, and in practice it often is. Thus scripts such as Gujarati, Bangla, and Oriya, as well as the major south Indian scripts, traditionally have been and often still are used in their proper territories for writing Sanskrit. Sanskrit, in other words, is not inherently linked to any particular script, although it does have a special historical connection with Nagari (see 2.1). This is presumably because its essential form tends to be conceived in oral rather than written terms (1.5.1).

Pali, as an MIA language which came to be the canonical language of the Theravāda Buddhist tradition of Sri Lanka and Southeast Asia, exhibits a similar pattern, presumably for the same or similar reasons. Pali has traditionally been written in the local scripts of the various regions in which it is the language of religion, namely Sinhala, Burmese, Thai, Lao and Khmer. More recently, in connection with efforts to publish and propagate Pali texts in India, Nagari has begun to be used for Pali, while in the west it is frequently printed in Roman script.

Thus it is for the most part only in connection with the development of the NIA languages that scripts and languages begin to be conceived as directly and inherently linked. In ancient and medieval times, the OIA and MIA languages, that is, Sanskrit and the Prakrits, at different times and places were written in a vast number of forms and derivatives of Brāhmī. In the premodern period, in other words, these languages would be written by a given scribe in whatever happened to be the current local script; there was no fixed or definitive form for the written language, at least as far as the outward shapes of the characters were concerned.

1.3 Systemic features of the Brāhmī-derived scripts

Many of the Brāhmī-derived scripts used for IA languages may appear quite different to the untrained eye, but ultimately the differences between them are mostly superficial, in that they all share essentially the same phonetic repertoire and systemic features. With small variations, they all have the same basic set of eleven vowels and thirty-three consonants, a repertoire which is largely determined by that of Sanskrit even where it is not always strictly applicable to the phonetics of the various NIA languages (see 2.3–2.4). Even more significantly, they share, again with only minor variations, the same basic graphic principles which are characteristic of Indian scripts generally. The principal features of this script type are:

(a) The basic unit is the graphic syllable or *akṣara*, with the phonetic structures V, CV, CCV, etc. The graphic syllable is understood by definition to always end with a vowel.

(b) An unmarked consonant sign is assumed to represent that consonant plus the 'inherent' vowel *a*, unless some other vowel or the absence of a vowel is explicitly marked on it.

(c) A set of diacritic or secondary marks is added to the consonant sign(s) to indicate vowels other than the 'inherent' *a* following the consonant in syllables of the type CV, CCV, etc.

(d) A separate set of 'full' or 'initial' vowel signs is used to represent syllables of the type V, most commonly (especially in Sanskrit) at the beginning of a word, but also medially in cases of vowel hiatus (mostly in MIA and NIA languages).

(e) Clusters of two or more consonants without an intervening vowel are represented by a conjunct syllable (*saṁyuktākṣara*) in which the consonant signs are physically joined together, usually with some abbreviation of one or both of them.

(f) In the case of a graphic 'syllable' of the type C (for instance, at the end of a word ending in a consonant), an additional diacritic sign, called in Sanskrit *virāma* 'stop' or *halanta* 'consonant-final', is attached to the consonant to indicate the cancellation of the inherent vowel.

The following are examples of the basic syllable types in the parent script, early Brāhmī, and in its most widespread derivative, Nagari:

Syllable type	Phonetic value	Brāhmī	Nagari
V	*a*	⅄	अ
C*a* (with inherent vowel)	*ka*	+	क
CV	*kā*	+̣	का
CCV	*kya*	⚓	क्य
C	*k*	[not used in early Brāhmī]	क्

The following are examples of complete words in Sanskrit exemplifying these syllabic types in Nagari. The divisions into graphic syllables are marked with a hyphen in the transliteration (for further details and examples see 2.1.1):

कुटुम्बकम्   *ku-ṭu-mba-ka-m* 'family' (nominative singular)
अर्थात्   *a-rthā-t* 'that is to say', 'i.e.'

This type of script, which combines some of the features of syllabic and alphabetic writing, is distinctive of and peculiar to Indian scripts in general, including the now defunct Kharoṣṭhī script (see 3.2) as well as Brāhmī and all of its derivatives, but is rare among scripts elsewhere in the world. Only in the Ethiopic scripts do we find an approximately similar system, though they lack some of the characteristic Indic features such as the special set of full vowel signs and the system of forming consonantal conjuncts to represent clusters. There is no consensus on what term should best be applied to scripts of this type. Among those which have been suggested are 'alpha-syllabary' (Daniels and Bright 1996: 384), 'neo-syllabary', or 'abugida' (Daniels and Bright 1996: 4; for further references see Salomon 1998a: 15–16). I would propose the more apposite and less ambiguous term 'akshara script'.

Nearly all of the scripts of the dominant Brāhmī group share the same alphabetic ordering, which, unlike the alphabets of most scripts of the world, follows a logical phonetic order; this presumably reflects the sophisticated awareness and understanding of language that prevailed from an early period in India. In this system, usually referred to as *varṇamālā* 'garland of letters', the characters are divided into vowels (*svara*) and consonants (*vyañjana*), and each major set is further divided into subgroups, again on phonetic principles. Thus the vowels are subdivided into simple vowels and diphthongs, each set up as short/long pairs (*a-ā-i-ī-u-ū*, etc.), while the consonants are classified into the groups *vargīya* (comprising stops, *sparśa*, including nasals, *anunāsika*), *antaḥstha* (semivowels), and *ūṣman* (spirants, including *ha*). Within each consonant subclass, the individual letters are arranged by place and manner of articulation. Thus the largest set, the twenty-five *vargīya*s, is divided into five sets (*varga*) of consonants with the same place of articulation, arranged from the back to the front of the mouth: *kaṇṭhya* 'velar', *tālavya* 'palatal', *mūrdhanya* 'retroflex' or 'cerebral', *dantya* 'dental' and *oṣṭhya* 'labial'. Each *varga* contains five types of consonants: unvoiced unaspirated, unvoiced aspirated, voiced unaspirated, voiced aspirated and nasal. This system may have originally been developed in a tradition of linguistic analysis before the use of writing, and only subsequently been applied to the written form of language in Brāhmī script. The earliest written specimens of the *varṇamālā* are found in terracotta plaques of about the second century BC showing a schoolboy's writing lessons (Salomon 1990: 271).

The written letters are usually referred to by adding the suffix element *-kāra* 'maker' to the sound value of the character; thus *a-kāra* 'the letter *a*' (literally, 'maker of [the sound] *a*), *ka-kāra*, 'the letter *ka*', etc. But the letters are also sometimes referred to by their sound value alone (*'a'*, *'ka'*), or in some regions by reduplicative names (see 2.2 and 2.5).

1.4 Overview of the history and family relationship of the Brāhmī-derived scripts

The earliest forms of Brāhmī script known to us, mainly from the Aśokan inscriptions (see 3.1.1), are more or less uniform throughout the South Asian subcontinent. Gradually, Brāhmī began to develop minor local variants, and these variations continued to diverge over the centuries until eventually, by about the second half of the first millennium AD, they have become what might be properly called separate scripts, in the sense that one would no longer be able to easily read one of them on the basis of a knowledge of another. Nevertheless, the underlying similarities of the corresponding letter forms become readily apparent when they are traced back through history to their Brāhmī prototypes.

Within the subgroup of the Brāhmī-derived scripts which are used for the IA languages, the differences are for the most part not very extensive, and some of them are even more or less mutually intelligible; for instance, anyone who knows Nagari script can pick up Gujarati script with little effort. In the case of scripts such as Gurmukhi, Bangla and Oriya, the differences are considerably more pronounced, and the Nagari reader would have trouble recognizing some, though not all of their letters without special study. Each Brāhmī-derived script has a characteristic stylistic format or ductus, which tends to exaggerate their apparent differences and mask their underlying similarities. For example, Nagari has a strong preference for symmetrical shapes, especially squared outlines and right angles, while Bangla tends toward forms with acute angles. Oriya, with its rounded shapes and large curved 'umbrella' above each letter superficially looks very different from Bangla, but closer examination and historical comparison show that they are actually very similar. Compare, for example, the forms of the consonants *ka* and *ṣa* in the three scripts:

	Nagari	Bangla	Oriya
ka	क	ক	କ
ṣa	ष	ষ	ଷ

Here we can see that the distinctive portion of the Oriya *ka* is essentially the same as that of the other two scripts, the main difference being its overall ductus and its large curved head, which is one of the various modern derivatives of the head mark or serif of early Brāhmī (see 4.1). Oriya seems anomalous among the north Indian scripts because its ductus is more typical of the south Indian scripts, most of which have a similar preference for curved and rounded rather than angular shapes.

1.5 Cultural and historical factors underlying script developments

1.5.1 The status of written vis-à-vis oral language

The tendency in Indian tradition generally, and particularly in the premodern period and the Sanskritic cultural milieu, to consider the oral form of a language as more primary than the written form (1.2) has had important effects on the development of script in India, and explains many of its peculiarities. In India, writing has traditionally tended to be viewed as an adjunct to or reflection of true language, that is, the spoken word. This attitude is manifested in a frequently casual attitude toward the aesthetic aspects of writing, such that calligraphy was, in pre-Islamic India, a minor art at best and never rose to anything approaching the level that it attained in cultural regions such as China or the Islamic world (Salomon 1984, Salomon 1998a: 68–70).

The secondary status of written language also explains the tendency, especially in the early period, towards defective (in the technical sense) forms of writing. Thus we find in the earliest surviving written documents, written in various MIA dialects, that orthography is often incomplete, for example in representing geminate consonants by the single consonant (see 3.1.3), and inconsistent in various ways. Although it is true that in later centuries, as Sanskrit became established as the major language of epigraphic and official documents, a more rigorous and standardized orthography came into play and greater attention was paid to the form and appearance of the documents, still the tendency toward casual writing remained strong in less formal types of writing, whether in Sanskrit or in regional languages.

The same cultural values may also explain, in part at least, the extreme regional diversity and lack of standardization among Indian scripts. Although this is admittedly a complex matter, involving political, geographical, and historical as well as cultural factors, the unrestricted development of local varieties and subvarities of scripts was influenced, if not determined, by the sense that writing is of secondary cultural value. This resulted in a vast proliferation, unparalleled elsewhere in the world, of script varieties in South Asia.

1.5.2 Problems of standardization and nomenclature of scripts

Presumably also related to the secondary status of writing in traditional Indian cultural values is the lack of standardization, not only of the forms of the scripts, but also of their nomenclature. In contrast to other traditions, for example in East Asia and the Islamic world, where variant styles of writing were a matter of prime importance in literary and cultural traditions, in premodern Indian literature very little is said about such matters. There are no ancient treatises on the art and forms of writing, and only a few lists of scripts (*lipi*) in Buddhist and Jaina texts tell us anything about the original names of the ancient scripts. In fact, it is only from these lists that we even know the names 'Brāhmī' and 'Kharoṣṭhī' for the two major ancient scripts, which appear as the first two names in the most extensive of these lists, found in the *Lalitavistara*, a biography of the Buddha. Although this list contains sixty-four names in all (see Salomon 1998a: 8–9 for details), only these two can be definitely identified with actual script forms that we know from ancient documents, a situation that reflects the lack of information about, and hence presumably of interest in script varieties in the tradition. It is noteworthy that what little information we do have comes almost entirely from the Buddhist and Jaina traditions, which tended to have somewhat more regard for the written word than the 'mainstream' Brahmanical literary tradition, which has virtually nothing on the subject.

The result is that in most cases we have no authoritative knowledge of the traditional names of the various premodern scripts, and indeed we are not even sure that all or even most of them ever had distinct or definitive names. Even in the case of an important exception like the 'Siddhamātṛkā' script (see 4.5), the clearest attestation of the term comes from a non-Indian source, namely Al-Bīrūnī's *India*. Therefore most of the premodern scripts are referred to by scholars by a hodgepodge of *ad hoc* linguistic, geographical, political or chronological terms such as 'Kuṣāṇa script', 'eastern Gupta script' or 'proto-Kannada-Telugu script'. Such terminology remains largely unstandardized, partly because much of the necessary detailed study of regional script styles still remains to be done, but also because clear lines of definition between the scripts and their variants are not always apparent and may never have existed. In other words, the absence of an indigenous terminology reflects the absence of a conscious standardization and categorization of styles. Until relatively recently (see 1.1), script forms tended to be fluid and variable, with gradual variations over small areas in time and space without clearly defined boundaries. In this respect, the behaviour of scripts mirrors typical patterns of distribution of languages and dialects in South Asia.

In view of these problems, it is impossible to be entirely consistent about the names of the scripts. It is not even clear, for example, where exactly the boundary lies between 'Brāhmī', taken as the name of the early prototype script, and its derivatives; that is to say, there is no single authority which tells us, for instance, when Brāhmī ends and Siddhamātṛkā begins. Therefore, as a matter of convenience, we follow in this article the standard established by D. C. Sircar (1970–1: 113), according to which 'Brāhmī' refers to scripts through the sixth century AD, and this period can be called the 'early' phase of the development of the Indic scripts. The period from the seventh to the tenth centuries could be called the middle or transitional phase, in which the local descendants of Brāhmī are beginning to take their distinct modern form, while from the eleventh century onwards we can speak of a modern period, during which the local scripts take on forms that are recognizably similar to their modern shapes.

1.6 Sources for the historical study of the Indian scripts

The history of the Indian scripts has been reconstructed by scholars over the past two centuries on the basis of inscriptions and manuscripts. For the earliest period, our knowledge of the Indian scripts is based entirely on inscriptions on stone, metal and other materials (see Salomon 1998a: 110–60 for a detailed survey). Only from about the second century do we begin to have any manuscripts, and these remain rare until about the tenth century, so that the study of the scripts up to this point is still mainly based on epigraphic materials. Due to the monsoon climate, manuscripts on perishable materials like palm leaf and birch bark rarely last more than a few centuries, and most of the early Indian manuscripts have been found either in the northwestern fringe of the subcontinent or in other parts of Asia, such as Afghanistan (Salomon 1999: 57–68) or the Tarim Basin in Chinese Central Asia (Sander 1968).

From about the beginning of the second millennium AD, manuscript materials from South Asia become more common, especially in Nepal, and enormous numbers of manuscripts from the past few centuries survive in all parts of India. These constitute a rich source of information for the study of the development of the scripts of the modern period, but very few detailed analyses of this material have actually been carried out. The field of Indian palaeography has been heavily dominated by studies with historical and antiquarian inclinations, so that in general the earlier the period, the better the documentation in scholarly literature. Indeed, the palaeographical development of the modern scripts on the basis of manuscript sources is still virtually an untouched field (cf. 4.6).

2 THE SCRIPTS USED FOR THE MAJOR MODERN IA LANGUAGES

2.1 Nagari (Devanagari) script

Nagari script has today, and to some extent has had in past times, a special status as the closest approximation to a 'national script' in India and the Indian cultural area. Unlike most of the other modern scripts, it is not linked with and limited to a single language, being used for Hindi, Marathi, Nepali and Sanskrit, among others, and has superseded several of the minor local scripts in recent years (Masica 1991: 144). Moreover, its supra-local status has historical roots in that early forms of Nagari and its prototypes were often used outside of north India. For example, a script known as Nandi-nāgarī and other similar northern-style scripts were sporadically used instead of, or in addition to, the local scripts for writing Sanskrit in the Deccan and south India from the seventh century onwards (Sivaramamurti 1952: 184–93; Maurer 1976: 104). Inscriptions in early or proto-forms of Nagari are also found outside of India, as far afield as Sri Lanka, Burma and Indonesia, and the Siddhamātṛkā script, from which Nagari developed, became a sacred form of writing for Buddhists in East Asia (van Gulik 1956). Thus, although Nagari has not supplanted the other major scripts, despite various recent reform movements which have proposed its universal adoption, it does have a special status as a sort of *primus inter pares* among the Indic scripts. In this way, Nagari can be said to have played a role among scripts that is in part analogous to that of languages such as Sanskrit, Persian and English, which at various times have served as linguae francae for the south Asian cultural region.

The origin and meaning of the terms *nāgarī* '(script [*lipi*]) of the city' and *devanāgarī* '(script) of the city of the gods', are uncertain. Maurer 1976 argues that the shorter form was the original one, though its original meaning is obscure. It has been suggested (Maurer 1976: 104) that it resulted from an association with the Nāgar brahmans of Gujarat.

2.1.1 Nagari for Sanskrit (table 3.1)

Nagari script as used for Sanskrit serves as the prototype for its application, with minor variations or additions, to other languages. The Sanskrit version of the script has the fullest repertoire of characters, including several such as the vowels *ṝ*, *l̥* and *l̥̄* and the supplementary character *visarga* (*ḥ*) which are either not used in other languages or appear only in highly Sanskritized literary styles. The letter *l̥̄* is not actually a primary phoneme of the Sanskrit language, but it usually included among the vowels in order to maintain the symmetry of short/long pairs (1.3). Nagari for Sanskrit has forty-seven primary characters, fourteen vowels and thirty-three consonants. For Vedic, there are two additional consonantal characters ळ *ḷa* and ळ्ह *ḷha*, which represent allophonic variants of *ḍa* and *ḍha* respectively in intervocalic position.

Despite efforts in recent decades toward standardization, there are variant forms for several of the basic characters of Nagari. In most of the examples given in Table 3.1, the

TABLE 3.1: NAGARI SCRIPT AS USED FOR SANSKRIT

Vowels (full form)

a	अ	i	इ	u	उ	$ṛ$	ऋ	$ḷ$	ऌ	e	ए	o	ओ	$aṁ$	अं
$ā$	आ	$ī$	ई	$ū$	ऊ	$ṝ$	ॠ	$ḹ$	ॡ	ai	ऐ	au	औ	$aḥ$	अः

Vowels (post-consonantal, with k)

ka	क	ki	कि	ku	कु	$kṛ$	कृ	$kḷ$	कॢ	ke	के	ko	को	$kaṁ$	कं
$kā$	का	$kī$	की	$kū$	कू	$kṝ$	कॄ	$kḹ$	कॣ	kai	कै	kau	कौ	$kaḥ$	कः

Vargīya consonants

	unvoiced unaspirated		unvoiced aspirated		voiced unaspirated		voiced aspirated		nasal	
velar	ka	क	kha	ख	ga	ग	gha	घ	$ṅa$	ङ
palatal	ca	च	cha	छ	ja	ज	jha	झ	$ña$	ञ
retroflex	$ṭa$	ट	$ṭha$	ठ	$ḍa$	ड	$ḍha$	ढ	$ṇa$	ण
dental	ta	त	tha	थ	da	द	dha	ध	na	न
labial	pa	प	pha	फ	ba	ब	bha	भ	ma	म

Semivowels

ya	य	ra	र	la	ल	va	व

Spirants

$śa$	श	$ṣa$	ष	sa	स	ha	ह

Representative examples of consonantal conjuncts

kya	क्य	$kṣa$	क्ष	$jña$	ज्ञ	tva	त्व	dga	द्ग
pra	प्र	rva	र्व	$ṣṭa$	ष्ट	$stra$	स्त्र	spa	स्प

first form is the more archaic one, the second the more modern, though regional variations also play a part (see Lambert 1953: 16–17):

a and $ā$:	ऋअ, ऋआ	अ आ
kha:	रव	ख
jha:	झ	झ
$ṇa$:	ए	ण
la:	ल	ळ
$śa$:	श	श.

The complete Nagari system for Sanskrit also involves several modifiers, extra characters, and punctuational symbols:

(a) *anusvāra* (ṁ) consists of a dot placed above the *akṣara* (full vowel or consonant) to indicate a nasal modification of its vocalic portion, for example, किं *kiṁ* 'what?'. It is often also used as a shorthand notation for a nasal consonant before a homorganic stop, as in अंग *aṁga* = more formal अङ्ग *aṅga* 'limb'. Sometimes the more emphatic form called *candrabindu* ('moon-and-dot') or *anunāsika* ('nasal') is used to mark a true nasalization, as in तॉल्लोकान् *tāṁl lokān* 'those worlds' (accusative). *Anusvāra* is not a primary phoneme, but generally results from sandhi combinations involving an original *m*.

(b) *Visarga* (*ḥ*) consists of two dots or circles arranged vertically at the right side of the *akṣara*, and is usually pronounced as a light aspiration, often followed by an echo of the preceding vowel; thus मुनिः *muniḥ* [munih[i]] 'the sage' (nominative). Like *anusvāra*, *visarga* is not a primary phoneme, but results from sandhi changes of an original *s*, or less commonly *r*, usually in word final position. In archaic forms of Nagari (and some other Brāhmī-derived scripts) there were distinct characters for the *jihvāmūlīya* (*ḫ*) and *upadhmānīya* (*ḫ*) varieties of *visarga* before velar and labial consonants respectively, but in modern usage these are not usually distinguished from ordinary *visarga*.

(c) The *virāma* or *halanta* sign (not usually represented in transcription), indicating the cancellation of the inherent vowel, consists of a short diagonal line sloping down from the lower right corner of a consonant, as in क् *k* (as opposed to क *ka*). In traditional usage, this sign is avoided wherever possible, even at the cost of suppressing word boundaries. Thus Sanskrit words ending in a consonant are joined in a syllabic unit with the first syllable of the following word, as in तत्किम् *tat kim* 'what is that?', so that *virāma* is usually found only at the end of a sentence or line of verse. In modern usage, however, especially in printing and computer fonts, *virāma* is often used to break up cumbersome conjuncts of three or more consonants; for example a Sanskrit word like भुङ्क्ष्व *bhuṅkṣva* 'eat!' may be printed as भुङ्क्ष्व. For the most part, *virāma* only appears in Sanskrit, though it is occasionally used in *tatsama* words in literary forms of NIA languages.

(d) *Avagraha* (') is a punctuational sign indicating the elision or coalescence of a vowel as a result of sandhi processes, as in एकोऽयम् *eko 'yam* (< *ekas* + *ayam*) 'this one'. An original long vowel lost by coalescence is sometimes indicated by a double *avagraha*, as in सदाऽऽत्मा *sadā ''tmā* (< *sadā* + *ātmā* 'always, the self').

Traditionally, punctuation was limited to the *daṇḍa* ('stick'), a vertical line marking a pause, often doubled to indicate a full stop. In modern printed usage, punctuation marks borrowed from Roman script, such as comma, question mark and exclamation mark, are sometimes employed, either as in western languages or with special adaptations, such as the exclamation mark to indicate a noun in the vocative form.

Besides the forty-seven basic characters and the various supplementary signs, Nagari script, particularly as used for Sanskrit, has a very large number of combined characters. There are two types of combinatory characters, which may occur together within a single syllabic *akṣara*:

(a) Combinations of consonants plus diacritic forms of the vowels (syllable type CV, where V ≠ *a*, the inherent vowel; see 1.3).

(b) Conjunct consonant combinations, with or without diacritic vowel signs (syllable types CCV, CCCV, etc., with subtypes CC*a* etc. and CCV[-a] etc.).

Given the permutations of these two combinational patterns within the same *akṣara*, the total number of syllabic combinations is very large. For the most part, this is not a practical problem, since the components usually combine in a predictable and recognizable fashion, but in both types of combinatory characters there are some anomalous formations resulting from conventional ligaturization or graphic difficulties in combining certain shapes. Thus, among type (a), the consonant + vowel combinations, the following are formed with some alteration of the basic shape of one or the other component: रु *ru* and रू *rū* (though in some modern fonts the regularized forms रु and रू have been introduced), दृ *dṛ*, शृ *śṛ*, हृ *hṛ*.

Type (b), the consonant conjuncts, are far more diverse and complicated. In general, the principle is that the component elements are joined horizontally in the case of combinations whose prior member has a vertical line on its right side, such as व्य *vya*, or vertically where this is not the case, as in ङ्क *ṅka*. Often the formation of conjuncts, especially of the first type, involves some abbreviation or alteration of one member, more commonly of the prior one, but not infrequently of the latter, or sometimes even of both. In quite a few cases, there are optional variants in the formation of conjuncts, such as ज्ज or ज्ज *jja*. Conjuncts of more than two consonants are made according to similar principles, as in न्त्य *ntya*, and conjuncts of up to five consonants are possible (र्त्स्न्य *rtsnya*, only in the word *kārtsnya* 'entirety').

The last example illustrates one of the special forms of the semivowel *r* in conjunct combination. In preconsonantal position, it is written as a hook attached to the top centre or upper right corner of the *akṣara*, for instance in र्प *rpa*. When it occurs in multiple consonant clusters as in the example in the previous paragraph, or in syllables with a diacritic vowel sign that is written above or to the right of the consonant portion as in the syllable र्पे *rpe*, *r* violates the normal order of reading sequence; that is to say, it is at the right side of the syllable, but is to be read as the first element of it. When *r* follows another consonant or consonants, it is abbreviated as a small diagonal line pointing down leftward from the bottom of the syllable, as in प्र *pra*. This form is also used when *r* comes between consonants, as in द्र्य *drya*. The special behaviour of *r* in conjunct formation is presumably due to its high frequency in consonant clusters in Sanskrit, and is reflected in the other Brāhmī-derived scripts as well (see 3.3).

Statistical frequency similarly explains the development of two other special consonantal ligatures, क्ष (older form क्ष) *kṣa* and ज्ञ *jña*. Although the component parts of these ligatures are no longer discernible in Nagari, they can be traced to their original forms as normal conjuncts in middle Brāhmī. However, as a result of having developed distinct shapes (and in some languages also special pronunciations), they are often considered as separate letters, placed at the end of the alphabet (Lambert 1953: 34).

There is also a substantial number of conjuncts in which the component parts are altered from their usual forms. The most common of these are:

त्र *tra*, where त *ta* is abbreviated before the post-consonantal *r*
त्त *tta*, with similar abbreviation of the first *ta* in the geminate conjunct
क्त *kta*, with abbreviation of *ka* in combination with *ta*
श्र *śra*, श्च *śca*, श्व *śva*, etc. with an optional alternative form of श *śa* before certain consonants (compare also शृ *śṛ* noted above).

2.1.2 Nagari for Hindi

Nagari script as used for Hindi and many related languages and dialects is essentially the same script as for Sanskrit, but with some deletions, additions and other changes. The Sanskrit vowels ṛ, ḷ, and ḹ are omitted from the Hindi *varṇamālā*. The consonants *ṅa*, *ña*, and *ṇa* and *ṣa* are retained, but appear only in Sanskrit loanwords (*tatsama*) in literary style. Symbols needed to represent sounds of Hindi not present in Sanskrit are created by adding a diacritic dot (*nuktā*) below the letters representing similar sounds. Thus ड़ *ṛa* and ढ़ *ṛha* represent the flapped pronunciation of ड *ḍa* and ढ *ḍha* respectively in non-initial position (compare the *ḷ* and *ḷha* of Vedic, 2.1.1). Several other such letters were introduced to render sounds occurring in loanwords from Arabic and Persian: क़ *ḳa* [qə], ख़ *ḳha* [xə], ग़ *ga* [ɣə], ज़ *ja* [zə], and फ़ *pha* [fə]. In theory, conjunct consonants operate as in Sanskrit, but in practice there are important differences. On the one hand, many of the conjuncts occurring in Sanskrit are absent or used only in Sanskritized literary style. On the other hand, new ones have come into use, mostly to represent loanwords from Arabic, Persian and English such as ब्त *bta* (e.g. in रब्त 'association', from Arabic), or स्ट *sṭa* (e.g. in स्टेशन *sṭeśan*, 'station'). However, the situation is actually more complicated than this, due to the fact that a historical inherent vowel *a* is often unpronounced in Hindi (as in most other NIA languages) in final position, at morpheme boundaries, and in medial syllables under certain conditions (see Lambert 1953: 62, 69). This means that not every consonant cluster of the spoken language is written with a conjunct consonant, as in करना *kar(a)nā* [kərnā] 'to do' (verbal base *kar-* + infinitive suffix *-nā*). Conjuncts are generally written only in loanwords or in native (*tadbhava*) words with clusters within a morpheme unit (e.g. ग्यारह *gyārah* 'eleven'). Thus the *tadbhava* word करता *kar(a)tā* 'does' (imperfective participle masculine) and the Sanskrit *tatsama* कर्ता *kartā* 'creator', though written differently, are homophonous [kərta]. In general, these rules do not introduce any ambiguity, but there are a few cases where the spelling is variable, for example बिलकुल or बिल्कुल *bilkul* 'entirely'.

2.1.3 Nagari for Marathi

As in the case of Hindi, Nagari adapted for writing Marathi involves some minor additions and subtractions. The Marathi *varṇamālā* omits the vowels *r̥*, *ḷ*, and *l̥* (as in Hindi), and adds the retroflex lateral ळ *ḷa*. The forms of the letters, including conjuncts, and the rendition of the inherent vowel are generally similar to those of Hindi, although the *r*-conjuncts are sometimes written differently, as in ऱ्ह *rha* and भ्र *bhra*.

In some modern fonts (Lambert 1953: 103; Masica 1991: 150) the full or initial vowel signs are written with the character for *a* plus the appropriate post-consonantal vowel diacritic, as in अि *i*, अु *u*. Curiously enough, this system is parallel to that of Kharoṣṭhī, where the full vowel sign for *a* similarly functions as a 'carrier' for the other vowels (see 3.2.1). It is also not without parallel in the other Brāhmī-derived scripts; note that in Nagari initial ओ *o* and औ *au* are written in this way, in contrast to the other initial vowels which are based on entirely separate character pairs. Earlier scripts had a separate character pair for *o* and *au*, but these fell out of use in Nagari, though the old *o* survives in the special character for the sacred syllable ॐ *oṁ*. In some modern scripts such as Bangla and Oriya (2.3, 2.4), the old separate characters for these vowels are retained, while others, such as Gujarati and Gurmukhi, have other irregular patterns among the full vowel signs (2.2, 2.5).

2.1.4 Nagari for Nepali

Nagari script as used for writing Nepali is essentially the same as that for Hindi. However, Nepali, unlike Hindi and most other NIA languages, explicitly marks the deletion in pronunciation of a historical inherent *a* vowel, either by forming conjunct consonants across morpheme boundaries (e.g. गर्नु *garnu* 'to do', in contrast to Hindi करना *kar(a)nā* 'ibid', cf. 2.1.2), or by the *virāma* sign marking the suppression of a final *a* (e.g. मन्दिर् *mandir* 'temple'; contrast Hindi मन्दिर *mandir(a)*). Thus *virāma* is seen much more commonly in Nepali than in the other NIA languages.

2.2 Gujarati script (table 3.2)

Gujarati script is in origin one of the many local informal varieties of Nagari. Attested since the sixteenth century, it developed in the nineteenth century into a regional script for printing and literature. Its most distinctive feature is the absence of the head mark, which reflects its origin in informal writing. Many of the letters forms, such as ત *ta*, થ *tha*, and ન *na*, are almost identical to those of Nagari, except of course for the lack of the head mark. Others, such as ક *ka*, ખ *kha*, and બ *ba*, are different, though close analysis reveals their kinship to the corresponding Nagari characters, the differences being typically the result of different stroke ordering (cf. 4.1).

The repertoire of characters is the same as Nagari as used for the neighbouring Marathi language; that is, it includes the retroflex lateral ળ *ḷa* but lacks the dotted (*nukṭā*) letters of Hindi. As in Gurmukhi (2.5, cf. also 1.3), the letters are referred to by reduplicative names: *ka* is *kakko*, *ta* is *tatto*, etc. A significant difference from Nagari is that the full forms of all four diphthong vowels (એ *e*, ઐ *ai*, ઓ *o*, ઔ *au*) are formed by placing diacritic vowel signs on the full form of અ *a*, which thus functions as a vowel carrier, whereas in Nagari this device is applied only to *o* and *au* (see 2.1.3).

The vowel repertoire of Gujarati script is theoretically imperfect in that it uses the same characters *e* and *o* to represent both the open and closed vowels ɛ/e and ɔ/o respectively, even though these pairs are phonemically distinct. Similarly, murmured vowels, also phonemically distinct in Gujarati, are not separately represented in the script (Daniels and Bright 1996: 393). Thus there is certain degree of lack of 'fit' between the Gujarati script and language, and although this does not cause any serious practical problem (being, after all, the rule rather than the exception in scripts all over the world), it is historically significant in showing how a standard phonetic repertoire based on that of Sanskrit became a conceptual straitjacket in the application of the Brāhmī-derived scripts to languages of the NIA family (cf. Masica 1991: 146). Indeed, the failure to develop new characters to represent new phonemes is the exception rather than the rule in this group (cf. 2.3 and 2.6).

2.3 Bangla (Bengali) script (table 3.2)

Bangla, unlike Gujarati, is distinctly a separate script from Nagari, with its own characteristic ductus emphasizing angular forms, and with many characters that are quite different from their Nagari correspondents, such as ত *ta* and ভ *bha*. Nevertheless, the broader family relationship is apparent from systemic parallels, from their common use of a full head mark over most of the characters, and from the more obvious resemblances of characters like ব *va*, with a typically angular form corresponding to the more rounded Nagari व, and ন *na*.

The post-consonantal vowel signs for *e* and *ai* are placed in Bangla to the left of the consonant, as in কে *ke* and কৈ *kai*, rather than above it as in Nagari (के *ke*, कै *kai*) and the other northern scripts (Gujarati and Gurmukhi). Similarly, one of the components of the compound diacritics for *o* and *au* is written to the left of the consonant (কো *ko*, কৌ *kau*) rather than above it (Nagari को *ko*, कौ *kau*). These vowel signs, known as *pṛṣṭhamātrā* 'back-strokes', were also sometimes used in archaic forms of Nagari and related scripts, and they anticipate the separated diacritic signs for the same vowels that are characteristic of the southern scripts (see 2.4).

The repertoire of characters is essentially the same as Nagari for Hindi, including the dotted ড় *ṛa* and ঢ় *ṛha*. There is no distinction between the labial stop ব *ba* and

TABLE 3.2: THE MAJOR SCRIPTS USED FOR NIA LANGUAGES

Vowels, anusvāra and visarga

Transliteration	Nagari	Gujarati	Bangla	Oriya	Gurmukhi	Sinhala
a	अ	અ	অ	ଅ	ਅ	අ
ā	आ	આ	আ	ଆ	ਆ	අා
i	इ	ઇ	ই	ଇ	ਇ	ඉ
ī	ई	ઈ	ঈ	ଈ	ਈ	ඊ
u	उ	ઉ	উ	ଉ	ਉ	උ
ū	ऊ	ઊ	ঊ	ଊ	ਊ	ඌ
ṛ	ऋ	ઋ	ঋ	ଋ		ඍ
e	ए	એ	এ	ଏ	ਏ	එ
ai	ऐ	ઐ	ঐ	ଐ	ਐ	ඓ
o	ओ	ઓ	ও	ଓ	ਓ	ඔ
au	औ	ઔ	ঔ	ଔ	ਔ	ඖ
aṁ	अं	અં	অং	ଅଂ	ਅਂ	අං
aḥ	अः	અઃ	অঃ	ଅଃ		අඃ

Consonants

ka	क	ક	ক	କ	ਕ	ක
kha	ख	ખ	খ	ଖ	ਖ	ඛ
ga	ग	ગ	গ	ଗ	ਗ	ග
gha	घ	ઘ	ঘ	ଘ	ਘ	ඝ
ṅa	ङ	ઙ	ঙ	ଙ	ਙ	ඞ
ca	च	ચ	চ	ଚ	ਚ	ච
cha	छ	છ	ছ	ଛ	ਛ	ඡ
ja	ज	જ	জ	ଜ	ਜ	ජ
jha	झ	ઝ	ঝ	ଝ	ਝ	ඣ
ña	ञ	ઞ	ঞ	ଞ	ਞ	ඤ
ṭa	ट	ટ	ট	ଟ	ਟ	ට
ṭha	ठ	ઠ	ঠ	ଠ	ਠ	ඨ
ḍa	ड	ડ	ড	ଡ	ਡ	ඩ
ḍha	ढ	ઢ	ঢ	ଢ	ਢ	ඪ
ṇa	ण	ણ	ণ	ଣ	ਣ	ණ
ta	त	ત	ত	ତ	ਤ	ත
tha	थ	થ	থ	ଥ	ਥ	ථ
da	द	દ	দ	ଦ	ਦ	ද
dha	ध	ધ	ধ	ଧ	ਧ	ධ
na	न	ન	ন	ନ	ਨ	න
pa	प	પ	প	ପ	ਪ	ප
pha	फ	ફ	ফ	ଫ	ਫ	ඵ
ba	ब	બ	ব	ବ	ਬ	බ
bha	भ	ભ	ভ	ଭ	ਭ	භ
ma	म	મ	ম	ମ	ਮ	ම
ya	य	ય	য	ଯ	ਯ	ය
ra	र	ર	র	ର	ਰ	ර
la	ल	લ	ল	ଲ	ਲ	ල
va	व	વ	ব	ଵ	ਵ	ව
śa	श	શ	শ	ଶ	ਸ਼	ශ
ṣa	ष	ષ	ষ	ଷ		ෂ
sa	स	સ	স	ସ	ਸ	ස
ha	ह	હ	হ	ହ	ਹ	හ
ṛa	ड़		ড়	ଡ଼	ੜ	
ṛha	ढ़		ঢ়			
ḷa	ळ	ળ		ଳ	ਲ਼	ළ
kṣa	क्ष	ક્ષ	ক্ষ	କ୍ଷ		ක්ෂ
jña	ज्ञ	જ્ઞ	জ্ঞ	ଜ୍ଞ		ඥ

the semivowel *ba*, historically *va* but pronounced [bɔ]. In several other cases, however, distinct graphic characters have been retained even where older phonetic distinctions have been lost in spoken Bangla. Thus the three sibilants of OIA, শ *śa*, ষ *ṣa*, and স *sa*, are retained in written form but are all pronounced [šɔ] in most environments. The distinction between the palatal consonant জ *ja* and the semivowel য *ya*, both pronounced [dʒɔ], is also lost, but a modified form of the latter called *antastha ya*, with a diacritic dot added below (য়), has been developed to represent the sound [y] which is retained in intervocalic and final post-vocalic position, for instance in মায়া *māyā*.

In these and other respects, Bangla script is highly conservative. The Bangla language has undergone more extensive phonetic restructuring than most of the other NIA languages, but is written under strong archaizing and Sanskritizing influences. The result is that the language and script are strongly diglossic, much more than most of the NIA languages, and more comparable to languages like French or Tibetan. This is also reflected in the treatment of conjunct characters in Bangla, especially in the very numerous Sanskrit loanwords, many of which are part of colloquial vocabulary and are not restricted to literary usage. Such words are spelled as in Sanskrit but pronounced according to the phonetic rules of Bangla, according to which many of the clusters represented as conjuncts in the script are geminated or otherwise simplified. For example, in written conjuncts consisting of C+*ya* the *ya* is not pronounced, and the cluster is rendered as [C] initially and [CC] medially; thus অন্য *anya* 'other' is pronounced [ɔnnɔ]. The situation is similar for most conjuncts of the type C+*ma* and C+*v/ba*; পদ্ম *padma* 'lotus' is pronounced as [pɔddɔ], and স্বামী *svāmī* 'husband' as [šāmī]. The conjunct ক্ষ *kṣa* is [khɔ] initially and [kkhɔ] medially, so that লক্ষ্মী *lakṣmī* 'proper name' is pronounced [lɔkkhī].

The first example cited above also shows that a special form (called *ya-phalā*) has developed for *ya* as the latter member of a conjunct, analogous to the special conjunct forms of *r* in Nagari and other scripts (2.1.1). Special forms for post-consonantal *y* are also found in middle and later Brāhmī, and are preserved in some southern scripts such as Kannada and Telugu. Bangla script also has a special character ৎ, called *khaṇḍa-ta* ('broken *ta*') to represent *t*, that is, ত *ta* without the inherent vowel. This is used instead of the vowel cancellation marker, called *hasanta* in Bangla, with *ta*, though *hasanta* can be used with other consonants. The *khaṇḍa-ta* is also used in conjunct clusters whose prior member is *t*, as in উৎপত্তি *utpatti* 'origination'.

As may be observed from the various examples cited above, the inherent vowel *a* is pronounced as [ɔ] or [ō] in Bangla, rather than as [ə] as in most IA languages. The distribution of the two pronunciations is determined by a complex set of factors involving etymology, position in the word, and vowel harmony, and cannot always be predicted from the written form of the word. Similarly, the written vowel *e* actually serves to represent three separate sounds, [ε], [e] or [æ]. As was the case in Gujarati (see 2.2), and presumably for the same reason, namely the Sanskritic 'straitjacket', Bangla script has not developed separate characters to express these distinctions, although they are to some extent phonemic.

Asamiya is written in essentially the same script as Bangla, with a few minor variations, mainly an alternative form of ৰ *ra* and a distinction between the stop consonant ব *ba* and the semivowel ৱ *va*.

2.4 Oriya script (table 3.2)

Oriya script exhibits a mixture of northeastern and southern, or more specifically Deccan features, appropriately in view of its geographical location. In ductus and general appearance it is distinctly southern, with rounded or curved forms typical of the south Indian scripts. Straight horizontal lines are conspicuously avoided, a pattern which is usually understood to have arisen out of the traditional practice of writing on palm leaf with a metal stylus, where straight horizontal lines would tend to split the leaf. The head mark has a particularly distinctive look in Oriya, consisting of a curved line at the top of or above the main part of the characters, in many cases (e.g. ଲ *ka*) forming a distinctive 'umbrella'. Also characteristically southern (cf. 2.6) are diacritic vowel signs for the diphthongs that are not connected to the consonantal character, as in *e* (e.g. ଡ଼ *ke*) and *o* (e.g. ଡ଼ି *ko*). But the forms of the distinctive portions of the letters, as opposed to their overall shapes and framing, are typically eastern; compare ଡ *ta* and ଭ *bha* with the corresponding Bangla letters (ত, ত), cited above (2.3) as characteristically eastern shapes.

The repertoire of Oriya script is essentially the same as that of Bangla, with the addition of the retroflex lateral ଳ *la*. Unlike Bangla, Oriya has a fairly close fit between the written and spoken language, although it does retain some distinctions in writing that are no longer pronounced; for example, all three sibilants, ଶ *śa*, and ଷ *ṣa*, and ସ *sa*, are pronounced [sɔ]. The inherent vowel is regularly pronounced as [ɔ], and unlike the other NIA languages, it is generally not deleted in pronunciation in final position and in medial syllables; thus ସୁନ୍ଦର sundara [sundɔrɔ] 'beautiful', in contrast to Hindi सुन्दर sundara [sundər].

As in Bangla, both *ra* and *ya* take special forms in conjuncts, as in ଙ *rka*, ଙ୍ *kra*, and କ୍ୟ *kya*. Some other consonants such as *t* also have distinct shapes in conjuncts, as in ସ *tpa* and ସ୍ *sta*. This is another characteristically southern feature, similar to patterns in Kannada and Telugu scripts. There are also a fairly large number of ligatured conjuncts in which the component members are altered so as to become more or less unrecognizable, such as ଙ୍କ *ṅka* or ଦ୍ଧ *ddha*.

2.5 Gurmukhi script (table 3.2)

Although the individual forms of the letters of Gurmukhi script are derived normally from local scripts of the northwestern group (of which it is the only important surviving member), its structure and system is in several respects anomalous among all the Indian scripts. There are two major reasons for this. First, the Panjabi language which it represents has some phonetic features, most significantly a tonal system, which are untypical of NIA languages. Second, the script was developed in cultural and historical circumstances quite different from those of the other scripts, and this had the effect of liberating it from the aforementioned Sanskritic straitjacket, allowing it to evolve unique features.

Gurmukhi script is believed to have been invented in the early sixteenth century by Guru Angad, the second guru of the Sikhs, whence its distinctive name 'script of those guided by the Guru', and it has always been closely associated with Sikh religion and cultural tradition. This tradition being much less Sanskritized than those which prevailed in most other parts of India, it is perhaps only natural that the script should have gone its own way in such features as repertoire and alphabetic order, as follows:

Vowels: *u, a, i.*
Fricatives: *sa, ha.*
The twenty-five *vargīya* consonants, ordered as in other scripts: *ka, kha, ga, gha, ṅa,* etc.
Semivowels: *ya, ra, la, va, ṛa.*
Supplementary characters: *ṣa, ja, pha, k̲ha, ga, ḷa.*

Although the influence of the standard Indic system is still very much perceptible, for instance in the ordering of the *vargīya* consonants, it is extensively reconceived and reordered. Particularly striking is the conception of the vowels as consisting of only three basic characters, of which the other seven are considered as variants, whereas in the other scripts each vowel is counted as a separate letter. Moreover, the order of the vowels, beginning with *u*, is unique, and the pattern of the building of the other vowels by the addition of diacritics to the base vowels is also unusual (although, as we have seen in 2.1.3 and elsewhere, similar patterns are found in other scripts). The modified vowels are graphically constructed as follows:

from ੳ *u:* ਊ *ū,* ਓ *o*
from ਅ *a:* ਆ *ā,* ਐ *ai,* ਔ *au*
from ੲ *i:* ਈ *ī,* ਏ *e.*

It has been noted (Masica 1991: 150–1) that the system of three base vowels resembles that of the Perso-Arabic scripts (see 5.1), and in this and other respects Gurmukhi seems to have been indirectly influenced by their model. We also see this in the sign called *addak*, indicating the doubling of a following consonant, for which there is no parallel in the Indic scripts but which recalls the Arabic *tashdīd.* The Perso-Arabic input is also reflected in five supplementary characters composed of basic characters with a diacritic dot (*nuk̲tā*) below to render sounds of Arabic and Persian loanwords, as in Hindi (see 2.1.2). These include *ṣa* to render [šə] in such loanwords, an addition which was not needed in Hindi because it had retained the Sanskrit *śa*; for Gurmukhi, alone among the scripts of NIA languages, had reduced the three sibilants of Sanskrit to the only one, *sa,* actually pronounced in native words, while the other scripts had retained them as spelling archaisms (see 2.3 and 2.4). This, of course, is yet another manifestation of Gurmukhi's unique independence from the Sanskritic model (cf. Masica 1991: 148).

The names of the letters are also unusual in Gurmukhi. The consonants are called *sassā, hāhā, kakkā, khakkhā,* etc. (as in Gujarati, 2.2), while the three basic vowels *u, a* and *i* have the anomalous names *uṛā, ayṛā,* and *iṛi.*

Also characteristic of the liberation from the Sanskritic model is the drastic reduction of conjunct consonants. These are limited to a set with subscript *h, r* and *v,* and of these, the second is rarely used, and the third is not really a conjunct but part of a complex set of graphic devices indicating the three tones of the Panjabi language. These are indirectly represented by the voiced aspirate consonants and *ha,* either written as a subscript or as independent consonant, in certain defined positions within a word. For example, voiced aspirates (which are never actually pronounced as such in Panjabi) in initial position are rendered as the corresponding unvoiced unaspirated consonant with the low tone, as in ਘੋੜਾ *ghoṛā* 'horse', pronounced [kòṛa]. (For a complete explanation of the tone marking system, see Daniels and Bright 1996: 397.) This indirect notation of phonemic tone probably reflects the actual historical origins of the Panjabi tones, which seem to have developed under the influence of old *h* and voiced aspirates, so that no need was perceived for a distinct set of new characters (Daniels and Bright 1996: 395).

2.6 Sinhala script (table 3.2)

The Sinhala script is used in Sri Lanka to write the Sinhala language as well as for Pali and, less frequently, Sanskrit. As would be expected from its location, it is very much a southern script in its overall ductus and system, although its history (see 4.5–4.6) involves complex interactions between a long-standing indigenous tradition and periodic influences from various parts of mainland India. Its southern character is manifested in the tendency toward rounded forms, including large semi-circular head marks above many of the consonants, the avoidance of straight horizontal lines, and the use of diacritic vowel signs separated from their consonant (in $\bar{a}$ and the diphthongs; cf. 2.4). Its basic repertoire is similar to that of the Indian scripts, including the retroflex lateral ළ *ḷa*, but it has several additional signs used to represent phonemes peculiar to the Sinhala language. These are:

The vowels *æ* and *ǣ* (also transliterated *ä, ā̈*) in both full (**ඇ, ඈ**) and diacritic (**කැ** *kæ*, **කෑ** *kǣ*) forms.

The vowels *ĕ* and *ŏ* in full (**එ, ඔ**) and diacritic forms (**කෙ** *kĕ*, **කො** *kŏ*), distinguished from **ඒ** *ē* and **ඕ** *ō* (as in some other south Indian scripts used for Dravidian languages).

Special signs to indicate the prenasalized stops or 'half-nasals' **ඟ** *ṅga*, **ඬ** *ṇḍa*, **ඳ** *ňda*, and **ඹ** *m̆ba*.

All of these additional characters are derived as modifications from characters of the standard Brāhmī-family repertoire (*æ* and *ǣ* from *a*, *ĕ* and *ŏ* from *e* and *o* respectively, etc.). Thus, although Sinhala script shows some independence from the Sanskritic model, it is still largely influenced by it, at least more so than Gurmukhi. Like other scripts such as Bangla, Sinhala script also retains graphic distinctions that are not rendered in the spoken language, such as those between non-aspirate and aspirate consonants and among the three sibilants, so that the relation between Sinhala language and script is significantly diglossic.

Conjunct consonants are formed in Sinhala according to the same general principles as in the other scripts, though the actual formations sometimes differ, particularly in the practice of rendering some conjuncts by writing the full form of their components in direct juxtaposition, without the small space that is normally left between separate *akṣara*s (e.g. රක්ත *rakta* 'red'). In modern printed usage, the inherent vowel cancellation marker, called *(h)al kirima*, is also frequently used instead of conjuncts and to mark final consonants; here one might suspect the influence of the neighbouring Tamil script, in which, alone among the Brāhmī-derived scripts, an inherent vowel canceller (*puḷḷi*) is used invariably, so that there are no conjuncts at all in Tamil. Like other scripts as Bangla and Oriya, Sinhala has special reduced forms for the liquids *r* (both pre- and post-consonantal) and *y* (post-consonantal) in conjuncts.

3 THE ORIGINS AND EARLY HISTORY OF THE INDIC SCRIPTS

An undeciphered prehistoric form of writing, the Indus Valley script, arose in South Asia in about the early third millennium BC, but then apparently died out entirely in the early second millennium BC. After a period of well over a millennium in which written materials were apparently completely absent, two new and evidently unrelated writing systems, Brāhmī and Kharoṣṭhī, come into view in the third century BC. While it is not impossible that the Indus script records an Indo-Aryan or related Indo-European language, nowadays most specialists think it more likely that the language of the Indus script is Dravidian (Parpola 1994: 123–75). Therefore, unless and until progress is made toward an understanding of the Indus script, the history of the written forms of the IA languages begins, in effect, with the first documents known in Brāhmī and Kharoṣṭhī.

3.1 Brāhmī script (table 3.3)

The overall visual impression of early Brāhmī is a strong, almost artificial regularity and symmetry (cf. 3.1.2). It is clearly monumental or epigraphic in ductus, as opposed to a cursive script script like Kharoṣṭhī, and this is in keeping with its earliest attested use in the Aśokan inscriptions and a few other early epigraphic records (see 3.1.1). Even in this earliest known form, Brāhmī already embodies all major features of the widespread family of scripts to which it gave rise (see section 4). Despite the superficial differences in the forms of the letters, the overall systemic principles of the Indic scripts (1.3) are in place from the beginning, and all of the diverse modern forms can be traced, through a

TABLE 3.3: EARLY BRĀHMĪ SCRIPT

(normalized forms from Aśokan and other early inscriptions, third century BC)

Vowels (full form)

a	Ⴘ	*i*	∴	*u*	L	*e*	Δ	*o*	⌐	*aṁ*	Ⴘ·
ā	Ⱶ	*ī*	∷	*ū*	Ŀ	*ai*	⌂				

Vowels (post-consonantal, with *k*)

ka	+	*ki*	✦	*ku*	✝	*ke*	✚	*ko*	✝	*kaṁ*	+·
kā	✦	*kī*	✦	*kū*	✝	*kai*	✝				

Vargīya consonants

	unvoiced unaspirated	unvoiced aspirated	voiced unaspirated	voiced aspirated	nasal
velar	*ka* +	*kha* ⎰	*ga* Λ	*gha* ℓ	
palatal	*ca* ♂	*cha* ♦	*ja* Ɛ	*jha* ℍ	*ña* Ⴌ
retroflex	*ṭa* Ϲ	*ṭha* Ο	*ḍa* ⌐	*ḍha* ♌	*ṇa* Ⴈ
dental	*ta* ⋏	*tha* ⨀	*da* ♭	*dha* D	*na* ⊥
labial	*pa* ℓ	*pha* ℓ	*ba* ☐	*bha* Π	*ma* Ϫ

Semivowels

ya ⚓		*ra* ⨏		*la* ⤳		*va* ♂

Spirants

śa ⬆		*ṣa* ⌊		*sa* ⟲		*ha* ⌐

Representative examples of consonantal conjuncts

khya ⤳		*tra* ⋏		*tva* ⋏		*mha* ⚭		*rva* ♂		*spa* ⚘

long series of intermediate steps, from early Brāhmī. The connections between the early and modern scripts can be seen, for example, in the forms and placement of the postconsonantal vowel signs. Their basic positions with regard to the consonant – $\bar{a}$ to the right, e to the left, u and $\bar{u}$ below, etc. – are stable through the entire family, although the shapes change and diverge extensively, usually by way of extension. Thus, for example, the $\bar{a}$ diacritic in Brāhmī is a short horizontal line added to the top right of the consonant; this gradually grew and bent downward in the later scripts, eventually forming the full-length vertical line in Nagari and most of the other modern scripts.

3.1.1 The antiquity of Brāhmī script

The antiquity of Brāhmī script is uncertain, mainly because the date of the earliest surviving inscriptions in it is highly controversial. What is beyond dispute is that the earliest definitely datable Brāhmī inscriptions are the rock and pillar inscriptions of the Mauryan emperor Aśoka, which were written around the middle of the third century BC. In this large corpus of thirty-seven inscriptions or sets of inscriptions spread out over almost all of the subcontinent, we seem to find, all of a sudden, a major form of writing without any evident prehistory. However, there is also a small but significant handful of other Brāhmī inscriptions (the Mahāsthān stone plaque, Sohgaurā bronze plaque, Piprāwā vase, etc.; Sircar 1965: 79–83) which, to judge from their palaeographic and linguistic character, are also very early, but which are not datable with any precision. Therefore it has long been a matter of controversy whether they are in fact earlier than the Aśokan inscriptions, or rather contemporary with or even later than them, and dates for the ultimate origin of Brāhmī as early as the ninth century BC (Bühler 1898: 80) have been proposed.

Such very early dates, however, are by now discredited for lack of corroboration or direct evidence, and the recent study by Falk (1993: 177ff.) has shown that there is no convincing palaeographic or historical evidence for dating any of these early Brāhmī inscriptions earlier than those of Aśoka. Recently, however, excavations at Anurādhapura in Sri Lanka have uncovered potsherds with fragmentary graffiti inscriptions in Brāhmī script from strata which have been dated to the fourth century BC, if not earlier (Allchin 1995: 165, 178–81, 209–11, Coningham, Allchin, Batt and Lucy 1996; see also Salomon 1998a: 12). Therefore it is still possible that Brāhmī script existed for a century or more before Aśoka, but the question remains controversial.

3.1.2 The origin of Brāhmī script

The problem of the date of the earliest surviving specimens ties in with the even more vexing problem of the origin of the script (for general discussion see Gupta and Ramachandran 1979, Falk 1993: 109–67, and Salomon 1998a: 19–30). Positions on this issue have tended to revolve around three theories:

(1) Brāhmī script is an indigenous Indian development which was ultimately derived, directly or indirectly, from the Indus Valley script.
(2) Brāhmī was borrowed from, adapted from, or modelled upon a Semitic prototype, either Phoenician or Aramaic script, at some time before the earliest datable inscriptions of the third century BC.
(3) Brāhmī was consciously invented *ex nihilo* or loosely modelled on another script such as Aramaic or Greek during the time of Aśoka, perhaps under his direct sponsorship.

The first theory is weakened by the absence of any convincing specimens of an intermediate form of writing between Indus script and Brāhmī. Although some graffiti on megalithic and chalcolithic potsherds have been proposed as such a link, the evidence is weak. Proponents of the Indus script theory have largely relied on comparisons of the outward shapes of the letters in the two scripts, but such comparisons are meaningless as long as the phonetic or semantic values of the supposed ancestor script are unknown. The only convincing hint of a possible relationship is the unusual pattern of multiple variant forms of many of the characters in the Indus script, which seems to resemble the diacritic vowel system of the later Indian scripts (Hunter 1934: 1, 51–8), but this too remains entirely speculative, pending decipherment of the former.

The theory of a Semitic origin has been generally favoured among European scholars since its classic formulation by Bühler (1898), but has been challenged on the grounds that the specific comparisons which he made between letters of the proposed Phoenician and Aramaic prototypes and those of early Brāhmī are often unconvincing. Certainly Bühler's formulation, tracing Brāhmī back to a very early borrowing (see 3.1.1) from Phoenician, is no longer credible. A derivation from a later form of Aramaic, as proposed by Diringer (1953: 336), is much more plausible on historical and geographical grounds, but the derivations of specific characters from Aramaic are not much more convincing than Bühler's. Moreover, since it is established that Kharoṣṭhī was derived from Aramaic (3.2.3), it is hard to explain why two separate Indic scripts would have developed from the same prototype at about the same time. The Semitic origin theories have also been criticized on the grounds that Brāhmī is normally written from left to right while all the Semitic scripts go from right to left, but since the direction of writing is typically unstable in early scripts, and since there are in fact numerous examples of Brāhmī written from right to left (Salomon 1998a: 27–8), this is hardly a persuasive criticism.

The third, or 'invention' theory has the advantages of accounting for the apparently sudden appearance of Brāhmī in the time of Aśoka, the unnaturally regular geometrical shapes of the earliest forms of the letters, and the lack of regional variation among the early inscriptions over a wide area of India (Upasak 1960). The invention theory is also historically plausible in view of parallel examples of other scripts, such as Old Persian cuneiform and Korean Hangul, having been invented by royal fiat. This theory was supported by, among others, S. R. Goyal (in Gupta and Ramachandran 1979: 1–53), and Falk in his comprehensive study (1993: 337–40) concluded that Brāhmī was developed during the reign of Aśoka with the Kharoṣṭhī and Greek script as models. However, the aforementioned discovery (3.1.1) of what seem to be earlier specimens of Brāhmī in Sri Lanka casts some doubt on the theory of its invention under Aśoka or his predecessors in the Mauryan dynasty.

In conclusion, it remains uncertain exactly when and how the Brāhmī script arose. All in all, however, the arguments for a Semitic, or more specifically an Aramaic prototype or model remain persuasive, though not conclusive. Such an inspiration is historically supportable in view of the wide use of Aramaic script under the Achaemenid emperors of Iran, whose territories included the western parts of the Indian subcontinent. Moreover, certain internal patterns of the Brāhmī script suggest a Semitic model. It is probably significant that the characters for the aspirate consonants *kha*, *gha* and *tha* are formed independently rather than as extensions or modifications of the corresponding non-aspirates as is the case with other aspirates, such as *cha* and *pha* (see table 3.3). This seems to reflect the influence of a Semitic script, presumably Aramaic, which had 'extra' guttural and dental consonants (i.e., *qoph*, *ḥet*, and *ṭet*) which did not correspond directly to any phonemes in the IA languages and which therefore could be used to represent aspirates (see Salomon 1998a: 29–30). Thus, even though it is not possible to convincingly derive all of the Brāhmī characters from Aramaic or any other Semitic script, there is both circumstantial and systemic evidence that points in favour of a connection, though perhaps an indirect one. Therefore the most likely explanation of the origin of Brāhmī is that it was created or developed for the writing of IA languages with Aramaic script as a model or inspiration. But it remains uncertain whether this event took place during Aśoka's reign or somewhat earlier, and we can only hope that further archaeological discoveries will clarify the issue.

The name 'Brāhmī' presumably refers to the traditional belief that the script was created by the god Brahmā (Salomon 1998a: 8 n.3), and hence sheds no light on the issue of its historical origin.

3.1.3 Brāhmī script and the IA languages

In any case, it is clear that Brāhmī script was invented or developed for MIA rather than OIA languages. This is not only apparent from the fact that all of its earliest documents are in MIA, but is also indicated by systemic features of the script such as the form of the conjunct consonants. On the surface, the system of conjuncts might seem to point in the opposite direction, since it is more appropriate to Sanskrit, which has many consonant clusters, than to MIA, in which the vast majority of clusters are geminates which can be conveniently represented by the single consonant (see 1.5.1), or nasal plus homorganic stop sequences, which can easily be written with the *anusvāra* diacritic.

However, there are several indications that the conjunct system in early Brāhmī is secondary, and perhaps was developed in connection with the semi-formal and partially Sanskritized orthography of the Aśokan inscriptions. For one thing, several of the conjuncts in Aśokan Brāhmī are imperfectly formed, with the proper phonetic order of their constituents reversed (e.g., ⟨ *pta* instead of the expected ⟩ *tpa*). For another, we find that the earliest inscriptions other than the Aśokan contain few if any conjuncts. Thus we can postulate an original variety of the script, more suited for writing MIA languages, in which the conjunct system had not yet been developed or was only present in a very rudimentary form.

If this interpretation of the conjunct consonant system as an early refinement of the original Brāhmī script is correct, it would be the first step in the well-attested process of gradual adaptation and supplementation in order to make the script adequate for the complete and accurate representation of Sanskrit. To judge by the epigraphic record (which is virtually all that we have to go by for the early period; see 1.6), this process took place very gradually over a period of five centuries or more, during which Sanskrit little by little superseded MIA as the principal language of inscriptions, and presumably of other official records and documents. During this long transitional period, we first see new characters needed for Sanskrit phonemes (Salomon 1998a: 37) that are absent from MIA (see 4.3). Most of these new signs first appear in or around the first and second centuries, when a language known as 'Epigraphical Hybrid Sanskrit', combining Sanskritized spellings with MIA morphology (Salomon 1998a: 81–6), was in wide use. By the time that Sanskrit was firmly entrenched as the language of inscriptions, in or around the fourth century AD, a complete repertoire of the characters needed to accurately represent it had developed in the various local forms of the Brāhmī script, and this now-standardized repertoire has served as a durable template for nearly all of the later derivative scripts, so that many scripts used for NIA retain Sanskrit characters that are no longer part of the phonetic repertoire of their languages, and conversely, new characters are only rarely developed to represent new sounds that have developed in NIA languages (see 2.2–2.5).

Thus we find that the early history of the writing of the IA languages, as embodied for the most part in the Brāhmī script and its derivatives, is not parallel to the history of the languages themselves; this, in contrast to the later patterns of development of the Indic scripts, which tend to parallel those of the languages (1.5.2). To judge from the limited material that we have, writing seems to have begun with MIA and only gradually spread to OIA. Of course it is possible that this peculiar situation – 'le grand paradoxe linguistique de l'Inde' in Renou's words (1956: 84) – is an illusion based on the limited type and amount of the material that has come down to us, and that there was actually a lost prehistory of writing Sanskrit in earlier forms of Brāhmī script. However, this seems not to be the case since, as we have seen above, early forms of Brāhmī appear to have been designed for MIA languages rather than for Sanskrit. This seemingly peculiar situation can once again be explained in view of the priority granted to the spoken rather than the written word in traditional Indian, especially Brahmanical culture (1.5.2). All indications are that writing was initially employed in the IA languages primarily in connection with practical matters such as record-keeping, official proclamations and legal procedures, rather than in cultural and literary pursuits, for which oral modes of learning and presentation were still preferred (though not necessarily to the total exclusion of writing). It is only in later centuries when the domain of the Sanskrit language expands into official and legal record-keeping that we find extensive records of it in written form.

3.2 Kharoṣṭhī script (table 3.4)

Although it shares most of its basic systemic features with Brāhmī, and hence is in essence an Indian script, Kharoṣṭhī is in many respects different from its more successful rival. Most strikingly, Kharoṣṭhī is written from right to left, like its presumptive Semitic ancestor, rather than from left to right like Brāhmī. Unlike the monumental Brāhmī, Kharoṣṭhī has a natural, cursive flow, and in its general ductus is again reminiscent of the Semitic scripts, particularly the later Aramaic that is its direct parent (3.2.3). Unlike Brāhmī, which from the very beginning of its attested history was a national script used almost all over the South Asian cultural region, Kharoṣṭhī was originally, and for the most part remained, a regional script of the northwest (3.2.2). And unlike Brāhmī which was to become the parent of a great family of scripts used in South, Central, and Southeast Asia, Kharoṣṭhī died out without an heir after some six centuries of use.

3.2.1 Systemic characteristics of Kharoṣṭhī

Despite its overall systemic similarity to Brāhmī, Kharoṣṭhī has significant differences from it in matters of detail. It shares with Brāhmī the quintessentially Indic features of the inherent vowel *a*, the representation of post-consonantal vowels by diacritic signs added to the consonant, and the use of conjunct characters to represent consonant clusters without intervening vowels. But it differs from Brāhmī in that it does not usually distinguish vowel length, except in some later documents where a supplementary stroke is occasionally added to the lower right corner of a syllable to mark its vowel as long. Thus in normal usage each vowel sign, whether full/initial or postconsonantal/diacritic, may represent either the short or long form, depending on context. The full/initial vowel

TABLE 3.4: KHAROṢṬHĪ SCRIPT

(representative manuscript forms of the middle period, *c.* first century AD)

Vowels (full form)

a	ʾ	*i*	ʾ	*u*	ʓ	*e*	ʾ	*o*	ʾ	*aṁ*	ʓ

Vowels (post-consonantal, with *k*)

ka	ƕ	*ki*	ƕ	*ku*	ƕ	*ke*	ƕ	*ko*	ƕ	*kaṁ*	ƕ

Vargīya consonants

	unvoiced unaspirated		unvoiced aspirated		voiced unaspirated		voiced aspirated		nasal	
velar	*ka*	ƕ	*kha*	ſ	*ga*	ƴ	*gha*	ƙ		
palatal	*ca*	ƴ	*cha*	ƛ	*ja*	ƴ	*jha*	ƴ	*ña*	ƒ
retroflex	*ṭa*	ƶ	*ṭha*	ʔ	*ḍa*	ƴ	*ḍha*	ʈ	*ṇa*	ſ
dental	*ta*	ƽ	*tha*	ƒ	*da*	ƒ	*dha*	ƹ	*na*	ſ
labial	*pa*	ƕ	*pha*	ƕ	*ba*	ƴ	*bha*	ƥ	*ma*	ʊ

Semivowels

ya	ʔ	*ra*	ʔ	*la*	ʔ	*va*	ʔ

Spirants

śa	ʼ	*ṣa*	ƿ	*sa*	ƽ	*ha*	ʔ

Representative examples of consonantal conjuncts

kṣa	ʎ	*tra*	ʔ	*tva*	ʔ	*tsa*	ƀ	*rva*	ƀ

signs also differ from those of Brāhmī, where each pair (short and long) of vowels has an entirely different shape (e.g. ℋ = *a*, ∴ = *i*), whereas in Kharoṣṭhī they are all formed from the basic vowel character ʾ *a/ā*, serving as a 'vowel carrier' to which is added the same set of diacritic signs which are attached to the consonants to form the other full vowel signs (e.g., ʾ = *i* or *ī*, ʓ = *u* or *ū*).

Similarly, the conjunct consonants of Kharoṣṭhī are formed under the same general principles as in Brāhmī, but have significant differences in their specific forms. Although some of them, such as *tma* (ℐ) or *spa* (ℛ) are transparent graphic combinations of the normal forms of the component consonants, in many other conjuncts such as *sta* (ℱ) or *kṣa* (ℽ) the presumptive components are not easily discernible. In fact, it is possible that these 'conjuncts' (which are conventionally transcribed according to their Sanskritic equivalents) are in origin not really graphic combinations, but were created as separate units expressly for the Gāndhārī language, in which they seem to have represented distinct phonemes (see Brough 1962: 72–3 and 75–7). Also in the course of the later development of the script, some new characters such as *ẓa* (ℰ) developed to represent new sounds of the language, in this case apparently [z]. In these and other respects, Kharoṣṭhī script shows itself to be mostly immune from the straitjacket that the phonetic system of Sanskrit imposed on the Brāhmī script and its derivatives, inhibiting their ability to accurately represent distinct phonetic features of the various local languages.

Another feature that sets Kharoṣṭhī off from all other Indian scripts is its alphabetical ordering. Instead of the standard order of the Brāhmī-derived group (see 1.3), the Kharoṣṭhī alphabet was arranged in a system known as 'Arapacana' after the first five letters of the sequence (i.e., *a-ra-pa-ca-na*; Salomon 1990, 2006). The underlying rationale of this system, which survives in later Buddhist tradition in ritual and mnenomic formulae, remains obscure.

3.2.2 Geographical and chronological range of Kharoṣṭhī

The use of Kharoṣṭhī script was centred in the Gandhāra region at the northwestern fringe of the Indian subcontinent, corresponding to the area around modern Peshawar in Pakistan's Northwest Frontier Province, and this presumably was also its place of origin. From this area, Kharoṣṭhī spread to adjoining regions of what is now northern Pakistan, northwestern and northern India as far as Mathurā, eastern and northern Afghanistan, and the southern parts of Uzbekistan and Tajikistan in ancient Bactria. Even beyond South Asia and its contiguous areas, Kharoṣṭhī came to be an important script of some of the oasis cities along the silk routes around the Tarim Basin in what is now the Xinjiang-Uighur Autonomous Region of the People's Republic of China.

As in the case of Brāhmī, the first datable specimens of Kharoṣṭhī script are Aśokan inscriptions, specifically the two sets of rock edicts inscribed at Shāhbāzgaṛhī and Mānsehrā in the Gandhāra region. But unlike Brāhmī, no other specimens of Kharoṣṭhī of comparable age are known, all other surviving inscriptions and documents in Kharoṣṭhī being of post-Mauryan age. Kharoṣṭhī records are in fact fairly rare until the first century BC, but thereafter become more common, especially in the first and second centuries AD, from which period the bulk of the known specimens of Kharoṣṭhī date. Thereafter, however, the script seems to have undergone a rapid decline, and virtually died out by the end of the third century in South Asia, though some of the provincial varieties in Bactria and Xinjiang seem to have survived for at least a century or two longer.

The spread and temporary popularity of Kharoṣṭhī script was closely linked to a series of powerful kingdoms founded by Greek, Scythian, Parthian and Kuṣāṇa immigrants from the west that were centred in the northwest. The last and greatest of these empires, the Kuṣāṇas, was instrumental in facilitating the spread of Kharoṣṭhī to the regions beyond South Asia which were under its control or within its sphere of influence. But with the decline of this empire in the third century, Kharoṣṭhī began to be supplanted by regional variants of Brāhmī-derived scripts, and after a transitional period in which the two were used simultaneously, Brāhmī gradually prevailed and Kharoṣṭhī died out, leaving no descendants among the modern scripts.

3.2.3 Origin and antiquity of Kharoṣṭhī

The derivation of Kharoṣṭhī from a Semitic prototype, more specifically Aramaic script, is far less controversial than that of Brāhmī, and is accepted by most authorities. Its geographical position in regions that were once part of the Achaemenid empire, where Aramaic was widely used, provides the historical background, and comparisons of the letter forms of Achaemenid Aramaic and early Kharoṣṭhī provide a much more cogent case for a close connection than in the case of Brāhmī, though even here not all of the characters of Kharoṣṭhī can be directly derived from Aramaic. Thus although some details are still subject to argument, the derivations worked out by Bühler (1895) have on balance stood the test of time, much more so than his derivations of the Brāhmī characters (see 3.1.2). In conclusion, the Kharoṣṭhī script must have arisen out of the application or adaptation of Achaemenid Aramaic script to the local language of northwestern India, that is, what we now know as Gāndhārī.

The date and process of such an adaptation, however, are less evident. As in the case of Brāhmī, we are not sure whether the oldest surviving specimens of Kharoṣṭhī, namely the Aśokan inscriptions, represent the earliest forms of the script. The more natural appearance of Aśokan Kharoṣṭhī, in contrast to the geometrically artificial look of Brāhmī, can be invoked in favour of a prehistory. The fact that its home territory was part of the Achaemenid empire as early as the fifth century BC seems to support this too, though it must also be noted that an Aramaic inscription, probably of the time of Aśoka, was discovered at Taxila in the Gandhāra region (Sircar 1965: 78–9), showing that Aramaic was still in use during the third century BC. Therefore all we can say with certainty is that it is likely, but not proven, that the origin of Kharoṣṭhī goes back before the time of Aśoka, to the fourth or perhaps even the fifth century BC.

Also problematic is the name of the script, which, if taken as an Indic word, would seem to mean, improbably, 'donkey's lip', but which is in all probability is actually of Iranian origin. Numerous etymologies have been proposed (see Salomon 1998a: 50–1), none of which is entirely convincing, but a connection with the Iranian *xšaθra* 'realm' seems most likely, and the word may have originally meant something like 'writing of the realm'.

3.2.4 The Kharoṣṭhī script and the Gāndhārī language

Unlike Brāhmī, Kharoṣṭhī script was, for the most part, intimately linked with a single language, namely the northwestern MIA dialect nowadays generally known as Gāndhārī, but also referred to, particularly in older publications, as Northwestern Prakrit. Gāndhārī was in several respects dialectally anomalous among the MIA languages, particularly in its phonetic repertoire, which preserved all three sibilants of OIA (*ś, ṣ, s*) more or less as they occur in Sanskrit, and which also retained certain consonant clusters, particularly those involving liquids (e.g. *tr, sv*), which in all other MIA dialects were reduced to single consonants (initially) or geminates (medially). Because of this dialectally distinct character, along with the use of a different script and a location on the margin of the South Asian area, the Kharoṣṭhī/Gāndhārī corpus of documents stands out as a cultural phenomenon distinct from, though of course related to, the mainstream corpus in Brāhmī-derived scripts. In the later stages, however, Kharoṣṭhī/Gāndhārī documents begin to be more and more Sanskritized, and there are even some specimens of documents written in the Sanskrit language in Kharoṣṭhī script (Fussman 1989: 439 and n.15; Salomon 1998b: 124–35).

Kharoṣṭhī script is attested in four classes of materials:

(a) Inscriptions, mostly on stone or metal and nearly all of Buddhist content, numbering in the hundreds (Konow 1929, updated list in Fussman 1989: 444–51).
(b) Legends on the coins of the Indo-Greek, Scythian, Kuṣāṇa and other dynasties.
(c) Documents on wood and leather, mostly secular and administrative, numbering nearly one thousand, found at Niya and other sites on the southern Tarim Basin silk roads (Boyer, Rapson and Senart 1920–29, Lin 1996).
(d) Manuscripts of Buddhist texts on birch bark and palm leaf (Brough 1962, Salomon 1999, Salomon 2000, Allon 2001, Lenz 2003).

Substantial amounts of new material in all four categories have come to light in recent years. In particular, new discoveries of large numbers of manuscripts in Kharoṣṭhī script, of which until recently a single specimen, the so-called Gāndhārī Dharmapada (Brough 1962) was known, are vastly enhancing our understanding of the history of the Kharoṣṭhī script (see, for example, Glass 2000). Thus the presently available presentations, principally Das Gupta 1958 and the relevant chapters in the standard handbooks of Indian palaeography (notably Bühler 1896, ch. 2, and Dani 1963, ch. 10), are outdated and incomplete, and will have to be supplemented by further studies in years to come.

3.2.5 Historical development of Kharoṣṭhī

The pattern of the historical development of Kharoṣṭhī is different from that of Brāhmī (see section 4) in that it never attained nearly the same degree of variety and diversification, nor did it ever develop into varieties that could be considered different scripts. This is in part, no doubt, because its entire attested period of existence, some six centuries in all, was much shorter, but equally important is the aforementioned cultural unity of the geographical area in which it was used. A distinct local variety did develop, not surprisingly, in the geographically isolated Tarim Basin region, but even this was not vastly different from the standard Indian form of the script.

In general, Kharoṣṭhī was stable and conservative, so that the differences between the oldest and latest forms are relatively minor. Certain letters, notably *sa*, *ca*, and *ya*, did change their shape over time, but not to the point of becoming unrecognizably diferent between their different stages. The *sa*, for example, has three distinct forms (𝖕, 𝖕, 𝖕) in the early, middle and late stages of the script, and while these and similar cases are useful for rough palaeographic dating of Kharoṣṭhī documents, older and later forms tend to overlap in the periods of their use, and hence cannot, in most cases, provide anything like exact dates.

4 THE HISTORICAL DEVELOPMENT OF BRĀHMĪ AND ITS DERIVATIVES (FIGURE 3.1)

4.1 General patterns and principles

The historical development of the Brāhmī-derived Indian scripts, and particularly of the subset used with the IA languages, is virtually limited to formal, as opposed to systemic changes. The graphic principles of the Brāhmī script group have been extraordinarily stable throughout history (1.3). In fact, among the scripts used for IA languages, there is only one example of what seems to be an incipient systemic change of type, and even this is short-lived and abortive. This is the anomalous system of post-consonantal vowel notation observed in a group of Buddhist stūpa inscriptions in Prakrit language from Bhaṭṭiprōḷu in Andhra Pradesh (Salomon 1998a: 34–5), dating from about the second century BC, wherein the vowel *a*, which is inherent in all other Indic scripts, is explicitly marked by a post-consonantal vowel diacritic. This system evidently developed under the influence of the better attested Tamil-Brāhmī inscriptions, which had similar variant systems of vowel notation. Thus it is surely no coincidence that the only significant variation in the vowel notation system used in a script recording an IA language comes from a period and region that was, in all likelihood, under the influence of variant systems developed in the Dravidian sphere.

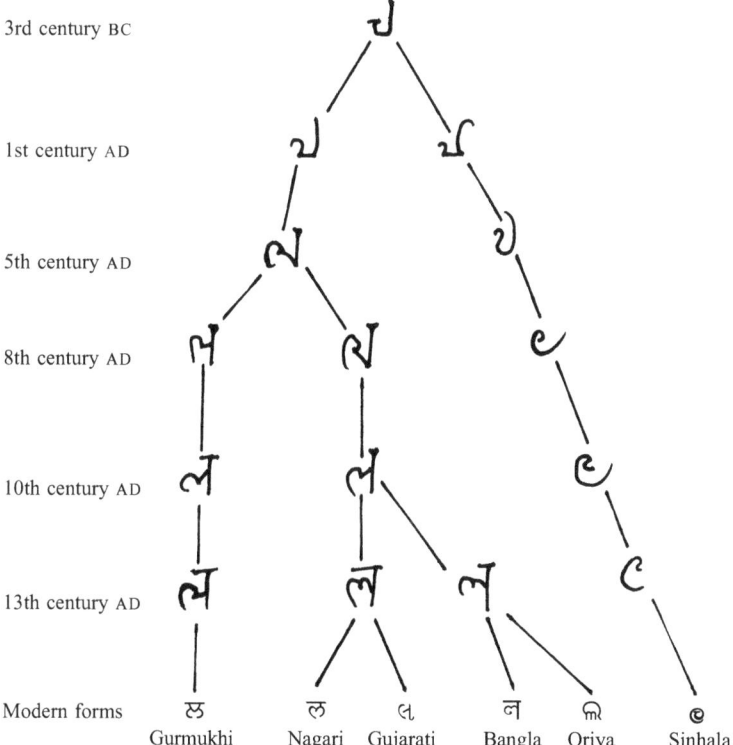

3rd century BC

1st century AD

5th century AD

8th century AD

10th century AD

13th century AD

Modern forms

Gurmukhi   Nagari Gujarati   Bangla Oriya   Sinhala

FIGURE 3.1: EXAMPLE OF SCRIPT DEVELOPMENTS FROM BRĀHMĪ TO THE MODERN SCRIPTS: THE CONSONANT *LA*

In fact, it was precisely when scripts of the Brāhmī family were adapted for use with non-IA languages such as Tamil, Tibetan or Thai that major systemic changes tended to make their appearance. The systemic stability within the IA group is only natural, in view of their overall phonetic similarities and general cultural cohesion. This pattern, moreover, is typical of the historical development of scripts worldwide, wherein major systemic alterations are apt to happen when scripts are borrowed and adapted to languages of other families. To cite one famous example, it was only when the Semitic Phoenician script was adapted to Greek that it was converted from a consonant syllabary to an alphabet.

Formal changes, however – that is, changes in the outward shapes of the individual letters – are extremely extensive throughout the history of the Brāhmī script group (this, in contrast to Kharoṣṭhī; cf. 3.2.5). These alterations began slowly and gradually in the first two or three centuries of Brāhmī's attested history, then became more rapid and radical with the development of distinct local varieties through the first millennium AD. Such changes were driven on the one hand by technological factors, that is, by the nature of the writing implements and materials, and on the other, by stylistic preferences or by changes in fashion. These two factors combined to produce three main types of changes in the letter forms:

(a) Changes resulting from cursivization or reduction in number of strokes.
(b) Changes resulting from alterations in the order or direction of strokes.
(c) Incidental changes resulting from the incorporation of (originally) graphically insignificant, mechanically conditioned changes in the letter forms.

The first type of formal change is illustrated by the development of *ka* from its original Brāhmī form of a cross written with two strokes (✝) into a single stroke shape with a loop at the lower left (↲), which arose when scribes wrote the second stroke rapidly, without lifting their pen from the surface. The old, so-called 'tripartite' form of *ya* (𝗝) similarly developed simplified forms such as 𝟚𝕁 when it was written written with one instead of two strokes.

The second type of change is observed in the history of letters such as *ṇa*, originally written as 𝕀 but later re-formed into shapes such as 𝕏 and 𝟚𝗋, eventually leading to modern forms like older Nagari ण (see Daniels and Bright 1998: 380, Salomon 1998a: 33). Similarly, the old *ma*, originally written with a single stroke crossing over itself (𝕏), was reconfigured into the so-called 'open' form 𝟚𝕁, which in due course developed into modern Nagari म.

While these two types of formal changes gradually led to extensive reconfigurations of individual characters, the third type of change tended to influence the entire ductus of a particular script. By far the most influential change of this type in the history of Brāhmī was the various developments of the original head line or top serif, which originally arose from the small blot of ink left by a split-reed pen at the commencing point of a letter. This incidental mark eventually came to be perceived as an inherent part of the letter, and then was intentionally written with a separate stroke. This head stroke, in turn, gradually became more and more pronounced, and moreover took on distinctive shapes or styles in the different regional scripts. In northern scripts such as Nagari, Gurmukhi and Bangla, it became a long horizontal line across the entire width of most of the letters, while in the southern scripts (except Tamil) it tended to take various rounded shapes such as the 'umbrella' of Oriya (2.4).

For detailed treatments of the history of the development of the Brāhmī-derived scripts, the reader is referred to the standard works on Indian palaeography such as Bühler 1896, Ojhā 1918 and Dani 1963. Helpful charts illustrating the development of individual letters are found in Ojhā 1918: plates 82–4, Sivaramamurti 1952: 56–154, Central Hindi Directorate 1967 (unnumbered plates at end), and all plates in Singh 1991.

4.2 Early developments: the first local variants (second to first centuries BC)

During the so-called Śuṅga period which followed the collapse of the Mauryan dynasty, Brāhmī began its gradual evolution and regional diversification. At this early stage, the formal changes were relatively minor, so that the script of the first century BC is not markedly different from that of the Mauryan period. However, some of these minor changes prefigure and determine more drastic ones in later centuries. For instance, it is during this period that the head marks which are to have such a major effect in the later developments of the regional scripts began to appear in the form of a small triangle at the top of the letters.

A few letters did undergo significant changes in form during this period, such as *dha* (𝗗 > 𝗗), which had a mirror-image shift. Some letters such as *ga* developed rounded shapes (⋀ > ⋂) under the influence of cursivization, yet at the same time a contrary tendency towards angular forms is exhibited in the changes of *ma* ($\curlyvee > \curlyvee$) and *va* ($\delta > \measuredangle$). Evidently, there was a dynamic tension between tendencies toward cursivization and monumental writing in this period.

While the north Indian scripts had not yet developed distinct subvariants, during this period broad regional differences between northern and southern scripts are becoming apparent. In south India, two important local variants, the Bhaṭṭiprōḷu script and the Tamil Brāhmī script, emerged. Besides their important systemic innovations (4.1), these also have some distinct formal characteristics, for instance the upside-down *ma* of Bhaṭṭiprōḷu ($\curlyvee$ in contrast to northern $\curlyvee$). In Sri Lanka too, Brāhmī developed some local peculiarities, including the habit of writing some inscriptions from right to left (3.1.2). All in all, at the end of the pre-Christian era Brāhmī is still a single script with only relatively minor variants, but the forces of graphic change and regionalization are beginning to show their effects.

4.3 The Middle Brāhmī period (first to third centuries AD)

During the early centuries of the Christian era, the centrifugal forces affecting Brāhmī progressed to the point that several local varieties become discernible. At this point, the terminological and analytic problems referred to in section 1.5.2 begin to become more serious, and the identification, classification and naming of the varieties becomes very much a matter of opinion. Dani's division (1963: 78–9, 100–1) of the major varieties of this period into the Kauśāmbī, Mathurā, western Deccan and eastern Deccan styles is influential and is the best we have to date, although more detailed analyses of the individual regional styles and their relationships remain to be done.

In this period, we begin to see linear, square, triangular, and other varieties of the head-line (for details see Dani 1963: 81), prefiguring the later regional developments. The same is true of the development of the diacritic vowel signs, which are now beginning to take on more rounded and extended forms such as $\mathfrak{I}$ *dī*, anticipating the longer vowel marks of the later and modern scripts (3.1). These extensions of the vowel marks are sometimes used for decorative effect, and other sorts of calligraphic elaborations are also coming into use in some regional styles, particularly in the eastern Deccan, where the tops and bottoms of many letters are sometimes extended with long decorative flourishes.

Formal changes in the various characters continue in this period, with *da* undergoing a mirror-image shift ($\flat > \natural$) like that of *dha* in the previous period. In general, we continue to see the operation of the contrary forces of monumental writing on the one hand, resulting in squared, angular shapes like E *ja*, and cursivization on the other, producing rounded and looped forms such as $\mathfrak{A}$ *sa* and $\mathfrak{d}$ *na*.

The repertoire of middle Brāhmī script is expanded in this period by the addition of characters such as *ṛ*, *au*, *ṅa* and *ḥ* (*visarga*) needed to represent Sanskrit, which is only now beginning to become the main epigraphic language (3.1.3). The first long formal inscription in classical Sanskrit is Rudradāman's Junāgaḍh rock inscription (Sircar 1965: 175–80) of about AD 150, but the predominant languages in this period are still Prakrits in the Deccan and the northwest and 'Epigraphical Hybrid Sanskrit' in the north. It is also because of the increasing Sanskritization of the inscriptional corpus that we now find more examples of consonantal conjuncts, including the development of special ligatures in which one of the component letters is altered or abbreviated. This is particularly the case with conjuncts involving the semivowel *r*, for which, no doubt due to their statistical frequency, special abridged forms emerge in both pre- and post-consonantal position (e.g. $𝑈$ *rpa* and $𝑌$ *pra*). This development prefigures patterns in later and modern scripts, in which certain common conjunct elements, especially *r*, take on special ligatured forms (2.1.1, 2.3, etc.).

4.4 The late Brāhmī period (fourth to sixth centuries AD)

In this period, we continue to see an increase in the number of regional and subregional varieties, both because of continuing differentiation and because of the larger number of inscriptional records available. Dani (1963: 109–14) enumerates 'nine main geographical divisions' in the scripts of this period, though as usual 'there is some overlapping' (ibid., p.109), and clear lines of demarcation and terminology are lacking. But formal changes are gradually becoming more extensive and regionally pronounced, such that we are now beginning to reach the point where we can speak of different scripts instead of varieties of one script. By now we can see in many of the new forms direct precursors of the modern letters; compare, for example, the new northern form of ᛜ *ga* with its ancestor ∧ and with modern Nagari ग. In the south, the preference for rounded forms and wavy lines that is so characteristic of most southern scripts is beginning to manifest itself.

4.5 The transitional scripts (seventh to tenth centuries AD)

During this period, the regional scripts become more and more distinct from each other in general ductus and in the forms of individual characters. In the north, the Siddhamātṛkā script (see 1.5.2), from which the modern northern and eastern scripts are largely derived, emerges. In it we see the development of cursivized forms like the looped *ka* (क) and the bipartite *ya* (य) that underlie the shapes of the letters in the modern scripts. The extension of the diacritic vowel signs that commenced in the middle Brāhmī period (4.3) now approximates its final result in the modern scripts, for example with the signs for *i* and *ī* curving over and alongside the full height of the consonant to which they are attached. In the northwest, an early form of the regional script which comes to be known as Śāradā (see Upadhyay 1998) has emerged. In south India, the regional scripts, especially those of the far south such as Tamil and Grantha, now have a distinct separate identity, and Sinhalese script is undergoing a major reconfiguration under their influence.

4.6 The emergence of the modern scripts

By the beginning of the second millennium, some of the major regional scripts, most notably Nagari, have reached a stage of development that is not drastically different from that of their modern forms, although some others, such as Gurmukhi and Gujarati, did not achieve a separate identity until the middle or second half of the millennium. In general, the developments of the individual modern scripts are not nearly as well documented as might be hoped or expected. Some of them, such as Bangla (Banerji 1919), Oriya (Tripathi 1962), and especially Nagari (Central Hindi Directorate 1967, Bhāṭiyā 1978, Singh 1991) have been separately studied on the basis of epigraphic and/ or manuscript materials, but completely definitive and comprehensive treatments are mostly lacking; Singh 1991 is a welcome exception.

In north India, by the beginning of this period the Siddhamātṛkā script has already evolved into an archaic form of Nagari (Salomon 1998a: 40–1), characterized by a horizontal top line across the entire width of the character, by predominantly square shapes and right angles, and by fully extended diacritic vowels *ā*, *i*, and *ī* reaching to the bottom level of the *akṣara*. In the northeast, Siddhamātṛkā meanwhile separately evolved into a form referred to as 'proto-Bengali' or 'Gauḍī', which prevailed until the fourteenth century, by which time it had begun to be differentiated into the modern eastern scripts, Bangla-Asamiya, Maithilī and Oriya. In the northwest, the early form of Śāradā had developed into a distinct subgroup comprising the many local scripts of Panjab, Kashmir and the western Himalayan regions, of which Śāradā and Gurmukhi are the most important representatives.

The Sinhala script developed in a more complex pattern, in part independently as befits its insular location, but also under the influence of several Indian scripts at various points in its history – five different varieties of far southern and peninsular Brāhmī according to Dani (1963: 216) – as would only be expected in view of Sri Lanka's long cultural and political interaction with the mainland. The Grantha script of far southern India had a particularly strong influence on the formation of modern Sinhala, which took shape in about the thirteenth century. Thus it is not surprising that in their general ductus the medieval and modern forms of Sinhala resemble the southern scripts.

5 NON-INDIAN SCRIPTS USED FOR IA LANGUAGES

5.1 Perso-Arabic scripts

In most parts of South Asia where substantial portions of the population converted to Islam in the medieval period, the local languages began to be written in Persian script (itself a modification of Arabic script), modified and adapted in various ways, though not always consistently across different regions. Given the strong identification among Muslims generally with the Arabic language and script, this is exactly what would be expected. Nonetheless there is a notable exception in East Bengal, where the Indic Bangla script was widely retained for the Bangla language (though a Perso-Arabic script was occasionally used) and continues to be the dominant script of modern Bangladesh despite a Muslim majority population of over ninety per cent.

The principal IA languages which are exclusively or widely written in a Perso-Arabic script are Urdu, Kashmiri, Panjabi (in Pakistan) and Sindhi. The alphabets of these languages follow the order and system of Persian, with the addition, by various kinds of diacritic modification, of several further letters needed to represent phonemes not occurring in Persian or Arabic. The orthography of the many Arabic and Persian loanwords in these languages is conservative, representing older phonetic distinctions, for example between ذ *ẓa* (*ẕāl*) and ز *za* (*ze*), that are not actually retained in pronunciation. The cultural forces at work here are analogous to those which preserve archaic Sanskritic spellings in Brāhmī-derived scripts such as Bangla (2.3; cf. Masica 1991: 151).

The forms of the additional characters are not consistent from language to language. For example, in Urdu (and, following its conventions, in Kashmiri), the aspirate consonants are indicated by writing the medial form (ﮭ) of the consonant *h* (ھ *he*) after the corresponding unaspirated consonant, as in پھ *ph*, whereas in Sindhi most of the aspirates are marked by the addition of two (ڌ *dh*) or four (ڦ *ph*) diacritic dots, though جھ *jh* and گھ *gh* are written with *he*, as in Urdu. In Urdu, the retroflex consonants are marked either by four diacritic dots (ٹ *ṭ*) or by the sign ◌ (ٹ *ṭ*, ڈ *ḍ*), while in Sindhi other combinations of diacritic dots are used: ٿ *ṭ*, ٽ *ṭh*, ڊ *ḍ*, ڍ *ḍh*. Also in Sindhi, the additional set of implosive consonants (*ɓ, ɗ,* and *ɠ*) are similarly represented through the addition of sets of diacritic dots (ٻ *ɓ,* ڐ *ɗ,* ڳ *ɠ*).

The Perso-Arabic scripts used for the IA languages are, like their prototypes, essentially consonant syllabaries with partial marking of vowels, mostly long vowels and diphthongs, by the *matres lectionis* system. Thus the consonant يے *y* (*ye*) serves to represent *ī, e,* and *ai* without distinction in most cases, while short *i* is left unmarked; similarly, و *v* (*wāw*) marks *ū, o* and *au,* but not *u.* All initial vowels are represented by ١ *alif,* originally glottal stop, but here, as in Kharoṣṭhī (3.2.1), serving as a vowel carrier. Initially, long *ā* is diacritically distinguished as آ, while medial *ā* is indicated by *alif* as a *mater lectionis.* Thus, for example, Urdu *sunār* 'goldsmith' is written سنار, transliterated *sn'r.* Special diacritics are available to mark the short vowels as well, but they are not used in ordinary writing; in this system, used mostly for pedagogical purposes, the same word would be written سُنار, with the vowel marker *zamma* or *pesh* indicating the *u.*

Because vowels are essentially marginal to the system of these scripts, the entire problem of conjuncts in the Indic scripts becomes irrelevant. The reader is expected to know, by acquaintance with the language, whether or not a vowel intervenes between two consonants in a word such as لڑکا *laṛkā* 'boy' (transliteration: *lṛk'*). Here again, there is a vowel cancellation marker (*jazm* or *sukūn*) available to make the absence of a vowel explicit, so that the word can be written لڑْکا, but this too is not normally used.

5.2 Roman script

Although Roman script is widely current in South Asia due to the use of English as a sort of lingua franca, and is widely employed for the rendition of Indian words therein as well as for scholarly and technical purposes, it has rarely been adopted in any systematic way for writing any of the major Indian languages. The only notable exception among the IA languages is Konkani, which has widely been written in Roman script, especially among Christian communities, since the sixteenth century (Masica 1991: 153). The orthography of Konkani in Roman script, which is influenced by Portuguese usage, does without diacritic marks. Vowel quantity is left unspecified, while retroflex consonants are distinguished from the corresponding dentals by being written as geminates.

The failure of Roman script to supplant any of the Indian scripts, despite proposals by various reformers to this effect, probably reflects the sense of personal, sentimental and patriotic attachment that people everywhere tend to feel for their familiar systems of writing. In South Asia, an additional factor comes into play, in that a distinctive script is often felt to be an intrinsic part of a language's identity (Masica 1991: 144).

ACKNOWLEDGEMENT

The tables in this article were prepared with the expert assistance of Andrew Glass.

REFERENCES

Allchin, F. R. (1995) *The Archaeology of Early Historic South Asia: The Emergence of Cities and States,* Cambridge: Cambridge University Press.
Allon, Mark (2001) *Three Gāndhārī Ekottarikāgama-type Sūtras: British Library Kharoṣṭhī Fragments 12 and 14* (Gandhāran Buddhist Texts 2), Seattle: University of Washington Press.
Banerji, R.D. (1919) *The Origin of the Bengali Script,* Calcutta: University of Calcutta.

Bhāṭiyā, O. (1978) *Nāgarī lipi kā udbhav aur vikās*, New Delhi: Sūrya Prakāśan.

Boyer, A. M., Rapson, E. J. and Senart, E. (1920–9) *Kharoṣṭhī Inscriptions Discovered by Sir Aurel Stein in Chinese Turkestan*, 3 parts (part 3 by Rapson and P. S. Noble), Oxford: Clarendon Press.

Brough, J. (1962) *The Gāndhārī Dharmapada* (London Oriental Series 7), London: Oxford University Press.

Bühler, G. (1895) 'The Origin of the Kharoṣṭhī Alphabet', *Wiener Zeitschrift für die Kunde des Morgenlandes* 9: 44–66. (Reprinted as Appendix 1 (pp. 92–114) of Bühler 1898.)

—— (1896) *Indische Palaeographie von circa 350 A. Chr. – circa 1300 P. Chr.* (Grundriss der indo-arischen Philologie und Altertumskunde 1.2), Strassburg: K. J. Trübner, 1896. English version (J. F. Fleet, tr.), *Indian Paleography From About B.C. 350 to About A.D. 1300*, Appendix to *Indian Antiquary* 33, 1904.

—— (1898) *On the Origin of the Indian Brāhma Alphabet* (Indian Studies No. III), 2nd ed., Strassburg: Karl J. Trübner.

Central Hindi Directorate (1967) *Devanagari through the Ages*, Delhi: Government of India.

Coningham, R. A. E., Allchin, F. R., Batt, C. M. and Lucy, D. (1996) 'Passage to India? Anuradhapura and the Early Use of the Brahmi Script', *Cambridge Archaeological Journal* 6: 73–97.

Dani, A. H. (1963) *Indian Palaeography*, Oxford: Clarendon Press, 2nd ed., New Delhi: Munshiram Manoharlal, 1968.

Daniels, P. T. and Bright, W. (eds.) (1996) *The World's Writing Systems*, New York: Oxford University Press.

Das Gupta, C. C. (1958) *The Development of the Kharoṣṭhī Script*, Calcutta: Firma K. L. Mukhopadhyay.

Diringer, D. (1953) *The Alphabet: A Key to the History of Mankind*, New York: Philosophical Library.

Falk, H. (1993) *Schrift im alten Indien: Ein Forschungsbericht mit Ammerkungen* (ScriptOralia 56), Tübingen: Gunter Narr Verlag.

Fussman, G. (1989) 'Gāndhārī écrite, gāndhārī parlée', in Caillat, C. (ed.) *Dialectes dans les littératures indo-aryennes*, Paris: Collège de France, pp. 433–501.

Glass, Andrew (2000) 'Paleography', in Salomon 2000: 53–74.

Grierson, G. A. (ed.) (1903–27) *Linguistic Survey of India*, 11 vols., Calcutta: Office of the Superintendent of Government Printing.

van Gulik, R. (1956) *Siddham: An Essay on the History of Sanskrit Studies in China and Japan* (Sarasvati-Vihara Series 37), Nagpur: International Academy of Indian Culture.

Gupta, S. P. and Ramachandran, K. S. (eds.) (1979) *The Origin of Brahmi Script* (History and Historians of India Series 2), Delhi: D. K. Publications.

Hunter, G. R. (1934) *The Script of Harappa and Mohenjodaro and Its Connection with Other Scripts*, London: Kegan Paul, Trench, Trubner & Co.

Konow, S. (1929) *Kharoshthī Inscriptions with the Exception of Those of Aśoka* (Corpus Inscriptionum Indicarum 2.1), Calcutta: Government of India.

Lambert, H. M. (1953) *Introduction to the Devanagari Script for Students of Sanskrit, Hindi, Marathi Gujarati and Bengali*, London: Oxford University Press.

Leitner, G. W. (1883) *A Collection of Specimens of Commercial and Other Alphabets and Handwritings as also of Multiplication Tables Current in Various Parts of the Panjab, Sind and the North West Provinces*, Lahore: Anjuman-i-Punjab Press.

Lin, Meicun (1996) 'Kharoṣṭhī Bibliography', *Central Asiatic Journal* 40: 188–220.

Masica, C. P. (1991) *The Indo-Aryan Languages* (Cambridge Language Surveys), Cambridge: Cambridge University Press.

Maurer, W. (1976) 'On the Name Devanāgarī', *Journal of the American Oriental Society* 96: 101–4.

Nowotny, F. (1967) 'Schriftsysteme in Indien', *Studium Generale* 20: 527–47.

Ojhā, G. H. (1918) *Bhāratīya Prācīn Lipimālā*, 2nd ed., Ajmer: Scottish Mission Industries Company.

Parpola, A. (1994) *Deciphering the Indus Script*, Cambridge: Cambridge University Press.

Renou, L. (1956) *Histoire de la langue sanskrite*, Lyons: Editions IAC.

Renou, L. and Filliozat, J. (1953) *L'Inde classique: Manuel des études indiennes*, vol. 2, Hanoi: École Française d'Extrême-Orient.

Salomon, R. (1984) 'Calligraphy in Pre-Islamic India', in Asher, Frederick M. and Gai, G. S. (eds.), *Indian Epigraphy: Its Bearing on the History of Art*, New Delhi: Oxford and IBH Publishing Co., pp. 3–6.

—— (1990) 'New Evidence for a Gāndhārī Origin of the Arapacana Syllabary', *Journal of the American Oriental Society* 110: 255–73.

—— (1998a) *Indian Epigraphy: A Guide to the Study of Inscriptions in Sanskrit, Prakrit, and the Other Indo-Aryan Languages* (South Asia Research Series), New York: Oxford University Press.

—— (1998b) 'Kharoṣṭhī Manuscript Fragments in the Pelliot Collection, Bibliothèque Nationale de France', *Bulletin d'Études Indiennes* 16: 123–60.

—— (1999) *Ancient Buddhist Scrolls from Gandhāra: The British Library Kharoṣṭhī Fragments*, Seattle/London: University of Washington Press/British Library.

—— (2000) *A Gāndhārī Version of the Rhinoceros Sūtra: British Library Kharoṣṭhī Fragment 5B* (Gandhāran Buddhist Texts 1), Seattle: University of Washington Press.

Sander, L. (1968) *Paläographisches zu den Sanskrithandschriften der Berliner Turfansammlung* (Verzeichnis der Orientalischen Handschriften in Deutschland, Supplementband 8), Wiesbaden: Franz Steiner Verlag.

Singh, A. K. (1991) *Development of Nāgarī Script*, Delhi: Parimal Publications.

Sircar, D. C. (1965/1983) *Select Inscriptions Bearing on Indian History and Civilization*, vol. 1: *From the Sixth Century B.C. to the Sixth Century A.D.*, 2nd ed., Calcutta: Calcutta University; vol. 2: *From the Sixth to the Eighteenth Century A.D.*, Delhi: Motilal Banarsidass.

—— (1970–1) 'Introduction to Indian Epigraphy and Paleography', *Journal of Ancient Indian History* 4: 72–136.

Sivaramamurti, C. (1952 [reprinted 1966]) *Indian Epigraphy and South Indian Scripts* (Bulletin of the Madras Government Museum, New Series, General Section, 3.4), Madras: Government of Madras.

Tripathi, K. ([1962]) *The Evolution of Oriya Language and Script*, Cuttack: Utkal University.

Upadhyay, Jiwan (1998) *Development of Śārdā Script (up to 13th Century A.D.)*, Delhi: Ramanand Vidya Bhawan.

Upasak, C. S. (1960) *The History and Palaeography of Mauryan Brāhmī Script*, Nalanda: Nava Nālandā Mahāvihāra.

FURTHER READING

Bühler, G. (1896) *Indische Palaeographie von circa 350 A. Chr – circa 1300 P. Chr.* (Grundriss der indo-arischen Philologie und Altertumskunde 1.2), Strassburg: K. J. Trübner, 1896. English version (J. F. Fleet, tr.), *Indian Paleography From About B.C. 350 to About A.D. 1300*, Appendix to *Indian Antiquary* 33, 1904.

Dani, A. H. (1963), *Indian Palaeography*, Oxford: Clarendon Press, 2nd ed., New Delhi: Munshiram Manoharlal, 1968.

Daniels, P. T. and Bright, W. (eds.) (1996) *The World's Writing Systems*, New York: Oxford University Press. Part VI, 'South Asian Writing Systems', pp. 371–441.

Das Gupta, C. C. (1958) *The Development of the Kharoṣṭhī Script*, Calcutta: Firma K. L. Mukhopadhyay.

Falk, H. (1993) *Schrift im alten Indien: Ein Forschungsbericht mit Anmerkungen* (ScriptOralia 56), Tübingen: Gunter Narr Verlag.

Lambert, H. M. (1953) *Introduction to the Devanagari Script for Students of Sanskrit, Hindi, Marathi Gujarati and Bengali*, London: Oxford University Press.

Masica, C. P. (1991) *The Indo-Aryan Languages*, Cambridge: Cambridge University Press. Chapter 6, 'Writing Systems', pp. 133–53.

Nowotny, F. (1967) 'Schriftsysteme in Indien', *Studium Generale* 20: 527–47.

Renou, L. and Filliozat, J. (1953) *L'Inde classique: Manuel des études indiennes*, vol. 2, Hanoi: École Française d'Extrême-Orient. Appendix 1, 'Paléographie', pp. 665–712.

Salomon, R. (1998) *Indian Epigraphy: A Guide to the Study of Inscriptions in Sanskrit, Prakrit, and the Other Indo-Aryan Languages* (South Asia Research Series), New York: Oxford University Press.

Sircar, D. C. (1965/1983) *Select Inscriptions Bearing on Indian History and Civilization*, vol. 1, *From the Sixth Century B.C. to the Sixth Century A.D.*, 2nd ed., Calcutta: Calcutta University; vol. 2, *From the Sixth to the Eighteenth Century A.D.*, Delhi: Motilal Banarsidass.

Sivaramamurti, C. (1952 [reprinted 1966]) *Indian Epigraphy and South Indian Scripts* (Bulletin of the Madras Government Museum, New Series, General Section, 3.4), Madras: Government of Madras.

SANKSKRIT

George Cardona

CONTENTS

LIST OF TABLES

1 INTRODUCTION

1.1 Sanskrit (*saṁskṛta* 'adorned, purified [by grammar]'; see Cardona 1997: 557–64) is a form of Old Indo-Aryan used over a wide area in the north of the Indian subcontinent from around the middle of the second millennium BC onwards.

Sanskrit has an extensive literature. The earliest texts are the four Vedas: *Ṛgveda*, *Sāmaveda*, *Yajurveda*, *Atharvaveda* in their continuously recited versions (*saṁhitā-pāṭha*). The Yajurveda is divided into two groups: the Śuklayajurveda and the Kṛṣṇayajurveda. The former is represented by the *Vājasaneyisaṁhitā*, the latter by the *Taittirīyasaṁhitā*, *Maitrāyaṇīsaṁhitā*, *Kāṭhakasaṁhitā* and *Kapiṣṭhalakaṭhasaṁhitā*. The texts of Kṛṣṇayajurveda reflect different branches (*śākhā*) represented by members of textual traditions (*caraṇa*); e.g. *taittirīyāḥ* (nom. pl. m.) refers to those who study the text as propounded by Tittiri. The other Vedic texts also come down in different 'recensions'. The Ṛgveda, Sāmaveda, Śuklayajurveda and Atharvaveda, respectively, are mainly represented by the Śākala, Kauthuma, Mādhyandina and Śaunaka branches. Many branches were recognized. Patañjali mentions numbers of such divisions for different Vedas – for example, twenty-one groups associated with the Ṛgveda – and cites the beginning of the *Atharvaveda* from the Paippalāda tradition. Also forming part of Vedic textual traditions are Brāhmaṇas, Āraṇyakas, Upaniṣads, Śrautasūtras, Gṛhyasūtras, Śulbasūtras and Prātiśākhyas.

The Vedas are known in versions that reflect speech habits of recitors later than the original authors. Thus, the text known from the time of the *Ṛgvedaprātiśākhya* at times has -*y*- and -*v*- where metrically one expects -*iy*- and -*uv*- (see section 2.5.1.4). The text represented in the analysed text (*padapāṭha*) composed by Śākalya and accounted for in the *Ṛgvedaprātiśākhya* is later accepted as authoritative.

Vedas are associated with ancillary works called *vedāṅgas*: ritual instruction (*kalpa*, in śrauta- and gṛhyasūtra texts); astronomy (*jyotiṣa*), used to assure the performance of rites at proper times; metrics (*chandoviciti*); grammar (*vyākaraṇa*); phonetics (*śikṣā*); and works explaining etymologically how particular words mean what they do (*nirukta*). Additional works constitute a set of ancillaries called *upāṅgas*: purāṇa (texts preserving traditional lore concerning topics such as ruling lineages, world creation and dissolution), nyāya (logic), mīmāṁsā – pūrvamīmāṁsā (dealing with exegetical principles for reconciling brāhmaṇa texts as they pertain to ritual) as well as uttaramīmāṁsā (which treats philosophical-religious ideas) – and dharmaśāstra (rules of duty and behaviour). Further, there are upavedas: āyurveda (medicine), dhanurveda (archery), gāndharvaveda (music) and arthaśāstra (government).

There is a large body of literature in both belles lettres and other spheres, ranging from works of drama and poetry – such as those composed by Bhāsa (e.g. *Svapnavāsavadatta*), Kālidāsa (e.g. *Śākuntala*, *Vikramorvaśīya*, *Kumārasambhava*, *Raghuvaṁśa*), Śūdraka (*Mṛcchakaṭika*), Bhavabhūti (*Mahāvīracarita*, *Mālatīmādhava*, *Uttararāmacarita*), Bhāravi (*Kirātārjunīya*) and Māgha (*Śiśupālavadha*) – and the epics *Rāmāyaṇa* and *Mahābhārata*, to didactic literature such as the *Pañcatantra* and *Hitopadeśa*, and treatises on logic, medicine and mathematics. Sanskrit is not restricted to Hindu works; Buddhist and Jain scholars used Sanskrit in original texts and commentaries. To this day, Sanskrit remains a vehicle for original literature as well as technical works such as modern commentaries, and periodicals are published in Sanskrit. It is officially recognized in the eighth schedule of the Indian constitution, is one of the languages in which denominations appear on Indian currency bills, and is used in daily newscasts on All India Radio and Doordarshan. In addition, speakers report Sanskrit as their mother tongue in the census of India. Moreover, due to factors that require study, the number of speakers has increased in recent years: 2212, 6106, and 49,736, respectively, for 1971, 1981, and 1991 (see Vijayanunni 1997:12, 23).

In this chapter, I avoid fine divisions of Sanskrit into categories such as classical and epic. I operate instead with a dichotomy between Vedic and non-Vedic, under the assumption that further subdivisions of the latter are predicated on matters of style and diction, not on basic points of grammar. Many of the usages usually labelled 'non-Pāṇinian' in epics and other works, moreover, do not truly qualify as such, since Pāṇini himself acknowledges broad and open-ended variation in some spheres of the language he describes, reflecting the fact that he speaks of a living language. Such variation comes under the rubric of liberty allowed to poets in later works, what is called *ārṣaprayoga*.

1.2 Pāṇini's grammar (*śabdānuśāsana*, *vyākaraṇa*), the core of which is a set of nearly four thousand rules in eight chapters – the *Aṣṭādhyāyī* – describes a spoken language (*bhāṣā*) current in the northwest of the subcontinent around 500 BC. Pāṇini recognizes dialectal differences. He notes (4.2.74: *udak ca vipāśaḥ*) a difference between usage north and south of the Vipāś river – corresponding to the modern Beas – concerning names of wells: to the north, terms such as *dátta*- ('built by Datta') are used, with high-pitch on the first syllable, but to the south corresponding oxytones (e.g. *dattá*-) are used. Pāṇini also mentions usages particular to northerners (*udīcām* [gen. pl.]) and easterners (*prācām*) and accounts for usage particular to Vedic. Vedic texts themselves were objects of linguistic study. The earliest analysis available is Śākalya's padapāṭha to the

Rgveda, which Pāṇini knew. There were also early works on phonetics (*śikṣā*), which inform us on the pronunciation of Sanskrit sounds and its tonal system. The earliest known of such descriptions are in works called prātiśākhyas, which also include rules for converting analysed texts (*padapāṭha*) into the continuously recited texts (*saṃhitāpāṭha*) of Vedas. Two of these – the *Rgvedaprātiśākhya* and *Taittirīyaprāti-śākhya* – are probably earlier than Pāṇini.

Prātiśākhyas mention pronunciation differences attributed to teachers associated with Vedic recitational traditions. Speech differences of various areas were known also to Patañjali in the mid-second century BC He remarks (Bh. I.9.25–10.1) that certain terms have restricted domains; e.g. the verb *śav* (*śavati*) 'go' is used in Kamboja (*kambojeṣu*), *hamm* (*hammati*) in Surāṣṭra (*surāṣṭreṣu*), *raṃh* (*raṃhati*) 'go' in the eastern and midland areas (*prācyamadhyeṣu*), but Āryas use *gam* (*gacchati*) in this meaning. Yāska, who antedates Patanjali, also mentions (Nir. 2.2) such differences. See General Introduction sections 1.4, 2.2.2.

There was diglossia from early on: a current language, from whose speakers Pāṇini assumed a native knowledge of usage conventions, coexisted with varieties of Indo-Aryan which differed by virtue of certain changes. In his discussion of *Aṣṭādhyāyī* 1.3.1, Kātyāyana (no later than third century BC) shows (1.3.1 vt. 12) that he knew terms like *āṇapayati*, equivalent to Skt. *ājñāpayati* 'commands'. In his commentary, Patañjali (Bh. I.259.6–7) adds *vaṭṭati, vaḍḍhati*, which are equivalent to *vartate* 'occurs, is', and *vardhate* 'grows'. These forms show Middle Indic phonological and grammatical developments, including the replacement of middle endings by active endings. Patañjali also brings up (Bh. I.11.11–14) something that is known from tradition (*śrūyate*): there were sages who instead of saying *yad vā naḥ* 'what (is) ours', *tad vā naḥ* 'that (is) ours' said *yar vā ṇas tar vāṇaḥ* – with *r* for *d* and *ṇ* for *n* – but they did not utter such incorrect speech (*nāpabhāṣante* [3sg. pres.]) at ritual performance. That is, in Kātyāyana's and Patañjali's times and places, speakers who commanded the accepted high speech also spoke vernaculars with Middle Indic features. There is good reason to consider that this situation existed much earlier also. Thus, a form like *vikaṭa-* 'deformed', attested already in the Ṛgveda (10.155.1a: *vikaṭe* [voc. sg. fem.]), admittedly represents a Middle Indic development of *vikṛta-*.

1.3 Pāṇini distinguishes between usages particular to Vedic (*chandasi* 'in sacred literature') and to the currently spoken language (*bhāṣāyām* [loc. sg.]), as opposed to usage common to both, and commentators distinguish between speech forms that pertain to the Vedas (*vaidikānām* [gen. pl. m.]) and those that occur in everyday usage (*laukikānām*). Modern scholars also commonly make a distinction between Vedic and Sanskrit. Some scholars use 'classical Sanskrit' with reference not only to the language of authors like Kālidāsa but also to the speech described in non-Vedic rules of the *Aṣṭādhyāyī*, although it has been demonstrated that the current language Pāṇini described bears close resemblance to the late Vedic Indo-Aryan represented in Brāhmaṇa texts such as the *Aitareyabrāhmaṇa*. In addition, it is customary to recognize a separate genre of 'epic Sanskrit' represented in the *Mahābhārata* and *Rāmāyaṇa*, and some scholars have devoted attention to what they term 'non-Pāṇinian' forms in these texts. Scholars also disagree concerning precisely how Sanskrit came to have its elevated status, just how it interacted with vernaculars, and whether at some time it ceased to be granted such status and was later revived (see Aklujkar 1996).

Leaving aside such disagreements, I think it is fair to say that post-Vedic Sanskrit literary compositions, although they are of various genres – poetry (*kāvya*), drama (*nāṭya*), stories (*kathā*), didactic compositions, technical treatises of various schools, and so on – and have different regional styles (*rīti*), share a common core of phonology, grammar and diction such that all these compositions can truly be considered to be in a single language, despite differences in vocabulary and adherence to relatively strict canons of grammar. Moreover, it is undeniable that the pre-eminent codifier of the language, Pāṇini, viewed the object of his description not as a frozen entity but as developing, subject to change.

In this chapter I describe briefly the phonetics, phonology and grammar of the Old Indo-Aryan common to the language current in Pāṇini's time as described in the *Aṣṭādhyāyī*, to the great majority of later Sanskrit literary compositions, and to Vedic, and indicate the major features particular to Vedic.

2 PHONETICS AND PHONOLOGY

2.1 Phonological system

The phonological system distinguishes vowels (*svara*) and consonants (*vyañjana*). Consonants are of three types: stops (*sparśa*), semivowels (*anta[h]sthā*), and spirants (*ūṣman*). Much is known about how these sounds were pronounced from information concerning their production found in works such as the *Taittirīyaprātiśākhya* and śikṣās. Traditional arrangements of the sound inventory are based on such phonetic knowledge; see section 4 with table 4.4.

2.2 Vowels

2.2.1 There are short (*hrasva*) and long (*dīrgha*) vowels: *a i u ṛ ḷ* and *ā ī ū ṝ e o ai au*, with the duration of one and two morae (*mātrā*), respectively. Extra-long (*pluta*) vowels, generally with three times the duration of a short vowel, occur under particular circumstances; e.g. the last vowel of *devadattā3* (voc. sg.), used to call from afar a person named Devadatta, is high pitched and trimoric. *ḷ* does not have a long counterpart, and *e o ai au* are long. All vowels occur between consonants, *ḷ* only in forms of the verb *kḷp* 'be fit, arrange'. All vowels except *ṝ ḷ* also occur as word-initial and prepause word-final segments. *-ṛ* occurs in the noun type *kartṛ-* 'doer' (nom.-acc. sg. nt. *kartṛ*) and before the word-boundary pause in the padapāṭha between members of compounds, as well as before certain suffixes.

Vowels are unnasalized (*ananunāsika, niranunāsika*) or nasalized (*anunāsika*); e.g. in *asmāñ ca tāṁś ca* 'both us (*asmān* [acc. pl.]) and (*ca ... ca*) them (*tān* [acc. pl. m.])', *asmāñ* has a clear vowel *ā* followed by *ñ*, but *tāṁś* has a nasalized vowel (*āṁ*) preceding *ś* (see section 2.5.2.5). There are also different pitches: high-pitched (*udātta*) and low-pitched (*anudātta*) vowels as well as vowels which combine high and low pitch (*svarita*), starting high and descending to low; e.g. the first and second vowels of *agni-* 'fire, Agni' are respectively low- and high-pitched and the vowel of *kvà* 'where?' bears a combination of high and low tones. Tone adjustments in continuous speech result in additional pitch variation, including super-high and super-low tones; see section 2.5.3.1.
2.2.2 *i ī, u ū* are pairs of high (*tālavya* 'palatal') and labial (*oṣṭhya*) vowels. *a ā* pair similarly, but differ qualitatively: *a* is a close (*saṁvṛta*) central vowel, *ā* a low open (*vivṛta*) vowel. *ṛ* and *ṝ* are metrically short and long and bear different pitches, but they are phonetically combinations of vowel and consonant segments: *r* flanked by very short segments which have different vowel colors in different dialects. In the dialect Śaunaka

represents, *ṛ* consists of a consonantal segment *r* – produced either at the roots of the teeth or the alveolae – flanked by segments *ă* (one-fourth of a mora) which are produced further forward than *a* due to the tongue positioning for *r*: *ără*. This accords with the statement that *ṛ* has the same place of production as velar (*jihvāmūlīya*) stops *k* and so on – in contrast to *a*, said to be produced further back – and with the *Ṛgvedaprātiśākhya* order of vowels: *ṛ* follows *a ā*. There is also evidence that *ṛ* was pronounced *ĕrĕ* and *ĭrĭ*. In descriptions where the place of the consonantal segment is assigned to *ṛ*, both this vowel and *r* are said to be retroflex elements. Modern pronunciations of *ṛ* vary; e.g. *ri* in the midlands, *ru* in the southwest.

e o ai au derive from Indo-Iranian diphthongs **ai au āi āu*, which source is reflected in the alternation of *e o ai au* with *ay av āy āv* before vowels (section 2.5.1.5), but according to the earliest descriptions, *e o* are monophthongs. *ai* and *au* are diphthongs consisting of a segment *a* followed by a palatal and labial segment. According to early descriptions, these constituents either have the same duration – one mora each – or the vowels consist of a half-mora of *a* followed by a mora and one-half of *i* and *u* respectively. In addition, the *Taittirīyaprātiśākhya* (2.27: *saṁvṛtakaraṇataram ekeṣām*) notes that according to some (*ekeṣām*) the segment *a* in *ai* and *au* is a closer (*saṁvṛtakaraṇataram*) vowel than the usual *a*.

2.3 Consonants

2.3.1 Stops are arranged in five groups, ordered in terms of speech production, from back to front: velar (*jihvāmūlīya*, *kaṇṭhya*), palatal (*tālavya*), located at the area immediately behind the alveolar ridge (*mūrdhanya* [usually translated 'retroflex']), dental (*dantya*, *dantamūlīya*), and labial (*oṣṭhya*). Each group is arranged in the following order: voiceless (*aghoṣa*) stops, with unaspirated (*alpaprāṇa*) stops followed by aspirated (*mahāprāṇa*) ones; voiced (*ghoṣavat*) stops, again in the order unaspirated and aspirated; and finally nasal (*anunāsika*) stops (see section 2.4). Palatal and retroflex stops are described (e.g. TPr 2.36–37) as produced by letting the mid-tongue (*jihvāmadhya*) make contact at the palate and by curling the tongue back (*prativeṣṭya*) and having the tip of the tongue (*jihvāgra*) make full contact at the mūrdhan, that is, behind the alveolar ridge; in articulating dental stops, one brings the tip of the tongue (*jihvāgra*) into contact with the roots of the upper teeth (*dantamūla*, TPr. 2.38: *jihvāgreṇa tavarge dantamūleṣu*).

2.3.2 The semivowels *y v* and *l* are respectively palatal, labiodental and dental. *r* is variously described as dental, alveolar (*vartsya*) or retroflex. Semivowels other than *r* have nasalized counterparts: *yṁ vṁ lṁ*. In the Mādhyandina tradition of the *Vājasaneyisaṁhitā*, utterance-initial *y* is realized as *j*, as is *y* in word-initial position after a vowel, and when doubling applies; e.g. in *yajñena yajñam atanvata* the first two words are pronounced with initial *j*-, and *vīryyam* is pronounced with *-rjja-*. In the same tradition, *v* has a strong pronunciation – *b* in some recitations – when initial and when subject to doubling; e.g. *vāyava stha* is recited with a strongly articulated *v*-, realized as a stop. These pronunciations are represented by special signs: the symbol for *y* with a stroke or a subscript dot (य य़) and doubled *v* (व्व).

2.3.3 The spirants *ś ṣ s* – respectively palatal, retroflex and dental – are voiceless; *h* is voiced. In the Mādhyandina tradition, *kh* is pronounced instead of *ṣ* except where it follows a velar stop. There is evidence for *kh* in place of *ṣ* in other dialects also.

2.3.4 *ḥ* (*visarjanīya*) is a voiceless spirant, restricted to word-final position, which is pharyngeal or takes the place of production of a preceding vowel. In modern pronunciation, prepause *ḥ* is accompanied by an echo of a vowel or the second part of a diphthong; e.g. *agneḥ, vāyoḥ, taiḥ, gauḥ* end with *-ehe, -oho, -aihi, -auhu*. ⵈ *k* and ⵈ *p*, respectively called *jihvāmūlīya* and *upadhmānīya* and represented by ⵈ (e.g. ⵈ क ⵈ ख ⵈ प ⵈ फ), are voiceless velar and bilabial spirants (= × φ) which occur only before voiceless velar and labial stops.

2.3.5 *ṁ* (*anusvāra*) is a nasal element that occurs only after vowels and has no specific oral point of production. Early descriptions reflect differences in how this was pronounced. In some dialects it was realized as a nasal offglide with the oral place of production of the preceding vowel; e.g. *taṁ, agniṁ, vāyuṁ, maṁsyate* contain pure vowels followed by a nasalized vocalic segment (*taã, agniĩ, vāyuũ, maãsyate*). In the *Ṛgveda* tradition represented by the *Ṛgvedaprātiśākhya*, anusvāra is described as a voiceless spirant, which accords with its occurring only before *r* and spirants. In recitations of the Kṛṣṇayajurveda, anusvāra preceding *r* and spirants is pronounced as a velar with an accompanying nasalized segment *u* (*gũ*), which I transliterate *ṃ*. In modern pronunciations, anusvāra is realized as *-ŋ*, nasalization of a vowel, nasalized *w*, or a stop homorganic with a following stop.

2.4 Inventory and arrangement of sounds

The inventory of Sanskrit sounds is traditionally arranged as follows: vowels: *a ā i ī u ū ṛ ṝ ḷ e ai o au*; consonants: velar stops: *k kh g gh ṅ*, palatal stops: *c ch j jh ñ*, retroflex: *ṭ ṭh ḍ ḍh ṇ*, dental stops: *t th d dh n*, labial stops: *p ph b bh m*; semivowels: *y r l v*; spirants: *ś ṣ s h*; dependent segments that do not occur in basic lexical items (*ayogavāhāḥ*): *ḥ* ⵈ *k* ⵈ *p ṁ*.

There are other orders. The *Ṛgvedaprātiśākhya* lists *ṛ ṝ* after *a ā*, which accords with the weight given to the vocalic segments of *ṛ* and *ṝ* (section 2.2.2), and some lists have *e o ai au* and pluta vowels *ā3 ī3 ū3*. Pāṇini's sound catalogue, which influenced later grammars, is shorter. Only *a i u ṛ ḷ e o ai au* are listed, and these are made class names for sets of vowels. Stops are arranged in accordance with phonological rules; by the same token, semivowels are ordered *y v r l*. *h* is listed twice, in accordance with its status as both a spirant and a voiced element and associated phonological operations. *ḥ* ⵈ*k* ⵈ*p ṁ*, accounted for solely as replacements for other sounds in specified contexts, are not included.

2.5 Phonological rules

Certain sounds are in complementary distribution or vary in given contexts. This system involves sounds pronounced in close juncture (*saṁhitā*), without any pause between them, a pronunciation that is obligatory within a simple word, between constituents of compounds, and between a preverb (*upasarga*) and the verb (*dhātu*) with which it is linked. Otherwise, pauses can occur between words in an utterance. Some alternations apply before pause (*avasāne*). There is also evidence of dialectal differences and historical change.

2.5.1 General

Sequences of vowels are generally not allowed. Single vowels or a sequence of a semivowel and a vowel occur instead of two contiguous vowels, although hiatus is allowed in certain instances at word boundaries (section 2.5.1.7). *titaü-* 'sieve' and *praüga-* 'yoke pole' – both attested in the *Ṛgveda* – are extraordinary.

2.5.1.1 The sounds that occur instead of sequences of vowels are as follows:

(a) $ă+ă$, $ĭ+ĭ$, $ŭ+ŭ$: $ā$, $ī$, $ū$ (b) $ă+ĭ$, $ă+ŭ$: e, o (c) $ă+e/ai$, $ă+o/au$: ai, au

Examples:

(a) *daṇḍāgra-*'tip (*agra*) of a staff (*daṇḍa-*)', *upāste* 'sits (*āste*) near (*upa*), waits upon, venerates', *kanyātra* 'the girl (*kanyā* [nom. sg.]) (is) here (*atra*)', *dadhīha* '(there is) yogurt (*dadhi* [nom. sg. nt.]) here (*iha*)', *strīkṣate* 'the woman (*strī*) is looking (*īkṣate*)', *pratīkṣate* '... awaits' (preverb *prati*), *madhūdake* (nom.-acc. du. nt.) 'honey (*madhu-*) and water (*udaka-*)'.
(b) *tavedam* 'this (*idam*) (is) yours (*tava* [gen. sg.])', *kanyeha* 'the girl is here (*iha*)', *kanyekṣate* 'the girl is looking', *tavodakam* 'your water (*udakam* [nom. acc. nt.])'.
(c) *ainàn devāsò amṛtāso asthuḥ* (RV 1.123.1) 'the immortal (*amṛtāsaḥ* [nom. pl. m.]) gods (*devāsaḥ*) have mounted (*ā ... asthuḥ* [3pl. aor. act. indic.]) it (*enam*)'.

In particular grammatical contexts sequences (b), (c) have different outcomes. The third singular corresponding to the 3pl. imperf. *āyan* 'went' is *ait*, with *ai* (← *ā* + *i*) instead of *e*; similarly, *aikṣata* 'looked, saw' (3sg. imperf.) has *ai* for *a* + *ī* (cf. *īkṣate*). Conversely, -*a* of a preverb and *e-*, *o-* of a following verb form combine to give -*e-* and -*o-* instead of -*ai-* and -*au-*; e.g. *preṣayati* 'sends' (*pra* + *eṣayati*), *proṣati* 'burns' (*pra* + *oṣati*). Certain verbs conform to the general rule; e.g. *upaiti* 'approaches' (*upa* + *eti*), *praidhate* 'thrives' (*pra* + *edhate*).

2.5.1.2 *ar* generally occurs instead of $ă+ṛ$, but in some dialects short *a* followed by *ṛ* occurs instead of $ă+ṛ$. Examples:

(1) *nardhyatĕ* (TS 1.5.2.2) 'does not (*na*) thrive (*ṛdhyate*)'
(2) *pra ṛbhubhyò dūtam ìvạ vācàm iṣye* (RV 4.33.1) 'I send forth (*pra ... iṣye*) my speech (*vācam* [acc. sg. f.]) to the Ṛbhus (dat. pl. m. *ṛbhubhyaḥ*) like (*iva*) a messenger (*dūtam*).'
(3) *yatrạ ṛṣayo jạggmuḥ* (VS 18.52) 'where (*yatra*) the ṛṣis (*ṛṣayaḥ* [nom. pl.]) went (*jaggmuḥ* [3pl. act. pfct.])'
(4) *viśśvakàrmmạ ṛṣiḥ* (VS 13.58) 'Viśvakarman (nom. sg. *viśvakarmā*) (is) the ṛṣi (*ṛṣiḥ* [nom. sg.]).'

In the Atharvaveda tradition accounted for by the *Śaunakīyā Caturādhyāyikā* and the Kṛṣṇayajurveda tradition with which the *Taittirīyaprātiśākhya* is associated, *ar* occurs instead of $ă+ṛ$, and this obtains also in other Kṛṣṇayajurveda traditions, but the traditions represented in the *Ṛgvedaprātiśākhya* and the *Vājasaneyiprātiśākhya* have a short *a* followed by *ṛ*. According to Pāṇini (6.1.128), in the dialect Śākalya records, a short vowel occurs instead of $ă$, $ĭ$, $ŭ$ followed by *ṛ*, as in

(5) *kanya ṛdhyate* 'The girl is thriving.'

Where -*a* of a preverb precedes *r̥*- of a verb, *ār* occurs instead of *a*+*r̥*, as in *upārcchati* (*upa* + *r̥cchati*)'comes up to'. Dialect differences are known. Pāṇini (6.1.92) notes that, in the speech Āpiśali records, *ar* or *ār* occurs if the *r̥*- following a preverb belongs to a denominative; e.g. *uparṣabhīyati/upārṣabhīyati* 'wishes a bull' (*r̥ṣabhīyati*).

2.5.1.3 Before dissimilar vowels, *y v r* occur instead of *ĭ ŭ r̥*; e.g. *dadhy atra* '(there is) yogurt here', *stry atra* 'the woman (is) here', *madhv atra* '(there is) honey here', *vadhvāgāra-* 'bride's (*vadhū-*) house (*āgāra-*)', *pitrartham* 'for the sake (-*artha*) of his father (*pitr̥-*)'.

In certain grammatical contexts, -*iy* and -*uv* occur instead of -*y* and -*v* before affixes beginning with vowels. This applies for verb bases, present-imperfect stems in -*nu*-, and certain nouns; e.g. *kṣiy-a-ti* 'dwells' (3sg. pres. act.), *ci-kṣiy-atuḥ* 'dwelt' (3du. pft. act.), *śak-nuv-anti* 'are capable, can' (3pl. pres. act.), *bhruv-au* 'brows' (nom.-acc. du. f.), *striy-au* 'women'. Verbs with -*ī* not preceded by a cluster have -*y*- in forms with more than one syllable, as in *ni-ny-atuḥ* 'led'; contrast *pu-puv-atuḥ* 'purified'. Under comparable conditions, root nouns in -*ŭ* have forms with -*v* before nominal endings; e.g. *khala-pvaḥ* (nom. pl.) 'men who clean a threshing floor', with -*pv*- instead of -*pū*- (nom. sg. *khala-pūḥ*). *i* 'go' has forms with *y*- before vowel-initial affixes; e.g. *yanti* (3pl. pres. indic.). *hu* 'offer oblations' has forms with *hv* before a vocalic ending in the present but *huv* before such an ending of the perfect, as in *ju-hv-ati* (3pl. pres. act.), *ju-huv-atuḥ* (3du. pft. act.). Stems with -*nu*- also have either -*nuv*- or -*nv*-, the former if the -*nu*- follows a consonant: *śaknuvanti* (3pl. pres. act.) versus *su-nv-anti* 'press juice out of something'.

2.5.1.4 In the spoken language Pāṇini describes, -*iy* and -*uv* occur instead of -*ī* and -*ŭ* under the conditions noted. Accordingly, *tryàmbakam* (acc. sg. m.) 'Tryambaka', and *svàpasyayà* (instr. sg. f.) 'with good artisanship, out of the wish to do work well', are pronounced with *y* and *v*, but the metres of RV 7.59.12a and RV 1.161.11b ideally require *triyàmbakam* and *suvàpasyayà*. The recitation handed down and maintained in the *R̥gvedaprātiśākhya* represents speech habits of recitors later than the original authors. Dialectal differences also are involved; e.g. instead of *indrāgnyoḥ* (gen. du. m.) 'of Indra and Agni' and *svargaḥ* (nom. sg. m.) 'heaven', the traditional recitation of the *Taittirīyasaṁhitā* has *indrāgniyoḥ* (e.g. 1.3.12.2) and *suvargaḥ* (e.g. 1.5.7.1).

2.5.1.5 Preconsonantal *e o ai au* alternate with prevocalic *ay av āy āv*. Corresponding to *nī* 'guide, lead' past ptcpl. *nī-ta*-) and *stu* 'praise' (*stu-ta*-), there are preconsonantal *ne nai*, *sto stau* and prevocalic *nay nāy*, *stav stāv*: *ne-tum* (inf.), *anai-ṣ-īt* ('[has] led, guided' [3sg. aor. act.]), *nay-a-ti* (3sg. pres. ind. act.), *nāy-ay-a-ti* ('has ... lead, guide' [3sg. pres. ind. act. caus.]); *sto-tum*, *stau-ti* (3sg. pres. ind. act.), *stav-ana*- ('praising' [nt. action noun]), *stāv-ay-a-ti*. Similarly, *agnau* (loc. sg. m.) 'in the fire' occurs before consonants or pause but *agnāv* occurs before a vowel; e.g. *agnāv iva* 'as in the fire'.

2.5.1.6 In the spoken language Pāṇini describes, a single vowel -*e*- or -*o*- occurs instead of word-initial *a*- and preceding -*e* or -*o*; e.g. *tevardhanta* 'they (nom. pl. m. *te*) grew (*avardhanta* [3pl. mid. imperf.])', *sobravīt* 'he (nom. sg. m. *so*) said (*abravīt* [3sg. act. imperf.])'. This collocation, called *abhinihita sandhi*, appears also in Vedic; e.g.

(1) *tèvardhantạ svatàvaso mahitvạnā* (RV 1.85.7a) 'They (the Maruts), strong of themselves (*svatavasaḥ* [nom. pl. m.]), grew in greatness (*mahitvanā* [instr. sg. nt.]).'

where the metre requires twelve syllables. But this is not the norm in early Vedic, where sequences *-e a-* and *-o a-* are retained; e.g.

(2) *sujā̱te̱ aśvàsūnṛte* (ṚV 5.79, fifth pāda of each verse) '(Dawn, you) who are well born (*sujāte* [voc. sg. f.]), generous with horses (*aśvasǜnṛte*).'

The vowels represented by *-e, -o* in instances like (2) must be scanned short. Moreover,

(3) *caràn va̱tso ... nìdā̱tāra̱n na vìndate* | *ve̱ti stotàva a̱mbyàm* (ṚV 8.72.5) 'As it wanders (*caran* [nom. sg. m. pres. ptcpl.]) the calf (*vatsah*) does not (*na*) find (*vindate*) one to tie it down (*nidātāram* [acc. sg. m.]), seeks (*veti*) a mother (*ambyam* scanned *ambiam*) to praise (*stotave*).'

has *-a* instead of *-e* before *a-*: *stotàva a̱mbyam*. Patañjali notes (Bh. I.22.21–3, 117.21–3) that short *ĕ* and *ŏ* occurred in a recitation tradition of the Sāmaveda; one of the examples he quotes is (2), recited with *ĕśva-* instead of *aśva-*. A pronunciation *-e ĕ-, -o ŏ-* in certain recitations is vouchsafed also by statements in the *Ṛgvedaprātiśākhya* and the *Taittirīyaprātiśākhya*. These facts are explained assuming that *-e, -o* originally alternated with *-ay, -av* in the same manner as *e* and *o* that are not word-final (section 2.5.1.5). *stotàva* then has *-a* from *-ay*, with a development of word-final *-y* known from other evidence (section 2.5.2.8). The phonological treatment of *-e a-* (→ *e*) and *-o a-* (→ *o*) reflects historical developments: the vowels of *-ay a-* and *-av a-* were colored to *ĕ* and *ŏ*, *-y* and *-v* were deleted, and the sequences *ĕĕ, ŏŏ* yielded single long vowels (section 2.5.1.1).

2.5.1.7 Vowel sequences can occur consequent on the deletion of word-final consonants (sections 2.5.2.7–8). Vowels of particular grammatical forms also are exempt from contextual operations which would otherwise apply, so that they occur in hiatus. Indian grammarians call these vowels and elements that end with them *pragṛhya* or *pragraha*. In the spoken language Pāṇini describes, dual forms in *-ī, -ū* and *-e* are pragṛhya; e.g. *agnī atra, agnī iha* '(there are) two fires (nom.-acc. du. m. *agnī*) here (*atra, iha*)', *śatrū atra* '(there are) two enemies (*śatrū*) here', *śatrū ūcatuḥ* 'the two enemies said (*ūcatuḥ* [3du. pfct. act.])', *pacete atra* 'they two are cooking (*pacete* [3du. pres. mid.]) here'. The final vowels of certain particles also are treated in the same manner. This treatment of duals in *-ī, -ū* and *-e* as well as particles in *-o* appears in earliest Vedic; e.g.

(1) *rājàntī a̱sya bhuvànasya* (ṚV 6.70.2c) '(heaven and earth) ruling (*rājantī* [nom. du. f. pres. ptcpl.]) over this (*asya*) world of beings (*bhuvanasya*.)'
(2) *indràvāyū i̱me su̱tāḥ* (ṚV 1.2.4a) 'Indra and Vāyu (*indravāyū* [voc. du.]), here are (*ime* 'these' [nom. pl. m.]) the pressed Soma juices (*sutāḥ* [nom. pl. m.]).'
(3) *te id viprā̃ ī̱late su̱mnam i̱ṣṭayè* (ṚV 6.70.4d) 'The inspired ones (*viprāḥ* [nom. pl.]) praise (*īlate* [3pl. pres. mid.]) those two (*te* [acc. du. f.]) to seek (*iṣṭaye* [dat. sg. f.]) (their) benevolence (*sumnam* [acc. sg.]).'
(4) *pro àyāsīd indu̱ḥ* (ṚV 9.86.16a) 'Soma (*induḥ* [nom. sg. m.] 'drop') has gone (*ayāsīt* [3sg. aor. act.]) forth (*pro*).'
(5) *indràś ca̱ yad yùyu̱dhāte̱ ahiś ca* (ṚV 1.32.13c) '... when (*yat*) Indra (*indrah* [nom. sg.]) and (*ca ... ca*) the serpent (*ahiḥ*) did battle (*yuyudhāte* [3du. pfct. mid.])'

Some forms in *-ī, -ū* and *-e* which occur only in Vedic, such as the locative singular type *gaurī* (f.) 'buffalo', are also pragṛhya; e.g.

(6) *somò ga̱urī adhì śri̱taḥ* (ṚV 9.12.3c) 'Soma (*somah*) has come to rest (*śritah* [nom. sg. m. past ptcpl.]) on the buffalo skin (*gaurī adhi*).'

Nominal duals in *-ī -ū -e* are well established pragṛhya elements from earliest Indo-Aryan, but dual verb endings in *-e* are not always so. Although the metre of (5) requires a sequence *yùyudhāte ahiṣ* with a long *-e*, the metre of

(7) *saparyantà śùbhe càkrāte aśvinà* (ṚV 8.26.13c) 'Honouring (*saparyantā* [nom. du. m. pres. ptcpl.]) (him), the Aśvins (*aśvinā* [nom. du. m.]) made (*cakrāte* [3du. pfct. mid.]) (him) to shine in splendour (*śubhe* 'splendour' [dat. sg.])'

requires the final of *cakrāte* to be a short vowel. That is, *-e* was originally subject to replacement by *-ay* (cf. section 2.5.1.6).

2.5.1.8 Certain alternations are associated with grammatical contexts. The base forms *ci-, śru-, kṛ-* occur before the suffix *-ta* (past ptcpl.), but *ce-, śro-* (prevocalic *cay-, śrav-*), *kar-* precede the agent suffix *-tṛ* and the action-noun suffix *-ana*, and *cai-, śrau-, kār-* precede the aorist suffix *-s-* in active forms: *cita-* 'heaped up, gathered', *cetṛ-* 'one who heaps up, gathers', *cayana-* 'heaping up, gathering', *acaiṣīt* (3sg. aor.) '(has) heaped up, gathered'; *śruta-* 'heard, famous', *śrotṛ-* 'hearer, listener', *śravaṇa-* 'hearing, listening', *aśrauṣīt; kṛta-* 'done, made', *kartṛ-* 'doer, maker, agent', *karaṇa-* 'doing, making', *akārṣīt.*

In Pāṇini's system, *a e o* and *ā ai au* are called *guṇa* and *vṛddhi*; accordingly, I speak of variants with *e o ar* and *ai au ār* as having guṇa and vṛddhi vowels. In modern terminology, such variants are also called full- and lengthened-grade forms, and the types *ci-, śru-, kṛ-* as well as variants like *s-* instead of *as-* in *asti* 'is' and *staḥ* 'they two are' (see section 3.1.1) are called zero-grade forms.

2.5.2 Consonants

2.5.2.1 The least restrictions apply to consonants between vowels within a word, although even here there are some restrictions in the current language: *ṅ, ñ* and single *ch* do not occur medially; *ḥ ⁚k ⁚p* and *ṁ* occur only as word-finals; *-jh-* is rare. Some dialects have *-ḷ-* and *-ḷh-* instead of intervocalic *-ḍ-* and *-ḍh-*. This is characteristic of the Ṛgveda recitation in the Śākala tradition, and the *Ṛgvedaprātiśākhya* (RPr. 1.52) notes that it is the pronunciation sanctioned by Vedamitra; e.g. *īḷe* (1st sg. pres. mid., ṚV 1.1.1) 'I praise' and *sāḷhā* (nom. sg., ṚV 7.56.23) 'one who overcomes' instead of *īḍe* (cf. 3sg. *īṭ-ṭe* [← *īḍ-te*]), *sāḍhā*. The change occurs elsewhere; the *Vājasaneyiprātiśā-khya* (4.146) notes that some Śuklayajurveda teachers have *-ḷ-* and *-ḷh-* for word-interior intervocalic *-ḍ-* and *-ḍh-*.

2.5.2.2 All consonants except *ḥ ⁚k ⁚p* and *ṁ* occur in word-initial position, though not in the same proportions. Early Vedic does not have terms with word-initial retroflex stops, but *ṣ-* occurs: *ṣaṣ-* 'six' (nom.-acc. *ṣaṭ*, instr. *ṣaḍbhiḥ*), *ṣaṣṭi-* 'sixty'. Later, retroflex stops other than *ṇ* do occur initially, albeit in a limited number of items.

2.5.2.3 Aspirates and palatals are not allowed as word-finals, before obstruents and *s* or in prepause position. Due to the different historical sources of *j* and *h*, as well as to certain sound changes and analogic developments, the synchronic distribution of elements is complex.

Stems with final aspirates before vocalic affixes have final unaspirated stops in the contexts noted; e.g. *uṣarbhut* (nom. sg.) 'one that awakens at dawn' (instr. pl. *uṣarbhudbhiḥ*, acc. sg. *uṣarbudham*), *bhotsyate* (3sg. fut. mid.) 'will be aware'; *triṣṭup* 'tristubh metre' (*tristubham*). Palatals alternate with velars; e.g. *vāc-/vāk-* 'voice, speech': *vāk* (nom. sg. f.), *vācam* (acc. sg., cf. *vaktṛ-* 'speaker', *vakṣyati* [3sg. fut. act.] 'will say'); *ūrj-/ūrk-* 'strength': *ūrk* (nom. sg. f.), *ūrje* (dat sg.); *yuj-/yug-/yuk-* 'join, yoke': *yoktum* (inf.), *yokṣyati* (3sg. fut. act.), *aśvayuk* (nom. sg.) 'one who yokes a horse', *-yujā* (instr. sg.). Some bases with such alternants have *-ṣ-* before suffixes with original *t-*; e.g. *sraṣ-ṭum* 'let loose, create', *srak-ṣyati*, *asrāk* (3sg. aor. act.), *sṛj-a-ti* (3sg. pres. act.). There are also bases with comparable forms that have word-final *-ṭ*; e.g. *yaṣ-ṭum* 'venerate, perform a rite', *yak-ṣya-ti*, *yāṭ* (2sg. inj.), *yaj-a-ti* (3sg. pres. act.).

Bases in *-ś, -ṣ* have similar alternants; e.g. *adarś-a-t* (3sg. aor. act.) 'saw, looked', *draṣ-ṭum, drak-ṣya-ti, tā-dṛk* (nom. sg. m.) 'such' (acc. *tādṛśam*); *vik-ṣu* (Ved. loc. pl.) 'settlement', *viṭ* (nom. sg.), *viś-am* (acc. sg.); *dveṣ-ṭi* (3sg. pres. act.) 'hates', *dvek-ṣi* (2sg.), *dviṭ* (nom. sg.) 'one who hates' (acc. sg. *dviṣ-am*).

Bases in *-h* that do not begin with *d-* have comparable alternants; e.g. *vah-a-ti* 'transports', *vakṣ-ya-ti, -vāṭ* 'one who transports'. Bases in *-h* with initial *d-* regularly have alternants with final velars; e.g. *duh-e* 'gives milk, milks', *dog-dhi* 'milks', *-dhuk* 'one that milks, gives milk' (e.g. *kāma-dhuk* 'wish-granting cow'). In the spoken language Pāṇini describes, *druh* 'wish harm to', *muh* 'be confused', *snuh* 'vomit' and *snih* 'be moist, unctuous' have alternants with either a retroflex or a velar; e.g. *mitra-dhruk/mitra-dhruṭ* (nom. sg.) 'one who deceives, harms a friend', *un-muk/un-muṭ* 'one who is confused'.

Dialects differ also concerning voiceless and voiced segments before pause. According to Pāṇini (8.4.56), voiceless and voiced unaspirated stops alternate in pre-pause final position; e.g. *uṣarbhud* and *triṣṭub* in addition to the forms cited. The *Ṛgvedaprātiśākhya* (1.15–16) notes that according to Gārgya voiced stops occur in this position while the dialect Śākaṭāyana represents has voiceless stops.

Word-final clusters are limited. Only one consonant is allowed in this position – subject to transitional phenomena such as doubling (section 2.5.2.14) – except for *r* followed by a stop; e.g. *ūrk, amārṭ* (3rd sg imperf.) 'wiped clean' (3sg. pres. *mārṣṭi*).

2.5.2.4.

Consonants assimilate to following elements. Some of the effects differentiate between word-interior consonants and consonants across word boundaries, others do not. There are also differences due to historical and dialectal factors.

Word-final stops regularly have the same voice feature as a following segment: voiced before a vowel or a voiced consonant, voiceless before a voiceless consonant; e.g. *tad ā naya* 'bring (*ā naya* [2sg. imp.]) that (*tad* [acc. sg. nt.])', *tad yathā* 'for example', *tat tatra* 'that (is) there (*tatra*)'. Nasal stops occur before nasals; e.g. *vāṅ me* 'my (*me* [encl. gen. sg.]) voice (*vāk*)', *tan na* 'not (*na*) that'. This is obligatory in the Vedic recitations described by all major prātiśākhyas but optional in the language of Pāṇini's time; e.g. *vāg/vāṅ me, tad/tan na*. Assimilation to a nasal does not apply across word-interior morpheme boundaries except in certain collocations ; e.g. *yat-na-* 'effort' (base *yat* 'make an effort') with *-t-* before the suffix *-na-*, but past participle *chin-na-* 'cut' to the base *chid*.

In some dialects a voiceless unaspirated stop is aspirated before a voiceless spirant. Kātyāyana (8.4.48 vt. 3) notes that this applies in the speech represented by Pauṣkarasādi, and Patañjali supplies the examples *vathsaḥ* 'calf' (*vatsaḥ* [nom. sg. m.]), *khṣīram* 'water, milk' (*kṣīram* [nom.-acc. sg. nt.]), *aphsarāḥ* 'Apsaras' (nom. sg. f.). This assimilation is also known from Vedic traditions; the *Ṛgvedaprātiśākhya* (6.54) says some teachers allow it.

In contact with palatal and retroflex segments, palatal and retroflex sounds occur instead of dentals; e.g. *tat tatra*: *tac ca* 'and (*ca*) that', *plakṣas tatra* '(there is) a plakṣa tree there': *plakṣaś ca nyagrodhaś ca* 'a plakṣa and a nyagrodha tree', *devadattas tatra* 'Devadatta (is) there': *devadattaś śete* 'Devadatta is lying (*śete*)', *devadattaṣ ṣaṣṭhaḥ* 'Devadatta is the sixth'.

Some assimilations occur only within words. Thus, a dental assimilates to a preceding retroflex stop within a word but not across a word boundary; e.g. *īṭ-ṭe* (3sg. pres. mid.) 'praises' (cf. 1sg. *īḍ-e*) has *-ṭe* instead of *-te* (cf. *śe-te*), but a sequence *-ṭ t-* occurs across a word boundary, as in *vaṣaṭ te* '(I say) '*vaṣaṭ*' to you'. Palatal stops do not occur in word-final position, but they do occur as finals of bases, so that following dentals can assimilate to them, as in *yāc-ñā-* 'request' (*yāc-a-te* 'requests'), *yaj-ña-* 'ritual' (*yaj-a-ti* 'performs a rite'), *rājñā* (instr. sg.) 'king' (voc. sg. *rājan*). *ś* does not condition palatalization of a following dental; e.g. *praś-na-* 'question' (see also section 2.5.2.16).

A dental stop assimilates to a following *l*, resulting in *-l l-*, *-lm̐ l-*; e.g. *tal lunāti* '... is cutting (*lunāti*) that (*tat*)', *bhavālm̐ lunāti* 'You (*bhavān* [nom. sg. m.]) are cutting'.

In most Vedic traditions, *-m* assimilates to a following stop; e.g.

(1) *tvaṅ kutsàṁ śuṣṇahatyèṣv āvitha* ... (RV 1.51.6a) 'You (*tvam* [nom. sg.]) helped (*āvitha* [2sg. pfct.]) Kutsa in the battles with Śuṣṇa (*śuṣṇahatyeṣu* [loc. pl.]).'
(2) *ghañ ca tvañ cà*... (RV 8.62.11a) 'I (*aham*) and (*ca*) you (*tvam*)'.
(3) *agnin dūtavm̐ vṛṇīmahe* (RV 1.12.1a) 'We choose (*vṛṇīmahe*) Agni (*agnim* [acc. sg.]) as messenger (*dūtam*).'

In the spoken language Pāṇini describes, this is optional, with *-m̐* also before stops: *tvaṁ kutsaṁ* and so on. Before *r* or a spirant, however, only *m̐* occurs instead of *m*, not only at a word boundary but also word internally; e.g.

(4) *ahaṁ rakṣāmi* 'I (*aham*) am protecting, keeping'.
(5) *ahaṁ śaye* 'I am lying'.
(6) *ahaṁ hasāmi* 'I am laughing'.
(7) *gaṁ-sya-te* (3sg. fut. pass.) 'will be understood' (3sg. pres. pass. *gam-ya-te*).

m̐ also occurs instead of *-n-* before a spirant, as in *maṁ-sya-te* 'will think' (3sg. pres. *man-ya-te*).

The treatment of *-m* before semivowels and spirants in Vedic shows much dialectal variation. The traditions of the Ṛgveda and the Śuklayajurveda have full assimilation to following semivowels *y l v*, but anusvāra (*m̐*) before *r* and spirants; e.g.

(8) *jaṭenà jātam ati sa pra sàrsṛte yaym̐ yaym̐ yujàṅ kṛṇute brahmàṇaspatiḥ* (RV 2.25.1cd) 'Whomever (*yam yam*) Brahmaṇaspati makes (*kṛṇute*) an ally (*yujam*), he (*sa*) surpasses (*pra sarsṛte* [3sg. pres. intens.]) the son born (*jātam*) of his son (*jātena* 'by the born' [instr. sg. m.]).'
(9) *yuñjāthāṁ rāsàbhaym̐ yuvam* (VS 11.13) 'You two (*yuvam* [voc. du.]), yoke (*yuñjāthām* [2nd. du. imper. mid.]) the donkey (*rāsabham* [acc. sg. m.]).'
(10) *bhadraiṣàlm̐ lakṣmīr nihitādhi vaci* (RV 10.71.2d) 'An auspicious (*bhadrā* [nom. sg. f.]) mark (*lakṣmīḥ*) is set down (*nihitā*) on their (*eṣām* [gen. pl. m.]) speech (*adhi vāci* [loc. sg. f.]).'
(11) *talm̐ lokam* (VS 20.25) 'that (*tam* [acc. sg. m.]) world (*lokam*)'
(12) *tavm̐ va indran na* (RV 6.48.14a) 'That (*tam* [acc. sg. m.]) (god) of yours (*vah* [encl. gen. pl.]), like (*na*) Indra (*indram* [acc. sg. m.]) ... .'

(13) *savm̐ vàpāmi* (VS 1.21) 'I put (*sam* [prev.]+ *vapāmi*) (the flour in the vessel).'

Kṛṣṇayajurveda traditions too observe such assimilation, but with considerable variation, as known from the *Taittirīyaprātiśākhya* (5.28, 30). Thus, in addition to *saym̐yàttā āsan̠* (TS 1.5.1.1) 'were (*āsan* [3d pl. imperf.]) arrayed (*saym̐-yàttāḥ* [nom. pl. m.])', with full assimilation of -*m* to a nasalized semivowel (*ym̐*), two other pronunciations are noted: *sam̐yàttā āsan̠*, with a nasalized vowel *am̐*, and *samyàttā āsan̠*, with anusvāra.

m̐ occurs for -*m* before *r*- and spirants in the Ṛgvedic tradition; e.g.

(14) *hotàram̐ ratnadhātàmam* (ṚV 1.1.1c) 'hotr̥ (*hotāram* [acc. sg. m.]) who best creates treasure'.

(15) *tvam̐ satya indra . . . tvam̐ ṣā | tvam̐ śuṣn̠àm . . .* (ṚV 1.63.3) 'Indra (*indra* [voc. sg.]), you (*tvam* [nom. sg.]) are the true one (*satyaḥ*) . . . you are one who overcomes (*ṣā*) . . . you (slew) Suṣn̠a. . . .'

(16) *tvām̐ ha tyad indrārn̠àsātau . . . hàvante* (ṚV 1.63.6ab) '(Men) call (*havante*) you (*tvām* [acc. sg.] *ha*) then (*tyad*), Indra, in the quest for winning the waters (*arn̠asātau* [loc. sg. f.]).'

In the spoken language Pāṇini describes, *m̐* is optional not only before word-initial *r* and spirants but also before semivowels other than *r*; e.g. *yam̐ lokam, tam̐ lokam*. The Śaunakīya branch of the Atharvaveda as represented in the *Śaunakīyā Caturādhyāyikā* (2.1.31–32, 1.3.5) has no anusvāra. -*m* assimilates to a following stop, but before semivowels and spirants it is dropped and the preceding vowel is nasalized.

2.5.2.5 As a result of sound changes that applied to Indo-Iranian complexes of long vowels followed by word-final *ns* (-*V̄ns*) as well as reanalyses and analogic extensions, a nasalized vowel or a vowel with anusvāra followed by a spirant occurs instead of -*n* preceded by a vowel (-*Vn*) before a voiceless stop other than a velar or labial, itself followed by a vowel; e.g. *tām̐ś ca/tām̐s ca* 'and (*ca*) them (*tān* [acc. pl. m.])', *bhavām̐s tarati/bhavām̐s tarati* 'you (*bhavān* [nom. sg. m.]) are crossing', *tasmim̐ś ca/tasmim̐ś ca* 'and in that' (*tamsin* [loc. sg. m.-nt.]), as opposed to *bhavān kiṅ karoti* 'what (*kim*) are you (*bhavān*) doing (*karoti* [3sg. pres. act.])?', *bhavān atra sīdatu* 'please sit (*sīdatu* [3sg. imp.]) here', *tasminn āgāre* 'in that house (*āgāre* [loc. sg. nt.])'.

Here too there is much variation. In Vedic -*V̄m̐* and -*V̄m̐r* occur before vowels; e.g. *sargàm̐ iva* (ṚV 8.35.20a) 'like (*iva*) flows (*sargān* [acc. pl.])', *raśmīm̐r iva* (ṚV 8.35.21a) 'like reins (*raśmīn* [acc. pl.])'. Alternations of the types *asmañ ca tām̐s ca* (ṚV 2.1.16c) 'both us (*asmān*) and them (*tān*)' and *tām̐ś ca/tām̐s ca* are attested in the earliest sources. The variant with a pure vowel followed by anusvāra calls for special comment. The *Taittirīyaprātiśākhya* (15.2–3) remarks that some allow this, and the *Vājasaneyiprātiśākhya* (3.131–132) says it is allowed in the speech represented by Aupaśavi. The *Ṛgvedaprātiśākhya* (14.37) notes the variant with anusvāra in its chapter on faults of pronunciation, showing that the tradition to which Śaunaka adheres condemns such a pronunciation.

2.5.2.6 -*ḥ*, which developed from -*s* and -*r*, occurs before pause and voiceless consonants. In the current language Pāṇini describes, -*ḥ* alternates with ꭥ *k*, ꭥ *p*, *ś* and *ṣ* before velar stops, labial stops, *ś* and *ṣ*; before other stops, spirants homorganic with the stops occur. Examples: *devadattaḥ* (nom. sg.) 'Devadatta', *prātaḥ* 'in the morning' (*prātar*), *yatiḥ* 'ascetic', *bandhuḥ* 'kinsman, relative'; *devadattaḥ/devadattaꭥk kiṅ karoti* 'what (*kim*) is Devadatta doing (*karoti* [3sg. pres.])?', *devadattaḥ/devadattaᵖ phalañ khādati* 'Devadatta is eating (*khādati*) a fruit (*phalam* [acc. sg. nt.])', *devadattaḥ/ devadattaś śayane śete* 'Devadatta is lying (*śete*) in the bed (*śayane* [loc. sg.])', *devadattaḥ/devadattas sīdati* 'Devadatta is sitting (*sīdati*)', *devadattas tatra* 'Devadatta is there', *devadattaś chatran dhārayati* 'Devadatta is holding (*dhārayati*) an umbrella (*chatram* [acc. sg. nt.])'. On the other hand, -*ḥ* precedes a voiceless stop followed by a spirant, as in *varcaḥ kṣatriyāya* 'splendour (*varcaḥ* [acc. sg. nt.]) to the Kṣatriya'.

There is general agreement on the occurrence of -*ś* and -*s* before palatal and dental stops, but much variation in other details. Thus, in the tradition described by the *Ṛgvedaprātiśākhya*, -*ḥ* alternates with ᵏ*k* and ᵖ*p* before velars and labials, and with -*ś* -*ṣ* -*s* before these spirants (RPr. 4.33–34, 36), but -*ḥ* is dropped before a cluster of a spirant and a following stop, as in *sàmudra sthàḥ* (RV 6.69.6) 'You (Indra and Viṣṇu) are (*sthaḥ* [2du. pres.]) the ocean (*samudraḥ* [nom. sg. m.])'. The same alternants are allowed for by the *Vājasaneyiprātiśākhya* (3.9–13) but this does not merely speak of variants; it mentions authorities who represent these ways of speaking: according to Śākaṭāyana -*ḥ* assimilates to these velars, labials and spirants, but Śākalya keeps -*ḥ*. Similarly, the *Taittirīyaprātiśākhya*, after stating (TPr. 9.3) that -*ḥ* does not assimilate to the velar of a cluster *kṣ*-, as in *varcàḥ kṣatriyàya* (TS 1.8.12.1) 'splendour for the Kṣatriya (i.e., the king)', notes (TPr. 9.4–6) that in the traditions represented by Agniveśya and Vālmīki assimilation does not take place before velars and labials, that this does not apply before a spirant according to some teachers, and that for Plākṣi and Plākṣāyaṇa it does not apply before any of these sounds, so that -*ḥ* is pronounced in all instances.

2.5.2.7 Corresponding to -*īḥ* and -*ūḥ* under the conditions given in section 2.5.2.6, -*īr* and -*ūr* occur before vowels and voiced consonants; e.g. *yatir asti* '... is (*asti*) an ascetic', *bandhur asti* '... is (*asti*) a relative', *yatir gacchati* 'the ascetic is going (*gacchati*)', *bandhur vrajati* 'the relative is going (*vrajati*)'. Instead of -*āḥ* and -*aḥ*, respectively, -*ā* and -*o* occur before voiced consonants; e.g. *puruṣā hasanti* 'the men (*puruṣāḥ* [nom. pl.]) are laughing (*hasanti*)', *puruṣo hasati* 'the man (*puruṣaḥ* [nom. sg.]) is laughing (*hasati*)'. Before vowels, there is variation. Pāṇini (8.3.17–19) notes three variants corresponding to -*āḥ*: -*āy*, -*ā*ʸ – with a very light glide – and -*ā*, the last two respectively in the speech areas Śākaṭāyana and Śākalya represent; e.g. *puruṣāy āsate, puruṣā*ʸ *āsate, puruṣā āsate* 'the men are seated (*āsate*)'. Similarly, -*ay*, -*a*ʸ, and -*a* occur for -*aḥ* before vowels other than *a*-; e.g. *devadatta*ʸ *iha, devadatta*ʸ *iha, devadatta iha* 'Devadatta is here (*iha*)'. But -*o*- occurs instead of -*as a*- (section 2.5.1.6). Such variation is vouchsafed for Vedic recitation also. The *Taittirīyaprātiśākhya* notes (9.10) that -*ḥ* changes to -*y* before a vowel and that prevocalic -*y* and -*v* are subject to various treatments; see section 2.5.2.8.

2.5.2.8 Word-final -*y* and -*v* also occur as part of prevocalic -*ay* -*av* -*āy* -*āv* corresponding to preconsonantal *e o ai au* (section 2.5.1.5). Pāṇini (8.3.18–19) notes that -*y* and -*v* before vowels are replaced by very lightly articulated glides ⁻ʸ ⁻ᵛ in Śākaṭāyana's speech but are dropped according to Śākalya. The *Taittirīyaprātiśākhya* (10.19–23) records several variations: -*y* and -*v* of -*āy* and -*āv* are generally dropped before vowels, but not according to Ukhya, and according to Saṅkṛtya -*y* is dropped but -*v* is not, while the tradition Vātsapra represents has light glides ⁻ʸ ⁻ᵛ, and in Mācākīya's tradition -*y* and -*v* drop before *u*- and -*au*-. In the Ṛgveda tradition represented by the *Ṛgvedaprātiśākhya* (2.25, 27, 31), -*av* and -*āv* from -*o* and -*au* occur before a vowel other than *ŭ*, and the Śuklayajurveda tradition represented in the *Vājasaneyiprātiśākhya*

(4.127–8) generally drops *-y -v* before vowels, although according to some *-v* is not dropped except before a labial. Variants with *-ay/-a* are found in Vedic texts:

(1) *táy ā́ vahante kavájyaḥ purāstāt* (MS 1.1.2) 'Those wise ones (*te kavayaḥ* [nom. pl. m.]) transport (the barhis) here (*ā vahante*) from the east (*purastāt*)'.

(2) *ta ā vàhanti kavayaḥ purastàt* (TS 1.1.2.1).

2.5.2.9 *-r* is dropped before *r-*, with compensatory lengthening of a preceding short vowel; e.g. *punā raktam* 'dyed (*raktam* [nom.-acc. sg. nt.]) again (*punar*)',

(1) *agnī rakṣā́ṁsi sedhati* (RV 7.15.10a) 'Agni (*agnir* [nom. sg. < *agnis*]) will drive away (*sedhati* [3sg. subj.]) demons (*rakṣāṁsi* [acc. pl. nt.])'.

2.5.2.10 *-s-* preceded within a word by a vowel other than *ă* or by a velar stop is retracted to *ṣ*; e.g. *agniṣu, vāyuṣu, pitṛṣu, deveṣu, vākṣu*, locative plurals of *agni-* 'fire', *vāyu-* 'wind', *pitṛ-* 'father', *deva-* 'god', *vāc-* 'voice, speech' (cf. *kanyāsu* 'girls'); *aśiṣat* (3sg. aor. act. of *śās* 'command, instruct'); *akṣan* (3pl. aor. act. of *ghas* 'eat'), *vak-ṣya-ti* (3sg. fut. of *vac* 'say'). In the current language Pāṇini describes, this retroflexion does not apply generally to word-final or word-initial *s*; e.g. *yatis tatra, bandhus tatra* (see section 2.5.2.6), *dadhi siñcati* '. . . is sprinkling on (*siñcati*) curds (*dadhi* [acc. sg. nt.])', *madhu siñcati* '. . . is pouring on honey (*madhu*)'. There are certain collocations in which word-initial retroflexion applies. For example, Pāṇini (8.3.66) notes that the *s-* of *sad* (pres. *sīda-*) is replaced by *ṣ-* after a preverb other than *prati*: *ni ṣīdati* 'sits down' versus *prati sīdati* 'abhors'. In Vedic, retroflexion applies to word-final *-s* before voiceless consonants, but not always, so that both *-iṣ ṭ-* (see section 2.5.2.4) and *-is t-* occur; e.g.

(1) *agniṣ ṭam . . . anīnaśat* (RV 10.162.2cd) 'Agni has destroyed (*anīnaśat* [3sg. caus. aor.]) that (*tam* [acc. sg. m.]) (illness).'

(2) *agnis tuviśràvastamam . . . putran dàdāti . . .* (RV 5.25.5) 'Agni gives (*dadāti*) a son (*putram* [acc. sg. m.]) of most powerful fame (*tuviśravastamam*).'

The details, doubtless reflecting historical developments, are sufficiently complex that prātiśākhyas enumerate contexts even in terms of particular words. See also General Introduction 2.2.3.

2.5.2.11 Another retroflexion involves *ṇ* instead of *n* preceded by *ṛ, ṝ, r* and *ṣ*, which may be separated from the nasal by a vowel, *h*, a semivowel other than *l*, a velar or labial stop, or a combination of these; e.g. *vṛ-ṇo-ti* 'covers', *bṛṁh-aṇa-* 'reenforcing, supporting', *pitṝ-ṇām* (gen. pl.) 'of the fathers', *vāri-ṇā* (instr. sg. nt.) 'with water', *puṣ-ṇā-ti* 'makes to thrive', *puruṣā-ṇām* 'of the men', as opposed to *su-no-ti* 'presses', *vac-ana-* 'saying', *devā-nām* 'of the gods', *agni-nā* 'with fire', *pu-nā-ti* 'purifies'. In particular collocations retroflexion applies across a word boundary; e.g. *pra ṇamati* 'bows' (*namati* 'bends'), *pra ṇayati* 'leads forth' (*nayati* 'guides, leads'). Vedic traditions concerning this retroflexion are also complex. At all stages, retroflexion was generally precluded for word-final *-n*; e.g. *girīn* 'mountains' (acc. pl. m.), *vṛkṣān* 'trees'. But there are some Vedic examples of *-ṇ*, as in *trīṇ imā́lṁ lokā́n* (MS 1.11.10) 'these (*imān* [acc. pl. m.]) three (*trīn*) worlds (*lokān*)', *soṇtárvāṇ abhavat* (MS 4.2.1) 'he (*saḥ*) (Prajāpati) became (*abhavat*) pregnant (*antarvān*)'. Moreover, Pāṇini (8.4.20: *antaḥ* [*aniteḥ* 19]) allows for *prāṇ* (voc. sg.) 'one who breathes'.

2.5.2.12 After a nonnasal stop, a voiced aspirated stop homorganic with the stop optionally occurs instead of *h-*, and in this context *ś* is optionally replaced by *ch* if a vowel or semivowel follows; e.g. *tad harati/dharati* '... is taking (*harati*) that (*tad* [acc. sg. nt.])', *tac śakyate/chakyate kartum* 'that can be (*śakyate* [3sg. pass.]) done (*kartum* [inf.])'.

2.5.2.13 A voiced unaspirated stop followed by *dh* occurs instead of a cluster in which *t* or *th* follows a voiced aspirated stop; e.g. *dugdha-* 'milked' (< *dugh-ta-* [past ptcpl.]), *baddha-* 'bound' (< *badh-ta-*), *abuddha* 'became aware' (< *abudh-s-ta* [3sg. aor.]), *abuddhāḥ* 'you became aware' (< *abudh-s-thās*). Due to analogic restructuring, this does not apply in reduplicated forms corresponding to the third singular *dadhāti* 'puts': *dhattaḥ* (3du.), *dhatthaḥ* (2du.), *dhattha* (2pl.).

2.5.2.14 At a word boundary, nasal stops except *ñ*, *m* are doubled if they follow a short vowel and precede a vowel; e.g. *pratyaṅṅ āste* '... is seated (*āste*) facing west (*pratyaṅ* [nom. sg. m.])', *kurvann api* 'even though (*api* 'and, also') acting (*kurvan* [nom. sg. m.] 'doing, making')'.

There are also particular transitions between word-final nasals and following spirants. In the current language Pāṇini describes, -*k*-, -*ṭ* and -*t*- respectively are optionally added when -*ṅ*, -*ṇ* and -*n* precede a spirant; e.g. *prāṅ/prāṅk śete* '... is lying (*śete*) facing east (*prāṅ*)', *vaṇ/vaṇṭ sāye* 'making a sound (*vaṇ* [nom. sg.]) in the evening (*sāye* [loc. sg.])', *bhavān/bhavānt samarthaḥ* 'you (*bhavān* [nom. sg. m.]) (are) capable (*samarthaḥ*)', *bhavān/bhavānt śete/chete* 'you are lying asleep'. Prātiśākhyas describe recitations in which these transitions apply in some traditions, to the extent that the texts have such sequences. Thus, the *Taittirīyaprātiśākhya* (5.32–33) says that *k* is inserted between -*ṅ* and *s*- or -*ṣ*- and *t* is inserted between -*ṭ*, -*n* and these spirants; the *Ṛgvedaprātiśākhya* (4.16–18) says that some teachers allow such transitions; and the *Vājasaneyiprātiśākhya* (4.15–16) says -*ṅ* and -*n* are respectively separated from a following *s*- by *k* and *t*, but that Dālbhya does not allow this.

2.5.2.15 Regardless of boundaries, certain consonantal doublings apply in particular dialects. According to Pāṇini's description (8.4.46–52), consonants other than *r* and *h* are optionally doubled after *r* or *h* preceded by a vowel, and doubling applies to consonants preceded by a vowel and followed by a consonant; e.g. *arka-/arkka-* 'ray, sun', *brahma-/brahmma-* 'Brahman', *apahnute/apahnnute* 'hides, denies' (3sg. pres. mid.), *madhya-/maddhya-* 'middle', *dadhy atra/daddhy atra* 'there are curds here', *madhv atra/maddhv atra* 'there is honey here'. Doubling does not apply to spirants followed by vowels; e.g. *ādarśa-* 'mirror', *karṣati* 'draws'. Nor was it prevalent in the speech areas represented by certain teachers. Śākalya disallows doubling in any of the contexts noted, while Śākaṭāyana does not allow it in clusters of three or more consonants; e.g *indra-* 'Indra', *candra-* 'moon', *uṣṭra-* 'camel', *rāṣṭra-* 'kingdom'. Some disallow it after long vowels; e.g. *dātra-* 'sickle', *sūtra-* 'thread, sūtra'.

In known Vedic traditions, doubling applies to initial consonants of clusters and consonants following *r*, *h*. Although this is generally not optional, there is also dialectal variation; e.g. according to the *Taittirīyaprātiśākhya* (14.2), Pauṣkarasādi allows doubling of a stop following *l* or *v*, as in *hiraṇyaśġlkkān* 'pieces of gold', *dadhikrāvṇṇaḥ-* 'of Dadhikrāvan'.

2.5.2.16 Prenasal consonants in clusters like -*kn*-, -*gm*-, -*ghn*- of *paliknīḥ* 'grizzled, aged' (nom. pl. f.), *pari gman* 'went round' (3pl. aor. act.) are checked; doubling applies (section 2.5.2.15), and the consonant that forms a transition to the following nasal acquires its nasality. The resulting pronunciations (*palikkm̐nīḥ, parì ggm̐man*) contain nasalized segments, pronounced in Vedic recitations, which are called *yama* ('twin'). Prātiśākhyas and śikṣās differ from each other in how they describe these segments and in the number of yamas recognized. I have followed the *R̥gvedaprātiśākhya* (6.17, 29).

2.5.2.17 There is general agreement that *r* before a consonant is released, with an anaptyctic vowel segment (*svarabhakti, bhakti*), generally said to have the duration of a quarter mora, whose colour varies in the same manner as that of *r̥*.

2.5.3 *Tone sandhi*

Sanskrit has a system of tone sandhi with three basic pitch levels: vowels are high-pitched, low-pitched or start high and descend to low (section 2.2.1). There is a dichotomy between accented and unaccented items. An accented item contains an udātta or svarita vowel, an unaccented one does not; e.g. *gr̥há-* 'house', *śā́lā-* 'house', and *svàr-* 'heaven, sun' are accented terms, but *ca* 'and' is unaccented. In addition, certain categories are associated with accentual properties. Finite verb forms that are not first elements of sentences or verse segments are usually unaccented (e.g. 2.5.3.1(1a): *īḷe*), though they are accented in certain contexts, such as relative clauses; non-initial vocative forms also are unaccented (e.g. 2.5.3.1(2): *gaṅge*) and utterance initial vocatives have initial high-pitched syllables (e.g. *ágne* 'Agni').

2.5.3.1 Once tone adjustments apply, there are four possible pitch levels in continuous speech: extra low, low, high and extra high. A low-pitched syllable following a high is converted to a svarita, and the high-pitched segment of this is raised to an extra high level in some dialects. A low preceding a high or a svarita is lowered to an extra low level. An original low that follows a svarita is raised to the level of a high unless a high or svarita follows. There can thus be one or more high-pitched syllables, which prātiśākhyas call *pracaya* ('accumulation') and Pāṇini refers to as *ekaśruti* ('mono-tone'). Such syllables are acoustically like a basic high, but they do not determine the conversion of a following low to a svarita. Thus, starting from

(1a) *agním īḷe puráḥ-hitam yajñásya devám r̥tvíjam*

phonological rules, including tone adjustments, apply to give

(1b) *àgnim īḷe pùrohìtaym̐ yàjñasyà d̥evam r̥tvìjàm* (R̥V 1.1.1ab) 'I praise (invoke) (*īḷe* [1st. sg. pres. mid.]) Agni (*agním* [acc. sg. m.]), the god (*devam*) set at the fore (*puráḥ-hitam*) as the priest (*r̥tvíjam*) of the rite (*yajñásya*).'

The low preceding the high in *agním* and *puráḥ-hitam* is made extra low. The first low-pitched vowels of *īḷe* and *hitam* are changed to a svarita, and the lows following these are raised to high. The low of *devám*, on the other hand, is not raised after the svarita of *yajñasyà*; it is made extra low because it is followed by a high, as is the low of *r̥tvíjam*. In

(2) *imàm mè gaṅge yamune sarasvati śutùdri stomàm̐ sacatā parúṣṇy ā | àsiknyā màrudvr̥dhe vitastàyārjīkīye śr̥ṇuhy ā suṣomàyā* ... ([R̥V 10.75.5] ← *imám me gaṅge yamune* ...) 'Gaṅgā, Yamunā, Sarasvatī, Śutudrī, Paruṣṇī, attend to (*sacata* ... *ā* [2pl. imper.]) this (*imam* [acc. sg. m.]) hymn of praise (*stomam* [acc. sg.]) of mine (*me* [gen. sg. encl.]); Marudvr̥dhā along with Asiknī, Arjīkīyā along with Vitastā and Suṣomā, harken (*śr̥ṇuhi ā* [2sg. imper.])'

the low of *imám* is made extra low before the following high, and the low of *me* is converted to a svarita, after which the low-pitched syllables of the vocative singular feminines *gaṅge* and *yamune* are raised; the vocative *śutudri* has high pitch on its first vowel, since it occurs at the beginning of a verse section, so that the final vowel of *sarasvati* is made extra low.

2.5.3.2 There is dialect variation involving tones and tone contours, mostly with respect to svarita syllables. One difference involves how much of a svarita is high. In some areas, the first half mora is high and the remainder is low, but in other areas the first half of the vowel is high, the second low; e.g. for some, *mè* has one mora high and one mora low, while others pronounce this with half a mora high and one and one-half morae low. In some dialects, the high of a svarita following a high is raised to extra high but not in others, and in some areas, the entire duration of a svarita is a descent from high. There is also a historical change involving svarita syllables. In some dialects, these were levelled to high, resulting in a system that has only high and low tones. Due to analogic changes prompted by this, a high here corresponds not only to a svarita but also to a low elsewhere and a low corresponds to a high elsewhere. This is best known from the tradition of the *Śatapathabrāhmaṇa*. For example:

(1) *pṛṣṭhe pṛthivvyāḥ sīda* ... (ŚBr. 9.2.3.34)

corresponds to

(2) *pṛṣṭtthe pṛthivvyāḥ sìda* . . . ([VS 17.72] ← *pṛṣṭhé pṛthivyáḥ sīda*) 'Sit (*sīda* [2sg. imp.]) on the back (*pṛṣṭhe* [loc. sg. nt.]) of the earth (*pṛthivyāḥ* [gen. sg. f.])'.

2.5.4 Grammatically determined adjustments

Some adjustments are determined by grammatical instead of phonological contexts. The following will serve to illustrate.

Certain grammatical categories – most perfects and certain presents – involve duplication. In reduplicated syllables, initial aspirates are deaspirated and velars replaced by palatals; e.g. *ca-kār-a*, *ja-gām-a*, and *ba-bhār-a*, third singular active perfects of *kṛ* 'do, make', *gam* 'go', and *bhṛ* 'bear, carry'; *ju-ho-ti*, third singular active present of *hu* 'offer oblations'.

An entire word is repeated to convey that the referent in question is associated repeatedly or constantly with an action or a property; for example, *yaym̐ yaym̐* (2.5.2.4(8)) 'whomever', *dive dive* (dat. sg.) 'day after day'. The second term in such a sequence is unaccented. The first vowel of *dive* has a svarita vowel because it follows the high-pitched vowel of the first term.

3 GRAMMAR

3.1 Verb system

3.1.1 Introduction

The basic unit of the verbal system is the base or root, called *dhātu* in Indian grammatical traditions. Affixes are added to bases to make different tense and modal forms. In western terms, the tense categories are present, aorist, imperfect, perfect, future; the modal forms are indicative, imperative, optative and subjunctive. There is also a conditional. The subjunctive and injunctive – formally an unaugmented secondary form – are Vedic (section 3.1.7), though the subjunctive leaves traces in the imperative (section 3.1.4.1). A trace of aspectual contrast persists in negative commands; e.g.

(1) *akṣair mā dīvyaḥ kṛṣim it kṛṣasva* (RV 10.34.13a) 'Stop playing (*mā dīvyaḥ*) at dice (*akṣaiḥ* [instr. pl.]), do (*kṛṣasva* 'draw, plough' [2sg. imper. mid.]) your ploughing (*kṛṣim* [acc. sg.]) alone (*it* [ptcle.]).'
(2) *mā nò vadhī rudra mā parā dāḥ* (RV 7.46.4a) 'Rudra (*rudra* [voc. sg.]), do not kill (*mā vadhīḥ*) us (*naḥ* [encl. acc. pl.]), do not forsake (*mā parā dāḥ*) us.'

The negative particle *mā* is used with the imperfect injunctive *dīvyaḥ* (2sg. imperf. *adīvyaḥ*) in a command to stop something that is going on – the gambler's dice playing – and *mā* is used with the aorist injunctives *vadhīḥ* (2sg. aor. indic. *avadhīḥ*), *parā dāḥ* in requesting that something should not be done to begin with. There are also remainders of a stative perfect and the creation of new presents to preterites of such perfects (section 3.1.7).

Some bases are suppletive. For example, *as* 'be', *brū* 'speak, say', and *han* 'strike, kill' occur in present and imperfect forms: 3sg. pres. act. *asti*, *bravīti*, *hanti*, imperf. *āsīt*, *abravīt*, *ahan*; but the corresponding aorists are from different bases: *bhū* (*abhūt*), *vac* (*avocat*), *vadh* (*avadhīt*).

There are sets of active and medio-passive endings, with distinct endings in the perfect (section 3.1.2). In agentive forms, some verbs take only active endings, others only middle endings; e.g. *asti* 'is', *tuṣyati* 'is pleased' and *āste* 'sits, is seated', *edhate* 'thrives', with the active and middle endings *ti*, *te* after the present stems of *as*, *tuṣ* and *ās*, *edh*. Some bases can be used with either set of endings, depending on whether the result of the act in question is intended for the agent performing it or someone else; e.g. *pacate* (3sg. mid.) 'cooks' is used if the agent is cooking something for himself, but *pacati* (3sg. act.) is used if this for someone else. The use of a verb with a particular preverb can determine diathesis. Thus, *kṛ* 'do, make' takes both active and middle endings under the conditions noted (*karoti*, *kurute*), but *adhi kṛ* 'prevail over' takes middle endings (*adhi kurute*) even if an agent performs the act for the sake of someone else, and *anu kṛ* 'imitate, quote' takes active endings (*anu karoti*) even if the agent performs the act for his own benefit.

A passive present-imperfect has medio-passive endings following a stem with -*ya*-, before which -*i* and -*u* are lengthened and -*ri*, -*īr*/-*ūr* occur for -*ṛ* and -*ṝ*; e.g. *pacyate* 'is cooked', *cīyate* 'is heaped up', *stūyate* 'is praised', *kriyate* 'is made, done', *kīryate* 'is scattered', *pūryate* 'is filled'. Identical forms serve as intransitives of the type *pacyate* 'is cooking, ripens', although some bases lack forms with -*ya*-; e.g. *namate* 'bends'. See also section 3.1.3.2.3b.

Verb endings designate both unspecified agents and objects and person and number, so that overt personal pronouns need not be used, although they may be used, as in section 3.1.7(4): *yuvam mahāni prathamāni cakrathuḥ*.

Certain finite verbal forms show vowel alternation: singular active forms with full-grade, other forms with zero-grade stems (section 2.5.1.8). Thus, sg. *as-ti* (3rd), *a-si* (2nd [← *as-si*]), *as-mi* (1st) have the full-grade stem *as*, with the vowel *a*-; the corresponding dual and plural forms have the zero-grade stem *s*-: *s-taḥ s-thaḥ s-vaḥ*, *s-anti s-tha s-maḥ*. Stems of the type *suno-/sunu*-, *ruṇadh-/rundh*-, *krīṇā-/krīṇī-/krīṇ*- (see section 3.1.3.1) have full-grade forms with -*no*-, -*na*-, -*nā*- and zero-grade forms with *-nu-*, *-n-*, and *-nī-/-n-*. Bases in *-u* of the second class have strong forms with *-au* before a consonant (*astaut astauḥ* [imperf.]), *-av* before a vowel (*astavam* [1sg. imperf.]). Stems of particular verbs lack zero-grade forms; e.g. *yā-ti yā-si yā-mi, yā-taḥ yā-thaḥ yā-vaḥ, yānti yā-tha yā-maḥ* 'go'; *ās-te ās-se āse, ās-āte ās-āthe ās-vahe, ās-ate ā-dhve* (← *ās-dhve*) *ās-mahe* 'sit, be seated'; *śe-te śe-ṣe śay-e, śay-āte śay-āthe śe-vahe, śe-rate śe-dhve śe-mahe* 'lie, sleep'. Some stems lack zero-grade alternants for phonological reasons and as a result of analogic developments; e.g. *at-ti at-si ad-mi, at-taḥ at-thaḥ ad-vaḥ, ad-anti at-tha ad-maḥ* 'eat'. Stems with a thematic vowel *-a-*, such as *bhava-ti* 'is, becomes' and *tuda-ti* 'shoves, goads, pricks' also have no root vowel alternation, but the stem vowel is *-ā-* before *-v-*, *-m-*.

In addition to primitive verb bases, there are derived bases, both deverbative and denominative (see section 3.1.6). Various nonfinite forms are associated with the verbal system, including participles, absolutives and infinitives (see section 3.2.4.1).

3.1.2 Endings

Primary and secondary endings are shown in table 4.1.

The perfect has a separate set of active endings: *a atus us, tha athus a, a va ma*; except after a small group of bases (e.g. *kṛ* 'do, make'), augmented *-iva, -ima* occur. The third singular and plural middle perfect endings are *e* and *ire*; others are identical with primary endings (section 3.1.3.2.4).

ati (3pl.) follows reduplicated stems, *-anti* other stems; e.g. *ju-hv-ati* 'offer', *s-anti* 'are'. Stems in *-a-* have *-anti* straddling the stem boundary; e.g. *bhavanti* 'are, become', *dīvyanti* 'gamble', *tudanti* 'shove, goad'. The corresponding secondary endings are *-us* and *-an* (← *-ant*); e.g. *ajuhav-uḥ, āsan* (3pl. imperf.). *-us* also occurs in sigmatic aorist and optative forms as well as root aorists of bases in *-ā*; see sections 3.1.3.2.3a, 3.1.4.2.

Instead of consonant-initial endings *-ti* etc., *-iti* and so on occur with certain verbs, which have *-īt* and *-īs* instead of *-t* and *-s*; e.g. *rod-iti rud-itaḥ rud-anti, rod-iṣi rud-ithaḥ rud-itha, rod-imi rud-ivaḥ rud-imaḥ; arod-īt arud-itām arud-an, arod-īḥ arud-itam arud-ita, arud-am arud-iva arud-ima* (*rud* 'cry weep'). *-īs, -īt* also occur in the imperfect of *as* 'be' (*ās-īt, ās-īḥ*) and in sigmatic aorist forms (e.g. *akār-ṣ-īt, akār-ṣ-īḥ* [*kṛ* 'do, make']).

-rate occurs in *śe-rate* 'lie, sleep'. The general primary third plural middle ending for stems that do not end in *-a-* is *-ate*; e.g. *ās-ate* 'are seated'. Stems in *-a-* have *-ante* parallel to active *-anti*; e.g. *edhante* 'they thrive'. The corresponding secondary forms are *aśe-rata, ās-ata, aidhanta*. *-ata* also occurs in sigmatic aorist forms such as *akṛ-ṣ-ata* 'did, have done, (have) made'.

TABLE 4.1: PRIMARY AND SECONDARY VERB ENDINGS

	Active							Medio-passive								
	Primary			Secondary				Primary			Secondary					
	Sg.	Du.	Pl.	Sg.	Du.	Pl.		Sg.	Du.	Pl.		Sg.	Du.	Pl.		
Person																
3	*ti*	*tas*	*anti ati*	*t*	*tām*	*an us*	*te*	*āte*	*ante ate rate*	*ta*	*ātām*	*anta ata rata*				
2	*si*	*thas*	*tha*	*s*	*tam*	*ta*	*se*	*āthe*	*dhve*	*thās*	*āthām*	*dhvam*				
1	*mi*	*vas*	*mas*	*m am va*		*ma*	*e*	*vahe*	*mahe*	*i*	*vahi*	*mahi*				

Certain modal forms have particular endings and some are restricted to Vedic; see sections 3.1.4.1–2, 3.1.7.

3.1.3 Tense forms

3.1.3.1 Present stems

Present stems consist of a root or a root with a particular affix. The nine major present-stem formations are as follows:

(1) Strong root with low-pitched suffix *-a-* (*-ā-* before *-v-* and *-m-*, *-e-* in 3du. and 2du. mid. forms); e.g. *bháv-a-* (base *bhū* 'be, become'), *édh-a-* 'thrive':

   bhava-ti -taḥ -nti, -si -thaḥ -tha, bhavā-mi -vaḥ -maḥ
   edhate edhete edhante edhase edhethe edhadvhe, edhe edhāvahe edhāmahe

(2) Root with vowel alternation in most instances, as in *as-ti* etc. (see section 3.1.1):

   e-ti i-taḥ y-anti, e-ṣi i-thaḥ i-tha, e-mi i-vaḥ i-maḥ (*i* 'go')
   stau-ti stu-taḥ stuv-anti, stau-ṣi stu-thaḥ stu-tha, stau-mi stu-vaḥ stu-maḥ; stu-te stuv-āte stuv-ate, stu-ṣe stuv-āthe stu-dhve, stuv-e stu-vahe stu-mahe (*stu* 'praise')

(3) Reduplicated root with vowel alternation:

   ju-ho-ti ju-hu-taḥ ju-hv-ati, ju-ho-ṣi ju-hu-thaḥ ju-hu-tha, ju-ho-mi ju-hu-vaḥ ju-hu-maḥ
   da-dhā-ti dha-t-taḥ da-dh-ati, da-dhā-si dha-t-thaḥ dha-t-tha, da-dhā-mi da-dh-vaḥ da-dh-maḥ (*dhā* 'put, make')

   Generally, the base vowel is echoed in the reduplicated syllable, with shortening, but there are exceptions; e.g. *bi-bhar-ti* (*bhṛ* 'bear, nurture').

(4) Accented root with suffix *-ya-*; e.g. *dī́vya-* (*div* 'gamble'):

   dīvya-ti -taḥ -anti etc.

(5) Stem with suffix *-no-/-nu-* (optionally *-n-* before *-v-* and *-m-*); e.g.

   suno-/sunu- (*su* 'press juice out of something'): *sunoti -nutaḥ -nvanti* etc. (*sunuvaḥ/sunvaḥ, sunumaḥ/sunmaḥ*), *sunute -nvāte -nvate* etc.
   śakno-/śaknu- (*śak* 'be able'): *śaknoti -nutaḥ -nuvanti* etc.
   āpno-/āpnu- (*āp* 'reach, obtain'): *āpnoti -nutaḥ -nuvanti* etc.

(6) Zero-grade root with accented suffix *-á-*; e.g.

   tudá- 'shove, goad': *tuda-ti -taḥ -nti; tudate tudete tudante* etc.

(7) *-na-/-n-* infixed to zero-grade root; e.g.

   ruṇadh-/rundh- (*rudh* 'hem in, obstruct'): *ruṇaddhi runddhaḥ rundhanti* etc., *runddhe rundhāte rundhate* etc.

(8) Suffix *-o-/-u-* after *kṛ*, with a strong form *kar-o-* and a weak form *kur-u-* (*kur-* before *-v-*, and *-m-*: *kurvaḥ kurmaḥ*), and bases with *-an*, of the type *tan-*, with optional deletion of *-u-* before *-v-* and *-m-* (*tan-u-vaḥ -maḥ/tan-vaḥ -maḥ*):

   karoti kurutaḥ kurvanti, kurute kurvāte kurvate etc.
   tanoti tanutaḥ tanvanti, tanute tanvāte tanvate etc.

(9) Suffix *-nā-/-nī-* (before consonants)/*-n-* (before vowels); in a subset of stems, the root vowel is shortened; e.g.

krīṇāti -ṇītaḥ -ṇanti, -ṇīte -nāte -ṇate (*krī* 'buy')
punāti, -nīte etc. (*pū* 'purify')

There is also a tenth group – of the type *coraya-ti -tas -anti* ('steal') etc. – which is like the first set except that the suffix *-a-* is preceded by another suffix, *-i-/-ay-*.

3.1.3.2 Preterit classes

3.1.3.2.1 Introduction
The current language Pāṇini describes distinguishes aorist, imperfect and perfect, the first two with stems augmented by initial *a/ā* and followed by secondary endings. These contrast as follows. Aorists are used with reference to actions that take place at a time in the past, possibly up to a moment in the day on which one speaks, imperfects with reference to actions performed in the past excluding this day; perfects are used of such past actions, with the added condition that the events in question are reported but were not witnessed by the speaker. This system is reflected also in some Vedic texts, e.g. the *Śāṅkhāyanaśrautasūtra* recounting of the Śunaḥśepa story (15.17–27, cf. AiBr. 7.13–18), which begins with a series of perfect forms: *āsa* (3sg.) 'was', *babhūvuḥ* (3pl.) 'were', *lebhe* (3sg. mid.) 'got', *ūṣatuḥ* (3du.) 'stayed', *papraccha* (3sg.) 'asked':

(1) *hariścandro ha vaidhasa aikṣvāko rājāputra āsa. tasya ha śataṁ jāyā babhūvuḥ. tāsu ha putraṁ na lebhe. tasya ha parvatanāradau gṛha ūṣatuḥ. sa ha nāradaṁ papraccha* ... (ŚŚS 15.17) 'King (*rājā* [nom. sg.]) Hariścandra, son of Vedhas (*vaidhasaḥ*), of the Ikṣvāku lineage (*aikṣvākaḥ*), was (*āsa*) sonless (*aputraḥ*). He had (*tasya ... babhūvuḥ* 'of him there were') a hundred (*śataṁ*) wives (*jāyāḥ* [nom. pl. f.]). He did not get (*na lebhe*) a son (*putram* [acc. sg. m.]) by them (*tāsu* [loc. pl. f.]). Parvata and Nārada (*parvatanāradau*) were staying (*ūṣatuḥ*) in his (*tasya*) house (*gṛhe* [loc. sg. nt.]). He asked Nārada....'

Nārada tells Hariścandra to approach Varuṇa for a son, and Hariścandra does this, promising Varuṇa he will offer his son to him. Hariścandra then puts off the sacrifice by making conditions. The story proceeds in a series of perfect forms narrating what happened and aorist forms used when Varuṇa tells Hariścandra that something has occurred; e.g.

(2) *tasya ha putro jajñe rohito nāma. taṁ varuṇa uvāca : ajani vai te putro yajasva māneneti* (ŚŚS 15.18) 'A son, Rohita by name (*rohito nāma*), was born (*jajñe* [3sg. pfct. mid.]) to him (*tasya* [gen. sg.]). Varuṇa said (*uvāca* [3sg. pfct. act.]) to him (*tam* [acc. sg.]): a son has indeed (*vai*) been born (*ajani* [3sg. aor. mid.]) to you (*te*). Sacrifice (*yajasva*) him (*anena* [instr. sg.]) to me (*mā* [acc. sg.]).'

Finally, Hariścandra yields. He summons his son and tells him what had happened:

(3) *sa tathety uktvā putram āmantrayāṁ cakre. tatāyaṁ vai mahyaṁ tvām adadāt* ... (ŚŚS 15.18) 'He agreed (*tathety uktvā* 'after saying "yes"') and summoned (*āmantrayāṁ cakre* [3sg. perf. mid.]) his son, (then said): son (*tata* [voc. sg.]), the fact is that this (*ayam*) (god Varuṇa) gave (*adadāt* [3sg. imperf.]) you (*tvām*) to me (*mahyam*)....'

The periphrastic perfect form *āmantrayāṁ cakre* is used in the narration, but the imperfect *adadāt* is used when Hariścandra speaks of what he himself experienced.

This system is not, however, the norm in Vedic, in epics or in other literary sources, where both the perfect and imperfect serve to narrate and report; see section 3.1.7.

3.1.3.2.2 Imperfect

Present and imperfect have the same stem. Present forms have primary endings but imperfects have secondary endings (section 3.1.2) and are augmented with *a* or *ā*, the latter with vowel-initial bases. Following are imperfects corresponding to the presents given in section 3.1.3.1:

(1) *abhava-t -tām -an, -ḥ -tam -ta, -m abhavāva -ma*
    aidhata aidhetām aidhanta, aidhathāḥ aidhethām aidhadvham, aidhe aidhāvahi aidhāmahi

(2) *ās-īt -tām -an, -īḥ -tam -ta, -am -va -ma*
    ait aitām āyan, aiḥ aitam aita, āyam aiva aima
    astaut astutām astuvan; astuta astuvātām astuvata etc.

(3) *ajuhot ajuhutām ajuhavuḥ, ajuhoḥ ajuhutam ajuhuta, ajuhavam ajuhuva ajuhuma.*

(4) *adīvya-t -tām -an* etc.

(5) *asunot asunutām asunvan; asunuta asunvātām asunvata* etc.

(6) *atuda-t -tām -an; atudata atudetām atudanta* etc.

(7) *aruṇat arunddhām arundhan; arunddha arundhātām arundhata* etc.

(8) *akarot akurutām akurvan; akuruta akurvātām akurvata* etc.
    atanot atanutaḥ atanvan; atanuta atanvātām atanvata etc.

(9) *akrī-ṇāt -ṇītām -ṇan; -ṇīta -ṇātām -ṇata*
    apunāt; apunīta etc.

3.1.3.2.3 Aorist

There are: (a) sigmatic aorists, (b) root aorists, (c) thematic aorists, (d) reduplicated root aorists.

3.1.3.2.3a Sigmatic aorist

Sigmatic aorists are of four types, with (1) *-s-*, (2) *-iṣ-*, (3) *-siṣ-*, and (4) *-sa-* after bases; the second type synchronically has *-s-* augmented with initial *i*. (3) and (4) are the most restricted. (3) supplies active forms of *yam* 'restrain, hold, stretch, offer', *ram* 'play', *nam* 'bend' and bases in *-ā*. *-sa-* occurs with roots whose final consonants and the *-s-* of the affix combine to give *-kṣ-*. This reflects the origin of the type: *aduhat* (Vedic 3sg. mid. imperf.): *aduhi* (1sg. mid. imperf.) 'milked' served as a model for *adhukṣat* in addition to *adugdha* (3sg. s-aor. mid.) corresponding to *adhukṣi* (1sg. s-aor. mid.). Forms with vocalic endings have *-s-* instead of *-sa-* and medio-passive endings beginning with dentals optionally follow *duh* 'milk', *dih* 'fashion', *lih* 'lick', *guh* 'hide' without *-sa-*. Some forms, such as *akṛta* (3sg. mid.), correspond to sigmatic forms like *akṛṣata* (3pl. mid.) but are historically root aorists. Examples of sigmatic aorists are:

-s-:
anai-ṣīt -ṣṭām -ṣuḥ, -ṣīḥ -ṣṭam -ṣṭa, -ṣam -ṣva -ṣma; ane-ṣṭa -ṣātām -ṣata, -ṣṭhāḥ -ṣāthām -ḍhvam, -ṣi -ṣvahi -ṣmahi (*nī* 'guide, lead')
aśrau-ṣīt -ṣṭām -ṣuḥ etc. (*śru* 'hear, listen')
asto-ṣṭa -ṣātām -ṣata etc. (*stu* 'praise')

akār-ṣīt -ṣṭām -ṣuḥ etc.; *akṛ-ta -ṣātām -ṣata, -thāḥ -ṣāthām -ḍhvam, -ṣi -ṣvahi -ṣmahi* (*kṛ* 'do, make')
apāk-ṣīt -tām -ṣuḥ, -ṣīḥ -tam -ta, -ṣam -ṣva -ṣma; apak-ta -ṣātām -ṣata etc. (*pac* 'cook, bake')
achait-sīt -tām -suḥ; achit-ta -sātām -sata etc. (*chid* 'cut, cut off, cut down, split')

-iṣ-:
apāv-īt -iṣṭām -iṣuḥ, -īḥ -iṣṭam -iṣṭa, -iṣam -iṣva -iṣma; apav-iṣṭa -iṣātām -iṣata, -ṣṭhāḥ -iṣāthām -iḍhvam/-idhvam, -iṣi -iṣvahi -iṣmahi (*pū* 'purify')
adev-īt -iṣṭām -iṣuḥ etc. (*div* 'gamble')
arāṇ-īt -iṣṭām -iṣuḥ etc. (*raṇ* 'tinkle, jingle')

-siṣ-:
anaṁ-sīt -siṣṭām -siṣuḥ, -sīḥ -siṣṭam -siṣṭa, -siṣam -siṣva -siṣma (*nam* 'bend')
ayā-sīt -siṣṭām -siṣuḥ etc. (*yā* 'go')

-sa-:
adhuk-ṣat -ṣatām -ṣan, -ṣaḥ -ṣatam -ṣata, -ṣam -ṣāva -ṣāma; adhukṣata/adugdha adhukṣātām adhukṣanta etc. (*duh* 'milk')

Sigmatic aorists with -*s*- and -*iṣ*- involve vowel alternation in bases. Roots with -*ĭ* -*ŭ* have the corresponding vṛddhi vowels (section 2.5.1.8) before -*s*- followed by active endings, but guṇa vowels before -*s*- and -*iṣ*- preceding medio-passive endings. Bases in -*ṛ* have -*ār* and -*ṛ* before -*s*- followed respectively by active and medio-passive endings. Consonant-final bases with penultimate -*a*-, -*ĭ*-, -*ŭ*- have vṛddhi vowels in active forms with -*s*-. In active forms with -*iṣ*-, bases in -*ŭ* have -*āv*-, the prevocalic variant of -*au*; consonant-final bases with penultimate -*ĭ*, -*ŭ* have -*e*- and -*o*-, while bases with penultimate -*a*- have either -*a*- or -*ā*-.

3.1.3.2.3b Root aorist
Active forms of several vowel-final verbs have endings directly following bases; e.g. *agā-t agā-tām ag-uḥ, agā-ḥ -tam -ta, -m -va -ma* (*gā* 'go'); similarly *asthāt* (*sthā* 'come to a stop, stand'), *adāt* (*dā* 'give'), *adhāt* (*dhā* 'put, make'), *apāt* (*pā* 'drink'), *abhūt* (*bhū* 'be, become', prevocalic *bhūv*- [e.g. 3pl. *abhūvan*]). For some bases in -*ā* root forms alternate with sigmatic forms; e.g. *aghrāt/aghrāsīt* (*ghrā* 'smell, sniff'). Bases of the eighth present group (section 3.1.3.1(8)) have such alternative third and second singular middle forms; e.g. *atata/ataniṣṭa, atathāḥ/ataniṣṭhāḥ*.
    There is also a third singular form, with -*i*, specific to passive and intransitive forms. Thus, *akāri* 'was made or done, has been made or done' is a passive aorist of *kṛ*. Such an aorist can be construed with an agentive instrumental, as in

(1) *astāvy agnir... ṛṣibhiḥ ...* (RV 10.45.12ab) 'Agni has been praised (*astāvi*) by the ṛṣis (*ṛṣibhiḥ* [instr. pl.]). . . .'

Some intransitives with -*i* alternate with sigmatic forms; e.g. *ajani* (section 3.1.3.2.1(2)), *ajaniṣṭa* 'has been born' (section 3.1.7(3)).

3.1.3.2.3c Thematic aorist
Thematic aorists have a stem in -*a*- (-*ā*- before -*v*-, -*m*-). These are predominantly active formations. Some have sigmatic medio-passive counterparts, others alternate with sigmatic aorists in medio-passive forms, still others alternate with active sigmatic

aorists. Examples: *apuṣa-t -tām -an, apuṣa-ḥ -tam -ta, apuṣ-a-m apuṣ-ā-va apuṣ-ā-ma* (*puṣ* 'thrive' [pres. *puṣyati*]); *agam-a-t* etc. (*gam* 'go'); *asic-a-t* etc., *asic-a-ta asic-e-tām asicanta* etc., *asik-ta asik-ṣ-ātām asik-ṣ-ata* etc. (*sic* 'sprinkle, irrigate'); *acchid-a-t/ acchait-s-īt* 'split'.

3.1.3.2.3d Reduplicated aorist

The reduplicated aorist, with a suffix *-a-*, serves to form agentive forms of some primitive bases; e.g. *aśi-śriy-a-t* (*śri* 'lean on, resort to'). Its major role, however, is to supply aorists to causatives; e.g. *acī-kar-a-t, ajī-gam-a-t, ajī-har-a-t*, third singular active aorists of the causatives *kāri* 'have ... do, make', *gami* 'have ... go, send', *hāri* 'have ... take' (section 3.1.6.1). The occurrence of *i* or *ī* in the reduplicated syllable is rhythmically determined: *i* before a cluster, *ī* to give a heavy syllable before a single consonant.

3.1.3.2.4 Perfect

Perfect forms are either simple or periphrastic. The simple perfect is characterized by reduplication, particular endings (section 3.1.2), and vowel alternation. The active and middle perfect forms of *nī* 'guide, lead', *lū* 'cut', *kṛ* 'do, make', *gam* 'go' are:

> *nināya ninyatuḥ ninyuḥ, ninetha ninyathuḥ ninya, nināya ninyiva ninyima*
> *ninye ninyāte ninyire, ninyiṣe ninyāthe ninyidhve, ninye ninyivahe ninyimahe*
> *lulāva luluvatuḥ luluvuḥ, lulavitha luluvathuḥ luluva, lulāva luluviva luluvima*
> *luluve luluvāte luluvire, luluviṣe luluvāthe luluvidhve, luluve luluvivahe luluvimahe*
> *cakāra cakratuḥ cakruḥ, cakartha cakrathuḥ cakra, cakāra cakṛva cakṛma*
> *cakre cakrāte cakrire, cakṛṣe cakrāthe cakṛdhve, cakre cakṛvahe cakṛmahe*
> *jagāma jagmatuḥ jagmuḥ, jagantha jagmathuḥ jagma, jagāma jaganva jaganma*
> *jagme jagmāte jagmire, jaganthāḥ jagmāthe jagandhve, jagme jaganvahe jaganmahe* (with preverb *sam: sam gam* 'come together')

Bases in *-ī̆, -ŭ* and *-ṛ* have these vowels or their prevocalic variants (section 2.5.1.3) in zero-grade forms (sections 3.1.1, 2.5.1.8) but guṇa vowels (*-e, -o* or their prevocalic variants *-ay, -av* and *-ar*) in other forms except for the third singular active, where *-āy, -āv* and *-ār* occur before the ending *-a*; in the first singular active, these are optional. Comparably, *gam* has zero-grade *gm-* with vocalic endings, but *gãm* elsewhere. Similarly, there is an alternation between *chid* 'split' and *ched*:

> *ci-cched-a ci-cchid-atuḥ ci-cchid-uḥ, ci-cched-itha ci-chid-athuḥ ci-chid-a, ci-cched-a ci-cchid-iva ci-cchid-ima*

Bases in *-ā* have third and first singular active perfects in *-au*; e.g. *dadau* 'gave', *dadhau* 'put, made', *tasthau* 'came to rest'.

As in reduplicated presents (section 3.1.3.1(3)), the reduplication involves repetition of the base vowels with shortening. Reflecting an older process, *a* occurs instead of *ṛ* and in the reduplicated syllable of *ba-bhūv-a* etc. (*bhū* 'be, become').

Some formal perfects lack reduplication. One of these is historically a perfect that functions as a present and alternates with forms having present endings: *ved-a vid-atuḥ vid-uḥ* etc. (*vet-ti vit-taḥ vid-anti* [*vid* 'know']). Bases with *-a-* flanked by single consonants such that the first consonant is not subject to modification in a reduplicated syllable have weak forms with *-e-* and no reduplicated syllable; e.g.

papāca pecatuḥ pecuḥ (*pac* 'cook, bake')
yayāma yematuḥ yemuḥ (*yam* 'restrain, hold')
sasāda, sedatuḥ seduḥ (*sad* 'sit')
lebhe lebhāte lebhire (*labh* 'gain')

The distribution of these forms reflects their source: the types *yem-*, *sed-*, where *-e-* flanked by simple consonants is a phonetic outcome: *yem-* < *ya-ym-*, *sed-* < *sa-zd-*.

In the introductory section to his *Mahābhāṣya*, Patañjali notes that second plural active perfect forms such as *ūṣ-a* (*vas* 'stay, dwell'), *ter-a* (*tṝ* 'cross'), *ca-kr-a* (*kṛ* 'do, make'), *pec-a* (*pac* 'cook, bake') were no longer used. Instead, one used past participles in *-ta* (*uṣita-*, *tīrṇa-*) for intransitives and verbs of motion and in *-tavat-* (*kṛtavat-*, *pakvavat-*) for other transitive verbs; e.g.

(1) *kva yūyam uṣitāḥ* 'Where (*kva*) did you stay (*uṣitāḥ* [nom. pl. m.])?'
(2) *kiṃ yūyaṃ tīrṇāḥ* 'What did you cross (*tīrṇāḥ*)?'
(3) *kiṃ yūyaṃ kṛtavantaḥ* 'What did you do (*kṛtavantaḥ*)?'
(4) *kiṃ yūyaṃ pakvavantaḥ* 'What did you cook (*pakvavantaḥ*)?'

The periphrastic perfect consists of a derivate in *-ām* – originally an accusative singular of an action noun – combined with a simple perfect of *kṛ*. This is the regular perfect formation for derived bases. Thus, *gamayāṃ cakāra* corresponds to *gamayati* 'has ... go', the causative of *gam*; *āmantrayāṃ cakre* (section 3.1.3.2.1(3)) and *lolūyāṃ cakre* are the perfects to *āmantrayate* 'invites, summons' and the intensive *lolūyate* 'cuts repeatedly, intently'. *kās* 'cough' (3sg. *kāsāṃ cakre*) and bases that begin with vowels other than *ă* as parts of heavy syllables (e.g. *īhāṃ cakre* 'exerted himself') also have this perfect. Some periphrastic perfects alternate with simple perfects; e.g. *bibhayāṃ cakāra/bibhāya* 'was afraid'.

3.1.3.3 Future

There are two future formations, associated with different time references, parallel to the contrast between aorist and imperfect (section 3.1.3.2.1). One formation has a suffix *-sya-/-iṣya-* and inflects in the same way as a present indicative: *dāsya-ti -taḥ -nti* 'will give'; *kariṣya-ti -taḥ -nti* 'will do, make', *lapsyate lapsyete lapsyante* 'will get, gain', and so on. This is used with reference to an act that will be performed at some time in the future, possibly including the day on which one is speaking; e.g. *staviṣyase* (2sg.) 'you will be praised' in

(1) *bhūribhiḥ ... ṛṣibhir barhiṣmàdbhiḥ staviṣyase* (ṚV 8.70.14ab) '(Indra,) you will be praised (*staviṣyase*) by many (*bhūribhiḥ* [instr. pl.]) ṛṣis with barhis.'

The other formation has active and middle forms as follows:

kartā kartārau kartāraḥ, kartāsi kartāsthaḥ kartāstha, kartāsmi kartāsvaḥ kartāsmaḥ
śayitā śayitārau śayitāraḥ, śayitāse śayitāsāthe śayitādhve, śayitāhe śayitāsvahe śayitāsmahe (*śī* 'lie, sleep')

This is used with reference to an act that will be performed in the future excluding the day on which one is speaking. For example,

(2) *yádi purắ saṃsthắnāad vīryetāadyá varṣiṣyatī́ti brūyāad yádi sáṃsthite śvó vraṣṭéti brūyāt* ... (MS 2.1.8) 'If (*yadi*) it should disperse (*vīryeta* [3sg. opt. mid.]) before

(*purā*) the completion (*saṁsthānāt* [abl. sg.]), he should say, 'It will rain today', if upon the completion (*saṁsthite* [loc. absol.]), he should say, 'It will rain tomorrow''

has *adya varṣiṣyati* and *śvo vraṣṭā*; *varṣiṣyati* and *vraṣṭā* are paired with *adya* 'today' and *śvaḥ* 'tomorrow'.

Though historically a combination of a noun in *-tṛ* and forms of *as* 'be', this is synchronically a formation with a suffix *-tā(s)*. For, whether the agent in question is male or female, it has no gender contrast comparable to the contrast between *kartṛ*- (nom. sg. m. *kartā*) and feminine *kartṛī*- (nom. sg. *kartrī*); *kartā* '... will do, make' is used regardless of gender. Moreover, although the third person forms *kartā kartārau kartāraḥ* formally are like the corresponding forms of *kartṛ*-, forms such as *kartāsthaḥ* (2du. act.), *kartāstha* (2pl. act.) do not contain dual and plural forms of a noun. In addition, *as* 'be' regularly inflects in the active, but the future type in question has middle forms with *-tāse* and so on; e.g *śayitāse* 'you will lie' in

(3) *sā hovāca savṁvatsarīṁ rātrim āgacchatāt taṇ ma ēkāṁ rātrim aṇtē śayitāse jāta u te'yan tarhi putrǫ bhaviteti* (SBr. 11.5.1.11) 'She (*sā*) (Urvaśī) said (*uvāca* [3sg.perf.]): 'Come (*āgacchatāt* [2sg. imper.]) on the night (*rātrim*) that will mark the completion of a year (*savṁvatsarīṁ*); then (*tat*) you will lie near me (*me ... ante*) for one night (*ekāṁ rātrim*), and then (*tarhi*) this son (*ayam ... putraḥ*) of yours (*te*) will be (*bhavitā*) born (*jātaḥ*)'.'

Finally, there is a first person middle form with *-he*. In

(4) *yaje'yakṣi yaṣṭāhe cà* (TĀr. 1.11.4)

yaṣṭāhe 'I will have a rite performed on my behalf' is paired with the present *yaje* and the aorist *ayakṣi*.

3.1.4 Non-indicative forms

Imperative, optative, and subjunctive are distinguished, though the last is not current in the language of Pāṇini's time. There is also a form called precative or benedictive, which is related to the optative.

3.1.4.1 Imperative

Imperatives are regularly formed from present stems (sections 3.1.3.1, 3.1.7). Third singular and plural active imperatives end with *-tu* and *-antu/-atu* as opposed to *-ti* and *-anti/-ati* of indicative forms: *as-tu, s-antu* 'should be', *bhavantu* 'should be(come)', *ju-hv-atu* 'should offer'. Corresponding medio-passive forms have *-ām* as opposed to *-e*; e.g. *ās-tām ās-atām* 'should sit, be seated' (indic. *ās-te ās-ate*), *edh-a-tām edh-antām* 'should thrive' (indic. *edh-a-te edhante*). Second singular active imperatives have either no overt ending or *-hi/-dhi*. Stems with a stem vowel *-a* or *-u* and with *-nu* following a vowel have no ending; e.g. *pac-a* 'cook, bake', *kur-u* 'do, make', *su-nu* 'press'. Stems with *-nā/-nī* (section 1.3.1(9)) following a consonant have imperatives with *-āna*; e.g. *gṛh-āṇa* 'grasp'. *-dhi* occurs after consonants and a subset of vowel-final stems, *-hi* after other vocalic stems; e.g. *rund-dhi* 'obstruct', *e-dhi* 'be', *śā-dhi* 'command, instruct', *ju-hu-dhi* 'offer', *āp-nu-hi* 'reach, obtain', *krī-ṇī-hi* 'buy'. Corresponding middle forms have *-sva*; e.g. *pac-a-sva, edh-a-sva, ās-sva* 'be seated, remain', *runt-sva* 'hem in, obstruct', *krī-ṇī-ṣva* 'buy'. Where vocalic alternation applies, zero-grade stems precede *-hi/-dhi* and *-sva*.

A suffix *-tāt* occurs in second and third singular active imperative forms expressing a wish; e.g. *jīv-a-tāt* 'may you (he/she) live', *ā gacch-a-tāt* (section 3.1.3.3(3)) 'you should come'. Such forms alternate with imperatives of the types noted above.

Reflecting their origins as subjunctives (section 3.1.7), first person imperatives have *-āni* in the singular active, *-āva* and *-āma* in the dual and plural active, and *-ai* in middle forms, all preceded by strong stems; e.g.

> *pac-āni* ('let me cook, may I cook') *pac-āva pac-āma*
> *yaj-ai yaj-āvahai yaj-āmahai*
> *kar-av-āṇi, kar-av-āva, kar-av-āma, kar-av-ai kar-av-āvahai kar-av-āmahai*

Other imperative forms have secondary endings; e.g. *gacch-a-tām* (3du.), *gacch-a-tam* (2du.), *gacch-a-ta* (2pl.).

3.1.4.2 Optative and precative

Optatives are characterized by *-ey-/-e-* for present stems in *-a*. Other present stems have active forms with *-yā-/-y-* and middle forms with *-īy-/-ī*. Third plural forms have endings *-us* (act.), *-ran* (medio-passive), and the first singular medio-passive has *-a*. Otherwise, secondary endings occur. Examples (*bhū, edh, as, ās, krī*) are given in table 4.2.

The precative is related to the optative with *-yā-* and *-ī-*, but is formed from the root and has forms with *-s-* that the optative lacks. Examples:

> *bhūyāt bhūyāstām bhūyāsuḥ, bhūyāḥ bhūyāstam bhūyāsta, bhūyāsam bhūyāsva bhūyāsma*
> *krīyāt krīyāstam krīyāsuḥ* etc.
> *edhiṣīṣṭa edhiṣīyāstām edhiṣīran, edhiṣīṣṭhāḥ edhiṣīyāsthām edhiṣīḍhvam, edhiṣīya edhiṣīvahi edhiṣīmahi*
> *kreṣīṣṭa kreṣīyāstām kreṣīran* etc.

3.1.4.3 Conditional

The conditional has a suffix *-sya/-iṣya*, as in the future (section 3.1.3.3), but with secondary endings and an augment; e.g.

TABLE 4.2: OPTATIVE FORMS

Active			Middle		
Sg.	Du.	Pl.	Sg.	Du.	Pl.
bhavet	*bhavetām*	*bhaveyuḥ*	*edheta*	*edheyātām*	*edheran*
bhaveḥ	*bhavetam*	*bhaveta*	*edhethāḥ*	*edheyāthām*	*edhedhvam*
bhaveyam	*bhaveva*	*bhavema*	*edheya*	*edhevahi*	*edhemahi*
syāt	*syātām*	*syuḥ*	*āsīta*	*āsīyātām*	*āsīran*
syāḥ	*syātam*	*syāta*	*āsīthāḥ*	*āsīyāthām*	*āsīdhvam*
syām	*syāva*	*syāma*	*āsīya*	*āsīvahi*	*āsīmahi*
krīṇīyāt	*krīṇīyātām*	*krīṇīyuḥ*	*krīṇīta*	*krīṇīyātām*	*krīṇīran*
krīṇīyāḥ	*krīṇīyātam*	*krīṇīyāta*	*krīṇīthāḥ*	*krīṇīyāthām*	*krīṇīdvham*
krīṇīyām	*krīṇīva*	*krīṇīma*	*krīṇīya*	*krīṇīvahi*	*krīṇīmahi*

abhaviṣya-t -tām -an, -ḥ -tam -ta, -m abhaviṣyā-va -ma
akreṣya-t -tām -an etc.; akreṣyata akreṣyetām akreṣyanta etc.

In the current language Pāṇini describes, such forms are used in stating contrary-to-fact conditions, whether the time reference is future or past. This usage is known also from Vedic texts. For example, after Aitaśa had started a certain recitation, one of his sons, thinking his father had gone mad, came up to him and covered his mouth (see section 3.1.7(6)–(8)). Aitaśa then cursed him and said:

(1) *yad vai me jālma mukhaṁ nāpy agrahīṣyaḥ śatāyuṣaṁ gām akariṣyaṁ sahasrāyuṣaṁ puruṣam* (KBr. 30.4.22–23) 'Wretch (*jālma* [voc. sg.]), if (*yad*) you had not (*na*) covered (*apy agrahīṣyaḥ*) my (*me*) mouth (*mukham* [acc. sg.]), I would have made (*akariṣyam*) the cow/ox (*gām*) to live a hundred years (*śatāyuṣam* [acc. sg.] 'with a life span of 100'), man (*puruṣam*) a thousand (*sahasrāyuṣam*).'

(2) *yadi jālma mukhaṁ na prāgrahīṣyaḥ śatāyuṣaṁ gām akariṣyaṁ sahasrāyuṣaṁ puruṣam* (GBr. 2.6.13)

The source of the conditional is a form of the type *akariṣyam* 'I was going to make', as in

(3) *taṁ hovāca apehy alaso'bhūr yo me vācam avadhīḥ. śatāyuṣaṁ gām akariṣyaṁ sahasrāyuṣaṁ puruṣam* (AiBr. 6.33) '(Aitaśa) said (*uvāca*) to him (*tam* [acc. sg. m.]), 'Be gone (*apehi*), you became (*abhūḥ*) negligent (*alasaḥ*), you who struck down (*avadhīḥ*) my speech (*me vācam*). I was going to make . . .'.'

3.1.5 Nominal forms associated with the verb system

Many nominals are formed from verbal bases; see section 3.2.4.1. As noted (section 3.1.3.3), nominal forms are incorporated in periphrastic verb forms and some finite verb forms were replaced by nominal ones (section 3.1.3.2.4). There is an extensive interplay between verb forms and nominal forms from earliest times.

3.1.5.1 Present, imperfect and future actives and passives have finite forms, as in

(1a)	*devdattaḥ*	*kaṭaṁ*	*karoti*	'Devadatta is making a mat.'
	nom. sg.	acc. sg. m.	3sg. indic. pres. act.	
(1b)	*devadattena*	*kaṭaḥ*	*kriyate*	'A mat is being made by Devadatta.'
	instr. sg.	nom. sg. m.	3sg. indic. pres. pass.	
(2a)	*devadattaḥ*	*kaṭam*	*akarot*	'Devadatta made a mat.'
			3sg. indic. imperf. act.	
(2b)	*devadattena*	*kaṭo*	*'kriyata*	'A mat was made by Devadatta.'
			3sg.indic. imperf. pass.	
(3a)	*devdattaḥ*	*kaṭaṁ*	*kariṣyati*	'Devadatta will make a mat.'
			3sg. fut. act.	
(3b)	*devadattena*	*kaṭaḥ*	*kariṣyate*	'A mat will be made by Devadatta.'
			3sg. fut. pass.	

In the aorist, both active and passive finite forms have participial equivalents; e.g.

(4a)	*devadattaḥ*	*kaṭam*	*akārṣīt*	'Devadatta (has) made a mat.'
			3sg. aor. act.	
(4b)	*devadattaḥ*	*kaṭaṁ*	*kṛtavān*	'Devadatta (has) made a mat.'
			nom. sg. m.	

(4c) *devadattena kaṭo*   *'kāri*   'A mat was (has been) made by Devadatta.'
                                         3sg. aor. pass.
(4d) *devadattena kaṭaḥ*   *kṛtaḥ*   'A mat was (has been) made by Devadatta.'
                                         nom. sg. m.

Examples (4a) and (4c) respectively contain the aorist active and passive forms *akārṣīt* and *akāri*, but (4b) and (4d) have the agentive past participle *kṛtavān* and the objective past participle *kṛtaḥ*, respectively coreferential with *devadattaḥ* and *kaṭaḥ*. Similarly, although

(5) *devadatto gacchati* 'Devadatta is going'
(6a) *devadatto 'gamat* 'Devadatta went (has gone)'

have the finite forms *gacchati* (3sg. pres. indic.) and *agamat* (3sg. aor. indic.),

(6b) *devadatto gataḥ* 'Devadatta went (has gone)'

uses the agentive past participle form *gataḥ*, coreferential with *devadattaḥ*. Verbs of movement, intransitives, and a small group of other verbs behave similarly.

    Absolutives and infinitives are also formed from verb bases; e.g. *ha-tvā* 'after killing' (section 3.2.2.3.7(1)), *ait-ya* 'after coming' (*ā + i*), *abhi-hā-ya* 'after approaching', *abhi-drut-ya* 'after running up to' (section 3.1.7(6)–(7)) are absolutives with *tvā* and *ya* (*-t-ya-* if a base ends in a short vowel) respectively after simple bases and compounds with preverbs; *han-tum*, *e-tum* are infinitives of *han* and *i*, formed with the suffix *tum* (see section 3.1.7(15)–(20)).

3.1.5.2 A derivate like *pāc-aka-* in

(1) *devadattaḥ pācako bhavati* 'Devadatta is a cook'
(2) *devadattaḥ pācako 'bhavat* 'Devadatta was a cook'

can refer to a person who cooks or may cook at any time. *pra-sād-aka-* (*pra sād-i* 'propitiate' [3sg. pres. indic. *prasādayati*]) is of the same formal type, but in

(3) *ahaṁ tu taṁ naravyāghram upayātaḥ prasādakaḥ | pratinetum ayodhyāṁ ca pādau tasyābhivanditum* (Rām. 2.84.17) 'But (*tu*), I (Bharata) have come (*upayātaḥ* [nom. sg. m. past ptcpl.]) to propitiate (*prasādakaḥ*) (Rāma), tiger among men (*naravyāghram*), to take him back (*pratinetum*) to Ayodhyā (*ayodhyām*), and (*ca*) to revere (*abhivanditum*) his feet (*tasya pādau*)'

prasādakaḥ (nom. sg. m.) is comparable in function to the infinitives *pratinetum* 'lead back' and *abhivanditum* 'to revere'. Pāṇini (Aṣṭādhyāyī 3.3.10) notes that derivates with *-tum* and *-aka* are used equivalently with reference to an action, to be done in the future, for the purpose of which another act is performed. Moreover, as *abhivanditum* occurs with the accusative *pādau*, so is *prasādakaḥ* construed with the accusative *naravyāghram*. Such a derivate in *-aka* differs from one that can be construed with an objective genitive, e.g. *odanasya pācakaḥ* 'one who cooks rice'.

3.1.6 Derived verbs

Sanskrit has a productive system of forming verbal bases from verbs and nominal items through affixation. Causatives, desideratives and intensives are formed from verb bases.

3.1.6.1 Causatives

The class of causatives includes factitives, such that a causative of an intransitive base like *sad* 'sit', *ās* 'sit, be seated', *śī* 'lie, sleep' is its transitive counterpart: *sād-i* (3sg. pres. indic. act. *sād-ay-a-ti*), *ās-i* (*ās-ay-ati*) 'cause to sit, seat', *śāy-i* (*śāy-ay-a-ti*) 'cause to lie'. Causatives are formed with a suffix *-i-/-e-*, which determines certain vowel alternations. Bases in *-ĭ̄ -ŭ̄ -ř̥* have alternants with vṛddhi vowels (section 2.5.1.8) before this suffix; bases with penultimate *i u ṛ* in light syllables have alternants with the corresponding guṇa vowels, and *ā* occurs for penultimate *a* except for particular bases. The following are additional pairs of primitive verbs and their corresponding causatives:

> *ci (ci-no-ti)* 'heap, gather, pluck': *cāy-i-* (*cāy-ay-a-ti, cāy-ay-a-te*), *nī* (*nay-a-ti*) 'lead, guide': *nāy-i-* (*nāy-ay-a-ti, -te*), *stu* (*stau-ti*) 'praise': *stāv-i-* (*stāv-ay-a-ti, -te*), *pū* (*pu-nā-ti*) 'purify': *pāv-i-* (*pāv-ay-at-i, -te*), *kṛ* (*kar-o-ti*) 'do, make': *kār-i-* (*kār-ay-a-ti, -te*), *kṝ* (*kir-a-ti*) 'scatter': *kār-i-* (*kār-ay-a-ti, -te*), *chid* (*chi-na-t-ti*) 'split, cut': *ched-i* (*ched-ay-a-ti, -te*), *tud* (*tud-a-ti*) 'goad, shove': *tod-i-* (*tod-ay-a-ti, -te*), *vṛdh* (*vardh-a-te*) 'grow, age': *vardh-i-* (*vardh-ay-a-ti, -te*), *jīv* (*jīv-a-ti*) 'live': *jīv-i-* (*jīv-ay-a-ti, -te*), *pac* (*pac-a-ti*) 'cook, bake': *pāc-i* (*pāc-ay-a-ti, -te*), *gam* (*gacch-a-ti*) 'go': *gam-i-* (*gam-ay-a-ti, -te*)

Active and middle causatives contrast in the same way as forms of the type *pacati, pacate* (section 3.1.1).

Causatives of bases in *-ā* have an augment *-p-*; e.g.

> *dā* (*da-dā-ti*) 'give': *dāp-i-* (*dāp-ay-a-ti*), *sthā* (*tiṣṭha-ti*) 'come to a stop, be in place, remain': *sthāp-i* (*sthāp-ay-a-ti*). *-p-* appears also with certain other bases; e.g. *ṛ* (*ṛcch-a-ti*) 'go, reach': *arp-i-* (*arp-ay-a-ti*), *hrī* (*ji-hre-ti*) 'be shy, abashed': *hrep-i-* (*hrep-ay-a-ti*)

Some bases with primitive vowels other than *-ā* have *-āp-* in causatives; e.g. *adhi i* (*adhīte*) 'study, learn': *adhy āp-i-* (*adhy āp-ay-a-ti*). This is optional in some instances; e.g. *cāp-i-* in addition to *cāy-i-* from *ci*. Some bases in *-ā* have causatives with *-āy;* e.g. *pā* (*piba-ti*) 'drink': *pāy-i-* (*pāy-ay-a-ti*).

3.1.6.2 Desideratives

A desiderative is used to signify that a given agent wishes to perform the act denoted by the base. Desideratives are formed with a suffix *-sa-/-iṣa-* that conditions reduplication and lengthening for a final vowel of a base as well as for penultimate *a* of some bases. Bases in *-ř̥* have *-īr* and *-ūr*, the latter when a labial precedes. Examples:

> *cicīṣa-* (*cicīṣati*) 'wish to gather, heap': *ci* (*cinoti*), *tuṣṭūṣa-* (*tuṣṭūṣati*) 'wish to praise': *stu* (*stauti*), *cikīrṣa-* (*cikīrṣati*) 'wish to do, make': *kṛ* (*karoti*), *mumūrṣa-* (*mumūrṣati*) 'wish to die, be about to die': *mṛ-* (*mriyate*), *jighāṁsa-* (*jighāṁsati*) 'wish to strike, kill': *han* (*hanti*)

-sa- and *-iṣa-* condition different effects; e.g. *yuyūṣa-/yuyaviṣa-* (*yuyūṣati, yuyaviṣati*) 'wish to bring together, blend': *yu* (*yauti*)

Due to historical and analogic developments, certain desideratives lack reduplicated syllables; e.g.

īpsa- (*īpsati*) 'wish to reach, obtain': *āp* (*āpnoti*), *dhīpsa-* (*dhīpsati*) 'wish to harm, deceive': *dabh* (*dabhnoti*), *lipsa-* (*lipsate*) 'wish to obtain': *labh* (*labhate*)

All desideratives, however, alternate with equivalent complexes of infinitives in *-tum* construed with forms of *iṣ* 'wish, desire' (*icch-a-ti*); e.g.

(1) *devadattaḥ kaṭaṁ kartum icchati*
(2) *devadattaḥ kaṭaṁ cikīrṣati* 'Devadatta wishes to make a mat.'

3.1.6.3 Intensives

Intensives, used to signify that an action is performed repeatedly or intensely, are of two types. Both involve reduplication, but one has a suffix *-ya-* and takes only middle endings while the other does not; e.g.

ce-cī-ya-te 'repeatedly heaps up', *lo-lū-ya-te* 'repeatedly cuts', *pā-pac-ya-te* 'cooks repeatedly'; *ro-rav-īti* 'roars', *jaṅ-gam-ya-te/jaṅ-gam-īti* 'constantly goes'

The reduplicated syllable has guṇa vowels *e* and *o* for *-ĭ* and *-ŭ*, *ā* for *-a-* except for bases that end with a nasal and a small group of other bases, such as *jap* 'mutter' (*jañjapyate/jañjapīti*).

3.1.6.4 Denominatives

Denominatives are regularly formed with *-ya-* following nominal forms and correspond to particular strings. Thus, *putrī-ya-* 'desire a son for oneself', 'treat like a son' corresponds to strings with *iṣ* 'wish' or *ā car* 'behave towards ...': *putrīyati = ātmanaḥ putram icchati* 'wishes a son (*putram*) of his own (*ātmanaḥ*)', *chātram putrīyati = chātram putram ivā carati* 'behaves towards his student (*chātram* [acc. sg.]) as (*iva*) towards a son'. Comparably, *vṛṣāyate* 'behaves like a bull' and *apsarāyate* 'behaves like an Apsaras' are equivalent respectively to *vṛṣa ivā carati* and *apsarā ivā carati*. There are other semantic groups. Some denominatives mean 'do, make ...', others 'experience ...', as in *śabdāyate = śabdaṁ karoti* 'makes noise', *namasyati devān = namas karoti devebhyaḥ* 'does reverence to the gods', *sukhāyate = sukhaṁ vedayate* 'knows happiness (of his own)'.

3.1.7 Dialectal and historical differences

Third plural forms of the type *aguḥ* 'went, have gone' are regular for root aorists of bases in *-ā* (section 3.1.3.2.3b), imperfects of which usually have third plural forms of the type *ayān* 'went' (pres. *yānti*). Pāṇini (Aṣṭādhyāyī 3.4.111–12) notes that in the dialect represented by Śākaṭāyana imperfects of bases in *-ā* also have forms of the type *ayuḥ* and that in this dialect the third plural imperfect active of *dviṣ* 'hate' is *adviṣuḥ* instead of *adviṣan*.

Although the language Pāṇini describes included perfect forms of the type *ūṣa* and *cakra*, in the accepted speech of Patañjali's time and area these were replaced by participial forms (section 3.1.3.2.4). There are also differences concerning the verb used in periphrastic perfect forms. In the language of Pāṇini's time and area, the regular auxiliary used is *kṛ* (section 3.1.3.2.4), as in *gamayāṁ cakāra*, the first such perfect attested in Vedic:

(1) *mṛtyur yamasyā́sīd dūtaḥ pracètā asū́n pitṛbhyò gamayāñ càkāra* (AV 18.2.27cd) 'Death (*mṛtyuḥ*) was the percipient (*pracetāḥ* [nom. sg. m.]) messenger (*dūtaḥ*) of Yama; he caused the living breaths (*asūn*) (of the corpse) to go to (join) the ancestors (*pitṛbhyaḥ*).'

Kātyāyana (3.1.40 vt. 3) knows of *as* and *bhū* 'be' as auxiliaries in addition to forms of *kṛ*: *gamayām āsa* and so on. Such differences are seen in Vedic texts. In the same context where the *Śāṅkhāyanaśrautasūtra* has *āmantrayāṁ cakre* (section 3.1.3.2.1(3)), the *Aitareyabrāhmaṇa* (7.14) has *āmantrayām āsa*:

(2) *sa tathety uktvā putram āmantrayām āsa ...*

The perfect shows other differences in usage and developments from early Vedic on. There were perfects such as *bibhāya* 'is afraid', which contrasted with presents (*bhayate* 'becomes afraid'). Such stative perfects persist in Vedic texts, and preterits were formed to them: *abibhet* 'was afraid'; similarly, *avet* 'knew' (*veda*). Such preterits, interpreted as imperfects, gave rise to new present forms: *bibheti* 'is afraid', *vetti* 'knows'. In the speech of Pāṇini's time and place, *vetti* alternates with *veda* and *bibhāya* has been assigned the preterital meaning 'was afraid' as opposed to the present *bibheti*.

In addition, there is variation in the use of imperfects and perfects as narrative forms. From earliest Indo-Aryan, the aorist was used with reference to events that took place at a past time which could include the present day, as in

(3) *ud u jyotìr amṛtàvm̐ viśvajànyavm̐ ... savitā́ devo àśret | ... devānā́m ajaniṣṭa cakṣùr āvir àkar bhuvànavm̐ viśvàm uṣāḥ* (RV 7.76.1) 'God (*devaḥ*) Savitṛ (*savitā*) ... has set up the deathless (*amṛtam*) light (*jyotiḥ* [acc. sg. nt.]) for all people (*viśvajanyam* [acc. sg.]); the eye (*cakṣuḥ*) of the gods (*devānām*) has been born, dawn (*uṣāḥ*) has made visible all (*viśvam*) being (*bhuvanam* [acc. sg. nt.])'

where the aorists *ud ... aśret* 'has set up', *ajaniṣṭa* 'has been born', and *āvir akaḥ* 'has made evident' are used. The perfect and imperfect could be used as narrative forms, referring to distantly past events, including mythological deeds; e.g.

(4) *indrā̀somā mahi tad vāṁ mahitvaym̐ yuvam mahāni prathamāni cakrathuḥ | yuvaṁ sūryàvm̐ vividathùr yuvaṁ svà̀1r viśvā̀ tamāṁsy ahatan nidaś cà* (RV 6.72.1) 'Indra and Soma (*indrāsomā* [voc. du.]), great (*mahi*) is that (*tad*) greatness (*mahitvam*) of yours (*vām*). You (*yuvam*) performed the first (*prathamāni* [acc. pl. nt.]) great deeds (*mahāni*). You found the sun (*sūryam*), you (found) the heaven (*svaḥ*). You struck down all (*viśvā*) darkness (*tamāṁsi* [acc. pl. nt.]) and denigrators (*nidaḥ*).'

(5) *yajño vai devebhya ud akrāmat na vo 'ham annaṁ bhaviṣyāmīti. neti devā abruvann annam eva no bhaviṣyasīti. taṁ devā vi methire. sa haibhyo vihṛto na pra babhūva. te hocur devā na vai na itthaṁ vihṛto'laṁ bhaviṣyati. hantemaṁ yajñaṁ sam bharāmeti. tatheti taṁ sam jabhruḥ* (AiBr. 1.18) 'The ritual (*yajñaḥ*) fled from the gods (*devebhyaḥ* [abl. pl.]), saying, "I will not (*na*) be (*bhaviṣyāmi*) your (*vaḥ*) food (*annam*)." The gods said, "No, you will be our food." The gods took it apart. Thus taken apart (*vihṛtaḥ*), it was not sufficient. The gods said, "Truly, thus taken apart, it will not be sufficient for us. Let us put together this ritual." They agreed and put it together.'

In (4), the great deeds are recounted using not only the second dual perfects *cakrathuḥ* 'performed, did', *vividathuḥ* 'found' but also the imperfect *ahatam* 'struck down'. In (5), the perfects *vi methire* (3pl. mid.) 'took apart', *pra babhūva* (3sg. act.) 'was sufficient', *ūcuḥ* (3pl. act.) 'said', and *saṁ jabhruḥ* (3pl. act.) 'brought together' are used, but so are the imperfects *ud akrāmat* (3sg. act.) 'strode up', *abruvan* (3pl.) 'said'.

In addition, there are indications of dialectal differences. Thus, the following occur in the story about Aitaśa (cf. section 3.1.4.3(3)):

(6) *tasyābhyagnir aitaśāyana etyākāle'bhihāya mukham apy agṛhṇāt* (AiBr. 6.33) 'Abhyagni, son of Aitaśa, came up (*etya* 'after coming') at an inopportune time (*akāle*), suddenly approached (*abhihāya*) (him), and covered up his (*tasya*) mouth (*mukham*).'

(7) *tasya hābhyagnir aitaśāyano jyeṣṭhaḥ putro'bhidrutya mukham api jagrāha* (GBr. 2.6.13) 'Abhyagni, eldest (*jyeṣṭhaḥ*) son of Aitaśa, ran up (*abhidrutya*) and covered up his mouth.'

(8) *tasya ha jyeṣṭhaḥ putro'bhisṛtya mukham api jagrāha* (KBr. 30.4.18) 'His eldest son ran up (*abhisṛtya*) and covered up his mouth.'

Example (6) has the imperfect *apy agṛhṇāt* but (7) and (8) have the corresponding perfect *api jagrāha*. Similarly, in the same story, *Aitareyabrāhmaṇa so'bravīt putrān* 'he said to his sons' contrasts with *sa ha putrān uvāca* of the *Gopathabrāhmaṇa* and the *Kauṣītakibrāhmaṇa*.

In the language of Pāṇini's time and place, aorist, imperfect and perfect were distinguished, and this has exact parallels in earlier Vedic texts (section 3.1.3.2.1). Given the preference for the imperfect when speaking of past events in the first person, even in early Vedic texts, and that the reportative perfect is not only characteristic of Pāṇini's speech but also found elsewhere in Brāhmaṇa texts, it is possible to say – although this is not the general view – that at an early stage of Indo-Aryan the contrasts Pāṇini describes were prevalent and that this state was retained longest in the peripheral northwest and east. The central area innovated by eliminating the contrast between perfect and imperfect, leaving a contrast between a narrative perfect/ imperfect and an aorist. Perfect and imperfect forms were also used according to metrical requirements. For example, *idaṁ vacanam abravīt* '... said this (*idaṁ vacanam* 'this statement' [acc. sg. nt.])', with the imperfect *abravīt*, is a common fourth pāda of anuṣṭubh verses in the *Rāmāyaṇa* and *Mahābhārata*; *tam uvāca . . .* '... said to him', with the perfect *uvāca*, is also a frequent beginning of an anuṣṭubh in the same texts. In the *Mahābhārata* the narrative is connected with . . . *uvāca* '... said' in prose introductions outside the scheme of metrical regulation. In a subsequent Middle Indic development the aorist alone persisted as the major preterit finite verb form in Pāli and Ardhamāgadhī.

One can also trace developments in the formation of aorists. Thus, in the language of Pāṇini's time and place, *gam* regularly forms a thematic aorist (*agamat, agamatām, agaman* etc.) and the aorist of *kṛ* is sigmatic (*akārṣīt, akārṣṭām, akārṣuḥ*). Both of these already appear in Vedic, but earliest Vedic also had root aorists; e.g. 2–3sg. *agan, akar*. Pāṇini (2.4.80) notes that the root aorists of these and several other verbs are limited to mantras. The interplay of such forms and their replacements is observable: Yāska (Nir. 4.10) and Patañjali (Bh. I.4.10, 13–14) cite ṚV 10.71.2, where the phrase *vācam akrata* 'produced speech' is used. In their exegesis, they replace the root aorist form *akrata* (3pl. mid.) with the current form *akṛṣata*.

In the language of Pāṇini's time, imperatives and optatives are regularly formed from present stems (sections 3.1.4.1–2). Such forms are known from the earliest Vedic texts. On the other hand, Vedic also allows such imperatives and optatives to be formed directly from a root; e.g. *gahi* (*gam* 'go'), *śrudhi* (*śru* 'hear, listen'), *gamyāḥ*.

Vedic also had some verbal categories that were gradually eliminated. One of these is the injunctive; e.g. *carat* and *bhūt* corresponding to the imperfect *acarat* 'go around, walk' and the aorist *abhūt* 'came about, became'. Unaugmented aorist forms of the type *kārṣīt* occur in the language of Pāṇini's time, but in construction with the negative particle *mā*, as in *mā kārṣīt* 'he should not do ...', *mā bhūt* 'let that not be'. Such constructions were known from earliest Indo-Aryan (section 3.1.1), but in Vedic injunctives were more widely used. Thus, in

(9) *agniḥ saptìvm̐ vājambhạran dàdāti ... agnī rodàsī vi carat ...* (RV 10.80.1a,c)
    'Agni gives a horse (*saptim* [acc. sg.]) that carries off the prize (*vājambharam*) ...
    Agni wanders about through the two worlds (*rodasī* [acc. du. nt.]). ...'

the injunctive *vi carat* 'wanders around' is coordinated with the present *dadāti* 'gives' in stating a general truth. Subjunctive forms also occur in such statements; e.g.

(10) *na dùṣṭutī martyò vindatẹ vasu na sredhàntam̐ rạyir nàṣat* (RV 7.32.21ab) 'A man (*martyah* [nom. sg.] 'mortal') does not (*na*) find (*vindate*) wealth (*vasu* [acc. sg. nt.]) through bad praise (*duṣṭutī* [instr. sg. f.]); wealth (*rayih* [nom. sg.]) does not reach (*naṣat*) one who is faulty in performing ritual (*sredhantam* [acc. sg. m.]).'

The aorist subjunctive active *naṣat* and the present indicative middle *vindate* are coordinated. Subjunctives occur also in purpose clauses, as in

(11) *tam īṣ̐āṅ jagàtas tạsthuṣạs patìm ... hūmahe vạyam | pūṣā nọ yathā vedàsām̐ asàd vṛdhe ràkṣitā pāyur adàbdhah svạstayè* (RV.1.89.5) 'We (*vayam*) call (*hūmahe*) that one (*tam*) who has power (*īṣānam* [acc. sg. m. pres. ptcpl.]) as master (*patim*) over what moves (*jagatah* [gen. sg.]), of what stands still (*tasthuṣah* [gen. sg.]), so that (*yathā*) Pūṣan might be (*asat*) keeper (*rakṣitā*) of possessions (*vedasām* [gen. pl.]) for growth (*vṛdhe*), undeceivable (*adabdhah*) protector (*pāyuh*) for well being (*svastaye*)'

with the present subjunctive *asat*. The subjunctive occurs in other kinds of dependent clauses, as well as independent clauses conveying commands; e.g.

(12) *ā ghà gamạd yadị śravàt sahạsraṇībhir ūtibhìh | vājèbhịr upà nọ havàm* (RV 1.30.8) 'Let (Indra) come (*ā ... gamat*) – if he hears (*yadi śravat*) – to our call (*havam*), with assistance (*ūtibhih* [instr. pl. f.]) that leads to thousands (*sahasraṇībhih*), with prizes (*vājebhih*)'

where *yadi śravat* and *ā ... gamat* have the root aorist subjunctives of *śru* and *gam*. In (11) and (12), subjunctives are used in subordinate clauses introduced by *yathā* 'so that' and *yadi* 'if'. The optative too occurs with *yathā* in purpose clauses; e.g.

(13) *ā daivyà vṛṇīmahe'vàm̐sị bṛhaspatir no mahạ ā sàkhāyah | yathā bhavèma mīḷhuṣẹ anã̀gā yo nò dā̀tā pàrāvatàḥ ppitevà* (RV 7.97.2) 'Friends (*sakhāyah* [voc. pl.]), we elect (*ā ... vṛṇīmahe*) the divine (*daivyā* [acc. pl. nt.]) help (*avām̐si* [acc. pl. nt.]) – Bṛhaspati grants (*mahe ā*) to us (*nah*) – so that we might be faultless (*anāgāh* [nom. pl. m.]) toward the generous one (*mīḷhuṣe* [dat sg. m.]) who (*yah* [nom. sg. m.]) grants (*dātā* 'giver' [nom. sg. m.]) us from afar (*parāvatah*) as (*iva*) a father (*pitā*) does'

with the optative *bhavema* (1pl.). Although in earliest Vedic *yadi* normally occurs with a subjunctive, it too came to be used with optatives, as in

(14) *yadi bibhīyād duścarmā bhaviṣyāmīti somāpauṣṇaṃ śyāmam ā làbheta* (TS 2.1.4.3)
'If one should fear being stricken by a skin disease (*duścarmā bhaviṣyāmīti* "I will become bad-skinned"), he should sacrifice (*ā labheta* [3sg. opt. mid.]) a black animal (*śyāmam* [acc. sg. m.]) dedicated to Soma and Pūṣan'

where *yadi bibhīyāt* 'if one should fear' is used.

The subjunctive was gradually replaced by presents, optatives and imperatives. Pāṇini (3.4.7) notes that subjunctives belong to Vedic usage. Subjunctive forms such as *karavāṇi* persist, integrated into the imperative system (section 3.1.4.1). As can be seen, the subjunctive has a stem vowel -*ǎ*- added to a full-grade base and either primary or secondary endings.

There are other categories which, though not eliminated in later Sanskrit, had more varied forms in Vedic. A derivate with -*tum* is used to refer to an act which is the purpose for which a related act is performed; e.g. *pratinetum* in *ahaṃ tu tam ... upayātaḥ pratinetum ... ayodhyāṃ* (section 3.1.5.2(3)) 'I have come to take ... back to Ayodhyā'. In such constructions a dative of an abstract action noun can be used alternatively, e.g.

(15) a. *devadatto bhoktuṃ gṛhaṃ gacchati*   b. *devadatto bhojanāya gṛhaṃ gacchati*
'Devadatta is going home to eat'

have *bhoktum* 'to eat' and the dative of *bhojana-* 'eating'; cf. 2.5.1.7(3): *iṣṭaye*. Infinitives like *bhoktum* are also used in constructions of the types

(16) *devadattaḥ kaṭaṃ kartum icchati* (section 3.1.6.2(1))

(17) *devadattaḥ kaṭaṃ kartuṃ śaknoti* 'Devadatta can make a mat.'

In (16), a given action is the object of desiring by the same agent; in (17), *kartum* 'make' occurs in construction with one of a specific set of verbs, including *śak* 'be able', *dhṛṣ* 'dare', and *jñā* 'know'. In Vedic, *śak* occurs also with root noun accusatives such as *vibhājam* 'divide', *āruham* 'mount, get on or in', *apalumpam* 'break away'; e.g.

(18) *agnív̇ṃ vai devā vibhājan nāśaknuvan* (MS 1.6.4) 'The gods were not (*na*) able (*aśaknuvan*) to divide Agni.'

(19) *na ye śekur yajñiyāṃ nāvàm āruhàm* (ṚV 10.44.6c) '... who were not able (*śekuḥ*) to get into the sacrificial boat.'

(20) *agnír vai sṛṣṭá úlbam apalúmpan nāśaknot* (MS 1.6.5) 'When Agni had been created (*sṛṣṭaḥ* [nom. sg. m. past ptcpl.]), he could not break away the embryonic cover.'

Vedic also has a series of infinitive forms which are not used in the language of Pāṇini's time and area; e.g. *jīvase* 'to live', *pātavai* 'to drink', *gantàve* 'to go', *prayai* 'to go to', *rohiṣyai* 'to grow'. The derivate with -*tum*, historically an accusative singular of an action noun in -*tu* – the dative corresponding to which ends in -*tave* – came to have separate status, but it nevertheless continued to alternate with dative forms of action nouns.

The absolutive shows a comparable development from Vedic to the later language, where it is formed with *tvā* after simple verb bases and in negative compounds and *ya* in other compounds (section 3.2.4.1). Vedic has additional formations, with -*tvāya* (e.g. *dattvāya* 'after giving'), -*tvī* (e.g. *pītvī* 'after drinking'). Pāṇini (7.1.47–9) notes these as well as *iṣṭvīnam* 'after venerating with a rite'.

There are also finite forms particular to Vedic. A group of variations concerns middle endings. Vedic has third person endings without *t*; e.g. *śaye* 'lies', *duhe* 'milks, gives milk', *aduha* 'milked, gave milk', besides *śete, dugdhe, adugdha*. The type *aduha* was subsequently marked for person by adding *-t* (*aduhat*), and the corresponding third plural ending *-ra* was marked for person by adding *-n* or *-m*: *aduhran* (*duh*), *asṛgran, asṛgram* ('have been let loose'). 3pl. mid. perf. *-re* (e.g. *cakre* [*kṛ* 'do, make']) occurs in addition to *-ire* (*cakrire*) and 2pl. imp. mid. *-dhvāt* occurs beside *-dhvam*; e.g. *vārayadhvāt* 'keep away', *antar... vārayadhvāt* 'hold in'. Other Vedic particularities are:

3sg.perf. *sasūva* 'engendered' equivalent to *suṣuve*
1sg. *-īm* corresponding to 2sg *-īḥ* and 3sg. *-īt*, e.g. *vadhīm* 'slew'
2pl. act. *-tana, thana*, e.g. *dadhātana* 'put', *niṣ kṛṇotana* (2pl. imper.) 'prepare', *sthana* 'you are', *iṣṭhana* 'send'
1pl. act. *-masi*, e.g. *dīpayāmasi* 'we make to shine'
2pl. imper. act. *-tāt*, e.g. *kṛṇutāt* 'make', *gamayatāt* 'make to go'
1sg. subj. act. *-ā*, e.g. *kim ... kṛṇavā* 'what will I do?'

Another development concerns passives. In early Vedic a form like *stave* could be passive ('is praised'), construed with an agentive instrumental form; e.g.

(21) *bhāsvatī ... divaḥ stàve duhitā gotàmebhiḥ* (ṚV 1.92.7) '(Dawn,) the effulgent (*bhāsvatī*) daughter (*duhitā*) of heaven (*divaḥ*) is praised by the Gotamas (*gotamebhiḥ*).'

In aorist and future passives also no special passive affix occurs with medio-passive endings; e.g. *astāvi* (section 3.1.3.2.3b(1)), *staviṣyase* (section 3.1.3.3(1)). For the present and imperfect passives, however, there was from earliest Vedic a marked form, with the suffix *-ya-*; e.g. *stūyase* 'you are praised' in

(22) *sahasriṇaṃ vājạm ... sasạvān tsan tstū̀yase jātavedaḥ* (ṚV 3.22.1) '(Agni) Jātavedas, (voc.sg. *jātavedaḥ*), you are praised, having won (*sasavān* [nom. sg. m. perf. ptcpl.]) prizes (*vājam* [acc.sg.m.]) in the thousands (*sahasriṇam* [acc. sg. m.] 'consisting of thousands').'

In the current language Pāṇini describes this had become regular for passive presents and imperfects of verbs, regardless of how they formed corresponding non-passive stems.

3.2 Nominal system

3.2.1 Introduction

The nominal system formally distinguishes nouns and adjectives on the one hand and pronouns on the other. There are three numbers – singular, dual, and plural – and seven cases in addition to a vocative. The nominal forms in their traditional order are: nominative (vocative), accusative, instrumental, dative, ablative, genitive, locative. Nouns generally have an assigned gender: masculine, feminine, neuter. There is no absolute distinction between nouns and adjectives with respect to inflection, but modifiers take the number and gender of the terms they qualify.

Pronouns are personal (first and second person), demonstrative (deictic), inter-rogative, and relative. Pronouns other than personal pronouns observe gender distinctions. There are also endings particular to pronouns (see section 3.2.2.4).

In addition, Sanskrit has indeclinable terms, including particles such as the connective *ca* 'and' (sentence and nominal connective) and the negative particle *na*, as well as terms such as *yad*, *yadi* 'if', *tad*, *tarhi* 'then', *karhi* 'when?', *tataḥ* 'thence', *yataḥ* 'whence', *kutaḥ* 'whence?', *yadā* 'when', *tadā* 'then', *kadā* 'when?', *yatra* 'where', *tatra* 'there', *kutra* 'where?', derived from pronominals (section 3.2.4.2). There are also preverbs, which regularly occur immediately preceding a verb or another preverb – although in Vedic they can be separated from a verb or follow it – as well as pre- and post-positional terms like *adhi*, *anu*, which co-occur with particular case forms.

Nominal bases can be derived from verbal bases (section 3.1.5). They are also derived from members of syntactic strings, forming secondary nominal derivates (*taddhitānta*) and compounds of four general types (section 3.2.4.3).

3.2.2 Case system, stems and endings

3.2.2.1 Case distinctions

All cases are formally distinguished only in the singular of masculine -*a*-stems. The dual has three groups of forms: nom.-voc.-acc., instr.-dat.-abl., gen.-loc. Dative and ablative plural forms are identical except for personal pronouns; feminine -*ā*-stems have identical nominative and accusative plural forms; neuter stems do not distinguish nominative and accusative. Forms of the following stems will serve as illustrations: *deva*- (m.) 'god', *phala*- (nt.) 'fruit'; *jihvā*- (f.) 'tongue'; *agni*- (m.) 'fire, Agni', *mati*- (f.) 'thought', *vāri*- (nt.) 'water', *tri*- (m., nt.) 'three', *vātapramī*- (m.) 'a swift antelope', *devī*- (f.) 'goddess', *strī*- (f.) 'woman, female', *śrī*- (f.) 'splendour'; *sūnu*- (m.) 'son', *dhenu*- (f.) 'cow', *madhu*- (nt.) 'honey'; *khalapū*- (m.) 'one who cleans a threshing floor', *vadhū*- (f.) 'bride', *bhrū*- (f.) 'eyebrow'; *pitṛ̣*- (m.) 'father', *kartṛ̣*- (m., nt.) 'doer', *mātṛ̣*- (f.) 'mother', *svasṛ̣*- (f.) 'sister', *tisṛ̣*- (f.) 'three'; *go*- (f., m.); 'cow, ox', *rai*- 'wealth' (m., f.); *rājan*- (m.) 'king', *nāman*- (nt.) 'name', *yaśas*- (nt.) 'fame'. These forms are summarized in table 4.3, where the stems listed in the first column are the items preceding final dashes: *deva*-, *phala*- and so on. Interior dashes (as in *dev-a*-, *phal-a*-) follow the segments which precede the elements shown in other columns as final parts of words: *devaḥ*, *deva*, *devam* and so forth. The chart is thus intended to illustrate forms, without regard to decisions concerning the precise shape of particular morphs; e.g *devam* leaves open whether the ending is -*am* in accordance with Pāṇini's system or -*m* in accordance with Western grammars.

Adjectives inflect similarly, although adjectival stems corresponding to all types are not found; e.g. *nava*- (m., nt.), *navā*- (f.) 'new', *śuci*- (m., f., nt.) 'bright, pure', *laghvī*- (f.), *laghu*- (m., f., nt.) 'light, short' inflect in the same manner as *deva*-, *jihvā*-, *agni*-, *mati*-, *vāri*-, *devī*-, *sūnu*-, *dhenu*-, and *madhu*-.

3.2.2.2 Nominal stem alternation

Stem forms vary, as noted in section 3.2.2.1. Some alternations depend on phonological contexts. Stems in final palatal and retroflex stops have alternations of the types *vāc-/vāg-/vāk*- (f.) 'speech, voice', *viś-/viḍ-/viṭ*- (f.) 'settlement', *tviṣ-/tviḍ-/tviṭ*- (f.) 'light, lustre'. The first variant occurs before vowels, the second and third respectively before voiced and voiceless consonants and as alternatives before pause; e.g.

TABLE 4.3: NOMINAL FORMS

Stem	Singular								Dual			Plural					
	N	V	A	I	D	Ab	G	L	NAV	IDAb	GL	NV	A	I	DAb	G	L
dev-a-	aḥ	a	am	ena	āya	āt	asya	e	au	ābhyām	ayoḥ	āḥ	ān	aiḥ	ebhyaḥ	ānām	eṣu
phal-a-	am	a	am	ena	āya	āt	asya	e	e	ābhyām	ayoḥ	āni	āni	aiḥ	ebhyaḥ	ānām	eṣu
jihv-ā-	ā	e	ām	ayā	āyai	āyāḥ	asya	e	e	ābhyām	ayoḥ	āḥ	āḥ	ābhiḥ	ābhyaḥ	ānām	āsu
agn-i-	iḥ	e	im	inā	aye	eḥ	āyāḥ / eḥ	au	ī	ibhyām	yoḥ	ayaḥ	īn	ibhiḥ	ibhyaḥ	īnām	iṣu
mat-i-	iḥ	e	im	yā	yai / aye	yāḥ / eḥ	yāḥ / eḥ	yām / au	ī	ibhyām	yoḥ	ayaḥ	īḥ	ibhiḥ	ibhyaḥ	īnām	iṣu
vār-i- (n.) / tr-i- (m.)	i	i	i / iyam	inā	ine	inaḥ	inaḥ	ini	inī	ibhyām	inoḥ	īṇi / ayaḥ / īṇi	īni / īn / īni	ibhiḥ	ibhyaḥ	īṇām	iṣu
-pram-ī	īḥ	īḥ	īm	yā	ye	yāḥ	yāḥ	ī	yau	ībhyām	yoḥ	yaḥ	īn	ībhiḥ	ībhyaḥ	yām	īṣu
dev-ī-	ī	i	īm	yā	yai	yāḥ	yāḥ	yām	yau	ībhyām	yoḥ	yaḥ	īḥ	ībhiḥ	ībhyaḥ	īnām	īṣu
str-ī-	ī	i	īm / iyam	iyā	iyai	iyāḥ	iyāḥ	iyām	iyau	ībhyām	iyoḥ	iyaḥ	īḥ / iyaḥ	ībhiḥ	ībhyaḥ	īnām	īṣu
śr-ī-	īḥ	īḥ	iyam	iyā	iyai / iye	iyāḥ / iyaḥ	iyāḥ / iyaḥ	iyām / iyi	iyau	ībhyām	iyoḥ	iyaḥ	iyaḥ	ībhiḥ	ībhyaḥ	īṇām / iyām	īṣu
sūn-u-	uḥ	o	um	unā	ave	oḥ	oḥ	au	ū	ubhyām	voḥ	avaḥ	ūn	ubhiḥ	ubhyaḥ	ūnām	uṣu
dhen-u-	uḥ	o	um	vā	vai	vāḥ	vāḥ	vām / au	ū	ubhyām	voḥ	avaḥ	ūḥ	ubhiḥ	ubhyaḥ	ūnām	uṣu
madh-u-	u	u	u	unā	une	unaḥ	unaḥ	uni	unī	ubhyām	unoḥ	ūni	ūni	ubhiḥ	ubhyaḥ	ūnām	uṣu
-p-ū	ūḥ	ūḥ	vam	vā	ve	vaḥ	vaḥ	vi	vau	ūbhyām	voḥ	vaḥ	vaḥ	ūbhiḥ	ūbhyaḥ	vām	ūṣu
vadh-ū-	ūḥ	u	ūm	vā	vai	vāḥ	vāḥ	vām	vau	ūbhyām	voḥ	vaḥ	ūḥ	ūbhiḥ	ūbhyaḥ	ūnām	ūṣu
bhr-ū-	ūḥ	u	uvam	uvā	uve	uvaḥ	uvaḥ	uvi	uvau	ūbhyām	uvoḥ	uvaḥ	uvaḥ	ūbhiḥ	ūbhyaḥ	uvām	ūṣu
pit-r̥-	ā	aḥ	aram	rā	re	uḥ	uḥ	ari	arau	r̥bhyām	roḥ	araḥ	r̥̄n	r̥bhiḥ	r̥bhyaḥ	r̥̄ṇām	r̥ṣu
kart-r̥-	ā	aḥ	āram	rā	re	uḥ	uḥ	ari	ārau	r̥bhyām	roḥ	āraḥ	r̥̄n	r̥bhiḥ	r̥bhyaḥ	r̥̄ṇām	r̥ṣu
māt-r̥-	ā	aḥ	aram	rā	re	uḥ	uḥ	ari	arau	r̥bhyām	roḥ	araḥ	r̥̄ḥ	r̥bhiḥ	r̥bhyaḥ	r̥̄ṇām	r̥ṣu
svas-r̥-	ā	aḥ	āram	rā	re	uḥ	uḥ	ari	ārau	r̥bhyām	roḥ	āraḥ	r̥̄ḥ	r̥bhiḥ	r̥bhyaḥ	r̥̄ṇām	r̥ṣu
tis-r̥-			raḥ						araḥ	r̥bhyām	roḥ	raḥ	raḥ	r̥bhiḥ	r̥bhyaḥ	r̥ṇām	r̥ṣu
g-o-	auḥ	auḥ	ām	avā	ave	oḥ	oḥ	avi	āvau	obhyām	avoḥ	āvaḥ	āḥ	obhiḥ	obhyaḥ	avām	oṣu
r-ai-	āḥ	āḥ	āyam	āyā	āye	āyaḥ	āyaḥ	āyi	āyau	ābhyām	āyoḥ	āyaḥ	āyaḥ	ābhiḥ	ābhyaḥ	āyām	āsu
rāj-an-	ā	an	ānam	ñā	ñe	ñaḥ	ñaḥ	ñi / ani	ānau	abhyām	ñoḥ	ānaḥ	ñaḥ	abhiḥ	abhyaḥ	ñām	asu
nām-an-	a	an	a	nā	ne	naḥ	naḥ	ni / ani	anī	abhyām	noḥ	āni	āni	abhiḥ	abhyaḥ	nām	asu
yaś-as-	aḥ	aḥ	aḥ	asā	ase	asaḥ	asaḥ	asi	asī	obhyām	asoḥ	āṃsi	āṃsi	obhiḥ	obhyaḥ	asām	assu / aḥsu

nom. sg. *vāk, viṭ, tviṭ*
nom.-acc. du. *vāc-au, viś-au, tviṣ-au*
nom.-acc. pl. *vāc-aḥ, viś-aḥ, tviṣ-aḥ*
acc. sg. *vāc-am, viś-am, tviṣ-am*
instr.-dat.-abl. du. *vāg-bhyām, viḍ-bhyām, tviḍ-bhyām*
loc. pl. *vāk-ṣu, viṭ-su, tviṭ-su*

Other alternations depend on grammatical contexts. A distinction is made between what western grammarians call strong and weak endings. All nominative endings and the accusative singular and dual count as strong endings after non-neuter stems, as do the nominative and accusative plural with neuter stems; the rest are weak. The nominative singular also has features of its own. Weak endings beginning with consonants other than *y* are treated phonologically as preceded by a word boundary.

Certain stems have vowel alternation. *-i-* and *-u-*stems of the types *agni-, sūnu-* have alternants with *-e-* and *-o-* (*-ay-* and *-av-* before vowels). *sakhi-* (m.) 'friend' differs: the nominative singular has *-ā* (*sakhā*), and other strong forms have *-āy: sakhāy-au, sakhāy-aḥ, sakhāy-am*, opposed to an *i-* stem *sakhi-* in the vocative singular *sakhe* and in weak forms (acc. pl. *sakhīn*, instr. sg. *sakhy-ā*, instr.-dat.-abl. du. *sakhi-bhyām*, loc. sg. *sakhy-au*, etc.). Non-neuter stems in *-ṛ-* have nominative singulars in *-ā* and *-ar-* or *-ār-* in other strong forms; *-ar* occurs in particular kinship terms (*pitṛ-, mātṛ-, bhrātṛ-*), *-ār* elsewhere. Stems in *-an* also have nominative singular forms in *-ā* (nt. *-a*) and other strong forms with *-ān-* or *-an-*, but *-n-* and *-a-* in weak forms with vocalic and consonantal endings respectively. Similarly, *-in-*stems, of the type *balin-* 'strong' (nom. sg. m. *balī*, nom.-acc. nt. *bali*), have preconsonantal weak forms in *-i* of the type *bali-bhyām, bal-ibhiḥ*. Stems with *-van* or *-man* such that *-v-* and *-m-* are parts of clusters do not have alternants with *-vn- -mn-*; e.g. *parvaṇ-ā* (instr. sg. nt.) 'joint, knot' (nom.-acc. sg. *parva*), *karman-ā* 'deed, action, object' (*karma*) as opposed to *rājñ-ā, nāmn-ā, takṣṇ-ā* 'carpenter' (nom. sg. *takṣā*). The type *śvan-/śva-/śun-* 'dog' (*śvā śvan śvān-am śun-ā śun-e śun-aḥ śun-i, śvān-au śva-bhyām śun-oḥ, śvān-aḥ śun-aḥ śva-bhiḥ śva-bhyaḥ śun-ām śva-su*) is restricted to a few nouns, including *yuvan-* 'youth' (m.): *yuvā, yū-naḥ, yuva-bhyām*.

Participles of the type *sat-/sant-* 'being', *bhavat-/bhavant-* 'being, becoming' also have forms with and without *-n-*: m. nom. sg. *san*, nom.-acc. du. *sant-au*, nom. pl. *sant-aḥ*, acc. sg. *sant-am*, acc. pl. *sat-aḥ*, instr. sg. *sat-ā; bhavan, bhavant-au, bhavant-aḥ, bhavant-am, bhavat-aḥ, bhavat-ā.*

Certain stems have augmented forms before strong endings. Neuters have alternants with a nasal augment in nom.-acc. pl. forms, *-n-* between vowels and anusvāra before *-s-*; e.g. *phalān-i* 'fruits', (nom.-acc. sg. *phalam*), *yaśāṁs-i* (nom.-acc. sg. *yaśaḥ*), *havīṁṣ-i* 'oblations' (*haviḥ*), *yajūṁṣ-i* 'ritual formulae' (*yajuḥ*). Some stems have a nasal augment in masculine strong forms. Perfect participles are formed with a suffix *-vas/-vad/-us* and *-vāṁs-* in prevocalic strong forms; e.g. m. nom. sg. *vidvān*, nom.-acc. du. *vidvāṁs-au*, nom. pl. *vidvāṁs-aḥ*, acc. sg. *vidvāṁs-am*, acc. pl. *vidus-aḥ*, instr. sg. *vidus-ā*, instr.-dat.- abl. du. *vidvad-bhyām* 'knowing, learned'. Similarly, derivates with *-īyas-* (section 3.2.4.2.3) have masculine strong forms with *-īyān, -iyāṁs-*; e.g. *paṭīyān* 'quite sharp', *paṭīyāṁs-au, paṭīyāṁs-aḥ, paṭīyāṁs-am, paṭīyāṁs-au paṭiyas-aḥ, paṭiyas-ā, paṭiyo-bhyām. -a*-stems have *-ā* in singular and dual forms of the type *devā-ya, devā-bhyām* and *-e* before plural endings with *bh-* and *s-* (→ *ṣ-*).

There are heteroclitic stems. *asthi-* 'bone', *dadhi-* 'yogurt, curds', *sakthi-* 'thigh', *akṣi-* 'eye', all neuter, occur in nominative and accusative forms and before consonantal endings, but forms of stems in *-an-* (*asthan-*, *dadhan-*, *sakthan-*, *akṣan-*) occur with other vocalic endings: *asthi*, *asthin-ī*, *asthīn-i*: *asthn-ā*, *asthi-bhyām*, *asthi-bhiḥ*, and so on. Some neuter stems with -*r̥*- in the nominative-accusative alternate with stems in *-an-*: *asr̥k*: *asn-ā* 'blood', *yakr̥t*: *yakn-ā* 'liver', *śakr̥t*: *śakn-ā* 'faeces'. *kroṣṭr̥-* 'jackal' occurs in strong forms (*kroṣṭā*, *kroṣṭār-au*, *kroṣṭār-aḥ*, *kroṣṭār-am*); *kroṣṭu-* occurs in the acc. pl. *kroṣṭūn* and in weak forms with consonantal endings (e.g. instr.-dat.-abl. du. *kroṣṭu-bhyām*); in other forms, the stems alternate (e.g. instr. sg. *kroṣṭr-ā*, *kroṣṭu-nā*). This alternation reflects a Middle-Indic development of -*u*- for -*r̥*-.

Certain alternations depend on gender. *tri-* 'three' is the masculine-neuter stem, in contrast to the feminine stem *tisr̥-*: nom. pl. *tray-aḥ*, acc. *trīn* (m.), nom.-acc. *trīṇ-i* (nt.), instr. *tri-bhiḥ*, dat.-abl. *tri-bhyaḥ*, gen. *tray-āṇām*, loc. *tri-ṣu*, feminine *tisr-aḥ* and so on (section 3.2.2.1). Similarly: *catvār-aḥ*, *catur-aḥ*, *catvār-i*, *catur-bhiḥ*, *catur-bhyaḥ*, *catur-ṇām*, *catur-ṣu* as against *catasr-aḥ*, *catasr̥bhiḥ* etc.

Some variations reflect dialectal and historical differences. In Vedic, the contrast between the types *śrī-* and *devī-* (section 3.2.2.1) had a larger domain than later. In addition to the type *devī-*, known from earliest Vedic onward, there were forms such as *vr̥kī-ḥ* (nom. sg.) 'she wolf', *nadiy-àm* (acc. sg. [*nady-àm*]) 'river', *nadiy-àḥ* (acc.pl. [*nady-àḥ*]), *veśiy-ā̀* (instr. sg. [*veśy-ā̀*]) 'needle', *vr̥kiy-è* (dat. sg. [*vr̥ky-è*]), *nadiy-àḥ* (gen. sg. [*nady-àḥ*]), *gaurī̀* (loc. sg., see 2.5.1.7(6)), *devīḥ* (nom. pl.), *mahīḥ* (nom.-acc. pl.) 'large, great'. The contrast was largely eliminated; the type *nadiyàḥ* was retained in some forms, although with a -*yà*-, -*yā̀* – also in the traditional Vedic recitations – for earlier -*iyà-*, -*iyā̀*. The svarita accentuation of nom.-acc. dual and nom. pl. forms of the type *devy-aù*, *devy-àḥ*, opposed to high-pitched vocalic endings in *devy-ā̀* and so on, reflects the earlier type diversity. The -*n*-stem of heteroclitics like *asthi-/asthan-* too had a wider range in Vedic: it occurred before consonant-initial endings, as in *asthabhiḥ*, *akṣa-bhiḥ*.

In the current language Pāṇini describes, the stem forms *pathi-* and *path-* 'path, way' occur respectively before consonantal and vocalic weak endings: *pathi-bhyām pathi-bhiḥ pathi-bhyaḥ pathi-ṣu*, *path-aḥ path-ā path-e path-aḥ path-oḥ path-ām path-i*. The nominative singular is *panthāḥ*, and *panthān-* precedes other strong endings: *panthān-au*, *panthān-aḥ*, *panthān-am*. Vedic differs in having nominative singular and plural *panthāḥ* and accusative singular *panthām*. In Vedic, a stem *rayí-* 'wealth' occurs before consonants (nom. sg. *rayíḥ*, acc. sg. *rayim*), with *rāy-* before vowels, as in the following forms attested in the Ṛgveda: *rāy-àḥ* (nom. pl.), *rāy-aḥ* (acc. pl., abl.-gen. sg.), *rāy-ā* (instr. sg.), *rāy-e* (dat. sg.), *rāy-ām* (gen. pl.). Due to analogic remodelling, the current language Pāṇini describes has *rā-* before consonants (*rāḥ* [nom. sg.], *rā-bhyām*, *rā-bhiḥ*, *rā-bhyaḥ*, *rāsu*) and *rāy-* before vowels, not only in *rāy-ā* and etc. but also in *rāy-am* (acc. sg.).

3.2.2.3 Pronominal stem alternation

3.2.2.3.1 Personal pronouns have *asmad-* (1p), *mad-* (1sg.), *yuṣmad-* (2p), *tvad-* (2sg.) in derivates such as *yuṣmadīya-*, *tvadīya-* 'of you, pertaining to you', *asmadīya-*, *madīya-*. Case forms of personal pronouns show complex alternation:

Sg. *aham mām mayā̀ mahyàm mat mamà mayi*, *tvam tvām tvayā̀ tubhyàm tvat tavà tvayi*
Du. *āvām āvā́bhyām āvayòḥ*, *yuvām yuvā́bhyām yuvayòḥ*
Pl. *vayam asmān asmā́bhiḥ asmabhyàm asmat asmā́kam asmāsù*
yūyam yuṣmān yuṣmā́bhiḥ yuṣmabhyàm yuṣmat yuṣmā́kam yuṣmāsù

The accusative, dative and genitive have unaccented enclitic forms, which occur only in sentence interior position. In the dual (*vām, nau*) and plural (*vas, nas*) there is one such form for each pronoun, but in the singular accusative (*mā tvā*) and dative-genitive (*me te*) clitic forms contrast.

There is another pronoun for the second person, which distinguishes between male and female reference: the polite pronoun *bhavat-* (f. *bhavat-ī-*), which also distinguishes different numbers. Except for the nominative singular masculine (*bhavān*), *bhavat-* inflects like a participle such as *bhavat-* 'being, becoming'; *bhavatī-* inflects like *devī-* (section 3.2.2.1). Unlike other personal pronouns, these occur with third person verb forms; e.g. *bhavān kutra gacchati* 'where (*kutra*) are you (*bhavān*) going (*gacchati* [3sg. pres.])?' *atrabhavat-* and *tatrabhavat-* also are used, with reference to persons held in high esteem.

3.2.2.3.2 Demonstrative pronouns are deictic, with a contrast between proximate and distant reference: *idam* 'this' and *adas* 'that yonder'. According to grammatical and lexicographic tradition, *etad* (nom.-acc. sg. nt.) has more proximate reference than *idam* 'this', and *tad* refers to something not in sight. In continuous discourse, *tad-* usually is coreferential with the immediate antecedent; e.g. *tasya* and *tāsu* in the second and third sentences of section 3.1.3.2.1(1) are coreferential with *hariścandraḥ* and *jāyāḥ* of the preceding sentences. *tad-* also supplies a correlative in construction with a relative pronoun. There is also a pronoun *tyad-* 'that'.

All these show stem alternation: *sa-/ta-* (*eṣa-/eta-*), *adas-/asau-/amū-/amī-*, *i-/ay-/id-/ima-/ana-/a-*. The following are their paradigms; except for the nominative-accusative forms shown, neuter and masculine forms are homophonous:

Sg. m. *saḥ tam tena tasmai tasmāt tasya tasmin, asau amum amunā amuṣmai amuṣmāt amuṣya amuṣmin, ayam imam anena asmai asmāt asya asmin* nt. *tad adaḥ idam*

f. *sā tām tayā tasyai tasyāḥ tasyāḥ tasyām, asau amūm amuyā amuṣyai amuṣyāḥ amuṣyāḥ amuṣyām, iyam imām anayā asyai asyāḥ asyāḥ asyām*

Du. m. *tau tābhyām tayoḥ, amū amūbhyām amuyoḥ, imau ābhyām anayoḥ* nt. *te amū ime*

f. *te tābhyām tayoḥ, amū amūbhyām amuyoḥ, ime ābhyām anayoḥ*

Pl. m. *te tān taiḥ tebhyaḥ tebhyaḥ teṣām teṣu, amī amūn amībhiḥ amībhyaḥ amībhyaḥ amīṣām amīṣu, ime imān ebhiḥ ebhyaḥ ebhyaḥ eṣām eṣu* nt. *tāni, amūni, imāni*

f. *tāḥ tāḥ tābhiḥ tābhyaḥ tābhyaḥ tāsām tāsu, amūḥ amūḥ amūbhiḥ amūbhyaḥ amūbhyaḥ amūṣām amūṣu, imāḥ imāḥ ābhiḥ ābhyaḥ ābhyaḥ āsām āsu*

Nominative singular masculine forms *sa, eṣa, sa* occur before consonants; before vowels, forms are like those of *deva-*. For example: *sa puruṣaḥ* 'that man' vs. *so 'śvaḥ* 'that horse'.

Certain other terms also have pronominal forms; e.g. *sarva-* (f. *sarvā-*) 'all', *eka-* (f. *ekā-*) 'one': *sarve sarvasmai sarvasmāt sarveṣām sarvasmin, sarvasyāḥ sarvāsām sarvasyām; eke* ('some'): *ekasmai* etc. The nominative plural masculine forms of *prathama-* 'first', *carama-* 'last', *alpa-* 'little, few', *katipaya-* 'some', and direction words such as *pūrva-* 'eastern, prior' are optionally of the type *prathamāḥ* or *prathame*.

3.2.2.3.3 Corresponding to accented forms of the proximate pronoun *ayam* etc. and to *etad-* there are unaccented anaphoric forms: from *ena-* in accusative, instrumental singular and genitive-locative dual forms, and from *a-* in other forms of the proximate pronoun except for nominative and accusative. For example:

(1) a.
asmai	*chātrāyà*	*kambạlan*	*dèhi*
dat. sg.	dat. sg.	acc. sg.	2sg. imper.
to this	student	blanket	give

b.
athò	*asmai*	*śātàkạm*	*api dehi*
ptcle.	dat. sg.	acc. sg.	ptcle.
and then	to him	cloth garment	also

'Give this student a blanket and then give him a cloth garment too.' (Kāś. 2.4.32)

(2) a.
asti	*somò*	*ạyaṁ*	*sụtaḥ*
3sg. pres.	nom. sg.	nom. sg.	nom. sg.
is	Soma	this	pressed

b.
pibànty	*asya*	*mạrutàḥ*
3pl. pres.	gen. sg.	nom. pl.
drink	of it	Maruts

'Here is the Soma that has been pressed; the Maruts drink of it.' (ṚV 8.94.4ab)

(3) a.
na ...	*indràvm̐*	*vṛtro*	*vi*	*bíbhayat*
ptcle.	acc. sg.	nom. sg.	prev.	3sg. inj.
not	Indra	Vṛtra	frightened	

b.
ạbhy	*ènavm̐*	*vajrà ...*	*āyạta ...*
prev.	acc. sg.	nom.sg.	3sg. imperf.
towards	him	vajra	came

'Vṛtra did not frighten Indra ...; the ... vajra came upon him.' (ṚV 1.80.12)

3.2.2.3.4 The relative pronoun is *yad-*, which inflects in the same way as *tad-* (section 3.2.2.3.2): *yaḥ yad yā, yam yad yām*, and so on. *ya-* occurs also in derivates with taddhita affixes (section 3.2.4.2): *yatra, yataḥ, yarhi, yadā. yā-* occurs in the quantitative derivate *yāvat-* 'of which quantity', which inflects like the polite pronoun *bhavat-* (section 3.2.2.3.1), and *yādṛś-* 'similar' (nom. sg. m. *yādṛk*, acc. *yādṛśam*), *yādṛśa-* 'similar'.

3.2.2.3.5 The interrogative pronoun is *kim-/ka-*. The former occurs as the nom.-acc. sg. nt. *kim* and in compounds (e.g. *kiṁsvarūpa-* 'of what form?'). Other forms are from a stem *ka-* (fem. *kā-*): *kaḥ kau ke, kam kau kān, kena kābhyām kaiḥ; kā ke kāḥ, kām ke kāḥ, kayā kābhyām kābhiḥ*, and so forth. *ka-* and *ku-/kva-* occur in derivates with taddhita affixes, as in *katham* 'how?' (Vedic also *kathā*), *kutra, kva* 'where?'

3.2.2.3.6 The interrogative serves to form complexes with indefinite reference in which *cid* or *cana* follows a form of *kim-/ka-* or a derivate of this, alone or preceded by a relative pronominal form in a generalized indefinite. For example: *kaścid, kaścana* 'some one' (instr. sg. *kenacid* etc.), *yaḥ kaścid* 'whosoever', *kadācid* 'at some time', *kutracid* 'somewhere', *kathañ-cid* 'in some way'.

3.2.2.3.7 *ātman-* 'self' serves as a reflexive; e.g. Rām. 3.28.16:

(1)
prākṛtān	*rākṣasān hatvā*	*yuddhe*	*daśarathātmaja*
acc. pl. m.	acc. pl. m. gerund	loc. sg.	voc. sg.
common	Rākṣasas after killing	battle	son of Daśaratha

ātmanā	*katham*	*ātmānam*	*apraśasyaṁ*	*praśaṁsasi*
instr. sg.		acc. sg.	neg. cpd. gerdv.	2sg. pres.
yourself	how?	self	not to be praised	praise

'Son of Daśaratha, after killing lowly Rākṣasas in battle, how do you praise yourself, you who should not be praised by yourself?'

In Vedic, *tman-* also occurs, instead of *ātman-*, as in the instrumental singular *tmanā̀*, and *tanū-* too serves as a reflexive.

3.2.2.4 Distribution of endings

Distinct endings are used with different stems, and several factors play roles.

Some distinctions pertain to grammatical classes. Pronominal forms of the type *tat anyat* ('other') *te ta-smai ta-smāt te-ṣām ta-smin* and *ta-syai ta-syāḥ tā-sām ta-syām* contrast with nominal forms of the type *phalam devāḥ devāya devāt devānām deve* and *jihvāyai jihvāyāḥ jihvānām jihvāyām*. -ṛ-stems have an ablative-genitive singular in *-us*, which contrasts with others. The same ending occurs with *sakhi-* (section 3.2.2.2): *sakhyuḥ*.

Distinctions can also be semantic. Thus, *pati-* used as a kinship term has an inflection that differs from *pati-* used otherwise; e.g. *patyuḥ* (gen. sg.) 'husband', opposed to *prajāpateḥ* (gen. sg.) 'Prajāpati (master of creatures)'; similarly *patyā patye patyau* opposed to *-patinā -pataye -patau*.

Some differences in endings are connected with variants of single items; e.g. *agneḥ sūnoḥ*, with *-s* after stem-final *-e-* and *-o-*, opposed to *-as* after consonant stems, as in *rājñ-ah nāmn-ah*.

Other contrasts are associated with gender distinctions. Accusative plurals of masculine vowel stems have long vowels followed by *-n*, but comparable feminines have *-s*; e.g *pitṝn, mātṝ́ḥ* (section 3.2.2.1). Except for the dual of *-a*-stems, nominative-accusative neuter duals and plurals have *-nī* and *-ni*, contrasting with the masculine types in *-au, -ī, -ū*. Feminine stems in *-ā, -ī̆, -ū̆* have endings that distinguish them from other classes, such as loc. sg. *-ām* (see section 3.2.2.1). Non-feminine stems in *-i* and *-u* generally have an instrumental singular with *-nā*, as in *agni-nā, sūnu-nā*, except for *pati-* and *sakhi-*.

Still other differences are due to dialectal and historical factors. Instrumental singular forms like *paty-ā, sakhy-ā* are more widely represented in Vedic (e.g. *pavy-ā* 'wheel rim'), which also has instrumentals such as *paśv-ā* (m.) 'animal', *madhv-ā̀* (nt.) 'honey' in addition to the usual *-u-nā* (*paśu-nā̀, madhù-nā*) and genitive singulars such as *avy-àḥ* (gen. sg. m.) 'sheep', *paśv-aḥ* 'animal', *madhv-àḥ* (gen. sg. nt.) 'honey', *madhòḥ* besides forms in *-es, -os, -u-nas*. In Vedic *-a*-stems have instrumental plurals like *karṇèbhiḥ* ('ears'), which were later eliminated. Nominative plural feminines of the type *devī́ḥ* equivalent to *devy-àḥ* are Vedic. In the language of Brāhmaṇas, there are ablative-genitive forms of the type *śvetāyai̇* 'white', identical with the dative. Also exclusively Vedic are certain nominal and pronominal forms with particular endings, as follows:

nom.-acc.-voc. du. *-ā* in addition to *-au*; e.g. *indrā̀somā* (section 3.1.7(4))
nom. pl. *-āsaḥ* in addition to *-āḥ;* e.g. *devāsàḥ* 'gods', *vā́srāsàḥ* (m., f.) 'resounding, roaring, bellowing'
nom.-acc. sg. nt. kad besides *kim*
nom.-acc. pl. nt. *-ā* as well as *-āni;* e.g. *havyā, havyāni* 'offerings'

instr. sg. -*ā* in addition to -*ena*: *yajñā* (*yajñā yàjñā* 'with each and every rite'), *vīryà* 'heroic might'

gen. pl. -*ām* besides -*ānām*: *devām* (*devāñ janmà* 'birth of the gods')

f. instr. sg. -*ī* in addition to -*yā*; e.g. *ūtī* 'help'

loc. sg. in -*ā* as well as in -*au*; e.g. *agnā*

-*n*-stem locatives in -*an*; e.g. *ahàn* 'day' in addition to *ahàni*

loc. sg. f. in -*ī* of the type *gaurī*

dat. sg. *tubhyà, mahyà* in addition *tubhyàm, mahyàm*

nom. du. *yuvam, āvam* besides *yuvām, āvām* and *āvoḥ* for *āvayoḥ*

loc. *tve, me*, dat.-gen.-loc. *yuṣme, asme* in addition to *tvayì, mayì, yuṣmabhyàm, asmabhyàm* and so forth

3.2.3 Number words

3.2.3.1 The cardinals one through ten are: *eka- dvi- tri- catur- pañcan- ṣaṣ- saptan- aṣṭan- navan- daśan-*. All inflect for case, and the first four also observe gender distinctions. *eka-* has pronominal forms (section 3.2.2.3.2). *dvi-* appears in compounds (see below), *dvā-* and *dve-* in dual case forms *dvau* (f., nt. *dve*) *dvā-bhyām dvay-oḥ*. *tri-* inflects as a masculine and neuter -*i*-stem; feminine forms are from a stem *tisṛ-* (section 3.2.2.1). *catur-* appears in *catur-bhiḥ catur-bhyaḥ catur-ṇām catur-ṣu* (m., nt.). Feminine forms are from *catasṛ-*, comparable to *tisṛ-*. The accusative plural masculine is *catur-aḥ*, but the corresponding nominative is *catvār-aḥ*, with -*ā*-, which also appears in the nominative-accusative neuter *catvār-i*. *pañcan-, saptan-, navan-, daśan-* inflect as -*n*-stems (*pañca-bhiḥ, sapta-bhiḥ, nava-bhiḥ, daśa-bhiḥ* etc.), except for the nominative-accusative, which is endingless (*pañca, sapta, nava, daśa*), and the genitive in -*ānām* (*pañcāmām* etc.). *ṣaṭ* (nom.-acc. pl.) too is endingless. Otherwise *ṣaṣ-* inflects like a consonant stem except for the genitive (*ṣaṇṇām*): *ṣaḍ-bhiḥ ṣaḍ-bhyaḥ ṣaṇ-ṇām ṣaṭ-su*. *aṣṭan-* has a nominative-accusative form *aṣṭau*. Other forms have -*a*- or -*ā*- except in the genitive: *aṣṭābhiḥ aṣṭābhyām aṣṭānām aṣṭāsu*.

ekādaśan- '11' has *ekā-*. *dvi-* appears in compound number words such as *dvi-catvāriṁśat-* '42', *dvy-aśīti-* '82', and *dvā* appears in certain other compound number words: *dvā-daśa-* '12', *dvā-viṁśati* '22', *dvā-triṁśat-* '32'. In compound number words from the forties to the nineties, except for the eighties, *dvi-* and *dvā-* alternate: *dvā-catvāriṁśat-* etc. *tri-* and *trayas-* occur in the contexts where *dvi-* and *dvā-* occur; e.g. *trayo-daśan-* '13', *trayo-viṁśati-* '23', *tri-catvāriṁśat-/trayaś-catvāriṁśat-* '43', *try-aśīti-* '83'.

viṁśati-, triṁśat-, catvāriṁśat-, pañcāśat-, saptati-, aśīti-, navati- designate decades from twenty to ninety. They form compounds with other number words to form terms such as *eka-viṁśati-, dvā-viṁśati-, trayo-viṁśati-, catur-viṁśati-, pañca-viṁśati-, ṣaḍ-viṁśati-, sapta-viṁśati-, aṣṭā-viṁśati-*. The number words from 11 to 18 too are compounds: *ekā-daśan-, dvā-daśan-, trayo-daśan-, catur-daśan-, pañca-daśan-, ṣo-ḍaśan-, sapta-daśan-, aṣṭā-daśan-*. The terms for 19, 29 and so on can be such compounds (e.g. *nava-daśan-, nava-viṁśati-*), but they are also commonly compounds with *ūna-* 'lacking', *ekona-* 'less by one'; e.g. *ekona-viṁśati-*, '19', *ekona-triṁśat-* '29'. Numbers above one hundred are expressed additatively, using *adhika-* 'more, greater' or *uttara-* 'beyond'; e.g. *pañcadaśādhikaśatam* '115'. Derivates from decade terms are used similarly; e.g. *ekādaśaṁ śatam* '111', *ekādaśaṁ sahasram* '1011'.

'100' is *śata-* (nt.: nom.-acc. *śatam*). There are also separate number words for 10^3, 10^4, and so on, up to 10^{17}: 1000: *sahasram*, 10,000: *ayutam*, 10^5: *lakṣam* ('a lakh'), 10^6:

prayutam, 10^7: *koṭiḥ* (f. 'a crore'), 10^8: *arbudam*, 10^9: *nyarbudam*, 10^{10}: *kharvaḥ*, 10^{11}: *nikharvaḥ*, 10^{12}: *śaṅkhaḥ*, 10^{13}: *padmaḥ*, 10^{14}: *sāgaraḥ*, 10^{15}: *antyam*, 10^{16}: *madhyam*, 10^{17}: *parārdham*. Some of these terms have alternants, including some that are semantically equivalent (e.g. *abjaḥ* = *padmaḥ*, *samudraḥ* = *sāgaraḥ*), and one term can be used instead of another (*niyutam* = *lakṣam* or *prayutam*; *vṛndam*, *abjaḥ* = *nyarbudam*).

3.2.3.2 Ordinals are derivates in -*a*, f. -*ī*. Derivates from *viṁśati*- through *pañcāśat*-have alternants of the types *viṁśa*-/*viṁśatitama*-, *ekaviṁśa*-/*ekaviṁśatitama*-, *triṁśa*-/*triṁśattama*-, *ekatriṁśa*-/*ekatriṁśattama*-. For *ṣaṣṭi*- and subsequent decade terms not preceded by other number words, -*tama*- is obligatory; e.g. *ṣaṣṭitama*- but *ekaṣaṣṭa*-/*ekaṣaṣṭitama*-. -*tama* is obligatory also for terms from *śata*- on: *śatatama*-, *ekaśatatama*- etc. Ordinals for cardinals from *ekādaśan*-, *dvādaśan*- and teens are of the type *ekādaśa*- (f. *ekādaśī*), *dvādaśa*- (*dvādaśī*). The ordinal corresponding to simple *daśan*- is *daśama*-/*daśamī*, and -*ma*- (f. -*mī*-) appear also in *pañcama*-, *saptama*-, *aṣṭama*-, *navama*-. The ordinals for *catur*- and *ṣaṣ*- have -*tha*-: *caturtha*- (*caturthī*), *ṣaṣṭha* (*ṣaṣṭhī*). Corresponding to *dvi*- and *tri*-, there are ordinals with -*tīya* (f. -*tīyā*): *dvitīya*-, *tṛtīya*-. The ordinal for *eka*- is *prathama*- (f. *prathamā*-).

3.2.3.3 Indeclinable derivates are used to count the times an action is performed. The general suffix is *kṛtvas*, as in *pañca-kṛtvas*- 'five times', *ṣaṭ-kṛtvas*- 'six times' and so on. The derivates corresponding to *dvi*-, *tri*- and *catur*- are *dvis*-, *tris*- and *catus*-; to *eka*-corresponds *sakṛt*- 'once'.

3.2.4 Derived nominals

Nominals are derived from verb bases or stems and from other nominal bases or syntactic terms.

3.2.4.1 Primary derivates from verbal bases

Derived nominals formed directly from verbal bases include action nouns like *kar-aṇa*-(nt.), *kṛ-ta*- (nt.), *kṛ-ti*- (f.) 'doing' from *kṛ* 'do, make', *gam-ana*-, *ga-ta*-, *ga-ti*- 'going' (*gam* 'go'); agent nouns like *kar-tṛ*- (f. *kar-tr-ī*-), *kār-aka*- (*kār-ikā*-) 'doer'; object nouns like *kar-man*- (nt.) 'deed, object'; instrument nouns such as *kar-aṇa*- (nt.) 'instrument'; locus nouns such as *doh-anī*- (f.) 'pail into which milk is milked'. Some derivates are best represented in particular grammatical classes; e.g. desideratives form agent nouns in -*u*, of the type *ci-kīr-ṣ-u*- 'one who wishes to make or do'.

Past participles of the types *kṛ-ta*- (f. *kṛtā*), *ga-ta*- 'gone', *bhin-na*- (*bhid* 'break'), *kṛ-tavat*- (f. *kṛtavatī*-) 'one who has done or made something' (nom. sg. m. *kṛtavān*), *ga-tavat*- 'one who has gone' are formed directly from bases, as are gerundives like *kar-tavya*- (f. *kartavyā*-), *kar-anīya*- (*karaṇīyā*-) 'to be done, doable'. Participles are formed also from stems. For example, *adat*- (nom. sg. m. *adan* [section 3.2.2.2], f. *adatī*-), *kurvat*- (*kurvatī*) are present participles corresponding to the present stems *ad*- 'eat' (3sg. *at-ti*), *karo*-/*kuru*- (*karoti*, *kurvanti* [3pl.]); *kariṣyat*- (*kariṣyatī*-) is a participle to the future stem *kariṣya*-; and *sedivas*- (nom. sg. m. *sedivān*, f. *seduṣī*-) is a participle to the perfect stem *sed*- from the base *sad* 'sit'.

Indeclinables that function as absolutives (section 3.3) and infinitives are formed from verb bases; e.g. *hatvā* 'after killing' (section 3.2.2.3(1)), *abhidrutya* 'after running up to' (3.1.7(7)), are absolutives with *tvā* and *ya* respectively after simple bases and bases combined with preverbs. There is also a derivate in *-am*; e.g. *smāraṁ smāraṁ* 'after repeatedly recalling'. *kartum* and so on are infinitives; see section 3.1.7(15)–(20).

3.2.4.2 Derivates with taddhita affixes

Secondary nominal derivates, formed with affixes traditionally called *taddhita*, are of several kinds.

Most correspond to syntactic strings. For example, there is a system of patronymics such as *gārg-i-* 'son of Garga', *gārg-ya-* 'oldest descendant of Garga starting with his son's son', *gārg-yāyaṇa-* 'younger descendant of the Garga lineage'. A form such as *gārgiḥ* is equivalent to *gargasya putraḥ* 'son (*putraḥ*) of Garga (*gargasya*)'. *gārgi-* and *gārgya-* are derivates with affixes *i* and *ya*; *gārgyāyaṇa-* combines the suffixes *-ya-* and *-āyana-*. Another formation with taddhita affixes is illustrated by *go-mat-* (nom. sg. m. *gomān*), *vahni-mat* (*vahnimān*), with the suffix *-mat-*. These refer to entities that have cows and on which smoke occurs, and are equivalent to strings in which nominative forms of *go-* 'cow, ox' and *vahni-* are used; e.g. *gomān devadattaḥ* 'Devadatta is rich in cows', *vahnimān parvataḥ* 'the mountain (*parvataḥ*) has smoke on it', equivalent to *gāvo devadattasya santi*, *vahniḥ parvate'sti*. Forms of *māthur-a-*, which refers to something born or located in the city of Mathurā, are equivalent to strings with a locative of *mathurā-* in construction with *jāta-* 'born' or *bhava-* 'located, occurring': *māthuraḥ* = *mathurāyāṁ jātaḥ*, *mathurāyāṁ bhavaḥ*. Similarly, *dantyaḥ* 'dental', with the suffix *-ya-*, is equivalent to *danteṣu bhavaḥ* 'located at the teeth', and *paurvaśālaḥ* is equivalent to *pūrvasyāṁ śālāyāṁ bhavaḥ* 'located in the eastern (*pūrvasyāṁ*) house (*śālāyām*); see section 3.2.4.3.

Ordinals such as *dvitīya-*, *caturtha-*, *pañcama-* and indeclinables such as *pañcakṛtvas-* (sections 3.2.3.2–3) contain taddhita affixes that occur with number words.

Some derivates are equivalent to certain case forms. Thus, derivates in *-tas* are equivalent to ablative forms; e.g.

(1) *rāmo ...*   *yo*   *nārāyaṇataḥ prati*
     nom. sg.   rel. pr. nom. sg.   ptcle.
     Rāma   who   Nārāyaṇa

'Rāma who is just like Nārāyaṇa' (BhK 8.89)

(2) *grāmataḥ/grāmād ā gacchati* '... is coming (*ā gacchati*) from the village'

where *nārāyaṇataḥ* construed with the particle *prati* is equivalent to the ablative singular *nārāyaṇāt*, and *grāmataḥ* is equivalent to *grāmāt*, an ablative construed with *ā gacchati* (3sg. pres.). Certain pronouns also form derivates equivalent to particular case forms. Thus, *ta-tas*, *tar-hi*, *ta-dā*, and comparable derivates with the relative and interrogative pronouns are equivalent to ablative and locative forms of these pronouns; e.g. *tataḥ*: *tasmāt*, *tasyāḥ*, *tābhyām*, *tebhyaḥ*, *tābhyaḥ*, *tatra*: *tasmin*, *tasyām*, *tayoḥ*, *teṣu*, *tāsu*. These derivates are neutral with respect to gender and number contrasts.

What western grammars call superlatives and comparatives also are formed with taddhita suffixes: *-iṣṭha-*, *-tama-* and *-īyas-/-yas-*, *-tara-*. The vowel-initial affixes are the more restricted: they occur with terms that designate qualities, as in *paṭ-iṣṭha-* 'most sharp, exceedingly sharp', *paṭ-īyas-* (see section 3.2.2.2) 'quite sharp, sharper' and *lagh-iṣṭha-* 'exceedingly light or short, lightest, shortest', *lagh-īyas-*, related to *paṭu-* and *laghu-*. Such terms may take *tama* and *tara* (*paṭu-tama-*, *paṭu-tara-*, *laghu-tama-*, *laghu-*

tara-), which can be used with other items also; e.g. *go-tara-* 'more of an ox (in that it can draw more)', *pācaka-tama-* 'one who is an exceedingly expert cook', *na-tarām* 'the more not so (because of an additional argument)', *na-tamām* 'all the more not so, absolutely not'. Moreover, *-tama-* and *-tara-* can occur not only in derivates like *natarām* and *natamām* but also with verb forms in derivates of the type *pacatitamām* 'cooks exceedingly well', *pacatitarām* 'cooks very well'.

-iṣṭha- and *-īyas-* in *paṭiṣṭha-* and *paṭīyas-* follow original bases, without affixes found in the corresponding absolute terms. Such derivates can also involve alternation in bases; e.g. *sthūla-* 'stout, thick': *sthav-iṣṭha-*, *sthav-īyas-*, *guru-* 'weighty': *gar-iṣṭha-*, *gar-īyas-*.

3.2.4.3 Compounds

Compounds can be assigned to four general classes, which in Indian grammatical traditions are called *avyayībhāva, tatpuruṣa, dvandva* and *bahuvrīhi.*

Avyayībhāvas are generally indeclinable; e.g. *adhi-stri* 'concerning women', *upāgni* (*upa-agni*) 'near the fire'. Some such compounds alternate with equivalent syntactic strings containing the constituents of the compound; e.g. *ākumāram* alternates with a string in which *ā* 'up to and including' is construed with an ablative *kumārebhyaḥ* (abl. pl.), as in

(1) *ākumāraṁ yaśaḥ pāṇineḥ*
(2) *ā kumārebhyo yaśaḥ pāṇineḥ* 'Pāṇini's fame (*yaśaḥ*) (extends) up to young boys (*kumārebhyaḥ*).'

Tatpuruṣa compounds are of several types. Some regularly alternate with equivalent strings in which the nominal that is the first constituent takes a particular ending. Thus, forms of *grāmagata-* 'gone to the village' alternate with strings containing an accusative of *grāma-*:

(3) a. *grāmagato devadattaḥ* b. *grāmaṁ gato devadattaḥ*

where (3b) has the accusative singular *grāmam* 'village' construed with the participle form *gataḥ* (nom. sg. m.), and (3a) has a compound form *grāmagataḥ* equivalent to *grāmaṁ gataḥ*. Similarly, forms of *ahihata-* 'slain (*hata-*) by a snake (*ahi-*)' alternate with strings in which an instrumental of *ahi-* is used (e.g. *ahinā hataḥ*), and forms of *rājapuruṣa-* 'king's servant' are equivalent to strings with genitive forms of *rājan-* 'king', as in *rājapuruṣaḥ* and *rājñaḥ puruṣaḥ*. In another subtype of tatpuruṣa, called *karmadhāraya*, the constituents are coreferential; e.g. forms of *nīlotpala-* 'blue (*nīla-*) lotus (*utpala-*)' alternate with strings containing coreferential terms: *nīlotpalam* (nom. sg.) = *nīlam utpalam*.

As shown in section 3.2.4.2, *paurvaśāla-* is semantically like *māthura-* but formally more complex. It is a derivate with a taddhita suffix following a compound that occurs in this formation: *pūrva-śālā-*, with coreferential constituents. In a comparable subtype of tatpuruṣa called *dvigu*, the first member is a number word; e.g. *dvigu-* 'bought for two (*dvi-*) cows', *pañcakapāla-* 'prepared in five cups'.

Though tatpuruṣa compounds usually alternate with equivalent syntactic strings, certain items form obligatory compounds and others are excluded from forming compounds. Consider *kumbhakāra-* 'pot maker'.

(4) *kumbhānāṁ kartā* 'a maker (*kartā* [nom. sg. m.]) of pots (*kumbhānām*)'

is possible, but a form of *kāra-* cannot be construed with *kumbhānām* or a comparable term: *kāra-* occurs only in compounds. Similarly, root nouns such as *-han* in *vṛtrahan-* '... who has slain Vṛtra' and *-sut* in *somasut-* 'one who has pressed Soma juice' are restricted to compounds. Conversely, agent nouns with *-tṛ-* and *-aka-* (such as *kartṛ-*, *kāraka-*) are generally excluded from compounds.

Dvandva compounds are equivalent to strings in which nominal forms are linked with *ca* 'and' or comparable connectives; e.g. *plakṣanyagrodhau* = *plakṣaś ca nyagrodhaś ca* 'a plakṣa and a nyagrodha tree', *indrāgnī* 'Indra and Agni' = *indraś cāgniś ca*. Some dvandva compounds alternate with dual forms of one of the constituents alone; e.g. *pitarau* 'parents' = *mātāpitarau* 'mother and father'.

Bahuvrīhi compounds are regularly exocentric. *bahuvrīhi-* 'someone who has much (*bahu-*) rice (*vrīhi-*)' is an instance of such a compound.

Compounds are syntactically and semantically separate units. Thus, there are strings like *ṛddhasya rājñaḥ puruṣaḥ* 'the servant of the rich (*ṛddhasya*) king', in which *rājñaḥ* is qualified by *ṛddhasya*, but *rāja-* in the compound *rājapuruṣa-* is not linked with such a qualifier. Similarly, *rājñaḥ rājñoḥ rājñām*, with singular, dual and plural genitive forms of *rājan-*, can be construed with forms of *puruṣa-*, but no number distinction can be made for the first constituent within the compound *rājapuruṣa-*. Case markings, number distinctions and qualifications apply to the compound as a unit. Tatpuruṣa and dvandva compounds regularly have a single gender, that of the final constituent, although a subgroup of dvandvas has the gender of the first constituent. Thus, *ardhapippalī-* 'half a pepper' is equivalent to *ardhaṁ pippalyāḥ*, with the neuter *ardha-* 'half' and feminine *pippalī-*; the compound is feminine Similarly, *kukkuṭamayūryau* (nom.-acc. du.) 'cock (*kukkuṭa-*) and peahen (*mayūrī-*) is feminine, but *aśvavaḍavau* 'horse (*aśva-*) and mare (*vaḍavā-*) is masculine. Compounds generally are accentually single units. The words in the string *rājñaḥ purùṣaḥ* have independent accents (bases *rā́jan-*, *púruṣa-*), but the compound *rājapuruṣá-* has a single accent.

There are exceptions. Consider *pitúḥ svasā̀* 'father's sister' and related compounds. The tatpuruṣa *pitṛ́ṣvasṛ-* has a single accent, and the *s-* of *-svasṛ-* is obligatorily changed to *ṣ-* after *-ṛ-* within the compound. There is also a compound *pituḥsvasṛ-/pituḥṣvasṛ-*. The accentual unity of the compound appears, but the ending of the first constituent is retained and the retroflexion is optional. Certain other compounds have separate accents for constituents; e.g. *śucī́páti-* 'master of Śucī, Indra' and dvandva compounds consisting of deity names, such as *índrā́sóma-* (nom. du. *indrā́somau̇*) 'Indra and Soma'.

3.2.5 Gender marking

In certain instances, a stem serves as both masculine and feminine; e.g. *sumanas-* 'happy' (nom. sg. m. f. *sumanāḥ*, du. *sumanasau*, pl. *sumanasaḥ*, instr. sg. *sumanasā* etc., nom.-acc. nt. *sumanaḥ, sumanasī, sumanāṁsi*). Some contrasts between male and female involve unrelated stems; e.g. *pitṛ-* 'father': *mātṛ-* 'mother', *bhrātṛ-* 'brother': *svasṛ-* 'sister'. There are also nominals to which affixes are added to form feminine derivates: *-ā-*, *-ī-*, and *-ū-*, variously accented. These derivates inflect like *jihvā-*, *devī-* and *vadhū-* (section 3.2.2.1). Nouns in *-a-* such as *aja-* 'goat' and qualifiers such as *nava-* 'new', *paṭutara-*, *paṭiṣṭha-* (section 3.2.4.2) form feminine stems with *-ā*: *ajā- navā-*, *paṭutarā-*, *paṭiṣṭhā-*. Particular *a*-stems have *-ī*; e.g. *deva-* 'god': *devī-* 'goddess', *naśvara-*: *naśvarī* 'perishable', *tādṛśa-*: *tādṛśī* 'such'. Derivates with *-īyas* also have *-ī* (e.g. *garīyas-*: *garīyasī* 'quite weighty'), as do the polite pronoun *bhavat-* (*bhavatī-* [section 3.2.2.3.1]), agent nouns in *-tṛ* (*kartṛ-*: *kartrī-*), participles in *-at* (pres. ptcpl.

bhavat-: *bhavantī-* 'being', *sat-*: *satī-* 'being') and *-vas* (e.g. *seduṣī-* [section 3.2.4.1]), derivates with *-in* (e.g. *balinī-* 'strong'), ordinals, patronymics of the type *gārgi-* (*gārgī-* 'daughter of Garga'), and compounds of the type *kumbhakāra-* (*kumbhakārī* [section 3.2.4.3]). *ū* appears in derivates such as *kurū-* 'daughter of the king of Kurukṣetra'. Terms in *-u* denoting qualities optionally form feminines with *-ī-*; e.g. *laghu-*: *laghu-/ laghvī-* 'short, brief'. Certain feminine formations involve an affix *-ī-* with an additional element; e.g. *indra-* 'Indra': *indrāṇī-* 'wife of Indra'.

3.3 Aspects of syntax

Case forms refer to participants in activities; verb endings, which can occur in verb forms without accompanying nominals, also designate agents and objects along with their numbers. In

(1) *tègnim àstuvạnt sa èbhyaḥ stụto rātrìyạ adhy ahàr ạbhi pạśūn nir ậrjat* (TS 1.5.9.3) 'They (the gods) praised Agni. When he had been praised (*stutaḥ* [nom. sg. m. past ptcpl.]), he led (*nir ārjat*) the animals (*paśūn* [acc. pl. m.]) from night (*rātriyā adhi*) unto day (*ahar abhi*) for them'

astuvan (3sg. imperf. act.) occurs with the accusative *agnim* referring to the object of praising and the nominative plural *te* referring to the agents. Accusatives signifying objects of actions appear also in: 2.5.1.6(3): *ambyam*, 2.5.2.4(14): *hotāraṁ ratnadhātamam*, 2.5.2.9(1): *rakṣāṁsi*, 2.5.2.10(1): *tam*, 2.5.2.10(2): *tuviśravastamam putram*; 3.1.1(1): *kṛṣim*, 3.1.1(2): *naḥ*, 3.1.5.1(1): *kaṭam*, 3.1.7(2): *putram*, 3.1.7(3): *jyotir amṛtam*, 3.1.7(4): *mahāni prathamāni*. Two accusatives occur where something is made into something else or modified; e.g. 3.1.4.3(1): *gāṁ śatāyuṣam akariṣyam*. An accusative can also refer to a goal of movement; e.g. 3.1.5.2(3): *ayodhyām*. In corresponding passives, nominative forms refer to objects and passive verb forms are construed with agentive instrumentals; e.g. 3.1.3.2.3b(1): *astāvy agnir ṛṣibhiḥ*, 3.1.3.3(1): *ṛṣibhir barhiṣmadhibiḥ staviṣyase*, 3.1.7(21): *divaḥ stave duhitā gotamebhiḥ*, (22): *sasavān tsan stūyase*.

Other major functions case forms serve are illustrated in examples cited earlier:

Accusative: space and time throughout which an act takes place: 3.1.3.3(3): *ekāṁ rātrim*, 3.1.7(9): *rodasī*.
Instrumental: (a) means: 3.1.1(1): *akṣaiḥ*, 3.1.7(10): *duṣṭutī*; (b) accompaniment: 3.1.7(12): *sahasraṇībhir ūtibhiḥ*, *vājebhiḥ*.
Dative: indirect object: 3.1.3.2.1(3): *mahyam*, 3.2.2.3.3(1): *asmai, sakhibhyaḥ* 'friends':

(2) *adhị sānạu ni jìghnatẹ vajrèṇa śạtaparvaṇā | mạndāna indrọ andhàsạh sakhìbhyo gātum icchati* (ṚV 1.80.6a–d) 'With his vajra (*vajreṇa*) of a hundred joints (*śataparvaṇā*) he strikes down (*nijighnate*) on (Vṛtra's) back (*adhi sānau*); drunk (*mandānaḥ*) (with Soma), Indra seeks (*icchati* 'wishes') a way (*gātum*) to the juice (*andhasaḥ* [gen. sg.]) for his friends (*sakhibhyaḥ* [dat. pl.])'

Ablative: point of departure: 3.1.7(5): *devebhyaḥ*.
Genitive: (a) relation between referents of nominals: 3.1.3.2.1(1): *tasya*, 3.1.7(1): *yamasya*; (b) direct object, if a nominal is construed with a verb derivate that includes a primary suffix: 3.2.4.3(4): *kumbhānāṁ kartā*; (c) direct object relative to particular acts: 3.1.7(11): *jagatas tasthuṣaḥ* (*īś* 'have power over, rule'), 3.2.2.3.3(2): *asya* (*pā* 'drink').

Locative: locus, whether spatial or temporal: 2.5.2.4(1): *śuṣṇahatyeṣu*, 2.5.3.2(1, 2): *pṛṣṭhe pṛthivyāḥ*, 3.1.3.2.1(1): *tāsu*, *gṛhe*, 3.1.3.2.4(1): *kva*, 3.1.7(6): *akāle*, 3.2.2.3.7(1): *yuddhe*.

The genitive and locative are also used absolutely; e.g. *saṁsthite* in 3.1.3.3(2) is a locative absolute.

Particular case forms also are construed with certain pre- and postpositional terms; e.g. *purā*, *prati*, *ā* (3.1.3.3(2), 3.2.4.2(1), 3.2.4.3(2)). Such terms can occur with case forms redundantly. In example (2) of this section, *adhi* is preposed to *sānau*, a locative that refers to the place on which the vajra is brought down in striking, and in

(3) *abhra āṁ apaḥ* (RV 5.48.1c) 'the waters (*apaḥ* [acc. pl. f.]) in the cloud (*abhra āṁ*)'

ā (nasalized in Vedic) is postposed to the locative *abhre*, which already contains an ending signifying a locus.

Absolutives (section 3.2.4.1) link clauses such that an agent performs one act prior to performing another; e.g. 3.1.3.2.1(3), 3.1.7(2): *uktvā*, 3.1.7(6): *etya*, 3.1.7(7): *abhidrutya*, 3.2.2.3.7(1): *hatvā*. Present participles, on the other hand, are used in clauses which speak of an action that serves to characterize another action or one that is the reason for another. Standard examples are

(4) *śayānā bhuñjate yavanāḥ* 'Yavanas eat (*bhuñjate*) while lying down (*śayānāḥ*).'
(5) *adhīyāno'tra vasati* '... is staying (*vasati*) here (*atra*) in order to study (*adhīyānaḥ*).'

Cf. 2.5.1.6(3): *caran ... na vindate*, 3.1.7(10): *na sredhantaṁ rayir naśat*. A participle can serve as a qualifier, equivalent to a relative clause, as in 3.1.7(11): *tam īśānañ jagatas tasthuṣas patim*.

Relative clauses can begin with forms of relative pronouns; e.g. 2.5.2.4(8): *yaṁ yaṁ yujaṅ kṛnute*, 2.5.1.2(3): *yatra ṛṣayo jaggmuḥ*. Temporal relative clauses are introduced by *yad* or *yadā*, purpose clauses by *yathā*, and conditional clauses by *yadi*; e.g. 2.5.1.7(5): *indraś ca yad yuyudhāte ahiś ca*, 3.1.7.(11): *yathā ... asat*, (13): *yathā ... bhavema*, 3.1.7(12): *yadi śravat*, (14): *yadi bibhīyāt*.

The particle *iti* is used in citing, as in 3.1.7(14): *duścarmā bhaviṣyāmīti*.

The common unmarked word order in both principal and subordinate clauses is verb final: subject-object-verb; e.g. 3.1.7(14): *somapauṣṇam śyāmam ā labheta*, (15): *devadatto ... gṛhaṁ gacchati*, (16): *devadattaḥ kaṭaṁ kartum icchati*, (20): *agnir vai ... ulbam apalumpan nāśaknot*. Fronting is also possible: 3.1.7(18): *agnivṁ vai devā vibhājan nāśaknuvan*. Stylistic factors can play a role in different word orders; e.g. 3.1.7(19) has *na ye śekur yajñiyān nāvàm āruham*, instead of which the neutral order would be *ye yajñiyān nāvam āruham na śekuḥ* or *ye ... na śekur āruham*.

Historical and dialectal factors are also involved. As in *ā labheta* (3.1.7(14)), some adverbial items are preverbs, immediately preceding verb forms to which they are linked. From earliest Indo-Aryan onwards, verb and preverb also form an accentual nexus. A finite verb form that is not initial in an utterance – or in a verse section – is unaccented except under particular circumstances, e.g. in a relative clause; if a verb is unaccented, an accompanying preverb that precedes is accented, but if the verb is accented, the preverb is unaccented. In the spoken language Pāṇini describes, preverbs immediately precede a verb to which they are attached. Earlier Vedic has tmesis and a preverb could follow a verb; e.g. 2.5.1.2(2): *pra ... vācam iṣye;* 2.5.3.1(2): *sacata ... ā*, *śṛṇuhy ā*.

4 SCRIPT

As a cultural vehicle transcending other linguistic borders, Sanskrit has been written in a variety of major scripts, from Śāradā in Kashmir to Grantha in the South. One major script that has been used in the relatively recent past at least for Sanskrit manuscripts throughout India is Devanāgarī. The Devanāgarī symbols representing the inventory of Sanskrit sounds are given in table 4.4. Consonants *k* and so on are cited with a default vowel *a*, which also is understood in running text unless another vowel is specified or the absence of a vowel is marked either by the use of the symbol ॒ (e.g., क्, त् in वाक् [*vāk*], तत् [*tat*]) or of a conjunct symbol (e.g. त्त in त्ते [*tat te*]); other consonant-vowel combinations are illustrated here with the consonants *k* and *p*. Nasalization is indicated by superscript ˘ (*candrabindu*), which I transliterate *m̐*; e.g. ताँश्च *tām̐s ca* 'and them'. There are also number symbols: १ २ ३ ४ ५ ६ ७ ८ ९ ०. For additional details and lists of conjunct consonants, see Whitney 1889: 3–18, Kale 1894: 1–12, Renou 1961: xi–xviii; for more information on the script and its history see Richard Salomon's contribution to this volume.

TABLE 4.4: DEVANĀGARĪ SYMBOLS

Vowels (*svarāḥ*)

अ [ऋ]आ [ऋा] इ ई उ ऊ ऋ [ऋृ] ॠ [ऋृ] ॢ ए ऐ ओ औ
a　　　*ā*　　　　*i ī u ū ṛ*　　　　*r̄*　　　*ḷ e ai o au*

Consonants (*vyañjanāni*)

Stops (*sparśāḥ*)

Velar	क	ख	ग	घ	ङ
(*jihvāmūlīya*)	*ka*	*kha*	*ga*	*gha*	*a*
Palatal	च	छ	ज	झ [भ्र]	ञ
(*tālavya*)	*ca*	*cha*	*ja*	*jha*	*ña*
Retroflex	ट	ठ	ड	ढ	ण [राा]
(*mūrdhanya*)	*ṭa*	*ṭha*	*ḍa*	*ḍha*	*ṇa*
Dental	त	थ	द	ध	न
(*dantya*)	*ta*	*tha*	*da*	*dha*	*na*
Labial	प	फ	ब	भ	म
(*oṣṭhya*)	*pa*	*pha*	*ba*	*bha*	*ma*

Semivowels (*anta[ḥ]sthāḥ*): य (य य़)　र ल व
　　　　　　　　　　　ya　　*ra la va*

Spirants (*ūṣmāṇaḥ*): श ष स ह
　　　　　　　　　śa ṣa sa ha

Dependent segments (*ayogavāhāḥ*): अः (अऽ अं अ ÷) ꞏक ꞏप अं (अँ अꙮ अ꣯ अ꣱)
　　　　　　　　　　　　　　　aḥ　　　　　　*ꞏka ꞏpa am̐ (am)*

Others: ꜣ ꜣह
　　　ḷa ḷha

Consonant-vowel combinations:

का कि की कु कू कृ कॄ कॢ के कै को कौ

kā ki kī ku kū kṛ kr̄ kḷ ke kai ko kau

पा पि पु पू पृ पॄ पॢ पे पै पो पौ

pā pi pu pū pṛ pr̄ pḷ pe pai po pau

Tones are represented differently in various traditions, as illustrated in:

(1) अग्निमीळे पुरोहितॠय्ञस्यं देवमृत्विजंम् । होतारं रत्नधातंमम् ॥ (ṚV 1.1.1 [sections 2.5.2.4(14), 2.5.3.1(1)])

(2) त आ वंहन्ति (TS 1.1.2.1 ([section 2.5.2.8(2)])

(3) तंयां बहन्ते (MS 1.1.2 [section 2.5.2.8(1)])

(4) अद्यं बर्षिष्यतींलि ब्रूयाद् ... श्वों व्रष्टेंलि ब्रूयात् (MS 2.1.8 [section 3.1.3.3(2)])

(5) यत्र ऋषंयो जग्मु ३ (VS 18.52 [section 2.5.1.2(3)])

(6) व्विश्श्वकंर्मं ऋष्षिं ÷ (VS 13.58 [section 2.5.1.2(4)])

(7) पृष्ठे पृथिव्या : सीद (ŚBr. 9.2.3.34 [section 2.5.3.2(1)])

(8) पृष्ठे पृथिव्या ३ सींद (VS 17.72 [section 2.5.3.2(2)]).

There are broader and narrower notations. In the former, horizontal strokes and superscript vertical strokes mark low-pitched and svarita syllables, high-pitched syllables are unmarked. The narrow notation used for the Maitrāyaṇīsaṃhitā marks all three. A superscript vertical stroke designates an udātta, a subscript horizontal stroke an anudātta, and different types of svarita are distinguished: one preceding an extra-low syllable is marked with three superscript vertical strokes, one preceding ekaśruti by a horizontal stroke through the akṣara. The Vājasaneyisaṃhitā notation similarly distinguishes svaritas, but with different symbols, and in this notation an udātta is unmarked. For additional details, see Yudhiṣṭhira Mīmāṃsaka 1985.

Yajurveda texts distinguish different types of anusvāra, and the notation used for the Vājasaneyisaṃhitā distinguishes three visarjanīyas, depending on the tone of the preceding vowel.

In this chapter, I have adhered to traditional notations found in manuscripts and transliterated accordingly (cf. Cardona 1997: li–lxiv). Printed editions differ, in particular by showing anusvāra instead of nasalized semivowels and by substituting the Vājasaneyisaṃhitā accent notations for those of the Maitrāyaṇīsaṃhitā (see Satavalekar 1983 introduction p. 24) or marking only udātta syllables and the particular svarita indicated by a numeral '3'.

ACKNOWLEDGEMENT

I am happy to acknowledge the help of Ashok N. Aklujkar and Edwin Gerow, who read drafts of this chapter and made valuable suggestions.

REFERENCES

AiBr   *Aitareyabbrāhmaṇa* (Malaviya)
AV   *Atharvaveda* (Vishvabandhu et al.)
Bh   *Mahābhāṣya* (Abhyankar)
BhK   *Bhaṭṭikāvya* (Joshi and Pansîkar)
GBr   *Gopathabrāhmaṇa* (Vijayapāla)
Kāś   *Kāśikāvṛtti* (Sharm et al.)
KBr   *Kauṣītakibrāhmaṇa* (Sreekrishna Sarma)
MS   *Maitrāyaṇisaṃhitā* (Satavalekar 1973)
Nir   *Nirukta* (Bhadkamkar)
Rām   *Rāmāyaṇa* (Bhatt et al.)
RPr   *Ṛgvedaprātiśākhya* (Varmā 1970)

RV   *Ṛgveda* (Sontakke et al.)
ŚBr   *Śatapathabrāhmaṇa* (Weber)
ŚŚS   *Śāṅkhāyanaśrautasūtra* (Hillebrandt)
TAr   *Taittirīyāraṇyaka* (Abhyankar and Joshi)
TPr   *Taittirīyaprātiśākhya* (Shama Sastri and Rangacarya)
TS   *Taittirīyasaṃhitā* (Satavalekar 1957)
VPr   *Vājasaneyiprātiśākhya* (Varmā 1975)
VS   *Vājasaneyisaṃhita* (Daulatram Gaur)

Abhyankar, Kashinath Vasudev (1962–72) *The Vyākaraṇa-mahābhāṣya of Patañjali, edited by Franz Kielhorn, third edition* ... (3 volumes), Poona: Bhandarkar Oriental Research Institute.
Abhyankar, Kashinath Vasudev and Joshi, G. A. (1967–9), *Kṛṣṇayajurvedīyaṃ Taittirīyāraṇyakam* (2 volumes, Ānandāśrama Sanskrit Series 36), Poona: Ānandāśrama.
Aklujkar, Ashok N. (1996) 'Sanskrit as supreme language', in Houben, Jan E. M. (ed.) *Ideology and Status of Sanskrit: Contributions to the History of the Sanskrit Language*, Leiden: Brill, pp. 59–85.
Aṣṭādhyāyī: References to chapter, quarter-chapter and rule according to the text in Cardona 1997: 607–731.
Bhadkamkar, H. M. (1918) *The Nirukta of Yāska (with Nighaṇṭu) edited with Durga's Commentary*, by ... assisted by R. G. Bhadkamkar, volume I (Reprinted (1985) Poona: Bhandarkar Oriental Research Institute).
Bhatt, G. H. et al. (1960–72) *The Vālmīki-Rāmāyaṇa Critically Edited for the First Time*, Baroda: Oriental Institute.
Cardona, George (1997) *Pāṇini: His Work and its Traditions, Part I: General Introduction and Background* (second edition, revised and enlarged), Delhi: Motilal Banarsidass.
Census of India: see Vijayanunni, M.
Daulataram Gaur Vedacharya (1965) *Śukla Yajurveda Saṃhitā*, Varanasi: The Chowkhamba Vidya Bhawan.
Deshpande, Madhav M. (1997) *Śaunakīyā Caturādhyāyikā, A Prātiśākhya of the Śaunakīya Atharvaveda with the commentaries Caturādhyāyībhāṣya, Bhārgava-Bhāskara-Vṛtti and Pañcasandhi, Critically edited* ... (Harvard Oriental Series 52), Cambridge, MA: Department of Sanskrit and Indian Studies, Harvard University.
Hillebrandt, Alfred (1885–99) *Śāṅkhāyana Śrauta Sūtra together with the Commentary of Varadattasuta Ānartīya and Govinda* (4 volumes), Calcutta: Asiatic Society of Bengal (Reprinted in 2 volumes (1981) Delhi: Meharchand Lachhmandas).
Joshi, Vinâyak Nârâyaṇa Shâstrî and Paṇsîkar, Wâsudev Laxmaṇa Shâstrî (1928) *The Bhaṭṭikâvya of Bhaṭṭi with the Commentary (Jayamangalâ) of Jayamangala* (seventh edition), Bombay: Nirṇaya Sāgara Press.
Kale, Moreshwar Ramchandra (1894) *A Higher Sanskrit Grammar (for the use of school and college students)* (Reprinted (1972) Delhi: Motilal Banarsidass).
Malaviya, Sudhakar (1980–3) *The Aitareya Brāhmaṇa of the Ṛgveda with the Vedārtha-Prakāśa of Sāyaṇācārya and the 'Sarala' Hindi Translation* (2 volumes), Varanasi: Tara Publications.
Pāṇini: see Aṣṭādhyāyī.
Renou, Louis (1961) *Grammaire sanscrite*, Paris: Adrien-Maisonneuve.
Śaunakīyā Caturādhyāyikā: see Deshpande.
Satavalekar, Shripad Damodar (1957) *Kṛṣṇayajurvedīya Taittirīyasaṃhitā*, Pardi: Svādhyaya Maṇḍala.
—— (1983) *Yajurvedīya Maitrāyaṇīsaṃhitā*, Pardi: Svādhyaya Maṇḍala.
Shama Sastri, R. and Rangacarya, K. (1906) *The Taittirīya-Prātiśākhya with the Commentaries: Tribhāṣyaratna and Vaidikābharaṇa* (Reprinted (1985) Delhi: Motilal Banarsidass).
Sharma, Aryendra, Deshpande, Khanderao and Padye, D. G. (1969–70) *Kāśikā : A Commentary on Pāṇini's Grammar by Vāmana and Jayāditya* (2 volumes, Sanskrit Academy Series 17, 20), Hyderabad: Sanskrit Academy, Osmania University.

Sontakke, N. S. et al. (1933–51) *Ṛgveda-Samhitā with the commentary of Sayaṇāchārya* (5 volumes), Poona: Vaidic Samshodhan Mandal.

Sreekrishna Sarma, E. R. (1968) *Kauṣītaki-Brāhmaṇa*, Wiesbaden: Steiner.

Varmā, Vīrendra Kumāra (1970) *Uvaṭa-Bhāṣya-Sahitam Ṛgveda-Prātiśākhyam*, Varanasi: Banaras Hindu University.

—— (1975) *Bhāṣyadvayasahitam Śuklayajurveda-Prātiśākhyam athavā Vājasaneyi-Prātiśā-khyam*, Varanasi: Jñānaprakāśa Pratiṣṭhāna.

Vijayapāla (1980) *Gopatha-Brāhmaṇam (mūla-mātram)*, Sonipat: Ram Lal Kapoor Trust.

Vijayanunni, M. (1997) *Census of India 1991, Series 1-India, Paper 1 of 1997: Language, India and States*, New Delhi: Government of India Press.

Vishva Bandhu, Bhīmdev and Munīshvar Dev (1960–4) *Atharvaveda (Śaunaka)* with *the Padapāṭha and Sāyaṇācārya's Commentary*, Hoshiarpur: Vishveshvaranand Vedic Research Institute.

Weber, Albrecht (1849) *The Çatapatha-Brâhmaṇa in the Mâdhyandina-çâkhâ with Abstracts from the Commentaries of Sâyaṇa, Harisvâmin and Dvivedagaṅga* (Reprinted (1964) Varanasi: Chowkhamba).

Whitney, William Dwight (1889) *Sanskrit Grammar Including both the Classical Language, and the older Dialects of Veda and Brahmana*, second edition, Cambridge, MA: Harvard University Press, London: Geoffrey Cumberlege, Oxford University Press (eighth impression 1955).

Yudhiṣṭhira Mīmāṁsaka (1985) *Vaidika-vāṅmaya meṁ prayukta vividha svarāṅkana-prakāra* [Various ways of Marking Accents in Vedic Literature], Sonipat: Ram Lal Kapoor Trust. [In Hindi]

FURTHER READING

Apte, Vaman Shivaram (1890) *The Student's Guide to Sanskrit Composition* (Reprinted (1970, 1984) Varanasi: The Chowkhamba Sanskrit Series Office).

Burrow, Thomas (1965) *The Sanskrit Language*, second edition, London: Faber and Faber.

—— (1969) 'Sanskrit', in Sebeok, Thomas A. (ed.) *Current Trends in Linguistics, volume 5: Linguistics in South Asia*, The Hague, Paris: Mouton, pp. 3–35.

Cardona, George (1990) 'Sanskrit', in Comrie, Bernard (ed.) *The Major Languages of South Asia, the Middle East and Africa*, London: Routledge, pp. 31–52.

—— (1993) 'The bhāṣika accentuation system', *Studien zur Indologie und Iranistik* 18: 1–40.

Coulson, Michael (1992) *Sanskrit: An Introduction to the Classical Language*, second edition revised by Richard Gombrich and James Benson, London: Hodder and Stoughton.

Debrunner, Albert (1954) *Altindische Grammatik, Band II, 2: Die Nominalsuffixe*, Göttingen: Vandenhoek & Ruprecht.

Debrunner, Albert and Wackernagel, Jakob (1930) *Altindische Grammatik, III. Band: Nominalflexion – Zahlwort – Pronomen*, Göttingen: Vandenhoek & Ruprecht.

Deshpande, Madhav M. and Hock, Hans Henrich (1991) 'A bibliography of writings on Sanskrit syntax', in Hock, Hans Henrich 1991: 219–44.

Hauschild, Richard (1964) *Register zur Altindischen Grammatik von J. Wackernagel und A. Debrunner (Bd. I–III)*, Göttingen: Vandenhoek & Ruprecht.

Hock, Hans Henrich (1991) *Studies in Sanskrit Syntax: A volume in honor of the centennial of Speijers Sanskrit Syntax (1886–1986)*, Delhi: Motilal Banarsidass.

Hoffmann, Karl (1967) *Der Injunktiv im Veda*, Heidelberg: Winter.

Macdonell, A. A. (1910) *Vedic Grammar* (Grundriss der indo-arischen Philologie und Altertumskunde I.4), Strassburg: Trübner.

Mayrhofer, Manfred (1986–2001) *Etymologisches Wörterbuch des Altindoarischen* (3 volumes), Heidelberg: Winter.

Renou, Louis (1956) *Histoire de la langue Sanskrite*, Lyon, Paris: IAC.

Speijer, J. S. (1886) *Sanskrit Syntax* (Grundriss der indo-arischen Philologie und Altertumskunde I.6), Leiden: Brill (Reprinted (1968) Kyoto: Rinsen-Shoten Bookstore, (1973)
Delhi: Motilal Banarsidass).

—— (1896) *Vedische und Sanskrit-Syntax*, Strassburg: Trübner

Wackernagel, Jakob (1896) *Altindische Grammatik, Band I: Lautlehre, Göttingen: Vandenhoek
& Ruprecht* (Reprinted (1957) with *Nachträge zu Band I* by Albert Debrunner and
Introduction générale by Louis Renou).

—— (1905) *Altindische Grammatik, Band II,1: Einleitung zur Wortlehre, Nominal-
komposition*, Göttingen: Vandenhoek & Ruprecht (Reprinted (1957) with *Nachträge zu
Band II,1* by Albert Debrunner).

Whitney, William Dwight (1885) *The Roots, Verb-Forms and Primary Derivatives of the
Sanskrit Language: A Supplement to his Sanskrit Grammar*, Leipzig: Breitkopf and Härtel
(Reprinted (1945), New Haven: American Oriental Society).

Werba, Chlodwig H. (1997) *Verba Indoarica: Die primären und sekundären Wurzeln der
Sanskrit-Sprache, Pars I : Radices Primariae*, Wien: Verlag der Österreichischen Akademie
der Wissenschaften.

CHAPTER FIVE

AŚOKAN PRAKRIT AND PĀLI

Thomas Oberlies

CONTENTS

LIST OF TABLES

1 INTRODUCTION

1.1 The Middle Indo-Aryan languages

The Indo-Aryan languages are commonly assigned to three major groups – Old, Middle and New Indo-Aryan –, a linguistic and not strictly chronological classification as the MIA languages are not younger than ('Classical') Sanskrit. And a number of their morphophonological and lexical features betray the fact that they are not direct continuations of Ṛgvedic Sanskrit, the main base of 'Classical' Sanskrit; rather they descend from dialects which, despite many similarities, were different from Ṛgvedic and in some regards even more archaic.

MIA languages, though individually distinct, share features of phonology and morphology which characterize them as parallel descendants of OIA. Various sound changes are typical of the MIA phonology:

(1) The vocalic liquids r and l are replaced by a, i or u;
(2) the diphthongs ai and au are monophthongized to e and o;
(3) long vowels before two or more consonants are shortened;
(4) the three sibilants of OIA are reduced to one, either $ś$ or s;
(5) the often complex consonant clusters of OIA are reduced to more readily pronounceable forms, either by assimilation or by splitting;
(6) single intervocalic stops are progressively weakened;
(7) dentals are palatalized by a following -y-;
(8) all final consonants except -$ṁ$ are dropped unless they are retained in *sandhi* junctions.

The most conspicuous features of the morphological system of these languages are: loss of the dual; thematicization of consonantal stems; merger of the f. i-/u- and $ī$-/$ū$- in one $ī$-/$ū$-inflexion, elimination of the dative, whose functions are taken over by the genitive; simultaneous use of different case-endings in *one* paradigm; employment of *mahyaṁ* and *tubhyaṁ* as genitives and *me* and *te* as instrumentals; gradual disappearance of the middle voice; coexistence of historical and new verbal forms based on the present stem; and use of active endings for the passive. In the vocabulary, the MIA languages are mostly dependent on OIA, with addition of a few so-called *deśī* words of (often) uncertain origin.

The most archaic of the MIA languages are the inscriptional Aśokan Prakrit on the one hand and Pāli and Ardhamāgadhī on the other, both literary languages. Two other stages of MIA may be distinguished, that of the Prakrits proper (excluding Ardhamāgadhī) and that of the Apabhraṁśa languages.

1.2 Aśokan Prakrit

The inscriptions of Aśoka – a king of the Maurya dynasty who reigned, based in his capital Pāṭaliputra, from 268 to 232 BC over almost the whole of India – were engraved in rocks and pillars, in various local dialects.

Like other MIA languages Aśokan Prakrit shows – compared with Old Indo-Aryan – processes of phonetic change, morphological simplification, and syntactic reconfigura-

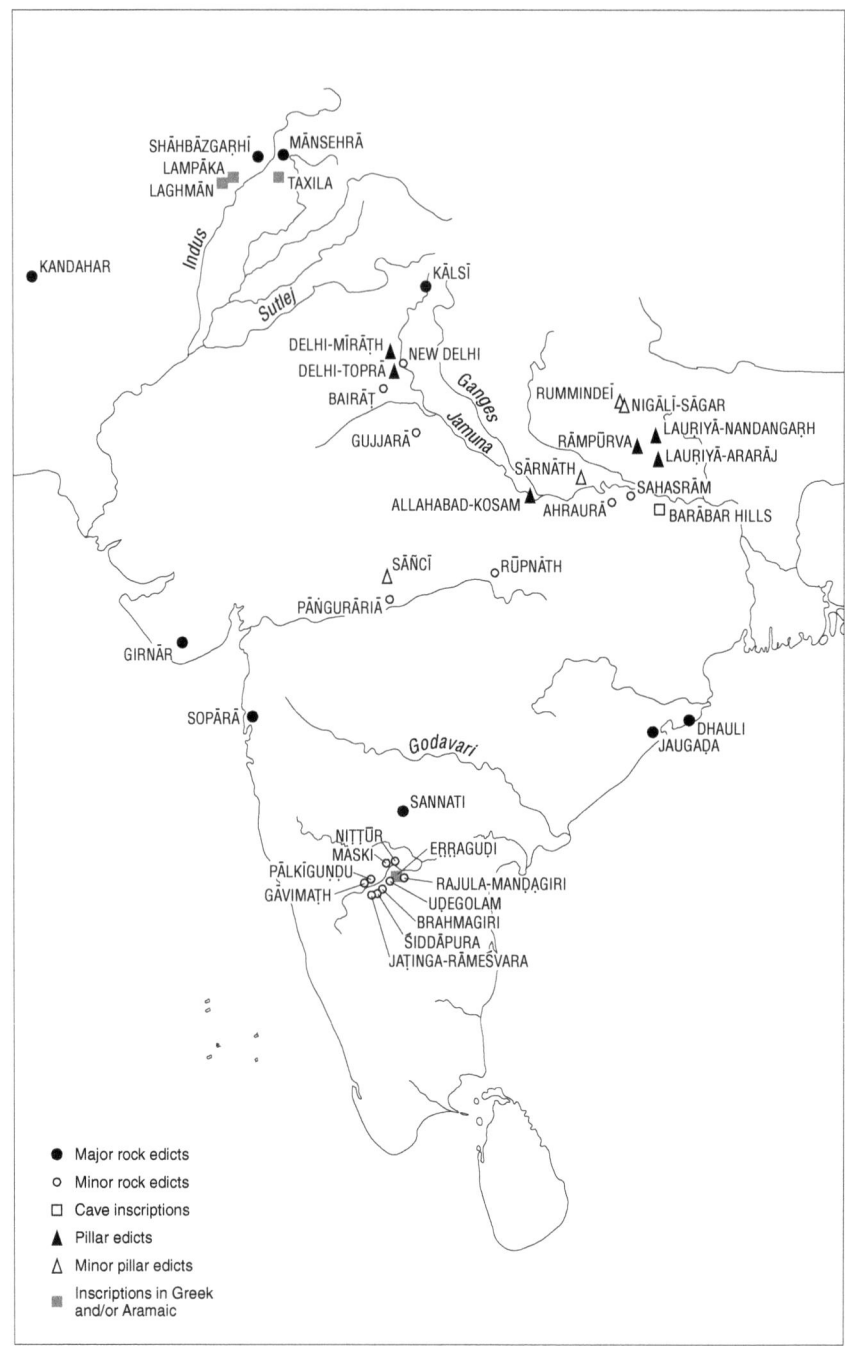

MAP 5.1: LOCATION OF AŚOKAN INSCRIPTIONS

Source: Richard Salomon, *Indian Epigraphy* (New York/Oxford: Oxford University Press, 1998), Map 3, p. 135.

tion. According to their language these inscriptions can be divided into three groups, (a) the western, (b) the northwestern and (c) the eastern; a central dialect group is *not* represented; those in its area are of eastern dialect type (in the Aśokan inscriptions, geminate consonants [letters] are represented by a single consonant [letter], and nasals are often left unindicated):

(a) The inscriptions of Girnār and the Bombay-Sopārā fragments keep the nasals *ñ, ṇ, n* distinct (*ñātika-* 'relative', *p(r)āṇa-* 'living being', *°anusāsanaṁ* 'instruction', *Taṁbapaṁni, aña-* '(an)other', *maṁñate* 'he thinks'), and retain both *r* and *l* (*karoti* 'he does', *rāja(n)-* 'king', *likhita-* 'written', *sīla-* 'virtue' [śīla-]) – Sopārā even has (un-etymological) *r* in place of OIA *l* (*phara-* 'result', *maṁgara-* 'ceremony' [phala-, maṅgala-]). They reduce the three OIA sibilants to *s* (*susrusā-* 'obedience' [śuśrūṣā-], *parisāyaṁ* 'in an assembly' [← parisad-]), have (normally) *-cch-* from *-kṣ-* (*vrac(c)ha-* 'tree' [vṛkṣa-]) and do not cerebralize a *t(h)* following *r̥/r* (*athāya* 'for [that] purpose' [arthāya], *kata-* 'made' [kr̥ta-]). The nominative sg. of masculine *a*-stems ends in *-o*, that of the neuter in *-aṁ* (*°(p)piyo* 'the beloved', *sādhu dānaṁ* 'good is a gift ...'), the locative in *-e* or *-aṁhi* (*vijite* 'in the kingdom', *dhaṁmamhi* 'in the law' [dharme]), and the accusative plural m. in *-e* (*yute* 'civil servants' [yuktān]). They use middle endings (*karote* 'he does', *anuvatare* 'they live according to ...') and have an absolutive in *-tpā* (written *-ptā*: *ārabhiptā* 'having killed', *paricajiptā* 'having abandoned').

(b) In the inscriptions of the northwest (Shāhbāzgaṛhī, Mānsehrā), written in Kharoṣṭhī script, the OIA sibilants survive (*priyadraśisa, suśruṣā-*), as do *r* and *l* (*arabhiyaṁti* 'they are killed', *maṁgala-* 'ceremony') and the nasals (*ñati-, praṇa-, dhramanuśaśanaṁ, Taṁbapa(ṁ)ṇi, aña-, mañati*). Liquids in consonant clusters are metathesized (*krama-* [karman-], *dhrama-* [dharma-]); historical remnants of this distinctive phonetic feature have been traced in the modern Dardic languages. The northwest has a loc. sg. of m./nt. *a*-stems in *-e*, *-asi* or *-aspi* (*vijite* 'in the kingdom', *rajaviṣavasi* id., *nivuṭaspi* 'for the success'); the future tense affix is *-iśa-* (*vaḍhiśati* 'it will grow' [(*)vardhiṣyati]) and the absolutive ends also in *-ti* (*tiṭhiti* 'having abided by', *vijiniti* 'having conquered').

(c) Inscriptions of all other rock edicts and of all pillar edicts, revealing a standard language (see below), have (throughout) *l* for *r* (*kaleti, lāja(n)-* [karoti, rājan-]), *n* for *ñ, ṇ* and *n* and *-ṁn-* as a rule for geminate nasals (*nāti-* 'relative' [jñāti-], *pāna-* 'living being' [prāṇa-], *dhaṁmānusāsanaṁ* 'instruction in the law' [dharmānuśāsanam], *Taṁbapaṁni* [Tāmraparṇī], *aṁna-* 'other' [anya-], *manati* 'thinks' [manyate]) and *-kkh-* from *-kṣ-* (*luk(k)ha-* [vṛkṣa-]); they cerebralize *t(h)* following *r̥/r* (*aṭhāya* 'for [that] purpose' [arthāya], *kaṭa-* 'made' [kr̥ta-]). They have a nominative sg. of the m. and nt. *a*-stems in *-e* (*°piye* 'the beloved', *sādhu dāne* 'good is a gift ... '), a loc. in *-asi* (*vijitasi* 'in the kingdom' [vijite], *olodhanasi* 'in the harem' [avarodhane]), an acc. pl. in *-āni* (*pulisāni* 'servants' [puruṣān], *yutāni* 'civil servants' [yuktān]), a present participle in *°mīna-* (*pakamamīna-* 'being zealous', *pāyamīna-* 'being suckled', *samīna-* 'being'), a 3pl. opt. in *-evŭ* (*vasevŭ* 'may they live!') and an absol. in *-tu* (*anusāsitu* 'having instructed'). Characteristic of this so-called 'administrative language' (*'Kanzleisprache'*) – in fact: the language of king Aśoka – are also forms like (3sg. ind.) *hoti* 'it is' (bhavati), (3sg. opt.) *siyā* 'it may be' (syāt), (acc.) *apheni* 'us' and *tupheni* 'you', *yeva* (eva), *hevaṁ* 'in this way' (evam), *hedisa-* 'such' (*edisa-* ← īdr̥śa-), and pronouns without initial *y-* (*e* < yaḥ, *āva* < yāvat).

Only Dhauli and Jaugaḍa are written in the pure eastern administrative language; all other edicts are more or less successful translations of this (or a similar) version. And the western dialect of Girnār is the one most similar to literary Pāli.

1.3 Pāli

The rise of MIA as inscriptional and literary language coincided roughly with the foundation of the new religions of Buddhism and Jainism round about 500 to 400 BC. Naturally the prestige of Sanskrit – the language of the Brahmins – was resisted by those who questioned the authority of the Vedas, and for this reason the early texts of the Buddhists and the Jains are in varieties of Middle Indo-Aryan. The Buddha is reported to have said that his teachings should be given to the people not in Sanskrit, but in their own language. This seems to be the reason for the multiplicity of languages the early Buddhism made use of. That of the texts of the Theravādins, an ancient school of Hīnayāna Buddhism, is called Pāli – a designation which originally meant 'text' and whose use as the name of a particular language seems not to antedate the sixteenth century. The Theravādin tradition has always claimed that the language the Buddha spoke was Māgadhī – i.e. a 'northeastern' language – and that this language was the same as that of its canonical texts, i.e. Pāli. And indeed we might expect that the language, the earliest Buddhism used, was essentially an eastern one, current in the Gangetic basin in the fifth century BC. Pāli as we have it, however, is basically a language of western India. With the help of the linguistic map (of India of the third century BC), which Aśoka's edicts allow us to draw (see 1.2.), the MIA languages can be localized geographically, Ardhamāgadhī and Māgadhī in the east, Śaurasenī and Pāli in the west of north India. Some of its salient features (retention of r and l, of ñ, ṇ and n, merging the sibilants into s, assimilation of consonant clusters, o- and am-nominatives of the a-stems, tvā-absolutive) Pāli shares with the (western) edicts of Girnār. But sporadically it presents features that belong to the eastern part of the linguistic area of India – l-forms, e-nominatives of a-stems, resolution of consonant clusters –, as evidenced by the edicts of (e.g.) Kālsī, Dhauli and of all pillars (see 1.2). Many Pāli words and forms – with 'frozen' phonetics – are relics from an earlier eastern dialect in which the 'texts' of early Buddhism were (orally) handed down and from which they were recast into their present 'western' linguistic shape. This proto-canonical language (which Heinrich Lüders called Alt-Ardhamāgadhī) – akin to the administrative language of Aśoka (see 1.2) and based on an artistic MIA 'Dichtersprache' which was in use long before the time of the Buddha – was in many ways, when compared with OIA, further advanced than the western dialects of its time: internal voiced occlusives had been lost, while the surds were voiced (-p- to -v-), original initial y- had (at least in some words) already become j-, and the gender distinction was about to break down, etc. That meant that the 'texts' were transformed into a more archaic language (unless the words were not taken over unaltered) as Buddhism spread westward. And that process over-reached itself in not a few instances, i.e. hyper-forms like Isipatana (Ṛṣyavṛjana) were created. In that way Pāli originated as a mixture of different dialects, as a kind of lingua franca.

From the west of mainland India – particularly from Vidiśā –, where the Buddhist communities using Pāli as their 'sacred' language settled, the 'texts' were brought to Ceylon during the reign of Aśoka (allegedly by his own nephew Milinda). In the monasteries of that island they were handed down orally – as they were before in India – until they were committed to writing during the council of Mātalē, held under the auspices of king Vaṭṭagāmaṇī Abhaya (27–19 BC). The main part in the tradition of the *Tipiṭaka* and its commentaries was played by the Mahāvihāra of Anurādhapura; this foundation of the Theravāda school was so dominant that another Pāli tradition independent of it is now documentable only in traces. The Pāli of the 'Mahāvihāra-texts' has phonetic features which it shares with no other form of MIA and which strongly suggest Sanskritization. This is the result of the great influence Sanskrit exercised on Pāli, notably in the twelfth century when the texts were revised on the basis of (the Burmese) Pāli grammars (e.g. the Saddanīti) which were heavily influenced by the works of Pāṇini and other Sanskrit grammarians. And also the orthography of our texts reflects the rules of these Pāli grammarians. The discrepancy between this orthography, which is historical and not phonetical, and the phonology of the original language of the canonical texts is considerable. Thus the anaptyctic vowels – to give just one example – often do not count as far as the metre is concerned. And we even have to assume that at one time a kind 'orthographical reform' took place. Generally, for example, *(kāla)par̥yaya-* ([-͜]-͜x), 'lapse of time', was replaced by *(kāla)pariyāya-* (see Ja IV 494,25*, V 367,2*), which, however, does not scan (cf. the coexistence of Skt. *kālasya paryayaṁ*, Mahābhārata 7,61.37d, and *kālasya paryāye*, ibid. 5,147.21a).

1.4 The Theravāda texts

Pāli is the language of (almost) all the texts of the Theravādins. These fall into two major groups, the 'canon' on the one hand and the non-canonical literature on the other. The latter comprises for the most part commentaries on the canonical texts the most famous of which were written by Buddhaghosa, who lived in the fifth century AD. Hence only very few texts – like the Dīpa- and Mahāvaṁsa, Ceylonese chronicles, and the Milindapañha – are not part of this canon, i.e. the 'canon' proper and the commentarial literature.

The canon – the only one of Buddhism that now exists in completeness in any Indian language – is formed by three aggregate collections, hence called *tipiṭaka* 'three baskets': (1) the *Vinayapiṭaka*, (2) the *Suttapiṭaka* and (3) the *Abhidhammapiṭaka*. The *Vinayapiṭaka* – two sections followed by a minor (younger) work – supplies the regulations for the management of the Order (*saṅgha*) and for the conduct of the daily life of monks and nuns. The *Suttapiṭaka* contains the discourses of Buddha. The first four of its five collections, called *nikāyas*, contain the *suttas*, the 'sermons' of Buddha. These are fairly homogeneous in character. The fifth *nikāya*, the *Khuddakanikāya*, is a miscellaneous collection of mostly verse texts. Its contents date from very different times; for, while several of its parts belong to the latest stratum of the Pāli canon, some go back to its earliest period. The third *piṭaka*, the *Abhidhammapiṭaka*, is basically a systematic arrangement of the contents of the *Suttapiṭaka* in the form of long lists of important terms of the doctrine.

Various stages of Pāli can be distinguished in the existing literature. Its oldest form is preserved in the verse portions of the canon. Many of these verses are very old, having parallels in Brahmanic and Jain texts – products of a post-Vedic 'Dichtersprache' –, and contain archaic grammatical forms, some of which are known in Vedic but have disappeared in Classical Sanskrit. The second stage is the language of the prose portions of the canon where the old forms are vanishing, being replaced by new formations. And the youngest stratum is the Pāli of the commentaries where the growing influence of literary Sanskrit caused the inclusion of numerous new words of that language disguised under a Pāli form.

In the following presentation, parenthetically cited OIA equivalents are *not* italicized. All *names* are written with a capital initial. The inscriptions of Aśoka write every geminate consonant with a single letter (in addition, Kharoṣṭhī does not distinguish vowel length). That has been retained unless it seemed advisable to indicate that a consonant actually stands for a geminate. In that case the second of the geminate consonants is given in parentheses (*aj(j)a, it(t)hī-*). In Kālsī no *ś* or *ṣ* appears in edicts I–IX while both characters are very frequently used in edicts Xff. This, however, is only an idiosyncrasy of the scribe of these edicts.

2 PHONOLOGY

2.1 The sound system

Aś Prakrit and Pāli possessed the following sounds:

Vowels: *a, ā, i, ī, u, ū, e, o*

Semivowels (counting as consonants): *y, r, l, v*

Consonants:	Stops	Spirants
Glottal		*h*
Guttural	*k, kh, g, gh, ṅ*	
Palatal	*c, ch, j, jh, ñ*	
Retroflex	*ṭ, ṭh, ḍ, ḍh, ḷ, ḷh, ṇ*	
Dental	*t, th, d, dh, n*	*s*
Labial	*p, ph, b, bh, m*	

In addition, there is a nasal called *anusvāra* or *niggahīta*: *ṁ*. The vowels *e* and *o* are generally long; allophonic *ĕ* and *ŏ* also occur, as a rule before double consonant. As to the survival of the sibilants *ś ṣ s* in northwestern Aś see 1.2.

2.2 Vowels

2.2.1 The system of vowels

The system of vowels (for consonants see 2.3) derived with certain modifications from that of OIA. Aśokan Prakrit and Pāli have lost the vowels (a) *ṛ, ṝ, ḷ* and the diphthongs (b) *ai* and (c) *au* which were replaced by (a) *a, i, u*, (b) *e, i* and (c) *o, u*. Examples:

(a) Aś RE V G *kaṭa-* 'made' (kṛta-), RE VII K *diḍha-* 'firm' (dṛḍha-), RE VIII G K *paripuchā-* 'inquiry' (paripṛcchā-), Pā. *gahita-* 'taken, seized' (gṛhīta-), *hadaya-* 'heart' (hṛdaya-), *kicca-* 'to be done' (kṛtya-), *siṅga-* 'horn' (śṛṅga-), *utu-* 'season' (ṛtu-), *pucchati* 'asks' (pṛcchati), *pitunnaṁ/pitūnaṁ* 'of the fathers' (pitṝṇām), *kutta-* 'arranged' (kḷpta-),

(b) Aś PE V *kevaṭa-* 'fisher' (kaivarta-), (inf.) °*tave* (°tavai), Pā. *pesuñña-* 'wickedness' (paiśunya-), *ucce* 'high' (uccaiḥ), *issariya-* '(royal) power, kingship' (aiśvarya-),

(c) Aś RE IV G *potra-* 'grandson' (pautra), Br *porāṇa-* 'old' (paurāṇa-), Pā. *orasa-* 'own' (aurasa-), *ratto* 'at night' (rātrau), *muñja-* 'made of *muñja* grass' (mauñja-).

The rules governing the substitution of OIA *ṛ* in Pāli – in word-initial position and in the neighbourhood of a palatal it generally results in *i*, in the neighbourhood of a labial in *u* (but if preceded by a consonant in word-initial position only after ≠*p*-), while *ṛ* not preceded or followed by a palatal or labial develops into *a* – are interfered with by numerous analogies: *diṭṭha-* 'seen' (< dṛṣṭa-) after *diṭṭhi-* 'view' (dṛṣṭi-) and *dissati* 'is seen' (dṛśyate) instead of expected **daṭṭha-*. And due to semantic differentiation *ṛ* can be represented in two different ways in one and the same OIA word: Pā. *maga-* 'wild beast', *miga-* 'gazelle', both < mṛga-, *vaḍḍhi-* 'profit, interest; welfare', *vuḍḍhi-* 'growth', both < vṛddhi-.

2.2.2 The law of mora

Due to the law of *mora*, according to which a syllable must not contain more than two *morae* (one *mora* is the length of time of a short vowel or of two consonants), the OIA long vowels – as such count also a short vowel plus *anusvāra* (*aṁ*, *iṁ*, *uṁ*), even if a vowel follows ([*sappaṁ ghora*]*visaṁ iva* 'like a very poisonous snake', Ja V 18,4*, scans ⌣---) – were (a) shortened before two or more consonants or else (b) the consonants (mainly *y*, *r* and sibilants) were reduced to one. Examples:

(a) Aś RE I G *devānaṁpriyo* '(Aśoka) beloved of the gods' (devānāṁ priyaḥ), Pā. *atta(n)-* 'self, soul' (ātman-), *maṁsa-* 'flesh' (māṁsa-), *ciṇṇa-* 'practised' (cīrṇa-), *puṇṇa-* 'full' (pūrṇa-), *upekkhā-* (i.e. *upĕkkhā-*) 'indifference' (upekṣā-), *oṭṭha-* (i.e. *ŏṭṭha-*) 'lip' (oṣṭha-),
(b) Aś PE I *palīkhāyā* 'observation' (instr. parīkṣayā), Br *dīgha-* 'long' (dīrgha-), Pā. *pāsa-* 'side' (pārśva-), *sīgha-* 'quick' (śīghra-), *apekhā-* 'attention' (apekṣā-), *vimokha-* 'deliverance' (vimokṣa-).

This shortening even occurs when the geminate consonant is split by a vowel (Aś Br *ācariya-* 'teacher' < ācārya-, PE VII *°suliyika-* 'pertaining to the sun' < * °sūryika-, Pā. *sukhuma-* 'soft' < sūkṣma-). Pāli words like *brāhmaṇa-* 'brahmin' or *svākkhāta-* 'well preached' violating this law are Sanskritisms (see 1.3); the 'etymologies' of *brāhmaṇa-* (e.g. *bāhitapāpo ti brāhmaṇo* 'He is called *brahmin* because his sins are [all] banished', Dhp 388) show that it was pronounced as *bāhaṇa-*.

A further effect of this law is the exchange of vocalic and consonantal length: Pā. *jaṇṇu(ka)-/jannu(ka)-* 'knee' (besides *jānu-*), *seyyo* (i.e. *sĕyyo*) 'better' (śreyaḥ), *yobbana-* (i.e. *yŏbbana-*) 'youth' (yauvana-).

Thus, the short vowels of Aśokan Prakrit and Pāli continue (a) OIA short vowels and (b) long vowels followed by two or more consonants. Examples:

(a) Aś RE IV Dh *abhisita-* 'anointed' (abhiṣikta-), Sār *bhikhunisaṁgha-* 'the order of the nuns' (bhikṣuṇī-saṅgha-), Pā. *abhiharati* 'brings' (abhiharati), *tiṭṭhati* 'stands' (tiṣṭhati), *ugga-* 'fierce' (ugra-),
(b) Aś MRE *pakaṁta-* 'practiced' (prakrānta-), RE XIII K *khaṁti-* 'forbearance' (kṣānti-), Pā. *aññā-* 'thorough knowledge' (ājñā-), *issā-* 'envy' (īrṣyā-), *uddhaṁ* 'above' (ūrdhvam).

Due to exchange of length (see above), a short vowel (followed by two consonants) may develop from

(c) a long OIA one followed by only one consonant: Pā. *kapalla-* 'bowl' (kapāla-), *vassita-* 'cry' (vāśita-).

Long vowels generally go back to OIA long vowels either followed by one or by more than one consonant: Aś RE I G *sūpāthāya* 'for curry' (sūpārthāya), MRE *lāti-* 'night' (rātri-), Pā. *ājānīya-* 'thoroughbred' (ājāney[y]a-), *kaññā* 'girls, daughters' (kanyāḥ), *(a)kāsi* 'he made' ([a]kārṣīt), *īdisa-* 'of such a kind' (īdṛś[a]-), *pīti-* 'joy' (prīti-), *pokkharaṇī* 'lotus ponds' (puṣkariṇīḥ), *kīrati* 'is scattered' (kīryate), *mūla-* 'root' (mūla-), *ahū* 'he was' (abhūt), *(deva)tūra-* 'heavenly music' (tūrya-), *lūkha-* 'rough' (rūkṣa-), *eti* 'goes', *ce* 'if' (ced), *ogha-* 'flood' (ogha-).

Compensatory lengthening of a short OIA vowel as a rule only occurs in connection with liquids, *-ṁ[s]-* (< -rś-, -ṁś-) and *-ṁh-* and at the boundary of prefix and root (in order not to obscure the root-initial sound, see 2.3.8): Aś RE IV G *avihīsā-* 'non-injuring' (avihiṁsā-), *vāsa-* 'year' (varṣa-), Rum *vīsati-* 'twenty' (viṁśati-), Pā. *kātuṁ* 'to do' (kartum), *sāsapa-* 'mustard' (sarṣapa-), *sārakkhati* 'wards off' (saṁrakṣati, see 2.3.6 end), *(aṅgāra)kāsu-* 'pit' (karṣū-), *sīha-* 'lion' (siṁha-), *cūḷa-* 'small' (kṣudra-), *ūhasati* 'breaks out into laughter' (uddhasati). Due to the similar pronunciation of both long vowel and short vowel followed by *-ṁ*, a long vowel, irrespective of whether primary or due to compensatory lengthening (mainly < *-Vr/lC-*), could be replaced before a single consonant by a vowel plus *-ṁ-* (and vice versa [see also above]): Aś RE XIII G *susuṁsā-* 'obedience' (śuśrūṣā-), RE IX K *khudā* 'futile' (~ Dh *khudaṁ* < kṣudram), Pā. *sanantana-* 'eternal' (sanātana-), *jigiṁsati* 'wishes to win' (~ *jigīsati*, Th 1110 [< jigīṣati]), *saṁvarī-* 'night' (śarvarī-), *(loma)haṁsa(na)-* 'causing horripilation' (harṣa[ṇa]-).

2.2.3 Word-final vowels

Except for *-(V)m* and *-(V)n*, which both resulted in *-(V)ṁ* (for the metrical value of *-ṁ* see 2.2.1), Aśokan Prakrit and Pāli have lost all final consonants unless they were retained in sandhi clusters (see 2.4.3). But due to analogies even *-ṁ* is dropped (Aś MRE *dāni* < idānīm 'now' after temporal adverbs in *-i*, Pā. *āyasmā* < āyasmān 'venerable one' after *rājā*). Final *-aḥ* (< -as/-ar) developed to *-o* – this sandhi form having been generalized – or to *-e* (see 3.2.1): Aś RE I G *samājo* 'assembly' (samājaḥ), RE IX K *tato* 'then' (tataḥ), Pā. *putto* 'son' (putraḥ), *bhikkhavo* 'monks' (bhikṣavaḥ), *mā pamādo* 'do not be indolent' (prāmadaḥ), *pāto* 'early' (prātaḥ); Aś RE I J *piyadasine* 'of (Aśoka) Priyadarśin' (°darśinaḥ), PE I *suve* 'tomorrow' (śvaḥ), Pā. *paṇḍitāse* 'wise men' ([Vedic] paṇḍitāsaḥ), *ante* 'inside' (antaḥ). And after vowels other than °*a-* the *visarga* is entirely lost: Aś PE I *vidhi* 'rule' (vidhiḥ), Pā. *jātī* 'births' (jātīḥ). Hence all words end in (short or long) vowels or else (due to the law of mora) in short vowels plus *-ṁ*: Aś RE I G *morā* 'peacock' (mayūrāḥ), Ko *bhikhu ... bhikhuni* 'monk and nun' (bhikṣuḥ ... bhikṣuṇī), RE IV K *āva* 'up to' (yāvat), Pā. *puttā* 'sons' (putrāḥ), *kaññā* 'girls, daughters' (kanyāḥ), *aggi* 'fire' (agniḥ), *dhī* 'shame!' (dhik), *āsi* 'was' (āsīt), *assā* 'from the horse' (aśvāt), *samantā* 'on all sides' (samantāt), *mayhaṁ* 'me' (mahyam). Final vowels may be 'nasalized' (by adding *-ṁ*) even after loss of a following consonant (this nasalization occurs sometimes analogically): Aś SE II J Sa *mamaṁ* 'my' (mama), RE XIII K *avaṁ* 'up to' (yāvat), Pā. *cirassaṁ* 'at last' (cirasya), *īsaṁ* 'a little' (īṣat), *puna-ppunaṁ* 'again and again' (punar), *asakkaccaṁ* 'carelessly' (asatkṛtya), *sakiṁ* 'once' (*saki < sakṛt).

In Pāli a long final vowel became shortened in polysyllabic words if the penultimate syllable was long whereas long finals remained in disyllabic words as well as in polysyllabic words with a short penult: *kaññāya* 'of the daughter' (kanyāyāḥ), *tassā* 'her' (tasyāḥ), *deviyā* 'of the queen' (dev₁yāḥ), *sīlavatā* 'by the virtuous' (śīlavatā), *abravī* 'he said' (abravīt), *atāri* 'he crossed' (atārīt). This accounts also for the sporadic absolutives in *-tva* (see 3.6.5). But possible unique forms, which this rhythmic law would have produced within a paradigm, were eliminated, e.g. *nattāro* (naptāraḥ) and *sakhāro* (see 3.2.6) on the model of *pitaro* (pitaraḥ); and a number of levellings (e.g. due to the frequent use of augment and preverb) affected this rule also in the verbal inflection. At some stage this rule ceased to operate; subsequently, new forms were created and redactional modernizations removed the old ones. That is the reason why the opposition of brevity and length seems to be neutralized in final vowels.

2.2.4 Assimilation and dissimilation of vowels

A number of (a) assimilations and (b) dissimilations affected the OIA vowels:

(a) Aś RE II J *udu°* 'water' (uda-), RE II G *osudha-* 'plant' (auṣadha), Pā. *kappara-* 'elbow' (kūrpara-), *pharati* 'pervades' (sphurati), *timissā-* 'darkness' (tamisrā-), *sirimsapa-* 'reptile' (sarīsṛpa-), *anusuyyaka-* 'not jealous' (anasūyaka-), *puthujjana-* 'a common man' (*puthajjana- < pṛthagjana-), *ucchu-* 'sugar-cane' (ikṣu-), *susu-* 'child' (śiśu-), *oṇojeti* 'pours out water' (avanejayati),

(b) Aś Tōp *kapīlikā-* 'ant' (pipīlikā-; see 2.3.2), Pā. *tad-aminā* 'by this' (iminā), *dakkhita-* 'consecrated' (dīkṣita-), *makula-* 'bud' (mukula-), *ahesum* 'they were' (*ahosum, cf. *ahosi*).

Vocalic assimilation was favoured by a differentiation of meaning: P. *pana* 'but', *puna* 'moreover' (both < punaḥ).

2.2.5 Colouring of vowels

OIA *a* and – though to a lesser degree – *ŭ* had a tendency to become palatalized to *i* in the vicinity of palatal sounds: Aś RE XII K *vaḍhiyati* 'makes prosper' (vardhayati), PE I *pulisa-* 'man' (*pulusa- < puruṣa-), Pā. *āsimsati* 'desires' (āśaṁsati), *dighañña-* 'inferior' (jaghanya-), *miñjā-* 'marrow' (majjan-/majjā-), *tissā* 'her' (tasyāḥ), *rajassira-* 'covered with dust' (*rajassila- < rajasvala-), *jigucchati* 'avoids' (jugupsate), *vālikā-* 'sand' (vāluka-), *bhiyyo* 'more' (bhūyaḥ). Such a (secondary) *i* could be written as *e*: Aś RE XIII Sh *meñati* 'thinks' (manyate), Tōp *seyaka-* 'porcupine' (śalyaka-), Pā. *pheggu-* 'wood that is not part of a tree's core' (phalgu-), *seyyā-* 'bed' (śayyā-). In the neighbourhood of a labial *ă* was liable to be coloured to *u*: Aś RE XIII K *(vedaniya)mute (gulu)mute* 'considered grievous, considered deplorable' ([vedanīya]-matam [guru]matam), RE IX K *ucāvuca-* 'high and low, various' (uccāvaca-), Pā. *navuti-* 'ninety' (navati-), *nimugga-* 'immersed' (nimagna-), *ummujjati* 'understands' ([ep.] unmārjati). OIA *i* and *u*, if followed by a cerebral that closes the syllable, could develop to *e* and *o*, respectively: Pā. *Vāseṭṭhī* (Vāsiṣṭhī), *Veṇhu* (Viṣṇu; cf. *Andhakaveṇhu*), *heṭṭhā* 'below' (*[a]dhiṣṭāt [adhastāt :: upariṣṭāt]), *oṭṭha-* 'camel' (uṣṭra-), *pokkharaṇī-* 'lotus pond' (puṣkariṇī-). Likewise *e* and *ai* before a palatal that closes the syllable resulted in *i* (here *i* represents *ĕ*): Pā. *ānissāmi* 'I shall bring' (*āneśyāmi < āneṣyāmi), *vissa-* 'abode' (veśman-), *issariya-* 'kingship' (aiśvarya-). And *u*, if preceded in word-initial position by a labial, sometimes developed to *o*: Pā. *pokkhara-* 'lotus' (puṣkara-), *potthaka-* 'book' (pustaka-), *poso* 'of a man' (puṁsaḥ), *bhogga-* 'bent' (bhugna-), *bondī-* 'body' (*bundī- < vṛndī-). On the other hand, MIA *o-* from OIA *ava-* could develop to *u-*: Pā. *uññā-* 'contempt' (avajñā-), *ujjhāyati* 'is annoyed' (avadhyāyati), *ussāva-* 'dew' (avaśyāya-), *ukkāra-* 'dung' (~ *avakkāra-* [ava[s]kara-]), *uttarati* 'descends' (~ *otarati* [avatarati]).

In the vicinity of palatals (*j, c, ñ, y, l, h*) the palatal colouring of the OIA vowels *ĭ ŭ* was only optionally expressed in writing (i.e. as *ĭ* or *e*); instead the vowel a was used: Pā.

ānañja- 'imperturbability' (*āniñjya-), *Koṇḍañña* (Kauṇḍinya), *kosajja-* 'indolence' (kausīdya-), *porohacca-* 'office of priest' (*paurohitya-), *Mucalinda* (Mucilinda), *rohañña-* 'redness' (rauhiṇya-), *āyasma(nt)-* 'venerable' (āyuṣmant-), *bāhusacca-* 'great learning' (bāhuśrutya-), *sakkhali-* 'ear orifice' (śaṣkulī-). Mainly before *-yy-*, however, *e* was used instead of *i*: Pā. *adejjha-* 'strung' (adhijya-), *apeyyamāna-* 'not drunk' (apīyamāna-), *atīraṇeyya-* 'impracticable' (°anīya-), *veyyatti-* cleverness' (*viyyatti- < vyakti-).

2.2.6 Changing vowel quantity/quality in foreign words

In Pāli changing vowel quantity and quality often occur in foreign words: *avāka-* 'a particular plant' (avakā̆-), *papphāsa-* 'the lungs' (pupphusa-), *mutiṅga-* 'drum' (mr̥daṅga-), *kaṇavera-* ~ *kaṇavīra-* 'oleander', *bella-* ~ *billa-* 'the fruit of the *vilva* tree'.

2.2.7 Contraction of vowels

The long vowels of Aśokan Prakrit and Pāli are also the result of various contractions: (a) *-ā-* < -ayā-, -āya- (especially after palatals and *-y-* and analogically to that kind of haplological contraction) and -avā-, (b) *-e-* (< [Aś] *-aï-*) < -aya-, -ayi-, *-ayir- (< -ar̥y-) and -avi-, (c) *(≠)o-* < (≠)ava- and -ayū-. Examples:

(a) (absent from Aś Pkt.) Pā. *katipāhaṃ* 'for a few days' (katipayâhaṃ), *upaṭṭhāka-* 'servant' (upasthāyaka-), *Kaccāna* (Kātyāyana), *pajjhāti* 'muses' (~ *pajjhāyati* < pradhyāyati), *pariyāgata-* 'reached' (*pariyāyagata-*), *vehāsa-* 'being in the air' (vaihāyasa-), *sampāyati* 'answers' (*sampāyayati* < sampādayati), *aññā* 'having realized' (ājñāya), *appaṭisaṃkhā* 'without reflecting' (°khyāya), *yāgu-* 'rice-gruel' (yavāgū-),

(b) Aś RE VIII *thaira-* 'elder' (sthavira-), RE V K *tedasa-* 'thirteen' (*trayadaśa- ~ trayodaśa-), SE I Dh *Ujjeni(te)* '(from) Ujjayinī' (Ujjayinī[taḥ]), Pā. *neti* 'leads' (nayati), *bhāveti* 'develops' (bhāvayati), *acceka-* 'extraordinary' (ātyayika-), *ācera-* 'teacher' (*ācayira- < ācariya- < ācārya-), *issera-* 'kingship' (aiśvarya-), *peyyāla-* 'repetition' (*payirāya- < paryāya-), *thera-* 'elder' (sthavira-), *hessati* 'will be' (bhaviṣyati),

(c) Aś RE VI K *olodhana-* 'harem' (avarodhana-), RE I G *mora-* 'peacock' (mayūra-), Pā. *oma-* 'inferior' (avama-), *olambati* 'hangs down' (avalambate), *koja-* 'armour' (kavaca-), *hoti* 'is, becomes' (bhavati), *uposatha-* 'day on which the *saṅgha* assembles to recite the *pātimokkha*' (upavasatha-), *poṇa-* 'sloping down' (pravaṇa-), *mora-* (see above).

Vowels are also contracted after the loss of an intermediary *-y-* or *-l-*: Aś RE IX K *kho* 'indeed' (khalu), MRE *vyūtha-* 'dawned' (< *vūtha- *vuyutha- < v̤yuṣṭa-), Pā. *vīti-* 'beyond' (*viyiti- < v̤yati-), *vūpa-* 'away' (*vu-y-upa- < v̤y-upa-).

2.2.8 Anaptyctic vowels

OIA conjuncts could be split up by anaptyctic vowels (see 2.3.3). *a* appears as such a vowel (called *svarabhakti*) between two consonants (at least) one of which contains an ā̆: Aś RE XII G K *garahati / galahati* 'reproaches' (garhati), Pā. *ratana-* 'gem' (ratna-), *pāsaṇī(ka)-* 'heel' (pārṣṇi-), *nahāpita-* 'bathed' (snāpita-). *i* functions as a *svarabhakti* sound between two consonants one of which has a palatal colouring: Aś RE IV Dh *diviya*- 'heavenly' (divya-), RE XIV Dh *lājinā* 'by the king' (rājñā), Bairāṭ °*pasina*- 'question' (praśna-), Pā. *aggini*- 'fire' (agni-), *kiloma*- 'bile' (kloman-), *gilāna*- 'sick' (glāna-), *sirī*- 'prosperity' (śrī-). Unconditioned -*i*- is an eastern feature: Aś RE XIII K *sineha*- 'affection' (sneha-), Pā. *tasiṇā*- 'thirst, passion' (tṛṣṇā-). And *u* figures as such a vowel between two syllables of which (at least) one contains a labial: Aś RE XIII G K *p(r)āpuṇāti* 'reaches' (prāpnoti), RE I J *puluvaṁ* 'formerly' (pūrvam), PE I *saḍuvīsati*° 'twenty-six' (ṣaḍviṁśati-), Pā. *sukhuma*- 'soft' (sūkṣma-), *sakkuṇāti* 'is able' (śaknoti), *sumarati* 'remembers' (smarati).

2.2.9 Prothetic vowels

For ease of pronunciation a vowel could be added word-initially: Aś RE IX Dh *ithī*- / Pā. *itthī*- 'woman' (strī-). *u*, however, is not used as a prothetic vowel (Pā. *umhayati* < ut-smayati 'smiles at' [and *not* < smayate]).

2.2.10 Saṁprasāraṇa

The so-called *saṁprasāraṇa* is a combined process of vocalic and consonantal assimilation. *i* resulted by it from OIA *(C)ya* in open and closed syllables (> *(C)yi* > *(CC)i*), a development partly favoured by analogies and folk etymologies: Aś Bar *nigoha*- 'Banyan tree' (nyagrodha-), PE I *majhima*- 'middle' (madhyama-), Pā. *abbhihāsi* 'offered' (abhyahārṣīt), *kāhiti* 'will make' (~ kariṣyati [see 3.5.5]), *sakkhi*- 'friendship' (sakhya-). In the same way *u* results from (< (CC)u < *(C)vu <) OIA *(C)va/i* and *(C)ma(__n)* (see 2.3.4): Aś PE VIII *su* (svid), SE I J *tul(an)āya* 'through haste' (tvaranayā), Pā. *turita*- 'quick' (tvarita-), *supina*- 'dream' (*svupina- < svapna-), *addhuno* 'of the time' (adhvanaḥ), °*khattuṁ* (: °kṛtvaḥ), *susāna*- 'cremation ground' (*śvaśāna- < śmaśāna-). In closed syllables, however, *o* results: Pā. *sotthi*- (svasti-), *sobbha*- (śvabhra-).

2.2.11 Changing vowel quantity/quality due to analogy etc.

Due to (a) analogical processes – often levellings within nominal and verbal paradigms – (b) blendings, (c) formations with 'new' suffixes (°*ima*-, -*ima[nt]*-), (d) adjustments to – what seemed – a regular form of suffix (°*ika*-, °*ita*-, °*iya*-) and (e) recomposition, the quantity and quality of the vocalism of cognate OIA/Sanskrit and Aśokan or Pāli words may differ. Examples:

(a) Aś RE XIII K *galu* °, Aś Br *garusu* '(towards the) teacher(s)' (guru[ṣu] :: garīyas-), RE VIII Dh *edisa*- 'such one' (īdisa- [īdṛśa-] :: *eta[d]*-), Pā. *pasibbaka*- 'bag' (*pasevaka [< prasevaka-] :: *sibbati* [< sīvyati]), *paputta*- 'grandson' (*papotta- [< prapautra-] :: *putta*- [< putra-]), *aggīhi, aggīsu* 'by/in fires' (:: *aggīnaṁ* < agnīnām), *bhikkhūhi, bhikkhūsu* 'by/with monks' (:: *bhikkhūnaṁ* < bhikṣūnām), (°)*rūhati* 'grows' ([rohati] : rūḷha- = gūhati : gūḷha-), *janettī*- 'mother' (janitrī- :: janeti), *dhovati* 'washes' (dhāvati :: *dhota*- [< dhauta-]),

(b) Aś RE VII Dh *munisa*- 'man' (manussa- [manuṣya-] x *pulisa*- [puruṣa-]), MRE *cu* 'but' (ca x tu), PE III *dekhati* 'sees' (dakkhati [√dṛś] x pekkhati [√īkṣ]), Pā. *pareta*- 'furnished with' (parīta- x upeta-),

(c) Pā. *carima*- 'last' (≠ carama-), *puttima(nt)*- 'having sons' (≠ putravant-),

(d) Aś *(aḍha)tiya-* 'two and a half' (see 2.3.10), Pā. *alika-* 'lie' (alīka-), *paccanika-* 'enemy' (pratyanīka-), *gahita-* 'grasped' (gṛhīta-), *khādaniya-* 'food' (khādanīya-), *pāniya-* 'water' (pānīya-), *dutiya-* 'second' (~ *dutīya-* < dvitīya-),

(e) Pā. *itarītara-* 'whatsoever' ([i.e. *itar'ītara-*, see 2.2.13] ≠ itaretara-).

2.2.12 Vṛddhi of primary and secondary a, i and u

In derivations *ā, e* and *o* are the *vṛddhi* vowels corresponding to primary and secondary *a, i* and *u*. The change of *ṛ* to *a, i* and *u* (see 2.2.1) led to new analogical *vṛddhi* formations. Examples: Aś Bairāṭ *gālave* 'respect' (← *galu-* [see 2.2.11a] < guru-), Pā. *sākhalya-* 'friendship' (← *sakhila-* [sakhi- x akhila-]), *bhākuṭika-* 'frowning' (← *bhakuṭi-* [bhṛkuṭi-]), *(pali)gedha-* 'greed' (← *giddha-* [< gṛddha-] = nisedha- : nisiddha- / bodha- : buddha-), *jeguccha-* 'loathsome' (← *jigucchati* [jugupsate]), *gelañña-* 'illness' (← *gilāna-*, see 2.2.8), *veyyāvacca-* 'service' (← **viyyāvata-* [< v₁yāpṛta-]), *opadhika-* 'pertaining to material objects' (← upadhi-), *dovārika-* 'door-keeper' (← dᵤvāra-), *dohaḷa-* 'longing of a pregnant woman' (← **duhaḷa-* ← dvihṛd[a]-), *pothujjanika-* 'common' (← *puthujjana-*, see 2.2.4), *phoṭṭhabba-* 'tangible' (← *phusati* [spṛśati]), *sosānika-* 'who lives near a burning-ground' (← *susāna-*, see 2.3.3 [end]).

OIA *ai, au* developed into *e, o,* and thus merged with original *e* and *o,* and OIA *ṛ* became *a, i* and *u* (see 2.2.1). Thus the three members of the characteristic vowel-alternations of OIA (*i : e : ai, u : o : au*) were reduced to two (*i : e, u : o*), while the alternation *ṛ : ar : ār* was upset altogether. This system was further confused by the shortening of all OIA long vowels in closed syllables (see 2.2.2), which caused, for example, the loss of all distinction between such pairs as OIA *candra-* 'moon' and *cāndra-* 'lunar'. As a consequence, Aśokan Prakrit and Pāli for the most part did without *vṛddhi,* especially in derivations from trisyllabic words whose first syllable is closed: Aś PE III *niṭhūliya-* 'harshness' (*niṣṭhurya-* [≠ naiṣṭhurya-]), PE V *puṁnamāsiya-* 'relating to the full moon' (≠ paurṇamāsya-), Pā. *sindhava-* 'belonging to Sindh' (≠ saindhava-), *ussukka-* 'eagerness' (≠ autsukya-).

2.2.13 Shortening and lengthening of vowels at the boundary of compounds

Long (OIA) vowels could be shortened at the boundary of a compound or of a stem and a suffix: Aś PE VII *devi-kumāla-* 'prince' (devī-kumāra-), Rum *Luṁmini-gāme* 'in the village of Lumbini' (Lumbinī-grāme), Pā. *māla+bhāri(n)-* 'one who bears a garland' (: *mālā-, pañña+va(nt)-* 'wise' (: *paññā-), itthi+ratana-* 'a jewel of a woman' (: *itthī-*, see 2.2.9), *siri+ma(nt)-* 'glorious' (: *sirī-*, see 2.2.8), *Bārāṇasi+to* 'from Benares' (: *Bārāṇasī-*). Conversely, (OIA) short vowels could be lengthened in this position as well as at the boundary of prefix and verb: Pā. *ratanā+maya-* 'consisting of gems' (ratnamaya-), *diṭṭhī+gata-* 'come into sight' (dṛṣṭigata-), *jutī+ma(nt)-* 'bright' (dyutimant-), *maṇī+maya-* 'made of jewels' (maṇimaya-).

Moreover, we have long Pāli vowels owing to a wrong resolution of compounds (Pā. *āgāra-* 'house' ← °âgāra-, *odaka-* 'water' ← [sīt]odaka-) and due to recomposition (Pā. *itarītara-* 'whatsoever', recomposed out of *itara+itara-* [see 2.2.11e] as *añña-m-aññam* also is recomposed).

2.3 Consonants

2.3.1 The system of consonants

Apart from *ḍ(h)*, *ś* and *ṣ*, simple initial and intervocalic consonants of OIA are generally preserved in Pāli (for Aś Pkt. see 1.2), which thus has by and large the same consonant system as OIA. Only *ṅ* is lost as a phoneme, whereas *ñ* has acquired phonemic status: *ñante* 'near-by' (nyante), *ñāṇa*- 'knowledge' (jñāna-). OIA *ś* and *ṣ* merged with *s*, and intervocalic *ḍ(h)* developed to *ḷ(h)*: *sisira*- 'cold season' (śiśira-), *osadhī*- 'medicinal herb' (oṣadhī-), *tāḷeti* 'beats' (tāḍayati), *aḷāra*- 'curved' (arāḍa-), *mūḷha*- 'confused' (mūḍha-). In word-initial position, however, ≠*s*- and ≠*ś(v)*- are sometimes represented by *ch*-: *cha*- 'six' (ṣaṣ-), *chāpa*- 'the young of an animal' (śāva-), *chap/vaka*- '(one who cooks dogs =) outcaste' (śvapaka-).

2.3.2 Consonantal sound change

There are, however, a number of exceptions to this general rule (2.3.1). Word-initial ≠*k*- ≠*t*-, ≠*p*- and ≠*b*- are often aspirated due to the presence of a following -*S*- or -*l*-: Aś SE I J *aphalusa*- 'not cruel' (aparuṣa-), Pā. *khuṁseti* 'scolds' (kutsayati), *thusa*- 'chaff' (tuṣa-), *pharasu*- 'axe' (paraśu-), *bhisa*- 'lotus fibre' (bisa-). In some words of eastern Aś Pkt. and of the 'eastern' stratum of Pāli intervocalic voiceless stops are voiced: Aś Bairāṭ *adhigicya* 'concerning' (adhikṛtya), Pā. *paṭigacca* 'previously' (~ *paṭikacca* < *pratikṛtya), *koja*- 'armour' (kavaca-), (*°)yādeti* 'gives' (yātayati), *medhaga*- 'quarrel' (methaka-), *thevati* 'trickles' (√stip). Quite often the -*k*- of the suffix *°ika*- is palatalized (see Aś RE IX K *akālikye* 'present-day' [akālike]) and subsequently dropped, a development due to terminal weakness that was favoured by the (partial) interchangeability of (*°iya*- <) *°ika*- and *°(i)ya*-: Aś RE XIII K *(pala)lokiya*- 'pertaining to the (other) world' ([para]laukika-), Pā. *adūsiya*- (~ *adūsika*-) 'innocent', *odariya*- (~ *odarika*-) 'gluttonous'. After *u* the hiatus left by a dropped consonant was bridged by *v*: Aś PE V *cāvudasa*- 'fourteen' (caturdaśa-), Pā. *suva*- 'parrot' (śuka-).

Sometimes intervocalic voiced stops and semivowels are lost – e.g. Aś RE VIII G *thaira*- 'elder' (sthavira-), Pā. *sārāṇīya*- 'ceremonious greeting' (saṁrāganīya-), *niya*- 'own' (nija-), *khāyita*- 'eaten' (khādita-) – while it is only in the numeral Aś Nig. *codasa*-, Pā. *cuddasa*- 'fourteen' (caturdaśa-) that a voiceless stop is dropped, favoured by the dissimilation of *t__d* (see Aś *cāvudasa*-, see above). 'Hyper-translations' (see 1.3) are responsible for the occasional representation of original voiced stops by voiceless stops: Pā. *vilāka*- 'slender' (*vilāga- < vilagna-), *palikha*- 'bar' (parigha-), *pāceti* 'drives on' (prājati), *(a)kusīta*-'(not) lazy' ([a]kusīda-), *jannutaggha*- 'reaching up to the knees' (jānudaghna-), *(a)pithīyati* 'is covered' (api-√dhā), *chāpa*- 'the young of an animal' (śāva-). And a genuine *°(i)ya*- may be rendered as *°ika*-: Pā. *rathikā*- 'road' (rath₁yā-).

OIA -*t(h)*- which follows a(n original) -*ṛ*- or an -*r*- is cerebralized, possibly an 'eastern' feature of Aś Pkt. and Pāli (see 1.2): Aś PE II *kaṭa*- 'made' (kṛta), *paṭipati*- 'behaviour' (pratipatti-), Pā. *uddhaṭa*- 'lifted up' (uddhṛta-), *paṭi+* 'towards, near' (prati+).

OIA -*n*- is sometimes cerebralized after *ū* or *o* or a palatal: Aś RE XIII G K *p(r)āpuṇāti* 'reaches' (prāpnoti), RE V G *Yoṇa* (~ K Dh *Yona*) 'Greek' (Yavana), Pā. *oṇata*- 'bent down' (avanata-), *oṇojeti* 'pours out' (avanejayati), *sakkuṇoti* 'is able' (śaknoti), *jaṇṇu(ka)*- 'knee' (jānu[ka]-), *(viñ)ñāṇa*- 'knowledge' ([vi]jñāna-). Conversely, -*ṇ*- is analogically decerebralized: Aś RE IX G *putena* 'by the son' (putreṇa), Pā. *sahassāni* 'thousands' (sahasrāṇi), *savana-* 'hearing' (śravaṇa-), *kubbāna-* 'doing' (kurvāṇa-).

In (eastern) Aśokan Prakrit an intervocalic *-y-* may develop to *-j-*: Aś RE I K *majūla-* 'peacock' (mayūra-). And initial *y-* of pronouns is dropped: Aś RE IV K *aṁ* 'which' (yat), RE VII Dh *asa* 'whose' (yasya). In (a) the vicinity of a palatal sound *y* is dissimilated to *v*, whereas it is (b) assimilated to a neighbouring *ŭ* or *o*. Examples:

(a) RE XIII K *lājaviśavaṣi* 'in the kingdom' (rājaviṣaye), Pā. *ussāva-* 'dew' (avaśyāya-), *kulāva(ka)-* 'nest' (kulāya-), *migavā-* 'hunting' (*migayā- < *mṛgayā-*; see Aś G/K RE VIII *migav[i]yā-* which goes back to *migavyā-* < *mṛgavīyā-* as does Pkt. *migavvā-*, Uttarajjhayaṇasutta XVIII,1),

(b) Aś MRE *dīghāvu(s)-* 'long life' (dīrghāyus-), RE VII K Dh. *vasevŭ* 'may they live!' (vaseyuḥ), PE VI *pāpovā* 'may he reach!' (*prāpnoyāt), Pā. *āvudha-* 'weapon' (āyudha-), *āvuso* 'friend(s)' (*āyuṣvaḥ).

Conversely, *v* is dissimilated to *y* in the vicinity of *v*: Pā. *lāyitvā* 'having cut' (*lāvitvā). *-y-* has a propensity for being geminated after *ĭ* and *e*: Pā. *bhiyyo* 'more' (*bhīyaḥ < bhūyaḥ), *koleyyaka-* 'of good breed' (kauleyaka-), *bhaveyya* 'may he be!' (*bhaveya ← bhavet :: bhaveyam). Only rarely is *-v-* geminated: Pā. *yobbana-* 'youth' (yauvana-).

In eastern Aś every *-r-* developed into *-l-*, while western Aś has retained old *-r-* (see 1.2), and Pāli has both old *r/l* and new (eastern) *l*, sometimes side by side: Pā. *antalikkha-* 'sky' (antarikṣa-), *ārabhati* 'sacrifices' (ā-√labh < √rabh), *(Isi)gili/giri-, pali+/pari+* 'around' (pari+). Sometimes *r* corresponds to an old *l* due to hyper-translation: Aś RE IX Sop *phara-* 'result' (phala-), *maṁgara-* 'auspicious ceremony' (maṅgala-), Pā. *suruddha-* 'very cruel' (sulubdha-).

Emphatic *h-* is prefixed to a number of words. They are frequent in the eastern versions of the Aśoka inscriptions: Aś RE I J *hida* 'here' (*hidha < idha), RE III K *hevaṁ* 'in that way' (evam), Pā. *hambho* 'look here!' (ambho), *hetaṁ* 'this' (etam).

Single consonants may arise from OIA clusters by (a) compensatory lengthening (see 2.2.2), (b) shortening of a geminate consonant when preceded by an originally long vowel (see 2.2.2) or (c) analogy (Pā. *dukha-* 'sorrow' < *dukkha-* [< duḥkha-] :: sukha- 'happiness').

A number of sound sequences were prone to (a) assimilation (mainly *p__p < p__v* and *vice versa*) and (b) dissimilation. Examples:

(a) Pā. *apilapati* 'floats before (one's mind)' (āplavate), *(a)palāpa-* '(free from) chaff' (palāva-), *vivina-* 'forest' (vipina-), *(a)vyāvaṭa-* '(not) occupied' ([a]vyāpṛta-);

(b) 1. one of two identical sounds is dissimilated (often *l__r < r__r, n__l < l__l* and *p__v < p__p*): Aś All *kipilikā-* 'ant' (pipīlikā-), RE XIII Sh *avatrapeyu* 'may they repent!' (apa-√trap), MRE Sah *pāvatave* 'to reach' (~ *pāpotave*), Pā. *kaṭhita-* 'boiling' (kvathita-), *daḍḍha-* 'burnt' (*daddha- < dagdha-), *naṅgala-* 'plough' (lāṅgala-), *nalāṭa-* 'forehead' (lalāṭa-), *vīmaṁsā-* 'reflection' (mīmāṁsā-), *Nerañjarā* (Nairañjanā), *Milinda* ([gr.] Μενάνδρος), *dalidda-* 'poor' (daridra-), *pūva-* 'cake' (pūpa-); 2. one of two similiar sounds is dissimilated (often *ṇ __ t < n__t, l__n/m < d__n/m, dh__p/bh/m < bh__p/bh/m, t__r < t__d*): Aś RE IV *ciṭhitu* 'having lived' (absol. of *ṭiṭhati [√sthā]), Pā. *khaṇati* 'digs' (khanati), *ālāna-* 'fetter' (ādāna-), *ālimpeti* 'kindles' (*ādimpeti < ādīpayati), *adhippāya-* 'intention' (abhiprāya-), *tārisa-* 'of this kind' (tādṛśa-), *sattarasa-* 'seventeen' (saptadaśa-), *tikicchā-* 'art of healing' (cikitsā-), *digucchā-* 'disgust' (jugupsā-), *dighañña-* 'inferior' (~ *jighañña-* < jaghanya), *pivati* 'drinks' (pibati).

Folk-etymologies and blends cause unetymological aspiration in medial syllables: Pā. *sunakha-* '(of good claw =) dog' ([*]śunaka- :: nakha-), *sukhumāla-* 'graceful' (*sukumāla-* [°kumāra] × *sukhuma-* [sūkṣma-]).

An OIA aspirate loses its occlusion only due to (a) dissimilation, (b) blending or (c) phonetical weakness of sounds at the end of a word (they are often subject to changes which do not take place elsewhere), and (d) in words which are used very frequently. Examples:

(a) Aś Bar *nigohakubhā-* 'Banyan grove' (*nigodhakubhā- < nyagrodha[kubhā]-), PE VI *vidahāmi* 'I ordain' (vidadhāmi), RE XIII K *lahuka-* 'little' (laghuka-), Pā. *dahati* 'puts' (*dadhati < dadhāti-), *pahu-* 'mighty' (prabhu-), *heṭṭhā* 'below' (*[a]dhiṣṭhāt),
(b) Pā. *ruhira-* 'blood' (rudhira- x lohita-),
(c) Aś / P. (instr. pl.) °ehi (°ebhiḥ),
(d) Aś RE IV K Dh *hoti* 'is, becomes' (bhavati), SE II Dh *lahevu* 'may they get' (labheyuḥ), Pā. *sāhu* 'well!' (sādhu).

An aspirate loses its aspiration due to dissimilation in the context of another aspirate inclusive of *h*: As RE IV K *kaṁdha-* 'mass' ([G] khamdha- < skandha-), RE I J *hida* 'here' (*h-idha ~ iha*), Pā. *khudā-* 'hunger' (ksudh[ā]-), *pihā-* 'longing' (*phihā- < spṛhā-). The correspondence of OIA -*h*- and a(n) Aśokan/Pāli aspirate is (apart from Pā. *idha*) only due to blending: Aś Sār *saṁnaṁdhāpayitu* 'having made to put on (clothes)' (sam-√nah × √bandh), Pā. *pilandhati* 'puts on (ornaments)' ([api]nandhati < °nahyati × °bandhati), *saṁgharati* 'collects' (saṁharati × saṁgṛhnāti).

The initial consonant of the second member of a compound (in the broad sense) is liable to be doubled (in analogy with an etymological geminate): Pā. *kummagga-* 'a bad way' (kumārga- [after *dummagga-*]), *niggilati* 'swallows' (nigirati [after *uggilati*]). This is one of the metrical licences of the poetic language of Pāli.

2.3.3 Development of OIA word-initial consonants

In word-initial position only single consonants are allowed; *nh*- and *mh*- (< sn-/sm-) are most probably unitary phonemes (viz. aspirates) and hence can occur initially: Pā. *nhāru-* 'sinew' (cf. snāyu-), *mhita-* 'smile' (smita-). Clusters are assimilated according to the rules of 2.3.4 (unless they are split up by a vowel [see 2.2.8] – the first a western, the latter an eastern feature of Pāli) but only the second sound is retained: Aś RE IV G *ñāti-* 'relative' (jñāti-), Nig *thuba-* 'Buddhist monument' (stūpa-), Pā. *khāyati* 'appears' (khyāyate), *ñāṇa-* 'knowledge' (jñāna-), *vajati* 'proceeds' (vrajati), *thana-* 'breast' (stana-), *ṭhāna-* 'place' (sthāna-). ≠C- as a rule corresponds to OIA ≠C(r/l/v)-: Aś PE V *gāma-* 'village' (grāma-), SE I Dh *sakhina-* 'mild' (ślakṣna-), Pā. *kamati* 'walks' (kramate), *kaṭhita-* 'boiling' (kvathita-), *semha-* 'phlegm' (ślesman-), *sita-* 'smile' (smita-). *hr-*, however, results in *r-* (Pā. *rassa-* 'short' < hrasva-) and *r(a)h-* (Pā. *r[a]hada-* 'lake' < hradas-). Initial palatals can result from ≠Cy-: Pā. *cavati* 'falls away, dies' (cyavate), *cāga-* 'liberality' (tyāga-), *jāni-* 'loss' (jyāni-), *jhāna-* 'meditation' (dhyāna-), *ñāya-* 'right manner' (nyāya-). Only very rarely was this group split up as was ≠Cl- regularly (if C ≠ S [cf. *semha-*, see above]) and others sporadically: Aś SE I J Dh *kilamatha-* 'fatigue' (klamatha-), MRE *sumi* 'I am' ([a]smi), Pā. *kilesa-* 'affliction' (kleśa-), *gilāna-* 'ill' (glāna-), *silesuma-* 'phlegm' (ślesman-), *sumarati* 'remembers' (smarati). An aspirate may go back to *SC(h)* or CS (for *ch*- and *jh*- see 2.3.6): Aś RE IV °*khaṁdha-* 'mass' (skandha-), Pā. *khambheti* 'supports' (skambhayati), *khalati* 'stumbles' (skhalati), *khīyati* 'is destroyed' (kṣīyate), *khudda-* 'small' (kṣudra-), *chāta-* 'hungry' (psāta-).

Initially and at the boundary of 'compounds' *sth-* may develop to *(t)ṭh-* (in analogy with Pā. *[ti]ṭṭh[ati]* 'stands' < tiṣṭhati and [e.g.] *adhiṭṭhāna-* 'support' < adhiṣṭhāna- [see Aś RE V G *adhiṣṭāna-* in contrast to K Y *adhithāna-*]): Aś RE VI K *uṭ(ṭ)hāna-* (~ G *uṣṭāna-,* see 2.3.5) 'exertion' (utthāna-), Pā. *ṭhita-* 'standing' (sthita-), *saṃṭhāna-* 'shape, appearance' (saṃsthāna-), *kūṭaṭṭha-* 'immovable' (kūṭastha-).

ś of word-initial *śm-* was dropped by dissimilation against a following *ś*: Pā. *massu-* 'beard' (śmaśru-). If, however, a nasal followed, the *m* was dissimilated to *v* (see 2.3.4) and **sva-* underwent *saṃprasāraṇa* (see 2.2.10): Pā. *susāna-* 'burning-ground' (śmāśana-). As to word-initial ≠*śv-* see 2.3.1, and as to ≠*kṣ-* and ≠*sk-* see 2.3.6.

2.3.4. Assimilation of OIA consonant clusters

Internally, clusters of two consonants can occur. These are, however, only of the following three types (but see 2.3.5):

(a) The second consonant is the same as the first,
(b) the second consonant is the aspirate corresponding to the first one,
(c) the first consonant is the homorganic nasal of the second (including the combination of geminate nasal, nasal/liquid plus *h* and *anusvāra* plus *s*).

Consonants of different classes are treated according to the rule that a consonant of lesser power of resistance is assimilated to one with greater power of resistance. The general principle is that an occlusive is dominant in all positions (Pā. *sappa-* 'snake' < sarpa-, *kibbisa-* 'fault' < kilbiṣa-, *magga-* 'immersed' < magna-); but the articulation of a dental (and *ṇ*) is adapted to that of a following *y*: Aś RE I G J *aj(j)a* 'nowadays' (adya), RE XII G *ithīj(j)hakha-* 'superintendent of the wives' (strī-adhyakṣa-), PE VII *nij(j)hati-* 'meditation as leading to comprehension' ([BHS] nidhyapti-), RE XI G *puṁña-* 'religious merit' (puṇya-), Pā. *sacca-* 'truth' (satya-), *vijjhati* 'pierces' (vidhyati), *añña-* '(an)other' (anya-), *puñña-* 'religious merit' (puṇya-). For the treatment of the groups *-tm-, -dm-* and *-sm-* see below.

A sibilant causes the aspiration of the assimilated cluster: Aś PE I *anusat(t)hi-* 'instruction' (anuśāsti-), PE V °*pak(k)ha-* 'half-month' (pakṣa-), Pā. *acchera-* 'marvel(lous)' (āścarya-, see 2.3.10), *sukkha-* 'dry' (śuṣka-).

The groups *ñc* and *jñ* result in *ññ*: Aś RE VI G *āñapayāmi* 'I order' (ājñapayāmi), Pā. *paññavīsati-* 'twenty-five' (pañcaviṃśati-), *aññā-* 'perfect insight' (ājñā-). In the east both these groups (also if secondary) ended in *-ṇṇ-* (*paṇṇuvīsa-, āṇā-* [see below]) or in *-nn-* (Aś PE V *paṁnaḍasa-* / Pā. *pannarasa-* 'fifteen' < pañcadaśa-, RE VI K *āṇapayāmi* 'I order', Pā. *saṁmannanti* 'decide together' < °manyante). A typical eastern feature seems to be the assimilation of a *-b-* to a following *-m-*: Aś Rum *luṁmini-gāme* 'in the village of Lumbinī' (see 2.2.13), Pā. *ārammaṇa-* 'mental object' (ārambaṇa-).

If two occlusives or two nasals are in contact, the first one is assimilated to the second as the stronger articulated: Aś Rum *ub(b)alika-* 'tax-free' (*udbalika-), SE I *ālad(d)hi-* 'obtaining' (*ālabdhi-), RE II Sh *vut(t)a-* 'sown' (upta-), Pā. *satthi-* 'thigh' (sakthi-), *ninna-* 'low land' (nimna-). Among the non-occlusives, sibilants and nasals dominate over liquids (as to OIA *-Sm-* > *-pph-* see below): Aś °*piyas(s)a* 'of the beloved' (°priyasya), RE IV G K *dhaṁma-* 'teaching (of the Buddha)' (dharma-), Pā. *assa-* 'horse' (aśva-), *kassaka-* 'ploughman' (karṣaka-), *kamma-* 'deed' (karman-), *kammāsa-* 'spotted' (kalmāṣa-). And within the liquids the power of resistance diminishes in the order *l, v, y, r*: Aś PE III *kay(y)āṇa-* 'good deed' (kalyāṇa-), MRE *ay(y)a-* (ārya-), Pā. *pallaṅka-* 'couch, a sitting position' (*palyaṅka- < paryaṅka-). In Pāli resulting *-vv-* (see Aś SE II Dh J *anuv(v)igina-* 'free from anxiety' < anudvigna-) is medially represented by *-bb-*, initially by *v-*, often written *vy-* (see 2.3.5): *kubbanti* 'they do' (kurvanti), (gerund) °*tabba-* (°tavya-), *vāḷa-* 'beast of prey' (vyāḍa-), *vyaggha-* 'tiger' (vyāghra-).

An *r* may cerebralize a following dental (see 1.2): Aś PE VII *aḍ(d)ha-* 'half' (ardha-), Pā. *aṭṭa-* 'plagued' (ārta-).

The groups *-tm-*, *-dm-* and *-sm-* are – as a rule – split up (and *-sm-* > *-mh-*). If, however, a nasal follows, *-m-* is dissimilated to *v* (see 2.3.3 end) which is subsequently assimilated to its neighbouring consonant according to the above rules: Aś RE XII K *ata(n)-* 'one's own' (*atvan- [see Aś G *ātpa-*] < ātman-), *aphe* 'us' (*ap[p]phe ← *asvaṁ < asmān), Pā. *vissa-* 'palace' (veśman-).

The possibility of multiple development (due to 'eastern' vs. 'western' features) was in Pāli also a means of differentiating meaning: *āṇā-* (ājñā-) 'order, command', *aññā-* 'thorough knowledge', *vaṭṭati* (vartate) 'is proper', *vattati* 'is, exists'.

Change of the class of consonants occurs as a rule only if the (proto-canonical) eastern language is involved (unless it is due to ass/dissimilations, see 2.3.2): Aś PE IV *caghati* 'will be able' (śakṣyati), PE VII *aḍha-* 'eight' (aṣṭa-), *niṁsiḍhi-* 'ladder' (*niśliṣṭi-), Queen *aṁbāvaḍikyā* 'mango-grove' (*āmravārtikā), Nig *thuba-* 'monument' (stūpa-), Pā. *sagghati* 'will be able' (śakṣyati), *aḍḍhuḍḍha-* 'three and a half' (ardha[ca]turtha-). 'Hyper-Pālisms" are a consequence of such sound changes: Pā. *vihañña-* 'faeces' (vihanna-), *manta(bhāṇin)-* 'friendly' (*manda- < mand[r]a-).

2.3.5 Retention/restoration of (OIA) consonant clusters

Sometimes clusters with (a) sibilants and (b) liquids are not assimilated in Aśokan Prakrit and Pāli. Examples:

(a) Aś RE VI G *usṭāna-* 'exertion' (see 2.3.3), Pā. *bhasma-* 'ashes', *(vaṅka)ghasta-* 'swallowed',

(b) *-ky-* (Pā. *vākya-* 'speech') *-my-* (Aś RE IX K *samyā* ° 'right', Pā. °*kamya[tā]-* 'desire'), *-vy-* (Aś RE IV K *divya-* 'heavenly', Pā. *[a]vyatta-* '[un]skilled'), *(-)d(h)r-* (RE I G *dhruvo* 'permanent', Pā. *gadrabha-* 'ass'), *pr-* (Aś Bairāṭ *prasāda-* 'faith'), *-ly-* (Pā. *kalyāṇa-* 'good deed'), *-tr-* (Pā. *tatra* 'there'), *br-* (Aś RE IV G *bramhaṇa-*, Pā. *brāhmaṇa-* 'brahmin'), *dv-* (Pā. *dvāra-* 'door'), *sv-* (Pā. *svāgataṁ* 'welcome!').

These conjuncts are merely orthographical as most of them do not make position in metrical Pāli texts. This points to their very feeble articulation, a fact that favoured their restoration.

2.3.6 Peculiar assimilation of OIA consonant clusters

The groups *-ts(y)-* and *-ps(y)-* result in *-c(c)h-* (*-ps-* by way of *-ts-*): Aś RE II G *cikīchā-* 'art of healing' (cikitsā-), PE V *ma(c)cha-* 'fish' (matsya-), Pā. *vaccha-* 'calf' (vatsa-), *accharā-* 'heavenly nymph' (apsaras-), *lacchāmi* 'I shall get' (lapsyāmi).

kṣ shows a twofold development. In the west it develops (by way of dissimilated *ṭs*) to *cch* (≠ *ch-*), and in the east to *kkh* (≠ *kh-*). This cluster, however, can also develop to *cch* in the environment of a dissimilating *k*: Aś RE II G *vra(c)cha-* 'tree' (vṛkṣa-), J *lu(k)kha-* id.,

RE XIII G *chāti-* 'forbearance', K *khaṁti-* id. (kṣānti-), Pā. *bhikkhu-* 'monk' (bhikṣu-), *chuddha-* 'rejected' (kṣubdha-), *chārikā-* 'ashes' (~ *khāra-*), *churikā-* 'knife' (kṣurikā-). The different development is used to differentiate meaning: Pā. *khaṇa-* (kṣaṇa-) 'moment', *chaṇa-* 'festival'. Also initial *sk-* shows this twofold representation: Pā. *khambha-* 'pillar' (skambha-), *chambhita-* 'stiff' (skambhita-). The correspondance of ≠*jh-* to Skt. ≠*kṣ-* (Aś PE V *jhāpetaviya-* 'to be inflamed' < kṣāpayitavya-, Pā. *jhāyati* 'burns' < kṣāyati, *jhāma-* 'burning' < kṣāma-) and that of *-ggh-* to *-kṣ-* (Pā. *paggharati* 'oozes' < prakṣarati) is due to a difference in the Vedic dialects on which the languages are based (see 1.1).

Clusters of *h* and nasals or semivowels are metathesized: Aś RE IX G *bamhaṇa-* 'brahmin' (brāhmaṇa-), Pā. *pubbaṇha-* 'forenoon' (pūrvāhṇa-), *jimha-* 'crooked' (jihma-), *sayha-* 'to be endured' (sahya-), *jivhā-* 'tongue' (jihvā-). Resulting *-uvh-* (< -uhv-) develops into *-ūh-*: Aś RE I G *prajūhitavyaṁ* 'what is to sacrificed' (← juhvati), Pā. *jūhato* 'of one who sacrifices' (juhvataḥ). As to *-hv-* > *-bbh-* see below. When in contact with nasals *s* develops to *h*, which is metathesized; an original *ś* palatalizes a following *n*: Pā. *pañha-* 'question' (praśna-), *kaṇha-* 'black' (kṛṣṇa-), *nhāyati* 'bathes' (snāyati).

Between *-m-* and *-r-* or *-l-* a *b* is inserted and only then is the cluster assimilated or split up: Aś PE VII *amba-* 'mango' (*ambra- < āmra-), RE II G *Taṁbapaṁṇī* (<*Tambra° < Tāmra°), Pa. *gumba-* 'thicket' (*gumbla- < *gumla- < gulma-). A similar insertion is seen in Aś RE IX K *bambhana-* ~ RE XIII K *bābhana-* 'brahmin' (brahmana-).

The *anusvāra* of the prefix *saṁ+* is elided before *-r-*, sibilants and *-h-* (Pā. *sārakkhati* 'wards off' < saṁrakṣati, see 2.2.2), while it is assimilated to a following *l* (Pā. *sallapeti* 'talks [with]', *sallitta-* 'smeared [with]').

v is able to labialize a preceding occlusive: P. *ubbha-* 'high' (ūrdhva-), *bārasa-* 'twelve' (dvādaśa-). Aś RE III G *dbādasa-* 'twelve' shows that *v* developed into a fricative **β*, which was assimilated. The cluster *-hv-* resulted in *-bbh-*: Pā. *abbheti* 'calls back (a monk who has been temporarily expelled)' (āhvayati), *gabbhara-* 'cavern' (gahvara-).

2.3.7 Assimilation of clusters of three consonants

Clusters of three consonants are assimilated according to the rules of 2.3.4, except that the last consonant is not taken into account unless it is a *-y-* following a dental: Aś RE IX Dh *ithī-* 'woman' (strī-, see 2.2.9), Pā. *aggha-* 'price' (arghya-), *ānañca-* 'boundlessness' (ānantya-). The groups *-kṣn/m-* and *-tsn-*, however, were assimilated as **-ṣṇ-/-sm-*: Pā. *tiṇha-* 'sharp' (tīkṣṇa-), *pamha-* 'eyelash' (pakṣman-), *juṇhā-* 'moonlight' (jyotsnā-). In the 'east' these clusters developed differently: Aś SE I Dh *sakhina-* 'mild' (ślakṣna-), Bairāṭ *abhikhinaṁ* 'constantly' (abhīkṣnam), Pā. *tikhiṇa-* 'sharp' (*tikhṇa- < tīkṣṇa-), *pakhuma-* 'eyelash' (*pakhma- < pakṣman-), *dosinā-* 'moonlight' (*josnā- < jyotsnā-).

2.3.8 Assimilation of consonant clusters at the boundaries of compounds

The rules of 2.3.4 and 2.3.6 are partly annulled at the boundaries of compounds in order not to obscure the initial sound of the posterior member especially if this is a verb(al derivative): Aś RE VI G K *uy(y)āna-* 'garden' (udyāna-), RE V G Sh *duk(k)ara-* 'difficult' (duṣkara-), PE I *us(s)āha-* 'endeavour' (utsāha-), RE X G K *us(s)aṭa-* 'high' (/ut+śrita-/), Pā. *duccarita-* 'bad behaviour' (duścarita-), *duttara-* 'difficult to cross' (dustara-), *samussaya-* 'body' (/sam-ut+śraya-/), *dovacassa-* 'bad conduct' (daurvaca-sya-), *vanappati-* 'tree' (vanaspati-), *ūhasati* 'breaks into a laugh' (/ud-hasati/). As to doubling of the initial consonant of the second member of a 'compound' see 2.3.2 (end).

2.3.9 Deaspiration of CCh-clusters

Due to (a) dissimilation of aspirates (see 2.3.2), (b) folk-etymologies, and (c) expressive articulation in affective usage, CCh-clusters may be deaspirated in Pāli. Examples:

(a) majjhatta- 'impartial' (*majjhattha- < madhyastha-), puṭṭha- 'touched' (*phuṭṭha- < spṛṣṭa-),

(b) catukka- 'square' (*catukkha- [< catuṣka-] × tika-), takkara- 'thief' (*takkhara- [< taskara-] × °kara-),

(c) ikka- 'bear' (*ikkha- < ṛkṣa-), babbu- 'cat' (*babbhu- < babhru-).

On the deaspiration of single aspirates see 2.3.2.

2.3.10 Irregular sound changes

Beside assimilation/dissimilation (see 2.2.4, 2.3.2, 2.3.9) Aśokan Prakrit and Pāli show other irregular sound changes. A special type of dissimilation occurs when a whole syllable is lost before or after a phonetically similar or identical one (so-called haplology): Aś Br aḍhatiya- 'two and a half' (*aḍha<ta>tiya- < ardhatṛtīya-), SE I J / PE I hemeva 'in that way' (e<ev>m-eva), Pā. cirattaṁ 'for a long time' (ci<ra>rātram), e<va>m-evâhaṁ … gacchissaṁ 'so I shall go …'. Haplology accounts also for 'shortened' case-endings: Pā. na kāme<na> haññate kvaci, Ja II 178,21*, mahāsālesu aḍḍhake<su>, Ap 75,10, bhāriyā<yā> yo padassati, Ja III 279,15*, mamaṁ rodantiyā sati<yā>, Ja VI 188,2*, bhikkhu<ni> nisinne, Vin III 189,6, raṭṭhe<hi> janapadehi vā, Ja VI 294,27*, vasanehi anūpame<hi>, Thī 374.

(Only) in words which are subject to abnormal shortenings – such as terms of address – does vowel loss occur in a medial syllable (so-called syncope): Aś Bairāṭ bhaṁte / Pā. bhante 'sirs!' < bhad(d)ante < bhaddaṁ te 'happiness to you', Ja III 77,10* (see bhaddaṁ vo, Th 402).

Transpositions of phonemes or syllables (metathesis) occur especially with sonants: Aś RE XIII G samacaira- 'mental control' (*°cayira- < °carya-), Pā. payirupāsanti 'they worship' (pariyupāsate), acchera- 'marvel(lous)' (*acchayira- < āścarya-, see 2.3.4.), duyhati 'is milked' (duhyate), vehāsaya- 'air' (vehāyasa-).

2.4 Sandhi

External sandhi in Aśokan Prakrit and Pāli differs fundamentally from that in Sanskrit. It is always optional and applies only to words which are syntactically closely connected. It permits all kinds of hiatus and elides and contracts initial as well as final vowels (including nasal ones). Therefore it is not always obvious what vowels suffered sandhi change, the more so as the law of mora can obscure vocalic length.

2.4.1 Vocalic sandhi

Vocalic sandhi is basically of two kinds, (1) elision and (2) contraction – both characterized by the replacement of two syllables by one. Each of these types exhibits several varieties:

(1) Otherwise than in Sanskrit, contiguous vowels (including vowels followed by an anusvāra) across a word boundary are subject to deletion:

(a) The final vowel of the preceding word or
(b) the initial vowel of the following word may be elided (for the elision of a vowel
     before or after a similar vowel see 2.b). Examples:
     (a) Aś RE IV Dh *c'eva* 'and' (ca+eva), IX Dh *paj'upadāye* 'at the birth of a child'
          (prajā+upa°), MRE *h'iyaṁ* 'because this ...' (hi+iyam), Sār *ik'ike* 'every
          single one' (*ike ike* ~ ekaikāḥ), SE I J *ev'e* (*ev[aṁ] e* < yaḥ), Sār
          tuphāk'aṁtikaṁ 'near (= with) you' (*tupkākam aṁtikaṁ*), Pā. *sīharāja v'*
          asambhīto 'unfrightened like a lion' (iva+asam°), *yath' odhikāni* 'in all parts'
          (yathā+o°), *anagāriy' upetassa* 'of one who has become homeless'
          (*anagāriyaṁ upe °*), *kath' eko ramasī araññe* 'why do you enjoy yourself
          alone in [this] forest?' (katham+eko), *sādh' āvuso* 'very well, my friend!'
          (*sādhu āvuso*), *mokkh' ito* 'liberation from here' (*mokkho ito*);
     (b) Aś RE XII G *ithī-jhakha °* 'superintendent of the wives' (strī+adhyakṣa-), VI K
          etāye 'ṭhāye 'for that purpose' (*etāye aṭhāye*), Pā. *karonti 'pāyaso* 'they made
          it in this way' (*karonti upā °*), *te 'bhirattā* 'they (are) affected (with passion)'
          (*te abhi °*), *me 'daṁ* 'this of me' (*me idaṁ*).
     If two identical vowels come together one is elided (this could be regarded as a peculiar
     contraction): Aś RE IX G *dham'nugaha-* 'help of the law' (dharma+anugraha-), Pā.
     kec' ime 'these (people) here' (*keci ime*), *m' etaṁ* 'this of me' (*me etam*);
(c) the remaining (short) vowel can be lengthened in both cases by compensatory
     lengthening unless a double consonant follows the elided vowel of the second word:
     (i)   Pā. *ken' īdha* 'by what ... here?' (*kena idha*), *c' ūpatapeti* 'and it torments
           (me)' (*ca upa°*), *y' ābhivadanti* 'who greet ... ' (*ye abhi°*),
     (ii) *Cundā ti* '[he said:] "Cunda! ... " ' (Cunda iti [as to this *sandhi* of *iti* see 2.4.5]).
(2) Taking into account type 1.c., it might be said that – otherwise than in Skt. – *all*
     vowels (including vowels followed by an *anusvāra*) can be contracted (and, indeed,
     some editors write *kenīdha* or *kenĭdha* [see Sn 793], etc.). But if we regard this
     sandhi as an elision with (compensatory) lengthening, we have in principle the
     same contractions as in OIA:
(a) Vowels, which differ in quantity only, coalesce to the corresponding long vowel
     (basically a *sandhi* of type 1.c): Aś RE XIII K *dhammānusathi-* 'instruction of the
     law' (dharma+anuśāsti-), Pā. *yassānusayā* 'whose dispositions' (yasya+anu°),
     gavaṁpatīdha 'the owner of the cows here ...' (*°pati+idha*). If a double consonant
     follows, this vowel is generally shortened (i.e. basically a *sandhi* of type 1.a): Aś RE I
     J *sūpaṭhāye* 'for curry' (sūpārthāya), P. *yassatthāya* 'because of ...' (*yassa+a°*), *yaṁ
     piccham na labhati* 'when one wishes [to attain] something [and] does not attain' (pi
     icchaṁ), *pañcasupādānakkhandhesu* 'in the five groups of grasping' (pañcasu+upā-
     dāna°). In the same way -*aṁ*, -*iṁ* and -*uṁ* are contracted: Pā *vācābhikaṁkhāmi* 'I
     long for your voice' (vācaṁ+abhi°), *munīdha* 'the sage here ...' (*muniṁ idha*);
(b) Like OIA, Pāli allows the contraction of final -*a* and -*ā* with a following dissimilar
     vowel into -*e*- and -*o*-: *nigrodhasseva* 'like ... of a Nigrodha tree' (*°assa iva*),
     nopalippati 'is not stained' (na+upa°).

These sandhis occur also (a) at the boundaries of (newly formed) compounds and (b)
within words (of usually more than three syllables). Examples:

(a) Pā. *mahodadhi-* 'great lake' (*mahā+udadhi-*), *mahesi-* 'great sage' (*mahā+isi-*
     [< ṛ̥ṣi-]), *sati'paṭṭhāna-* 'establishing of mindfulness'(*sati+upa°*), *udadh'ūpama-*
     'resembling a lake' (*udadhi+upa°*),

(b) Pā. *accāsana-* 'eating too much' (at$_i$yaśana-), *paccāmitta-* 'enemy' (prat$_i$y-amitra-).

2.4.2 Consonantal sandhi

If we disregard the preservation/restoration of (historically final) consonants as hiatus breakers (see 2.4.3), only *-ṁ ≠* can undergo consonantal sandhi within a sentence. Apart from its (frequent) replacement by *-ñ* before palatals (Pā. *bheriñ carāpetvā* 'having made the drum to be carried around'), it is only affected before enclitics (including vocatives) which form a whole with the preceding word, thus entailing a peculiar *sandhi*: Aś RE II G *evam-api* 'in the same way also …', Pā. *karissañ ca*, Ja III 437,25*, *evañ-hi*, Vin I 112,8, *kin ti*, *evam-eva*, *evam-me*, *evam-pi*, *yam-pi … tam-pi*. If followed by *y(eva)* it is assimilated to this: Pā. *tañ ñeva* (taṁ yeva).

Consonants at the boundaries within compounds and of prefix and 'root', and at the junction of a word and a following enclitic are assimilated, though in part according to special rules (see 2.3.8): Pā. *jaraggava-* 'an old cow' (jarad+g°), *punabbhava-* 'rebirth' (punar+bhava-), *tammaya-* 'made of that' (tad+maya-), *accuggamma* 'in a position raised above' (atyudgamya), *kaccin-nu* 'I suppose that …' (kaccid nu), *tayas-su* 'three [things]' (trayaḥ+su). This gemination of consonants is, however, often analogical (see 2.3.2 end).

2.4.3 Bridging of hiatus

A *hiatus*, though generally permitted (including in compounds), can be bridged by (a) a glide or (b) a (so-called) sandhi consonant, which may be a relic from OIA or analogically inserted.

(a) Glides break the hiatus inside words: Aś RE XII G *aṁña-m-aṁña-* 'each other' (: anyo'nya-), XIII K *di-y-aḍha°* 'one and a half' (dvyardha-), Pā. *piṇḍi-y-ālopa-* 'a morsel of food' (*piṇḍyālopa-), *anu-v-āsati* 'sits down after' (anu-√ās), *su-p-icchita-* 'well-wished' (*su-v-icchita-),

(b) The retention of final consonants before enclitics or in fossilized formulas (Pā. *pag-eva* 'not to speak of …', *sabbhir-eva* 'only by the virtuous', *etad-avoca* 'this he said', *pātur-ahosi* 'he appeared') is generalized and different (voiced) consonants (-*d*-, -*m*-, -*y*-, -*r*-, -*v*-) are inserted to break hiatus between two words: Aś RE VIII Dh *tadopaya-* 'corresponding to that' (~ Pā. *tadūpiya-*), Pā. *anva-d-eva* 'after-wards', *samma-d-aññāya* 'having understood [it] properly', *giri-m-iva* 'like a mountain', *mā … khaṇi-y-asmani* 'do not dig in the stone' (Ja III 433,11*), *dhi-r-atthu* 'woe upon …', *°dhammena-v-onatā* 'cast down by (anything) having the characteristic of …' (Th 662). Often historical sandhis (Pā. *aggir-iva* 'like a fire') furnish the pattern for new (sporadic) formations (*rājā-r-iva* 'like a king'), sometimes due to rhyme (*kata-r-asmāsu … bhatti-r-asmāsu* 'done towards us … devotion towards us' [kṛtam asmāsu … bhaktir asmāsu], Ja V 352,10*–11*). In a number of words these consonants have become fixed (Aś RE IX *vuta-* 'said' < ukta-, MRE *vivutha-* 'dawned' < [vy]uṣṭa-, Pā. *yiṭṭha-* 'sacrificed' < iṣṭa-, *vuppati* 'is sown' < upyate) – a process creating doublets (P. *[y]eva* < eva, *[v]ubho* 'both' < ubho).

Before sandhi consonants a long vowel can be shortened – *-e* and *-o* to *-a* – and a nasal vowel may lose its nasality: *(… bhariyā … / samuggapakkhitta) nikiṇṇa-m-antare* 'his wife) .... is put inside', Ja III 529,10*–11* (= *nikiṇṇā*, ct.), *hitva-m-aññaṁ* 'having left the other (state[s]) behind', Sn 1071, *tassa dajjaṁ imaṁ selaṁ jalanta-r-iva tejasā* '... this stone blazing with splendour', Ja VI 181,6* (jvalantam iva tejasā), *sarada-r-iv'* 'like ... in autumn', Sn 687 (°de+iva), *haṁsa-r-iv' ajjhapatto* 'like a goose ...', Sn 1134 (*haṁso iva*).

2.4.4 Lengthening of -aṁ before an enclitic

Final *-aṁ* can be lengthened before an enclitic, either to *-āṁ* or to *-aṁ-m*: Aś PE III *kayānaṁmeva* 'only the good', SE II Dh J *sukhaṁmeva* 'only happiness', Pā. *n' etaṁ ajjatanām-iva* (m.c. for *eva*) 'this does not hold true for today only', Dhp 227, *mam-m-iva* 'like me ...', Ja IV 71,23*. This sandhi – according to Aś an 'eastern' feature (see above) – seems to be analogical to the genuine sandhi *-ām-iva*: Pā. *asso ... kasām-iva* 'like a horse ... the whip', Dhp 143 (aśvaḥ ... kaśām iva), *āloko passatām-iva* 'for those who see [it is] ... like a light', Sn 763 (paśyatām iva).

2.4.5 Dropping of initial vowels in sandhi

In sandhi any initial vowel could be dropped (see 2.4.1), and such sandhi forms were sometimes generalized: Aś Sār *posatha-* 'the *uposatha* day' (upavasatha-), Pā. *(a)re* (interj. expressive of impatience or contempt), *(i)dāni(ṁ)* 'now', *(u)daka-* 'water', *(u)lūka-* 'owl'. With enclitics *aphaeresis* is particularly frequent: Aś / Pā. *pi* 'also' (api), *ti* 'thus' (iti). When *ti* follows a word ending in a vowel, that vowel is lengthened (see 2.4.1cII).

3 MORPHOLOGY

3.1 The noun

Like OIA, Aśokan Prakrit and Pāli distinguish three grammatical genders: masculine, feminine and neuter. The gender of a particular word is, in most cases, the same as the one current in OIA. Neuter nouns are inflected like masculines except for the nom./acc. sg. and pl., which are always identical. Aśokan Prakrit and Pāli have lost the dual (a process partly due to the development *au > o* [see 2.2.1]), which is replaced by the plural; and though the words for 'two, both' are a continuation of old forms, they do not represent a dual any longer: Aś RE I G *dvo morā* 'two peacocks', Pā. *dve pi cakkhūni* 'both eyes' (with plural noun forms).

In accordance with the tendency towards simplification of the morphological system of OIA, Aś Pkt. and Pā. changed consonant into vowel stems, mostly by generalizing a case form ending in a vowel (e.g. Aś *kamma-* ← *kamma* < karma, *vaca-* ← **vaco* < vacaḥ, Pā. *mana-* ← *mano* < manaḥ). Due to the elision of final consonants (see 2.2.3), the nominative of the old consonant stems ended in a vowel, becoming the source of new stems (*maru-*, *vijju-*) which normally retained their original gender (Aś PE V *parisā-* [f.] 'assembly' ← pariṣad-, Pā. *upanisā-* [f.] 'condition' ← upaniṣad-). Often, however, *-ā* or *-ī* are added (Aś RE X G *vaciguti-* 'control of speech' ~ K *vacaguti-* ← vāc-, Pā. *saritā-* 'river' ← sarit-, *sirasa-* 'head' ← śiras-) – a process that started from the acc. sg. (cf. Pā. *addhāna-* 'road' ← adhvānam, *vācā-* 'speech' ← vācam).

Seven of the eight OIA cases survived – the instr. and the abl. pl. have merged, while the dative disappeared in favour of the genitive. It is only preserved in the singular of the *a*-flexion as *dativus finalis* and *dativus temporis* (Aś RE III G *etāy' eva athāya*

TABLE 5.1: PARADIGMS OF PĀLI INFLEXION

	a-stems (see 3.2.1)	*ā*-stems (see 3.2.2)	*i/u*-stems (see 3.2.3)	*ī/ū*-stems (see 3.2.4)	cons. stems (see 3.2.5)
nom.sg.	*devo* (*-e*)	*kaññā*	*aggi*	*devī, jāti*	*-ø*
nom/acc.sg. nt.	*rūpaṁ* (nom. *-e*)	—	*akkhi(ṁ)*	—	*-ø*
acc.	*devaṁ*	*kaññaṁ*	*aggiṁ*	*deviṁ* (*-iyaṁ*)	*-aṁ*
instr.	*devena* (*-asā*)		*agginā*	*deviyā* (*-īyā, – CCā*)	*-ā*
dat.	= gen. (Pā. *arthāya*, Aś *athāye*)	*kaññāya* (instr. *-ā*, abl. *āto*)	= gen.		= gen.
abl.	*devā, devasmā, devamhā, devāto*		*aggismā, aggimhā, agginā, aggito*		= instr.
gen.	*devassa*		*aggissa, aggino*		*-o*
loc.	*deve, devasmiṁ, devamhi*	*kaññāya(ṁ)* (*-āye*)	*aggismiṁ, aggimhi*	*deviyā, deviyaṁ* (*-CCaṁ*)	*-i*
voc.m./n.	*deva*	*kaññe*	*-i* (*-e; -o*)	*devi*	= nom.

	a-stems	*ā*-stems	*i/u*-stems	*ī/ū*-stems	cons. stems
nom/voc.pl.	*devā* (*-āso, -āse*)	*kaññā, kaññāyo*	*aggayo, aggī, bhikkhavo; bhikkhū* (*-iyo, -uyo; voc. -ave*)	*deviyo* (*-īyo*)	*-o*
acc.	*deve* (*-āni*)				*-o*
nom/acc.pl.nt.	*rūpāni* (*-ā*, acc. *-e*)		*akkhīni, akkhī*		—
instr./abl.	*devehi*	*kaññāhi*	*aggīhi* (*-ibhi, -ihi*)	*devīhi*	*-(b)hi*
dat.-gen.	*devānaṁ*	*kaññānaṁ*	*aggīnaṁ* (*inaṁ*)	*devīnaṁ* (*inaṁ*)	*-aṁ*
loc.	*devesu*	*kaññāsu*	*aggīsu* (*-isu*)	*devīsu* (*-isu*)	*-su*

'for that purpose', Pā. *jahassu rūpaṁ apunabbhavāya* 'abandon your body for the sake of non-renewed existence' [Sn 1121], *ajjatanāya* 'for today').

The suffix *-to* (in Aś with an 'eastern' by-form *-te*) is added to any stem to form an ablative (Pā. *hatthito* 'from the elephant' [← *hasti(n)-*], *rājato* 'from the king' [← *rāja(n)*]); sometimes the stem final is lengthened (Pā. *°bandhanāto* 'from binding' – a blending of *°bandhanā* < *°bandhanāt* and *°bandhanato* < *°bandhanataḥ*), sometimes it is shortened (Aś SE I *Ujjenite* 'from Ujjenī', Pā. *jihvato* 'from the tongue', *Bārāṇasito* 'from Benares', see 2.2.13).

3.2 Paradigms

Nouns are organized mainly into five paradigms, all of which are inherited types. The Pāli case terminations of these declensions are as follows (only the endings of the *i*- and *ī*-stems are listed, as *u*- and *ū*-stems take corresponding ones) (see table 5.1).

3.2.1 *a-inflexion*

The case-endings of the *a*-inflexion are partly (a) historical, partly (b) transferred from the pronominal or other inflexions and partly (c) due to paradigmatical analogy. Examples:

(a) The nom. sg. m. of the Pāli *a*-inflexion in *-e* is characteristic for the proto-canonical eastern language (see 1.2). Also the nom. sg. nt. in *-e* (*dullabbhe ... dassane* 'difficult to obtain is the sight [of ...]', Ja VI 263,13*) is a feature of the eastern language, where it stood beside an acc. in *-aṁ* (see Aś PE II nom. *dāne* 'generosity', PE IV acc. *dānaṁ* 'gift'). The 'eastern' Aś Pkt. dative in *°āye* owes its *-e* to a strict phonetic development. The (Pā.) nom. pl. in *-āso* (*samuppilavāso* 'jumping up and down', Sn 670) is a continuation of Vedic *-āsaḥ*, and *-āse* is the corresponding 'eastern' form (*paṇḍitāse* 'wise men', Sn 875). The same holds true for the acc. pl. in *-āni* (Pā. *puttāni āmantaya tambanette* 'call the copper-eyed boys', Ja VI 290,9*) as Aś proves (PE IV *pulisāni* 'the servants' ~ *puruṣān*; see RE IV Dh *hathīni* [acc.] 'elephants'). The nom/acc. nt. pl. ends also in *-ā*. The ending of the instr. and abl. pl. *-ehi* developed out of OIA *-ebhiḥ* found in Vedic.

(b) The Pāli instr. in *-asā* (*kāmasā* 'through greed', Ja VI 182,14*, *balasā* 'with strength', Th 1141) is taken over from the *as*-stems, the abl. (*°asmā, °amhā*) and loc. sg. (*°asmiṁ, amhi*) from the pronominal flexion (for *-mh-* < *-sm-* see 2.3.6, for *-sm-* see 2.3.5). The ending *-e* of the acc. pl., which is called for by the instr. in *-ehi* and the loc. in *-esu* (due to the analogy with *kaññā – kaññāhi – kaññāsu* or *aggī/ bhikkhū – aggīhi/bhikkhūhi – aggīsu/bhikkhūsu*), is taken over from the pronominal flexion (see 3.3.1).

(c) The gen. pl. lost (perhaps under the influence of the corresponding ending of the sg., *-assa*) its final *-ṁ*: Aś RE XII K *°pasaḍāna* 'of the sects', Pā. *devāna* 'of the gods', Th 1266.

3.2.2 *ā-infexion*

The instr. *-āya* (< *-āyāḥ*, see 2.2.3) of the *ā*-stems – instead of the expected **-ayā* – reflects generalization of a single oblique form (likewise the loc. in *-āya* < *-āyām*), as does 'eastern' Aś Pkt. *-āye* (< *-āyai*). The (Pā.) instr. in *°ā* (*appaṭipucchā* 'without inquiry' [: *appaṭipucchā<ya>*], Vin I 325,33) is originally due to a haplology of -*ā <ya>*, but was also generalized: *saddhā* 'with faith' (: *saddhāya*), S I 198,9* (so read). The rare loc. in -*āye* (Aś RE VI K °*saṁtilanāye* 'in the conclusion', PE V *Tisāye* 'under [the *nakṣatra*] Tiṣyā', Pā. *sabhāye* 'in the assembly', Vin III 200,19) is a contamination of (f.) -*āya* and (m.) -*e*. The nom./acc./voc. pl. Aś RE X G *(mahiḍ)āyo*, Pā *(kaññ)āyo* 'daughters' is formed analogically to the *ī*-stems (proving their ending -*īyo*, see 3.2.4) to differentiate it from the sg. (both OIA *kanyā* and *kanyāḥ* > *kaññā*).

3.2.3 *i/u-inflexion*

The paradigm of the *i/u*-stems is composed of forms continuing the old *i/u*-flexion (Pā. *aggi, aggiṁ, agginā, aggayo, aggīnaṁ*, nt. *akkhi, akkhīni; bhikkhu* etc.) and of forms built analogically to *a*-stems (Pā. *aggismā, aggimhā, aggissa, aggismiṁ, aggimhi*, nt. sg. *akkhiṁ*, pl. *akkhī*, f. *ī-* (Pā. [acc. pl. → nom.] *aggī :: jātī*) and the nt. *i-/u*-stems (Pā. *aggino, bhikkhuno*; see Aś PE V [loc.] *Punāvasune*, PE VII *bahune*). Due to the forms of the nominative and the accusative plural being confused the nom. pl. ends in -*ī* -*ū* (see above). Instr. and loc. pl. °*ī/ūhi*, °*ī/ūsu* are analogical to the gen. *(agg)īnaṁ (bhikkh)ūnaṁ*. The plural forms with short stem-vowels (°*i/uhi*, °*i/unaṁ*, °*i/usu*), on the other hand, have the vocalism of the singular, thus (apparently) preserving – as far as the instr. and the loc. are concerned – the old vowel length: Pā. *akkhihi* 'with the eyes', Sn 608, *usuhi* 'with arrows', M I 86,31, *ñātinaṁ* 'of the relatives', Th 240, *bhikkhunaṁ* 'of the monks', S I 190,15, *asisu* 'on the swords', M I 87,1, *bhikkhusu* 'with the monks', Th 241. The voc. pl. Pā. *bhikkhave* 'monks!' showing -*e* < -*aḥ* is the 'eastern' form corresponding to 'western' *bhikkhavo*.

Apart from the historical form of the nom. sg. (in -*ū*) the Pā. m. *ū*-stems – all *nomina verbalia* – are inflected as *u*-stems: (sg.) *mataññu, abhibhuṁ, sayambhunā, abhibhussa, amattaññuno, abhibhusmiṁ*, (pl.) *vadaññū, viññūhi, viññūnaṁ, viññūsu*. The nom./acc. pl. in -*uno* is analogical to the *in*-stems (see 3.2.7): *vedaguno* 'the knowers of the *veda*'. In the same way *(a)vidū*- and *(a)viddasū*- (based on the acc. [a]vidvāṁsam) are inflected: (nom. pl. m.) °*viduno* 'those who know', Vin II 241,7.

3.2.4 *ī-/ū-inflexion*

The OIA f. *i-/u*- and *ī-/ū*-inflexions (of mono- and poly-syllabic nouns) have merged in Pā. and Aśokan Prakrit in one *ī-/ū*-class (only the nom. sg. has -*i/u* or -*ī/ū*) which has only one oblique form in the singular (in 'eastern' Aś Pkt. in -*iye*, -*uye*). The *ū*-stems take over the glide consonant -*y*- from the *ī*-stems: Pā. (sg.) *dhenuyā / dhenuyaṁ*, (pl.) *dhenuyo*. Under the influence of the *ā*-inflexion the nom. pl. in -*iyo / -uyo* (in 'eastern' Aś Pkt. -*iye*) was used also as acc. and vice versa the acc. in -*ī/ū* as nom.: Aś RE XIII Sh (nom.) *aṭavi* 'forests' ~ G *aṭaviyo*, Pā. (nom.) *pokkharaṇī* 'lotus ponds', Vv 1168 (if not a sg.), *puthū* 'many', Th 1190, (acc.) *pokkharaṇiyo* 'lotus ponds', D II 178,23, *dhenuyo* 'cows', Vv 1157. The regularity of the paradigm is disturbed by historical forms: Pā. (acc. sg.) *ajiyaṁ* 'a she-goat', Ja V 241,24*, *nadiyaṁ* 'a river', D II 135,3*, (instr.) *jaccā* 'by birth', Dhp 393 (*jātyā*), *sammuccā* 'by common assent', Sn 648 (*saṁmatyā*), (gen.) *najjā* 'of the river', D II 112,22 (*nadyāḥ*), (loc.) *Naliññaṁ*, Ja VI 313,9*, *Bārāṇassaṁ*, Ja II 435,14*, (nom. pl.) *dasso* 'female servants', Ja IV 53,29* (*dāsyaḥ*), *najjo* 'rivers', S III 202,6 (*nadyaḥ*). The oblique case ends (in Pāli) also in -*īyā* and -*ūyā*, foreshadowing the Pkt. endings -*īe* and -*ūe* (see Aś Pkt. [cas. obl.] -*āye -īye*): *kumārīyā* 'of the girl', Ja VI 65,11*, *brāhmaṇīyā* 'of the brahmin woman', Ja VI 524,15*, *kāsūyā* 'in the pit', Ja

VI 12,20* (Ee throughout metrically faulty -*i/uyā*). The nom./acc. pl. ends (in Pāli) also in -*īyo*, a forerunner of Pkt. -*īo*: *jātīyo* 'births', Thī 511, *pokkharaṇīyo* 'lotus ponds', A I 145,10, *saṁgītīyo* 'songs', Ja VI 528,30* (Ee except A I 145,10 *°iyo*). And the vocalism of the plural may conform to that of the singular: Aś PE VII *devinaṁ* 'of the wives of the king', MRE *pavatisu* 'in the mountains', Pā. *anudiṭṭhīnaṁ* (‿‿‿‿‿) 'of the theories', Th 754, *jātisu* 'in (my) births', Th 346, *nārisu* 'with the women', Dhp 284.

3.2.5 Consonantal inflexion

Only traces of the consonant stems without vowel alternation – mainly nt. nouns in -*as*, -*is* and -*us*, and very few m./f. *as*-nouns – have survived: Aś RE X G *yaso* 'fame' (*yaśaḥ*), SE I Dh *daviye* 'to agreeable extent, more' (*davīyaḥ* 'farther'), PE VII *bhuye* 'more' (*bhūyaḥ*), Pā. *ayo* 'iron' (*ayaḥ*), *mano* 'mind', *vaco* 'speech', (instr.) *jarasā* 'due to old age', (gen.) *jagato* 'of the world', *manaso* 'of the mind', (loc.) *sarasi* 'in the lake', (acc. pl.) *sarado satam* 'a hundred autumns', (gen.) *saritam* 'of the rivers'; (nom.) *candimā* 'the moon', (acc.) *vyāsattamanasaṁ* 'whose mind is attached to [worldly pleasures]', (gen.) *ananvāhatacetaso* 'of one whose mind is not perplexed', (gen. pl.) *accharasaṁ* 'of the heavenly nymphs', Ja IV 450,11* (so read).

The nom. in *°o* was a favourable basis for transferring the neuter *as*- into *a*-stems (see 3.1), and the compounds with *as*-stems as posterior members followed this development: Aś PE IV (nom. pl.) *avimanā* 'those who are not confused', Pā. (nom. sg.) *dummano* 'dejected', (nom. pl.) *sumanā* 'happy', (acc.) *muditamane* 'whose mind is delighted'.

3.2.6 Inflexion of sakha-/sakha(r)- 'friend'

The Pāli stems *sakha-*, *sakha(r)-* 'friend' (abstracted from the nom. *sakhā* after the pattern *pitā* : *pita[r]-*) and *sakhāra-* (formed according to the proportion *x* : *sakhā* = *satthāraṁ* : *satthā*) supplement the paradigm of *sakhi-* which inflects as an *i*-stem (see 3.2.3): nom./voc. sg. *sakhā* (voc., Ja III 295,20*), *sakho* (Th 648), acc. *sakhaṁ* (Ja II 299,13*), *sakhāraṁ*, abl. *sakhārasmā*, nom. pl. *sakhā*, *sakhāro*, gen. pl. *sakhānaṁ*.

3.2.7 i(n)-inflexion

The old endings of the *i(n)*-stems are preserved throughout: (Aś = Pā.) sg. m. *°ī*, *°inaṁ*, *°inā*, *ino* (eastern Aś *°ine*), *°ini*, pl. *°ino* (eastern Aś [acc. m.] *°īni*), *°ibhi*, *°inaṁ*, *°isu*; nt. nom. sg. *°i*, pl. (Aś) *°īni*; f. nom. sg. *°inī-*. Besides, the *in*-stems inflect in analogy to the *i*-stems, since some cases (instr. sg./pl., loc. pl.) were homophone: Pā. *jhāyiṁ* 'meditator' (≠ dhyāyinam), Aś RE II Sh *priyadraśisa* (≠ *°darśinaḥ*), Pā. *seṭṭhimhi* 'with the merchant' (≠ śreṣṭhini), (nom. pl.) *pāṇayo* 'living creatures' (≠ prāṇinaḥ), (acc. pl.) *pakkhī* 'birds' (pakṣiṇaḥ). Starting from the acc. sg. in -*inaṁ* the *in*-stems were thematicized: Pā. (loc. sg.) *yasassine* 'with one who is renowned', (acc. pl.) *māladhārine* 'those who wear a garland', (loc. pl.) *verinesu* 'towards people who are full of hatred' (cf. Aś PE V *Punāvasune* ~ OIA punarvasau).

3.2.8 Inflexion of diphthong-stems

Of the OIA diphthong-stems only *go*- survived, and this only in some historical forms: Pā. (sg.) *go*, Sn 580, (pl.) *gāvo*, M I 225,10, *gohi*, S I 6,9*, *gavaṁ(pati)*, Sn 26–27. The new stem *gava*- is based on the instr. *gavā*, which evidently was understood as an abl.;

the corresponding feminine is *gāvī-* which got its -*ā-* from the old nom./acc. plural *gāvo*. Another stem, *goṇa-*, was extracted from the (newly created) feminine *goṇī-*: Aś PE V *gone*, Pā. *goṇo*, Vin IV 7,16, *goṇaṁ*, M I 10,36, nom. pl. *goṇā*, M III 167,24.

3.2.9 *n-inflexion*

The paradigm of the *n-*inflexion is composed of

(1) historical forms, eastern ones with epenthetic vowel – they are also to be found in Aś K and Dh which only have final *°e* < *°aḥ* –, western ones with assimilated consonants (= Aś G), and

(2) innovations which are based

    (a) on the proportion (e.g.) Pā. *rājū(hi/naṁ)* / Aś PE VII *lājīhi* : *rājā* / *lājā* = *pitū(hi/naṁ)* / *pitisu* : *pitā* (see 3.2.10),

    (b) abstracted from nominal compounds (*rāja+*, *mahārāja-*), and

    (c) though only sporadically, forms of the stem *rañña-*.

TABLE 5.2: PARADIGMS OF *N*-INFLEXIONS

nom.	(1) *rājā*, (nt.) *nāma*	(1) *rājāno*
	(2c) Pā. *rañño*	(2b) *rājā*
voc.	(2b) *rājǎ*; (*°*)*rāje*	(1) *rājāno*
acc.	(1) *rājānaṁ*, (nt.) *nāma*	(2) *rājāno*
	(2b) *rājaṁ*	
instr. / abl.	(1) *raññā*, *rājinā* (abl. *rājato*)	(2a) *rājūhi*, Aś *lājīhi*
		(2c) *raññehi*
gen.	(1) *rañño*, *rājino* (Aś *lājine*)	(1) *raññaṁ*
	(2b) *rājassa*	(2a) *rājūnaṁ*
loc.	(1) *rājini*	(2a) *rājūsu*
	(2c) *raññe*	

The analogy of the *r-*stems (see above 2a) was especially effective when a -*m-* preceded -*an*: Pā. *brahmunā*, *brahmuno*, *kammunā*, *kammuno* (but see *brahmani* ~ *satthari*). Vocatives like Pā. *nāgarāje* 'o king of the water snakes' and *brahme* 'o brahmin' have the generalized ending -*e*.

Stems with *°an-* after a double consonant (< *°Cman-/van-*, also *muddha[n]-*) retain -*a-* in the weak cases: Aś PE VI *atanā*, SE I *atane*, Pā. *attanā*, *kammanā*, *attano*, *attani*, *asmani*, *kammani*. In the case of neuter *an-*stems the nom. sg./pl. in *°a/°āni* was the base of a new stem (see 3.1): Aś RE III K *kaṁmaye*, G *kaṁmāya*, Pā. *kammena*, *kammesu*, (nom. sg.) *nāmaṁ*, (nom./acc.) *muddhaṁ*.

Most of the OIA comparatives in *°(i)yas-* are transferred to the *a-*inflexion, with only few historical forms surviving (Aś PE VII *bhuye* 'more' < *bhūyaḥ*, Pā. *seyyo* 'better' < *śreyaḥ*, *bhiyyo* 'more' < *bhūyaḥ*). The comparative is usually formed with the suffix *°tara-* (Aś RE XIII K *galumatatale* 'considered more grave', Pā. *mahattara-* 'greater'), which was even added to old comparatives (Pā. *bhiyyatara-* 'more').

3.2.10 a(r)-inflexion

In Pāli the distinction between *nomina agentis* and kinship terms has been retained with the *a(r)*-stems (Aś Pkt. has no relevant forms): (nom.) *satthā* 'teacher', (acc.) *satthāraṁ*, (nom./voc. pl.) *satthāro* (see Aś RE IV K *natāle* 'grandsons' < naptāraḥ) vs. (nom.) *pitā* 'father', (acc.) *pitaraṁ*, (nom./voc. pl.) *pitaro*. The nom. sg. in °*ā* was used as vocative, the nom. pl. as accusative (Pā. *nattāro* 'grandsons'). Also the gen., loc. and voc. sg. (and the instr. in Aś Pkt.) and the loc. pl. are historical forms (Aś RE IX *bhātrā* [instr.], Queen °*mātu* [gen.], RE III *mātari*, *pitari* [loc.], Pā. *satthu*, *sattari*, *sattha*; *pitu*, *pitari*, *pita*, *pitusu*). The instr./abl., Pā. *satthārā*, *pitarā*, however, is analogical to the loc. (*satthari*, *pitari*), while the younger form in °*ārā* shows the vocalism of the accusative. Other forms were based on the gen. sg. in -*u*, which itself was reinforced; also on the plural forms in **-ubhi* / **-unaṁ* / **-usu* which had generalized *u* < ṛ: Aś RE IX Sh *pituna*, MRE *mātāpitūsu*, Pā. (instr.) *satthunā*, (gen.) *satthuno*, *pituno*, *satthussa*, *mātuyā*, (nom. pl.) *bhātuno*, (instr./abl. pl.) *satthūhi*, (gen.) *satthūnaṁ*, *pitūnaṁ*, (loc.) *satthūsu*. Eastern Aś has the corresponding *i*-forms, while in Pāli this vowel appears – as a rule – only in compounds and suffix derivations: Aś RE IX K *pitinā*, *bhātinā*, RE V K *bhātinaṁ*, RE III K *mātāpitisu*; Pā. *piti+*, *(a)pitika-*, *pitito*, *bhātika-* (side by side with *dhītu+*, *bhātuka-*).

3.2.11 ma(nt)-/va(nt)-/-a(nt)-inflexion

The paradigm of the °*m/va(nt)*-stems (and of the word *mahant-*) is composed of (a) historical and (b) newly created forms based on the acc. sg. (°*[m/v]anta-* ← °*[m/v]antaṁ*); however in the plural only nom./voc. (= acc.) and gen. pl. have survived:

(a) (sg.) nom./voc. Pā. *sīlavā* 'virtuous', acc. °*vantaṁ*, instr. °*vatā*, gen. °*vato*, loc. °*vati*, voc. °*va* (< °*van* [?]), (pl.) nom.-voc./acc. °*vanto*, gen. °*vataṁ*,
(b) (sg.) Pā. °*vanto* ([eastern] Aś RE XIV Dh *mahaṁte* 'great'), °*vantena*, °*vantā*, °*vantassa*, °*vante/* °*vantamhi/* °*vantasmiṁ*, °*vanta*, (pl.) °*vante*, °*vantehi*, °*vantā-naṁ*, °*vantesu*, °*vantā* (for the forms see 3.2). The feminines are derived from the weak stem (P. *sīlavatī-*).

The present participle in °*a(nt)-/* °*e(nt)-* inflects in the same way, except for the nom. sg. which – as a historical form – ends in -*aṁ* < -an (a peculiar form of the nom. sg. is Aś G RE XII *evaṁ-karuṁ*). And the paradigm of this participle has occasionally preserved the historical instr. pl. (Pā. *sabbhi* 'by the good ones' [SI 17, 3*] < sadbhiḥ). Pāli *araha(nt)-* 'saint' (not attested in Aś Pkt.) and Aś Pkt. *bhagava(nt)-* 'venerable' follow either inflexion (nom. sg. *arahaṁ*, *arahā*; Aś Rum *bhagavaṁ*). The paradigm of Pā. *bhava(nt)-* 'sir', used for addressing people, shows some contracted forms (instr. sg. *bhotā*, gen. *bhoto*, voc. *bho*, voc. pl. *bhonto* [bhavantaḥ]).

3.3 Pronominal inflexion

The pronouns have marked peculiarities of inflexion, which entail a transfer to the nominal inflexion by adding the suffix °*ka-* (Aś RE XIV G *etaka-*, Pā. *amuka-* 'such and such a thing'). They are especially liable to wear and tear and consequently to renewal (e.g. Aś RE VI G *tāya athāya* / SE II Dh J *etāye ca aṭhāye* 'to that purpose' ~ /tasmai arthāya/). Their inflexion, on the other hand, has preserved archaic characteristics such as the use of the dative (partly as genitive). A number of adjectives, such as Aś *aṁna-* /

TABLE 5.3: PERSONAL PRONOUNS (FIRST AND SECOND PERSON)

	1st person			2nd person		
	Pāli	Western Aś	Eastern Aś	Pāli	Western Aś	Eastern Aś
nom. sg.	*aham*	*amhe*	*hakam*	*t(u)vam*	—	—
nom. pl.	*mayam*, *amhe*	—	*maye*	*tumhe*	—	*tuphe*
acc.sg.	*mam*, *mamam*	—	*mam*	*tam* *t(u)vam*	—	—
acc.pl.	*amhe, asme, no*	—	*aphe, apheni*	*tumhe, vo*	—	*tuphe, tupheni*
instr.-abl. sg.	*mayā, me, mamato*	*mayā*	*mamayā, mamiyā, me, mamate*	*t(v)ayā, te*	—	—
instr.-abl. pl.	*amhehi, no*	—	—	*tumhehi, vo*	—	*tuphehi*
dat.-gen.sg.	*mama(m), mayha(m), me*	*mama, me*	*mamam, me, hamā*	*tava(m), tuyha(m), tumham, te*	—	—
dat.-gen. pl.	*amhākam, asmākam, amham, no*	—	*aphāka(m), ne*	*tumhākam, tumham, vo*	—	*tuphākam*
loc. sg.	*mayi*	—	—	*t(v)ayi*	—	—
loc. pl.	*amhesu*	—	*aphesu*	*tumhesu*	—	*tuphesu*

aña- 'other', *sava-* 'all', Pā. *añña-* 'other', *itara-* 'other' and *sabba-* 'all' are inflected, in part or wholly, according to the pronominal declension.

3.3.1 Inflexion of the personal pronoun (1st and 2nd person)

The personal pronouns show a great number of forms which are due to analogies between the cases as well as between the numbers. The pronouns of the first and second persons have no distinction of gender.

Aś Pkt. (gen.) *hamā* (see table 5.3) is probably a contamination of *mamā* and **ha(ka)m* (< aham). The bases of *apheni*, *tupheni* (with hyper-characterized endings: *aphe* ← asmān *plus -ni*; see acc. *pulisāni*, 3.2.1), *tuphehi*, *aphāka(m)*, *tuphākam*, *aphesu*, *tuphesu* are **aph-* and **tuph-* (< asmad- / **tuṣma-*, a remodelling of *yuṣmad-* after *tvad-*). The gen. *mama* and *tava* are the bases for the acc. (Pā.) *mamam* and *tavam*, for the abl. *mamato* (~ Aś *mamate*) and for the instr. (Aś) *mamayā*. The nom. Aś *maye* / Pā. *mayam* (OIA vayam) takes its *m-* from the oblique cases of the singular, and the initial *t-* of the plural of the second person stems from the singular (see above), while the *-e-* of the instr. and loc. (see OIA *asmābhiḥ, asmāsu*) is analogical to the corresponding forms of the third-person pronoun (see 3.3.2). It was called for by the nom./acc. (Aś) *maye*, (P.) *amhe*. This (as nom.) is formed according to the proportion (*amhe* <) **asme : asmān = te : tān*. Later on the ending *-ān* was replaced by *-e*, which is the general substitution in the acc. pl., and the acc. was also (Pā.) *amhe/asme*. Based

TABLE 5.4: PERSONAL PRONOUNS (THIRD PERSON)

	Western Aś ~ Pāli	Eastern Aś
nom. sg.	*sa, so* (nt. *taṁ*); *sā*	*se* (nt. *se*); *sā*
nom. pl.	*te* (nt. *tāni*); *tā, tāyo*	*te*
acc. sg.	*taṁ* (all three genders)	*taṁ* (all three genders)
acc. pl.	*te* (nt. *tāni*); *tā, tāyo*	*tāni; tā*
instr. sg.	*tena; tāya*	*tena*
instr. pl.	*tehi; tāhi*	*tehi*
abl. sg.	*tamhā, tasmā; tāya*	*taphā*
abl. pl.	*tehi; tāhi*	
gen. sg.	*tassa; tassā, tissā, tāya*	*tasa*
gen. pl.	*tesaṁ; tāsaṁ*	*tesa(ṁ), tānaṁ*
loc. sg.	*tamhi, tasmiṁ; tassaṁ, tāsaṁ, tissaṁ*	*tasi*
loc. pl.	*tesu; tāsu*	*tesu*

on *amhe* the gen. *amhaṁ* was formed analogical to *mamaṁ* (the same holds good for *tumhaṁ*).

3.3.2 Inflexion of the personal pronoun (3rd person)

The third-person pronoun distinguishes gender. The paradigm is composed of historical and newly created forms. In table 5.4, the forms before the semicolon belong to the masculine, those after it to the feminine (if only one form is given it is the masculine).

The acc. pl. (Aś) *tāni* has the neuter ending transferred to masculines (see 3.2.1). Aś *taphā* is the regular outcome of (OIA) *tasmāt*. In Pāli, the nom. sg. m. *sa* – in OIA only allowed before consonants – stands beside *so*, which becomes the dominant form (as is *se* < *saḥ* in eastern Aś Pkt.). The instr. f. sg. *tāya* (tayā) is borrowed from the nominal type *kaññāya* – as is nom./acc. pl. *tāyo* (see 3.2.2) – to avoid homonymity with the 2nd person pronoun *tayā* (tvayā). On *tissā* (tasyāḥ) see 2.2.5, on *tāsaṁ* (tasyām) see 2.2.2.

3.3.3 Inflexion of eta(d), ya(d) and (e)na(d)-

The stems *eta(d)*- and *ya(d)*- inflect in the same way; the latter has lost in eastern Aś Pkt. its initial *y*- (eastern Aś *e* < *yaḥ* / *yat*). In Pāli, the pronoun *ena(d)*- is used only as acc. of all three genders (*enaṁ*). And after the pattern of *ta(d)*- : *eta(d)*- a new stem *na*- is created to *ena(d)*- which inflects like *(e)ta(d)*-.

3.3.4 Inflexion of ki(m)-

The stem *ki(m)*- of the interrogative pronoun is not only used for the nom./acc. sg. nt. but forms derived from it supplement the *ka*-paradigm ([Pā.] abl. sg. m. *kismā*, gen. *kissa*, loc. *kimhi, kismiṁ*) which inflects as *ta(d)*- does (Aś Bairāṭ *ke-ci* 'whatever' <

*kam-cit). This contributes to the mingling of the masculine and neuter forms, which is complemented by a levelling of sing. and pl. forms (Pā. *ko nu tumhe* 'Who are you?', Ja V 390,18*). Aś Pkt. *kāni*, however, seems to be a fossilized form which does not succumb to grammatical congruency.

3.3.5 Inflexion of ida(m)-

In the paradigm of *ida(m)*- historical forms ([m. sg.] *ayaṁ* [in Pāli also f.; Aś Pkt. has *ayaṁ* and *iyaṁ* for all three genders], *imaṁ, asmā, assa, asmiṁ*, [m. pl.] nom./acc. *ime*, gen. *esaṁ*, [f. sg.] obl. *assā*, [f. pl.] nom./acc. *imā*, gen. *āsaṁ*, [nt.] *idaṁ, imāni*) are complemented by new ones based on the old acc. *imaṁ*: (m. sg.) gen. *imassa*, loc. *imasmiṁ*, (pl.) instr. *imehi*, gen. *imesaṁ*, loc. *imesu*, (f. sg.) obl. *imāya*, loc. *imāyaṁ*, gen. *imissā*, (pl.) nom./acc. *imāyo*, instr. *imāhi*, gen. *imāsaṁ*, loc. *imāsu*, (nt.) *imaṁ*. Since the enclitic gen. pl. Pā. *esaṁ* and *āsaṁ* – both used for m. *and* f. – can lose their initial vowel in *sandhi* (*na 'saṁ*) these forms were reinforced (Pā. *esānaṁ, āsanaṁ*). The instability of the initial, however, remained.

3.3.6 Inflexion of amu-

The singular of both masculine and feminine of the paradigm of Pā. *amu-* 'that' is a direct continuation of that of OIA *adas-*. The *-u* of Pā. *asu* (nom. sg. m.) and of (nom./ acc. sg. nt.) *aduṁ – amuṁ* is used besides – is due to the influence of *amu-*. The plural is built up exclusively from forms of this stem, which encroached likewise on the nom. sg. m. (*amu*).

3.4 Numerals

(1) The numeral *eka-* inflects as a pronominal adjective (see 3.3), i.e. (nom. pl.) Pā. *eke*, Aś Sār *ik'ike*, (gen.) Pā. *ekesaṁ*, (obl. f.) *ekissā/ekissaṁ*.

(2) Due to the loss of the dual the numeral 'two' (with the stems *d[u]vā-, d[(u)v]i-, d[v]e-, du[v]-* and *bā-*) had to be remodelled. The form of the nom./acc. f. and nt., *d(u)ve*, was transferred to the masculine, the ending being identical to that of *ime, te, sabbe*. It is only in the western Aśoka inscriptions that the inflexion of masculine and feminine is kept apart (RE I G *dvo morā*, RE II *dve cikīch[ā]*). In Pāli, the remaining cases are formed analogical to those of the numeral 'three' (as is the gen. of *ubha-*, see below): *dvīhi, dvinnaṁ, dvīsu* (Aś PE instr. *duvehi*). *ubha-* has generalized the *o* of the nom. (< ubhau): Pā. nom./acc. *ubho*, instr./abl. *ubhohi*, gen. *ubhinnaṁ*, loc. *ubhosu*.

(3) In Pāli, the numeral *ti-* 'three' (with the stems *ti-* and *te-*) distinguishes in the nom./ acc. all three, and in the genitive two genders; both these genitives were modelled after *catunnaṁ* and *channaṁ*, the feminine one receiving its geminate *-ss-* from (nom./acc.) *tisso*: nom./acc. m. *tayo* (trayaḥ), f. *tisso* (tisraḥ), nt. *tīṇi* (trīṇi), gen. m./nt. *tiṇṇaṁ*, f. *tissannaṁ* (< *tisanaṁ* < tisṛṇām). The instrumental/ablative and locative identical for all genders, show the inflexion of an *i*-stem (with *-ī-* in accord with *tīṇi*): *tīhi, tīsu*. The gen. also has a double ending (*tiṇṇannaṁ*), by analogy with *pañcannaṁ, channaṁ, sattannaṁ*.

(4) 'Four' (*catu[r]-*) has two forms for nom. *and* acc. m. (owing to case confusion and after the model of the feminine); also the other cases are historical forms whose compensatory lengthened *-ū-* conforms to the vocalism of 'three': Pā. (nom./acc.) *cattāro, caturo* (Aś RE XIII G nom. *captāro* ~ Sh *cature*), (instr./abl.) *catūhi, catubbhi*, (gen.) *catunnaṁ, catūsu*. The feminine has as nom./acc. and gen. the historical forms

(Pā. *catasso, catassannaṁ* [< *catasanaṁ : tissannaṁ]), whereas the remaining cases are supplied by the masculine. The nom./acc. nt. is an historical form too (Pā. *cattāri*; Aś RE XIII K *catāli*, used for m.).

(5–10) The numerals 'five' to 'ten' continue the old forms; as a rule only the instrumental has the ending *-ahi*, while the gen. regularly has *-annaṁ* by analogy and 'six' has *s-* and *ch-* (with *cha[t]-* as stem) as its initial (see 2.3.1).

(11–18) In Pāli, the numerals 'eleven' to 'eighteen' have a by-form *°rasa-* (see Aś K *duvādasa-*), which probably originated in 'seventeen' by dental dissimilation (*sattarasa-* < saptadasa-) to then spread by analogy: *ekādasa-/rasa-, dvā°/(bā°), te°, pañca°, soḷasa-/°rasa-, satta°, aṭṭhā°*. 'Thirteen' also has a form with *-ḷ-* < *-ḍ-* (*[aḍḍha]teḷasa-*; see Aś RE V M *tredaśa°*), as has 'forty' (*cattāḷīsa-*), while 'fourteen' also shows abnormal loss of *-t-* (*cuddasa-*, Aś Nig *codasa°* < PE V *cāvudasa-*) and the genuine MIA forms of 'fifteen' are (Pā.) *paṇṇarasa-* and *pannarasa-* (see Aś PE V *paṁnaḍasa-*).

(19/29 [etc.]) 'Nineteen' is (Pā. / Aś) *ekūnavīsati-*, 'twenty-nine' (Pā.) *ekūnatiṁsa-* (etc.).

(20/30) 'Twenty' took over the ending of 'thirty' (and sometimes also vice versa): (Pā. / Aś) *vīsati-*, (Pā.) *vīsa(ṁ)-, vīsā-, tiṁsa(ṁ)-, tīsā-, chattiṁsati-* (viṁśati-, triṁśat-).

(21–28/31–38) *°vīsa(ṁ)-* and *°vīsati-, tiṁsa-* and (sporadically) *tiṁsati-* are the bases of the numerals '21–28' and '31–38' ('33' with analogical levelling: *tettiṁsa-* < *tetthiṁsa-* < trayastriṁśat-).

(40) (Pā.) *cattārīsa-* has by-forms with *-l-* and *-ḷ-* (see above); compounded with other numerals, it is sometimes shortened to *°tālīsa-*.

(50) (Pā.) *paññāsa-/paṇṇāsa-* 'fifty' shows the same development of *-ñc-* as 'fifteen'.

(60) The initial of Pā. *saṭṭhi-* contrasts with that of *cha-* 'six'.

The other numerals continue the OIA forms.

The numerals 'one' to 'eighteen' are used as adjectives, unless they inflect as neuters (sg.) in analogy with *vīsaṁ* (< *viṁśat). The numerals 'nineteen' and upwards are neuter or feminine substantives in *-aṁ* or *-ā* and *-ti* respectively. When connected with substantives, they may be used appositionally in the same case as the substantive, or else the qualified substantive may be put in the genitive plural. Often, however, the numerals are not inflected at all. Finally, a determinative compound may be formed.

The ordinals continue – *mutatis mutandis* – the OIA ones (as to *dutīya-* and *tatīya-* see 2.2.11[d]). The higher numbers (except for '60th') may be formed by adding *°ma-* to the cardinal: *vīsa-, vīsatima-* (viṁśa-, viṁśatitama-), *saṭṭhitama-*. They are all inflected as *a*-stems. Their feminine is always in *-ā*, while those in *-ī* are used to denote dates.

3.5 The verb

Compared with the verb system of OIA, the systems of Aś Pkt. and Pāli have undergone extensive reorganization. The dual has been completely lost, and the middle survives only in some forms (in 'western' Aś Pkt. and Pāli to a higher degree than in 'eastern' Aś Pkt.). The system of tenses has been simplified: it comprises the present, the future (and conditional) and a combined preterite consisting of (former) imperfect, aorist and perfect. The subjunctive is missing from the moods. Of derived present stems only the causative and the denominative are productive categories, while the desiderative and the intensive have been preserved in just a few historical forms: Aś RE X Dh *susrusatāṁ* 'may he obey' (śuśrūṣatām), Pā. *jigucchati* 'loathes', *tikicchati* 'cures' (cikitsati), *lālappati* 'talks too much' (lālapyate), *caṅkamati* 'walks up and down' (caṅkramīti [patterned after *kamati* 'walks']).

The focus of the verbal conjugation is no longer the root but the present stem, i.e. the third singular of the indicative without the ending -ti. All regular verb forms are based on it; forms that are not so constructed are chiefly historical relics. According to its stem-final, two 'conjugations' can be distinguished. In one type (the more numerous) the present stem ends in -a (the OIA present classes I, VI and IV, the latter as a rule with characteristic -CCa- < -Cya-); in the other, it ends in a long vowel, most commonly -e (see 3.5.2), fairly often -ā, rarely -ī or -o. This 'second' conjugation comprises the old athematic presents now made uniform by suppressing alternations, this as a consequence of generalizing a frequent form (Pā. *eti* 'he goes' ... *enti* 'they go' [OIA *eti* ... *yanti*], *suṇomi* 'I listen' ... *suṇoma* 'we listen' [OIA *śṛṇomi* ... *śṛṇumaḥ*]); or which were thematized, i.e. transferred to the 'first' conjugation – a process based on a form constantly used (thus all verbs of class VII were thematized forming a group with *muñcati*, etc.): Pā. (1sg.) *dadhāmi* → *da(d)hanti* (≠ OIA *dadhati* 'they put'), (3sg.) *seti* (*śete*) → *senti* (≠ OIA *śerate* 'they lie'), (3pl.) *chindanti* → *chindati* (≠ OIA *chinatti* 'he cuts'), *kubbanti* (kurvanti) → *kubbati* (≠ OIA *karoti* 'he makes'), *gaṇhanti* (gṛhṇanti) → *gaṇhati* (≠ OIA *gṛhṇāti* 'he grasps'). Or alternatively, a new stem was extracted from such forms as (3sg.) *jūhati* 'he sacrifices' (see Aś RE I G *prajūhitavyaṃ*) and *jaggati* 'he wakes up' from (OIA) 3pl. *juhvati* and *jāgrati*. Verbs of the old 5th class were often transferred to the 9th class: Aś RE XIII K *pāpuṇāti* 'he reaches' (≠ OIA prāpnoti), Pā. *sakkuṇāti* 'he is able' (≠ OIA śaknoti), *suṇāti* 'he listens' (≠ OIA śṛṇoti). Thus the *o*-present, which disturbs the verbal system of *a*- and *e*-presents, was gradually superseded by the *(n)ā*-present which fitted in better. And even the small difference in vocalism (°ati :: °āti) was finally levelled: Aś Bairāṭ *suneyu* 'may they listen' (← *sunati* [≠ śṛṇuyuḥ]), Pā. *pāpuṇa* 'obtain!', (Thī 432), (opt.) *suṇe* 'may he listen' (Ja IV 240,29*). A number of verbs were supplemented or replaced by new creations based (e.g.) on the imperative (Pā. *[ā]deti* / °dheti ← dehi / dhehi [√dā / √dhā]) or aorist (Pā. *pāheti* ← *pāhesi* [√hi]).

3.5.1 atthi, bhavati, dad(h)āti, karoti, tiṭṭhati

The old forms were, however, preserved to a great extent: (class II) Pā. *sināhi* 'take a bath!' (snāhi), (class III) *jahāti* 'he leaves', (class V) *suṇomi* 'I listen', *pappoti* 'he obtains', (class IX) *jināti* 'he deprives'. And especially verbs like (1) *atthi* 'is', (2) *bhavati* 'is', (3) *dadāti* 'gives', *dahāti* 'puts', (4) *karoti* 'does, makes', (5) *tiṭṭhati* 'stands' retained their old inflexion (beside numerous neo-forms):

(1) After the pattern °āma : °āmase, °anti : °ante a medium is formed in Pāli based on 1pl. *asmā̆, amhā̆* 'we are' – themselves analogical to *asmi* (and its by-form *amhi*-) and 3pl. *santi* 'they are': (1pl.) *smase, amhase*, (3pl.) *sante*. The 1st and 2nd persons tend to join the preceding word, which led to the loss of the initial *a*-: *ummaggapaṭipanna mhi* 'I have entered upon the wrong road' (Thī 94), *sītibhuta mha* 'I have become tranquillized' (Thī 66). (3sg.) *atthi* 'is', which never lost its *a*-, and univerbated *natthi* 'it is not' are used as petrified forms also with a plural subject: *natthi khandhādisa dukkhā* 'No misery (pl.) is like that of the *skandhas*' (Dhp 202). Of the imperative – apart from some sporadic forms – only (3sg.) *atthu* and (3pl.) *santu* are preserved. The optative has two paradigms, one with the stem *ass*-, the other with *siy*- (see 1.2).

(2) In Pāli, *bhava(ti)* 'is, becomes' has this uncontracted form with *bh*- and a form with initial *h*- and contracted -o- < -ava-. The first one is used in Girnār, the latter in the

eastern Aśokan inscriptions, while Shāhbāzgaṛhī has forms with both character-istics (*bhoti, bhotu*). It is only in some compounds that such forms are used in Pāli: *anubhoti* 'obtains', *saṃbhoti* 'arises'.

(3) Beside (a) *dadāti* 'gives' and (b) *dahāti* 'puts' (see 2.3.2 [p. 177]) Pāli has a number of new stems:

    (a) (1) *dada-* (extracted from *dadāmi*), the base of (e.g.) the optative *dadeyyaṃ* (*dadeyyāsi, dade[yya]* ...), (2) *de-* (see above, 3.5), (3) *dajja-* (abstracted from the optative *dajjaṃ* < dadyām), (4) 1sg. *dammi* (analogical to *kummi* 'I make', see below);

    (b) (1) *daha-*, (2) *dhe-* (see above, 3.5).

(4) The present (Pā.) *karoti/kurute* 'makes' (and its opt. *kuriyā, kuyirā* < *kuryāt*) is retained and has influenced other parts of the paradigm: *karoti ... karomase ... karonti*, (imp.) *karohi ... karontu*, (opt.) *kariyǎ* (*kuriyā x kar* °), (ind.) *kuruse, kurute*, (imp.) *kuru, kurutu, kurutaṃ*. The 3pl. (OIA) *kurvanti* 'they make' (→ *kurvati*) was the base of the present *kubbati* and its optative (3sg.) *kubbetha*. The 1sg. *kummi* 'I make' goes back to (Epic) Skt. *kurmi*, which is based on (1pl.) *kurmaḥ*. From the future (OIA) *kariṣyati* 'will make' a new stem *kara-* was abstracted (cf. Aś / Pā. *dakkhati* 'sees' < drakṣyati). It served as the base of an imperative (2sg. *kara* / *karassu* 'make!') and of an optative ([1sg.] *kareyyāmi, kareyyaṃ*, [3pl.] *kareyyuṃ*, [all persons] *kare*). Moreover 'eastern' Aś has *kaleti*, an *e*-verb (see 3.5.2).

(5) Besides *tiṭṭha(ti)* 'stands' Aś Pkt. and Pā. have the present *ṭhāyati* (analogical to *sayati* 'lies' and influenced by *ṭhāyi[n]-* < sthāyin-) – Aś SE I J *uthāye* 'may he stand up!', Pā. *ṭhāyāmi*, Th 888–, Pāli also has *ṭhāti, ṭhahati* and *ṭheti*.

The possible contraction of *-aya-* > *-e-* and *-ava-* > *-o-* (see 2.2.7) led to various doublets: Pā. *jeti* ~ *jayati* 'wins', Aś / Pā. *hoti* ~ *bhavati* (see above). And in line with that model, even primary *-e-* could be resolved into *-aya-*: Pā. *seti* 'lies' (śete) → *sayati*. All this lent the verbal system its variegated appearance.

3.5.2 e-verbs

Many verbs were transferred to the *e*-class. For the most part this transference started from the verbal adjective in °*ita-*: Pā. *uṭṭheti* 'stands up' (← *uṭṭhita-*), *phuseti* 'touches' (← *phusita-*). These *e*-verbs are often distinguished from *e*-causatives by their *a*-vocalism (Pā. *vadeti* 'speaks'~ *vādeti* 'plays'), though causatives were also used instead of the simple verbs, i.e. as 'common' *e*-verbs (then their causative is formed with *-āpaya-/-āpe-*, see 3.5.8).

3.5.3 The verbal endings

The endings of the (1) indicative present and the future (for the use of 1sg. *-aṃ* in the future see below) are (sg.) *-mi, -si, -ti*, (pl.) *-ma, -tha, -nti* (the secondary ending *-ma* has replaced primary **-mo* < *-maḥ*); the 1sg. of the indicative has in Pāli a by-form *-ǎhaṃ* (*palāyahaṃ*, Ja II 340,9*). The corresponding *ātmanepada* endings of the singular are *-e, -se, -te* (in Pāli often replaced by *-sī, -tī: pekkhasī* 'you look at' < prekṣase, *jāyatī* 'he is born' < jāyate), while of the plural only *-nte* is preserved. The last one has a by-form °*are* (Pā. *upapajjare* 'they are reborn', *socare* 'they mourn') – known from Aś RE XIII G (*anuvatare*) – which is used for the aorist and the future as well (see 3.5.5).

(2) The imperative endings (sg.) *-mi* and (pl.) *-tha* are transferred from the indicative; its 2sg. has *-ø* (i.e. the pure stem vowel) and after long vowels *-hi* – borrowed from OIA athematic *ā*-roots –, its 3sg. *-tu* and its 3pl. *-ntu*. The stem vowel can be lengthened before these endings (and it has been surmised that the imperative endings *-āhi/-ātu/ -ātha*, attested also with Aś, are remains of an historic subjunctive). The rare 1pl. in *-mu* (frequently attested in 1pl. opt. *-emu*, see below) is a remodelling of *-ma* after (3sg.) *-tu* and (2sg. mid.) *-ssu*. The *ātmanepada* endings, which are frequently used, are (2sg.) *-ssu* (by *samprasāraṇa* < -sva), (3sg.) *-taṁ*, (1–3pl.) *-mase, -vho, -ntaṁ*. In the 3sg. passive, younger *(haññā)tu* supersedes older *(āharīya)taṁ*.

(3) The optative has two sets of suffixes – one with generalized *-e-* (based on OIA 3sg. *-et*), one with *-eyya-* (a contamination of the OIA thematic and athematic endings, starting from 1sg./3pl. *-eyam/-eyuḥ*) –, and two sets of endings, (a) the old optative endings (the *-ā[≠]* of the athematic ones, supported by that of the second set of endings [*-eyyāmi, -eyyāma*], was retained except for the 3sg.) and (b) those of the indicative present (with substitution of secondary *-ta* by primary *-tha*): (1sg.) *-eyyaṁ, -eyyāmi, -e*, (2sg.) *-eyya, -eyyāsi, -esi*, (3sg.) *-eyya, -eyyāti, -e*, (1pl.) *-eyyāma, -ema, -emu*, (2pl.) *-eyyātha, -etha*, (3pl.) *-eyyu(ṁ)* ('eastern' Aś *-evu*, see 2.3.2). The medium has (2sg.) *-etho, -etha, -eyyātho*, (3sg.) *-etha*, (1pl.) *-emase, -emasi, -emahe*. Corresponding to the analytical form *-ahaṁ* of the indicative (see above), the optative has (1sg.) *-eyyāhaṁ* and (2sg. middle) *-eyyāhe*: Pā. *jāneyyāhaṁ* 'I would know', M I 487,13, *vareyyāhe* 'I would choose for me', D II 267,11*. *ālabhehaṁ*, Aś Sep I, has this form with the alternative optative suffix *-e-*. The regular optative of both 'conjugations' is that in *-e(yya)-*. But some historical forms of the optative of athematic verbs were preserved: Aś RE XII Sh *siya*, G *assa* 'it may be' (see 1.2), Pā. *dajjaṁ/dajjāsi/dajjā* ' ... may give', *kayirā* 'he may do'. And these relics were the pattern for new 'athematic' optatives like (Pā.) *vajjā* 'he may say' (← vadati).

(4) The endings of the *preterite* are those of the tenses which merged into it (see 3.5.4).

3.5.4. The preterite

The preterite replaced the (OIA) aorist, imperfect and perfect, supplemented by the verbal adjective (with or without *hoti*) used as *verbum finitum*. The core of this tense is the (OIA) aorist; historical forms of the imperfect and perfect were integrated into its paradigms: (imperfect) Aś RE VIII G *ayāya* 'he went' (*ayāyat), Pā. *adadam* 'I gave', *abravī* 'he said' (abravīt), *āsī* 'it was' (āsīt), (perfect) Aś RE III G *āha* 'he said', Pā. *āsa* 'he was', *jagāma* 'he went', *vidu(ṁ)* 'they knew' (viduḥ). Of the OIA aorist types five have survived in Pāli, of which two (3 and 4) are productive:

(1) The root-aorist (*akā* 'he made', *aṭṭhā* 'he stood'),
(2) the thematic aorist (*agamaṁ* 'I went', *acchida* 'he cut', *avoca* 'he said'),
(3) the *s*-aorist (*aññāsi* 'he knew', *pāyāsi* 'he went', *assosi* 'he heard', *addakkhi* 'he saw'; cf. Aś RE VIII G *ñayāsu* 'they went out' < *nyayāsuḥ),
(4) the *iṣ*-aorist (*akkamī* 'he went', *avadhī* 'he killed', *acāri* 'he went'; cf. Aś RE VIII K *nikhamisu* 'they went out'),
(5) the reduplicated aorist (*udapatto* 'he flew up' < udapaptat [rebuilt after *patto* < prāptaḥ]).

Beside historical forms, which were partly analogically rebuilt (*adāsi* 'he gave' [≠ adāt], *akkocchi* 'he scolded' [≠ akrukṣat]), the Pāli aorist has new formations based on the present stem: Those of the 'first conjugation' (see 3.5) built an aorist of the fourth type (1sg. *pucchi[ṁ]* 'I asked', 3sg. *ajāni* 'he knew'; cf. Aś PE VII *ichisu* 'they wished', Pāṅg *pāpunitha* 'he reached'), those of the 'second' one of the third type (*kathesi* 'he narrated', *pūjesi* 'he honoured', *māresi* 'he killed').

The endings of the preterite are basically those of the OIA *a-/s-/(s)iṣ-* and root-aorist:

(a) (type I: *dadāti* 'gives') *adaṁ, adā, adā, adamha, adattha, adū/aduṁ*;

(b) (type II: *gacchati* 'goes') *agamaṁ, agamā, agamā, agamāma/agamamha, agamat(t)ha, agamuṁ,* (3sg. middle) *abhāsatha* 'he said', (1pl.) *akaramhase* 'we made', (3pl.) *amaññaruṁ* 'they thought', *abajjhare* 'they were bound';

(c) (type III: *karoti* 'makes') *akāsiṁ, akāsi, akāsi* (with *-i* < [akārṣ]īḥ, *-īt* according to the rhythmic rule [see 2.2.3]), *akamha, akattha* (instead of expected *-ṭṭha* < [akār]ṣṭa), *akāsuṁ,* (3sg. middle) *alattha* 'he obtained' (alabdha);

(d) (type IV: *gacchati* 'goes') *agamisaṁ/agamiṁ, agami, agami, agamimha, agamittha, agamisuṁ/agamiṁsu/agamuṁ,* (2sg. med.) *paṭisevittho* 'you indulged in', (3sg.) P. *sandittha* '[the river] flew' (cf. Aś RE VIII K *nikhamithā* 'he went out').

In Pāli, the augment *a-* is prefixed when the aorist would be monosyllabic without it (*adā* 'he gave'). And it is used (at least in the language of the canon) with all disyllabic aorists except for continuations of the *iṣ*-aorist (type IV) where it is facultative (*[a]labhi* 'he obtained'). It is facultative also with polysyllabic aorists, apart from those which were enlarged within Pāli (*agamāsi* 'he went') or which continue old imperfects or thematic aorists.

3.5.5 The future

Historical forms of the future and new formations based on the present-stem (including the passive stem: Aś RE I K *alābhiyisanti* 'they will be killed', Pā. *kariyissati* 'it will be done') stand side by side (Aś Sh and M have *-is-* [< *-iṣy-*] as suffix; see *manusa-* 'man' < manuṣya-). Both have the endings of the indicative present (the medium is attested in the forms *-se, -te, -mase* and *-are*, see 3.5.3), the 1sg. *-aṁ* in addition to *-āmi* (Aś RE XIV G *likhāpayisaṁ* 'I shall order that ... is inscribed'). The close relationship of future and aorist, which gave rise to future stems such as (Aś. / Pā.) *kass-/kās-* (*kārṣy-* < [a]kārṣ- x kariṣy-), points to the fact that this ending is taken from the aorist. The *-ss-* could be weakened to *-s-* and further to *-h-* (primarily after a long stem vowel): Aś PE IV *dāhaṁti* 'they will give' (dāsyanti), SE II Dh Sa *ehatha* 'you will come' (eṣyatha), Pā. *kāhiti* 'he will make' (*kārṣyati). Only sporadically is a periphrastic future attested: Pā. *gantā* 'he will go', Ja IV 273,17*, *āgantā* 'he will come', Ja II 420,3*.

3.5.6 The conditional

The conditional, used as *irrealis*, is formed from the (almost exclusively) augmented future stem by adding the endings of the second aorist (3sg *-issa*), except that the 3pl. has *-aṁsu*: Pā. (3sg., pl.) *abhavissā, abhavissaṁsu*. Of the medium only the 3sg. is attested: Pā. *okkamissatha*, D II 63,3.

3.5.7 The denominative

Denominatives are formed from 'nominals' (a) without or (b) with suffixes (1. *-aya-/-e-* [with a causative in *-āpaya-/-āpe-*, see 3.5.8], 2. *-āya-*, 3. *-ya-*, 4. *-ĭya-*). Historical forms stand beside new formations:

(a) Pā. *laggati* 'sticks to' (← *lagga-* < lagna-), *sukkhati* 'is dried up' (← *sukkha-* < śuṣka-), *sajjhāyati* 'studies' ([BHS] svādhyāyati),

(b) (1) Pā. *patthayati* 'desires' (prārthayati), *baleti* 'has strength' (balayati), *sukheti* 'makes happy' (sukhayati),

    (2) Aś RE VI K *sukhāyāmi* 'I make happy' (~ G *sukhāpayāmi*), Pā. *cirāyati* 'delays' (cirāyati), *saddāyati* 'makes a sound' (śabdāyati), *mamāyati* 'is attached to' (mamāyate [← gen. *mama*]),

    (3) Pā. *namassati* 'pays honour to' (namasyati),

    (4) Aś SE I Dh *dukhīyati* 'suffers' (cf. PE IV *sukhīyana-dukhīyanaṃ*), Pā. *aṭṭīyati* 'is worried' (← *aṭṭa-*).

3.5.8 The causative

Aś Pkt. and Pāli have causatives formed with the suffix -aya-/-e- from the root (Aś RE IV K *pravaḍhayati* 'makes grow', Pā. *sāveti* 'recites') or – though rarely – from the present stem (Pā. *nacceti* 'makes dance', *laggeti* 'fastens'). The causative-stem may show a vowel grade different from its base (*CVCC-* and *[C]V̄C*-bases usually remain):

(1) *CaC*-roots generally have *ā*-vocalism as against -*a*- of the simplex (see Aś RE III Dh *nikhamāvū* vs. SE I Dh *nikhāmayisāmi*, Pā. *nikkhāmeti* vs. *kamati* [< krāmati]); only *Can/m*-bases do not have vowel alternation (Pā. *gameti* 'sends', *janeti* 'produces');

(2) *Ci/eC-* and *Cu/oC*-bases have *e*- and *o*-vocalism (Pā. *deseti* 'teaches', *codeti* 'impels') and

(3) *Cĭ/ŭ*-bases result in *Cāy/v*- (Pā. *bhāyayate* 'frightens', *cāveti* 'makes fall').

(Mostly) added to *Cā*-bases – which sometimes shorten their radical vowel – is the suffix -*paya-/-pe*: Aś PE IV *nijhapayisaṃti* 'they will cause amnesty' (*nidhyāpayi-ṣyanti), Pā. *jāpeti* 'makes deprive' (jyāpayati), *ropeti* 'plants' (ropayati [√ruh]). This suffix was abstracted and added to any verb stem to form causatives (very frequently to present stems): Pā. *laggāpeti* 'makes stick' (based on *laggati*). If the base itself was a causative, the derivation had a 'double causative' meaning: Aś RE II G *ropāpeti* (*ropāpita-* is attested) 'makes plant' (based on *ropeti* 'plants'), PE VII *likhāpāpeti* (*likhāpāpita-* is attested) 'orders that [the inscriptions] is caused to be engraved', Pā. *ṭhapāpeti* 'orders to be erected' (based on *ṭhapeti* 'erects').

3.5.9 The passive

The opposition of active and passive is shown not by the endings – the passive, too, has active endings –, but by the stems: Aś *anuvidhīyaṃtī* 'act in conformity with' versus *vidahāmi* 'I instruct', Pā. *bajjhati* 'is bound' versus *bandhati* 'binds', *harīyati* 'is taken' versus *harati* 'takes'. (a) Historical forms are preserved to a great extent (*[C]V/V̄C*-bases have *[C]VCC*-passive stems), partly (b) remodelled after the present stem. Examples:

(a) Aś RE I G *ārab(b)hare* 'are killed' (ālabhyante), RE XIII Sh *vuc(c)ati* 'is said' (ucyate), Pā. *paññāyati* 'is perceived' (prajñāyate), *dīyati/diyyati* 'is given' (dīyate), *ḍayhati* 'is burnt' (dahyate),

(b) Aś RE I J *āla(ṃ)bhiyaṃti* 'are killed', Pā. *kariyati/kayirati* 'is made' (k$_i$riyate x karoti).

Additionally, new passive stems are formed with the suffix -*īya*- (a contamination of -*[i]ya*- and -*īya*- [from *(d)īya(ti)* etc.]) which is added to the present stem, especially to that in -*e*-: Aś PE V *khādiyati* 'is eaten' (← *khādati*), Pā. *pucchīyati* 'is asked' (← *pucchati*), *posiyati* 'is nourished' (← *poseti*). New aorists are formed from the passive stem: Pā. *chijjiṃsu, haññiṃsu.*

3.6 The verbum infinitum

The coexistence of historical forms and new forms based on the present stem characterises also the *verbum infinitum.*

3.6.1 The present/future particle

The present/future participle (see 3.2.11) is formed by adding -*nt*- to the present/future stem (with only a few historical forms surviving like *kubba[nt]*- and *sa[nt]*-): Pā. *tiṭṭha(nt)*- 'standing', *jāna(nt)*- 'knowing', (pass.) *khajja(nt)*- 'being eaten', (fut.) *marissaṃ*. Frequently it is thematized: Aś RE XII G *karo(ṃ)ta*- 'making', Pā. *hananta*- 'killing'. As the middle voice was no longer used as a living category and the passive had active endings (see 3.5.9), the suffixes °*māna*- (in eastern Aś Pkt. °*mīna*-, see 1.2) and °*āna*- – though often concealed by the first one – became true alternatives (e.g. Pā. *bhuñjāna*-, Ja II 262,28*, where the PTS edition has unmetrical *bhuñjamāna*-): Aś RE VI G *bhuṃjamāna*- 'eating' (~ Sh *aśamana*-), SE I *saṃpaṭipajjamīna*- 'addicting oneself to' (sampratipadyamāna-), Gav *samīna*- 'being', Pā. *caramāna*- 'walking', *kubb(am)āna*- 'making', *apekhāna*- 'looking for' (apekṣamāṇa-), (pass.) *vuccamāna*- 'being called'.

3.6.2 The gerundive

The *participium necessitatis* is formed with the suffixes °*(i)tabba*- (°[i]tavya-), °*anīya*- / °*aṇīya*- (with its variants °*aniya*- / °*aṇiya*- and °*aneyya*- / °*aṇeyya*-), °*teyya*-, °*tayya*- / °*tāya*-, °*ya*- and °*a*-. Beside numerous historical forms of the two first-named gerundives (Aś RE XIII G *vijetavya*-, SE I *sotaviya*-, Pā. *gantabba*-, *labhanīya*-, *dassaneyya*-) there are many based on the present stem (Aś RE I G *prajūhitavya*-, PE IV *ichitavya*-, Pā. *pucchitabba*-, *sāretabba*-, *avissāsaniya*-, *avedaniya*-). The suffix (OIA) °*ya*- lost its clarity due to the (usual) assimilation of -*y*- to the preceding consonant and has consequently survived mainly (cf. Aś PE III *dekhiya*-) in historical forms: Aś RE IX G *kaca*- (kṛtya-), SE II Dh *cakiya*- (śakya-), Pā. *kāriya*- (kārya-), *(a)garahiya*- ([a]garhya-), *kicca*- (kṛtya-), *viññeyya*- (vijñeya-). The suffix °*a*- was added to present stems to form gerundives (type OIA *duṣkara*-): Aś RE V *supadālaya*-, PE I *dusaṃpaṭipādaya*-, Pā. *dukkara*-, *sulabha*-, *atappaya*-, *dudamaya*-, *duviññāpaya*-.

3.6.3 The verbal adjective

As the verbal adjective is preserved largely in historical forms, it has become the most frequent irregular form of the verb system (especially in the 'first conjugation'; see 3.5), very often unconnected with the present stem: Aś *kaṭa*- (*kaleti*), *pakaṃta*- (*pakamati*), Pā. *bhūta*- (*bhavati/hoti*), *laddha*- (*labhati*), *pakka*- (*pacati*), *jāta*- (*jāyati*), *iṭṭha*- (*icchati*), *sitta*- (*siñcati*), *kata*- (*karoti*), *ñāta*- (*jānāti*). Only the derived verbs have a consistent form in °*ita*-: Aś PE VII *ānapita*- (*ānapayati*), Pā. *kārita*- (*kāreti*), *kathita*-

(*katheti*), *jighacchita-* (*jighacchati*). Following this pattern 'new' verbal adjectives were derived from present stems: Pā. *āharita-* (*āharati*), *supita-* (*supati*). Thus two verbal adjectives often appear side by side: Pā. *puṭṭha-/pucchita-* 'asked' (*pucchati*), (*pa*)*muñcita-/pamutta-* 'released' (*muñcati*). Only sporadically the suffix °*ta-* is substituted by °*na-*: Aś PE IV *diṁna-* 'given' (datta-), Pā. *dinna-* 'given' (datta-).

By adding the suffix °*va(nt)-* to a verbal adjective an active participle is formed: Pā. *bhuttava(nt)-* 'having eaten'. The suffix °*āvin-*, a continuation of Vedic °*āvín-*, has the same function: Pā. *katāvi(n)-* 'having made', *bhuttāvi(n)-* 'having eaten' (inflected according to 3.2.7).

3.6.4 The infinitive

The most usual infinitive suffix is °*(i)tuṁ*. In historical forms it is added to the root (Pā. *ketuṁ* 'to buy' < kretum, *sotuṁ* 'to hear' < śrotum), in new formations to the present stem (Pā. *pappotuṁ* 'to reach' [≠ prāptum], *pucchituṁ* 'to ask' [≠ praṣṭum], [pass.] *pamuccituṁ* 'to be freed'). Sometimes it is enlarged by the particle *-ye* (with sporadic dropping of *-ṁ*): Pā. *kātuṁ-ye* 'to make' (kartum), *hetu-ye* 'to be' (bhavitum). The suffix °*tave* is inherited from Vedic Sanskrit. Historical forms served as models for new ones: Aś RE XIII G *chamitave* 'to forgive' (*kṣamitavai), Bairāṭ *vatave* 'to say' (*vaktavai), Pā. *kātave* 'to make', *gantave* 'to go', *dharetave* 'to carry'. Another rare suffix is °*tāye* of unknown origin: Pā. *dakkhitāye* 'to see', *pucchitāye* 'to ask'. And the acc. and dat. of *a*-stems were used as infinitives: Pā. *niyyāhi abhidassanaṁ* 'go out to see ...', Ja VI 193,22*, *na ca mayaṁ labhāma bhagavantaṁ dassanāya* 'we did not receive an opportunity to see the Holy one', Vin I 253,11.

3.6.5 The absolutive

The absolutive shows a similar variety of formations: (1) °*(i)tvā*, (2) °*(i)tvāna(ṁ)*, (3) °*(t)tu* (< * °*tvu* < °*tva*, see 2.2.3), (4) °*tūna(ṁ)*, (5) °*(i)yǎ*, (6) °*(i)yānǎ(ṁ)*, (7) °*eyya*, (8) °*aṁ* and – peculiar to northwestern Aś Pkt. – (9) °*ti*. All these suffixes *can* be added to the present stem. Examples:

(1) Aś RE I G *ārabhiptā* 'having killed' (see 1.2), Pā. *ñātvā*, *jānitvā* (both) 'having known' (jñātvā), *gantvā* 'having gone' (out of OIA *gatvā* analogical to inf. *gantuṁ*), *katva* 'having done' (kṛtvā), *chetva* 'having cut' (chittvā),
(2) Pā. *yajitvānaṁ* 'having sacrificed', Ja VI 136,25* (Ee °*tvāna*),
(3) Aś RE I K J *ālabhitu* 'having killed' (*ārabhitvā), PE VII *sutu* 'having heard' (śrutvā), Pā. *daṭṭhu* 'having seen' (dṛṣṭvā),
(4) Aś Bairāṭ *abhivādetūnaṁ* 'having greeted', Pā. *hātūna* 'having killed', Ja IV 280,17*,
(5) Aś Nig *āgac(c)a* 'having come' (āgatya), Bairāṭ *adhigicya* 'concerning' (adhikṛtya), Pā. *āmanta* 'having addressed' (āmantrya), *dajjā* 'having given' (← dadāti), *kariya* 'having done' (← karoti), *sakkacca(ṁ)* 'having honoured' (satkṛtya), *khādiyā* 'having eaten',
(6) Pā. *paribhuñjiyāna* 'having enjoyed', Ja V 505,28*, *khādiyānaṁ* 'having eaten', Ja V 24,4*,
(7) Pā. *vineyya* 'having removed', *viceyya* 'having considered',
(8) Pā. *samācāraṁ* 'having performed', *saṁsaraṁ* 'having moved about',
(9) Aś RE XIII Sh *vijiniti* 'having conquered', RE XIV Sh *aloceti* 'not regarding'.

PĀLI TEXTS (quoted according to the edition of the Pali Text Society)

A   Aṅguttaranikāya
Ee   Pali Text Society editions
Ja   Jātaka
Th   Theragāthā
Thī   Therīgāthā
D   Dīghanikāya
Dhp   Dhammapada
M   Majjhimanikāya
S   Saṁyuttanikāya
Sn   Suttanipāta
Vin   Vinayapiṭaka

AŚOKAN INSCRIPTIONS AND THEIR SITES
(For transcription conventions see section 1.2, p. 165.)

RE   Rock Edicts
SE   Separate Edicts
PE   Pillar Edicts
MRE   Minor Rock Edicts

All   Allahabad
Bairāṭ   Bairāṭ
Bar   Barābar
Br   Brahmagiri
Dh   Dhauli
G   Girnār
Gav   Gavīmaṭh
J   Jaugaḍa
K   Kālsī
Ko   Kosam
M   Mānsehrā
Nig   Nigālīsāgar
Pāṅg   Pāṅgurāriā
Queen   The Queen's Edict
Sa   Sannati
Sah   Sahasrām
Sār   Sārnāth
Sh   Shāhbāzgaṛhī
Sop   Sopārā
Tīp   Delhi-Toprā
Y   Yerraguḍī (= Erraguḍi)

SIGLA

V   vowel
C   consonant
S   sibilant
≠   word initial/final position
+   boundary of preverb/verb, stem/suffix or a compound
:   instead of, a substitute for

```
::      analogical to
~       alternating with
x       blended with
<       dcrivcd from
←       based on
```

REFERENCES

Berger, Hermann (1955) *Zwei Probleme der mittelindischen Lautlehre*, München: Kitzinger.

Bloch, Jules (1950) *Les inscriptions d'Asoka*. Paris: Les Belles Lettres (Collection Émile Senart).

—— (1965) *Indo-Aryan. From the Vedas to Modern Times*, Paris: Adrien-Maisonneuve (English translation of *L'Indo-Aryen du Véda aux temps modernes*, Paris 1934).

Caillat, Colette (1970) *Pour une nouvelle grammaire du Pāli*, Torino: Istituto di Indologia della Università di Torino (Conferenze IV).

Geiger, Wilhelm (1994) *A Pāli Grammar*. Translated into English by Batakrishna Ghosh, revised and edited by K. R. Norman, Oxford: The Pali Text Society.

von Hinüber, Oskar (2001) *Das ältere Mittelindisch im Überblick*, Wien: Verlag der Österreichischen Akademie der Wissenschaften.

Insler, Stanley (1994) 'Rhythmic Effects in Pali Morphology', *Die Sprache* 36 (1994) 70–93.

Lüders, Heinrich (1954) *Beobachtungen über die Sprache des buddhistischen Urkanons*, Berlin: Akademie-Verlag (Abhandlungen der Deutschen Akademie der Wissenschaften zu Berlin. Klasse für Sprachen, Literatur und Kunst. Jahrgang 1952, Nr. 10).

Oberlies, Thomas (1996) 'Stray remarks on Pali phonology, morphology, and vocabulary', *Münchener Studien zur Sprachwissenschaft* 56 (1996) 91–130.

—— (2001) *Pāli – A Grammar of the Language of the Theravāda Tipiṭaka*. Berlin – New York: de Gruyter.

Sakamoto-Goto, Junko (1988) 'Die mittelindische Lautentwicklung von *v* in Konsonantengruppen mit Verschluβlaut bzw. Zischlaut', *Indo-Iranian Journal* 31 (1988) 87–109.

Smith, Helmer (1952) 'Le futur moyen Indien et ses rythmes', *Journal Asiatique* 1952, 169–83.

Trenckner, Vilhelm (1908) 'Critical and philological notes to the first chapter (*bāhirakathā*) of the Milinda-Pañha', *Journal of the Pali Text Society* 1908, 102–51.

Turner, Ralph Lilly (1960) *Some Problems of Sound Change in Indo-Aryan*, Poona: Bhandarkar Oriental Institute (P. D. Gune Memorial Lectures 1).

—— (1975) *Collected Papers 1912–1973* (ed. by John Brough), London: School of Oriental and African Studies.

CHAPTER SIX

PRĀKRITS AND APABHRAṀŚA

Vit Bubenik

CONTENTS

LIST OF TABLES

1 A SURVEY OF MIDDLE INDO-ARYAN DIALECTS

It is customary to divide the long MIA period of *c*. fifteen centuries (fourth century BC–twelfth century AD) into three stages: Old (Early), Middle and New (Late). The Old stage (represented by writings in Pāli and inscriptional Aśokan Prākrits) was dealt with in the previous chapter.

1.1 Prākrits of the middle stage of Middle Indo-Aryan

The following are the most important literary Prākrits documented in Sanskrit drama, Prākrit poetry, Jain writings and statements by the grammarians:

(i) Māhārāṣṭrī, Śaurasenī and Māgadhī (used in Sanskrit drama, Māhārāṣṭrī also in poetry);
(ii) Ardha-Māgadhī (in Jain Canon), Jain-Māhārāṣṭrī and Jain-Śaurasenī (in post-canonical writings)
(iii) so-called Paiśācī is known to us only through statements by grammarians.

1.1.1 Literary and stage Prākrits

Māhārāṣṭrī (Mah), according to the grammarians, was the Prākrit par excellence, the 'standard' Prākrit. While the grammarians describe its features, in the case of other Prākrits they mention only how they deviate from the 'standard' Prākrit. According to Daṇḍin (sixth century c. AD), Māhārāṣṭrī was the most 'excellent' Prākrit. It was based on the living tongue of the northwestern part of the Deccan (along the river Godāvarī) and the beginnings of its literary cultivation go back to the fourth century AD. Its prestige might be due to the fact that it was spoken in the dominions of the powerful dynasty of Sātavāhanas (the Andhra dynasty) which established itself in this part of India with the capital city Pratiṣṭhāna (the modern Paiṭhan on the north bank of the Godāvarī in the Aurangābād district). In the second century AD the Sātavāhanas ruled over Mahārāṣṭra, Kāthiāwār, Central India, Berar and Mālwā; their Prākrit inscriptions were found at Nāsik, Nānāghaṭ, Sāñci, Kārle, Kaṇheri, Amarāvati and Cina. Only Māhārāṣṭrī among the other Prākrit dialects used in Sanskrit drama became literary *koine* and various magnificent poetic works were composed in this dialect. *Setubandha* (or *Rāvaṇavaha*) relates the story of Rāma, but is supposed to commemorate the building of a bridge of boats by the king of Kashmir, Pravarasena, in Srinagar. The *Gauḍavaho* celebrates the conquest of Bengal by Yaśovarman of Kanauj (the end of the seventh century AD). *Sattasaī (Saptaśatakam)* of Hāla, identified with the king Sātavāhana (second century AD), is an anthology of lyric verses composed by many poets.

Māhārāṣṭrī is the most advanced dialect of the middle stage. Some of its salient features are the following:

(i) The three sibilants of OIA, *s* (dental) *ś* (palatal) and *ṣ* (retroflex), merged into one dental sibilant *s*.
(ii) All intervocalic voiceless stops were voiced and spirantized (cf. section 3.2.6.). Subsequently, the resulting voiced fricatives were reduced to zero: OIA *prākṛta* > Mah *pāua* 'Prākrit'. Similarly, all murmured voiced stops were spirantized and ultimately lost their consonantal component but kept their murmur as a segment: OIA *mukham* 'face' > Mah *muhaṁ*; *katham* 'how' > *kahaṁ*; *dadhi* 'curds' > *dahi*. Intervocalic voiced retroflex stops do not undergo spirantization: *prābhṛta* 'present, offering' > *pāhuḍa* as against *pāua* (< *prākṛta*).
(iii) Final -*aḥ* of OIA becomes -*o* in Mah.

Śaurasenī (Ś) is deemed to be the Prākrit of the Madhyadeśa (Śūrasena was the name of the country around Mathurā). Unlike for Māhārāṣṭrī and Māgadhī, we have absolutely no inscriptional evidence for this Prākrit. In Sanskrit drama it is spoken by women and the *Vidūṣaka* 'clown, jester'. Apart from these dramatic passages, there are no independent literary works in Śauraseṇī. The following are its main phonological and morphological features:

(i) The three sibilants of OIA merged into one dental sibilant *s*.
(ii) Its intervocalic stops were reduced to zero as in Mah with the exception of the voiced dental stop (plain or murmured) whether the original or arising from the voiceless one: *t(h)* > *d(h)*. Thus we find Ś *jāṇādi* 'he knows' (< OIA *jānāti*) as against Mah *jāṇaï*; Ś *jīvadha* 'you live' (< *jīvatha*) as against Mah *jīvaha*.
(iii) Final *-aḥ* of OIA becomes here *-o* as in Mah.

Māgadhī (Mg), reflecting the dialects of eastern India, possesses rich inscriptional evidence. In Sanskrit drama Māgadhī is spoken by people of low social status. Sanskrit drama supplies us with precious evidence for a number of its regional and occupational varieties (e.g. Śākārī, Cāṇḍālī, Ḍhakkī). Its salient phonological features are:

(i) The three sibilants of OIA merged here into one palatal sibilant *ś* (< *ś, ṣ, s*): *śuṣka* 'dry' > Mg *śuśka* (but see section 3.2.1.)
(ii) The two liquids of OIA *r* and *l* merged into *l*: *rājā* 'king' > *lājā*.
(iii) Intervocalic stops in Mg are reduced to zero as in Ś (with the exception of the voiced dental stop): *bhaviṣyati* 'he will be' > *bhaviśśaï* (cf. Ś *bhavissadi*). However, the environment for spirantization in Mg includes also the voiced palatal affricate (plain or murmured). Thus we find Mg *ayya* 'today' as against Mah *ajja* (< OIA *adya*).

It is generally assumed that Prākrits used in Sanskrit drama do not represent the actual speech of the people they are supposed to typify. Nevertheless, they are based upon it and they remain for us pieces of valuable evidence regarding phonology, morphology and syntax of Middle Aryan dialects. This value diminishes with time. The later dramas, written by playwrights who learnt their Prākrits as a 'classical' language, present us with Prākrits following strictly the rules of Prākrit grammarians. For instance, the 'tyrannic' use of the passive causative in Sanskrit and Prākrit sections of Mudrārākṣasa (*c.* 800) shows the pervasive influence of Sanskrit (cf. section 5.5). Hemacandra (twelfth century) composed *Kumārapālacarita* mainly to illustrate the rules of his grammar (cf. section 2.1.)

1.1.2 Prākrits used by Jainas

Ardha-Māgadhī (AMg) and Māhārāṣṭrī were cultivated above all by the religious sects of Jainas who made them a linguistic medium for their literary works, rejecting Classical Sanskrit linked with Hindu scriptures. The earliest Jain sūtras (second century AD) were composed in Ardha-Māgadhī. Its salient features are the following:

(i) The nominative singular of masculine *a*-stems ends in *-e*.
(ii) The locative singular of *a*-stems adopted the pronominal suffix *-ṁsi*.
(iii) *-ittha* is the singular suffix of the preterite in all persons, and *-iṁsu* is its counterpart in plural.

These sūtras form the Canon (arranged by Devaḍḍhi Gaṇin in the fifth century in forty-five *āgamas*) of the Śvetāmbara sect. The exegetical texts of the Śvetāmbaras (so called *niryuktis* and *bhāṣyas*) were written in a form of Māhārāṣṭrī, called Jain Māhārāṣṭrī (JM). The Jainas had been using this variety for literary purposes since *c.* AD 300 until it was replaced in this function by Apabhraṁśa during the eighth–ninth centuries. Jain Māhārāṣṭrī used by the Jain authors in their secular writings was for all purposes identical with 'general' Māhārāṣṭrī. One of the few differences, noticed by Jacobi (1886: XXII), was the use of the palatal glide to avoid the hiatus in the environment after vowels before *a*: Mah *gaa* vs. JMah *gaya* 'gone', Mah *hiaa* vs. JMah *hiyaya* 'heart'. The Canon of the Digambara sect was written in a dialect which in some respects resembles Śaurasenī and has therefore been termed Jain Śaurasenī (JŚ).

At the beginning of the secular literature in Jain Māhārāṣṭrī we find a vast epic in more than 9000 verses, the celebrated *Paumacariya* 'The Life of Padma' by Vimalasūri. Vimalasūri (*c*. AD 300) stands at the beginning of a new literary tradition, part epic and part poetic, but corresponding more closely to the *kāvya* style. He picked up a well known subject, the story of Rāma called Padma in Jain mythology. It underwent various changes to suit Jainism (for instance, Rāvaṇa is killed by Lakṣmaṇa, and the gold deer incident is omitted). Vimalasūri's Māhārāṣṭrī shows a number of Apabhraṁśa features. The salient ones are the gerund in *-evi*, the pronoun *kavana* 'who' (cf. H *kauṇ*, Gu *kɔṇ* vs. Skt *kaḥ*), and the negative particle *navi* (< *na api*) 'not' (cf. R *navi*). In addition, many *deśī* 'local, provincial' words are used to make the epic more understandable to the common people.

Another early major work in prose, composed in archaic Māhārāṣṭrī in the seventh century, *Vāsudevahiṇḍī* 'Transmigratory wanderings' narrates the life of Vāsudeva and Kṛṣṇa on the model of the famous *Bṛhatkathā* by Guṇādhya. To the next century belong two romances: Haribhadra's *Samarādityakathā* (on the model of Sanskrit *mahākāvyas*) and Uddyotanasūri's *Kuvalayamālakathā* (written in 779 during the reign of Vatsarāja of the Pratihāra dynasty). The latter work in addition to Jain Māhārāṣṭrī makes use of Paiśācī and Apabhraṁśa.

1.1.3 *Paiśācī*

Paiśācī (Pai) with its subdialect Cūlikāpaiśācī (CP) is considered to be an archaic MIA dialect which is known to us only through statements by the grammarians, most notably Vararuci (Book X) and Hemacandra in 25 sūtras [8.4.303–28]. There are several reasons for allocating this dialect to the Northwest India. The major literary work composed entirely in Paiśācī was (nowadays lost) Guṇādhya's *Bṛhatkathā* (first/second centuries AD). Indian tradition considered Paiśācī to be *bhūtabhāṣā* 'language of the demons' (e.g. Bhāmaha in his commentary on Vararuci X.1). The following features may be gleaned from Hemacandra:

(i) The three sibilants of OIA merged into one dental sibilant *s* (as in Mah and Ś).
(ii) The voiced dental stop was devoiced; hence the 'archaic' 3rd Sg present *-ati* (cf. Pāli) as against AMg, Mah, Ap *-aï*.
(iii) Retroflex *ṇ* > *n* (Instr Sg *nena* 'with this' as against AMg *ṇeṇa*); and, vice versa, *l* was retroflexed.
(iv) The clusters *jñ*, *ny*, *ṇy* ended up as the geminate *ññ*.

Cūlikāpaiśācī, according to Hemacandra [8.4.325], at variance with all the other MIA dialects, devoiced systematically all the voiced and murmured stops: OIA *madanaḥ* 'god of love' > CP *matano*; *vyāghraḥ* 'tiger' > *vakkho*; *bhagavatī* > *phakkavatī*; etc. In India the devoicing of murmured stops took place only in Dardic and Romani languages (e.g. OIA *dhūma* 'smoke' > European Romani *thuv*; *bhūmi* 'earth' > *phuv*).

1.2 Apabhramśa – the late stage of Middle Indo-Aryan

The late stage of MIA (fifth to twelfth centuries) is represented by writings in Apabhramśa (Ap) and Avahaṭṭha (Av). The term *Apabhramśa* is used as the name of a literary dialect in which Jain authors composed their poetic works between the fifth and twelfth centuries AD (virtually no prose works in Apabhramśa have come down to us). Among ancient Indian grammarians and rhetoricians the term *Apabhramśa* was used contemptuously to denote all deviations from Pāṇinian Sanskrit, descended from the divine language of the Vedic texts. For instance, Patañjali (second century BC) in his *Mahābhāṣya* [1.1.1] labels all the dialectal forms of Sanskrit go 'cow' (*gāvī, goṇī, gotā*, etc.) as *apabhramśa* 'aberant, off standard'. *Bhāratīya Nāṭyaśāstra,* the famous treatise of dramaturgy of the second century AD, describes *Apabhramśa* as *vibhraṣṭa* 'fallen down', as a dialect abounding in -*u* and as the dialect of the *Ābhīras*. The Ābhīras were a west Indian nomadic tribe whose roaming grounds stretched from Mathurā to the western sea. (There is some evidence that Ābhīradeśa must have been a part of Sindhudeśa extending from the Indus delta to the Rann of Kutch, and that Ābhīra Apabhramśa could have been identical with Vrācaḍa Apabhramśa, known only through later grammarians.) Their political history is virtually unknown. Ptolemy mentioned them under the name of Abiria and at the beginning of our era there were Ābhīra rulers as far east as Nepal. Samudra Gupta (fourth century AD) recorded their name as one of the conquered nations on the stone pillar at Allahabad. At the time of Islamic invasions they held Khandesh and Nimar (between contemporary Surat and Nagpur).

Given the fact that some Apabhramśa words appear in Vimalasūri's *Paumacariya,* composed otherwise in Jain Māhārāṣṭrī in the third century, we may agree with Tagare (1948: 1) that Apabhramśa was a linguistic stage as early as AD 300. As of the sixth century there is indirect evidence that Apabhramśa achieved the status of a literary dialect, furnished by statements of Bhāmaha and Daṇḍin, and the inscription of the Vallabhī king Dharasena II (referring to his father Guhasena (559–69) as one proficient in composing works in three languages: Sanskrit, Prākrit and Apabhramśa). The only direct piece of evidence for the early period of Apabhramśa are Kālidāsa's Apabhramśa songs, assuming their genuineness. To the eighth century belong presumably the epics of Svayaṁbhūdeva (*Paumacariu* and *Riṭṭhanemicariu*). Another great poet was Puṣpadanta (tenth century), an author of a monumental epic depicting the lives of 63 *mahāpuruṣas*, edited under the title *Mahāpurāṇa.* During the tenth century various biographic tales, such as those by Kanakāmara, Dhanavāla and others, were written. Haribhadra's story of Sanatkumāra, the *cakravartin* 'sovereign of the world', and Somaprabha's story of the conversion of the king Kumārapāla are representative of the late Apabhramśa works of the twelfth century. And finally we may mention Addahamāṇa's *Saṁdeśa Rāsaka* (twelfth/thirteenth centuries) as a sole specimen of the late secular Apabhramśa poetry.

During the centuries of Islamic invasions, when NIA languages started emerging, Apabhramśa became another classical language of India in addition to Sanskrit and Prākrit. Its rise from the regional dialect of Jain epic poetry culminated in the normative work of the greatest Prākrit grammarian, Hemacandra Sūri (1088/89–1172/73). Kramadīśvara (Eastern grammarian of the twelfth century) was the first to mention three varieties of Apabhramśa [*Prākṛtādhyāya* v 66–7]: *Vrācaṭa, Nāgara* and *Upanāgara.* Jacobi and Bhayani identified *Vrācaṭa* with *Ābhīra* as its main variety. Late eastern grammarians (of the seventeenth century) located *Vrācaḍa* in the valley of Indus. Its salient phonological feature was the preservation of *r* in consonant clusters (cf.

Sindhi *ṭre* 'three' as against Hindi *tīn* < Pkt *tīṇi* < OIA *trīṇi*). *Nāgara*, according to Bhayani (1947: 306), is to be understood as a cover term for all sorts of regional Apabhraṁśas which had developed in northern and western India in opposition to Vrācaṭa. From its beginnings Apabhraṁśa was located in Gujarat, Rajputana and Malwa and thence it spread through the whole of north India and ultimately became north India's literary koine. Given the number of Apabhraṁśa works which originated in Gujarat, we may be justified in postulating a regional variety called Gurjara Apabhraṁśa even though there are no extant works in this variety earlier than the twelfth century (with a possible exception of Dhanavāla's *Bhavisattakahā* dated to the tenth century).

From the point of view of later developments seen in early NIA languages, it was proposed by Alsdorf that there were two varieties within Apabhraṁśa. The 'classical' Apabhraṁśa variety which bore certain affinities with Old Gujarati and Marwari was labelled Śvetāmbara Apabhraṁśa, and another, closer allegedly to Old Braj and Western Hindi, was labelled Digambara Apabhraṁśa. However, we may agree with Bhayani that this dichotomy is rather untenable for a simple reason of the eclectic character of Apabhraṁśa literature borrowing freely from earlier Prākrits and Sanskrit. More importantly, we have some evidence for the existence of Eastern Apabhraṁśa (EAp) known to us through the *Dohākoṣas* of Kāṇha and Saraha (edited by Shahidullah in 1928).

2 PREVIOUS STUDIES OF THE MIDDLE INDO-ARYAN PERIOD

2.1 Evidence from medieval Indian grammarians

The earliest pieces of Prākrit grammar are the fragments preserved in Chapter XVII of the *Bhāratīya-Nāṭyaśāstra*. Its present text existed in the second century AD but it appears to be a compilation from previous works going back to a period as early as the first century BC. It considers Prākrit to be 'disfigured' in comparison with Sanskrit and lacking in the proper grammatical processes and qualities. In Chapter XVII (XVIII).47, seven *bhāṣās* 'major dialects' are enumerated (Māgadhī, Āvantī, Prācyā, Śaurasenī, Ardha-Māgadhī, Bāhlīkā and Dākṣiṇātyā), and the rules for their use on the stage are given.

Apart from these fragments which do not offer any grammatical analyses, the first treatise on Prākrit grammar is the *Prākṛta-prakāśa* attributed to Vararuci (another title is *Prākṛta-lakṣaṇa-sūtra*) whose dates remain unknown. The eight books of his treatise (of *c*. 430 sūtras) deal with Māhārāṣṭrī: I–III with phonology, IV with morphophonemics, V with nominal declension, VI with pronominal declension, and VII–VIII with conjugation. According to Scharfe (1977: 192), Vararuci's rules were probably abstracted from a collection of popular songs with regional dialectal differences such as the famous collection *Sattasaī* (ascribed to King Hāla of the second century AD).

Sometime in the seventh century AD the rhetorician Bhāmaha commented on the *Prākṛta-prakāśa* but the text in his possession included two additional books: one on the Paiśācī and another on the Māgadhī dialect. Sometime after Bhāmaha another book on the Śaurasenī dialect was added, and book V was split in two. Thus in Cowell's 1868 edition, book IX deals with particles, X with Paiśācī, XI with Māgadhī, and XII with Śaurasenī, for the total of twelve books.

Vararuci's Prākrit grammar presupposes knowledge of Pāṇini's Sanskrit grammar. Its descriptive technique consists of transfer rules that convert the Sanskrit 'underlying' forms into the 'surface' Māhārāṣṭrī forms. Vararuci gives often a number of variants for the same grammatical function. For instance, the genitive singular of the 1st Pers pronoun is specified as follows (with an English paraphrase):

(1) *me mama maha majjha asi*   [Vararuci VI. 50]
     '(The pronoun *asmad* [from Sūtra 40] has the substituents) *me, mama, maha, majjha* in the genitive singular.'

The post-Vararuci grammatical tradition is dichotomized into the Eastern and Western School of Prākrit grammarians (cf. Banerjee 1977b; Scharfe 1977: 192–4). Among the earliest grammarians, i.e. those who are relatively close to the Apabhramśa stage, the following may be mentioned: in the east, Kramadīśvara and Puruṣottama (twelfth century); Hemacandra (eleventh–twelfth centuries) and Trivikramadeva (thirteenth century) in the west. Their evidence is sometimes at variance with that of the preserved Apabhramśa literature, and one is faced with a serious problem of 'how far we should go in correcting the Prākrit literature to conform with the rules of the grammarians' (Scharfe 1977: 193).

The most influential among them was Jain Hemacandra Sūri (1089–1172), an author of *Siddha-hema-śabdānuśāsana* 'Hema(candra)'s grammar' (literally, that by means of which speech forms are explained). *Siddha-* reflects the name of his illustrious patron, the Cālukya king Jayasiṁha-Siddharāja of Gujarat. Hemacandra composed his opus in eight books (of four chapters each) consisting of *c.* 4500 sūtras. Its first seven books are devoted to the grammar of Sanskrit and the eighth book deals with the Prākrit dialects (Māhārāṣṭrī, Māgadhī, Paiśācī, Śaurasenī), which are derived from Sanskrit by means of transfer rules. Hemacandra taught Apabhramśa (contained in sūtras 329–446 of the fourth chapter of his last book) in the same manner as the above Prākrits by means of transfer rules. His dependance on Vararuci is obvious. As an example of his descriptive technique let us examine his derivation of the Apabhramśa forms of the genitive singular of the 1st Pers pronoun from Sanskrit *asmad*; compare (2) with (1):

(2) *mahu majjhu ṅasi-ṅasbhyām*   [Hc 8.4.379]
     Apabhramśe asmado ṅasinā ṅasā ca saha pratyekaṁ mahu majjhu ity ādeśau bhavataḥ
     'In Apabhramśa *mahu* and *majjhu* substitute for *asmad* together with *ṅasi* (Abl Sg) and *ṅas* (Gen Sg)'

One of the major problems for the grammarians was the coexistence of older Sanskritic and Prakritic forms with those of contemporary Apabhramśa. For instance, the Instr Sg of *a*-stems could be either -*eṁ* (< *en* < *ena*) or Sanskritic -*eṇaṁ*, e.g. *deveṁ* or *deveṇaṁ* 'by/with god'. This state of affairs was described without any comments regarding their distribution in the following fashion by Hemacandra:

(3) *eṭṭi (= et ṭā-[pratyaye])*   [Hc 8.4.333]
     Apabhramśe akārasya ṭāyām ekāro bhavati
     'In Apabhramśa the -*a* of a stem is replaced by -*e* before the ending *ṭā* (Instr Sg)'

A *dohā* 'couple' [in 333.1] containing the instrumental form *daieṁ* 'by the lover' (*daie* according to manuscripts A and B) is added as an illustration.

(4) *āṭṭo ṇānusvārau*   [Hc 8.4.342]
     (= a[-ant]āt ṭā-[pratyayasya] ṇaḥ anusvāraḥ [ca ādeśau])
     Apabhramśe akārātparasya ṭā-vacanasya ṇānusvārāvādeśau bhavataḥ
     'In Apabhramśa the ending *ṭā* (Instr Sg) is replaced by -*ṇa* or *anusvāra* after -*a*'

Daieṁ (cited in 333.1) and *pavasanteṇa* 'sojourning abroad' are added as an illustration.

2.2 Contemporary Indian and western scholarship

There are two comparative grammars of MIA. The earlier was published in the frame of the *Grundriss der indo-arischen Philologie und Altertumskunde* by R. Pischel at the beginning of the twentieth century (1900) and since 1965 it has been available in S. Jha's English translation. The later one was written and published in India in 1960 by Sukumar Sen. Pischel's monumental *Grammatik der Prakrit-Sprachen* has the character of a loose compilation of phonological and morphological data (with no section on syntax) which methodologically does not proceed beyond their collection and classification. In phonetics the orthographic and phonetic (not to mention phonological) facts are often confused; in morphology pandialectal MIA paradigms are presented and their individual forms are discussed atomistically in terms of sound changes from their OIA ancestors. In terms of coverage Pischel did not include Pāli and inscriptional Prākrits into his work; for Apabhraṁśa he relied solely on Hemacandra. A wealth of new texts, especially in Apabhraṁśa, were published in the meantime. Nevertheless, Pischel's opus remains valuable for its rich documentation and references to MIA texts available to him.

In 1934 J. Bloch's masterpiece *Indo-Aryan from the Vedas to Modern Times* appeared. (Its English version, enlarged and revised by A. Master, was published in 1965.) Bloch's introduction of the diachronic dimension into Indo-Aryan studies set up an example for the studies of individual NIA languages on historical principles in India. His monograph is organized into three sections (Sanskrit, Middle Indian and Neo-Indian). In the paragraphs dealing with Middle Indian the main attention is paid to the 'phonetic origin' of the endings and their 'alternation'. The short section dealing with the sentence (Part Three, pp. 303–19) is devoted to: (i) verb 'to be' and the nominal sentence, (ii) word order, and (iii) linking of sentences (subordination). Bloch viewed the MIA period only as a transitional stage between OIA and NIA and did not try to elaborate on MIA dialects systematically. Their data are presented atomistically in terms of the phonetic origin of individual forms (paradigmatic relations obtaining in MIA after various sound changes have taken place are rarely considered). Some of his non-descriptive statements à propos Apabhraṁśa being 'only a disfigured Sanskrit' (p. 29) undergoing 'phonetic deterioration' (p. 141) are inappropriate.

The comprehensive study of MIA by S. Sen, *A Comparative Grammar of Middle Indo-Aryan* (1960), presents a detailed classification of MIA dialects (Chapter III); devotes a rather short section to phonology (Chapter III, pp. 34–73), where the OIA sources of MIA vowels, consonants and consonant clusters are listed; Chapters IV–IX are devoted to morphology of noun, pronoun, verb, and nominal stem formation and composition. *Historical Syntax of Middle Indo-Aryan* by the same author appeared earlier in *Indian Linguistics* (1952/53). Sen's treatment of MIA morphology – as that of Bloch – emphasizes heavily the phonetic aspect. The individual dialects are presented without paradigms and their individual forms are analysed piecemeal in terms of sound changes from OIA proto-forms.

An earlier comprehensive study by G. V. Tagare, entitled *Historical Grammar of Apabhraṁśa* (1948), devotes one chapter to Apabhraṁśa phonology and three chapters to morphology (declension, conjugation and nominal-stem formation). Tagare applied what he calls a 'chrono-regional' method of study to the available Apabhraṁśa literature and presented his findings in a number of diachrono-diatopical tables which allow the reader to trace the history of a particular Apabhraṁśa feature through the entire period of AD 500–1200.

Other Indian scholars devoted their energy to the editing of Prākrit and Apabhraṁśa manuscripts; their editions usually contain very useful grammatical sketches and lexica. Suffice it to mention H. C. Bhayani's edition of Svayaṁbhūdeva's *Paumacariu* (1953–60) and P. L. Vaidya's *Grammar of Hemacandra* (1958). The editorial activity of H. L. Jain, M. Shahidullah, P. L. Vaidya and others (in India) and that of H. Jacobi and L. Alsdorf (in Europe) belongs to the period before the Second World War.

A number of articles dealing with MIA phonology, morphology, semantics and various literary problems were written during the previous decades by H. C. Bhayani, A. M. Ghatage, S. N. Ghosal (and others) in India, and K. D. Vreese, K. R. Norman, L. Schwarzschild (and others) in the west.

Syntactic matters of MIA were seriously neglected. Bender's bibliography of Middle Indo-Aryan studies (1969) lists 147 titles but only one devoted to syntax: Sukumar Sen's *Historical Syntax of Middle Indo-Aryan*, published in 1953. Sen's work is valuable for its extensive documentation (with emphasis on the early and middle periods) but the author does not use any particular syntactic theory in his explications. S. K. Sen's study of *Proto-New Indo-Aryan* (1973) focuses on the transition from late MIA to early NIA in the areas of phonology and morphology and makes a few scattered comments on historical syntax. R. A. Singh's *Syntax of Apabhraṁśa* (1980) contains a wealth of morphosyntactic data from the final stages of MIA, but in the vein of S. Sen's study (1953) does not offer any syntactic framework for their evaluation. In spite of its title, Singh's study deals predominantly with morphology (syntax is dealt with by providing textual examples for nominal and verbal categories under traditional classificatory labels). In none of the above studies is there any attempt to outline morphosyntactic trajectories into the early NIA period (eleventh/twelfth centuries) when the real break with the synthetic typology of earlier MIA begins.

More recently, A. Breunis (1990) devoted a monograph to the study of the nominal sentence containing the verbal adjective (the *ta*-form) in OIA and MIA (Pāli and Māhārāṣṭrī) but stopped short of examining the crucial formative period of NIA, that is of Apabhraṁśa. C. Masica (1991) in his *Indo-Aryan Languages* devoted Chapter 7 (historical phonology) to MIA Prakritic developments and their consequences for the NIA state of affairs. Syntactic matters of NIA are dealt with synchronically in Chapter 10, with occasional references to the earlier stages of MIA and OIA (e.g. in the sections dealing with word order and the ergative construction).

In India S. S. Misra and H. Misra published a historical grammar of Ardhamāgadhī (limited to phonology and morphology) in 1982. H. C. Bhayani published a monograph devoted to the study of Hemacandra's *Deśīnāma-mālā* (a lexicon of a certain class of Prākrit words), entitled *Studies in Deśya Prakrit* (1988). Another work by Bhayani, *Apabhraṁśa Language* (with the section on language limited to nine pages) appeared in 1989. Another short study of Apabhraṁśa (of 59 pages), based exclusively on the examples supplied by Hemacandra in his grammar, was published by M. Mishra in 1992 (unlike similar treatments his study contains a section on syntax).

More recently, V. Bubenik attempted to synthesize the previous research in a monograph (1996) dealing with phonology, morphology and syntax of Aśokan Prākrits, Pāli, Ardha-Māgadhī, Māhārāṣṭrī and Apabhraṁśa. Another monograph, *A Historical Syntax of Late Middle Indo-Aryan* (1998), exploring the issues of the restructuring of the nominal and pronominal systems, the evolution of the grammatical and lexical aspect, the emergence and development of the ergative construction and the scope of the causative, was designed to fill in the gap in MIA syntactic studies.

In the field of lexicography, a Prakrit-Hindi and an Apabhraṃśa-Hindi dictionary were published in 1987. K. R. Chandra re-edited an improved version of H. Sēṭh's dictionary, *Prākṛta-Hindī Koś* and N. Kumār brought out *Apabhraṃśa-Hindī Koś*. A large Prakrit–English dictionary remains a major desideratum of MIA studies. This gap will be filled in by the output of the Prakrit Dictionary Project at Bhandarkar Oriental Research Institute headed by A. M. Ghatage.

It goes without saying that the above survey is not meant to be exhaustive and an interested reader will have to consult various earlier bibliographies such as Bender's (1969), Banerjee's (1977a) and references to later monographs quoted above.

The whole field of MIA studies is clearly in need of a new comprehensive study cast in the framework of contemporary historical and comparative linguistics.

3 PHONOLOGY

3.1 Vowels

The OIA triangular system possessed vowels of three heights on both axes. The feature of length was phonemic on high and low vowels (and diphthongs); however, no contrast existed with mid vowels which were only long in both open and closed syllables. OIA diphthongs were monophongized in MIA: *ai* >, *ē*, *au* > *ō*. If the diphthong occurred in a closed syllable the resulting long mid vowel was shortened (section 3.1.2) and later on raised (section 3.1.3). For instance, OIA *vairamaṇī* 'abstinence' > Pāli *vēramaṇī*, but *vaidya* 'doctor' > Pāli, Mah *vejja*.

Early MIA completed this diagram by creating short mid vowels. These resulted from OIA long mid vowels *ē* and *ō*, either original ones or those monophthongized in overweight and pretonic/posttonic heavy syllables (section 3.1.2.) Short mid vowels could be phonemicized only if they appeared in open syllables, where they could arise in several ways:

(i)   If the double consonant in heavy syllables was degeminated without compensatory lengthening

(ii) If the syllable boundary was moved after the rule of metathesis had applied in clusters of *h* + nasals or liquids (cf. section 3.2.3). Thus when the structure of Ś, Mg *geṇ$hadi* 'takes' (< OIA *gṛhṇāti*) changed to *ge$ṇhadi*, we find a short mid vowel in an open syllable.

(iii) If the dyadic cluster was resolved by epenthesis. For instance, OIA *jyōtsnā* 'moonlight' underwent shortening of the vowel and simplification of the triadic cluster yielding *j(y)os$nā*. This form developed in two directions: AMg *do$siṇā* shows the epenthesis of *i* while preserving short *o* which now appears in an open syllable; Mah *jo$nhā* underwent the fricative weakening of *s*, metathesis of *hn* and resyllabification: *joh$nā* > *jon$nhā* > *jo$nhā* (cf. Pāli *juṇhā*).

(iv) Finally, a short vowel could arise in an open syllable if the shortening of an originally long mid vowel was not accompanied by the compensatory gemination of the following consonant. In middle and late MIA dialects the shortening process spread to heavy syllables, especially if the OIA accent was located on the preceding or the following syllable. The shortening in this environment might have been accompanied by compensatory gemination of the following consonant (section 3.1.2). If the gemination did not take place, the mid vowel would appear in an open syllable: OIA *ēvám* 'thus' > Mah *ev$vaṃ* ~ *e$vaṃ*.

In the late MIA vocalic space short *i* and long *ē* became closer to one another than to long *ī* and short *e,* respectively; and the same is true about the back axis. It will be argued (in section 3.1.3) that the MIA spellings with Ē (*ē-kāra*) and Ō (*ō-kāra*) for [i] and [u] may be interpreted as indicating that the value of short *i* and *u* was lax [ɪ] and [ʊ], i.e that Ap had already reached a NIA state of affairs with four degrees of aperture.

3.1.1 Compensatory lengthening of short vowels

Two types of OIA consonant clusters were assimilated and the resulting geminate (preserved in Pāli) was degeminated with a concommitant compensatory lengthening of the preceding short vowel:

(a) *r* followed by a consonant (esp. sibilant): OIA *kartum* 'to make' > Ś, Mag *kāduṁ;* Mah, AMg, JMah *kāuṁ.*
(b) *s* followed by glides, *r* and a sibilant: OIA *paśyati* 'sees' > (Pāli *passaï*) AMg, JMah *pāsaï.*

In grammatical morphology the degemination had significant consequences for the remodelling of nominal (section 4.1) and verbal paradigms (section 4.3.4) .

3.1.2 Shortening of long vowels

There are two environments for the shortening of OIA long vowels: overweight syllables and pre-/posttonic heavy syllables. The change in the syllabic pattern of MIA vis-à-vis that of OIA is explained by the 'Law of Mora' (Geiger, 1916/1943: 63–4); most importantly, one mora is lost in trimoraic syllables: OIA *gātra* 'limb' > MIA *gatta;* *grīṣma* 'sommer' > *gimha.*

In middle and late MIA dialects the shortening process spread from the overweight syllables to the heavy ones. In these dialects the long vowels are often shortened if the OIA accent was located on the preceding or the following syllable: OIA *kúlāla* 'owl' > AMg *kulala;* *sthāpáyati* 'stop' > Mah, AMg, JMah *ṭhavei.*

The shortening process of the long vowels may be accompanied by the compensatory lengthening of the following consonant if the word was accented on the ultima: OIA *ēvám* 'thus' > Mah, Ś, Mg *evvaṁ* (but also *evaṁ*).

3.1.3 Raising of short mid vowels

Short mid vowels arising through the shortening of OIA long vowels before consonant clusters (section 3.1.2) were raised during the middle period of MIA. Our evidence comes from the spellings with graphemes I (*i-kāra*) and U (*u-kāra*) for *e* and *o* found in AMg, Ś, Mah, JMah: AMg *miccha* 'barbarian' vs. Mg, JM, Ś, Ap *meccha* (OIA *mlēccha*); JMah *uṭṭha* 'lip' AMg *huṭṭha* vs. AMg, Mah, JM *oṭṭha* (< OIA *ōṣṭha*).

In our data from the middle period of MIA there are also examples which seem to indicate an opposite process of the lowering of high short vowels: OIA *itthā* 'thus' as against Mah, AMg, JMah, Mg *ettha,* Ap *etthu;* *āgamiṣyant* 'go' (Part Fut) AMg *āgamessa;* *puṣkara* 'lotus', Ś *pokkhara.* From the way these facts are presented in Pischel (1900: 96 ff.) and Tagare (1948: 59) one might conclude that we are dealing with a phonological process of the lowering of short high vowels in the environment before consonant clusters.

I argued (1996:32–3) that there was no lowering process of high short vowels of a phonological nature in MIA, and that we are only dealing with attempts at the phonetic spelling of high lax vowels [ɪ] and [ʊ] by graphemes Ē(ē-kāra) and Ō (ō-kāra). My main point was an assumption that the products of the raising rule were not identical with short OIA vowels (i and u) but that they were lax, that is, realized lower and more towards the centre than i and u. Hence the suitability of the graphemes Ē and Ō for the products of the raising rule.

It is tempting to hypothesize that here Apabhraṁśa inaugurates the development of the NIA phonological type based on four degrees of aperture instead of three as in the previous OIA type. It goes without saying that its exact phonetic reconstruction is beyond the powers of historical linguistics. Thus it is conceivable that phonetically the four degrees of aperture on the front axis could be [i, ɪ, e, æ] (as in Modern Panjabi or Hindi) or [i, e, ɛ, a] (as in Modern Gujarati).

3.2 Consonants

MIA dialects were remarkably stable in their system of plosives vis-à-vis that of OIA. The basic pattern of five articulatory positions combined with features of voice, aspiration and murmur remained unchanged during the MIA period, and it survived, with various additions or losses, until NIA times. Major changes, in terms of loss and acquisition of phonemes, took place in the subsystems of syllabic liquids, sibilants and nasals.

(i)   There are three vocalic reflexes of /r̥/: a, i, and u depending on the dialect and environment (in the west only a is found). In Pāli we find i before i, u before u and after labials, and a elsewhere; long /r̥̄/ becomes ī and ū in identical environments with some vacillation as in AMg piūnaṁ ~ piīnaṁ 'fathers' (Gen) < OIA pitr̥̄ṇām.
(ii) The three sibilants of OIA s (dental), ś (palatal) and ṣ (retroflex), merged into one dental s (in most MIA dialects) or into palatal ś (in eastern Prākrits). (Only in Niya and Aśokan northwestern inscriptional Prākrits are all three preserved.)
(iii) With the exception of Sanskrit as a metalanguage, palatal [ñ] was only an allophone of /n/ in the environment of palatal affricates. In several MIA dialects this allophone was phonemicized as a result of various phonological processes. In Pāli the OIA cluster jñ became ññ (by regressive assimilation) and the geminate ññ was simplified in the initial position: OIA jñāpayati > Pāli ñāpeti. In Cūlikāpaiśācī ñ appears intervocalically in grammatical forms such as rāciñā 'king' (Instr). This 'deviant' dialect devoiced all the voiced stops (section 1.1.3); hence the trajectory from OIA rājñā > rājiñā > rāciñā.
(iv) In OIA the feature of murmur was contrastive in the subsystem of stops; elsewhere, it appears only with retroflex ḷ in isolated lexical items (cf. RV voḷhṛ 'draught horse' ~ voḍhṛ). In MIA murmured nasals and the lateral liquid resulted through metathesis from OIA clusters hm, hn, hṇ and hl: brāhmaṇa 'brahman' > Ś, Mg bamhaṇa; madhyāhna 'midday' > Mah, AMg, JM, JŚ, Ś majjhaṇha.

3.2.1 MIA consonant clusters

A high number of dyadic and triadic consonant clusters was typical of OIA. Their number was drastically limited in MIA by epenthesis and various assimilations in place and manner of articulation. The resulting geminates could be simplified (with a concomitant lengthening of the preceding short vowel).

In Pāli in non-geminate clusters whose second member is a stop the first member is typically a nasal (as in Sanskrit); the only other possibility is the combination of the sibilant with the labial stop *sm*. According to the grammarians, in Māgadhī the sibilants could form clusters with the stops in all the five articulatory positions, and the glottal fricative could occur before the velar stop (*hk*). Evidence of stage Māgadhī is ambivalent; thus at variance with *sk(h)* of the grammarians we find *kkh* (also *kk*) in our manuscripts; instead of *st* we find *tth* or *śt*; instead of *sp(h)* we find *pph* or *sp* (data and other details in Pischel, 1900: 207–14). The most sensible explanation of this state of affairs would seem to assume an existence of two dialects of Māgadhī; the dialect which is described by the grammarians did not change OIA clusters of the sibilant + stop, whereas the other one, in agreement with the other MIA dialects, metathesized the sequence $s + C > C + s$ and weakened the sibilant $s > h$. The Māgadhī cluster *śc* continues OIA *śc*, e.g. *aścalia* 'marvellous' (< OIA *āścārya*), while the other dialects show here the effects of metathesis and fricative weakening (Mah, Ś *accharia*). According to Hemacandra [8.4.289] Māgadhī possessed also the clusters of the type sibilant + nasal (*sn* and *sm*): *Visnu* (OIA *Viṣṇu*), *usma* 'vapour' (OIA *ūṣman*). Stage Māgadhī displays only forms showing effects of fricative weakening: *panha* 'question' (OIA *praśna*), *gimha* 'summer' (OIA *grīṣma*).

The final position was heavily constrained in OIA. No dyadic clusters (with the exception of *r* + voiceless unaspirated stops) were allowed in this position; and among single consonants only oral and nasal stops (with the exception of *c* and *ñ*) and voiceless velar fricative (*visarga*) were allowed before the pause. In MIA absolutely no consonants were tolerated in final position; consequently, we find only open syllables before the pause. This constraint had, of course, far-reaching consequences for the fate of OIA consonant stems (section 4.1).

3.2.2 Geminate clusters

With the exception of *n, r, v, h* all consonants (especially in Pāli) may occur geminated (pertinent examples are in the chapter on Aśokan Prakrit and Pāli, 2.3.4). Several phonological processes are responsible for their appearance:

(i)   regressive and progressive assimilation in place and manner of articulation in OIA clusters containing stops, nasals, liquids and glides (with the exception of iii);
(ii) fricative weakening in OIA clusters containing the sibilant as a first or second member (section 3.2.3);
(iii) and dental palatalization in OIA clusters containing the dental or retroflex stop as a first member and palatal glide as a second member (cf. section 3.2.4). Also *ts* (the original one or that arising through metathesis or epenthesis, cf. section 3.2.3) undergoes dental palatalization.

Under (i) we may distinguish between assimilatory processes taking place in (a) homorganic and (b) heterorganic clusters (from the point of view of manner of articulation).

(a) Homorganic clusters underwent regressive assimilation (that is, they were reduced to the geminate form of the second member).
(b) Heterorganic clusters were reduced to the geminate form of the 'stronger' consonant from the point of view of its occlusion: (oral) stop–nasal (stop)–liquid–glide (in descending order). Consequently, the clusters of the type (oral or nasal)

stop + nasal, liquid or glide; liquid + glide; and also sibilant + liquid or glide underwent progressive assimilation. In the case of the cluster *tm* the expected reflex is *tt*, cf. Pāli *atta(n)* 'self' < OIA *ātman* 'soul'. Māhārāṣṭrī and Apabhraṁśa, however, show almost always *appa*, which can be explained by coalescence: (dental) stop + labial (nasal) = labial stop.

The development of the cluster *ry* was exceptional in that it shows regressive assimilation: *r* > *y*/ — *y*. Resulting *yy* remained in Pāli and Māgadhī but it was affricated in other dialects: *yy* > *jj*: OIA *ārya* 'lord' > Pāli and Mg *ayya* as against *ajja* in Mah (and other dialects).

3.2.3 Fricative weakening in MIA dialects

This process of the weakening of the sibilant into the glottal fricative (*s* > *h*) is responsible for some of the most drastic changes which remodelled the morphophonemic pattern of OIA. Its environment was primarily the postconsonantal position: OIA *bhikṣu* 'monk' > Pāli *bhikkhu*. However, even clusters of the type sibilant + stop underwent this process after the sequence sibilant + stop had been metathesized: OIA *śuṣka* 'dry' > Pāli *sukkha* (via *sukṣa*).

In the environment before nasals there is some evidence that during the earlier stages of MIA this development did not proceed further. Thus in Bhāsa's dramas we find forms such as *hṇāīadi* 'bathing takes place' (vs. Ś *ṇhāīadi* < OIA *snāpyate*). Later on metathesis followed the fricative weakening quite regularly: OIA *praśna* 'question' > *paṇha*.

The rule of fricative weakening did not operate intervocalically during the middle stage of MIA. Thus in Māhārāṣṭrī there are only several lexical items which show its effect: *dhaṇuha* 'bow' (< thematized *dhanus-*), *paccūha* 'morning sun' (< *pratyūṣa*), *pāhāṇa* 'stone' (< *pāṣāṇa*; cf. Hindi *pāhān*).

In grammatical morphology the earliest examples are found in the genitive singular of *a*-stems in the Māgadhī passages of *Mṛcchakaṭikā* (the pronominal form *tāha* and nominal forms in -*āha* go back to OIA -*asya*).

3.2.4 Dental palatalization in MIA dialects

Another far-reaching morphological process which remodelled the morphophonemic pattern of OIA was palatalization. This process was limited to dental stops before the palatal glide: OIA *nitya* 'permanent' > Pāli *nicca*, *mithyā* 'falsely' > *micchā*. (Retroflex oral stops did not undergo this process: OIA *nāṭya* 'dancing' > Ś *ṇaṭṭaa*, *kuḍya* 'wall' > Mah *kuḍḍa*). Also the cluster retroflex nasal + glide developed in the same fashion. In Pāli (and Mg according to Hemacandra) the result is the palatal geminate *ññ* versus retroflex geminate *ṇṇ* in other dialects.

There was no velar palatalization in MIA. The development of the cluster *kṣ* > *ch*, which looks superficially as velar palatalization, can actually be explained by assimilation in the place of articulation *k* > *c* / — *ṣ* (i.e. velar > palatal / — retroflex).

3.2.5 Affrication

During the middle stage of the MIA period the palatal glide in initial position changed into the palatal affricate (with the exception of Mg and P): OIA *yadi* 'if' > Ś, Ap *jai* but

Mg *ya(d)i*. Also the geminate *yy*, which arises medially through compensatory gemination, was affricated: OIA *dēyāt* 'give' (Opt) > Mg *dejjā*. Although early MIA displays *y*-, in OIA in *Śuklayajurveda* recitation tradition (as known from the *Pratijñāsūtra*) *j*- was pronounced initially and when doubling took place.

3.2.6 Lenition and spirantization

Lenition (voicing) affected all the articulatory positions of both plain and aspirated stops in intervocalic position. In the same environment spirantization operated on the output of lenition (but also the original voiced stops were affected) with the exception of the retroflex stop *ḍ*. The output of spirantization was not stable and the resulting voiced fricatives *γ*, *ð*, *y*, *v/β* were deleted in most dialects. Here are some examples from Mah: *uaa* 'water' (< *uðaya* < *udaga* < *udaka*), *gaa* 'elephant' (< *gaya* < *gaja*), *riu* 'enemy' (< *riβu* < *ribu* < *ripu*); also the original palatal and labiodental fricatives were deleted: *chāā* 'shade' (< *chāyā*), *jīa* 'alive' (< *jīva*). In AMg, JM and JŚ there appeared a phonetic glide in hiatus which arose as a consequence of the deletion of the voiced fricative (indicated by *ẏ* in the editions of manuscripts). According to Hemacandra [8.1.180] *y* arose in the environment of low vowels, but he also acknowledged its existence before/after *i*: *piẏai* [piyai] 'drinks' (*piβaði* < *pibadi* < *pibati*), *sariẏā* [sariyā] 'river' (< *sariðā* < *saridā*, cf. OIA *sarit*). The earliest manuscripts spell *ẏ* after all vowels before *a*: *hiẏaẏa* 'heart', *loẏa* 'world'. The deletion rule did not operate with equal force in all articulatory positions. The peripheral fricatives *γ* and *β/v* are reduced to zero in all stage Prākrits but the dental fricative underwent deletion only in Māhārāṣṭrī.

In Apabhraṁśa the situation with respect to deletion is similar to that found in Māhārāṣṭrī. Hemacandra [8.4.355, 373, 380, 427] lists some Apabhraṁśa lexical items which show voiced plain and murmured stops in intervocalic position; *nāyagu* 'leader' (< OIA *nāyakaḥ*), *āgado* 'come' (< OIA *āgataḥ*). Here we may assume that in some dialects the voiced fricatives were more stable, in that the spirantization was not followed by the deletion: [nāyaγʊ], [āγaðʊ].

In the case of murmured stops (the original ones or those arising through lenition of voiceless aspirated stops) spirantization did not affect the palatal and the retroflex stops.

The rule of lenition was blocked if the original accent was located on the following syllable. In this case the intervocalic voiceless stop is geminated: OIA *ukhá* 'boiler' > AMg *ukkhā*; *nakha* 'nail' > Mah *ṇakkha*.

3.2.7 Retroflexion

In OIA retroflexion affected only two consonants: the dental stop and the sibilant (*n* and *s*) in very restricted environments:

(i)   *s* was retroflexed after high vowels (*i* and *u*), *r* and *k* (by the so-called *ruki*-rule);
(ii) *n* was retroflexed after *r* and *ṣ* (which results from *s* through the *ruki*-rule).

In MIA the scope of retroflexion became much wider in that in addition to *n* all dental stops were affected (*n*, however, more regularly than the other dental stops). Furthermore, while in OIA retroflexion had a character of progressive assimilation, in MIA retroflexion acquired also a character of regressive assimilation.

In Pāli we find this state of affairs in its initial stage. Data from later MIA dialects demonstrate further spread of the retroflexion rule. In AMg *nijjūḍha* 'ousted' (< OIA *niryūtha*) *th* was retroflexed after the high vowel (and after *r*); *ḍh* in AMg *ḍhaṅka*, Mah *ḍhaṅkha* 'crow' (< OIA *dhvāṅkṣa*) may be explained as resulting from the anticipation of *k* or, perhaps, by 'spontaneous' retroflexion in initial position. *ḍh* in Mah *ḍhakkai* 'covers' (< OIA *sthagáyati* with the pretonic reduplication of the consonant, cf. section 3.1.2) can be explained similarly.

The dental nasal was most susceptible to retroflexion in most dialects. In Ś, Mah, Mg, Ap (less in AMg, JM, JŚ) *n* was retroflexed initially and medially even in the environment of *a*. In AMg *n* is retroflexed before the palatal glide (whereas in Pāli it is palatalized): OIA *rājñā* > *raynā* > *rayṇā* > *raṇṇā* 'king' (Instr) as against Pāli *raññā*.

In AMg and also in JM the effects of retroflexion are noticeable in the passive participle of some of the roots which ended in *ṛ* in OIA. Thus we find *kaḍa* 'made' (< OIA *kṛta*), *haḍa* 'taken' (< OIA *hṛta*), *maḍa* 'dead' (< OIA *mṛta*). Here we possess precious evidence that the process of retroflexion preceded that of the vocalization of syllabic *ṛ* (this process could run its course only after *ṛ* had retroflexed the following dental stop).

In many cases retroflexion cannot be explained in terms of retroflexing environment and we have to assume either spontaneous retroflexion or various analogical processes (or interplay of both). For instance, both *gada* and *gaḍa* 'gone' (< OIA *gata*) are found in *Mṛcchakaṭika*; the latter form could have arisen by analogy with *maḍa* 'dead' (where *t* > *ṭ* / *r* —).

3.3 Accent

In middle and late MIA dialects (Mah, AMg, JMah, JŚ, Ap) long vowels in open syllables are often shortened if found in posttonic or pretonic syllables (cf. section 3.1.2). The shortening process of the long vowels may be accompanied by the compensatory gemination of the following consonant if the word was accented on the ultima: OIA *yauvaná* 'youth' > *yōvaná* > *yovvaná* > *jóvvana* (Mah and other dialects). If compensatory gemination is really conditioned by the following accent we might be in the possession of a piece of evidence for the survival of the OIA accent into the MIA period (in addition to certain other phenomena such as the 'weakening' of posttonic short *a* to *i* in Pāli).

4 MORPHOLOGY

Morphology and morphosyntax underwent far-reaching changes which altered fundamentally the synthetic morphology of earlier Prākrits in the direction of the analytic typology of NIA.

4.1 Nouns

The nominal system of the late MIA underwent a considerable erosion of case contrasts and Apabhraṁśa ended up with only one form for earlier nominative and accusative, instrumental and locative, and genitive and ablative. Table 6.1 puts these matters into diachronic perspective of earlier Prākrits represented by Pāli and Ardha-Māgadhī.

In general terms, earlier Prākrits created a new type of the opposition of the direct (Nom, Acc) to the oblique cases (Instr, Gen, Abl, Loc) in both numbers: a monosyllabic ending in the direct case and a disyllabic ending in the oblique case (trisyllabic in the ablative in AMg). In Apabhraṁśa, in addition, a new opposition of the singular to the

TABLE 6.1: NOMINAL FORMS

	OIA	Pāli	Ardha-Māgadhī	Apabhraṃśa
Sg Nom	*putr -aḥ*	*putt -o*	*putt -o/e*	*putt -u*
Acc	-am	-aṁ	-aṁ	-u
Instr	-eṇa	-eṇa	-eṇa(ṁ)	-e(ṁ)
Dat	-āya	-assa/āya	-assa	-aho/ahu
Abl	-āt	-asmā/ato	-ā(o)	-ahe/ahu
Gen	-asya	-assa	-assa	-aho/ahu
Loc	-e	-e/asmi(ṁ)/amhi	-aṁsi/ammi	-e/i(ṁ)
Pl Nom	-āḥ	-ā	-ā	-a
Acc	-ān	-e	-ā/e	-a
Instr	-ebhiḥ (Ved)	-ehi	-ehiṁ	-ahiṁ/ehiṁ
Dat	-ebhyaḥ	-āṇaṁ	-āṇaṁ	-ahaṁ
Abl	-ebhyaḥ	-ehi	-ehiṁto	-ahuṁ/ahaṁ
Gen	-āṇām	-āṇaṁ	-āṇaṁ	-ahaṁ
Loc	-eṣu	-esu	-esuṁ	-ahiṁ

Note: In the instrumental plural Classical Sanskrit displays the suffix *-aiḥ* (< PIE *-ōis*) with nouns and pronouns; Vedic *-ebhiḥ* (< PII *-aibhis*) also persists in the pronominal declension.

plural in the oblique cases based on the presence of the nasalized vowel started emerging: plain as against nasalized ultima of the ending signalized the opposition between the singular as against the plural oblique case (here we are reaching the NIA state of affairs). At the end, the nasalization of the ultima became more or less consistent in the oblique plural cases in Apabhraṃśa.

i- and *u*-stems underwent thematization, that is they started being declined more and more as *a*-stems.

	Sg *i*-stems	Sg *u*-stems	Pl *i*-stems	Pl *u*-stems
Instr	*giri -eṁ/ṇa*	*guru -eṁ/ṇa*	*giri -hiṁ*	*guru -hiṁ*
Abl/Gen	-he	-he	-huṁ/haṁ	-huṁ/haṁ
Loc	-hi	-hiṁ	-hiṁ	-hiṁ
Voc			-ho	-ho

The following observations may be made:

(i) In the instrumental singular the *a*-stem suffix *-eṁ* (< *en* < *ena*) replaced the original *i-/u*-stem suffixes *-inā/-unā*.
(ii) The Abl/Gen Sg suffix *-he* was used also with *a*-stems.
(iii) In the plural subparadigm several suffixes were transferred from *a*-stems: Instr *-hiṁ*, Abl *-huṁ* and Gen *-haṁ*.

4.2 Pronouns

4.2.1 Personal pronouns

The development of the pronominal system may be studied by means of the juxtapositions of our three representative dialects in Tables 6.2–6.8 (based on Hemacandra's grammar, Ghatage 1941/1993, Pischel 1900/1965 and Tagare 1948/1987).

TABLE 6.2: PRONOMINAL FORMS OF THE 1ST SG

	AMg	Mah	Ap
Nom	*ahaṁ, haṁ*	*ahaṁ*	*hauṁ*
Acc	*mamaṁ, maṁ*	*mamaṁ*	*mai(ṁ)*
Instr	*mae, mai*	*mae*	*mai(ṁ)*
Dat	*majjha, maha*	*majjha, maha*	*mahu(ṁ), majjhu*
Abl	*mamāo, matto*	*mamāo* [JM]	
Gen	*mama*	*majjha, maha*	*mahu(ṁ), majjhu*
Loc	*mamaṁsi, mai*	*mai, mamammi*	*maiṁ*

TABLE 6.3: PRONOMINAL FORMS OF THE 2ND SG

	AMg	Māh	Ap
Nom	*tumaṁ, taṁ, tume*	*tumaṁ*	*tuhuṁ*
Acc	*tumaṁ*	*tumaṁ*	*paiṁ, taiṁ*
Instr	*tu(m)e, tumae, tae*	*tue*	*paiṁ, taiṁ*
Dat	*tujjha, tu(m)ha*	*tujjha, tuha*	*tau, tujjha, tudhra* [Hc]
Abl	*tumāo, tumatto*	*tumāo*	
Gen	*tava*	*tujjha, tuha*	*tau, tujjha, tudhra* [Hc]
Loc	*tumaṃsi, tumammi, tai*	*tumammi, tai*	*paiṁ, taiṁ*

The general Ap form *hauṁ* (found in texts from 500 to 1200 AD) can be traced back to OIA *ahakam* (cf. Aśokan *hakaṁ*). The initial *a-* is preserved in WSAp *ahaya*.

OIA Instr Sg *mayā* is continued in Pāli and AMg (*may-ā > mai*); AMg and Mah *mae* is according to Bloch either a combination of *mayā* and the clitic form *me* or an imitation of the nominal instrumental *-eṇa*.

The AMg ablative singular form *mamāo* displays the nominal suffix *-āo* with the Gen Sg *mama* as the base; *matto* is rather from *mat* (Abl) plus *-taḥ*.

The OIA dative form *mahyam* was metathesized (cf. Pāli *mayhaṁ*) and the palatal glide was affricated in AMg and Mah *majjha*.

The suffix of the AMg Loc Sg *mam-aṁsi* is adopted from the demonstrative pronoun *so-* (cf. section 4.2.2).

In the nominative and accusative AMg and Mah continue the disyllabic Vedic form *tuvam* with *-m-* by extension from the 1st Pers *mamaṁ* (Acc).

The initial *p-* in Ap *paiṁ* (Acc/Instr) continues the OIA cluster *tv-* seen also in Pāli *tvaṁ* (~ *tuvaṁ*) 'thou'; *taiṁ*, on the other hand, continues the *v*-less forms seen in Pāli doublets *taṁ* ~ *tvaṁ* (Acc) and *tayā* ~ *tvayā* (Instr).

Pāli Gen/Dat *tuyhaṁ* is a further development of OIA *tubhyam* (by metathesis); AMg and Mah further affricated the palatal glide (*y > j*) *tubhyam > tuhyam > tuyhaṁ > tujjha*. Pāli and AMg *tumhaṁ* is formed from the plural stem *tumh-* (similarly *amhaṁ*). The simplified form *tuha* in AMg and Mah is influenced by the 1st Pers *maha*.

While Pāli continues the OIA Loc *tvayi*, both AMg and Mah adopted here the endings of the 3rd Pers *-aṁsi* and *-ammi* (cf. section 4.2.2).

h in Ap *tuhū* 'thou' is by extension from the 1st Pers *aha-* 'I'.

The accusative plural form *amhe* corresponds to OIA *asmān* as *deve* (Acc Pl) to *devān* (and *te* to *tān*). Already in AMg there is a single direct form of *amhe* 'we' in the plural. In Ap this form takes the nominal neuter plural suffix *-aiṁ*; in the instrumental and locative there is a form *amha(h)iṁ* whose *-ahiṁ* might be by an extension from the

TABLE 6.4: PRONOMINAL FORMS OF THE 1ST PL

	AMg	Mah	Ap
Nom/Acc	amhe	amhe	amhe, amhaiṁ
Instr	amhehiṁ	amhehiṁ	amhehiṁ, amha(h)iṁ
Dat	amhaṁ	amh(āṇ)aṁ	amhaha(ṁ), amha
Abl	amhehiṁto		
Gen	amha	amh(āṇ)aṁ	amhaha(ṁ), amha
Loc	amhesuṁ	amhesu	amha(h)iṁ

TABLE 6.5: PRONOMINAL FORMS OF THE 2ND PL

	AMg	Mah	Ap
Nom/Acc	tumhe, tujjhe, tubbhe	tumhe	tumhe, tumhaiṁ
Instr	tumhehiṁ, tujjhehiṁ, tubbhe(hiṁ)	tumhehiṁ	tumhehiṁ tumhaiṁ
Dat	tumh(āṇ)aṁ, tubbhaṁ	tumh(āṇ)aṁ	tumhaha(ṁ), tumha
Abl	tumhehiṁto, tubbhehiṁto		
Gen	tumh(āṇ)aṁ, tubbhaṁ	tumh(āṇ)aṁ	tumhaha(ṁ), tumha
Loc	tumhesuṁ, tujjhesuṁ tubbhesuṁ	tumhesu	tumhāsu [Hc]

nominal or the pronominal locative -ahiṁ (< OIA-asmin). In the genitive both forms amhahaṁ (WAp) and amhaha (SAp) appeared at about the same time (c. AD 1000 according to Tagare, 1948: 210). It would seem that -ha (from the singular form ma-ha?) was added to the stem amha- and was nasalized in WAp.

OIA had two forms of the stem in the plural: yū- and yuṣm-. MIA adopted the initial t- from the singular: *tusme > *tumse (by metathesis) > tumhe (by fricative weakening). Whereas in Pāli, Mah and Ap all the cases are based on only one form, AMg uses three bases: tumh-, tujjh- and tubbh-.

In OIA the only difference between the orthotonic and clitic forms in the accusative in the first and second person is the presence of a nasal element mām/tvām against mā/ tvā. Other orthotonic forms were typically disyllabic (or trisyllabic in the case of the genitive and dative plural) versus monosyllabic clitic forms. In MIA the phonological difference between māṁ against mā was lost – thus in Pāli maṁ is both an orthotonic and a clitic form. Only OIA and Pāli show the formal distinction between the direct and oblique forms in the system of clitics (OIA me against mā). In AMg and Ap me functions as a general oblique case form (that is in all grammatical functions with the exception of the subject). In the plural the instrumental forms are identical with those of the genitive (in AMg in the 1st Pl only ṇe is documented as the instrumental, whereas both ṇo and ṇe appear in the genitive and the accusative). A remarkable innovation of AMg is the plural clitic form bhe (Gen/Acc/Instr).

At the end of the MIA period Apabhraṁśa appears to make four formal distinctions in the first and second person pronouns: nominative as against accusative/instrumental as against locative (in the singular), and nominative/accusative as against instrumental as against ablative/genitive as against locative (in the plural). In semantic terms, both subsystems differentiate between the agent/subject and patient; the notions of spatial removal and appurtenance are syncretized (Abl/Gen); and there was the general locative case. A salient feature of this Western Apabhraṁśa system was the existence of the morphological syncretism of the accusative and instrumental singular: *mai(ṁ)* and *paiṁ/ taiṁ*. In Bubenik (1998:89) I used the term double-oblique for this phenomenon. The same phenomenon is observable in some Iranian languages such as Pashto and Kurdish, and Pamir languages. The double-oblique system did not exist in OIA; as far as I can tell it made its first appearance in the Ardha-Māgadhī texts of the fourth to third centuries BC Diachronically speaking, its appearance in AMg was only an extension of the situation which had already existed in the plural subparadigm of pronominal clitics in OIA. The conservative Prākrit dialects, such as Pāli, preserved the OIA accusative forms *maṁ* and *taṁ* in the singular subparadigm but AMg started using the universal clitic forms *me* and *te* instead. Analogy with the plural subsystem could have been operative here.

4.2.2 Demonstrative pronouns

As in many other IE languages, the pronominal declension proved to be much more resistant to phonological and analogical changes than the nominal one throughout the history. Within the pronominal system this state of affairs is particularly observable in the third person, where the MIA dialects continue the OIA heteroclisis of the stem *sa-* versus *ta-*.

The great variety of forms found in the locative singular is explainable by the interplay of several phonological processes (metathesis, progressive and regressive assimilation, fricative weakening, nasalization and denasalization).

The AMg Abl Sg *tāo* (as against Pāli *tasmā* and Ap [Hc] *tahāṁ*) is identical with nominal *devāo*, which is explained as a contamination of the Abl Sg *devā* (< *devāt*) and adverbial *-o* (< *-taḥ*).

The Ap genitive displays both earlier forms with *-s-* (*tāsu*) and later forms showing the effects of fricative weakening (*taho/u*). The earliest pieces of evidence for the fricative weakening in the genitive singular appear in Mg passages in *Mṛcchakaṭikā* (*tāha* and nominal *-āha* as against Mah *tāsa*).

The accusative plural is identical with the Nom Pl *te* (as against OIA *tān*). This ending *-e* was extended to the nominal declension (*deve* = Nom and Acc Pl).

The oblique forms in Pāli are derivable from their OIA ancestral forms, whereas AMg developed a new pattern of marking for the plurality by the nasalization of the

TABLE 6.6: PRONOMINAL FORMS OF THE 3RD PERSON MASCULINE

	AMg	Mah	Ap
Sg Nom	*so, se*	*so*	*so, su*
Acc	*taṁ*	*taṁ*	*taṁ*
Instr	*teṇa*	*teṇa*	*teṇa, te(ṁ), ti(ṁ)*
Dat	*tassa*	*tassa*	*taho/tahu*
Abl	*tāo*		*tahāṁ* [Hc]
Gen	*tassa*	*tassa*	*taho/tahu*
Loc	*taṁsi, tammi*	*tammi*	*tahiṁ*
Pl Nom/Acc	*te, se*	*te*	*te*
Instr	*tehiṁ*	*tehiṁ*	*tehiṁ*
Dat	*tesiṁ*	*tāṇam*	*tāhaṁ*
Abl	*tehiṁto*	*tehiṁ*	
Gen	*tesiṁ*	*tāṇam*	*tāhaṁ*
Loc	*tesuṁ*	*tesu*	*tahiṁ* [Hc]

ultima of the ending (*tehiṁ*, *tesiṁ*, *tesuṁ*). In AMg this nasalization was only optional in the nominal declension but it became obligatory in Ap (*-ahiṁ*, *-ahaṁ*, *-ahuṁ*). The genitive plural form *tesiṁ* is a peculiar innovation of AMg (found also in JMah), the Abl Pl *tehiṁto* (as against Pāli *tehi*) is a contamination of the Instr Pl *tehiṁ* and the Abl suffix *-to* (< *-taḥ*).

The Instr *tāe* and Abl *tāo* in AMg are of nominal origin. The dative/genitive and locative singular show alternative forms with the root *ti-* which seems to be extended from the interrogative pronoun *ki* 'what' (*ka* 'who'). Earlier forms are seen in Pāli *tissā* (Gen) and *tissaṁ* (Loc). AMg forms show further development from *tissV* > *tīse* (by compensatory lengthening) > *tīe* (by fricative weakening and the loss of intervocalic *h*).

AMg again shows the typical nasalization of the ultima of the ending in the oblique cases as in their masculine counterparts. The genitive plural with the nasalized ultima is found in JMah and JŚ. In AMg both *tesi* ~ *tesiṁ* (and *tāsi* ~ *tāsiṁ*) occur.

Ap created a real direct case by extending the nominative singular form *sā* to the accusative. One of the most remarkable archaisms is the clitic form of the third person pronoun (Gen/Dat) *se* (< PII *sai*, cf. Avestan *he*). It is not found in Vedic (which,

TABLE 6.7: PRONOMINAL FORMS OF THE 3RD PERSON FEMININE

		AMg	Mah	Ap
Sg	Nom	*sā*	*sā*	*sā*
	Acc	*taṁ*	*taṁ*	*sā*
	Instr	*tāe, tīe*	*tīe*	*tāe, tīe*
	Dat	*tāe, tīe, tīse*	*tīe*	*tāhe/i*
	Abl	*tāo*	*tāe*	*tāha*
	Gen	*tāe, tīe, tīse*	*tīe*	*tāhe/i*
	Loc	*tīe, tīse*	*tīe*	*tahiṁ*
Pl	Nom/Acc	*tāo*	*tāo*	*tāu*
	Instr	*tāhiṁ*	*tāhiṁ*	*tāhiṁ*
	Dat	*tāsiṁ*	*tāṇaṁ*	*tāhaṁ*
	Abl	*tāhiṁto*	*tāhiṁ*	*tāhiṁ*
	Gen	*tāsiṁ*	*tāṇaṁ*	*tāhaṁ*
	Loc	*tāsuṁ*	*tāsu*	*tāhiṁ*

TABLE 6.8: DEMONSTRATIVE PRONOUN 'THIS' (MASCULINE)

		AMg	Ap
Sg	Nom	*ayaṁ, ime, iṇamo*	*āyau, āu*
	Acc	*imaṁ*	*āyau, āu*
	Instr	*ṇeṇa, imeṇa, imiṇā*	*(ā)eṁ, (ā)eṇa*
	Dat	*(im)assa*	*āyaho*
	Abl	*imāo*	
	Gen	*(im)assa*	*āyaho*
	Loc	*imaṁsi, assiṁ*	*āyahiṁ*
Pl	Nom/Acc	*ime*	*āyaiṁ* (Neuter)
	Instr	*imehiṁ*	
	Dat	*(im)esiṁ*	*āyahaṁ*
	Abl	*imehiṁto*	
	Gen	*(im)esiṁ*	*āyahaṁ*
	Loc	*imesuṁ*	

however possesses clitic forms *sīm* and *īm* in the accusative); neither is *se* found in Pāli and Classical Sanskrit (but it occurs in Buddhist Sanskrit). In MIA the following dialects possess *se*: Mah, AMg, JM, Ś, and Mg (*śe*). In AMg (and Buddhist Skt) even the form *si* (with raised *e*) has been recorded (cf. Pischel 1900: 299). This form is used without distinction of gender. Thus Ś (in *Mṛcch*) *dehi se āsanam* may be translated – depending on the context – as either 'give him a seat!' or 'give her a seat!' Ultimately, *se* replaced the OIA neuter form *tad* and in AMg spread even to the nominative plural.

The OIA ancestral paradigm was built on three bases: *a(y)-* ~ *i(m)-* ~ *a(n)-* (the first two continue the PIE pronominal root **ei-* ~ **i-*). At a certain point in time the accusative form *imam* was resegmented and the new stem *ima-* adopted in all cases. Pāli and AMg Nom Sg *ayaṁ* is the only exception. AMg, apart from a few surviving forms, inflects the stem *ima-* identically with *ta-* 'that, he'. The instrumental form *iminā* got its *-i-* by an extension from the interrogative pronoun *ka-* 'who' (Gen *kissa*).

During the last stage, however, the whole paradigm could be built around the base *a(y)-*, which previously had appeared only in the nominative singular masculine. The Ap form of the Nom Sg *āyau* goes back to **aya-ka*, and the Instr Sg *eṁ* (in *Vikr*) arose by contraction *ā-eṁ*; elsewhere, the usual nominal and pronominal suffixes are found.

4.3 Verbs

Already in OIA the aspectual character of the basic system (Imperfect-Aorist-Perfect) was essentially eliminated (with the exception of the contrast of perfectivity in injunctives), yielding a temporal system. From the rich system of OIA modal forms (injunctive, subjunctive, optative) only the optative survived into MIA. Also the middle voice (*ātmanepada*) was eliminated and the passive established itself. Glancing at Pāli we observe first of all an almost complete loss of the perfect forms and the merging of the OIA aorist and imperfect into a single past tense (preterite). A further simplification took place in AMg. The forms of the past started being used without the augment and consequently some forms of the conditional became homophonous with those of the future; ultimately, the conditional was eliminated. The past possessed only two forms: the singular *-itthā* and the plural *-iṁsu*. In Māhārāṣṭrī this system was further simplified by a complete loss of the synthetic morphology of the past and its place was taken by analytic expressions with the agent expressed by the instrumental and the verb by the past participle, e.g. *mae kaaṁ* lit. by me done 'I did' (cf. section 5.4.) Finally, in Apabhraṁśa the optative was lost (one of the reasons being the homophony of certain of its forms with the passive, cf. sections 4.3.5. and 4.3.6.). Table 6.9. visualizes the gradual reduction of aspectual and modal morphology during the long MIA period.

MIA dialects were, of course, not only 'losers' and the categories which were formerly expressed by synthetic morphology started being expressed analytically by participial constructions; cf. section 5.3. for perfect and progressive aspect.

4.3.1 Thematic and athematic conjugations

Early MIA reduced considerably the ten conjugations of OIA (for details cf. Aśokan Prākrit and Pāli 3.5–3.5.2 in this volume). Athematic conjugations lost their ablaut and were thematized (with some relics such as 'to be' surviving until Ap). In the case of thematic conjugations, we cannot be sure how long the OIA contrast between the first and sixth conjugation (based on the accent on the root as against the thematic vowel) remained viable in Pāli and AMg (e.g. OIA *píbati* 'drinks' as against *diśáti* 'shows' >

TABLE 6.9: GRADUAL REDUCTION OF ASPECTUAL AND MODAL MORPHOLOGY DURING THE MIA PERIOD

	Present	Past	Future
Pāli			
Indicative	*karomi*	*akāsi*	*karissāmi*
Optative	*kare(yyaṁ)*	*akarissaṁ* (Cond)	
Ardha-Māgadhī			
Indicative	*kuvvāmi*	*kuvvithā* (Pl *kariṁsu*)	*karissāmi* ~ *kāhimi*
Optative	*kujjā~karejjā*		
Māhārāṣṭrī			
Indicative	*karemi*	*(mae kaaṁ)*	*karissaṁ*
Optative	*karejja*		
Apabhraṁśa			
Indicative	*karauṁ*	*(maiṁ kiyau)*	*karissami* ~ *karihimi*

AMg *pivai* and *disai*). The fourth conjugation lost its identity as a result of the palatalization of the stem-forming element *-ya* to the root: OIA *krudh-ya-ti* 'is angry' > AMg *kujjh-ai*; *nr̥t-ya-ti* 'dances' > *nacc-ai*.

In athematic conjugations, the seventh conjugation gave up its ablaut (of the type *chi-ná-t-ti* 'cuts off' vs. *chi-n-d-ánti*) and thematized the zero-grade; hence Pāli *chind-ati*. Its passive counterpart was formed from the *n*-less form *chid-ya-ti*, resulting in *chijj-ai* 'is cut off'. Similar strategy was used in AMg *muñc-ai* 'liberates' versus *mucc-ai* 'is liberated'.

Another remarkable innovation of AMg and Mah was a new type of the thematic conjugation in *-e* which continues the OIA causative: *kar-ei* 'does' (< *kār-aya-ti*). Here all the MIA dialects got rid of the OIA allomorphy caused by ablaut: *kar-ó-mi* vs. *kur-máḥ*. Pāli rebuilt its paradigm on the basis of the singular form, *kar-o-mi* and *kar-o-ma*; AMg on the basis of the plural form *kuvv-* (< *kur-u*), *kuvv-ā-mi* and *kuvv-ā-mo*; and Mah uses the stem in *-e*, *kar-e-mi* and *kar-e-mo*.

The verb 'to be' remained athematic in all MIA dialects, but its paradigm was levelled in favour of the full grade *as-* in Pāli (*as-mi* and *as-mā*) or the zero-grade *s-* in inscriptional and stage Māgadhī (*s-mi* and *s-ma*) and AMg (*mi* and *mo*). The cluster *-sm-* could be metathesized giving **amsi* as shown by AMg *aṁsi*, Pāli *amhi* and Ap *mhi* 'I am'. The AMg optative *siyā* is built on the zero-grade *s-* (continuing OIA *s-yā-t*) while Pāli also developed forms built on the full grade: *assa* (< **as-yā-t*).

4.3.2 Personal endings

Personal endings of thematic verbs in early and middle MIA after all the phonological changes described above took place are still very much the same as in OIA:

	Sg 1	2	3	Pl 1	2	3
Pāli	*-āmi*	*-asi*	*-ati*	*-āma*	*-atha*	*-anti*
Ś	*-āmi*	*-asi*	*-adi*	*-āmo*	*-adha*	*-aṁti*
Amg	*-āmi*	*-asi*	*-ai*	*-āmo*	*-aha*	*-anti*
Mah	*-āmi*	*-asi*	*-ai*	*-āmo*	*-aha*	*-aṁti*
Ap	*-auṁ*	*-ahi,-asi*	*-ai*	*-ahuṁ*	*-ahu*	*-ahiṁ*

The early stage of MIA (Pāli) differs from OIA in adopting the secondary ending *-ma* in the first plural (all other MIA dialects show the appropriate reflex *-o* of OIA *-aḥ*). The middle stage shows the effects of typical MIA phonological developments: the voicing of intervocalic voiceless stops *t(h)* > *d(h)* – represented by Śaurasenī – and their subsequent reduction to zero *d(h)* > *ð(h)* > *Ø(h)* – represented by Ardha-Māgadhī and Māhārāṣṭrī. This still essentially OIA system receives a new look during the final stage of MIA.

In Apabhraṁśa the first singular *-auṁ* can be derived (with Pischel) from the secondary ending *-am* preceded by the stem enlarging suffix *-k* (*-ak-am*). According to Sen (1960: 150), the ending may have come from the pronominal form *mama* (Gen), and according to Tagare (1948: 287) its source is the pronoun *hauṁ* 'I'.

In the second singular *-asi* may be considered a Prākritism (with Tagare, 1948: 288), while *-ahi* represents a genuine development of Apabhraṁśa. Bloch (1934/1965: 244) explains *-ahi* from the imperative suffix *-dhi*. I would prefer to trace it back to *-asi* by the historical process of fricative weakening (cf. section 3.2.3.).

There are various difficulties connected with explaining the origin of the plural suffixes in Apabhraṁśa. *u* in *-ahu* in the second person, as suggested by Bloch (1934/1965:244), comes probably from the suffixes of the third person imperative *-a(h)u* (< *-atu*) and *-antu*. *-h-* in *-ahuṁ* in the first person may have been extended from the second person; in addition, as suggested by Bloch, *-h-* found in various forms such as the pronoun 'we' (Ap *amhaiṁ*) and the copula 'we are' (Mah *mho*; not found in Ap) could have reinforced this extension. The third person suffix *-ahiṁ* cannot be derived phonologically from *-anti* and the proportional analogy with the first person (following Bloch 1934/1965: 245) might be the most likely explanation.

It should be mentioned that Prākrits did away with the phenomenon (found in Sanskrit and most IE languages) of having no overt indication of person in the second singular imperative. In Mah the endings of the imperative *-hi* and *-su* spread even to the optative (cf. Jacobi 1886/1967: LXIII).

4.3.3 Preterite

MIA dialects lost the distinction of the OIA aorist and imperfect by syncretizing them into a single past tense, usually called preterite. Pāli possesses four classes of the preterite, continuing the OIA root aorist, thematic aorist and imperfect, *s*-aorist and *iṣ*-aorist. In AMg there are relics of the *s*-aorist (*akāsī* 'made' < OIA *akār-ṣ-īt*, cf. Pāli *akāsi*) but the only productive formation is that continuing the OIA *iṣ*-aorist; its two suffixes are *-itthā* (Sg) and *-iṁsu* (Pl). Both suffixes are also found in Pāli in addition to the more original form *-is-uṁ* (by metathesis). The AMg singular suffix *-itthā* corresponds to the Pāli mediopassive singular suffix *-ittha* (*dīy-ittha* 'was given'); the latter is derivable from OIA *-iṣ-ṭa* in spite of the objections by Misra and Misra (1982: 109) that the phonologically regular outcome would have to be *-iṭ-ṭha*; Mayrhofer (1951: 157–8) suggested prophylactic influence of other aorist types (e.g. *agama-ttha* 'you went').

4.3.4 Future

In MIA the future is formed by adding the suffix *-iss* (< OIA *-iṣy*) to the root. In Apabhraṁśa we encounter its degeminated form *-is* whose *s* could undergo weakening *s* > *h* yielding future forms marked by *h*:

	s-future	*h*-future
Pāli	*karissāmi/aṁ*	
Amg	*karissāmi/aṁ*	*kāhimi*
Mah	*karissam*	*gacchihāmi/imi* [Hc]
Ap	*kare/isami*	*karīhimi*

AMg *kāhimi* derives presumably from **kar-(i)ṣy-imi* (via *kar-ṣ-imi > kā-s-imi*); Ap *karīhimi* is an innovative *h*-future with the suffix *-h* added to the root *kar-*.

The derivational base of the future (and also the aorist in early MIA) became increasingly identical with that of the present, e.g. Pāli and AMg *gacchissāmi* 'I will go' (vs. OIA *gamiṣyāmi*). The OIA forms with consonant plus *-s* undergo fricative weakening and palatalization, e.g. AMg *checchai* 'will split'(< OIA *chet-sy-ati*); *dacchai* 'will see' (< OIA *drak-ṣy-ati*). In Apabhraṁśa the *s*-future predominates in SAp (cf. Mn Marathi); in WAp both types are found (cf. the *s*-future in Gujarati and Lahnda, and the *h*-future in Marwari, Braj, Awadhi and Bundeli).

4.3.5 Optative

The MIA suffix of the optative, Pāli *-ĕyy*, AMg and Mah *-ĕjj*, continues the OIA suffix – *ēy* (found in the first singular and third plural). Its long ē was shortened in pre/posttonic position (cf. section 3.1.2.) and the glide geminated (in Pāli) and subsequently affricated (in AMg and Mah): OIA *páśy-ēy-am* 'may I see' > Pāli *pass-ĕyy-aṁ* > AMg *pās-ĕjj-ā(mi)*. Pāli also possessed another form, *pass-e*, which continues the OIA suffix *-ē* (found in all other persons, *paśy-ē-*); this form could be used in any person in the singular (as AMg *pās-ĕjj-ā*). In AMg there are also relics of the OIA optative formed by the suffix *-ya*: OIA *de-yá̆-t* 'may he give' > AMg *dĕ-jj-ā*; *kur-yā-t* 'may he do' > *ku-jj-ā* (beside innovative *kar-ejj-ā*).

4.3.6 Passive

The OIA passive suffix *-ya* appears unchanged if added to vocalic roots in Pāli: OIA *śru-ya-te* 'is heard' > *sū-ya-ti*; *dī-ya-te* 'is given' > *dī-ya-ti*. It may be assumed (with Mayrhofer 1951: 160) that one of the very common forms, such as *dī-ya-ti,* was resegmented into *d-īy-ati*, its *ī* shortened and *y* geminated, yielding *d-iyy-ati*; and *-iyy* became the source of the MIA passive suffix *-ijj* (through affrication). Hence AMg *suṇ-ijj-ai* 'is heard' (replacing inherited *suvvai*, cf. Pāli *suyyati ~ sūyati*), Ap *kar-ijj-ai* 'is made' (earlier Pāli *kar-īy-ati* vs. OIA *kri-ya-te*). The inherited passive forms of athematic verbs show the effects of palatalization and assimilation (*chid-ya-* 'cut' > *chijja-*, *han-ya-* 'kill' > *hañña-*). In the case of the verbs with nasal infix its presence could maximize the contrast between the active and the passive: AMg *muñcai* 'liberates' vs. *muccai* 'is liberated'; Pāli *chindati* 'cuts' versus *chijjati* 'is cut'. In the absence of the middle voice the passive is conjugated actively. The similarity of the passive and the optative suffixes (*-ijj* and *-ejj* respectively) contributed to the loss of the synthetic morphology of these two categories in Ap. Already in Mah certain persons (first and second plural) were almost identical; both *pucchejjaha* 'may ye ask' and *pucchijjaha* 'ye are asked' may have sounded approximately [pʊtːʃhɪdːʒaha], cf. section 3.1.3.

4.3.7 Causative

The OIA causative in *-aya* is continued in Pāli and other MIA dialects. The roots in long *-ā* form their causative, as in OIA, with the suffix *-paya* > *-pē*, e.g. *dāpēti* 'make X give Y', *ñāpēti* 'make X know Y'. The latter strategy became a source of numerous formations in MIA in that the inherited causatives, such as *dā-pē-ti*, were resegmented into *d-āpē-ti*, and the formative *-āpē* started being used even with roots ending in a consonant: *pac-āpē-ti* 'make X bake Y'. The suffix *-āpē* could be added to lengthened roots, yielding a double causative: *kār-ē-ti* 'cause X make Y' vs. *kār-āpē-ti* 'cause X make Y make Z'.

With further phonological changes (*p* > *v* through voicing and spirantization) these formations were continued during later MIA stages: AMg *ṭhāvei* 'make X stand' (cf. Pāli *ṭhāpēti* < OIA *sthā-paya-ti*); JMah *jāṇāvēi* 'make X know Y' (vs. Pāli *ñāpēti*). Double causatives (with the lengthened root plus the suffix *-āvē*) are also very common; contrast the passive causative participle *jīv-āv-idā* 'resuscitated' (Ś in *Mṛcch*) with OIA *jīv-i-tā*, and the finite passive causative *jīv-āv-ī-adi* '(she) is resuscitated' with OIA *jīv-ya-te* (in *jīv-āv-ī-adi* *-āv* marks the causative and *-ī* the passive).

In Apabhraṁśa the markers of the causative are *-a* (and *-āva*) instead of general MIA *-ē* (and *-āve*); contrast Ap *mārai* 'make X die' with Mah *mārei*; Ap *karāvai* 'make X make Y' with JMah *karāvei*.

4.3.8 Participles

The rich participial system of OIA continued to be reduced during the MIA period. At its beginning (Pāli) the system was dichotomized into the active and the passive with three forms in each set: present (imperfective), past (perfective) and future. The past participle with intransitive verbs possesses active meaning (*gata* 'gone') and passive meaning with transitive verbs (*kṛta* 'done'). A major innovation of Classical Sanskrit and Pāli was the past active participle formed by the possessive suffix *-vant* attached to the inherited past participle in *-ta*: *uṣ-ita-vant* (Sanskrit) *vus-ita-vant* (Pāli) 'who has lived', *bhut-ta-vant* 'who has enjoyed'. (This formation replaced aorist and perfect participles, *kr-ant* and *ca-kṛ-vāṁs*, lost at the end of the Vedic period). Another major innovation observable in AMg was the reshaping of the present (imperfective) participle by replacing the OIA mediopassive suffix *-māna* with the active suffix *-anta*: OIA *kr-iya-māna* > AMg *kar-ijja-māna* but also *kar-ijj-anta*. Ap further simplified the participial system by dropping the future active participle *kar-iss-anta* (documented in Mah). On the other hand, the gerundive survived through the whole MIA period: OIA *-tavya* > AMg *-yavva* > Ap *-(v)va*; *-anīya* > Ap *-aṇijja*.

4.3.9 Infinitive

Prākrits continued the two main infinitival suffixes of OIA: *-tum* (Pāli) and *-tave/ai* (AMg). In AMg the infinitive in *-tuṁ* is relatively rare: *dāuṁ* 'to give', *bhāsiuṁ* 'to speak'. The regular suffix is *-ittae* is traceable back to *-etavaí* (seen in double-accented Vedic forms such as *étavaí* 'to go' or *dátavaí* 'to give') whose geminate *-tt-* is according to section 3.1.2. This suffix is attached above all to the present stem: *hottae* ~ *bhavittae* 'to be', *sumarittae* 'to remember', *gacchittae* 'to go'.

A remarkable innovation of Prākrits is the passive infinitive formed by attaching the suffix *-iuṁ* (< OIA *-itum*) to the passive stem in *-ijj* (cf. the situation in early MIA where the present stem served as the derivational base of the aorist and the future as mentioned in section 4.3.4). Contrast the AMg innovative infinitive *marijjiuṁ* 'to die' with the inherited form *mariuṁ* (< OIA *martum*); or the JMah passive infinitive *dijjiuṁ* 'to be given' with the active infinitive *dāuṁ* 'to give'. A remarkable form is Mah *dīsiuṁ* 'to be seen' (in *Rāvaṇavaha* 4.51; 8.30) which does not show the passive marker *-ijj* (it appears to be built on the OIA finite passive *dṛśyate* 'is seen').

In Ap a great variety of infinitival suffixes is found. From the point of view of subsequent developments the WAp set *-aṇa/u* and *-aṇahaṁ/iṁ* is most important. *-aṇa* is the primary derivational suffix of deverbative action nouns (e.g. *darś-ana* 'sight'); *-aṇahaṁ* is formally the genitive plural and *-aṇahiṁ* the locative singular (or instrumental plural) of this action noun. Another characteristic of WAp (unknown in EAp) is the use of the absolutive for the infinitive. In SAp the commonest suffix of the infinitive was *-huṁ* (> Old Marathi *-ūṁ*).

4.3.10 Absolutive

The OIA suffix *-tvā* > MIA *-ttā* (*-tā* after nasals) remained the most productive suffix in AMg: *caittā* 'having abandoned' (versus OIA *tyaktvā*); *gantā* 'having gone' but also *gacchittā*. Another AMg suffix is *-ttāṇaṁ* (< *-tvānam*): *bhavittāṇa* 'having been', *caittāṇa* 'having abandoned'.

The commonest suffixes in Mah, JM, JŚ, Pai (and also in AMg) are *-tūṇaṁ* and *-ūṇaṁ* (*tūṇa* in Pai, *-dūṇa* in JŚ): *āgantūṇa* 'having come' (but also *gamidūṇa* and *gacchidūṇa*), *pekkhiūṇa* 'having seen'. There are also forms in *-ccā(ṇa)* which arose through the contamination of *-tvā* and *-ya*: AMg *hoccā* 'having been', *peccā* 'having drunk'.

Vedic absolutive suffixes *-tvī* and *-tvīnam* are regarded as the source of the Ap suffixes *-ep(p)i*, *-ep(p)iṇu*, *-evi*, *-eviṇu*. They are usually attached to the present stem: *kareppi(ṇu)* ~ *karevi* 'having made'; *gampi* 'having gone' (< *gan-tvī*, cf. Vedic *ga-tvī*) but also *gameppi(ṇu)* [Hc 8.4.442].

5 SYNTAX

5.1 Word order

The canonical word order in Classical Sanskrit prose was SOV. It is generally known that during the previous periods (Brāhmaṇa and Vedic Sanskrit) and in MIA dialects word order was not as rigid as in Classical Sanskrit. VS (verb-initial) and VO (postverbal object) characteristics of Brāhmaṇa Sanskrit were studied by Canedo (1937: 28–36) and Gonda (1959: 7–69). Their findings may be summarized in the following five points:

(i) The sentence initial position of the verb is common in narrative passages.
(ii) The verb tends to be placed immediately after the sentence initial adverbial expression.
(iii) The verb occurs initially in imperative sentences.
(iv) In the expressions of volition the dative of purpose and the infinitive (expressing the realization of the wish) appear often postverbally.
(v) In Brāhmaṇa-Sanskrit, as in Vedic Sanskrit, Wackernagel's Law may place the verb in second sentential position (e.g. the verb may be cliticized to the sentence-initial adverbial particle).

MIA narrative passages usually display the verb in final position (SV and SOV); the initial position (VS and VSO) may be exploited for pragmatic and stylistic purposes.

However, there are passages/stories where VS(O) order predominates. For instance the story of Double-face [No.V] and the story of beggar-thief Maṇḍio [No. IX] in JM (Jacobi 1886) differ strikingly in this respect. Statistically, the 71 sentences in either story break down as follows:

	S(O)V	SVO	VS(O)
Story V	35	11	44
Story IX	61	1	9

The only SVO sentence in the narrative of Maṇḍio was (1):

(1) *so   vi   ṇa   sakkati coraṁ   geṇhiuṁ*   [Erz IX 65.24]
      he   also   not   can   thief-acc. catch-inf.
      'He also is unable to catch the thief'

This sentence displays the infinitival object in sentence final position (cf. iv) and one justifiably wonders why not *so vi ṇa coraṁ geṇhiuṁ sakkai* (with the finite verb at the end of the sentence). In stage Prākrits infinitival objects appear in both postverbal and preverbal position (the overall ratio for *Mudrārākṣa, Mṛcchakaṭikā* and *Vikramorvaśīya* is roughly 1:1):

(2) *icchadi   sappaṁ   daṁseduṁ*   [Mudr 2.10.17]
      want-3sg.pres. snake-acc. see-caus.-inf.
      'He wishes to exhibit snakes.'

Apropos (iii), it seems to be the case that in MIA prose we find instances of genuine linear indeterminancy (cf. Patañjali's comment that the command 'fetch the bowl' may be expressed either way in Sanskrit: *āhara pātram ~ pātram āhara*). For instance, Cārudatta (in *Mṛcch*) commands his servants in Sanskrit using either sequence (VO or OV):

(3) *Radanike Maitreyam anugaccha*   [Mṛcch 1.38.4]
      'Radanikā, follow Maitreya!'

(4) *Maitreya anugaccha tatrabhavatīm*   [Mṛcch 1.56.33]
      'Maitreya, follow her ladyship!'

I studied these matters statistically (Bubenik 1996: 138–50) on the basis of Prākrit passages in several Sanskrit dramas. It appeared that nominal and pronominal objects may occur in both preverbal and postverbal positions, but in contradistinction to Classical Sanskrit the postverbal position was the preferred one in imperative sentences. More specifically, in Prākrit declarative sentences with nominal objects the sequence OV predominated more than 10:1 over the VO. But the situation was clearly different in imperative sentences where the postverbal position of both nominal and pronominal objects was preferred. This is shown in (5):

(5) Imperative sentences:

	Nominal objects		Pronominal objects	
	VO	OV	VO	OV
Mṛcchakaṭikā	68	56	17	6
Mudrārākṣasa	10	6	7	2
Vikramorvaśīya	14	10	8	3
Vetālapañcaviṁśatikā	4	29	4	20

The OV word order of Classical Sanskrit, exemplified by *Vetālapañcaviṁśatikā*, displays ratios which are diametrically opposite.

5.2 Phrasal case

Given the drastic reduction from the seven fusional cases of OIA to four by the end of the MIA period (cf. section 4.1) the postpositions grew steadily in importance in denoting relational aspects of their head nouns.

5.2.1 Source

As a consequence of phonological changes the synthetic morphology of the ablative became insufficient. This happened already in Early MIA, where the old ablative *devāt* lost the final -*t* and and became homophonous with the nominative plural. Pāli helped the situation by adopting the pronominal ablative suffix -*asmā* (< OIA *tasmāt*) ~ *amhā*, or the adverbial suffix -*to* (< *tas*). The latter suffix is continued in Middle Prākrits in the form -*āo* (cf. section 4.2.1). In Māhārāṣṭrī, in addition to the ablative suffixes -*ā* (< *āt*) and -*āo* (<*āt* + *tas*), there was a peculiar suffix -*ahi*, which is well documented in Hāla's *Sattasaī* ; for -*āhi* in Pāli cf. Oberlies (1996).

In Late MIA there arose a need to differentiate between the function of source (ablative) and appurtenance (genitive) by analytic means. Apabhramśa used two postpositions, *honta(u)* and *ṭhiu*, for this purpose. Both are participial forms: *honta(u)* is the present participle of the verb *ho* 'be' (< OIA *bhū*) and *ṭhiu* is the past participle of the verb *ṭhā* 'remain, stay' (< OIA *sthā*).

(6) hiaya-ṭṭhiu   jai   nīsarahi   [Hc 8.4.439]
    heart-remain-PP if   out-go-2sg.pres.
    'If you get out of [my] heart'

(Its Sanskrit rendition would be *hṛday-ād yadi niḥsarasi* with *hṛday-ād* in the ablative.)

5.2.2 Appurtenance

Earlier Prākrits continued the synthetic genitive case; at the end of the MIA period Apabhramśa ended up with two genitival postpositions, *kera* and *tana*, which display full adjectival agreement with the possessed object. At that point Apabhramśa reached the NIA state of affairs, where the genitival postposition displays adjectival agreement with the possessed object (the pronominal possessor, however, is not marked for gender):

(7) Apabhramśa   Hindi
    tao kerau bhāū   *is = kā bhāī*   'his brother'
    tao kerī dhūya   *is = kī beṭī*   'his daughter'
    tahe kerau bhāū   *is = kā bhāī*   'her brother'
    tahe kerī dhūya   *is = kī beṭī*   'her daughter'

In historical perspective, Hindi possessive (genitival) pronominal forms preserved adjectival characteristics and Apabhramśa shows matters *in statu nascendi*. The adjectival form *kera* (etymologically, the gerundive *kārya* 'to be done, made') was cliticized to the pronoun and underwent some phonological erosion.

In OIA and the earlier Prākrits agreement with the possessed object could not be shown because the pronoun referring to the possessor was in the genitive case:

(8)   Sanskrit   Prākrits
      tasya bhrātā   *tao bhāū*   'his brother'
      tasya duhitā   *tao dhūya*   'his daughther'
      tasyā bhrātā   *tahe bhāū*   'her brother'
      tasyā duhitā   *tahe dhūya*   'her daughter'

5.2.3 Reference

As Table 6.1 shows, the MIA dialects syncretized the dative with the genitive. In Apabhraṁśa the sense of reference came to be expressed by one of the postpositions attached to the genitive form or the stem of the noun. Hemacandra [8.4.425] mentions five postpositions without specifying their semantic difference or the range of their usage:

(9)   *tādarthye kehiṁ-tehiṁ-resi-resiṁ-taṇeṇāḥ*   [Hc 8.4.425]
      apabhraṁśe tādarthye dyotye kehiṁ tehiṁ resi resiṁ taṇeṇa ity ete paṁca
      nipātāḥ prayoktavyāḥ
      'In Apabhraṁśa when the sense of reference is to be indicated the five *nipātas* (here, postpositions) are to be used: *kehiṁ, tehiṁ, resi, resiṁ* [and] *taṇeṇa.*'

The postposition *kehiṁ* (~ *kihiṁ*) corresponds to Hindi *lie* 'for (the sake of)'. Formally, it is the masculine instrumental plural form of *ka-* 'who' (similarly, *tehiṁ* is the masculine instrumental plural form of *ta-* 'that').
    Resiṁ can be traced back to the genitival postposition *kera* via the longer form *keresiṁ*, and *taṇeṇa* is the instrumental form of the genitive postposition *taṇa*.
    Examples of both *kehiṁ* and *resi* are found in the illustration to Hemacandra [8.4.425]:

(10) *ḍhollā eha parihāsaḍī ai bhaṇa kavaṇahiṁ desi*   [Hc 8.4.425.1]
      hauṁ jhijjauṁ tau kehiṁ pia tuhuṁ puṇu annahi resi
      he nāyaka, eṣā paribhāṣā ayi bhaṇa kasmin deśe
      ahaṁ kṣiye tava arthe, tvaṁ punaḥ anyasyāḥ arthe
      'O dear, tell me in what place is this practice in vogue
      (that) I am pining for you, while you are pining away for someone else?'

5.2.4 Location

In OIA it was enough to say *gṛh-e* 'in the house' with the locative suffix *-e*; in MIA it became necessary to use the adverb *majjhe/i* 'inside' as an adposition (< OIA *madhy-e* 'in the middle') with the noun in the genitive: *majjhe gharaho* ~ *gharaho majjhe* 'in the house'. In Apabhraṃśa both the constructions (with the head *majjhe* before or after its modifier) are available:

(11) *majjhi   hiyayaha*   [Sc 707.5]
      middle-loc. heart-gen.
      'in the heart'

In NIA the case of the noun has been lost and the adverb *majjhe* has been reduced to the postposition *meṁ* which is cliticized to the noun: *ghar = meṁ*. Put differently, the fusional case of OIA has been replaced by the phrasal (postpositional) case in MIA.
    The locative postposition *par* 'on' in Hindi goes back to the adverb/adposition *upari* which could be used with the noun in various cases: N-acc. 'above, over'; N-loc. 'upon,

at the head of'; N-abl. 'with regard to, after', and, of course, also with the genitive. In Apabhramśa literature all sorts of examples are available ranging from (a) *upari/uvari* detached from its (pro)nominal modifier to (b) the immediately following one (N-gen. *upari*) to (c) the quasi-'compound' N=*upari*. Representative examples are provided in (12):

(12) (a) *iyarassu   kassu   vi   uvari*   [Sc 693.2]
         another-gen. who-gen. prt.   on
         'on whoever else'

   (b) *acchai kailāsaho   upari sāhu*   [Pc 13.2.6]
       is   Kailasa-gen. on   saint
       'The saint is on the Kailasa'

   (c) *iyar'uvari*   [Sc 694.8]
       another on
       'on another (one)'

5.2.5 Accompaniment/instrumentality

The most common adpositions expressing these two notions in Apabhramśa are *samau* (also *samāṇu*) and *sahuṁ* (also *sahu/sau/saiṁ/sai*, cf. Old Hindi *se*). They may precede or follow the noun in the instrumental.

In later documents, such as *Saṁdeśa Rāsaka*, the postposition *sau* may be attached as a clitic to the noun in the absolute form (i.e. here we reach the early NIA state of affairs):

(13) *pahiya   ṇa   sijjhai   kiri balu   maha Kaṁdappasau*   [SR 99]
     traveller not succeed–3sg. prt. strength I-gen. Cupid=with
     'O traveller, my strength cannot compete with Cupid/proves of no avail against Cupid.'

The ancestor of the Hindi postposition =*ke sāth* 'with' is Ap *satthihi* from OIA *sa artha* lit. having [its] object attained → 'successful, wealthy' (cf. its OIA derivatives such as *sārthaka* 'profitable, significant', *sārthika* 'travelling with a caravan, travelling merchant'). It appears in *Saṁdeśa Rāsaka* where its -*hi* seems to be identical with the marker of the oblique case. It is attached to the nouns in the absolute form and it may be spelled separately or together with its noun (the latter option undoubtedly indicates its status of a postpositional clitic as in NIA):

(14) *viviha-viakkhaa satthihi jai pavisai   ṇiru*   [SR 43]
     various-clever=with   if   enter–3sg.   continuously
     'If in the company of clever persons one takes a stroll [in the city]'

5.3 Evolution of the grammatical and lexical aspect

5.3.1 Grammatical aspect

We saw in section 4.3.3 that the OIA aorist was recategorized as the preterite in early Prākrits (Pāli and Ardha-Māgadhī); in later Prākrits (Māhārāṣṭrī and Apabhramśa) the synthetic preterite was replaced by analytic formations based on the past participle (of the type *tena kiau* lit. by him done). The OIA perfect with its complex morphology survived in a handful of relics in Pāli (*āha* 'he (has) said', *vidu* 'they know/have known'); otherwise, it was replaced by analytic formations based on the past participle. With intransitive verbs the OIA construction PPP plus pronoun (*āgato 'ham* lit. come I 'I have come') provided the pattern for PPP plus copula: MIA *āgato 'mhi* lit. come I am 'I have come'; in the pluperfect with the copula in the past form *āsi* (unmarked for person).

At the end of the MIA period the expressions of the perfect were systematized in the following fashion:

Present perfect PPP + copula *acch-* in the present
Past perfect   PPP + copula *acch-* in the preterite (*āsi*)
                 PPP + *ṭhiu* (of *thā-* 'stand')

Pertinent Ap examples are in (15) and (16):

(15) *acchai   āsaṇapatti   ṇisaṇṇau*   [Bk 74.2]
     is   seat-slab-loc. sit-PPP
     'He is seated on the seat.'

(16) *gayau   asi*   [Pc 36.4.6]
     go-PPP   was
     'He had gone.'

In Pāli and other MIA dialects one occasionally encounters combinations of the present participle of the main verb with the verb *tiṣṭhati* 'stand' or *vicarati* 'walk' which may be interpreted as an incipient category of the progressive aspect. These rare constructions were continued and further developed during the late MIA period (to compensate, presumably, for the loss of the OIA imperfect, cf. 4.3.3). Here are some Ap examples: Present progressive:

(17) *acchai   duri   bhamantu*   [Pd 4.17.2]
     be-3sg.   far   wander-part.
     'He is wandering far away.'

(18) *vollau   savvu haseppiṇu   acchami*   [Pc 38.19.2]
     say-PP   all   laugh-ger. be-1sg.
     'I am laughing at all [that has been] said.'

Past progressive:

(19) *bhavakaddami   hauṁ hiṇḍantu   acchiu*   [Jc 4.17.2]
     world-mud-loc.   I   wander-part.   be-PPP
     'I was wandering in the mud of the world.'

(20) *vaṇe   vijjau   ārāhanta   thiu*   [Pc 9.8.9]
     forest-loc. *vidyā* worship-part. stand+PPP
     'He was worshipping *vidyā* in the forest.'

Instead of the participle we also encounter the gerund in *-eppi(ṇu)* or *-evi*; in the past the preterite form of the copula (*āsi*) may be replaced by its PPP *acchiu* or the PPP *ṭhiu-* (< OIA *sthita-* 'stood') with the latter form heralding the NIA state of affairs.

Summarily, at the end of the MIA period we encounter a rich system of periphrastic constructions which could adequately express aspectual contrasts of retrospectivity (perfect) and progressivity:

(21)		Perfect	Progressive	
		PPP + copula	Pres Part + copula	Gerund + copula
	Present	*gayau acchai*	*karantu acchai*	*kareppi(ṇu) acchai*
	Past	*gayau āsi~ṭhiu*	*karantu acchiu~ṭhiu*	*kareppi(ṇu) ṭhiu*

5.3.2 Lexical aspect

MIA data contain examples of verbal compounds expressing several categories of *Aktionsart* (= lexical aspect). As in NIA languages, these are composites of main verbs with one of a small number of the auxiliary verbs. The lexical meaning of the auxiliary is not present fully in the compound or rather it is present only 'figuratively'; the auxiliary simply modifies or makes more specific the basic meaning of the main verb.

At the end of the MIA period our Apabhraṁśa data allow us to identify exponents of the notions of inception and completion, expressed by the *Aktionsart* auxiliaries *lag(g)*- 'begin' and *jā* 'go' (and perhaps also *ā*- 'come'). There is also some evidence for another pair, that of version (movement 'towards') and ablation (movement 'away') expressed by the auxiliaries *le*- 'take' (also *nī*- 'take') and *de*- 'give'. According to Singh (1980: 164–7) there were other *Aktionsart* nuances, such as intensive and continuative, expressed by the auxiliaries *ā-/nī*- and *rah*- 'remain', respectively. In my analysis *ā*- is rather completive and *nī*- versive; apropos the continuative, none of Singh's examples is satisfactory. The main verb is realized by the gerund (-*vi(ṇu)*, -*eppi(ṇu)*), the infinitive (-*aṇaham*, -*aṇahiṁ*, -*ahuṁ*) or the gerundive (-*ev(v)ae*). Here are some representative examples:

(22) *daddura raḍevi lagga*   [Pc 28.3.2]
frog   cry-ger.   attach-PPP
'The frog began to weep.' (inception)

so jāu jji muu   [Pc 36.5.9]
he   go-PP   prt.   die-PPP
'He has died.' (completion)

vijjulaṅgu ṇiu āliṅgeppiṇu   [Pc 25.4.9]
Vidyudaṅga   take-PP   embrace-PPP
'[The king] embraced Vidyudanga.' (version)

nimmala-guaṇhaṁ bhareviṇu dehu   [Bk 21.9]
pure-quality-gen.pl.   fill-ger.   give–2sg.imp.
'Fill with good qualities!' (ablation)

5.4 Passive constructions and the emergence of the ergative construction

5.4.1 Passive constructions

The passive could be expressed in three ways during the MIA period. The synthetic passive in -*ijja* continues the OIA passive in -*ya* (cf. section 4.3.6). Its use is practically limited to the present tense with innovative forms in the future (AMg *mucc-ih-ii*) and the aorist (AMg *mucc-iṁsu*), cf. Pischel 1900/1965: 379–80). The other way was to combine the past (passive) participle with the copula:

(23) *jam jehau*   *diṇṇau   āsi*   [Riṭṭha 6.14]
     what which manner   give-PPP was
     'What was given in which manner ...'

And finally, at the end of the MIA period there appeared examples of the innovative *go*-passive heralding the NIA state of affairs (cf. Hindi *kiyā gayā* lit. do-PPP go-PPP 'was done'). An earliest isolated example was spotted in Svayaṁbhūdeva's *Paumacariu*:

(24) *so   vane   diṭṭhu   gau*   [Pc 19.17.5]
     he   forest-loc. see-PPP   go-PPP
     'He was seen in the forest.'

Another isolated example with the auxiliary 'to go' in the future tense was found in Haribhadra's *Sanatkumāracarita* (twelfth century):

(25) *kaha maiṁ   diṭṭhau   jāisai   ehu*   [Sc 631.8]
     how   I-instr. see-PPP   go–3sg.fut.   this
     'How will I be able to see this city?'

5.4.2 Emergence of the ergative construction

The ambiguity between the passive and the active interpretation of the same construction with the PPP is symptomatic of the shift towards ergative typology in late MIA. One of the contributing factors in this process was the elimination of the contrast between the nominative as against the accusative in Ap (OIA *naraḥ* vs. *naram* > Ap *naru* 'man'). The resulting absolutive form allows for the active interpretation of the passive construction when its agent is specified:

(26) *naru   māri(y)a(u)*
     man-abs.   kill-PPP
     'The man was killed' (passive interpretation)

   mae   naru   māri(y)a(u)
   I-instr.   man-abs.   kill-PPP
   'I killed the man' (active interpretation)

   mayā   naro   māritaḥ   [OIA]
   I-instr.   man-nom.   kill-PPP
   'The man was killed by me.'

Nevertheless, depending on the context, even the Ap construction *mae naru māri(y)a(u)* may be interpreted passively and it was only during the NIA period after the crystallization of the *go*-passive and the establishment of two different agentive postpositions (=*ne* for the agent in the ergative construction vs. =*se* for the agent in the passive construction, as in Hindi) that this ambiguity was sorted out; contrast Ap *amhahiṁ ki(a)u* '[It] was done by us' ~ 'We did [it]' with Hindi *ham=ne kiyā* 'We did [it]' as against *ham=se kiyā gayā* '[It] was done by us'.

Using the verb *kar-* we may outline the system of voice in Apabhraṁśa as follows:

(27) | | Active | Passive |
     |---------|--------------------------|------------------|
     | Present | *kar-ai* | *kar-ijj-ai* |
     | Past | *tena ki(a)u* | *ki(a)u gau* |
     | Future | *kar-is-ai* ~ *kar-ih-ii* | *ki(a)u jā-is-ai* |

5.5 Causative constructions

Extensive use of causative constructions was one of the salient features of IA syntax during all its periods. In all the Prākrit works one observes the pervasive influence of Sanskrit causative syntax in its main principles: the causer agent is the grammatical subject in the active causative construction; in the passive construction it is the causee agent or the logical object which is the grammatical subject; the causee agent may function as the grammatical object (accusative in Sanskrit) or it may be realized by the instrumental; and if the logical object functions as the grammatical subject both the causer and the causee may be expressed by the instrumental.

5.5.1 Finite causatives

In MIA the causatives are formed freely from both intransitive and transitive verbs in the present and the future tenses, as in the following Apabhraṁśa example:

(28) *jovai   bāla dhāi   darisāvai*   [Riṭṭha 3.1.1]
     watch-3sg. girl   nurse   see-caus.-3sg.
     'The girl watches, the nurse shows'

The finite passive causative appears rarely in imitation of Sanskrit as in (29):

(29) *jaṁ   uppajjai   bālu   saihi   mi   ṇiyabhattāreṁ*   [Riṭṭha 1.9]
     when be-born–3sg. son   wife-gen. prt. own-husband-instr.
     'When the wife has a son by [her] own husband'

The form *uppajjai* is ambiguous between non-causative *ut-pad-ya-te* 'is born' and causative *ut-pād-ya-te* 'is caused to be born' distinguished solely by length in OIA.

5.5.2 Non-finite causatives

As in section 5.4.2, these could be interpreted actively or passively. Progressing through the MIA period, the ergative interpretation became more and more likely as a consequence of the overall increase in ergative typology. The earliest signs of it might be the use of the causative PPP in the first and second person where one can legitimately maintain that the spontaneous use of language in conversation does not favour the passive (and *a fortiori* the passivized causative). Other reasons, as in the case of the ergative interpretation of non-causative PPPs, were pragmatic (postulates of Functional Sentence Perspective) and syntactic (problems with conjoining intransitive and transitive predicates). Representative Ap examples are provided in (30):

(30) *avuhu   padarisiu   appaṇau*   [Pc 1.3.12]
     ignorance   see-caus.-PPP own
     'I manifested my ignorance.'

     bhaṇu keṇa   karāviu   ihu   layaṇu   [Kc 5.1.1]
     tell   who-instr. make-caus.-PPP this   cave
     'Tell [me], who built this cave?'

On the other hand, agentless constructions are best interpreted passively:

(31) *paḍilāhiu   risi   vaisavaṇa-ghare*   [Hv 82.12.1]
     obtain-caus.-PPP seer Vaiśravaṇa-house-loc.
     'The seer was given alms in Vaiśravaṇa's house.'

Examples of double causatives are common in MIA. The following is an example of a double passive causative from the *Erzählungen* in Māhārāṣṭrī:

(32) *eeṇa*   *pagāreṇa*   *savvaṁ*   *davvaṁ*   *davāvio*   [Erz 66.19]
     this-instr.   manner-instr.   all-acc.   wealth-acc. give-caus.-caus.-PPP
     'In this manner he was made to give all (his) wealth away.'

In practice one would expect various cases of 'disagreement' of the type two causees but the verb in a single causative, or one causee but the verb in a double causative (or even non-causative). These indeed can be documented from Aśokan Prākrits which show a bewildering variety of non-causative, causative and double causative passive participles with the verb *likh* 'write'. The alternation between *likhite* 'incised', *likhāpitaṁ* and *lekhāpitaṁ* 'caused to be incised' should not be taken literally as implying that Aśoka himself incised some of the inscriptions whereas had the others inscribed through his stonemasons who were commanded to do so by him directly or through an intermediary. The conclusion is rather that the 'agreement' (1 causee – causative, 2 causees – double causative) was far from being of categoric nature in spoken language.

5.6 Modal constructions

We saw in section 4.3.5 that the earlier Prākrits (Pāli, AMg and Mah) continued the OIA optative morphology. In Ap there are only relics of it above all with the verb 'to be': *acch-ijja-hi/u* 'may you be'. In the third person another optative form of 'to be', *hojja* 'let him be/may he be' (from the aorist optative *bhū-yā-t*), functions as the modal form expressing contrafactive utterances (wishes):

(33) *piya-bhattāru*   *hojja*   *mahu*   *lakkhaṇu*   [Pc 29.5.3]
     dear-husband   be-3sg.-opt.   I-gen./dat.   Lakṣmaṇa
     'May Lakṣmaṇa be my dear husband.'

In Apabhraṁśa we witness a further development of the gerundive from the statements of deontic modality to the future. During the twelfth century, especially in the east, to judge by evidence from Kāṇha's and Saraha's *Dohākoṣa*, the gerundive *maiṁ karevvau* 'I have to do [it]' (< *mayā kartavyam* '[it is] to be done by me') had already been recategorized as the future tense 'I will do it' (inherited by Bengali *ami kariba*).

This shift might be linked with the 'weakening' of the future tense morphology by phonological attrition (*s* > *h*) in that the gerundive supplied new more distinctive morphology for it. Nevertheless, the sigmatic future is found in western IA languages such as Lahnda and Gujarati (*calīś* 'I will go', *calśe* 'you will go', etc.); and its weakened counterpart with *h* in certain eastern Hindi dialects (e.g. Bundeli *calahaũ* 'I will go' < OIA *cariṣyāmi, calahai* 'you will go' < *cariṣyasi*).

5.7 Absolute constructions

OIA possessed absolute constructions involving the noun and its participial attribute in the locative and less commonly in the genitive ('the genitive of disrespect'). These constructions were used when the subjects of two clauses were not coreferential. The absolute construction could express an event contemporary with the main clause (using the present active participle) or anterior to that in the main clause (using the past passive participle). In MIA the construction involving the genitive became as common as that involving the syncretic instrumental/locative case.

Given the fact that the main function of the instrumental case in late MIA was agentive (ergative), frequent Ap examples of absolute constructions involving the instrumental may be viewed as Sanskritisms.

One of the striking Sanskritisms is the absolute construction involving the passive imperfective participle. As explained in section 4.3.8, its morphology is peculiar in combining the inherited passive marker -*ya* > -*ja* and the suffix of the active participle -*anta*, which replaced the OIA medio-passive suffix -*māna*: OIA *dī-ya-māna* > Ap *di-jj-anta* 'being given'. All the examples I came across in Svayaṃbhūdeva and the late Sanskritizing poet Haribhadra (twelfth century) were of the type shown in (34):

(34) *gīyahiṃ*   *gijjantaehiṃ*   [Pc 21.14.7]
song-instr./loc.pl. sing-pass.-part.-instr.pl.
'while the songs were being sung'

In my Apabhraṃśa data I have not found any instances of the 'genitive of disrespect'. For instance, 'while he was ruling' may be expressed indiscriminately by either the instrumental/locative or the genitive absolute in identical contexts:

(35) *rajju*   *karaṃte*   [Riṭṭha 1.4.1]
kingdom do-part.-instr./loc.

rajju   *karaṃtaho*   [Riṭṭha 6.13.6]
kingdom do-part.-gen.
'while [X] was ruling'

The subordinate clause may also be realized by the absolute construction with the participle and its head noun in the nominative/accusative (or rather absolutive, cf. sections 4.1 and 5.4.2). Its existence may be taken as symptomatic of the continuing demise of the morphology of the synthetic case and its replacement by analytic formations as described in section 5.2.

5.8 Complementation

The main verb complementing the modal verb *sakkai* 'can' (or the adjective *samathu* 'capable') is expressed by the past participle or the gerund in Apabhraṃśa:

(36) *ko*   *sakkai*   *rāya*   *gaṇevi*   *tāiṃ*   [Pc 37.5.8]
who can–3sg. king count-ger. those
'King, who can count them?'

After the verbs of motion the complement (= verbal noun) appears in the genitive/dative or it may be realized by the gerund:

(37) *dāmodara-halayara jāyavā* *vi* *gaya*   *naṃdaho* *goula*
Kṛṣṇa-Balabhadra Yādava and go-PPP Nanda-gen. cattle-pen
    pekkhaṇevi   [Riṭṭha 6.4.1]
    see-ger.
'Kṛṣṇa, Balabhadra and Yādava went to see Nanda's cattle-pen.'

(-*n*- in *pekkhaṇevi* could be by contamination with the infinitive *pekkhaṇa*).

In Ap texts there are also examples of complementation by means of the Sanskritizing infinitive in -*u* (< -*tum*). Complementary clauses are introduced by the quotative particle *ema* (from the OIA adverb *evam* 'thus') after *verba dicendi et sentiendi.* It functions in approximately the same fashion as its OIA counterpart *iti*, but it differs from it in being placed usually before the complementary clause:

(38) *paṇaveppiṇu*   *teṇa*   *vi*   *vuttu*   *ema*   *gaya*   *diyahā*
     bow-with-respect-ger. he-instr. prt. say-PPP   quot.prt. go-PPP days
        jovvaṇu lhasiu   deva   [Pc 22.2.1]
        youth   wither-PPP lord
     'Having bowed with respect he said: "Lord, [my] days are gone [and my] youth has withered".'

5.9 Relative clauses

Relative clauses in MIA are very much like their OIA and NIA counterparts in presenting the characteristic relative – correlative construction of the type '(Which girl we saw), she came from the village' (*yā kanyā asmābhir dṛṣṭā*) *sā grāmād āgatā.* The relative clause is introduced by a member of the *j*-set of relative pronouns (adverbs and conjunctions), and is represented by its correlative counterpart in the main clause.

5.9.1 Subordinate clauses introduced by relative pronouns

Subordinate clauses introduced by relative pronouns function as a modifier of the head noun or pronoun in the main clause.

As in many other languages, in Apabhraṁśa it was possible to relativize on both the subject and the object with the result that the relative and correlative pronouns might be in a different case (as in the Sanskrit construction of the type *yām apaśyāma sā mama sakhī*, lit. whom we saw she is my friend). This is shown in (39):

(39) *so ṇa johu ... jaṁ   vasueu-sarehiṁ   ṇa   viṁdhau* [Riṭṭha 3.6]
     he not warrior who-acc. Vasudeva-arrow-instr.pl. not pierce-PPP
     'There was no such a warrior who(m) Vasudeva did not pierce with [his] arrows'

The relative – correlative pair *jaṁ-taṁ* (< OIA *yam-tam* 'whom' – 'that') could also fulfil the function of the adverbial pair *jāba – tāba* (EAp) 'when' – 'then' (< OIA *yāvat-tāvat*). Its relative pronoun *jaṁ* was reduced to the temporal conjunction 'when' through the process of grammaticalization.

5.9.2 Subordinate clauses introduced by relative adverbs

Adverbial clauses of place, time and manner are realized as relative clauses introduced by a number of adverbs. As in the case of relative pronouns these adverbs begin with *j*- (< OIA *y*-), and their main clauses are usually introduced by a corresponding correlative adverb beginning with *t*- (< OIA *t*-).

The following are the representative relative – correlative pairs of MIA adverbs

of place: *jattha – tattha*, Ap *jahāṁ – tahāṁ, jahiṁ ~ tahiṁ* 'where' – 'there';
of time: *jabba – tabba*, EAp *jāba – tāba*, WAp *jāma – tām/va*, Ap *jā – tā* 'when' – 'then';
of manner: *jahā – tahā, jidha – tidha*, Ap *jiha – tiha, jāvehiṁ – tāvehiṁ* 'in which manner' – 'in this manner'.

In Ap the pair *jet(t)ā – tet(t)ā* 'as many' – 'so many' appears also in the compound *jettavāra – tettavāra* 'as many times' – 'so many times'. Late Ap forms, such as *jima –*

tima 'as, like' – 'so', cannot be traced back directly to OIA *yathā* – *tathā*; they appear to result from the contamination with temporal *jāma* – *tāma* or the particle *eva/ema* whose *-m-* is justifiable phonologically.

ACKNOWLEDGEMENT

The author wishes to acknowledge the help of G. Cardona with translating and interpreting several passages from Hemacandra's grammar in (2)–(4).

REFERENCES – PRIMARY LITERATURE

Acharya, K. C. (1968) *Mārkaṇḍeya's Prākṛta-sarvasva* (Prakrit Text Series XI, Prakrit Grammar Series 1), Ahmedabad: Prakrit Text Society.

Alsdorf, L. (1928) *Der Kumārapālapratibodha. Ein Beitrag zur Kenntnis des Apabhraṁśa und der Erzählungsliteratur der Jainas* (Alt- und Neu-Indische Studien 5), Hamburg: Friedrichsen, de Gruyter.

—— (1936) *Harivaṁśapurāṇa. Ein Abschnitt aus der Apabhraṁśa-Welthistorie 'Mahāpurāṇa Tisaṭṭhimahāpurisaguṇālaṁkāra' von Puṣpadanta. Als Beitrag zur Kenntnis des Apabhraṁśa und der Universalgeschichte der Jainas herausgegeben*, Hamburg: Friedrichsen, de Gruyter.

Banerjee, S. R. (1980) *Prākṛtādhyāya by Kramadīśvara*, Ahmedabad: Prakrit Text Society.

Bhayani, H. C. (1953–60) *Svayambhūdeva's Paümacariu* (3 vols., Singhi Jain Series 34, 35, 36), Bombay: Bharatiya Vidya Bhavan.

—— and Modi, M.C. (1974) *Haribhadra's Sanatukumāra-cariya (a section of his Nemināhacariya). (L. D. Series, 42)*, Ahmedabad: L. D. Institute of Indology.

Cowell, E. B. (1868) *The Prākṛita-Prakāśa: or The Prākṛit Grammar of Vararuchi with the Commentary (Manoramā) of Bhāmaha*, London: Trübner (Reprinted (1962), Calcutta: Punthi Pustak).

Jacobi, H. (1882) *The Āyāraṁga Sutta of the Çvetāmbara Jains*, London: Pāli Text Society.

—— (1886/1967) *Ausgewählte Erzählungen in Māhârâshṭrî: zur Einführung in das Studium des Prâkṛit*, Leipzig: Hirzel (Reprinted (1967) Darmstadt: Wissenschaftliche Buchgesellschaft).

—— (1918) *Bhavisatta Kaha von Dhaṇavāla. Eine Jaina-Legende in Apabhraṁśa* (Abhandlungen der Kgl. Bayerischen Akademie der Wissenschaften, Philos.-philol. u. hist. Klasse 29.4), München: Bayerische Akademie der Wissenschaften.

—— (1921) *Sanatkumāracaritam ein Abschnitt aus Haribhadras Nemināthacarita. Eine Jaina-Legende in Apabhraṁśa* (Abhandlungen der Kgl. Bayerischen Akademie der Wissenschaften, Philos.-philol. u. hist. Klasse 31.2), München: Bayerische Akademie der Wissenschaften.

—— (1962–8) *Ācārya Vimalasūri's Paumacariya* (2 vols., Prakrit Text Society Series, 6, 12.). Varanasi: Prakrit Text Society. (2nd ed. revised by Muni Punyavijayaji; translated into Hindi by Shantilal M. Vora.) [Originally published in 1914]

Jain, D. K. (1958) *Paumcariu of Kavirāja Svayambhūdeva*, Kāshī: Bhāratīya Jñānapīṭha.

—— (1985) *Kavirāja Svayambhūdeva's Riṭṭhaṇemi-cariu (Arishtanemi-charita)*, Kāshī: Bhāratīya Jñānapīṭha.

Jain, H. L. (1932) *Sāvayadhammadohā of Devasena*, Karanja, Berar: Karanja Jaina Publication Society.

—— (1933) *Muni Rāmasiṁha viracita pāhuḍadohā*, Karanja, Berar: Karanja Jaina Publication Society.

—— (1934) *Kanakāmara's Karakaṇḍacariu*, Karanja, Berar: Karanja Jaina Publication Society.

Jain, V. P. (1968) *Jaṁbūsāmi Cariu of Virakavi*, Kāshī: Bhāratīya Jñānapīṭha.

Śrī Jina, Vijaya Muni (1945) *The Saṁdeśa Rāsaka of Abdul Rahman*, Bombay: Bharatiya Vidya Bhavan.

Kāle, M. R. (1900) *Mudrārākshasa*, Bombay: Śāradākrīḍanamudrāyantrālaya (Reprinted (1976), Delhi: Motilal Banarsidass).

—(1925) *Daśakumāracarita of Daṇḍin*, Bombay: Gopal Narayana & Co. (Reprinted (1979), Delhi: Motilal Banarsidass).

Karmarkar, R. D. (1932) *Vikramorvaśīya of Kālidāsa*, Poona: Karmarkar.

—— (1937) *Mṛcchakaṭikā*, Poona: Karmarkar.

—— (1952) *Abhijñāna-Śākuntala of Kālidāsa*, Poona: Sharangpani.

Konow, S. (1901) *Rāja-çekhara's Karpūra-mañjarī, A Drama by the Indian Poet Rājaçekhara (about 900 AD), Critically Edited ... and Translated into English by Charles Rockwell Lanman* (Harvard Oriental Series IV), Cambridge: Harvard (Reprinted (1963), Delhi: Motilal Banarsidass).

Laddu, R. D. & Gore, N. A. (1941) *Paumacariya of Vimalasūri* (Cantos 33–5), Poona: Venus Book Stall.

Leumann, E. (1897) *Āvaśyaka-Erzählungen*, Leipzig: Hirzel.

Modi, P. K. (1965) *Ācārya Padmakīrti's Pāsaṇāhacariu*, Varanasi: Prakrit Text Society.

Modi, P. K. & Bhayani, H. C. (1948) *Paumasiri-cariu of Dhāhila*, Bombay: Bharatiya Vidya Bhavan.

Nitti-Dolci, L. (1938) *Le Prākṛtānuśāsana de Puruṣottama* (Cahiers de la Société Asiatique VI), Paris: Société Asiatique.

Pandit, S. P. (1887) *The Gaüḍavaho. A Prakrit Historical Poem by Vākpati*, Poona: Bhandarkar Oriental Research Institute. (Re-edited (1927) by Narayan B. Utgikar.)

Pischel, R. (1877/1880) *Hemacandra's Grammatik der Prâkritsprachen (Siddhahemacandram Adhyâya, VIII)*, Halle: Waisenhaus (Reprinted 1880).

Shahidullah, M. (1928) *Les chants mystiques de Kāṇha et de Saraha*, Paris: Adrien-Maisonneuve.

Tieken, H. J. T. (1983) *Hāla's Sattasai. Stemma and Edition of Gāthās 1–50, with Translation and Notes*, Utrecht. (Dissertation.)

Upadhye, A. N. (1973) *Śrī Yogīndudēva's Paramātmaprakāśa and also Yogasāra*, Shrimad Rajachandra Ashrama AGAS: Śrīmad Rājachandra Jaina Śāstra-mālā 3.

Vaidya, P. L. (1931) *Jasahara-cariü of Puṣpadanta, an Apabhraṁśa Work of the 10th Century*, Karanja, Berar: Karanja Jaina Publication Society (2nd ed. (1972) with Hindi translation by Hiralal Jain, Delhi: Bhāratīya Jñānapīṭha Prakāśana).

—— (1937–41/1979) *Mahākavi Puṣpadanta's Mahāpurāṇa*, Bombay, New Delhi: Bhāratīya Jñānapīṭha. (2nd ed. (1979) with Hindi translation by Devendra Kumar Jain.)

—— (1954) *Prakrit Grammar of Trivikrama* (Jīvarāja Jaina Granthamālā 4), Sholapur: Jaina Sanskriti Samrakshaka Sangha.

—— (1958/1980) *Prakrit Grammar of Hemacandra being the eighth Adhyāya of his Siddha-hema-śabdānuśāsana* (Bombay Sanskrit and Prakrit Series No. LX [Appendix]), Poona: Bhandarkar Oriental Research Institute (Reprinted 1980).

Vyas, B. S. (1959–62) *Prākṛita-Paiṅgalaṁ* (*A Text on Prākṛita and Apabhraṁśa Meters*) 2 vols. (Prakrit Text Society Series 2, 4), Varanasi: Prakrit Text Society.

Vyas, K. B. (1982) *Apabhraṁśa of Hemacandra* (Prakrit Text Series 23), Ahmedabad: Prakrit Text Society.

FURTHER READING

Alsdorf, L. (1937) *Apabhraṁśa Studien*. Abhandlungen für die Kunde des Morgenlandes XXII.2, Leipzig: Deutsche Morgenländische Gesellschaft.

Bubenik, V. (1996) *The Structure and Development of Middle Indo-Aryan Dialects*, Delhi: Motilal Banarsidass.

—— (1998) *A Historical Syntax of Late Middle Indo-Aryan (Apabhraṁśa)*, Amsterdam/Philadelphia: John Benjamins.

Pandit, P. B. (1961) *Prākṛta bhāṣā* [Prākrit]. Banaras: Śrīpārśvanāthavidyāśrāma. [In Hindi]

Pischel, R. (1900) *Grammatik der Prakrit-Sprachen*, Strassburg: Trübner (English translation by S. Jha (1965), *Comparative Grammar of the Prākrit Languages*, Delhi: Motilal Banarsidass, 1965).
Sen, S. (1953) 'Historical syntax of Middle Indo-Aryan', *Indian Linguistics* 13: 355–473 (Reprinted (1995) in Sen, Sukumar *Syntactic Studies of Indo-Aryan Languages*, Tokyo: Institute for the Study of Languages and Cultures of Asia and Africa, Tokyo University of Foreign Studies, pp. 255–402).
—— (1960) *A Comparative Grammar of Middle Indo-Aryan*, Poona: Deccan College.
Singh, R. A. (1980) *Syntax of Apabhraṁśa*, Calcutta: Simant Publications India.
Tagare, G. V. (1948/1987) *Historical Grammar of Apabhraṁśa*, Poona: Deccan College (Reprinted (1987), Delhi: Motilal Banarsidass).
Upadhye, A. N. (1975) *Prākrit Languages and Literature*, Poona: University of Poona.
Vertogradova, V. V. (1978) *Prakrity*, Moskva: Nauka.
Woolner, A. C. (1928/1975) *Introduction to Prakrit*, Varanasi: Panna Lal. (Reprinted (1975), Delhi: Motilal Banarsidass).

REFERENCES

Av *Āvaśyaka-Erzählungen* (M. Leumann)
Bk *Bhavisatta Kaha* (H. Jacobi)
Erz *Ausgewählte Erzählungen in Mâhârâshṭrī* (H. Jacobi)
Hc *Prakrit Grammar of Hemacandra* (P. L. Vaidya)
Hv *Harivaṁśapurāṇa* (L. Alsdorf)
Jc *Jasahara-cariü* (P. L. Vaidya)
Kc *Karakaṇḍacariu* (H. L. Jain)
Mṛcch *Mṛcchakaṭikā* (R. D. Karmarkar)
Mudr *Mudrārākṣasa* (M. R. Kale)
Pc *Paümacariyu* (H. C. Bhayani)
Pd *Pāhuḍadohā* (H. L. Jain)
Riṭṭha *Riṭṭhanemi-cariu* (D. K. Jain)
Sc *Saṇatukumāra-cariya* (H. C. Bhayani and M. C. Modi)
SR *Saṁdeśa Rāsaka* (Śri Jina Vijaya Muni)
Vikr *Vikramorvaśīya* (R. D. Karmarkar)
Alsdorf, L. (1974) *Kleine Schriften:* see Wezler.
Banerjee, S. R. (1977a) *A Bibliography of Prakrit Language*, Calcutta: Sanskrit Book Depot.
—— (1977b) *The Eastern School of Prakrit Grammarians*, Calcutta: Vidyasagar Pustak Mandir.
Bender, E. (1969) 'Middle Indo-Aryan', in Sebeok, T. E. (ed.) *Current Trends in Linguistics, Volume 5: Linguistics in South Asia,* The Hague: Mouton, pp. 46–54.
Bhayani, H. C. (1947) 'Language of Gujarat from earliest times to *c.* 1300 AD', *Bhāratīya Vidyā* 8: 289–318.
—— (1988) *Studies in Deśya Prakrit*, Ahmedabad: Kalikala Nidhi.
—— (1989) *Apabhraṁśa Language and Literature*, Delhi: B. L. Institute of Indology.
Bloch, J. (1934) *L'indo-aryen du véda aux temps moderne*, Paris: Adrien-Maisonneuve. (English translation by A. Master, Paris: Adrien Maisonneuve, 1965.)
Breunis, A. (1990) *The Nominal Sentence in Sanskrit and Middle Indo-Aryan*, Leiden: Brill.
Bubenik, V. (1996) *The Structure and Development of Middle Indo-Aryan Dialects*, Delhi: Motilal Banarsidass.
—— (1998) *A Historical Syntax of Late Middle Indo-Aryan (Apabhraṁśa)*. Amsterdam/Philadelphia: Benjamins.
Canedo, I. (1937) *Zur Wort- und Satzstellung in der alt- und mittelindischen Prosa. Zeitschrift für vergleichende Sprachforschung.* Ergänzungsheft, 13, Göttingen: Vandenhoeck & Ruprecht.

Chandra, K. R. (1987) *Sva. Paṃ. Hargovindadās Trikamacaṃd Sēṭh kṛta Pāia-sadda-mahaṇṇavo kiñcit parivartit āvṛtti Prākṛta-hindī kōś*, Ahmedabad: Prākṛta Jaina Vidyā Vikās Phaṇḍ.

Geiger, W. (1916) *Pāli: Literatur und Sprache,* Strassburg. (English translation by B. Ghosh (1943), Calcutta: University of Calcutta).

Ghatage, A. M. (1941) *Introduction to Ardha Māgadhī,* Kolhapur: School & College Book-Stall (Reprinted (1993), Pune: Sanmati Teerth).

Gonda, J. (1959) *Four Studies in the Language of the Veda,* The Hague: Mouton.

Jacobi, H. (1886/1967) *Ausgewählte Erzählungen in Mâhârâshṭrî: zur Einführung in das Studium des Prâkrit,* Leipzig: Hirzel (Reprinted (1967), Darmstadt: Wissenschaftliche Buchgesellschaft).

Kumar, N. (1987) *Apabhraṁśa-Hindī Kośa,* Ghaziabad: Indo-Vision.

Masica, C. (1991) *The Indo-Aryan Languages,* Cambridge: Cambridge University Press.

Mayrhofer, M. (1951) *Handbuch des Pali I/II,* Heidelberg: Winter.

Mishra, M. (1992) *A Grammar of Apabhramsha,* Delhi: Vidyānidhi Prakāshan.

Misra, S. S. and Misra H. (1982) *A Historical Grammar of Ardhamāgadhī,* Varanasi: Ashutosh Prakashan Sansthan.

Oberlies, T. (1996) 'Stray remarks on Pali phonology, morphology and vocabulary', *Münchener Studien zur Sprachwissenschaft* 56: 91–130.

Pischel, R. (1900) *Grammatik der Prakrit-Sprachen,* Strassburg: Trübner. (English translation by S. Jha (1965), Delhi: Motilal Banarsidass).

Scharfe, H. (1977) *Grammatical Literature. A History of Indian Literature* Vol. 5, Fasc.2., Wiesbaden: Harrassowitz.

Sen, S. (1953) 'Historical syntax of Middle Indo-Aryan', *Indian Linguistics* 13: 355–473 (Reprinted (1995) in Sen, Sukumar *Syntactic Studies of Indo-Aryan Languages.* Tokyo: Institute for the Study of Languages and Cultures of Asia and Africa, Tokyo University of Foreign Studies, pp. 255–402).

Sen, S. K. (1973) *Proto-New Indo-Aryan,* Calcutta: Eastern Publications.

Sheth, H. D. T. (1928) *Pāia-sadda-mahaṇṇavo. A Comprehensive Prākrit Hindi Dictionary with Sanskrit Equivalents, Quotations and Complete References,* Calcutta: Prakrit Text Society (Second edition (1963) (Prakrit Text Society 7), Varanasi: Prakrit Text Society).

Singh, R. A. (1980) *Syntax of Apabhraṁśa,* Calcutta: Simant Publications India.

Tagare, G. V. (1948) *Historical Grammar of Apabhraṁśa,* Poona: Deccan College (Reprinted (1987), Delhi: Motilal Banarsidass).

Wezler, A. (1974) *Ludwig Alsdorf. Kleine Schriften, herausgegeben von A.Wezler* (Glasenapp-Stiftung 10), Wiesbaden: Steiner.

SELECT BIBLIOGRAPHY

Alsdorf, L. (1937) *Apabhraṁśa-Studien. Leipzig: Brockhaus in Komm. Abhandlungen für die Kunde des Morgenlandes* XXII.2, Leipzig: Deutsche Morgenländische Gesellschaft (Reprinted (1966) Nendeln, Liechtenstein: Kraus).

Ananthanarayana, H. S. (1977) 'Structure of verbal constructions in Prakrit', *Osmania Papers in Linguistics* 3: 13–32.

Badiger, P. B. (1972) *Noun Morphology in Middle Indo-Aryan.* (Ph.D. Thesis, D. B. F. Dayand College, Sholapore).

Balbir, N. (1989) 'Morphological Evidence for Dialectal Variety in Jaina Māhārāṣṭrī', in Caillat, C. (ed.) *Dialectes dans les littératures indo-aryennes,* Paris: Collège de France, pp. 503–25.

Berger, H. (1955). *Zwei Probleme der mittelindischen Lautlehre,* München: Kitzinger.

—— (1957) 'Bemerkungen zur Endung der 1 pl. präs. im Mittelindischen', *Münchener Studien zur Sprachwissenschaft* 11: 109–12.

Bhayani, H. C. (1943) 'Apabhraṁśa gleanings', *Bhāratīya Vidyā* 4: 222–4.

—— (1945a) 'Two Apabhraṁśa citations', *Bhāratīya Vidyā* 6: 13–15.

—— (1945b) 'Endingless genitive in Apabhraṁśa', *Bhāratīya Vidyā* 6: 103–4.

—— (1951) 'Some interesting features of the Prākrit of the Nāṇapañcamīkahā', *Bhāratīya Vidyā* 12: 153–62.

—— (1957) 'Apabhraṁśa and Old Gujarātī Studies', *Bhāratīya Vidyā* 17: 122–6.

—— (1958a) 'Chaturmukha, one of the earliest Apabhraṁśa epic poets', *Journal of the Oriental Institute, Baroda* 7: 214–24.

—— (1958b) 'Apabhraṁśa and Old Gujarātī studies', *Bhāratīya Vidyā* 18: 67–73, 91.

—— (1959) 'Analogical replacement in MIA past passive participle bases: replacive -*gga*-, -*ḍha*- and a few others', *Bhāratīya Vidyā* 19: 111–15.

—— (1961) 'The late MIA suffix -*āṇa*-', *Adyar Library Bulletin* 25: 313.

—— (1962) 'Studies in Hemachandra's Deśīnāmamālā', *Bhāratīya Vidyā* 22: 51–6.

—— (1963) 'Apabhraṁśa *uviṭṭha*- "lost taste", "become insipid"', *Journal of the Oriental Institute, Baroda* 13: 17–20.

—— (1965) 'The narrative of Rāma in the Jain tradition', *Bhāratīya Vidyā* 25: 18–25.

—— (1971) 'Jambūsāmi-cariya of Vīra', *Journal of the Oriental Institute, Baroda* 20: 347–56.

Bubenik, V. (1987) 'Passivized causatives in Sanskrit and Prakrits', *Linguistics* 25: 687–704.

—— (1989) 'On the origins and elimination of ergativity in Indo-Aryan languages', *Canadian Journal of Linguistics* 34: 377–98.

—— (1991) 'Nominal and pronominal objects in Prākrit', in Hock, H. H. (ed.) *Sanskrit Syntax: Traditional and Modern Approaches*, Delhi: Motilal Banarsidass, pp. 19–30.

—— (1992) 'On the use of pronominal clitics in Late Middle Indo-Aryan', *Wiener Zeitschrift für die Kunde Südasiens und Archiv für indische Philosophie* XXXVI (Supplement) 7–18.

—— (1993a) 'Morphological and syntactic change in Late Middle Indo-Aryan', *Journal of Indo-European Studies* 21: 259–81.

—— (1993b) 'Restructuring of the nominal system and the evolution of phrasal case in Late Middle Indo-Aryan', *South Asian Horizons* 1: 229–48, Ottawa: Carleton University.

Bubenik, V. and Paranjape C. (1996) 'Development of pronominal systems from Apabhraṁśa to New Indo-Aryan', *Indo-Iranian Journal* 39: 111–32.

Chatterji, S .K. and Sen, S. (1957) *A Middle Indo-Aryan Reader*, Calcutta: Calcutta University.

Deshpande, N. A. (1967) 'Chronology of Apabhraṁśa works', *Bhāratīya Vidyā* 27: 104–8.

Edgerton, F. (1954) 'The Middle Indic verb system', *Asiatica. Festschrift Friedrich Weller.* Lepzig, pp. 78–81.

Ghatage, A. M. (1946) 'An unassimilated group in Apabhraṁśa', *Proceedings and Transactions of the All-India Oriental Conference (Benares Hindu University, 1943–1944)*, pp. 444–63.

Ghosal, S. N. (1952) 'References to other works in the Prākṛta-Paiṅgala – an Apabhraṁśa text', *Journal of the Oriental Institute, Baroda* 2: 174–6.

—— (1953) 'Dr. H. Jacobi's introduction to the Bhavisattakahā', *Journal of the Oriental Institute, Baroda* 2: 236–42, 346–58, 3: 84–94, 164–8, 269–76, 345–56, 4: 37–45, 176–89, 358–71, 5: 29–43, 140–68. (Translated from original German)

—— (1955) 'A note on the nasals in contact with aspirates in Prākrit', *Journal of the Oriental Institute, Baroda* 5: 360–5.

—— (1957) 'Dr. H. Jacobi's introduction to the Sanatkumāracaritam', *Journal of the Oriental Institute, Baroda* 6: 3–21, 89–101, 250–71, 7: 36–43. (Translated from original German)

—— (1960) 'A Prākrit word and some linguistic phenomena at the background of its origin', *Journal of the Oriental Institute, Baroda* 10: 289–82.

—— (1963) 'The stage of development of the Prākrit of Bhāsa's dramas and his age', *Journal of the Oriental Institute, Baroda* 13: 48–53.

—— (1966) 'The Apabhraṁśa elements in the Mṛcchakaṭikā', *Journal of the Oriental Institute, Baroda* 16: 124–30.

—— (1969) 'The Ārṣa Prākrit as Hemacandra viewed it', *Journal of the Oriental Institute, Baroda* 28: 304–14.

—— (1972) *The Apabhraṁśa Verses of the Vikramorvaśīya from the Linguistic Standpoint.* Calcutta: The World Press.

—— (1976) 'The genitive form as the basis of some pronominal bases in Prākrit', *Journal of the Oriental Institute, Baroda* 25: 343–8.

Hiän-lin, D. (1944) *Die Umwandlung der Endung -aṃ in -o und -u im Mittelindischen.* Göttingen: Vandenhoeck & Ruprecht.

Hiersche, R. (1960) 'Zu mi. *gacchati*, u. ä. als "Futurum", *Sprache* 4: 33–8.

Insler, S. (1993) 'The Prakrit ablative in *-ahi*', *Annals of the Bhandarkar Oriental Research Institute* LXXII and LXXIII: 15–21.

Jacobi, H. (1898) 'Der Akzent im Mittelindischen', *Zeitschrift für Vergleichende Sprachforschung* 35: 563–8.

Jain, D. K. (1983) *Apabhraṃśa aur hindī*, Jaipur: Rājasthān prākṛt bhāratī saṃsthān.

Jain, J. C. (1973) 'Is Vāsudevahiṇḍī a Jain version of the Bṛhatkathā?', *Journal of the Oriental Institute, Baroda* 23: 59–63.

Jha, M. (1967) *Māgadhī and Its Formation*, Calcutta: Sanskrit College.

Katre, S. M. (1939–1940) 'A new approach to the study of Middle and Modern Indo-Aryan', *Bhāratīya Vidyā* 1: 135–43.

—— (1964) *Prakrit Languages and Their Contribution to Indian Culture*, Poona: Deccan College.

—— (1965) *Some Problems of Historical Linguistics in Indo-Aryan*, Poona: Deccan College.

Kochaṛ, H. (1972) *Apabhraṃśa-Sāhitya*, Dillī: Bhāratīya sāhitya mandir.

Kuiper, F. B. J. (1957) 'The Paiśācī fragment of the *Kuvalayamālā*', *Indo-Iranian Journal* 1: 229–40.

—— (1963) 'Paiśācī *kaṭāpa-* bundle', *Indo-Iranian Journal* 6: 296–97.

Kulkarni, V. M. (1952) 'The Rāmāyaṇa version of Saṅghadāsa as found in the *Vasudevahiṇḍi*', *Journal of the Oriental Institute, Baroda* 2: 128–38.

Lesný, V. (1918). 'Die Entwicklungsstufe des Prākrits in Bhāsa's Dramen und das Zeitalter Bhāsa's', *Zeitschrift der Deutschen Morgenländischen Gesellschaft* 72: 203–8.

Mehendale, M. A. (1975) Review of S. K. Sen, 'Proto-New Indo-Aryan', *Indian Linguistics* 36: 63–5.

Morgenroth, W. (1981) 'Zur Position der mittelindoarischen Literatursprachen in der indischen Sprachgeschichte', *Zeitschrift für Phonetik, Sprachwissenschaft und Kommunikationsforschung* 34: 59–64.

Nara, Tsuyoshi (1979) *Avahaṭṭha and Comparative Vocabulary of New Indo-Aryan languages*, Tokyo: Institute for the Study of Languages and Cultures of Asia and Africa.

Nitti-Dolci, L. (1938) *Les grammairiens prakrits*, Paris: Société asiatique. (English translation by P. Jhā (1972), *The Prākṛita Grammarians*, Delhi: Motilal Banarsidass).

Norman, K. R. (1958) 'Some absolute terms in Ardha-Māgadhī', *Indo-Iranian Journal* 2: 311–15.

—— (1960–74) 'Middle Indo-Aryan studies I–XI', *Journal of the Oriental Institute, Baroda.*

—— (1960) 'Some vowel values in Middle Indo-Aryan', *Indian Linguistics* 21: 104–7.

—— (1990–93) *Collected Papers* (4 Vols), Oxford: The Pāli Text Society.

Pischel, R. (1902) *Materialien zur Kenntnis des Apabhraṃśa*, Berlin: Weidmann.

Prakash, R. (1974) *Verb Morphology in Middle Indo-Aryan*, New Delhi: Munshiram Manoharlal.

Pray, B. R. (1976) 'From passive to ergative in Indo-Aryan', in M. K.Verma (ed.), *The Notion of Subject in South Asian Languages* (*South Asian Studies Publication Series*, 2), Madison: University of Wisconsin, pp. 195–211.

Printz, W. (1921) *Bhāsa's Prākrit*, Frankfurt am Main. (Dissertation)

Rocher, L. (1986) *The Purāṇas. A History of Indian Literature* Vol. 3, Fasc. 3., Wiesbaden: Harrassowitz.

Sandesara, B. J. (1960) 'Cultural data in the *Vasudeva-hiṇḍi*, a Prākṛt story-book by Saṅghadāsagaṇi (circa 5th AD)', *Journal of the Oriental Institute, Baroda* 10: 7–17.

Scheller, M. (1967) 'Das mittelindische Enklitikum *se*', *Zeitschrift für Vergleichende Sprachforschung* 81: 1–53.

Schokker, G. H. (1969–70) 'The *jānā*-passive in the NIA languages', *Indo-Iranian Journal* 12: 1–23.

Schwarzschild, L. A. (1955) 'Notes on the history of the infinitive in Middle Indo-Aryan', *Indian Linguistics* 16: 29–34.

—— (1956) 'Some forms of the absolutive in Middle Indo-Aryan', *Journal of the American Oriental Society* 76: 111–15.

—— (1957) 'Notes on some Middle Indo-Aryan words in *-ll-*', *Journal of the American Oriental Society* 77: 203–7.

—— (1958) 'Gleanings from the *Vasudeva-hiṇḍi*', *Bhāratīya Vidyā* 18: 22–6.

—— (1959) 'Notes on two postpositions of Late Middle Indo-Aryan: *taṇaya* and *resi, resammi*', *Bhāratīya Vidyā* 19: 77–86.

—— (1962) 'The Middle Indo-Aryan prefix *vo-* "off" and some phonological problems associated with it', *Journal of the American Oriental Society* 85: 350–67.

Sen, S. (1962) 'Three lectures on Middle Indo-Aryan', *Journal of the Oriental Institute, Baroda* 11: 193–216.

Sen, S. K. (1973) *Proto-New Indo-Aryan*. Calcutta: Eastern Publications.

Shriyan, R. N. (1965) 'Some foreign loanwords in Puṣpadanta's Apabhraṁśa', *Bhāratīya Vidyā* 25: 26–37.

Siṁha, Ś. (1955) *Kīrtilatā aur avahaṭṭha bhāṣā*, Ilāhābād: Sāhitya Bhavan.

Sircar, D. Ch. (1943) *A Grammar of the Prakrit Language Based Mainly on Vararuchi, Hemachandra and Purushottama*, Calcutta: University of Calcutta. (2nd enlarged edition (1970) Delhi: Motilal Banarsidass).

Smith, H. (1932) 'Désinences du type apabhramça en pali', *Bulletin de la société de linguistique* 33: 169–72.

Tessitori, L. P. (1914–1916) 'Notes on the grammar of the Old Western Rajasthani with special reference to Apabhraṁśa and to Gujarātī and Maṛwāṛī', *The Indian Antiquary* XLIII–XLV.

Turner, R. L. (1926) 'The position of Romani in Indo-Aryan', *Journal of the Gypsy Lore Society* 5(4): 145–189 (Third series).

—— (1960) *Some Problems of Sound Change in Indo-Aryan*, Poona: University of Poona.

—— (1966, 1969, 1971, 1985) Vol. I: *A Comparative Dictionary of the Indo-Aryan Languages*, London: Oxford University Press. Vol. II: *Indexes*. Compiled by Dorothy Rivers Turner. Vol. III: Turner, R. L. and D. R. Turner, *Phonetic Analysis*. Distributed by the School of Oriental and African Studies. Vol. IV: *Addenda and Corrigenda*. Edited by J. C. Wright. London: School of Oriental and African Studies (All four volumes reprinted (1999), Delhi: Motilal Banarsidass).

—— (1985) *Indo-Aryan Linguistics. Collected Papers 1912–1973*, Delhi: Disha Publications.

Upadhye, A. N. (1931) 'Joindu and his Apabhraṁśa works', *Annals of the Bhandarkar Oriental Research Institute* XII: 132–63.

Vaidya, P. L. (1941) *A Manual of Ardhamāgadhī Grammar*, Poona: Wadia College.

—— (1952) 'On the use of Prākrit dialects in Sanskrit dramas', *Annals of the Bhandarkar Oriental Research Institute* XXXIII: 15–25.

Vertogradova, V. V. (1963) 'A classification of Ardhamāgadhī phonemes based on a classification of their distribution', *Kratkie soobščenija Instituta narodov Azii, Moskva* 61: 125–41.

de Vreese, K. (1954) 'Apabhraṁśa studies I & II', *Journal of the American Oriental Society* 74: 1–5, 142–6.

—— (1955) 'Did Middle Indian know an abl. sg. m. n. in *āṃ* ?', *Bulletin of the School of Oriental and African Studies* 17: 369–71.

—— (1959) 'Apabhraṁśa studies III', *Journal of the American Oriental Society* 79: 7–16.

—— (1961) 'Apabhraṁśa studies IV', *Journal of the American Oriental Society* 81: 13–21.

Vyas, K. (1984) 'Apabhraṁśa – its origin, literature and grammatical structure', *Bhāratīya Vidyā* 44: 1–38.

HINDI

Michael C. Shapiro

CONTENTS

LIST OF TABLES

1 INTRODUCTION

Hindi, generally considered by language statisticians to be anywhere from the third to the fifth most widely spoken language in the world, is spoken natively by upwards of

300 million people. The language is, along with English, one of the two officially recognized national languages of India. The major concentration of speakers of the language is in the Indian states of Uttar Pradesh, Uttaranchal, Madhya Pradesh, Chhattisgarh, Bihar, Jharkhand, Haryana, Rajasthan, Himachal Pradesh and Delhi, although not insignificant numbers of speakers of the language can be found throughout all of India. Distinctive non-standard varieties of Hindi are found in large urban areas of India outside of the so-called 'Hindi belt', with those spoken in Mumbai, Hyderabad (V. Sharma 1981), and Calcutta (Chatterji 1931, Jagannathan 1981) especially noteworthy. Various forms of Hindi are spoken as a second or subsequent language throughout South Asia and by many millions of people of north Indian extraction as part of a worldwide Indian diaspora. Several overseas forms of Hindi, particularly those spoken in Guyana, Suriname (where the language is known as Sarnami (Gambhir 1981, Damsteegt 1990) , Trinidad, Fiji (Moag 1977, 1986), Mauritius, and South Africa either have some order of political recognition (e.g. Fiji, Mauritius, Suriname) or are spoken by significant populations (Barz and Siegel 1988). In recent years the spread of this diaspora also has resulted in the establishment of communities of Hindi speakers in Europe, the United States and Canada. Hindi, together with its sister language Urdu, is spoken as a second or subsequent language by tens of millions of people in South Asia. The language also serves as a lingua franca in emigrant Indian communities throughout the world.

Providing speaker estimates for Hindi has been rendered difficult for several reasons. In the past, practice has been inconsistent with regard to how returns involving regional forms of Hindi, including the so-called 'Rajasthani' and 'Bihari' languages, are recorded and classified. There has been much inconsistency, not to mention political and bureaucratic controversy, on how returns involving such rubrics as 'Hindustani' and 'Urdu' are to be handled. The official 1991 returns for India show 337,272,114 speakers for Hindi (Vijayanunni 1997: 11), a 27.5% increase over the 264,514,177 figure obtained in the 1981 Census (Singh and Manoharan 1993: 292–4; Breton 1997: 192). Both the 1991 and 1981 figures, however, include returns entered under four dozen different rubrics, including not only those designating regional dialects of Hindi (e.g. Braj, Avadhi), but also some referring to speech varieties that from a strict linguistic point are languages distinct from Hindi (e.g. Maithili, Marwari).

2 MAJOR DIALECTS AND CLASSIFICATION WITHIN INDO-ARYAN

There are many factors that have complicated the enumeration of Hindi dialects and their classification. These have included confusion and inconsistency in the use of such terms as 'Hindi', 'Hindustani', 'Urdu' etc., variation as to which north Indian vernacular languages and dialects are to be allowed to fall under the umbrella of 'Hindi', the existence of a complex network of literary languages/traditions (e.g, Braj, Avadhi, Maithili, etc.) which at one time or another have been subsumed under the rubric of 'Hindi', the existence of different and sometimes conflicting schemata for the overall classification of Indo-Aryan languages, shifting practices and assumptions on the part of governmental bodies, language planners and commissions, and educational organizations as to what constitutes Hindi, and a complex and highly nuanced state of affairs with regard to socially determined registers of the language.

If there is anything approaching a consensus concerning the dialectology of Hindi, it is that there are two sets of dialects, referred to as 'western' and 'eastern' respectively, that constitute Hindi proper (Dh. Varma 1971: 16–20, Shapiro 1989: 3–5). Other speech varieties that are sometimes claimed for Hindi, i.e. the 'Bihari', 'Rajasthani', and

'Pahari' languages/dialects are excluded from Hindi proper. The western dialects of Hindi include Braj (western Uttar Pradesh and adjacent districts of Haryana and Rajasthan (Dh. Varma 1935, Liperovskij 1988)), Bundeli (west-central Madhya Pradesh (Jaiswal 1962)), Harianvi (also known as Bangaru, spoken in Haryana and some outlying areas of the National Capital Territory of Delhi (N. C. Sharma 1968)), Kanauji (west-central Uttar Pradesh, considered by some a form of eastern Braj), and Vernacular Hindustani (also called Kauravi, spoken to the north and northeast of Delhi). Eastern Hindi comprises three major dialects, Avadhi (north-central and central Uttar Pradesh (B. R. Saksena 1971), Bagheli (north-central Madhya Pradesh and south-central Uttar Pradesh), and Chhattisgarhi (southeast Madhya Pradesh and northern and central Chhattisgarh). The relationship between Avadhi and Bagheli is a particularly close one, causing Grierson (*LSI* VI:1) to consider separation of the two into separate dialects to be based primarily upon 'popular prejudice'.

An additional dialect of Hindi or Urdu that deserves mention is that of Dakhini (and sometimes called Dakhini Hindi or Dakhini Urdu). Although the language is centred in Hyderabad, capital of the modern state of Andhra Pradesh, it is also spoken in other urban areas of the Deccan Plateau with significant Muslim populations (Masica 1991: 426). The language has enjoyed status as the bearer of a substantial body of literature, particularly in the fifteenth to eighteenth centuries (Schmidt 1981: 1–13, Masica 1991: 426). The language continues to be spoken as a distinct regional dialect of Hindi or Urdu (V. Sharma 1981), with considerable influence noticeable from Telugu (Schmidt 1981: 58–64, Subbarao and Arora 1988).

The standard variety of Hindi, recognized by the Government of India and promulgated by educational agencies and organizations dedicated to the promulgation of the language, is based upon a western Hindi dialect, generally identified with the grammatical core of vernacular Hindustani, but also demonstrating features from other regional dialects (Harris 1966, Nespital 1990), adjoining Indo-Aryan languages, and even such non-Indo-Aryan languages as Persian. There are several names under which the standard variety of the language is or has been known. Although the 'official' name of the language is simply 'Hindi', in many grammar books the terms Standard Hindi, Modern Standard Hindi, or *Kharī Bolī* (lit. 'standing language') are used. The term *Kharī Bolī* is often subject to misinterpretation or confusion. As used by some writers the term can also refer to a particular regional dialect, Vernacular Hindustani, in the specific sense employed by George Grierson (Bahri 1980: 40, Masica 1991: 433). In this chapter the normative variety of Hindi is referred to as Modern Standard Hindi (MSH).

The grammatical core of Hindi is generally thought to be essentially the same as that around which standard Urdu evolved. The position within Indo-Aryan as a whole assigned to Hindi has varied in the highly divergent overall taxonomies proposed for Indo-Aryan. This is complicated by the fact that in some schemata for Indo-Aryan the western and eastern dialect groups do not occupy a single taxonomic node. In the *LSI*, for instance (as reported by Shapiro and Schiffman 1981: 79), western Hindi dialects constitute a subgroup (one of six) of a larger 'Central Group' of an 'Inner Sub-branch' of Indo-Aryan. The eastern dialects, by contrast, constitute a 'Mediate Group' of a 'Mediate Sub-branch' of Indo-Aryan. In Cardona (1974), by contrast, a 'Midland Group' of Indo-Aryan is postulated, within which both eastern and western Hindi, are contained.

The term 'Hindi' has in both popular and technical usages often been used in varied (and often contradictory) senses, thus complicating the description of the dissemination of the language. The term has frequently been used with reference to the vernacular languages of Rajasthan (Marwari, Mewari, etc.) as well as to the so-called 'Bihari' languages (i.e., Bhojpuri, Maithili, Magahi), despite the fact that these languages are linguistically independent of western and eastern Hindi. The term is commonly applied to the diaspora languages of Fiji, Mauritius, Trinidad, etc., even though the grammatical cores of these speech varieties is often derived from Bhojpuri or other 'Bihari' languages. In addition, the term 'Hindi' has been used indiscriminately with reference to speech varieties used in Indian cinema and popular music, even in cases where the vocabulary and idiom of the language employed more closely resemble the norms of Urdu than they do MSH.

3 REGISTERS AND STYLES OF THE LANGUAGE

A noteworthy characteristic of Hindi, in the most generic sense of the term, is the existence of a network of registers or styles. One of the most important cases of this concerns the dichotomy between Hindi and Urdu. There is substantial controversy, among professional linguistics, politicians, writers and members of the general public, as to how this dichotomy is to be analyzed. For some, Hindi and Urdu are two stylistic poles of a single language, Hindi-Urdu. Urdu is held to be that style of the language written in Perso-Arabic script, showing a high degree of learned vocabulary, a lesser degree of morphological and syntactic features, and a limited number of phonemes, borrowed from Persian and Arabic. Hindi is taken to be that style of the language, written in Devanāgarī, deriving its learned vocabulary primarily from Sanskrit, possessing some phonemes lost in the gradual evolution from OIA to NIA, but reintroduced in the modern period, and influenced to a considerable degree by Sanskrit processes of compound formation, derivational morphology, and sandhi. Countering this view is a opinion, which has gained an increasing number of adherents after the partition of India and Pakistan, that Hindi and Urdu, as bearers of distinct literary and cultural traditions, should be considered fully separate languages.

Further complicating the discourse concerning the relations among various styles or registers of Hindi/Urdu (or Hindi and Urdu) is the use of the term 'Hindustani' in any of a number of separate senses. Frequently the term has been used as a synonym for Urdu (C. R. King 1994: 198). In addition, the term has been used with regard to stylistically neutral speech variety of H/U, shorn of either the strongly Persian or Arabic linguistic correlates of literary Urdu or heavily Sanskritized features of *śuddh* 'pure' Hindi. This was the sense of the term used by Gandhi and Nehru with regard to a national language for independent India. To advocates of a view that sees Hindi, Urdu and Hindustani as stylistic variants of a common language, matters of script and literary history are of less importance than the shared grammatical, lexical features of the vernacular languages of the upper Gangetic valley, not to mention the unifying aspects of shared cultural traditions.

Although the main body of literature on varieties of Hindi has focused on regional dialects and definable registers related to the Hindi/Urdu/Hindustani nexus, it is possible to discuss varieties of the language in still other terms. It is possible to draw distinctions between urban and rural styles of the language, between formal and informal styles (Gumperz and Naim 1960), between educated and non-educated varieties, and among styles used in bi- and multilingual households, where different Indian languages coexist along with Hindi (i.e., Panjabi influenced Hindi, Bangla influenced Hindi, etc.). In addition, the types of Hindi used for specific purposes or in specific social milieus (governmental Hindi, newspaper Hindi, the Hindi of popular film and film songs, the Hindi of children, slang, etc.) have been described as possessing salient linguistic features of different kinds.

4 LITERARY TRADITIONS AND LINGUISTIC DEVELOPMENT

Writing a history of the Hindi language is rendered complex by a pronounced disjunction between the known facts of the literary traditions that are subsumed under the broad umbrella of the cultural history of the language and the linguistic data that are the raw material for historical linguistic reconstruction. The immediate roots of MSH are relatively young (dating back only to the early and middle decades of the nineteenth century). For the earlier sources of the language, however, one must look to a complex array of literary texts and textual traditions, for all of which, however, positing a direct path of evolution leading to MSH is problematic. Both within the Hindi and Urdu literary traditions many scholars attempt to assign as early a date as possible for the inception of Hindi, Urdu, or a common Hindi-Urdu literature. R. A. Dwivedi (1966: 5), for instance, sees the earliest period of Hindi literature as extending from 760 AD and extending up to the eleventh century. Such an early date for the inception of a Hindi literature, one made possible only by subsuming the large body of Apabhraṁśa literature into Hindi, has not, however, been generally accepted by scholars. A more prudent position (expressed in McGregor 1984: 3–9) sees the emergence of a Hindi-like NIA literature taking place in a highly complex and fluid context, within which Aprabhraṁśa played some role in influencing and helping to shape the nascent 'Hindi' vernacular. The more generally agreed upon starting places for 'Hindi' literatures several centuries later (twelfth–fourteenth centuries), lie in several bodies of texts. These include bardic epics of Rajasthan (of which the story of Ḍholā-Mārū is well known), some of which are believed to have been current as early as the late twelfth or early thirteenth century, and the so-called *rāsau* literature, involving panegyric verses, intended for recitation, concerning the exploits of well-known kings. One of these works, the *Pṛthvīrāj Rāsau*, of Chand Bardāī, a court poet to Pṛthvīrāj Cauhān, the last Hindu king of Delhi, is considered by some to be the first epic poem in Hindi (Handa 1978: 40). A different strand in the complex web of early 'Hindi' texts is to be found in the compositions of Amīr Khusrau (1253–1325), who wrote in a mixed style of Delhi, that has been claimed to be the precursor of both literary Urdu and MSH. Lastly, a body of devotional poetry was composed in the Mithila region of what is today north Bihar by Vidyāpati in the late fourteenth and early fifteen centuries. This body of devotional poetry, some of the most famous of which was written in the *pada* genre and much of which deals with the love of Rādhā and Kṛṣṇa, has been appropriated as an early milestone for each of Hindi, Bengali and Maithili literatures.

When looking at pre-modern Hindi literary dialects as a whole, it has been common to enumerate five such dialects of greatest importance, each of which can be conventionally associated with sets of texts and literary or cultural traditions. These dialects consist of

(1) Ḍingal (sometimes also called Old Rajasthani), associated with the Bardic traditions of Rajasthan and adjoining areas;
(2) Braj, strongly connected with the Vaiṣṇava traditions of Kṛṣṇa worship;
(3) Avadhi, associated with Sufi allegorical romances dating as early as the fourteenth century (Maulānā Dāūd's *Candāyan* (1379)) , and with the most renowned work of Rāma worship, and perhaps of all of Hindi literature, the Rāmāyaṇa version of Tulasīdās (*Rāmacaritamānasa*);
(4) *Sādhū Bhāṣā* (also called *Sant Bhāṣā* or *Sādhūkāṛī*), seen in the western recension of the works of the poet saints of the *nirguṇa bhakti* tradition (most particularly Kabīr (fifteenth century) and Nānak (1469–1539)); and

(5) Maithili, seen in the devotional tradition of north Bihar, as given highest expression in the works of Vidyāpati (b. 1360–80).

Although each of these five literary traditions can be understood as having a basis in the vernacular dialects of a particular region of north India, it need also be understood that some of them transcended the confines of single geographical areas of, and became literary vehicles extending broadly over, northern India. This is especially so of Braj, which served well into the nineteenth century across north India as a vehicle of literary expression for large segments of the population, both Hindu and non-Hindu. In this capacity Braj competed in a literary arena which also contained such other broad-based vehicles of literary expression as Sanskrit, Urdu and Persian.

To a great extent the emergence of MSH can be seen as a phenomenon that is thoroughly intertwined with the sweeping political, social and communal changes that took place in North India between the establishment of the British Rāj in 1858 in the wake of the Great Rebellion of 1857–8 and the granting in 1947 of independence to India and Pakistan. The roots of these changes, of course, go back earlier. The emergence of MSH cannot be fully understood except in reference to the prior forging of a literary Urdu, which took place in the sixteenth and seventeenth centuries, first in the Islamic courts of South India, most particularly Golconda and Bijapur, but later in such centres as Aurangabad in the Deccan and Lucknow and Delhi in the north. Although it is a commonplace to say that the grammatical core of this newly emergent literary Urdu was the language of the military camps in the Delhi area (often pointing to the fact that the word *Urdū* itself is a Turkic loanword, having the original sense 'encampment'), the identification of a specific linguistic system as the core for this putative language of the imperial camps is problematic. Some scholars see this language to be a composite, having a western 'Hindi' grammatical core, but with considerable admixture from Panjabi, Braj, local dialects and Persian. Others see the dialect of the camps to be firmly rooted in a regional dialect, in particular that of Delhi and regions to the north of it, and referred to as Vernacular Hindustani in one of the senses of that term.

In the nineteenth century, a complex array of forces served as an impetus for the establishment of a literary Hindi. One of these was the conscious effort to develop prose literature – medieval literary dialects such as Braj, Avadhi, etc. were used primarily for poetry – in a style of *Kharī Bolī*. This movement was given explicit sanction by the British with the establishment of Fort William College in Calcutta in 1800, and with commissioning of prose texts in *Kharī Bolī*. In the early decades of the century little theoretical importance was accorded to matters of script and, although actual practice tended to favour the use of Perso-Arabic script, both Perso-Arabic script and Devanāgarī were used for the writing of prose texts. By the third decade of the nineteenth century concerted efforts began to be made to cultivate a style of *Kharī Bolī* written in Devanāgarī (as opposed to Perso-Arabic) script. At the end of the nineteenth and beginning of the twentieth century these efforts were given added impetus by the establishment of a movement for the propagation of a Sanskritized register of Hindi. Two prominent organizations playing an active role in advocacy for a this new style of Sanskritized Hindi were the Nāgarīpracāriṇī Sabhā in Banaras (founded 1893) and the Hindī Sāhitya Sammelan in Allahabad (founded 1910) (C. R. King 1994). Towards the end of the nineteenth and early decades of the twentieth century the cause of Hindi was taken up by many talented writers, literary critics and journalists, among whom Bhāratendu 'Hariścandra' (1850–85), Mahāvīr Prasād Dvivedī (1864–1938), and the renowned novelist and short story writer Dhanpat Rai 'Premchand' (1880–1936) are noteworthy (Gaeffke 1978).

Efforts for advancing the cause of Hindi attained a plateau of success when the Eighth Schedule of the Indian Constitution of 1950 provided that the national language of the independent Republic of India was to be Hindi, written in the Devanāgarī script (R. D. King 1997: 74). This decision was not made, however, without substantial debate concerning what particular register within the so-called Hindi/Urdu/Hindustani nexus was to form the basis of the national language. Although all evidence points to Gandhi and Nehru having favoured a style of the language neither heavily Sanskritized nor excessively Perso-Arabicized, and written in either Devanāgarī or Perso-Arabic script, in the years subsequent to independence, Hindi was increasingly cast in a heavily Sanskritized mould. That form of the language taught in government schools, for which grammars and teaching materials were developed by newly established agencies and commissions, for which new vocabulary was coined in specialized and technical material, and in which much newspaper publication and television and radio broadcasting took place, bore the stamp of Sanskrit in terms of phonology, morphology, and particularly vocabulary and idiom.

In recent years the situation in India with regard to the status of Hindi has continued to evolve. At the beginning of the twentieth century, and even as late as the 1950s and 1960s, it was generally the case that there existed few genuine native speakers of *Kharī Bolī*. Most so-called Hindi speakers were actually native speakers of one or another regional dialects of Hindi, but with some degree of competence in the standard language learned through formal education. At present the effects of a half century of effort by the Government of India have clearly been felt. There are now tens of millions of people, including many living in geographical areas which would have been thought of as the heartlands of Braj, Avadhi, Bhojpuri, etc. whose native language is some variety of MSH. In addition, the massive spread of modern technologies of communication, including radio, television, film, and now the Internet, have had a standardizing effect, and brought heavy exposure of MSH to significant portions of the population in north India. There have also been noticeable changes that have taken place in the registers or styles of Hindi that are used for various functions and in different contexts. The new technologies of cable television and the Internet, together with an extraordinary growth in publications of all sort, have hindered the ability the Government of India to dictate the form of Hindi that is used throughout the nation. Thus efforts on the part of official institutions and Hindi advocacy organizations that lead towards increased Sanskritization of MSH are often contravened by tendencies, percolating up from the use of Hindi in various public spheres, towards a less Sanskritic and more heterogeneous register of the language.

5 SCRIPT, PHONETICS AND PHONOLOGY

Today MSH is conventionally written in the Devanāgarī syllabary. In earlier periods, varieties of Hindi were also written in different local scripts including Kaithī, Śāradā and Mahājanī. Prior to independence the use of Perso-Arabic script was common for many registers in the Hindi/Urdu/Hindustani nexus. At early stages in the development of many Hindi dialects manuscripts of important works of literature existed in both Devanāgarī and Perso-Arabic script. As late as the early decades of the twentieth century important 'Hindi' writers employed Devanāgarī and Perso-Arabic scripts interchangeably. The linkage of Hindi exclusively with Devanāgarī (as reflected in the occasionally encountered term *Nāgarī Hindī*) is a phenomenon that owes its origins primarily to the politics and sentiments of the past century.

The way in which Devanāgarī is used to write MSH is a modification of the use of Devanāgarī for representing Sanskrit. These modifications by and large reflect the ways in which Hindi's phonological system have evolved from the phonological systems of OIA and MIA. They also reflect the addition to Hindi's phonological inventory of phonemes borrowed from such non-Indo-Aryan languages as Arabic, Persian, Portuguese and English. To a great extent these modification are carried out by the addition of diacritics to Devanāgarī characters used in Sanskrit. Unfortunately, practice with regard to the use of diacritics to indicate loan phonemes is not always consistent. Some writers are meticulous in their use, others disregard them altogether, and still others are haphazard in their employment. Both Devanāgarī and Arabic numerals are available for Hindi, although the Constitution of India stipulates that only the Arabic numerals are sanctioned for official use. Punctuation in early Hindi Devanāgarī texts by and large follows Sanskrit usage. In the modern period punctuation has begun to follow English, with the exception of the use of *daṇḍa* (|) as a full stop. In the usage of contemporary magazines, newspapers and the Internet, however, the *daṇḍa* has begun to give way to the period. Despite inconsistencies in the usage of diacritics, the existence of overlapping phonological inventories in dialects and registers of the language, a considerable degree of biuniqueness exists between basic graphemes of Devanāgarī and phonemes of Hindi.

The phonemic inventory of MSH is best understood as consisting of a core of native Indo-Aryan phonemes, augmented by a set of loan phonemes (Mathews 1964; Kelkar 1968; Kostić, Mitter and Rastogi 1975, Mehrotra 1980). The precise enumeration of the set of core phonemes is complicated by several factors. Some Sanskrit phonemes (e.g., the retroflex sibilant *ṣ* , the vocalic *ṛ*, visarga) were eliminated in the course of the development of Hindi from OIA and MIA, but reintroduced as a result of learned borrowings of Sanskritisms back into Hindi. Likewise, phonemic contrasts that were productive in Sanskrit, were neutralized in Hindi in some word positions (e.g., short versus long vowel distinctions word-finally). Sanskritization of Hindi in the modern period has led to a situation in which there is for many speakers a disjunction between the set of phonemes in their operative phonemic systems and the set of phonemes necessary for the learned vocabulary in the educated register of the language. Such a disjunction also occurs with regard to permissible consonant clusters, where learned borrowings from Sanskrit, Arabic, English, etc. require a more extensive inventory than exist in the native Hindi stratum of the language.

The core phonemic inventory of MSH is generally held to consist of eleven vowels and thirty-five consonants. The analysis and schematization of vowels varies considerably in the scholarly literature, depending on whether one is choosing to represent output phonetic forms or more underlying abstract levels of structure. The first six phonemes have the phonetic (IPA) values [ə] or [ʌ], [a], [I], [i], [U] and [u] respectively, but often, following Sanskrit (and followed in this article), are taken to consist of three pairs of vowels, low back /a ā/, high front /i ī/, and high back /u ū/ respectively, with the first of each pair phonologically short and the second long. The seventh vowel, occurring only in learned Sanskrit borrowings, is the vocalic-r, transcribed generally as *ṛ*, and commonly pronounced in standard Hindi as an apical tap followed by the lax high front vowel [I], i.e., as [rI]. The remaining four vowels are /e/, /ai/, /o/, and /au/. /e/ and /o/ are monophthongal mid tense vowels, front and back respectively. The pronunciation of /ai/ and /au/ are variable, although monophthongal realizations as [æ] and [ɔ] based upon the pronunciation of educated Delhi usage, are standard. Diphthongal realizations of these ranging from [əI] to [aI] in the case of /ai/ and [əu] and [au] in the case of /au/ are common in eastern dialects and many non-standard western dialects. Vowel nasalization is phonemic for all vowels except /r̥/, and is represented in Devanāgarī by either of two diacritics, anusvāra ˙ and candrabindu ˜ (e.g. ई or ईँ). A summary of basic Hindi vowel phonemes, giving their phonetic values and their representation in Devanāgarī, is given in table 7.1.

Several additional features of Hindi segmental vowel phonemes are noteworthy. The phoneme /a/ (phonetically [ə] or [ʌ]) has a phonologically conditioned front allophone [ɛ] in proximity to /h/ (e.g., kahnā [kɛhna] 'to say'. The same /a/ phoneme is normally deleted in several predictable environments (Pandey 1980, Ohala 1983: 117–54, Ohala 1989), including:

(1) word-finally (e.g, *phal* 'fruit' [*phala*, as in Skt.]), except after consonant clusters having a glide as their final member (e.g., *bhrātratva* 'brotherhood');
(2) at the end of a nominal or verbal stem before a derivational or inflectional suffix (e.g. *miltā* [*milatā*] m.sg.imperfective particle of *milnā* 'to be available');
(3) when serving as the vowel of the second syllable of what is in writing a trisyllabic nominal base, if the vowel of the third syllable is other than *a* (e.g, *kursī* [*kurasī*] 'chair');
(4) when the vowel of the second syllable of a trisyllabic verbal stem, before a termination beginning with a vowel (e.g. *samjhī* [< *samajh-* + -*ī*] 3 sg.f. simple perfective of *samajhnā* 'to understand', not *samajhī*); and
(5) when the final sound in a stem standing as the first member of a compound (e.g. *ās-pās* [*āsa-pās*] 'close at hand, near'.

The phonemic opposition between the members of the pairs *i* and *ī* and *u* and *ū* is neutralized in word-final position. Words with inherited -*i* and -*u* (virtually all of which are direct borrowings from Sanskrit are pronounced with the tense vowels [i] and [u] respectively (e.g. *šakti* 'power, energy' is pronounced with a final [i] in place of the predicted [I], and *vastu* 'thing, item' with [u] in place of [U]). Lastly, nasalization of non-nasal vowels takes place in numerous environments (Narang and Becker 1971,

TABLE 7.1: VOWEL PHONEMES

Phoneme and Devanāgarī representation	Phonetic transcription	Phonetic description
a (अ)	[ə] or [ʌ]	mid central, tense or lax depending on position
ā (आ)	[a]	low back unrounded
i (इ)	[I]	high front unrounded lax
ī (ई)	[i]	high front unrounded tense
u (उ)	[U]	high back rounded lax
ū (ऊ)	[u]	high back rounded tense
r̥ (ऋ)	[rI]	apical tongue tap followed by short [I]
e (ए)	[e]	mid front unrounded tense
ai (ऐ)	[æ]	low front unrounded; diphthongal pronunciations in eastern and non-standard dialects
o (ओ)	[o]	mid back rounded tense
au (औ)	[ɔ]	low back rounded

TABLE 7.2: CONSONANT PHONEMES

	Bilabial	Labio-dental	Dental	Pre-palatal (retroflex)	Palatal (affricated)	Velar	Uvular	Glottal
PLOSIVES								
Voiceless, non-aspirated	p (प)		t (त)	ṭ (ट)	c (च)	k (क)	(q) (क़)	
Voiceless, aspirated	ph (फ)		th (थ)	ṭh (ठ)	ch (छ)	kh (ख)		
Voiced, non-aspirated	b (ब)		d (द)	ḍ (ड)	j (ज)	g (ग)		
Voiced, aspirated (=murmured)	bh (भ)		dh (ध)	ḍh (ढ)	jh (झ)	gh (घ)		
NASALS	m (म)		n (न)	ṇ (ण)	ñ (ञ)	ṅ (ङ)		
FRICATIVES								
Non-Sibilant, voiceless		(f) (फ़)				(x) (ख़)		h (ह) (ḥ) :
Non-sibilant, voiced							(ɣ) (ग़)	
Sibilant, voiceless			s (स)	ṣ (ष)	ś (श)			
Sibilant, voiced			(z) (ज़)					
APPROXIMANTS	v (व)				y (य)			
LATERAL APPROX.			l (ल)					
TAP				r (र)				
FLAPS: Non-aspirated				ṛ (ड़)				
Aspirated				ṛh (ढ़)				

Note: Loan phonemes are given in parentheses.

Ohala 1983: 77–116, Ohala 1989, Ohala and Ohala 1991), some instances of this having natural motivation in the course of Hindi's evolution from OIA (e.g, *cãd* 'moon' : Pkt. *canda*, Skt. *candra*), and others classified as 'sporadic' (e.g., *hãsī* 'laughter' : Skt. *hāsya*).

The basic set of thirty-five core consonantal phonemes consists of thirty-three consonants inherited from earlier Indo-Aryan, augmented by two additional consonants that represent internal developments of Sanskrit consonants in specific word medial contexts.

The traditional analysis of Hindi consonants closely follows that used for Sanskrit, dividing them into a sequence of five sets of five consonants, with the five sets arranged according to place of articulation, working from the rear of the oral cavity to the front. The first four of each set of five are stop consonants, and the fifth is a homorganic nasal. The five places of articulation are velar, palatal (phonetically realized as affricates), apical prepalatals (commonly referred to as retroflex), dentals and labials. In addition to the twenty-five so-called *vargīya* consonants (i.e. consonants arranged into *varga*s 'classes'), Hindi has four semivowels (Srivastava 1970), three sibilants, and an *h* sound. To these sounds can be added an unaspirated and an aspirated flap, which represent native Hindi developments of retroflex stop consonants in defined phonetic environments.

The loan phonemes that exist in the pronunciation of some Hindi speakers, and which are sometimes recorded in careful writing, are a uvular voiceless stop /q/, voiceless velar fricative /x/ a voiced uvular fricative /ɣ/, a labio-dental voiceless fricative /f/ (which for many Hindi speakers is completely replacing /ph/ in native Hindi words), and the voiced groove sibilant /z/. Sanskrit *visarga* (*ḥ*), occurring only in a limited number of direct Sanskrit loanwords (e.g. *ataḥ* 'hence') within the most Sanskritized register of the language, can be assigned a marginal status within Hindi's phonemic inventory. A summary of Hindi consonant phonemes is given in table 7.2.

Within the set of inherited phonemes several points are noteworthy. Hindi, in common with most Indo-Aryan languages, has a productive contrast between dental and retroflex stops. This same contrast in place of articulation is also found in the nasal series, although the retroflex nasal /ṇ/ has as a common allophone a nasalized flap [r̃]. Aspiration is phonemic for stops and the flaps. In the majority of studies of Hindi grammar the aspiration present in the voiceless stops (e.g. /kh/) is treated as if it were the same as that in analogous voiced stops (e.g. /gh/). Evidence from experimental phonetics, however, has demonstrated that the two types of sounds involve two distinct types of voicing and release mechanisms. The series of so-called voiced aspirates should now properly be considered to involve the voicing mechanism of murmur, in which the air flow passes through an aperture between the arytenoid cartilages, as opposed to passing between the ligamental vocal bands.

Several of the phonemes given in the basic inventory are not productive in a full range of environments. Three of the five nasals have limited distributions. The retroflex nasal /ṇ/ does not occur initially and the palatal and velar nasals (/ñ/, /ṅ/) occur only in consonant clusters preceding homorganic stop clusters, as variants of sequences of a nasal vowel followed by a stop consonant (e.g. *aṅg* 'limb' ~ *ãg*). The phonemic contrast between palatal and retroflex sibilants (/ś/, /ṣ/) is not operational in anything but the most Sanskritized registers of the language in extremely formal contexts. The phonemic status of the two flaps is marginal. It is possible to consider *r̤* and *r̤h* to be phonologically conditioned (i.e., word medial or word final) allophones of the retroflex voiced stops *ḍ* and *ḍh* if only native Indo-Aryan vocabulary are considered. The existence in Hindi of retroflex consonants as a result of the adaptation of English alveolar stops, however, has led to the existence of sets of contrasting forms such as *heḍ* 'head (of a department, organization, etc.') ~ *her* 'flock' (regional) ~ *her* 2 sg. imp. of *hernā* 'to seek, search'.

In the usage of some Hindi speakers neutralizations further reduce the inventory of phonemes. For some non-standard speakers all three sibilants are reduced to a single sibilant phoneme. The neutralization of *v* (pronounced as a bilabial voiced approximant, a bilabial voiced fricative, or a labio-dental voiced fricative) and *b* is common (e.g. MSH *bīvī* 'wife' ~ *bībī*). Likewise, retroflex nasals are often rendered as dentals in some varieties of non-standard Hindi.

An additional area of variability in Hindi phonology concerns the treatment of loan phonemes. Some speakers do not pronounce any or all of *q*, *x*, *ɣ*, *z* or *f*, and realizations are common that represent that pronunciation indicated by the Devanāgarī spelling of the word, with the subscript dot removed (e.g. [badʒar] instead of [bazar] for बाज़ार *bāzār*). In some instances, hypercorrect pronunciations are heard in which native Hindi words are pronounced with loan phonemes, as though the items were foreign borrowings (e.g., [fɪr] instead of [phɪr] for फिर *phir*).

In its formal registers MSH possesses a rich array of consonant clusters in initial, medial and final word positions (K. C. Bhatia 1964). The richness of the combinatorial possibilities can be attributed to the existence in Hindi of loan vocabulary from Sanskrit, Arabic, English and to a lesser extent Persian, in each of which a wide range of consonant clusters is possible. The introduction (or in the case of Sanskrit loans, reintroduction) of consonant clusters into Hindi, contravenes a broad historical tendency in the native core of Hindi vocabulary to eliminate consonant clusters through such processes as cluster reduction and epenthesis.

Although MSH demonstrates a range of phenomena roughly subsumed under the term 'stress', a precise characterization of Hindi stress (or accentuation) has proven difficult to formulate. Most attempts to formulate algorithms for the assignment of stress (e.g. Grierson 1895, Ray 1966, A. Sharma 1969, Pandey 1989, Shukla 1990) have been stated with reference to underlying configurations of syllables, described as short or long in terms of one or another theory of syllabic length or weight. The earliest of these formulations, by Grierson, was intended to describe stress not only in MSH, but in vernacular NIA languages as a whole. As summarized by Ohala (1983: 83), Grierson's stress rule, which is quite similar to rules commonly postulated for both Sanskrit and Latin, can be stated as follows:

> assign stress to the penultimate syllable if it is long, if it isn't, keep moving backward until you find a long syllable. (If no such syllable is found, the accent is thrown back as far as possible but no further than pre-antepenultimate if the word ends in a short vowel and antepenultimate if it ends in a long vowel.)

More recent formulations represent progressively more refined varieties of what is essentially the method of analysis set down by Grierson.

The phonemic status of stress is a matter of considerable controversy. Pairs of words have been adduced (Ohala 1986: 82) whose members are claimed to de differentiated solely by stress (e.g. *báhā* 'flowed' (simple perfective) versus *bahá* 'cause to flow' (imperative); *gálā* 'throat' versus *galá* 'melt' (imperative). It has been argued, however, that the according of phonemic status for putative stress differences in the members of pairs such as these cannot be supported by experimental acoustic data or empirical testing of Hindi speakers (Ohala 1983, 1986, 1991, 1999). This rejection of phonemic status for word stress in Hindi has itself been challenged by some scholars

(Fairbanks 1987, cited in Hayes 1995: 162–7) who find evidence for productive rules for stress assignment in Hindi, which ultimately are based on complex patterns of syllabic weight.

6 MORPHOLOGY AND SYNTAX

6.1 Morphology

In terms of its degree of overt morphological complexity, MSH represents a type of internal linguistic structure intermediate between that of such so-called 'analytic' languages as Thai and Chinese and 'polysynthetic' or 'agglutinative' ones such as Turkish and many native American Indian languages. A language of the so-called 'inflecting' type, MSH expresses grammatical categories through a mixture of means, including affixation (generally involving suffixes, which frequently express more than one grammatical category), word position, the use of free-standing grammatical function words (e.g. postpositions, particles), and compounding of different kinds (including the use of auxiliary forms). The morphology of the language includes both processes of inflection (which affect all members of a given grammatical class or part of speech) and those of derivation (through which new lexical stems are derived from other, underlying stems (Singh and Agnihotri 1997). The degree of complexity with regard to inflectional and derivational morphology exhibited by Hindi is roughly comparable to that of German, but considerably less than that of Latin, Classical Greek, Old English, or Sanskrit. Although there is a high degree of standardization in the core inflectional morphology of MSH, the terminology used by writers of reference and pedagogical grammars of the language (e.g, Kellogg 1875, A. Sharma 1858, Vajpeyi 1858, Shapiro 1989, McGregor 1995) to characterize and schematize these constructions varies greatly from writer to writer.

6.1.1 Nouns

All nouns in Hindi belong to one of two grammatical genders, masculine and feminine, each of which is further subdivided into two major declensional subtypes, which can be referred to as type-I and type-II respectively. Nouns are further marked with regard to the categories of number (singular versus plural) and case. Two cases (direct and oblique) are distinguished through affixation. In addition, the syntactic functions served by nouns relative to verbs (e.g. direct object, agent, indirect object, locus) often also are indicated by a distinct set of words, called postpositions, that are analogous to prepositions in English and many European languages. For the most part, the oblique case form of a noun is the form in which the noun appears when it is followed by a postposition. The form in which a noun appears when it is not followed by a postposition is in most circumstances the direct case. In addition to direct and oblique cases, all nouns referring to human beings may also have a special vocative case form in the plural, and in the singular of masculine type-I nouns. The singular direct case form of a noun is the form in which the noun is normally listed in dictionaries and by which it is generally cited.

Masculine type-I nouns show the characteristic ending -*ā* in the dir. sg., which becomes -*e* in the dir. pl., obl. sg., and voc. sg., -*õ* in the oblique plural, and -*o* in the voc. pl. A small number of masc. type-I nouns display nasalization of all terminations. Masculine type-II nouns have no distinct markings in the direct singular and may show any ending, including -*ā*. The direct singular and oblique singular is identical to the direct singular, while the oblique plural has the suffix -*õ* and the vocative plural -*o*. Masculine type-II nouns whose stems end in -*ū* generally shorten this vowel to -*u* before the terminations -*õ* and -*o* of the oblique plural and vocative plural respectively. Comparable nouns with stems ending in -*ī*, shorten the vowel to -*i* and insert the semivowel -*y*- before obl. and vocative plural terminations.

Feminine type-I nouns show any of the characteristic terminations -*ī*, -*i* and -*iyā* in the direct singular, which do not change in the obl. sg. Terminations for the direct plural, oblique plural and vocative plural are -*iyã*, -*iyõ* and -*iyo* respectively. Feminine type-II nouns show no characteristic termination in the direct singular (excepting the -*ī*, -*i* and -*iyã* of type-I feminine nouns) and the oblique singular is identical to the direct singular. The terminations of the direct plural, oblique plural, and vocative plural are -*ẽ*, -*õ*, and -*o* respectively. Example nouns representing these declensional patterns are given in table 7.3.

The rather sparse set of morphologically distinct cases exhibited by the above paradigms is inadequate to the task to denoting all the grammatically relevant case functions served by nouns relative to verbs. A set of independent words or multi-word units, referred to as postpositions, is employed in Hindi to specify many basic nominal (and pronominal) cases. These postpositions occur directly after nouns, which are placed in their oblique forms, and form with the nouns tightly bound syntactic units that function as basic sentence constituents. Hindi possesses several dozen common postpositions, of which those most often playing a role in delimiting basic case functions are *mẽ* 'in, among', *se* 'from, by means of', *par* 'on, at', *ko* (marks indirect object and, under specified conditions, direct object), *tak* 'as far as, up to', *ke liye* 'for the benefit of', and *ne* (indicates agent in defined environments). An additional postposition, which has the variable form *kā/ke/kī*, has a special role in the formation of possessive phrases. The use of specific postpositions for indicating case functions in Hindi is quite complex and it is not possible to establish one-to-one linkages between particular postpositions and particular case functions. In many instances the selection of postpositions to express case functions is lexically determined.

The variable postposition *kā/ke/kī* mentioned above is the dominant mechanism employed in Hindi in the formation of possessive phrases (Kachru 1970a). The schema

TABLE 7.3: NOUN DECLENSIONS

	Dir. sg.	Obl. sg.	Dir. pl.	Obl. pl.	Voc. pl.
Masc. Type-I	*larkā* 'boy' (voc.sg. *larke*)	*larke*	*larke*	*larkõ*	*larko*
	kuã 'well'	*kuẽ*	*kuẽ*	*kuõ*	——
Masc.Type-II	*seb* 'apple'	*seb*	*seb*	*sebõ*	——
	pitā 'father'	*pitā*	*pitā*	*pitāõ*	*pitāo*
	ādmī 'man'	*ādmī*	*ādmī*	*ādmiyõ*	*ādmiyo*
	cākū 'penknife'	*cākū*	*cākū*	*cākuõ*	——
Fem. Type-I	*larkī* 'girl'	*larkī*	*larkiyā*	*larkiyõ*	*larkiyo*
	śakti 'power'	*śakti*	*śaktiyā*	*śaktiyõ*	——
	dariyā 'river'	*dariyā*	*dariyā*	*dariyõ*	——
Fem. Type-II	*kitāb* 'book'	*kitāb*	*kitābẽ*	*kitābõ*	——
	mātā 'mother'	*mātā*	*mātāẽ*	*mātāõ*	*mātāo*

for such phrases is X *kā/ke/kī* Y, having the sense 'X's Y', with the *kā/ke/kī* element agreeing in gender, number and case with the following Y (e.g. *rām kā beṭā* 'Ram's son', *rām kī beṭī* 'Ram's daughter', *rām ke beṭe se* 'from Ram's son'). This construction, in which the adjectival modifier precedes the head noun of the phrase, contrasts with the so-called '*izāfat*' construction (e.g. *śer-e-pājāb* 'lion of the Panjab' [cf. MSH *pājāb kā śer*]), borrowed into Urdu (and, on rare occasions, into Hindi) from Persian and Arabic, in which the head noun precedes the qualifier.

6.1.2 Adjectives

Adjectives in Hindi are divided into two types, referred to as declinable and indeclinable. Declinable adjectives are marked for gender (masc./fem.), number (sing./pl.), and case (dir./obl./voc.). The terminations for masculine forms of declinable adjectives are -*ā* in the dir. sg. and -*e* in the obl. sg., dir. pl., obl. pl., voc. sg., and voc. pl. Feminine forms of declinable adjectives display the termination -*ī* throughout the entire paradigm. A small number of declinable adjectives display nasalization of all terminations. Paradigms for declinable adjectives are given in table 7.4.

Indeclinable adjectives show no particular base forms, and examples can be found ending in either consonants and vowels (e.g. *lāl* 'red', *bhārī* 'heavy'), including -ā (e.g. *zindā* 'alive').

Declinable adjectives agree with the nouns they modify in gender, number and case (e.g. *lambā laṛkā* '(a/the) tall boy', *lambe laṛke* 'tall boys', *lambe laṛke se* 'from a/the tall boy', *lambe laṛkõ se* 'from (the) tall boys', *lambī laṛkī* 'a/the tall girl', *lambī laṛkiyõ se* 'from (the) tall girls'. All adjectives can be used either attributively or predicatively (e.g. *lambā laṛkā* 'tall boy' versus *laṛkā lambā hai* 'the boy is tall'. In some circumstances, adjectives, as a result of the ellipsis of the nouns they are understood as modifying, may take the place of nouns, in which case they are declined as nouns rather than as adjectives (e.g., *baṛõ kī ādar karo* 'respect (your) elders' [cf. *baṛā* 'large, old']).

6.1.3 Pronouns

The pronominal system of MSH is rich in morphologically distinct forms. The language possesses personal pronouns, demonstrative pronouns (which also assume the functions of personal pronouns in the third person), interrogative pronouns, relative pronouns, and reflexive pronouns. The majority of these pronouns display distinctions of case and number. In addition, the pronominal system is susceptible at many points to contraction, and suppletive forms exist that take the place of particular pronouns followed by specific postpositions.

Hindi personal pronouns can be categorized in terms of person (1/2/3) and number (sg./pl.). The forms that serve as third person pronouns are actually demonstrative (or

TABLE 7.4: ADJECTIVE DECLENSIONS

	Dir. sg.	Obl. sg.	Voc. sg.	Dir. pl.	Obl. pl.	Voc. pl.
Masculine	*lambā* 'tall'	*lambe*	*lambe*	*lambe*	*lambe*	*lambe*
Feminine	*lambī*	*lambī*	*lambī*	*lambī*	*lambī*	*lambī*

deictic) forms, which can be categorized as proximate and non-proximate. In the second person, three separate pronouns are distinguished, *tū*, *tum* and *āp*, the first grammatically singular and the second and third grammatically plural. These three pronouns are further categorized as intimate, familiar, and polite respectively, with regard to a sociolinguistic scale of formality. The analysis of Hindi personal and/or demonstrative pronouns conventionally admits of a direct case form, an oblique form, an optional contraction equivalent to the simple oblique + *ko*, a possessive form and an agentive form incorporating the postposition *ne*. Relative and interrogative pronouns display full declensional paradigms that closely mirror those of personal and demonstrative pronouns. A small number of Hindi quantifier pronouns (*kuch* 'some', *kaī* and *anek* 'several') are indeclinable. The indefinite sg. pronoun *koī* 'some one person or thing' has a distinct oblique form *kisī*. The reflexive pronoun is the declinable *apnā*, which has a variant form *apne āp*. The form *apnā* also functions as an adjectival possessive flexive pronoun with the sense 'one's own'. A summary of the basic paradigms of common Hindi pronouns is given in table 7.5.

In most registers of Hindi the comparative and superative degrees of adjectives are formed by multi-word phrases involving the postposition *se* (e.g., *aśok lambā hai* 'Ashok is tall'; *aśok ajay se lambā hai* 'Ashok is taller than Ajay', *aśok ajay kā sab se lambā bhāī hai* 'Ashok is Ajay's tallest brother'). In Sanskritized and Persianized registers of the language, however, comparative and superlative adjectival forms showing the Sanskrit and Persian-derived suffixes *-tar/-tam* and *-tar/tarīn* respectively (e.g. *priya/priyatar/priyatam* 'dear/dearer/dearest'; *nek/nektar/nektarīn* 'refined, more refined, most refined' are also encountered. The Sanskrit-derived superlative suffix *-iṣṭh* appears in a limited number of Sanskrit loanwords, although sometimes lacking specifically superlative sense (e.g. *kaniṣṭh* 'younger, youngest').

TABLE 7.5: PRONOMINAL PARADIGMS

		Direct	Oblique	Obl. + *ko* (optional)	Possessive	Agentive
Personal and Demonstrative						
1. sg.		*maĩ*	*mujh*	*mujhe*	*merā*	*maine*
2. sg.	(int.)	*tū*	*tujh*	*tujhe*	*terā*	*tūne*
3. sg.	(prox.)	*yah*	*is*	*ise*	*iskā*	*isne*
	(non.prox.)	*vah*	*us*	*use*	*uskā*	*usne*
1. pl.		*ham*	*ham*	*hamẽ*	*hamārā*	*hamne*
2. pl.	(fam.)	*tum*	*tum*	*tumhẽ*	*tumhārā*	*tumne*
	(pol.)	*āp*	*āp*	*āpko*	*āpkā*	*āpne*
3. pl.	(prox.)	*ye*	*in*	*inhẽ*	*inkā*	*inhõne*
	(non.prox.)	*ve*	*un*	*unhẽ*	*unkā*	*unhõne*
Other						
Relative						
sg.		*jo*	*jis*	*jise*	*jiskā*	*jisne*
pl.		*jo*	*jin*	*jinhẽ*	*jinkā*	*jinhõne*
Interrogative						
sg.		*kyā* 'what?'/ *kaun* 'who?'	*kis*	*kise*	*kiskā*	*kisne*
pl.		*kyā* 'what?/ *kaun* 'who?/	*kin*	*kinhẽ*	*kinkā*	*kinhõne*

6.1.4 Adverbs

The class of Hindi adverbs, comprising adverbs of place (e.g. *yahā̃* 'here', *idhar* 'in this direction'), time (*āj* 'today', *hāl mẽ* 'recently'), manner (*aise* 'in this manner, thus', *jaldī se* 'quickly', degree (*bahut* 'very', *atyant* 'exceedingly'), affirmation and negation (*hā̃* 'yes', *nahī̃* 'no, not'), does not normally display any single inflectional marking. Many adverbs are freestanding single words, while others are postpositional phrases of one kind of another (A. B. Singh 1977), with postpositional phrases involving *se* very commonly (e.g. *rāt ko* 'at night', *ghar par* 'at home', *xuśī se* 'happily' [cf. *xuśī* 'happiness']). In some instances a noun or noun phrase in the oblique case, but not followed by a postposition, may function as an adverb (e.g. *savere* 'in the morning' [cf. *saverā* 'morning'], *is taraf* 'in this direction'. In formal registers of Sanskritized Hindi and Perso-Arabicized Urdu single-word adverbs are found that incorporate adverb-forming suffixes in Sanskrit and Persian or Arabic respectively (e.g. *sābhavataḥ* 'possibly' [= Skt. *saṁbhava* 'possible' + *-taḥ*]; *ittifāqan* 'by chance' [= Ar. *ittifāq* 'chance' + *-an*]). An additional type of adverbial phrase can also be formed in Hindi through reduplicative or quasi-reduplicative expressions of many kinds, including reduplicating forms of participles (Abbi 1977, 1980) and echo forms (A. B. Singh 1969).

6.1.5 Verbs

MSH possesses a wide variety of distinct verbal constructions, although very few of them can be said to embody only a single verbal category. The majority of verbal constructions can be seen to represent concatenations of verbal categories, which interact with each other to form a highly geometric verbal network (Allen 1950–1, Bahl 1967b: 174–479). At least in the modern standard language, the amount of morphological irregularity in the verbal system is relatively small, and even those irregularities that occur can be grouped into 'regular' patterns.

Unlike English, for which it can be plausibly argued that the single most productive verbal category is that of tense, the Hindi verbal system is largely structured around a combination of aspect and tense, with many verbal constructions morphologically marked for both of these categories (Lienhard 1961). The category of aspect, which provides a fundamental axis around which the verbal system is structured, is to be understood as indicating properties of a verbal action with regard to the beginning, duration, repetition or completion of an action, but without reference to the location of that action in time. Hindi contains three such aspects, referred to as the habitual, progressive (sometimes also called continuous) and perfective. Each of these aspects has overt morphological correlates. The habitual is formed from the so-called imperfective particles, which consist of the verbal stem, plus the suffix *-t-*, plus a vowel displaying gender, number agreement with the subject. The progressive is built upon a combination of the verbal stem, which occurs as an independent verb, plus the stem of the verb *rahnā* 'to remain', followed by a vowel showing gender and number agreement. The perfective is built upon the perfective participle which, although it displays a fair number of irregularities and morphophonemic adjustments, consists essentially of the stem plus a vowel indicating gender and number agreement.

The copula in Hindi *honā* 'to be' occupies a position in Hindi distinct from all other verbs (Kachru 1968). It occurs in four sets of forms, referred to as present, past, presumptive, and subjunctive respectively, which are grouped together under the category of 'tense', despite the fact that only the first two of these categories have anything to do with time. The four sets of forms of the copula, in addition to being used in basic predicative or existential sentences, serve as verbal auxiliaries in a wide variety of complex verbal constructions. The standard forms of the four sets of copula forms are given in table 7.6.

In characterizing the Hindi verbal system as a whole (excluding forms of the copula), it is useful to divide verbal constructions into aspectual ones and non-aspectual ones. Each of the three aspects described about can occur in conjunction with each of the four 'tenses' (manifest through the selection of an appropriate form of the copula), thus leading to the production of twelve aspectual tenses (present-habitual, past-progressive, presumptive perfective, etc.). In addition, the verbal system also allows the formation of a 'simple perfective', in which specification is given for aspect (i.e. perfective), but not for tense. A summary of aspectual verb forms, using the 3. sg. masc. forms of *calnā* 'to move' for example, is given in table 7.7.

Non-aspectual verb forms in MSH include the infinitive (which ends in *-nā* and functions as a masculine type-I verbal noun), the stem (formed from the infinitive by the removal of *-nā*), the root-subjunctive (as opposed to the subjunctive used in conjunction with verbal aspects), the future, and the imperative. The root subjunctive is formed by adding a special set of vowels ($\tilde{u}$ 1 sg.; *-e* 2/3 sg; *-ẽ* 1 pl., 2 pl. (pol), 3 pl., *-o* 2 pl. (fam.) to the verbal stem. The future (which is but one from among a large number of constructions available for indicating future time (Nespital 1981)) is formed by the addition of the suffix *-gā*(m.sg.)/*-ge*(m.pl.)/*-gī*(f.) (with appropriate gender/number

TABLE 7.6: FORMS OF THE COPULA (*HONĀ*) 'TO BE'

Description	Pronoun	Present	Past	Presumptive	Subjunctive
1 sg.	*mãĩ*	*hũ*		m. *hoũgā*	*hoũ*
			m.sg. *thā*	f. *hoũgī*	
2 sg. (int.)	*tū*	*hai*	f.sg. *thī*	m. *hogā*	*ho*
3 sg.	*yah/vah*	*hai*		f. *hogī*	
1 pl.	*ham*	*hãĩ*		m. *hõge*	*hõ*
			m.pl. *the*	f. *hõgī*	
2 pl. (fam.)	*tum*	*ho*	f.pl. *thĩ*	m. *hoge*	*ho*
				f. *hogī*	
(pol.)	*āp*	*hãĩ*		m. *hõge*	*hõ*
3 pl.	*ye/ve*	*hãĩ*		f. *hõgī*	

TABLE 7.7: ASPECTUAL VERB FORMS

	Habitual	Progressive	Perfective
	stem + *-t-* + V ## *honā*	stem## *rah* + V ## *honā*	stem + V ## (*honā*)
Simple			*calā*
Present	*caltā hai*	*cal rahā hai*	*calā hai*
Past	*caltā thā*	*cal rahā thā*	*calā thā*
Presumptive	*caltā hogā*	*cal rahā hogā*	*calā hogā*
Subjunctive	*caltā ho*	*cal rahā ho*	*calā ho*

Note: ## represents a word boundary; V indicates a vowel marking gender/number agreement; forms are cited in the masculine singular.

agreement) to the subjunctive. A small number of verbs (*lenā* 'to take', *denā* 'to give', *honā* 'to occur') show irregular subjunctive and future paradigms. MSH recognizes five so-called 'imperative' verb forms, referred to as intimate, familiar, polite, deferred and deferential, and manifest by the bare stem, the stem + *-o*, the stem + *-iye*, the infinitive, and the polite imperative + *-gā* respectively. The selection of the first three of these is linked directly to the selection of options from among the three second person pronouns *tū, tum* and *āp*. The verbs *lenā* 'to take' and *denā* 'to give' show the irregular fam. imperatives *lo* and *do*. The polite imperatives for *lenā, denā, karnā* 'to do', and *pīnā* 'to drink/smoke' are likewise irregular (*lījiye, dījiye, kījiye, pījiye*). A summary of non-aspectual verb forms is given in table 7.8.

The greatest number of grammatical peculiarities in the core verbal morphology of MSH is to be found in the perfective aspect (Pořízka 1967–9). Some of these involve irregularities in the perfective participles of some common verbs (e.g. *gayā/gaye/gaī/gaĩ* from *jānā* 'to go', *huā/hue/huī/huĩ* from *honā* 'to occur', *kiyā/kiye/kī/kĩ* from *karnā* 'to do'). More noteworthy, however, is the existence in MSH of the so-called 'ergative' construction (S. M. Gupta 1986a, Montaut 1989, 1992) wherein the verbs in the perfective aspect agree not with their grammatical subjects, as is the case with other verbal constructions, but rather with their direct objects. When this occurs, the subject is followed by the 'ergative' postposition *ne* and placed in the oblique case. If the direct object is itself followed by a postposition (as is often the case when it refers to humans, the verb occurs in its 3 masc. sg. form by default:

> *rām   ne   xūb   miṭhāiyā̃ khāī hõgī*
> Ram   erg. a lot sweets   must have eaten
> m. sg.   f. pl.   3 pl. f. presumpt. perf. of *khānā* 'to eat'
> 'Ram must have eaten a lot of sweets'.

> *anitā   ne   soniyā ko   skūl mẽ   dekhā thā*
> Anita   erg. Sonia dir.obj. school in had seen
> f. sg.   f. sg.   m. sg. past. perf. of *dekhnā* 'to see'
> 'Anita had seen Sonia in school.'

but

> *anitā   abhī   soniyā   ko   dekh rahī hai*
> Anita   right now   Sonia   direct object is looking at
> f. sg.   f. sg.   3. sg. f. pres. prog. of *dekhnā*
> 'Anita is looking at Sonia right now.'

TABLE 7.8: NON-ASPECTUAL VERB FORMS

Stem	*cal*
Infinitive (= stem + *-nā*)	*calnā*
Root subjunctive	*cale* (3. sg.)
Future	*calegā*
Imperative: Intimate (=stem)	*cal*
Familiar (= stem + *-o*)	*calo*
Polite (= stem + *-iye*)	*caliye*
Deferred (= infinitive)	*calnā*
Deferential (= pol. imperative + *-gā*)	*caliyegā*

In addition to a core verbal morphology as described above, MSH possesses several other constructions worthy of note. Perfective and imperfective participles, often extended with some form of the simple perfective of *honā* (i.e., *huā, hue,* etc.) or reduplicated, are used in a wide variety of adjectival and adverbial functions (Pořízka 1950, 1952, Burton-Page 1957b). 'Compound' aspectual constructions exist, wherein the perfective or imperfective participle is followed by either *rahnā* or *jānā* (e.g. *baiṭhā* 'to remain seated', *jātā rahnā* 'to keep on going', *baṛhtā jātā* 'to keep on (gradually) advancing'). The language possesses a 'frequentative' construction in which a verbal noun, formed from the stem of a verb (with occasional modification) by addition of the invariable suffix *-ā*, is followed by *karnā* 'to do' (e.g. *paṛhā karnā* 'to make a habit of studying'). A combination of a special declined form of the infintive (ending in *-ne* and referred to as the oblique infinitive) and the declinable adjective-forming suffix *-vālā* is used in several distinct senses. It can serve as an agentive noun (as in *hindī bolnevālā* 'Hindi speaker' [cf. *bolnā* 'to speak']) and it can serve as a quasi predicate adjective indicating the imminent onset of an action in sentences such as *rām jānevālā hai* 'Ram is about to go'. The oblique infinitive followed by *lagnā* (literally 'to adhere') constitutes a quasi-aspectual inception (e.g. *jāne lagnā* 'to begin to go'). There are two separate voices in MSH, active and passive, with the passive formed from the perfective participle by the addition of the auxiliary *jānā* (e.g. *xarīdā jānā* 'to be bought' [cf. *xarīdnā* 'to buy'] (Gaeffke 1967: 39–94, Shapiro 1974: 193–210, A. Saksena 1978, Pandharipande 1979, 1981. Davison 1982, Montaut 1990, 1991). There are many complexities in the use of the so-called passive in MSH, however, and many applications are passive in form only, with representation of negative capability one of the most common:

kal	*rāt ko*	*mujh se*	*soyā nahī̃ gayā*
yesterday	at night	me-by	was not slept
			3 sg. m. simple perf. pass. of *sonā* 'to sleep'

'I couldn't manage to get to sleep last night.'

Three common modal constructions are formed in Hindi by the use of auxiliary verbs *saknā, pānā,* and *cuknā,* the first two indicating capability to carry out an action (although the second is generally restricted to the negative), and the third indicating the prior completion of an action (e.g. *khā saknā* 'to be able to eat' [cf. *khānā* 'to eat'], *nahī̃ khā pānā* 'not to be able to eat', *khā cuknā* 'to have already eaten').

Several other aspects of Hindi verbal grammar are quite distinctive and have been the subject of much investigation by past linguists and grammarians. Particularly noteworthy are conjunct verbs, compound verbs and morphologically related verb sets. Conjunct verbs (Burton-Page 1957a, Hacker 1961, Gaeffke 1967: 95–207, Van Olphen 1973, Bahl 1974, 1979, Shapiro 1974: 211–31, Kachru 1982) comprise either a noun or adjective plus a verbal element, most commonly *karnā* 'to do' or *honā* 'to be', with the entire combination functioning in the place of a single unified verb (e.g. [X *kī*] *pratīkṣā karnā* 'to wait [for X]' [cf. *pratīkṣā* n.f. 'waiting, expectation']; [X *kī*] *pratīkṣā honā* ['for X] to be waited for'; cf. *ṭhaharnā* 'to wait, stay'). Compound verbs (also called V_1V_2 compounds) consist of a verbal stem V_1, which comprises the lexical core of the compound, and a subsidiary verb V_2 referred to by grammarians variously as an auxiliary, an explicator verb, or a vector verb (Hacker 1958, 1961, Bahl 1967: 328–459, Hook 1974, 1978, Shapiro 1974: 129–92). Virtually any main verb in MSH can serve as a V_1, but the class of V_2 elements is limited, with only *ānā, jānā, lenā, denā, rakhnā, baiṭhnā, paṛnā, uṭhnā, pahucnā, calnā, ḍālnā, marnā* and *mārnā* occurring with any degree of productivity. Considerable attention has been paid by scholars to determining the semantic properties contributed by the selection of particular V₂ verbs for use in particular compounds (Burton-Page 1957a, Hook 1974, 1978). In many cases, the meaning contributed by V₂ element bears scant resemblance to the literal meaning of the V₂ element when it occurs as an independent verb. Thus for example, it is not possible to explain the semantic difference between *uṭhnā* 'to rise, get up' and *uṭh baiṭhnā* 'to get up suddenly, to spring up' in terms of the semantics of *baiṭhnā* 'to sit down'.

A highly visible aspect of the verbal grammar of MSH, and one that is shared with other NIA languages, is the presence of morphologically related verb sets, often including a distinct 'causal' member (Kachru 1966: 62–80, Bahl 1967a, Upadhyaya 1970, Shapiro 1976). The members of each set share a common semantic core as well as shared phonological features. In the case of some such sets it is possible to divide the members into analogous intransitive, transitive and causal verbs (e.g. *jalnā* v.i. 'to burn, ignite' : *jalānā* v. tr. to burn, ignite: *jalvānā* v. caus. 'to cause to burn, to have someone else burn something'). Unfortunately, the phonological and semantic traits displayed by many other verb sets cannot be so simply characterized. Some sets have members whose phonetic shapes that are related by complex rules of derivation. Derivational rules that suffice to relate the members one set to one another often do not hold for other sets. The intransitive/transitive/causative pattern is not exhibited in some sets. Sets exist that can have as many as four of five distinct members (e.g. *dikhnā/dīkhnā* v. i. 'to seem, appear' : *dekhnā* v. tr. 'to see, look at' : *dikhānā* v. tr. 'to show' : *dikhvānā* v. caus. 'to cause to show') or as few as one (e.g. *jānā* 'to go'). The meanings of certain members of given sets may be idiosyncratic. Thus, *mārnā*, which is the transitive analogue to *marnā* 'to die', has the meaning 'to strike, beat, hit', rather than the predicted meaning 'to kill', for whose expression the V₁V₂ compound verb *mār ḍālnā* is required. A list of some representative verb sets is shown in table 7.9.

6.2 Syntax

As applied to Hindi, the term 'syntax' refers to a disparate set of linguistic phenomena, many of whom need also be understood with reference to, or have implications for, morphology, pragmatics, sociolinguistic considerations and the like. The notion of a level of 'autonomous syntax', wherein it is possible to generate formal strings of syntactic elements, without reference to semantics and morphological features such as case marking, inflection and agreement, is of only marginal utility for the language.

TABLE 7.9: MORPHOLOGICALLY RELATED VERB SETS

girnā 'to fall (intr.)'	*girānā* 'to fell (tr.)'	*girvānā* 'to have something felled'
bannā 'to be made (intr.)'	*banānā* 'to make (tr.)'	*banvānā* 'to cause to make'
khulnā 'to open (intr.)'	*kholnā* 'to open (tr.)'	*khulvānā* 'to cause to open'
sīkhnā 'to learn (tr.)'	*sikhānā* 'to teach (tr.)'	*sikhvānā* 'to cause to learn'
khānā 'to eat (tr.)'	*khilānā* 'to feed (tr.)'	*khilvānā* 'to have someone feed'
biknā 'to be sold (intr.)'	*becnā* 'to sell (tr.)'	*bikvāna* 'to cause to be sold'
dikhnā/dīkhnā (intr.) 'to seem, appear'	*dekhnā* (tr.) 'to see'	*dikhānā* (tr.) 'to show' *dikhvānā* 'to cause to show'
kahnā 'to say (tr.)'		*kahlānā* 'to be called (intr.)'

For purposes of exposition it is useful to divide the syntax of Hindi into that which is applicable at the level of the individual clause and that whose domain is bi- and multi-clausal structures. At the level of the individual clause noteworthy syntactic features of MSH include word order, a contrast between what has been referred to as 'direct' versus 'indirect' syntax (Van Olphen 1973), question formation (Nespital 1994), negation (T. K. Bhatia 1973), reflexivization (Davison 1965, Kachru 1977, Kachru and Bhatia 1977, Saxena 1985b, Mayee 1987) and some additional properties of constructions (e.g. conjunct and compound verbs, ergatives, passives) that have already been discussed with regard to their purely morphological properties.

In terms of basic word order, Hindi has generally been considered to be an SOV language. With regard to directionality of branching, MSH is neither purely left-branching nor right-branching, and phenomena can be found that are of both these types. There are no hard and fast rules governing the order of constituents in sentences as a whole, and frequent deviations are found from putative 'normative' word position, which can be described in terms of a small number of rules, which account for facts over and beyond those implicit in the SOV formulation:

(1) when both a direct object and an indirect object are present, the latter precedes the former;
(2) attributive adjectives precede the nouns they modify;
(3) adverbs modifying adjectives precede the adjectives;
(4) negatives markers (*nahī̃, na, mat*) and question words (e.g. *kab* 'when', *kyõ* 'why', *kidhar* 'in which direction') precede the verb;
(5) if both a question marker and a negative are present, the question marker precedes the negative;
(6) the yes–no question marker *kyā* (which is not to be confused with the homophonous question word meaning 'what') occurs at the beginning of a clause.

These principles are illustrated in the following sample sentence:

kal	*āp-ne*	*mere ghar par*	*kiśor ko*	*nayā upanyās*	*kyo nahī̃*	*diyā?*
yesterday	you-erg.	my house par (adv.)	Kishor to	new novel	why not	gave
Adv.-time	S	Adv.-place	IO	DO	Inter. neg.	V

'Why didn't you give the new novel to Kishor yesterday at my house?'

The so-called 'indirect verb construction' represents an important and interesting feature of MSH syntax. This construction for the most part is used to represent psychological states or conditions, physical sensations, judgements or perceptions and other internal states of different kinds. In this construction, the noun indicating the animate (and most often human) being or beings having the psychological state, sensation, etc. appears in the oblique case and is followed by the postposition *ko*. The animate parties in such structures are sometimes known as dative subjects, patients or experiencers (Kachru 1970b, Van Olphen 1976, Davison 1985) to differentiate them from the subjects in sentences displaying direct syntax. The noun indicating the emotion, psychological state, sense perception, etc. appears as the grammatical subject of the sentence, whose verb is usually one of the common intransitive verbs *honā* 'to be', *lagnā* 'to adhere', *paṛnā* 'to fall', *milnā* 'to be available', or *ānā* 'to come'. Some representative indirect verb constructions include the following: X *ko pyās lagnā* 'for X to feel thirsty' (cf. *pyās* n.f. 'thirst'); X *ko āśā honā* 'for X to hope' (cf. *āśā* n.f. 'hope'); X *ko buxār ānā* 'for X to come down with a fever' (cf. *buxār* n.m. 'fever'); X *ko* Y *kā patā honā* 'for X to know about Y' (cf. *patā* n.m. 'information'); X *ko* Y *pasand honā* 'for X to like Y' (cf. *pasand* 'pleasing').

A productive sub-system of indirect verb constructions in Hindi pertains to sentences indicating obligation or necessity (Shapiro 1989: 132–5). One type of such construction involves a verbal marker *cāhiye* (which is a fossilized reflex of a passive form of a verbal root *cāh-* 'to wish, desire, lack') and has the schematic form X *ko* Y *cāhiye*, where Y can stand for either a simple noun phrase or an entire infinitival form:

mātājī	*ko*	*ṭhāḍā*	*pānī*	*cāhiye*
mother-honorific	to	cold	water	is needed

'Mother needs cold water.'

mātājī	*ko*	*ṭhāḍā*	*pānī*	*pīnā*	*cāhiye*
mother-honorific	to	cold	water	to drink (inf.)	is needed

'Mother ought to drink cold water.'

Similar constructions can be formed if the infinitive element is followed either by some form of *honā* 'to be' or *paṛnā* 'to fall', both indicating the necessity for carrying out the action specified by the infinitive, but with the construction with *paṛnā* implying that the obligation arose as a result of external circumstances:

pichle	*hafte*	*pitā-jī*	*ko*	*kānpur*	*jānā thā/paṛā*
last	week	father	to	Kanpur	had to go

'Father had to go to Kanpur last week.'

At the bi- and multi-clausal level, important areas of Hindi syntax concern the means by which clauses standing in various relations to one another are joined together. These include devices of coordination and subordination, with the overwhelming majority of types of clausal linkage involving subordination of one type or another. Complex multi-clausal sentences include linking with those in which the clauses preserve much of their independent structure when they are linked together, usually by means of subordinating conjunctions or other overt morphology and sentences in which the dependent clause is, in effect, nominalized and used to replace a constituent in the main (or 'matrix' clause). In complex sentences involving subordination, it is possible for the dependent clause to either precede or follow the independent clause (Donaldson 1971, Klaiman 1976, S. M. Gupta 1986b). This is quite evident in complex sentences involving relative clauses:

jis	*kursī*	*par*	*dīdī-jī*	*baiṭhī hai*	*vah*	*banāras*	*mē*	*banī thī*
which	chair	on	big sister-hon.	is seated	it	Banaras	in	was made

vah	*kursī*	*banāras*	*mē*	*banī thī*	*jis*	*par*	*dīdī-jī*	*baiṭhī hai*
this	chair	Banaras	in	was built	which	on	big sister-hon.	is seated

'The chair on which Big Sister is sitting was made in Banaras.'

In many sentences containing predicates of saying, thinking, reading, understanding, etc. – i.e. predicates capable of having objects representable in the form of sentential propositions – the clause representing the sentential proposition is introduced by the 'complementizer' *ki* (Subbarao 1976, 1984), which is a historical borrowing from Persian:

laṛkā	*soctā hai*	*ki*	*yah*	*film*	*acchī hai*
boy	thinks	that	this	film	good is

'The boy things that this film is good.'

mujhe   mālūm nahĩ   thā   ki dukān   āj   khulī   nahĩ   hai
to me   known not   was that store today   open   not   is
'I didn't know that the store isn't open today.'

This *ki* element is found incorporated in several subordinating conjunctions, including *kyõki/cũki* 'because', *hālãki* 'even though, and *is liye ki* 'for this reason, because'. The complementizer *ki* can also serve as a replacement for other subordinating elements, such as *jab* 'when' and *yā* 'or'.

   A further productive means for achieving bi-clausal linkages is the so-called '*kar*' structure, which is used for a number of functions of which the most frequent is temporal subordination (Dwarikesh 1971, Abbi 1984, Davison 1986). In this construction, the verb in the first of two clauses, which generally must share a common subject, is given in stem form followed by the grammatical marker *kar* (under certain conditions also *ke* or Ø). The subject shared by the two clauses is given only once and full verbal inflections are added to the verb in the temporally subsequent clause. The inflectional categories provided for this second clause is understood as pertaining to the verbs in both the prior and subsequent clauses:

rūpal   kām   se   vāpas   ā-kar   ṭī vī   dekhne lagī
Rupal   work from   back   having come   t.v.   started to watch
'Rupal returned from work and started to watch t.v.'

In some instances *kar* constructions become dislodged from their origins and clausal connecting devices and take on the function of fixed manner adverbials (e.g. *xuś ho-kar* 'happily' [cf. *xuś* adj. 'happy'], *do do kar ke* 'two at a time' [cf. *do* 'two']).

7 LEXICON

Given the prominence that MSH, its precursors, and stylistic variants have enjoyed within South Asian society and culture, it is no surprise that the lexicon reflects the diversity of the languages with which Hindi, in its various guises, has come in contact over the past centuries. The lexicon of Hindi, as reflected in standard dictionaries of the language (e.g. Platts 1884, Das 1965–75, McGregor 1993) is extraordinarily rich, abounding in a multiplicity of synonyms (Barannikov 1961, Bahl 1974, 1979), near-synonyms, and words evoking specific cultural, intellectual or specialized associations. Educated speakers of Hindi, who command a broad band of the lexical resources available to Hindi speakers, draw upon, manipulate, and even play with these resources as they use the language for diverse purposes.

   The conventional way of characterizing the lexical stock of MSH is to divide it into lexemes of Indo-Aryan origin and non-IA loan lexemes of various kinds. The Indo-Aryan stratum conventionally is further broken down into words of 'native' Hindi origin, i.e., words that although they ultimately can be derived from OIA forms, have undergone a continuous and unbroken path of evolution from OIA through MIA, and direct borrowings from Sanskrit, unmediated by MIA and early NIA. The native lexemes, designated *tadbhava* (literally 'located in that [i.e., Sanskrit]') and which constititute the lexical core of the language, permeate Hindi in all its stylistic variants, regional dialects and social registers. Common examples include such words as *āg* 'fire' (OIA *agni:* MIA *aggi*); *ãkh* 'eye' (OIA *akṣi*: MIA *akkhi*), *āj* (OIA *adya*: MIA *ajja*), and *bhāt* 'boiled rice' (OIA *bhakta*: MIA *bhatta*) (Tiwari 1969: 200–11, Shackle and Snell 1990: 28–9). *Tadbhava* lexemes are generally held in contradistinction to another class of lexemes, designated *tatsama* (lit. 'the same as that [i.e. Sanskrit]'), which refer to learned borrowings directly from Sanskrit, which have not undergone gradual modification throughout the history of IA. The term *tatsama* can be somewhat misleading, however, as it is sometimes used to refer both to actual attested words in Sanskrit (e.g. *karma* 'action, karma', *kṣetra* 'field', *guru* 'heavy', *atyanta* 'exceedingly', *nakṣatra* 'asterism'), but also to modern neologisms and loan translations formed out of Sanskrit building blocks (e.g. *dūrdarśan* television (especially the state-owned national television network in India; cf. *dūra* 'distant' + *darśana* 'viewing'), *gṛha-mantrī* 'Home Minister' (= *gṛha* 'house' + *mantrī* 'minister'), *vidyut-cālita* 'electrically propelled' (cf. *vidyut* 'electricity' + *cālita* 'propelled'), *kāryakārī* 'acting, pro tem' (= *kārya* 'action, deed' + *kārī* 'doing'), *madhyāvakāś* 'intermission, half-time' (= *madhya* 'mid, middle' + *avakāś* 'leisure'). As a result of the existence of both of these types of lexical items, MSH often possesses pairs of *tadbhava/tatsama* doublets (e.g. *varṣ* [*tatsama*] ~ *baras* [*tadbhava*] 'year').

The primary sources of non-IA loans into MSH are Arabic, Persian, Portuguese, Turkic and English. Conversational registers of Hindi/Urdu (not to mentioned formal registers of Urdu) employ large numbers of Persian and Arabic loanwords, although in Sanskritized registers many of these words are replaced by *tatsama* forms from Sanskrit. The Persian and Arabic lexical elements in Hindi result from the effects of centuries of Islamic administrative rule over much of north India in the centuries before the establishment of British rule in India. Although it is conventional to differentiate among Persian and Arabic loan elements into Hindi/Urdu, in practice it is often difficult to separate these strands from one another. The Arabic (and also Turkic) lexemes borrowed into Hindi frequently were mediated through Persian, as a result of which a thorough intertwining of Persian and Arabic elements took place, as manifest by such phenomena as hybrid compounds and compound words. Moreover, although the dominant trajectory of lexical borrowing was from Arabic into Persian, and thence into Hindi/Urdu, examples can be found of words that in origin are actually Persian loanwords into both Arabic and Hindi/Urdu. The common noun *daftar* 'office', for example, is actually an old Greek loanword (having the sense 'hide'/animal skin) into Persian, from which it was borrowed into Arabic and Hindi/Urdu, where its sense shifted to 'file' (i.e. group of documents bound with a hide) and eventually 'office' (i.e. place where files are stored).

The Arabic component of the MSH lexicon includes a large number of words in common use, in addition to the myriad lexemes that are restricted to Perso-Arabicized registers of the language. Some representative examples include *kursī* 'chair', *kitāb* 'book', *sāhab* 'sir, gentleman, Mr.', *qilā* 'fort', *xayāl* 'idea, intention', *imtahān* 'examination', *istemāl* 'use, utilization', *mālūm* 'known', *taraf* 'direction', *imārat* 'building', *fauran* 'immediately', *aksar* 'immediately', *vaqt* 'time', *muqāblā* 'comparison, confrontation', *bilkul* 'entirely', *zarūr* 'certainly', *śurū* 'beginning', *savāl* 'question', *śakal* 'form, appearance', and *inām* 'prize'. In some instances, Arabic loanwords into Hindi/Urdu incorporate elements of the inflectional or derivational morphology of Arabic (Shackle and Snell 1990: 49–59), including dual and plural markers (e.g. *vālidain* 'parents' [cf. *vālid* 'father'], *imtahānāt* 'examinations'), gender markers (e.g. *sāhibā* 'Mrs.'), and prepositions (*fī śaxs* 'per person' [= Ar. *fī* + *śaxs* 'person').

The contribution of Persian to the lexical composition of MSH is immense (Bahri 1960). In the course of the history of the language many native IA words have been replaced by Persian loanwords, a process facilitated no doubt by the existence in both IA and Iranian of lexical doublets arising from the status of IA and Iranian as parallel divisions of the overarching Indo-Iranian sub-branch of Indo-European. Loanwords from Persian into Hindi took place in diverse semantic spheres ranging from government and administration (*śāh* 'king', *darbār* 'royal court', *farmān* 'decree') the arts (*sitār* 'sitar', *kārīgar* 'craftsman'), agriculture and horticulture (*bādām* 'almond', *gulāb* 'rose, rose-water'), household realia (*darvāzā* 'door', *śīśā* 'mirror, glass'), geography and topography (*pājāb* 'Panjab', *dariyā* 'river'), common descriptive adjectives (*xūb* 'abundant, good', *kam* 'few', *xuś* 'happy', *kamzor* 'weak'), parts of the body (*sīnā* 'chest', *kamar* 'waist', *dil* 'heart', and animalia (*śer* 'lion'), to family members (*baccā* '[male] child') and even the name *hīdī* 'Hindi' itself. In addition, many Persian derivational morphomes can be seen in areas of the lexicon, not only in combination with other Persian morphemes (e.g. *bandargāh* 'port' [= *bandar* 'port' + -*gāh* 'place'], *kośiś* 'attempt' [= *koś* 'trying' + -*iś* forms abstract nouns]), but also in combination with Arabic or native Hindi elements (e.g. *be-īmān* 'dishonest' [= *be-* 'without, in-, un-, dis-' + Ar. *imān* 'honest'], *beḍaul* 'misshapen' (= *be-* + *ḍaul* [*tadbhava* Hindi] 'shape, form'). In Persian, many derivational suffixes are in origin present stems of verbs. Many of these are borrowed into Hindi/Urdu where they retain their productivity (Shackle and Snell 1990: 65–6) (e.g. -*bīn* [from *dīdan* 'to see'] in *dūrbīn* 'telescope', *māl-* [from *malidan* 'to rub'] in *rūmāl* 'handkerchief' [cf. *rū* 'face']).

The Turkic component in Hindi/Urdu is significantly more restricted than that of either Arabic or Persian. The Turkish loan stratum in NIA has been so thoroughly mediated through Persian that it is often difficult to disentangle Turkic lexemes from Iranian ones. Of the Turkic lexical borrowings that have been enumerated for Hindi, Urdu, Hindustani etc. (Spies 1955), a relatively small number are current in MSH. Some of these in most general use are *beg* (fem. *begam*) 'man (woman) of high status', *kāīcī* 'scissors', *top* 'field gun, cannon', *coya* 'a type of cloak' and *urdū* 'camp, encampment, the Urdu language'.

European languages too have left their mark on the Hindi lexicon, the two major sources being Portuguese and English. From Portuguese were borrowed such common terms as *almārī* 'cupboard', *kamrā* 'room', *cābī* 'key', *mistrī* 'artisan, mechanic', and *girjā* 'church'. The English contribution, of course, has been far more extensive and pervasive and, given the popularity of English medium education, of the spread of global television networks and the Internet, and the international dominance of English in the spheres of science and technology, shows no signs of abating. The English contribution to Hindi vocabulary can be seen in many aspects of the Hindi lexicon. It appears in well-established and thoroughly nativized loan items that are used by virtually all members of the Hindi-speaking community (e.g. *hoṭal* 'hotel', *fon* 'telephone (call)', *skūl* 'school', *lāin* 'line', *reḍiyo* 'radio', *ījīniyar* 'engineer', *sṭeśan* 'station'). It can also appear in the form of newer loans arising from the worldwide spread of new technology and popular culture (e.g., *kampyūṭar*, *ḍisko*,), some of which even appear in hybrid complex words, parts of which derive from other strata of the vocabulary (e.g., *kampyūṭīkaraṇ* 'computerization' [*kampyūṭar* + -*īkaraṇ* Skt. suffix indicating 'transformation into']).

The effects of English on the Hindi lexicon in many instances go behind direct borrowing of words or derivational elements (Snell 1990). Loan translation based from English models is a frequent phenomenon, whether in the case of single words (e.g. *stambh*, literally 'pillar, column' for newspaper column, *sitārā* 'star' [itself a Persian loan into Hindi] for film star), phrasal idioms, or entire sentential patterns as when, for example, a sentence such as *tum baṛī jaldī mẽ ho* (lit. you-fam. big hurry in are) 'You are in a great hurry' uses the phrase *baṛī jaldī mẽ* 'in a big hurry', clearly based upon an

English model, as a variant of the sentence *tumko baṛī jaldī hai* (lit. to you big hurry is) with indirect syntax (i.e. having a dative subject with *ko*).

8 DISCOURSE GRAMMAR

MSH possesses many linguistic devices by which sentences (and, in some instances, clauses or isolated phrases) are woven together in the formation of large chunks of discourse. For the most part, the use of such devices is dependent upon forms that have already been enunciated in prior discourse. An important example of the class of discourse markers in MSH is the set of so-called particles (Kaul 1990), comprising *hī*, *bhī*, and *to* (each of which has several additional functions). The particle *to*, for example, is frequently used to pose a constituent of a sentence in contradistinction to a constituent already operative in discourse from an immediately preceding sentence (Shapiro 1999). Thus in the sequence

> *rājū   śikāgo mẽ   rahtā hai, gopāl to   vahā̃   nahī̃   rahtā*
> Raju   Chicago in   lives   Gopal *to* there   not   lives
> 'Raju lives in Chicago, [but] Gopal [by contrast] doesn't live there.'

the element *to* serves to introduce a new subject, Gopal, who is held in contrast to the earlier subject Raju. The particles *hī* and *bhī* can function within discourse either to mark a linguistic constituent as a unique member of a set of comparable entities or to include an item into such a set, which is already known from discourse:

> *ãjulī hī /   ãjulī bhī   mere fon   kā nambar jāntī hai*
> Anjuli only/ Anjuli also   my   phone of   number knows
> 'Only Anjuli/ Anjuli also knows my telephone number.'

Devices that are used to link sentences together go beyond sentence particles. Several words or phrases are employed, often in senses different from their literal meanings, in sentence final (or sometimes initial) position in such as way as to affect linkages between speakers taking part in multi-speaker verbal interactions. Such markers include the indeclinable *zarā* (as opposed to the homophonous declinable adjective meaning 'little, a little bit [of]'), *na, kyõ na, kyā,* and *vaise to*. In addition, MSH, at least in its spoken variety, employs a complex and subtle system of syntactic displacements from normative word order. Some of the most common of rules are those whereby a word or phrase is placed after the verb in sentence final position:

> *bahut kām   kiyā āp-ne*
> much work   did you-erg
> 'You did much work'

where an attributive adjective, frequently in the form of a possessive phrase, is moved after the noun it modifies (e.g. *dost āp-kā* in place of *āp-kā dost* 'your friend'), or where a structural element, including even the copula is moved to the beginning of a sentence:

> *is tarah   kī hindī   yahā̃ log   nahī̃ bolte*
> this kind of Hindi here   people not   speak
> 'People don't speak this kind of Hindi here.'

> *hai to   vah   hindustānī lekin lagtā hai jāpānī*
> is *to* he   Indian   but   seems   Japanese
> '[It's true] he's Indian, but he seems Japanese.'

A further type of discourse-related phenomenon in Hindi concerns the matter of pronominal selection with regard to the complex interrelationships holding among the persons who engage in verbal interaction. This is an exceedingly complex and understudied area of grammar, involving not only purely linguistic consideration, but factors of pragmatics, social structure, and interpersonal dynamics. As mentioned earlier, MSH possesses three distinct second-person pronouns, the grammatically singular intimate form *tū* and the plural forms *tum* (int.) and *āp* (pol.). Only *tum* and *āp* can be used in specifically plural senses; all three, however, can be used to refer to a single person. The selection of a specific pronoun in a specific context is sensitive to a complex array of factors, including the degree of respect being accorded to the addressee, relationship between the speaker and addressee (in terms of relative age, social status), the social context (i.e. whether informal or formal), whether anyone else is present, and the temporary disposition of the speaker towards the addressee (i.e., whether being warm, distant, angry, sarcastic, etc.), and semantic factors (Jain 1973, Sinha 1987). It is not infrequently the case that between given pairs of speakers, any of the three pronouns may be employed in different circumstances. Similar considerations arise with regard to selections between the singular and plural pronouns in both the first- and third-persons.

Related to matters of pronominal selection are issues pertaining to the selection among competing verb forms. A prominent example concerns ways of issuing commands or making requests. Hindi possesses abundant means for making utterances whose pragmatic function is to cause a listener to carry out some course of action. This class of utterances subsumes what are conventionally referred to as commands and those referred to as requests, differing primarily in the degree of politeness with which the statements are made. In MSH such occurrences include not only the five types of imperatives, but also sentences in the subjunctive (and often the passive subjunctive), indirect verb constructions involving infinitive + *cāhiye/honā/paṛnā* etc., and rhetorical questions involving tag markers. The selection from among these options is highly nuanced and involves the manipulation of a subtle set of sociolinguistically determined politeness distinctions (Jain 1969, 1975, S. M. Gupta 1980). These distinctions are manifest even in such matters as whether traffic instructions on road signs in Hindi-speaking areas are to be given in the subjunctive, *tum* imperative, or *āp* imperative, where actual practice often varies from region to region, and where gradual changes are taking place with regard to preferred usage (e.g. the replacement of the polite imperative by the root subjunctive).

9 HISTORICAL DEVELOPMENTS

Constructing a coherent narrative describing the historical pathways by which MSH developed from earlier stages of IA is by no means an easy task. It is complicated by any number of factors. First there is the eclectic nature of the standard language itself, based upon a historical dialect of 'Western' Hindi dialect, but incorporating features from non-western dialects, adjacent IA languages, and even non-IA languages such as Persian. Related to this is the fact that the set of dialects that comprise Hindi, even in the strict sense that includes only Western and Eastern Hindi, cannot be shown to derive from any single Prakrit or Apabhraṃśa dialect. In at least one important scholarly analysis (Chatterji 1926 I: 6), the immediate precursor of the Western Hindi dialects is said to be Śaurasenī Apabhraṃśa, while that for the Eastern Hindi dialects is Ardha-māgadhī Apabhraṃśa. Further complicating matters are the pervasive and long-lasting effects of

Sanskrit on Hindi and other NIA languages. In many instances natural developments affecting one or another level of the language have been offset by the reintroduction of Sanskrit forms or constructions, thus reintroducing contrasts that were lost earlier. In addition, relatively few changes that have taken place in the evolution of Hindi have been limited only to Hindi. Many are common to NIA as a whole or to subgroups within NIA. Unfortunately, it is not possible to establish a constant subset of NIA languages which share a major portion of the developments that affect Hindi (Masica 1991: 187–211). The type of taxonomic grouping in which dialect (and eventually) language divisions within a language family are determined by the relative thickness of bundles of isoglosses (marking the limits of shared linguistic innovations) is notoriously hard to do with regard to Hindi and other NIA languages.

At the phonological level, MSH exhibits a wide variety of changes affecting the nature and distribution of segmental phonemes. Many of these changes are common to the majority of NIA languages and have been described in standard comparative grammars of NIA (e.g. Beames 1882–9, Bhandarkar 1877, Hoernle 1880, Bloch 1934) and modern studies of the historical phonology of Hindi (Misra 1967, Učida 1977, 1978). Some of the most common of these changes are the following:

(1) the loss of final vowels, including some long vowels, which are believed to have become short in Apabhraṁśa (Masica 1991: 188) (e.g. MSH *khet* 'field' : MIA *khetta* : OIA *kṣetra*; MSH *rāt* 'night' : MIA *rattī* : OIA *rātri*; MSH *lāj* 'shame', MIA, OIA *lajjā*);

(2) degemination of MIA medial geminate consonants with compensatory lengthening of a preceding short vowel (e.g. MSH *sāṭh* 'sixty' : MIA *saṭṭhī* : OIA *ṣaṣṭi*; MSH *sūt* 'thread' : MIA *sutta*: OIA *sūtra*; MSH *īkh* 'sugar cane' : MIA *ikkhu* : OIA *ikṣu*; MSH *hāth* : MIA *hattha*: OIA *hasta*); in some cases nasalization, sometimes referred to as 'spontaneous', takes place even where no historical nasal consonant was present (e.g. MSH *ĩṭ* 'brick' : MIA *iṭṭā* : OIA *iṣṭakā* ; MSH *kãc* 'glass' : MIA *kacca* : OIA **kācca*);

(3) in the case of medial consonant clusters whose first member is a nasal, dropping of the nasal consonant, with compensatory nasalization of the preceding vowel (e.g. *cãd* 'moon' : MIA *canda* : OIA *candra*; MSH *bãdh* 'dam' : MIA, OIA *bandha*; MSH *dãt* 'tooth' : MIA, OIA *danta*);

(4) coalescence into long vowels and diphthongs of sequences of vowels resulting from the loss of intervocalic single consonants (Masica 1991: 189–91, Učida 1977) (e.g. MSH *dūnā* 'double' : MIA *dūṇa* : OIA *dviguṇa* ; MSH *mor* 'peacock' : MIA *maūra* : OIA *mayūra*);

(5) the development of the flap consonants *ṛ* and *ṛh* from several different intervocalic consonants or consonant sequences (e.g. *thoṛā* 'a little, few' : MIA *thogā* : OIA *stoka* 'drop' : MIA *baṛā* 'large, old' : MIA *vaḍḍa* : OIA *vaḍra*; MSH *baṛhaī* 'carpenter' : MIA *vaḍḍhaki* : OIA *vardhaki*); and

(6) the substitution of *b* for *v*, the effects of which are obscured by the reintroduction into MSH of *tatsama* lexemes containing *v* (e.g. MSH *byāh* 'wedding' : MIA, OIA *vivāha*, but also MSH *vivāh*).

In the evolution of the morphological system of MSH some of the most important changes have concerned the means by which basic morphological categories have been expressed. With regard to nouns, pronouns, and adjectives, this has involved the gradual decrease in importance of inflectional case endings (a tendency already well established in the transition between OIA and MIA) and the increased use and functional importance of postpositions, words that for the most part owe their origins to OIA inflected nouns or nominal expressions (e.g. MIA *mẽ* 'in, among', ultimately from OIA *madhye*; (*ke*) *pās* 'in the possession of, near', from OIA *pārśve*) (Oberlies 1998: 11). In early stages of Hindi we find an extraordinary diversity of postpositional forms, with different early NIA texts displaying different sets of competing forms, alternating with inflected forms, both with and without attached postpositions (Ridgeway 1986). Gradually the situation tilted in the direction of postpositional usages, with inflected cases severely limited. The emergence of the so-called agentive form of nouns and pronouns, marked with *ne* (together with the distinctive pattern of object-verb agreement), is a particularly important historical development in Hindi.

In the verbal system, noteworthy developments include the following:

(1) the elaborate system of $V_1 V_2$ compounds, used to express subtle shadings of meanings ways broadly similar to the use of prefixes (*upasarga*) plus verbal root combinations in OIA and MIA (e.g. MSH *baiṭh jānā* 'to sit down' : OIA *upa* + *viś*-);

(2) the development and spread of N or Adj. + verb conjuncts, originally under Persian influence, and with the noun or adjective element frequently calqued from Persian or Arabic into a *tatsama* Sanskrit form (e.g. Pers. *rāzī kardan* 'to satisfy' > Urdu *rāzī karnā* > Hindi *santuṣṭ karnā* (Shackle and Snell 1990: 72));

(3) the development of a periphrastic passive using the auxiliary *jānā*, first alongside of and then in place of an historical passive formed with reflexes of the Skt. passive suffix -*ya* (e.g. *pāyā jātā hai* 'is found' : Braj *pāīai* : OIA *prāpyate*);

(4) the use of an originally periphrastic future in -*g* formed from an incorporated use of a derivative of the root *gam*- 'to go', gradually replacing historical futures formed with -*h*- or -*s*-, which are the reflexes of future terminations in OIA and MIA (e.g. *karegā* 3. sg. masc. fut. of *kar*- 'to do': *karasī* [Guru Nānak]/ *kariha* [Braj] : OIA *kariṣyati*);

(5) the gradual shift in meaning and function of the old historical present indicative to that of the subjunctive, with the place of historical tenses taken over by newer aspectual tenses (MSH *cale* 'he/she might go' [= 3 sg. subj. of *calnā* 'to move, go'] : *caltā hai* 'he (habitually) goes [3. sg. masc. pres. hab.] : MIA *calaï* : OIA *calati*);

(6) the drastic simplification of complex allomorphic variation in the perfective forms of verbs (e.g. in Nānak *kītā*, *kīā*, *kīnhā* alternate as m. sg. perf. of *kari*- 'to do', whereas in MSH the standard form is only *kiyā* [cf. OIA *kṛta*]).

In terms of syntax, the single most notable historical development in MSH is the shift from an older left-branching pattern of quotation with markers such as *iti* to one in which quoted information is extraposed to the right and introduced complementizers such as *ki*, borrowed from Persian. The extension right-branching patterns of syntax in complex sentences, in which extraposed clauses of various kinds are introduced by means of complementizers, is an extremely prominent development in Hindi, as well as in many other NIA languages. Lastly, the spread of patterns of indirect syntax, involving constructions of many different types (e.g. X *ko* Y *pasand honā* 'for Y to be pleasing to X', X *ko hindī ānā* 'for X to be able to speak Hindi', X *ko* infinitive (=Y) + *honā* 'for X to have to do Y'), is highly characteristic of the development of MSH.

ACKNOWLEDGEMENTS

I am most grateful to David Smith for research assistance he provided with regard to the bibliography for this chapter. I would also like to thank Professors Paul R. Brass, Manjari Ohala and Bernard Comrie for insights they provided in discussions of specific points raised in this chapter. I am, of course, solely responsible for all errors and inaccuracies.

REFERENCES

Abbi, A. (1977) 'Reduplicated adverbs in Hindi', *Indian Linguistics* 38: 125–35.
—— (1980) *Semantic Grammar of Hindi: A Study in Reduplication*, New Delhi: Bahri Publications.
—— (1984) 'The conjunctive participle in Hindi-Urdu', *International Journal of Dravidian Linguistics* 13: 252–63.
Aggarwal, N. K. (1985) *A Bibliography of Studies on Hindi Language and Linguistics* (2nd ed.), Gurgaon: Indian Document Service.
Allen, W. S. (1950–51) 'A study in the analysis of Hindi sentence structure', *Acta Linguistica* 6.2–3: 68–86.
Bahl, K. C. (1967a) 'The causal verbs in Hindi', in *Languages and Area Studies: Studies Presented to George V. Bobrinskoy*, Chicago: University of Chicago, Division of the Humanities: 6–27.
—— (1967b) *A Reference Grammar of Hindi: A Study of Some Selected Topics in Hindi Grammar*, Chicago: University of Chicago, Department of South Asian Languages and Civilization, mimeographed.
—— (1974, 1979) *Studies in the Semantic Structure of Hindi: Synonymous Nouns and Adjectives with* karanā), Vol. 1, Delhi: Motilal Banarsidass, Vol. 2, Delhi: Manohar.
Bahri, H. (1960) *Persian Influence on Hindi*, Allahabad: Bharati Press.
—— (1980) *Grāmīṇ Hindī Boliyā̃*, Allahabad: Kitāb Mahal.
Balachandran, L. B. (1971) *A Case Grammar of Hindi with a Special Reference to the Causative Sentences*, unpublished Cornell University Ph.D. dissertation.
Barannikov, P. A. (1961) 'Style synonyms in modern Hindi', *Indian Linguistics* 22: 64–81.
Barz, R. K. and J. Siegel (eds.) (1988) *Language Transplanted: The Development of Overseas Hindi*, Wiesbaden: Otto Harrassowitz.
Beames, J. (1872–9 [repr. 1970]) *A Comparative Grammar of the Modern Aryan Languages of India*, New Delhi: Munshiram Manoharlal.
Bhandarkar, R. G. (1877 [repr. 1974]) *Wilson Philological Lectures on Sanskrit and the Derived Languages*, Poona: Bhandarkar Oriental Institute.
Bhatia, K. C. (1964) 'Consonant sequences in Standard Hindi', *Indian Linguistics* 25: 206–12.
Bhatia, T. K. (1973) 'On the scope of negation in Hindi', in Kachru, B. B. (ed.) *Papers on South Asian Linguistics (Studies in the Linguistic Sciences* 3.2), pp. 1–27.
—— (1987) *A History of the Hindi Grammatical Tradition*, Leiden: E. J. Brill.
Bloch, J. (1934 [tr. 1965 by A. Master]) *Indo-Aryan: From the Vedas to Modern Times*, Paris: Adrien-Maisonneuve.
Breton, R. J.-L. (1997) *Atlas of the Languages and Ethnic Communities of South Asia*, Walnut Creek: AltaMira Press.
Burton-Page, J. (1957a) 'Compound and conjunct verbs in Hindi', *Bulletin of the School of Oriental and African Studies* 19: 469–78.
—— (1957b) 'The syntax of participial forms in Hindi', *Bulletin of the School of Oriental and African Studies* 19.1: 94–104.
Cardona, G. (1974) 'The Indo-Aryan Languages', *Encyclopedia Britannica*, 15th ed., 9: 439–50.
Chakroborty, J. (1992) 'Perfectivity and the resultive state in Hindi', *South Asian Language Review* 2: 55–67.

Chatterji, S. K. (1926 [repr. 1970]) *The Origin and Development of the Bengali Language*, London: George Allen and Unwin.
—— (1931) 'Calcutta Hindustani: A Study of a Jargon Dialect', *Indian Linguistics* 1: 2–4.
—— (1960) *Indo-Aryan and Hindi* (2nd ed.), Calcutta, K. L. Mukhopadhyay.
Damsteegt, T. (1990) 'Hindi and Sarnami as literary languages of the East Indian Surinamese', in M. Offredi (ed.), *Language Versus Dialect: Linguistic and Literary Essays on Hindi, Tamil, and Sarnami*, Delhi: Manohar, pp. 47–63.
Dās, S. S. (1965–75) *Hindī Śabdsāgar* (rev. ed.), Varanasi: Nāgarī Pracāriṇī Sabhā.
Davison, A. (1965) 'Reflexivization and movement rules in relation to a class of Hindi psychological predicates', *Chicago Linguistics Society* 5: 37–52.
—— (1982) 'On the form and meaning of Hindi passive sentences', *Lingua* 58: 149–79.
—— (1985) 'Experiencers and patients as subjects in Hindi-Urdu', in Zide, A. R. K. Magier, D. and Schiller, E. (eds.), *Proceedings of the Conference on Participant Roles: South Asia and Adjacent Areas*, Bloomington, IN: Indiana University Linguistics Club, pp. 160–78.
—— (1986) 'Hindi *-kar*: the problem of multiple syntactic interpretation', in Krishnamurti, Bh., Masica, C. P. and Sinha, A. K. (eds.), *South Asian Languages: Structure, Convergence and Diglossia*, Delhi: Motilal Banarsidass: 1–14.
Donaldson, S. K. (1971) 'Movement in restrictive relative clauses in Hindi', in Kachru, Y. (ed.), *Papers on Hindi Syntax* (*Studies in the Linguistic Sciences* 1.2), pp. 14–74.
Dwarikesh, D. P. S. (1971) *Historical Syntax of the Conjunctive Participle Phrase in New Indo-Aryan Dialects of Madhyadeśa (Midland) of Northern India*, unpublished University of Chicago Ph.D. dissertation.
Dwivedi, R. A. (1966) *A Critical Survey of Hindi Literature*, Delhi: Motilal Banarsidass.
Fairbanks, C. (1987) 'Hindi stress: a new approach through meter', unpublished ms., University of Minnesota, Department of Linguistics.
Gaeffke, P. (1967) *Untersuchungen zur Syntax des Hindi*, The Hague: Mouton.
—— (1978) *Hindi Literature in the Twentieth Century*, Wiesbaden: Otto Harrassowitz (Gonda, J. (ed.), *A History of Indian Literature*, Vol. VIII, fasc. 5).
Gambhir, S. (1981) *The East Indian Speech Community in Guyana*, unpublished University of Pennsylvania Ph.D. dissertation.
Grierson, G. A. (1895) 'On the stress-accent in the modern Indo-Aryan vernaculars', *Journal of the Royal Asiatic Society of Great Britain and Ireland* 1895: 139–47.
—— (1903–28 [repr. 1967]) *Linguistic Survey of India*, Delhi: Motilal Banarsidass.
Gumperz, J. J. and Naim, C. M. (1960) 'Formal and informal standards in the Hindi regional language area', in Ferguson, C. A. and Gumperz, J. J. (eds.) *Linguistic Diversity in South Asia* (= *International Journal of American Linguistics* 26.3), pp. 92–118.
Gupta, S. M. (1980) 'Indirect request in Hindi: a pragmatic approach', *Indian Linguistics* 41.2: 85–90.
—— (1986a) 'Development of ergativity in Hindi', *Indian Journal of Linguistics* 13: 89–110.
—— (1986b) *Discourse Grammar of Hindi: A Study in Relative Clauses*, New Delhi: Bahri Publications.
Guru, K. P. (1920) *Hindī Vyākaraṇ*, Vārāṇasī: Nāgarīpracāriṇī Sabhā.
Hacker, P. (1958) *Zur Funtion einiger Hilfsverben im modernen Hindi*, Wiesbaden (Abhandlungen der Akademie der Wissenschaften und der Literaturs in Mainz, Geistes- und Sozialwissenschaftliche Klasse, Jahrgang 1958, No. 4).
—— (1961) 'On the problem of a method for treating the compound and conjunct verbs in Hindi', *Bulletin of the School of Oriental and African Studies* 24: 484–51.
Handa, R. L. (1978) *A History of Hindi Language and Literature*, Bombay: Bharatiya Vidya Bhavan.
Harris, R. W. (1966) 'Regional variation in urban Hindi', *Indian Linguistics* 27.1: 58–69.
Hayes, B. (1995) *Metrical Stress Theory: Principles and Case Studies*, Chicago: University of Chicago Press.
Hoernle, A. F. R. (1880 [repr. 1975]) *A Comparative Grammar of the Gauḍian (Aryo-Indian) Languages*, Amsterdam: Philo Press.

Hook, P. E. (1974) *The Compound Verb in Hindi*, Ann Arbor: Center for South and Southeast Asian Studies, University of Michigan.
—— (1978) 'The compound verb in Hindi: what it is and what it does', in Singh, K. S. (ed.), *Readings in Hindi-Urdu Linguistics*, Delhi: National Publishing House, pp. 129–54.
Jagannathan, V. R. (1981) *Prayog aur Prayog*, Delhi: Oxford University Press.
Jain, Dh. (1969) 'Verbalization of respect in Hindi', *Anthropological Linguistics* 11.3: 79–97.
—— (1973) *Pronominal Usage in Hindi: a Sociolinguistic Study*, unpublished University of Pennsylvania Ph.D. dissertation.
—— (1975) 'The semantic basis of some Hindi imperatives', *Indian Linguistics* 36.2: 173–84.
Jaiswal, M. P. (1962) *A Linguistic Study of Bundeli: A Dialect of Madhyadeśa*, Leiden: Brill.
Kachru, Y. (1966) *An Introduction to Hindi Syntax*, Urbana: Department of Linguistics, University of Illinois.
—— (1968) 'The copula in Hindi', in Verhaar, J. W. M. (ed.) *The Verb 'be' and its Synonyms (Foundations of Language,* Supplementary Series) 6, pp. 35–59.
—— (1970a) 'A note on possessive construction in Hindi-Urdu', *Journal of Linguistics* 6: 37–45.
—— (1970b) 'The syntax of *ko* sentences in Hindi-Urdu', *Papers in Linguistics* 22: 299–314.
—— (1977) 'On reflexivization in Hindi-Urdu and its theoretical implications', *Indian Linguistics* 38: 21–38.
—— (1980) *Aspects of Hindi Grammar*, Delhi: Manohar.
—— (1982) 'Conjunct verbs in Hindi-Urdu and Persian', in Mistry, P. J. (ed.), *South Asian Review*, Jacksonville, FL: South Asia Literary Association, pp. 117–26.
Kachru, Y. and Bhatia, T. K. (1977) 'On reflexivization in Hindi-Urdu and its theoretical implications', *IL* 38.1: 21–38.
Kaul, O. N. (1990) 'The use of the particles in Hindi', *International Journal of Dravidian Linguistics* 19.1: 22–36.
Kelkar, A. R. (1968) *Studies in Hindi-Urdu, I: Introduction and Word Phonology*, Poona: Deccan College (Building Centenary and Silver Jubilee Series, 35).
Kellogg, S. H. (1875) *A Grammar of the Hindí Language* (2nd ed.), London: Routledge & Kegan Paul.
King, C. R. (1994) *One Language, Two Scripts: The Hindi Movement in Nineteenth Century North India*, Bombay: Oxford University Press.
King, R. D. (1997) *Nehru and the Language Politics of India*, Delhi: Oxford University Press.
Klaiman, M. H. (1976) 'Topicalization and relativization in Hindi', *Indian Linguistics* 37: 315–33.
—— (1990) 'The prehistory of noun incorporation in Hindi', *Lingua* 81.4: 327–50.
Kostić, D., Mitter, A. and Rastogi, K. G. (1975) *A Short Outline of Hindi Phonetics*, Calcutta: Indian Statistical Institute.
Lienhard, S. (1961) *Tempusgebrauch und Aktionsartenbildung in der modernen Hindi*, Stockholm: Almqvist & Niksell.
Liperovskij, V. P. (1988) *Očerk grammatiki covremennogo braža*, Moscow: 'Nauka'.
Masica, C. P. (1991) *The Indo-Aryan Languages*, Cambridge: Cambridge University Press.
McGregor, R. S. (1969) *The Language of Indrajit of Orchā: A Study of Early Braj Bhāṣā Prose*, Cambridge: Cambridge University Press.
—— (1974) *Hindi Literature of the Nineteenth and Early Twentieth Centuries*, Wiesbaden: Otto Harrassowitz (Gonda, J. (ed.), *A History of Indian Literature*, Vol. VIII, fasc.3).
—— (1984) *Hindi Literature from its Beginnings to the Nineteenth Century*, Wiesbaden: Otto Harrassowitz (Gonda, J. (ed.), *A History of Indian Literature*, Vol. VIII, fasc. 6).
—— (ed.) (1993) *The Oxford Hindi–English Dictionary*, Oxford: Oxford University Press.
—— (1995) *Outline of Hindi Grammar*, 3rd ed., Oxford: Oxford University Press.
Mathews, W. K. (1964) 'Phonetics and phonology in Hindi', *Le Maître Phonétique* 102: 18–22.
Mayee, J. (1987) 'Reflexivization and passivization in Hindi', *Indian Linguistics* 48.1–4: 109–115.

Mehrotra, R. C. (1980) *Hindi Phonology: A Synchronic Description of the Contemporary Standard*, Raipur: Bhashika Prakashan.

Miltner, V. (1969) 'Hindi', in Sebeok, T. A. et. al. (eds.), *Current Trends in Linguistics,* Volume 5, *Linguistics in South Asia*, The Hague: Mouton, pp. 55–84.

Misra, B. G. (1967) *Historical Phonology of Modern Standard Hindi*, unpublished Cornell University Ph.D. dissertation.

Moag, R. F. (1977) *Fiji Hindi: A Basic Course and Reference Grammar*, Canberra: Australian National University Press.

—— (1986) 'Diglossia versus bidialectalism: Hindi in Fiji and in Eastern Uttar Pradesh', in Krishnamurti, Bh., Masica, C. P. and Sinha, A. K. (eds.) *South Asian Languages: Structure, Convergence and Diglossia*, Delhi: Motilal Banarsidass, pp. 350–70.

Montaut, A. (1989) 'On the temporal reference of some peculiar uses of the perfective forms in Modern Hindi', *IL* 50.1–4: 95–112.

—— (1990) 'La construction passive en hindi moderne' *Bulletin de la Société de Linguistique de Paris* 85: 91–136.

—— (1991) *Aspects, voix et diathèses en hindi moderne: Syntaxe, sémantique, énonciation*, Louvain: Peeters.

—— (1992) 'L'Interprétation de l'ergativité dans les structures verbales du hindi', *Modèles Linguistiques* 14.2: 89–104.

Narang, G. C. and Becker, D. (1971) 'Aspiration and nasalization in the general phonology of Hindi', *Language* 47: 646–67.

Nespital, H. (1981) *Das Futursystem im Hindi und Urdu* (Schriftenreihe des Südasien-Instituts der Universität Heidelberg, 29), Wiesbaden: Steiner Verlag.

—— (1990) 'On the relation of Hindi to its regional dialects: the impact of dialects on the standard language in the speech of Hindi speakers (with regard to lexical, morphological, and syntactic features', in M. Ofredi (ed.), *Language Versus Dialect: Linguistic and Literary Essays on Hindi, Tamil and Sarnami*, Delhi: Manohar, pp. 3–23.

—— (1994) 'Fragesätze im Hindi und Urdu', *Studien zur Indologie und Iranistik* 19: 173–98.

—— (1998) 'The linguistic structure of Hindavī, Dakkhinī, early Urdu and early Kharī Bolī Hindī', *Berliner Indologische Studien* 11/12: 195–217.

Oberlies, T. (1998) *Historische Grammatik des Hindi*, Reinbek: Dr. Inge Wezler, Verlag für Orientalistische Fachpublikationen.

Ohala, M. (1983) *Aspects of Hindi Phonology*, Delhi: Motilal Banarsidass.

—— (1986) 'A search for the phonetic correlates of Hindi stress', in Krishnamurti, Bh., Masica, P. and Sinha, A. K. (eds.), *South Asian Languages: Structure, Convergence and Diglossia*, Delhi: Motilal Banarsidass, pp. 81–90.

—— (1989) 'Schwa deletion and vowel nasalization in Hindi by linear and non-linear routes: a reassessment', *IL* 50: 173–86.

—— (1991) 'Phonological area features of some Indo-Aryan languages', *Language Sciences* 13.2: 107–24.

—— (1999) 'The syllable in Hindi', in van der Hulst, H. and Ritter, N. (eds.), *The Syllable: Views and Facts*, Berlin: Mouton de Gruyter, pp. 93–112.

Ohala, M. and Ohala, J. (1991) 'Nasal epenthesis in Hindi', *Phonetica* 48.2–4: 207–20.

Pandey, P. K. (1980) 'Hindi schwa deletion', *Lingua* 82.4: 277–311.

—— (1989) 'Word accentuation in Hindi', *Lingua* 77: 37–73.

Pandharipande, R. (1979) 'Postpositions in passive sentences in Hindi', *Studies in the Linguistic Sciences* 9: 172–88.

—— (1981) 'Exceptions and rule government: the case of passive rule in Hindi', in Koul, O. N. (ed.), *Topics in Hindi Linguistics-2*, New Delhi: Bahri Publications, pp. 93–121.

Platts, J. T. (1884) *A Dictionary of Urdū, Classical Hindī, and English*, Oxford: Oxford University Press.

Pořízka, V. (1950) 'Hindi participles used as substantives', *Archiv Orientální* 18: 166–87.

—— (1952) 'The adjectival and adverbial participles in Hindi syntax', *Archiv Orientální* 20: 524–38.
—— (1967–9) 'On the perfective verbal aspect in Hindi', *Archiv Orientální* 35: 64–88, 36: 233–51, 37: 19–47.
Pray, B. R. (1970) *Topics in Hindi-Urdu Grammar*, Berkeley: Center for South and Southeast Asia Studies, University of California.
Rai, A. (1984) *A House Divided: The Origin and Development of Hindi/Hindavi*, Delhi: Oxford University Press.
Ray, P. S. (1966) 'Hindi-Urdu stress', *Indian Linguistics* 27: 95–101.
Ridgeway, T. B. (1986) *The Syntax of Case in Medieval Western Hindi*, unpublished University of Washington Ph.D. dissertation.
Sahai, R. N. and Narain, V. J. (1964) 'The structure of nounphrase in Hindi', *Indian Linguistics* 25: 111–18.
Saksena, A. (1978) 'A reanalysis of the passive in Hindi', *Lingua* 46: 339–53.
Saksena, B. R. (1971) *Evolution of Awadhi: A Branch of Hindi*, 2nd ed., Delhi: Motilal Banarsidass.
Saxena, A. (1985a) 'Intensifiers in Hindi', *International Journal of Dravidian Linguistics* 14.1: 566–8.
—— (1985b) 'Reflexivization in Hindi: a reconsideration', *International Journal of Dravidian Linguistics* 14.2: 224–37.
Schmidt, R. L. (1981) *Dakhini Urdu: History and Structure*, New Delhi: Bahri Publications.
Shackle, C. and R. Snell. (1990) *Hindi and Urdu since 1800: A Common Reader*, London: School of Oriental and African Studies, University of London.
Shapiro, M. C. (1974) *Aspects of Hindi Abstract Verbal Syntax*, unpublished University of Chicago Ph.D. dissertation.
—— (1976) 'The Analysis of Hindi morphologically related verb sets', *Indian Linguistics* 35: 1–44.
—— (1978) 'Current trends in Hindi syntax: a bibliographic survey', *Studien zur Indologie und Iranistik* 3: 3–53.
—— (1989) *A Primer of Modern Standard Hindi*, Delhi: Motilal Banarsidass.
—— (1999) 'Hindi *to* as discourse marker', in Mistry, P. J. and Modi, Bh. (eds.), *Vidyopaasanaa: Studies in Honour of Harivallabh C. Bhayani*, Mumbai and Ahmedabad, Image Publications, pp. 179–89.
Shapiro, M. C. and Schiffman, H. (1981) *Language and Society in South Asia*, Delhi: Motilal Banarsidass.
Sharma, A. (1958) *A Basic Grammar of Modern Hindi*, English Version, New Delhi: Government of India, Ministry of Education and Scientific Research.
—— (1969) 'Hindi word-accent', *Indian Linguistics* 30: 115–18.
Sharma, D. N. and Tripathi, R. D. (1971) *Hindī Bhāṣā kā Vikās*, Delhi: Rādhākṛṣna Prakāśan.
Sharma, N. C. (1968) *Hariyāṇvī Bhāṣā kā Udgam aur Vikās*, Hoshiarpur: Vishvesvaranand Vedic Research Institute.
Sharma, V. (1981) '*Hindī–Haidarābād*', in V. R. Jagannathan *Prayog aur Prayog*, Delhi: Oxford University Press, pp. 428–36.
Shukla, S. (1990) 'Syllable structure and word stress in Hindi', *Georgetown Journal of Language and Linguistics* 1: 235–47.
Singh, A. B. (1969) 'On echo-words in Hindi', *Indian Linguistics* 30: 185–95.
—— (1977) 'On time and place postpositions in Hindi', *Indian Linguistics* 38.1: 12–20.
Singh, K. S. and Manoharan S. (1993) *Languages and Scripts* (Anthropological Survey of India, People of India, National Series Volume IX), Delhi: Oxford University Press.
Singh, R. and Agnihotri. R. K. (1997) *Hindi Morphology: A Word-based Description*, Delhi: Motilal Banarsidass.
Sinha, A. K. (1987) 'The semantic implications of variables of switching address forms in Modern Hindi', *Indian Journal of Linguistics* 14: 1–24.
Snell, R. (1990) 'The hidden hand: English lexis, syntax, and idiom as determinants of modern Hindi usage', *South Asia Research* 10: 53–68.

Spies, O. (1955) 'Türkische Sprachgut im Hindustani', in O. Spies (ed.), *Studia Indologica: Festschrift für Willibald Kirfel*, Bonn: Selbstverlag des Orientalischen Seminars der Universität Bonn, (= *Bonner Orientalistische Studien*, Neue Serie, 3) pp. 321–43.

Srivastava, R. N. (1970) 'The problem of the Hindi semivowels', *IL* 31: 129–37.

Subbarao, K. V. (1974) 'Phrase-structure rules for noun phrase in Hindi', *IL* 35.3: 173–84.

—— (1976) 'Complementizers in Hindi', *Indian Linguistics* 37.2: 115–32.

—— (1984) *Complementation in Hindi Syntax*, Delhi: Academic Publications.

Subbarao, K. V. and Arora, A. (1988) 'On extreme convergence: the case of Dakkhini Hindi-Urdu', *Indian Linguistics* 49: 92–108.

Tiwari, U. N. (1969) *Hindī bhāṣā kā Udgam aur Vikās*, Allahabad: Bhāratī Bhādār.

Učida, N. (1977) *Hindi Phonology: A Study of the Treatment of Indo-Aryan Vowel Sequences in Hindi*, Calcutta: Simant Publications.

—— (1978) *Studien zur Hindi-Vokalphonologie*, Wiesbaden: Steiner Verlag.

Upadhyaya, S. N. (1970) *Causal Constructions in Hindi*, unpublished University of Wisconsin Ph.D. dissertation.

Vajpeyi, K. D. (1958) *Hindī Śabdānuśāsan*, Kāśī: Nāgarīpracāriṇī Sabhā.

Van Olphen, H. H. (1970) *The Structure of the Hindi Verb Phrase*, unpublished University of Texas Ph.D. dissertation.

—— (1973) 'Functional and non-functional conjunct verbs in Hindi', *Indian Linguistics* 34: 237–50.

—— (1975) 'Aspect, tense, and mood in the Hindi verb', *Indo-Iranian Journal* 16.4: 284–301.

—— (1976) 'The Hindi verb in indirect constructions', *Indian Journal of Dravidian Linguistic* 5: 224–37.

Varma, Dh. (1933) *Hindī Bhāṣā kā Itihās.* Allahabad: Hindustani Academy.

—— (1935) *La langue Braj: Dialecte de Mathurā*. Paris: Adrien Maisonneuve.

—— (1971) *Grāmīṇ Hindī.* Allahabad: Sāhitya Bhavan (repr. ed.).

Verma, M. K. (1971) *The Structure of the Noun Phrase in English and Hindi*, Delhi: Motilal Banarsidass.

Vijayanunni, M. (1997) *Census of India 1991, Series 1-India, Paper 1 of 1997: Language, India and States*, New Delhi: Government of India Press.

SUGGESTED READING

For further information on the literary history of Hindi, including both MSH and earlier literary dialects, Dwivedi 1966, Gaeffke 1978 and McGregor 1974, 1984 are recommended. The single most comprehensive study of Hindi phonology is that by Manjari Ohala (1983). Outlines of the core inflectional and derivational morphology of MSH is found in many reference and pedagogical grammars, of which Guru 1920, A. Sharma 1958, Vajpeyi 1958, Shapiro 1989, McGregor 1995 are representative. Kellogg's classic grammar of Hindi (1875), although outdated in many respects, is still an important source of information on Hindi dialects. For an overview of Hindi syntax, the reader is referred to the useful digest of the subject by Yamua Kachru (1966). Overviews of Hindi nominal and verbal syntax can be found in M. K. Verma 1971 and Van Olphen 1970 respectively. A useful outline of the historical phonology of MSH is contained in Mishra 1967 and of historical morphology in Oberlies 1998. An important comparative study of grammatical features of early Hindi-like speech varieties is Nespital 1998. A broader history of the language as a whole is contained in Chatterji 1960. A stimulating, although polemical, overview of the history of the language that deals in depth with the relationship between Hindi and Urdu is that by Rai (1984). The standard study of the history of the Hindi grammatical tradition is that by T. K. Bhatia (1987). For detailed bibliographic information for research on Hindi linguistics, see Miltner 1969, Shapiro 1978 and Aggarwal 1985.

URDU

Ruth Laila Schmidt

CONTENTS

LIST OF TABLES

1 BRIEF HISTORY AND GEOGRAPHY OF URDU

1.1 History and sociocultural position

1.1.1 The speech of Delhi

Historically, Urdu has developed primarily from the sub-regional language of the Delhi area, which has been variously called Kharī Bolī, Zabān-e-Dehlavī ['language of Delhi'], or Hindavī ['Indian']; with influences from the regional dialects spoken in the vicinity of Delhi: Kauravī, Hariyāṇvī, Mevāṭī, eastern Panjābī and western Braj Bhāṣā. All these dialects are closely related and have developed out of the Middle Indo-Aryan vernacular speeches represented by the literary language Śaurasēnī Apabhraṁśa, which is a late variety of Śaurasēnī Prākrit.

The earliest texts containing elements of Kharī Bōlī are of devotional poetry, written in the mixed speech (Sādhukkaṛī) of the itinerant yogīs and preachers of that time. The poems of Amīr Khusrau (AD 1236 to 1324) are usually considered the first real Kharī Bōlī texts, although these also show traces of Braj Bhāṣā (Rai 1984: 136, quoting Gyan Chand). It is reasonable to assume that in the absence of a written standard, a certain amount of convergence between Kharī Bōlī and its neighbours took place.

1.1.2 Dakhanī

Under the Delhi Sultanate (AD 1211 to 1504), the Zabān-e-Dehlavī or Kharī Bolī was carried throughout most of India with the Muslim armies and their attached Hindu traders, as well as by sūfī mystics and preachers, establishing it as a lingua franca. In AD 1327 Panjābī-influenced Kharī Bolī was transplanted to the south of India along with the migration of the inhabitants of Delhi to Aurangabād in the Deccan, at the order of Sultan Muhammad bin Tughlaq. In the fifteenth century it became a literary language, known as Dakhanī ('southern'), Hindavī, Hindī, or Dehlavī, in the Deccan kingdoms of Gōlkundā and Bījāpur. Aside from a few specifically Panjābī features, Dakhanī is an archaic form of Urdu showing strong affinities to the modern spoken Urdu of the artisans of Old Delhi, which is also known as Karkhandārī Urdu (Schmidt 1981: 57–8). Both Karkhandārī Urdu and Old Dakhanī show a number of phonological and grammatical similarities which have disappeared from modern Urdu and Hindi.

Dakhanī is a distinct dialect of Urdu, not at present used for literary purposes. It diverges from standard Urdu with respect to phonology, morphology, syntax and lexicon. A brief description of its major points of divergence with standard Urdu is provided under 1.1.6.

1.1.3 The development of modern Urdu

When the capital of the Mughal Empire (AD 1526 to 1757; see 6. 'Remarks') was shifted from Agra to Delhi in 1648 (and named Shāhjahānābād after the emperor Shāh Jahān), the royal court of about 10,000 people migrated from Agra, which was the centre of Braj Bhāṣā. While the elites spoke and wrote Persian, the rank-and-file presumably spoke a form of Braj Bhāṣā. There was also an influx of people from the surrounding areas, mostly speaking the Kauravī and Hariyāṇvī dialects, and in smaller numbers, from the Panjāb and Braj Bhāṣā regions. The language which developed in the Red Fort, or Urdū-e-mucallā ['the exalted camp'], gradually diverged from the Old Delhi dialect, or Karkhandārī (Nespital 1994: 310–11). The language of the Red Fort (called variously and confusingly Hindavī, Rekhta, or Zabān-e-Urdū-e-Mucallā) shows greater influence from Braj Bhāṣā than does the Old Delhi dialect (Rai 1984: 123–9). The name 'Urdu' is derived from the descriptive term Zabān-e-Urdū-e-Mucallā, or 'language of the exalted camp', and is seen for the first time in a couplet written by the poet Muṣḥafī (مصحفى 1750–1824), dated to c. 1776.

The language of the Red Fort first began to be used as a literary language in compositions in which it was mixed with Persian (hence the term Rekhta, which means 'scattered' or 'mixed'). Nespital (1994: 313) has divided the history of classical Urdu literature into five periods. The first period (1648–1700) is characterized by the Rekhta poetry of sūfī mystics. The second (1700–20) begins with the arrival in Delhi of the poet Valī Dakhanī from Aurangabād, bringing his works of Dakhanī poetry with him. Valī stimulated the composition of poetry in 'Urdu' (the Zabān-e-Urdū-e-Mucallā or late Hindavī), unmixed with Persian. Persianization of the vocabulary of Urdu poetry composed in Delhi soon began however (Rai 1994: 226–7; Nespital 1994: 320).

The third period (1720–40) saw movement toward standardization of the grammar of the new literary language. During this period the old finite present tense forms (such as karē 'does', āvē 'comes', jānē 'knows') shifted to subjunctives, the formation of continuous tense forms with rahā (the perfective participle of rahnā 'to remain') became more common, and the use of the ergative construction with the postposition nē began to stabilize. However the formation of the present tense with imperfect participles + auxiliaries (*kartā hai* 'he does'; *caltā hū̃* 'I go'), characteristic of modern Urdu and also of Dakhanī, had not entirely displaced an older formation with finite verbs + auxiliaries: (*karē hai, calū̃ hū̃*):

Old	Modern
vo kar-e h-ai	*vo kar-t-ā h-ai*
he do-3sg. AUX-3sg.	he do-IMPV-m.sg. AUX-3sg.
he does	he does
vo kar-e th-ā	*vo kar-t-ā th-ā*
he do-3sg. AUX-p.m.sg.	he do-IMPV-m.sg. AUX-p.m.sg.
he did, was doing, used to do	he was doing, used to do

Hindavī tadbhava words began to be replaced with Perso-Arabic ones, and these began to be spelled as they were written in Persian and Arabic, and not according to their pronunciation (Nespital 1994: 318–20).

The fourth period (1740–80) is the golden age of the Delhi School of Urdu poetry, with the great masters Saudā, Mīr Taqī Mīr and Mīr Dard; but it was ironically also a period of rapid disintegration of the Mughal Empire, in which Delhi was repeatedly occupied and looted by armies contending for the imperial throne (Russell and Islam 1968: 22–36). A consequence of the decline of the Mughal power was the reduced importance of Persian as a literary and culture language, and greater scope for Urdu to flourish. Linguistically this period is a continuation of the previous one, with the ergative construction and present tense verb forms still somewhat in flux (Nespital 1994: 320–1). Although Perso-Arabic vocabulary is used, there are relatively few borrowed Persian and Arabic grammatical forms, and the poetry of this period is more accessible than that of the later Lucknow School. By the fifth period (1780–1810) the standardization process was nearing completion; the poet Inšā published his work on Urdu grammar and dialects, *Daryā-e-Laṭāfat*, in 1807, in which he discourages the use of forms such as *calū̃ hū̃* 'I go' (for *caltā hū̃*) or *kisū* 'some (obl.)' (for *kisī*) (Nespital 1994: 321–3).

The constant warfare over Delhi left it in ruins, and most of the poets moved eastward, particularly to Lucknow, capital of the province of Avadh (nominally subject to Delhi but in fact virtually autonomous since 1723). By the early nineteenth century the language of the Lucknow School of Urdu was Standard Urdu, no longer associated with regional Delhi usages. Delhi poets in the period 1820–50 continued to use regionalisms; Nespital 1994: 324 supplies an example from Ghālib:

> *īmān mujh-ē rōk-ē h-ai, tō khĕc-ē h-ai mujh-ē kufr*
> faith me-obl.-DAT stop-3sg-AUX-3sg. TOP pull-3sg. AUX-3sg. me-obl.-DAT disbelief
> 'Faith stops me, while disbelief attracts me.'

However, Delhi was to develop its own standard form of Urdu, which avoided the extreme Persianization of the Lucknow School, but which was otherwise quite similar to the Lucknow School so far as the grammar of Urdu is concerned.

Urdu also began to be used for prose, especially after 1830. The impetus given to modern Urdu literature by the reformer and modernizer Sir Syed Ahmad paved the way for the re-examinations of Urdu literary history and Muslim civilization by Hālī and Āzād in the second half of the nineteenth century, and also for the social realism of the prose writers Nazīr Ahmad and Prem Chand. Hālī's vision of Islam in decline called for a new vision of Islam in South Asian society, which was offered by the poet Iqbal in the early twentieth century.

In the generation between 1827 and 1857, Delhi College contributed to the development of Urdu prose through its teaching, sponsorship of translations, and the publications of its students, and encouraged the development of new literary forms such as the novel, short story, essay and literary criticism. Sir Syed Ahmad collaborated with Delhi College's Maulvi Imām Baxš to produce his study of the topography of Old Delhi, and Nazīr Ahmad and Āzād were graduates of the college (Minault 1999: 132–4).

From its establishment in 1903, the Anjuman-e-Taraqqi-e-Urdu (Society for the Development of Urdu) under the leadership of Maulvi Abdul Haqq played an important role in adapting Urdu to the requirements of a contemporary national language. Abdul Haqq's pioneering work in Urdu lexicography, grammar, textual commentaries and studies of the early sūfīs earned him the title *Bābā-e-Urdū* (the father of Urdu) (Matthews 1994: 94).

The departure in 1947 of large numbers of educated Muslims from Uttar Pradesh reduced Urdu to a minority language in its home state. Sanskritized Hindi was made the state's official language, and Muslims only managed to win approval for Urdu as the state's second official language in 1998. In Pakistan, where Urdu was formerly nowhere an indigenous mother tongue, it has become the official language, and is used in most government schools, at the lower levels of administration, in mass media and in all the major cities of the country (Rahman 1996: 1).

In the multilingual state of Kashmir, Urdu superseded Persian as the administrative language in the second decade of this century (Sufi 1974: 812–13), and this policy was continued after 1947 on both sides of the Line of Control.

1.1.4 Hindustani

In the early 1800s, the British chose the Kharī Bolī lingua franca, which they called Hindustani, as their medium for administration, and sponsored the composition of Hindustani prose texts in both the Persian and Dēvanāgarī scripts. The Hindi variant of Kharī Bōlī, hitherto seldom written (Nespital 1998: 214) now began to emerge as a literary language. In the course of the nineteenth century, it was to rival not only Urdu, but claim other languages in north India as its 'dialects' (Srivastava 1995: 229), and in due course to inherit the literary traditions of its Hindi sister dialects Braj Bhāṣā and Avadhī.

Grierson comments that the Hindustani *Prem Sāgar*, or 'Ocean of Love' composed by Lallūjī Lāl in the Dēvanāgarī script, was:

> so far as the prose portions went, practically written in Urdū, with Indo-Aryan words substituted wherever a writer in that form of speech would use Persian ones ... The language fulfilled a want. It gave a *lingua franca* to the Hindus. It enabled men of widely different provinces to converse with each other without having recourse to the (to them) unclean words of the Musalmāns (Grierson 1916: 46).

Urdu was already Persianized. Kharī Bolī Hindi was now made acceptable by preferring tadbhava Hindi words over, or substituting tatsama Sanskrit words for, Perso-Arabic ones.

Hindustani officially disappeared after 1947; neither Schedule VIII of the Constitution of India, which enumerates the languages of India, nor the official documents of Pakistan make even a cursory mention of it (G. C. Narang, personal communication). Unofficially, the Hindustani lingua franca is a fully functioning vernacular link language in India, Pakistan and among the South Asian diaspora (1.3.1).

1.1.5 Modern Urdu and Hindi

Kharī Bōlī's period of convergence and absorbing linguistic features from its neighbours had come to an end with Inšā's *Daryā-e-Laṭāfat*. The forces of divergence now began to gather strength, and crystallized in what has come to be known as the Hindi-Urdu controversy.

Christopher R. King (1994) documents the movement for the establishment of Kharī Bōlī Hindi in the Dēvanāgarī script as the pre-eminent language of literature, education and official administration for Hindus in north India, which began in the United Provinces [modern Uttar Pradesh] in the 1860s. In the rhetoric of the Hindi movement, Kharī Bōlī Hindi and Dēvanāgarī assumed the status of central symbols of Hindu cultural identity, opposed to Urdu and the Persian script, seen as symbols of Muslim cultural identity. In this context, the replacement of Persian and Arabic words with Sanskrit ones served to differentiate Hindi from Urdu (King 1994: 181). In the samples provided in Grierson's Linguistic Survey of India, collected around 100 years ago (Vol. 9, Part 1, pp. 100, 137, 165), there is already considerable divergence between the common Kharī Bōlī base (known as Ṭhēṭh Hindī) and its Persianized and Sanskritized variants:

Ṭhēṭh Hindī	Urdu	Hindi	
mānus	*šaxs*	*manuṣya*	'person'
bēṭā	*bēṭā*	*putra*	'son'
bāp	*bāp*	*pitā*	'father'
dēs	*mulk*	*dēś*	'country'
bakhᵃrā	*hissa*	*aṁś*	'share'

Although the formal literary Urdu and Hindi variants of Kharī Bōlī still share most major grammatical features, on the lexical level they have diverged to such an extent that an Urdu speaker needs a dictionary to read modern Hindi literature even if he has learned the Dēvanāgarī script. A Hindi speaker has a similar problem with Urdu literature, although to a lesser extent since many Perso-Arabic words are still common in spoken Hindi.

1.1.5.1 Writing systems

The most obvious and irreducible difference between Urdu and Hindi is found at the level of orthography. Urdu is written in a modified form of the Arabic script, as adapted for Persian and later for Urdu. Arabic and Persian loanwords are spelled as they are in the original languages, and not according to their pronunciation. Hindi is written in the Dēvanāgarī syllabary used for Sanskrit, and Sanskrit loans are also spelled as they are in Sanskrit. 'While both languages are very careful about the spelling of their "own" loanwords, and careful speakers often attempt their original pronunciation, each is equally careless about the other's' (Shackle and Snell 1990: 27). Persianized Urdu *imtihān* 'examination' and *ixtiyār* 'authority' become Hindi *imtahān* and *akhtiyār* (Thiesen 1990: 358). Sanskritized Hindi *janma* 'birth' becomes Urdu *janam* (Shackle and Snell 1990: 28).

1.1.5.2 Phonological differences

Urdu and Hindi have different normative subsets of phonemes which have been acquired along with borrowed vocabulary (Gumperz and Naim 1960: 105–12, Shackle and Snell 1990: 24–5). Normative Urdu has acquired the phonemes / f x š z ž γ q / from Persian and Arabic, while normative Hindi has acquired / ṇ š ṣ / from Sanskrit. The Urdu subset is partially shared by Hindi, as educated Hindi speakers often distinguish / f š z /. In the Hindi subset, only / š / is shared by Urdu, although retroflex / ṇ / occurs before a retroflex consonant, e.g. *aṇḍā* 'egg'. The distribution of phonemes also varies. Final short / a i u / occur in Hindi, but Urdu allows only final short / a /. Urdu / -a / is not identical with Hindi / -a /: Urdu *camca* corresponds to Hindi *camcā* 'spoon', Urdu *bacca* corresponds to Hindi *baccā* 'child'. Borrowing of vocabulary from different sources also leads to differing inventories of permitted consonant clusters. Among the distinctive Hindi clusters are initial / kr kš, st sv šr sn ny / and final / tv šv ny ly rv jy ry /: *kripā* 'kindness', *kšamā* 'forgiveness', *šrī* 'Mr.', *mahatv* 'importance', *rājy* 'rule'. Distinctively Urdu are final / ft rf mt mr ms kl tl bl sl tm lm hm hr /: *barf* 'snow', *umr* 'age', *šakl* 'shape', *xatm* 'finished', *ilm* 'knowledge, *šehr* 'city'.

With Sanskrit loanwords Hindi has acquired a full range of vowel and consonant sandhi (or assimilation). In Urdu, vowel sandhi occurs mainly in the derivation of transitive and causative stems, and although other examples of vowel and consonant sandhi survive, they are not recognized as such. The following examples from Hindi (McGregor 1972: 185–7) are illustrative of the way in which the processes of word-compounding and sandhi give rise to new (often not easily recognized) vocabulary in Hindi:

$a + ā = ā$: *hima* 'snow' + *ālaya* 'abode' → *himālaya* 'Himalaya'
$a + u = ō$: *grāma* 'village' + *udyōga* 'endeavour' → *grāmōdyōg* 'village industry'
s before a vowel/voiced consonant = *r*: *dus* 'bad' + *daiv* 'fate' → *durdaiv* 'evil fate'
a voiceless stop before a voiced stop is assimilated: *bhagavat* 'divine being + *gītā* 'song' → *bhagavadgītā* 'Song of the Lord'

1.1.5.3 Grammatical differences

The grammatical differences between Urdu and Hindi are minimal. Normative Hindi distinguishes singular and plural third person demonstrative pronouns in the nominative case: *yah* 'this', *yē* 'these'; *vah* 'that', *vē* 'those'. Urdu distinguishes only *ye* 'this, these' and *vo* 'that, those' (3.3.1). Hindi (and early Urdu) permits the use of the verb root without the extending suffix *kar* (3.5.5) as an absolutive, but normative modern Urdu does not, except in proverbs. The following example is taken from Naim (2000: 97).

Early Urdu: *ghar sē nikal bāhar jā baiṭh-ī*
               house from emerge outside go sit-PFV-f.sg.
               She came out of the house and sat down outside.
Modern Urdu: *ghar sē nikal kar bāhar jā baiṭh-ī*
               house from emerge CP outside go sit-PFV-f.sg.
               She came out of the house and sat down outside.

The future suffix, conjunctive participle and the suffix *vālā* are treated as bound morphemes in written Hindi, but as separate words in written Urdu. Postpositions are treated as bound morphemes after pronouns in Hindi, but as separate words in Urdu.

Urdu	Hindi	
āp kō	*āpkō*	'to you'
jāū̃ gā	*jāū̃gā*	'(I) will go'
jā kar	*jākar*	'having gone'
jānē vālā	*jānēvālā*	'going', 'one who goes'

1.1.5.4 Lexical differences

The amount of lexical difference between Urdu and Hindi is least at the informal spoken level, and greatest in formal speech, literature and official communications. As a rough index of the minimum lexical difference between Urdu and Hindi, this writer made a count of the Hindi words (both tadbhava and tatsama) in the textbook *Teach Yourself Hindi* (Snell and Weightman 1992), which are not shared by Urdu, or which are sufficiently uncommon that Urdu equivalents would need to be supplied if the textbook were used for a first-year course in which Hindi and Urdu students were taught together. The authors have chosen to present the variety of Hindi that is most useful for communication purposes, and the book includes many words that are common to Urdu and Hindi: 'The language of this course is that which is used unselfconsciously by Hindi speakers and writers in the various, mainly informal situations which are introduced' (Snell and Weightman 1992: 1). Approximately ten per cent of the vocabulary in the book is not shared with Urdu.

The lexical differences between Hindi and Urdu often reflect different cultural paradigms, so that the Perso-Arabic and Sanskrit equivalents are not always freely substitutable. Shackle and Snell (1990: 31) comment that

> While it is often the case that the PA [Perso-Arabic] word represents the colloquial norm in both U [Urdu] and H [Hindi], the semantic field of any particular word is likely to have some specific cultural implication which affects usage: H *sevā karnā* implies a piety deriving from Hindu ideals of religious service which makes it semantically distinct from the more neutral U *xidmat karnā*.

Another pair of this type is Hindi *yātrā*, which means both 'journey' and 'pilgrimage', and Urdu *safar*, which lacks the connotation of a pilgrimage. Other pairs are more nearly synonymous:

Urdu	Hindi	
kitāb	*pustak*	'book'
xabar	*samācār*	'news'
dōst	*mitra*	'friend'
vaqt	*samay*	'time'
xūbsūrat	*sundar*	'beautiful'

However, the associations called forth by Urdu's Perso-Arabic vocabulary belong to a different world view and find their place in a different cultural history than those echoing from Hindi's Sanskritic vocabulary.

In the case of both Urdu and Hindi, the borrowed vocabulary consists predominantly of nouns and adjectives. Finite verbs are not borrowed, and verb coinages consist of denominative noun + verb or adjective + verb sequences, in which the verbs are often the same in both Urdu and Hindi. Examples:

Urdu	Hindi	
šurū karnā	*ārambh karnā*	'to begin (do beginning)'
istēmāl karnā	*prayōg karnā*	'to use (make use)'
madad dēnā	*sahāyatā dēnā*	'to help (give help)'
ijāzat dēnā	*āgyā̃ dēnā*	'to permit (give permission)'

Differing inventories of derivational affixes have come into Urdu and Hindi along with the borrowed vocabulary. A few illustrative examples are:

Urdu		Hindi	
bad- 'bad'	*badbaxt* 'ill-fated'	*dus-* 'bad'	*durdaiv* 'evil fate'
ɣair- 'not, un-'	*ɣairhāzir* 'absent'	*nis-* 'not'	*nisphal* 'fruitless'
-mand 'possessing'	*aqlmand* 'wise'	*-mān* 'possessing'	*buddhimān* 'wise'

Some common Perso-Arabic affixes are shared:

Urdu-Hindi
bē- 'without, -less'   *bēkār* 'unemployed, useless'; *bēṭikaṭ* 'ticketless'
-dār 'having'   *dukāndār* 'shopkeeper', *samajhdār* 'intelligent'

A number of common conjunctions are borrowed from different sources (Gumperz and Naim 1960: 115–16):

Normative Urdu	Normative Hindi	
agar	*yadi*	'if'
agarce	*yadyapī*	'although'
kī vajah sē	*kē kāraṇ*	'because of'
magar, lēkin	*parantu*	'but'
aur	*ēvam, tathā*	'and'

1.1.6 Modern Urdu and Dakhanī

Schmidt (1981) studied the modern Dakhanī dialect of Hyderabad as it was spoken in the early 1960s. Matthews (1976) analysed Dakhanī texts composed in the period AD 1500–1700, and sampled modern speech from Nalgunda District of Andhra Pradesh. Both writers point to numerous similarities between modern and seventeenth century Dakhanī, despite the increasing influence of Standard Urdu. The features described below represent the modern Dakhanī of Hyderabad as described by Schmidt, unless otherwise indicated. Dakhanī Urdu shows great variation, and most of the forms and examples shown below represent those of Schmidt's (1981: 44–7) 'primary system', which is the form of Dakhanī containing the maximum number of historically derived contrasts, and the minimum number of loans or innovations showing influence from neighbouring languages.

No more recent study of modern Dakhanī phonology has come to the attention of this writer, however the papers by Pray (1980) and Kachru (1986) describe aspects of grammatical and syntactic convergence between Dakhanī and neighbouring languages (1.3.3, 1.3.4). See 'Recommended Reading' for bibliographic references.

Convergence between Dakhanī and neighbouring languages is discussed under 1.3.3 and 1.3.4.

1.1.6.1 Phonological differences

Loss of /h/ and aspiration
Intervocally, before consonants and in final position, /h/ is often lost, or is realized as aspiration (Schmidt 1981: 19–20). This also occurs intervocally across morpheme boundaries, and accounts for the bound form of the auxiliary *hōnā* described by Schmidt (1981: 32). (Intervocalic /h/ is unstable in Standard Urdu also; see 2.2.3.2.) Kachru (1986: 171) provides an example of /-h-/ = [y], *khēl rayā thā* 'was playing' (=*khēl rahā thā*). Examples: *maīnā* 'month' (=*mahīna*), *cāiyē* 'is wanted' (=*cāhiē*), *baiṭ jāō* 'sit down' (=*baiṭh jāō*), *katē* (reported speech operator, =*kahtē*), *bhen* 'sister' (=*bahen*).
    Voiced aspirates may lose aspiration: *bī ~ bhī* 'also', *bajjiyā ~ bhajjiyā* 'vegetable fritter', *samaj ~ samajh* 'understand'.
    Matthews (1976: 181–2) cites examples of loss of both /h/ and aspiration from older texts: *naī̃* 'not' (=*nahī̃*), *pennā* 'to wear' (=*pahennā*), *liknā* 'to write' (=*likhnā*).

Loss of nasalization
In final position, nasalization is lost in the speech of some speakers: *nī̃ ~ nī* 'not', *hāī̃ ~ hai* 'are' (Schmidt 1981: 20). Matthews (1976: 182) finds both nasalization of historically oral long vowels and loss of nasalization: *dunyã* 'world' (=*dunyā*), *tũ* 'you (sg.)' (=*tū*), *dōnō* 'both' (=*dōnõ*).

Consonant assimilation
/n/ occurring before or after /t/ is usually assimilated to it. Assimilation of a voiceless to a voiced consonant also occurs (Schmidt 1981: 21). Examples: *kittā* 'how much?' (=*kitnā*), *uzzamānē mẽ* 'in that time' (=*us zamānē mẽ*).

Reduction of vowel length
Long vowels are frequently shortened (Schmidt 1981: 22): *admī* 'person' (=*ādmī*), *accha* 'good' (=*acchā*). Matthews (1976: 180) states that 'vowel length is variable. The most common tendency is for vowels, which are long in modern Urdu, to be shortened.' Examples: *lak(h)* 'hundred thousand' (=*lākh*), *asmān* 'sky' (=*āsmān*). But Matthews also finds some examples of lengthening of short vowels: *rākhnā* 'to put' (=*rakhnā*), *chīn* 'moment' (=*chin*).

Loss of postvelar stop /q/
The Standard Urdu phoneme /q/ is replaced in Dakhanī by a voiceless velar spirant /x/, varying with /k/ (Schmidt 1981: 19). According to Qadri (1930: 82) /x/ is assimilated to a voiced consonant. Examples: *vaxt* 'time', *faxat* 'only', *haxdār* 'deserving'. Matthews (1976: 183) finds an example of *vaqt* which was clearly intended to rhyme with *taxt* 'throne', in the seventeenth-century text *Sab Ras* by Mullā Vajhī.

1.1.6.2 Grammatical differences

Nouns and postpositions
As in Standard Urdu, two genders are distinguished. Based on noun morphology there are three classes of Dakhanī nouns: (1) marked masculine taking the plural in *-ē*; (2) marked/unmarked feminine and unmarked masculine taking the plural in *-ã*, and (3) unmarked masculine/feminine taking no plural suffix. Examples:

(1) *bacca* 'child' → *baccē* 'children'
     kapṛā 'cloth' → *kapṛē* 'clothes'

(2) *piyālī* (f.) 'cup' → *piyāliyā̃* 'cups'
     bhen (f.) 'sister' → *bhenā̃* 'sisters'
     ghar (m.) 'house' → *gharā̃* 'houses'

(3) *xālā* (f.) 'aunt' → *xālā* 'aunts'
     ām (m.) 'mango' → *ām* 'mangoes'

Only Class 1 nouns show the oblique singular case: *baccē kū* 'to the child', but *ghar kū* 'to the house', *xālā kū* 'to auntie'. The oblique plural suffix is -*õ* ~ -*ã̃*: *baccõ kū* 'to the children', *gharõ/gharā̃ kū* 'to the houses', *laṛāiyā̃ mẽ* 'in the disputes'.

At the time of the study Class 3 was expanding at the expense of the other classes, and noun-verb agreement patterns showed a weakening of the masculine/feminine gender distinction, with some speakers treating only animate feminine nouns and marked feminine nouns ending in -*ī* as feminine. Matthews (1976: 188–9) finds a masculine plural suffix -*e* and a masculine/feminine plural suffix -*ã̃* ~ -*yã̃*. He also comments that:

> Gender of nouns in Dakanī tends to be somewhat erratic, and occasionally the same word may be assigned both genders by the same writer. There is, however, a greater tendency to treat feminine nouns as masculine, rather than the other way around (1976: 188).

The oblique plural suffix in Matthews' text corpus was almost always -*ã̃*, although he finds the suffix in -*õ* occurring occasionally in later texts, as well as used instrumentally in all periods:

akēlā dukhõ beqarār
alone sorrow-obl.pl. anxious
'alone, anxious with grief'

Schmidt's (1981: 26) Hyderabad corpus contains the primary postpositions *kā* (possessive), *kū* ~ *kō* (dative), *mẽ* 'in', *pe* 'on', *sē* 'by/from', *tak* 'until' and *kanē* 'near' (the Standard Urdu equivalent of *kanē*, *kē pās*, also occurs). The Standard Urdu ergative marker *nē* does not occur. The older speech as attested in Matthews (1976: 202–3) corpus shows a greater variety of postpositional forms, including *karā* (possessive, =*kā*); *kõ* (dative, =*kō*); *manē/manẽ/myānē* 'in' (=*mẽ*), *pe* 'on', *sõ/sētē/sēthē/sitē/thē/tē* 'by/from' (=*sē*), *lag/lagan/talag* 'until' (=*tak*) and *kan/kanē* 'near' (=*kē pās*).

Pronouns

The possessive pronoun is sometimes used as a base for postpositions (*mērē kū* 'to me', *mērē sē* 'from me'), and the occurrence of the alternate suffixal forms (3.1.1.3.2) is sporadic. The disappearance of the ergative construction with *nē* in perfective tenses (3.1.1.3.3) has given rise to alternates of third person pronouns (Schmidt 1981: 28–9), and in the speech of some speakers, the development of a new contrast between personal and demonstrative third person pronouns.

The honorific pronoun *āp* (3.3.2) occurs only in the speech of those who have learned Standard Urdu.

1st pers. nom. *mãĩ* sg., *ham* ~ *hamẽ* pl.; obl. *muje* ~ *mije* sg., *ham* ~ *hamẽ* pl.
2nd pers. nom. *tū* sg., *tum* ~ *tumẽ* ~ *tumhẽ* pl.; obl. *tuje* sg., *tum* pl.

3rd pers. prox.: nom. *inē ~ ye* sg., *inõ̃ ~ ye lōkã̄* pl.; obl. *ise ~ is* sg., *inhē̃ ~ inã̄ ~ in* pl.
3rd pers. rem.: nom. *unē ~ vo* sg., *unõ̃ ~ vo lōkã̄* pl.; obl. *use ~ ũs* sg., *unhē̃ ~ unã̄ ~ un* pl.

In the speech of most speakers, *ye* and *vo* are demonstratives, whereas *inē/unē, inõ̃/unõ̃* are personal pronouns. The oblique plural forms *inhē̃, unhē̃* are subject to loss of aspiration and nasalization, resulting in the loss of the distinction between nominative and oblique forms. Schmidt's corpus does not show an unambiguous distinction between proximate and remote demonstratives.

The interrogative pronouns *kyā* and *kaun* and the relative pronoun *jō* occur in the corpus. *jukōī* 'whoever' shows vowel reduction (*=jō kōī*). The oblique form of *kaun*, *kis* occurs in *kis kū* 'to whom'. The reflexive adjective *apnā* 'own' occurs, used in the same way as in Standard Urdu; a variant *apē* also occurs, which does not seem to inflect.

Examples (from Schmidt 1981: 78–9):

inē/unē hamār-ī sār-ī šakkar lē li-y-ā
he our-f. all-f. sugar take take-PVF-m.sg.
'He has taken all our sugar.'

tumē̃ mer-ī bahut madad kar-ē
you my-f. much help do-PVF-AUX-m.pl.
'You have helped me a lot.'

inē apē̃ ammã̄ kī bahut madad kar-ī-e
she own mother POSS much help do-PFV-AUX-f.-sg.
'She has helped her mother a lot.'

vo lōk-ã̄ pūch-nē ā-ē tak hamē̃ apn-ā ghar bēc ḍāl-ē
those people-pl. ask-INF-obl. come-PVF-obl. until we own-m. house sell pour-PFV-AUX-m.pl.
'We had already sold our house when they came to ask about it.'

Matthews' (1976: 193–5) corpus shows most of the above pronouns with some variations: *munj, munje* (=*muje*), *hamē, hamnē* (=*hamē̃*), *tumē, tumnē* (=*tumē̃*).

Verb morphology and agreement

The verb system (Schmidt 1981: 31–43) shows imperfective, perfective and continuous aspects just as in Standard Urdu (3.5.2). The formation of the imperfective and perfective participles is the same as in Standard Urdu, however the regular form of *karnā* is used in the perfective participle (*karā ~ karē ~ karī ~ karī̃*). The continuous participle shows loss of /h/: *rā ~ rē ~ rī ~ rāī*.

The construction PRESENT PARTICIPLE + AUXILIARY is an indefinite tense, describing all non-past actions except continuous ones. The future tense in *gā* (~ *gē ~ gī*) does not occur in the speech of all speakers. When it occurs it is usually formed as in Standard Urdu; however sometimes the suffix *-gā* does not inflect.

In perfective tenses, *nē* does not occur, and the verb invariably agrees with the subject.

The infinitive suffix *-nā* varies with *-ōnā ~ -unā*: *karnā ~ karōnā* 'to do', *banānā ~ banaunā* 'to build'.

The extension of the conjunctive participle (3.5.5) is *kō ~ kē*.

Perfective and imperfective participles occur as modifiers. Participial phrases are formed with the invariant modifier *sō*, which is added to oblique participles. The corpus contains no examples of participial phrases with stative verbs (for example, *baiṭhā hūā hai*).

Examples (Schmidt 1981: 76–8):

mãĩ khā kō ā-y-ā
I eat CP come-PFV-m.sg.
'I have already eaten.'

ammã̄ khō-ē sō rūpiyā ḍhū̃ḍ r-ī-ē
mother lost-obl. MOD rupee search CON-AUX-f.sg.
'Mother is searching for a rupee she lost.'

mãĩ kacc-ā huv-ā tō kyā ām khā r-ā-õ̃
I unripe-m.sg. having-been-m.sg. so what mango eat CON-AUX-m.sg.-1
'I'm eating the mango even though it's unripe.'

ham tumārī intizārī mẽ baiṭh-ẽ
we your-f.sg. waiting in sit-PFV-AUX-m.pl.
'We're sitting here waiting for you.'

ham tum ɣaltiy-ã̄ kart-ē nĩ ḍã̄ṭ-ē
we you mistake-pl. doing-m.pl. not scold-PFV-m.pl.
'We didn't scold you when you made mistakes.'

The loss of intervocalic /h/ has given rise to a bound form of the auxiliary verb, occurring after the imperfective, perfective and continuous participles (Schmidt 1981: 32–9): first person. sg. m./pl. -ũ̃ ~ -ũ ~ -õ̃, second/third person sg. m./pl.) -ē, first/second/ third person m.pl. -ẽ, f.pl. -aĩ. The last form is rare, occurs only with imperfect and continuous participles and is usually replaced with -ẽ. Examples:

mãĩ jātaũ ~ jātõ̃ 'I (m.) go' (=*mãĩ jātā hũ*), *mãĩ jātĩũ* 'I (f.) go' (=*mãĩ jātī hũ*); *mãĩ gayũ̃* 'I (m./f.) have gone' (=*mãĩ gayā/gaī hũ*); *mãĩ jā rāũ̃* 'I (m.) am going' (=*mãĩ jā rahā hũ*), *mãĩ jā rĩũ* 'I (f.) am going' (=*mãĩ jā rahī hũ*).

tū/une jātāē 'you (m.sg.) go/he goes' (=*tū/vo jātā hai*), *tū/une jātīē* 'you (f.sg.) go/ she goes' (=*tū/vo jātī hai*), *tū/une karāē* 'you (m.sg.)/he did' (=*tū/us nē kiyā hai*), *tū/une karīē* 'you (f.sg.)/she did' (=*tū/us nē kiyā hai*), *tū/une jā rāē* 'you (m.sg.)/he are/is going' (=*tū/vo jā rahā hai*), *tū/une jā rīē* 'you (f.sg.)/she are/is going' (=*tū/ vo jā rahī hai*).

ham/tum/unõ jātẽ 'we/you/they (m.pl.) go' (=*ham/tum/vo jātē hãĩ*), *ham/tum/unõ jātāĩ* 'we/you/they (f.pl.) go' (=*ham/tum/vo jātī hãĩ*), *ham/tum/unõ baiṭhẽ* 'we/ you/they (m./f.pl.) sat down' (=*ham/tum/vo baiṭhē hãĩ*), *ham/tum/unõ jā rẽ; 'we/ you/they (m.pl.) are going' (=ham/tum/vo jā rahē hãĩ), ham/tum/unõ jā rāĩ 'we/ you/they (f.pl.) are going'* (=*ham/tum/vo jā rahī hãĩ*).

The auxiliary is dropped in negative sentences. Examples:

tū/une nĩ jātā 'you (m.sg.)/he do/does not go' (=*tū/vo nahĩ jātā*), *tū/une nĩ karā* 'you (m.sg.)/he did not do' (=*tū/us nē nahĩ kiyā*).

Matthews (1976: 207–13) finds in his text corpus the following differences between Dakhanī and Standard Urdu: an infinitive suffix *-n ~ -an: pālan* (=*pālnā*) 'to protect, rear', the conjunctive participle extension *kar ~ kō*, and a future tense stem ending in *-v-*: *jāvēgā* 'he will go', *hōvũ̃gā* 'I will be'. The perfective participle has the suffixes *yā ~ yē/ē ~ ī ~ iyā/ī: dēkhyā, dēkhyē/dēkhē, dēkhī, dēkhiyã̄/dēkhĩ*, which according to Chatterji (1960: 204–5) points to affinities with Panjabi and Bangaru (Hariyāṇvī).

Matthews observes that *nē* is seldom employed, and that even when it is, the verb invariably agrees with the subject. Matthews does not find the bound forms of the auxiliary in his text corpus, but records modern speech in which they are apparent:

yã kē lōg-ã dakanī bi bol-t-ēĩn, telugu bi bol-t-ēĩn
here POSS people-pl. Dakhanī also speak-IMPV-AUX-m.pl. Telugu also speak-IMPV-AUX-m.pl.
'The people here speak both Dakhanī and Telugu.'

Matthews (1976: 214) also finds *achnā* 'to be' used as a synonym of *hōnā*. This did not occur in the Hyderabad corpus.

Examples (Schmidt 1981: 77–9):

mãĩ dar hamēš rēl sē jā-t-aũ
I in always rail by go-IMPV-AUX-1m.sg.
'I always go by rail.'

inē navā ghar banā r-ā-ē
he new-m. house build CON-AUX-m.sg.
'He is building a new house.'

inõ haft-ē haft-ē kō sinēmā jā-t-ẽ
they week-obl.sg. week-obl.sg. DAT cinema go-IMPV-AUX-m.pl.
'They go to the cinema every week.'

bas mẽ lōk-ã yek hī wakat dhas-t-ẽ
bus in people-pl. one-EMPH time crowd-IMPV-AUX-m.pl.
'Everybody crowds into the bus at the same time.'

vo cōkriy-ã samjh-t-ãĩ aur bōl-t-ãĩ bhī
those girl-pl. understand-IMPV-AUX-f.pl. and speak-IMPV-AUX-f.pl. also
'Those girls understand as well as they speak.'

mãĩ ēk ēk bacc-ē kū nav-ē kitāb-ã dī-ũ
I one one child-obl.sg. DAT new-pl. book-pl. give-PFV-AUX–1sg.
'I gave new books to each child.'

inē/unē hamār-ī sār-ī šakkar lē li-y-ā
he our-f. all-f. sugar take take-PFV-m.sg.
'He has taken all our sugar.'

inē ais-ē wakat po ā-ē
he such-obl.sg. time at come-PFV-AUX-m.sg.
'He came at such a time.'

piyāliy-õ mẽ dhūl bhar-i-ē
cup-obl.pl. in dust be-filled-PFV-AUX-f.sg.
'The cups are dusty.'

1.1.6.3 Lexical differences

The vocabulary in Schmidt's (1981) corpus is a mixture of Urdu-Hindi tadbhava words and Perso-Arabic loans of the type common to both Urdu and Hindi, with a sprinkling of Telugu loanwords. Matthews comments at length on the vocabulary in his texts:

One striking feature which distinguishes Dakanī from the Urdu written at later periods in northern India is the wide and varied vocabulary, which was drawn from several different sources.

The Dakanī written at Bījāpur and Golkuṇḍa during the seventeenth century possesses a relatively high proportion of words taken over from Sanskrit (*tatsama* words) and Hindi or one of the Hindi dialects (*tadbhava* words) which are not found, or rarely found, in other forms of Urdu. The majority of these words, however, have always been common in Hindi writing.

A large number of Persian and Arabic words are found even in the works of the earliest Dakanī writers, and in the seventeenth century, when Persian literary forms were widely adopted by Dakanī writers, the number of Persian words increased. Indeed some Arabic/Persian words which occur fairly frequently in Dakanī works, are rather rare in the works of later Urdu writers.

The number of *tatsama* and *tadbhava* words, which are not found in later forms of Urdu, at a rough estimate account for about fifteen percent of Dakanī vocabulary, and this element remained more or less constant throughout the seventeenth century. (Matthews 1976: 218–19)

1.2 Geographical distribution and number of speakers

The Summer Institute of Linguistics (*Ethnologue*) provides an estimate of 54,584,000 Urdu speakers worldwide. The accuracy rating given by the SIL for most of the country data for Urdu is 'B', which means 'based on good published sources but with need for further investigation by linguists in the field'. Statistics for the geographic distribution of Urdu are unsatisfactory for several reasons. Urdu is a symbol of cultural and religious identity, thus South Asian Muslims may return their mother tongue as Urdu even when a different language is spoken in the home, or conversely, governments sometimes underestimate Urdu speakers for political reasons. For Pakistan, the census data available at this writing are out of date. The 1991 Census of India is relatively up to date, but there have been complaints that census enumerators in North India reported Hindi as the mother tongue of Urdu speakers without consulting them (Farouqui 1994b: 783). The census could not be conducted in Kashmir in 1991, and so the 1981 figures are shown.

1.2.1 India

The 1991 Census of India (1997: 39) enumerated 43,406,932 speakers of Urdu in India (5.13% of the population). The Summer Institute of Linguistics provides the figure of 43,773,000 Urdu speakers in India. States or territories reported as having more than 2000 speakers of Urdu are shown in Table 8.1 in descending order. The percentages are not shown in the Census documents and have been calculated by this writer.

1.2.2 Pakistan

The 1981 Census of Pakistan provides the percentage (but not the number) of Urdu speakers in the country as a whole and in the provinces. There was no census between 1981 and 1998, and the findings of the 1998 census are not available at this writing. The total number of speakers in 1981 may be estimated at 6,403,228 by taking 7.6% of the

TABLE 8.1: NUMBER OF URDU SPEAKERS IN INDIA (AS PERCENTAGE OF POPULATION)

India	43,406,932	5.13%
Uttar Pradesh	12,492,927	8.98%
Bihar	8,542,463	9.89%
Maharashtra	5,734,468	7.26%
Andhra Pradesh	5,560,154	8.36%
Karnataka	4,480,038	9.96%
West Bengal	1,455,649	2.13%
Madhya Pradesh	1,227,672	1.86%
Tamil Nadu	1,036,660	1.86%
Rajasthan	953,497	1.71%
Gujarat	547,737	1.24%
Delhi	512,990	5.45%
Orissa	502,102	1.59%
Haryana	261,820	1.59%
Goa	39,944	3.41%
Punjab	13,416	6.61%
Kerala	12,625	4.34%
Himachal Pradesh	8,252	1.60%
Jammu and Kashmir (1981)	6,315	1.05%
Pondicherry	6,170	7.64%
Chandigarh	4,570	7.12%
Assam	3,935	1.76%
Meghalaya	2,863	1.61%

total population of 84,253,000. The *Encyclopedia Britannica* (*Britannica Online*) however provides the figure of 6,700,000 speakers in 1981, and adds in Table 4 that Urdu is spoken by a further 5,900,000 as an additional language. The Summer Institute of Linguistics (*Ethnologue*) provides the figure of 10,719,000 Urdu speakers in 1993, with the percentage at 7.57% of the population.

The 1981 census data (percentage of speakers of Urdu in Pakistan) is shown below for the country as a whole and province by province. The estimated number of speakers has been calculated by this writer (see 6. 'Remarks'). A reasonable estimate of the current number of Urdu speakers cannot be projected using the annual growth rate for the country as a whole of 3.1%, since the predominantly urban Urdu-speaking Muhajir population probably has a lower growth rate than the rural population. (*Muhājir* [refugee] is a term referring to all those who migrated to Pakistan at Partition, whether speakers of Urdu or of some other language. Not all Muhajirs are mother-tongue Urdu speakers, but mother-tongue Urdu speakers are still predominantly Muhajirs, despite the adoption by some non-Muhajirs of Urdu as the language of the home.) The larger number of Urdu speakers in Sindh, Islamabad and Punjab reflects the settlement of Muhajirs in the large cities of Karachi, Hyderabad, Islamabad and Lahore.

1.2.3 Bangladesh

At the time of the first census in Bengal in 1872, Muslims formed 48% of the population. The elite, or *ašrāf*, often spoke Urdu. Two contradictory movements arose, one promoting Urdu and the other Bengali. After the establishment of Pakistan, Bengali nationalists were provoked by the declaration of Mohammad Ali Jinnah that the state language of Pakistan would be Urdu and no other language (Rahman 1996: 87), and

TABLE 8.2: PERCENTAGE OF URDU SPEAKERS IN PAKISTAN (AS PERCENTAGE OF TOTAL POPULATION)

Pakistan	6,403,228	7.6%
Sind	4,308,166	22.64%
Islamabad	38,182	11.23%
Punjab	2,019,368	4.27%
Baluchistan	59,348	1.37%
North West Frontier Province	91,806	0.83%
Federally Administered Tribal Areas	2,199	0.01%

insistence on the equal status of Bengali and Urdu became a conspicuous feature of Bengali nationalism. The *Encyclopedia Britannica* (*Britannica Online*) provides a figure of 240,000 Urdu speakers for Bangladesh in 1981. The Summer Institute of Linguistics provides a figure of 600,000 Urdu speakers in 1993. Urdu speakers in Bangladesh are for the most part Muhajirs from Bihar.

1.2.4 Urdu worldwide

Urdu has become the culture language and lingua franca of the South Asian Muslim diaspora outside the subcontinent. The Summer Institute of Linguistics has attempted to compile the statistics of this population, and their figures are provided below. In addition to the countries mentioned by the Summer Institute of Linguistics, Urdu is also spoken in Afghanistan, Denmark, Sweden, the United Kingdom, the United States and Thailand.

It should be noted that overseas Pakistani or Indian Muslims often report their mother tongue as Urdu even when a different language is spoken in the home, as Urdu is their literary, cultural and religious language as well as a unifying force in the community. This makes it difficult to define what an Urdu speaker is. A good example is the Urdu-speaking community in Norway. There are approximately 20,000 people of Pakistani origin in Norway (Vassenden 1997), of whom the overwhelming majority come from the Panjab. Thus it is likely that even fewer than 7.6% of them originally spoke Urdu in the home. The mother-tongue education provided to them by the Norwegian school system, and other facilities such as mother-tongue radio broadcasts, is however in Urdu, and few report their mother tongue as Panjabi. There are as yet no studies of how this situation affects actual language use.

TABLE 8.3: NUMBER OF URDU SPEAKERS OUTSIDE SOUTH ASIA

Country	Number	Source
Nepal	54,000	*Encyclopedia Britannica*
Mauritius	64,000	Summer Institute of Linguistics
South Africa	170,000	Summer Institute of Linguistics
Fiji	3,562	Summer Institute of Linguistics
Oman	30,000	Summer Institute of Linguistics
Bahrain	20,000	Summer Institute of Linguistics
Qatar	19,950	Summer Institute of Linguistics
Germany	23,000	Summer Institute of Linguistics
Norway	14,000	Summer Institute of Linguistics

1.3 Diglossia

Information about diglossia among Urdu speakers is relatively scarce. However, the fact that they are everywhere a minority of the population implies a high rate of bilingualism and even trilingualism in the population as a whole.

1.3.1 Nonstandard speech styles

Before the introduction of education for women, the speech style of women, or *Bēgamātī zabān* ['ladies' Urdu'] differed from that of men due to the segregation of women (Minault 1984: 157; see 6. 'Remarks' for bibliographic information.). Women spent most of their time in the company of other women, where men were not party to the conversation. *Bēgamātī zabān* was an unwritten dialect, but was eventually captured in a number of lexicons and Urdu novels in the late nineteenth century. It was characterized by a straightforward and idiomatic style without the flowery and polite phrases of Persianized Urdu. Often tadbhava vocabulary items from the vernaculars, such as Braj Bhāṣa, Avadhī and Dakhanī, are used rather than Persian loans: *bhāg* 'fate' (rather than *qismat*) and *bēlajjā* 'shameless' rather than *bēšarm*. Some examples of women's speech occur in *Umrāō Jān Adā*, by Rusvā, for example *mūā* 'wretch (lit. 'dead')'. A specimen of *Bēgamātī* Urdu preserved by Grierson (1916: 128–33) shows an unvarnished colloquial style which derives much of its liveliness from the exploitation of reduplicatives and compounds of various kinds: *bak bak jhak jhak* 'continually talking nonsense' (lit. 'babble-babble chatter-chatter'), *ɣul ɣapārā* 'uproar' (lit. 'noise-clamour'), *kōī bāt na cīt, bēkār bēkār* 'without even a word, for no reason' (lit. 'any word not thought, useless useless').

A relatively unPersianized Urdu (or unSanskritized Hindi) is used in the cinema, television dramas and popular music industries, in both India and Pakistan. A speech style approximating more or less to it (with more Panjabi vocabulary in Pakistan and more Hindi vocabulary in India) functions as a lingua franca for informal communication between speakers of different languages. This speech style is not taught in the schools, and is seldom written, as it is unacceptable to the purists. It is, however, a major factor in inhibiting divergence between Urdu and Hindi.

1.3.2 Multilingualism

Urdu exists in a multilingual environment almost everywhere, the inevitable result of historical dislocations and the educational policies of both India and Pakistan.

In Pakistan, Urdu is the major language of the mass media, and government schools are supposed to use Urdu as the medium of instruction. Thus Urdu has become a second language for Panjabi, Sindhi, Pashto and other speakers. Urdu has not succeeded in displacing English as the medium of instruction in elitist schools however (Rahman 1996: 228–47), and 'even diehard supporters of Urdu do not take the risk of educating their own children in Urdu-medium schools, if they can afford English-medium ones' (Rahman 1996: 245). In Pakistan, Urdu and English are dominant in the workplace, the schools and the media, while the regional languages are the languages of the home.

India has a three-language policy for education, in which Hindi, English and one modern regional language are supposed to be taught in the schools. Urdu was envisioned as an optional choice under this formula, but according to Farouqui (1994b: 782), only in Maharashtra and Bihar is there satisfactory provision for education in Urdu, while in Andhra Pradesh it is available, though not satisfactory. Media reports suggest that Indian Urdu speakers who can afford to do so prefer to educate their children in English medium schools rather than Urdu medium schools. Thus the majority of Indian Urdu speakers acquire a second language through their education. For employment in white collar jobs, knowledge of Hindi and English is essential in the north, and regional languages and English are essential in the south. The dominant languages of the mass media are English and Hindi in the north, and English and the regional languages in the south. Lack of education in Urdu has resulted in a paucity of readers for the Urdu press in India, which (unlike the Urdu press in Pakistan) does not have an all-India circulation (Farouqui 1994a: 361–2). The only Urdu newspaper in Lucknow ceased publication in 1998.

In India Urdu is the language of the home, the *dīnī madrasa* (Islamic religious school) and restricted cultural institutions such as *mušāiras* (poetry readings) and an Urdu press limited in scope and relevance. (However even in the religious school, the place of Urdu is not secure, as the Jamaat-e-Islami in India have adopted a policy of publishing religious books in Hindi in North India and regional languages in South India (Farouqui 1992).) In the school and the workplace, Hindi, English and the regional languages are dominant.

1.3.3 Grammatical convergence between Urdu and other languages

Phenomena of convergence of Pakistani Urdu with Panjabi and other languages of Pakistan are usually dismissed as 'bad Urdu', while scientific studies of diglossia have focused mainly on the Urdu dialects of South India, or Dakhanī. Schmidt (1981: 59–61) points to three areas of the grammar where Dakhinī has converged with Telugu: (a) loss of the ergative construction with transitive verbs in perfective tenses; (b) weakening of the masculine/feminine gender distinction, with the tendency of the feminine gender to subside into an inanimate and (c) extension of the indefinite tense (the imperfective participle with or without an auxiliary) to include future actions.

Kachru (1986) says that many Dakhanī features at all levels show influence from Marathi, Kannada and Telugu, and identifies two syntactic constructions in the spoken language of Hyderabad which show convergence with Marathi and Dravidian. The first is the use of a periphrastic causal construction with an oblique infinitive + *lagvāī*, which suggests influence from Marathi.

mãĩ naukar sē kamrā sāf karnē lagvāī
I servant by room clean do engaged
'I had the servant clean the room.' (Kachru 1986: 168)

The standard Urdu construction would use *sāf karvānā* 'cause to clean':

mãĩ nē naukar sē kamrā sāf karvā-y-ā
I ERG servant from room clean cause-to-do-PFV-m.sg.
'I had the servant clean the room.'

Note also that while in standard Urdu, the pronoun is followed by *nē* and the verb agrees with the object, in Dakhanī, perfective verbs agree with the subject (Schmidt 1981: 36; Kachru 1986: 173).

The second of Kachru's examples of convergence is a relative clause construction which is closer to a participial construction, with a preference for the relative clause preceding the main clause, a usage which is very similar to the participial modifier construction in Dravidian languages (Kachru 1986: 170–3).

khēl rayā thā sō laṛkā gir gayā
playing was C boy fall went
'The boy who was playing fell down.' (Kachru 1986: 171)

Schmidt (1981: 36–7) also provides examples with *sō* used to form participial modifiers:

ammā̃ khō-ē sō rūpiyā ḍhū̃ḍ r-ī-ē
mother lost-obl.sg. MOD rupee search CON-AUX-f.sg.
'Mother is searching for a rupee she lost.'

In the Dakhanī of Bhongir, about thirty miles from Hyderabad, Pray (1980: 91–4) found more extensive convergence with Telugu than Schmidt (1981) found in Hyderabad city. Examples include (a) distinction between an exclusive and inclusive first person plural pronoun, (b) replacement of the reflexive possessive adjective *apnā* with the non-reflexive possessive, (c) loss of gender contrast in plural verbs, (d) a split between the demonstratives *ye/vo* and the third person personal pronoun *unē*, and (e) loss of the oblique case in pronouns. Examples:

(a)   *ham lōgā̃* '(exclusive) we'
      apan/apal lōgā̃ '(inclusive) we'

(b)   *maĩ mēr-ē kitāb-ā̃ bēc-ũ gā* (= Standard Urdu *maĩ apnī kitābē̃ bēcũ gā*)
      I my-m.pl. book-pl. sell-1sg. FUT-m.sg.
      'I will sell my books.'

(c)   *bacciyā̃ āē* 'the girls came' (= Standard Urdu *bacciyā̃ āĩ*)

(d)   *vo kitāb* 'that book'
      unē āyā 'he came' (= Standard Urdu *vo āyā*)

(e)   *ye kitāb mē̃* 'in this book' (= Standard Urdu *is kitāb mē̃*)

There are usage shifts at the grammatical level in the Urdu of Pakistan which may be due to Panjabi influence. Bashir (1999) presents data showing that in that dialect, *nē* (rather than *kō*) marks the subject of impersonal verbal constructions when external necessity or compulsion is not involved (see 3.5.10.2.4. Bashir's 'marker of source'). Divergence between the Urdu of Pakistan and the Urdu of India is only beginning to receive scholarly attention.

1.3.4 Lexical convergence between Urdu and other languages

Introduction of Perso-Arabic vocabulary continues, particularly of Arabic vocabulary under the stimulus of official and religious sources (such as state-sponsored media and textbooks in Pakistan, or religious textbooks in both countries), but seems to have less impact on the spoken language than borrowing from English, which is universally pervasive at the lexical level (for example, in Norway, Urdu speakers often continue to use assimilated English loanwords instead of replacing them with Norwegian loanwords).

Schmidt (1981: 53) provides some miscellaneous examples of lexical influence on Dakhanī from Marathi (*nako* 'no' [=*nahī̃*]), *navā* 'new' [=*nayā*]), and *-c* [emphatic enclitic, ex. *vahīc* 'right there']).

Pray (1980: 97) identifies several Dakhanī words which, while not themselves borrowed, express the same lexical functions as Telugu words. The Dakhanī indefinite particle *kī* corresponds to the Telugu enclitic particle *-ō* which forms indirect questions. *kī* is suffixed to interrogatives to form indefinites: *kyā kī* 'something', *kaun kī* 'someone'. The Dakhanī reported speech operator *katē* (the only form of Standard Urdu *kahnā* 'to say' surviving in Dakhanī) corresponds to Telugu *aṭa*. The Dakhanī quotative *bōlkē* 'having said' corresponds to the Telugu quotative particle *ani*. Examples:

> *une ā-y-ā katē*
> he come-PFV-m.sg. RSO
> 'They say he came.'

> *unē ye kām kar-ā bōlkē mērē kū mālūm hai*
> he this work do-PFV-m.sg. QUOT my DAT known is
> 'I know that he did this work.'

(Further references are provided under 'Dakhanī Urdu' in Further reading'.)

In the Urdu of Pakistan, Panjabi influence is common at the lexical and grammatical levels. The following examples of borrowing from English and Panjabi are taken from a short story by Mazhar ul Islam. The loans are bolded and the source (E = English, P = Panjabi) given in brackets.

> *ḍākṭar* [E] *kōī **aukh-ā** [P] sā angrēzī nām lē-t-ē h-aĩ*
> doctors some hard-m.sg.-very English name take-IMPV-m.pl. AUX-3pl
> 'The doctors use a hard English name.'

In the last example, *aukhā sā* evokes the Panjabi *aukhā jā*, which is more forceful than Urdu *muškil sā* (Bashir 1998, personal communication).

> *cūhā ... **ṭuk ṭuk** [P] rōṭiy-ã̄ kutar-nē lag-ā*
> rat ... munch munch bread-nom.f.pl. gnaw-INF-obl. begin-PFV-m.sg.
> 'The rat ... began to gnaw the rotis, munch munch.'

> *piyāla bacc-õ kē **vārḍ** [E] mẽ lag-ē bijlī kē **mīṭar** [E] kē ḍibb-ē kē ūpar paṛ-ā th-ā*
> cup child-obl.pl. POSS ward in apply-PFV-obl.sg. electricity POSS meter POSS box-obl.sg. POSS above lie-PFV-m.sg. AUX-PAST-m.sg.
> 'The cup was on top of the meter-box (attached) in the children's ward.'

Bashir considers the preference for *paṛā thā* 'was lying' in the last example as an instance of convergence with Panjabi; in standard Delhi Urdu, *rakhā thā* 'was put' would be preferred for an object which has been deliberately placed in a location. In Panjabi, *pyā e* (corresponding to Urdu *paṛā hai*) is the normal way of saying that something is (lying) in some position or location (Bashir 1998, personal communication).

2 PHONOLOGY

2.1 Classical phonemes

TABLE 8.4: THE PHONEMIC INVENTORY OF STANDARD URDU

	Bilabial	Labio-dental	Dental	Post-alveolar	Alveo-palatal	Dorso-velar	Postvelar
Consonants							
Stops							
voiceless	/ p		t	ṭ	c	k	q
voiced	b		d	ḍ	j	g	
Fricatives							
voiceless		f	s		š	x	
voiced			z		ž	γ	h
Nasals	m		n				
Lateral			l				
Tap			r				
Flap				ṛ			
Semivowels		v			y /		

	Front	Central	Back
Vowels			
High	/ i		u
Mid	e		o
Low	ai		au
		a	ɑ /

Coarticulation and suprasegmentals
Aspiration, occurs with /p t ṭ c k b d ḍ j g ṛ /
Nasalization, occurs with all vowels except /ɑ/
Vowel length, occurs with all vowels

(Adapted from Kelkar 1968: 79 and Gumperz and Naim 1960: 102–3)

2.2 Phonological contrasts and realizations

Contrasts are illustrated below for the consonants, with allophonic variation mentioned. The vowels and semivowels are described in detail. Data have been taken from a variety of sources, including Kelkar 1968, Gumperz and Naim 1960, Barker 1975 and Singh 1966, supplemented by data recorded from a mother-tongue Urdu speaker who moved from Delhi to Lahore at the age of ten, and spent his adult life in Lahore. Individual pronunciations may vary considerably from region to region.

2.2.1 Consonants

The five-way contrast in stops, with voicing and aspiration, is well attested in all dialects of Urdu (see however 1.1.6.1.). A comprehensive list of minimal pairs is beyond the scope of this chapter; the following list is illustrative.

2.2.1.1 Place of articulation and voicing

pal 'moment', *tal* 'low', *ṭal* 'withdraw', *cal* 'walk', *kal* 'yesterday'
bal 'strength', *dal* 'army', *ḍal* 'be put', *jal* 'burn', *gal* 'melt'

2.2.1.2 Aspiration and /h/

pāl 'bring up', *phāl* 'ploughshare', *tāl* 'musical measure', *thāl* 'platter', *ṭāl*
'stack', *ṭhāl* 'idleness', *ḍāl* 'pour', *ḍhāl* 'shield', *kāl* 'famine', *khāl* 'hide (of an
animal)', *gāl* 'cheek', *ghāl* 'ruin', *hāl* 'condition', *paṛ* 'fall', *paṛh* 'read'.

The distribution of aspirated consonants stated in table 8.4 under 'Coarticulation and
suprasegmentals' predicts that /h/ does *not* represent aspiration in the following items:
/tashīh/ 'correction', /mazhab/ 'religion', /mashūr/ 'famous'. When /h/ occurs after
consonants which may occur aspirated, it may be realized as aspiration: /sab+hī/ =
[səbʰiː] 'all (emphatic)', /nibāhnā/ = [nɪbaːhnaː] ~ [nɪbʰaːnaː] 'to carry through'.
    Geminated consonants are aspirated as a single unit (when an aspirated consonant is
doubled, only the second consonant is aspirated): /citthī/ 'letter'.
    Final /h/ may be realized as (nonphonemic) aspiration or lost: /gunāh/ = [gʊnʰaː] ~
[gʊnaːh]) 'sin', /sahīh/ = [səhiː] ~ [səhiːh] 'correct'.
    /ph/ occasionally alternates with /f/: /phir/ ~ /fir/ 'again'.

2.2.1.3 Nonphonemic gemination

Gemination or doubling of consonants is usually phonemic in Urdu: /pakā/ 'cooked',
/pakkā/ 'ripe'. But a consonant preceded by a short vowel and followed by a long vowel
may be doubled nonphonemically: /uṭhō/ → /uṭṭhō/ 'get up!' In some Urdu dialects,
including Old Delhi Urdu and Panjabi-influenced Urdu, the sequence: long vowel +
(unaspirated) consonant is changed to short vowel + geminate consonant: /cādar/ →
/caddar/ 'sheet, veil', /darvāza/ → /darvazza/ 'door'.

2.2.1.4 Nasals and nasalization

/n/ = [ṇ] before post-alveolar stops, and [ŋ] ~ [̃] before dorso-velar stops: /ghanṭa/ =
[ghaṇṭa] 'clock, hour', /rang/ = [rəŋg] 'colour', /rangīn/ = [rəŋgiːn] ~ [rə̃giːn]
'colourful', /mangnā/ = [maːŋgnaː] ~ [mãːgnaː] 'to ask for'. [ṇ] and [ŋ] do not occur
initially.
    The contrast between a homorganic nasal stop and a nasalized vowel can be
identified, but is unstable, particularly with long vowels: [samjʰaːna:] 'to explain',
[sãbʰaːlna:] 'to take care of', [caːnd] ~ [cãːd] 'moon'. Final long vowels ending in /n/
may be reduced to nasalized long vowels, particularly in poetry: [jəhãː] 'world' (=
/jahān/), [aːsmãː] 'heaven' (= /āsmān/).

2.2.1.5 Illustration of contrast between oral and nasalized vowels

hai 'is', *haĩ* 'are', *kahā* 'said', *kahā̃* 'where?', *vahī* 'that very one', *vahī̃* 'right there', *hō*
'(you) are', *hō̃* '(they) might be'.

2.2.1.6 Marginal phonemes

/q/ occurs most commonly in the speech of educated speakers. In the speech of uneducated speakers, or in fast speech, it may be realized as [k], as [x] before a voiceless stop, and as [k] ~ [ɣ] before a voiced stop: [qəri:b] ~ [kəri:b] 'near', [wəqt] ~ [vaxt] 'time', [həqda:r] ~ [həɣda:r] 'deserving'.

The contrast between /ḍ/ and /ṛ/ is only partial. /ṛ/ does not occur initially. Medially, /ḍ/ occurs only doubled, following close juncture, and in loanwords from English. Finally, /ḍ/ occurs following a nasal and in loanwords from English. [həḍḍi:] 'bone', [nă+ḍər] 'do not fear', [so:ḍa:] 'soda', [dʰũ:ḍ] 'look for!', [mu:ḍ] 'mood'. Compare [muṛ] 'turn'.

A glottal stop is sometimes heard in hypercorrect speech, where it represents ع ᶜain in the spelling: [jəma:ʔət] ~ [jəma:t] 'class' (جماعت).

/ž/ occurs only in a few words borrowed from Persian or English: /miža/ 'eyelash', and /z/ is often substituted by speakers who are not well-educated in Perso-Arabic usage.

2.2.2 Semivowels

There has been considerable debate as to whether the sounds classed as semivowels here (/v/, /y/) are to be handled as consonants or vowels. Scholars who favour handling them as vowels distinguish in transcription between /v/ with consonantal friction, and /w/ realized as a glide or short vowel. They also define /y/ as a glide before and after vowels, and a short vowel elsewhere. Thus Barker's (1975, Vol. 1: 13) transcriptions:

/yəhã/ 'here' (*yahā̃* [i̯əhã:])
/nəya/ 'new' (*nayā* [nəi̯a:])
/kya/ 'what?' (*kyā* [ke̯a:])
/ysm/ 'noun, name' (*ism* [ɪsm])

Barker (ibid.) distinguishes between a short lower-high-back rounded vowel, /w/, and a voiced labio-dental fricative, /v/:

/wrdu/ 'Urdu' (*urdū* [ʊrdu:])
/twm/ 'you' (*tum* [tʊm])
/vw/ 'that' (*vo* [βo])
/vəhã/ 'there' (*vahā̃* [vəhã:])
/həva/ 'wind' (*havā* [həβa:])

This is not merely a question of transcription; for Barker, /y/ and /w/ are phonemic vowels.

This solution is economical, but tends to obscure the role played by the *y*-glide in syllabification. Barker's /y/ is syllabic in /ysm/, but nonsyllabic in /nəya/. In addition, the *w*-glide ([ʊ̯], [o̯]) appears to be an allophone of /v/ (see phonetic statements for /v/, below). In this chapter, the vowels /i/, /u/ are treated as phonetic units with syllabic properties, and /y/ and /v/ are handled as semivowels.

The following statements cover the above occurrences of /y/ and /v/.

/y/ = [i̯] initially, before /u e o/ or after /i/: [i̯əhã:] 'here', [i̯ũ:] 'like this', [ki̯i̯e:] 'did (m.pl.)', [ki̯õ:] ~ [ki̯ũ:] 'why?', [ni̯i̯ət] 'intention'.

= [ɪ̯] after [ə]: [nəi̯a:] ~ [nɛi̯a:] 'new'.

= [e̯] before or after /a/: [a:e̯a:] 'came', [ke̯a:] 'what?'.

/v/ = [v] ~ [β] initially: [vəhã:] 'there', [βo] 'that'.

= [v] before /i/, /e/: , [bi:vi:] 'wife', [həve:li:] 'mansion', [mɔ:lvi:] 'religious scholar'.

= [β] ~ [ʋ] intervocalically after [ə]: [nəʋãː] 'ninth', [təʋəjjõh] 'attention', [jəβaːniː] ~ [jəʋaːniː] 'youth', [qəββaːliː] 'religious song'.
= [β] ~ [o̥] intervocalically before or after /a o/, [ləgaːβət̪] ~ [ləgaːo̥ət̪] 'attachment'.
= [β] ~ [o̥] in the environment C<u>v</u>ā: [bʊlβaːnaː] ~ [bʊlo̥aːnaː] 'to summon'.
=[β] ~ [ʋ] in the environment C<u>v</u>ə: [rɪʂβət] ~ [rɪʂʋət] 'bribe'.

2.2.3 Vowels

The phonetic values are shown in the examples below. Note that in phonemic transcription, long vowels are shown with a macron (ā ū ī) and short vowels without (a u i). Short /i/ and /a/ are neutralized before a tautosyllabic /h/: /mihnat/ → [mɛhnət] 'effort'; /pahinnā/ → [pɛhnna] 'to wear'. /i/ is also often lowered when preceding ع (the Arabic character ᶜain). While short [e] is usually considered an allophone of /i/, in the speech of speakers who pronounce ک as [kẽ] there is a minimal set for /e/ : /ē/ : /ī/: [kẽ], 'that'; [keː], m. pl. poss. postposition; [kiː], f. poss. postposition. Short /i/ and /u/ do not occur finally.
   Note that the eight-vowel analysis offered here treats length as a phoneme, and the distinction between short and long vowels as a quantitative rather than a qualitative one. In point of fact, short vowels are qualitatively different from long vowels, and an eleven-vowel system (i ɪ u ʊ ə a ɑ e o ɛ ɔ) could be offered instead. In the latter analysis, length would be a property of vowel quality. The reason for rejecting the second approach is that most analyses of Urdu treat length as phonemic, and length is traditionally regarded as contrastive; and one of the purposes of this chapter is to introduce the reader to the linguistic study of Urdu. The solution of the problem of the semivowels and syllabification, mentioned under 2.2.2, also points to an analysis in terms of vowel length.
   The transcription used here distinguishes short and long /e/ and /o/: e ē o ō, even though short e o are allophones of /i a u/, as detailed below. The purpose for offering this slightly overdifferentiated transcription is that the environments of short e o are many, complex, and often require a knowledge of the spelling of the word, or its origin. Thus it is helpful to the reader to transcribe short e o.

2.2.3.1 Phonetic values of vowels

/i/ = [ɪ] in short syllables (does not occur in final position): [dɪn] 'day'.
   = [ẽ] finally in monosyllables, the final syllable of Persian loanwords and as izāfat (see 6. 'Remarks'): [yẽ] 'this', [ki̯õ:+kẽ] ~ [ki̯õ:+kẽh] 'because', [əgərcẽ] 'although', [dərd+ẽ+dɪl] 'heartache'.
   = [ɛ] in short syllables before tautosyllabic /h/ or adjacent to ع ᶜain: [mɛhnət] 'effort', [ɪstɛmaːl] (استعمال) 'use' (also [ɪsteːmaːl]).
   = [i] in long syllables: [diːn] 'religion', [kiː], f. poss. postposition.
/e/ = [e] in long syllables only: [deːn] 'giving', [keː], m. pl. poss. postposition.
   = [ɛ] (in loanwords from English): [fɑːrɛn] 'abroad', [kɑːlɛj] 'college'.
/ai/ = [æ] in long syllables only: [hæː] 'is', [hæ̃ː] 'are', [bæːl] 'ox'.
/a/ = [ə] in short syllables, except finally: [əgərcẽ] 'although', [kəm] 'less'.
   = [ă] in final short syllables or in monosyllables: [naʔ] 'not', [bəccă] 'child'.
   = [ẽ] ~ [ɛ] in short syllables before tautosyllabic /h/: [kẽhaː] 'said', [pɛhlaː] 'first'. In some dialects, /-ayā/ = [ɛi̯aː]: [nɛi̯aː] 'new', [gɛi̯aː] 'went'.
   = [ə] ~ [ø] in short syllables before tautosyllabic /h/ followed by a short vowel (see also note on medial /h/, below: [bəhʊt] ~ [bʰõt] ~ [bʰɔt] 'many, very', [məhɛl] ~ [mʰɛl] 'palace'.

= [a] in long syllables: [baːl] 'hair', [bəcaː] 'saved', [kaːm] 'work'.
/a/ = [ɑ] in long syllables in loanwords from English: [bɑːl] 'ball', [kɑːlɛj] 'college'.
/u/ = [ʊ] in short syllables (does not occur in final position): [ʊn] 'them', [sʊkʰ] 'happiness'.

= [o] ~ [ŏ] finally in monosyllables, in short syllables before tautosyllabic /h/, and as the Persian copula -o- : [vŏ] 'that', [sohbət] 'companionship', [təʊəjjŏh] 'attention', [aːb+ŏ+həβaː] 'climate (water and wind)'.

= [u] in long syllables: [uːn] 'wool', [suːkʰ] 'dry'.
/o/ = [o] in long syllables only: [joː] 'who (relative)', [koːnaː] 'corner'.
/au/= [ɔ] ~ [əo] in long syllables only: [kɔːn] 'who?', [jəo] 'barley'.

2.2.3.2 Intervocalic /h/

Intervocalic /h/ is unstable, and may be reduced to aspiration in fast speech. Here it is hard to formulate universally applicable rules, since register must be taken into account. Some examples are given below.

/ahi/ → [əhĕ] ~ [øhɛ]: /bahin/ → [bəhen] ~ [bʰɛn] 'sister', /pahilā/ → [pɛhla] ~ [pʰɛla] 'first'.
/ahu/ → [əhʊ] ~ [øhŏ] ~ [øhɔ̃]: /bahut/ → [bəhʊt] ~ [bəhŏt] ~ [bʰɔ̃t] 'many, very'.
/aha/ → [əhĕ] ~ [øhɛ]: [mahal] → [məhĕl] ~ [mʰɛl] 'palace'.

When the vowel following /h/ is long, it usually remains unaffected, but in fast speech medial /h/ is reduced: /jā rahā hai/ → [jaː rʰaːe], '(he) is going'.

2.2.3.3 Reduction of short root vowels

When suffixes consisting of long vowels are added to roots of the CVCVC pattern (in which the vowels are short), the penultimate short vowel of the root is reduced or lost.

aurat 'woman' + *-ẽ* (f. pl. nom. suffix) → *aurtẽ* 'women'
bahen 'sister' + *-õ* (obl. pl. suffix) → *bahnõ* 'sisters (oblique plural)'
pakaṛ 'catch' + *ā* (causative affix) → *pakṛā* 'give to hold'

This also applies in some cases where the first vowel is long: *vālid* 'father' + *-ain* (Ar. dual suffix) → *vāldain* 'parents'.

3 GRAMMAR

(Where not otherwise indicated, data are taken from Schmidt 1999.)

3.1 Nominal structures

3.1.1 Nouns

3.1.1.1 Gender and number

Two genders are distinguished, masculine and feminine; and two numbers, singular and plural. These distinctions are shown, where they are marked, by means of suffixes.

Some nouns are marked, i.e., they have gender-suffixes: *-ā* for masculine nouns and *-ī* for feminine nouns. However many nouns are unmarked (have no gender-suffix).

Massive borrowing from other languages, particularly Persian, Arabic and English, has greatly increased the number of unmarked nouns, reducing the functional load on the old case system. Examples:

laṛk-ā 'boy' (masculine marked)
laṛk-ī 'girl' (feminine marked)
mard 'man' (masculine unmarked; loan from Persian)
aurat 'woman' (feminine unmarked; loan from Arabic)

Perso-Arabic nouns ending in final unpronounced *h* (ه) are handled as masculine marked nouns with the gender suffix *-a*. Not all speakers distinguish between final *-a* (ه) and final *-ā* (ا) in pronunciation: *bacc-a* 'child' (masculine marked) = [bəccă ~ bəccaː].

The gender suffixes inflect to show singular and plural: *laṛk-ē* 'boys', *bacc-ē* 'children', *laṛkīy-ā̃* 'girls'.

Unmarked masculine nouns have no plural suffix. Unmarked feminine nouns have the plural suffix *-ẽ̃*: mard 'men', *aurt-ẽ̃* 'women'.

3.1.1.2 Case

The masculine gender-suffix inflects to show three cases: nominative (also called direct), oblique and vocative. The feminine gender suffix does not inflect to show case, and unmarked nouns have no case suffixes in the singular. All nouns, marked and unmarked, take an oblique plural suffix, *-õ̃*, and a vocative plural suffix, *-ō* (the vocative with animates only).

Nominative nouns occur most commonly as the subjects of verbs. Oblique nouns are usually followed by postpositions: words which function similarly to English prepositions (3.1.1.3), but which follow nouns or pronouns. They may also be used without postpositions as locatives or illatives.

An adjective which qualifies an oblique or vocative noun also becomes oblique (3.2).

Nominative

laṛk-ā yahã̄ rah-t-ā h-ai
boy-nom.sg. here live-IMPV-m.sg. AUX-3sg.
'The boy lives here' (nominative sg. of *laṛkā*).

laṛk-ē yahã̄ rah-t-ē h-ãĩ
boy-nom.pl. here live-IMPV-m.pl. AUX-3pl.
'The boys live here' (nominative pl. of *laṛkā*).

Oblique before a postposition

laṛk-ē kā ghar yahã̄ hai
boy-obl.sg. POSS home here is
'The home of the boy is here' (obl. *laṛkē* followed by postposition *kā* 'of').

laṛk-õ̃ kā ghar yahã̄ hai
boy-obl.pl. POSS home here is
'The home of the boys is here' (obl. *laṛkõ̃* followed by postposition *kā* 'of').

Oblique used as illative

> *kyā āp ḍāk xān-ē jā rah-ē h-ãĩ?*
> INTER you-L3 post house-obl. go CON-m.pl. AUX-pl. (see 3.3.2)
> 'Are you going to the post office?'

Marked masculine nouns ending in short -*a* pattern like nouns ending in -*ā*:

> *bacc-a yahā̃ rah-t-ā h-ai* 'The child lives here.'
> *bacc-ē yahā̃ rah-t-ē h-ãĩ* 'The children live here.'
> *bacc-ē kā ghar* 'the home of the child'
> *bacc-õ kā ghar* 'the home of the children'

Compare the uninflecting feminine and the unmarked nouns:

> *laṛk-ī kā ghar* 'the home of the girl'
> *mard kā ghar* 'the home of the man'
> *aurat kā ghar* 'the home of the woman'

The oblique plural suffix is added to all nouns except borrowed Arabic and Persian duals and plurals:

> *laṛkiy-õ kā ghar* 'the home of the girls'
> *mard-õ kā ghar* 'the home of the men'
> *aurt-õ kā ghar* 'the home of the women'

But:

> *vālid-ain kā ghar*
> parent-dual POSS house
> 'the home of (one's) parents' (*vālid+ain* [Arabic dual suffix])

Vocative
Only marked masculine nouns show the vocative singular suffix -*ē*. All nouns show the vocative plural -*ō*. The noun *bēṭā* 'son' is however commonly used in the nominative singular to address both boys and girls. This seems to be an urban phenomenon.

> *bacc-ē, sun-ō!*
> child-m.-voc.sg. listen-IMP-2
> 'Listen, child!'

> *bacc-ō, sun-ō!*
> child-m.voc.pl. listen-IMP-2
> 'Listen, children!'

> *bhāiy-ō aur bahn-ō!*
> brother-voc.pl. and sister-voc.pl.
> 'brothers and sisters!'

3.1.1.3 Postpositions

Urdu postpositions function similarly to prepositions in European languages, but follow nouns or pronouns, and mark (a) grammatical functions, (b) location, movement or extent in space and time. In Urdu they are written as separate words. The grammatical functions of possession, object marking, agent, locative and ablative functions are all marked by postpositions. While nominative, oblique and vocative case marking is limited to marked masculine nouns in the singular, and to plural nouns, postpositions are added to all nouns, marked or unmarked, singular or plural. This has led some grammarians to treat the postpositional system as a case system, and to speak of the ergative case, dative case, and so on. Masica (1991: 231–48) speaks of three layers of forms with case-like functions. Layer I consists of the old case-affixes (in Urdu, nominative, oblique and vocative); layer II consists of the primary postpositions with grammatical functions, and layer III consists of phrases composed of the primary postposition *kā* plus a noun, adjective or adverb ('compound postpositions').

Postpositions, unlike cases, are added only to nouns and pronouns (if a postposition is added to an adjective, the adjective is treated as a noun), and normally only to the last in a series of nouns. Before postpositions, nouns and pronouns occur in the oblique case:

mēr-ē bhāiy-ṍ aur bahn-ṍ kō
my-pl. brother-obl.pl. and sister-obl.pl. DAT
'to my brothers and sisters'

The primary postpositions are:

kā (~ *kē* ~ *kī*), possessive postposition
kō 'to (dative)'
nē, ergative marker
sē 'from, by, with'
mẽ 'in'
par 'on, at'
tak 'till, until, as far as'

3.1.1.3.1   *kā* (~ *kē* ~ *kī*) shows a possessive relationship (POSS) between two nouns. It agrees with the noun it qualifies in gender, number and case, like an adjective:

mã̄ k-ā dūdh
mother POSS-m. milk (m.)
'mother's milk'

mã̄ k-ī duā
mother POSS-f. prayer (f.)
'mother's blessing'

3.1.1.3.2   *kō* is the dative postposition, marking objects (DAT). *kō* marks direct objects normally only with nouns denoting animate creatures:

bair-ē kō bulā-ō
waiter-obl.sg. DAT call-IMP-2
'Call the bearer.'

us kō ciṭṭhī dī-j-iē
him-obl.sg. DAT letter give-IMP-3
'Please give him the letter.'

The subjects of impersonal verbal constructions take the dative postposition *kō*. Impersonal constructions include expressions of sensation (often with *lagnā* 'to be applied'), liking/disliking, knowing, getting (with *milnā* 'to meet'), and the impersonal modal constructions with infinitives (3.5.10.2.2). The verb is always in the third person, and agrees with the object. Dative subjects (4.2.3) have been characterized as experiencers rather than agents and are discussed by Kachru (1990a: 59–75), Abbi (1990: 253–65) and Magier (1987: 192), among others:

> *munīr kō sardī lag-ī h-ai*
> Munir DAT coldness applied-PFV-f. AUX–3sg.
> 'Munir is feeling cold.'

> *muhj-ē ye bāt mālūm hai*
> I-obl.-DAT this thing known is
> 'I know this.'

> *ham-ẽ āp kī ciṭṭhī mil-ī*
> we-obl.-DAT you-L3 POSS letter receive-PFV-f.sg.
> 'We received your letter.'

Following pronouns (including personal, demonstrative, interrogative and relative pronouns) *kō* has the alternate suffixal forms *-ē* (following singular pronouns) and *-(h)ẽ* (following plural pronouns):

> *mujh kō* → *mujhē*
> *tujh kō* → *tujhē*
> *us kō* → *usē*
> *ham kō* → *hamẽ* (with dissimilation)
> *tum kō* → *tumhẽ*
> *un kō* → *unhẽ*

For example:

> *us-ē ciṭṭhī dī-j-iē*
> him-obl.-DAT letter give IMP-3
> 'Please give him the letter.'

The honorific second person pronoun *āp* does not have an alternate suffixal form.

3.1.1.3.3 *nē* is the ergative postposition (ERG). The syntax of perfective tenses is partially nominative and partially ergative (split ergativity). Only intransitive verbs agree with the subject, which is in the nominative case. Transitive verbs agree with the object (unless it is marked with *kō*), and the subject is followed by the ergative postposition *nē* (3.5.2.3, 4.2.2):

> *us nē mujh-ē ciṭṭhī dī*
> him-obl. ERG me-obl.-DAT letter (f.sg.) give-PFV-f.sg.
> 'He gave me a letter.'

> *us nē mujh-ē lifāfa di-y-ā*
> him-obl. ERG me-obl.-DAT envelope (m.sg.) give-PFV-m.sg.
> 'He gave me an envelope.'

Some studies of the Urdu of Pakistan point to a shift in the function of *nē* in that dialect. There is a class of intransitive verbs (the size of which varies according to region) in which the use of *nē* is optional. Bashir 1999 (quoting Tuite et al. 1985: 264 and Butt

1995: 110) argues that the use of * nē* with such verbs expresses conscious choice, and goes on to present data showing that in the Urdu of Pakistan, the subject of impersonal verbal constructions may take *nē* (rather than *kō*) when external obligation or compulsion is not involved (see examples under 3.5.10.2.4).

3.1.1.3.4 *sē* shows movement away from something, or lapse of time. It may also mark the instrument of the passive, involuntary subjects or causative agents (3.5.9). Comparison of adjectives (3.2) is expressed with *sē*. (In the examples which follow, nouns showing units of measure, time or money preceded by numbers do not take the oblique plural suffix.) Examples:

ye bas kahā̃ sē ā-t-ī h-ai?
this bus where from come IMPV-f. AUX-3sg.
'Where does this bus come from?'

mãĩ dō din sē bīmār hū̃
I two days from sick am
'I have been sick for two days.'

qalam sē dastxat kar-nā
pen with signature do-INF
'Sign it with a pen.'

ōhō, mujh sē kyā hō ga-y-ā?
alas I-obl. from what be go-PFV-m.sg.
'Oh no, what have I done?'

3.1.1.3.5 *mē̃* and *par* express location in, on or at a point in space or time:

kamr-ē mē̃
room-obl. in
'in the room'

ēk din mē̃
one day in
'in one day'

rāst-ē par
road-obl. on
'on the road'

darvāz-ē par
door-obl. at
'at the door'

3.1.1.3.6 *tak* expresses extent or limit:

ye bas sadar tak jā-t-ī h-ai
this bus center till go-IMPV-f. AUX-3sg.
'This bus goes as far as the center (of town).'

cār baj-ē tak ā-iyē
four strike-PFV-m.pl. till come-IMP-3
'Come by (at or before) four o'clock.'

3.1.1.4 Compound postpositions

Compound postpositions are postpositional phrases consisting of *kā* + a noun, adjective, adverb or more complex construction. The nouns and adjectives are very often Perso-Arabic loans. Some of the more common types are:

kā + oblique noun: *kē vāstē* 'for, in order to' < *vāsta* (m.) 'connection, reason'
kā + oblique noun + postposition: *kē muqābilē mẽ* 'in comparison with' < *muqābila* (m.) 'comparison'
kā + adjective: *kē munāsib* 'appropriate to' < *munāsib* 'proper, appropriate'
kā + adverb: *kē pīchē* 'behind, after' < *pīchē* 'behind, after'
kā + Persian preposition + oblique noun: *kē bāvujūd* 'in spite of' < *bā* 'with' + *vujūd* (m.) 'existence'

3.2 Adjectives

Adjectives, like nouns, belong to either marked or unmarked classes. Marked adjectives have the suffixes -*ā* (m. sg.), -*ī* (f. sg./pl.) and -*ē* (m. pl., m. obl. sg.). Unmarked adjectives do not inflect. There is no oblique plural suffix for adjectives. In the examples below, *baṛā* is a marked adjective and *sāf* is an unmarked one. Examples:

ēk baṛ-ā, sāf ghar
one big-m.sg.nom. clean house
'a big, clean house'

ēk baṛ-ē, sāf ghar mẽ
one big-m.sg.obl. clean house in
'in a big, clean house'

dō baṛ-ē, sāf ghar
two big-m.pl. clean house
'two big, clean houses'

dō baṛ-ē, sāf gharõ mẽ
two big-m.pl. clean house-obl.pl. in
'in two big, clean houses'

There are no derivative affixes showing the comparative and superlative of adjectives, which are expressed with the postposition *sē* 'from':

tumhār-ā ghar mēr-ē ghar sē baṛā hai
your-m.sg. house my-m.sg.obl. house from big is
'Your house is bigger than mine.'

un kā ghar sab sē baṛā hai
they-obl. POSS house all from big is
'Their house is biggest.'

The reflexive possessive adjective *apnā* is treated under 3.3.5.

3.3 Pronouns

3.3.1 Parameters of the pronoun system

The Urdu pronoun system distinguishes two degrees of number (singular and plural) and two degrees of distance (proximate and remote). Deictics have replaced the old third person pronouns, so that demonstrative pronouns also serve as the third person personal pronouns. Gender is not shown in pronouns.

The nominative third person pronouns do not show number (the same word is used for both singular and plural), but the oblique third person pronouns do show it. Most of the pronouns inflect for case (3.3.3). Examples:

ye ghaṛ-ā hai
this-PROX water-pot-sg. is
'This is a water pot.'

ye ghaṛ-ē hãĩ
these-PROX water-pot-pl. are
'These are water pots.'

ye cāē banā-ē g-ī
she-PROX tea make-3sg. FUT-f.
'She (close at hand) will make tea.'

vo pānī lā-ē g-ī
she-REM water bring-3sg. FUT-f.
'She (at a distance) will bring water.'

vo lakṛī lā-ē g-ā
he-REM wood bring-3sg. FUT-m.sg.
'He (at a distance) will bring wood.'

us kō bulā-ō
him-REM-obl. DAT call-IMP-2
'Call her/him.'

un kō bulā-ō
them-REM-obl. DAT call-IMP-2
'Call them.'

3.3.2 Honorific levels in the pronoun system

In the second person, the old number distinctions have been almost entirely replaced by distinctions in honorific level, or grade of respect.

Level 1: The second person singular pronoun *tū* is very intimate. It is used only when addressing animals, a small child in one's own family, one's beloved, God, as an insult, or as a reproof to a subordinate. It occurs commonly in poetry (where according to convention, the poet addresses his beloved); see example from the poet Faiz, below.

Level 2: The second person plural pronoun *tum* is nonhonorific, and is used when addressing one or more persons of lower status, children, close family members younger than oneself, or by equals in informal social situations.

Level 3: *āp* (originally a reflexive pronoun) is honorific. It is used when addressing one or more persons of higher status, persons to whom respect is due, elders, skilled persons, and by parents to children, to teach them good manners. Persons of equal status generally address each other as *āp* in formal situations.

āp is also used as a third person polite plural pronoun, referring to people to whom a high degree of respect is due (including revered religious personages, especially the Prophet).

The imperative or request forms (3.5.8) show corresponding grades of respect. Examples:

mãĩ nē samjh-ā ke tū hai tō daraxšã̄ hai hayāt
I ERG understand-PFV-m.sg. that you-L1 are so resplendent is life
'I thought that because you exist, life is resplendent.' (Faiz 1943)

tum itnī rāt ga-ē kahã̄ jā rah-ī h-ō?
you-L2 so-much night go-PFV-m.obl. where go CON-f. AUX-pl.
'Where are you going so late at night (to a younger family member)?'

āp baiṭh-iē
you-L3 sit-IMP-3
'(You) please sit (to an elder).'

āp sē darxāst hai ke ham-ẽ apn-ē fann sē navāz-ẽ
he-L3 from request is that us-obl.-DAT own-obl. art from favour-SUBJ-3pl.
'He is requested to favour us with his art (to an honoured poet).'

3.3.3 Inflection of pronouns

Pronouns occur in the oblique case before postpositions except *nē* (3.1.1.3.3). *ham*, *tum* and *āp* have no oblique forms. Before *nē*, first and second person pronouns occur in the nominative case; third person singular pronouns occur in the oblique case and third person plural pronouns have special forms. Table 8.5 shows the nominative, oblique and possessive forms of the pronouns, including the form of the pronoun used before *nē*.

The plural third person pronouns may refer to natural plural (more than one person), or respectful plural (referring to a singular subject respectfully).
Examples:

nasīm sāhib is daftar mẽ kām kar-t-ē h-āĩ
Nasim sir this-obl. office in work does-IMPV-m.pl. AUX-pl.
'Mr Nasim works in this office.'

is mẽ kōī šak nahī̃
this-PROX-obl. in some doubt not
'There is no doubt about (lit. in) this.'

un par zimmedārī hai
them-REM-obl. on responsibility is
'The responsibility is his/theirs.'

TABLE 8.5: PRONOUNS

	Nominative	Oblique	+ *nē*	Possessive
Personal pronouns				
Singular				
1st person	*mãĩ* 'I'	*mujh*	*mãĩ nē*	*mērā*
2nd person	*tū* 'you'	*tujh*	*tū nē*	*tērā*
3rd person	*vo* 'he, she, it'	*us*	*us nē*	*us kā*
	ye 'he, she, it'	*is*	*is nē*	*is kā*
Plural				
1st person	*ham* 'we'	*ham*	*ham nē*	*hamārā*
2nd person	*tum* 'you'	*tum*	*tum nē*	*tumhārā*
	āp 'you'	*āp*	*āp nē*	*āp kā*
3rd person	*vo* 'they'	*un*	*unhõ̃ nē*	*un kā*
	ye 'they'	*in*	*inhõ̃ nē*	*in kā*
Interrogative pronouns				
Singular	*kyā* 'what?'	(*kis*)	(*kis nē*)	(*kis kā*)
	kaun 'who'?	*kis*	*kis nē*	*kis kā*
Plural	*kyā* 'what?'	*kin*	——	——
	kaun 'who'?	*kin*	*kinhõ̃ nē*	*kin kā*
Relative pronoun				
Singular	*jō* 'who, which'	*jis*	*jis nē*	*jis kā*
Plural	*jō* 'who, which'	*jin*	*jinhõ̃ nē*	*jin kā*

Notes: The modern oblique form of *kyā* 'what', is *kis* (identical with the oblique of *kaun* 'who'). The old oblique form *kāhē* survives in the phrase *kāhē kō* 'why, for what reason' (= *kis liē*). In Pakistan it is heard mainly in Karachi, among Muhajirs. The oblique forms of *kyā* occur mainly as adjectives, meaning 'which'.

3.3.4 Possessive pronouns

The possessive pronouns are grammatically marked adjectives, and agree with the nouns they qualify in gender, number and case:

mēr-ā bhāī 'my brother'
mēr-ī bahen 'my sister'
mēr-ē vālid-ain 'my parents' (*vālid* 'father' + *ain*, Arabic dual suffix)

3.3.5 The reflexive possessive adjective *apnā*

The possessive adjective *apnā* 'one's own' is substituted for the possessive forms of personal pronouns when the subject of the sentence possesses the object. *apnā* agrees with the noun it qualifies:

ahmad apn-ī gharī dēkh rah-ā h-ai
Ahmad own-f.-watch look CON-m.sg. AUX-3sg.
'Ahmad is looking at his (own) watch.'

The postposition *kō* has the alternate forms *-ē* ~ *-(h)ē̃* after some personal pronouns (see 3.1.1.3.2).

3.3.6 The parameters PROXIMATE-REMOTE-INTERROGATIVE-RELATIVE

Table 8.5 shows that proximate third-person pronouns begin with *y ~ i*, remote third person pronouns begin with *v ~ u*, interrogative pronouns begin with *k*, and relative pronouns begin with *j*. Similar *y-v-k-j*-sets may also be found among adjectives and adverbs (3.4). Indefinite pronouns also begin with *k*:

> *kuch* 'some (with mass nouns)'
> *kōī* 'some, any; someone, anyone (with count nouns)'

For example:

> *kuch pānī*
> 'some water'

> *kōī darvāz-ē par hai*
> someone door-obl. at is
> 'Someone is at the door.'

kuch has no oblique form. The oblique of *kōī* is *kisī*.

3.4 Adverbs

Urdu has few underived adverbs. Most adverbs are derived from:

3.4.1 Adjectives or nouns, by making them oblique: *nīcē* 'down' (< *nīcā* 'low'), *sāmnē* 'before, in front' (< *sāmnā* 'encounter'), *āhestē* 'slowly' (< *āhesta* 'slow');

3.4.2 Nouns, by adding the postposition *sē* or a postpositional phrase: *ehtiyāt sē* 'carefully' (lit. 'with care'), *xās taur par* 'especially' (lit. 'on a special way');

3.4.3 Arabic nouns, by suffixing the Arabic suffix *-an* (*tanvīn*): *fauran* (فوراً) 'immediately' (< *faur* 'hurry, haste');

3.4.4 Verbs, by making conjunctive participles:

> *vo ghabrā kar bōl-ā . . .*
> he be-anxious ABS say-PFV-m.sg.
> 'He said anxiously . . .'

Original adverbs include modal adverbs and some common adverbs of time and place. Several have been borrowed:

> *nahī̃, na, mat* 'not, do not'
> *bhī* 'also'
> *šāyad* 'maybe' (loan from Persian)
> *sirf* 'only' (loan from Arabic)
> *zarūr* 'certainly' (loan from Arabic)
> *āj* 'today'
> *kal* 'tomorrow; yesterday'
> *ūpar* 'up'

Some underived adverbs belong to the *y-v-k-j* (NEAR-FAR-INTERROGATIVE-RELA-TIVE) sets mentioned under 3.3.6. See table 8.6.

TABLE 8.6: ADVERB SETS

	Proximate	Remote	Interrogative	Relative
Time	*ab* 'now'	(*tab* 'then')	*kab* 'when?'	*jab* 'when'
Place	*yahā̃* 'here'	*vahā̃* 'there'	*kahā̃* 'where?'	*jahā̃* 'where'
	idhar 'hither'	*udhar* 'thither'	*kidhar* 'whither?'	*jidhar* 'whither'
Manner	*yū̃* 'thus'	(*tū̃* 'so', 'thus')	*kyõ ~ kyū̃* 'why?'	*jū̃* 'as'

Notes: *tab*, 'then' and *tū̃* 'so', 'thus' are not actually members of the 'remote' category, but surviving members of a nearly obsolete category, the *t*-set, or correlative set. *tab* is still most frequent in correlative clauses, but has also acquired the function of expressing a point in remote time (past or future). *tū̃* occurs in the compounds *jū̃ tū̃* 'somehow or the other' and *jū̃ kā tū̃* 'verbatim'.

3.5 Verbal structures

Urdu verbs, like Urdu nouns, are formed by the suffixation of elements to the root, or lexical base (Masica 1991: 257). A complex system of verb tense and aspect is elaborated with participles and auxiliaries (see table 8.8 under 3.5.2 'Aspect'). The participle (imperfect, perfect or *rahā*-form) determines the aspect of the verb, while the form of the auxiliary determines its tense.

The modern verbal system based on participles has replaced an older one based on finite tense forms. This process is illustrated by the displacement of the old present, or aorist, (*karē* 'does', *āvē* 'comes', *jānē* 'knows') by a construction of IMPERFECT PARTICIPLE + PRESENT AUXILIARY. However texts show that for centuries the participle-based system coexisted with constructions based on finite verbs: *karē hai* 'he does', *calū̃ hū̃* 'I go', were used along with *kartā hai*, *caltā hū̃* even in the nineteenth century. Platts (1920: 143–4) remarks:

> The present tense is sometimes formed by adding the [present auxiliary] to the aorist of a verb; as هوں چلوں *chalūṅ hūṅ*, 'I go or am going.' This form, which is properly an indefinite present, was at one period general; numerous instances of its use occur in the poets, and it is still very common in the tract of country extending from Agra to Sindh, but in other parts of Northern India it is now seldom used, except by the uneducated.

The aorist is now found only in the subjunctive mood and in proverbs, so that in modern Urdu finite verbs with person-number suffixes are found only in the present and subjunctive forms of the auxiliary verb, and in the subjunctive mood of other verbs. The participial suffixes which have replaced them show agreement in gender and number, like adjectives.

The auxiliary verb (*hōnā* 'to be') has two moods: indicative and subjunctive; in the indicative it has three tenses: present, past and future. These four conjugations elaborate the dimensions of tense and mood in the verbal system.

3.5.1 The auxiliary verb

The present and subjunctive tenses of *hōnā* are finite and have person-number suffixes; the past tense is adjectival and has gender-number suffixes. The future tense of *hōnā* is formed by adding the future suffix *gā* (~ *gē* ~ *gī*) to the subjunctive forms. *gā* is a contraction of *gaā* (=*gayā*, the perfective participle of *jānā* 'to go') (Platts 1920: 142).

TABLE 8.7: THE PRESENT, PAST, SUBJUNCTIVE AND FUTURE FORMS OF THE AUXILIARY VERB

	Present	Past	Subjunctive	Future
Singular				
1st person (*maĩ*)	*hũ*	*thā* m. *thī* f.	*hũ*	*hũ gā* m. *hũ gī* f.
2nd person (*tū*)	*hai*	*thā* m. *thī* f.	*hō*	*hō gā* m. *hō gī* f.
3rd person (*vo*)	*hai*	*thā* m. *thī* f.	*hō*	*hō gā* m. *hō gī* f.
Plural				
1st person (*ham*)	*haĩ*	*thē* m. *thī̃* f.	*hō*	*hõ gē* m. *hõ gī* f.
2nd person (*tum*)	*hō*	*thē* m. *thī̃* f.	*hō*	*hō gē* m. *hō gī* f.
2nd person (*āp*)	*haĩ*	*thē* m. *thī̃* f.	*hõ*	*hõ gē* m. *hõ gī* f.
3rd person (*vo*)	*haĩ*	*thē* m. *thī̃* f.	*hõ*	*hõ gē* m. *hõ gī* f.

Note: The verb *hōnā*, like other verbs, also has participles: imperfective (*hō-t-ā*), perfective (*hū-ā*) and conjunctive (*hō kar*). The perfective participle *hūā* is used as a simple past meaning 'became' (process), contrasting with *th-ā* 'was' (state).

Although *gā* is a suffix, it is written as a separate word in Urdu. *gā* is also adjectival, and agrees with the noun or pronoun in gender and number.

3.5.2 Aspect

The participle-based verb system is capable of showing precise distinctions of tense and mood in three aspects: durative, imperfective, and perfective, as outlined in table 8.8. The participles are aspect markers, while the auxiliaries make temporal tenses (present and past) or modal tenses (conditional with the subjunctive of the auxiliary, and presumptive with the future of the auxiliary). The form of the negative (*nahī̃* or *na*) used with each construction is shown in parentheses.

3.5.2.1 Continuous tenses

Durative (or continuous) tenses describe actions or states which are incomplete and in progress at the time (or in the mood) shown by the auxiliary. They have the structure: VERB ROOT + INFLECTED PARTICIPLE *rahā* + AUXILIARY. (*rahā* is the perfective participle of *rahnā* 'remain'.) The participle is the aspect marker; or to be more precise, {*rah-*} (partially lexically emptied) is the aspect marker, since *-ā* is an inflectional suffix which shows the gender and number of the subject. Examples:

CONTINUOUS :   *farīda cāē pī rah-ī h-ai*
PRESENT   Farida tea drink CON-f. AUX-3sg.
             'Farida is drinking tea.'

CONTINUOUS   *zāhid cāē pī rah-ā th-ā*
PAST   Zahid tea drink CON-m.sg. AUX-PAST-m.sg.
             'Zahid was drinking tea.'

CONTINUOUS   *agar salmā kām kar rah-ī hō, us-ē taklīf na dō*
CONDITIONAL   if Salma work do CON-f. AUX-SUBJ-3sg. her-DAT trouble not give-
             IMP-2
             'If Salma is working, don't bother her.'

TABLE 8.8: OVERVIEW OF ASPECT, TENSE AND MOOD

Infinitive *ānā*, to come **Basic form of verb**	ROOT *ā*	IMPERFECTIVE PARTICIPLE *ātā*	PERFECTIVE PARTICIPLE *āyā*
Simple constructions	SUBJUNCTIVE *(agar) vo āē (+ na)* (if) he comes; he might come FUTURE *vo āē gā (+ nahī̃)* he will come	IRREALIS *(agar) vo ātā (+ na)* (if) he had come	SIMPLE PAST *vo āyā (+ na, nahī̃)* he came
Aspect	CONTINUOUS TENSES (durative aspect)	HABITUAL TENSES (imperfective aspect)	PAST TENSES (perfective aspect)
Complex constructions			
PRESENT Temporal tenses	CONTINUOUS PRESENT *vo ā rahā hai (+ nahī̃)* he is coming	HABITUAL PRESENT *vo ātā hai (+ nahī̃)* he comes	IMMEDIATE PAST *vo āyā hai (+ nahī̃)* he has come
PAST Temporal tenses	CONTINUOUS PAST *vo ā rahā thā (+ nahī̃)* he was coming	HABITUAL PAST *vo ātā thā (+ nahī̃)* he used to come	REMOTE PAST *vo āyā thā (+ nahī̃)* he had come, he came
CONDITIONAL Modal tenses	CONTINUOUS CONDITIONAL *(agar) vo ā rahā hō (+ na)* (if) he is coming	HABITUAL CONDITIONAL *(agar) vo ātā hō (+ na)* (if) he comes	CONDITIONAL PAST *(agar) vo āyā hō (+ na)* (if) he has come
PRESUMPTIVE Modal tenses	CONTINUOUS PRESUMPTIVE *vo ā rahā hōgā (rare with neg.)* he must be coming	HABITUAL PRESUMPTIVE *vo ātā hōgā (+ nahī̃)* he must come	PRESUMPTIVE PAST *vo āyā hōgā (+ nahī̃)* he must have come
IRREALIS (Unfulfilled conditions)	CONTINUOUS IRREALIS *(agar) vo ā rahā hōtā (+ na)* (if) he were coming	HABITUAL IRREALIS *(agar) vo ātā hōtā (+ na)* (if) he came (regularly)	PAST IRREALIS *(agar) vo āyā hōtā (+ na)* (if) he had come

(From Schmidt 1999)

CONTINUOUS   *nasīm is silsil-ē mẽ kām kar rah-ē h-ȭ g-ē*
PRESUMPTIVE   Nasim this-obl. connection-obl. in work do CON-m.pl. AUX-3pl. FUT-m.pl.
              'Nasim must be working in this connection.'

3.5.2.2 Habitual tenses

Imperfective (or habitual) tenses describe actions or states which occur generally or
regularly at the time (or in the mood) shown by the auxiliary. They have the structure:
IMPERFECTIVE PARTICIPLE + AUXILIARY. The imperfective participle is the aspect
marker, or to be more precise, {-*t*-} is the aspect marker, since -*ā* is an inflectional suffix
which shows the gender and number of the subject.

The habitual present also expresses close future and willingness. Examples:

HABITUAL :   *mãĩ nāzimābād mẽ rah-t-ā h-ũ*
PRESENT   I Nazimabad in live-IMPV-m.sg. AUX-1sg.
                'I live in Nazimabad.'

HABITUAL   *us vaqt mãĩ qarōl bāg mẽ rah-t-ī th-ī*
PAST   that-obl. time I Karol Bagh in IMPV-f. AUX-PAST-f.sg.
                'At that time I lived in Karol Bagh.'

HABITUAL   *mumkin hai ke vo lōg kisī aur saṛak par rah-t-ē h-ȭ*
CONDITIONAL   possible is that those people some-obl. other street on live-IMPV-
                m.pl. AUX-SUBJ-3pl.
                'It's possible that those people live on some other street.'

HABITUAL   *vo lōg kisī aur saṛak par rah-t-ē h-ȭ g-ē*
PRESUMPTIVE   those people some-obl. other street on live-IMPV-m.pl. AUX-3pl.
                FUT-m.pl.
                'Those people must live on some other street.'

3.5.2.3 Past tenses

Perfective (or past) tenses describe actions or states which occur once in the past. They
have the structure: PERFECTIVE PARTICIPLE + AUXILIARY. The perfective participle is
the aspect marker, or to be more precise, {-*y*- ~ ø} is the aspect marker, since -*ā* is an
inflectional suffix which shows the gender and number of the subject. Note that the
habitual and continuous pasts are not perfective tenses.

{-*y*-} is the 'euphonic' glide that is inserted in perfective participles between
prohibited vowel clusters. Historically it is the remnant of the old perfective marker.

ā + *ā* → *āyā*   *khā* 'eat' → *khāyā* 'eaten' (m.sg.)

Elsewhere there is no phonological element which marks the perfective, so it is
considered to have zero marking, or {ø}.

The immediate past describes an action or state which is completed, but which still
affects the present situation, and is sometimes called the present perfect. The remote
past describes something which was completed in the past and no longer affects the
present situation. It is sometimes called the past perfect, but unlike the past perfect in
English, it is unimportant in the chronological sequencing of past events (Masica 1991:
276–7), because this function belongs to the conjunctive participle (3.5.5) and to the
modal verb *cuknā* (3.5.10.1).

The syntax of perfective tenses is partially nominative and partially ergative (split ergativity). Only intransitive verbs agree with the subject, which is in the nominative case. Transitive verbs agree with the object (unless it is marked with *kō*), and the subject is followed by the ergative postposition *nē* (4.2.2). Examples:

IMMEDIATE : PAST	*bāriš hū-ī h-ai, saṛak gīlī hai* rain be-PFV-f. AUX-3sg. street wet is 'It has rained, the street is wet.'
REMOTE PAST	*kal bāriš hū-ī th-ī* yesterday rain be-PFV-f. AUX-PAST-f.sg. 'It rained yesterday.'
CONDITIONAL PAST	*mumkin hai ke un lōg-ṍ nē ghar badal-ā hō* possible is that those-obl. people-obl-pl. ERG house change-PFV-m.sg. AUX-SUBJ-3sg. 'It's possible that those people have moved.'
PRESUMPTIVE PAST	*us nē zarūr āp kī bāt mahsūs k-ī hō g-ī* him-obl. ERG certainly you-L3 POSS matter feel do-PFV-f. AUX-3sg. FUT-f.sg. 'He must certainly have have been hurt by what you said.'

3.5.3 Other uses of the participles

The imperfective participle is used without an auxiliary in contrary-to-fact conditional sentences (irrealis), describing a failed or impossible condition. It is also used in past narration (MacGregor's [1972: 170] 'routine imperfective'). Example:

agar āp ehtiyāt kar-t-ē, tō hādisa na hō-t-ā
if you-L3 care do-IMPV-m.pl. so accident not be-IMPV-m.sg.
'If you had been careful, (then) there would not have been an accident.'

The perfective participle is used without an auxiliary in the simple past, showing the completion of a single action or state at a point in the past, without reference to the context of prior or subsequent events; e.g.

pahāṛ-ṏ mẽ bahut bāriš hū-ī
mountain-obl.pl. much rain be-PAST-f.sg.
'In the hills it rained a lot.'

3.5.4 Irregular verbs

The verbal system of Urdu is by and large regular. Five verbs have irregular perfective stems, and four have alternate stems before the polite request form suffix *-iē* (3.5.8). The formation of the perfective participles from the irregular perfective stems, as well as the occurrence of the irregular polite request stems, can in fact be predicted by phonological rules, which are presented in the notes following table 8.9.

The verbs *hōnā* 'to be', *dēnā* 'to give'; and *lēnā* 'to take' are irregular in the subjunctive and future (table 8.10).

TABLE 8.9: IRREGULAR VERB STEMS

Root	Perfective Stem	Perfective participle				Request Stem	Polite Request
		m.sg.	m.pl.	f.sg.	f.pl.		
hō 'be'	*hū-*	*hūā*	*hūē*	*hūī*	*hūī̃*	(regular)	(not used)
jā 'go'	*ga-*	*gayā*	*gaē*	*gaī*	*gaī̃*	(regular)	(regular)
kar 'do'	*ki-*	*kiyā*	*kiyē*	*kī*	*kī̃*	*kīj-*	*kījiē*
dē 'give'	*di-*	*diyā*	*diyē*	*dī*	*dī̃*	*dīj-*	*dījiē*
lē 'take'	*li-*	*liyā*	*liyē*	*lī*	*lī̃*	*līj-*	*lījiē*
pī 'drink'	(regular)					*pīj-*	*pījiē*

Phonological rules for predicting perfective participles and polite request stems:

ā + ā →	*āyā*	*khā-* 'eat' →		*khāyā* 'eaten' (m.sg.)	
a + ā →	*ayā*	*ga- < jā-* 'go' →		*gayā* 'gone' (m.sg.)	
ō + ā →	*ōyā*	*sō-* 'sleep' →		*sōyā* 'slept' (m.sg.)	
ī + ā →	*iyā*	*pī-* 'drink' →		*piyā* 'drank' (m.sg.)	
ī + ī →	*ī*	*pī-* 'drink' →		*pī* 'drank' (f.sg.)	
i + ī →	*ī*	*di- < dē* 'give' →		*dī* 'gave' (f.sg.)	
ī + iē →	*īj*	*dī- < dē* 'give'+ *-iē* →		*dījiē* 'please give' (Level 3)	

3.5.5 Conjunctive participle

The conjunctive participle in Urdu is homophonous with the verb root (or more precisely, the verb stem, in the case of derived transitives and causatives), and has the extension *kar ~ kē*. Conjunctive participles transform two separate but related clauses into a single sentence which shows two actions or events happening in sequence. The underlying clauses must have the same subject, and verbs in the same tense. The conjunctive clause may show an earlier event, the cause or means of a later event, or the manner of a later event (see Schumacher 1977 for more functions). Examples:

paṛh kar ārām kar-ō!
study CP rest do-IMP-2
'Study before you rest!' (Temporal sequence: study first)

vo pān bēc kar kamā-t-ā h-ai
he betel-leaf sell CP earn-IMPV-m.sg. AUX-3sg.
'He earns (a living) by selling *pān*.' (Instrument: by means of selling *pān*)

us nē ghabrā kar javāb di-y-ā ...
he be-anxious CP answer give-PFV-m.sg.
'He replied anxiously ...' (Manner: becoming anxious)

The verb in the main clause determines the transitivity of the sentence: in the previous example, *dēnā* is transitive, so the subject takes *nē* although *ghabrānā* is intransitive.

The alternate form of the extension, *kē*, is required after the conjunctive of the verb *kar* ('do'), and is an optional, rather idiomatic variant after other verbs:

kām kar kē ārām kar-ō
work do CP rest do-IMP-2
'Work before you rest.'

TABLE 8.10: SUBJUNCTIVE AND FUTURE

karnā
Singular
1st person	*mãĩ karũ*	I may do (m.f.)
2nd person (level 1)	*tū karē*	you may do (m.f.)
3rd person	*vo karē*	he, she, it may do (m.f.)

Plural
1st person	*ham karẽ*	we may do (m.f.)
2nd person (level 2)	*tum karō*	you may do (m.f.)
2nd person (level 3)	*āp karẽ*	you may do (m.f.)
3rd person	*vo karẽ*	they may do (m.f.)

dēnā
Singular
1st person	*mãĩ dũ*	I may give (m.f.)
2nd person (level 1)	*tū dē*	you may give (m.f.)
3rd person	*vo dē*	he, she, it may give (m.f.)

Plural
1st person	*ham dẽ*	we may give (m.f.)
2nd person (level 2)	*tum dō*	you may give (m.f.)
2nd person (level 3)	*āp dẽ*	you may give (m.f.)
3rd person	*vo dẽ*	they may give (m.f.)

Future: *mãĩ karũ gā* 'I (m.) will do', *mãĩ karũ gī* 'I (f.) will do', *ham karẽ gē* 'we (m.) will do', *ham karẽ gī* 'we (f.) will do', *vo karē gā* 'he will do', *vo karē gī* 'she will do'.

3.5.6 Subjunctive mood

The subjunctive (table 8.10) is formed from the verb root. In modern Urdu it is not a tense, but a mood describing a non-factual action or state, such as something which is uncertain or contingent on something else. It is often used in conditional sentences or when asking for permission. Certain conjunctions, adverbs and phrases describing wish, necessity, possibility, inquiry and result require the subjunctive. It is also used as a request form (3.5.8). The forms of the subjunctive are finite and agree with the subject in person and number. They do not show gender. The negative used with the subjunctive is always *na*.

> *kyā mãĩ andar ā-ũ?*
> INTER I inside come-SUBJ-1sg.
> 'May I come in?'

> *šāyad āj šām kō cãd nazar ā-ē*
> maybe today evening DAT moon sight come-SUBJ-3sg.
> 'Maybe this evening the moon will be visible (sighted).'

> *zarūrī hai ke āj hī pais-ē adā kar-ũ*
> necessary is that today EMPH money-pl. payment do-SUBJ-1sg.
> 'It's necessary that I pay the money today.'

3.5.7 Future

The future tense is formed by adding the future suffix *gā ~ gē ~ gī* to the subjunctive forms of a verb (table 8.10). The future suffix is adjectival and agrees with the noun or pronoun in gender and number.

mãĩ āj hī pais-ē adā kar-ū̃ g-ā
I today EMPH money-pl. payment do-SUBJ-1sg. FUT-m.sg.
'I will pay the money today.'

3.5.8 Imperative (request forms)

The imperative or request forms show grades of respect corresponding to the honorific levels in the second person pronouns (3.3.2).

Corresponding to the second person singular pronoun *tū*, the low-level request form, homophonous with the suffixless verb root (or stem), is used:

bēṭ-ē, khānā khā
son-voc.sg. food eat-IMP-1
'Son, eat (your) food (to a small child).'

Corresponding to the second person plural pronoun *tum*, the mid-level request form, consisting of the verb root with the suffix *-ō* (homophonous with the second person plural subjunctive) is used:

khānā khā lō
food eat take-IMP-2
'Eat (your) food.'

Corresponding to the second person plural pronoun *āp*, the polite request form, consisting of the verb root with the suffix *-iē* (*-iyē* following roots ending in *-ā, -ō, -ū*) is used. The irregular verbs use the stem in *-īj* (3.5.4). Example:

ab khānā khā-iyē ~ ab khānā khā lī-j-iē
now food eat-IMP-3 ~ now food eat take-IMP-3
'Please eat (food) now.'

In Pakistan, the subjunctive plural form (3.5.6) corresponding to *āp* is also used as a polite request.

bã̄ taraf cal-ē̃
left direction go-SUBJ-2pl.
'Please drive on the left.'

Courteous formal requests at the *āp*-level can be made by suffixing the future suffix, *gā* (which does not inflect) to the polite request form, or using a phrase with *tašrīf* 'one's honourable self'. The request with *gā* appears to be interpreted by some as a courteous question and by others as a courteous future imperative.

yahã̄ baiṭh-iē g-ā
here sit-IMP-3 FUT-m.sg.
'Would you please sit here?' (You will please sit here.)

janāb, yahã̄ tašrīf rakh-iē
your-honour here honourable-self place-IMP-3
'Sir, please sit here (= Place your honourable self here).'

ā-iyē, tašrīf lā-iyē
come-IMP-3 honourable-self bring-IMP-3
'Please come in, please come in! (= Please come, bring your honorable self).'

3.5.9 Voice and valence

Urdu verbs are inherently transitive or intransitive. A very few verbs, including *badalnā* 'to change' and *bharnā* 'to fill/be filled' may function both transitively and intransitively. A few transitive verbs function nominatively in perfective sentences: they agree with the subject, which does not take *nē*. This group includes *bōlnā* 'to speak', *bhūlnā* 'to forget', *milnā* 'to meet' and *lānā* 'to bring'. *samajhnā* 'to understand', may be used either nominatively or ergatively in perfective tenses.

3.5.9.1 Passive

There is no morphologically marked passive. A periphrastic passive construction is derived by adding an inflected form of *jānā* to the perfective participle of the main verb. The instrument of the action is not usually specified, but may be marked with *kē zarīē or kē hāth* 'by means of' (preferred if the instrument is human), or the postposition *sē* 'from'. Examples:

kām ki-y-ā jā-ē g-ā
work do-PFV-m.sg. go-3sg. FUT-m.sg.
'The work will be done.'

kām mazdūr-ō̃ kē zarī-ē ki-y-ā jā-ē g-ā
work labourer-obl.pl. POSS means-obl. do-PFV-m.sg. go-3sg. FUT-m.sg.
'The work will be done by the labourers.'

kām jādū sē ki-y-ā jā-ē g-ā
work magic with do-PFV-m.sg. go-3sg. FUT-m.sg.
'The work will be done by magic.'

Both transitive and intransitive verbs may be passived to show physical or psychological incapacity, usually in negative sentences. The person or inanimate creature who is incapable is expressed as an instrument marked by *sē*:

mujh sē itnā kām nahī̃ ki-y-ā jā-t-ā
me-obl. from so-much work not do-PFV-m.sg. go-IMPV-m.sg.
'I can't possibly do so much work.'

mujh sē šarāb nahī̃ pī jā-t-ī
me-obl. from wine not drink-PFV-f. go-IMPV-f.sg.
'I can't possibly drink wine.'

Intransitives often have a passive sense, or express unintentional action.

āp kā kām hō jā-ē g-ā
your-L3 POSS work be go-3sg FUT-m.sg.
'Your work will be done (successfully).'

ōhō, mujh sē kyā hō ga-y-ā?
alas I-obl. from what be go-PFV-m.sg.
'Oh no, what have I done?'

3.5.9.2 Causative

A 'causative' affix, -*ā*, derives transitive and causative stems from verb roots. The derivational process is complex, involving reduction of the root vowel, or in cases where -*ā* is infixed into the verb root, lengthening of the root vowel (with modification of vowel quality), but may be summarized briefly as follows.

(a) -*ā*- is suffixed or infixed to an intransitive root to derive a transitive stem:

> *bannā* 'to form, be made' → *banānā* 'to make'
> *bacnā* 'to escape' → *bacānā* 'to save'
> *sūkhnā* 'to dry up' → *sukhānā* 'to dry something' (with reduction of stem vowel)
> *kaṭnā* 'to be cut' → *kāṭnā* 'to cut, disconnect' (-*a*- + -*ā*- → *ā*)
> *ruknā* 'to stop' → *rōknā* 'to stop (something)' (-*u*- + -*ā*- → *ō*)
> *biknā* 'to be sold' → *bēcnā* 'to sell' (-*i*- + *ā* → *ē*)

(b) -*ā*- is suffixed to a transitive root to derive a double transitive stem (one which takes both a direct and an indirect object):

> *sunnā* 'to hear, listen to' → *sunānā* 'to tell'
> *dēkhnā* 'to see, look at' → *dikhānā* 'to show' (with reduction of stem vowel)

(c) -*ā*- is added to an intransitive or a transitive root to derive a causative stem (with reduction of long root vowels). An alternate causative affix -*lā*- occurs with a class of roots ending in long vowels. An instrument may be be specified and is marked with *kē zarīē* or *kē hāth* 'by means of', or the postposition *sē* 'from'; but is usually omitted. (Kachru [1986: 168] calls these 'direct causatives'.)

> *kaṭnā* 'to be cut' → *kaṭānā* 'to have cut'
> *baiṭhnā* 'to sit' → *biṭhānā* 'to seat, cause to sit'
> *tōṛnā* 'to break (tr.)' → *tuṛānā* 'to get broken, break loose' (with reduction of stem vowel)
> *dēnā* 'to give' → *dilānā* 'to have given' (alt. *lā* with reduction of stem vowel)
> *rōnā* 'to cry' → *rulānā* 'to make cry' (alt. *lā* with reduction of stem vowel)

> *nāhīd nē mujh-ē xabar sun-ā-ī*
> Nahid ERG me-obl.-DAT news tell-CAUS-PFV-f.sg.
> 'Nahid told me the news (double transitive).'

> *māngnē vāl-ē kō ēk rūpaya di-lā dō*
> beg-INF agent-obl DAT one rupee give-CAUS give-IMP-2
> 'Have someone give the beggar a rupee (causative).'

(d) The suffix -*vā* can be added to the roots of most verbs to make indirect causatives (excepting verbs already derived with -*ā*, or intransitives which cannot be transitivized, such as *jānā* 'to go'). Causatives with -*vā* more often take an instrument (a noun followed by *kē zarīē* or *kē hāth* 'by means of', or the postposition *sē* 'from').

> *karnā* 'to do' → *karvānā* 'to cause to do'
> *bannā* 'to be made' → *banvānā* 'to cause to be made'

> *ham bāɣ mālī sē sāf kar-vā-t-ē h-aĩ*
> we garden gardener from clean do-CAUS-IMPV-m.pl. AUX-pl.
> 'We have the garden cleaned by the gardener.'

3.5.10 Modality

Modality, as expressed in English by verbs like 'can', 'may', 'must' is expressed in Urdu by diverse types of constructions.

3.5.10.1 Modal verbs

There are two verbs which function like English modal verbs: *saknā* 'to be able', and *cuknā* 'to be finished (showing temporal sequence)'. The verb *pānā* 'to find, get' may also be used as a modal. Modal verb phrases have the structure: VERB ROOT + inflected MODAL VERB. The modal verbs are intransitive and agree with the subject; *nē* is not used even if the verb root belongs to a transitive verb. *pānā* is intransitive as a modal even though it is transitive as a sentence verb.

> *mērā bacc-ā cal sak-t-ā h-ai*
> my child-m. walk-ROOT can-IMPV-m.sg. AUX-3sg.
> 'My child can walk.'

cuknā shows the completion of an action or event prior to a second one. It sometimes means 'already', but often corresponds to an English pluperfect.

> *meharbānī, mãĩ cāē pī cuk-ā h-ũ̃*
> kindness I tea drink-ROOT complete-PFV-m.sg. AUX-1sg.
> 'Thank you, I have already had tea.' (A polite refusal to a second cup)

pānā expresses feasibility (often in negative sentences). The oblique infinitive may be used instead of the root if a second clause (usually with a verb of motion) follows.

> *vo masrūf hai, kal kī dāvat mẽ nahĩ ā pā-ē g-ā*
> he busy is tomorrow POSS invitation in not come-ROOT find-3sg FUT-m.sg.
> 'He is busy (and) won't be able to come to tomorrow's party.'

> *agar mãĩ jā-nē pā-y-ā tō us sē mil kar jā-ũ̃ g-ā*
> If I go-INF-obl. find-PFV-m.sg. so him-obl. with meet CP go-1sg. FUT-m.sg.
> 'If I manage to go I will meet with him before I go.'

3.5.10.2 Modal infinitival constructions

Many modal functions are expressed by infinitival constructions. They are of two types, personal constructions and impersonal constructions.

3.5.10.2.1 Personal infinitive constructions

'want'
The NOMINATIVE INFINITIVE + an inflected form of *cāhnā* expresses 'to want (to)'. The subject is in the nominative case (except when followed by *nē-* [3.1.1.3.3.]. If the infinitive has an object, the infinitive optionally agrees with it, like an adjective:

> *mãĩ bhī jā-nā cāh-t-ā h-ũ̃*
> I also go-INF-m.sg. want-IMPV-m.sg. AUX–1sg.
> 'I also want to go.'

mãĩ sair kar-nā (~ kar-nī) cāh-t-ā h-ũ̃
I stroll do-INF-m.sg. (~ do-INF-f.) want-IMPV-m.sg. AUX-1sg.
'I want to go for a walk.'

'let'
The OBLIQUE INFINITIVE + an inflected form of *dēnā* 'to give' expresses 'to let'.

macchar- õ̃ nē mujh-ē sō-nē nahĩ̃ di-y-ā
mosquito-obl.pl. ERG me-obl.-DAT sleep-INF-obl. not give-PFV-m.sg.
'The mosquitoes didn't let me sleep.'

chuṭṭiy-ã̃ ā-nē dō, ham lakhnau kā daura kar-ẽ̃ g-ē
holiday-pl. come-INF-obl. give-IMP-2 we Lucknow POSS tour do-3pl. FUT-m.pl.
'Let the holidays come, we'll make a tour of Lucknow.'

3.5.10.2.2 Impersonal infinitive constructions
Impersonal modal constructions with dative subjects have the structure NOMINATIVE
INFINITIVE + IMPERSONAL VERB, and express several degrees of external necessity
ranging from advisability to lack of choice. The verb is always in the third person. The
subject usually takes the dative case (*kō* or its variant forms, 3.1.1.3.2). If the infinitive
has an object, the verb agrees with it, unless the object is followed by a postposition. The
infinitive usually agrees with it as well, however the force of the agreement weakens in
longer sentences, and there are dialects of Urdu in which the infinitive remains
masculine singular.

'should, ought to'
NOMINATIVE INFINITIVE + *cāhie* expresses advisability. *cāhie* is historically an old
passive form meaning 'is wished, is necessary'. It agrees with the object of the infinitive
in number, unless the past auxiliary is added to the phrase.

mujh-ē sair kar-nī (~ kar-nā) cāh-ie
I-obl.-DAT stroll do-INF-f. (~ INF-m.sg.) wished-sg.
'I should go for a walk.'

mujh-ē cīnī xarīd-nī (~ xarīd-nā) cāh-ie
I-obl.-DAT sugar buy-INF-f. (~ INF-m.sg.) wished-sg.
'I should buy sugar.'

us-ē aṇḍ-ē xarīd-nē (~ xarīd-nā) cāh-iẽ̃
he-obl.-DAT egg-pl. buy-INF-m.pl. (~ INF-m.sg.) wished-pl.
'He should buy eggs.'

mujh-ē kal aṇḍ-ē xarīd-nē (~ xarīd-nā) cāh-ie th-ē
I-obl.-DAT yesterday egg-pl. buy-INF-m.pl. (~ INF-m.sg.) wished AUX-PAST-m.pl.
'I should have bought eggs yesterday.'

'have to'
NOMINATIVE INFINITIVE + AUXILIARY expresses necessity. If the subject is inanimate,
the dative case marking is not required.

mujh-ē vo kitāb paṛh-nī (~ paṛh-nā) h-ai
I-obl.-DAT that book read-INF-f. (~ INF-m.sg.) AUX-3sg.
'I have to read that book.'

mujh-ē vo kitāb paṛh-nī (~ paṛh-nā) h-ō g-ī
I-obl.-DAT that book read-INF-f.sg (~ INF-m.sg.) AUX-3sg. FUT-f.sg.
'I will have to read that book.'

mujh-ē vo axbār paṛh-nē (~ paṛh-nā) th-ē
I-obl.-DAT those newspapers read-INF-m.pl (~ INF-m.sg.) AUX-PAST-m.pl.
'I had to read those newspapers.'

musībat ā-nī h-ai
misfortune come-INF-f. AUX-3sg.
'Misfortune is bound to strike.'

3.5.10.2.3 Agha's 'telic aspect'
Agha (1998) considers the *-n-* in *paṛh-nī*, *ā-nī* (in the examples above) as an aspectual marker {*-n-*}, which he calls TELIC aspect. For Agha, the *-nā* in *paṛhnā hai* is homophonous with the infinitive marker *-nā*, but has a different morphological composition.

mujh-ē vo kitāb paṛh-n-ī h-ai
I-obl.-DAT that book read-TEL-f. AUX-3sg.
'I have to read that book.'

mujh-ē vo axbār paṛh-n-ē th-ē
I-obl.-DAT those newspapers read-TEL-m.pl AUX-PAST-m.pl.
'I had to read those newspapers.'

Agha also argues that the split in case inflection (dative with [+ animate] and nominative with [- animate]) is aspectually driven and thus comparable to the split ergative of the perfective aspect. *musībat*, being inanimate, takes the nominative:

musībat ā-n-ī h-ai
misfortune come-TEL-f. AUX-3sg.
'Misfortune is bound to strike.'

Agha does not go so far as to call the construction a 'telic participle', but the agreement of the infinitive with its object is a pattern usually associated with participles, not with infinitives, which are basically verbal nouns.

3.5.10.2.4 Bashir's 'marker of source'
Bashir 1999, using transcripts of television dramas, provides examples of NOMINATIVE INFINITIVE + AUXILIARY with ergative case marking (*nē*) of the subject, in the Urdu of Pakistan. With first person subjects, a subject marked by *nē* may express the speaker's conscious choice. With (animate) second and third person subjects, the speaker makes an assumption or has an expectation about another person's conscious choice. Bashir analyses *nē* as a marker of SOURCE in the generalized sense. In

āj mãĩ nē zarūr jā-nā h-ai
today I ERG certainly go-INF AUX-3sg.
'Today I am definitely going to go [+ conscious choice].'

volition is involved and the speaker is its source. By contrast the dative subject is unmarked for SOURCE, therefore the issue of speaker volition does not arise:

āj mujh-ē zarūr jā-nā h-ai
today I-obl.-DAT certainly go-INF AUX-3sg.
'Today I definitely have to go [- conscious choice].'

This new data suggests that the parameters EXTERNAL SOURCE : INTERNAL SOURCE may form an unexplored dimension of the modal system, at least in the Urdu of Pakistan.

'must'
NOMINATIVE INFINITIVE + inflected form of *paṛnā* 'to fall, befall' expresses external compulsion or lack of choice:

mujh-ē ye kaṛv-ī davā khā-nī (~ khā-nā) paṛ-ī h-ai
I-obl.-DAT this bitter-f. medicine eat-INF-f. (~ INF-m.sg.) befall-PFV.-f. AUX-3sg.
'I must take this bitter medicine.'

3.5.11 Compound verbs

Compound verbs are nuanced verb sequences with a structure similar to ROOT + *saknā* or ROOT + *cuknā*:

VERB ROOT + inflected VECTOR VERB

Nespital (1997: v) identifies the first element of the compound verb with the simple absolutive (the bare conjunctive participle [3.5.5] without the extension *kar* ~ *kē*; see 'Remarks'), rather than the verb root. It is for practical purposes called the main verb, and provides the lexical meaning of the sequence. The second element has been variously called the 'vector verb', 'intensifying verb', 'compound auxiliary', or 'explicator verb'. It loses its lexical meaning to a greater or lesser extent, but contributes contextual information to the verb phrase.

A number of scholars (including Hook 1974, Butt 1995 and Nespital 1997) have pointed to quasi-aspectual functions of compound verbs, but Masica (1991: 262–8 and 326–30) objects to this for several reasons, most importantly the existence of a morphologically based aspectual system (3.5.2) and its pivotal role in the predicting whether a subject takes the nominative or ergative case (split ergativity). Masica follows Lienhard (1961) in designating the quasi-aspectual functions of compound verbs as Aktionsart rather than aspect.

There has been extensive research on vector verbs using Hindi data, but only one work based specifically on Urdu data (Butt 1995 examined complex predicates in the Urdu of Lahore, Pakistan). Lexicographers such as Abdul Haqq (1994) do document many individual compound verb combinations, but without examples which would clarify the definitions. Therefore, while one may anticipate that compound verbs are used similarly in both Urdu and Hindi, at least in India, one cannot say with certainty that all the semantic functions of Hindi compound verbs are covered in the same way by Urdu compound verbs, particularly in the Urdu of Pakistan.

For Hindi, Hook (1974: 119) identifies 24 vectors, and Nespital (1997: xvii) identifies 47. Kachru 1990b: 66–7 identifies 13 'main explicator [vector] verbs' in 'Hindi-Urdu'. For Urdu, the nine vector verbs mentioned here cover the bulk of compound sequences occurring in a fairly large sample of third-year pedagogical texts; but additional vector verbs certainly exist, particularly when one includes one-of-a-kind compound sequences with unique definitions).

Simple verb:	*baiṭhnā* 'to sit'
Compound verb:	*baiṭh jānā* 'to sit down'
Simple verb:	*paṛhnā* 'to read'
Compound verb:	*paṛh dēnā* 'to read to someone'

3.5.11.1 Function of compound verbs

A simple verb shows only that an action or event takes place. Compound verbs show the unfolding of an action, or provide contextual information. Example:

kyā āp nē ciṭṭhī paṛh-ī h-ai?
INTER you-L3 ERG letter read-PFV-f. AUX-3sg.
'Have you read the letter?' (Simple verb)

maĩ nē ciṭṭhī ammā̃ kō paṛh d-ī
I ERG letter mother DAT read give-PFV-f.sg.
'I read that letter (completely) to mother.' (Compound verb, vector *dēnā*)

maĩ nē ciṭṭhī paṛh l-ī
I ERG letter read take-PFV-f.sg.
'I finished reading the letter (to myself).' (Compound verb, vector *lēnā*)

The commonest vector verbs are *jānā* 'to go', *dēnā* 'to give', and *lēnā* 'to take'. Hook (1979: 63–4) describes *dēnā*, *lēnā* and *jānā* as the 'least marked' of the vectors, that is, lexically nearly colourless. *dēnā* and *lēnā* occur with transitive verbs. Both show the completion of an action, but *dēnā* implies an action done for someone else, directed away from the self, or affecting the external environment, while *lēnā* implies an action done for the self, on the self, directed toward the self, or coming from the external environment and affecting the self. Both *dēnā* and *lēnā* may show completion.

jānā occurs with intransitive verbs, and implies a transition from one state to another. In the following example about the sinking of a boat (a metaphor for a misfortune), Hook 1979: 233 says that a simple verb (*dubāī*) is used when the question concerns only the agent of the sinking. But when the context of the sinking is brought into focus, the transition between the prior state (when it is afloat) and the subsequent one (being sunk) requires a compound verb (*ḍūb gaī*).

kisī nē (nāō) ḍubā-ī hō, ab tō ḍūb hī ga-ī (Prem Chand, Gōdān)
someone ERG (boat) sink-PFV-f. AUX-SUBJ-3sg. now TOP sink EMPH go-PFV-f.sg.
'Whoever sank the boat, now it has really sunk.'

3.5.11.2 Intransitive vectors

Intransitive vectors occur mainly with intransitive main verbs. In addition to *jānā* 'to go', *paṛnā* 'to fall, befall'; *nikalnā* 'to come out'; *baiṭhnā* 'to sit'; and *uṭhnā* 'to rise' also occur as intransitive vectors, but retain more lexical colour and have a much lower functional load. *paṛnā* connotes something which happens involuntarily, suddenly, or unavoidably. *nikalnā* shows suddenness, but also motion out or away. *uṭhnā* functions like an intensifier, and *baiṭhnā* shows speaker disapproval of an impulsive or involuntary action. Examples:

laṛkā cal-t-ī rēl gāṛī sē gir paṛ-ā
boy move-IMPV-f. rail vehicle from fall befall-PFV-m.sg.
'The boy fell off the moving train (an accident).'

bail gāṛī cal nikl-ī
bullock vehicle move come-out-PFV-f.sg.
'The bullock cart set off quickly.'

mulāzim malik sē laṛ baiṭh-ā, aur naukarī ga-ī
employee boss with fight sit-PFV-m.sg. and job go-PFV-f.sg.
'The employee (foolishly) quarrelled with the boss, and lost his job.'

3.5.11.3 Transitive vectors

Transitive vectors occur mainly with transitive main verbs. In addition to *dēnā* and *lēnā*, *ḍālnā* 'to put, pour', and *rakhnā* 'to put, place' also occur. *ḍālnā* has a higher functional load than *rakhnā*. It is an intensifier and shows intensity, urgency, completeness or violence.

bacc-õ nē baraf kā ādmī banā ḍāl-ā
children-obl. ERG snow POSS person build pour-PFV-m.sg.
'The children made a snowman (when they got the chance).'

pōlīs vāl-ē na ā-t-ē tō ḍākū us-ē mār ḍāl-t-ē
police agent-pl. not come-IMPV-m.pl. so bandits him-obl.-DAT beat pour-IMPV-m.pl.
'(If) the police had not come, the bandits would have killed him.'

According to Butt 1995: 108–10, *ḍālnā* shows volition, and thus contrasts with *paṛnā*, which shows absence of volition. *rakhnā* occurs with the main verbs *dēnā* and *lēnā*, meaning 'to give/take (as a loan)', and with other semantically appropriate main verbs showing an action performed beforehand.

us nē apnā makān hamẽ dē rakh-ā h-ai
he-obl. ERG own house us-obl.-DAT give put-PFV-m.sg. AUX-3sg.
'He has given us his house (allowed us to use it).'

Butt 1995: 111 includes an example of *mārnā* as a transitive vector.

us nē xat likh mār-ā
he-obl. ERG letter write hit-PFV-m.sg.
'He dashed off a letter.'

While most Urdu grammars mention *choṛnā* as a transitive vector, and Hook 1974 gives an example for Hindi, Schmidt 1999 (working with Gopi Chand Narang) did not find a grammatically correct example of *choṛnā* as a vector in the Standard Urdu of Delhi.

3.5.11.4 Mixed transitivity in compound verbs

Compound verb sequences with mixed transitivity occur (and are grammatically intransitive). The result is usually compounds with unique lexical meanings and limited recombinability. Here we are in the realm of idiom, where new coinages occur. Some common combinations are illustrated below.

Transitive main verbs with intransitive vectors

>*lē jānā* 'to take away'
>*lē calnā* 'to take someone somewhere'
>*khā jānā* 'to eat up'
>*kar jānā* 'to accomplish'
>*kar baiṭhnā* 'to do as a blunder'
>*kar guzarnā* 'to do (in spite of obstacles)'
>*sīkh jānā* 'to learn (quickly)'

Example:

>*vo naša kar-nē kē liē kuch bhī kar guzar-t-ā h-ai*
>he intoxication do-INF-obl. POSS for something also do pass-IMPV-m.sg. AUX-3sg.
>'In order to get high, he (an addict) will do anything at all.'

Intransitive main verbs with the transitive vector *dēnā*
This class includes mainly *calnā* 'to go', *hãsnā* 'to laugh' and *rōnā* 'to cry':

>*cal dēnā* 'to set off, depart, leave'
>*hãs dēnā* 'to burst into laughter'
>*rō dēnā* 'to burst into tears'

>*rēl gāṛī cal d-ī*
>rail vehicle move give-PFV-f.sg.
>'The train departed.'

4 SYNTAX

4.1 Basic word order

The basic word order in Urdu sentences is SUBJECT - PREDICATE. However, since defining the subject is not a straightforward matter in Urdu, this initial generalization is better formulated as: the basic sentence consists of a noun phrase and a verb (formulations adapted from Masica 1991: 332–3).

NP + Vb (intransitive):

>*laṛkā khēl rah-ā h-ai*
>boy play CON-m.sg. AUX-3sg.
>'The boy is playing.'

If there is an object, it comes between the noun phrase (subject) and verb (predicate). Objects with *kō* precede simple objects.

NP + NP + Vb (transitive):

>*ārif xabrẽ sun rah-ā h-ai*
>Arif news listen CON-m.sg. AUX-3sg.
>'Arif is listening to the news (a broadcast).'

NP + NP + NP Vb (double transitive):

ārif hamẽ xabar sunā-ē g-ā
Arif us-obl.-DAT news tell-3sg. FUT-m.sg
'Arif will tell us the news (what he heard).'

Adverbs and postpositional phrases precede the verb. The unemphatic word order for simple declarative sentences is:

SUBJECT - OBJECT + *kō* - TIME ADVERB - PLACE ADVERB - SIMPLE OBJECT - VERB

For example,

mãĩ āp kō kal urdū bāzār mẽ ēk acchī dukān dikhā-ũ g-ā
I you DAT tomorrow Urdu Bazaar in one good shop show-1sg. FUT-m.sg.
'I will show you a good shop in the Urdu Bazaar tomorrow.'

Interrogatives and negatives immediately precede the verb; interrogatives precede negatives:

us nē mujh-ē dukān nahĩ dikhā-y-ā
he-obl. ERG me-obl.-DAT shop not show-PFV-m.sg.
'He didn't show me the shop.'

us nē mujh-ē dukān kyõ nahĩ dikhā-y-ā?
he-obl. ERG me-obl.-DAT shop why not show-PFV-m.sg.
'Why didn't he show me the shop?'

In actual discourse, the order of adverbs changes very flexibly, reflecting nuances of emphasis. An adverb of time is often given prominence by placing it right after the subject, or even first in the sentence. An adverb of place may also be given prominence by moving it to the left. The order of the subject, object and verb are more rarely changed, but examples may be found where the verb is moved to the left to emphasize it.

If the verb provides the necessary information about the person, number and gender of the speaker, the subject may be omitted:

kal (mãĩ) āp kō urdū bāzār mẽ ēk acchī dukān dikhā-ũ g-ā
tomorrow (I) you DAT Urdu Bazaar in one good shop show-1sg FUT-m.sg
'Tomorrow (I) will show you a good shop in the Urdu Bazaar.'

4.2 Types of subject marking

4.2.1 Nominative subjects

In imperfective tenses, the verb agrees with the subject, which is in the nominative case. As mentioned above (3.5.2.3), the syntax of perfective tenses is partially nominative and partially ergative (split ergativity): intransitive verbs agree with the subject, which is in the nominative case (but see 4.2.2). For example,

laṛk-ā gẽd phẽk rah-ā h-ai
boy-nom. ball throw CON-m.sg. AUX-3sg.
'The boy is throwing the ball.'

4.2.2 Ergative subjects

In perfective tenses, transitive verbs agree with the object (unless it is marked with *kō*), and the subject takes the ergative postposition *nē* (3.1.1.3.3):

laṛk-ē nē is taraf gẽd phẽk-ī th-ī
boy-obl. ERG this-obl. direction ball throw-PFV-f. AUX-PAST-f.sg.
'The boy had thrown the ball this way.'

How do we know that *laṛkē nē* is the subject of the last sentence? Aside from the fact that it has been transformed from the previous non-perfective one, *laṛkē nē* here functions grammatically and syntactically as a subject. It is the first NP in the sentence, the agent of the action (throwing the ball), requires the reflexive pronoun *apnā* (if the boy owns the ball), and is also the agent of conjunctive clauses:

laṛk-ē nē apn-ī gẽd phẽk-ī h-ai
boy-obl. ERG own-f. ball throw-PFV-f. AUX.sg.
'The boy has thrown away his ball.'

laṛk-ē nē gẽd pakaṛ kē phẽk-ī
boy-obl. ERG ball catch CP throw-PFV-f.sg
'The boy caught the ball and threw it.'

4.2.3 Dative subjects

The subjects of impersonal verbal constructions take the dative postposition *kō* (or its alternate forms, 3.1.1.3.2). Impersonal constructions include expressions of sensation (often with *lagnā* 'to be applied'), liking/disliking, knowing, getting (with *milnā* 'to meet'), and the impersonal modal constructions with infinitives (3.5.10.2.2). The verb is always in the third person, and agrees with the object:

bacc-ī kō ḍar lag rah-ā th-ā
child-f. DAT fear applied CON-m.sg. AUX-PAST-m.sg.
'The little girl was feeling frightened.'

mujh-ē samōs-ē pasand hãī
I-obl.-DAT samosa-pl. liked are
'I like samosas.'

āj ham-ẽ tanxāh mil-ē g-ī
today we-obl.-DAT pay meet-3sg. FUT-f.sg.
'Today we will get (our) pay.'

Many scholars (3.1.1.3.2) consider dative subjects experiencers rather than agents, but like ergative subjects, they take the reflexive pronoun *apnā* and may be agents of conjunctive clauses.

mujh-e apn-ā nay-ā makān pasand hai
I-obl.-DAT own-m. new-m. house liked is
'I like my new house.'

āj ham-ẽ apn-ī tanxāh mil-ē g-ī
today we-obl.-DAT own-f. pay meet-3sg. FUT-f.sg.
'Today we will get our pay.'

(*mērā ghar and *hamārī tanxāh would be incorrect in the above examples; mujhē and hamē̃ are the subjects of the sentences and own the house and the pay, respectively.)

> vahā̃ jā kar ham-ē̃ aur bhī acch-ē samōs-ē mil-ē̃ g-ē
> there go CP we-obl.-DAT and also good-pl. samosa-pl. meet-3pl. FUT-m.pl.
> 'We'll get even better samosas if we go there.'

In the above sentence, the subject of the conjunctive clause is a deleted ham, corresponding to hamē̃ in the main clause.

4.2.4 Subjects marked by sē

As mentioned under 3.1.1.3.4, subjects of involuntary actions take the postposition sē. This usage is similar to the passive instrument marked by sē, and it may be preferable to treat all such cases as instruments. In the following examples, the instrument becomes the subject of the English translation.

Intransitive:

> bacc-ē sē camca gir ga-y-ā
> child-m.obl. from spoon fell go-PFV-m.sg.
> 'The baby dropped the spoon (accidentally).'

Passive of incapacity

> pērū sē uṛā nahī̃ jā-t-ā
> turkey from fly-PFV-m.sg. not go-IMPV-m.sg.
> 'A turkey is unable to fly.'

5 WRITING SYSTEM

Urdu is written in a modified form of the Arabic script, as adapted for writing Persian, and which, including characters developed for representing Urdu sounds not found in Persian, contains 38 linear characters. It is written from right to left (except for numerals, which are written from left to right). Its cursive, multilevel form is known as Nastaᶜliq. It is originally derived from a less cursive, less multilevel, form called Naskh, which is still used for some typeset printing. Arabic and Persian loanwords are spelled as they are in the source languages, and not according to their pronunciation, which accounts for the large number of characters and the many sets of characters with identical pronunciations (MacGregor 1992: xiii; Naim 1975: 41).

Both Nastaᶜliq and Naskh differ from Roman orthography in one important respect. In the latter, both consonants and vowels are represented sequentially in horizontally arranged characters (segmental characters). In the Perso-Arabic orthography, consonants and semivowels are represented segmentally, but short vowels, if they are represented, are added by three signs written above or below the line. They are usually not written unless they are necessary for the recognition of words. Long vowels are represented by the Arabic character for a glottal stop, | alif, or the semivowels ی yē and و vāō, (initial long vowels by | alif plus the semivowels ی yē and و vāō), but there is no one-to-one correspondence between the pronunciation and the written representation, except in the case of final -ī and -ē. Initial vowels must be shown by | alif, plus the appropriate vowel sign if necessary for recognition.

Many consonant characters have identical segmental shapes and are distinguished by dots or groups of dots written above or below the line. There are two types of letters, 'connectors' and 'non-connectors'. 'Connectors' may be joined from both the left and right, while 'non-connectors' are joined only from the right. The forms of the characters are given below in their traditional order, along with their traditional transliteration. Non-connectors are indicated by empty columns under the 'Medial' and 'Initial' forms of the characters (in initial position the independent form of the character is used).

5.1 Characters of the Urdu script

(See Table 8.11)

5.2 Samples of the Urdu script

بتاتا ہے *batātā hai* '(he) tells', جاتا تھا *jātā thā* '(he) used to go', وہ جاتی تھی *vo jātī thī* 'she used to go', ہم جائیں گے *ham jāẽ gē* 'we will go', ہم لوگ کھانا کھائیں گے *ham lōg khānā khāẽ gē* 'we (people) will eat food', میں کھانا کھاؤں گا *mãĩ khānā khāũ gā*, 'I will eat food', اب کھانا کھا لو *ab khānā khā lō* 'eat food now', اب کھانا کھا لیجئے *ab khānā khā lījiē* 'please eat food now', میری والدہ یہ کہتی ہیں *mērī vālida ye kahtī hãĩ* 'my mother says this', نسیم صاحب اِس دفتر میں کام کرتے ہیں *nasīm sāhib is daftar mẽ kām kartē hãĩ* 'Mr Nasim works in this office', مجھے سموسے پسند ہیں *mujhē samosē pasand hãĩ* 'I like samosas', اگر آپ احتیاط کرتے تو حادثہ نہ ہوتا *agar āp ehtiyāt kartē, to hādisa na hōtā* 'If you had been careful, (then) there would not have been an accident.'

5.3 Comments

ا *alif* (a glottal stop in Arabic) represents an initial vowel at the beginning of a word, but a long *ā* medially or finally. If an initial long *ā* is to be written a superscript called *mad* is written over *ali* آ. The short vowels *zabar*, *zēr* and *pēš* may be written over initial *alif* to indicate an initial *a-*, *i-* or *u-*: اُ اِ اَ اِس طرف *is taraf* '(in) this direction', اُس طرف *us taraf* '(in) that direction'. Initial long vowels are written with *alif* ا plus ی *yē* and و *vāō*:

اور	*aur*	'and'
ایک	*ēk*	'one'
اون	*ūn*	'wool'

ع *ᶜain* (a glottal fricative in Arabic) is realized as zero or (in pedantic or careful speech) a glottal stop. The quality of original Arabic *i* and *u* is lowered in Urdu preceding a zero-realized *ᶜain*. A short vowel in the Arabic original becomes a long vowel in Urdu when followed by *ᶜain*. Final *ᶜain* following a consonant is realized as *-a* or *ā*.

عورت	*ᶜaurat → aurat*	'woman'
جماعت	*jamā ᶜat → jamā'at, jamāt*	'class'
بعد	*baᶜd → bād*	'after'
معلوم	*maᶜlūm → mālūm*	'known'
موقع	*mauqaᶜ → mauqā*	'occasion'

TABLE 8.11: CHARACTERS OF THE URDU SCRIPT

Name	Independent	Final connected	Medial connected	Initial connected	Transliteration
alif	ا	ـا	—	—	See comments
bē	ب	ـب	ـبـ	بـ	b
pē	پ	ـپ	ـپـ	پـ	p
tē	ت	ـت	ـتـ	تـ	t
ṭē	ٹ	ـٹ	ـٹـ	ٹـ	ṭ
sē	ث	ـث	ـثـ	ثـ	s̱
jīm	ج	ـج	ـجـ	جـ	j
cẹ	چ	ـچ	ـچـ	چـ	c
baṛī hē	ح	ـح	ـحـ	حـ	ḥ
xē	خ	ـخ	ـخـ	خـ	x, ḵẖ
dāl	د	ـد	—	—	d
ḍāl	ڈ	ـڈ	—	—	ḍ
zāl	ذ	ـذ	—	—	z̲
rē	ر	ـر	—	—	r
ṛē	ڑ	ـڑ	—	—	ṛ
zē	ز	ـز	—	—	z
žē	ژ	ـژ	—	—	ẓ̌
sīn	س	ـس	ـسـ	سـ	s
šīn	ش	ـش	ـشـ	شـ	š
svād	ص	ـص	ـصـ	صـ	ṣ
zvād	ض	ـض	ـضـ	ضـ	ẓ
tōē	ط	ـط	ـطـ	طـ	ṭ
zōē	ظ	ـظ	ـظـ	ظـ	ẓ̤
ain	ع	ـع	ـعـ	عـ	c
ɣain	غ	ـغ	ـغـ	غـ	g, ɣ
fē	ف	ـف	ـفـ	فـ	f
qāf	ق	ـق	ـقـ	قـ	q
kāf	ک	ـک	ـکـ	کـ	k
gāf	گ	ـگ	ـگـ	گـ	g
lām	ل	ـل	ـلـ	لـ	l
mīm	م	ـم	ـمـ	مـ	m
nūn	ن	ـن	ـنـ	نـ	n
nūn-e-ɣunna	ں	ـں	—	(not initial)	nasalization
vāō	و	ـو	—	—	v, ū, ō, au
chōṭī hē	ہ	ـہ	ـہـ	ہـ	h, -a
dō cašmī hē	ھ	ـھ	ـھـ	ھ	aspiration
chōṭī yē	ی	ـی	ـیـ	یـ	y, -ī, ai
baṛī yē	ے	ـے	ـیـ	(not initial)	ē
hamza	ء (superscript)		ـئـ	—	vowel glide

Notes: The short vowels *a, u, i* can be indicated by the superscript signs *zabar*, *zēr* and *pēš*: ـٔ but are usually omitted. Aspiration as a phonetic phenomenon cannot occur syllable-initially. But if *dō cašmī hē* is written following a non-connecting character and prior to a connecting character, its initial form is written.

استعمال	$isti^c m\bar{a}l \rightarrow ist\bar{e}m\bar{a}l$ 'use' (sometimes shortened to $istem\bar{a}l$)
اعتراض	$i^c tir\bar{a}z, \rightarrow etir\bar{a}z$ 'objection'
توقع	$tavaqqu^c \rightarrow tavaqqo$ 'expectation'
شمع	$šam^c \rightarrow šama$ 'candle'

5.4 Arabic roots

Because Arabic loanwords are spelled as they are written in Arabic, the writing system permits the identification of semantic relationships between words derived from a single three-consonant Arabic root.

محنت	امتحان	محن
meḥnat	*imtiḥān*	*meḥan*
effort	examination	sufferings

علم	عالم	معلوم	تعليم	معلم
$^c ilm$	$^c\bar{a}lim$	$m\bar{a}^c l\bar{u}m$	$t\bar{a}^c l\bar{\imath}m$	$mu^c allim$
knowledge	scholar	known	education	teacher

6 REMARKS

Dakhanī (1.1) This word is spelled in various ways: Persianized, as Dakanī; Sanskritized, as Dakkhinī. Schmidt 1981 follows Grierson in calling it Dakhinī. In this chapter however, the usage of the authorititive writer on Dakhanī, S. G. Mohiuddin Qadri 'Zor', is followed.

The Mughal Empire (1.1.3) The Mughal Empire survived in a weakened form after 1757 (the Battle of Plassey) until 1857 (the suppression of the Rebellion), and some scholars give the dates of the Mughal Empire as 1526 to 1857. Richards (1998: xv) treats the collapse of Mughal centralized power, apparent in 1720, as the end point.

The Census of Pakistan (1.2.2) The percentages supplied in the Census of Pakistan have been rounded off to two digits, and the population figures have been rounded off in thousands. The total of the number of province-wise estimated speakers comes to 6,519,069, a difference of 115,841 from the estimated number of speakers for the country as a whole.

Bēgamātī ẓabān (1.3.1) Lexicons cited by Minault include: Munshi Chiranji Lal Dehlavi, *Hindūstānī Makhzan ul Muhāvarāt* (Delhi: Imperial Book Depot, 1898); M. Munir Lakhnavi, *Muhāvarāt-e-Nisvã va Khās Bēgamāt kī Zabān* (Kanpur: Majidiya Press, 1930); Sayyid Ahmad Dehlavi, *Lughat-un-Nisā* (Delhi: Daftar-e-Farhang-e-Asafiya, 1917); and Sayyid Amjad Ali Ashhari, *Lughat al Khawātīn* (Lahore: Khādim ut-Ta^c līm Press, 1907). The following linguistic studies are also cited: Mīr Inshāullāh Khān 'Inshā', *Daryā-e-Laṭāfat*, Urdu tr. by Brajmohan Dattatreya 'Kaifī' Dehlavī, ed. by Abdul Haqq (Aurangabad: Anjuman-e-Taraqqi-e-Urdu (Dakkhan), 1935); Muhiyuddin Hasan, *Dillī kī Bēgamātī Zabān* (New Delhi: Nayi Avaz, 1976) and Wahida Nasim, *Urdū Zabān aur Aurat* (Karachi: Intikhab-e-Nau, 1963).

izāfat (2.4.1) izāfat is the Persian enclitic which shows (a) possession, or (b) modification of a noun by an adjective. It is written as a *zēr* (short *i*) beneath the preceding consonant.

Simple absolutive The simple (or short) absolutive consists of the conjunctive participle without the extension *kar* ~ *kē*. Short absolutives are allowed in Hindi, when the first action in some way causes the second action. This usage is incorrect in modern Standard Urdu, but may nevertheless be found in texts, particularly older ones.

ACKNOWLEDGEMENTS

The author wishes to thank Knut Kristiansen, Finn Thiesen and Razwal Kohistani for reading the draft of this chapter and making many corrections and offering useful information. I am also grateful to Elena Bashir for responding to email requests for information and bibliographic references. Errors and omissions which may remain are my own.

REFERENCES

Abbi, Anvita (1990) 'Experiential constructions and the "subjecthood" of the experiencer NPs in South Asian languages', in Verma, Manindra and Mohanan, K. P. (eds.) *Experiencer Subjects in South Asian Languages*, Stanford, CA: Center for the Study of Language and Information, Stanford University, pp. 253–67.

Agha, Asif (1998) 'Form and function in Urdu-Hindi verb inflection', in Singh, Rajendra, Dasgupta, Probal and Mohanan, K. P. (eds.) *The Yearbook of South Asian Languages and Linguistics*, New Delhi, London: Sage Publications, pp. 105–33.

Bashir, Elena (1999) 'The Urdu postposition *ne*: its changing role in the grammar', in Singh, Rajendra, Dasgupta, Probal and Mohanan, K. P. (eds.) *The Yearbook of South Asian Languages and Linguistics*, New Delhi, London: Sage Publications, pp. 11–36.

Butt, Miriam (1995) 'The Structure of Complex Predicates in Urdu', in Bresnan, Joan et al. (eds.) *Dissertations in Linguistics*, Stanford, CA: Center for the Study of Language and Information, Stanford University.

Census of India (1991) *Paper 1 of 1997, Language*: see Vijayanunni, M.

Census of Pakistan (1981) 1983, *Main Findings*.

Chatterji, Suniti Kumar (1960) *Indo-Aryan and Hindi*, Calcutta: Firma K. L. Mukhopadhyaya.

Encyclopedia Britannica. Languages of the World: INDO-EUROPEAN LANGUAGES: Indo-Iranian Languages: The Indo-Aryan Languages: The modern Indo-Aryan stage.' *Britannica Online*.
    <http://www.eb.com:180/cgi-bin/g?DocF=macro/5003/62/63.html> [Accessed 30 November 1998].

Faiz Ahmad Faiz (1943) 'Mujh sē pahlī sī muhabbat merē mahbūb na māng', *Naqś-e-Faryādī*, p. 47.

Farouqui, Ather (1992) 'Future prospects of Urdu in India', *Mainstream Annual* 1992.

—— (1994a) 'The emerging dilemma of the Urdu press in India', *American Journal of Economics and Sociology* 53.3: 360–2.

—— (1994b) 'Urdu Education in India', *Economic and Political Weekly* April 2, 1994: 782–5.

Grierson, George (1916) *Linguistic Survey of India, Vol. 9, Part 1, Western Hindī and Pañjābī*, Calcutta: Superintendent Government Printing, India. (Reprinted (1968) Delhi: Motilal Banarsidass).

Grimes, Barbara F. (ed.) (1996) *Ethnologue: Languages of the World*, 13th edition, Houston: Summer Institute of Linguistics.

Gumperz, John and Naim, C. M. (1960) 'Formal and informal standards in the Hindi regional language area', in Ferguson, Charles A. and Gumperz, John J. (eds.) *Linguistic Diversity in South Asia (International Journal of American Linguistics*, 26.3), pp. 92–118.

Haqq, Abdul (1994) *Standard Twentieth Century Dictionary, Urdu into English*, Delhi: Educational Publishing House.

Hook, Peter E. (1974) *The Compound Verb in Hindi*, Ann Arbor: University of Michigan, Center for South and Southeast Asian Studies.

—— (1979) *Hindi Structures: intermediate level*, Ann Arbor: University of Michigan, Center for South and Southeast Asian Studies.

Islam, Mazhar ul (1988) 'Sargōšiyõ kī õṭ mẽ baiṭhā xākrōb [Sweeper sitting in the screen of whispers]', in *Guṛiyā kī ãkh sē šahr kō dēkhō* [Look at the city from the eyes of the doll], Lahore: Sang-e-Meel, pp. 101–112.

Kachru, Yamuna (1986) 'The Syntax of Dakkhini: a study in language variation and change', in Krishnamurti, Bh. (ed.) *South Asian Languages: Structure, Convergence and Diglossia*, Delhi: Motilal Banarsidass, pp. 165–78.

—— (1990a) 'Experiencer and other oblique subjects in Hindi', in Verma, Manindra and Mohanan, K. P. (eds.), *Experiencer Subjects in South Asian Languages*, Stanford, CA: Center for the Study of Language and Information, Stanford University, pp. 59–75.

—— (1990b) 'Hindi-Urdu' in Comrie, Bernard (ed.) *Major Languages of South Asia, the Middle East and Africa*, London: Routledge, pp. 53–72.

Kelkar, Ashok R. (1968) *Studies in Hindi-Urdu, I. Introduction and Word Phonology*, Poona, India: Deccan College Postgraduate and Research Institute.

King, Christopher R. (1994) *One Language, Two Scripts: the Hindi Movement in Nineteenth Century North India*, Bombay: Oxford University Press.

Lienhard, Siegfried (1961) *Tempusgebrauch und Aktionsartenbildung in der modernen Hindi*, Stockholm: Almqvist & Wiksell.

Magier, David (1987) 'The transitivity prototype: evidence from Hindi', *Word* 38.1: 187–99.

Masica, Colin P. (1991) *The Indo-Aryan Languages*, Cambridge University Press.

Matthews, D. J. (1976) *Dakanī Language and Literature*, Thesis submitted for the degree of Ph.D., School of Oriental and African Studies, University of London.

—— (1994) 'Eighty years of Dakani Scholarship', *Annual of Urdu Studies* 9: 91–107.

McGregor, R. S. (1972) *Outline of Hindi Grammar*, New Delhi: Oxford University Press.

—— (1991) *Urdu Study Materials* for use with *Outline of Hindi Grammar*, New Delhi: Oxford University Press, India.

Minault, Gail (1984) 'Begamati zuban: women's language and culture in nineteenth century Delhi', *India International Center Quarterly* (New Delhi) 11.2: 155–70.

—— (1999) 'Delhi College and Urdu', *Annual of Urdu Studies* 14: 119–34.

Naim, C. M. (1975) *Introductory Urdu*, 2 vols, Chicago: University of Chicago, Committee on Southern Asia Studies.

Nespital, Helmut (1994) 'The development of literary Urdu in Delhi in the 17th and 18th centuries with regard to changes of its language structure', in Chitre, Dilip et al. (eds.), *Tender Ironies. A Tribute to Lothar Lutz*, New Delhi: Manohar, pp. 308–25.

—— (1997) *Dictionary of Hindi Verbs*, Allahabad: Lok Bharti Prakashan.

—— (1998) 'The linguistic structure of Hindavī, Dakkhinī, early Urdu and Early Khaṛī Bōlī Hindi', *Berliner Indologische Studien* 11/12: 195–217.

Platts, John T. (1920) *A Grammar of the Hindūstānī or Urdū Language*, London: Crosby Lockwood and Son.

Pray, Bruce R. (1980) 'Evidence of grammatical convergence in Dakhini Urdu and Telugu', *Proceedings of the Sixth Annual Meeting of the Berkeley Linguistic Society*, pp. 90–9.

Pritchett, Frances (1998) *Inventory of Language Materials*, at the web site: gopher://gopher.cc.columbia.edu:71/11/clioplus/scholarly/SouthAsia/Teaching/ILM.

Qadri, S. G. Mohiuddin 'Zor' (1930) *Hindustani Phonetics*, Villeneuve-Saint Georges: Imprimerie l'Union Typographique.

Rahman, Tariq (1996) *Language and Politics in Pakistan*, Karachi: Oxford University Press.

Rai, Amrit (1984) *A House Divided*, Delhi: Oxford University Press.

Richards, John F. (1993) *The Mughal Empire*, Cambridge: Cambridge University Press.

Russell, Ralph and Islam, Khurshidul (1968) *Three Mughal Poets*, Cambridge, MA: Harvard University Press.

Schmidt, Ruth (1981) *Dakhini Urdu: History and Structure*, New Delhi: Bahri Publications.

—— (1999) *Urdu: An Essential Grammar*, London: Routledge.

Schumacher, Rolf (1977) *Untersuchungen zum Absolutiv im modernen Hindi. Ein Beitrag zur semantischen Syntax*, Frankfurt am Main: Peter Lang.

Shackle, C. and Snell, R. (1990) *Hindi and Urdu since 1800. A Common Reader*, London: School of Oriental and African Studies.

Singh, Bahadur (1966) *The Dialect of Delhi*, South Asian Studies III, New Delhi: South Asia Institute, University of Heidelberg.

Snell, Rupert and Weightman, Simon (1992) *Teach Yourself Hindi*, Sevenoaks, Kent (UK), Teach Yourself Books.

Srivastava, Sushil (1995) 'Christopher R. King. One Language, Two Scripts (review article)' *The Annual of Urdu Studies* 10: 222–33.

Sufi, Al Haji Dr. G. M. D. (1974) *Kashir, A History of Kashmir*. (Reprinted New Delhi: Light and Life Publishers; originally published Lahore: Punjab University, vol. 1, 1948: vol. 2, 1949.)

Thiesen, Finn (1990) 'Participles and verbal nouns formed from the derived forms of the Arabic strong triliteral verb and their treatment in Urdu', in Keck, Egon et al. (eds.), *Living Waters. Scandinavian Orientalistic Studies*, Copenhagen: Museum Tusculanum Press.

Times of India, October 10, 1994 'A language under siege'.

Tuite, Keven J., Agha, Asif and Graczyk, Randolph (1985) 'Agentivity, transitivity and the question of active typology', *Chicago Linguistic Society* 21.2: 252–70.

Vassenden, Kåre (ed.) (1997) *Innvandrere i Norge. Hvem er de, hva gjør de og hvordan lever de?* [Immigrants in Norway: who are they, what do they do, and how do they live?], in the Series: *Statistical Analyses 20*, Oslo Central Bureau of Statistics.

Vijayanunni, M. (1997) *Census of India 1991, Series 1-India, Paper 1 of 1997: Language, India and States*, New Delhi: Government of India Press.

FURTHER READING

Selected and expanded from Frances Pritchett, *Some Useful Sources on Hindi/Urdu Language and Literature*, at the website:

http://www.columbia.edu/itc/mealac/pritchett/00urduhindilinks/index.html

TEXTBOOKS

Barker, M. A. R., *et al.* (1975) *Spoken Urdu*, 3 vols. (with cassettes), Ithaca, NY: Spoken Language Services.

Bhatia, Tej K. and Koul, Ashok (1999) *Colloquial Urdu: A Complete Language Course*, London: Routledge.

Glassman, Eugene H. (1995) *Spoken Urdu: A Beginning Course* (11th ed., with cassettes), Lahore, Pakistan: Nirali Kitaben Publishing House.

Grainger, Peter L. (1986) *Making A Sound Start In Urdu* (with cassettes), Lahore, Pakistan: Nirali Kitaben Publishing House. (Pronunciation drills, explanations, dialogues; correlates with Barker, *Spoken Urdu*.)

Matthews, D. J. and Dalvi, Mohamed Kasim (1999) *Teach Yourself Urdu*, Sevenoaks, Kent (U.K.), Teach Yourself Books.

Matthews, D. J. and Shackle, C. (1982) *Introduction to Urdu*, London: School of Oriental and African Studies.

Naim, C. M. (1999) *Introductory Urdu*, 2 vols., Chicago: University of Chicago, Committee on Southern Asia Studies.

Russell, Ralph (1981–6) *A New Course in Urdu and Spoken Hindi* (vol. 1); vol. 2, *An Outline of Grammar and Common Usage*; vol. 3, *Rapid Readings*; vol. 4, *The Urdu Script*, London: School of Oriental and African Studies.
Schmidt, Ruth Laila (1999) *Urdu: An Essential Grammar*, London: Routledge.

URDU WRITING SYSTEM

Hanaway, William L. and Spooner, Brian (1995) *Reading Nastaᶜliq. Persian and Urdu Hands from 1500 to the Present*, Costa Mesa, California: Mazda Publishers.
McGregor, R. S. (1992) *Urdu Study Materials* for use with *Outline of Hindi Grammar*, New Delhi: Oxford University Press.
(See also sections of textbooks by Barker 1993, Naim 1999 and Russell 1986 which are devoted to the writing system.)

GLOSSED READERS AND GLOSSARIES FOR PUBLISHED SHORT STORIES

Ahmad, Mumtaz (1985) *Urdu Newspaper Reader* (with cassettes), Wheaton, MD: Dunwoody Press.
Barker, M. A. R. et al. (1968) *An Urdu Newspaper Reader*, Ithaca, NY: Spoken Language Services.
Kalsi, A. S. et al. (1991) *Modern Urdu Texts. Urdu Short Stories*, London: School of Oriental and African Studies. (A glossary to accompany selected short stories by Prem Chand, Manto, Krishan Chandar, Bedi, Intizar Husain, and Mazhar ul Islam.)
Matthews, D. J. (1994) *Ghalib: Eight Letters and Fifteen Ghazals*, London: School of Oriental and African Studies.
Matthews, D. J. and Shackle, C. (1991) *A Selection of Twentieth Century Urdu Verse*, London: School of Oriental and African Studies.
Shackle, C. and Snell, R. (1990) *Hindi and Urdu since 1800: A Common Reader*, London: School of Oriental and African Studies.
Taj, Afroz (1996) *Tanhaiyan, Ankahi and Ahsas* (*Companion*), Raleigh, NC: Hillsborough Street Textbooks. (Summaries of Pakistani television series, episode by episode, with brief vocabularies, followed by discussion questions, in both Urdu calligraphy and typeset Devanagari script.)

DICTIONARIES AND GLOSSARIES

Ferozsons Urdu–English Dictionary; A Comprehensive Dictionary of Current Vocabulary, (1983, revised ed.), Lahore, Pakistan: Ferozsons.
Kitabistan's Twentieth Century Standard Dictionary (Urdu–English and English–Urdu), Lahore, Pakistan: Kitabistan Publishing Company.
Platts, John T. *A Dictionary of Urdu, Classical Hindi, and English*. Reprint (1977) of 1930, New Delhi, India: Oriental Books Reprint Corp. (Also: reprint [1994] of 1911, Lahore, Pakistan: Sang-e-Meel. Original edition 1884).

(الحاج مولوی فیروز الدین (۱۹۸۷) جامع فیروزاللغات ـ دہلی ، بھارت: انجم بک ڈپو)

[Alhaj Maulvi Firozuddin (1987) *Jame Firoz-ul-Lughat*, Delhi, India: Anjum Book Depot.]
Schomer, K. et al. (1983) *Basic Vocabulary for Hindi and Urdu* (2nd ed.), Berkeley, CA: Center for South Asia Studies, University of California.

DAKHANĪ URDU

Arora, Harbir (1986) *Some Aspects of Dakkhini Hindi-Urdu Syntax with Special Reference to Convergence*. (University of Delhi Ph.D. thesis).

Kachru, Yamuna (1986) 'The Syntax of Dakkhini: a study in language variation and change', in Krishnamurti, Bh. (ed.) *South Asian Languages: Structure, Convergence and Diglossia*, Delhi: Motilal Banarsidass, pp. 165–78.

Matthews, David (1976) *Dakanī Language and Literature 1500–1700* AD (University of London Ph.D. thesis).

Pray, Bruce R. (1980) 'Evidence of grammatical convergence in Dakhini Urdu and Telugu', *Proceedings of the Sixth Annual Meeting of the Berkeley Linguistic Society*: 90–4.

Schmidt, Ruth (1981) *Dakhini Urdu: History and Structure*, New Delhi: Bahri Publications.

Shamatov, A. N. (1974) *Klassicheski dakkhini (iuzhnyi khindustani)*, 17 vols., Moscow: Nauka.

CHAPTER NINE

BANGLA

Probal Dasgupta

CONTENTS

LIST OF TABLES

1 GENERALITIES

Bangla, or Bengali, at the most recent census in 1991, had 58,541,519 speakers in West Bengal (88,752 sq. km.) plus 11,054,219 other Indian speakers, and an estimated 107 million speakers in Bangladesh (143,998 sq. km.), a total of 177 million subcontinental speakers in 1991, plus diasporic speakers for whom systematic figures are unavailable. For comparison, consider the West Bengal plus residual India figures for speakers of Bangla in 1961 (29,435,928 + 4,453,011), 1971 (37,805,905 + 6,986,407), and 1981 (46,347,935 + 4,950,384). In the absence of Bangladesh language data, the total Bangladesh population figures for 1974 (76,398,000), 1981 (89,912,000), and 1991 (111,455,185) may be taken into account; but these numbers need to be interpreted on the basis of the general conjecture that, consistently, over 96% of the Bangladeshi population has been Bangla-speaking.

West Bengal and Bangladesh together constituted a continuous Bangla-speaking region commonly called Bengal. This region crystallized as a language-based province in British India's twentieth century map. The Britons departing in 1947 who oversaw the partition of the subcontinent left West Bengal as part of India and East Bengal as the sole province of East Pakistan. Early Pakistani language policy favoured Urdu as a symbol of Muslim identity. But a movement for giving Bangla equal status, culminating in a major 21 February 1952 demonstration in Dhaka that the police fired on, killing seven university students, forced a settlement making Bangla and Urdu the official languages of Pakistan. Ever since, 21 February has been *bhāšā dibaš* 'language day' in East Bengal. Emerging in this Pakistani context, the transition in English usage from the colonial designation for the language, Bengali, to the indigenous form Bangla – analogous to the transition from, say, Canarese to Kannada – spread to India during the 1971 upheavals that led to the independence of Bangladesh. The transition is not yet complete, but the postcolonial form Bangla has become more frequent than the colonial form Bengali in linguistic English usage in recent years. The language itself distinguishes *bāŋlā*, the language, from a *bāŋāli*, a member of the speech community. English renders the latter as Bengali (the archaic spelling Bengalee for this is obsolete). Hindi likewise distinguishes *baṁglā* (by now the standard designation for the language in educated circles) from *baṁgālī*.

Within the Eastern Indic language family the history of the separation of Bangla from Oriya, Assamese, and the languages of Bihar remains to be worked out carefully. Scholars do not yet agree on criteria for deciding if certain tenth century AD texts were in a Bangla already distinguishable from the other languages, or marked a stage at which Eastern Indic had not finished differentiating. Such agreement may emerge once the contemporary enterprise of producing serious descriptions of the modern languages has achieved its objectives. The priorities may then permit greater attention to the unfinished task of drawing rigorous maps of the past. As research perspectives stand, researchers wishing to examine the history of Bangla find that the present speech community which they have to speak to and for is segmented. Language standardization efforts in sectors like education and publishing are not coordinated across the Indo-Bangladesh border. This may initially appear a long-term obstacle. However, the unsettlement of the forms of Bangla spoken and written in West Bengal has been due in part to the growing numbers and influence of waves of East Bengali migrants. This unsettlement made its impact right after the rise in the early twentieth century of the new Colit standard – also called the Standard Colloquial variety of Bangla, or the L(ow) term of a diglossia – which had favoured the pre-1947 southwestern dialects of the language.

In other words, scholarship taking the new influences on West Bengal into account will be compelled, because of the linguistic material to be handled, to narrow the gap between Indian and Bangladeshi work. For example, in order to examine the sources of what the migrants have wrought, scholars concerned with each side will have to engage with dialect geography on the other side of the India–Bangladesh border. For the moment, we need to note that speakers perceive Bangla as divided both horizontally, into geographical dialects, and vertically, into 'codes', or varieties classifiable in terms of a moribund High versus living Low dichotomy usefully called a 'diglossia'.

On both the geographical and the diglossic dimension, speakers have stereotyped views about what kinds of variation exist and how they co-articulate with other factors. The popular perception of geographical and diglossic differentiation has consistently influenced the directions of standardization throughout Bengal. Speakers of Bangla tend to oversimplify the geographical differentiation in terms of a dichotomy of Easterner or bāṅāl versus Westerner or ghoṭi. These stereotypes correspond to a rural–urban divide. Urbanization and industrialization did come relatively early to the southwestern region surrounding Calcutta. It was the capital of British India until 1911. Subsequent events reinforced such stereotypes in at least West Bengal. Refugees from the East experienced serious rehabilitation problems, often confining them to physical or social ghettoes and preserving the bāṅāl or ex-Eastern identity. However, the socio-political power in West Bengal of many former Easterners and their mostly left-wing spokesmen has partially easternized the Calcutta-based Indian standard. In the other direction, publications and media material from the West have continued to enjoy a reasonable public reception in the East. Such mitigating factors have worked to maintain a high density of serious linguistic communication across the border. The two standards have not yet seriously diverged. Educated Bengalis perceive the diglossic differentiation of their language into H(igh) and L(ow) codes in terms of the way the inflectional and pronominal systems in the sādhu or H code of standard written Bangla contrast with those in the colit or L code.

These codes publicly competed for ascendancy in the twentieth century. The H norm steadily retreated in several domains of use, especially in West Bengal, where only editorials in a major daily are written in H, for reasons of symbolic continuity, but otherwise no author uses H any more. The use of H for erudite lecturing, even in the form of reading from a prepared text, ceased entirely in the 1950s. As for Bangladesh, Singh and Maniruzzaman (1983) find the presence of H there limited and beleaguered, but still a factor affecting trends of standardization. The formation of the H written prose norm for Bangla in the early nineteenth century reflected that period's Sanskritization process which was later to become a tributary feeding the much more powerful current of the Bengal renaissance (or 'enlightenment', as a different reading of history would have it). Inflectional and pronominal choices made at that juncture gave the written prose code some continuity with verse composition traditions modelled on much earlier spoken forms, but sharply separated it from recent or current Bangla speech. For example, H conjunctive participles like *bhāśiyā* 'floating' corresponded to some speech model current in the sixteenth or at best the seventeenth century – not to the modern period, whose dialects, ranging from the core eastern Dacca–Mymensingh region exhibiting *bhāiš(š)ā*, through the intermediate Jessore–Khulna region with *bhæeše*, to the southwestern districts using the form *bheše*, all represent various degrees of change from that old model. H pronominal forms like *āmādiger* 'our', also associable with spoken models of late middle Bangla, again failed to reflect the realities on the modern ground, ranging from the eastern *āmāgo* to the intermediate and southwestern *āmāder*.

The L written norm, which became a serious option for general use only in the early twentieth century, uses the southwestern morphology (*bheše* and *āmāder* in the cases just mentioned) which had become the common currency of cross-dialect elite conversation in the nineteenth century. It is thus an important and initially surprising fact that, after half a century of separate development, the L norms of the two Bengals are still substantially the same.

In the present chapter, I describe, except in passages with explicit disclaimers, the L standard of Bangla as used in the standard-setting region of West Bengal. Throughout, for reference, I provide [[H]] forms for comparison, using double brackets [[ ]] to identify them. Where no H form is given, it may be presumed that the L form provided is common property.

For reasons given above, it is important to be agnostic about crucial issues in the history of Bangla that can only be settled when research perspectives become more balanced. In particular, one avoids listing specific texts to avoid even the appearance of postulating a 'canon' which inevitably biases one's view. However, an uninformed reader who wishes to use this source for reference purposes is entitled to be told what is uncontroversial.

There was an early New Indic language spoken around AD 1000 that can be called Old Bangla, or alternatively some Old X within the Magadhan (Eastern Indic) branch of the Indic (or Indo-Aryan) subfamily of the Indo-European language family. This Old X subsequently branched out, in a way no research has been able to specify in detail as yet, into several languages which can now legitimately regard Old X as a common initial form. Then there was a language spoken from around AD 1300 that marks the beginning of what can usefully be called the Middle Bangla period. It differs from Old X most crucially in that it lacks all traces of grammatical gender and of ergativity. Middle Bangla comes into its own amidst Muslim rule in Bengal (a conventional characterization that poses unresolved problems but has found no satisfactory replacement as yet), a period during which large numbers of Bengalis converted to Islam. (About seventy per cent of the speakers of Bangla today are Muslims.) As the language grew, its lexicon drew heavily on Sanskrit and (Turko-)Perso-Arabic sources, for the administrative language of the region was Persian. The landmarks of this period include: devotional movements in Hinduism (*bhakti*) and mystical trends in Islam that encouraged the use of regional languages and public participation in religious life; a broad-basing of music leading to more verse compositions and their wider accessibility, including verse translations of the Hindu epics *Rāmāyaṇa* and *Mahābhārata* into Bangla; major breakthroughs by Sanskrit-speaking Bengali scholars in logic who changed the terms and issues of scholastic disputation, and also left their mark on the vocabulary and locutions of Bangla.

The transition from Middle to Modern Bangla occurs in the seventeenth century. Shortly after Modern Bangla comes into its own as a literary language, the British win a crucial battle at Plassey in 1757. British rule proper – another term that serious historians will find unsatisfactory, as the mercantile capitalism of the eighteenth century was domestically and geopolitically very different from the industrial imperialism of the nineteenth – begins only in 1770, and takes off only in the early nineteenth century, ending centuries of Turko-Perso-Arabic superstratum influence and starting a series of games for which satisfactory accounts do not yet exist.

2 PHONOLOGY AND SCRIPT

2.1 Vowels

Bangla's seven vowels /i e æ ā a o u/ are high front, mid front, low front, low back unrounded, low back rounded, mid back rounded, and high back rounded. The mid vowels are phonetically mean-mid to higher-mid. The low round /a/ is treated as a default vowel, left unmarked in the script when it serves as nucleus for a consonantal onset. Thus, a graphic *kh* is to be pronounced as /kha/ unless 'silenced', the way other scripts in the Devanagari family treat the schwa. One standardly represents graphic *kh* as graphemic *kha*, even word-finally, where, as in other modern Indic languages, the default vowel is typically silent. The script marks contrasts now lost between short and long high vowels. That the orthography of particular words uses long vowel symbols has to be rote-learnt, as in *dina* 'day' and *dīna* 'poor', both phonologically /din/. Other features of the way the script treats vowels become clear in the discussion of vowel harmony in subsection 2.3.

Nasalization is significant, occurs with all the vowels, and has a consistent written correlate, the candrabindu, distinguished from the anusvara, on which more anon (subsection 2.4.)

Lacking a monographemic symbol of its own, /æ/ is written variously as *e, yā*, or *ya*: *becā, byākarana, byasta* for /bæcā, bækoron, bæsto/ 'selling, grammar, busy'. The vowel quality distinctions are exemplified below (throughout this section, the H forms are provided only as collateral information, not to illustrate any parallel H phonology; H is hardly a spoken variety for which an independent phonology exists): /gilo/ 'swallow' (ImpFut-2PN, H[igh] form [[giliyo]]); /gelo/ 'swallow' (Pres-2PN [[gilo]]); /gælo/ 'went' (3PN [[jāilo]]); /gālo/ 'strain (the rice)' (Pres-2PN); /galo/ 'melt' (Pres-2PN intr.); /golo/ 'stir' (Pres-2PN [[gulo]]); /gulo/ 'stir' (ImpFut-2PN [[guliyo]]).

As for nasalization versus orality: /sī̃thi/ 'hair parting': /šithil/ 'loose'; /bẽte/ 'short (not tall)': /bete/ [[bāṭiyā]] 'having ground'; /šæ̃k/ 'roast' (Imp-2PI): /šækrā/ 'goldsmith'; /ghā̃t/ 'mix-up' (Imp-2PI): /ghāt/ 'ghat'; /pācāši/ 'eighty-five': /pacā/ 'rotten'; /šõke/ [[šũke]] 'sniffs, smells': /šoke/ 'in grief'; /šũko/ [[šũkiyo]] 'sniff' (ImpFut-2PN): /šuko/ [[šukā]] 'dry' (Imp-2PI).

Certain words in the tatsama lexical stratum (see section 4 [Lexis]) with what in Sanskrit was a consonant plus non-dental nasal sequence such as /jñ, sm, tm/ have nasalization (plus, if metrically appropriate, compensatory consonant gemination) in Bangla, whose conservative graphism therefore has *jijñāsā, smaraṇa, jībāśma, bartma, bismita* for /jiggæ̃šā, šāron, jibæ̃šs̃o, bartõ, biššĩto/ 'query, inquiry; memory; fossil; road; surprised'. (For more, see subsection 2.8.)

Vowel length is phonologically non-significant. Phonetic length is a function of position. Typical contexts for phonetically longer vowels include monosyllables like /gāl/ 'cheek' (in contrast with the phonetically short /ā/ in /gālo/ 'strain' [Pres-2PN]), where length is mandatory, and final syllables like /gælo/ 'went', whose final /o/ can be lengthened for prosodic or emotional reasons.

Stress and tone do not distinguish words in Bangla. Phonetic 'stress' is a component of the prominence of word-initial syllables. The distinction between low /a/ and mid /o/ is associated with patterns of such prominence. For details, see section 2.3.

Nasalization as a phonetic spread feature affects pre- and post-nasal vowels. Therefore no phonologically nasalized vowel occurs right before or after a nasal consonant. Sister languages are different. Hindi-Urdu, which replicates the Bangla pattern only pre-nasally, distinguishes post-nasal /e/ from /ẽ/ in verbs like /pahne/ 'wear' (Opt-3PSg) vs /pahnẽ/ 'wear' (Opt-3PPl). Unlike many nasalized vowel languages, Bangla distinguishes ṼP from VNP, P a plosive and N a homorganic nasal, for both voiced and voiceless P, as in /pãjā/ 'pile (of bricks)' versus /pānjā/ 'arm wrestling', or /šā̃tār/ 'swimming' versus /šāntār/ 'Shanta's'. A nasalized vowel in Bangla does not force a homorganic nasal transition into a voiced plosive in the manner of Hindi-Urdu /cā̃dī/ 'silver', which thus contrasts with Bangla /cā̃di/ 'silver'. The only type of stop that a nasalized vowel in Bangla never precedes is /g, gh/, a gap reflecting the velar nasal's special status. But even there, arguably, pairs like /šaŋge/ 'with' versus /šaŋe/ 'clown' (Loc) or /šā̃ŋghātik/ 'terrible' versus /šāŋhāi/ 'Shanghai' really instantiate VNP versus ṼP, if the phonotactics makes Vŋ(h) count as representing the equivalent but never phonetically realized Ṽg(h).

2.2 Semivowels

We may usefully describe as y-type and w-type semivowels the intervocalics in sequences like /dušo [[duišato]] (y) āṭ/ 'two-hundred eight' (inter-word intrusives are consistently of the y-type) and words like /di(y)o/ 'give' (ImpFut-2PN), /sthāni(y)o/ 'local', /khe(y)o/ [[khāi(y)o]] 'eat' (ImpFut-2PN), /prode(y)o/ 'payable', /bæ(y)e/ 'expense' (Loc), /bæyām/ 'exercise', /bāyu/ 'wind', /bayon/ 'weaving', /moyur/ 'peacock', /šuyo/ [[šuiyo]] 'lie-down' (ImpFut-2P); /mewā/ 'dried fruit', /de(w)ul/ 'temple', /khāwā/ 'to eat', /bā(w)ul/ 'member of the Baul sect', /bawā/ 'to carry', /šo(w)ā/ 'to lie down', /hālu(w)ā/ 'sweet semolina dish'.

As illustrated, y-glides contiguous to /i, e/ and w-glides next to /u, o/ are consistently optional. The w-glide may be absent – this varies across speakers and across tokens – in /de(w)āl/ 'wall' and, for some speakers, even /de(w)ā/ 'to give' and /ne(w)ā/ 'to take'; when the words omit this glide, they often substitute /y/. The orthography omits inter-word intrusives: *duśo* [[*duiśata*]] *āṭa* 'two-hundred eight'. Written *y* is optional only between stem-final *i, e* and desinential *o*. Otherwise – partly due to a convention of inserting a graphic *y* between any vowel and a following vowel other than *u, o* – nearly every potential /y/ is written as a mandatory *y*, as in *sthānīya, pradeya, byaye* among the forms listed above. In this context it is important to note the exceptionally optional written *y* in verbs like *di(y)o* and *khe(y)o* [[*khāi(y)o*]], future imperative forms mentioned above. All verbs of these canonical shapes fall under that exception. The orthography implements /w/ systematically as *oy* (as in *deoyā* for /dewā/ 'to give') between non-round vowels, treats the *o* in that *oy* as optional if preceded by *o* (thus *śo(o)yā* for /šo(w)ā/ 'to lie down', and omits it in contiguity to *u*, whence *hāluyā, bāula* for /hālu(w)ā, bā(w)ul/ 'semolina dish, Baul'.

Any account of intervocalic glides must note the unavailability of semivowel onsets. Items like /yār/ 'mate', /yārki/ 'jest', /wāriš/ 'heir', /wāṛ/ 'pillow-case' can be pronounced with initial semivowels. But most speakers and all writers substitute /i(y)ā/, /o(w)ā/, *iyā, oyā*. We conclude that intervocalic semivowels count as interludes. The language has no true onset semivowels.

The treatment of the offglides /i e u o/ as second elements in diphthongal nuclei – but note that rime-final /e/ is conventionally written as *ya* – usefully insulates the diphthong-final high /i u/ vs mid /e o/ contrast from the height-neutralizing intervocalics /y/ and /w/, and facilitates the coexistence of optional /i, e/-contiguous /y/ or /u, o/-contiguous /w/ with non-optional offglides in /ii, ei, ee, ou, oo/. Examples are classified by second elements. Ending in /i/: /dii/ 'I give', /nei/ 'there isn't' [[nāi]],

/khāi/ 'I eat', /doi/ 'yoghurt', /dui/ 'two'; ending in /u/: /miu/ 'mew', /gheu/ 'bow-wow', /jhāu/ 'type of pine', /mou/ 'honey'; ending in /e/ (written *ya*): /mejhee/ 'on floor', /dæe/ 'gives', /khāe/ 'eats', /hae/ 'is', /šoe/ 'lies down'; ending in /o/: /šæola/ 'moss', /khāo/ 'eat' (Pres-2PN), /hao/ 'you are', /šoo/ 'lie-down' (Pres-2PN). Crucial contrasts that the orthography conceals distinguish diphthongs as in /deule/ 'bankrupt' or /pāonā/ 'debt due' from sequences with an optional semivowel buffer as in /de(w)ule/ 'temple-Loc' and /šā(w)oner/ 'Shaon's'. Spellings betoken the reality of the contrast but mark its incidence only variably. Orthography records an obligatory *y* in /dā(y)i/ 'responsible' and no *y* in /dāi/ 'nurse'. But one writes /gā(y)e/ 'body' (Loc) always as *gāye* and /gāe/ 'sings' only as *gāya*. No devices exist to mark a contrast like /deule/ vs /de(w)ule/.

2.3 Synthesis

This subsection is placed where it is because word integration phenomena have to do with how vowels (and semivowels) are handled. Bangla is a Vowel Harmony language. Compare /pācāši/ 'eighty-five' with /põciš/ 'twenty-five' and /kenār/ 'to buy' with /kini/ '(I) buy' to see that a lone vowel 'eligible' nucleus – of low or mid default height and having (unlike /ā/) the same value for rounding and backness (back rounded or front unrounded) – is 'raised' by a contiguous high trigger, compelled to climb up one notch to non-default mid and high respectively. A two-vowel 'eligible' nucleus obeys the same pressures; compare /pāetālliš/ 'forty-five' with /põitriš/ 'thirty-five', /bāper ba(y)eš/ 'father's age' with /bāper boiši/ '(someone who is your) father's age', and /apobbæe/ 'wasteful expenditure' with /apobbe(y)i/ '(one) given to wasteful expenditure'. Low vowels represented in writing by the default vowel do not indicate the vowel harmonic raising: the first syllables of /põciš/ 'twenty-five', /põitriš/ 'thirty-five', /boiši/ '(who is . . .) age', /bbe(y)i/ '(one) given to (. . .) expenditure' are written as if they contained low vowel nuclei – one source of the speech-writing gap in Bangla.

As one sees, in this normal or dominant vowel harmony pattern, a triggering high vowel on the right raises a left-hand eligible. This norm is absolute and strong in the conjugation: the verb /lekh/ 'write', instantiating this bare form in the imperative, comes out raised in /likhi/ '(I) write'. Among non-verbs, the norm is absolute only if a low must be raised to mid, as in the reciprocity reduplicates /balāboli/ 'speaking with each other', /ghæšāghêši/ 'rubbing shoulders with each other', where the second copy must have a mid nucleus. These contrast with /lekhālekhi/ 'writing back and forth' and /cokhācokhi/ 'eye contact', where the second copy cannot raise from mid to high. The existence of /ṭhokāṭhuki/ 'bumping into each other' or /mešāmiši/ 'mixing with each other', with a second copy that does raise the vowel, shows that (non-verb) lexical items idiosyncratically choose whether to raise or not. There are words which choose both, reserving the default preservation pattern for the conservative or H pole of the diglossia and the vowel harmony pattern for the informal or L register. (However, in L writing, one can draw on the H register without incongruity; it is H writing that cannot use the L forms in these cases.) The adjective from /deš/ 'country, nation' has a formal variant /deši/ and a less formal variant /diši/, 'indigenous'; from /iŋrej/ [[iŋrej, iŋrāj, the latter confined to H]] 'English(wo)man' and /bilet/ [[bilet, bilāt, the latter confined to H]], a cultural (not geographical) and somewhat old term for 'England', one derives the more formal and less formal variants /iŋreji [[iŋrāji even more formal, confined to the H register entirely]], iŋriji/ 'English (the language)', /bileti [[bilāti even more formal, etc.]], biliti/ 'English (cooking, law etc.)'.

The Bangla vowel harmony system also exhibits a counter-normal pattern, where a preceding trigger affects a right-hand eligible /ā/, with verb and non-verb subpatterns. The latter turns the target /ā/, which we see intact in the adjectives /phāṭā/ 'burst', /bhāṇā/ 'broken', /pākā/ 'ripe', /pacā/ 'rotten', into a mid vowel copying the backness of the trigger: /bhije/ [[bhijā]] 'wet', /bhulo/ 'forgetful', /ḍubo(jāhāj, pāhār)/ 'underwater (ship, mountain)'. The subpattern for verbs turns /ā/ uniformly, if unexpectedly, into /o/. The stem formative that appears as /ā/ in triggerless /pālā/ 'run away' or /cæ̃cā/ 'shout' comes out as /o/ [[does not change, in H Bangla]] after a raising trigger: /phuro/ [[phurā]] 'be finished, used up', /cibo/ [[cibā]] 'chew', /douṛo/ [[douṛā]] 'run'. The verb subpattern equally unexpectedly treats mid /e/ as a raising trigger: /bero/ 'go out', /ego/ 'go ahead', /pero/ 'cross'. [[H has /āgā/ for L /ego/ and simply avoids the other forms of this template, employing synonyms to skirt the problem.]] The verb subpattern is unexpectedly also active outside the conjugation, in reciprocal reduplicates like /jhulojhuli/ 'insistence', /mukhomukhi/ 'face to face', /culoculi/ 'hair-pulling combat', /piṭhopiṭhi/ 'back to back, one after the other', a template characterized, as cases given earlier show, by an inter-copy default /ā/ [[preserved unaltered in H: /jhulājhuli/ etc.]]. The counter-normal pattern is, like the normal pattern, omnipotent in the conjugation and a lexical choice ridden set of tendencies outside it. Both the patterns of vowel harmony refrain from touching English loans: /afis/, /bæṭiŋ/ and the like violate the norms with impunity.

In addition to vowel harmony, Bangla exhibits prosodic patterns associating low vowels with positional prominence. Thus, only a root-initial syllable can host /æ/: /æk/ 'one' contrasts with its formal negation /anek/ 'many', where the low vowel is raised to mid /e/. As for /a/, it is allowed only in root-initial syllables and at strong niches in the rhythm, giving way to its weak congener /o/ elsewhere, whence the alternation between the initial syllable's /a/ in /parājito/ 'defeated' and /o/ in its morphological negation /aporājito/ 'undefeated'. Another indicator of the prominence of the initial syllable is its tendency to attract nasalization, which, in general, is allowed in non-word-initial syllables only rarely, and in non-root-initial syllables never. (French loans are exempt.) This has a tangible effect on the exceptional words /ãttā, ãtto, ãttiyo/ 'soul, self, relative'. Because of their Sanskrit-based orthographies with a consonant plus non-dental nasal sequence ātmā, ātma, ātmīya, one would have expected to pronounce these words as /āttã; āttõ; āttĩyo/ (and indeed some stage accents which follow the orthography pedantically do use these spelling pronunciations) in accordance with the treatment of such Sanskrit sequences explained above, at the start of the vowels section. That the nasalization, breaking this expectation, jumps to the initial syllable, must reflect a powerful tendency. Its force affects even the French loan /restorã/, usually pronounced as /restõrā/, moving the nasalization leftwards, if not far enough for total naturalization.

2.4 Sonorants

The basically alveolar /n/ has palatalized, retroflex, and dental allophones in appropriate consonantal contexts. This is also true of the lateral /l/. Examples: alveolar in /nun/ 'salt', /lāl/ 'red'; dental in /bārāndā/ 'verandah', /šolte/ [[šolitā]] 'wick'; retroflex in /ghanṭā/ 'bell', /ulṭo/ [[ulṭā]] 'opposite'; palatalized in /inci/ 'inch', /lālce/ 'reddish'. The bilabial /m/, as in /mom/ 'wax', requires no comment. The velar /ŋ/, as in /rāŋā/ 'reddish (said of sky)', /aŋko/ 'arithmetic', /rāŋtā/ '(aluminium) foil', contrasts with /n/ and /m/, as in /rānā, rāmā/, names, /āŋkhā/ 'superfluous, out of place', /ṭhunko/ 'fragile, cheap', /ācomkā/ 'suddenly', /pāntā (bhāt)/ '(rice) kept overnight', /komti/ 'lack, deficit'. But it cannot serve as a pure (non-interlude) onset of a syllable.

The dependent nasal or the anusvara in the alphabet (traditionally called that in Bengal, rather than the anusvāra) is treated as simply a silenced (rather than default-vowel-endowed) /ŋ/, which means that forms with an unambivalent velar nasal like /šaŋšār, šaŋšac, šaŋbād, šaŋboron, šaŋhār, šoŋhitā/ 'domesticity, doubt, news, restraint, destruction, code-book' in Bangla correspond to a wide range of contemporary Indic renderings of the older, slightly mysterious dependent nasal.

The liquid /r/, an advanced alveolar approximant in normal standard speech with a postdental tap allophone (but consistently a tap or trill in many non-standard varieties and in much stage enunciation), remains distinct from the (always non-initial, and otherwise limited in distribution) retroflex flap /ṛ/ in the Western standard. But in all Eastern varieties, /ṛ/ becomes /r/ unconditionally. Even in the West, /ṛ/ tends to approach /r/ in words like /ãcṛāno/ 'to comb', /hātṛāno/ 'to grope'. Speakers of Bangla have no doubt that /ṛ/ contrasts with the plosive /ḍ/, and the availability of direct evidence bears them out, unlike many other South Asian languages. Though somewhat far-fetched, the minimal pair /kānāḍā/ 'Canada' versus /kānāṛā/ 'Kannada' is surely decisive. If common nouns are preferred, there is /reṛio/ 'even castor' versus /reḍio/ 'radio'.

The 'aspiration' element /h/ has occasioned much discussion. We may take the convenient stand that it is murmured intervocalically and voiceless elsewhere, leaving these characterizations for careful clarification at the phonetics–phonology interface. The visarga in the alphabet serves as a final /h/ in exclamations like /bāh/ 'bravo', /uh/ 'ouch'; see section 2.7.2 for some complications.

The script, by using a single symbol for it, appears to postulate greater unity for the aspirated flap phoneme /ṛh/ in /gurho/ 'profound' than in the /rh/ sequence which the script shows as two graphemes in /gorhit/ 'despicable'. We return to the matter after finishing with the true consonants.

2.5 Plosives and affricates

Every stop series displays a voiceless and a voiced pair of simple versus 'aspirated' stops. Neither the traditional term 'aspirated stop' implying one segment nor conventional transcriptions like /kh gh/ implying two segments need be construed as encoding any specific analysis. The velar series /k kh g gh/ is exemplified in /kā/ 'caw', /khā/ 'please eat', /gā/ 'body', /ghā/ 'wound'. The series of alveolo-palatal affricates /c ch j jh/, as in /cā/ 'tea', /chā/ 'offspring', /jā/ 'husband's brother's wife', /jhā/ 'a surname', shows considerable variation. Some of this variation is phonological: the series tends to become /ts dz s z/ before dentals and liquids, raising the issue of whether, say, the word for 'to choose' written as *bāchate* and thought to be phonemically /bāchte/, but standardly rendered as [bāste], perhaps actually has the same phonology as *āste* /āste/ 'slowly'. [[No H equivalent; the issue does not arise; 'to choose' is /bāchite/, with a buffer vowel, which is typical of H.]] Some of the relevant variation is subphonemic. It is a familiar shibboleth that many Eastern dialects use alveolars as the principal allophones and have been making an impact on the Western standard. Sociolinguistic work on this impact is long overdue.

The series of retroflex plosives /ṭ ṭh ḍ ḍh/ is more apico-alveolar in Bangla than the true apico-palatals of sister languages to the west. (This could be why the plosive /ḍ/ in Bangla is not phonologically close to the flap /ṛ/ the way it is in many other South Asian languages where the retroflex plosives are truly apico-palatal.) To the east of Bangla lies Assamese, where these plosives and the dentals merge in an alveolar series. Examples of the retroflex series in Bangla: /ṭak/ 'sour', /ṭhak/ 'a cheat', /ḍāk/ 'mail', /ḍhāk/ 'drum'.

Skipping the alveolar position, unutilized in Bangla, we have a dental series /t th d dh/ as in /tān/ 'tune', /thān/ 'white cloth', /dān/ 'donation', /dhān/ 'paddy'. In the labial series /p ph b bh/ as in /pāl/ 'sail', /phāl/ 'ploughshare', /bāl/ 'child (learned form)', /bhāl/ 'forehead (learned form)' the unstable aspirated /ph/ is often realized, under sociolinguistic and phonotactic conditions not yet examined, as [f]. Less often, [bh] likewise gives way to a [v] which is in any case required in /āovān/ 'call', a point taken up presently.

2.6 Fricatives and aspiration

The conjunct letter *hb* (encoding an older /hw/) in a few tatsama words like *gahbara* 'abyss', *āhbāna* 'call', *bihbala* 'upset', *jihbā* 'tongue' is rendered by careful speakers as a labio-dental /v/ (otherwise available only in foreign loans) preceded by a w-type coda: /gaovar, āovān, biuval, jiuvā/. (Some users of /v/ strengthen it to [vh], a matter of subphonemic taste; many users don't.) The less careful /gaobhar, āobhān, biubhal, jiubhā/ are tolerated. Such variants as /ābbhān, āohān/ have fallen into disuse. But /bh/ users appear to differ from /v/ users at the shibboleth level. Hence our decision to record a cross-speaker /v/ vs /bh/ contrast here rather than treat the matter as subphonemic. The language certainly has no general [v-bh] allophony under /bh/ on a par with [f-ph] under /ph/. Based on these facts, some authors have introduced *hb* to represent foreign /v/ quite generally, in a *hbalphagāŋ* 'Wolfgang' or a *hbebāra* 'Weber'. Others still use *bh* for foreign /v/, as speakers of Bangla unable to handle [f, v] routinely substitute [ph, bh] in foreign vocables.

The /z/ of foreign loans has the similar routine substitute /j/ in the case of Perso-Arabic origin. But the Islamic context, and the coincidentally correlated dominance of [z] over [j] in the eastern speech region, once led to some use in Eastern Bengal of the semivowel-derived special /j/ grapheme – our system's *yj* – to represent /z/ in words like *hayjarata* /hazrat/ 'Hazarat'. This practice is now obsolete to the point of unrecognizability in Western Bengal; current proposals for [z] include *j* plus underdot or afterdot; no firm decisions have emerged. With the spread of English, some Bangla speakers now tend to preserve /z/ and even /ž/ in loanwords. Even for them, the [z] of a [māzlo] 'brushed (teeth)' [[unavailable in H, whose /mājilo/ interposes a buffer vowel]] still counts, along with [mādzlo], as a subphonemic allegro variant of lento phonology's /mājlo/, quite remote from the /z/ of a /māzl/ 'muzzle' which is [z] even in lento speech.

Velar fricatives have no significant past in Bangla, even in loans, and no foreseeable future. That they occur in allegro speech, intervocalically, has had no impact on the system.

Bangla has two sibilants, alveolar /s/ and palato-alveolar /š/, contrasting in pairs like /āste/ 'slowly' vs /āste/ 'to come' in standard speech [[but not in H, with its buffer vowel /i/ before /te/ 'to' in /āšite/]], a contrast strengthened by the growth of English literacy. In many Southern dialects, including working class speech in the towns whose elite speech defines the standard, they merge into /s/. Contiguity with this fact puts some sociolinguistic pressure on the contrast. The contrast is phonotactically weak even in Standard Bangla, where the sibilants can contrast only between a vowel and a /t, n, r, l/. The rough generalization is that syllable-initially, only /sk, st, sp, sr, sn, sl, sm/ clusters are possible; elsewhere, basically only /š/ is possible, with some lexical exceptions: /bās/ 'bus' contrasts with /bāš/ 'residence'.

We turn now from fricatives to aspiration. The phonological unity and phonetic diversity of aspiration across the voiced–voiceless boundary in the system are an area inviting research. Even if the phonetics of normal /ghā/ 'wound' exhibits murmur and is quite distinct from the true aspiration of /khā/ 'eat', the two seem to fall together in whispered speech. The phonology seems to treat what have traditionally been called voiced and voiceless aspirated stops alike: both sets effectively lose their aspiration word-finally, and if no sonorant follows also syllable-finally. Is an aspirated plosive (or affricate) best described as one segment, as the term 'aspirated stop' suggests, or as a sequence of two, as the transcription suggests? Only time and phonological research will tell. One systemic fact that speaks against the one-segment view is the total non-existence in Bangla of any pair of morphemes /AX'B/ vs /AXhB/ where /X/ is a plosive or affricate, /X'/ is a true single segment aspirated congener of /X/, and the sequence /Xh/ is a clearly bisegmental sequence placing that /X/ in contiguity with an independent /h/ after it. If 'aspirated stops' are single segments, this gap in the system remains unexplained. Holders of the single segment view who provide an explanation of this gap are likely, in their explanation, to approach the essence of the segment sequence view. As in many other descriptive controversies, not much divides the two views.

2.7 Script

2.7.1 Basics

The Bangla alpha-syllabic writing system, which belongs to the Devanagari family, uses the following symbols, which we transliterate as shown in table 9.1 (default vowel omitted in transcription). Vowel symbolization and other basic architectural features are

TABLE 9.1: BANGLA SCRIPT

অ	আ	ই	ঈ	উ	ঊ	ঋ	এ	ঐ	ও	ঔ							
a	ā	i	ī	u	ū	ṛ	e	ai	o	au							
ক	খ	গ	ঘ	ঙ	কা	কি	কী	কু	কূ	কৃ	কে	কৈ	কো	কৌ	ক্
k	kh	g	g	ṅ	kā	ki	kī	ku	kū	kṛ	ke	kai	ko	kau	k
চ	ছ	জ	ঝ	এঞ											
c	ch	j	jh	ñ											
ট	ঠ	ড	ঢ	ণ											
ṭ	ṭh	ḍ	ḍh	ṇ											
ত	থ	দ	ধ	ন											
t	th	d	dh	n											
প	ফ	ব	ভ	ম											
p	ph	b	bh	m											
য	র	ল													
yj(/j/)	r	l													
শ	ষ	স	হ	য়	ড়	ঢ়									
ś (/š/)	ṣ (/š/)	s (/š/)	h	y	ṛ	ṛh									
ৎ	অং		অঃ	অঁ											
t	ṁ (/ŋ/)		ḥ	(nasalization)											

as in the other members of this script family. Elaborate coverage is beyond the scope of this chapter.

2.7.2 Orthography

The script has no explicit space for the vowel phoneme /æ/. But Sanskrit words with an orthographic *Cyā* are pronounced /Cæ/; so the use of this graphism for /æ/ – and of a special conjunct vowel, with dependent *-yā* attached to the normal *a* – has become standard. This amendment is not taught as part of the normative alphabetical listing yet.

The silencer is used sparingly. Speakers are expected to know that *na* comes out as /n/ in *bhinadeśī* /bhindeši/ 'foreigner' but as /na/ in *anara* /anaṛ/ 'unmoving' and /no/ in *anabarata* /anobaroto/ 'continuously'. No known rules reliably map the written *a* to these and other phonemic correlates and back in Bangla orthography. This single biggest problem in the system has been compounded by the transition from the H(igh) to the L(ow) norm in Bangla writing. The H system was conceptualized on a Sanskrit foundation and used graphemic *o* sparingly, making it obligatory to write /dito/ 'used to give' as *dita*, for instance. But the L system suggests a closeness to speech that has led many authors to switch to *dito* in such cases. This switchover has not been complete or consistent in anyone's usage, and remains an area of contestation. Another contested area is a spelling reform measure eliminating the speech-unfaithful long *ī* in favour of short *i* wherever this can be done without directly confronting the tatsama doctrine (discussed in section 4 below). Some authors have been resisting this reform in the case of feminines like *māmī* 'mother's brother's wife' (derived from *māmā* 'mother's brother'), for which the long *ī* is an established feminine marker. The fact that feminines ending in *ī* are frequent in the tatsama sublexicon, a fact that underlies this resistance, is left untouched by spelling reforms that do not tackle the tatsama doctrine itself. In such contested areas, the dust is unlikely to settle in the foreseeable future.

Apart from these areas of systemic uncertainty, there are a few unpredictable and thus truly exceptional speech-writing correlations as in cases like *padma* /paddo/ 'lotus' (the non-nasalized final vowel is unpredictable), *gardabha* /gardhob/ 'donkey' (one would have expected /gardobh/ with a possibly weakened final aspiration, instead of this throwback of the aspiration to the next plosive to the left), *ēṭo* /ēṭho/ 'food touched' (with an unexpected aspiration), *smita* /smito/ 'smiling', and *smārta* /smārto/ 'smriti-erudite' (the only words with an initial /sm/ left intact in speech; the regular pattern is shown in *smāraka* /šãrok/ 'memorial'). These are not a problem. The areas of systemic uncertainty are large enough to give rise to a persistent malaise.

I conclude with some formulas to bridge the orthography-speech gap caused mainly, but not exclusively, by the vagaries of tatsama words. In the statements I provide, positions (initial, medial, final) are defined within the orthographic word; for this purpose, a word remains a word even if a prefix is attached to it.

Cb, for any *C* [onsonant] except *g, m, r, h*, is single /C/ if initial and geminated /CC/ if medial. For *g, m, r, Cb* is simply /Cb/. For *hb* /v/, see subsection 2.4 above. Some cases of *db* are to be read as /db/ on the basis of idiosyncratic lexical knowledge, but in such cases most writers today use a silencer *d\b* and not the *db* conjunct consonant.

Cya, Cyā for any *C* other than *b, h* are respectively /Ca, Cæ/ initially (the /a/ but not the /æ/ is liable to be raised by a vowel harmony trigger) and /CCo, CCā/ medially. In eastern speech, such consonant gemination CC is preceded by a postvocalic intrusive /i/. For the purpose of this formula – and other purposes, for that matter – *jñV* counts as if it was *gyV̆*. The formula holds for a medial sequence with *C = b*; but initial *bya, byā* are

BANGLA 363

both /bæ/, with the further embedded exception that *bya* /bæ/, but not *byā* /bæ/, raises to /be/ if a trigger follows, as in /bekti/ realizing *byakti* 'individual'. The principle that prefixation leaves a word-initial boundary intact is mitigated only to the extent that gemination applies, as in *bikhyāta* /bikkhæto/ 'renowned', which differs only in this respect (not in its vocalism) from the unprefixed *khyāta* /khæto/ 'famous'. Compare the vocalism with *ākhyā* /ākkhā/ (not /ākkhæ/) 'epithet'. For C = *h*, the formula works if C is initial. If it is medial, *hy* is always realized as /jjh/: *sahya* /šojjho/ 'tolerance'.

Final *a* observes what one might call Indic Silence if preceded by a non-cluster, non-*h* consonant, unless it forms part of a tatsama past participial *(i)ta* affix (the general deletion principle overrides this exception clause if the word is a proper noun). In an even-numbered or final syllable (but only if the preceding syllable nucleus is not /i/), *a* reduces to /o/, and a *Cra* sequence anywhere is rendered as /Cro/, both of these reductions subject to the mitigator *ya* /e/ which, if it follows an *a* liable to reduce to /o/, overrides the reduction and makes it come out intact, as /a/: hence unmitigated *āpada* /āpod/ 'trouble' (but *bipada* /bipad/ 'danger') and *āśrama* /āsrom/ 'ashram, hermitage', but mitigated *āśaya* /āšae/ 'receptacle', *āśraya* /āsrae/ 'asylum'.

An *a* followed (not across word boundary, and this includes a boundary between a prefix and a recognizable word) by a syllable with a high vowel or by a *Cy* cluster or by *kṣ* raises to /o/: *ati* /oti/ 'very', *gadya* /goddo/ 'prose'.

A *CmV* sequence where V is any vowel and C is a coronal (dental, retroflex, palatal) plosive or affricate comes out as initial /CṼ/ and medial /CCṼ/, provided that a preceding vowel enables the gemination to surface. One case where the absence of a vowel prevents it is *bartma* /bartõ/ 'road'. These and other vowel nasalization markings are subject to the steady erosion of nasalized vowels throughout western speech under the influence of Eastern varieties that lost it long ago.

The visarga (ḥ) is implemented as /h/ only in interjections like /uh oh āh/. In regular words, visarga plus C is rendered as /CC/: *duḥkha* /dukkho/ 'suffering', *niḥsīma* /niššim/ 'limitless'. Word-final visarga in tatsamas, long treated as silent, fell into disuse in twentieth century Bangla orthography, an unusual departure from the tatsama doctrine: *kramaśaḥ* /kromošo/ 'gradually', *prathamataḥ* /prothomoto/ 'firstly'.

In careful speech, *VCṛ* with vocalic *ṛ* places a syllable boundary between V and C, whereas *VCrī* with the consonant *r* places it after *C* (some speakers exaggerate this by geminating a *C* in every *CL* cluster, *L* any liquid). It remains to be seen if this type of care can survive such demographic realignments as the community of literates is now experiencing.

A conjunct consisting of a non-retroflex sibilant plus *t, d, n, r, l*, vocalic *ṛ* implements the sibilant as /s/, though spelling pronunciation for some speakers preserves the palatal sibilant if conjoined with *n, l* (but the switch to /s/ is absolute before *r* and *ṛ*). A conjunct of *s* with *p, ph, k, kh* realizes the sibilant medially as /š/ and tends to realize it initially as /s/, with /š/ a marginal variant. A conjunct of *s* with a retroflex always implements it as /s/. The retroflex sibilant is always rendered as /š/, except in the cluster *kṣ*, which maps into /kh/ initially and /kkh/ medially. That cluster plus *m* have varying fates, but always lose the /m/: *lakṣmī* /lokkhi/ 'Lakshmi' shows no nasalization, *pakṣma* /pakkhõ/ 'eyelash' does, and with *lakṣmaṇa* [lakkhõn] 'Lakshmana' it is unclear, due to the interference of the phonetic nasalization imposed anyway by the following [n], if phonetic [õ] here counts as phonological /õ/.

3 MORPHOLOGY

3.1 Inflection

3.1.1 Nouns and pronouns

All nouns and pronouns inflect for case: nominative /grām/ 'village', accusative-dative (or 'objective') /grāmke/, genitive /grāmer/, locative /grāme/. The genitive suffix /er/ loses its vowel postvocalically: /cākā/ 'wheel', /cākār/. The locative suffix has an allomorph /te/, mandatory after a high vowel, optional after a non-high: /bāli/ 'sand', /ālu/ 'potato', /bālite, ālute/; /mejhe/ 'floor', /ālo/ 'light', /mejhee, mejhete, āloe, ālote/. For further allomorphy, see below.

The locative has a locational reading only for inanimates. The ambiguous word /pātro/ 'bowl; potential bridegroom' provides a minimal pair, /pātre dhulo lāgbe/ [[pātre dhulā lāgibe]] 'dust will fall on the bowl' versus /pātrer gāye dhulo lāgbe/ [[pātrer gāye dhulā lāgibe]] 'dust will fall "on the body of" (= on) the potential bridegroom'; animates require the circumlocution device /gā/ 'body'. Inanimate locatives also have an instrument reading with non-volitional verbs: /churite āŋul keţe jete pāre/ [[churite āŋul kāţiyā jāite pāre]] 'your finger may get cut (injured) on a knife', but /churi diye āpel keţo/ [[churi diyā āpel kāţiyo]] 'cut apples with a knife'.

The Bangla genitive covers some uses of the dative in other Indic languages, as in the experiencer subject construction: /robir rākāke bhālo lāge/ 'Robi likes Raka, lit. Robi-Gen Raka-AccDat good feels', cf. Hindi-Urdu *ravi ko rākā acchī lagtī hai*, lit. 'Ravi Dat Raka good feel does' where the patient is in the nominative (not the accusative) and triggers verb agreement (the Bangla verb is in the default third person). The genitive in Bangla, as in the rest of Indic, works with the copula to express possession: /rākār sāikel āche/ 'Raka has a bicycle'. The genitive in Bangla /or šāhoš āche/ 's/he-Gen courage is, s/he has courage' corresponds to the locative in Hindi-Urdu *us mẽ himmat hai* 'in him/her there is courage', for: 's/he has courage', a fact related to the absence of true locatives for Bangla animates. These nouns, and first and second person pronouns, do use the locative suffix (a) for coupled reciprocals, a frozen construction: /rājāe rājāe juddho/ 'a war between king and king', /māye jhiye jhagrā/ 'a quarrel of mother with daughter', /tomāe āmāe milan/ 'union between you and me'; (b) in generics expressing a natural kind and a typical activity: /gorute ghāš khāe/ 'cows(Loc) eat grass'; (c) exceptionally, as a variant of the accusative-dative for /āmi/ 'I' and /tumi/ 'you Neutral Singular': /uni tomāe /tomāke cān, āmāe /āmāke nā/ 's/he wants you, not me'. The decision to classify (a) and (b) as locatives and (c) as a variant accusative-dative seems most congruent with general usage.

The genitive and the locative share formal irregularities in a class of nouns ending in older /a/, modern /o/, which if deleted triggers the choice of the genitive /er/ and the locative /e/: /groho/ 'planet', /grohe, groher/; /rakto/ 'blood', /rakte, rakter/. In this class, proper nouns have the option of keeping /o/ intact in the genitive, and forcing the choice of /r/ which is the normal postvocalic allomorph: /šukro/ 'Venus': unambiguous Loc /šukre/, but Gen either /šukrer/ or /šukror/. The homonymous common noun /šukro/ 'semen' permits only the expected irregular genitive /šukrer/. Irregularities of a rather different sort occur in the genitive for a few nouns of space and time: for the expected /ājer, kāler, ækhoner, ekhāner/ etc. we observe instead /ājker, kālker, ækhonkār, ekhānkār/ 'of today, of yesterday/tomorrow, of the present, of this place'; and alongside the phrasal variants /še diner, o diker/ etc. with regular genitive morphology for 'of that day, of that direction' we find also the compounds /šedinkār, odikkār/ etc. with the irregular /-kār/ genitive. It is possible that the forms /ājker, kālker/ in the L norm should be treated not in terms of a doubly irregular /-ker/ variant of the /-kār/ variant, but instead as the genitives of /ājke, kālke/ 'today, tomorrow' rather than of their shorter and apparently non-inflectable versions /āj, kāl/. [[In H the descriptive situation is different. The longer version /ājike/ 'today' can be the base only for the variant /ājiker/ 'today's', not for /ājikār/, which also exists. As for 'tomorrow', /kollo/ is preferred to the /kālke/ that counts as a borrowing from L, and /kollokār/ 'tomorrow's' corresponds to the equally erudite /oddokār/ 'today's' which tends to be upstaged by the more readily available /ājikār/. The L-borrowed form /kālker/ for 'tomorrow's' is possible in the less heavy uses of H, but only as a case of 'slumming', un-H-like borrowing from L.]]

Under coordination, overt case manifestation is mandatory only for the last conjunct and optional for the non-finals: /grām(ke) ār šahorke ālādā bhābā/ [[grām(ke) o šahorke ālādā bhābā; H avoids /ār/ 'and' and prefers /o/, which in turn is avoided in L]] 'to view the village and the city as different'; /grām(er), jelā(r), prodeš(er) bā dešer prošāšon/ 'the village('s), the district('s), the state('s), or the country('s) administration'; /āmār nijer grām(e) bā pāšer grāme/ '(in) my own village or in the next village'. The status of non-final conjuncts lacking overt case marking awaits clarification; the following remarks only serve to point up the problem.

Animate nouns and personal pronouns inflect not just for case but also for number: singular /āmi/ 'I', /mohilā/ 'woman'; plural /āmrā/ 'we', /mohilārā/ 'women'. In the Western Bangla standard, which is what I am describing unless otherwise specified, the plural provides a syncretistic form for the genitive and the accusative-dative: /āmāder/ 'us /our', /mohilāder/ 'the women('s)' and no form at all for the locative. The Eastern Bangla standard tends to reserve this form for the genitive and features a distinct accusative-dative: /āmāderke/ 'us', /mohilāderke/ 'the women'. The Eastern dialects in the influential Dhaka-Mymensingh region use /go/ and /go-re/ for these functions: /āmāgore/'us', /āmāgo/'our' (less preferred: 'us'); cf. the singular accusative-dative / āmāre/ 'me'. All spoken varieties of Bangla seem to feature the syncretistic plural conflating the genitive with the accusative-dative. [[In H, there is a more conservative variant which distinguishes the two, as /āmādigoke/ 'us' vs /āmādiger/ 'our', and a less conservative variant which does not, which copies the L form /āmāder/ 'us, our'. Nouns behave identically.]]

Some personal pronouns distinguish a nominative singular weak stem as in /tui/ 'you-SgIntim' from a strong stem occurring elsewhere as in /tor/ 'your-SgIntim', /torā/ 'you-PlIntim', /toke/ 'you-SgIntim-AccDat'. One might prima facie suspect that case-dropping non-final conjuncts are bare strong stems, call them 'strong forms'. But the language forces all conjuncts to show case-marking in pronominal examples that would be decisive (/toke bā āmāke/ 'you-SgIntim-AccDat or me'), leaving this suspicion unconfirmed. The fact that pronominal strong stems appear both in non-nominatives and in plurals may be relevant to the issue of why animate nouns make plurality marking as optional as case marking for nonfinal conjuncts: /bāccā chele(rā), bāccā meye(rā), buṛo(rā) ār buṛirā āge khābe/ 'little boy(s), little girl(s), old ma(/e)n, and old women will eat first'; /bāccā chele(der) ār meyeder āge bolbo/ 'we will tell little boy(s) and girls first'. Again, pronouns always mark plurality overtly (/torā ār āmrā āge khābo/ [[torā o āmrā āge khāibo]] 'you-PlIntim and we will eat first'), making it impossible to test the suspicion that bare conjuncts might be tacitly strong forms.

One might expect Bangla nouns that exhibit strong morphology, like /lok/ 'man' vs /loke-/ in /lokerā/ 'men', /lokeder/ 'men-Gen/AccDat', /loker/ 'man's', or /bhritto/

'servant' vs /bhritte-/ in /bhritterā/ 'servants', /bhritter/ 'servant's', to permit direct examination of bare conjuncts as to their possibly strong status. The fact is that bare conjuncts from such paradigms exhibit the weak form: one says /mitro ār bhritter taphāt/ [[mitro o bhritter pārthokko]] 'the difference between a friend and a servant', never /mitre ār bhritter/ with the strong form /mitre/ for 'friend'. But this observation is not decisive. All Bangla nouns use the weak stem for the AccDat Sg: /lokke, bhrittoke, mitroke/. Nouns with a deletable final /o/ use it also for the Gen/Acc/Dat Pl: /bhrittoder, mitroder/. Noun declensions with a strong form distribute it unevenly over the paradigm. This may be why it is unavailable for syntactic use in bare conjuncts. Future work on the Bangla strong form will need to distinguish it from the superficially comparable oblique case phenomenon in the more richly inflected Indic languages. True obliques are consistently non-nominative, differ from direct forms in nouns as sharply as in pronouns, and can occur alone in conjuncts (Hindi-Urdu *kuttõ yā billiyõ se* 'from dogs-Obl or cats-Obl').

Turning to a cognate phenomenon, Bangla (animate) nouns modified by a plural quantifier always revert formally to the singular: 'many women' comes out as /anek mohilā/. No plural variant of the /anek mohilārā/ type exists. For a numeral to modify a noun, normally a classifier must intervene: /pā̃ctā grām/ 'five-Ta village(s)', /tinjon mohilā/ 'three-Jon wom(e)n', /cārkhānā ciṭhi/ 'four-Khana letter(s)'. The classifier-supported numeral can occur alone with noun ellipsis: /āmi cārkhānā peyechi/ 'I've got four (letters)'. The default classifier, /ṭā/ ('Ta' in our glosses), has contextual allomorphs in /duṭo, tinṭe/ 'two-Ta, three-Ta', but the quasi-diminutive in /ekṭi chele/ 'one-Ti boy' or /cheleṭi/ 'the boy' and the true diminutive in /ekṭu dudh/ 'one-Tu milk, a little milk'or /dudhṭuku/ 'milk-Tuku, the bit of milk' differ from the default classifier grammatically rather than just phonologically. For example, the default classifier, like hard core inanimate classifiers, is incompatible with formal verb forms. If one says /pā̃ctā netā/ 'five-Ta leader, five leaders' with the default classifier to disparage leaders for whom the human classifier would normally be expected (/pā̃cjon netā/ 'five-Jon leader'), for instance, the default classifier compels the use of an informal verb as a matter of grammar, not pragmatics. Pragmatics allows both /pā̃cjon netā jābe/ 'five leaders will go' with the informal verb /jābe/ [[jāibe]] and the morphologically formal /pā̃cjon netā jāben/ 'five leaders will go'. But once the default classifier steps in, grammar permits only the informal /pā̃ctā netā jābe/ 'five leaders will go'. Here it becomes crucial that the quasi-diminutive classifier in /bhadromohilāṭi/ 'the lady' – used instead of the default classifier because the intrinsic formality of the noun /bhadromohilā/ 'lady' sounds dissonant with the neutrality of the default marker – permits the formal noun to elicit formal verb agreement in a sentence like /bhadromohilāṭi jāben/ 'the lady will go'. How does the true diminutive in /ekṭu dudh/ 'one-Tu milk, a little milk' differ grammatically from the default classifier? Where the default item can occur with numerals, the true diminutive occurs only with /ek/ to the point of forcing us to doubt if this is an instance of the singular numeral or some sort of homonym. My own view is that this /ek/ is best treated as part of a semi-opaque word /ekṭu/ which means 'a little' and contains a classifier equatable with the suffixed element in the definite /dudhṭuku/ 'milk-Tuku, the bit of milk'. If I were forced to place this fragment /ek/, I would call it a mass quantifier like the /khānik/ of /khānikṭā dudh/ 'some-Ta milk', not a count quantifier like the /kayek/ of /kayekjon mohilā/ 'a few women'.

Numerals and count quantifiers use the same classifiers and treat them the same way: /anekgulo khām/ 'many-Gulo envelope(s)', /kayekjon mohilā/ 'some-Jon wom(e)n'. The absence of a classifier in /anek mohilā/ 'many women', an example given above, reflects the idiosyncratic unacceptability of /anekjon/ 'many-Jon', a form presumably blocked by the morphologically more specific variant /aneke/ 'many (people)' which occurs only as a complete nominal, not as a noun modifier. The form /kayekjon/ 'some-Jon' has no such variant and can be used alone or as a modifier. A noun followed by an inanimate (animacy-neutral) classifier conveys definiteness: /grāmṭā/ 'the village', /ciṭhikhānā/ 'the letter'. The nonhuman classifier /gulo/ combines this positional definiteness with plurality: /khāmgulo/ 'the envelopes'. Small numbers may occur in this structure: /grām-tinṭe/ 'the three villages', /khām-dukhānā/ 'the two envelopes'. With or without a supporting morpheme, the human classifier /jon/ is generally unavailable in this position: /meye-jon/ for 'the girl' is unacceptable in all varieties of Bangla, and only some speakers have /meye-dujon, meye-tinjon/ for 'the two/three girls'. Speakers who lack this option are forced to use /meye-duṭo/ 'girl-two-Ta' and the like, with the default classifier. The interrogative count quantifier /ka/ combines with a classifier to yield / kajon meye, kakhānā khām/ 'how many girls, how many envelopes'. These and other interrogatives allow an indefinite declarative interpretation 'some girls, some envelopes' if supported by appropriate intonation. Suffixed to a noun, /ka/ plus classifier expresses definiteness and plurality with a suggestion that the number is not large: /khām-kakhānā/ 'the (not many) envelopes', /grām-kaṭā/ 'the (couple of) villages'. Suffixed to /šab/ 'all', /kaṭā/ alternates with the non-human plural classifier /gulo/: /šabgulo boi, šabkaṭā boi/ 'all the books'.

Bangla exhibits no case or number agreement, and no grammatical gender phenomena at all. Personal pronouns establish points on a formality scale, but there is no Noun-Determiner agreement for this. The agreement that the verb exhibits with its subject for Person and Formality conflates 2PF (Second Person Formal) with 3PF, as subsection 3.2 will illustrate.

	Formal	Neutral	Intimate
2nd Person Singular	āpni	tumi	tui
2nd Person Plural	āpnārā	tomrā	torā
3rd Person Singular	tini	še	—
3rd Person Plural	tā̃rā [[tāhārā]]	tārā [[tāhārā]]	—

The forms shown as Third Person in this chart figure also in an orthogonal set of Demonstrative pronouns – the Proximals /ini, e, ẽrā, erā [[ini, e, ĩhārā, ihārā]]/; the Distals /uni, o, õrā, orā [[uni, o, ūhārā, uhārā]]/; and the Sequents, just given as 'Third Person' forms in the chart, where the term Sequent expresses the fact that these are follow-up Demonstratives, not pointing to the external world, but sending us back to a first reference to the entity in the sentence or the discourse. One could decide, in a radical and basically terminological gesture, to deny that there are any true Third Person Pronouns in the language, and thus to classify all these forms as being only deictic or pointing expressions. A decision more likely to survive scrutiny would bring all Demonstrative Pronouns under a widened Third Person umbrella. We leave the question open, tentatively cross-classifying the Sequents as true Third Person Pronouns and as Demonstrative Pronouns of one type.

In the eastern standard, the three sets come out as follows: Proximal /ini, e, enārā, erā/; Distal /uni, o, onārā, orā/; Sequent /tini, še, t(en)ārā, tārā/. For Proximals and Distals, these more regular forms have been rapidly supplanting the conventional Western standard forms described here even in the urban heartland of the Western standard, most rapidly in colloquial speech. This morphological change is helped along by the fact that the older system depends on the oral versus nasalized vowel contrast, which is lost in the phonology of the Eastern standard, rendering the crucial distinctions between /tārā, orā, erā/ and /tā̃rā, õrā, ẽrā/ inaudible and the morphology of Formality obscure.

The Demonstrative Determiners – Proximal /e(i)/, Distal /o(i)/, Sequent /še(i)/ – whether endowed with the individuation-emphasizing Fortifier /-i/ or not, freely occur with inherently informal nouns like /kukur/ 'dog', inherently formal nouns like /prodhānmontri/ 'prime minister', and negotiable nouns like /chātro/ 'student', without any change in the shape of the Determiner to reflect the formality level of its companion: /ei kukur jābe, oi prodhānmontri jāben, šei chātro jābe(n)/ 'this dog will go, that prime minister will go, that student will go'. It is the character of the noun that triggers appropriate formality agreement on the verb, observed in the presence or absence of /n/ in the word /jābe(n)/ 'will go' in the examples just given. This take-over of the noun phrase by the noun if present also means that the deictic or 'pointing' nature of the phrase is optionally suspended. If an entity is introduced by a Demonstrative Pronoun, any follow-up must preserve the type of pointing (Proximal, Distal, Sequent): /e bolechilo e jābe/ (not: /še jābe/) 's/he (Proximal) had said s/he (Proximal) would go (not: s/he [Sequent] would go)', /uni bolechilen uni jāben/ (not: /tini jāben/) 's/he (Distal, Formal) had said s/he (Distal, Formal) would go (not: s/he [Sequent] would go'. But if an entity is introduced by a Demonstrative Determiner plus a Noun, a follow-up can appeal either to the Demonstrative, preserving its deixis, or to the Noun, using the default Sequent: /ei oddhāpok bolechilen ini jāben/ (or: /tini jāben/) 'this professor had said he (Proximal, Formal) would go (or: he (Sequent, Formal) would go)'.

The inherent or negotiable formality levels that the noun colours its noun phrase with are contributed not by the noun lexeme alone but also by any classifiers present.

3.1.2 Verbs

Finite verbs agree with the nominative subject for person and formality. For 'you came' we have: singular /āpni elen, tumi ele, tui eli/, plural /āpnārā elen, tomrā ele, torā eli/.

Verbs inflect as shown in tables 9.2 and 9.3 for the simple consonant-final stem (/ken/) verb /kenā/ 'to buy', the simple vowel-final stem (/khā/) verb /khāwā/ 'to eat, drink', and the extended stem (/kenā/) verb /kenāno/ 'to cause to buy'. I am following the convention of citing verbs in their Gerciple form. In table 9.2, 1P, 2P, 3P stand for the three Persons. I(ntimate), N(eutral), F(ormal) are points on the formality scale. The Pres[ent], Past, Fut[ure] tenses interact with moods, namely the Imp[erative] and the unmarked Indicative, and with aspects, namely Simp[le], Prog[ressive], Perf[ect], Hab[itual]. The Progressive and Perfect aspect forms are morphologically tight and half-loose compounds respectively, which I discuss in section 3.3. That the Formal Imperative form /kinun/ merges into the Formal Present Simple form /kenen/ is a shibboleth marking the Eastern Bangla standard. The existence of a sibilant-final option alongside the V-final variant of the Past Habitual 2PI is likewise a shibboleth that still marks the Western Bangla standard but is likely to give way completely to the Eastern form. In the shorter nonfinite charts, the Conjunctive is the typical South Asian adverbial (perfect) participle construction and requires no comment.

The Conditional /VB-le/ 'if Subject VBs, when Subject VBs' is unusual in consistently licensing nominative subjects. The Ger[und-Parti]ciple form is usable as a Gerund as in /rupener ei boi kenā/ 'Rupen's buying this book' and as a Perfect Participle as in /rupener kenā ei boi/ 'this book bought by Rupen', a syncretism that invites

TABLE 9.2: BANGLA FINITE VERB FORMS

Category	1P	2PI	2PN	2/3PF	3PN
Simple consonant-final stem /ken/:					
Pres Simp	*kini*	*kiniš*	*keno*	*kenen*	*kene*[1]
Pres Prog	*kinchi*	*kinchiš*	*kincho*	*kinchen*	*kinche*
	[[*kinitechi*	*kinitechiš*	*kinitecho*	*kinitechen*	*kiniteche*]]
Pres Perf	*kinechi*	*kinechiš*	*kinecho*	*kinechen*	*kineche*
	[[*kiniyāchi*	*kiniyāchiš*	*kiniyācho*	*kiniyāchen*	*kiniyāche*]]
Imper Pres	—	*ken*	*keno*	*kinun*	*kinuk*[2]
Past Simp	*kinlām*	*kinli*	*kinle*	*kinlen*	*kinlo*
	[[*kinilām*	*kinili*	*kinile*	*kinilen*	*kinilo*]]
Past Prog	*kinchilām*	*kinchili*	*kinchile*	*kinchilen*	*kinchilo*
	[[*kinitechilām*	*kinitechili*	*kinitechile*	*kinitechilen*	*kinitechilo*]]
Past Perf	*kinechilām*	*kinechili*	*kinechile*	*kinechilen*	*kinechilo*
	[[*kiniyāchilām*	*kiniyāchili*	*kiniyāchile*	*kiniyāchilen*	*kiniyāchilo*]]
Past Hab	*kintām*	*kinti(š)*	*kinte*	*kinten*	*kinto*
	[[*kinitām*	*kinitiš*	*kinite*	*kiniten*	*kinito*]]
Fut Simp	*kinbo*	*kinbi*	*kinbe*	*kinben*	*kinbe*
	[[*kinibo*	*kinibi*	*kinibe*	*kiniben*	*kinibe*]]
Imper Fut	—	*kiniš*	*kino*	*kinben*	*kinbe*
	[[—	*kiniš*	*kiniyo*	*kiniben*	*kinibe*]]
Simple vowel-final stem /khā/:					
Pres Simp	*khāi*	*khāš*	*khāo*	*khān*	*khāe*
	[[*khāi*	*khāš*[3]	*khāo*	*khān*[4]	*khāe*]]
Pres Prog	*khācchi*	*khācchiš*	*khāccho*	*khācchen*	*khācche*
	[[*khāitechi*	*khāitechiš*	*khāitecho*	*khāitechen*	*khāiteche*]]
Pres Perf	*kheyechi*	*kheyechiš*	*kheyecho*	*kheyechen*	*kheyeche*
	[[*khāiyāchi*	*khāiyāchiš*	*khāiyācho*	*khāiyāchen*	*khāiyāche*]]
Imper Pres	—	*khā*	*khāo*	*khān*	*khāk*[5]
Past Simp	*khelām*	*kheli*	*khele*	*khelen*	*khelo*
	[[*khāilām*	*khāili*	*khāile*	*khāilen*	*khāilo*]]
Past Prog	*khācchilām*	*khācchili*	*khācchile*	*khācchilen*	*khācchilo*
	[[*khāitechilām*	*khāitechili*	*khāitechile*	*khāitechilen*	*khāitechilo*]]
Past Perf	*kheyechilām*	*kheyechili*	*kheyechile*	*kheyechilen*	*kheyechilo*
	[[*khāiyāchilām*	*khāiyāchili*	*khāiyāchile*	*khāiyāchilen*	*khāiyāchilo*]]
Past Hab	*khetām*	*kheti(š)*	*khete*	*kheten*	*kheto*
	[[*khāitām*	*khāitiš*	*khāite*	*khāiten*	*khāito*]]
Fut Simp	*khābo*	*khābi*	*khābe*	*khāben*	*khābe*
	[[*khāibo*	*khāibi*	*khāibe*	*khāiben*	*khāibe*]]
Imper Fut	—	*khāš*[6]	*kheyo*	*khāben*	*khābe*
	[[—	*khāš*[7]	*khāiyo*	*khāiben*	*khāibe*]]
Extended stem:					
Pres Simp	*kenāi*	*kenāš*	*kenāo*	*kenān*	*kenāe*
	[[*kināi*	*kināš*[8]	*kināo*	*kinān*	*kināe*[9]]]
Pres Prog	*kenācchi*	*kenācchiš*	*kenāccho*	*kenācchen*	*kenācche*
	[[*kināitechi*	*kināitechiš*	*kināitecho*	*kināitechen*	*kināiteche*]]
Pres Perf	*kiniyechi*	*kiniyechiš*	*kiniyecho*	*kiniyechen*	*kiniyeche*
	[[*kināiyāchi*	*kināiyāchiš*	*kināiyācho*	*kināiyāchen*	*kināiyāche*]]
Imper Pres	—	*kenā*	*kenāo*	*kenān*	*kenāk*
	[[—	*kinā*	*kināo*	*kinān*	*kināk*]]
Past Simp	*kenālām*	*kenāli*	*kenāle*	*kenālen*	*kenālo*
	[[*kināilām*	*kināili*	*kināile*	*kināilen*	*kināilo*]]
Past Prog	*kenācchilām*	*kenācchili*	*kenācchile*	*kenācchilen*	*kenācchilo*
	[[*kināitechilām*	*kināitechili*	*kināitechile*	*kināitechilen*	*kināitechilo*]]

Category	1P	2PI	2PN	2/3PF	3PN
Past Perf	*kiniyechilām*	*kiniyechili*	*kiniyechile*	*kiniyechilen*	*kiniyechilo*
	[[*kināiyāchilām*	*kināiyāchili*	*kināiyāchile*	*kināiyāchilen*	*kināiyāchilo*]]
Past Hab	*kenātām*	*kenāti(š)*	*kenāte*	*kenāten*	*kenāto*
	[[*kināitām*	*kināitiš*	*kināite*	*kināiten*	*kināito*]]
Fut Simp	*kenābo*	*kenābi*	*kenābe*	*kenāben*	*kenābe*
	[[*kināibo*	*kināibi*	*kināibe*	*kināiben*	*kināibe*]]
Imper Fut	—	*kenāš*	*kiniyo*	*kenāben*	*kenābe*
	[[—	*kināš*[10]	*kināiyo*	*kināiben*	*kināibe*]]

Notes:
1 H accepts these; conservative H or 'HH' prefers *kino, kinen, kine*.
2 Okay in H; conservative H or 'HH' prefers *kino*.
3 'HH' *khāiš*.
4 'HH' *khāen*.
5 Okay in H; 'HH' prefers *khāun, khāuk*.
6 'HH' *khāiš*.
7 'HH' *khināiš*.
8 'HH' *kināiš*.
9 Some users of H, towards the end of its active life, had switched over to /kenāi/ etc. throughout the chart; others preserved the /i/ here but had switched over to /keno, kene/ etc. in the simple stem conjugation.
10 'HH' prefers *kināiš*.

TABLE 9.3: NON-FINITE FORMS

Stem type (and ending in -C/-V)	Simple (-C)	Simple (-V)	Extended
Gerciple (Gerund-Participle)	*kenā*	*khāwā*	*kenāno*
	[[*kenā*[1]	*khāwā*	*kināno*]]
Dependent Gerund	*kinbār, kenbār*	*khābār*	*kenābār*
	[[*kinibār*	*khāibār*	*kināibār*]]
Conjunctive Participle	*kine*	*kheye*	*kiniye*
	[[*kiniyā*	*khāiyā*	*kināiyā*]]
Infiniciple (Infinitive-Participle)	*kinte*	*khete*	*kenāte*
	[[*kinite*	*khāite*	*kināite*]]
Conditional Participle	*kinle*	*khele*	*kenāle*
	[[*kinile*	*khāile*	*kināile*]]

Note:
1 'HH' *kinā*.

research. The intrinsically genitive Dependent Gerund occurs in a narrow range of contexts, typically governed by a postposition like /jonne/ 'for' or /āge/ 'before', and is consistently interchangeable with a genitive Gerciple. The Infini[tive-Parti]ciple, another case of research-worthy syncretism, is infinitival as a single verb in /jiten māch khete cāe/ 'Jiten wants to eat fish' and an active adverbial progressive participle as an iterated verb in /khete khete rupen boi kinte pāre nā/ 'while eating, Rupen cannot buy books'. In these typical uses the Infiniciple takes no overt subject. When it licenses an overt nominative subject, it may appear either iterated or single but reinforced by the emphasizer clitic /-i/, as in /jiten bolte-i rupen rāji holo/ 'the moment Jiten told him, Rupen agreed'; /jiten āšte āšte rupen beriye jābe/ 'By the time Jiten comes (lit. Jiten coming), Rupen will leave'. For discussion of the interaction between the copula and the non-finite Conjunctive and Infiniciple forms in the tight progressive and half-loose perfect compound tenses, see subsection 3.3.

Vowel harmony along the height dimension, visible in /kini, kinuk/ vs. /kenen, keno/ above, is a pervasive fact of Bangla discussed earlier. A high vowel like /i, u/, or a morphologically opaque trigger that contained an appropriately placed high vowel in an earlier period (like the Simple Future marker, now /b/, earlier /ib/) raises a vowel that precedes it from mid /e, o/ to high /i, u/ (thus turning /ken/ into /kin/) or from low /æ, a/ to mid /e, o/. Only certain strong raising triggers, the Imp Fut 2PN ending /(y)o/ and the Conjunctive Participle ending /(y)e/, can raise a preceding stem extension /ā/ (otherwise impervious to vowel harmony) to /i/, which then triggers raising further to the left to yield a Conjunctive Participle like /kiniye/. Local details, like the contrast between the Dependent Gerund marker /bār/ which induces vowel raising variably and the Simple Future marker /b/ which does it consistently, or like the unusual vowel harmony patterns of the V-final simple conjugation (including the failure of the Simple Future to trigger raising in these stems), do not lend themselves to general statement.

3.2 Derivation

Productive affixation, which can be freely used to form new derivatives, is a rare commodity in the language. The set of words is basically frozen, with exceptions in the sector of technical term coinage. Word-level novelty is possible not in derivation proper, but in phrasal verb formation, a matter discussed in subsection 3.3 below. Under derivation, then, I can only review some sets of words interrelated via word formation strategies that were once truly productive, choosing as far as possible models that are sometimes followed in the occasional (rare) new formation.

Simple verbs regularly map into causative verbs, /kenā/ 'to buy' into /kenāno/ 'to make (someone) buy', /khāwā/ 'to eat, drink' into /khāwāno/ 'to feed'. But there are also non-causative extended stem verbs like /pātāno/ 'to start (an interpersonal relationship)' with no morphologically simple counterpart. Some of these extended stem verbs are based on nominals and may be called denominal verbs: /hātāno/ 'to grab' is related to /hāt/ 'hand', /jutono/ 'to beat with a shoe' to /juto/ 'shoe'. But the process is not productive; no new verb stems are entering the language, except in the expressive or ideophonic domain. See the discussion of compounds in subsection 3.3 for more.

Turning to nominals, masculine bases yield feminine nouns in /i/, as in /morog, murgi/ 'cock, hen', /pæcā, pēci/ 'he-owl, she-owl', /jæthā, jethi/ 'father's elder brother, father's elder brother's wife'. Some bases use instead the strategy of /ni/ or /ini/ suffixation, as in /māšṭār, māšṭārni/ 'male teacher, female teacher', /bāgh, bāghini/ 'tiger, tigress'.

A second /i/ forms adjectives and inhabitant/language names from place names: /pānjāb, pānjābi/ 'Panjab, Panjabi', /multān, multāni/ 'Multan, Multani'. Yet another /i/ nominalizes adjectives: /cālāk, cālāki/ 'clever, cleverness'; /bekār, bekāri/ 'unemployed, unemployment', a much less productive strategy in Bangla than in sister languages.

The paucity of Perso-Arabic loans in ordinary written and spoken Bangla and relative abundance of Sanskrit loans has meant that the privative prefix /be/ of a few words such as /bewāriš/ 'ownerless' and /bešāmāl/ 'not in control of one's faculties' has not prospered, whereas the privative suffix /hin/ has: /grihohin/ 'homeless', /šoŋgihin/ 'companionless', etc. is a productive model.

While adjectives formed with /hin/ nominalize in /tā/, /grihohinotā, šoŋgihinotā/ 'homelessness, companionlessness', the favourite nominalizing suffix for adjectives in Bangla is /(t)to/ (*tba*) from Sanskrit *tva*. It is productive enough to be usable in a nonce formation context like /hātir hātitto, murgir murgitto, bāgher bāghotto/ 'an elephant's elephanthood, a hen's henhood, a tiger's tigerhood', where no other affix is possible.

The process or action nominal formative affix of choice is the equally Sanskritic /āyon/, as in /šobujāyon/ (which has the feel of 'greenation') 'afforestation'. The change of state nominal affix in default cases is again from Sanskrit, /(i)karon/, as in /ādhunikikaron/ 'modernization', /ṭikākaron/ 'vaccination'.

The Bangla cognates of non-Sanskrit affixes that rule the roost in sister languages carry various nuances which confine them to specific word types. For example, /panā/ marks /āllādipanā/ 'the quality of expecting to have one's least whim instantly satisfied', /ādekhlepanā/ 'a tendency to ask at once, insistently, for any even remotely desirable object that comes into view', and the like as undesirable qualities.

English prefixes like /nan, eks/ are widely used and understood in ordinary educated circles. The suffix /ifãi/ is doing well. But all this is in colloquial speech that its users would not admit to if pressed. The purism that has put the Sanskrit affixes in power is still the norm.

3.3 Compounds

Bangla compounds involving nouns and/or adjectives exhibit no features that call for comment in the context of other Indic languages. Suffice it to say that they are all 'tight' compounds in the sense that they cannot be interrupted even by an Associative or Dissociative Emphasizer /o, i/. I shall here look at tight, half-loose, and loose compounds involving one or more verbs.

A Progressive verb form is a tight compound of the progressive stem of the verb with the light copula element /ch/: no Emphasizer /i/ or /o/ can interrupt /khācche/ 'is-eating', for example. [[Note of dissent from H: /khāiteche/ can be interrupted by /i, o/.]] But a Perfect form is a half-loose compound of the perfect stem of the verb with the light copula element: /kheyeche/ 'has-eaten' can be interrupted by an Emphasizer, as in /kheyeiche/ 'has indeed eaten', /kheyeoche/ 'has also eaten', and by nothing else. [[/khāiyāche, khāiyāiche, khāiyāoche/ are similar.]] Particularly colloquial speech, at least in the Calcutta standard-setting area, permits constructions like /kheye-to-che/ (the clause-internal particle /to/ 'of course' is discussed in section 5) or /kheye-ki-che?/ 'Has s/he eaten?' with the clause-internal alternative question particle /ki/, but only as a case of stretching the language. [[H has never heard of these phenomena.]]

Loose compounds involving two verbs are called compound verbs, the first or contentive member (regularly in the Conjunctive participle form) a 'Pole' and the second or semi-auxiliary member a 'Vector': /bole dewā/, lit. say-Conjunctive to-give, 'to say for someone's benefit' is a typical example. Equally typical is its interruptibility: /āmi bole kichui dii ni/, lit. I say-Conjunctive anything-Emph give NegPerf, 'There's nothing I told them for free'. The compound verb formation is productive in the sense of being a site of speaker creativity. The number of combinations is large enough that compound verb use is at the borderline between choosing a word from the lexicon and freely constructing a syntactic phrase.

Non-verb plus verb Composite Verbs like /protibād karā/ lit. protest to-do, 'to protest', also loose, are productive in another sense: loanwords, technical coinages etc. find a verb innovation site here. Bangla no longer permits the formation of denominal verb stems, except marginally from ideophones. The normal way to make new verbs is to add a 'light verb' like /karā/ 'to do' or /hawā/ 'to be', as appropriate, to the relevant content word and form a Composite Verb: /ziraks karā/ 'to xerox', /mægnifāi karā/ 'to magnify', etc.

4 LEXIS

Bangla has a segmented lexis along several dimensions of segmentation. It distinguishes conventional (arbitrary) words like /kālo/ 'black' from expressive (onomatopoeic or otherwise iconic) words like /kuckuce/ as in collocations like /kuckuce kālo/ 'pitch black', /dhabdhobe šādā/ 'sparkling white'. Among conventionals, speakers can tell non-naturalized borrowings of English origin (even these exemplify several strata: /lāin/ 'line' does not stand out as a loan, whereas /saṭoeyār/ 'software' does, with the semi-naturalized /jiraks, jeraks/ and the non-naturalized /ziraks/ for 'xerox' marking points on the continuum between them) from 'native' vocables like /holde/ 'yellow'. Even this vocabulary is stratified, making the invidiously pure term 'native' a misnomer. If loans are visualized as accretions to some pre-existing turf, it may be useful to use the term 'turf vocabulary' to characterize that to which loans are added, without prejudice to heterogeneity within this turf. Erudite words adopted directly from Sanskrit into the learned stratum of Bangla stand out and are confined to the written mode, subject to some inter-speaker variation as to which ones count as erudite.

All direct adoptions from Sanskrit – traditionally called tatsama words (*sama* 'equal' to *tat* 'that, Sanskrit') – take part, regardless of how erudite they are, in the classical systems of derivation and compound (*samāsa*) formation and of the morphophonemic processes of sandhi that cement some of these compounds. The classical sandhi rules, handed down to Bangla school grammar pedagogy together with a classical taxonomy of compounds, are opaque to the untrained speaker because of the speech-writing mismatch described in connection with orthography earlier, which makes the school grammar pedagogy a major problem for Bangla. The educated speaker's understanding of the lexis, shaped by such a pedagogy, puts the claims of Sanskrit first. The tatsama theology at the heart of this pedagogy treats all Sanskrit nominative singulars (minus any final dependent nasal or aspiration) as actual or potential Bangla words of the tatsama type. The tatsama ideology has blocked any readjustment of their spellings. By the same token, the pedagogy that forms educated speakers treats words derived from Sanskrit with sound change as tad-bhava 'that-derived' words. Remaining words count as either 'native' or 'foreign'. Words presumed to be either of South Asian but non-Indo-European origin or of unknown origin, and expressives, are called native. The rubric of foreign words includes not only identifiably English words, but also Dutch and Portuguese loans whose origins users have forgotten and Turko-Perso-Arabic items that a characterization of Bangla can treat as foreign only on a skewed reading of what is native and what is foreign in the history of Bengal.

The tatsama doctrine also underlies technical term creation initiatives throughout the last two centuries. Tatsama derivational mechanisms have become opaque, however, with the decline and loss of Sanskrit in the school curriculum. Many technical coinages and even long established tatsama words of the erudite stratum have become inaccessible with the demographic realignment of the set of educated speakers. Neo-literates from a whole range of marginal backgrounds have begun to alter acceptability or comprehensibility thresholds. These and other factors have eroded the tatsama ideology.

Among the other factors are certain counter-hegemonic pressures. There have been arguments in favour of the systematization and use of tadbhava derivational strategies; in favour of a restoration of the rights of the Turko-Perso-Arabic sublexicon plus its derivational systems; in favour of accepting and taking seriously the abundant expressive or ideophonic vocabulary; in favour of a pragmatic legitimization even in the written standard of the many non-naturalized English loans already accepted in speech, especially among the educated. But these arguments have not added up to a coherent critique of the dominant theory and practice with viable alternative proposals for pedagogy, term coinage policy, a word classification to replace the foursome of tatsama, tadbhava, native, foreign, or other relevant problem domains. The tatsama hegemony may yield to a well-argued successor, if one with a serious constituency does emerge. To consider one case of the lexical diversity of the language, I take a look at its numerals.

The cardinals are tatsama at zero and one, tadbhava from two to a hundred: 0 /šunno/, 1 /æk/, 2 /dui/, 3 /tin/, 4 /cār/, 5 /pãc/, 6 /chae/, 7 /šāt/, 8 /āṭ/, 9 /nae/, 10 /daš/, 11 /ægāro/, 12 /bāro/, 13 /tæro/, 14 /coddo/, 15 /ponoro/, 16 /šolo/, 17 /šatoro/, 18 /āṭhāro/ (variants of 15–18 ending in /-ero/ instead also fall within the standard in Western speech and, in the case of 15 and 17, even in writing), 19 /uniš/ (Eastern spoken standard /unniš/), 20 /kuṛi, [variant used only in restricted contexts in the standard: biš]/, 21 /ekuš/, 22 /bāiš/, 23 /teiš/, 24 /cobbiš/, 25 /põciš/, 26 /chābbiš/, 27 /šātāš/, 28 /āṭ(h)āš/, 29 /untriš/, 30 /tiriš/, 31 /ektriš/, 32 /botriš/, 33 /tetriš/, 34 /coutriš/ ('spontaneous' nasalization of /cou/ here and in 64 still occurs in Western speech, but under the influence of Eastern migrants and spelling pronunciation it is no longer regarded as exclusively standard), 35 /põitriš/, or spelling pronunciation /pãetriš/, 36 /chotriš/, 37 /sãitriš/, 38 /āṭtriš/, 39 /unocolliš/, 40 /colliš/, 41 /ekcolliš/ (former Western standard /ækcolliš/ moribund under Eastern impact), 42 /biyālliš/, 43 /tetālliš/, 44 /cuālliš/, 45 /pãetālliš/, 46 /checolliš/, 47 /sātcolliš/, 48 /āṭcolliš/, 49 /unopancāš/, 50 /pancāš/, 51 /ækānno/, 52 /bāhānno/ (Eastern /bāānno/ *bāyānna*), 53 /tippānno/, 54 /cuānno/, 55 /pancānno/, 56 /chāppānno/, 57 /šātānno/, 58 /āṭānno/, 59 /unošāṭ/, 60 /šāṭ/, 61 /ekšoṭṭi/ (former Western standard /ækšoṭṭi/, see comment at 41), 62 /bāšoṭṭi/, 63 /tešoṭṭi/, 64 /coušoṭṭi/ (comment at 34 applies here), 65 /pãešoṭṭi/, 66 /chešoṭṭi/, 67 /šātšoṭṭi/, 68 /āṭšoṭṭi/, 69 /unošottor/, 70 /šottor/, 71 /ækāttor/, 72 /bāhāttor/ (cf. comment at 52), 73 /tiyāttor/, 74 /cuāttor/, 75 /pãcāttor/, 76 /chiyāttor/, 77 /šātāttor/, 78 /āṭāttor/, 79 /unoāši/, 80 /āši/, 81 /ækāši/, 82 /birāši/, 83 /tirāši/, 84 /curāši/, 85 /pãcāši/, 86 /chiyāši/, 87 /šātāši/, 88 /ašṭoāši/, 89 /unonobboi, -nobbui/, 90 /nobboi, nobbui/ (the /nobbui/ variant, older and moribund, is not repeated throughout the series), 91 /ækānobboi/, 92 /birānobboi/, 93 /tirānobboi/, 94 /curānobboi/, 95 /pãcānobboi/, 96 /chiyānobboi/, 97 /šātānobboi/, 98 /āṭānobboi/, 99 /nirānobboi/, 100 /ækšo [or, in certain modes of counting: ša; but not used to modify a noun]. 1000 is /æk hājār/, of Persian origin. The tatsama words available for 1,000, /šahosro/, and for 10,000, /ojut/, are not actively used any more. Nor are the tatsama cardinals for 1,000,000, /nijut/, for 100,000,000, /orbud/, for 1,000,000,000, /brindo/, for 10,000,000,000, /kharbo/, or for 100,000,000,000, /nikharbo/, though arithmetic primers continue to teach them. The tatsama numbers still in use in the cardinal system are /æk lokkho/ for 100,000 (also called /æk lākh/, using the tadbhava form), and /æk koṭi/ for 10,000,000. There are tatsama alternatives for the cardinals from eleven onwards, very seldom used nowadays: 11 /ækādaš/, 12 /dādaš/, etc. The regular ordinals from 1 to 10, however, are tatsama: 1st /prothom/, 2nd /ditiyo/, 3rd /tritiyo/, 4th /coturtho/, 5th /pancom/, 6th /šošṭho/, 7th /šaptom/, 8th /ašṭom/, 9th /nabom/, 10th /dašom/. These ordinals are used in forming small number fractions: two-thirds is /dui tritiyāṇšo/, for example. (Larger fractions are managed phrasally; see next paragraph.) Also tatsama is the device used for larger ordinals like 90 /nobboitamo/ or 91 /ækānobboitamo/. While this affix is normal for those higher numbers for which contemporary speakers no longer remember the tatsama ordinals, many users prefer the regular tatsama ordinals from 11 to 20: 11 /ækādaš/, 12 /dādaš/, 13 /trayodaš, troyodaš/, 14 /coturdaš/, 15 /pancodaš/, 16 /šoṛaš, šoṛoš/, 17 /šaptodaš/, 18 /ašṭādaš/, 19 /unobiṇšo/, 20 /biṇšo/. There is a 'native' turn of phrase that expresses ordinals: /šāt diner din/, lit. 'the day of seven days', for 'the seventh day'. These phrasal ordinals are obsolescent. The phrasal fractions, as in /pācer bāro/ for 5/12, are struggling for the right to coexist with /pāc bāi bāro/, which borrows the English *by*.

Date ordinals used for dates of the month are an entirely different, tadbhava set: 1 /paelā/, 2 /došrā/, 3 /tešrā/, 4 /couthā/, 5 /pācoi/, 6 /chooi/ (obsolescent Western standard form /chõoi/ with spontaneous nasalization, possibly by contamination from the phonetically triggered nasalization of [nõoi] three slots down]), 7 /šātoi/, 8 /āṭoi/, 9 /nooi/, 10 /dašoi/, 11 /ægāroi/, 12 /bāroi/, etc. up to 18, then 19 /uniše/, 20 /biše/, 21 /ekuše/, 22 /bāiše/, etc. And then there are the equally tadbhava playing card ordinals. After /ṭekkā/ 'ace', which of course belongs in no morphological series, we have 2 /duri/, 3 /tiri/, 4 /couko/, 5 /pānjā/, 6 /chakkā/, 7 /šātā/, 8 /āṭā/, 9 /naholā/, 10 /daholā/. For academic and other competitive contexts, salient in the political economy of contemporary Bengal, ranking uses semi-naturalized English ordinals: /phārsṭ, sekenḍ, thārḍ, phorth, phiphth, siksth, sebhenth, eiṭth, nāinth, ṭenth, ilebhenth, ṭuelbhth/, etc. This microcosm is fairly representative of the lexical arrays available in contemporary Bangla. Comparative linguistic work has always found numerals a convenient starting point.

5 SYNTAX

5.1 Basic features

The basic constituent order of the clause is Sentence Adjunct, Subject, Predicate Adjunct, Indirect Object, Direct Object, Complement Verb (preceded by its own dependents if any), Finite Main Verb, Negation:

(1) kono kārone brotin āj šunilke šomae dite cāe nā
     some reason-Loc Brotin today Sunil-Obj time give-Inf wants not
     'For some reason, Brotin does not want to spend any time with Sunil today.'

Negation is preverbal in non-finite constructions as in (2), and in related constructions to which we return in subsection 5.4:

(2) brotin kāj nā korle šuniler-i ašubidhe [[H: ... nā korile ... ašubidhā]]
     Brotin work not do-Cond Sunil-Gen-Emph problem
     'If Brotin does not work, Sunil is the one who has a problem.'

The example just given also illustrates certain typologically significant features relevant to a comparison of Bangla with its neighbours: the conditional participle, the experiencer subject construction (a descriptive term not intended to preclude the possibility that the experiencer is not technically a subject), the emphasizer clitic, and the zero copula construction.

The conditional participle is non-finite in that it is invariant, but assigns nominative even to an agentive or volitional subject, as in the example above, in contrast to the common South Asian conjunctive participle, which in Bangla prefers a null subject as in (3) and at best permits only a non-volitional nominative subject as in (4):

(3) roj ghum theke uṭhe mukh dhuye ḍim-ruṭi kheye āmi kāje jāi [[roj ghum hoite
     uṭhiyā mukh dhuiyā ḍim-ruṭi khāiyā āmi kāje jāi]]
     daily sleep from rise-Conj face wash-Conj egg-bread eat-Conj I work-Loc go
     'Every day I get up, wash my face, have breakfast, and go to work.'

(4) brotin eše šuniler kono šubidhe holo nā [[brotin āšiyā šuniler kono šubidhā hoilo nā]]
Brotin come-Conj Sunil-Gen any advantage happened not
'That Brotin came didn't help Sunil.' (lit.: 'Brotin having come, Sunil gained nothing.')

The experiencer subject construction, which in Bangla has the experiencer in the genitive and the theme in the objective rather than the more usual dative and nominative respectively, occurs not just with the zero copula as in (2), but also with the standard set of psychological predicates:

(5a) oder āmāke bhālo lāge nā [[uhāder āmāke . . .]]
they-Gen I-Obj good feels not
'They do not like me.'

(5b) tomār kæno rāg holo? [[. . . hoilo?]]
you-Gen why anger happened
'Why did you get angry?'

A particular instance of the experiencer subject construction in Bangla plays roughly a passive-like functional role in the Bangla syntactic system, although it seems fair to say that the language does not have a true passive:

(6a) āmār ækkhānā probondho lekhāo holo, rāješke dābāe hāriye dewāo holo, mondo nā [[. . . hoilo, . . . hārāiyā dewāo hoilo . . .]]
I-Gen one-Cla article write-Gerc-Emph got, Rajesh-AccDat chess-Loc defeat Aux-Gerc-Emph got, bad not
'(This week . . .) I got an article written and Rajesh beaten at chess, not bad.'

(6b) ebār tāhole šampādokke šei probondhokhānā diye dewā gælo [[ebār tāhā hoile . . . probondhokhānā jamā dewā gælo]]
this-time then editor-AccDat that article-Cla give Aux-Gerc went
'This time, then, that article of mine (at last) got submitted to the editor.'

Note the unsuppressed object case marking of /rāješke/ in (6a), comparable to that of /āmāke/ in (5a). If one assumes for these constructions a semantics along the lines of that of the English 'get-Passive' in the gloss of (6b) and its active counterpart, which has no standard designation, in the English gloss of (6a), then the syntax of (6) can be viewed as instantiating nothing more or less than the experiencer subject construction of (5). In that case it becomes appropriate to state that Bangla has no grammatical passive, but can partly mimic the passive effect by using its experiencer subject construction. The obligatory absence of the agent (with any case marking) in the /jā/ ('go') version (6b) then counts as analogous to the non-canonical (subjectless) impersonal construction in /rākāke khāšā dækhācche/ [[. . . dækhāiteche]] for 'Raka is looking fine', where the beholder nominal cannot be syntactically present with any case marking, and where Raka nevertheless appears in the Accusative-Dative case. A passive subsystem would be worth postulating only if it had independent properties that needed to be stated.

Bangla has two emphasizers, the Dissociative clitic /i/ 'indeed, alone' illustrated in (2) above and the Associative clitic /o/ 'even, also':

(7a) brotin kāj nā korle šunil-o nācār [[. . . nā korile . . .]]
Brotin work not do-Cond Sunil-Emp helpless
'If Brotin does not work, Sunil too is helpless.'

(7b) kājer jāegāe procur jhāmelā
work-Gen place-Loc plenty trouble
'There is plenty of trouble at the workplace.'

The zero copula is illustrated in (2) and (7). This invisible finite verb – like an overt Bangla copula in this respect – corresponds to *be* when coupled with a nominative as in (7a, b), and to *have* when coupled with a genitive as in (2).

Compound verbs, consisting of a contentive 'pole' or main verb in the conjunctive participle form and a nuance-bearing 'vector' or semi-auxiliary, are a common South Asian trait which Bangla shares:

(8) hiteš jāniye debe ke rāji [[... jānāiyā dibe ...]]
Hitesh inform-Conj give-Fut who willing
'Hitesh will inform (you) who (is) willing.'

Other typologically salient features illustrated in (8) include the zero copula construction, the omissibility of contextually identifiable arguments like the object 'you', and causative verbs like /jānāno/ 'to inform' morphologically derived from /jānā/ 'to know'.

Causatives stand in a regular morphological relationship to their bases, as in (9) and (10). What are morphologically single causatives can syntactically function as double causatives, as in (11), but Bangla has no double causative morphology:

(9) æto jiniš bākše ḍhukbe nā [[... ḍhukibe nā]]
so-many things box-Loc enter-Fut not
'So many things won't go into the box.'

(10) āmi nije jiniš ḍhukiye nebo [[... ḍhukāiyā loibo]]
I self things pack-Conjunctive take-Fut
'I myself will pack (cause-to-go-in) the things.'

(11) cākorke diye jiniš ḍhukiye nāo [[... ḍhukāiyā lao]]
servant-Obj by things pack-Conjunctive take-Imp
'Get the servant to pack the things.'

A complement clause is marked either by an opening particle /je/, typical of Indo-European, or by a closing quotative /bole/ [[boliyā]] which is formally the conjunctive of /bal/ 'say', typical of Dravidian:

(12) biren thākbe bole šabāi bhebechilo, kintu āmi jāntām je thākbe nā [[biren thākibe boliyā šabāi bhābiyāchilo, kintu āmi jānitām je thākibe nā]]
Biren stay-Fut Quot everybody thought,but I knew that stay-Fut not
'Everybody thought that Biren would stay, but I knew he wouldn't.'

5.2 Case phenomena

The syntax of case assignment in Bangla shows several unusual traits. Some have already been discussed in the context of (5) and (6) above and in the morphology section. The absolute nominative with a non-finite in (2) needs to be seen in the wider context of the absolute nominative with a locative-bearing noun as in (13), or a locative-bearing gerciple as in (14), or an adjunct construction involving gerciple plus postposition as in (15). No rigorous account of this broad spectrum of nominatives is available at the moment of writing.

(13) jholā kā̃dhe ṭarc hāte dhireš cole elo [[... coliyā āśilo]]
side-bag shoulder-Loc torch hand-Loc Dhiresh over came
'Side bag on shoulder, torch in hand, Dhiresh came over.'

(14) dhireš cæ̃cāmeci karāe śuren ekṭu muškile poṛlo [[... poṛilo]]
Dhiresh fuss making -Loc Suren a-bit embarrassed was
'On Dhiresh making a fuss, Suren was a bit embarrassed.'

(15) dhireš cæ̃cāmeci karā śatteo śuren bhrukkhep korlo nā [[... korilo nā]]
Dhiresh fuss making despite Suren bother-in-the-least did not
'Despite Dhiresh making a fuss, Suren wasn't bothered in the least.'

Bangla case markers, as their morphological description above indicates, morpho-
tactically resemble Hindi-Urdu or Marathi markers that fuse gender and number with
obliqueness. For Bangla case markers too are phonologically integrated into the noun
word. But they morpho-syntactically parallel the case particles proper of those
languages in that they have consistent, invariant shapes and are not copied onto
dependents of the nominal. Since Bangla has no obliqueness or number in the Hindi-
Urdu sense and no morphological gender, the upshot is that dependents like
demonstratives and adjectives do not agree with the head noun on any grammatical
dimension; they thus carry no inflectional features:

(16) ei lambā chelegulo oi lambā meyeguloke cene ki? [[... chelegulā/guli ...
meyegulāke/gulike ...]]
this tall boy-Cla those tall girl-Cla-Obj know Q
'Do these tall boys know those tall girls?'

Given that adjectives do not inflectionally agree with nouns in Bangla, how they are to
be identified becomes an open question. One diagnostic that distinguishes the noun
/buddhijibi/ 'intellectual' from the adjective /buddhimān/ 'intelligent' is that
comparison targets adjectives alone. The comparative construction, as in /birener ceye
(beši) buddhimān/ [[biren hoite (odhik) buddhimān]] '(more) intelligent than Biren',
features an obligatory particle and an optional intensifier. This intensifier is best glossed
'much' when used outside the comparative construction, as in /biren beši khāe ni/
[[biren odhik khāe nāi]] 'Biren hasn't eaten much', and is also used, optionally, in the
superlative: /šabceye (beši) buddhimān/ [[šarbāpekkhā (odhik) buddhimān, šarbādhik
buddhimān]] 'most intelligent, lit. than-all (much) intelligent'.

Many adverbs are derived from adjectives by the very productive adverbializing
element /bhābe/, now an affix, once a separate word denoting 'in an [Adjective]
fashion': thus, /bektigatobhābe/ 'personally', /sthāyibhābe/ 'permanently', /spašṭobhābe/
'clearly', /bhadrobhābe/ 'politely' etc. from the adjectives /bektigato/ 'personal' etc.

Phrasal adverbs that use the slightly less productive adverbializing particle /kore/
[[koriyā, not repeated throughout paragraph]] (formally the conjunctive participle of /karā/
'to do') sometimes target the same adjectives /bhābe/ does, as in /spašṭo kore/ 'clearly' or
/bišeš kore/ 'especially', and sometimes different adjectives, as in /ālādā kore/
'separately'. Adverbs that affix a locative /e/ to adjectives, like /dure/ 'far away', /šahoje/
'easily', form a compact set, transparently derived but not a productive template (even
simple extensions like /šarole/ 'naively' from /šarol/ 'naive' are inconceivable). This holds
a fortiori of the set that uses the archaic tatsama derivational affix /to/: /bišešoto/
'especially', /šādhāronoto/ 'ordinarily', /spašṭotoi/ 'clearly' (with the mandatory
dissociative emphasizer /i/), etc., including the locally productive set /prothomoto/

'firstly', /ditiyoto/ 'secondly' etc. based on the learned ordinals. The slight meaning differences in cases where more than one adverbializing strategy exists, like /spaṣṭo kore/, /spaṣṭobhabe/, /spaṣṭotoi/ for 'clearly', seem word-bound, hard to generalize.

Items like /kāche/ 'near' that can occur alone or with a complement may be treated, depending on descriptive decisions, as transitive adverbs when they take a complement like 'road' in /rāstār kāche/ 'near the road', or – this is my preference – as an adposition taking this genitive complement. Bangla adpositions are overwhelmingly often postpositions like /kāche/. It seems likely that the only apparent preposition /binā/ 'without' found in /binā rojgāre/ 'without income', /binā nāliśe/ 'without complaint' etc., governing as it does the locative, is to the privative prefixes in the locative-ending adverbs /nirbhaye/ 'fearlessly', /nirdidhāe/ 'unhesitatingly', /anāyāśe/ 'effortlessly', /akleśe/ 'without difficulty', /nikharcāe/ 'without expenditure' what the word-external adverbializing particle /kore/ is to the affixal adverbializer /bhābe/ in the instances discussed above. In other words /binā/ is not a true preposition, but a phrasal adverb introducer. One argument in favour of this analysis is the otherwise inexplicable unusability of adjectives between /binā/ and the locative: one cannot say /binā jorālo nāliśe/ for 'without strident complaint', or /binā bhadro rojgāre/ for 'without a decent income'. If this account of /binā/ is granted, then every adposition in Bangla follows its complement and is a 'post'-position.

Certain adpositions, unlike the typical /kāche/ 'near', take a complement in the objective case, like /niye/ [[loiyā]] 'about', as in /tomār bābā-ke niye/ [[tomār bābā-ke loiyā]] 'about your father(-ke)' and /tomār rojgār-0 niye/ [[tomār rojgār-0 loiyā]] 'about your income(-0)', examples which illustrate the standard /ke-0/ variability of objective case marking. A few adpositions take consistently zero case marked complements, e.g. /oder śiddhānto onuśāre/ [[uhāder śiddhānto …]] 'according to their decision/s', /āin motābek/ 'according to law'. And the adposition /kore/ [[koriyā, not repeated throughout paragraph]] 'by', distinct from the adverbializer /kore/ [[koriyā]], takes a locative complement denoting a means of storage or transport: /hāte kore/ 'by hand', /bāse kore/ 'by bus', /mājhāri bāltite kore/ 'in medium-sized bucket/s'.

5.3 Indefiniteness/definiteness phenomena

It is convenient to describe referential definiteness phenomena in Bangla in terms of the use of classifiers and other devices to express Ordinary In/Definiteness (presence or absence of a specific/definite interpretation) and Antidefiniteness (imprecise quantification plus emphatic indefiniteness).

Nominal constructions distribute In/Definiteness information over three choice points: DemQ, Dem[onstrative] and Q[uantifier] choice; NumCla, the choice and positioning of a Num[eral]-Cla[ssifier] complex; and OZC, overt versus zero Case. Of these factors, NumCla is the most important. For the dominant definite template in Bangla involves certain Classifiers which, either alone or with a small Num prefixed, can occur encliticized to a Noun, and are interpreted as definitizing: /boi-ṭā/ 'book-Neut[er]Cla[ssifier], the book', /boi-du-ṭo/ [[boi-dui-ṭā]] 'book-two-NeutCla, the two books'. At the indefinite end of the spectrum, the prenominal position and internal Classifier-Numeral sequencing of certain NumCla complexes expresses 'antidefiniteness', as in /khān-dui ciṭhi/ 'Seg[mental]Cla-two letter, two letters or so', and contrasts with the normal order Num-Cla N, which expresses ordinary indefiniteness: /du-khānā ciṭhi/ [[dui-khānā…]] 'two-SegCla letter, two letters'. Examples illustrating the choice points and their consequences for the expression of in/definiteness:

(17) boi āmār kāje lāgbe nā (bare N; indefinite) [[... lāgibe nā]]
book my work-Loc be-useful-Fut not
'A book/Books will be of no use to me.'

(18) ei boi āmār kāje lāgbe nā (Dem /ei/; definite) [[... lāgibe nā]]
this book my work-Loc be-useful-Fut not
'This book will be of no use to me.'

(19) kono boi āmār kāje lāgbe nā (Q /kono/; indefinite) [[... lāgibe nā]]
any book my work-Loc be-useful-Fut not
'No book/s will be of use to me.'

(20) duṭo boi āmār kāje lāgbe (Num-Cla /du-ṭo /pre-N; indef) [[duiṭā ... lāgibe]]
two-Cla book my work-Loc be-useful-Fut
'Two books will be of use to me.'

(21) boi-duṭo āmār kāje lāgbe (Num-Cla post-N clitic; definite) [[... duiṭā ...
lāgibe]]
book-two-Cla my work-Loc be-useful-Fut
'The two books will be of use to me.'

(22) ækṭā boi āmār kāje lāgbe (Num-Cla /æk-ṭā/ pre-N; indefinite) [[... lāgibe]]
one-Cla book my work-Loc be-useful-Fut
'One/A book will be of use to me.'

(23) boiṭā āmār kāje lāgbe (Cla /ṭā/ post-N clitic; definite) [[... lāgibe]]
book-Cla my work-Loc be-useful-Fut
'The book will be of use to me.'

(24) tumi beṛāl dekhte cāo (null case; indefinite) [[... dekhite cāo]]
you cat to-see want
'You want to see a cat.'

(25) tumi beṛālke dekhte cāo (overt case; definite) [[... dekhite cāo]]
you cat-Obj to-see want
'You want to see the cat.'

(26) beṛāl niye tumi kichu jāno nā (null case; indefinite) [[... loiyā tumi ...]]
cat about you anything know not
'You know nothing about any cat/s.'

(27) beṛālke niye tumi kichu jāno nā (overt case; definite) [[... loiyā tumi ...]]
cat-Obj about you anything know not
'You know nothing about the cat.'

These are the primary phenomena in the study of ordinary in/definiteness. And the phenomenon of antidefiniteness is observable in the following pairs:

(28a) cār-jon chātro   b) janā-cār-ek chātro
      four-HumCla student   HumCla-four-Aug student
      'four students'   'about four students'

(29a) tin-khānā ciṭhi   b) khān-tin-ek ciṭhi
      three-SegCla letter   SegCla-three-Aug letter
      'three letters'   'about three letters'

(30a) pãc-ṭā boi   b) goṭā-pãc-ek boi
       five-NeutCla book   NeutCla-five-Aug book
       'five books'   'about five books'

In the a-examples, the Num-Cla N sequence bears an Ordinary Indefinite interpretation. In the b-examples, we have instead Cla-Num-Aug N and unusual Cla allomorphs, associated with the Antidefinite readings.

I first consider the factors that place a nominal expression on the ordinary in/definiteness spectrum. DemQ: As (17)–(19) show, certain choices of Dem, especially in the form with the fortifier /i/ – Proximal /e(i)/, Distal /o(i)/, Sequent /še(i)/, Relative /je/ – yield a definite reading. It is of some typological significance that there is no bleached Dem of the canonical Definite Article variety familiar from European languages. Dasgupta (1992) provides a formal account of the way /i/-fortified Dems emphasize referential individuation. Certain choices of Q – /anek/ 'plenty', /kichu/ 'some (amount)', /kono/ 'some (particular)', etc., – make the nominal indefinite. NumCla: A NumCla complex in prenominal position induces an indefinite reading, as exemplified above at (20) and (22), which employ /ṭā/, a default or maximally Neutral Classifier that does not occur in an environment requiring grammatical Formality. If a non-singular Num plus non-human Cla complex, or a nonhuman Cla acting alone but with a default singular reading, is encliticized to the N, this yields a definite reading, as in (21) and (23). For all Bangla speakers, an enclitic Num must be a small number. Some varieties permit even a human Cla to participate in the pattern. But note that, while Count Quantifiers may occur in a QuaCla N construction as in (31):

(31) kayek-jon netā 'some leaders'
      some-HumCla leader

– nonetheless, they do not occur as postnominal clitics, and preclude definiteness.

OZC: A direct object with an overt case affix can, unlike one without, have a definite reading, as exemplified above at (24) versus (25). Generic or indefinite contexts may force overtly case-marked nominals to bear appropriate non-definite readings, as in:

(32) ei kukurṭā ækṭā berālke beš bhae pāe
      this dog-Cla a-Cla cat-Obj really fear gets
      'This dog is really scared of a (particular) cat.'

(33) bāgherā berālder bhae pāe nā
      tigers cats-Obj fear get not
      'Tigers don't fear cats.'

But no context can definitize a null case object. Furthermore, when a prenominal NumCla complex forces indefiniteness even in the presence of the overt case marker, this marker's presence signals specificity, as in:

(34) āmi duṭo berāl dekhi ni [[... duiṭā ... dekhi nāi]]
      'I didn't see two cats (i: I didn't see any pair of cats; ii: there are two cats I haven't seen)'

(35) āmi duṭo berālke dekhi ni [[H: as in (34)]]
      'There are two cats I haven't seen.'

I turn to the expression of Antidefiniteness. The prototypical cases, shown above at (28)–(30), are morphologically augmented. But antidefinites that exhibit an unaugmented Cla-Num sequence also exist:

(36) khān-dui bāṭi,(slightly marginal variant:) bāṭi khān-dui
    SegCla-two bowl, bowl SegCla-two
    'about two bowls'

(37) ghaṇṭā khān-ek (the only sequence possible)
    hour SegCla-one
    'an hour or so'

Only the typical patterns can consistently feature numbers bigger than one or two:

(38a) janā-pãc-ek kormi
    HumCla-five-Aug employee
    'about five employees'

(39a) khān-cār-ek ciṭhi
    SegCla-four-Aug letter
    'about four letters'

(40a) goṭā-du-ek botol
    NeutCla-two-Aug bottle
    'two bottles or so'

(41a) khān-kay-ek biškuṭ
    SegCla-some-Aug biscuit
    'a couple of biscuits'

(42a) goṭā-kato-k / guṭi-kato-k churi
    NeutCla-some-Aug /IndivCla-some-Aug knife
    'a couple of knives'

(43a) guṭi-chay-ek šamoššā
    IndivCla-six-Aug problem
    'six problems or so'

The Classifier allomorph alternations across the ordinary versus antidefinite divide are even more striking than the Neutral Classifier /ṭā/'s vowel-harmonic alternation [[unavailable in H]] with /ṭo/ in /duṭo/ [[duiṭā]] 'two NeutCla' and /ṭe/ in /tinṭe/ [[tinṭā]] 'three-NeutCla'. Note the way the Cla morphs in the antidefinite (38a)–(43a) above contrast with the regular Cla morphs in the ordinary indefinite (38b)–(43b), noting also the persistence of the /-(e)k/ augment in the quantifiers at (42b), (43b), the only non-numerals that participate in the antidefinite paradigm:

(38b) pãc-jon kormi 'five employees'

(39b) cār-khānā ciṭhi 'our letters'

(40b) du-ṭo botol 'two bottles' [[dui-ṭā ...]]

(41b) cha-ṭi šamoššā 'six problems' [[chae-ṭi ...]]

(42b) kay-ek-khānā biškuṭ (cf. ka-khānā 'how many', dialectally kae-khānā)
    how-many-Aug-SegCla biscuit
    'some biscuits'

(43b) kato-k-gulo/guli churi (cf. kato-gulo/guli 'how many')
    how-many-Aug-CollCla knife
    'some knives'

While antidefiniteness plays no role outside the nominal system, definiteness does. It appears in a clausal construction exemplified in /tumi jācchoṭā kothāe/ [[unavailable in H]] 'you are-going-NeutCla where, where is it that you are going?', consisting of gapped clause plus default Cla plus gap-filling focal interrogative. One might conclude from this that the default Cla as a general purpose definiteness marker serves to mediate between the Given clause-body, which it definitizes, and the New focus. There is something to ponder also in the adjectival system. Some adjectives, especially ordinals, welcome the Human Cla /jon/ to form individual aggregation definites: /prothomjon jāe ni, ditiyojon gæche/ [[prothomjon jāe nāi, ditiyojon giyāche]] 'The first one didn't go, the second one has gone'. This is mysterious in view of the fact that nouns do not accept /jon/ to form individual aggregation definites in Bangla (*/oddhāpokjon/ 'professor-Jon' would mean 'the professor' if it was even remotely acceptable; such forms are routine in Assamese).

Even for nouns, there are some loose ends. I have so far concentrated on the definitizing role of a post-nominal Cla that either clearly belongs to the count category, like /khānā/, or at least, like the NeutCla /ṭā/, does not distinctly contrast with it. But there is also the noncount classifier /ṭu(ku)/, with a clipped allomorph in /ek-ṭu tel/ 'a little bit of oil' (where the least numerical Num /æk/ 'a, one' has its /æ/ harmonically raised to /e/ by the high /u/), which does definitizing work and displays an unreduced allomorph in /tel-ṭuku/ 'the little bit of oil'. To this we may add the use of the NeutCla in /kichuṭā tel/ 'some oil' and /telṭā/ 'the oil'. The evidence for its non-count character in these contexts comes from the unavailability here of the individuating alternant /ṭi/: */kichuṭi tel/, */telṭi/.

Follow-up work will wish to explore in detail the individual aggregation classifiers Human /jon/, Segmental /khānā/ (diminutivized variant /khāni/), Neutral /ṭā/, Individuative /ṭi/ [[which carries a more neutral nuance in H]]; and the collective aggregation ones, including at least the Collective Neutral /gulo/ (with the ill-understood variant /guli/, mainly restricted to the H pole of the diglossic system) and the possible Collective Animate classifier /rā/ whose Pickwickian variant /der/ (combining the features of /rā/ with the neutralized Case features of Acc-Dat and of Gen) may indicate that it is a true inflectional ending rather than a Cla.

There is no way to factor out the /i/ of the Cla variants /khāni/, /guli/, /ṭi/ synchronically. But follow-up workers may find that the Fortifier /i/ in Dem elements like /ei, oi/ has some focalizing element in common with a dissociative emphasizer particle. Such a finding would create a bridge between the noun phrase and our next domain, the clause.

The reason for providing this unusually detailed coverage of one aspect of Bangla syntax is of course that, for the foreseeable future, the way Classifiers and other noun-related formal phenomena interact with the syntax and semantics of reference – in a sense that will no doubt be broadened, to include the time reference of the verb's tense-aspect-mood system – is obviously going to engage a disproportionate amount of the attention of most researchers.

5.4 Clause structure

The resources of morphological agreement are limited in the Bangla clause, whose organization is therefore governed by a variety of clause particles. We have already seen the clitic emphasizers that accord focal status to their host constituent. If a constituent is immediately followed by a particle like /to/ 'of course, as you know', /nāki/

'apparently', /ki/ 'Q' (turns what without it would be a declarative clause into a yes–no question), /je/ 'TopCompC' (marks a clause as a topicalized complement clause), then that constituent counts as a topic or as 'given' information relative to which the 'new' information in the message becomes salient, peaking at the focus, which is marked by an emphasizer in (44):

(44) biren to ækhon brotin-ke-o cene
      Biren of-course now Brotin-Obj-Emph knows
      'Biren, of course, now knows Brotin too.'

Sentence (45) shows that a given constituent can serve as both focus and topic:

(45) brotin-o to birenke bohudin dhore cene [[... dhoriyā ...]]
      Brotin-Emph of-course Biren-Obj long-time for knows
      'Brotin also, of course, has known Biren for a long time.'

A focus, regardless of whether it is also a topic, tends to gravitate towards and is always acceptable at the slot immediately to the left of the finite verb, like the emphasizer-marked foci in (44) and its reordered variant (46):

(46) birenke bohudin dhore brotin-o to cene [[... dhoriyā ...]]
      Biren-Obj long-time for Brotin-Emph of-course knows = '(44)'

An Interrogative constituent is always intrinsically focal in character, and falls under this rule:

(47) niren je brotinke kothāe dekheche, tā tār mone nei [[... dekhiyāche, tāhā tāhār mone nāi]]
      Niren TopCompC Brotin-Obj where has-seen, that he-Gen mind-Loc isn't
      'Just where Niren has seen Brotin, he can't remember.'

Notice that the constituent in (47) which the clause-internal particle /je/ marks as topicalized, /niren/, must not follow such an intrinsically focal constituent. If it does, the result is sharply unacceptable, as in (48), which presents two impossible first halves for the sentence for which (47) is the only viable sequence:

(48) *kothāe niren je brotinke dekheche /*brotinke kothāe niren je dekheche ... [[... dekhiyāche]]
      where Niren TopCompC Brotin-Obj has-seen / Brotin-Obj where Niren TopCompC has-seen ...

Focalizing and topicalizing particles, with supporting intonation contours, have grown in importance as the H pole of the diglossic system recedes into history and the more speechlike L pole becomes prominent. One particularly interesting type of particle that organizes the information sectors of the clause is the inflected clause-internal element that I will call the Positive Polarity Copula (PPC) because of its copular character and its mandatory positive value, avoiding both negation and interrogation. The PPC is a clause-internal topicalizing particle comparable to /to/ 'of course', and yet agrees with the subject for person and formality, as shown in (49)–(51). The focus, following the pattern shown above, either follows the topic as in (49) and (50) or is identical to the topic as in (51):

(49) biren holo tomār-i ābiškār [[... hoilo ...]]
      Biren PPC your-Emph discovery
      'Biren is your discovery (no one else's).'

(50) uni holen birener-i guru [[... hoilen ...]]
s/he PPC-Formal Biren's-Emph guru
'S/he is Biren's guru (nobody else's).'

(51) tumi-i hole birener āšol puroškār [[... hoile ...]]
you-Emph are Biren's real prize

Had the PPC been a verb, as its inflectability might lead one to speculate, then one would have expected it to be able, if not bound, to occur in the clause-final position of the typical South Asian verb. But the PPC is unacceptable there:

(52) *biren tomār-i ābiškār holo [[*... hoilo]]
Biren your-Emph discovery PPC (cf. (49))

Tentatively, I therefore conclude that it is an inflected clause-internal particle.

One clause particle, the Exhortative /jæno/, is of syntactic interest because of its interaction with the mood of the verb:

(53) rājā-rāni jæno ānonde thāken
ing-queen Exh happiness-Loc stay
'May the king and the queen live in happiness.'

Exh, like the clause particles /jāte/ 'so that', /jodi/ 'if', /pāche/ 'lest' and such matrix verbs as /cāwā/ 'to want', selects a verb in the subjunctive mood. The subjunctive in Bangla is not an overtly morphological phenomenon, but a syntactic one. The subjunctive mood borrows the indicative present simple endings in their entirety. But one can distinguish it from the indicative because a subjunctive clause systematically substitutes the heavy quasi-copula stem /thāk/ for the indicative's light copula element /ch/ in the compound tenses and the true light copula /āch/, as we see when we compare the a- and b-indicatives below with the corresponding c-subjunctives:

(54a) a. rājā-rāni bhālo āchen
king-queen fine are (the true light copula /āch/)
'The king and queen are (now) fine.'

(54b) rājā-rāni bhālo thāken
king-queen fine stay
'The king and queen are (normally) fine.'

(54c) rājā-rāni jodi bhālo thāken/*āchen
king-queen if fine stay/*are
'If the king and queen (a) are now fine or (b) are normally fine.'

(55a) rājā phire gæchen [[... phiriyā giyāchen]]
king back has-gone(to wit:go-Conjunctive+ light copula element /ch/)
'The king has gone back.'

(55b) *rājā phire giye thāken [[*... phiriyā giyā thāken]]
king back go-Conjunctive stays

(55c) rājā jodi phire giye thāken
king if back go-Conjunctive stays
'If the king has gone back.'

(56a) rājā bicār korchen [[... koritechen]]
       king judgement is-doing(to wit:do-Infiniciple+ light copula element /ch/)
       'The king is meting out judgement.'

(56b) rājā bicār korte thāken [[... korite ...]]
       king judgement do-Infiniciple stays
       'The king keeps on meting out justice.'

(56c) rājā jodi bicār korte thāken [[... korite ...]]
       king if judgement do-Infiniciple stays
       'If the king (a) is or (b) keeps on meting out justice.'

We are at last ready to state the basic distribution of the various Neg[ative] particles in the Bangla clause, a topic adumbrated at the outset of this syntax section. Recall, from the discussion of (1) and (2) in subsection 5.1 above, that Neg is preverbal with non-finites and postverbal with a finite indicative. Now, the Subjunctive as in (54c') given below, the negation of (54c), patterns with non-finites in requiring preverbal placement of Neg, and contrasts in this respect with the Indicative in (54b') given below, the negation of (54b):

(54b') rājā-rāni bhālo thāken nā
        king-queen fine stay Neg
        'The king and queen don't keep well.'

(54c') rājā-rāni jodi bhālo nā thāken /*thāken nā
        king-queen if fine Neg stay /*stay Neg
        'If the king and queen are not (a) now or (b) normally fine.'

What about the negation of (54a)'s true light copula /āch/? The answer is the agreement-invariant Neg /nei/ in (54a') given below:

(54a') rājā-rāni bhālo nei /*āchen nā /*nā āchen [[... bhālo nāi/...]]
        king-queen fine aren't /*are Neg/ *Neg are
        'The king and queen aren't well.'

I turn to the negation of (55a)'s Present Perfect with its word-embedded light copula element /ch/. What we encounter is

(55a') rājā phire jān ni [[... phiriyā jān nāi]]
        king back goes NegPerf
        'The king hasn't gone back /hadn't gone back /didn't go back.'

a general purpose NegPerf which displaces the Person and Formality agreement marking job leftwards, to the verb. This phenomenon remains poorly understood. [[The Eastern standard and H use the same /nāi/ both for the NegPerf function illustrated in (55a') and as the negative of the existential 'be', as in /ghare keu nāi/ 'There isn't anybody in the room', where the Western L standard uses the distinct form /nei/ 'isn't'.]]

The negation of (56a), to finish the set, is a straightforward indicative negation:

(56a') rājā bicār korchen nā [[... koritechen nā]]
        king judgement is-doing Neg
        'The king is not meting out judgement.'

Imperatives pattern with Indicatives in opting for Verb Neg order, but stage a different drama by conflating the two Imperative tenses in the negative:

(57) p (pres) āmāke bhāt dāo
me rice give-ImpPres
'Give me rice (now).'

f (fut) āmāke bhāt diyo
me rice give-ImpFut
'Give me rice (when it is due).'

n (neg) āmāke bhāt diyo nā
me rice give-ImpFut Neg
'Don't give me rice((p)now/(f)when due).'

These puzzles point up the importance of relating the study of the written language more closely to that of speech, in syntax no less than in phonology.

6 SEMANTIC AND PRAGMATIC EFFECTS

6.1 Iterations and echo words

There is an impression of direct contact between speech and meaning in ideophonic or expressive words like /kuckuce (kālo)/ 'pitch (black)' (cf. section 4 above). But the argument that the formal structure refers some aspect of the message content to the boundary between formal linguistics and the substantive cognitive or cultural support systems of language becomes more concrete in the study of partly or wholly 'iconic' phenomena such as the iterations in (1) or the echo words in (2):

(1) Iterations

(a) holde holde phul
yellow yellow flower 'yellow flowers'
(b) šādhu šādhu bhāb
saint saint impression 'a vague impression of saintliness'
(c) cā khete khete probondho lekhā [[. . . khāite khāite. . .]]
tea drinking drinking article writing 'writing an article while drinking tea'
(d) āmlāder kāche giye giye phāiler khõj newā [[. . .jāiyā jāiyā . . . khõj lawā]]
officials to going going file-Gen information seeking 'seeking information about the file on repeated visits to officialdom'
(e) golite golite jene gæche [[. . .jāniyā giyāche]]
alley-Loc alley-Loc knowing has-gone
'They already know, all over the alleys.'

(2) Echo words

(a) boi-khātā, lit. book-notebook: 'books etc.'
(b) ṭākā-koṛi, lit. money-cowrie-shell: 'money etc.'
(c) bāšon-košon, lit. dish-'kish': 'dishes etc.'
(d) botol-ṭotol, lit. bottle-'tottle': 'bottles etc.'
(e) botol-photol, lit. bottle-'phottle': 'bottles etc., said disparagingly'

(1a–e) exemplify the South Asian phenomenon of iteration, or the syntactic reduplication of entire words. All five cases present syntactically identical surfaces. They differ functionally, in a way that the absence of syntactically differentiated devices leads us to assign to the semantic/pragmatic domain. Iteration conveys plurality in (1a);

vagueness in (1b); the adverbial participle (rather than infinitival) role of the Infiniciple in (1c); repeated action in (1d) whose Conjunctive (unlike the Infiniciple, see discussion of non-finites in subsection 3.1.2 above) could have avoided this iteration (at the cost of losing the repeated action meaning); and spatial dispersion in (1e).

In (2) we observe another areal feature Bangla shares – echo words. The echo word is a current contentive in (2a), an obsolete contentive in (2b), semi-schematized in (2c) (/bāšon/ lexically selects the idiosyncratic echo /košon/ – alongside the fully schematic echo options /ṭāšon, phāšon/ and the contentive option /patro/), and schematized as deprecative in (2e). The morphosyntax, again, is uniform throughout (2), relocating the rich differentiation in a direct or 'iconic' dialogue between speech and content.

I did not place this discussion under section 4, as the traditional treatment of the lexis has proceeded in terms of ethno-historical segmentations of sublexica within the conventional or contentive sector. But the principles of ideophonic creativity surely have something in common with the iconic phenomena just reviewed, and lie outside the Lexis proper.

6.2 Exclamations

Having considered the syntactically unmediated interpretive properties of some word pairings, I turn to single clauses in this subsection and clause pairings in 6.3. Exclamation clauses universally arrange direct dialogue between spoken tone and intended prominence, of course. Bangla deserves attention because it distributes its wh-word exclamations among the two major wh-word classes, k-interrogatives like /ke, ki, kato, kirakom/ 'who, what, how much, how' and j-relatives like /je, jā, jato, jerakom/ 'idem'. K-word-based exclamations such as /tomār jonne kato apekkhā korte hae!/ lit. you for how-much wait to-do one-has, 'What a lot one has to wait for you!' coexist with j-word-based ones: /tomār jonne jā apekkhā korte hae!/ [[...jonno...korite...]] lit. you for what wait to-do one-has, more like 'The waiting that one has to do for you!'

The phenomena are of considerable theoretical interest. As we see in subsection 6.3, Bangla relative (j-word-based) clauses fall into two broad types, one which fronts the wh-word as in English or French and one which does not; and j-word-based exclamations select the non-fronting type, a matter that awaits elucidation. Disparagement-type emotions show up as relatives: /rājjer jato āborjonā ene [[āniyā]] phælo!/, lit. kingdom's whatever rubbish bring in, 'You bring in all this rubbish!', apparently because a relative sweeps up the material and puts it in a package you can then trash. Open-ended emotions of wonder, as in /orā [[uhārā]] kirakom gādā-gādā biddut kharoc kare!/, lit. they how heap-heap electricity spend do, 'Look how they spend heaps of electricity!', prefer the interrogative vehicle. Other Indic languages, which retain the Indo-European morphological contrast between relatives and interrogatives, provide opportunities to extend such inquiry in a comparative direction.

6.3 Parataxis and relatives

The preference for parataxis and the avoidance of explicit coordination devices beyond bare necessity are features that make the echo word phenomenon possible at the lexical level. The same traits are at work sententially, where interclausal coordination markers are little used. Often a clause-internal particle shows how this clause feels about its neighbours. In relative clauses this work is done not by a particle but by the Relative grammatical features of j-words.

Like other Indic languages, Bangla has two types of relatives, adnominal and adsentential. Bangla tends to confine adnominal relatives to the extraposed position seen in /āmi tār kathā bolchi je gatokāl dǽkhā korechilo/ [[...tāhār...bolitechi...koriyāchilo]], lit. I him/her about am-talking who yesterday meeting did, 'I am talking about the person who met (you) yesterday'.

Bangla adnominal relatives, like all such relatives that have overt relative words, place them in clause-initial position. Unlike many other languages, however, Bangla avoids placing adnominal relatives in direct contact with the antecedent nominal as in the marginal example (which would be fine in, say, Hindi-Urdu) /āmrā šei šahore jekhāne tomrā āger bār korechile šāmner māše kanferens korte cāi/ [[... koriyāchile ... korite cāi]], lit. we that city-Loc where you last time had-done next month-Loc conference to-do want, 'We want to have a conference next month in that city where you had done it last time'.

Adsentential relative clauses, unlike adnominal ones, are free to have multiple relative phrases, and free not to front them within the clause: /tomrā jāke jekhāne thākte debe, še šekhānei thākbe, bǽs/ [[...jāhāke...thākite dibe...thākibe, bās]], lit. you-people whom where to-stay will-let, s/he there-Emph will-stay, period 'Whoever you put up, wherever, they are going to stay there, that's final'.

There is some evidence for the view that this looseness within the adsentential relative clause is related to the non-regimented paratactic relationship that such a relative clause, which comes first, strikes up with the neighbouring clause containing the so-called 'antecedents', better called Sequents in this type of construction. One piece of evidence comes from the coordinative emphasizer couple /...o...o.../ in an example like /orāo ješab šubidhe cāe, āmrāo ābār šeguloi cāi/, lit. they-too which-all advantages want, we-too then-again those-very-ones want, 'The advantages that they want, we too want'. If the adsentential relative clause is a coordinated sister of the other clause here, it must be capable of being so in general; and the default assumption is that it always is, in the absence of evidence for subordination - and there is no independent evidence for subordinate status.

We can safely conclude that, here and elsewhere, Bangla makes considerable use of looseness in ways that will no doubt repay careful study, as it lacks many of the explicit formal devices of languages more given to tighter structures in words and sentences.

ACKNOWLEDGEMENTS

I have had to draw on everything I ever learnt, through my own work and that of countless others, and cannot usefully – or justly – itemize, but can only offer a very general thanksgiving. I have chosen, in this piece, to address facts and issues rather than address colleagues who have addressed them elsewhere, mainly due to space constraints forcing a choice. I hereby explicitly disclaim any credit claims readers might otherwise think I was tacitly making.

REFERENCES

Dasgupta, P. (1983) 'On the Bangla classifier /Ta/, its penumbra, and definiteness', *Indian Linguistics* 44: 11–26.
—— (1985) 'On Bangla nouns', *Indian Linguistics* 46: 37–65.
—— (1992) 'Pronominality and deixis in Bangla', *Linguistic Analysis* 22.1–2: 61–77.

Singh, Udaya Narayana and Maniruzzaman (1983) *Diglossia in Bangladesh and Language Planning*, Calcutta: Mithila Darshan.

FURTHER READING

Azad, Humayun (1984) *Bākkotatto* (*Syntax*), Dhaka: Bangla Akademi (In Bangla).
—— (1988) *Tulanāmulak o aitihāsik bhāṣābijñān*, Dhaka: Bangla Akademi (In Bangla).
Bender, Ernest and Riccardi, T., Jr. (1978) *An Advanced Course in Bengali*, Philadelphia: South Asia Regional Studies, University of Pennsylvania.
Bhattacharja, Shishir (1998) *Sañjanani Byākaraṇ* (*Generative Grammar*), Dhaka: TCAROU (In Bangla).
Chaki, Jyotibhushan (1996) *Bāṇlābhāṣābyākaraṇ* (*Grammar of the Bangla language*), Calcutta: Ananda (In Bangla).
Chatterji, Suniti-Kumar (1926) *The Origin and Development of the Bengali Language* (2 vols.), Calcutta: Calcutta University Press.
—— (1963) *Languages and literatures of modern India*, Calcutta: Prakash Bhavan.
Chattopadhyay, Suniti-Kumar (1988) *Bhāṣā-prakāś Bāṁlā Byākaraṇ* (*Language-clarifying grammar of Bangla*), Calcutta: Rupa (In Bangla).
Čižikova, Ksenija L. and Ferguson, Charles A. (1969) 'Bibliographic Review of Bengali Studies' in Thomas A. Sebeok (ed.), *Current Trends in Linguistics, vol. 5: Linguistics in South Asia*, The Hague: Mouton, pp. 85–98.
Dasgupta, Probal (1987) *Kathār kriyākarma*, Calcutta: Dey's (In Bangla).
Dimock, Edward C., Jr., et al. (1964) *Introductory Bengali, vol. 1*, Honolulu: East-West Center Press (Reprinted 1976, Columbia, Mo.: South Asia Books).
Radice, William (1994) *Teach Yourself Bengali*, London: Hodder Headline; Lincolnwood (Chicago): NTC Publishing.
Ray, Punya Sloka, Ray, Lila, and Hai, Muhammad Abdul (1966) *Bengali Language Handbook*, Washington, D.C.: Center for Applied Linguistics.
Sen, Sukumar (1975) *Bhāṣār itibṛtta* (*The story of language*), Calcutta: Eastern (In Bangla).
Singh, Udaya Narayana (1986) *Bibliography of Bengali Linguistics*, Mysore: Central Institute of Indian Languages.
Tagore, Rabindranath (1984) *Bāṇlā śabdatattva*, Calcutta: Visvabharati (In Bangla).

CHAPTER TEN

ASAMIYA

G. C. Goswami and Jyotiprakash Tamuli

CONTENTS

LIST OF TABLES

LIST OF FIGURES

1 INTRODUCTION

1.1 The name Asamiya: its derivation

Asamiya, pronounced *ɒxɒmia,* is the major language spoken in the northeastern part of India beyond West Bengal. It is the language of Assam which is pronounced *ɒxɒm* by the native speakers and the word Asamiya has been derived from Assam (*ɒxɒm*) with the adjectival affix *-īyā,* meaning 'of', 'relating' or 'belonging to'. Assam (*ɒxɒm*), the name of the state, is of recent origin; and so is Asamiya (*ɒxɒmia*), the name of the language (Kakati 1972: 1–4).

1.2 Language situation and position of Asamiya

The northeastern part of India has been a veritable Tower of Babel. There are languages belonging to all the four major language families spoken in the subcontinent: Indo-European represented by Asamiya, Bangla, Hindi, etc., Sino-Tibetan, Austric and

Dravidian. The Khasi language in the Khasi Hills constitutes an island of Austric speech surrounded by Asamiya and some Tibeto-Burman languages. Bodo, Rabha, Karbi, Mising, Deuri-Chutiya, etc. belong to the Tibeto-Burman branch of the Sino-Tibetan family. The Ahoms in the eastern Assam districts speak one or the other dialect of the same family. Besides these dialects, a sizable population in the tea-garden areas speaks Dravidian languages of Central and South India.

However, Asamiya is the major language spoken in Assam, and serves almost as a lingua franca among the different speech communities in the whole area. According to Census of India (1991), 1,29,58,088 persons out of a total population of 2,24,14,322 all over Assam speak Asamiya as their mother tongue, besides a sizable population that speaks it as a second language in and around the State. It is spoken in all the states of Assam, Meghalaya, Arunachal Pradesh and Nagaland. In Assam, it is spoken primarily in all the Brahmaputra Valley districts. It is the mother tongue in some areas in the Surama Valley districts as well. Asamiya is also the common language of Arunachal Pradesh in the areas bordering the plains. Arunachal Pradesh is a land of numerous dialects and subdialects, most of them mutually unintelligible. Virtually every tribe or clan speaks a dialect of its own, and uses Asamiya as a link language for inter-tribe communication. The British administrators, anthropologists and foreign travellers in the past had to be assisted by Asamiya interpreters. After the creation of the separate State of Arunachal Pradesh, All India Radio broadcast common news bulletins and programmes for the people of the state in a hybrid form of Asamiya mixed with elements from the native dialects.

The situation in Nagaland is no different. All Naga tribes, except those of the areas bordering northern Myanmar, speak another form of hybrid Asamiya, very appropriately called Nagamese (Naga + Assamese), a harmonious blend of Naga dialects and Assamese, the anglicized name for Asamiya. The Bhutanese people of southern Bhutan areas communicate in Asamiya for business and other purposes. And thus, the status of Asamiya in the northeastern states of the Indian Union may be realized.

2 ORIGIN AND HISTORY OF THE LANGUAGE

2.1 Indo-Aryan origin

Asamiya has historically originated from the Old Indo-Aryan dialects, but the exact nature of its origin and growth is not very clear as yet. It is supposed that Asamiya evolved from a Magadhi Prakrit in the east that gave rise to four Apabhraṁśa dialects: Rāḍha, Vaṅga, Vārendra and Kāmarūpa (Chatterji 1970: 140). The Kāmarūpa Apabhraṁśa spread to the east keeping north of the Ganges, and is represented in north Bengal at present by North Bengal dialects, and in the valley of Assam by Asamiya. 'North Bengal and Assam did not get their language from Bengal proper but directly from the west' (Kakati 1972: 3). In early times, North Bengal and Assam constituted a single dialect group which continued to be the same even as the different dialectical offshoots penetrated far into the eastern states of Assam, Meghalaya, Manipur, Nagaland and Arunachal Pradesh. History tells us how the Kocha kings of Koch-Behar, now in West Bengal, patronized the Asamiya language and literature during the time of Maharaja Naranarayana and his illustrious brother Chilaraya in the sixteenth and seventeenth centuries AD. But during the twentieth century, the language of North Bengal has been influenced to a great extent by its neighbour Bangla, and after political amalgamation of the areas with West Bengal, the process of change has accelerated.

2.2 Kāmarūpa Apabhraṁśa

The history of Asamiya may be traced back to very early times. It has, to its credit, an indirect reference by Hiuen T'sang, who visited Kāmarūpa, the ancient name by which Western Assam was referred to, in AD 643 during the reign of Kumara Bhaskara Varma. He recorded that the language of Kāmarūpa 'differed a little from that of mid-India' (Beal 1980: 404). A question may arise here as to what that language of Kāmarūpa might be, that was different from the language of 'mid-India'? Could it be some language of Austric or Tibeto-Burman origin, and hence, structurally quite different from the Aryan language? Or could it be some Aryan language which might have undergone tremendous modifications due to linguistic acculturation in this predominantly non-Aryan country? The second proposition seems to be more probable.

It should be pertinent to note at this point that 'a silent Aryanization of Assam was evidently taking place during the time extending over one millennium from 1000 BC onwards' (Chatterji 1959: 2). It should also be remembered that Kumara Bhaskara Varma was a Brahmin king who patronized Sanskrit learning and culture. Therefore, by the seventh century AD the kingdom of Bhaskara Varma, which extended to a considerable part of Bengal in those days, must have been populated by a large number of Aryans, who, by virtue of their superiority, spread their language among the aboriginal people speaking non-Aryan languages. The native population gave up their undeveloped and unwritten languages in favour of a much more developed Aryan tongue. It is probable that the non-Aryan population preferred to learn Asamiya first as a second language which in course of a few generations replaced the native dialects altogether, and became monolingual in Asamiya. Thus, Asamiya became the dominant language with the number of speakers swelling as the language penetrated deeper and deeper into the Brahmaputra Valley and the neighbouring hills. It is in this way that the entirely different speech habits of the local population must have moulded the Kāmarūpa Apabhraṁśa – for, those were the days of Apabhraṁśa stages of the Aryan languages all over the country – into a unique shape, and attributed such a distinct character to the language that the great Chinese traveller could not pass over it unnoticed. There is no systematically recorded evidence of the language as characterized by the Kāmarūpa Apabhraṁśa, but the copper-plate and stone inscriptions of the ancient Kāmarūpa kings from the fifth to the thirteenth centuries AD, though written in Sanskrit, throw some interesting light as to the various typical phonological and quite a few morphological peculiarities of the language that gave birth to Asamiya later on (Sharma 1981: 169).

3 EXOGENOUS PRESSURES AND INDIVIDUALIZATION

3.1 Special features

The impact of the Austric and Tibeto-Burman languages in individualizing Asamiya can never be over-emphasized. The language as it stands today is distinguished by many special features all its own. It presents tremendous modifications in phonology, morphology, syntax and vocabulary.

3.1.1 Phonology

The Sanskrit cerebral and dental series of stops totally disappeared in Asamiya and a completely different set of alveolar stops evolved instead. This means that both the cerebral and the dental series merged into a single alveolar series not available in any of the Aryan languages of India. Likewise, Sanskrit palatal *c* and *ch* merged into alveolar *s*, and *j* and *jh* into alveolar *z*, and *zh* in certain areas of western Asamiya dialect. The Sanskrit sibilants *ś* *ṣ* and *s* merged into velar voiceless fricative *x* which is a development unique, inexplicable and indigenous in nature, neither insititious nor effect of external forces. This with certain other features, such as diametrically opposing stress systems and the use of aspirated and unaspirated consonants in the two major dialect groups of eastern and western Asamiya only reminds us of our inadequacies in the approach to the evolution of Asamiya in the extreme east of the Indian subcontinent.

It is thus evident that the number of phonemes is drastically reduced: only twenty-three consonants and eight vowels remain. While there is a phonemic merger in consonants, there is split in case of the vowels.

3.1.2 Morphology

The OIA language was highly inflectional. Its later developments in MIA retained the synthetic character in some simplified forms, but Asamiya became much more analytical. For example, number and gender categories no longer remained grammatical. That is, the subject and the verb agreement in number, unlike in Sanskrit or Hindi, has become irrelevant. Likewise, number and gender agreement between the adjunct and the substantive qualified is lost.

3.1.3 Other features

There are two more distinguishing features of the language, which have been ascribed to extra-Aryan influences: the inflections for four persons of the nouns of relationship and the use of the enclitics and numeral definitives (12.1.1–2).

The nouns of relationship are a small class of words which undergo twofold inflections, viz., the inflection for personal relationship as well as for the cases. The entire class of words expressing personal relations, such as *deuta* 'father', *ma* 'mother', *baideu* 'elder sister', *bʰɒni* 'younger sister', including terms for addressing friends such as *xɔkhi* or *mita* constitute this class of nouns. It should be noted that the terms of relationship are different according to the seniority or juniority of the persons related. There are words for elder brother or younger brother, but no word for brother in general. For example, *bʰai* 'younger brother', *kɒkaideu* 'elder brother', *bʰɒni* 'younger sister', and her husband *bɔinai*; *baideu* 'elder sister', and her husband *bʰiinifii*; mother's younger sister is *mafii*, her husband *mɒfia*, etc. It is evident from the above that every relationship is expressed by different words. This method of using different words to denote differences in seniority or juniority has been ascribed to Kolarian influences. The words are Aryan, but the way they are used is extra-Aryan (Kakati 1972: 28–9, 284–9).

This class of nouns undergoes case inflections like any other noun of the general class with the case endings added at the end of the forms (12.1.3).

The enclitics and numeral definitives are forms which express the size, shape and form of the nominals to which they are suffixed. Numeral definitives are free forms, the enclitics are not. These forms denote definiteness in men and things; and hence, may be looked upon as comparable to the article in English.

It is thus evident that far-reaching changes and innovations in the Indo-Aryan speech were the result of a fusion of Aryan and extra-Aryan speakers into a common fold and medium, viz., Asamiya, and that this fusion occurred very early was evidenced by Hiuen T'sang in his remarks on the language (section 2.2).

4 EARLIEST SPECIMEN OF ASAMIYA

The earliest specimen of Asamiya language and literature is available in the *dohās*, known also as *Caryās*, written by the Buddhist Siddhacharyas hailing from different parts of eastern India. Some of them are identified as belonging to ancient Kāmarūpa by the Sino-Tibetologists (Kakati 1972: 10–11).

The language of the *Caryās* is late Apabhraṁśa, and represents the formative period of the NIA languages including Asamiya. Some typical Asamiya features are recorded in the *Caryās*. One such phonological feature is the shortening of an anterior *ā* before a following *ā* in the next or succeeding syllable. For example, *pakhā* (As. *pɒkha*) 'feather'; *cakā* (As. *sɒka*) 'wheel'; *bapā* (As. *bɒpa, bopa, bɒpai*) 'dear boy'.

Some typical Asamiya morphological features are as follows:

Case endings: Nominative *-e* (As. *-e*): *kumbhire khāa*, As. *kumbfiire khae* 'crocodile eats'; *bhāde bhanai*, E.As. *bhāde bhanai*, Mod. As. *bfiade bfiɒne* 'Bhāda says'; *core nila*, As. *sore nile* 'thief stole', etc.

Dative *-lai* (As. *-lɔi*): *meruśikharalai*, As. *meruxikhɒrɒlɔi* 'to the mountain top'; *kulalai*, As. *kulɒlɔi* 'to the bank', etc.

Locative *-ta* (As. *-t*): *bāṭata*, As. *batɒt* 'on the way'; *duārata*, As. *duarɒt* 'at the door'; *hāḍīta*, As. *fiarit* 'in the cooking pot'; *ṭālata*, As. *tilat* 'at the hill-top', etc.

The negative verb: In most of the verbs the negative particle *na* is a preposition as in E. As. This *na* is prefixed and the vowel of the particle gets assimilated in Mod. As. For example, *najānai*, E. As. *najānai*, Mod. As. *nazane* 'does not know'; *na jāi*, E. As. *najāi*, Mod. As. *nazae* 'does not go'.

One idiomatic expression shared by the *Caryā* is *apaṇā māṁse hariṇā bairī*, Mod. As. *apon mɒŋɒfiei fiɔrinar bɔiri*, or *fiɔrinar mɒŋɒfiei bɔiri* 'enemy of the deer is its own flesh'.

Some of the words which are same in form and meaning with Asamiya are – *mai* (As. *mɒe*) 'I', *mor* (As. *mor*) 'my', *ghar* (As. *gfiɒr*) 'house', *hāḍī* (As. *fiari*) 'cooking pot', *uju* (As. *uzu*) 'easy', *rāti* (As. *rati*) 'night', *bāṭ* (As. *bat*) 'path', etc.

Besides the linguistic features noted above, the literary form of the *Caryās*, the *dohā* is also the precursor of Asamiya *Bargīt* 'the song celestial' composed by the early saint-poets of Assam.

However, the earliest literary work available which may be claimed as distinctly Asamiya is the *Prahrāda Carita* written by a court poet named Hema Sarasvatī in the latter half of the thirteenth century AD. The language of this short poem seems to have been still nurtured in the cradle of its Apabhraṁśa mother. Ever since the fourteenth century to modern times there has been a continuous stream of literature in the language.

5 DISTINCTIVE PERIODS OF ASAMIYA

Asamiya has been divided into the following three periods:

(a) Early period from the fourteenth to the end of the sixteenth century, which has been split into the Pre-Vaishnavite and the Vaishnavite sub-periods.

(b) Middle period from the beginning of the seventeenth to the beginning of the nineteenth century.

(c) Modern period from the early nineteenth century to the present times.

In the early period itself the language became mature enough in the hands of quite a few distinguished court poets of the time. It emerged as the most powerful vehicle of expression in the Rāmāyaṇa rendered into Asamiya by Kavirāja Mādhava Kandali, the greatest wizard of the Asamiya idiom of early times. The language of this period is marked by the use of certain archaic forms and conjunctive particles which were absent in the Vaishnavite sub-period.

Śaṅkaradeva (1449–1567) brought about a Vaishnavite revival accompanied by a revival of the language and literature. *Brajabuli* forms and expressions were introduced by Śaṅkaradeva in his one-act plays and in the *Bargīt*, which were carried on by his followers. Moreover, Śaṅkaradeva was the first writer to create a prose style of writing in his one-act plays. Early Asamiya prose developed to fuller strength and glory in the hands of Vaikuṇṭhanātha Kaviratna, who translated the entire *Bhāgavata Purāṇa* and the *Gītā*, besides several other scriptures, into a masterly prose. Kaviratna's was a classical prose, highly restrained and selective in the use of words, phrases and idioms, a style all his own. He made plenteous use of Sanskrit forms and expressions harmoniously blended in an Asamiya syntax. His supreme command over Sanskrit and Asamiya helped him achieve brevity and clarity all at once, even in highly abstruse philosophical discussions. Others tried to continue his style, but failed to maintain the high dignity and strain so characteristic of the master writer.

Middle Asamiya is the period of secular prose that became the main vehicle of expression for all purposes. Different styles of prose developed, such as the colloquial prose of the biographies of the religious gurus, the archaic prose of the books on charms, the conventional prose of utilitarian literature, such as medicine, astrology, arithmetic, dance and music and commentaries on religious scriptures, and above them all, the standardized literary prose of high standing used in the diplomatic writings, administrative records and regular history known as the *Burañjī* in Asamiya. The prose of the *Burañjīs* is a standardized literary prose in the true sense of the term. It is through this prose that Arabic and Persian elements crept into the language in abundance. This prose comes very near to the literary language of the modern period.

The modern period of the language began with the translation and publication of the Bible in Asamiya in AD 1813. It was the American Baptist Missionaries who laid the foundation of the modern Asamiya literary idiom. They learnt the dialect of the area around Sivasagar in eastern Assam and wrote as they heard the speech of the people in a new orthography. This new idiom lost all the vigour and vitality of the well-developed literary language that had grown during the long period of its evolution. It became soft and delicate, relying entirely on indigenous *tadbhava* elements. This was evident in the language of the *Arunodai* and other Christian literature of the time. The Assamese intelligentsia accepted this, being totally demoralized after losing not only political independence after the treaty of Yandabu in AD 1826, but also their own speech from the schools and courts in 1836.

Asamiya, for the first time in its long history, met with a tragedy that brought about a serious set-back in its development for several decades to come. The British, being ignorant of the separate identity of the language of the newly acquired territory, considered Asamiya to be a local variant of Bangla, which was already familiar to them in Bengal. The British administration introduced Bangla in all offices, in the courts and schools of Assam. The Assamese people struggled for the reintroduction of their own language; and Asamiya could stand the ordeal at last. The British administrators realized their mistake, and corrected it by reinstating Asamiya in 1873, thanks to the untiring efforts of the missionaries assisted by the Assamese elite of that time.

The coming of the British and the English language heralded a new era of renaissance in Assam. Waves of modern thoughts, ideas and literary forms swept the land through English language and literature. Assamese scholars acquainted with English found the missionary idiom wanting in all respects: it was hardly capable of standing the stress and strain of the western impact. Confronted with such a situation, they realized what was amiss. They looked back to the fully mature prose of the historical writings of earlier periods, which possessed all the strength and vitality to stand the new challenge. Hemchandra Barua and his followers immediately reverted to the syntax and style of that prose, and Sanskritized the orthography and spelling system entirely. He was followed by one and all including the missionaries themselves, in their later writings. And thus, the solid plinth of the modern standard language was founded and accepted as the norm all over the state.

6 THE VOCABULARY

The largest number of Asamiya words are *tadbhavas*, besides a fairly large number of *tatsama*, semi-*tatsama* and *deśya* words. Asamiya has been a borrowing language; during its growth, it enriched its vocabulary by acquisition from all the non-Aryan languages and dialects. Ever since the Middle period, it started borrowing from Hindi and other northern Indian languages; and the process of borrowing gained momentum with the contact and conflict of the Mughals and the Ahoms, when words of Persian and Arabic origin entered through Hindi. Foreign words from European languages, such as English, Portuguese, etc. began their journey even before the British entered Assam. A good number of early borrowings have been assimilated and naturalized beyond recognition. The coming of the British opened the flood-gate of English words and expressions in the early part of the nineteenth century. Words used in the courts are all foreign: English, Persian and Arabic. With the spread of knowledge and contact with foreign countries, words from foreign languages are creeping in almost daily and adding to the vitality of the language. Science and technological development have widened the horizon of human knowledge, and radio, television and the electronic media have accelerated the process of borrowing beyond imagination.

7 DIALECTS AND DIALECTICAL DIVERGENCES

7.1 Dialectal regions

Banikanta Kakati (1972: 18–21) divided all the dialects of Asamiya into two broad groups, Eastern Asamiya and Western Asamiya. According to him, Eastern Asamiya, spoken in the area from Sadiya down to Guwahati constitutes a single homogeneous unit which 'hardly presents any notable points of difference from the spoken dialect of Sibsagar'. But a close scrutiny of the phonology and morphology of the dialect reveals that the Eastern Asamiya of this vast area may also be divided into two dialect groups: the Eastern and Central dialects. As such, the dialects of Asamiya may be regrouped as the Western, Eastern and Central or rather, the Intermediate dialects. According to this regrouping, Eastern Asamiya is spoken in the districts of Sivasagar and Lakhimpur, shading off in the contiguous areas of Arunachal in the east and down to the districts of Sonitpur and Nowgong in the west. Western Asamiya covers a fairly big area from a little east of Guwahati in the south and the Darrang district in the north, and down to the district of Goalpara in the west. The Central or Intermediate dialect occupies the area in between the two regions mentioned above, i.e. the entire Morigaon district extending to a little east of Guwahati.

The Eastern and Central dialects may be regarded as uniform to a certain extent in their respective areas, while Western Asamiya is heterogeneous in character, with large regional variations in the east, west, north and south. There must have been, in early times as well, diverse dialects and dialect groups as at present. But then, there seems to be only one dominant literary language prevailing over the whole area; and that was Western Asamiya, the sole medium of all ancient Asamiya literature including the *Burañjīs* written in the Ahom courts. This was because the centre of all literary activities in early times was in western Assam; and the writers were patronized by the kings and local potentates of that region. In the later period, however, even though the centre of literary activities moved to eastern Assam in the Ahom period, the writers continued to accept and use the existing model of the literary style of that time.

In the early nineteenth century, for some important historical reasons, the Eastern Asamiya dialect attained the status of standard literary language. Now, Dispur, the Capital city being around Guwahati, as also with the spread of literacy and education in the western Assam districts, forms of the Central and Western dialects have been creeping into the literary idiom and reshaping the standard language during the last few decades.

7.2 Nature of dialectical variations

Eastern and Western Asamiya are sharply differentiated in phonology and intonation including speech tempo, morphology, morphophonemic changes, and vocabulary. As a result, speakers of either group, at times find it difficult to understand one another. The differences among the Western dialects are confined mainly to phonology, intonation specifically, and to vocabulary occasionally.

Central Asamiya stands as an intermediate dialect with a few distinct features of its own. This dialect shares some characteristics of the other two dialect groups. The following is a comparative study of only a few of the distinguishing features of the dialects.

7.2.1 Phonological

(a)   Stress. Eastern and Central Asamiya have medial stress, whereas Western Asamiya has a strong initial stress. Owing to the influence of Western Asamiya dialect in recent times, the medial stress is optionally being shifted either to the first or the second syllable from the left, and never beyond.

The strong initial stress of Western Asamiya generally shortens words, the medial syllables being slurred over owing to want of stress. In the other two dialects, words are not shortened, but the nucleus of the syllable immediately following the stressed one is attenuated in timbre. For example, Eastern *komóra* 'pumpkin', *kɔribɒ* '(he/she) will do'; Central *kumúra, kɔríbɔu*; Western *kúmra, kɔ́rbo*.

In words of more than three syllables, the third syllable is very short; e.g. *mɒɦápṷrux* 'great man', *ɒxɒ́ntṷxia* 'discontented'.

(b) Simple vowels. There appears to be a predominance of high vowels in Western (and often in Central) Asamiya as opposed to higher-mid and low vowels to the lower-mid vowels of Eastern dialects; e.g. Eastern *kapór* 'cloth', *nemú* 'lemon'; Central *kapór/kapúr, nemú*; Western *kápur, nímu*.

Eastern and Central Asamiya have lower-mid front / ɛ / in place of Western Asamiya higher-low front / æ /. Moreover, there is no phonemic contrast between / ɒ / and / ɔ / in Western Asamiya. That means, this dialect has a seven-vowel system in place of the eight-vowel system of the other two dialects.

(c) Diphthongs are common in all the dialects, but their quality and distribution are different; in Eastern and Central dialects they are generally falling, whereas the Western dialects have both the falling and the rising ones, e.g. Eastern *láthua* 'wicked', *kátia* 'born in the month of *Kāti* '; Central *láthua, kátia;* Western *láutha, káita.*

The final diphthong / ɔu / is common and prominently articulated in Eastern and Central Asamiya. / ɔi / has a tendency to become / ɔ / medially and / e / or / ee / finally in certain forms in Eastern Asamiya. In the Western dialects the final / ɔu / and / ɔi / either become monophthongs / o / and / e /, or change in quality and become / ɔo / and / ee /, respectively.

(d) Triphthongization, a very common feature of Western Asamiya is entirely absent from the other two dialects.

(e) The most important feature of the Western Asamiya consonant system is the considerable palatalization of all oral consonants before the vowels / i æ / and before / j / in clusters. The velar and alveolar stops are more palatalized than the rest. In the other two dialects / s z / only are palatalized in clusters with a following / j /.

(f) Another contrasting feature of Eastern and Central Asamiya with the Western dialects is the deaspiration of medial aspirated consonants when they are preceded by another aspirate or by the spirants / s x ɦ / and occasionally by / z /. Western Asamiya always retains the aspirates of the earlier stage of the language in like environments. The occurrence of two aspirates in the neighbouring syllables in *tadbhava* words in Eastern and Central dialects is extremely rare; e.g. Eastern and Central *sɔku* 'eye', *ɦati* 'elephant', *xitan* 'head (of a bed)'; Western *sɔkhu* (< *cakkhu-*< *cakṣu-*), *ɦathi* (< *hatthi-* < *hasti-*), *xithan* (< *śirasthāna*).

(g) Conjunct consonants in *tadbhava* words are rare in the Eastern and Central dialects; but Western Asamiya has a predominance of conjuncts medially owing to the strong initial stress.

(h) Assimilation of consonants, specially of / r / before an unaspirated stop in word boundary and medially is common in the Western dialects; e.g. *tar dɒre* 'like him' is *táddɒre; bɒrali* 'a kind of fish' is *bálli* or *bɒ́lli*.

(i) The syllable structure (C)VCe(C)i (where C represents any consonant and V represents any vowel except / e ɛ /), a very common feature in Western Asamiya, is not favoured in the other two dialects.

(j) The intonation patterns of all the three dialect groups are different. The speech tempo which is very fast and forceful in the Western dialects is rather slow in Eastern Asamiya, and medium in the Central one.

7.2.2 *Morphological*

There are quite a few differences in nominal and verbal inflections, in pronominal and plural derivations, as also in the choice of definitives and numeratives among the dialect groups. For example:

(a) Nominal inflection. The initial vowel of the ending is lost after the final vowel of the preceding form as shown in table 10.1.

(b) In verbal conjugation, the third person ending is different in all the dialect groups in different tenses and moods. In the future tense, it is zero (after the future tense affix *-ibɒ*) in the Eastern, *-ɔu* in the Central and *-o* or *-u* in the Western dialects; e.g. Eastern *kɔribɒ* '(he/she) will do'; Central *kɔribɔu;* Western *kɔ́rbo/kɔ́rbu.*

The third person ending added after the *-il* past is *-e* in the Eastern, *-a* in the Central, and *-a/-ak* in the Western dialects; e.g. Eastern *kɔrile* '(he/she) did'; Central *kɔrila*; Western *kɔrila/kɔ́rilak/kɔ́illak.*

The same endings in the progressive are *-e* in the Eastern, *-ei* in the Central and *-i* in the Western dialects. In the present tense also Central Asamiya has *-ei*, whereas the other two dialects have *-e*; e.g. Eastern *kɔrise* '(he/she) is doing', *pɔrfie* '(he/she) reads'; Central *kɔrisei, pɔrfiei*; Western *kɔ́risi, pɔfire.*

There are differences in the first person endings, the progressive affix and the verbal post-positions as well.

(c) In plural derivation, Eastern Asamiya uses *-bor, -bilak* and *-fiõt*, Central Asamiya adds one more, viz., *-gɛla*, and Western Asamiya has *-gila, -gilan, -gilak*, etc.

(d) The pronominal derivatives of time and place are the same for the Eastern and Central dialects, but different for the Western dialects; for example, *kɔt* 'where', *zɔt* 'where (relative)' *tɔt* 'there' and *ɔt* 'here' are respectively *kɒfiẽ/kɒfiãi, zɒfiẽ/zɒfiãi, xɒfiẽ/xɒfiãi* and *ɒfiẽ/ɒfiãi* in Western Asamiya. Likewise, *ketia* 'when', *zetia* 'when (relative)', *tetia* 'then' and *etia* 'now' are *kethen, zethen, tethen* and *ethen*, respectively, in Western Asamiya.

(e) Morphophonemic changes are also different for different dialects.

7.2.3 *Glossarial*

The dialects of the two major groups – Eastern and Western Asamiya – except for a small part of the total nominal vocabulary, use entirely different words and idiomatic expressions in common parlance. In this respect, the Central dialect plays the real intermediate role, sharing equally with both the dialect groups. For example, Eastern

TABLE 10.1: DIALECTICAL DIFFERENCES IN NOMINAL INFLECTION

Case ending	Eastern	Central	Western
Accusative	-ɒk	-ɒk	-ɒk
Dative	-ɒlɔi	-ɒk ~ -ɒk + lagi	-ɒk ~ -ɒk + lagi ~ -ɒk + lɔgi
Instrumental	-ere ~ -ere + xɔte	-ɒre ~ -ɒre + xɔti ~ -ɒr + xɔti	-ɒre ~ -ɒr + xɔti

kũwa 'well', *gamosa* 'towel', *dfiɒpat* 'tobacco', *ɛral* 'tether'; Central *nad/patki, gamosa/ phali, dfiɒpat, ɒral/dɒrɒx*; Western *pátki/láfinda/índra, múksa/pháli, taŋkhu, dɒrɒx/ dɒrɒkh*.

7.2.4 Conclusion

The above is a brief note on the salient features of differences among the dialects of Asamiya discussed on a regional basis. Social or class dialects are not very clearly marked from the regional variations. It should be of sociolinguistic interest to note that there are no distinct caste dialects in Asamiya to distinguish a higher caste person from a lower caste one. There are, however, certain community dialects that cut across all regional dialects. One such speech form is used by the religious Vaishnavite sattra circle all over the state. It is a highly polite and most respectful form that uses entirely different sets of nominals, pronominals and verbal forms. Sanskrit *tatsama* words are preferred to the *tadbhava* words that are used in a special idiomatic expression only. For example, *bfiat* 'rice' is *prɒsad/saul xizoa* 'food offered to a deity /cooked rice'; *ga dfioa* 'bath' is *snan*, (Skt. *snāna*) or *ga tioa* 'wetting of the body'; *bfiɔri* 'feet' is *srisɒrɒn/ sɒrɒn* (Skt. *śrīcaraṇa/caraṇa*); *pita/deuta* 'father' is *ata*; *ma/mai/ai* 'mother' is *ai*; *deuta* 'Sir' is *bap*; *ɛõ/ekhet* 'this person (hon.)' is *ɔt*, '(the august presence) here'; *tɛõ/tekhet* 'that person (hon.)' is *tɔt* '(the august presence) there'; etc.

Another important feature of this dialect is the preference for indirect and passive expressions. For example, *ɔt bɒfia fiɒok* '(please) be seated', [lit. (the august presence) here sitting be done (3hon.)]; *tɔt ba ki kɒe*, '(wonder) what he would say!', [lit. (the august presence) there *(tɔt)*, uncertainty *(ba)* what *(ki)* says *(kɒ-3.* present indefinite)], etc.

A notable feature of the standard dialect is that a speaker would often refer to or address a highly respectable person not in the second person (hon.), but in the third person only! For example, *etia sare kɔbɒ lage* 'Now *(etia)* Sir *(sare)* should *(lage)* to say *(kɒ-*inf.)'; that means, 'Now, you please say'.

A community dialect is prevalent among the fisherman community in the middle and upper Assam districts. The very same Asamiya words are differently pronounced with a significant intonation of their own. Educated persons of the community communicate with other people in the standard colloquial, but the uneducated ones use their own speech on all occasions.

There is yet another secret language used by the astrologer community of the Darrang district. It is known as *thar*, i.e. 'hint or indication'. This community uses a disguised vocabulary prepared and chosen from the common language itself, which can hoodwink the people around. Asamiya is a fit case for studies in language-in-contact and theories of communication. The virgin field of socio- and ethnolinguistic interest is yet to be explored.

8 PHONOLOGY

8.1 Inventory

There are twenty-three consonant and eight vowel phonemes in standard colloquial Asamiya. The consonants may be grouped into two broad divisions as stops and continuants. Stops contrast in three points of articulation: the lips, the alveolae and the velum; and they present four-way contrasts in every point as to the presence or otherwise of voice and aspiration. Therefore, a stop may be voiced or voiceless, aspirated or unaspirated.

There are eleven continuants: semivowels / w j /, spirants / s z x ɦ /, lateral / l /, trill / r /, and nasals / m n ŋ /.

There are eight vowels, contrasting as front, central, back, and high, higher-mid, lower-mid and low.

The consonants and vowels are shown in table 10.2 and table 10.3 respectively.

TABLE 10.2: ASAMIYA CONSONANTS

	Bilabial		Alveolar		Palatal	Velar		Glottal
	Vl.	Vd.	Vl.	Vd.	Vd.	Vl.	Vd.	Vd.
Unaspirated	p	b	t	d		k	g	
Aspirated	ph	bɦ	th	dɦ		kh	gɦ	
Spirants			s	z		x		ɦ
Nasals		m		n			ŋ	
Lateral				l				
Trill				r				
Frictionless continuants		w			j			

TABLE 10.3: ASAMIYA VOWELS

	Front	Central	Back
High	i		u
Higher-mid	e		o
Lower-mid	ɛ		ɔ
Low		a	ɒ

Other features are:

Nasalization			/ ˜ /.
Open juncture			/ + /.
Word stress:	(i)	Primary stress	/ ′ /,
	(ii)	Secondary stress	unmarked.
Utterance stress:	(i)	Sentence stress	/ ' /,
	(ii)	Emphatic stress	/ " /.
Phrase terminals:	(i)	Single bar	/ | /,
	(ii)	Hyphen	/ - /.
Utterance terminals:	(i)	Falling	/ ‖ /,
	(ii)	Rising	/ ? /,
	(iii)	Abrupt rising	/ ʒ /,
	(iv)	Holding	/ # /,
	(v)	Surprise	/ ! /.

8.2 Consonants

8.2.1 Consonant contrasts

The initial commutations, shown in table 10.4, establish the consonants.

8.2.2 Distribution of the consonants

Initially, all consonants except / ŋ w j / occur before vowels, and / p t k b d g bɦ dɦ gɦ kh m n s z ɦ / occur before consonants. All consonants save / w j / occur medially and finally after vowels. The phonemes / p t d dɦ s z ɦ / occur finally after consonants which are sonorants. The aspirated stops are not frequent finally: the voiceless are less frequent than the voiced ones.

All aspirated stops, finally, are lenis. There is a tendency to spirantize, in some of the dialects, all except / dɦ gɦ / into their homorganic spirants, viz. / ph th kh bɦ / have final allophones [ɸ θ x β], respectively.

Two aspirates in immediately neighbouring syllables in a word with or without intervening V or VC are extremely rare in the standard colloquial language.

8.2.3 Allophones of the consonants

Environments for allophonic variations are as follows:

(1) When followed by a nasal in a cluster: unaspirated stops have nasal release in this environment.
(2) When preceded by a vowel and followed by / j /. All consonants except / ŋ w x ɦ / have half-long allophones; in case of the aspirates the stop element is slightly long. / k kh s z / are a bit palatalized also.
(3a) When preceded by a vowel and followed by / r /; and
(3b) When preceded by / r / and followed by a vowel.

TABLE 10.4: CONSONANT CONTRASTS ILLUSTRATED

/p/	/ph/	/b/	/bɦ/
/pat/	/phat/	/bat/	/bɦat/
'leaf'	'crevice'	'way, path'	'rice'
/t/	/th/	/d/	/dɦ/
/tat/	/thak/	/dãt/	/dɦak/
'there'	'steps'	'teeth'	'cover'
/k/	/kh/	/g/	/gɦ/
/kat/	/khat/	/gãt/	/gɦat/
'cut'	'bedstead'	'hole'	'ferry'
/s/	/z/	/x/	/ɦ/
/sat/	/zat/	/xat/	/ɦat/
'cover'	'caste'	'seven'	'hand'
/m/	/n/	/r/	/l/
/mat/	/nat/	/rakh/	/lakh/
'voice'	'drama'	'keep'	'1/10th of a million'

In both these environments, consonants occur in half-long allophones in free variation with those without length. All alveolar consonants except / s z / are slightly retroflex in environment (3b).

(4) As a first member of a cluster following a stressed vowel, all consonants are slightly long.

(5) Initially, when preceded by any juncture and followed by vowels, the voiced aspirates have slightly glottalized allophones which freely vary with allophones without glottalization.

All consonants are tense initially. The consonants / z ɦ r l / start voiceless and become fully voiced immediately.

(6) Final occurrences. Consonants are long in varying degrees before junctures. The continuants are longer than the stops if they are unreleased. / z ɦ r l / end voiceless.

(7) Intervocally, the aspirated stops are more lenis than the unaspirated ones.

(8) All consonants have lip rounding when they are immediately followed by the higher back vowels / o u /; lip rounding being a little more when flanked by / o u / intervocally. The spirants / s z x ɦ / have comparatively more lip rounding than other consonants.

(9) / k kh x / are palatalized before / i /; / x / is palatalized also after / i / finally.

8.2.4 The aspirates

The aspirates / ph th kh bɦ dɦ gɦ / have been interpreted as phonetically complex unit phonemes. They occur initially before vowels, intervocally, in clusters medially and after vowels finally. / dɦ / occurs in final cluster after / n / (Goswami 1982: 95–6).

8.2.5 The frictionless continuants

The frictionless continuants / w j / have been treated as rare phonemes in Asamiya because of their limited distribution. They do not occur initially before vowels, and present contrasts with the vowels / o u / and / e i /, respectively, after consonants only. Intervocally and finally in unstressed positions there are no contrasts between / w / = [w] and / o / = [o̞] or / u / = [u̞]; and between / j / = [j] and / i / = [i̞] or / e / = [e̞].

It is clear from the above that although / w / and / j / have contrasts with the vowels and consonants, these contrasts are neutralized, or they overlap with / o u / and / e i /, respectively, in all other positions before vowels where / w / and / j / never occur (Goswami 1982: 81–2).

8.2.6 Consonant clusters

Consonant clusters in standard Asamiya are not many, whereas they are numerous in the Western and Central dialects. The discussions on clusters below mainly relate to *tatsama* words, i.e. words directly borrowed from Sanskrit, and also to foreign words.

Clusters occur initially, medially and finally. Clusters of two or three consonants may be permitted initially and medially, while clusters of two consonants only may occur finally.

Initial clusters are few. The following shows the nature of initial clusters in the language.

	First member	Second member
(a)	/ p t k b d g kh bɦ dɦ gɦ m n s ɦ /	/ r /
(b)	/ p k b g m s /	/ l /
(c)	/ t b g kh dɦ m n s z /	/ j /
(d)	/ s /	/ p t k ph th kh m n r l j w /
(e)	/ d s /	/ w /

Final clusters are very few and limited in nature: all the permitted clusters have a sonorant as the first member; e.g.

(a) / mp mbɦ /
(b) / nt nd ndɦ ns /
(c) / rt rs rz rɦ /
(d) / lk /

All final and initial clusters along with some others are permitted medially.

There are clusters of three consonants where the first member may be either / s /, / r / or a nasal. / p t k m / may be preceded by / s / and followed by / r /.

Phonemic gemination of consonants occurs with the following consonants:

/ p t k b d g m n ŋ l s z /

All consonants save the aspirates when preceded by a syllable with emphatic stress may be optionally doubled. The stop element of the aspirates is lengthened in a like environment.

8.3 Vowels

8.3.1 Types of vowel contrasts

The eight vowels present three types of contrasts as follows:

(1) Eight-way contrasts in closed syllables and in open syllables when / i u / do not follow in the next syllable with intervention of a single consonant except the nasals.
(2) Six-way contrasts in open syllables with / i / occurring in the following syllable with intervention of any single consonant except the nasals, or when the preceding vowel is nasalized.
(3) Five-way contrasts in open syllables when / u / occurs in the following syllable with a single consonant intervening.

The contrasts between / e ɛ / and / ɔ ɒ / in B, and / e ɛ /, / ɒ ɔ / and / o u / in C are neutralized.

The various contrast types and examples of the contrasts are shown in table 10.5 and table 10.6.

TABLE 10.5: CONTRAST TYPES FOR VOWELS

Contrast types	Vowels								Total
	i	e	ɛ	a	ɒ	ɔ	o	u	8
A	i	e	ɛ	a	ɒ	ɔ	o	u	8
B	i	e		a		ɔ	o	u	6
C	i	e		a		ɔ		u	5

TABLE 10.6: VOWEL CONTRASTS ILLUSTRATED

	A Eight-way contrasts	B Six-way contrasts	C Five-way contrasts
/i/	/bil/ 'small lake'	/bɦiinifii/ 'brother-in-law'	/ritu/ 'season'
/e/	/bel/ 'bell (Eng.)'	/abeli/ 'afternoon'	/renu/ 'pollen'
/ɛ/	/bɛl/ 'wood apple'		
/a/	/bal/ 'pubic hair'	/mɒdafii/ 'drunkard'	/ranu/ a proper name
/ɒ/	/bɒl/ 'strength'		
/ɔ/	/bɔl/ 'Let's go!'	/rɔdali/ 'sunny'	/pɔtu/ 'expert'
/o/	/bol/ 'colour'	/bɦogi/ ~ /bɦugi/ 'one who enjoys'	
/u/	/bul/ 'walk'	/bɦugi/ 'having suffered'	/buku/ 'breast'

TABLE 10.7: DISTRIBUTION PATTERNS FOR VOWELS

Vowels	VCi	VCe	VCɛ	VCa	VCɒ	VCɔ	VCo	VCu
i	i	i	i	i	i	i	i	i
e	e	e ⤴	?	e	e	e ⤴	e ⤴	e
ɛ		ɛ ⤴	ɛ	ɛ	ɛ	ɛ ⤴	ɛ ⤴	
a	a	a	a	a	a	a	a	a
ɒ		ɒ	ɒ	ɒ	ɒ	ɒ ⤵	ɒ ⤵	
ɔ	ɔ	ɔ	?	ɔ	ɔ	ɔ ⤵	ɔ ⤵	ɔ
o	o ⤵	o	o	o	o	o	o	
u	u ⤵	u	u	u	u	u	u	u

the arrow indicates direction of free variation

8.3.2 Distribution of the vowels in open syllable

Table 10.7 presents the distributional pattern of the vowels.

8.3.3 Vowel allophony

The following generalizations can be made:

All vowels are nasalized after the nasal consonants, nasal vowels and / ɦ / following a nasal vowel. All nasalized high and higher-mid vowels are slightly lowered in quality. / e ɛ a ɒ ɔ o u / have allophones with a palatal glide when they are followed by a consonant cluster with / j / as the last member. (The consonant before / j / is also lengthened in a like environment); e.g.

| /besja/ | [beᵉssja] 'prostitute' | /alɛkhjɒ/ | [alɛᵉkkhjɒ] 'picture' |
| /bakjɒ/ | [baᵉkkjɒ] 'sentence' | /punjɒ/ | [puⁱnnjɒ] 'virtue', etc. |

All vowels start voiceless when preceded by / s x /. Vowels have different degrees of length according to their position in a word. They are tense in closed syllables. / i e / are [j] and / o u / are [w] respectively after a vowel in unstressed position. / i e ɛ / and / u o ɔ / are accompanied by [i̯ = j] and [u̯ = w], respectively, when they are followed by lower vowels in sequences. / a / is [aᵉ] and [aᵒ] before / e ɛ / and / ɒ ɔ /, respectively.

8.3.4 Vowel sequences

Sequences of two vowels are shown in table 10.8.

Phonemically there are no diphthongs, although /i e o u/ form phonetic diphthongs in unstressed positions after another vowel.

The geminates /ii ee oo uu/ may not, and /aa/ never, form two-syllable nuclei each: one member becomes syllabic and the other occurs as a glide.

The following sequences form two-syllable nuclei in all occurrences: e.g. / ie iɛ ia iɒ iɔ ɛa ɛɒ aɛ aɒ aɔ /, and / ɒɒ oe oa oɒ oɔ ue ua uɒ uɔ /.

The phoneme of nasalization /~/ may occur with all vowels except /ɔ/. It nasalizes vowels in sequence.

TABLE 10.8: VOWEL SEQUENCES

Vowels	i	e	ɛ	a	ɒ	ɔ	o	u
i	ii	ie	iɛ	ia	iɒ	iɔ	io	iu
e	ei	ee				eɔ	eo	eu
ɛ				ɛa	ɛɒ		ɛo	
a	ai	ae	aɛ	aa	aɒ	aɔ	ao	au
ɒ		ɒe			ɒɒ		ɒo	
ɔ	ɔi							ɔu
o		oe		oa	oɒ	oɔ	oo	
u	ui	ue		ua	uɒ (?)	uɔ	uo	uu

8.3.5 Syllable structure

The canonical form of the syllable is (C) (C) (C) V (V) (C) (C).

There are twenty-four possibilities out of which vowel nucleus with consonant clusters as coda or onset are very rare.

The forms in CCCVV(C) and (C)CCV(V)CC do not occur in the language.

9 WORD STRESS

There are two word stresses: (i) Primary stress / ´ /, and (ii) Weak stress, phonemically unmarked. There is contrast in position rather than degree of stress in a word as both the stresses do not occur in the same environment. The position of the primary stress is either the first or the second syllable.

There are two stresses at the utterance level: (i) Sentence stress / ' /, and (ii) Emphatic stress / " /. Phonetically there seems to be no difference between the emphatic and sentence stress.

10 MORPHOPHONEMICS

10.1 Introduction

Consonantal alternation is rare in Asamiya morphophonemics. There is vowel harmony among the lower and higher vowels: the lower vowels give place to the next higher vowels of both the front and back series occurring in the immediately following syllable: /ɛ/ is realized as /e/, /ɒ/ is realized as /ɔ/, and /o/ is realized as /u/.

10.2 Conditions for vowel harmony

Occurrences of /i u ɔ/ in the following environments:

(a) occurrence as a following member in vowel sequences;
(b) occurrence in the following syllable with intervention of (i) any single consonant, (ii) any single consonant except a nasal, (iii) any nasal consonant;
(c) vowels with nasalization. Nasalized /ɛ̃ ɒ̃/ are not affected by occurrences of high vowels in the environments (a) and (b) above.

10.3 The vowel morphophonemes

10.3.1 ɛ

(i)   ɛ is realized as /e/ when followed by /i u/ in environment (b) (ii); e.g.
      pɛti   :   /peti/ 'belt', cf. *pɛt* 'belly'
      khɛluɔi   :   /kheluɔi/ 'player', cf. *khɛl* 'play'
      bʰɛkoli   :   /bʰiekuli/ 'frog', cf. *bʰɛkola* 'male frog'
(ii) *ɛCɛCi/u* : /ɛCeCi/u ~ /eCeCi/u; e.g.
      sɛreli   :   /sɛreli/ ~ /sereli/ 'emaciated woman', cf. *sɛrela* 'emaciated man'
      dʰɛmɛlia   :   /dʰiɛmelia/ ~ /dʰiemelia/ 'farcical, playful', cf. *dʰɛmali* 'play, fun'
(iii) *ɛCɔ* : /eCɔ/ ~ /ɛCɔ/, e.g.
      bʰɛlɔfiu   :   /bʰɛlɔfiu/ ~ /bʰelɔfiu/ a proper name (male), cf. *bʰɛlɛŋa* a proper name (male)

10.3.2 ɒ

(i)   *ɒa* : /oa/; e.g.
      lɒa   :   /loa/ '(you, fam.) take', cf. *lɒ* 'take'
      kɒa   :   /koa/ '(you, fam.) say', cf. *kɒ* 'say'
(ii) *ɒɒ* : /ɒoɒ/ ~ /ɒɒ/ ~ /ɒ/, e.g.
      lɒɒ   :   /lɒoɒ/ ~ /lɒɒ/ ~ /lɒ/ '(you, inf.) take'
      kɒɒ   :   /kɒoɒ/ ~ /kɒɒ/ ~ /kɒ/ '(you, inf.) say'
(iii) *ɒi* : /ɔi/ in environment (a); e.g.
      kɒi   :   /kɔi/ 'having said', cf. *kɒ* 'speak'
      fiɒisil   :   /fiɔisil/ 'had become', cf. *fiɒ* 'become'
(iv) *ɒCi* : /ɔCi/ in environment (b) (ii); e.g.
      mɒti   :   /mɔti/ 'mind', cf. *mɒt* 'consent'
      pɒthia   :   /pɔthia/ 'send', cf. *pɒtha* 'send', *pɒthaõ* '(I) send'

(v)   *ɒCu* : /ɔCu/ in environment (b) (i); e.g.

bɒfiua   :   /bɔfiua/ 'cause to sit', cf. *bɒfi* 'sit'

rɒnua   :   /rɔnua/ 'warrior', cf. *rɒn* 'war'

(vi)   *ɒCɒCi/u* : /ɒCɔCi/u/ ~ /ɔCɔCi/u/; e.g.

khɒrɒsi   :   /khɒrɔsi/ ~ /khɔrɔsi/ 'extravagant', cf. *khɒrɒs* 'expenditure'

zɒgɒru   :   /zɒgɔru/ ~ /zɔgɔru/ a proper name for man, 'offender, accused', cf. *zɒgɒr* 'offence'

(vii)   *ɔCɒ* : /ɔCɔ/; e.g.

fiɔbɒla   :   /fiɔbɔla/ 'perhaps'

kɔbɒ   :   /kɔbɔ/ '(he) will say'; but *zabɒ* '(he) will go'

(viii) *ɒCɔ* : /ɔCɔ/ ~ /ɒCɔ/; e.g.

zabɒlɔi   :   /zabɔlɔi/ ~ /zabɒlɔi/ 'to go (infinitive)', cf. *zabɒ* 'to go (also, infinitive)'

kɒribɒlɔi   :   /kɔribɒlɔi/ ~ /kɔribɔlɔi/, 'to do (infinitive)'

(ix)   *ɒCi* : /ɒCi/ ~ /ɔCi/ in environment (b) (iii); e.g.

dfiɒni   :   /dfiɒni/ ~ /dfiɔni/ 'rich', cf. *dfiɒn* 'money, riches, wealth'

mɒrɒmial :   /mɒrɒmial/ ~ /mɒrɔmial/ ~ /mɔrɔmial/ 'kind', cf. *mɒrɒm* 'kindness'

(x)   *õCi* : /õCi/ in environment (c); e.g.

zõtia   :   /zõtia/ 'tangled, knotty' cf. *zõt* 'knot'

diõti   :   /diõti/ 'a giver (female)'

10.3.3 *o*

o(C)i/ɔ : /u(C)i/ɔ/; e.g.

xoi   :   /xui/, 'having slept', cf. *xo*, 'sleep'

xãtori   :   /xãturi/ 'having swum', cf. *xãtor* 'swim'

dopɒria   :   /dupɔria/ 'noon', cf. *dopɒr* 'noon'

kõɒri   :   /kũɔri/ 'princess', cf. *kõɒr* 'prince'

10.3.4 *i*

(i)   *ii* : /ī/ ~ /i/; e.g.

diise   :   /dīse/ ~ /dise/ '(he) is giving', cf. *di* 'give'

niisil   :   /nīsil/ ~ /nisil/ '(he) took', cf. *ni* 'take'

(ii)   *aiɛ* : /aiɛ/ ~ /aɛ/; e.g.

baiɛk   :   /baiɛk/ ~ /baɛk/ 'elder sister', cf. *bai* 'elder sister', *-ɛk* 3(n)

momaiɛr :   /momaiɛr/ ~ /momaɛr/ '(your, fam.) maternal uncle,' cf. *momai* 'maternal uncle'

10.3.5 *a*

(i)   *aa* : /oa/ when they are not preceded by /i u/; e.g.

khaa   :   /khoa/ 'eating', cf. *kha* 'eat'

pɒrfiaa   :   /pɒrfioa/ 'teaching', cf. *pɒrha* 'teach', *pɒrfi* 'read'

(ii)   *aɒ* : /aoɒ/ ~ /aɒ/; and /aoɔ/ ~ /aɔ/ when they are followed by /i/ in environment (b) (ii); e.g.

khaɒn   :   /khaoɒn/ ~ /khaɒn/ 'act of eating', cf. *kha* 'eat'

khaɒria   :   /khaoɔria/ ~ /khaɔria/ 'voracious eater'

(iii)   *i/u aa* : /i/u oa/ ~ /i/u ua/ e.g.
   sɔtiaa   :   /sɔtioa/ ~ /sɔtiua/ 'act of sprinkling', cf. *sɔtia* 'sprinkle'
   xunuaa   :   /xunuoa/ ~ /xunuua/ 'act of causing to hear', cf. *xunua* 'to cause to listen'
(iv)   *a (C)ia* : /ɔ(C)ia/ in environment (a) and (b) (ii); e.g.
   gɦaia   :   /gɦɔia/ 'strike with a knife', cf. *gɦa* 'cutting wound'
   ɛkatia   :   /ɛkɔtia/ 'one sided, slanting', cf. *kati* 'side', *ɛkati* 'one side'
(v)   *aCia* : /ɒCia/ in environment (b) (iii); e.g.
   pania   :   /pɒnia/ 'tasteless', cf. *pani* 'water'
   aokania   :   /aokɒnia/ 'indifferent, inattentive', cf. *aokan* 'indifference'
(vi)   *aCua* : /ɔCua/ in environment (b) (i); e.g.
   dɦarua   :   /dɦɔrua/ 'debtor, borrower', cf. *dɦar* 'debt'
   pɒtharua :   /pɒthɔrua/ 'wild, of the field', cf. *pɒthar* 'field'
(vii)   *aC(C)a* : /ɒC(C)a/; e.g.
   saka   :   /sɒka/ 'wheel', cf. *sak* 'round mould'
   kanda   :   /kɒnda/ 'crying', cf. *kand* 'cry, weep'
(viii)   *aCɒCa* : /ɒCɒCa/; e.g.
   ãkɒra   :   /ɵ̃kɒra/ 'obstinate', cf. *ãkɔri* 'obstinate (woman)'
   batɒra   :   /bɒtɒra/ 'news', cf. *batɔri* 'news'

10.3.6 *A*

   A : / a / always in all environments: e.g.
   xArua   :   /xarua/ 'fertile', cf. *xar* 'manure'
   zAloa   :   /zaloa/ 'fisherman who catches fish with nets'
   kAnia   :   /kania/ 'opium eater', cf. *kani* 'opium'
   zAgialia :   /zagiɔlia/ 'belonging to *Jāgī*'
   dÃtialia :   /dãtiɔlia/ 'residing at the border,' cf. *dãti* 'border'

Morphophoneme *A* answers some of the exceptions to the morphophoneme *a*.

10.4 Consonant alternation

Consonant alternation is rare. The following have been noticed:

10.4.1 *k*

It is replaced alternatively by / g / when it is followed by / g gɦ / in open juncture; e.g.

   dak gari   :   /daggari/ 'mail coach, mail train'
   dak gɦɒr :   /daggɦɒr/ 'post office'
   pak gɦɒr :   /paggɦɒr/ 'kitchen', cf. *pak xala* 'kitchen'; *pak* 'cooking', etc.

10.4.2 *t*

It is optionally replaced by / d / when followed by / d b /, and occasionally dropped before / d /; e.g.

   xat din   :   /xaddin/ ~ /xadin/ 'seven days'
   xat dinia :   /xaddinia/ ~ /xadinia/ 'weekly'
   xat bar   :   /xadbar/ 'seven times'

10.4.3 dɦ

It is optionally replaced by /d/ when followed by consonants in open juncture; e.g.

budɦibar	:	/budbar/, 'Wednesday'
adɦia+	:	/admɔɦia/, 'a two-anna piece', cf. *mɒɦa* 'a four-anna piece'
adɦi+	:	/adkɒpali/ 'headache', cf. *kɒpal* 'forehead'

11 WRITING SYSTEM

In Asamiya, there are forty consonant and eleven vowel letters in the alphabet. The fifty-one letters represent twenty-three consonant and eight vowel phonemes of the language.

The Asamiya script with the letters according to their traditional order are shown in table 10.9 along with the phonemes and Roman transliteration.

All vowel letters, except অ, have two forms, one primary that occurs after any juncture or after another vowel, and the other a secondary form that occurs after consonants. The secondary form for অ, which is zero, accompanies all consonant symbols when they are not followed by any other vowel, except finally where, barring a few cases, it is lost (see Kakati 1972: 154–67).

(a) The vowel letters and their associated phonemes and Roman transliteration are shown in table 10.10.
(b) The secondary forms for আ and ঈ follow, and those for ই, এ and ঐ precede the consonant after which they occur; e.g.

―া	:	মালা	*mālā*	'garland'
―ী	:	মালী	*mālī*	'gardener'
ি―	:	ভিনিহি	*bhiniɦi*	'brother-in-law'
ে―	:	সেমেকে	*semeke*	'gets moistened'
ৈ―	:	মাদৈ	*mādai̱*	'queen'

(c) The secondary forms for ও and ঔ have two parts that flank the consonant letter; e.g.

| ে―া | : | কোনো | *kono* | 'anybody' |
| ে―ী | : | মৌ | *mau̱* | 'honey' |

TABLE 10.9: CONSONANT LETTERS, TRANSLITERATION AND PHONEMES

Letter	ক	খ	গ	ঘ	ঙ	চ	ছ	জ	ঝ	ঞ
Transliteration	k	kh	g	gh	ṅ	c	ch	j	jh	ñ
Phoneme	k	kh	g	gɦ	ŋ	s	s	z	z (zh)	n
Letter	ট	ঠ	ড	ঢ	ণ	ত	থ	দ	ধ	ন
Transliteration	ṭ	ṭh	ḍ	ḍh	ṇ	t	th	d	dh	n
Phoneme	t	th	d	dɦ	n	t	th	d	dɦ	n
Letter	প	ফ	ব	ভ	ম	য	ৰ	ল	ৱ	
Transliteration	p	ph	b	bh	m	z	r	l	w	
Phoneme	p	ph	b	bɦ	m	z	r	l	w	
Letter	শ	ষ	স	হ	ক্ষ	ড়	ঢ়	য়	ৎ	
Transliteration	ś	ṣ	s	h	kṣ	ḍ	ḍh	y	t	
Phoneme	x	x	x	ɦ	khj	r	rɦ	j	t	

TABLE 10.10: VOWEL LETTERS, TRANSLITERATION AND PHONEMES

Asamiya script		Roman transliteration	Phonemes
Primary form	Secondary form		
অ	zero	a (á for the zero form)	ɒ
অ', অ	zero or –'	a, a'	ɔ
আ	–ꠣ	ā	a
ই,ঈ	ি– –ী	i, ī	i
উ,ঊ	ু– ূ–	u, ū	u
এ	ে–	e	e, ɛ
ঐ	ে–ꠣ	o	o
ঔ	ে–	ai	(ɔi)
	ে–ꠣ	au	(ɔu)

(d) উ and ঊ have the forms ু and ূ , which occur below the consonants; e.g.

| ু | : | কুকুৰ | kukur | 'dog' |
| ূ | : | সূত্ৰ | sūtrà | 'definition' |

উ and ঊ have special forms with the following consonants; e.g.

ৰ+ ু	:	গৰু	gàru	'cow'
গ+ ু	:	শগুণ	śàgun	'vulture'
শ+ ু	:	শুন	śun	'to hear'
হ+ ু	:	হুল	hul	'thorn'
ৰ+ ূ	:	ৰূপ	rūp	'beauty'

After *r* in a cluster, ু and ূ are represented as – ৹ , and – ী ; e.g.

– ৹	:	ত্ৰুটী	trūṭī	'shortcomings'
		ভ্ৰুকুটি	bhrukuṭi	'joking'
– ী	:	শুশ্ৰুষা	śuśrūṣā	'treatment'

(e) ঋ , pronounced as *ri* is symbolized as ৃ , written below the consonants; e.g.

| ঋ | : | তৃণ | tṛṇ | 'grass' |
| হ + ৃ is হৃ ; e.g. | | হৃত | hṛtà | 'stolen' |

There are 143 two-phoneme clusters symbolized by 174 conjunct letters. Three phoneme clusters are 21 in number which are written by 27 conjunct letters. Most of the letters undergo modification in conjunction; quite a few are changed beyond identification; e.g. হ (*h*) + ম (*m*) = হ্ম (*hm*), ক (*k*) + ষ (*ṣ*) = ক্ষ (*kṣ*), ব (*b*) + ধ (*dh*) = ব্ধ (*bdh*), etc.

Consonants in cluster with a preceding *r* were reduplicated since the formative period of the language, which has been discarded now from the middle of the present century.

Writing starts from the left and moves horizontally to the right.

The following is a para from G. C. Goswami's article, *Bāṇīkāntà Kākàtir gàdyàrīti*, i.e., Prose style of Banikanta Kakati, published in the *Madhulipi*, Guwahati, 1963.

The Asamiya text (a) is followed by Roman transliteration (b) and a free translation in English (c):

(a) গৱেষণামূলক সাহিত্য প্রণেতা আৰু চিন্তাশীল প্রবন্ধ লিখক হিচাবে স্বর্গীয় বাণীকান্ত কাকতি প্রসিদ্ধ। মৌলিক গৱেষণা, গভীৰ তত্ত্বানুসন্ধিৎসা আৰু বৈজ্ঞানিক দৃষ্টিভঙ্গীৰ কাৰণে অসমীয়া সমালোচনা সাহিত্যত তেওঁ শ্রেষ্ঠ আসন লাভ কৰিছে। তেওঁৰ ৰচনাৱলীয়ে আধুনিক অসমীয়া সমালোচনা সাহিত্যত এক নতুন ভাৱধাৰাৰ সূচনা কৰে। ভাৱপ্ৰৱণতাৰ পৰা আঁতৰি বাস্তৱ দৃষ্টিভঙ্গীৰে সমালোচনাত প্ৰবৃত্ত হৈছিল দেখি ডঃ কাকতি অসমীয়া ভাষা আৰু সাহিত্যৰ ক্ষেত্ৰত দিগ্বিজয়ী হ'ব পাৰিছিল।

(b) gàweṣàṇāmūlàk sāhityà prāṇetā āru cintāśīl prābàndhà likhàk hicābe swàrgīyà bāṇīkāntà kākàti prāsiddhà. maulik gàweṣàṇà, gàbhīr tàttwānusàndhitsā āru baijñānik dṛṣṭibhàṅgīr kārāṇe asàmīyā sàmālocànā sāhityàt teõ śreṣṭhà āsàn lābh kàriche. teõr ràcànāwàlīye ādhunik asàmīyā sàmālocànā sāhityàt ek nàtun bhāwàdhārār sūcànā kàre. bhāwàpràwàṇàtàr pàrā ātàri bāstàw dṛṣṭibhàṅgīre sàmālocànāt prābṛttā haichil dekhi ḍàḥ kākàti asàmīyā bhāṣā āru sāhityàr kṣetràt digwijàyī hà'bà pārichil.

(c) The late Banikanta Kakati is well known for his research publications and thought-provoking essays. His original research, scientific outlook and keen inquisitiveness made him the greatest literary critic in Asamiya. His writings, detached, disinterested and objective in outlook, initiate new trends in the history of Asamiya literary criticism, and raise him to very high stature.

12 MORPHOLOGY

Asamiya morphology is simple, as it does not involve inflections for number and gender. Derivation is effected by various processes that include prefixation, suffixation, zero modification (Bloch and Trager 1942: 59), compounding and change of consonant and vowel phoneme. As far as inflection is concerned, the relevant categories are definiteness and case for nominals in general, and additionally, personal deixis for a small class of nouns of relation. The correlatable categories for the verb are aspect, tense and person.

12.1 Nominal morphology

The relevant grammatical categories for Asamiya nouns and nominals are personal deixis (12.1.1) for the subclass of relational nouns, and definiteness and case (12.1.2–3) for nouns/nominals generally. The personal and other subtypes of the pronominal subclass are discussed in 12.1.4.

12.1.1 Personal deixis

The inflection of a small class of nouns of relationship with regard to personal deixis constitutes an important typological characteristic of Asamiya. The various deictic affixes that serve to mark relational nouns for the category of person (cf. 12.2.1) and their illustrations are shown in tables 10.11 and 10.12 respectively.

As the examples show, personal deixis is morphologically expressed in Asamiya, as opposed to its expression through analytic means in other languages. The formal contrast is neutralized between the deictic centres of second person honorific and third person (for a similar neutralization between verbal personal inflections, see 12.2.1).

Nouns of relationship can take regular case inflections – with or without the definitives (cf.12.1.2) – only after taking the personal deictic inflectional suffixes.

TABLE 10.11: DEICTIC AFFIXES: ALLOMORPHS AND DISTRIBUTION

Person	Affixes	After forms ending in -a	After forms ending in i/u and consonants
1(n).	-Ø	-Ø	-Ø
2inf(n).	-ɛr	-r	-ɛr
2fam(n).	-ɛra	-ra	-ɛra
2hon(n).	-ɛk	-k	-ɛk
3(n).	-ɛk	-k	-ɛk

TABLE 10.12: NOMINAL DEICTIC AFFIXES: ILLUSTRATIVE EXAMPLES

Deictic centre	Respect grading	Deictic affix	Examples ending in:			Consonant
			Vowel			
			-a	-i	-u	
First person		-Ø	pita-Ø father-1(n). 'my father'	zi-Ø daughter-1(n). 'my daughter'	xafiu-Ø mother-in-law-1(n). 'my mother-in-law'	xɔfiur-Ø father-in-law-1(n). 'my father-in-law'
Second person:	Inferior	-(ɛ)r	pita-r father-2inf(n). 'your father'	zi-ɛr daughter-2inf(n). 'your daughter'	xafiu-ɛr mother-in-law-2inf(n). 'your mother-in-law'	xɔfiur-ɛr father-in-law-2inf(n). 'your father-in-law'
	Familiar	-(ɛ)ra	pita-ra father-2fam(n). 'your father'	zi-ɛra daughter-2fam(n). 'your daughter'	xafiu-ɛra mother-in-law-2fam(n). 'your mother-in-law'	xɔfiur-ɛra father-in-law-2fam(n). your father-in-law'
	Honorific	-(ɛ)r	pita-k father-2hon(n). 'your father'	zi-ɛk daughter-2hon(n). 'your daughter'	xafiu-ɛk mother-in-law-2hon(n). 'your mother-in-law'	xɔfiur-ɛk father-in-law-2hon(n). 'your father-in-law'
Third person		-(ɛ)k	pita-k father-3(n). 'his father'	zi-ɛk daughter-3(n). 'his daughter'	xafiu-ɛk mother-in-law-3(n). 'his mother-in-law'	xɔfiur-ɛk father-in-law-3(n). 'his father-in-law'

12.1.2 Definiteness

Asamiya has a set of definitive morphemes that are suffixed to nominals, numerals and demonstrative pronouns of the language. These definitives then serve to identify the status of the referent of the resulting expression in discourse.

In addition to signalling definiteness, definitives simultaneously serve to impose a classification on the nouns, demonstrative pronouns, etc. to which they are attached, based on semantic features that range from inanimate–animate, male–female, dimensionality (e.g. long, flat, thin, etc.), size (normal, diminutive) to respect-gradation and emotional colouring (polite, neutral, pejorative). Moreover, they also signal number. Depending upon whether the definiteness indicated relates to single or multiple referents, the definitive affixes of Asamiya belong to two classes – singular definitives and plural definitives. Distributionally, the singular definitives are mutually exclusive with the plural definitives: the latter are suffixed to all nominals and pronominals of the third person.

TABLE 10.13: THE SINGULAR DEFINITIVES

Definitive	Context of occurrence	Illustrative examples	
zɒn	human male, respect/polite	manufi-zɒn man-def. 'the man'	dɒfi-zɒn num-def. 'ten (men)'
zɒni	human female, lack of respect	manufi-zɒni man-def. 'the woman'	sari zɒni num-def. 'four (females)'
	non-human female	gai-zɒni cow-def. 'the cow'	sagɔli-zɒni she-goat-def. 'the she-goat'
gɒraki	human, respect	manufi-gɒraki man-def. 'the gentleman/lady'	sari-gɒraki num-def. 'four (gentlemen/ladies)'
to	inanimate, non-human male	xadfiu-to story-def. 'the story'	bɒlɒdfi-to bull-def. 'the bull'
	human male (impolite)	manufi-to man-def. 'the man'	musi-to cobbler-def. 'the cobbler'
ta	after numerals (allomorph of to) (impolite when used with human male referents)	ɛ-ta num.-def. 'one (story, man, etc.)'	dɒfi-ta num.-def. 'ten (bulls, men, etc.)'
ti	same as to, but diminutive, endearing	zuri-ti stream-def. 'the little stream'	lɔra-ti boy-def. 'the (dear) little boy'
khɒn	dimensional (space, time)	kitap-khɒn book-def. 'the book'	natɒk-khɒn play-def. 'the play'
khɒni	same as khɒn, but diminutive, endearing	nɔi-khɒni river-def. 'the river'	natika-khɒni playlet-def. 'the playlet'
khini	non-count (mass) nouns and pronouns	pani-khini water-def. 'the water'	xei-khini that-def. 'that (place/thing)'
dal	inanimate, flexible/stiff, oblong human (pejorative)	lathi-dal stick-def. 'the stick'	manufi-dal man-def. 'the man'

TABLE 10.14: THE PLURAL DEFINITIVES

Definitive	Context of occurrence	Illustrative examples	
bor, bilak	animate, inanimate	*manufi-bor* man-pldef. 'the men'	*kitap-bilak* book-pldef. 'the books'
fiõt	human	*lɔra-fiõt* boy-pldef. 'the boys'	*xi-fiõt* he (dist.)-pldef. 'those (people)'
	non-human (pejorative reference to humans)	*gɔru-fiõt* cow-pldef. 'fools'	*gadfiɒ-fiõt* ass-pldef. 'fools'
lok	human, respect (occurs with select pronouns)	*toma-lok* you (fam.)-pldef. 'you'	*cõ-lok* he/she (prox.)-pldef. 'these (people)'
xɒkɒl	human, respect (occurs with select nouns and pronouns)	*xikhyɒk-xɒkɒl* teacher-pldef. 'the teachers'	*tekhet-xɒkɒl* he/she (dist.)-pldef. 'those (ladies/gentlemen)'

The function of class- and number-marking is limited to the nominal and pronominal word forms, since there are no patterns of verbal concord that further signal the class membership of nouns, nor do verbs exhibit any inflection for number (cf. 12.2.1). The singular and plural definitives form a more-or-less closed set. Some of the more important and frequently occurring examples are cited in tables 13 and 14 respectively.

Another important strategy of plural formation in Asamiya is the use of an indefinite plural morpheme *kei-* that is in a mutually exclusive relationship with the numerals and which takes the singular definitive suffix like the latter. This results in a set of plural expressions corresponding exactly to the set of singular expressions in definiteness, semantic classification and respect grading, as shown in table 10.15.

One clear evidence of the pluralizing indefinite function of the formative *kei-* is its relationship of mutual exclusion with the other plural definitives and numerals illustrated earlier.

TABLE 10.15: THE PLURAL INDEFINITIVE *KEI-*

Definitive	Context of occurrence	Illustrative examples	
zɒn	human male, respect/polite	*manufi-zɒn* man-def. 'the man'	*manufi-kei-zɒn* man-indefpl.def. 'the men'
gɒraki	human, respect	*manufi-gɒraki* man-def. 'the gentleman/lady'	*manufi-kei-gɒraki* man-indefpl.def. 'the gentlemen/ladies'
khila	sheet, leaf-like	*kagɒz-khila* paper-def. 'the (sheet of) paper'	*kagɒz-kei-khila* paper-indefpl.def. 'the sheets of paper'

12.1.3 Case

The grammatical category of case is correlatable with the various classes of nouns and pronouns, including the various subclasses of the latter (cf. 12.1.4). In Asamiya, it is both a morphological and a syntactic category. All nominals with or without the definitives, both singular and plural, and the personal endings of nouns of relationship must undergo case inflections to become eligible for use in a sentence. The various cases are given in table 10.16 with their traditional nomenclature, along with a few paradigms.

TABLE 10.16: CASE INFLECTIONS

| | Case forms | Illustrative paradigms | | |
		Common noun	Relational noun	Pronoun
Nominative	-e, Ø	manufi-zɒn-e man-def.nom. 'the man'	ma-ra-e mother-2fam(n).nom. 'your mother'	xi 3rd person pronoun 'he'
Accusative	-(ɒ)k	manufi-zɒn-ɒk man-def.acc. 'to the man'	ma-ra-k mother-2fam(n).acc. 'to your mother'	ta-k he-acc. 'to him'
Instrumental	-(e)re	kitap-khɒn-ere book-def.instr. 'by the book'	ma-ra-re mother-2fam(n).instr. 'by your mother'	ta-re he-instr. 'by him'
Dative	-(ɒ)lɔi	kitap-khɒn-ɒlɔi book-def.dat. 'to the book'	ma-ra-lɔi mother-2fam(n).dat. 'to your mother'	ta-lɔi he-dat. 'to him'
Genitive	-(ɒ)r	kitap-khɒn-ɒr book-def.gen. 'of the book'	ma-ra-r mother-2fam(n).gen. 'of your mother'	ta-r he-gen. 'his'
Locative	-(ɒ)t	kitap-khɒn-ɒt book-def.loc. 'in the book'	ma-ra-t mother-2fam(n).loc. 'in your mother'	ta-t he-loc. 'in him'

As the examples show, case inflections are the rightmost elements in the nominal and pronominal forms. Apart from the typical function of expressing the notion of possession, the genitive and locative cases have a facultative function of allowing certain postpositions to occur after the nominal/pronominal forms. The genitival and locative forms, along with the postpositional element then express a variety of functions, as the following examples illustrate:

(a) genitive case

form		function	form		function
gfiɒr-ɒr home-gen. 'from home'	pɒra from	ablative	ram-ɒr Ram-gen. 'with Ram'	lɒgɒt/xɔite with	comitative
gfiɒr-ɒr home-gen. 'like home'	dɒre/nisina like	adjectival comparative	ram-ɒr Ram-gen. 'by Ram'	dara/fiɔtuai by	instrumental

(b) locative case

form		function	form		function
ram-ɒt	*kɔi*	adverbial	*atai-t*	*kɔi*	adverbial
Ram-loc.	than	comparative	all-loc.	than	comparative
'than Ram'			'than all'		
zo-a-t	*kɔi*	adverbial	*mo-t*	*kɔi*	adverbial
go-denom.loc.	than	comparative	I (obl.)-loc.	than	comparative
'than going'			'than me'		

12.1.4 Pronouns

Most members of the subclasses of pronouns in Asamiya have a distinction between oblique and direct bases. The variant forms of the personal pronouns, along with the distinct proximal and distal forms of the third person pronouns are shown in table 10.17.

Most personal pronouns are regulated by an elaborate set of sociolinguistic norms such as age, social and educational status, role-relationship, etc., which govern pronominal usage. Since the choice of personal pronouns influences verbal inflection (cf. 12.2), a few observations on the norms underlying their choice are in order.

The complex nature of role-relationship between speaker and hearer in Asamiya is reflected in the norms that govern the choice of the second person pronouns *tɒe* (inferior), *tumi* (familiar) and *apuni* (honorific). *tɒe* is used with those who are relatively lower in status than the speaker, but also used between intimates. It is found to be used with servants as well as childhood friends, though it is in reciprocal use between the latter. *tumi* is used with God. It is reciprocally used between spouses in a less formal

TABLE 10.17: THE PERSONAL PRONOUNS

				Singular		Plural	
				Base form	Oblique form	Base form	Oblique form
First person				*mɒe* 'I'	*mo-*	*ami* 'we'	*ama-*
Second person	inferior			*tɒe* 'you'	*to-*	*tɒɦɒt* 'you'	
	familiar			*tumi* 'you'	*toma-*	*tomalok* 'you'	
	honorific			*apuni* 'you'	*apona-*	*aponalok* 'you'	
Third person	inferior	masc.	prox. dist.	*i* *xi* 'he'	*ia-* *ta-* 'he/it'	*iɦɒt* *xiɦɒt* 'they'	
		fem.	prox. dist.	*ei* *tai* 'she'		*iɦɒt* *xiɦɒt* 'they'	
	honorific		prox. dist.	*cõ, ekhet* *tɛõ, tekhet* 'he/she'		*cõlok, ekhetxɒkɒl* *tɛõlok, tekhetxɒkɒl* 'they'	

relationship, and non-reciprocally by the husband in a formal relationship where he gets addressed with *apuni*. Interaction with people who are older in age and of equal or higher status invariably requires the non-reciprocal use, with the person in the relatively junior position using *apuni*. The reverse can happen when the hearer is lower in status even though older in age (e.g. peons, labourers on daily wage, rickshaw pullers, etc.). In such situations, the speaker uses *tumi* (and less frequently, *toe*) and is addressed with the higher form *apuni*. Friends at college and university use *tumi* reciprocally. There is reciprocal use of *apuni* between colleagues who are equal in status, at the place of work, though there is a tendency towards reciprocal *tumi* among younger people.

What adds to the complexity of the social norms governing the choice of second person pronouns is that these tend to fluctuate with the developing social situation. For instance, the older person may realize that he used to be at school together with the hearer's father. Despite the formal nature of the situation, he may decide to switch to *tumi* after having used *apuni* initially. This transition from a reciprocal *apuni–apuni* situation to a non-reciprocal *tumi–apuni* one, signals a change in the role-relationship. Often, responding to established conventions, the hearer initiates the transition himself by requesting the older person to use the *tumi* form with him. If a situation becomes charged with tension, reciprocal *apuni–apuni* gives way to reciprocal *toe* or non-reciprocal *apuni–toe* depending on the power equation between the interlocutors. An initially reciprocal *apuni* is likely to be replaced eventually by *tumi* as initial acquaintance develops into a familiar and intimate relationship. The written medium also influences dyadic pronominal usage. While a father-and-son pair uses *toe* and *tumi* with each other, respectively, in spoken discourse, this is often found to change to *tumi* and *apuni* in written correspondence.

Other pronoun subtypes are the K-initial interrogative and indefinite pronouns, and the Z-initial relative pronouns. All these pronoun subtypes have distinct forms for human and non-human referents. In addition, indefinite pronouns have distinct affirmative and negative forms. The different subtypes of pronouns are shown in table 10.18.

TABLE 10.18: THE INTERROGATIVE, RELATIVE AND INDEFINITE PRONOUNS

| | Interrogative pronouns | | Relative pronouns | | Indefinite pronouns | | | |
| | | | | | Affirmative | | Negative | |
	human	non-human	human	non-human	human	non-human	human	non-human
Base form	*kon*	*ki*	*zi*	*zifi*	*konoba*	*kiba* *kifioba*	*kono*	*εko*
Oblique form	*ka-*	*kifi-*	*za-*		*karoba*	*kifioba*	*ka-*	
	'who'	'what'	'who'	'what'	'someone'	'something'	'no one'	'nothing'

The pronouns share all the case inflections of the nouns. However, most of the base forms, particularly those of the singular personal pronouns, do not take the nominative case.

12.2 Verbal morphology

We shall begin by discussing the morphology of finite verbs, which are distinguished from non-finite verbs by their personal inflections. The positions of the various grammatical categories relative to the verb stem in Asamiya finite verbs can be set out as follows (for a discussion on how the various sets of stems are formed with one or more of these categories, see Goswami 1982: 249–52) – verbal base + aspect + tense + person. The various finite verb forms are derived both through paradigmatically substitutable elements within each category, as well as through the inclusion/omission of one or more of these categories (except for the inflectional category of person, which obligatorily occurs with the finite verb).

12.2.1 Finite forms

We shall consider the finite verb in terms of the various grammatical categories correlatable with it. The morphology associated with each category will be briefly introduced followed by a presentation of their full array in verbal paradigms.

The morphology of the category of aspect in Asamiya is complementary to its expression through periphrasis (12.2.5). Morphologically, imperfective aspect is expressed by –*is*. It combines with the base to form the present imperfective stem (*likh-is-* write-impv.) and past imperfective stem (*likh-is-il* write-impv.past). Imperfective aspect is also periphrastically expressed by the auxiliary verb *as* 'BE' through analytic stems of the form *likh-i as* write-conj. BE (cf. 12.2.5). Habitual aspect has no overt markers, but is covertly expressed with present indefinite stems (*likh* write) and past imperfective stems (*likh-is-il* write-impv.past). Similarly, the perfective aspect is co-expressed in simple past stems *(likh-il-* write-past).

As far as tense is concerned, the past and future tense morphemes are –*il* and –*ib*, respectively. –*il* forms simple past stems as well as past imperfective stems (see above). –*ib* is directly added to the verbal base to form future stems (*likh-ib* write-fut.). Although there are no overt markers for the present tense, the verbal base itself (*likh* write) and the present imperfective stem (*likh-is* write-impv.) are associated with this tense.

Person is the only category that is inflectionally marked in the Asamiya verb. The personal suffixes shown in table 10.19 mark the first and third person pronouns, as well as the three-way distinction of personal pronouns in the second person.

TABLE 10.19: THE VERBAL PERSONAL SUFFIXES

	Future	Present indefinite	Present imperfective	Simple past	Past imperfective
First person	-*im* *	-ɔ̃	-ɔ̃	-ɔ̃	-ɔ̃
Second person (inferior)	-*i*	-ɒ	-ɒ	-*i*	-*i*
Second person (familiar)	-*a*	-*a*	-*a*	-*a*	-*a*
Second person (honorific)	-ɒ	-*e*	-*e*	-*e*	Ø
Third person	-ɒ	-*e*	-*e*	-*e*	Ø

* represents fusion of future marker -*(i)b* and person marker -ɔ̃

The person markers are the rightmost elements in the verb. As can be seen, the distinction between second person (honorific) and third person is neutralized in all the tenses. The third person marker alternates between -*e* and Ø (zero) depending on the transitivity status of the stem.

The morphology of the twenty-five finite verb forms with regard to tense, aspect and person are shown in table 10.20.

TABLE 10.20: FINITE VERB FORMS IN DECLARATIVE SENTENCES (AFFIRMATIVE)

			Illustrative verb: *likh* 'write'		
	Future	Present indefinite	Present imperfective	Simple past	Past imperfective
First person	*likh-im* write-fut.+1	*likh-ō* write-1	*likh-is-ō* write-impv.1	*likh-il-ō* write-past.1	*likh-is-il-ō* write-impv.past.1
Second person (inferior)	*likh-ib-i* write-fut.2inf.	*likh-ɒ* write-2inf.	*likh-is-ɒ* write-impv.2inf.	*likh-il-i* write-past.2inf.	*likh-is-il-i* write-impv.past.2inf.
Second person (familiar)	*likh-ib-a* write-fut.2fam.	*likh-a* write-2fam.	*likh-is-a* write-impv.2fam.	*likh-il-a* write-past.2fam.	*likh-is-il-a* write-impv.past.2fam.
Second person (honorific)	*likh-ib-ɒ* write-fut.2hon.	*likh-e* write-2hon.	*likh-is-e* write-impv.2hon.	*likh-il-e* write-past.2hon.	*likh-is-il* write-impv.past
Third person	*likh-ib-ɒ* write-fut.3	*likh-e* write-3	*likh-is-e* write-impv.3	*likh-il-e* write-past.3	*likh-is-il* write-impv.past

The following examples show the finite verb forms in imperative sentences:

	Second person (inferior)	Second person (familiar)	Second person (honorific)	Third person
Present imperative	*likh* write write!	*likh-a* write-2fam.(imp.) write!	*likh-ɒk* write-2hon.(imp.) write!	*likh-ɒk* write-3.(imp.) let him/her write!

Apart from their forms in affirmative sentences, Asamiya finite verbs have a set of distinct negative forms in affirmative and imperative sentences (12.2.3).

12.2.2 Non-finite forms

The various non-finite forms have nominal, adjectival and adverbial functions. Some of the more important formatives suffixed to Asamiya verbal bases are discussed here.

The denominative suffix *-a* is added directly to either primary or derived verbal bases. Besides their subject and object functions, denominatives can take case inflections and have various adnominal functions. The nominalized verb in the passive is also formed by *-a* as shown below:

dɔur-a-to   *bɦal*
run-denom.def.   good
'Running is good.'   (subject)

ram-e   *dɔur-a-lɔi*   *mɒe* *nɒ-rɒ-õ*
Ram-nom.   run-denom.dat.   I   neg.wait.1
'I won't wait till Ram's running.'   (adnominal)

ram-ɒr   *kho-a*   *fɔ-l*
Ram-gen.   eat-denom.   be-past
'Ram has finished eating.'   (passive)

Non-finite forms ending in denominative -*a* have adjectival functions as well. These, as well as verbal stems ending with the suffix -*(i)bɔlɔgia*, are used both attributively and predicatively:

| *ei-khɒn* | *mɒe pɒrfi-a* | *kitap* / | *ei-khɒn* | *kitap mɒe pɒrfi-a* | | (attr./pred.) |
| this-def. | I read-denom. | book / | this-def. | book I read-denom. |

'I have read this book.'

| *ei-to* | *pɒk-a* | *phɒl* / | *ei* | *phɒl-to pɒk-a* | (attr./pred.) |
| this-def. | ripe-denom. | fruit / | this | fruit-def. ripe-denom. |

'This is a ripe fruit/this fruit is ripe.'

| *ei-khɒn* | *sa-bɒlɔgia sinema* / | *ei* | *sinema-khɒn sa-bɒlɔgia* | (attr./pred.) |
| this-def. | see-adjvl. cinema / | this | cinema-def. see-adjvl. |

'This film is worth watching.'

There are several non-finite suffixes that are added to verbal bases to form adverbials. Three of them are – the contingent -*ōte*, future conditional -*(i)le* and past conditional -*(i)lɒt*. Some examples of these adverbial forms are given below, along with sentences illustrating their occurrence:

za-ōte	*pɔrfi-ile*	*pɔrfi-ilɒt*
go-contin.	read-cond(f).	read-compl.
'while going'	'if (one) reads'	'on having read'

kha-ōte	*kha-le*	*kha-lɒt*
eat-contin.	eat-cond.	eat-compl.
'while eating'	'if (one) eats'	'on having eaten'

| *ram-e* | *bɒzar-ɒlɔi* | *za-ōte* | *fiɔri-k* | *dekh-il-e* |
| Ram-nom | market-dat. | go-contin. | Hari-acc. | see-past.3 |

'Ram saw Hari while going to the market.'

| *ram-e* | *sɛsta* | *kɔr-ile* | *par-ib-ɒ* |
| Ram-nom. | effort | do-cond(f). | be able-fut.3 |

'Ram will be able to if he makes the effort.'

| *ram-e* | *sɛsta* | *kɔr-ilɒt* | *par-il-e* |
| Ram-nom. | effort | do-cond(p). | be able-past.3 |

'Ram was able to, on making the effort.'

Infinitive -*i* has a range of functions. As a conjunctive participle, it is attached to simple and conjunct verb stems immediately preceding the vector verb and forms compound verb stems (see table 10.27 and section 12.2.5). Infinitive -*i* also functions as an adverbial formative and as a marker of prior action. The various uses of -*i* are illustrated below:

| *ram-e* | *sithi* | *likh-i* | *uth-il* |
| Ram-nom. | letter | write-conj. | RISE-past |

'Ram wrote up the letter.'   (conjunctive -*i*)

| *ram* | *dɔur-i* | *afi-il* |
| Ram | run-inf. | come-past |

(i) 'Ram came running.'   (adverbial formative -*i*)
(ii) 'Having run, Ram came.'   (prior action marking -*i*)

The potential ambiguity among the various uses of infinitive -*i* is prevented by the distributional and functional differences of the verb sequences they serve to concatenate (for a set of criteria that distinguishes compound verbs from other main verb sequences in Asamiya, see Tamuli 1998: 161–8). Such a sequence as *dɔur-i afi-il* run-inf. come-past, which is potentially ambiguous between an adverbial+V reading and a V+V reading, have distinct correlates:

> *ram dɔur-i dɔur-i afi-il*
> Ram run-inf. run-inf. come-past
> 'Ram came running.'

> *ram dɔur-i uth-i afi-il*
> Ram run-inf. RISE-conj. come-past
> 'Having run, Ram came.'

The infinitive -*(i)bɒ* has at least two functions. It functions as a nominal formative, as in the following examples:

> *za-bɒ-r xɒmɒj-ɒt mo-k mat di-b-a*
> go-inf.gen. time-loc. I(obl.)-acc. call give-fut.2fam.
> 'See me when you are about to leave.'

> *kha-bɒ-r babe ruti as-e*
> eat-inf.gen. for bread be-3
> 'There is bread to eat.'

> *kɒtha-to xun-ibɒ-r-e pɒra ram-ɒr mɒn bɛa*
> matter-def. hear-inf.gen.emph from Ram-gen. mind bad
> 'Ram has been feeling dejected ever since he heard about the matter.'

> *ram-e xɒdae xãtur-ibɒ-lɔi za-e*
> Ram-nom. daily swim-inf.dat. go-3
> 'Ram goes to swim every day.'

Elsewhere infinitive -*(i)bɒ* serves to concatenate the main verb stems to which it is attached, with a following modal verb (cf. 13.4):

> *xi saikel sɒla-bɒ par-e*
> he cycle ride-inf. be able-3
> 'He can ride a bicycle.'

Because of the distinct forms of the infinitives -*(i)bɒ* and -*i* and conjunctive -*i*, verb stem + modal verb sequences are formally set apart from both compound verbs and main verb sequences:

MV-*ibɒ* + modal verb		MV-*i* + vector verb		MV-*i* + MV	
dɔur-ibɒ	*par*	*dɔur-i*	*uth*	*dɔur-i*	*afi*
run-inf.	be able/may	run-conj.	RISE	run-inf.	come
'be able to run/may run'		'finish running'		'come running'	
mat-ibɒ	*khoz*	*mat-i*	*di*	*mat-i*	*an*
call-inf.	want	call-conj.	GIVE	call-inf.	bring
'want to call'		'call (as a favour)'		'call-and-bring over'	

12.2.3 Negatives

Negation in Asamiya is expressed by prefixing a negative morpheme *na-* to the verbal base. A unique feature of this process, quite novel in Indo-Aryan, consists in the assimilation of the vowel of the negator to the non-initial first vowel of the verb. With vowel-initial verbs, the negator's vowel is deleted as illustrated in table 10.21.

The negative forms of the verbs *par* 'be able to' in all the tenses and *as* 'be' in the present imperfective represent a fusion between the negative element and the verbal stem, e.g.:

TABLE 10.21: NEGATIVE VERB FORMS

Affirmative	Negative	Affirmative	Negative
kɒr-e do-3 'does'	*nɒ-kɒr-e* neg.do-3 'does not do'	*an-e* bring-3 'brings'	*n-an-e* neg.bring-3 'does not bring'
kin-e buy-3 'buys'	*ni-kin-e* neg.buy-3 'does not buy'	*ur-e* fly-3 'flies'	*n-ur-e* neg.fly-3 'does not fly'
khol-e open-3 'opens'	*no-khol-e* neg.open-3 'does not open'	*ola-e* emerge-3 'emerges'	*n-ola-e* neg.emerge-3 'does not emerge'
bɛs-e sell-3 'sells'	*nɛ-bɛs-e* neg.sell-3 'does not sell'	*kat-e* cut-3 'cuts'	*na-kat-e* neg.cut-3 'does not cut'

TABLE 10.22: CONTRASTS BETWEEN NEGATION BY (A) PERIPHRASIS AND (B) PREFIXATION

	Affirmative	Negation by periphrasis	Negation by prefixation
Present imperfective	*kɔr-is-e* do-impv.3 'has done'	*kɒr-a nae* do-denom. neg.+be 'has not done'	*nɒɔ-kɔr-is-e* neg.do-impv.3 'is not about to do'
	fiɔ-is-e become-impv.3 'has become'	*fio-a nae* become-denom. neg.+be 'has not become'	*nɔ-fiɔ-is-e* neg.become-impv.3 'is not about to become'
	kɔ-is-e tell-impv.3 'has told'	*ko-a n-ae* tell-denom. neg.+be 'has not told'	*nɔ-kɔ-is-e* neg.tell-impv.3 'is not about to tell'
Past imperfective	*kɔr-is-il* do-impv.past 'had done'	*kɒr-a n-as-il* do-denom. neg.be-past 'had not done'	*nɔ-kɔr-is-il* neg.do-impv.past 'did not use to do'
	fiɔ-is-il become-impv.past 'had become'	*fio-a n-as-il* become-denom. neg.be-past 'had not become'	*nɔ-fiɔ-is-il* neg.become-impv.3 'did not use to become'
	kɔ-is-il tell-impv.past 'had told'	*ko-a n-as-il* tell-denom. neg.be-past 'had not told'	*nɔ-kɔ-is-il* neg.tell-impv.past 'did not use to tell'

par-e	*no-war-e*	*as-e*	*nae*
may/be able-3	neg.be able-3	be-3	neg. + be
	'is not able to'	'is'	'is not'

The present and past imperfective forms of the negative existential – *nae* 'is not' and *n-as-il* 'was not' occur in periphrasis along with verbs undergoing negation in the present and past imperfective tenses. The regularly formed negative verbs continue to be available in these two tenses along with those formed periphrastically, though these latter are more marked in their uses. The various present and past imperfective forms are shown in table 10.22.

The contrast between future and indefinite present forms is neutralized in first person and second person (honorific)/third person under negation. These neutralized forms serve to regularly negate the senses of the corresponding affirmative verb forms, while the negated forms morphologically congruent with the future forms of the affirmative have come to additionally express dubitative overtones. These are illustrated in table 10.23.

TABLE 10.23: NEUTRALIZED NEGATIVE AND DUBITATIVE NEGATIVE CONTRASTS

		Future	Present indefinite
First person	affirmative	*kɔr-im* do-fut.+1 'I/we will do'	*kɒr-õ* do-1 'I/we do'
	regular negative		*nɒ-kɒr-õ* neg.do-1 'I/we will not/do not do'
	marked negative (dubitative)	*nɔ-kɔr-im* neg.do-fut.+1 'perhaps I/we will not do'	
Second person (honorific)	affirmative	*kɔr-ib-ɒ* do-fut.2hon. 'you will do'	*kɒr-e* do-2hon. 'you do'
	regular negative		*nɒ-kɒr-e* neg.do-2hon. 'you will not/do not do'
	marked negative (dubitative)	*nɔ-kɔr-ib-ɒ* neg.do-fut.2hon. 'perhaps you will not do'	
Third person	affirmative	*kɔr-ib-ɒ* do-fut.3 '(s)he will do'	*kɒr-e* do-3 '(s)he/ does'
	regular negative		*nɒ-kɒr-e* neg.do-3 '(s)he/ will not/does not do'
	marked negative (dubitative)	*nɔ-kɔr-ib-ɒ* neg.do-fut.3 'perhaps (s)he will not do'	

12.2.4 Morphologically related stems

In its simplest form, the verbal base consists of just the verb root, with its valence (e.g. transitive/intransitive) inherently specified. However, this basic valence can be increased by the suffixation of the causative morphemes -a and -oa, resulting in secondary stems. Depending on whether the root verb is primarily transitive or intransitive, two sets of morphologically related stems are available as shown in table 10.24 (for the nature of morphophonemic alternation induced in the root vowel by the process of causative formation, see section 10).

The examples cited in table 10.24 illustrate stems that are related by a fairly regular morphological process. Less regular are instances such as those illustrated in table 10.25 where a variety of strategies are involved.

12.2.5 Compound stems

Another way that secondary stems are formed in Asamiya is by a process of verbal compounding, whereby the non-finite form of a main verb is followed by a finite or non-finite auxiliary verb (termed 'vector' verb in the relevant literature), as shown.

TABLE 10.24: CAUSATIVELY RELATED PRIMARY AND SECONDARY STEMS

Primary intransitives	Derived transitives	Indirect causative	Primary transitives	Direct/indirect causatives
uth 'rise'	uth-a 'lift'	uth-oa 'cause to be lifted'	mar 'kill'	mɒr-a/mɒr-oa 'cause to be killed'
gus 'move over'	gus-a 'remove'	gus-oa 'cause to be removed'	kat 'cut'	kɒt-a/kɒt-oa 'cause to be cut'
baz 'ring'	bɒz-a 'ring (something)'	bɒz-oa 'cause to be rung'	pɒrfi 'read'	pɒrfi-a/pɒrfi-oa 'cause to be read'
bfiiz 'get wet'	bfiiz-a 'soak (something)'	bfiiz-oa 'cause to be soaked'	kɒr 'do'	kɒr-a/kɒr-oa 'get x to do something'
			tan 'pull'	tɒn-a 'cause to be pulled'

TABLE 10.25: CAUSATIVIZATION STRATEGIES

Intransitive	Transitive	Causative
khol kha 'open'	khol 'open (something)'	khol-a 'cause to be opened'
fiɒ 'become'	kɒr 'do'	kɒr-a/kɒr-oa 'cause to be done'
thak 'stay'	thɒ 'keep'	thɒ-a 'cause to be kept'
bfiaŋ 'break'	bfiaŋ 'break (something)'	bfiɒŋ-a 'cause to be broken'
phat 'split'	phal 'split (something)'	phɒl-a 'cause to be split'

ram-e   am-to   kha-i   pɛla-l-e
Ram-nom. mango-def. eat-conj. THROW-past-3
'Ram ate up the mango.'

mohɒn-e   siɔr-i   di-ōte   sor-to   pɒla-l
Mohan-nom. shout-conj. GIVE-contin. thief-def. flee-past
'The thief fled as soon as Mohan gave a shout.'

Such analytic stems as *kha-i pɛla* eat-conj. THROW and *siɔr-i di* shout-conj. GIVE have come to be known as compound verbs, because although they are made up of two distinct verbs, these verbs nevertheless denote a single event (as distinct from ordinary V-conj.+V sequences which denote events-in-series). The MV constituent of a compound verb belongs to an open-ended class, while vector verbs constitute a more-or-less close set. Nearly all of the vector verbs have homophonous main verb counterparts with which they bear an interesting syntactic–semantic relationship that varies from a relatively opaque to a more transparent one depending on the degree of grammaticalization of individual vectors.

While there are constraints on the kinds of main verbs that can co-occur with kinds of vectors, there are still a considerable number of acceptable combinations in Asamiya. The numerous choices open to either of its constituents of combining with one another suggests that a possible way of looking at the function of the compound verb is in terms of the oppositions involving each of its constituents. For both kinds of oppositions, one involving the main verb and the other involving the vector, it is useful to consider the different parameters of variation proposed for the temporal–causal structure of situations (for more details on such an approach to Asamiya, see Tamuli 1998: 178–254). The temporal features relate to subtypes of lexical aspect or *Aktionsart* such as inceptive, iterative, egressive, etc., while the causal features include agentive, affective, benefactive, causative, experiencer and other features. Figure 10.1 indicates how some of these parameters serve to highlight the causal and temporal features of the main verb articulated by the three vectors in opposition.

Vectors 1–3 (*za* GO, *pɛla* THROW and *thak* STAY) on the right of figure 10.1 represent three choices open to the MV *bfiaŋ* 'break', giving rise to the three CV oppositions: *bhaŋ-i za*, *bhaŋ-i pɛla* and *bfiaŋ-i thak*, as illustrated below:

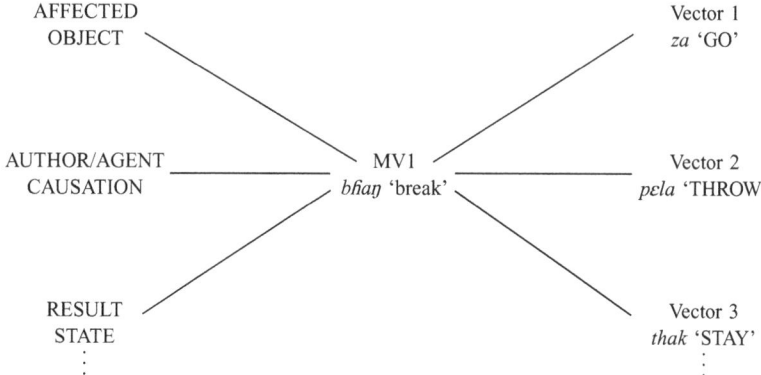

FIGURE 10.1: VECTORS AND THE TEMPORAL–CAUSAL STRUCTURE OF MAIN VERBS

gilas-to   bɦaŋ-i   gɔ-l
tumbler-def. break-conj. GO-past
'The tumbler broke.'
(focus on entry into event and affected object)

ram-e   gilas-to   bɦaŋ-i   pɛla-l-e
Ram-nom. tumbler-def. break-conj. THROW-past.3
'Ram smashed up the tumbler.'
(focus on result state and causative subject)

gilas-to   bɦaŋ-i   thak-il
tumbler-def. break-conj. STAY-past
'The tumbler suddenly broke.'
(focus on result state and affected object)

The expressions on the left of figure 10.1 are characterizations of the opposing CVs. These characterizations are based on the different temporal and causal parameters along which the structure of situations can vary. What figure 10.1 highlights is the way in which the temporal and causal focus of the situation keeps shifting (exemplified by the expressions on the left) depending on which particular vector verb co-occurs with the main verb.

For the other kind of CV opposition involving the choice of MVs, the temporal–causal perspective suggests a relatively detailed format for capturing the various senses of the vector teased out by different kinds of co-occurring MVs. Figure 10.2 illustrates the polysemic variation of the vector *thak* resulting from the choice of MVs.

MVs 1-3 (*bɔɦi* sit, *mɔr* die and *baz* ring) in figure 10.2 represent three choices open to the vector *thak* STAY, allowing three CVs opposed to one another with regard to the MV constituent: *bɔɦi-i thak*, *mɔr-i thak* and *baz-i thak*, illustrated in the following sentences:

ram   sɔki-khn-ɒt   bɔɦi-i   thak-il
Ram chair-def.loc. sit-conj. STAY-past
'Ram kept sitting on the chair.'
(focus on internal stages of event and affected experiencer)

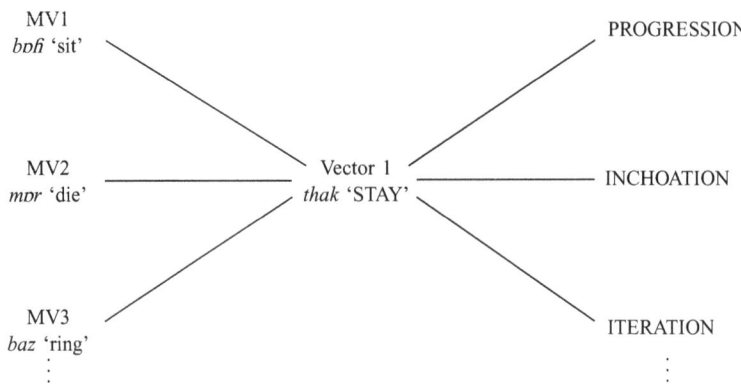

FIGURE 10.2: THE POLYSEMIC VARIATION OF VECTOR VERBS

manuɦ-to mɔr-i   thak-il
man-def. die-conj. STAY-past
'The man suddenly died.'
(focus on result state and affected experiencer)

bel-to   baz-i   thak-il
bell-def. ring-conj. STAY-past
'The bell kept ringing.'
(focus on internal stages of event and affected object)

Table 10.26 is a summary of some of the compound verb stems illustrated so far. The parenthesized comments on the temporal–causal focus provided by them are indicated by a system of two-term labels.

TABLE 10.26: TEMPORAL–CAUSAL FOCUS OF COMPOUND VERBS

Compound verb		Temporal–causal function
Main verb	Vector verb	
bhaŋ-i break-conj.	*za* GO-past	inceptive–affective
bɦaŋ-i break-conj.	*pɛla* THROW	inchoative–causative
bɦaŋ-i break-conj.	*thak* STAY	inchoative–affective
bɔɦ-i sit-conj.	*thak* STAY	progressive–experiencer
mɔr-i die-conj.	*thak* STAY	inchoative–experiencer
baz-i ring-conj.	*thak* STAY	iterative–affective

13 SYNTAX

13.1 Word order

As most of the other Indo-Aryan languages, word-order in Asamiya has the pattern S–O–V. While word-order among the immediate constituents of the sentence is relatively free, Asamiya can be regarded as a head-final language since this characteristic is exemplified in various constructions of the language. For instance, noun modifiers precede the noun, noun phrases precede postpositions and objects precede the verb.

Even though the verb can appear in non-final positions, there are clear phonological and semantic consequences when it does so. Therefore, in addition to contributing to the generalization that heads occur finally, the clause-final position is clearly the unmarked one for verbs.

13.2 Subjects and objects

The nominative subject occurs in transitive sentences. It is overtly marked by the nominative case in transitive sentences, and unmarked in intransitive ones:

ram-e   kitap-khɔn pɔrfi-il-e   (transitive)
Ram-nom. book-def.   read-past.3
'Ram read the book.'

ram   xu-l-e
Ram   sleep-past.3
'Ram slept.'

However, certain intransitive verbs that are, potentially or actually, of the conjunct subtype, take the overt nominative case:

ram-e   bfiɐe kha-l-e   (conjunct verb)
Ram-nom. fear   eat-past.3
'Ram got scared.'

ram-e   xãtur-il-e   (potentially conjunct verb)
Ram-nom. swim-past.3
'Ram swam.'

ram-e   xãtor mar-il-e   (actually conjunct verb)
Ram-nom. swim beat-past.3
'Ram did a swim.'

The accusative subject occurs in sentences with the verb *lag* 'want/need', which is invariably in the third person:

ram-ɒk tɒka   lag-e
Ram-acc. money want-3
'Ram needs money.'

The genitive subject occurs with psychological predicates and in passive constructions. The psychological predicates typically express sensory, mental, emotional and physical experiences and occur in conjunct forms. The genitive subject of these predicates is semantically an experiencer, and lacks volitionality. This semantics of experiencer subjects is congruent with the lack of personal concord with the verb, which is invariably in the third person:

ram-ɒr   khɒŋ uth-is-e
Ram-gen. anger rise-impv.3
'Ram is angry.'

mo-r   sinta fiɔ-is-e
I(obl.)-gen. worry become-impv.3
'I am worried.'

The genitive subject also occurs in passive constructions with complex predicates consisting of a nominalized construction co-occurring with the matrix predicate *fiɒ* 'become'. The matrix verb always takes the third person and the tense is that of the corresponding active sentence:

ram-e   kam-to   kɔr-il-e   (active)
Ram-nom. job-def. do-past.3
'Ram did the job.'

ram-ɒr   kam-to   kɔr-a   fiɔ-l   (passive)
Ram-gen. job-def. do-denom. become-past
'The job was done by Ram.'

ram-e   sɔbi-khɒn kalilɔi   ãk-ib-ɒ
Ram-nom. picture-def. tomorrow draw-fut.3
'Ram will draw the picture tomorrow.'

ram-ɒr   sɔbi-khɒn kalilɔi   ɒ̃k-a   fiɔ-b-ɒ
Ram-gen. picture-def. tomorrow draw-denom. become-fut.3
'The picture will be drawn tomorrow by Ram.'

Objects take the accusative case -(ɒ)k when the referent is a human noun. Otherwise they are not formally marked:

ram-e   mo-k   pafiɔr-is-e
Ram-nom. I(obl.)-acc. forget-impv.3
'Ram has forgotten me.'

ram-e   kɒtha-to   pafiɔr-is-e
Ram-nom. matter-def. forget-impv.3
'Ram has forgotten the matter.'

Even with human noun objects, the referent's identity is relevant. Thus, pronouns and proper nouns regularly take the accusative -(ɒ)k:

bagfi-e   manufi kha-l-e   (referent unidentified)
tiger-nom. man   eat-past.3
'The tiger ate men.'

bagfi-e   manufi-zɒn-ɒk / ram-ɒk   khed-il-e   (referent identified)
tiger-nom. man-def.acc. / Ram-acc. chase-past.3
'The tiger chased the man/Ram.'

13.3 The noun phrase

The basic noun phrase in Asamiya is left branching, with modifiers preceding the noun. The order of the constituents is roughly as below:

ram-ɒr   ei   tini-khɒn dami   kitap
Ram-gen. this three-def. costly book
'these three costly books of Ram'

The numeral definitive can either precede or follow the head noun. When the numeral expression precedes, the referents are unidentified:

> *du-zɒn   manuɦ aɦi-is-e*
> two-def. man   come-impv.3
> 'Some two men have come.'

> *mɒe zi kono pãs-ta   nam bisar-is-õ*
> I   any   five-def. name search-impv.1
> 'I am looking for any five names.'

When the numeral expression follows the head noun with the two forming a numeral compound, the referents are identified:

> *manuɦi-du-zɒn   aɦi-is-e*
> man-two.def.   come-impv.3
> 'The two men have come.'

> *tumi kali   bisɒr-a   kitap-sari-khɒn pa-l-õ*
> you yesterday search-denom. book-four.def. get-past-1
> 'I found the four books you were looking for yesterday.'

Alternatively, the numeral definitive has a partitive function in the post-nominal position:

> *manuɦ du-zɒn   aɦi-is-e*
> man   two-def. come-impv.3
> 'Two of the men have come.'

> *tɒrkari   du-bidɦi-ɦe   an-il-õ   baki-bor-ɒr   bɒr dam*
> vegetables two-kinds.emph. bring-past-1 rest-pldef.gen. very price
> 'I brought just two kinds of vegetables – the rest are very costly.'

The singular numeral expression is indefinite both pre- and post-nominally:

> *ɛ-zɒn   manuɦ aɦi-is-e /   manuɦ ɛ-zɒn   aɦi-is-e*
> one-def. man   come-impv.3 / man   one-def. come-impv.3
> 'A man has come.'

13.4 The verb phrase

In the verbal phrase, the main verb stem occupies the leftmost place, and the places to its right are occupied by members of the categories of aspect, tense and person, in their permissible combinations (12.2.1). The main verb stem can take various forms, ranging from a simple verb root to complex stems consisting of conjunct and compound verb, with or without the causative morpheme. Some of these possibilities are shown in table 10.27.

Modal verbs immediately precede the bound elements of aspect, tense and person. *par* be able/may, *khoz* want, *lag* need/may, *pa* may, *bisar* want, are among the important modal verbs in Asamiya. The concatenation of a modal verb regularly triggers the ante modal suffix *-(i)bɒ* on the preceding verb stem. The following examples illustrate:

TABLE 10.27: MAIN VERB STEM TYPES

		Illustrative examples		
Simple stem	primary intransitive	*bagɒr* fall 'fall'	*kɒm* lessen 'become less'	
	derived transitive	*bɒgɒr-a* fall-caus. 'cause to fall'	*kɒm-a* less-caus. 'cause something to become less'	
	primary transitive			*dfiak* cover 'cover something'
Conjunct stem	primary intransitive	*bagɒr kha* fall eat 'suffer a fall'	*kɒm fiɒ* less become 'become less'	*dfiak kha* cover eat 'become covered'
	primary transitive		*kɒm kɒr* less do 'make something less'	
	derived transitive	*bagɒr khu-a* fall eat.caus. 'cause something to fall'		*dfiak khu-a* cover eat.caus. 'cause something to be covered'
	direct/ indirect causative		*kɒm kɒr-a* less do-caus. 'cause something to become less'	
Simple-compound stem	primary intransitive	*bagɔr-i za* fall-conj.GO 'fall'	*kɔm-i za* lessen-conj.GO 'lessen'	
	derived transitive	*bɒgɒr-a-i di* fall-caus.conj. GIVE 'cause something to fall'	*kɒm-a-i di* lessen-caus.conj. GIVE 'cause something to lessen'	
Conjunct-compound stem	primary intransitive	*bagɒr kha-i za* fall eat-conj. GO 'suffer a fall'	*kɒm fiɔ-i za* less become-conj. GO 'become less'	*dfiak kha-i za* cover eat-conj. GO 'become covered'
	primary transitive		*kɒm kɔr-i di* less do-conj. GIVE 'make something less'	
	direct/ indirect causative	*bagɒr khu-a-i di* fall eat-caus.conj. GIVE 'cause something to fall'	*kɒm kɒr-a-i di* less do-caus.conj. GIVE 'cause something to become less'	*dfiak khu-a-i di* cover eat-caus.conj. GIVE 'cause something to be covered'

ram-e   bakɒs-to daŋ-ibɒ par-e
Ram-nom. box-def. lift-inf. be able-3
'Ram can lift the box.'

ram-e   fiɔri-r   fiɔtuae bakɒs-to daŋ khu-a-i   di-bɒ   par-e
Ram-nom. Hari-gen. by   box-def. lift eat-caus.conj. GIVE-inf. be able-3
'Ram can have the box lifted up by Hari.'

13.5 Clauses

Asamiya allows nominal clauses to be formed by both clause-initial and clause-final subordinators; the subordinate clause is placed rightward or leftward of the verb accordingly. The subordinators *ze* and *buli* are illustrated below:

> *ram-e   bɦab-il-e   (ze) fiɔri   n-afi-e*
> Ram-nom.   think-past.3 sub. Hari   neg.come-3
> 'Ram thought that Hari wouldn't come.'

> *fiɔri n-afi-e   buli ram-e   bɦab-il-e*
> Hari neg.come-3 sub. Ram-nom.   think-past.3
> 'Ram thought that Hari wouldn't come.'

The parentheses around *ze* are meant to signal the optionality of this subordinator, which appears to be a loan translation of English 'that'.

Other devices for forming nominals have been discussed already in the section on non-finite forms (12.2.2).

Relative clauses in Asamiya are formed by gapping – there is no overt indication of the role of the head within the relative clause:

> *kali   ɒfi-a   manufi-zɒn-ɒk ram-e   sin-il-e*
> yesterday come-denom. man-def.acc.   Ram-nom. recognize-past.3
> 'Ram recognized the man who came yesterday.'

Positions not accessible to relativization by gapping (e.g., the possessor) can be relativized by a correlative clause which uses one of the Z-initial relative pronouns:

> *za-r   pɒra kɒtha-to   xun-is-il-õ   xei manufi-zɒn dɦuka-l*
> who-gen. from matter-def. hear-impv.past.1 that man-def.   die-past
> 'The man from whom I heard the story died.'

13.6 Interrogative clauses

There is no auxiliary/wh-movement in the formation of yes–no/wh-questions in Asamiya. For the former, an interrogative particle, *-ne* or *-neki* is cliticized to the finite verb:

> *ram bia-lɔi   za-b-ɒ-ne/neki*
> Ram wedding-dat. go-fut.3.inter.
> 'Will Ram go to the wedding?'

Interrogation is also shown by a rising intonation at the end of the structurally declarative sentence, without *-ne* or *-neki*:

> *ram bia-lɔi   za-b-ɒ*
> Ram wedding-dat. go-fut.3
> 'Will Ram go to the wedding?'

TABLE 10.28: NEGATIVE INTERROGATIVES

Affirmative interrogative	Negative interrogative	Marked negative interrogative
ram-e bfiat kha-b-ɒ-ne Ram-nom.meal eat-fut.3-inter. 'Will Ram have a meal?'	*ram-e bfiat na-kha-e-ne* Ram-nom.meal neg.eat-3-inter. 'Won't Ram have a meal?'	*ram-e bfiat na-kha-b-ɒ-ne* Ram-nom.meal neg.eat-fut.3-inter. 'Won't Ram have a meal (even if I request him)?'
tumi kam-to kɔr-ib-a-ne you work-def. do-fut.2fam.inter. 'Will you do the work?'	*tumi kam-to nɒ-kɒr-a-ne* you work-def. neg.do-2fam.inter. 'Won't you do the work?'	*tumi kam-to nɔ-kɔr-ib-a-ne* you work-def. neg.do-fut.2fam.inter. 'Won't you do the work (even though you are pressed for time)?'
apuni za-b-ɒ-ne you go-fut.2hon.inter. 'Will you go?'	*apuni na-za-e-ne* you neg-go-2hon.inter. 'Won't you go?'	*apuni na-za-b-ɒ-ne* you neg.go-fut.2hon.inter. '(Just because I am not accompanying you) won't you go?'

Wh-questions are formed by replacing the relevant constituent with a K-initial interrogative pronoun that is compatible in terms of animacy, case etc:

ram   gari-t   gɔ-is-e
Ram   car-loc. go-impv.3
'Ram has gone by car.'

ram   kifi-ɒt   gɔ-is-e?
Ram   what-loc. go-impv.3
'In what has Ram gone?' (i.e., how has Ram gone?)

Compared with their affirmative counterparts, negative interrogatives have overtones of expectation. Marked negative interrogatives, formed with dubitative negative forms (table 10.23) express a further dimension of meaning which presupposes a conditional or circumstantial antecedent clause. Examples of both types of negative interrogatives are shown in table 10.28 along with the corresponding affirmative interrogatives.

13.7 Negation

The distinct forms of affirmative and negative third person indefinite pronouns in Asamiya (12.1.4) occur in affirmative and negative sentences:

konoba   afi-is-e   (affirmative)
someone come-impv.3
'Someone has come.'

kono ɒfi-a   n-ae   (negative)
none come-denom. neg.be+3
'No one has come.'

TABLE 10.29: THE NEGATION OF MODAL VERBS

Modal	Affirmative	Negative
khoz	*di-bɒ khuz-il-e* give-inf. want-past.3 'wanted to give'	*di-bɒ nu-khuz-il-e* give-inf. neg.want-past.3 'didn't want to give'
bisar	*kɔr-ibɒ bisar-il-e* do-inf. want-past.3 'wanted to do'	*kɔr-ibɒ ni-bisar-il-e* do-inf. neg.want-past.3 'didn't want to do'
pa *	*za-bɒ pa-e* go-inf. may-3 'would have gone'	*na-za-bɒ pa-e* neg.go-inf. may-3 'wouldn't have gone'
lag **	*kɔr-ibɒ lag-e* do-inf. need/may-3 'needs to do/might do'	*kɔr-ibɒ na-lag-e* do-inf. neg.need-3 'doesn't need to do' *nɔ-kɔr-ibɒ lag-e* neg.do-inf. may-3 'might not do'
par	*pɔrfi-ibɒ par-e* read-inf. may/be able-3 'might read/is able to read'	*nɔ-pɔrfi-ibɒ par-e* neg.read-inf. may-3 'might not read' *pɔrfi-ibɒ no-war-e* read-inf. neg.be able-3 'is not able to read'

* *pa* has limited distribution, and only allows the present indefinite forms
** *lag* allows only the third person forms. Its use in the present imperfective is also rather restricted

ram-e   kiba   kha-b-ɒ   (affirmative)
Ram-nom. something eat-fut.3
'Ram will eat something.'

ram-e   ɛko   na-kha-e   (negative)
Ram-nom. nothing neg.eat-3
'Ram won't eat anything.'

ram-e   karoba-k   dekh-il-e   (affirmative)
Ram-nom. someone(obl.)-acc. see-past.3
'Ram saw someone.'

ram-e   ka-k-o   ne-dekh-il-e   (negative)
Ram-nom. who(obl.)-acc.indef. neg.see-past.3
'Ram didn't see anyone.'

In sequences consisting of the main verb stem + modal verb, the modals behave differently with regard to the placement of the negative marker, as shown in table 10.29.

13.8 Discourse markers

There exist certain 'floating' particles in Asamiya whose functions go beyond the clausal/sentential context. In terms of distribution, these particles are capable of being attached as enclitics to almost all the constituents of a clause, thereby suggesting that the proper level of syntactic operation is that of discourse. More research is required in this area, but the following can be distinguished. In the following sections the neutral sentence generally precedes the sentences that illustrate the various possibilities of focus inherent in the neutral sentence. The context of the focus is provided within parentheses.

13.8.1 The exclusive particle fie

This particle serves to flag the constituent which is the focal point of contrast:

mɒe bɒzar-ɒlɔi gɔ-is-il-õ
I   market-dat. go-impv.past.1
'I had gone to the market.'

(ram nɒ-fiɒe) mɒe-fie bɒzar-ɒlɔi gɔ-is-il-õ
Ram neg.be I-excl. market-dat. go-impv.past.1
'I was the one who had gone to the market (not Ram).'

mɒe (phur-ibɒ-lɔi   nɒ-fiɒe)   bɒzar-ɒlɔi-fie   gɔ-is-il-õ
I   outing-inf.dat neg-be   market-dat.excl.   go-impv.past.1
'I had gone to the market (not for an outing).'

mɒe bɒzar-ɒlɔi gɔ-is-il-õ-fie   (ubfiɔt-ibɒ-r   fiɔ-l-ei)
I   market-dat. go-impv.past.1.excl. return-inf.gen. become-past-emph.
'I had just gone to the market (and it is already time to return).'

13.8.2 The particle to

This particle indicates contradictive focus of the constituent to which it is attached:

mɒe ram-ɒk   ne-dekh-il-õ
I   Ram-acc. neg.see-past.1
'I didn't see Ram.'

mɒe-to ram-ɒk   ne-dekh-il-õ (an-e   fiɒeto   dekh-is-e)
I-contr. Ram-acc. neg.see-past.1 other-nom. possibly see-impv.3
'But I didn't see Ram (maybe someone else did).'

ram-ɒk-to   mɒe ne-dekh-il-õ (fiɔri-k-fie   dekh-il-õ)
Ram-acc.contr. I   neg.see-past.1 Hari-acc.excl. see-past.1
'It wasn't Ram I saw (but I saw Hari).'

ram-ɒk mɒe ne-dekh-il-õ-to   (thak-il-e dekh-il-õ-fiēten)
Ram-acc. I   neg.-see-past-1.contr. stay-past.3 see-past.1.counter.
'But I didn't see Ram (I would have if he were there).'

In interrogative sentences, the particle *to* is attached to the verb, and indicates confirmative focus:

ram   afi-ib-ɒ-to
Ram   come-fut.3.conf.
'Is it certain that Ram will come?'

tɛõ   kam-to   kɒr-is-e-to
he   work-def. do-impv.3.conf.
'Is it certain that he has done the job?'

13.8.3 The remonstrative particle no

The remonstrative particle *no* occurs in interrogative sentences. It suggests that the speaker has some reservation or psychological distance regarding the item highlighted:

ram-e   ki   kam   kɔr-is-e
Ram-nom. what   work do-impv.3
'What work is Ram doing?'

ram-e-no   ki   kam kɔr-is-e   (fiɔri-e-fie   xɒkɒlo sa-is-e)
Ram-nom.rem. what work do-impv.3 Hari-nom.excl. all   see-impv.3
'What work has Ram done? (Surely Hari's the one looking after everything?)'

(agɒte-to   bɔfi-i-e   kha-l-e)   etia ram-e   ki-no   kɔr-is-e
earlier-contr. sit-inf.emph. eat-past.3 now   Ram-nom. what-rem. do-impv.3
'(Having sat idle earlier on,) what work is Ram doing these days?'

ram-e   ki   kɔr-is-e-no   (ta-k-son   bɒfi-a-ke   dɛkh-õ)
Ram-nom. what   do-impv.3.rem.   he(obl.)-acc.contraf. sit-denom.emph. see-1
'What would Ram be doing? (I see him just sitting idle.)'

13.8.4 The particle son

son has a dual function. With verbs in imperative form, it expresses a polite directive function:

apuni   kitap-khɒn pɒrfi-ɒk-son
you(hon.) book-def.   read-2hon(imp.).dir.
'Please read the book.'

Elsewhere *son* expresses contrafactivity, i.e. an attitude that is in contrast with the state of affairs expressed:

ram-e   safi kha-l-e
Ram-nom. tea eat-past.3
'Ram had tea.'

ram-e-son   safi kha-l-e /   ram-e   safi kha-l-e-son
Ram-nom.contraf. tea eat-past.3 / Ram-nom. tea eat-past.3.contraf.

(*etia an   kiba   kha-b-ɒ-ne*)
now other something eat-fut.3.inter.
'Ram has already had tea, (will he have anything else now).'

NOTE

Jyotiprakash Tamuli wrote sections 12 (Morphology) and 13 (Syntax) and the remaining chapter was written by G. C. Goswami.

REFERENCES

Beal, S. (1980) *Buddhist Records of the Western World*, Vol. IV, Reprinted Delhi: Bharatiya Publishing House.
Bloch, B. and Trager, G. L. (1942) *Outline of Linguistic Analysis*, Baltimore: Linguistic Society of America, Waverly Press.
Chatterji, S. K. (1959) 'Assam and India', in *The Heritage of Assam*, Guwahati: Indian History Congress.
—— (1970) *The Origin and Development of the Bengali Language*, 3 vols., London: George Allen and Unwin.
Goswami, G. C. (1963) 'Bāṇīkāntà Kākàtir gàdyàrīti', in *Madhulipi*, published by K. Khakhlari, Guwahati.
—— (1982) *Structure of Assamese*, Guwahati: Gauhati University.
Kakati, B. (1972) *Assamese, Its Formation and Development*, edited and revised by G. C. Goswami, reprint of 2nd edition, Guwahati: Lawyer's Book Stall.
Sharma, D. (1981) *Kāmarūpa Śāsanāvalī*, Guwahati: Assam Publication Board.
Tamuli, J. (1998) *The Compound Verb in Assamese*, Ph.D. dissertation, University of Reading.

FURTHER READING

General and history and development of Asamiya

Barua, B. (1964) *History of Assamese Literature*, Delhi: Sahitya Akademi.
Bora, M. (1981) *The Evolution of Assamese Script*, Jorhat: Asam Sahitya Sabha.
Downs, F. S. (1978) 'Missionaries and the language controversy in Assam', *Journal of the University of Gauhati*, Vol. XXVIII–XXIX, Arts: 122–59.
Goswami, U. (1970) *A Study on Kāmarūpī: A dialect of Assamese*, Guwahati: Department of Historical and Antiquarian Studies.
—— (1978) *An Introduction to Assamese*, Guwahati: Mani Manik Prakash.
Grierson, G. A. (1903–28) *Linguistic Survey of India* Vol. 5 Part I, Calcutta. Reprinted Delhi: 1968: Motilal Banarsidass.
Hazarika, B. (1985) *Assamese Language: Origin and Development*, Guwahati: Joya Publication.
Kakati, B. (ed.) (1950) *Aspects of Early Assamese Literature*, Guwahati: Gauhati University.

Medhi, Kaliram (1936) *Assamese Grammar and Origin of the Assamese Language*, Guwahati: Kaliram Medhi, Panbazar, Guwahati.

Moral, D. (1996) 'North-east India as a linguistic area', *Mon Khmer Journal of S. E. Asian Languages*, Vol. 27.

Pattanayak, D. (1966) *A Controlled Historical Reconstruction of Oriya, Assamese, Bengali and Hindi*, Mouton: The Hague.

Sen, N. (1978) *Caryāgīti Koṣ*, Kalyani: Dipali Sen.

Verma, T. P. (1976) *Development of Script in Ancient Kāmarūpa*, Jorhat: Asam Sahitya Sabha.

STRUCTURE AND GRAMMAR

Bora, S. (1964) *Bahal Vyākaraṇ*, Guwahati: Jnananath Bora, 2, Earle Road.

Chowdhary, R. (1995a) *Assamese Verbs: A Study in the Structural Paradigm*, Guwahati: Anundoram Barooah Institute of Language Art and Culture.

—— (1995b) 'On some aspects of reflexivization in Assamese', *Gauhati University Journal of Arts*, Vol. XXXVII: 130–40.

Dutta Baruah, P. N. (1978) *A Comparative Analysis of the Morphological Aspect of Assamese and Oriya*, Ph.D. dissertation, Gauhati University.

—— (1980) *An Intensive Course in Assamese*, Mysore: Central Institute of Indian Languages.

—— (1994) *A Contrastive Analysis of the Syntactic Aspects of Assamese and Bengali*, Ph.D. dissertation, Mysore University.

Goswami, G. C. (1959) 'Assamese verb morphology: derivation', *Journal of the University of Gauhati*, Vol. X, Arts: Guwahati.

—— (1966) *An Introduction to Assamese Phonology*, Poona: Deccan College.

—— (1968) 'Classifiers and quantifiers in Assamese' in *Studies in Indian Linguistics*, Poona: Deccan College.

—— (1971) 'Eastern and central Assamese dialects', *The Assam Academy Review*, New Series 1, Guwahati.

—— (1993) *Asamīyā Vyākaraṇar Maulik Bicār*, Guwahati: Bina Library.

—— (2000) *Asamīyā Vyākaraṇ Praveś*, Guwahati: Bina Library.

Goswami, U. (1975) 'A grammatical sketch of Assamese', in A. Mitra, Registrar-General of India (ed.) *Grammatical Sketches of Indian Languages with Comparative Vocabulary and Text*. Calcutta: A. Mitra.

—— (1981)) *Asamīyā Bhāṣār Vyākaraṇ*, Guwahati: Mani Manik.

Mahanta, R. K. (1970) *Assamese in the Firthian Model of Analysis*, Ph.D. dissertation, University of London.

—— (1976) 'The category of case in Assamese: a phonological study', *Journal of the University of Gauhati*, XXVI–XXVII: Arts: 79–94.

Moral, D. (1992) *Phonology of Asamiya Dialects: Contemporary Standard and Mayong*, Ph.D. dissertation, Poona: Deccan College Post Graduate and Research Institute.

—— (1996) 'Consonant gemination and compensatory lengthening in Asamiya dialects: contemporary standard and central Assam', in *Pan Asiatic Linguistics*, Vol. I, Salaya, Thailand: Institute of Language and Culture for Rural Development, Mahidol University: 151–63.

Tamuli, J. (1995) 'Aspect and the Assamese verb', *Gauhati University Journal of Arts*, Vol. XXXVII: 31–43.

DICTIONARIES

Barua, Hemchandra (1998) *Hema-Kosha: Assamese–English Dictionary*, 10th edition, Guwahati: Hemakosha Printers and Publishers.

Deka, P. (1990) *Jyoti Dvibhāṣik Abhidhān* (English–Assamese), 1st edition, Guwahati: P. Deka, Kanvacal Road, Guwahati.

Gauhati University (1962) *Chandrakānta Abhidhān*, 2nd edition, Guwahati.

Publication Board, Assam (1994) *Ādhunik Asamīyā Abhidhān*, Revised edition, Guwahati.

CHAPTER ELEVEN

ORIYA

Tapas S. Ray

CONTENTS

LIST OF TABLES

1 BACKGROUND

Oriya, called *oḍia* by native speakers, is the official language of the eastern Indian state of Orissa. It is one of the eighteen languages specified in the Eighth Schedule of the Constitution of India.

According to the 1991 Census, there are 28 million speakers of Oriya in India. The major concentration of Oriya speakers has been reported from Orissa. According to the 1991 Census, 93.33% of the Oriya speakers live in Orissa. The other states which have reported more than a hundred thousand Oriya speakers are: Madhya Pradesh (721,348), Bihar (404,443), Andhra Pradesh (259,947), West Bengal (170,001) and Assam (140,782). In Andhra Pradesh, the Oriyas have mainly settled in the neighbouring coastal areas. In Madhya Pradesh, their largest concentration is in the Chhattisgarh basin. A large number of Oriyas have migrated to Calcutta and its suburbs, and the Damodar Valley, where they work in factories. Plantations in North Bengal Terai, the Assam foothills, upper Brahmaputra Valley, Cachar and Tripura have also attracted many Oriyas (Breton 1997: 95).

Oriya belongs to the eastern group of the Indo-Aryan family and is believed to have developed from Magadhan Apabhramsha (Chatterjee 1926: 105–8). Bangla, Assamese, Magahi, Maithili and Bhojpuri are the other languages which belong to the Magadhan subfamily. Of these, Bangla and Assamese are considered to be the closest to Oriya.

Traces of Oriya words and expressions have been found in inscriptions dating from the seventh century AD. For example, the Oriya word *kumbharɔ* 'potter' occurs in a copperplate inscription 'belonging to a date not later than the seventh century AD' (Tripathi 1962: 2). Similarly, in inscriptions of 991 AD Oriya words like *bhituru* 'from inside' and *pɔndɔrɔ* 'fifteen' (Tripathi 1962: 2–3) can be found. 'An Oriya passage' also has been found in another inscription of about 715 AD (Tripathi 1962: 383, Pattanayak 1969: 127).

Like most other languages, Oriya has been enriched by inheritance from the ancestral languages and also by borrowings from other languages. The contribution of both the sources can be easily seen in the vocabulary of the language. In the context of the Indo-Aryan languages, however, the normal practice is to analyse the sources of vocabulary under four headings: *tatsama*, *tadbhava*, *deśaja* and *videśi*. A *tatsama* is a word which has the same form as it has in Sanskrit. In practice, however, *tatsama* is used for a word which has the same spelling (but not necessarily the same pronunciation) as in Sanskrit. The following are a few examples of *tatsama* words in Oriya: *ɔgni* 'fire', *nɔgɔrɔ* 'city', *nɔdi* 'river', *hɔsti* 'elephant', *citrɔ* 'picture', *kɔrmɔ* 'action'.

A *tadbhava* is a word which, having originated from old Indo-Aryan, now has a different form. The following are some examples of *tadbhava* words in Oriya: *kaṭhɔ* 'wood', *kanɔ* 'ear', *nacɔ* 'dance', *hati* 'elephant', *machɔ* 'fish', *miṭha* 'sweet'.

Deśaja words can neither be easily related to Sanskrit nor to any foreign language like English, Arabic, etc. These words are believed to have originated locally but have been used in Oriya for ages. The following are some examples of *deśaja* words in Oriya: *goḍɔ* 'leg', *mɔlatɔ* 'cover', *cerɔ* 'root', *kuṭa* 'straw', *khaṇṭi* 'pure', *ṭapɔra* 'joke'. *Deśaja* words also include words assimilated into Oriya from Dravidian and Austroasiatic languages, since Oriya has always come in close contact with both these groups of languages. Before Orissa became an independent state, the southern districts of Orissa were part of the Madras Presidency. From the twelfth to the fifteenth century AD, Orissa was ruled over by the kings of the Ganga dynasty, who came from Dravidian-speaking areas. Austroasiatic languages are spoken by the tribals living in Orissa. The following are some examples of Oriya words which are believed to have originated from Dravidian and Austroasiatic languages: *pila* 'child', *sanɔ* 'small', *bilɔ* 'field' (Dravidian); *baṭi* 'pot', *boka* 'foolish', *koḍi* 'twenty' (Austroasiatic).

Videśi words are those which are believed to have come from foreign languages like Persian, Arabic, Turkish, English and Portuguese. Perso-Arabic words are likely to have entered Oriya when Orissa was under the Mogul administration. English words must have entered during the British rule. Portuguese words are believed to have been borrowed through trade and commerce. The following are some examples of foreign words in Oriya (these and the earlier examples of *tatsama*, *tadbhava* and *deśaja* words are from Mohanty 1970, Mahapatra and Das 1978, Padhi 1988, Pradhan et al. 1995, Mahapatra 1997, Sarangi 1998): *gɔribɔ* 'poor', *mɔida* 'flour', *cɔsɔma* 'spectacles' (Persian); *kɔlija* 'liver', *umɔrɔ* 'age', *ɔkɔlɔ* 'intelligence' (Arabic); *kuli* 'coolie', *caku* 'knife', *bɔburci* 'cook' (Turkish); *kɔp* 'cup', *ṭebul* 'table', *kɔlej* 'college' (English); *acarɔ* 'pickles', *tɔmakhu* 'tobacco', *balti* 'bucket' (Portuguese).

Different languages have not only contributed to the growth of the Oriya language, but they are also partly responsible for stylistic and dialectal variations within the language. Stylistically, two varieties within the Oriya language that have been usually distinguished are formal and informal. One notable difference between the two varieties is that the former makes a greater use of *tatsama* words than the latter (see Mahapatra et al. 1989: 388). The formal variety is restricted to formal writings and speeches. But, even in these domains, the formal variety is gradually being replaced by a less formal variety, which is seen as a 'compromise' between the formal and informal varieties (see Mahapatra 1984; Mahapatra et al. 1989: 389).

Dialectally, there seem to be four major varieties: standard dialect spoken in the districts of Cuttack, Puri and surrounding areas, Western (or Sambalpuri) dialect spoken in western Orissa, Southern dialect spoken in southern Orissa, and Northern (or Baleswari) dialect spoken in northern Orissa (Dhall 1957, Mahapatra et al. 1989: 388). The three non-standard dialects are spoken in areas adjoining the three neighbouring states where these languages are spoken: Telugu in the south, Hindi in the west, and Bangla in the north. This chapter will describe the standard dialect.

2 SCRIPT

The modern Oriya script, like the Devanagari script, is a descendant of the Brahmi script. It is related to the Brahmi script through the following intermediate states: (i) transitional Oriya, (ii) Proto-Oriya, (iii) *Kuṭila*, and (iv) Gupta scripts (Tripathi 1962: 32).

Oriya letters are quite distinctive in their appearance. Unlike Devanagari and Bangla letters, they do not hang from a horizontal line. In place of a horizontal line there is a half-circle. This quality of the Oriya script seems to have developed from writing on palm leaves, which were basic writing material in the earlier times. Palm leaves being extremely fragile, drawing horizontal lines on them while writing was avoided to save the leaves from splitting (Grierson 1903: 375). In another view, however, this quality of the Oriya letters is seen as an influence of the Dravidian writing system (Mohanty 1996: 25–31).

Unlike English writing, there is a great deal of correspondence between Oriya writing and pronunciation. This correspondence, however, is not total. To cite a few examples: there are two letters ଶ and ଯ, called *bɔrgyɔ jɔ* and *ɔntɔsthɔ jɔ*, respectively. Both, however, are usually pronounced alike. ଶ and ଯ have separate historical sources. ଯ has the same source as the letter ୟ, which is called *yɔ*. Usually, ୟ does not occur in word-initial positions, where ଯ occurs. There are, however, some exceptions. Similarly, there are three letters in Oriya for the three sibilant sounds: ସ for dental [s], ଶ for palatal [š] and ଷ for retroflex [ṣ]. However, in common Oriya speech, all the three are pronounced alike.

Oriya letters for consonant sounds are always pronounced with the inherent vowel [ɔ]. For example, କ, the letter for the sound [k], is usually read as [kɔ] and ପ, the letter for the sound [p], is usually read as [pɔ]. When a letter for a consonant sound is to be pronounced without this inherent vowel, a special diacritic called *holɔnt* is used as a guide to pronunciation. In other words, when କ, the letter for the sound [k], occurs without any combining form used for vowel sounds or without any diacritic, it is to be pronounced as [kɔ]. But when it occurs with the diacritic *holɔnt,* it is to be pronounced as [k]. Thus କ and କ୍ are to be pronounced as [kɔ] and [k], respectively. In practice, however, the use of this diacritic is not very common. For example, a word like ଚୁପ୍ *cup* 'keep quiet' will be pronounced [cup] whether ପ, the letter for the sound [p], is used with or without the diacritic *holɔnt.*

In Oriya, there are also independent letters representing vowels. The letters are used when a syllable begins with a vowel sound, e.g. for ଆ [a] in ଆସ୍ *as* 'come', or consists of only a vowel sound, as for [a] in ଆ *a* 'come'. In other cases, the combining forms are used. For example, for the vowel [a] in କାମ *kamɔ* 'work' a combining form is used. (The vertical line after କ in କାମ *kamɔ* is the combining form for the vowel [a].) But with neither the letter nor the combining form, there is one-to-one correspondence between the sound and the letter or form. For example, there are separate letters as well as combining forms for long and short vowels. In common speech, however, both are usually pronounced alike. For example, the [i] sound in ଭାଇ *bhai* 'brother' is represented by the letter ଇ, called 'small i'. The [i] sound in ଗାଈ *gai* 'cow' is represented by a different letter ଈ, called 'long i'. Both are, however, usually pronounced alike. Similarly, there are two letters and combining forms for the two diphthongs [ɔi] and [ɔu]. In common speech, however, the letter or combining form for a diphthong is often pronounced as two monophthongs.

In Oriya orthography, special characters are usually used to represent consonant clusters. Like the letters for consonant sounds, these characters are supposed to be pronounced with the inherent vowel [ɔ], if they occur without any combining form used for vowel sounds or without the diacritic *holɔ nt*. For example, ସ୍କ, the special character used for [sk], is supposed to be read as [skɔ], unless it occurs with a combining form for a vowel sound or the diacritic *holɔ nt*.

These special characters usually consist of a letter and one or two combining forms. For example, ସ୍କ, the special character used for [skɔ], consists of ସ, the letter used for [sɔ] and a combining form for କ [kɔ]. ଷ୍ଟ୍ର, the special character used for [ṣṭrɔ], consists of ଷ, the letter used for [ṣɔ] and combining forms used for ଟ [tɔ] and ର [rɔ]. Since the letter for [ṣɔ] is usually pronounced as [sɔ], the special character meant for [ṣṭrɔ] is usually read as [stro]. ସ୍ତ୍ର, the special character used for [strɔ], consists of ସ, the letter used for [sɔ] and a combining form for ତ୍ର [trɔ]. In most cases, the first consonant in a consonant cluster is represented by a letter, and the other consonant(s) by combining form(s). In some cases, however, the first consonant is represented by a combining form. For example, ର୍ଗ, the special character used for [rgɔ], consists of ଗ, the letter for [gɔ] and a combining form for [r]. Thus, while [rgɔ] is written as ର୍ଗ, [grɔ] is written as ଗ୍ର.

The special characters for consonant clusters, however, do not always consist of a letter and one or two combining forms. Some of them are actually special letters, which do not contain any combining form. For example, ଣ୍ଡ, the special character used for [ndɔ], does not contain any combining form.

3 PHONOLOGY

Table 11.1 lists the sounds which are considered to be the segmental phonemes of standard Oriya (see Pattanayak 1966, Pattanayak and Das 1972, Mahapatra et al. 1989: 389, Pradhan et al. 1995).

All the vowels listed in table 11.1, except /o/, can be nasalized and the nasalized vowels contrast with their oral counterparts: *nia* 'take-suffix', *niã* 'fire'; *diɔ* '(you) give', *diɔ̃* 'deity'; *kua* 'crow', *kuã* 'tender branch of a tree'. Nasalized vowels, however, do not always contrast with their oral counterparts (Pattanayak 1959: 163 and 1966: 16).

Of the six vowels listed in table 11.1, /o/ is found to have a restricted distribution. It rarely occurs in word-final position. Even in initial and medial syllables, it sometimes freely varies with /u/ or /ɔ/: *koɳɔ* / *kɔɳɔ* 'corner', *mote* / *mɔte* 'me', *pɔkoḍi* / *pɔkuḍi* 'fritter', *bhugoḷɔ* / *bhugɔḷɔ* 'geography', *bɔndobɔstɔ* / *bɔndɔbɔstɔ* 'arrangement' (Mohanty 1986: 12).

Most Oriya words end with a vowel sound. This becomes obvious when a comparison is made with cognate languages: *ghɔrɔ* (Oriya) and *ghɔr* (Bangla) 'house/room', *phulɔ* (Oriya) and *phul* (Bangla) 'flower', *dinɔ* (Oriya) and *din* (Bangla) 'day' (Bhattacharya 1993: 50). Words ending with consonant sounds are, however, not rare in Oriya. A number of borrowed words, imperative verbs, and other words end with a consonant sound. But there are also many instances of the vowel /ɔ/ being added to borrowed words ending with consonant sounds: *dokanɔ* (Oriya) from *dukan* (Persian) 'shop', *nɔrɔmɔ*

TABLE 11.1: PHONEMES OF ORIYA

Vowels

	Front	Centre	Back
High	i		u
Mid	e		o
Low		a	ɔ

Consonants

	Labial	Dental	Retroflex	Palatal	Velar	Glottal
Stop Voiceless Unaspirated	p	t	ṭ	c	k	
Stop Voiceless Aspirated	ph	th	ṭh	ch	kh	
Stop Voiced Unaspirated	b	d	ḍ	j	g	
Stop Voiced Aspirated	bh	dh	ḍh	jh	gh	
Nasal	m	n	ṇ		ŋ	
Flap		r				
Lateral		l	ḷ			
Fricative		s				h
Semivowel	w			y		

(Oriya) from *nərm* (Persian) 'soft', *ḍaktərɔ* (Oriya) from *doctor* (English), *bhoṭɔ* (Oriya) from *vote* (English) (Mohanty 1986: 36). For certain words, both types of pronunciations are heard, i.e. with and without the word-final /ɔ/. For example, *kɔlɔmɔ* and *kɔlɔm* 'pen', *kɔbaṭɔ* and *kɔbaṭ* 'door', *nɔrɔmɔ* and *nɔrɔm* 'soft', *ḍaktərɔ* and *ḍaktɔr* 'doctor', *sundɔrɔ* and *sundɔr* 'beautiful'. For certain words, pronunciations are also heard with and without word-medial /ɔ/. For example, *sɔrɔkar* and *sɔrkar* 'government', *dɔrɔkari* and *dɔrkari* 'necessary', *bɔdɔ mas* and *bɔdmas* 'wicked', *malɔpua* and *malpua* 'a type of sweet'.

Now, coming to the consonant phonemes listed in table 11.1, it must be noted that there is some disagreement regarding the phonemic status of the velar nasal /ŋ/ and also regarding the description of certain phonemes. For example, in some descriptions, /r/, /l/ and /s/ are considered to be alveolar phonemes and /w/ to be a labio-velar phoneme.

Most consonant phonemes listed in table 11.1 occur word-initially. The consonants which do not occur word-initially are: /ṇ,ŋ,ḷ/. If, in a consonant cluster, a nasal consonant occurs as the first member and a stop as the second member, the nasal consonant is pronounced as a homorganic nasal (Pattanayak 1966: 15–16).

Aspirated stops rarely occur in consecutive syllables. Retroflex stops, particularly the voiced ones, do not usually occur in consecutive syllables (see Mahapatra et al. 1989: 359). Voiced retroflex stops /ḍ/ and /ḍh/ have flap allophones [ṛ] and [ṛh], respectively. The flap allophones occur intervocalically and word-finally (Pattanayak 1966: 15). The following are some examples of the occurrence of the allophonic variants of the retroflex stops: *ḍɔrɔ* 'fear', *pɔṇḍitɔ* 'scholar', *ḍhɔmɔna* 'a type of snake', *kuṇḍheiba* 'to embrace' (voiced retroflex stops); *baṛɔ* 'fence', *chaṛ* '(you) leave', *daṛhi* 'beard', *baṛh* '(you) serve' (flap allophones). Notice in the examples given for flap allophones that the allophones ([ṛ] and [ṛh]) occur either intervocalically or word-finally.

There are, however, certain exceptions. For example, *cɔṛcɔṛi* 'lightning' and *ghɔṛghɔṛi* 'thunder'. These exceptions have been explained by assuming that *cɔṛcɔṛi* and *ghɔṛghɔṛi* are underlyingly *cɔṛɔcɔṛi* and *ghɔṛɔghɔṛi*, respectively (Mohanty 1986: 30–7). This assumption has been made on the basis of the observation that these words were earlier pronounced as and even now are pronounced by some speakers as *cɔṛɔcɔṛi* and *ghɔṛɔghɔṛi*.

Although flap allophones occur intervocalically, they do not occur morpheme-initially: *niḍɔrɔ* 'fearless', *sudhɔḷɔ* 'beautifully proportioned'. *niḍɔrɔ* consists of the morphemes *ni* and *ḍɔrɔ*, *sudhɔḷɔ* consists of *su* and *ḍhɔḷɔ* (Mohanty 1986: 37–8).

In loanwords, retroflex stops can occur intervocalically: *reḍio* 'radio'; *biḍio* 'B.D.O., i.e. Block Development Officer' (Bhattacharya 1993: 30). Some speakers, however, use a flap allophone even in these loanwords, e.g. *reṛio* and *biṛio*.

Deaspiration is another interesting aspect of the Oriya sound system. A consonant is often deaspirated by many speakers if it is preceded by a syllable consisting of /s/ and a vowel, and followed by a vowel. For example, *subhila / subila* 'heard', *sijha / sija* 'boiled', *sujhibɔ / sujibɔ* 'will repay' (Mohanty 1986: 41–51). There are, however, exceptions to the pattern observed in the preceding examples. For example, *sidha* 'straight' is never pronounced as *sida*.

A consonant is also often deaspirated by many speakers when it is preceded by /s/ and followed by a vowel (Mohanty 1986: 45–6). For example, *pruṣṭha / pruṣṭa* 'page', *upɔsthit / upɔstit* 'present', *ɔbɔsthitɔ / ɔbɔstitɔ* 'situated'.

Another speaker-variation that is noticed in Oriya is concerned with the use of geminate consonants (see Pattanayak and Das 1972: 15). In the speech of some speakers, geminate consonants contrast with single consonants. For example, *mɔllɔ* 'wrestler' and *mɔlɔ* '(you) died', *pɔṭṭɔ* 'silk' and *pɔṭɔ* 'side', *mɔlli* 'a type of flower' and *mɔli* '(I) died'. In the speech of many other speakers, however, the geminate consonants are usually replaced by a single consonant.

4 GRAMMAR

4.1 Nominal forms and categories

4.1.1 Gender

Oriya does not have grammatical gender. It is not like Hindi, in which every noun belongs to a grammatical gender, masculine or feminine. In Oriya, gender is basically used for semantic purposes, that is, to distinguish a male member of a class from its female member. For example, different forms are used to distinguish a male teacher (*sikhyɔkɔ*) from a female teacher (*sikhyɔyɔtri*) or a male doctor (*ḍaktɔr*) from a female doctor (*ḍaktɔraṇi*). Feminine forms of nouns and adjectives are usually derived from their masculine forms by using suffixes like /-a/, /-i/, /-ṇi/, /-aṇi/, /-uṇi/, etc. For example, *dusṭa* (F) from *dusṭɔ* (M) 'wicked', *sundɔri* (F) from *sundɔrɔ* (M) 'beautiful', *muliaṇi* (F) from *mulia* (M) 'labourer', *barikaṇi* (F) from *barikɔ* (M) 'barber', *bhikharuṇi* (F) from *bhikhari* (M) 'beggar'.

Feminine forms are not available for all adjectives. A few examples of such adjectives are: *bhɔlɔ* 'good', *khɔrap* 'bad', *bɔḍɔ* 'big', *sanɔ* 'small', *kamika* 'hardworking', *pɔrisrɔmi* 'industrious'. These adjectives can be used with both masculine and feminine nouns. The following examples illustrate this.

bɔḍɔ	*puɔ*		*bɔḍɔ*	*jhiɔ*
eldest	son		eldest	daughter
'eldest son'			'eldest daughter'	
pɔrisrɔmi	*baḷɔkɔ*		*pɔrisrɔmi*	*baḷika*
industrious	boy		industrious	girl
'industrious boy'			'industrious girl'	

Even where feminine forms of adjectives are available, masculine forms can be used with feminine nouns. This is illustrated by the following examples.

(1) *mũ goṭe sundɔrɔ   jhiɔ dekh -il -i*
     I   one beautiful (M) girl see   PST 1P SG
     'I saw a beautiful girl.'

(2) *mũ goṭe sundɔri   jhiɔ dekh -il -i*
     I   one beautiful (F) girl see   PST 1P SG
     'I saw a beautiful girl.'

It is interesting to note that (1) is more commonly used than (2). Although masculine adjectives are often used with feminine nouns there are a few exceptions to it (see Mohanty 1986).

Personal pronouns in Oriya are not marked for masculine or feminine gender. Irrespective of whether one is referring to a man or a woman, the same pronoun is used. Personal pronouns are, however, sensitive to status/familiarity differences and differences between humans and non-humans. Table 11.2 lists some of the singular personal pronouns which are commonly used in Oriya.

TABLE 11.2: SINGULAR PERSONAL PRONOUNS

Person	Human / Non-human	Honorificity	Distal/Proximal	Pronoun
First	–	–	–	mũ
Second	–	Non-honorific	–	tu
		Mid-honorific	–	tume
		Honorific	–	apɔnɔ
Third	Human	Non-honorific	Distal	se
			Proximal	ye
		Honorific	Distal	se
			Proximal	ye
	Non-human	–	Distal	seiṭa
			Proximal	eiṭa

First person pronouns are not usually marked for status/familiarity differences. But second person pronouns are marked for a three-way distinction for familiarity/status or honorificity: non-honorific, mid-honorific and honorific. Non-honorific pronouns are usually used for younger relatives or socially 'inferior' people, mid-honorific for equals and friends, and honorific for older relatives and socially 'superior' people. Third person pronouns are marked for human and non-human differences, and human third person pronouns for a further two-way distinction for familiarity or honorificity: honorific and non-honorific. The honorificity differences for third person pronouns are not shown overtly on the pronouns. They are shown, in sentences, on the verbal agreement markers (see 4.2.2). Deictically, third person pronouns are also marked for proximal and distal differences. For non-deictic references, the distal pronoun is used. It may be noted here that human and non-human pronouns are not strictly used for humans and non-humans, respectively. A human pronoun may be used for a pet dog out of affection, similarly a non-human pronoun may be used for a person to show disrespect.

4.1.2 Number

The Oriya grammatical system has two numbers: singular and plural. The suffixes that are commonly used for pluralizing human and non-human nouns are *-mane* and *-guḍikɔ* or *-guḍakɔ*, respectively. For example, *ḍaktɔrmane* 'doctors' and *bɔhiguḍikɔ* 'books'. It is also possible to use *-guḍikɔ* or *-guḍakɔ* with human nouns, who are not held with respect in the society. For example, *pilaguḍakɔ* 'children' and *corɔguḍakɔ* 'thieves'. If *-guḍikɔ* or *-guḍakɔ* is used with people who are held with respect it may imply disrespect or even pity:

bɔdɔmas ḍaktɔr-guḍakɔ	*bicɔra ḍaktɔr-guḍakɔ*
wicked doctor PL	poor doctor PL
'wicked doctors'	'poor doctors'

It is, however, impossible to use *-mane* with inanimate nouns: **bɔhimane* 'books'.

Words like *sɔbu* 'all' and numbers like *dui jɔnɔ* 'two (person)' or *tiniṭa* 'three-suffix' can also be used to pluralize nouns. They can be used either before the noun or after the noun:

sɔbu bɔhi	*bɔhi sɔbu*
all book	book all
'all books'	'all books'

dui jɔnɔ ḍaktɔr	*ḍaktɔr dui jɔnɔ*
two person doctor	doctor two person
'two doctors'	'two doctors'

tini-ṭa kukurɔ	*kukurɔ tini-ṭa*
three SFX dog	dog three SFX
'three dogs'	'three dogs'

A numeral with the suffix -ṭa or -ṭi is usually used with non-human nouns. It is, however, possible to use it with a human noun, although it will imply disrespect to the persons referred to: *tiniṭa ḍaktɔr* 'three doctors'. But it is impossible to use a numeral with *jɔnɔ* with a non-human noun: **dui jɔnɔ gai* 'two cows'.

Some pronouns are also pluralized with the help of suffixes like *-mane* and *-guḍikɔ* and words like *sɔbu*, *dui jɔnɔ* and *tiniṭa*. As with the nouns, *-mane* or a numeral with *jɔnɔ* is used with only human pronouns, and *-guḍikɔ* or *-guḍakɔ* or a numeral with the suffix *-ṭa* or *-ṭi* is usually used with non-human pronouns: *se* 'he/she', *semane* 'they', *se dui jɔnɔ* 'they two', *seguḍikɔ* 'those', *se tiniṭa* 'those three', *se sɔbu* 'all of those'. However, unlike nouns, pronouns cannot follow words like *sɔbu*, *tini jɔnɔ* or *tiniṭa*: **sɔbu se*, **tiniṭa se*, **tini jɔnɔ se*.

Count nouns without any suffixes clearly express neither singularity nor plurality. For example, in (1), it is not clear whether one book or more than one book is to be bought.

(1)   *se   bɔhi kiṇ-iba-ku   ja -u   -ch -ø   -i*
      he/she book buy SFX to   go PROG AUX PRES 3P SG NON-HON
      'He/she NON-HON is going to buy a book/books.'

To express singularity unambiguously, suffixes like *-ṭa, -ṭe, -ṭi, -ṭae, -ṭie* and numerals like *goṭe* 'one' or *jɔne* 'one person' are used. Numerals can be used before or after the noun. *goṭe* can be used with either non-human or human nouns. But *jɔne* must be used only with human nouns. The following examples illustrate this.

bɔhi-ṭe	*goṭe sapɔ*	*pila jɔne*
book INDEF	one snake	child one (person)
'a book'	'one snake'	'one child'

For numerals, Oriya uses the well-known decimal-positional system. Table 11.3 lists some examples of how numerals are written and read in Oriya.

Some numerals are also read slightly differently from what has been indicated in table 11.3. For example, ୧ is read both as *ek* and *ekɔ* 'one', ୩ as *tin* and *tini* 'three' and ୪ as *car* and *cari* 'four'.

The numerals from 11 to 18, from 21 to 28, from 31 to 38 and so on are usually expressed in words as one to eight (plus) ten, one to eight (plus) twenty, one to eight (plus) thirty, respectively. Thus, as shown in the examples, the Oriya word for 31 is *ektiris*, where *ek*, the first part of the word refers to one and *tiris*, the second part of the word, refers to thirty. Numerals such as 19, 29, 39 and so on, to 99 are, however, expressed in words as 'prefix-twenty', 'prefix-thirty', 'prefix-forty' ... and 'prefix-one hundred', respectively. Thus the Oriya word for 39 is *ɔncaḷis*, where *ɔn*, the first part of the word is a prefix and *caḷis*, the second part of the word refers to forty. Similarly, forty-one in Oriya is *ekcaḷis*, literally 'one-forty', but forty-nine is *ɔnpɔcas* 'prefix-fifty'.

TABLE 11.3: ORIYA NUMERALS

Arabic numerals	Oriya numerals (in figures)	Oriya numerals (in words)
0	୦	sun
1	୧	ek
2	୨	dui
3	୩	tin
4	୪	car
5	୫	panc
6	୬	chɔ
7	୭	sat
8	୮	aṭh
9	୯	nɔ
10	୧୦	dɔs
11	୧୧	egarɔ
20	୨୦	koḍie
21	୨୧	ekois
30	୩୦	tiris
31	୩୧	ektiris
40	୪୦	caḷis
41	୪୧	ekcaḷis
50	୫୦	pɔcas
51	୫୧	ekabɔn
60	୬୦	saṭhie
61	୬୧	eksɔṭhi
70	୭୦	sɔturi
71	୭୧	ekɔstɔri
80	୮୦	ɔsi
81	୮୧	ekaɔsi
90	୯୦	nɔbe
91	୯୧	ekanɔbe
100	୧୦୦	sɔhe/ekɔ sɔhɔ
101	୧୦୧	sɔhe ek/ekɔ sɔhɔ ek
371	୩୭୧	tini sɔhɔ ekɔstɔri
1,000	୧,୦୦୦	hɔjare/ekɔ hɔjar
4,650	୪,୬୫୦	cari hɔjar chɔ sɔhɔ pɔcas
10,000	୧୦,୦୦୦	ɔyute/ekɔ ɔyutɔ
1,00,000	୧,୦୦,୦୦୦	lɔkhe/ekɔ lɔkhyɔ
10,00,000	୧୦,୦୦,୦୦୦	niyute/ekɔ niyutɔ
1,00,00,000	୧,୦୦,୦୦,୦୦୦	koṭie/ekɔ koṭi

There are, however, certain exceptions. For example, although 20 is called *koḍie*, 19 is not called **ɔnkoḍie*. It is called *uṇeis*, where *is* refers to 20. Similarly, 21 is not called **ekkoḍie*, but *ekois*, where *is* also refers to 20. As a matter of fact, *koḍie* does not occur in any of the words used for the numerals from 21 and 28. All of them have *is* instead.

Numerals from 101 to 999 are expressed in words as a *sɔhɔ* 'hundred' or a multiple of *sɔhɔ* (plus) the remaining number. Thus, as shown in table 11.3, a numeral such as 371 is expressed in words as *tini* 'three' *sɔhɔ* 'hundred' *ekɔstɔri* 'seventy-one'. Similarly, numerals which are more than a *hɔjarɔ* 'thousand' but less than a *lɔkhyɔ* 'hundred thousand' are usually expressed in words as a *hɔjarɔ* or a multiple of *hɔjarɔ* (plus) the remaining number. Thus, as shown in the table, a numeral such as 4650 is expressed in words as *cari* 'four' *hɔjar* 'thousand' *chɔ* 'six' *sɔhɔ* 'hundred' *pɔcas* 'fifty'.

Although the words *ɔyutɔ* (10,000) and *niyutɔ* (10,00,000) have been used in the table, they are rarely used in Oriya. An *ɔyutɔ* is usually expressed as a multiple of *hɔjarɔ* 'thousand' and a *niyutɔ* as a multiple of *lɔkhyɔ* 'lakh'. Thus, a numeral such as ୧୫,୦୦୦ (15,000) will be usually read as *pɔndɔr* 'fifteen' *hɔjar* 'thousand' and not as *ekɔ ɔyutɔ pancɔ hɔjar* 'one *ɔyutɔ* and five thousand'. Similarly, a numeral such as ୨୪,୦୦,୦୦୦ (24,00,000) will usually be read as *cɔbis* 'twenty-four' *lɔkhyɔ* 'lakh' and not as *dui* 'two' *niyutɔ* 'million' *cari* 'four' *lɔkhyɔ* 'lakh'.

Although the use of the decimal system is very common in Oriya, in the rural areas, *koḍi* 'twenty' is also used as the base unit for counting. In this system, a numeral such as 45 is expressed as *di koḍi panc*, literally 'two twenties (and) five' and 70 as *tini koḍi dɔs*, literally 'three twenties (and) ten'.

4.1.3 Case

It can be assumed that Oriya has three cases: nominative, genitive and objective (see Mohanty 1986). Usually, the nominative case marker is null; the genitive case marker is *-rɔ*; and the objective case marker is *-ku*. The following are some examples of nouns and pronouns in the three cases: *ramɔ* (NOM) 'Rama NON-HON', *ramɔrɔ* (GEN), *ramɔku* (OBJ); *bɔhi* (NOM) 'book', *bɔhirɔ* (GEN), *bɔhi(ku)* (OBJ); *tume* (NOM) 'you MID-HON', *tumɔrɔ* (GEN), *tumɔku* (OBJ); *se* (NOM) 'he/she NON-HON', *taarɔ* (GEN) *taku* (OBJ). The following are, however, some well-known exceptions to the pattern illustrated in the preceding examples: *mũ* (NOM) 'I', *moorɔ* (GEN), *mote* (OBJ); *tu* (NOM) 'you NON-HON', *toorɔ* (GEN), *tote* (OBJ). It is not possible to say **moku* for 'me' or **toku* for 'you (OBJ)'.

With plural and honorific nouns and pronouns, genitive and objective cases are usually realized as *-ŋkɔrɔ* and *-ŋku*, respectively. The following examples illustrate this: *ramɔbabu* (NOM) 'Ramababu HON', *ramɔbabuŋkɔrɔ* (GEN), *ramɔbabuŋku* (OBJ); *se* (NOM) 'he/she HON', *taŋkɔrɔ* (GEN), *taŋku* (OBJ); *apɔnɔ* (NOM) 'you HON', *apɔnɔŋkɔrɔ* (GEN), *apɔnɔŋku* (OBJ); *semane* (NOM) 'they', *semanɔŋkɔrɔ* (GEN), *semanɔŋku* (OBJ).

When a noun or pronoun in the genitive form is used attributively *-rɔ* is often deleted:

Genitive form with -rɔ	Attributive use without -rɔ
ramɔrɔ	*ramɔ bɔhi*
'Rama's NON-HON'	'Rama's NON-HON book'
ramɔbabuŋkɔrɔ	*ramɔbabuŋkɔ bɔhi*
'Ramababu's HON'	'Ramababu's HON book'
moorɔ	*mo bɔhi*
'my'	'my book'
semanɔŋkɔrɔ	*semanɔŋkɔ bɔhi*
'their'	'their book'

Although *-rɔ* can be and is commonly deleted when a noun or pronoun in the genitive form is used attributively, it cannot be deleted when it is used predicatively. The following examples illustrate this.

(1) *ei   bɔhi-ṭa   ramɔrɔ/*ramɔ*
     this   book DEF   Rama's NON-HON
     'This book is Rama's NON-HON.'

(2) *ei*   *bɔhi-ṭa*   *ramɔbabuŋkɔrɔ/*ramɔbabuŋkɔ*
     this   book DEF   Ramababu's HON
     'This book is Ramababu's HON.'

(3) *ei*   *bɔhi- ṭa*   *moorɔ/*mo*
     this   book DEF   my
     'This book is mine.'

(4) *ei*   *bɔhi-ṭa*   *semanɔŋkɔrɔ/*semanɔŋkɔ*
     this   book DEF   their
     'This book is theirs.'

So, it can be said that the genitive has two forms in Oriya: attributive and predicative. The attributive form is without *-rɔ*, which is commonly used in the attributive position. The predicative form is with *-rɔ*, which must be used in the predicative position.

Postpositions like *dwara* 'by', *paĩ* 'for', *ṭharu* 'from', *pakhɔre* 'near', *lagi* 'for', etc. are usually used with the attributive form of the genitive:

ta	*pakhɔre*	*ramɔbabuŋkɔ*	*paĩ*
his/her NON-HON	near	Ramababu's HON	for
'near him/her NON-HON'		'for Ramababu HON'	
mo	*lagi*	*semanɔŋkɔ*	*ṭharu*
my	for	their	from
'for me'		'from them'	

It can therefore be said that, in Oriya, the attributive genitive form is usually used as the oblique form.

4.1.4 Definiteness

In Oriya, the suffixes that are usually used for making a singular noun or an noncount noun definite are: *-ṭa*, *-ṭi* and *-kɔ*. *-ṭa* or *-ṭi* is normally used with a non-human noun:

bɔhi-ṭa	*phulɔ- ṭi*	*dudhɔ- ṭa*
book DEF	flower DEF	milk DEF
'the book'	'the flower'	'the milk'

-kɔ is generally added to the word *jɔṇɔ* 'person', which is used after a human noun to express definiteness:

     ḍaktɔr   jɔṇɔ-kɔ
     doctor person DEF
     'the doctor'

-ṭa or *-ṭi* is also used for human nouns, for persons who are not held with respect in the society:

pila- ṭa	*cakɔrɔ-ṭa*	*corɔ-ṭa*
child DEF	servant DEF	thief DEF
'the child'	'the servant'	'the thief'

If *-ṭa* or *-ṭi* is used with people who are normally held with respect, it may imply disrespect or even pity:

bɔdɔmas ḍaktɔr-ṭa   bicɔra ḍaktɔr-ṭa
wicked   doctor DEF   poor   doctor DEF
'the wicked doctor'   'the poor doctor'

In certain contexts, a singular noun or an uncount noun can also express definiteness
even without a suffix:

(1a) ḍaktɔr kah-   ø-   anti ?
     doctor where PRES   3P SG HON
     'Where is the doctor HON?'

(1b) se   ḍaktɔr ḍak- iba- ku
     he/she doctor call SFX to
     ja- u-   ch- ø-   i
     go PROG AUX PRES 3P SG NON-HON
     'He/She NON-HON is going to call a doctor.'

(2a) se   dudhɔ kɔuṭhi rɔkh- i-   ch- ø-   i ?
     he/she milk   where keep   PFTV AUX PRES 3P SG NON-HON
     'Where has he/she NON-HON kept the milk?'

(2b) se   dudhɔ kiṇ- iba- ku
     he/she milk   buy   SFX to
     ja- u-   ch- ø-   i
     go PROG AUX PRES 3P SG NON-HON
     'He/She NON-HON is going to buy milk.'

For making plural nouns definite, usually a demonstrative pronoun is used:

se   ḍaktɔr- mane   se   bɔhi- guḍakɔ
those   doctor PL   those   book PL
'those doctors'   'those books'

se   dui jɔṇɔ ḍaktɔr   se   dui-ṭa   bɔhi
those   two person doctor   those   two SFX   book
'those two doctors'   'those two books'

se   ḍaktɔr dui jɔṇɔ   se   bɔhi dui-ṭa
those   doctor two person   those   book two SFX
'those two doctors'   'those two books'

Four of the six preceding examples, where the plural markers occur after the noun, can
also express definiteness without the demonstrative pronoun. These four are:
ḍaktɔrmane, ḍaktɔr dui jɔṇɔ, bɔhiguḍakɔ, and bɔhi duiṭa. But the meaning of
definiteness will depend on the context. This is illustrated by the following examples:

(3a) ḍaktɔr-mane kah-   ø-   anti ?
     doctor PL   where PRES   3P PL
     'Where are the doctors?'

(3b) ḍaktɔr-mane aji- kali   bɔhut
     doctor PL   today tomorrow a lot of
     pɔisa ne- u-   ch- ø-   ɔnti
     money take PROG AUX PRES 3P PL
     'Doctors are taking a lot of money these days.'

(4a) *ḍaktɔr   dui jɔṇɔ   kuaḍe gɔ- l-   e ?*
     doctor two person where go   PST 3P PL
     'Where did the two doctors go?'

(4b) *ḍaktɔr   dui jɔṇɔ*
     doctor two person
     pɔṭha- ib-   u-   ki ?
     send   FUT 2P SG NON-HON QUES PTCLE
     'Will you NON-HON send two doctors?'

The words or suffixes usually used for making a singular noun indefinite are *jɔṇe* 'one person', *goṭe* 'one', *-ṭe, -ṭie,* and *-ṭae. jaṇe* is used with only human nouns; others are normally used with non-human nouns but they can also be used with human nouns. The following examples illustrate this:

jɔṇe	*ḍaktɔr*	*ḍaktɔr*	*jɔṇe*
one (person)	doctor	doctor	one (person)
'a doctor'		'a doctor'	

goṭe	*bɔhi*	*bɔhi*	*goṭe*
one	book	book	one
'a book'		'a book'	

bɔhi-	*ṭe*	*bɔhi-*	*ṭie*
book	INDEF	book	INDEF
'a book'		'a book'	

Plural numbers like *dui jɔṇɔ* 'two persons' or *duiṭa* 'two-suffix' usually make plural nouns indefinite, but they must be used before the noun to avoid any possibility of expressing definite meaning:

dui jɔṇɔ	*ḍaktɔr*	*dui-*	*ṭa*	*bɔhi*
two person	doctor	two	SFX	book
'two doctors'		'two books'		

4.2 Verbal forms and categories

4.2.1 Aspect, tense and mood

The meanings of time, mood and aspect are intricately interlinked in the Oriya verbal system. One way of understanding this system is to look at the inflectional suffixes taken by the verb root in a finite verbal paradigm.

In a finite verbal paradigm, there are usually five slots for inflectional suffixes. Of these five slots, the last or the outermost slot is meant for the suffix indicating subject-verb agreement. For example, in a finite verbal paradigm like *kha-u-tha-ø-ant-a* 'would have been eating', which consists of the verb root *kha-* 'to eat' and suffixes *-u-, -tha-, -ø-, -ant-* and *-a*, the last suffix, *-a,* indicates agreement with subject.

Just before the agreement morpheme, occurs the conditional mood morpheme *-ɔnt-,* whose allomorphs are *-ant-* and *-nt-.* For example, in *kha-u-tha-ø-ant-a, -ant-* is the conditional morpheme.

Immediately before the agreement morpheme, occurs the tense morpheme. In *kha-u-tha-ø-ant-a, -ø-* indicates tense. In Oriya, there are three types of tense morphemes:

(i) -il- and its allomorph -l-, (ii) -ø- and (iii) -ib- and its allomorph -b-. Based on these three types of tense morphemes, Oriya can be said to have three tenses: (i) past, (ii) present, and (iii) future. The conditional morpheme occurs only with present tense. The following are examples of verbs in the three tense forms.

> Past: *kha-u-th-il-a*
> Present: *kha-u-tha-ø-ant-a*
> Future: *kha-u-th-ib-ɔ*

Just before the tense marker there is a slot for auxiliary verbs like -ɔch- or its common variant -c(h)-, and -tha- or its allomorph -th-. The auxiliary verb that we have in *kha-u-tha-ø-ant-a* is -tha-. -ɔch- can occur only with present tense, but -tha- can occur with all the three tenses. -tha- can occur with the conditional mood morpheme, but -ɔch- cannot. -nãh- and -n- are the common negative variants of -ɔch- (see examples (12) and (13) in section 4.3.7.). Like the English 'be' verbs, ɔch- and tha- can also be used as main verbs.

-u- in *kha-u-tha-ø-ant-a* is an aspect marker. The innermost slot in the finite verbal paradigm is for the aspect marker -i- or -u- While -i- implies a perfective meaning, -u- implies a progressive meaning.

Of the five slots meant for suffixes, the slots meant for tense and subject-verb agreement suffixes are obligatorily filled in a finite verbal paradigm. The different types of combinations of tenses, aspect markers, auxiliary verbs and the conditional mood morpheme give Oriya a variety of finite verbal paradigms, some of which are illustrated in the following examples.

(i)   Simple Past
    se   kha- il-   a
    he/she eat   PST 3P SG NON-HON
    'He/She NON-HON ate.'

(ii) Simple Present
    se   kha- ø-   e
                    PRES 3P SG NON-HON
    'He/She NON-HON eats.'

(iii) Simple Future
    se   kha- ib-   ɔ
                    FUT 3P SG NON-HON
    'He/She NON-HON will eat.'

(iv) Simple Conditional
    se kha- ø-   ant-   a
              PRES COND 3P SG NON-HON
    'He/She NON-HON would eat.'

(v)   Past Continuous
    se kha- u-   th-   il-   a
             PROG AUX PST 3P SG NON-HON
    'He/She NON-HON was eating.'

(vi) Present Continuous

se kha- u-   ch- ø-   i
        PROG AUX PRES 3P SG NON-HON
'He/She NON-HON is eating.'

(vii) Future Continuous

se kha- u-   th- ib-   ɔ
        PROG AUX FUT 3P SG NON-HON
'He/She NON-HON will be eating.'

(viii) Conditional Continuous

se kha- u-   tha- ø-   ant- a
        PROG AUX PRES COND 3P SG NON-HON
'He/She NON-HON would have been eating … (if) … '

(ix) Past Perfect

se kha- i-   th- il- a
        PFTV AUX PST 3P SG NON-HON
'He/She NON-HON had eaten.'

(x) Present Perfect

se kha- i-   ch- ø-   i
        PFTV AUX PRES 3P SG NON-HON
'He/She NON-HON has eaten.'

(xi) Future Perfect

se kha- i-   th- ib-   ɔ
        PFTV AUX FUT 3P SG NON-HON
'He/She NON-HON will have eaten.'

(xii) Conditional Perfect

se kha- i-   tha- ø-   ant- a
        PFTV AUX PRES COND 3P SG NON-HON
'He/She NON-HON would have eaten … (if) … '

(xiii) Narrative Continuous

se kha- u-   tha- ø-   e
        PROG AUX PRES 3P SG NON-HON
'(At that time) he/she NON-HON used to eat.'

(xiv) Narrative Perfect

se kha- i-   tha- ø-   e
        PFTV AUX PRES 3P SG NON-HON
'(At that time) he/she NON-HON had eaten.'

The following are some of the combinations of aspect markers, tenses and the conditional mood morphemes that are not possible.

(1) *se kha- u-   ø-   ant- a
            PROG PRES COND 3P SG NON-HON

(2) *se kha- i-   ø-   ant- a
            PFTV PRES COND 3P SG NON-HON

(3)   *se   kha- u-   il-   a
              PROG PST   3P SG NON-HON

(4)   *se   kha- u-   ø-   e
              PROG PRES 3P SG NON-HON

(5)   *se   kha- i-   ø-   e
              PFTV PRES 3P SG NON-HON

(6)   *se   kha- u-   ib-   ɔ
              PROG FUT   3P SG NON-HON

However, as shown in the fourteen verbal paradigms listed earlier, these combinations
will be acceptable if the auxiliary -tha- is inserted. For comparison, -tha- is inserted in
the (a) counterparts of the unacceptable six combinations given in examples (1)–(6).

(1a) se kha- u- tha- ø- ant- a
(2a) se kha- i- tha- ø- ant- a
(3a) se kha - u – th - il - a
(4a) se kha - u - tha - ø - e
(5a) se kha - i - tha - ø - e
(6a) se kha - u - th - ib - ɔ

The combinations (4a) and (5a) will also be acceptable if the auxiliary -tha- is replaced
by the auxiliary -ɔch-:

(4b) se kha - u - ch - ø - i
(5b) se kha - i - ch - ø - i

This shows certain restrictions in the use of the aspect markers. The aspect markers
cannot be used without the auxiliary suffixes. As a matter of fact, the aspect markers and
the auxiliary suffixes go together. The following examples illustrate that the auxiliary
suffixes -tha- or -ɔch- cannot be used without the aspect markers.

(7)   *se   kha- th-   il-   a
              AUX PST   3P SG NON-HON

(8)   *se   kha- ch-   ø-   i
              AUX PRES 3P SG NON-HON

In most verbal paradigms, the outermost inflection indicates subject-verb agreement.
With certain paradigms, however, it indicates both subject-verb agreement and the
imperative/subjunctive mood. Consider, for example, the following sentences.

(9a) se   kha- ø-   u
      he/she eat   PRES   IMP/SUBJ+3P SG NON-HON
      'Let him/her NON-HON eat.'

(9b) se   kha- ø-   antu
      he/she eat   PRES   IMP/SUBJ+3P SG HON
      'Let him/her HON eat.'

(10a) se   kha- u-   tha- ø-   u
      he/she eat   PROG AUX PRES IMP/SUBJ+3P SG NON-HON
      'Let him/her NON-HON continue to eat.'

(10b)*se   kha- u-   tha-   ø-   antu*
    he/she eat   PROG AUX   PRES IMP/SUBJ+3P SG HON
    'Let him/her HON continue to eat.'

Like the conditional mood morpheme, the imperative/subjunctive mood morpheme occurs only with present tense. Further, as in the case of the conditional mood morpheme, the auxiliary *-tha-* can occur with the imperative/subjunctive morpheme, but *-ɔch-* cannot.

4.2.2 Concord

The concord inflection, which is usually the outermost inflection in the finite verbal paradigm, reflects the person, number and honorificity features of the subject. It also reflects the hearer inclusive-exclusive feature of the first person plural subject. Table 11.4 gives the verbal agreement inflections that occur with the future tense marker *-ib-* or *-b-*. The agreement inflections do not necessarily vary from one tense to another. But they may vary for certain person, number and honorificity features. For example, for first person plural hearer-inclusive and third person singular non-honorific features, the agreement inflections for the future tense and past tense are different. But for these two tenses, they are the same for all other person, number and honorificity features. The agreement markers vary most for the third person singular non-honorific features. This is illustrated in the examples of verbal paradigms given in the last section. Within the present tense, agreement inflections often vary from one auxiliary to the other and from one mood to the other.

For inanimate nouns, whether singular or plural, third person singular non-honorific agreement inflections are used:

(1) *bɔhi- ṭa   kɔuṭhi ɔch- ø-   i   ?*
     book DEF   where   be   PRES 3P SG NON-HON
     'Where is the book?'

(2) *bɔhi- guḍakɔ kɔuṭhi ɔch- ø-   i   ?*
     book PL   where   be   PRES 3P SG NON-HON
     'Where are the books?'

TABLE 11.4: VERBAL AGREEMENT INFLECTIONS FOR FUTURE TENSE

Person	Number	Honorificity	Hearer inclusive–exclusive	Agreement inflection
1P	SG	–	–	-i
1P	PL	–	INCL	-a
1P	PL	–	EXCL	-u
2P	SG	NON-HON	–	-u
2P	SG	MID-HON	–	-ɔ
2P	SG	HON	–	-e
2P	PL	NON-HON	–	-ɔ
2P	PL	MID-HON	–	-ɔ
2P	PL	HON	–	-e
3P	SG	NON-HON	–	-ɔ
3P	SG	HON	–	-e
3P	PL	NON-HON	–	-e
3P	PL	HON	–	-e

4.2.3 Non-finite forms

In Oriya, some of the suffixes used for deriving non-finite forms from the root forms of the verbs are: -u, -i, -ile, and -iba. For example, the following non-finite verbs can be derived by adding the suffixes to the verb as- 'to come'.

> as- + -u   = asu
> as- + -i   = asi
> as- + -ile = asile
> as- + -iba = asiba

Although all of them can be used as non-finite forms, they do not necessarily have the same syntax or semantics.

A non-finite verb formed with the suffix -u has to be reduplicated to be used and it implies a meaning of continuity of the action:

(1) tɔme   as-   u   as- u   ta   gitɔ
     you MID-HON come SFX come SFX his/her NON-HON song
     sɔr-   i-   gɔ- l-   a
     finish SFX go   PST 3P SG NON-HON
     'His/her NON-HON song got over before you MID-HON came/before you MID-HON could come/as soon as you MID-HON came.'

Here, the meaning of the continuity of the action seems to come from the suffix -u, which is used as a progressive aspect marker.

A non-finite verb formed with the suffix -i implies a meaning of the completion of the action. This meaning seems to come from the use of the suffix -i, which is used as a perfective aspect marker:

(2) se   ghɔrɔ-ku as-   i
     he/she   home to   come SFX
     ta   bapa- ku   dekh- il- a
     his/her NON-HON father OBJ NON-HON see   PST 3P SG NON-HON
     'He/she NON-HON saw his/her NON-HON father NON-HON after coming home.'

Non-finite verbs formed with the suffix -ile imply a meaning of conditionality or sequence. Here -il in -ile is probably related to the past tense inflection:

(3) se   as-   ile mũ j-   ib- i
     he/she   come SFX I   go   FUT 1P SG
     'I will go if he/she comes.'
     or
     'I will go after he/she comes.'

Non-finite verbs formed with the suffix -iba are used in clauses which usually take postpositions like -ku 'to', -pɔre 'after', paĩ 'for', etc. Here, -ib in -iba may be related to the future tense morpheme -ib:

(4) se   mote as-   iba- ku   kɔh- il- a
     he/she   me   come SFX   to   say   PST 3P SG NON-HON
     'He/she NON-HON asked me to come.'

Although the non-finite verbs seem to contain tense or aspect inflections, none of them can be inflected for agreement with the subject.

4.2.4 Compound verbs and causatives

In Oriya, as in other Indo-Aryan languages, formation of compound verbs and causal verbs is a very productive process.

Oriya compound verbs are of two types: (i) those that involve a nominal or an adjectival and a verbal, and (ii) those that involve verbs in a series. The following are some examples of the first type.

bhrɔmɔnɔ	*kɔ-*	*l-*	*a*
travelling	do	PST	3P SG NON-HON
(N)			
'travelled'			

pɔsɔnd	*kɔ-*	*l-*	*a*
appreciation	do	PST	3P SG NON-HON
(N)			
'appreciated'			

rɔndhɔnɔ	*he-*	*b-*	*ɔ*
cooking	happen	FUT	3P SG NON-HON
(N)			
'will be cooked'			

pɔtitɔ	*he-*	*l-*	*a*
fallen	happen	PST	3P SG NON-HON
(ADJ)			
'fell'			

pɔrastɔ	*kɔ-*	*l-*	*e*
defeated	do	PST	3P SG HON
(ADJ)			
'defeated'			

pɔrastɔ	*he-*	*l-*	*e*
defeated	happen	PST	3P SG HON
(ADJ)			
'was defeated'			

As shown in the examples, *kɔr-* 'to do' and *he-* 'to happen' are the two verbs that are (usually) used in the compound verbs of the first type. While *kɔr-* assigns an agentive role, *he-* assigns a patient role to the subject of these compound verbs. Compound verbs of this type are not very commonly used in the informal variety. This is because, for many of these verbs, 'simpler' verbs with 'equivalent' meaning are available in the informal variety. For example, *bulila* for *bhrɔmɔnɔ kɔla, pɔɗila* for *pɔtitɔ hela* and *hɔraila* for *pɔrastɔ kɔla*.

Compound verbs of the second type are more commonly used in Oriya than those of the first type. A few examples of this type are:

hɔs-	*i*	*de-*	*l-*	*a*
laugh	SFX	give	PST	3P SG NON-HON
'laughed'				

taṇ-   i   *aṇ-*   *il-*   *a*
draw   SFX   bring   PST   3P SG NON-HON
'drew'

pɔḍ-   i   *gɔ-*   *l-*   *a*
fall   SFX   go   PST   3P SG NON-HON
'fell'

kheḷ-   i   *par-*   *il-*   *a*
play   SFX   be able   PST   3P SG NON-HON
'was able to play'

so-   i   *pɔḍ-*   *il-*   *a*
sleep   SFX   fall   PST   3P SG NON-HON
'fell asleep'

so-   i   *pɔḍ-*   i   *sar-*   *i-*   *th-*   *il-*   *a*
sleep   SFX   fall   SFX   finish   PFTV   AUX   PST   3P SG NON-HON
'had fallen asleep'

As the examples show, compound verbs of this type consist of two or more verbs. If there are two verbs, the first verb, usually called the main verb, consists of the root form of the verb and the suffix *-i*. For example, *hɔsi* in *hɔsi dela* consists of *hɔs-* 'to laugh' and *-i*. The second verb, often called the explicator verb, functions like a simple verb, that is, it is marked for tense and agreement and can also take aspect and mood markers. If there are more than two verbs, the last verb carries tense, agreement, etc. and the other verbs take the suffix *-i*. Whether there are two or more verbs, the meaning largely comes from the first verb, but it is modified or restricted by the other verb(s). The following are some of the explicator verbs that are commonly used in Oriya: *deba* 'to give', *jiba* 'to go', *pɔḍiba* 'to fall', *pariba* 'to be able to do', *sariba* 'to finish', *aṇiba* 'to bring', *pɔkeiba* 'to drop', *asiba* 'to come', *bɔsiba* 'to sit', *neba* 'to take', *dhɔriba* 'to hold' and *uṭhiba* 'to rise'.

The use of causal verbs is also very common in Oriya. They are derived from the root forms of verbs. The following examples compare some causal verbs with their simple (non-causal) counterparts.

(i)   Root: *hɔs-*
          'to laugh'
      Simple verb: *hɔs-*   *il-*   *a*
          laugh   PST   3P SG NON-HON
          'laughed'
      Causal verb: *hɔs-*   *a-/e-*   *il-*   *a*
          laugh   SFX   PST   3P SG NON-HON
          'made (somebody) laugh'

(ii) Root: *rag-*
          'to get angry'
      Simple verb: *rag-*   *u-*   *ch-*   *ø-*   *i*
          get angry   PROG   AUX   PRES   3P SG NON-HON
          'is getting angry'
      Causal verb: *rɔg-*   *ɔ-/a-*   *u-*   *ch-*   *ø-*   *i*
          get angry   SFX   PROG   AUX   PRES   3P SG NON-HON
          'is making (somebody) angry'

(iii) Root: *bɔs-*
                         'to sit'
       Simple verb: *bɔs- ib-   ɔ*
                         sit   FUT 3P SG NON-HON
                         'will sit'
       Causal verb: *bɔs- a-/e- ib-   ɔ*
                         sit   SFX   FUT 3P SG NON-HON
                         'will make (somebody) sit'

The syntax of a verb also changes when it is causativized. For example, intransitive verbs become transitive and transitive verbs become ditransitive when they are causativized. The following sentences illustrate the change in the syntax of the verbs when they are causativized.

(1a) *sita hɔs- u-   ch- ɵ-   i*
     Sita laugh PROG AUX PRES 3P SG NON-HON
     'Sita NON-HON is laughing.'

(1b) *sita   ta   puɔ- ku*
     Sita   her NON-HON son   OBJ NON-HON
     hɔs- ɔ-/a- u-   ch- ɵ-   i
     laugh SFX   PROG AUX PRES 3P SG NON-HON
     'Sita NON-HON is making her NON-HON son NON-HON laugh.'

(2a) *sita paṇi pi-   u-   ch- ɵ-   i*
     Sita water drink PROG AUX PRES 3P SG NON-HON
     'Sita NON-HON is drinking water.'

(2b) *sita   ta   puɔ- ku   paṇi*
     Sita   her NON-HON son   OBJ NON-HON water
     pi-   ɔ-/a- u-   ch- ɵ-   i
     drink SFX   PROG AUX PRES 3P SG NON-HON
     'Sita NON-HON is making her NON-HON son NON-HON drink water.'

hɔsiba 'to laugh' is an intransitive verb (as in (1a)), but it becomes transitive (as in (1b)) when it is causativized. *piiba* 'to drink', which is a monotransitive verb (as in (2a)), becomes ditransitive (as in (2b)) when it is causativized.

4.3 Sentence and sentence modifications

4.3.1 Word order

Oriya is an SOV language. The following examples show the word order in sentences of four basic types.

(1) Intransitive
     (subject–verb)
     se   hɔs- u-   ch- ɵ-   i
     he/she laugh PROG AUX PRES 3P SG NON-HON
     'He/She NON-HON is laughing.'

(2)   Monotransitive
      (subject–object–verb)
      se   bhatɔ kha- u-   ch-   ɵ-   i
      he/she rice   eat   PROG AUX PRES 3P SG NON-HON
      'He/She NON-HON is eating rice.'

(3)   Ditransitive
      (subject–indirect object–direct object–verb)
      se   mote goṭe bɔhi de-   l-   a
      he/she me   one   book give PST 3P SG NON-HON
      'He/She NON-HON gave me a book.'

(4)   Complex transitive
      (subject–object–object complement–verb)
      se   mote bɔhut bhɔlɔ bhab- ɵ-   e
      he/she me   very good think PRES 3P SG NON-HON
      'He/She NON-HON considers me very good.'

Adjuncts usually occur between subject and verb:

(5)   *se   kali   as-   ib-   ɔ*
      he/she tomorrow come FUT 3P SG NON-HON
      'He/She NON-HON will come tomorrow.'

(6)   *se   kɔlikɔta- re cakiri kɔr- ɵ-   e*
      he/she Calcutta in job   do PRES 3P SG NON-HON
      'He/She NON-HON works in Calcutta.'

Oriya, however, does not have a rigid word order. The word order that has been illustrated in examples (1)–(6) is used most frequently. Stylistically, it is probably most neutral.

It is, however, not impossible for a sentence such as (7) to have any of the word orders given in sentences (8)–(11).

(7)   *ramɔ   sita- ku   bhɔlɔ- pa- ɵ-   e*
      Rama Sita OBJ NON-HON good   get PRES 3P SG NON-HON
      'Rama NON-HON loves Sita NON-HON.'

(8)   *ramɔ   bhɔlɔpae   sitaku*
      'Rama NON-HON loves Sita NON-HON.'

(9)   *sitaku bhɔlɔpae   ramɔ*
      'Rama NON-HON loves Sita NON-HON.'

(10) *bhɔlɔpae   ramɔ   sitaku*
      'Rama NON-HON loves Sita NON-HON.'

(11) *bhɔlɔpae   sitaku ramɔ*
      'Rama NON-HON loves Sita NON-HON.'

All the sentences have been given the same gloss to indicate that the grammatical relations of the constituents in the sentences remain the same. Stylistically, of course, the sentences will have different meanings. For example, (8) will mean something like: 'It is Sita whom Rama loves.' But the point that is being made is that all of these are possible, although not all are equally acceptable; (10–11) in particular are deviant.

4.3.2 Passive

The passive verb in Oriya is formed with the passive participle and the passive auxiliary -*he*- 'to happen' or -*ja*- 'to go'. The passive participle is usually formed by adding the suffix -*a* to the verb root, or to a form derived from the verb root, for example, *kɔra*- from *kɔr*- 'to do', or *dia*- from *de*- 'to give'. The passive auxiliary, like any ordinary verb, can be marked for aspect, tense and agreement and can occur with the mood markers. So the passive verb can occur in all the verbal paradigms. To give a few examples: *kɔrahue* 'is done', *kɔrajauchi* 'is being done', *kɔrajaithaanta* 'would have been done'.

Formal passive has a low acceptability in Oriya. What is commonly used in place of formal passive is impersonal passive. Consider the following for comparison.

(1)   *hɔri   ramɔbabu-   ŋku   bɔmbe*
      Hari   Ramababu   OBJ HON   Bombay
      ne-   l-   a
      take   PST   3P SG NON-HON
      'Hari NON-HON took Ramababu HON to Bombay.'

(2) ? *ramɔbabu   bɔmbe   ni-   a-   he-   l-   e*
      Ramababu   Bombay   take   SFX   SFX   PST   3P SG HON
      'Ramababu HON was taken to Bombay.'

(3)   *ramɔbabu-   ŋku   bɔmbe*
      Ramababu   OBJ HON   Bombay
      ni-   a-   he-   l-   a
      take   SFX   SFX   PST   3P SG NON-HON
      'Ramababu HON was taken to Bombay.'

Sentence (2) is an example of formal passive and (3), of impersonal passive. The low acceptability of (2) is indicated by the question mark that occurs before the sentence. Both (2) and (3) use passive verbs. The syntactic role of *ramɔbabu*, however, is different in the two sentences. In (2), it is the grammatical subject: it is in nominative case and the verb agrees with it. In (3), however, it functions like a grammatical object: it is in objective case, as in (1), and the verb does not agree with it. The verb in Oriya impersonal passive actually does not agree with any noun phrase in the sentence, it is always marked for third person singular non-honorific subject by default.

4.3.3 'Dative subject' constructions

The subject of the so-called 'dative subject' construction is not always marked dative or objective case in Oriya. In certain cases, it is assigned genitive case. In certain other cases, it is assigned either genitive or nominative case. It may be therefore more appropriate to call them affective constructions. The following are some examples of affective constructions.

(1)   *ramɔ-   ku   bhokɔ*
      Rama   OBJ NON-HON   hunger
      lag-   u-   ch-   ɵ-   i
      appear   PROG   AUX   PRES   3P SG NON-HON
      'Rama NON-HON is hungry.'

(2) *hɔri- ku*   *nidɔ*
     Hari OBJ NON-HON sleep
     maḍ- u-   ch- ø-   i
     appear PROG AUX PRES 3P SG NON-HON
     'Hari NON-HON is feeling sleepy.'

(3) *moorɔ goṭe bɔhi dɔrɔkar*
     my   one   book necessary
     'I need a book.'

(4) *sitarɔ   /   sita kɔṭɔk*
     Sita's NON-HON Sita Cuttack
     j- iba- rɔ   ɔch- ø-   i
     go SFX GEN be   PRES 3P SG NON-HON
     'Sita NON-HON is to go to Cuttack.'

In an affective construction, the verb (if a verb is used) does not agree with the affective subject. It is marked for third person singular non-honorific subject by default. The affective construction cannot take a volitional adverb. The affective subject, however, can act as an antecedent for the reflexive *nijɔ*, which is known for its inability to take a non-subject noun phrase as its antecedent:

(5) **hɔri- ku*   *jaṇ- i   jaṇ- i*
     Hari   OBJ NON-HON   know SFX know SFX
     ragɔ maḍ- ø-   e
     anger appear PRES 3P SG NON-HON
     'Hari NON-HON deliberately gets angry.'

(6) *hɔri- ku*   *nijɔ upɔre- bi*
     Hari OBJ NON-HON self on   also
     ragɔ maḍ- ø-   e
     anger appear PRES 3P SG NON-HON
     'Hari NON-HON gets angry even with himself.'

4.3.4 Complement clauses

Finite complement clauses in Oriya occur with *boli*, *je*, or without either of them. While *boli* occurs clause-finally, *je* occurs clause-initially or medially. *boli* has been accepted as a clause-final complementizer, but the status of *je* as a complementizer has been questioned (see Patnaik 1976, Pattanaik 1987, Nayak 1987, Bal 1990). *boli*-clauses usually precede the main clause, but can also follow it or occur within it. *je*-clauses follow the main clause when *je* occurs clause-initially, but they precede it when *je* occurs clause-medially. When *je* occurs clause-medially, the main clause has to be related to a phrase like *e kɔtha* 'this fact'. The following examples illustrate this.

(1) *se   as- ib- ɔ*   *boli   mũ*
     he/she come FUT 3P SG NON-HON COMP I
     jaṇ- ø-   e
     know PRES 1P SG
     'I know that he/she NON-HON will come.'

(2) *mũ   se   as- ib-   ɔ*
    I   he/she come FUT 3P SG NON-HON
    boli jaṇ- ø-   e
    COMP know PRES 1P SG
    'I know that he/she NON-HON will come.'

(3) *mũ jaṇ- ø-   e   se   as- ib-   ɔ*
    I   know PRES 1P SG he/she come FUT 3P SG NON-HON
    boli
    COMP
    'I know that he/she NON-HON will come.'

(4) *mũ jaṇ- ø-   e   je se   as- ib-   ɔ*
    I   know PRES 1P SG   he/she come FUT 3P SG NON-HON
    'I know that he/she NON-HON will come.'

(5) *se   je as- ib-   ɔ   e*
    he/she   come FUT 3P SG NON-HON this
    kɔtha mũ jaṇ- ø-   e
    fact   I   know PRES 1P SG
    'I know that he/she NON-HON will come.'

Non-finite complement clauses take a verb formed with *-iba* (as shown in 4.2.3) and occur with a postposition like *-ku* or *paĩ*. With certain verbs, however, they can occur without a postposition:

(6) *se   mote kɔlikɔta j- iba- ku*
    he/she me   Calcutta go SFX   to
    kɔh- il-   a
    say   PST 3P SG NON-HON
    'He/She NON-HON asked me to go to Calcutta.'

(7) *se   mũ ḍaktɔr- i   pɔḍh- iba*
    he/she I   doctor SFX study SFX
    pɔsɔnd   kɔr- ø-   e
    appreciation do   PRES 3P SG NON-HON
    'He/She NON-HON likes my studying medicine.'

4.3.5 Relative clauses

Relative clauses commonly used in Oriya are of the relative–correlative type. *jie, jeũmane, jeũṭa, jeũguḍikɔ*, etc. are usually used as the relative pronouns. *jie* is used for singular human nouns, *jeũmane* for plural human nouns, *jeũṭa* for singular non-human nouns and *jeũguḍikɔ* for plural non-human nouns. Like personal pronouns, they also have different case forms. *jeũ* is used as the modifier for the noun to be relativized. The relative clause (also called the modifying clause or J-clause) usually precedes the main clause:

(1) *jie   kali   as- i-   th- il-   a*
    REL PR yesterday come PFTV AUX PST 3P SG NON-HON
    sie   e   bɔhi- ṭa lekh i-   ch- ø-   i
    he/she this book DEF write PFTV AUX PRES 3P SG NON-HON
    'He/She NON-HON who NON-HON came yesterday has written this book.'

(2) *jeŭ*　　　　　*pila- ţa　　sethi*
　　REL modifier boy　DEF　there
　　kheḷ- u-　　ch-　ø-　　i
　　play PROG AUX PRES 3P SG NON-HON
　　sei pila- ţa / 　sie rɔmarɔ　　　　　　puɔ
　　that boy DEF he Rama's NON-HON son
　　'The boy NON-HON who is playing there is Rama's NON-HON son.'

The relative clause, however, does not always precede the main clause:

(3) *sei　pila- ţa　jie　　　　sethi*
　　that boy DEF REL PR there
　　kheḷ- u-　　ch-　ø-　　i　　　　　　　　sie
　　play PROG AUX PRES 3P SG NON-HON he
　　rɔmarɔ　　　　　　puɔ
　　Rama's NON-HON son
　　'The boy NON-HON who NON-HON is playing there is Rama's NON-HON son.'

Non-restrictive relative clauses are rarely used in the informal variety. But they are not so uncommon in the formal variety:

(4) *bhagirɔthi　das, jie　　　amɔ sɔhɔrɔ paĩ*
　　bhagirathi das REL PR our town for
　　ete　　　kamɔ kɔr- i-　　th- il-　e
　　so much work do PFTV AUX PST 3P SG HON
　　(se) aji　au　　nah- ø　　anti
　　he today more NEG PRES 3P SG HON
　　'Bhagirathi Das HON, who HON had done so much for our town, is no more.'

4.3.6 Conditional constructions

Conditional constructions in Oriya can be structurally divided into two types: (i) *-ile* type, and (ii) *jɔdi* 'if' type. The *-ile* type uses the non-finite *-ile* verb in the conditional clause and cannot use the word *jɔdi* with the conditional clause. The *jɔdi* type uses a finite conditional clause and must use the word *jɔdi* with the conditional clause. The following examples illustrate this.

(1) *se　　as-　ile　mŭ j-　ib-　i*
　　he/she come SFX I go FUT 1P SG
　　'If he/she comes then I will go.'
　　or
　　'After he/she comes I will go.'

(2) *jɔdi se　　as- ø-　e　　　　　　　　　　ta　he-　le*
　　if he/she come PRES 3P SG NON-HON that happen SFX
　　mŭ j-　ib-　i
　　I go FUT 1P SG
　　'If he/she NON-HON comes, then I will go.'

In the *-ile* type, the conditional verb can have only two forms: with or without the auxiliary *-tha-*. In sentence (1), the conditional verb is without *-tha-* The following is an example with *-tha-*.

(3) *se*   *as-*   *i-*   *th-*   *ile*
    he/she come PFTV AUX SFX
    mũ ja- i-   *tha- ø-*   *ant-*   *i*
    I   go PFTV AUX PRES COND 1P SG
    'If he/she had come, I would have gone.'

In the *jɔdi* type, however, the conditional verb can occur in any tense:

(4) *jɔdi se*   *as-*   *ø-*   *ɔnt-*   *a*
    if   he/she come PRES COND 3P SG NON-HON
    ta he-   *le*   *mũ ja- ø-*   *ant-*   *i*
    that happen SFX I   go PRES COND 1P SG
    'If he/she NON-HON would come, then I would go.'

(5) *jɔdi se*   *as-*   *ib-*   *ɔ*
    if   he/she come FUT 3P SG NON-HON
    ta he-   *le*   *mũ j-*   *ib-*   *i*
    that happen SFX I   go FUT 1P SG
    'If he/she NON-HON will come, then I will go.'

(6) *jɔdi se*   *as-*   *i-*   *th-*   *il-*   *a*
    if   he/she come PFTV AUX PST 3P SG NON-HON
    ta he-   *le*   *ramɔ-*   *ku*
    that happen SFX Rama   OBJ NON-HON
    bhet- i-   *th-*   *ib-*   *ɔ*
    meet PFTV AUX FUT 3P SG NON-HON
    'If he/she NON-HON had come, then he/she NON-HON must have met Rama
    NON-HON.'

4.3.7 Negation

In Oriya, the following are commonly used as negation markers: *-nahĩ* and *nɔ-*. *-nahĩ*
and its common variant *-ni* are used only with a finite verb:

(1) *se*   *j*   *ib-*   *ɔ-*   *ni*
    he/she go FUT 3P SG NON-HON NEG
    'He/she NON-HON will not go.'

When the finite verb has the auxiliary *-tha-*, the negative marker that is commonly used
is *nɔ-*:

(2) *se*   *ja- i-*   *nɔ-*   *th-*   *il-*   *a*
    he/she go PFTV NEG AUX PST 3P SG NON-HON
    'He/She NON-HON had not gone.'

With non-finite verbs, only *nɔ-* is used as the negative marker. Here, the negative marker
is used immediately before the verb:

(3) *se*   *mote nɔ- j- iba-*   *ku*
    he/she me   NEG go SFX to
    kɔh- i-   *ch- ø-*   *i*
    say PFTV AUX PRES 3P SG NON-HON
    'He/She NON-HON has asked me not to go.'

nɔ- is also used with the conditional clauses. If the verb of the conditional clause does not have the auxiliary *-tha-*, *nɔ-* is used immediately before the verb:

(4) *se   nɔ- gɔ- le   mũ j- ib-   i-   ni*
     he/she NEG go SFX   I   go FUT 1P SG NEG
     'If he/she does not go, I will not go.'

(5) *jɔdi se   nɔ- ja- ø-   ant-   a*
     if   he/she NEG go PRES COND 3P SG NON-HON
     ta   he- le   mũ ja- ø-   ant-   i
     that happen SFX I   go PRES COND 1P SG
     'If he/she NON-HON did not go, I would go.'

But if the verb of the conditional clause has the auxiliary *-tha-*, *nɔ-* can be used either immediately before the verb or immediately before *-tha-*:

(6) *se   nɔ- ja- i-   th-   ile*
     he/she NEG go PFTV AUX SFX
     mũ ja- i-   tha- ø-   ant-   i
     I   go PFTV AUX PRES COND 1P SG
     'If he/she had not gone, I would have gone.'

(7) *se   ja- i-   nɔ- th-   ile*
     he/she go PFTV NEG AUX SFX
     mũ ja- i-   tha- ø-   ant-   i
     I   go PFTV AUX PRES COND 1P SG
     'If he/she had not gone, I would have gone.'

nɔ- can also be used with imperative/subjunctive verbs:

(8) *semane nɔ- ja- ø-   antu*
     they   NEG go PRES IMP/SUBJ + 3P PL
     'Let them not go.'

nɔ- can also be used before the existential copula *tha-* to express negative meaning:

(9) *se   ghɔr- e nɔ- th- il-   a*
     he/she house in NEG be PST 3P SG NON-HON
     'He/She NON-HON was not at home.'

nũh- and *nãh-* are used as the negative counterparts of the equative copula *ø/ɔṭ-* and the existential copula *ɔch-*, respectively:

(10) *se   ḍaktɔr nuh- ø-   ẽ*
     he/she doctor NEG PRES 3P SG NON-HON
     'He/She NON-HON is not a doctor.'

(11) *se   ghɔr- e nah- ø-   ĩ*
     he/she house-in NEG PRES 3P SG NON-HON
     'He/She NON-HON is not at home.'

-nãh- is also used as the negative counterpart of the auxiliary *-ɔch-*:

(12) *se   ja- u-   nah- ø-   anti*
     he/she go PROG AUX PRES 3P SG HON
     'He/She HON is not going.'

In certain cases, -n- can also be used as a variant of the negative auxiliary -nãh-:

(13) *tu   ja- u-   n-   ø-   u*
     you NON-HON   go   PROG AUX PRES 2P SG NON-HON
     'You NON-HON are not going.'

4.3.8 Question formation

The 'WH-question' words in Oriya are: *kie* 'who', *kɔɔṇɔ* 'what', *kahaku* 'whom', *kebe* 'when', *kuaḍe* 'where', *kete* 'how much', *kete(ṭa)* 'how many', *kete jɔṇɔ* 'how many [human]', *ka(h)a(rɔ)* 'whose', *kahĩki* 'why', etc. *ka(h)a* is usually used as the oblique form, e.g. *kaha paĩ* 'for whom', *kaha pakhɔre* 'near whom'.

In short WH-questions, the WH-word usually occurs immediately before the verb, *in situ*, or sentence-initially.

(1) *tu   se   bɔhi- ṭa   kahaku*
    you NON-HON   that book DEF whom
    de- l-   u   ?
    give PST 2P SG NON-HON
    'Whom did you NON-HON give that book?'

(2) *tu   kahaku se   bɔhi- ṭa*
    you NON-HON   whom that book DEF
    de- l-   u   ?
    give PST 2P SG NON-HON
    'Whom did you NON-HON give that book?'

(3) *kahaku tu   se   bɔhi- ṭa*
    whom you NON-HON   that book DEF
    de- l-   u   ?
    give PST 2P SG NON-HON
    'Whom did you NON-HON give that book?'

In long WH-questions, the question word or the clause containing the question word usually occurs sentence-initially:

(4) *kahaku se   bhɔlɔ- pa- ø-   e*
    whom he/she good   get PRES 3P SG NON-HON
    boli tɔme   bhab- u-   ch- ø-   ɔ   ?
    COMP you MID-HON   think PROG AUX PRES 2P SG MID-HON
    'Whom do you MID-HON think he/she NON-HON loves?'

(5) *se   kahaku bhɔlɔ- pa- ø-   e*
    he/she whom good   get PRES 3P SG NON-HON
    boli tɔme   bhab- u-   ch- ø-   ɔ   ?
    COMP you MID-HON   think PROG AUX PRES 2P SG MID-HON
    'Whom do you MID-HON think he/she NON-HON loves?'

(6) *kahaku tɔme   bhab- u-   ch- ø-   ɔ*
    whom you MID-HON   think PROG AUX PRES 2P SG MID-HON
    se   bhɔlɔ- pa- ø-   e   boli ?
    he/she good   get PRES 3P SG NON-HON COMP
    'Whom do you MID-HON think he/she NON-HON loves?'

Yes/no questions are usually asked by using the question-marker particle *ki*, a combination of the negative marker *ni* and *ki*, a combination of the negative markers *na* and *nahĩ*, a combination of the negative marker *na* and *kɔɔnɔ* 'what', an emphasis marker such as *tɔ*, etc. sentence-finally, or by using *kɔɔnɔ* sentence-initially or medially:

(7) *tu   j- ib- u   ki   ?*
    you NON-HON go FUT 2P SG NON-HON QUES PTCLE
    'Will you NON-HON go?'

(8) *tu   j- ib- u-   ni   ki   ?*
    you NON-HON go FUT 2P SG NON-HON NEG QUES PTCLE
    'Won't you NON-HON go?'

(9) *tu   j- ib- u   na   nahĩ ?*
    you NON-HON go FUT 2P SG NON-HON NEG NEG
    'Will you NON-HON go or not?'

(10) *tu   j- ib- u   na   kɔɔnɔ ?*
    you NON-HON go FUT 2P SG NON-HON NEG what
    'Will you NON-HON go?'

(11) *tu   j- ib- u   tɔ   ?*
    you NON-HON go FUT 2P SG NON-HON EMPHT
    'Will you NON-HON really go?'

(12) *tu   kɔɔnɔ j- ib- u   ?*
    you NON-HON what go FUT 2P SG NON-HON
    'Will you NON-HON really go?'

(13) *kɔɔnɔ tu   j- ib- u   ?*
    what you NON-HON go FUT 2P SG NON-HON
    'Will you NON-HON really go?'

It is also common to ask yes/no questions without using any of the forms illustrated in (7)–(13) and simply by intonation:

(14) *tu   j- ib- u   ?*
    you NON-HON go FUT 2P SG NON-HON
    'Will you NON-HON go?'

(15) *tu   j- ib- u-   ni   ?*
    you NON-HON go FUT 2P SG NON-HON NEG
    'Won't you NON-HON go?'

Although (7)–(15) ask the same question, they are likely to have different presuppositions, which is partially indicated by the glosses given.

ACKNOWLEDGEMENT

I am grateful to Panchanan Mohanty for helpful comments and suggestions.

REFERENCES

Bal, B. K. (1990) *Comp and Complementizers in Oriya and English*, Unpublished Ph.D. dissertation, CIEFL, Hyderabad.

Bhattacharya, K. (1993) *Bengali–Oriya Verb Morphology*, Calcutta: Das Gupta & Co. Private Limited.

Breton, Roland J.-L. (1997) *Atlas of the Languages and Ethnic Communities of South Asia*, New Delhi: Sage Publications India Pvt Ltd, CA: Sage Publications Inc, London: Sage Publications Ltd.

Chatterji, S. K. (1926) *The Origin and Development of the Bengali Language*, 3 vols. Calcutta: Calcutta University Press (Reprinted (1970), London: George Allen and Unwin Ltd).

Comrie, B. (ed.) (1990) *The Major Languages of South Asia, the Middle East and Africa*, London: Routledge.

Dash, G. N. (1971) 'Structure of verb stem in Oriya', *Indian Linguistics* 32: 207–12.

—— (1982) *Descriptive Morphology of Oriya*, Santiniketan: Visva-Bharati Research Publications Committee.

Dhall, G. B. (1957) 'The languages and dialects spoken in Orissa', *Indian Linguistics* 17: 39–43.

—— (1966) *Aspiration in Oriya*, Bhubaneswar: Utkal University.

Grierson, G. A. (1903) *Linguistic Survey of India, volume V: Indo-Aryan Family (Eastern Group)*, Part II: *Bihari and Oriya Languages,* Govt. of India (Reprinted (1968), Delhi: Motilal Banarasidass).

Kachru, Y. (1980) *Aspects of Hindi Grammar*, New Delhi: Manohar.

Mahapatra, B. P. (1984) 'Language modernization in Oriya newspapers', in Krishnamurthi, Bh. and Mukherjee, A. (eds.) *Modernization of Indian Languages in News Media*, Hyderabad: Department of Linguistics, Osmania University.

Mahapatra, B. P. et al. (1989) *The Written Languages of the World*: *A Survey of the Degree and Modes of Use*, Volume 2: *India*, Book I: *Constitutional Languages*, India: Office of the Registrar General and Canada: International Centre for Research on Bilingualism, Laval University.

Mahapatra, D. (1997) *Oriya Dhwanitattwa o Sabda Sambhar*, Cuttack: Friends' Publishers.

Mahapatra, N. and Das, S. (1978) *Sarbasara Byakarana*, Cuttack: New Students' Store.

Majumdar, P. C. (1970) *A Historical Phonology of Oriya*, Calcutta: Sanskrit College.

Masica, C. P. (1991) *The Indo-Aryan Languages*, Cambridge: CUP.

Mishra, B. (1972) *Odiya Bhasara Puratattwa*, Cuttack: Friends' Publishers.

—— (1975) *Odiya Bhasara Itihasa*, Cuttack: Cuttack Students' Store.

Misra, H. (1975) *Historical Oriya Morphology*, Varanasi: Bharata Manisha.

Mohanty, B. (1970) *Odiya Bhasara Utpatti o Kramabikasa*, Cuttack: Friends' Publishers.

Mohanty, P. (1986) *Aspects of Oriya Language: Phonology and Morphology*, Unpublished Ph.D. dissertation, Berhampur University, Berhampur.

—— (1996) 'Pandit Nilakhantha Das and the reformation of Oriya script', in Mohanty, P. (ed.) *Essays on Linguistics and Folkloristics*, Bhubaneswar: Mayur Publications.

Nanda Sharma, G. (1927) *Odiya Bhasatattwa,* Cuttack: New Students' Store.

Nayak, R. (1987) *Nonfinite Clauses in Oriya and English*, Unpublished Ph.D. dissertation, CIEFL, Hyderabad.

Padhi, B. (1988) *Oriya Bhashara Roopatattwa*. Cuttack: New Students' Store.

Patnaik, B. N. (1976) *Complementation in Oriya and English*, Unpublished Ph.D. dissertation, CIEFL, Hyderabad.

Patnaik, B. N. and Pandit, I. (1986) 'Englishization of Oriya', in Krishnamurthi, Bh. (ed.) *South Asian Languages: Structure, Convergence and Diglossia*, Delhi: Motilal Banarasidass.

Pattanaik, U. P. (1987) *Distribution of Empty Categories in Oriya and English*, Unpublished Ph.D. dissertation, CIEFL, Hyderabad.

Pattanayak, D. P. (1959) 'Nasal phonemes in Oriya', *Indian Linguistics* 20: 159–64.

—— (1966) *A Controlled Historical Reconstruction of Oriya, Assamese, Bengali and Hindi*, The Hague: Mouton.

—— (1969) 'Oriya and Assamese', in Sebeok, T. (ed.) *Current Trends in Linguistics, Volume 5: Linguistics in South Asia,* The Hague: Mouton.

Pattanayak, D. P. and Das, G. N. (1972) *Conversational Oriya*, Mysore: Smt. Sulakshana Pattanayak.

Pradhan, S. C. et al. (1995) *Byakarana*, Cuttack: Board of Secondary Education, Orissa.

Ray, T. S. (1982) *The Form and Function of the Passive in English and Oriya*, Unpublished M.Litt. dissertation, CIEFL, Hyderabad.

—— (1987) *Binding Principles in Oriya and English*, Unpublished Ph.D. dissertation, CIEFL, Hyderabad.

—— (2000) 'Lexical anaphors and pronouns in Oriya', in Lust, Barbara C. et al. (eds.) *Lexical Anaphors and Pronouns in Selected South Asian Languages*, Berlin, New York: Mouton de Gruyter.

Sarangi, N. (1998) *Bruhat Oriya Byakarana*, Cuttack: Satyanarayan Book Store.

Tripathi, K. B. (1962) *The Evolution of Oriya Language and Script*, Cuttack: Utkal University.

Young, A. H. (1935) *First Lessons in Oriya*, Cuttack: Orissa Mission Press.

FURTHER READING

Bhattacharya, K. (1993) *Bengali–Oriya Verb Morphology*, Calcutta: Das Gupta & Co. Private Limited.

Dash, G. N. (1982) *Descriptive Morphology of Oriya*, Santiniketan: Visva-Bharati Research Publications Committee.

Dhall, G. B. (1966) *Aspiration in Oriya*, Bhubaneswar: Utkal University.

Majumdar, P. C. (1970) *A Historical Phonology of Oriya*, Calcutta: Sanskrit College.

Misra, H. (1975) *Historical Oriya Morphology*, Varanasi: Bharata Manisha.

Mohapatra, B. P. (1961) *The Verb-piece in Oriya*, Unpublished M.A. dissertation, University of London.

Mohanty, P. (1986) *Aspects of Oriya Language: Phonology and Morphology*, Unpublished Ph.D. dissertation, Berhampur University, Berhampur.

Pattanayak, D. P. (1966) *A Controlled Historical Reconstruction of Oriya, Assamese, Bengali and Hindi*, The Hague: Mouton.

—— (1969) 'Oriya and Assamese', in Sebeok, T. (ed.) *Current Trends in Linguistics, volume 5: Linguistics in South Asia*, The Hague: Mouton.

Pattanayak, D. P. and Das, G. N. (1972) *Conversational Oriya*, Mysore: Smt. Sulakshana Pattanayak.

Tripathi, K. B. (1962) *The Evolution of Oriya Language and Script*, Cuttack: Utkal University.

Young, A. H. (1935) *First Lessons in Oriya*, Cuttack: Orissa Mission Press.

CHAPTER TWELVE

MAITHILI

Ramawatar Yadav

CONTENTS

LIST OF TABLES

1 BACKGROUND

Maithili, a descendant of the Māgadhī Apabhraṁśa, is an eastern Indo-Aryan language. According to an estimate (Davis 1973: 316), it is spoken by approximately 21 million people in the eastern and northern regions of the Bihar State of India and the southeastern plains, known as the *tarāī*, of Nepal. Short of carrying out a new linguistic survey of Bihar, it is not easy to ascertain the exact number of speakers of Maithili in contemporary Bihar. Current censuses of India tend to underreport the figure for Maithili – Maithili being erroneously viewed as a dialect of Hindi, or of a spurious language called Bihari.

For example, the 1961 census figure of less than 5 million (4,982,615) Maithili speakers in Bihar seems grossly inaccurate when compared with the figure of more than 9 million (9,389,376) given by Sir George Abraham Grierson as early as 1891 (Brass 1974: 64). In a guesstimate of the raw 1971 census figure arrived at by adding up the population of the districts of Purnea, Saharsa, Darbhanga, Muzaffarpur, Bhagalpur, Monghyr (half) and Santhal Pargana (half), G. Jha (1974: 4–6) argues that around 23 million (22,998,706) people speak Maithili in Bihar. Adding up the Nepal 1971 census figure of 1,327,242 Maithili speakers to the population of Maithili speakers of Bihar, a total of more than 24 million (24,325,948) persons may be said to speak Maithili in India and Nepal. In a survey of the 50 most-spoken languages in the world, carried out by Grimes (1996: 588) and reported on the Internet (*http://infoplease.com/ipa/A0774735.html*), Maithili ranks as the fortieth most-spoken language in the world and that it is spoken by 24.3 million 'first language speakers' in India and Nepal. The 2001 census of Nepal reports that a total of 2,797,382 persons (i.e. twice the number of speakers as of the 1971 census) speak Maithili natively in Nepal. No such census figure is available for Bihar in India. Nevertheless it may be safely asserted that currently there are about 30 million native speakers of Maithili in India and Nepal.

Demographically, Maithili is the second most widely spoken language of Nepal, and the Constitution of Nepal recognizes it as one of the 'languages of the nation' (*rāṣṭrīya bhāṣā*) of Nepal. Maithili is now also included in the Eighth Schedule of the Constitution of India as the 20th major language. Maithili is not yet recognized as an official language of Bihar; it has, however, been recognized as an autonomous modern Indo-Aryan language by the Indian branch of the P.E.N. since 1947 and as the sixteenth largest language of India by the Sahitya Akademi (Academy of Letters) since 1965. Today, Maithili is recognized as a distinct language and taught as such in the Indian universities of Calcutta, Patna, Bihar, Bhagalpur, Mithila and Benares, and the Tribhuvan University and the Nepal Sanskrit University. Maithili is also taught as a school subject in the secondary schools of India and Nepal.

Since Hindi is used as the medium of instruction in the schools of north Bihar, most literate Maithili speakers of Bihar are bilingual in Hindi. By the same token, the literate Maithili speakers of Nepal are bilingual in Nepali – this being the medium of instruction in the schools of Nepal. Literate Maithili speakers in the Nepal *tarāī* also tend to be bilingual in Hindi due to constant travel across the border to India for social commerce and preponderant use of Hindi newspapers, magazines and films. However, the illiterate rural masses of Maithili speakers in India and Nepal are by and large monolingual.

On the boundaries of Maithili, a number of modern Indo-Aryan languages are spoken: Bangla in the east, Bhojpuri in the west, Nepali in the north, and Magahi in the south. Within its own territory in India, Maithili has both contiguity and contact with Santhali – a Munda language. During the fourteenth to early eighteenth centuries, Maithili also came in close contact with Newari (a Tibeto-Burman language spoken in the Kathmandu Valley) and in fact occupied the pride of place in the royal court of the Malla Kings of Nepal.

Within the boundaries of India and Nepal, Maithili is characterized by considerable internal, regional and social (especially caste) variations (Yadav 1995, 1999) – the full extent of which has not been adequately surveyed since Grierson (1883–7). The standard of spoken Maithili is tacitly identified with the speech of the towns of Madhubani in Bihar and Rajbiraj in Nepal.

In the course of its history, Maithili has developed a number of innovations that set it apart from other neighbouring languages. For instance, Maithili has almost lost the OIA gender system. Modem Maithili has no grammatical number either. It has also developed overwhelming honorificity distinctions in its pronominal system as well as an uncharacteristically complex verbal agreement morphology, not shared by other Indo-Aryan languages of India and Nepal.

References to Maithili as a language date back to 1801 (Colebrooke 1801). However, serious interest in the Maithili language and linguistics began in the early 1880s, when Grierson published a series of scholarly books and papers on Maithili. In 1881, Grierson published the first grammar of Maithili entitled: *An Introduction to the Maithilī Language of North Bihār*. The major contribution of Grierson, however, lies in the very extensive dialectal survey of what he somewhat erroneously called Bihari (i.e. Maithili, Magahi and Bhojpuri), published during 1883–7 as the *Seven Grammars of the Dialects and Sub-dialects of the Bihārī Language*. A consummate summary of all the major findings was later published in Grierson's (1903) *Linguistic Survey of India 5:2*. Several native scholars have also published book-length grammatical studies of Maithili. Prominent among these are: D. Jha 1946, S. Jha 1958, G. Jha 1974, 1979, Yadav 1984d, 1996, Yadava 1998 and S. K. Jha 2001. The only unpublished doctoral dissertation that deserves mention is Singh 1979. Maithili, however, continues to remain a less-known and less-studied language. Lexicographical study of Maithili has also suffered from neglect, and as of today no satisfactory Maithili–English, English–Maithili, Maithili–Hindi, Hindi–Maithili, Maithili–Nepali, Nepali–Maithili dictionaries are available. The three well-known monolingual dictionaries in existence are: D. Jha 1950, G. Jha 1992, 1993 and M. N. Mishra 1998, and the only bilingual (i.e. Maithili–English) dictionary in existence is G. Jha 1999.

Maithili has a long literary tradition dating back to the thirteenth century. The *Varṇa–Ratnākara* of Jyotirīśvara-Kaviśekharācārya (Chatterji and Misra 1940) is the oldest extant prose text of the Maithili language; it dates back to the early fourteenth century and is preserved in a manuscript written in 1507. Some Maithili scholars (J. Mishra 1949: 101–18, S. Jha 1958: 32–6) claim unreservedly that the *Caryāpada* hymns (*c*. 900–1200) are also written in some form of Old Maithili, while many Bangla scholars, including S. K. Chatterji, argue that the *Caryāpada* hymns were written in Old Bangla. The controversy rages on to include other Indian languages such as

TABLE 12.1: MAITHILI PHONEMES

	Consonants					
	Bilabial	Dental	Retroflex	Palatal	Velar	Glottal
Stops	p	t	ṭ		k	
	ph	th	ṭh		kh	
	b	d	ḍ		g	
	bh	dh	ḍh		gh	
Affricates				c		
				ch		
				j		
				jh		
Nasals	m	n	(ṇ)		(ŋ)	
Taps		r	(ṛ)			
Fricatives		s	(ṣ)	(š)		h
Approximants	(w)			(y)		

	Vowels		
	Front	Central	Back
High	i		u
Mid	e	ɔ	o
Low	æ	a	ɔ

+/- ~ (nasalization)

Old Assamese and Old Oriya as well. The greatest Maithili poet is Vidyāpati (*c.* 1350–1438), whose *Padāvalī* is the finest specimen of graceful lyrics written in Maithili.

2 SOUND SYSTEM AND SCRIPT

The inventory of Maithili consonant and vowel phonemes is shown in table 12.1. Phonemes enclosed in parentheses are marginal.

2.1 Vowels

The eight oral vowel phonemes in Maithili are: /i/ high front, /e/ mid front, /æ/ low front, /ə/ mid central, /a/ low central, /u/ high back, /o/ mid back, and /ɔ/ low back. All vowels can be nasalized. Lip rounding is not distinctive in Maithili; only the back vowels are rounded. Length is also not distinctive in Maithili, although the Devanāgarī script in

TABLE 12.2: EXAMPLES OF VOWEL CONTRASTS

Front vowels /i e æ/
/i/ 'this' /piʈ/ 'beat (IMP)' /ki/ 'what'
/ek/ 'one' /peʈ/ 'stomach' /ke/ 'who'
/æb/ 'defect' /pær/ 'feet' /gæ/ 'cow'

Central vowels /ə a/
/ən/ 'grain' /phər/ 'fruit' /kərə/ 'do (IMP)'
/an/ 'bring!' /phar/ 'ploughshare' /kəra/ 'hard'

Back vowels /u o ɔ/
/us/ 'whitener' /kus/ 'a kind of grass used for worship' /kəru/ '(chilli) hot'
/os/ 'dew' /kos/ 'two miles' /koro/ 'bamboo pole used in a thatched house'
/ɔrh/ 'out of sight' /lɔr/ 'male organ' /sərɔ/ 'wrestling'

High vowels /i u/
/inar/ 'well' /mit/ 'friend' /tari/ 'palm juice'
/unar/ 'unbalanced' /mut/ 'urine' /daru/ 'alcohol'

Mid vowels /e ə o/
/ena/ 'like this' /khet/ 'field' /he/ 'a vocative form used for God'
/əna/ 'a coin denomination' /khət/ 'scar mark' /hə/ 'oh'
/ona/ 'like that' /khod/ 'dig (IMP)' /ho/ 'become (IMP)'

Low vowels /æ a ɔ/
/æs/ 'luxury' /pær/ 'feet' /bhæ/ 'brother'
/as/ 'hope' /par/ 'across' /ba/ 'open (IMP)'
/ɔtah/ 'will come (3p HON)' /hɔda/ 'elephant seat' /bhɔ/ 'pretence'

Nasalized vowels
/ĩʈ/ 'brick' /chĩʈ/ 'a dyed garment' /kəhĩ/ 'what if'
/ẽr/ 'heel' /kẽt/ 'cane' /pærẽ/ 'on foot'
/æ̃/ 'what!' /kæ̃kæ̃/ 'bitter cry' /sæ̃/ 'husband'
/ɔ̃/ 'yes!' /hɔ̃s/ 'laugh' /hɔ̃/ 'yes'
/ãʈ/ 'courage' /bãs/ 'bamboo' /kəhã/ 'where'
/ɔ̃ʈəl/ 'boiled' /gɔ̃t/ '(cattle) urine' /bhɔ̃/ 'eyebrow'
/õ/ 'groaning sound' /ghõʈ/ 'swallow (IMP)' /khõkhõ/ 'cough'
/ũʈ/ 'camel' /sũra/ 'grain bug' /kəhũ/ 'what if'

which Maithili is now written does provide separate graphemes for long and short vowels. Examples of contrasts among vowels are given in table 12.2.

/æ/ is a defective phoneme, and is diphthongized as [əë], [aë] or [aï], e.g. /pær/ [pəër] 'feet', /mæ/ [maë] 'mother', /bhæ/ [bhaï] 'brother'. /ə/ occurs primarily in non-final positions. In final position, it appears mainly in the imperative construction where it is a contracted form of the verbal agreement affix -əh for second person mid-honorific. It is worth noting here that the traditional descriptions of Maithili (and of other Indo-Aryan languages) transcribe all final consonants as if they were followed by a schwa /ə/, e.g. /babhən/ 'brahmin' is written as [babhənə]. There is no empirical reason for continuing to do so, since these 'inherent vowels' were dropped centuries ago (Yadav 1984b).

Of the back vowels, /ɔ/ is a defective phoneme, and it varies with [o] and [əŭ]; e.g. [sərɔ] ~ [səro] 'wrestling', [ɔtah] ~ [əŭtah] 'will come (3p HON)', [kɔr] ~ [kor] 'morsel'.

Not only does Maithili have nasalized vowels but vowel nasalization is also phonetically conditioned within a syllable and occasionally even across a syllable boundary; e.g. [nãk] 'nose', [hə̃m] 'I', [tõ + hu] ~ [tõhũ] 'even you', [hə̃m + hi] ~ [hə̃mhĩ] 'only I'.

Diphthongization in Maithili is closely related to vowel clustering (Yadav 1984d, 1996). Most diphthongs are rising diphthongs. For example:

[əi]	[kəĭl]	'brown'	[əu]	[kəŭa]	'crow'
[ai]	[kaĭlh]	'yesterday, tomorrow'	[au]	[jaŭt]	'husband's brother's son'
[oi]	[koĭli]	'cuckoo'	[ui]	[buĭr]	'vagina'
[iu]	[piŭsi]	'father's sister'	[ou]	[hoŭ]	'become (IMP, 2p HON)'
[eu]	[ḍeŭṛhi]	'court'			

There are constraints on diphthongization; such diphthongs as *æi, *æu, *ɔi, *ɔu, *ei, *ii, *uu are not permissible in Maithili.

2.2 Consonants

Maithili stops are bilabial, dental, retroflex, palatal and velar. As in most Indo-Aryan languages, there is a four-way contrast between voiced and voiceless and aspirated and unaspirated stops. Examples of consonantal contrasts are given in table 12.3.

Phonologically, affricates also behave like stops. Phonetically, the taps, laterals and nasals also show a two-way contrast between aspirated and unaspirated. Aspiration thus is an overriding characteristic of the Maithili sound system (Yadav 1976). The results of a fibre-optic and acoustic study (Ingemann and Yadav 1978, Yadav 1984a, c, d) conducted to investigate the temporal course and width of the glottis during the production of four types of Maithili stops and affricates and two types of resonants occurring in various positions show that the voiced–voiceless distinction correlates with the adduction–abduction gesture of the larynx. The study also suggests that glottal width is the key factor for aspiration and that sounds which are produced by a combination of vibrating vocal cords and aspiration should, in fact, be called 'voiced aspirated' consonants.

A few words about the 'marginal' phonemes of Maithili are in order. All these so-called marginal phonemes are in fact phonemes of Sanskrit and it has been customary to treat them as phonemes of various modern Indo-Aryan languages, including Maithili. Such a practice is further strengthened by the fact that the Devanāgarī script provides separate letters for all these sounds. There is, however, some justification for omitting these sounds from the inventory of Maithili phonemes.

TABLE 12.3: EXAMPLES OF CONSONANT CONTRASTS

Bilabials /p ph b bh/

/par/ 'across'	/nəpa/ 'measure'	/sãp/ 'snake'
/phar/ 'ploughshare'	/nəpha/ 'profit'	/saph/ 'clean'
/bar/ 'pubic hair'	/səbək/ 'lesson'	/kheb/ 'sail'
/bhar/ 'load'	/səbhək/ 'of all'	/khebh/ 'plant seeds'

Dentals /t th d dh/

/tan/ 'music'	/poti/ 'granddaughter'	/bat/ 'talk (n)'
/than/ 'yards of cloth'	/pothi/ 'book'	/bath/ 'pain'
/dan/ 'charity'	/udar/ 'generous'	/bad/ 'after'
/dhan/ 'paddy'	/udhar/ 'credit'	/badh/ 'lands surrounding a village'

Retroflex /ṭ ṭh ḍ ḍh/

/ṭik/ 'pigtail'	/kəṭgər/ 'shapely'	/ḍãṭ/ 'scold'
/ṭhik/ 'true'	/kəṭhgər/ 'hard'	/ḍhaṭh/ 'fence'
/ḍol/ 'a small bucket'	/ənḍa/ 'egg'	/dənḍ/ 'punishment'
/ḍhol/ 'drum'	/ṭhənḍha/ 'cold'	/ṭhənḍh/ 'cold'

Palatals /c ch j jh/

/cor/ 'thief'	/ɔcar/ 'pickle'	/bic/ 'centre'
/chor/ 'edge'	/əchar/ 'shower'	/bich/ 'pick up'
/jor/ 'strength'	/bajəl/ 'spoken'	/bij/ 'seed'
/jhor/ 'soup'	/bajhəl/ 'entangled'	/bijh/ 'rust'

Velars /k kh g gh/

/kam/ 'work'	/kəkri/ 'a cucumber-like vegetable'	/bik/ 'sell'
/kham/ 'pole'	/khəkhri/ 'paddy without rice'	/bikh/ 'poison'
/gam/ 'village'	/gəgri/ 'a small pitcher'	/bag/ 'garden'
/gham/ 'sweat'	/ghəghri/ 'skirt'	/bagh/ 'tiger'

Nasals /m n/

/mam/ 'mother's brother'	/mami/ 'mother's brother's wife'	/kam/ 'work'
/nam/ 'name'	/nani/ 'mother's mother'	/kan/ 'ear'

Liquids /r l/

/rer/ 'crowd'	/baru/ 'light (IMP 2P HON)'	/cir/ 'a garment'
/ler/ 'saliva'	/balu/ 'sand'	/cil/ 'eagle'

Fricatives /s h/

/sar/ 'wife's brother'	/pəsar/ 'spread' (IMP 2P NON-HON)	/ghas/ 'grass'
/har/ 'garland'	/pəhar/ 'mountain'	/ghah/ 'wound'

The velar nasal [ŋ] occurs only non-initially and is followed by a homorganic stop, which if voiced and non-final may be deleted in some dialects. The voiced stop is always deleted in the final position. Examples:

/jəngəl/	[jəŋgəl] ~ [jəŋəl] 'forest'	/ṭang/	[ṭaŋ] 'leg'
/kənghi/	[kəŋghi] ~ [kəŋhi] 'comb (n)'	/mung/	[muŋ] 'a lentil'
/ḍənka/	[ḍəŋka] 'huge drum'	/ənk/	[əŋk] 'number'
/pənkha/	[pəŋkha] 'fan (n)'	/pənkh/	[pəŋkh] 'wings'

The retroflex nasal [ṇ] also occurs only before /ḍ/ (except in highly literary styles in borrowed words): /ənḍa/ [əṇḍa] 'egg', /ṭhənḍha/ [ṭhəṇḍha] 'cold', /dənḍ/ [dəṇḍ] 'punishment', /dənḍa/ [dəṇḍa] 'heavy staff'. The position taken here is that the velar nasal [ŋ] and the retroflex nasal [ṇ] should be derived from underlying /n/ before a velar stop and a retroflex stop, respectively. In less literary styles, the original pronunciation of [ŋ] in words borrowed from Sanskrit is abandoned. This is evident in the variation that occurs between the final retroflex nasal [ṇ] and the dental nasal [n]: [baṇ] ~ [ban] 'arrow', [praṇ] ~ [pran] 'life', [koṇ] ~ [kon] 'angle'.

Similar stylistic variations also occur in the cases of [š] and [ṣ], which are replaced by dental [s], of [ṛ], which is replaced by a non-retroflex tap [r], and of [w], which is replaced by [b]. [y] and [j] vary freely in colloquial styles. Examples: [šəbd] ~ [səbd] ~ [səbəd] 'word', [šawas] ~ [sabas] 'bravo', [kəṣṭ] ~ [kəst] 'pain', [nəṣṭ] ~ [nəst] 'ruin', [kəṛa] ~ [kəra] 'hard', [maṛ] ~ [mar] 'liquid accompanying boiled rice', [əwətar] ~ [əbətar] ~ [əptar] 'incarnation', [yadəb] ~ [jadəb] 'a family name', [cərya] ~ [cərja] 'routine'.

2.3 Stress and intonation

2.3.1 Stress

Stress has little significance in Maithili, playing only a marginal role in distinguishing words. In brief, despite a few exceptions, the general pattern is for most words of Maithili to receive stress on the penultimate syllable (Yadav 1984d).

2.3.2 Intonation

Declarative sentences and polite commands in Maithili have a falling intonation, e.g.

(1) *həm   əkhbar   pəiṛh   rəhəl   ch-i*
     I   newspaper read   PROG   AUX-PRES-1p
     'I am reading a newspaper.'

(2) *a-u   ne*
     come-IMP-2p HON   DEF
     'Come on in, please!'

Information questions containing *k-* 'who' question words have a falling intonation:

(3) *tõ   ke   ch-əh?*
     you_MID-HON who   AUX-PRES-2p MID-HON
     'Who are you?'

Similarly, yes-no questions formed with the use of a sentence-initial question word *ki* 'what' also have a falling intonation:

(4) *ki   o   cəil   ge-l-ah?*
     what he_HON walk   go-PST-3p HON
     'Did he go away?'

Yes-no questions containing no sentence-initial question word *ki* 'what' have a rising intonation:

(5) *jənəkpur   jae-b?*
     Janakpur go-FUT-2p HON
     'Would you like to go to Janakpur?'

2.4 Morphophonemics

The two morphophonemic alternations that are very productive and regular in Maithili are schwa deletion and replacement of *a* by schwa.

(a)   Schwa deletion: ... *VCəCV* ... → ... *VCØCV* ...

Schwa deletion in Maithili occurs in words/stems containing a schwa as the second vowel when a vowel-initial suffix is added; e.g. *həmər-o* → *həmro* 'even mine', *sərək-e* → *sərke* 'only the road', *ṭəhəl-ət* → *ṭəhlət* 'will walk (3p NON-HON)', *pəsər-əit* → *pəsrəit* 'spreading'.

(b)   *a* → *ə*

Stem internal *a* occurring in the first syllable of a word/stem is changed into *ə* upon the addition of an affix containing a vowel. For example: *babhən* 'brahmin', but *bəbhinia* 'brahmin (F, IMPOL)'; *mar* 'kill', but *məra* 'cause to kill', and *mərba* 'cause to kill (through someone)'. For more information on idiosyncratic morphophonemic alternations in Maithili, see Yadav 1996: 51–9.

2.5 Script

Mithilākṣara, Kaithī and Devanāgarī are the three scripts associated with Maithili. Mithilākṣara is derived from the ancient Brāhmī script, and no books are printed in this script nowadays. Brahmins and Kayasthas use it in rituals for decoration; occasionally, book titles are printed in ornate Mithilākṣara letters.

As the name suggests, Kaithī was used by Kayasthas for record-keeping in government offices during the British regime in India; its use also spread to the Nepal *tarāī*. According to Grierson (1881b), most non-Brahmins used the Kaithī character and found it extremely easy to read and write. Kaithī symbols with their Devanāgarī equivalents and Roman transliterations are given in table 13.1 of the Magahi chapter in this volume.

Towards the turn of the twentieth century, Maithili began to be written in the Devanāgarī script, which is also the script associated with classical Sanskrit and a number of modern Indo-Aryan languages such as Nepali and Hindi. One specific shortcoming of the Devanāgarī script is its inability to represent the vowel [æ] in Maithili; thus, a word like [bhæ] 'brother' is written variously as *bhāe*, *bhāya* and *bhāi*.

3 MORPHOLOGY

3.1 Nominals

Gender, number and case are the morphosyntactic categories by which Maithili nouns may be classified. Modern Maithili, however, has no grammatical gender and number. The gender of a noun is simply inherent, receiving no overt expression on the noun itself, being instead expressed, though restrictedly, in the agreement of verbs. Number is marked only periphrastically by *səb/səbh* 'all' or *lokəin* 'all (HON)', while case is marked inflectionally.

Five cases are distinguished as opposed to the traditional eight cases: nominative (NOM), accusative–dative (ACC-DAT), instrumental (INSTR), genitive (GEN), and locative (LOC). Case relations are expressed in the following ways:

(a) by the absence of a case marker, e.g. the nominative case,
(b) by the suffixation of a case marker, e.g. the genitive case marker *-ək* when the noun phrase ends in a consonant, *-k* when it ends in a vowel, and the instrumental case marker *-e/-ẽ* provided that the noun is not a human proper noun,
(c) by the use of a postposition, e.g. instrumental *sə/sə̃*, locative *me/pər*, and accusative–dative *ke/kẽ*.

For example: *ram* (Ram-NOM), *ram-ək* (Ram-GEN), *rani-k* (queen-GEN), *hath-ẽ* (hand-INSTR), *hath-sə̃* (hand-INSTR), *ghər me* (house-LOC), *raja kẽ* (king-ACC-DAT). Several complex postpositions or combinations of case markers and postpositions indicate specific shades of meaning; e.g. *gam pər sə̃* (village at from) 'from the village', *həm-ra me sə̃* (I-ACC-DAT in from) 'from among mine', *ghər-ək lel* (house-GEN for) 'for the house'.

Adjectives in Maithili precede nouns and show no number or case distinctions. Gender distinctions are shown, but only marginally. Thus, definite adjectives modifying nouns which are animate in reference show masculine and feminine forms; e.g. *moṭ-ka chõra* 'the fat boy', *moṭ-ki chəuri* 'the fat girl'. However, non-definite adjectives do not vary according to gender; e.g. *kari ghoṛa* 'a black horse', *kari ghoṛi* 'a black mare'.

Maithili pronouns are marked for three persons (first, second and third); four grades of honorificity (high honorific, honorific, mid-honorific and non-honorific) for the second person and two grades of honorificity (honorific and non-honorific) for the third person; two numbers (singular and periphrastic plural marked by *səb/səbh* or *lokəin* 'all'); and case. They are not marked for gender. The first person is indeterminate as to honorificity. The Maithili personal pronouns are: *həm* 'I', *əpne* 'you (high honorific)', *əhã* 'you (honorific)', *tõ* 'you (mid-honorific)', *tõ* 'you (non-honorific)' (distinguished by verbal endings), *o* 'he (honorific)', and *u/o* 'he (non-honorific)'.

The case system of the pronouns is more complex than that of the nouns. As a matter of fact, the case morphology of the first and second (mid-honorific and non-honorific) persons is alike (and quite different from that of Maithili nouns), while the case morphology of the second person (high honorific and honorific) pronoun forms is quite regular (and therefore similar to that of the nouns). Examples: *həm-ra* 'to me', *to-ra* 'to you', but *həm-ra səb kẽ* 'to us', *to-ra səb kẽ* 'to you'; *həm-ər* 'mine', *toh-ər* 'yours', but *həm-ər səbh-ək* 'ours', *toh-ər səbh-ək* 'yours', *əpne-k*, *əpne səbh-ək*, *əhã-k*, *əhã səbh-ək* 'yours'.

The third person pronouns are the same as the proximate and remote demonstrative pronouns. The demonstrative pronouns also show the honorific : non-honorific contrast; e.g. *i* 'this' (honorific proximate), *o* 'that' (honorific remote), *i* 'this' (non-honorific proximate) and *u/o* 'that' (non-honorific remote). The declension of the proximate demonstrative *i* is given for illustration in table 12.4.

The interrogative pronouns in Maithili are *ke* 'who' and *ki/kəthi* 'what'. *ke* alone refers to humans, and thus has both honorific and non-honorific forms; e.g. *ke* (NOM); *kin-ka* (ACC-DAT, HON), *kek-ra* (ACC-DAT, NON-HON); *kin-ka sə̃* (INSTR, HON), *kek-ra sə̃* (INSTR, NON-HON); *kin-k-ər* (GEN-HON) *kek-ər* (GEN, NON-HON), *kin-ka me* (LOC, HON), *kek-ra me* (LOC, NON-HON). *ki/kəthi*, on the other hand, is used for non-human (and inanimate) objects, hence does not have honorific distinctions.

The relative pronouns are *je* 'who' (used for humans with honorific : non-honorific forms) and *je* 'what' (used for non-humans with no honorific : non-honorific forms); e.g. *je* (NOM, HON), *jin-ka* (ACC-DAT, HON), *jin-k-ər* (GEN, HON); but *je* (NOM, NON-HON), *jek-ra* (ACC-DAT, NON-HON), *jek-ər* (GEN, NON-HON), and so on. The correlative pronoun is *se*.

TABLE 12.4: DECLENSION OF THE PROXIMATE DEMONSTRATIVE PRONOUNS IN MAITHILI

| | Honorific | | Non-honorific | |
	Singular	Plural	Singular	Plural
Nom	*i*	*i səb*	*i*	*i səb*
Acc-Dat	*hin-ka*	*hin-ka səb kẽ*	*ek-ra*	*ek-ra səb kẽ*
Instr	*hin-ka sə̃*	*hin-ka səb sə̃*	*ek-ra sə̃*	*ek-ra səb sə̃*
Gen	*hin-k-ər*	*hin-k-ər səbh-ək*	*ek-ər*	*ek-ər səbh-ək*
	hin-ək	*hin-ka səbh-ək*		*ek-ra səbh-ək*
Loc	*hin-ka me*	*hin-ka səb me*	*ek-ra me*	*ek-ra səb me*

Like *je, se* has distinct forms depending on whether it is human or non-human in reference; e.g. *se* (NOM), *tin-ka* (ACC-DAT, HON), *tek-ra* (ACC-DAT, NON-HON), *tin-k-ər* (GEN, HON), *tek-ər* (GEN, NON-HON), and so on.

The reflexive pronoun is *əpne* 'self'. The declension of the reflexive pronoun is quite regular, except that the reflexive possessive form is *əpən*, and the accusative-dative and locative forms are *əpna kẽ* and *əpna me*, respectively.

The indefinite pronouns are *keo* 'someone, anyone' (used for humans, with honorificity distinctions) and *kichu* 'something, anything' (used for inanimate objects, with no honorificity distinctions); e.g. *keo* (NOM), *kin-ko* (ACC-DAT, HON), *kek-ro* (ACC-DAT, NON-HON), *kin-ko sə̃* (INSTR, HON), *kek-ro sə̃* (INSTR, NON-HON), *kin-kə-ro* (GEN, HON), *kek-ro* (GEN, NON-HON), and so on.

3.2 Verb morphology

Finite verb forms in Maithili are conjugated for aspect, tense, mood, person and honorificity. Modern Maithili makes no distinction of number (i.e. singular and plural) and gender in the verb system. In highly formal and literary contexts, however, a gender distinction between masculine and feminine is shown by intransitive verbs in non-present tense forms of the third person honorific and by transitive verbs in future tense forms of the third person honorific. Examples:

(6) *raja   əe-l-ah*
king   come-PST-3p HON M
'The king came.'

(7) *rani   əe-l-ih*
queen   come-PST-3p HON F
'The queen came.'

(8) *raja   əu-t-ah*
king   come-FUT-3p HON M
'The king will come.'

(9) *rani   əu-t-ih*
queen   come-FUT-3p HON F
'The queen will come.'

(10) *raja   khǝe-t-ah*
     king   eat-FUT-3p HON M
     'The king will eat.'

(11) *rani   khǝe-t-ih*
     queen   eat-FUT-3p HON F
     'The queen will eat.'

Three aspects can be distinguished in modern Maithili. These are marked as follows:

(i)   imperfective *-ǝit* when the verbal base ends in a consonant, and *-it* when it ends in a vowel,
(ii) perfective *-ne* (transitive) and *-ǝl* (intransitive),
(iii) progressive *rǝhǝl*.

Unless a modal or a compound verb intervenes, the aspect markers are attached directly to the verb stems themselves. Examples:

(12) *ram   ja-it   ch-ǝith*
     Ram   go-IMPERF AUX-PRES-3p HON
     'Ram goes/ is going.'

(13) *ram   khǝe-ne ch-ǝith*
     Ram   eat-PERF AUX-PRES-3p HON
     'Ram has eaten.'

(14) *ram   ge-l   ch-ǝith*
     Ram   go-PERF AUX-PRES-3p HON
     'Ram has gone.'

(15) *ram   kha rǝhǝl ch-ǝith*
     Ram   eat PROG AUX-PRES-3p HON
     'Ram is eating.'

The auxiliary in Maithili requires an aspect marker to appear on the verb stem. Since the auxiliary occurs after the aspect marker, the tense, mood, honorific and agreement markers are all attached to the auxiliary itself. The auxiliary forms in Maithili are: present tense third person non-honorific *ǝich*, present tense elsewhere *ch-*; past tense *ch-*; future tense *rǝh-* and *ho-*. Thus, the auxiliary forms are by their nature tense carriers, and their grammatical function is to provide finiteness to the verbal constellation.

Maithili verbs conjugate for three tenses – past, present and future. The tense markers are: past *-ǝl-* when the verbal base ends in a consonant and *-l-* when it ends in a vowel; future *-ǝb-* (first and second persons) and *-ǝt-* (elsewhere) when the verbal base ends in a consonant, *-b-* and *-t-* when it ends in a vowel; and present *-Ø-*. Note that no overt tense marker is used in the present tense; in other words, in present tense constructions the auxiliary itself serves the function of the tense. Examples:

(16) *tõ   ge-l-ẽ*
     you_NON-HON   go-PST-2p NON-HON
     'You went.'

(17) *tõ   jǝe-b-ẽ*
     you_NON-HON   go-FUT-2p NON-HON
     'You will go.'

(18) *tõ*   *ja-it*   *ch-ẽ*
you_{NON-HON} go-IMPERF AUX-PRES-2p NON-HON
'You go.'

In Maithili, five moods are distinguished: indicative, imperative, optative, presumptive and conditional. On purely morphosyntactic grounds, however, only three moods can be distinguished: imperative, optative and conditional.

As in many natural languages of the world, the unmarked imperative forms of Maithili are the affixless verb stems themselves. However, overt morphological devices are employed in order to indicate honorificity. Unlike in most Indo-Aryan languages, imperative forms are also available in Maithili for the first and third person subject pronouns. The markers of the imperative mood are: *-u* (1p); *-ə, -u* (2p HON); *-əh* (2p MID-HON); *-Ø, -o* (2p NON-HON); *-əuth* (3p HON); and *-ɔ~ -o* (3p NON-HON). Examples:

(19) (*həm*) *ja-u*
I   go-IMP-1p
'May I go!'

(20) (*əhã*)   *ja-u*
you_{HON} go-IMP-2p HON
'(You) go!'

(21) (*əhã*)   *li-ə*
you_{HON} take-IMP-2p HON
'(You) take!'

(22) (*tõ*)   *ab-əh*
you _{MID-HON} come-IMP-2p MID-HON
'(You) come!'

(23) (*tõ*)   *a-Ø*
you _{NON-HON} come-IMP-2p NON-HON
'(You) come!'

(24) (*tõ*)   *kh-o*
you _{NON-HON} eat-IMP-2p NON-HON
'(You) eat!'

(25) (*o*)   *baj-əuth*
he_{HON} speak-IMP-3p HON
'He may speak (Let him speak)!'

(26) (*u*)   *baj-ɔ*
he_{NON-HON} speak-IMP-3p NON-HON
'He may speak (Let him speak)!'

Maithili also has 'future' imperative constructions involving second person mid-honorific and non-honorific subjects alone. For the future imperative, Maithili uses a distinct morphological marker *-ih-* which conveys that the speaker asks the addressee categorically to perform the task at a time later than the time of asking. Examples:

(27) *rəu*   *chõṛa tõ*   *kailh*   *jə-ih-e*
VOC-2p NON-HON boy   you _{NON-HON} tomorrow go-FUT IMP-2p NON-HON
'Boy, go tomorrow!'

(28) *həu   bhəiya tõ   ghər dekh-ih-əh*
VOC-2p MID-HON brother you_{MID-HON} house see-FUT IMP-2p MID-HON
'Brother, keep an eye on the house!'

In impersonal imperative constructions, the markers of the imperative mood is invariably *-i*, as in

(29) *ena   nəi baj-i*
this way not speak-IMP
'One should not talk like this!'

The markers of the optative mood are: *-i* (1p and 2p HON), *-əh* (2p MID-HON), *-o* (2p NON-HON), *-əith* (3p HON), *-əe ~ -ɔ* (3p NON-HON). For example:

(30) *he bhəgban həm pas bhə   ja-i*
VOC god   I   pass become go-OPT–1p
'May I pass, O Lord!'

(31) *raja dirghau ho-ith*
king longlife become-OPT-3p HON
'May the king live long!'

A typical conditional sentence consists of an antecedent (or a condition) clause with *jɔ̃* (or *jədi*) 'if' and a consequent clause with *tə* 'then':

(32) *jɔ̃ həm ṭhaṛh bhe-l-əhũ   tə   əhã   cheka jae-b*
if I   stand become-PST-1p then you_{HON} block go-FUT-2p HON
'If I stood, you would be blocked.'

The marker of the counterfactual conditional mood in Maithili is basically *-it* for all persons. Tense distinctions may not be shown, but the honorificity distinctions are obligatorily maintained even in counterfactual conditionals, e.g.

(33) *jɔ̃ o   həm-ər bat suin-t-əith   tə*
if he_{HON} I-GEN talk hear-COND-3p HON then
   hun-ka   ena   nəi ho-it-əinh
he_{HON}-ACC-DAT this way not be-COND-3p HON
'Had he listened to me, he wouldn't have suffered so.'

Maithili has one of the most complex agreement systems of the Indo-Aryan languages and probably of all the languages of the world (Stump and Yadav 1988, Yadav 1996). In Maithili, the agreement rules function to copy features from the noun phrase onto verbal inflections. In a thorough description of Maithili verb morphology, two kinds of agreement inflections must be distinguished. A verb's *primary* agreement inflection encodes the features of person and honorific grade of the subject noun phrase which is in the nominative case, and is obligatory. The inflectional affixes vary according to tense and transitivity, as shown in table 12.5.

A few examples will serve to illustrate:

(34) *həm ja-it   ch-i*
I   go-IMPERF AUX-PRES-1p
'I go/am going.'

TABLE 12.5: 'PRIMARY' AGREEMENT AFFIXES OF MAITHILI VERBS

	1p	2p HON	2p MID-HON	2p NON-HON	3p HON		3p NON-HON
Present	-i	-i	-əh	-e/-ẽ		-əith	-Ø ~ -əik
						(-əthinh)	
Past	-əhũ/-i	-əhũ/-i	-əh	-e/-ẽ	tr	-əinh	-ək
						(-əith)	
						(-əthinh)	
						(-əkhinh)	
					intr	-ah	-Ø
						(-əith)	
						(-əthinh)	
						(-əkhinh)	
Future	Ø/-əik	Ø/-əik	-əh	-e/-ẽ		-ah	-Ø ~ -əik
						(-əthinh)	

(35) *həm   ge-l-əhũ*
     I   go-PST-1p
     'I went.'

(36) *həm   jae-b-Ø*
     I   go-FUT-1p
     'I will go.'

(37) *tõ   ja-it   ch-əh*
     you_MID-HON go-IMPERF   AUX-PRES-2p MID-HON
     'You go/are going.'

(38) *tõ   ge-l-əh*
     you_MID-HON go-PST-2p MID-HON
     'You went.'

(39) *tõ   jəe-b-əh*
     you_MID-HON go-FUT-2p MID-HON
     'You will go.'

(40) *o   ja-it   ch-əith/əthinh*
     he_HON   go-IMPERF   AUX-PRES-3p HON
     'He goes/is going.'

(41) *o   ge-l-ah*
     he_HON   go-PST-3p HON
     'He went.'

(42) *o   jəe-t-ah*
     he_HON   go-FUT-3p HON
     'He will go.'

In addition to its primary inflection, a Maithili verb may also bear a *secondary* agreement inflection. In such an instance, where the primary dimension of agreement is nominative, the secondary dimension is controlled by the person and honorific grade of the verb's object arguments encoded with the accusative-dative case. Thus in sentences

(43)–(46), the verb bears a secondary agreement inflection controlled by the direct object noun phrase:

(43) *həm   to-ra*   *kəh-əl-iəuk*
    I   you_{NON-HON}-ACC-DAT say-PST-1p+2p NON-HON
    'I told you (NON-HON).'

(44) *həm   to-ra*   *kəh-əl-iəh*
    I   you_{MID-HON}-ACC-DAT say-PST-1p+2p MID-HON
    'I told you (MID-HON).'

(45) *həm ok-ra*   *kəh-əl-iəik*
    I   he_{NON-HON}-ACC-DAT say-PST-1p+3p NON-HON
    'I told him (NON-HON).'

(46) *həm   hun-ka*   *kəh-əl-iəinh*
    I   he_{HON}-ACC-DAT say-PST-1p+3p HON
    'I told him (HON).'

The agreement affixes may vary with the tense of the verb, as shown in tables 12.6–8.

TABLE 12.6: 'SECONDARY' VERB AGREEMENT INFLECTIONS FOR PRESENT TENSE IN MAITHILI

Object	1p	2p NON-HON	2p MID-HON	2p HON	3p NON-HON	3p HON
Subject						
1p	–	iəuk	iəh	∅	iəik/∅	iəinh
2p NON-HON	∅	–	–	–	əhik/∅	əhunh
2p MID-HON	∅	–	–	–	əhək	əhunh
2p HON	∅	–	–	–	iəik/∅	iəinh
3p NON-HON	∅	əuk	əh	∅	əik/∅	əinh
3p HON	∅	əthunh	əthunh	∅	əthinh	əthinh

Notes: ∅ = no overt marking; – = does not apply

TABLE 12.7: 'SECONDARY' VERB AGREEMENT INFLECTIONS FOR PAST TENSE IN MAITHILI

Object	1p	2p NON-HON	2p MID-HON	2p HON	3p NON-HON	3p HON
Subject						
1p	–	iəuk	iəh	∅	iəik (∅)	iəinh
2p NON-HON	∅	–	–	–	əhik	əhunh
2p MID-HON	∅	–	–	–	əhək	əhunh
2p HON	∅	–	–	–	iəik	iəinh
3p NON-HON	∅	əkəuk	əkəh	∅	əkəik	əkəinh
		(əuk)	(əh)		(əik)	(əinh)
3p HON	əinh	əkhunh	əkhunh	əinh (∅)	əkhinh	əkhinh
		əkhuhunh	əkhuhunh		əthinh	əthinh
		əthunh	əthunh		(əinh)	əkhihinh
		əthuhunh	əthuhunh			əthihinh
						(əkəinh)
						(əinh)

TABLE 12.8: 'SECONDARY' VERB AGREEMENT INFLECTIONS FOR FUTURE TENSE IN MAITHILI

Object	1p	2p NON-HON	2p MID-HON	2p HON	3p NON-HON	3p HON
Subject						
1p	–	ɔuk	əh	Ø	əik (Ø)	əinh
2p NON-HON	Ø	–	–	–	əhik	əhunh
2p MID-HON	Ø	–	–	–	əhək	əhunh
2p HON	Ø	–	–	–	əik	əinh
3p NON-HON	Ø	ɔuk	əh	Ø	əik	əinh
3p HON	Ø	əthunh	əthunh	Ø	əthinh	əinh
						əthinh

A few examples are given below for illustration.

Present tense

(47) *həm hun-ka kitab də-it ch-iəinh*
   I he_HON-ACC-DAT book give-IMPERF AUX-PRES-1p+3p HON
   'I give him a book.'

(48) *o to-ra kitab də-it ch-əthunh*
   he_HON you _NON-HON-ACC-DAT book give-IMPERF AUX-PRES-3p HON+2p NON-HON
   'He gives you a book.'

Past tense

(49) *tõ ok-ra kitab de-l-hək*
   you_MID-HON he _NON-HON-ACC-DAT book give-PST-2p MID-HON+3p NON-HON
   'You gave him a book.'

(50) *o hun-ka kitab de-l-thihinh*
   he_HON he_HON-ACC-DAT book give-PST-3p HON+3p HON
   'He gave him a book.'

Future tense

(51) *əhã hun-ka kitab de-b-əinh*
   you_HON he_HON-ACC-DAT book give-FUT-2p HON+3p HON
   'You will give him a book.'

(52) *o to-ra kitab de-t-əthunh*
   he_HON you _NON-HON-ACC-DAT book give-FUT-3p HON+2p NON-HON
   'He will give you a book.'

The person and honorific grade of the genitive noun phrase modifying the subject noun phrase also trigger the secondary verb agreement. The genitive modifiers, however, behave like ordinary non-subject noun phrases in controlling the secondary verb agreement. For example:

(53) *toh-ər pita ji əe-l-thunh*
   you _NON-HON-GEN father HON come-PST-3p HON+2p NON-HON
   'Your father came.'

(54) *hun-k-ər   nokər   khəe-l-kəinh*
he_{HON}-GEN   servant   eat-PST-3p NON-HON+3p HON
'His servant ate.'

Genitive noun phrases modifying the direct object noun phrases also trigger the secondary verb agreement:

(55) *o   toh-ər   babu-o   kẽ   dekh-əl-thunh*
he_{HON} you_{NON-HON}-GEN father_{HON}-EMPHT ACC-DAT see- PST-3p HON+2p NON-HON
'He saw even your father.'

(56) *u   toh-ər   bet-o   kẽ*
he _{NON-HON} you_{NON-HON}-GEN son _{NON-HON}-EMPHT ACC-DAT
dekh-əl-kəuk
see-PST-3p NON-HON+2p NON-HON
'He saw even your son.'

The person and honorific grade of 'dative subjects' may seem to trigger the secondary verb agreement. However, if the dative subject construction is interpreted as a regular SOV construction in which the DO equals S, and the 'dative' S equals DO, then the general rules of secondary verb agreement apply:

(57) *hun-ka   həsi   laig   ge-l-əinh*
he_{HON}-ACC-DAT laughter attach go-PST-3p NON-HON+3p HON
'He felt like laughing.'

(58) *jənardən kẽ   radha nik   ləg-əl-khinh/khihinh*
Janardan ACC-DAT Radha good attach-PST-3p HON+3p HON
'Janardan liked Radha.'

For more information on the complex verb agreement system in Maithili, the reader is referred to Stump and Yadav 1988 and Yadav 1996.

Maithili verbs are involved in two highly productive processes of derivation. The first is causativization, which is mainly suffixal. For example: *mər-əb* 'to die' (intr), *mar-əb* 'kill/cause to die' (tr), *mər-a-eb* 'cause to kill' (caus I), and *mər-ba-eb* 'have (someone) kill' (caus II); *pərh-əb* 'read/study (tr)', *pərh-a-eb* 'teach/cause to read' (caus I), and *pərh-ba-eb* 'have (someone) teach' (caus II).

The second derivational process is the formation of compound verbs, which in linear terms consist of a sequence of a main verb plus an appropriately inflected finite form of a second verb – from a limited set – that modifies or adds a specific nuance to the meaning of the main verb. For example: *kha le-l-əinh* (eat take-PST-3p HON) 'he ate up', *lə l-e* (take take-IMP-2p NON-HON) 'take yourself!', *mair ge-l-ah* (die go-PST-3p HON) 'he died', *bhag pər-o* (run away lie-IMP-2p NON-HON) '(you) get out of here!'

An equally productive verbal compounding involves a set of complex predicates, popularly known as conjunct verbs, which consist of a nominal followed by a rather small set of verbs; e.g. *pəsin kər-əb* (liking do-INF) 'to like', *gor lag-əb* (feet attach-INF) 'to greet (by touching the feet)', *khəbər de-b* (news give-INF) 'to inform'.

4 SYNTAX

The basic unmarked word order of the major constituents of the sentence in Maithili is Subject, Object, Verb (SOV) in that order. Within a noun phrase, attributive adjectives

(ADJ) and genitive modifiers (GEN) precede head nouns (N), while in a relative clause construction the head noun predominantly precedes the relative clause (REL). Postpositions (PP) follow the noun phrase. In the verb phrase, auxiliary verbs typically follow the main verbs, while the adverbial modifier and the negator are preverbal in Maithili. Adverbials can also precede sentences. In sum, Maithili is a nominative-accusative rather than an ergative language; it shows SOV, GEN N, ADJ N, N REL, VB AUX and N PP ordering, and it is a suffixing language.

Maithili has both periphrastic and inflectional passive constructions. The periphrastic passive is formed by using the past participle stem of the main verb plus an auxiliary verb of motion *ja* 'go', to which are affixed all the inflectional endings. The inflectional passive is formed by adding -*a* to the main verb. A passive sentence with the ex-subject/agent (marked with the instrumental postposition *sə/sə̃*) present conveys a capabilitative meaning; the passive with agent is usually in the negative and expresses the agent's inability to do something. For example:

(59) *həm-ra   sə̃   nəi hə̃s-ae-l*   (inflectional passive)
I-ACC-DAT   INSTR not laugh-PASS-PST-3p NON-HON+1p
'I was not able to laugh.' (lit 'It was not laughed by me.')

(60) *həm-ra   sə̃   nəi hə̃s-əl   ge-l*   (periphrastic passive)
I-ACC-DAT INSTR not laugh-PST PTCPL go-PST-3p NON-HON+1p
'I could not laugh.' (lit 'It was not laughed by me.')

Agentless passive sentences, on the other hand, do not convey the capabilitative meaning and have meanings similar to those of their English equivalents:

(61) *ghər   bənae-l   ge-l*
house   build-PST PTCPL go-PST-3p NON-HON
'The house was built.' (* 'The house could be built.')

Coordination in Maithili involves the linking of two (or more) categories of expression with the use of the coordinator *a*. Examples:

(62) *əhã   [$_{AP}$ dhənik a nami] dunu ch-i*
you$_{HON}$ rich and famous   both AUX-PRES-2p HON
'You are both rich and famous.'

(63) *[$_S$ tren khuj-əl   a   həm hath hilɔ-l-əhũ]*
train open-PST-3p NON-HON and I   hand shake-PST-1p
'The train started and I waved.'

(64) *[$_{NP}$ ram a   mohən] pəhũc ge-l-ah*
Ram   and Mohan   arrive go-PST-3p HON
'Ram and Mohan arrived.'

(65) *əhã   [$_{PP}$ həm -ra (sə̃) a   beṭi   sə̃]   nəi baj-u*
you$_{HON}$ I-ACC-DAT from and daughter from not speak-IMP-2p HON
'Please do not talk to me and (my) daughter.'

Three types of subordinate clauses may be recognized in Maithili: complement clauses, relative clauses, and adverbial clauses. A complement clause in Maithili is formed by the use of a number of complementizers: *je*, *ki* or *jeki* – all meaning 'that'. *je*, however, is the most common complementizer:

(66) *o   jən-əit   ch-əith   [je   əhã   gayək ch-i]*
he_{HON} know-IMPERF AUX-PRES-3p HON COMPZ you_{HON} singer AUX-PRES-2p HON
'He knows that you are a singer.'

(67) *i   bat   [je   həm jərmən bəj-əit   ch-i]   səb*
this matter COMPZ I   German speak-IMPERF AUX-PRES-1p all
kẽ   bujh-əl   ch-əinh
ACC-DAT know-PST PTCPL AUX-PRES-3p NON-HON+3p HON
'The fact that I can speak German is known to all.'

A relative clause in Maithili is formed by the use of a relativizer *je* 'who', which serves as a determiner when the noun is present in the subordinate clause. The noun phrase of the relative clause is correferential with the head noun phrase of the main clause. The head noun phrase consists of a correlative pronoun *se* or the demonstrative pronoun *i/u*:

(68) *[je nəṭua rait nac-əl]   se/u ekhən sutəl*
REL dancer night dance-PST-3p NON-HON COR now   asleep
əich
be-PRES-3p NON-HON
'The dancer who danced last night is now asleep.'

(69) *u   chɔ̃ra [je kailh   ae-l   ch-əl]*
that boy   REL yesterday come-PST PTCPL be-PST-3p NON-HON
(se) ok-ər   jəmae   ch-əl-əik
COR he _{NON-HON}-GEN son-in-law be-PST-3p NON-HON
'The boy who had come yesterday was his son-in-law.'

Adverbial clauses in Maithili can be divided into the following types: time, location, manner, reason, result, purpose, simultaneity, condition, counterfactual condition, and converbal. A few examples are given below for illustration.

Time

(70) *jəhiya əhã   əe-l-əhũ   təhiya həm gam   ch-əl-əhũ*
when   you_{HON} come-PST-2p HON then   I   village be-PST-1p
'When you arrived, I was in the village.'

Location

(71) *jətə   kəh-əb   tətə həm jae-b*
where say-FUT-2p HON+1p there I   go-FUT-1p
'I will go wherever you ask me to go.'

Purpose

(72) *həm əŋreji pəṛh-ə bilaet   ge-l-əhũ*
I   English read-INF England go-PST-1p
'I went to England (in order) to study English.'

Simultaneity

(73) *chɔ̃ra hə̃s-əit   hə̃s-əit   kan-ə   lag-əl*
boy   laugh-IMPERF laugh-IMPERF weep-INF attach-PST-3p NON-HON
'The boy began to cry while laughing.'

Finally, converbal adverbial clauses are formed by adding the converbal affix *kə* to the verb stem of the subordinate clause. For more information on Maithili converbal constructions and their diachronic origins, see Yadav 2004.

(74) *həm   nəha kə   bhojən kər-əit   ch-i*
     I   bathe CONV meal   do-IMPERF AUX-PRES-1p
     'I bathe before eating.' (lit 'Having bathed, I have my meal.')

(75) *u   məugi səb sə̃   hə̃is kə   gəp kər-əit   əich*
     that woman all from laugh CONV talk do-IMPERF AUX-PRES-3p NON-HON
     'The woman talks to everyone smilingly/pleasantly.'

5 CONCLUSION

Maithili shares a common core vocabulary with other Indo-Aryan languages such as Hindi and Nepali. Over ninety percent of Modern Maithili vocabulary is Indo-Aryan. Modern Maithili, however, diverges from the earlier Indo-Aryan in a number of ways, in that a few newer traits have emerged. Modern Maithili is characterized by loss of number and gender; it has developed profusely overwhelming honorific distinctions; and, at the same time, it has developed a highly complex verbal agreement system. These recent developments have led modern-day linguists to conclude that Maithili is a distinct language. As early an investigator as Grierson (1881b 'Preface': v–vi) observed that:

> The native language of every Bihārī is as different from Hindī as French is from Italian ...
> ... but it [Hindi] is not, never was, and never can be the vernacular of Bihār. History and the laws of philology alike decide against it, and experience has shown how Norman-French never became the vernacular of England.

REFERENCES

Brass, Paul R. (1974) *Language, Religion and Politics in North India*, Cambridge University Press.
Chatterji, S. K. and Misra, B. (eds.) (1940) *Varṇa-Ratnâkara of Jyotirīśvara-Kaviśekharâcārya* (Bibliotheca Indica 262), Calcutta: Royal Asiatic Society of Bengal.
Colebrooke, H. T. (1801) 'On the Sanscrit and Prácrit languages', *Asiatic Researches* 7: 199–231.
Davis, Alice I. (1973) 'Maithili sentences', in Hale, Austin (ed.) *Clause, Sentence, and Discourse Patterns in Selected Languages of Nepal* 1, University of Oklahoma, Norman: Summer Institute of Linguistics, pp. 259–319.
Grierson, George A. (1881a) *An Introduction to the Maithilī Language of North Bihār*, Part 1, 'Grammar', Calcutta: Asiatic Society of Bengal.
—— (1881b) *A Handbook to the Kaithi Character*, Calcutta: Thacker, Spink & Co. (Second revised edition 1899).
—— (1883–7) *Seven Grammars of the Dialects and Subdialects of the Bihārī Language*, Parts 1–8, Calcutta: Bengal Secretariat Press.
—— (1903) *Linguistic Survey of India, Volume V, Indo-Aryan Family, Eastern group, Part II: Specimens of the Bihārī and Oriyā languages*, Calcutta: Office of the Superintendent of Government Printing (Reprinted (1968), Delhi: Motilal Banarsidass).
Grimes, Barbara F. (ed.) (1996) *Ethnologue: Languages of the World* (13th Edition), Dallas, Texas: Summer Institute of Linguistics.
Ingemann, Frances and Yadav, Ramawatar (1978) 'Voiced aspirated consonants', in Lance, D. M. and Gulstad, D. E. (eds.) *Papers from the 1977 Mid-America Linguistics Conference*, Columbia: University of Missouri, pp. 337–44.

Jha, Dinabandhu (1946) *Maithilī-Bhāṣā-Vidyotana* (Maithili Grammar), Darbhanga: Maithilī Sāhitya Pariṣada. (In Maithili)
—— (1950) *Mithilā Bhāṣā Koṣa* (Maithili Dictionary), Patna: Sri Rambhajan Press. (In Maithili)
Jha, Govind (1974) *Maithilī Bhāṣā kā Vikāsa* (Development of the Maithili Language), Patna: Bihar Hindi Granth Academy. (In Hindi)
—— (1979) *Uccatara Maithilī Vyākaraṇa* (Higher Maithili Grammar), Patna: Maithili Academy. (In Maithili)
—— (1992) *Maithilī Śabdakośa* (Maithili Dictionary), Part 1, Patna: Maithili Academy. (In Maithili)
—— (1993) *Maithilī Śabdakośa* (Maithili Dictionary), Part 2, Patna: Maithili Academy. (In Maithili)
Jha, Subhadra (1958) *The Formation of the Maithilī Language*, London: Luzac.
Jha, Sunil K. (1984) 'A Study of Some Phonetic and Phonological Aspects of Maithili', Unpublished Ph.D. Thesis, University of Essex.
Mishra, Jayakanta (1949) *A History of Maithili Literature* 1, Allahabad: Tirbhukti Publications.
Mishra, Mati Nath (1998) *Maithilī Śabda Kalpadruma* (Maithili Dictionary), Jamuthari, Jhanjharpur, Madhubani: Mishra Bandhu Publications. (In Maithili)
Nepāla Adhirājyako Saṁvidhāna 2047 (The Constitution of Nepal 1990). (In Nepali)
Singh, U. N. (1979) 'Some Aspects of Maithili Syntax: A Transformational-Generative Approach', Unpublished Ph.D. Dissertation, University of Delhi.
Stump, Gregory T. and Yadav, Ramawatar (1988) 'Maithili verb agreement and the control agreement principle', *Chicago Linguistics Society Parasession on Agreement in Grammatical Theory* 24.2: 304–21.
Yadav, Ramawatar (1976) 'Generative phonology and the aspirated consonants of colloquial Maithili', *Contributions to Nepalese Studies* 4.1: 77–91.
—— (1984a) 'Voicing and aspiration in Maithili: A fiberoptic and acoustic study', *Indian Linguistics* 45: 1–30.
—— (1984b) 'Maithili phonology reconsidered', *Studien zur Indologie und Iranistik* 10: 155–68.
—— (1984c) 'Laryngeal behavior and stop and affricate distinctions in Maithili: A fiberoptic and acoustic study', in Rajpurohit, B. B. (ed.) *Papers in Phonetics and Phonology*, Mysore: Central Institute of Indian Languages, pp. 43–75.
—— (1984d) *Maithili Phonetics and Phonology*, Mainz: Selden und Tamm.
—— (1995) 'Sā̃ya-bahume gappasappa konā karī: Mahendra Malaṅgiyāka nāṭakaka sandarbhame', (How to talk to your husband/wife in Maithili: with reference to Mahendra Malaṅgiya's plays), *Sayapatrī* (Journal of the Royal Nepal Academy) 1.2 (2053 V.S./1995 AD): 131–42. (In Maithili)
—— (1996) *A Reference Grammar of Maithili* (Trends in Linguistics: Documentation 11), Berlin and New York: Mouton de Gruyter.
—— (1999) 'Maithilīka bhāṣika vaividhya: Aupabhāṣika o mānaka svarūpa', (Linguistic variations in Maithili: Standard and dialectal forms), *Jijñāsā* (Journal of the Centre for the Study of Indian Traditions, Ranti, Madhubani, India) 4.6: 73–89. (In Maithili)
Yadava, Yogendra P. (1998) *Issues in Maithili Syntax*, München: Lincom Europa.

FURTHER READING

Jha, Govind (1979) *Uccatara Maithilī Vyākaraṇa* (Higher Maithili Grammar), Patna: Maithili Academy. (In Maithili)
Jha, Subhadra (1958) *The Formation of the Maithilī Language*, London: Luzac.
Yadav, Ramawatar (1996) *A Reference Grammar of Maithili* (Trends in Linguistics: Documentation 11), Berlin and New York: Mouton de Gruyter.

CHAPTER THIRTEEN

MAGAHI

Sheela Verma

CONTENTS

LIST OF TABLES

1 INTRODUCTION

Magahi is one of the three commonly recognized principal languages under the rubric of Bihari languages, Bhojpuri and Maithili being the other two. From the time of

Grierson's Survey (Grierson 1903–28), these languages have been assumed to represent one branch of an Eastern group of languages, namely, the Māgadhī group of the Middle Indo-Aryan, which includes Bangla, Asamiya, and Oriya. This view has generally been subscribed to by many scholars including Chatterji (1926) and Katre (1968). More recently, though, other scholars, such as Cardona (1974) and Jeffers (1976), have argued for a modified sub-grouping. Cardona attaches it to the Central group with Eastern Hindi and Western Hindi; Jeffers goes a step further and would prefer to posit a Bihari subgroup itself within New Indo-Aryan, independent of the Hindi languages on the one hand, and the Bangla languages on the other. At any rate, the speakers of Magahi, and other Bihari languages, have a sense of identity and a great deal of cultural affinity with the Hindi group in various ways. Very often they will identify their language as Hindi in response to census questions, thereby skewing the figures for the speakers of the language. Hindi is the formal language of the region, used in schools and law courts. Magahi today uses the Devanagari script borrowed directly from Hindi in place of the Kaithi script used earlier. Both in vocabulary and phonology, it has a greater alignment with Eastern Hindi (in addition to the inevitable lexical borrowing from the formal, administrative, and literary varieties of Western Hindi as the state language). It is essentially in morphology that it has some crucial affinity with Bangla and the Eastern group, though it has Eastern flavours in some aspects of phonology too. Within the Bihari group itself, from all accounts, Magahi and Maithili are closer together forming an eastern branch of the Bihari as opposed to Bhojpuri as its western branch.

2 MAGAHI SPEECH AREA

Unlike Bhojpuri, which is prominently spoken in significant portions of two Indian states, namely, Bihar and Uttar Pradesh, Magahī is essentially restricted to the state of Bihar, though there are mixed varieties of the language found in the adjoining regions of Bengal and Orissa. The name Magahi is a direct derivative of the name Māgadhī itself and many educated speakers of Magahi prefer to call it Magadhī rather than Magahi. Magahi, in the sense of the language of the Magadh country, should very well be expected to cover the currently reorganized districts of Patna, Gaya, Nalanda and Nawada in Bihar, which would roughly correspond to that historical territory, and so it does. This area may be interpreted as defining the focal area for what may be termed 'Standard Magahi'. The structural description of the Magahi language attempted in this chapter relates to this standard variety of Magahi.

The total geographical area covered by Magahi today is much larger. In a very broad sense, the river Ganga may be seen as marking a linguistic boundary making Magahi the language of South Bihar as opposed to Maithili as the language of North Bihar (with the river Son marking a western border to separate it from Bhojpuri). In the west it extends to the eastern part of the district of Palamu, in the east to portions of the districts of Munger and Bhagalpur, in the south to Singhbhum, and in the southeast to Dhanbad, all in the state of Bihar. Magahi does, however, extend beyond Bihar, even though marginally, into Bengal in the district of Purulia (which was part of the state of Bihar until 1956), and into Orissa in the districts of Mayurbhanj and Bamra. In fact, there is another region in Bengal, Malda in its northern part, where Magahi coexists with Bangla. It is referred to in almost all discussions on Magahi, including Grierson (1903). Since this area is not contiguous to any other Magahi speaking area, it is perhaps a case of a migrant Magahi community, though there are other theories (Grierson 1903: 179, Pandeya 1980: 8).

3 DIALECTS OF MAGAHI

Grierson (1903) and Aryani (1976) both essentially identify two basic dialects of Magahi, standard Magahi and eastern Magahi. From its focal area, standard Magahi, with possible local variations, extends to Aurangabad and the eastern border of Palamu in the west, and Hazaribagh and Giridih in the south and southeast. In the northeast, it extends to the western portions of the districts of Munger and Bhagalpur.

Eastern Magahi is the name given to a collection of subdialects on the eastern and southern border of South Bihar where Magahi meets Bangla (in Purulia) and Oriya (in Mayurbhanj and Bamra). It starts along the eastern border of the Ranchi plateau and goes through the Bangla speaking Manbhum area and then turns west, skirting the southern part of the plateau through the Oriya elements of Singhbhum. The Magahi of Malda in upper Bengal is also treated as part of eastern Magahi by Grierson (1905). In addition, eastern Magahi is also spoken in the southeast of Hazaribagh, in the extreme east of the Ranchi district, and in Kharsawan of the Singhbhum district, and all of them have been heavily influenced by their neighbouring languages. While the regional varieties of standard Magahi are all called Magahi, the subdialects of eastern Magahi have various names. The prominent ones are *Kurmālī* in Mayurbhanj and Kharsawan, *Kurmālī Ṭhār*, *Khoṭṭā* in the Manbhum region, Sadrī Kol in Bamra, *Khonṭai* in Malda, and *Pãc Parganiā* or *Tamariā* in the extreme East of the Ranchi district. Each name has its own logic, which also allows for the name 'Hindi' (as opposed to Bangla) in Malda, and 'Bangla' (because of heavy borrowing and the script from Bangla) in the southeast of the Hazaribagh district, in addition to the usual name Magahī or Magahiyā as in the Dhanbad area.

4 SPEAKERS OF MAGAHI

It is not easily possible to indicate the number of Magahi speakers because dependable statistics are not available. This is so for two reasons. In the standard Magahi region, in response to census questions, most educated speakers of Magahi name Hindi as their language since that is what they use in formal contexts and so consider it to be the appropriate response. The uneducated and the rural population of Magahi speakers return Hindi, as the generic name for their language. In the eastern Magahi area, as discussed above, subdialectal names such as *Kurmālī*, *Khoṭṭā*, *Pãc Parganiā*, and even *Hindi* are used more often than Magahi in census responses.

Aryani (1965), on the basis of several data, estimated the number of Magahi speakers at approximately 9,900,000 for 1951. Surprisingly enough, the 1971 Census figures show only 6,638,495 speakers for Magahi. This discrepancy can be understood in the context of the sociolinguistic phenomenon of educated urban speakers naming their language of schooling, namely Hindi, as their mother tongue. Obviously, the number of Magahi speakers did not really decline between 1951 and 1971 but was simply swallowed up by the census figures for Hindi. Breton (1997) estimates the number at 9 million. Grimes (1996), however, provides the figure 10,821,000 for 1994, and further gives Magahi the seventy-fifth position among the top 100 languages of the world by population, with the figure of 12 million speakers as currently updated.

5 SCRIPT AND LITERARY TRADITION

In one sense, Magahi is written in four scripts, Devanagari, Kaithi, and also Bangla and Oriya. Bangla and Oriya scripts are employed in writing the forms of eastern Magahi current in the Manbhum area, such as Purulia but also in the southeastern part of the Hazaribagh district that borders on the Manbhum region. The Oriya script is used, expectedly, in areas where it coexists with Oriya, such as Mayurbhanj. Devanagari is the script for whatever is sought to be published today, or has been sought to be published since the early part of the twentieth century. Part of the reason may be simply the unavailability of typesetting for Kaithi. But more importantly, Devanagari in the greater Hindi area has a more scholarly image and is perceived as the right instrument for any kind of activity that has any claim to being literary. It is the script used in books written for the educated and in writing by the educated. Devanagari as the 'metropolitan' script (as the name implies) has increasingly become the script of the new literatures of Bihari and other 'regional' language and also replaced the earlier scripts such as Maithili, Newari and Dogri. The use of the Devanagari for Magahi presents a slight problem, though. The pronunciation convention associated with the Devanagari in the greater Hindi area (as also Nepali) drops the inherent vowel of the last consonant character of a word. Quite a number of verbal forms in Magahi end in that inherent vowel /a/. Therefore, the Devanagari for Magahi has been slightly modified with the addition of a word-final character, namely the 'avagraha' <S>, to provide for that vowel word finally. (Nepali, which also is faced with the same situation, solves the problem by the use or absence of the 'halanta'.) Thus, second person imperative form, such as *ihā̃ baiṭha* 'sit here' will be written in Devanagari as इहां बइठS; similarly, in other verbal forms including the auxiliary, as in तू का कर रहलS हS *tu kā kar rahla ha* 'What are you doing?' No further discussion or display of the Devanagari alphabet is provided here since it is found elsewhere in this volume.

The traditional script for Magahi has been Kaithi, which is still used in personal communication, and sometimes in semi-legal transactions. The Kaithi script gets its name from the word 'Kāyath' < 'Kāyastha', the caste of writers in Northern India, and has been current until recently in Bihar and Eastern Uttar Pradesh. It derives from early Nagari and is closely related to the current Gujarati script which replaced the Devanagari only in the nineteenth century. Table 13.1 gives the Kaithi alphabet (Grierson 1903).

There has been some effort on the part of scholars in the Magahi area to explore and identify a literary tradition for Magahi and, in fact, to go as far back as the Siddha Sahitya of the eighth century, and the subsequent Nathpanth Sahitya and the Sant Sahitya traditions the same way as Hindi literature does (e.g., Aryani 1976: 28–31, Pandeya 1982, Singh 1982). More relevantly, Magahi is quite rich in its folk literature, and in modern times, there have been various activities in the publication of creative writings. A great deal of enthusiasm has been shown in organizing literary activities. An organization called Magahi Parishad was established in Patna in 1952, which was later renamed Bihar Magahi Mandal. A monthly journal called Magadhi was started at the same time, which was later renamed *Bihān*. Both these events have been in the nature of growing efforts towards the linguistic and literary promotion of Magahi.

6 PHONOLOGY

The phonemic inventory of Magahi is given in tables 13.2 and 13.3. Certain aspects of the system are noteworthy. Because of the use of the Devanagari for scholarly approaches to Magahi, most language related discussions on Magahi routinely posit the same phonemic inventory for Magahi as the Devanagari alphabet implies. The phonemic inventory of Magahi can best be viewed as a somewhat reduced version of the core of the New Indo-Aryan inventory in a systematically statable manner.

TABLE 13.1: KAITHĪ OR KĀYATHĪ SCRIPT WITH DEVANĀGARĪ EQUIVALENTS AND TRANSLITERATIONS

Vowels

अ	अ	*a*	आ	आ	*ā*	इ	इ	*i*	ई	ई	*ī*
उ	उ	*u*	ऊ	ऊ	*ū*	ए	ए	*e*	ऐ	ऐ	*ai*
ओ	ओ	*o*	औ	औ	*au*						

Consonants

Stops

Velar	क	क	*k*	रव	रव	*kh*	ग	ग	*g*	घ	घ	*gh*		
Palatal	च	च	*c*	छ	छ	*ch*	ज	ज	*j*	झ	झ	*jh*		
Cerebral	ट	ट	*ṭ*	ठ	ठ	*ṭh*	ड	ड	*ḍ*	ढ	ढ	*ḍh*		
Dental	त	त	*t*	थ	थ	*th*	द	द	*d*	ध	ध	*dh*	न	*n*
Labial	प	प	*p*	फ	फ	*ph*	ब	ब	*b*	भ	भ	*bh*	म	*m*

Semivowels

य	य	*y*	र	र	*r*	ल	ल	*l*	व व *v*

Spirants

श	श	*ś*	ष	ष	*ṣ*	स	स	*s*	ह	ह	*h*

Others

Anusvāra	अं	अं	*aṁ*
Visarga	अः	अः	*aḥ*

6.1 Consonants

As regards the consonants, Magahi has retained the same contrasts of place and manner features, except in the categories of nasals and fricatives. Instead of the five-way distinction for the nasals, Magahi has retained only two, the labial /m/ and the dental /n/. Others occur only homorganically before stops and the sibilant /s/. In that sense, they could simply be considered allophones of /n/. As regards the sibilants, Magahi has participated in the typical NIA syncretism resulting in a single sibilant, the dental fricative /s/, as in most other languages. Thus, /sankar/ (Sanskrit /śaṅkara/) 'Lord Shiva', /kisun/ (Sanskrit /kṛṣṇa/) 'Lord Krishna', etc. Even though it has its fair share of Arabo-Persian and English (as also Sanskrit) loanwords, Magahi does not, unlike Modern Standard Hindi, admit any of the Arabo-Persian or English fricatives /f/, /v/, /š/, /z/, /x/, or /ɣ/, or the Sanskrit sibilants /ś/ and /ṣ/. There is massive phonological reshaping of words involving these sounds whereby all voiceless sibilants are reduced to the dental /s/, and all other fricatives are replaced by homorganic stops. Thus, /philam/ 'film', / bhoṭ/ 'vote', /sahar/ for Persian /śahr/ 'city' or /sāsan/ for Sanskrit /śāsana/ 'government', /kasṭ/ for Sanskrit /kaṣṭa/ 'suffering', /janānā/ for Persian /zanāna/ 'feminine', /jid/ for Arabic /zidd/ 'stubbornness', /jon/ for English 'zone' in the sense of a specified administrative area, /kharāb/ for Persian /xarāb/ 'bad', /garib/ for Arabic / ɣarīb/ 'poor'. Magahi also does not use the uvular voiceless stop /q/ found in many commonly used Arabic loanwords, and replaces it with /k/, e.g. /kisim/ for Arabic /qism/ 'variety', /kasam/ for Arabic /qasm/ 'oath', /kasur/ for Arabic /quṣūr/ 'shortcoming', etc.

TABLE 13.2: CONSONANTS

		Labial	Dental	Retroflex	Palatal	Velar	Glottal
Stops	vl.unasp	p	t	ṭ	c	k	
	vl.asp.	ph	th	ṭh	ch	kh	
	vd.unsap	b	d	ḍ	j	g	
	vd.asp.	bh	dh	ḍh	jh	gh	
Nasals		m	n				
		mh	nh				
Fricatives			s				h
Flaps (Liquids)			r	ṛ			
			rh	ṛh			
Laterals (Liquids)			l				
			lh				
Glides		w			y		

TABLE 13.3: VOWELS AND DIPHTHONGS

	Front	Central	Back
High	i		u
Mid	e	a	o
Low		ā	
Diphthongs	ai		au

Note: Magahi has no phonemic length distinction in vowels, though allophonic variations in length do operate. The central vowel transcribed here as /a/ has the phonetic value of a somewhat rounded [ʌ] in stressed positions and [ə] in unstressed positions. The diphthongs /ai/ and /au/ are truly diphthongal and have a more central initiation point, phonetically [əi] and [əu].

6.2 Glides

The glides /y/ and /w/ occur in Magahi but essentially intervocalically. Just about all cases of word initial /y/ and /w/ have been replaced by /j/ and /b/ respectively, as in Bangla. For example, /jantar/ 'instrument', /jag/ 'big religious ceremony', /jam/ 'death god' /jug/ 'era' as opposed to Sanskrit /yantra, yajña, yama, yuga/, respectively. Similarly, /bans/ 'lineage', /bansi/ 'flute', /bacan/ 'word, promise', /bajar/ 'thunderbolt', in contrast to Sanskrit /vaṃśa, vaṃśī, vacana, vajra/, respectively. Glides as the second element of a consonant cluster are, as a general rule, replaced by their corresponding vocalic forms /i/ and /u/ (or /e/ and /o/, see below for vowel harmony and lowering of high vowels), which is in the general spirit of the simplification of consonant clusters in Magahi. Thus, /teohār/ 'festival', /piās/ 'thirst', /ciũṭi/ 'ant', for standard Hindi /tyohār, pyās, cyũṭī/, respectively. Similarly, /goālā/ 'milkman', /kūār/ 'unmarried', /subhāw/ 'nature' for standard Hindi /gwālā, kwārā, swabhāwa/, respectively. In more recent loans, initial /y/ and /w/ are also more likely to be replaced by their corresponding vocalic forms, as in /iāri/ for Persian /yārī/ 'friendship', /okālat/ for Arabo-Persian /wakālat/, /ojah/ for Arabic /wajh/ 'reason'. Word-final and syllable-final /y/ and /w/ invariably have a vocalic pronunciation even though they may be transcribed with a य or

व, and also word-initially as in the loans referred to above यारी /iāri/ or वकालत /ukālat/ and गांव /gão/ 'village' or ठांव /ṭhão/ 'place'.

6.3 Liquids

Like many NIA languages, Magahi also has developed the retroflex flap phoneme /ṛ/. It has a limited privilege of occurrence, occurring essentially intervocalically, but also word-finally. It is phonologically possible to consider it an allophone of the retroflex stop /ḍ/ except for some marginal contrasts in loanwords. The liquids and nasals all have an aspirated counterpart phoneme, /rh/, /ṛh/, /lh/, /nh/ and /mh/. All of them are limited to word-medial or final position, as in /muri/ 'a place name' but /murhi/ 'roasted rice', /morhā/ 'sitting stool', /tilhā/ 'mound', /cinhā/ 'sign', and /tumhī/ 'a musical instrument'. The liquids /l/ and /r/ do show some interchangeability and one could get both /phal/ and /phar/ for 'fruit'. The situation seems to be that as a general rule the inherited medial /-l-/ in Magahi (and other Bihari languages) changes to a /-r-/, or a final /-r/ after the loss of the vowel. Thus /karia/ 'black', /har/ 'plow', /phār/ 'plowshare', as opposed to Hindi /kālā, hal, phāl/, respectively. /phal/ 'fruit' in Magahi is a borrowing from Hindi. Magahi also shows some interchangeability between /l/ and /n/: /nẽgā/ as also /langā/ or /lāgaṭā/ 'naked', /nukānā/ as also /lukānā/ 'to hide', /nãgaṛ/ as also /lãgar/ 'lame', etc.

6.4 Clusters

The canonical form of the syllable in Magahi is essentially of the CV or VC type, and the language shows a marked penchant for simplifying consonant clusters in both inherited and borrowed forms. A largely valid generalization could be made to say that Magahi just does not have any syllable-initial or word-initial clusters. Syllable-final or word-final clusters are either geminates or of the sibilant/nasal+stop type. The nasal+stop type is essentially homorganic, and a final cluster with a stop as the first element is simply not possible. Even the generally common type of a cluster with a liquid as the first member is not acceptable to a Magahi syllable and tends to be simplified by an epenthetical vowel in borrowed words; thus /karam/ 'destiny' for Sanskrit /karma/, /darad/ 'pain' for Persian /dard/, /philam/ for English 'film', and /silik/ for English 'silk'. Word-medial clusters are all across syllables anyway, but even so they are essentially of the sibilant/liquid/nasal+stop type. Medial clusters with a stop as the first element appear to be possible in the speech of Hindi-educated speakers, but in the speech of the rural native speakers a possible cluster tends to be interrupted by an attenuated /ã/. The simplification of a cluster involving a glide has already been referred to above. The cluster is simplified by changing the glide into its corresponding vocalic form, as in /jeonār/ for Hindi /jyonār/ 'feast'. In the phonological reshaping process of Magahi, the completely unacceptable existence of initial clusters is remedied by anaptyxis (svarabhakti) or prothesis in borrowed words (from English or Sanskrit, for that matter). If the cluster begins with a /s/, then a prothetic front vowel /i/ or /e/ is used to transform it into a more acceptable medial cluster with /s/. Thus, /iskul/ for 'school', /isṭesan/ for 'station'. (Even a complete elimination of /s/ to avoid a cluster can be found sporadically, as in /ṭesan/ for 'station'.) A cluster beginning with a stop is broken up with an anaptyctic /a/, as in /garhan/ for Sanskrit /grahaṇa/ 'eclipse', /ṭaraikṭar/ for 'tractor', /balaik/ for 'black' as in black market, etc.

6.5 Vowels

As regards the vowels, Magahi has lost the phonemic contrast of length in the high vowels, both front /i/ and back /u/. The question of phonemic length in the vowels (as inherited) arises only in the case of high vowels anyway, and the phonemic inventory implied in the Devanagari alphabet commonly used in the scholarly use of the language encourages many to posit phonemically long and short high vowels almost routinely. Phonetic variation in length related to variational syllabic structure of morphologically related forms in statable phonological contexts does arise, but so does it also for the vowels /e/ and /o/, which have been treated as undistinguished in regard to length for the Hindi area in general (and for most of native Indo-Aryan). All these vowels are essentially long, that is, the base allophone is the long one. In native Magahi lexicon, it is only the long version of all these vowels that appears in monosyllables. There is no contrast in word-final position and it is hard to find minimal pairs elsewhere or in general. The central vowels [ʌ] and [a] (transcribed in this discussion as /a/ and /ā/), though in phonemic contrast, have a parallel behaviour morphophonemically, and could very well be considered systematically related to each other in terms of length, that is to say, /a/ as the shorter version of /ā/. However, /a/ as a vowel in its own right, like other vowels in definable phonological contexts, also has its own shorter allophonic version whose phonetic nature is [ə]. (Incidentally, the basic allophone of the central vowel /a/, that is, the long allophone under stress, is phonetically a somewhat rounded vowel like [ɔ], more like Bangla than Hindi, though not quite that rounded.) The shorter counterparts of Magahi vowels can better be looked upon as 'attenuation' conditioned by statable phonological conditions and will be shown as ă, ŭ, ĕ, ŏ, and ă as necessary in the discussion. The term short may be used interchangeably for the attenuated quality of these vowels.

The front and back diphthongs /ai/ and /au/ respectively are more diphthongal than in a language like Hindi and have essentially a central starting point as in [əi] and [əu]. Nasalization is phonemic, which provides for the nasalized counterparts for all of the eight vocalic nuclei / i, e, a, ā, o, u, ai and au/. In Kaithi, the nasalization is indicated with an anusvāra rather than a candrabindu.

6.6 Stress and vowel shortening

Vowel shortening in Magahi is intimately related to syllabic structure and stress placement. As a general rule, stress falls on the penultimate in disyllabic words, and on the antepenultimate in words of more than two syllables, unless other factors such as syllable weight and derivational structure intervene. In general, a vowel in a stressed syllable has the longer allophone and an unstressed vowel has the shorter one. CVCC, as also CVC with V representing a diphthong or /ā/, act as heavy syllables. A heavy final syllable in a disyllabic word would shift the stress to the final syllable, and a heavy penultimate syllable in a trisyllabic word will shift the stress to the penultimate. Thus, /káha/ 'say' 2p.Imp., /sáṛal/ 'rotten', /ṭhélā/ 'pushcart', /bójhā/ 'load', /kóṛā/ 'whip', but /ba.sánt/ 'spring', /tõdáil/ 'fat-bellied', /dokắn/ 'store'. The shifting of the stress and the resulting attenuation can be seen in such pairs as [lóhā] 'iron' but [lŏhár] 'blacksmith', [sónā] 'gold' but [sŏnár] 'goldsmith', [ḍắkā] 'robbery' but [ḍakáit] 'robber' (/a/ behaving as the short version of /ā/ in derivation, as mentioned above). In trisyllabic words, the stress is on the antepenultimate, as in /láṛikā/ 'boy', /nókari/ 'job'. With the stress on the antepenultimate, the vowel in the penultimate is attenuated, but if a longer related word makes the penultimate syllable antepenultimate, then the stress will shift and make the erstwhile attenuated vowel a regular vowel. Thus, [lárĭkā] 'boy' but [lăríkawā] 'the boy', [mótări] 'bundle' but [mŏtáriyā] 'the bundle', [lárĭki] 'girl' but [lăríkiyā] 'the girl'. The shift in stress (and vowel quality) can be seen in a series like

> *nókar* (penult)   *nókări* (antepenult)   *nŏkáriyā* (shifted antepenult)
> 'servant'   'service'   'the service'

Vowel attenuation in Magahi operates morphophonemically also. Magahi has a derivative suffix in stressed -ắ which, among other things, derives intransitive passive verb stems and denominatives. Thus, [dho-] 'wash': [dhoắ-] 'to be washed'. This is against the usually expected stress pattern of penultimate stress in disyllabic words and can provide nice minimal pairs, such as [jhúlā] 'a swing': [jhŭlắ-] 'to cause to swing' from the verb stem [jhúl-] 'to swing'. As can be seen, it also causes attenuation in the vowel from where the stress shifts. Similarly, [bŏắ-] 'to be sown' from [bo-] 'to sow', [dĕkhắ-] 'to cause to see' from [dekh-] 'to see', [likhắ-] 'to be written' from [likh-] 'to write', and the denominatives from nouns [tatắ-] 'to become too dry and hard' from [tāt] 'hard canvas', [cĭnhắ-] 'to be recognized' from [cinh-] 'to recognize', and denominatives from adjectives: [mŏtắ-] 'to become fat' from [mot] 'fat', [pĭyărắ-] from [piyar] 'yellow', etc. Other derivational suffixes with a stressed initial /ā-/, such as /-āi/ as in [līkhắi] 'writing' from [likh] 'to write' and /-ār/ as in [camắr] 'leather worker' from [cām] 'leather' also trigger the same effect.

The stressed penultimate vowel of a disyllabic word will retain the stress when it becomes the antepenult vowel of a trisyllabic word through suffixation (which is in agreement with the general stress pattern of trisyllabic words), but will become attenuated even when stressed. Thus, [dékha] 'look' 2p.Imp., [dĕkhăla] '(you) saw', [dĕkhălā] infinitive oblique, [máli] 'gardener' but [máliyā] 'the gardener', [páwa] '(you) get', but [páwăla] '(you) got'; the last two examples showing /a/ as the derivational short version of /ā/. In all this, the penult has to have an attenuated vowel, so much so that in the speech of some, and in fast speech, there may be complete elision of that attenuated penult vowel resulting in the forms [dĕkhla] and [dĕkhlā]. In that case, the word becomes disyllabic, with the predictable stress on the penult but on an attenuated penult vowel, provided the syllabic structure is CVC-CV. It turns out that this syllabic structure becomes a general phonological condition for the occurrence of an attenuated vowel and stress for words ending in such a syllabic structure. Thus, [chot] 'little' but [chŏtkā] 'the little one', [mũh] 'mouth' but [mŭhwặ], [deh] 'body' but [dĕhwā] 'the body', [kúsum] 'safflower' but [kŭsmi] 'reddish-yellow'. This vowel shortening does not happen if the penult in the disyllabic word has the structure CV, as we find in a word like [chu] 'to touch' but also [chúla] '(you) touched'.

6.7 Vowel harmony

Magahi also seems to evince a process of vowel harmony, whereby high vowels are lowered when followed by a low vowel. Earlier, we noted the conversion of glides /y/ and /w/ into their corresponding high vowels /i/ and /u/ in clusters, such as /swabhāwa/ 'natural disposition' becoming /subhāw/, but then also /sobhāw/ as a doublet, lowering the high vowel /u/ to the mid /o/ with the low vowel /ā/ following. Numerous examples can be found, such as /teohār/ with a /e/ from /tyohār/, and /goālā/ from /gwālā/ 'milkman', /soāmi/ for /swāmi/ 'master', etc. with the mid /o/ in place of the high vowel /u/. This is obviously a general process and can be seen even in more recent loans (involving no original cluster situation) as in /bemāri/ for /bimāri/ 'sickness', /dokān/ for /dukān/ 'store', and /okālat/ < /ukālat/ < /wakālat/ 'legal profession', while /ukil/ 'lawyer' can keep its high vowel.

7 MORPHOLOGY

Magahi has no grammatical gender for agreement, though sex-related gender derivation for animate nouns is commonly possible; thus, /maugā/ (masc.) 'an effeminate person', /maugi/ (fem.) 'woman'; /buṛhā/ (masc.) 'old man', /buṛhiyā/ (fem.) 'old woman'. Magahi has two numbers, singular and plural. Grammatical functions are essentially expressed through the use of postpositions and also through case forms for both nouns and pronouns. While there is no agreement forms of the verb based on gender, Magahi has a system of agreement based on person and politeness for both the subject and the object simultaneously, which is rather uncharacteristic of Indo-Aryan languages in general.

7.1 Nouns

Noun stems in Magahi can end in a consonant or a vowel but vowels /e/ and /o/ are rare as final vowels for noun stems. Stems can be classified as basic or derived. Derived noun stems are obtained from adjectives, verbs, as well as other basic nouns. They are in conformity with the phonological structure described above. Particularly, if the suffix involves a stressed vowel /ā/, then there will be shortening of the preceding vowels in accordance with what has been described; thus adjective [sāph] 'clean' and noun [saphāi] 'cleaning', verb [pis] 'to grind' and noun [pīsāi] 'grinding', noun [sonā] 'gold' and derived noun [sŏnār] 'goldsmith', noun [gãw] 'village' and derived noun [gãwār] 'an uncouth person'. Suffixes with other initial vowels do not cause this attenuation; both [cor] 'thief' and [cori] 'thievery' have the same vowel phonetically without involving any shift in the stress.

Other types of noun stems involve various derivationally related masculine and feminine 'animate' nouns (with no agreement consequences) such as /beṭā/ 'son' and /beṭī/ 'daughter', thematically related compounds /dāl-bhāt/ 'everyday meal (literally, lentil soup and cooked rice)', translation compounds with two semantically same or similar words from two different linguistic stocks /sādi-biyāh/ 'weddings and related things' (phonologically reshaped Magahi forms of Persian /śādī/ 'marriage' and Sanskrit /vivāha/ (Hindi /byāh/) 'marriage'. The most conspicuous and productively derived form of nouns in Magahi is formed with the suffix /-wā/ or its variant /-yā/ as in /laṛikawā/ 'the boy' and /laṛikiyā/ 'the girl'. Phonologically conditioned distribution provides for /-yā/ occurring after the nouns ending in the vowel /i/ and /-wā/ occurring elsewhere. As the translation implies, this suffix expresses 'definiteness' morphologically (not found in a language like Hindi, though found in a language like Bangla (/-ṭā/ or /-ṭī/). It may have other marginal uses, too, such as dimunition and disparagement coupled with definiteness. /-wā/ can be suffixed to any noun, in the singular as well as the plural. This suffix can bring about vowel attenuation in the preceding syllable in accordance with the principles described above; e.g. /rājā/ but /rajāwā/.

7.1.1 Plural forms

Plurality is the only morphologically productive category for noun inflection and is expressed by the suffix /-an/ (with necessary changes in the stem), as in /bail/ 'bull',

/bailan/ 'bulls'; /bailawā/ 'the bull' /bailawan/ 'the bulls'. However, a periphrastic pluralization with the word /sab/ (or /log/ with human nouns) added to the singular form is very common: /laṛikā/ 'boy' /laṛikan/ 'boys' but also /laṛikā sab, laṛikā log/ 'boys, children'. The plural is really a marked form, the singular is both more general as well as the form of the generic noun, as in /hamārā santarā$_{sg.}$ khūb pasand ho/ 'I like oranges very much'.

7.1.2 Case forms

Magahi is not very rich in its nominal inflectional case system; however, it does have an inflected locative (as in Bangla) more readily available than in Hindi. The form is the suffix /-e/, as in /ham ghar-e jā hi/ 'I am going home'. The suffix /-e/ is also used for the expression of instrumentality or reason: /bhukh-e hamar hālat kharāb ho gelo/ 'I was in bad shape due to hunger'. Other case functions on nouns are accomplished with the use of postpositions. Apart from the inflected locative, which expresses general location, two other locatives could be considered, with the postpositions /mẽ/ 'in' and /par/ 'on'. There is a benefactive postposition /lā/ as in /hamārā lā/ 'for me'. /ke/ is the most versatile postposition, used for the dative, accusative and genitive functions: /laṛikā ke da/ 'give to the boy', /laṛikā ke dekha/ 'see the boy', /laṛikā ke bāp/ 'the boy's father'. /se/ is another versatile postposition used in several constructions including the comparative (as in Hindi) as also the instrumental and the ablative: /torā se baṛhiyā/ 'better than you', /cābhī se/ 'with a key', /laṛikā se/ 'from the boy'.

7.1.3 Pronouns

Personal pronouns in Magahi exhibit a paradigm for three persons and two numbers. They do inflect for case but essentially only two, the nominative and the genitive. The genitive has an oblique form used before postpositions. Thus /ham/ nominative 'I', /hamar/ genitive 'my', and its oblique form /hamārā/, which is used with postpositions to obtain various periphrastic case functions such as /hamārā se/ 'from me', /hamārā lā/ 'for me', and /hamārā ke/ for the accusative and the dative. A noteworthy fact in this regard is that Magahi, unlike Hindi but like Bangla, uses the genitive, and not the dative, in 'experiencer' subject constructions (Verma 1990). More specifically, it uses the genitive oblique without any postposition for this purpose: Magahi /hamārā ḍar lāga hai/ and Bangla /āmār$_{gen.}$ bhōy lāgce/ 'I am afraid'. However, the genitive form is available only to the singular and not to the plural pronouns, which results in the plural pronoun occurring in a single case form. The genitive, as well as the 'experiencer' case, in the plural is accomplished with the use of the postposition /ke/, e.g. /hamni ke/.

It also needs to be noted that apart from the distinction of proximate and non-proximate third person pronouns (which are employed also as deictically contrasted demonstratives to mean 'this' and 'that', including their attributive function as in /i laṛikā/ 'this boy' and /u laṛikā/ 'that boy'), the distinction of honorificity is an important grammatical entity in Magahi and has extensive agreement consequences. It operates in both second person and third person. Personal pronouns are illustrated in Table 13.4.

It should be noted that even though the forms in second and third person singular do not show different forms for the honorific; honorificity is operative in verbal agreement for them. The honorific genitive and oblique do show separate forms. Second person may have variant forms /tū/ or /tõ/ in the speech of some. There is also a reflexive

TABLE 13.4: PERSONAL PRONOUNS

Person		Singular	Sg. Genitive	Sg. Oblique	Plural
First		*ham*	*hamār*	*hamărā*	*hamăni*
Second		*tu*	*tor*	*torā*	*tohăni*
	Honorific		*tohār*	*tohărā*	
Third Proximate		*i*	*ekar*	*ekărā*	*i (sab)*
	Honorific		*inkar*	*inkărā*	
Third Non-Prox.		*u*	*okar*	*okărā*	*u (sab)*
	Honorific		*unkar*	*unkărā*	

pronoun /apane/ 'self' which is used for extra respect in second person and has separate verbal agreement. All these together result in three degrees of respect for second person.

7.1.4 Demonstratives and related paradigms

The forms of the interrogative and relative pronouns are more or less exact copies of the demonstrative/third person personal pronoun with the morpheme /k-/ for the interrogative and the morpheme /j-/ for the relative. Magahi also has correlatives, in /s-/ or /t-/ (cf. the Bangla correlatives /śe/ and /tārā/, etc.) comparable to the Hindi /wo/ in /jo ... wo/. Furthermore, they have their various adjectival, adverbial and other modifier counterparts, too, as seen in table 13.5.

Other pronominals and modifiers include the indefinite pronoun /koi/, the indefinite attributive /kauno/ (/bhore kauno laṛikā āil halo/ 'Some boy had come early in the morning'), the indefinite numeral /kai/ (/kai go laṛikā āil halo/ 'Several (indefinite number) of boys had come'), and the indefinite quantitative /kuch/ 'some'.

An important aspect of the noun phrase structure in Magahi is the use of the numeral classifiers /go/, /ṭho/ (cf. the Bangla classifier /ṭā/). They essentially occur with numerals in attributive function and strictly denote countability. Thus /pãc rupiyā/ 'five rupees' is a total of five rupees in any combinations, but /pãc ṭho rupiyā/ is a count of five rupee pieces.

The noun phrase in Magahi is a left-branching, head final structural unit with all modifiers including long participials and relatives occurring prenominally unless

TABLE 13.5: DEMONSTRATIVES AND RELATED PARADIGMS

	Demonstrative	Interrogative	Relative	Correlative
Nominative	*i/u*	*kā/ke (human)*	*je*	*se/te*
Genitive	*ekar/okar*	*kekar*	*jekar*	*sekar/tekar*
Oblique	*ekarā/okarā*	*kekarā*	*jekarā*	*sekarā/tekarā*
Attributive	*i/u*	*ke/kaun*	*je/jaun*	*se*
Adjectival	*aisan/oisan*	*kaisan*	*jaisan*	*taisan*
Quantitative	*etanā/otanā*	*ketanā*	*jetanā*	*tetan*
Manner adv.	*aise/oise*	*kaise*	*jaise*	*taise*
Place adv.	*ihã/uhã*	*kahã*	*jahã*	*tahã*
Time adv.	*ab*	*kab*	*jab*	*tab*

scrambled: /sūtal laṛikā/ 'the sleeping child', /bagal ke kamarā mẽ sūtal laṛikā/ 'the child sleeping in the adjoining room' (lit. 'in the adjoining room sleeping child'), /jekrā ham paisā deliyo, ū ādmi ailo he/ 'the man to whom I gave the money is here' (lit. 'to whom I gave the money, that man is here').

7.2 Verbs

A brief description of the structure of the Magahi verb follows (for a detailed description, see Sheela Verma 1985). Verb stems in Magahi can be divided into three basic categories: (i) primitive, (ii) derivative, and (iii) complex. Primitive stems are monomorphic and could also be considered basic; e.g. /khā-/ 'eat', /dekh-/ 'see', /sun-/ 'hear'. Derivative stems are polymorphic and are forms obtained by adding various kinds of derivative suffixes to stems, verbal as well as non-verbal, such as /khiā-/ 'to feed' from the verb /khā-/ 'eat', /batiyā-/ 'to chat' from the noun /bāt/ 'talk', and /piyarā-/ 'to turn yellow' from the adjective /piyar/ 'yellow'. The derivative stems may involve well-defined morphophonemic alternation according to the principles discussed above in the section on phonology. Complex stems are formed by adding various kinds of modals to the primitive and derivative stems, which can be subdivided into various types commonly recognized for South Asian languages, namely, conjunct verbs, such as /biyāh kar-/ 'to marry', compound verbs, such as /mar jā-/ 'to die', modal verbs, such as /paṛh sak-/ 'to be able to read', and aspectual verbs, such as /jāe da-/ 'to let go'. Complex stems, though internally complex, form a unit just like the primitive and derivative stems and enter the tense and various other constructions just like them.

Verbs occur in finite and non-finite forms. Unlike Hindi, which has only one nominal non-finite form (the infinitive), Magahi has several; they are aspectually distinguished like their participial counterparts, and they have their oblique forms, too. Magahi can be interpreted to have three types: (i) neutral in [-ø] or [-a], (ii) imperfective in [-t], and (iii) perfective in [-l], in their basic forms; for example, neutral: /tu dekh-a ha/ 'You see' with the habitual aspect, imperfective: /tu dekh-ai-t ha/ 'you are looking' with the progressive aspect, and perfective: /to sut-a-l ha/ 'you are asleep' with the stative aspect. In fact there is a fourth one in [-b], as in /u sut-b-e kari/ literally 'He will certainly do the sleeping'. Even though it is slightly limited in distribution (occurring only as a complex stem with the light verb /kar/ and only in the emphatic form with the emphatic suffix /-e/), this nevertheless completes the picture. To the extent the imperfective and the perfective have the present and the past tense connotations (with the neutral providing for the 'timeless' habitual), this one, which could be named the 'proximate', has the connotation of the future tense, thereby completing the tense picture even for the non-finites. The following are some of the examples of nominal non-finites with their oblique counterparts, using the verb /dekh-/ 'see':

Neutral:	*hamrā se dekh-dākh-ø nā howa ho* 'I cannot manage the task of looking after.'
Oblique:	*hamarā dekh-e se kuch nā hoto* (before postposition) 'Nothing will be accomplished by my examining it.'
Perfective:	*dekh-a-l jaruri ho* 'It is important to see.'
Oblique:	*dekhlā ke bād* 'after looking'

The finite verb forms have two patterns, Type I: one word finite verbs of the structure Stem-Tense/Mode-Personal Ending, and Type II: two-word finite verbs of the structure Stem-Aspect-Auxiliary. In the latter, the auxiliary carries the tense and the mode. Magahi truly provides a very patterned picture. The auxiliary as the carrier of tense/ mode in effect becomes a finite verb construction in Type I format itself using the same endings. When the tense/mode endings are applied to a main verb stem, we get five finite forms with the five tense/mode suffixes (illustrated with the verb /sun-/ 'hear' in the First Person):

Injunctive:	*sun - ø - iyo*
Past simple:	*sun - l - iyo*
Past subjunctive:	*sun - t - iyo*
Future:	*sun - b - o*
(Future imperative:	*sun - ih - a* (second person))

It may be noted that the regular imperative, in this scheme of things, is simply the injunctive for second person /sun - ø - a/. Also not discussed in any detail here is the past simple ending, which has the form /-lk/ with transitive verbs in the third person, as in /u baiṭh-l-o/ 'he sat', but /u kaha-lk-o/ 'he said'.

The auxiliary actually employs two separate stems /ha-/ and /ho-/. The constructions with /ha-/ provide the tenses, and the constructions with /ho-/ provide the modes.

Present tense:	*h- ø - iyo*
Past tense:	*ha - l - iyo*
Past subjunctive mode:	*ho - t - iyo*
Injunctive (present subjunctive) mode:	*ho - ø - iyo*
Presumptive mode:	*ho - b - o*

These auxiliary forms then combine with the participial forms of the main verb for aspect giving various possible strings of Type II. The auxiliary can, of course, stand all by itself in which case it acts as the copula. Incidentally, in the forms given above, it can be noticed that, unlike standard Hindi, Magahi uses *l*-past and *b*-future like Bangla.

Aspect is provided by participial endings as follows: neutral [-ø] or [a] for the habitual, imperfective [-t] for the progressive, and perfective [-l] for the stative. Thus main verbs in three possible participial forms combining with the five auxiliary forms provide for fifteen verbal strings (leaving out the variations due to agreement). They can be named appropriately on the basis of the particular combinations of the participial main verb plus the particular form of the auxiliary, such as habitual present, habitual past, habitual past subjunctive, habitual subjunctive, habitual presumptive, progressive present, progressive past, and so on.

There are still other finite verbal strings in the following way. The present and past tense forms of the auxiliary can be added to the past simple form of the main verb (which is already finite and carries the agreement features). This results in present and past perfective verbal strings in which this added auxiliary is in the frozen form for person agreement (since it is already there on the main verb); thus, /ham sutli/ 'I slept' and /tu sutla/ 'you slept', but the same form of the auxiliary in /ham sutli he/ 'I have slept' and /tu sutla he/ 'you have slept'. This construction is different from the one in which the main verb occurs in the frozen perfective participial form with the auxiliary carrying the tense and person agreement features, as in /tu sutal ha/ 'you are asleep', which is a stative present construction.

Another significant finite verbal form in Magahi involves a Type II construction. In this construction, the perfective participle on the main verb has two forms, /-al/ with intransitive verbs and generally, but /-le/ with transitive verbs, as in /ham sut-al hi/ 'I am asleep' but /ham khai-le hi/ 'I have eaten'. As pointed out above, this construction has a stative flavour, naturally with most intransitive verbs but in a marked way with the transitives: 'I have eaten' in the sense that I am in the state of having had the experience of eating it. This use of /-le/ then is employed also with intransitive verbs to bring out this extra stative meaning resulting in a contrastive finite string, such as

ham sut-al hi   'I am asleep.'
ham sut-le hi   'I have had the experience of sleeping
              (in a bed/place like this)'

Transitivity turns out to be a crucial parameter in Magahi in various ways including the points made in the preceding discussion, and the fact, as pointed out earlier, that it seeks to distinguish between transitive and intransitive verbs in the morphological selection of the past tense suffix /-l/ vs /-lk/ for third person. This is reflected also in the transitivity series of morphologically related verbs (intransitive-transitive-causative type) that it shares with Indo-Aryan languages in general. What is interesting, though, is the fact that it is a little more pervasive than in a language like Hindi, providing more intransitive-passive counterparts than available in Hindi. In fact, one could profitably posit a de-transitivising suffix to productively obtain intransitive counterparts of transitive verbs which are not available for their cognates in Hindi (Sheela Verma 1985).

8 SYNTAX

The syntactic structure of Magahi is comparable to that of the general NIA languages. In this section, attention will be drawn only to those aspects of Magahi syntax that present interestingly different things. In accordance with the general NIA typology, Magahi is a head-final language with Subject-Object-Verb as the unmarked word order and the use of postpositions rather than prepositions, as also 'experiencer' subject constructions (Verma 1990) and topic orientation in sentence structure (Verma 1991b). Another significant feature of syntax shared with NIA languages is the heavy use of long participial phrases, in place of embedded relative or adverbial clauses, in nominal modification and adverbial function. The relatively ready availability of morphological passive-intransitive verbs reduces the need for passive constructions periphrastically compared to a language like Hindi; the familiar NIA 'jā-passive' (Verma 1971) is used essentially in the imperative for politeness, as in /baiṭhal jāe/ 'please be seated', /calal jāe/ 'let's go, please'.

8.1 Verb agreement

This is where Magahi presents a picture very different from just about all NIA languages including its sister language Bhojpuri (though not Maithili). Magahi has simultaneous subject and object agreement with the verb in the sentence (see Verma 1991a for details). This is a feature not very commonly found in the languages of the world either, with some such exceptions as the Bantu languages of East Central Africa (e.g. Swahili), and the Mayan languages of Central America (e.g. Mam). The following are illustrative examples which break down the tense, subject agreement and object agreement morphemes in the verb:

(i)	*ham dekha-l-i*	'I saw' – neutral object
(ii)	*ham okrā dekha-l-i-ai*	'I saw' – 3P object, – honor
(iii)	*ham unkā dekha-l-i-ain*	'I saw' – 3P object, + honor
(iv)	*ham torā dekha-l-i-au*	'I saw' – 2P object, – honor
(v)	*ham to(h)rā dekha-l-i-o*	'I saw' – 2P object, + honor

In fact this is not the complete picture. Magahi can also have alternative sentences for the same English glosses, as in

(i)	*ham dekhali / dekhalio*	'I saw' – neutral object
(ii)	*ham okrā dekhaliai / dekhalio*	'I saw' – 3P object, – honor
(iii)	*ham unkā dekhaliain / dekhalio*	'I saw' – 3P object, + honor
(iv)	*ham torā dekhaliau / dekhalio*	'I saw' – 2P object, – honor
(v)	*ham to(h)rā dekhalio*	'I saw' – 2P object, + honor

It seems that Magahi syntax involves an abstract entity like an 'addressee component' which gets into the agreement system. This addressee component has the force of co-opting the listener as a silent participant or witness to what is being stated. Its illocutionary force could be paraphrased something like 'let me tell you', or 'this may be of interest to you'; and just in case the addressee has different agreement features, the sentences will have still other forms, as in

(i)	*ham okrā dekhalio*	'I saw him' object – honor, addressee + honor
	ham okrā dekhaliau	same	object – honor, addressee – honor

(ii)	*ham unkā dekhalio*	'I saw him' object + honor, addressee + honor
	ham unkā dekhaliau	same	object + honor, addressee – honor

REFERENCES

Aryani, Sampatti (1965) *Magahī: Vyākaraṇ, Koś*, Patna: Hindi Sahitya Sammelan.
—— (1976) *Magahī-Bhāṣā aur Sāhitya*, Patna: Bihar Rashtrabhasha Parishad.
Breton, Roland J.-L. (1997) *Atlas of the Languages and Ethnic Communities of South Asia*, Walnut Creek, CA: AltaMira Press.
Cardona, G. (1974) 'The Indo-Aryan languages', *Encyclopedia Britannica*, 15th ed., 9: 439–50.
Chatterji, Suniti Kumar (1926) *The Origin and Development of the Bengali Language*, 3 vols., London: George Allen and Unwin. (Reprint 1970).
Grierson, George A. (1903–28) *Linguistic Survey of India*, (11 vols. in 19), Calcutta: Office of the Superintendent of Government Printing. (Reprinted (1967–73), Delhi: Motilal Banarsidass).
—— (1903) *Linguistic Survey of India, Vol. V: Indo-Aryan Family, Eastern Group, Pt. II: Specimens of the Bihari and Oriya Languages*, Delhi: Motilal Banarsidass. (Reprint 1967).
Grimes, Barbara F. (1996) *Ethnologue*, Houston: Summer Institute of Linguistics.
Jeffers, Robert J. (1976) 'The position of the Bihārī dialects in Indo-Aryan', *Indo-Iranian Journal* 18: 215–25.
Katre, S. M. (1968) *Problems of Reconstruction in Indo-Aryan*, Simla: Indian Institute of Advanced Study.
Pandeya, Ras Bihari (1982) 'Magahī Bhāṣā ke Ādi Kavi Sarahapād', in Ras Bihari Pandeya (ed.) *Magahī-Bhāṣā-Sāhityik-Nibandhāwalī*, Patna: Lok-Sāhitya-Saṅgam.
Singh, Dr. Talakeshwar (1982) 'Siddha Sāhitya Aur Magahī', in Ras Bihari Pandeya (ed.) *Magahī-Bhāṣā-Sāhityik-Nibandhāwalī*, Patna: Lok-Sāhitya-Saṅgam.
Sinha, Dr. Lakshaman Prasad (1969) *Rūpvijñān kī Dṛṣṭi se Magahī aur Bhojpūrī*, Patna: Aṃśukamal Prakashan.

Verma, Manindra K. (1971) *The Structure of the Noun Phrase in English and Hindi*, Delhi: Motilal Banarsidass.

—— (1990) 'Experiencer subjects in Bhojpuri and Magahi', in Manindra K. Verma and K. P. Mohanan (eds.) *Experiencer Subjects in South Asian Languages*, Stanford: CSLI, Stanford University, pp. 85–103.

—— (1991a) 'Exploring the parameters of agreement', *Language Sciences* 13.2: 125–43.

—— (1991b) 'Topic and Subject', in V. Prakasam (ed.) *An Encyclopaedia of the Linguistic Sciences*, Delhi: Allied Publishers, pp. 210–18.

Verma, Sheela (1985) *The Structure of the Magahi Verb*, New Delhi: Manohar.

Verma, Sheela and Verma, Manindra K. (1983) 'The auxiliary with special reference to Magahi', *Indian Linguistics* 44: 97–101.

FURTHER READING

Dass, Thakur (1976) Position of Eastern Hindi-Bihari Dialects in Indo-Aryan, Ph.D. dissertation, Delhi: University of Delhi.

Grierson, George A. (1883–7) *Seven Grammars of the Dialects and Subdialects of the Bihari Languages, Parts I–VIII*, Delhi: Bharatiya Publishing House. (Reprint 1980)

—— (1903–28) *Linguistic Survey of India*, 12 vols. Delhi: Motilal Banarsidass. (Reprint 1967–8)

Masica, Colin P. (1991) *The Indo-Aryan Languages*, Cambridge: Cambridge University Press.

Nalin, Dr. Brajmohan Pandeya (1982) *Magahī Arthavijñān: Viśleṣnātmak Nirvacan*, Allahabad: Abhinav Bharati.

Pandeya, Ras Bihari, ed. (1980) *Magahī Bhāṣā Kā Itihās*, Gaya: Lok-Sāhitya-Saṅgam.

—— ed. (1982) *Magahī-Bhāṣā-Sāhityik-Nibandhāwalī*, Patna: Lok-Sāhitya-Saṅgam.

Yugeshwar, Dr. (1969) *Magahī Bhāṣā*, Varanasi: Bharatiya Sahitya Asthan.

Zograph, Georgii A. (1982) *Languages of South Asia*, London: Routledge & Kegan Paul Ltd.

CHAPTER FOURTEEN

BHOJPURI

Manindra K. Verma

CONTENTS

LIST OF TABLES

LIST OF MAPS

1 INTRODUCTION

Bhojpuri is the westernmost member of the Eastern group of languages that Grierson (1927: 5) chose to group together as deriving from Māgadha Apabhraṁśa (and Māgadhi Prakrit) that includes not only the other Bihari languages but also Bangla, Asamiya, and Oriya. In fact, the term 'Bihari' was first used by Grierson (1883–87) to mean a single language, with Bhojpuri, Magahi and Maithili as its three dialects. Both Chatterji (1926) and Tiwari (1960) treat them as separate languages in which Magahi and Maithili are sub-grouped together separately from Bhojpuri, sharing, among other things, a rather complex system of verbal conjugation.

As the westernmost member of the Māgadhi group, Bhojpuri is in direct contact with Avadhi and other languages of what is known as the Eastern Hindi group, with mutual intelligibility. It shares with them such grammatical features as the 'redundant' (Tiwari 1960: 104) nominal and adjectival stems and the pronominal system. Such similarities coupled with the speakers' sentiments about cultural and political ties and a lack of a clearly defined geographical boundary between them led scholars like Beams (1872: 96) and Kellogg (1875: 65) to regard Bhojpuri as an eastern variety of Hindi, a position expressly attacked by Grierson (1927: 148). In fact, another scholar, Hoernle (1880: viii), even used the term 'Eastern Hindi' to mean primarily Bhojpuri. Chatterji (1926) essentially supported Grierson's basic conclusion. More recently, however, Grierson's grouping has been questioned by scholars like Cardona (1974), Jeffers (1976) and Dass (1976). On the basis of comparative reconstruction in terms of 'shared innovation' and not just 'shared retention', Dass concludes that 'Bihari does not constitute a sub-group with Bengali …' (1976: 294), and that 'Bihari and Eastern Hindi belong to one group … distinct from Bengali or Hindi on the basis of shared phonological innovations …' (1976: 295).

Of the three Bihari languages, Bhojpuri covers much the largest territory consisting of an area of approximately 73,100 square kilometers of western Bihar and eastern Uttar Pradesh and also the southwest part of Nepal (Ranjan 1997). Thus, unlike other 'Bihari' languages, Bhojpuri is spoken in two adjoining states in India, and two contiguous countries of South Asia, India and Nepal. Furthermore, it is also the chief lingua franca of sizeable communities of Bhojpuri speaking settlers in Mauritius (Ranjan 1997), Trinidad (Mohan 1978), Guyana (Gambhir 1981), and Surinam (Damsteegt 1988). Mesthrie (1992) discusses Bhojpuri spoken in South Africa, and Fiji Indians are fond of saying that their 'Hindi' is derived from Bhojpuri. (Moag 1978). All this does in a way accord Bhojpuri the status of an international language.

The geographical spread of the Bhojpuri speech area occupies the western districts of the state of Bihar west of the river Son and the western parts of the Ranchi plateau, and

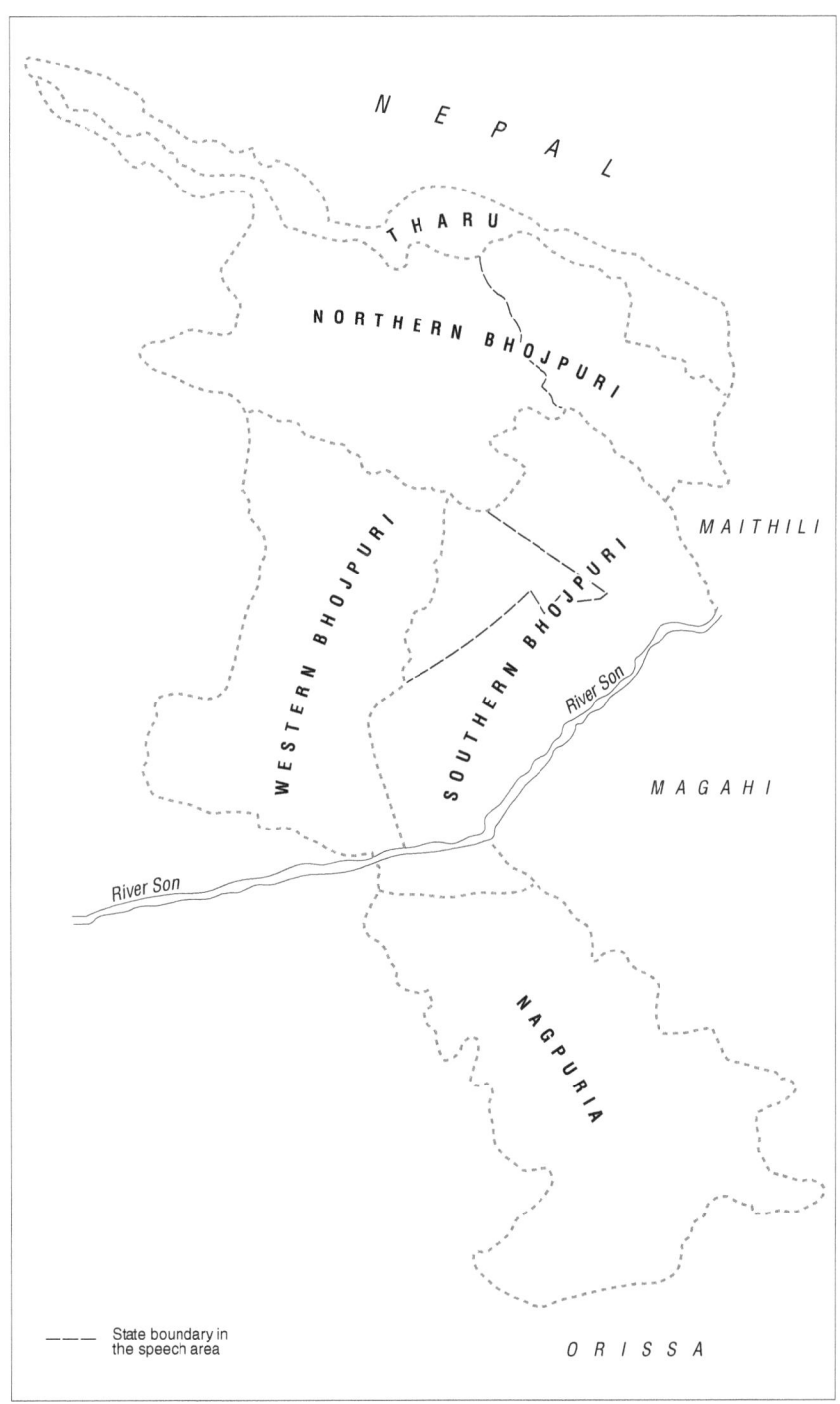

MAP 14.1: BHOJPURI SPEECH AREA

extends to the eastern districts of Uttar Pradesh with roughly the districts of Basti, Azamgarh, Varanasi, and Mirzapur marking the western flank. In Nepal, Bhojpuri is spoken in the Tarai tract bordering India from Baharaich in Uttar Pradesh to Champaran in Bihar, and includes such places in Nepal as Kailali on the west and Mahottari on the east. On its western border, Bhojpuri meets Avadhi, with a transition area roughly along the 83° E meridian. Saksena (1937: 2) identifies some isoglosses which serve to distinguish the Bhojpuri area there, such as the present (habitual) tense with the enclitic /la/, the past tense in /-l/, and the dative postposition /lā/.

Bhojpuri gets its name from a place called Bhojpur in Bihar, now also the name of the district where it is situated. It is believed that Ujjain Rajputs claiming their descent from Raja Bhoj of Malwa had established an important principality here which fought the Mughals of Delhi in the 16th century and the British in 1857. The name Bhojpuri for the language seems to be established by the 17th century and first appears in writing in 1789 (Tiwari 1960). It is denoted by other local names, too, as we will see below.

As a language spread over an area of almost 45,000 square miles, Bhojpuri obviously has dialects, essentially four of them, identified in the literature as 1. Standard Bhojpuri (also referred to as Southern Standard), 2. Northern Bhojpuri, 3. Western Bhojpuri, and 4. Nagpuria. A fifth one, 'Thāru' Bhojpuri, is also recognized as the Bhojpuri spoken in the Nepal Terai and the adjoining areas in the upper strips of Uttar Pradesh and Bihar, from Baharaich to Champaran. Some of the places in the Nepal Terai, from west to east, are Kailali, Dang, Rupandehi, Bhairawa, Butwal, Chitwan, and Mahottari.

Southern Standard covers the areas of Bhojpur, Rohatas, Saran, parts of Champaran in Bihar, and Ballia and eastern Ghazipur in Uttar Pradesh. The description of Bhojpuri in this chapter essentially relates to this variety. One may come across a local name 'Chaparahiyā' in Saran.

Northern Bhojpuri covers the areas of Deoria, Gorakhpur, and Basti in Uttar Pradesh, and parts of Champaran in Bihar. Local names include 'Gorakhpuri' for the language in Deoria and eastern Gorakhpur, and 'Sarwariyā' (< saruār < sarayu-pār) for the language in western Gorakhpur and Basti. The variety spoken east of Gandak river between Gorakhpuri Bhojpuri and Maithili in Champaran has a local name 'Madhesi' (< madhya desīya; 11,029 returns by that name in 1971, most likely under-represented).

Western Bhojpuri includes the areas of Varanasi, Azamgarh, Ghazipur, and Mirzapur in Uttar Pradesh. 'Banārasi' is a local name for the Banaras Bhojpuri. There is a very popular general name 'Purabiyā' for (curiously enough) Western Bhojpuri, obviously used by Hindi speakers to the west of them.

Nagpuria is the dialect spoken to the south of the river Son, in the Palamu and Ranchi districts in Bihar. It has Chattisgarhi contact and may have a Chattisgarhi flavor in its nominal forms. It is also called 'Sadāni' or 'Sadri' (1,142,310 returns by these names and Nagpuria in 1971), as also 'Diku Kāji' by the Munda population there.

Dependable population figures for Bhojpuri, as for other Bihari languages, are hard to come by. Part of the reason, of course, is the designation 'Hindi' used by its speakers for one reason or another in response to census questions. The 1961 census lists the figure at 7, 964,755, and the 1971 census figure is 14,340,564. For 1994, Grimes (1996) provides the figures 23,375,000 for India, and 1,370,000 for Nepal, bringing the total to 25 million and making it the 37th most spoken language in the world. However, taking into account the long-time overseas settlers using Bhojpuri extensively as a lingua franca in their communities in Mauritius, Trinidad & Tobago, Guyana, and Surinam, we can add at least another 2 million to bring the total to 27 million.

Some scholar enthusiasts like to trace the literary history of Bhojpuri from Siddha Sahitya itself, as early as 8th century A.D. (Upadhyay 1972: 39). The so-called Bhojpuri forms that they may find that early may be nothing more than common developments shared by the whole northern complex of language-dialects stretching from the Midlands to the East. However, Kabir's contribution of 'nirgun' poetry to Sant Sahitya certainly qualifies as recorded literature in Bhojpuri in the 15th century. Kabir's language was Western Bhojpuri, more specifically, 'Banarasi' (notwithstanding some edited conformity to the preferred literary diction). The nineteenth century has such works as *Devākṣaracarita by* Ramdatta Shukla (1884), *Badmāśdarpan* by Teg Ali Teg (1895), and *Jangal mē Mangal* and *Nāgari Vilāp* by Ram Garib Chaube in the later half of the nineteenth century. Publication activity in Bhojpuri has been significant, both in volume and quality. The script for them, of course, is Devanagari. Kaithi, the script originally used, is restricted to informal family communication. (A discussion and display of the Kaithi and Devanagari scripts are to be found in the Magahi and Sanskrit chapters of this volume.) Bhojpuri is very actively used by its educated speakers in just about all situations except formal education and government. Folk literature, with characteristic Bhojpuri genres like 'Kajari' songs, 'Bidesiyā' dramas, and 'Baṭohiyā' poems are well-recognized even among the non-Bhojpuri speakers. Unlike the situation in other Bihari languages, there are very popular full length feature films in Bhojpuri shown beyond the Bhojpuri speech area (with songs sung by all-India level singers). In this context, it is very interesting to note that the Hindi cinema (and also the stage play) has created a stylized character – a relatively un-urban, simple-hearted, caring attendant – who speaks Bhojpuri. Bhojpuri in a way has become a character delineator and in this sense the 'Prakrit' of Hindi plays.

2 PHONOLOGY

Bihari languages have a great deal of unity in their phonological structure. In fact, it is this unity in phonology that makes them different as a group from Bangla, a point significantly noted by scholars like Jeffers (1976) and Dass (1976), which even persuades them to consider setting them up in some NIA subgroup to which Bangla does not belong. We note below some of the essential features of Bhojpuri phonology.

Features which are distinctive in identifying and contrasting phonemic segments in the phonological system of Bhojpuri can be read from tables 14.1 and 14.2. Treating Hindi as representing the normative NIA system for ease of discussion (see the Hindi phoneme charts in this volume, pp. 258–9), one may note the following points. While Bhojpuri shows the same place, manner, laryngeal (voice, aspiration), and dorsal (tongue height and position) features, the total number of contrasts is smaller. That may, however, be in tune with the inherited phonology of Hindi, too, shorn off the reintroduced contrasts from Sanskrit tatsamas and Arabo-Persian and English loanwords. Bhojpuri, too, has its share of loanwords from Sanskrit, Persian and English, but while Hindi tends to create an assimilated phonological subsystem with a sociolinguistic flavour, Bhojpuri simply resorts to 'phonological reshaping'; for example, Hindi /das/ 'ten' but /daśāwatār/ 'having ten avatārs, an epithet for Viṣṇu', with two different sibilants for the same morpheme without the benefit of any morphophonemic conditioning, whereas Bhojpuri has /das/ as also /dasāwatār/, both with a dental sibilant.

TABLE 14.1: BHOJPURI CONSONANTS

		Labial	Dental	Retroflex	Palatal	Velar	Glottal
Stops	vl.unasp	p	t	ṭ	c	k	
	vl.asp.	ph	th	ṭh	ch	kh	
	vd.unsap	b	d	ḍ	j	g	
	vd.asp.	bh	dh	ḍh	jh	gh	
Nasals		m	n			ŋ	
		mh	nh			ŋh	
Fricatives			s				h
Flaps (Liquids)			r	ṛ			
			rh	ṛh			
Laterals (Liquids)			l				
			lh				
Glides		w			y		

2.1 Consonants

Bhojpuri does, however, show an extension of the feature of aspiration to nasals and liquids, e.g., /barmā/ 'Verma, a surname', /barmhā/ 'Brahma'; /kānā/ 'one-eyed', /kānhā/ 'Lord Kṛṣṇa'; /kāl/ 'death', /kālh/ 'yesterday'; /(mārā)-māri/ 'fight', /mārhi/ 'a kind of grain'. The velar nasal in Bhojpuri does behave as a distinctive consonantal segment as in /maṇani/ '(I) asked' versus /manani/ '(I) admitted'. Thoughts of its possible subphonemic status as a cluster phenomenon in /ŋg/ can be countered by the presence of forms like /phungi/ 'tip of a branch', /kankhi/ 'squint' (as opposed to /paŋkhi/ 'bird'), even though statistically marginal. Besides, it has its aspirated counterpart, too, like the other nasals in Bhojpuri, as in /siŋh/ 'horn'.

2.2 Clusters

Consonant clusters in Bhojpuri are very limited both in type and position of occurrence. The canonical shape of the Bhojpuri syllable could be represented as (C)V(C)(C). Word initially, the inherited (as also the borrowed) clusters are reduced by svarabhakti (/bharam/ for /bhram-/ 'misapprehension'), or prothesis (/asnān/ for /snāna/ 'bath'), or the conversion of a semivowel into a vowel (/beohār/ for /vyavahāra/ 'behaviour'). Word-finally, they are essentially restricted to a stop (or the lone sibilant /s/) preceded by a homorganic nasal. Medially, a sibilant could also precede a stop. However, Bhojpuri shows a penchant for geminates word-medially and tends to retain them in inherited forms where both Hindi and Bangla, for example, prefer simplification with compensatory lengthening. Some examples are Bhojpuri /ujjar/ 'white, bright', Hindi /ujalā/ (Bangla /ujɔl/, Sanskrit /ujjvala/); Bhojpuri /pittar/ 'brass', Hindi /pītal/ (Bangla /pitɔl/, Pkt. /pittala/); Bhoj. /bajjar/ 'thunderbolt', Bangla /bāj/ (Sanskrit /vajra/, Pkt. /vajja/); Bhoj. /buttā/ 'strength', Hindi /būtā/ (Sanskrit /vr̥tta/, Pkt. /vutta/); Bhojpuri /suttal/ 'sleeping state', Bangla /śutā/ (Pkt. /sutta/). For many words in Hindi with a medial consonant preceded by a long vowel, Bhojpuri will have an attenuated vowel followed by a geminate: Bhoj. /sujji/ 'cream of wheat', Hindi /sūjī/; Bhoj. /ghussā/ 'a fist blow', Hindi /ghũsā/; Bhoj. /banaccar/ 'a wild wayward person', Hindi /bancar/; Bhoj. /juttā/ 'shoe', Hindi /jūtā/. Bhojpuri also shows a somewhat different development for the Nasal+Consonant clusters, changing them into nasal geminates (rather than single consonants with (nasalized) long preceding vowels), as in the following tadbhava Bhojpuri forms uninfluenced by Hindi: Bhoj. /sunnar/ 'beautiful', Bangla /sũdɔr/ (Hindi /sundar/); Bhoj. /tammā/ 'copper', Hindi /tāmbā/ (Sanskrit /tāmra/), Bhoj. /alamm/ 'support' (Sanskrit /ālamba/), as also Bhojpuri /punn/ 'meritorious act' (Sanskrit /puṇya/), /sonnā/ 'zero' (Sanskrit /śūnya/), and even /innar/ 'Indra' and /demennar/ 'Devendra'. Aspirated stops in such situations lead to the relatively rich availability of aspirated nasals in Bhojpuri: Hindi /ādherā/, Bangla /ãdhār/ but Bhoj. /anhār/ 'darkness'; Hindi /bā̃dh-/, Bangla /bā̃dhā-/ but Bhoj. /bānh-/ 'bind'; Sanskrit /skambha/, Hindi /khambhā/, Bangla /khāmbā/ but Bhoj. /khāmhā/ 'pillar'; Sanskrit /skandha/, Hindi /kandhā/, Bangla /kã̃dh/ but Bhojpuri/kānhā/ 'shoulder'.

2.3 Vowels

Bhojpuri has essentially a system of six vowels, with nasalized counterparts. There are two additional vowels – high short ones – shown in parentheses in Table 14.3 to provide for what is claimed for Northern Bhojpuri in general and Gorakhpuri in particular (Shukla 1981: 27–8). Since they have well-defined positional restrictions (Tiwari 1960: 4, 7), they have to be treated as subphonemic. The reduction of phonological contrasts vis-à-vis the normative NIA thus applies also to the Bhojpuri vowel inventory, eliminating the length contrast (which, even in the normative NIA, is relevant only in the case of the high vowels anyway and, from most accounts, neutralized in the final position in Hindi, too). Bhojpuri does have allophonic length reduction, though, which may be called 'attenuation'. It may be noted that it is a phenomenon that is not segment determined but has the syllable, or the word, or even the derivation as its domain. It is related to stress, which in turn is related to syllabic structure, or derivation resulting in a stem or word. It turns out that in Bhojpuri /a/ is the only truly short vowel and /ā/ is the only truly long vowel. Others are indeterminate. All vowels are capable of receiving the word stress, and all vowels have their attenuated counterparts in statable conditions. Only /ā/ has an attenuated counterpart which is a phoneme in its own right, namely /a/ (/rājā/ 'king' but /rajawā/ 'the king'); all other attenuations are allophonic, which may be represented in the discussion as / ˘ / over the vowel symbol (e.g. [moti] 'pearl' but [mŏtiyā] 'the pearl'). Notwithstanding loan elements or native elements of marginal

TABLE 14.2: BHOJPURI VOWELS AND DIPHTHONGS

	Front	Central	Back
High	i		u
	(I)		(U)
Mid	e	a	o
Low		ā	
Diphthongs	ai		au

Note: Central vowel transcribed here as /a/ has the phonetic value of [ʌ] in stressed positions and [ə] in unstressed positions. In the eastern half of the Bhojpuri region this [ʌ] has a somewhat rounded quality. The diphthongs /ai/ and /au/ are truly diphthongal and have a more central initiation point, phonetically [əi] and [əu].

status incidentally vitiating an abiding pattern, the overall system of stress placement in Bhojpuri is that the penult in a disyllabic word and the antepenult in a longer word is tonic, unless other factors, phonological such as relative syllable weight, or morphological such as derivation or inflection, intervene. In general, a vowel in a stressed syllable has the basic long allophone and an unstressed vowel has its attenuated counterpart. A syllable of the type CVCC or CVC with /ā/ or a diphthong is always heavy (/gí-na/ 'count' but /u-dās/ 'sad'). CVC with an /a/ makes it as heavy as other vowels by themselves, which is still less heavy than a CVC with any of the other vowels. All these get into the determination of stress placement and movement, as seen in /gó-rakh/ 'a name' with no movement, but shifted stress in /par-dés/ 'foreign land'. Derivation with a heavy (stressed) vowel or heavy syllable will always shift the stress: /ká-hā̃/ 'where' with the expected stress on the penult, but with the passive derivative suffix /-ā̃/ as in /ka-hā̃/ 'said' (/galati se ka-hā̃ gail/ 'got said by mistake'), the stress shifts. The changing syllabic weight in an inflected form, however, will not allow stress shift: /kár/ 'do' as also /ká-reb/ 'will do' even though the last syllable turns up heavy, whereas in a non-inflected word like /ha-rék/ 'each one' the syllable weight can move the stress on to the last syllable. Similarly, the stress is on the heavy syllable in /ma-hín/ 'fine, subtle' but is unshifted, regardless of the syllabic weight, in the inflected verb form /rá-hit, ú-ṭhit/ 'would have stayed/gotten up' from the verbs /rah-/ 'to remain' and /uṭh-/ 'to get up'. In the syllabic sequence CVC-CV in a word, the preceding V even when stressed will have the attenuated allophone, as in [móṭ] 'fat' but [móṭ-kā]. Further details of attenuation may be seen in section 6.6 of the chapter on Magahi in this volume, another Bihari language which shares this feature with Bhojpuri along with the feature of vowel harmony.

3 MORPHOLOGY

The internal structure of word forms in Bhojpuri involves a consideration of word derivation processes in the various lexical categories, and the forms of words in grammatical subclasses marked by inflection in those categories.

3.1 Derivation

Bhojpuri productively uses formative prefixes and suffixes to derive words from basic words within and across lexical categories. However, suffixes are more numerous than prefixes. Some illustrative examples are: within categories, by prefixation, nouns /dharam/ 'right act' /adharam/ 'sinful act', /lacchan/ 'characteristics', /kulacchan/ 'ominous characteristics'; adjectives /subh/ 'auspicious' /asubh/ 'inauspicious'; adverbs /bāte/ 'with substance, reason' /bebāte/ 'unreasonably'. Examples of derivation by suffixation are seen in nouns /karani/ 'deed' /karanihār/ 'doer'; adjectives /choṭ/ 'small' /choṭkā/ 'the small (one)'; adverbs /upar/ 'above' /upare/ 'at the very top'; verbs /paṛh-/ 'read' /paṛhāw-/ 'teach'. Derivation across categories are illustrated as follows: nouns: /laṛāi/ from the verb /laṛ-/ 'to fight', /khusi/ 'happiness' from the adjective /khus/ 'happy'; adjectives: /beimān/ 'dishonest' from the noun /imān/ 'honesty', /khāu/ 'voracious' from the verb /khā-/ 'to eat'; verbs: /latiyā-/ 'to kick, insult' from the noun /lāt/ 'leg', /moṭā-/ 'to fatten up' from the adjective /moṭ/ 'fat'; and adverbs: /goṛe/ 'on foot' from the noun /goṛ/ 'foot', and /ĩhā̃/ 'here' from the pronoun /i/ 'this'.

It may be noted that the formative affixes in Bhojpuri, as in its lexicon, include (apart from the inherited NIA stock) borrowed elements of Arabo-Persian origin, as also tatsama elements, with phonological reshaping wherever applicable. This may be seen in the Persian adjectival suffix /-i/ as in /hisāb/ 'calculation' and /hisābi/ 'the calculating one', or the Persian prefix /be-/ 'without' as in /bebāt/ 'without substance or reason'. It is interesting to note that Persian affixes occur not only with borrowed Persian bases but can be used productively with words of native origin too, as in /samajhdār/ 'the perceptive one', with NIA /samajh/ and Persian /-dār/. The negative prefixes /a-, an-, ku-, dus-, dur-/ in words like /adharam/ 'contrary to virtue', /anek/ 'not just one, many', /kucāl/ 'depraved conduct', /durbhāg/ 'misfortune' illustrate affixes of tatsama origin. In fact, prefixes in Bhojpuri are more likely to be borrowed than native. It may also be noted that while Bhojpuri has vocabulary items borrowed from English, it does not use affixes from that source.

Derivational processes in Bhojpuri also include reduplication and compounding. Reduplication is an important feature of the structure of Bhojpuri as it is in South Asian languages in general. In Bhojpuri, it is a rather productive process and can have related but subtly differentiated semantic functions in different lexical categories. Basically, it has a distributive function, which may also imply plurality or intensity depending on the lexical category and the context; thus, quality adjective /niman/ 'good' /niman niman/ 'various good ones', colour adjective /hariyar/ 'green' /hariyar hariyar khet/ 'a very green field', /thoṛ/ 'little' /thoṛ thoṛ/ 'little by little'. The last one also effects category change, an adverb from an adjective. Reduplication of imperfective forms of verbs and oblique nouns yields adverbs very productively, as in /u rowat rowat kahlas/ 'lit. 'she said it cryingly (while crying)' from the verb /ro-/ 'cry', and /u goṛe goṛe cal āil/ 'He managed to arrive on foot' from the noun /goṛ/ 'foot'.

Compounding yields various types of derived words in Bhojpuri. The interesting ones include 'translation compounds' in which two semantically same or similar words from different linguistic stocks are compounded almost as an explanation of a loanword, such as /pāw-roṭi/ 'a loaf of (as opposed to flat) bread' from Portuguese /pão/ 'bread' + NIA /roṭi/ 'bread', /sāg-sabji/ 'vegetables' from NIA /sāg/ 'greens'+ Persian /sabzi/ 'greens'. Most such compounds in Bhojpuri assume the flavour of an aggregative copulative compound (*samāhāra dwandwa*), as in /kāgaj-pattar/ 'papers, documents and such' from Persian /kaɣaz/ 'paper' and Sanskrit /pattra/ 'leaf, sheet', /khel-tamāsā/ 'spectacles and such' from NIA /khel/ 'sport' and Persian /tamāsā/ 'exhibition'. Such aggregative meaning can also be obtained in dwandwa compounds involving stems with different or even opposite meanings but thematically related, such as /niman-bāur/ 'good-bad, all kinds whatever', /māi-bāp/ 'mother-father, a protector like one's parents', /dāl-roṭi/ 'lentil-bread, essential provision'. While dwandwa compounds are very productive in Bhojpuri, we do find some frequently used bahuvrīhis (attributive compounds) in religious contexts which are essentially borrowed from Sanskrit through Hindi. Some examples are /pitāmbar/ 'Vishnu-Krishna', /nilkanṭh/ 'Lord Shiva'. To be sure, there are some NIA type Bhojpuri bahuvrīhis, such as /ṭuṭpūjiyā/ 'a trader of smaller means' or /bahurupiyā/ 'a mimic in funny disguises'. However, there is a particular kind of reciprocity denoting bahuvríhi (vyatihāra bahuvrīhi) which is very common in Bhojpuri. It is formed by reduplicating a noun with templatic final vowels (/ā – i/) to characterize the nature of an event, as in /lātā-lāti/ lit. 'leg-leg', i.e. 'reciprocal kicking', /kānā-kāni/ lit. 'ear-ear', i.e., 'secretly' (by sharing one another's ears), /muhā̃-muhī̃/ lit. 'mouth-mouth', i.e. 'squabble, wrangle', /jhõṇṭā-jhõṇṭi/ lit. 'hair-hair', i.e. 'a scuffle with mutual tugging at one another's hair'.

It may be noted that while there are tatpuruṣa (determinative) compounds with a noun as the first element in Bhojpuri (most of them, of course, in the well-established inherited vocabulary as single words, such as /bailgāṛi/ 'bullock-cart' or /gaṅgājal/ 'Ganges water'), they are not characteristic of Bhojpuri. Thus a Sanskrit type Hindi expression like /bālikā vidyālaya/ could not find a Bhojpuri equivalent like /laṛki iskul/. It would be more natural to have a noun phrase with the genitive postposition /ke/ as in /laṛkian ke iskul/, or /dil ke daurā/ for 'heart attack' even if High Hindi could opt for a possible Sanskritized /hṛdpāt/.

3.2 Inflection

The forms that a Bhojpuri word takes for its participation in larger structures creates certain inflectional categories marking its relations within those structures. The ones which are relevant for Bhojpuri are number, gender and person for nouns and pronouns, and mood, aspect, tense and agreement for verbs. Some adjectives are also inflected for agreement. The inflectional elements in Bhojpuri are all suffixes. The inflected forms may vary depending on the nature of the bases.

3.3 Noun morphology

Nominal bases that participate in nominal inflection can be basic simple stems or derived complex stems, such as /pujā/ 'worship' /pujāri/ 'worshipper'. The derived noun stems can be obtained from the bases of various lexical categories. In so far as the main stock of Bhojpuri vocabulary is the inherited NIA, supplemented by the more commonly used higher register complex stems borrowed from a language like Hindi (with phonological reshaping wherever applicable, as in /durdassā/ 'woeful condition', /canarmukhi/ 'the moon-faced one'), its derivational morphology, for a large part, is quite akin to what we may find in a language like Hindi. What is being attempted here is an account of the more characteristic, and productive, aspects of the derivational morphology of Bhojpuri.

A derived noun stem of Bhojpuri that is quite significant is the so-called 'redundant' form (Tiwari 1960: 104) of the noun typically ending in /-wā/, as in /camarwā/ 'the cobbler' from /camār/ 'cobbler' (with morphophonemic vowel shortening/attenuation as applicable). As can be seen from the glosses, it is hardly a redundant form; this suffix accomplishes a grammatical task not commonly found in NIA languages, namely coding 'definiteness' in a noun morphologically. It has two other variations /-ā/ and /-yā/, as in /camarā/ 'the cobbler' and /maliyā/ 'the gardener'. They are neatly distributed. /ā/ has a very restricted distribution. It occurs only with nouns that satisfy two conditions, a grammatical condition of possessing the feature [+animate], and a phonological condition of having the disyllabic structure CV-CVC. Semantically, it adds the nuance of good-natured pejoration and possibly diminution. Most of these nouns have /-ār/ as the final VC deriving agentive nouns indicating trade, such as /sonār/ 'goldsmith', /komhār/ 'potter' (from OIA /-kāra/ as in /suvarṇakāra, kumbhakāra/) and yield such forms as /sonarā/ 'the goldsmith', /komharā/ 'the potter'. But this is not quite exclusively so, as we also find /bānar/ 'monkey', /banarā/ 'the monkey', /damād/ 'son-in-law', /damadā/ 'the son-in-law'.

The suffix /-yā/ is added to stems ending in /-i/; these include a lot of feminine nouns, but also nouns which have the feature [+feminine] without ending in /-i/ . In the latter cases an epenthetical /-i/ is added to make the rule apply regularly. Examples are masculine /ādami/ 'man', /admiyā/ 'the man'; marked feminine /beṭi/ 'daughter' /beṭiyā/, unmarked feminine /aurat / 'woman' /aurat-i-yā/ 'the woman'. The variant

/-wā/ is essentially the 'elsewhere' allomorph applying even to forms already derived by the other variants, in effect creating doublets, /sonarā/ and /sonarwā/ from /sonār/, and /bhaiyā/ and /bhayawā/ from /bhāi/ 'brother'.

The pejorative nature of this derivation can be noted in the fact that verbal agreement, which involves the feature [± honorific] will disallow [+honorific] verb form with a subject noun in /-wā/, as in the unacceptable */unkar beṭwā āil rahan/ with an honorific 3p. aux. /rahan/ instead of the non-honorific 3p. aux. /rahe/. The feature of definiteness in this form can be seen in the acceptable /u kamijwā kin la/ 'Buy that shirt' with a definite determiner vs. the unacceptable */e-go kamijwā kin la/ to mean 'Buy a shirt' with an indefinite determiner.

Another significant derivational process in Bhojpuri is the extensive use of the suffix /-wālā/ to derive 'characterizing' nouns. This is available in a language like Hindi, too, but its productivity is larger in Bhojpuri, to the degree that it can be substituted for borrowed items of a higher register which use such characterizing suffixes as /-dār, -bāz, -xor/, as in /izzatdār, daγābāz, naśāxor/ to result in /ijjatwālā, dagā dewe wālā, nasā kare wālā/ 'honourable, deceitful, drunkard'. Another productive characterizing suffix is /-iyā/ (with possible variations in /-aiyā/, /vaiyā/, or /iyā̃/), as in /kalkatiyā/ 'characteristic of or belonging to Calcutta', /īnjoriyā/ 'characterized by light', /laṭpaṭiyā/ 'a tangler', /purbaiyā/ 'easterly', /paṛhwaiyā/ 'one who indulges in reading a lot', /puraniyā̃/ 'an older person, one characterized by old age'.

3.3.1 Gender

Animate nouns in Bhojpuri are gender distinguished for agreement. So are some animate personal pronouns. Nouns referring to females are feminine, all others are masculine. Gender derivation is possible for animate nouns, with /-i/ being the most typical feminine suffix, followed by /-in/ and /-ni/, as in the /dādā – dādi/ type (grandfather–grandmother), the /camār–camārin/ type (cobbler–cobbler woman), and the /babuā–babuni/ type (boy–girl). The last is quite popular in loanwords: /ḍākṭar–ḍākṭarni/, /māsṭar– māsṭarni/ (male and female doctors and teachers, respectively). While the masculine noun is generally the base for gender derivation, the kinship terms use the primary female relationship as the base and derive the masculine counterpart wherever possible, as in /bahin–bahnoi/ (sister–her husband), /nanad–nandoi/ (husband's sister–her husband), /phuā–phuphā/ (father's sister–her husband).

3.3.2 Number

Number has agreement consequences in Bhojpuri and nouns and pronouns inflect for number. /-an/ (or some variation of it) is the most common plural suffix and can be added to simple as well as derived stems; e.g., in nouns: /sonār–sonār-an/ 'goldsmith– goldsmiths', /sonarā–sonar-an/ 'the blighted goldsmith–the blighted goldsmiths' /sonarwā–sonarw-an/ '(that) goldsmith–(those) goldsmiths'; in pronouns: /ham– hamani/ 'I–we', /u–okani/ 'he–they'. However, periphrastic plurals are very common in Bhojpuri. These are made by adding /log/ to human nouns and personal pronouns, and /sab/ to all nouns and pronouns. In general, the inflected plural and the periphrastic plural are mutually exclusive, avoiding a periphrastic plural form on an inflected plural form: /laṛikā–laṛikan–laṛikā log/ but not */laṛikan log/ for 'children'.

3.3.3 Case

Case by inflection is not a prominent feature of the Bhojpuri noun, and is marginally so for the pronoun. However, case as a syntactically relevant thing is provided for by the use of postpositions. Unlike Hindi, the noun in Bhojpuri does not have an oblique form before a postposition; however pronouns, all of them – personal, demonstrative, interrogative, relative and correlatives – have an oblique form counterpart of the inflected genitive. Nouns have neither an inflected genitive nor an oblique form of it, though they may be interpreted to have the inflected locative and instrumental with an inflectional suffix /-e/ on an appropriately restricted set. In fact, it seems more fruitful to consider this /-e/ a derivational suffix to derive adverbs from nouns indicating place or manner. The latter interpretation seems more appropriate also because, depending on the nature of the noun, it may also have the interpretation of reason or time, as seen in the examples below:

u bhor-e aile	He came in the morning
bhukh-e hamār hālat kharāb ho gail	I am in bad shape due to hunger
dằt-e tura	Break it by (using your) teeth
ghar-e cala	Let's go home

The postpositions used to obtain case functions for nouns are as follows: dative with /ke/ or /lā/, ablative and instrumental with /se/, locative with /mẽ/ 'in', /par/ 'on', /le/ 'up to', and genitive with /ke/. The nominative is always unmarked, and the accusative is generally unmarked but marked with /ke/ for animateness or specificity (see section 4.4). The same postpositions are used with pronouns for their respective case functions, but the pronouns, all of them, use the oblique form of the genitive before a postposition, as in /ham, hamār, hamarā se/ 'I, my, from me', respectively.

3.4 Pronouns

Bhojpuri has an extensive set of pronominal classes whose members are very symmetrically patterned in relation to each other. The set consists of personal, demonstrative, interrogative, relative, correlative and reflexive pronouns. The personal pronouns appear in three persons, with various degrees of honorificity in second and third persons with agreement consequences. Third person and demonstratives are further distinguished for proximity. There are some dialectal variations (see Tiwari 1960: V for details). We will essentially list the Standard Southern Bhojpuri forms. Table 14.3 displays the patterns of inflectional endings.

It may be noted that plurality in the pronouns is indicated by a form of the genitive postposition /ke/ or /kā/ (much like the Bangla plural in the genitive /āmi -āmrā/). Third

TABLE 14.3: PERSONAL PRONOUNS

	Singular			Plural		
	I	II	III	I	II	III
Direct	*ham*	*tu*	*u*	*hamani kā*	*tohani kā*	*okani kā*
Genitive	*hamār*	*tohār*	*unkar*	*hamani ke*	*tohani ke*	*okani ke*
Oblique	*hamarā*	*toharā*	*unkarā*	*hamani ke*	*tohani ke*	*okani ke*

TABLE 14.4: SECOND AND THIRD PERSON HONORIFICS AND PROXIMATES

	II			III			
	Neutral	-Hon	Hon	Neutral	-Hon	Prox	-Hon Prox.
Direct	*tu*	*tẽ*	*rauā*	*u*	*u*	*i*	*i*
Genitive	*tohār*	*tor*	*rāur*	*unkar*	*okar*	*inkar*	*ekar*
Oblique	*toharā*	*torā*	*raurā*	*unkarā*	*okarā*	*inkarā*	*ekarā*

person pronoun /u/ shown above can be treated as neutral in terms of proximity. The proximate pronominal /i/ is the marked member of the pair. Its plural form, following the pattern, is /ekani kā/. Table 14.4 displays the pattern of pronouns, in the singular, distinguished for honorificity and proximity.

The pronouns /tu/ and /u/ are treated as 'neutral' also in the sense of being not non-honorific without being overly honorific. They could be considered 'familiar' honorific. In fact, both second person and third person have a still higher level of honorificity, a kind of super-honorific /apne kā/ for second, and /ihãkā, uhãkā/ for third person with agreement consequences in the verb.

Bhojpuri has indefinite pronouns /kucho/ 'some' for the inanimate and /kauno/ for the non-honorific animate. /kehu/ is the form for the honorific as also for the oblique of the animate. The demonstratives are /hai/ proximate 'this' and /hau/ non-proximate 'that'(alternatively, also just its /i/ and /u/ parts). They all can have only the periphrastic plural in /sab/. The large set of Bhojpuri deictics are based on the demonstrative stems and provide the patterns for the corresponding forms of the interrogative set in /k-/, the relative set in /j-/, and the correlative set in /t-/ (or /s-/ unlike Hindi, a holdover from Sanskrit /sas/). Each of them has its corresponding set of various pronominal, adjectival and adverbial forms, e.g., adjectival /aisan, oisan, kaisan, jaisan, taisan/, and manner adverbial /aise, oise, kaise, jaise, taise/, and place adverbial /ihã, uhã, kahã, jahã, tahã/, etc.

3.5 Adjectives and adverbs

Basic adjectives in Bhojpuri are typically consonant-final, as in /baṛ, choṭ, ũc, nic/ (cf. Hindi /baṛā, choṭā, ũcā, nicā/) 'big, small, high, low', and they do not involve agreement /baṛ laṛikā/laṛiki/ 'older son/daughter'. However, unlike Hindi, it provides for the feature [+definite] by adding a suffix /-kā/ as in /baṛkā, choṭkā/ and then it involves agreement /baṛkā laṛikā, baṛki laṛiki/ implying 'the one who is older'. Derived adjectives, from nouns (/dukhi/ 'suffering'), from verbs (/bahat/ 'flowing'), from adverbs (/pichilā/ 'preceding'), and the comparative constructions using a postposition (/hamarā se baṛhiyã/ 'better than me') are all structures comparable to those of NIA languages like Hindi. Derived adverbs, except for those resulting from a class of nouns in the locative/ instrumental as noted above, are essentially of the same types as found in a language like Hindi (such as adverbs made on abstract nouns, as in /arām se/ 'comfortably', and onomatopoetic adverbs such as /dhaṛām se/ 'crashingly').

3.6 The noun phrase

In accord with the typological make up of South Asian languages, Bhojpuri has head-final phrasal structures. The structure of a simple noun phrase is the noun head preceded by a determiner. Regardless of the fact that it does not have a system of articles per se as in English, various parameters of definiteness are operative in Bhojpuri. Nouns may occur with indefinite determiners /kauno/ 'some, a certain' with the oblique in /kehu/, as in /kauno nadi/ 'some river' but /kehu nadi mẽ/ 'in some river'. In contrast, definiteness, as also genericity, is expressed by a zero marker in the Bhojpuri determiner system, as in the definite /larikā ā gail/ 'The boy has arrived' or the generic /hamār bhāi māstar ha/ 'My brother is a teacher'. The generic noun occurs in the singular /i larikan$_{pl.}$ sab kuli$_{sg.}$ bāran sab/ 'These boys are coolies'. A noun may also be preceded by 'quantifiers' of various kinds, with some co-occurrence and ordering restriction (see Verma 1971: 75–99 for applicable details). The quantifier that deserves special notice in Bhojpuri is the category 'numeral'. Numerals in attributive constructions take the classifier /go/ or /ṭho/, which emphasizes countability as opposed to just the totality. The noun phrase may also contain 'limiter' expressions (Verma 1971: 85–95), but unlike the Hindi particles /hi/ and /bhi/ used for this function, Bhojpuri has them marked morphologically by the suffixes /-e/ and /-o/ to express 'exclusiveness' and 'inclusiveness', as in /ham ām-e khāeb'/ 'I will eat only mangoes' versus '/ham ām-o khāeb/ 'I will eat mangoes, too'. These suffixes are very productive in Bhojpuri and can be added also to other lexical categories such as numerals, adjectives, adverbs and verbs.

In a complex noun phrase, the noun heads can be modified by adjectives, participial phrases, and full relative clauses, but in keeping with the structural scheme of head-final phrases, all of them in Bhojpuri precede the noun head. An important aspect of the Bhojpuri noun phrase is the fact that unlike many languages (including high register Hindi), it does not allow a noun to modify a noun head. The modifier noun has to occur with the genitive postposition /ke/ or the particle /wālā/ to modify a noun. The noun+wālā/ke form in Bhojpuri may very well be interpreted as a productive adjectival derivation from a noun; thus, /lohā ke phāṭak/ 'an iron gate', /pakāwe-wālā soḍā/ 'baking soda'.

3.7 Verb morphology

Bhojpuri has an elaborate inflectional system to indicate tense, aspect and mode on the finite verb forms, which are further marked for agreement in terms of person and honorificity, as also gender and number. In fact, a further parameter of transitivity also gets into the inflectional system of Bhojpuri in a rather significant way. For example, the 3p.perf. on an intransitive verb gives us /u baiṭh-al/ 'he sat' with the expected /-al/, but with a transitive verb it needs an additional ending in /-as/, as in /u dekh-al-as/ 'he saw' (*/u dekh-al/ unacceptable). In the verb string involving the perfective participial and an auxiliary, the transitive has to have the ending /-le/ : /u baiṭh-al bā/ 'he is seated' but /u dekh-le bā/ 'he has seen it' (*/u dekh-al bā/ unacceptable).

3.7.1 Verb stems

Bhojpuri verb stems can be *basic*, such as /ban-/ 'to be made', or morphologically *derived*, such as /banā-/ 'to make', or *complex*, involving a basic or derived verb followed by one of the various kinds of modals but behaving as a single unit for inflectional and tense/mode constructions.

Derived verb stems can be based on a verb itself, as /banā/ from /ban-/, or on a noun, as in /khīsiyā-/ 'to anger' from /khis/ 'anger', or on an adjective /patarā-/ 'to thin down' from /pātar/ 'thin'. As already noted, derivative suffixes with a stressed initial /-a̍/ cause attenuation of the preceding vowel, changing /ā/ to /a/ phonemically and shortening others allophonically. Bhojpuri also participates in the well-known derivationally related NIA transitivity series of intransitive, transitive and causative verbs, as in /ban-, banā-, banwā-/, with systematic rules of derivation. However, what is somewhat special about Bhojpuri in this regard is a productive process of passive (and ipso facto intransitive) derivation with a suffix /-a̍/, as in /khĩcā-/ 'to be pulled' from /khĩc/ 'to pull', /bānhā-/ 'to be bound' from /bã̄nh-/ 'to bind', /sunā-/ 'to be audible' from /sun-/ 'to hear', /kahā-/ 'to be called' from /kah-/ 'to say'. Such intransitive forms are not available in Hindi.

Complex stems can be classified as (i) modals, (ii) aspectual modals, (iii) compound verbs, and (iv) conjunct verbs. In all of them the first element is the carrier of the basic meaning and the second element is the carrier of the inflection and agreement. The latter is a verb from a very restricted set which adds a modality of some sort. The internal structures of these types are respectively as follows:

(i)   verb stem + modal (/khā sak/ eat – modality of ability, 'can eat'),
(ii) aspectually inflected invariant verb + verb (/bol-at rah/ speaking – modality of progressive state 'continue to speak', or /bol-e lag/ speaking – modality of initiation, 'to start speaking'),
(iii) verb stem + verb (/sut jā/ sleep – modality of change of state, 'go to sleep'), and
(iv) noun/adjective + verb (/bakherā-kar/ obstacle – verbalizer modality 'to effect obstacles').

Bhojpuri verb stems are very often listed the way Hindi verb stems are listed, e.g. intr. /ban-/, tr. /banā-/, caus. /banwā-/. This creates a needlessly unpredictable allomorphic problem. While many ā-final stems simply add an inflectional ending without any change (as the imperfective /pakaṛā-t/ on /pakaṛā-/ 'to be caught'), others – which turn out to be transitives – will need to add a /w/, as in the imperfective /banā-w-at/ on the stem /banā-/ 'to make'. The conclusion is straightforward. The derived transitive verbs in Bhojpuri take the suffix /-āw/, and the stems should simply be listed as /banāw-/ 'to make' and /banwāw-/ 'to cause to make' (unlike the Hindi listing); similarly, /uṭhāw-/ 'to raise' or the denominatives /latiyāw-/ 'to kick' or /garmāw-/ 'to heat'. The inflected forms, then, would automatically be whatever is regular for a consonant-final stem. A vowel-final intransitive stem like /jā-/ 'go' or an underived transitive stem like /khā-/ 'eat' does not change in the imperfect /jā-ø-t, khā-ø-t/. Thus, for inflectional purposes, Bhojpuri verb stems are principally divided into consonant-final and vowel-final stems. As a very general rule, vowel-final stems either cause the elision of an initial vowel in the suffix or trigger a homorganic glide between the stem-final vowel and the suffix-initial vowel; examples are /jā-ø-t, chu-w-at, pi-y-at/ for /jā-/ 'go', /chu-/ 'touch', and /pi-/ 'drink'. Incidentally, it seems Hindi has a pervasive rule of eliding derived stem-final /w/ in verbs before inflectional endings; Bhojpuri has a more restricted rule, of eliding it only when the stem form occurs as a word, as in /ham samjhāw-at bāni/ 'I am explaining it' versus /ham samajhā ke hār gaini/ ' I am tired of explaining it'.

3.7.2 Non-finites

Bhojpuri non-finites are of two kinds, nominal and participial. Participial non-finites are clearly aspectually distinguished, apparently with tense correlations: the imperfective (present) participle in /-t/, and the perfective (past) participle in /-l/. It turns out that for

Bhojpuri there are two more, the neutral in /-ø/ (with the variant /-e/ after consonants, as in /u khā-ø-lā/ 'He eats' but /u dekh-e-lā/ 'He looks'), and the other, the proximate in /-b/, as in /u khai-b-e kari/ 'lit., He will certainly do the eating'. The proximate aspect here ties in with the Bhojpuri future tense suffix /-b/. This way, they together provide a neatly complete picture of aspect/tense as follows:

Imperfective – Present:	/-t/
Perfective – Past:	/-l/
Proximate – Future:	/-b/
Neutral – Habitual:	/-ø/ or /-e/

The systematic nature of these endings is seen in the fact that they turn out to be the endings (with morphophonemic variations, if any) for the mutual correlations of participle, aspect and tense in both finite and non-finite forms. It should also be noted here that the perfective/past and the proximate/future endings in Bhojpuri are forms in /-l/ and /-b/, respectively like Bangla and unlike Hindi.

Bhojpuri has also nominal non-finite forms which are aspectually distinguished like the participial ones (unlike the solitary Hindi nominal non-finite infinitival in /-nā/ , as in /bananā, dekhnā/). They are also distinguished in terms of their functional and structural distribution (see Verma 1992 for details). Like other nominals, they have their oblique forms, too, as shown below:

Neutral:	*hamār kah-sun māf kariha*
	lit. 'Don't mind my say and listen.'
Neutral Oblique:	*kuch kahe ke pahile soce ke cāhĩ*
	'One should think before saying anything.'
Imperfective:	*hamarā i kahat jamānā ho gail*
	lit. 'Ages have passed my saying this.'
Imperf. Oblique:	*hamrā i kahte hi u uṭh ke cal gail*
	'He left soon after my saying this.'
Perfective:	*i kahal moskil bā*
	'It is difficult to say this.'
Perf. Oblique:	*i kahalā khātir u bahut gussā kailan*
	'He was very annoyed with my saying this.'

3.7.3 Finite verb forms

The overall structure of the finite verb forms in Bhojpuri is Stem + Aspect/Tense + Person. The personal ending is, in fact, a complex of person and honorificity. Gender is distinguished in a limited way, only in the neutral second and neutral third person, for example, /tu gail-a/ 'you (masc.) went', /tu gail-u/ 'You (fem.) went'; /u gail-an/ 'He went', /u gail-i/ 'She went'. Number is expressed optionally and periphrastically in some dialects through the use of the particles /jā/ and /san/ after the verb. /san/ is a strong marker of solidarity in first person but non-honorificity in second and third persons. The neutral (honorific) 3p. ending seen in the example above /gail-an/ could very well be plurality marker used for honorificity, as in /u sab gail-an/ 'They all$_{\text{hon}}$ went', but when used with /san/, it is transformed into a non-honorific plural /u sab gail-an san/ 'They all$_{\text{non hon}}$ went.'

3.7.4 Personal endings

Personal endings have some dialectal variations (see Tiwari 1960 and Ranjan 1997 for details), but they are basically as follows:

First Person	/-ĩ/
Second Person [-Hon]	/-e/
Second Person Neutral	/-a/
Second Person Neutral Feminine	/-u/
Third Person [-Hon]	/-ø/, /-as/
Third Person Neutral	/-an/
Third Person Neutral Feminine	/-i(n)/

The honorific second persons /rauā, apane kā/ and third person /ihā̃ kā, uhā̃ kā/ all take the same ending /-ĩ/.

3.7.5 Simple finites

The set of personal endings when added to the verb stem in the various participial forms generate the following single word finite forms shown in the second person masculine:

Perfective participle /-l/:	Simple Past	*tu dekh-l-a*
Imperfective participle /-t/:	Counterfactual	*tu dekh-t-a*
Proximate participle /-b/:	Future	*tu dekh -b-a*
Neutral participle /-e/, (/-ø/):	Habitual	*tu dekh-e-l-a (jā-ø-l-a)*

The last one above is a sort of simple present construction with a habitual present particle in /la/. There also is a special future imperative participle /-ih/ of limited use used only with second and third persons, /tu dekh-ih-a, u dekh-ih-an/ with the import '(Make sure) you/they see it sooner or later'.

Essentially the same set of personal endings, different only in 2p.-Hon and 3p.-Hon & Neutral (using /-ø, /-o/, and /-as/, respectively), when added directly to the verb stem with no participial ending, create 'injunctives'. The regular 'imperatives' are really a function of the injunctive in second person (/tu dekh-a, tẽ dekh-ø/ 'You look').

3.7.6 Auxiliaries

The other pattern for the Bhojpuri finite verb is a construction with the main verb in a frozen participial form followed by an auxiliary. It is the auxiliary which occurs in the finite form with the personal endings. When the auxiliary occurs all by itself it behaves as a copula. Bhojpuri is quite prolific in its auxiliaries and has more of them than in a sister language like Magahi or in Hindi. They are formed on five bases, /ha-, ho-, hokh- bāṭ- and rah-/ . They are related in the following way. /bāṭ-/ and /hokh-/ are the principal auxiliary stems forming additional tenses and modes in construction with the participial forms of the main verb. /bāṭ-/ forms provide for the tense and /hokh-/ forms provide for the modes. /ho-/ is a restricted alternate form of /hokh-/; /rah- /is the past tense stem version of /bāṭ-/. Unlike /bāṭ-/, /ha-/ occurs in a limited way, basically in a single form, with the finite perfective form of the main verb which has all the agreement features on it, e.g., /tẽ dekh-le ha, tu dekh-la ha, u dekh-las ha/. As a copula, it is 'identificational' as opposed to the copula /bāṭ-/ which behaves as 'existential' (see the discussion in section 4.6.).

3.7.7 String finites with auxiliaries

The finite verb strings involving a participially frozen form of the verb followed by auxiliaries give us the following, displayed with the verb /sut-/ 'sleep' with the subject /tu/ 'you':

TABLE 14.5: STRING FINITES

Non-finite main verb		Auxiliary	Tense/Mode
Imperfective: Progressive:	*sut-at*	*bāṛ-a*	Present Tense
Perfective: Stative:	*sut-al*	*rah-a*	Past Tense
		hokh-ø-a	Subjunctive
		hokh-t-a	Counterfactual
		hokh-b-a	Presumptive

Table 14.5 generates ten finite constructions (with their appropriate agreement versions), which could receive such labels as Present Progressive, Past Progressive, Present Perfective/Stative, etc. It may be noted that the auxiliary /hokh-/ used above is a main verb, inchoative in nature, with regular conjugation. Three of its possible forms are used in this setup; they provide for the modes only and no tense. The tenses – present and past – are provided for by /bāṭ-/ and its past tense allomorph stem /rah-/.

4 SYNTAX

The syntax of Bhojpuri fully conforms to the typology of NIA syntax. The highlights are given below along with the features that deserve special notice for Bhojpuri. Bhojpuri is a verb-final SOV language, with postpositions and left-branching head-final phrasal syntax. Variations, by and large, are structurally motivated, and apply not to words but to constituent phrases.

4.1 Declarative and interrogative sentences

Word order in declarative and interrogative sentences is the same without, for example, subject verb inversion or question word movement to the clause initial position as in English. Bhojpuri question words (k-words) are *in situ*, that is, the question word fills the same positional slot in the sentence as the questioned element of that class would in the declarative sentence, as in

(1)   *u kalkattā gail*
      he Calcutta went
      'He went to Calcutta.'

(2)   *u kahā̃ gail*
      he where went
      'Where did he go?'

The yes–no question is obtained simply by the use of a rising intonation on the last syllable of its declarative counterpart, with an optional interrogative particle /kā/ added sentence finally: /tu jāt bāṛa (kā)?/ 'Are you going?'

4.2 Negative sentences

Negation divides the sentences in Bhojpuri into two separate groups. Sentences with the present tense auxiliary/copula /bāṭ-/ or a verb string involving /bāṭ-/ replace it with a form in /naikh-/ in their negative counterparts: /u ihẫ bā, u ihẫ naikhe/ 'He is here, He is not here'. In that sense, Bhojpuri also has a negative auxiliary in the present tense, with the stem /naikh-/, which like other auxiliaries takes on the personal agreement features of the subject (the main verb occurring in a frozen participial form and, uncharacteristically, coming after the auxiliary), as in /ham naikh-ī jāt, tu naikh-a jāt, u naikh-e jāt, u_hon_naikh-an jāt/. 'I/you/he/ he_hon_ is not going'. Sentences with the same constructions in the past tense, as also others, will take /nā/, as in /ham nā jāt rahī/ 'I was not going'.

4.3 Passive sentences

The syntactic passive in Bhojpuri is formed by using a special auxiliary /jā-/ with the perfective form of the main verb; /dekhal jāi/ 'It will be seen'; but it is likely to be used only when some agency is implied, /dokān bihān khuli/ 'The store will open tomorrow' versus /dokān bihān kholal jāi/ 'The store will be opened (by someone) tomorrow'. In the habitual tense, it is used to make a statement about the order of things: /ghar roj bahāral jālā/ 'The house is to be/should be cleaned everyday', or for 'prescriptive' constructions in subjectless passives: /baṛ log se aise bāt nā kail jālā/ 'It is not right to talk to the elders like this'.

In Bhojpuri, the syntactic passive is productively used also as an 'abilitative' construction, and in that function it happily uses even intransitive verbs: /hamarā se etnā jaldi jaldi nā calal jālā/ 'I am not able to walk this fast.' The passive imperative is a very favoured construction in Bhojpuri for avoiding any peremptory flavour in imperative sentences: /baiṭhal jāo/, a kind of abstract or impersonal voice 'let sitting be done'. Understandably, it is used with the super honorific form of the second person pronoun /apane kā/.

The syntactic passive in Bhojpuri, thus, has a rather limited use as a putative passive. As noted previously, Bhojpuri has a productive device for the morphological derivation of passive verbs. Also, passivization as a structural strategy for topicalization (as in English, by changing the object into the subject to topicalize it) has a limited use in a relatively topic-oriented language like Bhojpuri (see section 4.7 below) where topicalization is effected by word order shift. In the situation where Rama killed Ravana, in answer to the question 'what happened to Ravana?', the only felicitous answer in English would be in the passive 'Ravana was killed by Rama.' In Bhojpuri the voice does not change; the object phrase is simply moved to the fore of the sentence in the active voice itself: /rāwanwā ke rāmji mār dele/ (see Verma 1991).

4.4 Object in Bhojpuri

The general pattern is to have no object postpositional marking for inanimate direct object nouns. Direct object nouns which are animate and human are marked. Object marking obviously has implications of specificity. Because of this, the general pattern can be reversed when the human noun is used generically (i.e. non-specifically), as in /ham torā larki ke ṭhik se dekhab/ 'I will look after your daughter well' but /ham larki dekhe jāt bāni/ I am going looking for a girl (for marriage)'. However, when the inanimate noun is indirect object in the dative case, it has to have an object marking: /roj paudhā ke pāni diha/ lit. 'give water to the plants everyday'. The marked object noun precedes the direct object or object complement, as in /tu i phul ke (specified object) gulāb (object complement) bujhala/ 'you thought this flower a rose'.

4.5 Subject in Bhojpuri

As an eastern NIA language, Bhojpuri has no agentive/ergative marking for the subject (cf. Marathi, Hindi *-ne* or Nepali *-le*). Its agentive subjects are all in direct case. It does, however, have what may be called non-nominative or 'indirect' subjects of various kinds, marked so morphologically. These indirect subjects in Bhojpuri (and NIA languages in general) provide for a very useful distinction between 'subject as actor' on the one hand and the non-agentive, non-volitional participant in an event structure on the other, including the phenomenon of 'experiencer' subjects (see Verma 1990 for details). A language like English, for example, may have the same subject construction for both the agentive and the non-agentive readings (leading to a great deal of skewing of theta roles and syntactic roles), as in 'he smelled the flowers' and 'he smelled gas (when he entered the room)'. Bhojpuri, on the other hand, will have a separate 'experiencer' subject coding for the latter as in /unkā gais mahakal/ as opposed to /u phul mahakalan/. This is a feature of other NIA languages, too, such as Hindi, but whereas Hindi and most NIA languages use a subject in the dative case to encode this, Bhojpuri uses a very special coding, the oblique of the genitive, as in /hamarā iād bā/ and /hamarā-ke iād karawalan/ with two separate subject forms versus the single indirect subject form in Hindi /ham-ko yād hai/karāyā/ 'I remember/was reminded.'

The non-volitionality of an act is also expressed by coding the subject indirectly, in the instrumental case, with an intransitive verb (which is non-volitional vis-à-vis its transitive counterpart), as in /hamarā-se pleṭ ṭuṭ gail/ 'I broke the plate (by mistake)'. A volitional statement would simply use the transitive counterpart of the verb and use the subject in the direct case, as in /ham pleṭ ṭuṭ deni/ 'I broke the plate (and meant to do it)'. Transitive verbs in Bhojpuri are intrinsically volitional and, accordingly, would not allow a sentence with an inappropriate subject form in that sense. If a man hits a ball with a bat and breaks a window, there may be two ways to encode it in English: 'The man broke the window' or 'The ball broke the window'. While an exact translation of the first one is possible in Bhojpuri, none is available for the second one. The second one will have to use an intransitive verb with the ball in the instrumental, as in /baul-se khiṛki ṭuṭ gail/ and not */baul khiṛki ṭuṭ delas/ (unless you personify the ball and imbue it with volition).

4.6 Stative constructions in Bhojpuri

'Experiencer' subject constructions turn out to be stative, and stativity turns out to be an important grammatical entity in Bhojpuri (and NIA languages in general) in other ways, too. The grammatical structure of Bhojpuri seeks to make and express that distinction in various ways, including the various forms of the subject. For example, Bhojpuri makes a distinction between alienable and inalienable possession, in which obviously a distinction of 'transient state' and 'permanent state' comes into play (indicating a state of affairs in one's life's situation), as in being born with and possessing two eyes or two hands as opposed to possessing two books by acquisition.

Bhojpuri captures this distinction by encoding the possessor subject differently: (alienable) /hamarā pās du ṭho kitāb bā/ versus (inalienable) /hamarā du ṭho hāth bā/ 'I have two books/hands'.

In fact, in Bhojpuri (though not in Hindi), even an auxiliary can be selected varyingly to express stativity and non-stativity. The Bhojpuri auxiliary/copula /bāṭ-/, which can be considered an 'existential' copula, contrasts with /ha-/ which functions as an 'identificational' copula, as in /i kā ha/ 'what is this?' as opposed to /i kahā̃ bā/ 'where is this?' The use of /bāṭ-/ as opposed to /ha/ also ties in with the structural distinction made in expressing the idea of 'the existence of a state', which can be seen in their differential use as an auxiliary in finite verb strings /ham khaini hã/ and /ham khaile bāni/ both translated in English as 'I have eaten.' They are not equivalent, though. Constructionally, the second one uses /bāṭ-/ and an invariant form of the participle. Semantically, this second type can be used to assert, for example, that I have eaten pizza, I know what it is, etc. It is stative.

4.7 Topic orientation in Bhojpuri

Some aspects of the discussions above begin to tie in with the nature of Bhojpuri as a language that is more topic-prominent than subject-prominent (see relevant discussion in Verma 1991). Bhojpuri, among other things, has a 'pro-drop' phenomenon whereby the subject of a sentence does not have to be present overtly, unlike in a language like English which is very clearly a subject-oriented language with its insistence on an overt subject leading not only to 'dummy' subjects (as in It is raining, There is a man there) but also to a great deal of skewing of theta roles and syntactic roles as briefly seen above. Bhojpuri, on the other hand, seems to satisfy just about all the criteria for topic-prominence discussed in Li and Thompson (1976), such as the marginality of the passive construction, absence of dummy or empty subjects, tendency to be verb-final, word order variation to provide for the positional distribution of topic and focus (without in any way flagging them as marked or unusual). In Bhojpuri, topic, which may or may not be the grammatical subject, occurs in the sentence-initial position and is the definite noun phrase par excellence, as in /capāti ke banā rahal bā/ 'Who is making the chapatis?' Furthermore, Bhojpuri does also have a particle like /ta/ as a topic marker (comparable to a marker like /wa/ in Japanese), as in /ām ta ājkal nā mili/ 'As for mangoes, you cannot find them these days'). In fact, the Bhojpuri pronominal form /je/ in a non-relative function does act as a deictic and functions as a topic marker: /ham okarā ke jhā̃paṛ je deni ta u .../ 'When I administered him that big blow, he ...'.

It may be noted that the recognition of topic orientation in Bhojpuri may also explain and help us understand the phenomenon of (non-nominative) indirect subjects better. Topic-prominent languages have been famous for their pervasive so-called 'double subject' constructions, as found in Japanese, Korean, Mandarin, Lahu, etc. (Li and Thompson 1976). It seems that Bhojpuri and other South Asian languages can fruitfully be interpreted as belonging to that group. Their indirect subjects are indirect only in the sense that the (nominative) direct case marking and the verb agreement control is with the other subject, but the control for reflexivization and coreferential constituent deletion properties of the subject still resides with the so-called indirect subjects. In so far as these are viewed as extremely important properties characterizing subjects, it seems that the two subjects in Bhojpuri and other South Asian languages are simply structured to share the totality of the responsibilities of subjecthood.

REFERENCES

Beames, John (1872) *A Comparative Grammar of the Modern Aryan Languages of India.* (Reprinted (1966), Delhi: Munshiram Manoharlal).

Breton, Roland J.-L. (1997) *Atlas of the Languages and Ethnic Communities of South Asia,* Walnut Creek, CA: AltaMira Press.

Cardona, G. (1974) 'The Indo-Aryan Languages', *Encyclopedia Britannica,* 15th ed., 9: 39–50.

Chatterji, Suniti Kumar (1926) *The Origin and Development of the Bengali Language,* 3 vols. London: George Allen and Unwin (Reprinted 1970).

Damsteegt, T. (1988) 'Sarnami: A Living Language', in Barz, Richard and Siegel, Jeff (eds.) *Language Transplanted: The Development of Overseas Hindi,* Wiesbaden: Otto Harrossowitz.

Dass, Thakur (1976) *Position of Eastern Hindi-Bihari Dialects in Indo-Aryan,* Ph.D. Dissertation, Delhi: University of Delhi.

Gambhir, Surendra K. (1981) *The East Indian Speech Community in Guyana: A Sociolinguistic Study with Special Reference to Koine Formation,* Ph.D. Dissertation, Philadelphia: University of Pennsylvania.

Grierson, George A. (1883–7) *Seven Grammars of the Dialects and Subdialects of the Bihari Languages,* Parts I–VIII. (Reprinted (1980), Delhi: Bharatiya Publishing House.)

—— (1903) *Linguistic Survey of India, Vol. V. Indo-Aryan Family, Eastern Group, Pt. II: Specimens of the Bihari and Oriya Languages,* Calcutta: Office of the Superintendent of Government Printing. (Reprinted (1967), Delhi: Motilal Banarsidass.)

—— (1927) *Linguistic Survey of India, Vol. I, Part I,* Calcutta: Office of the Superintendent of Government Printing. (Reprinted (1967), Delhi: Motilal Banarsidass.)

Grimes, Barabara F. (1996) *Ethnologue* 13th edition, Houston: Summer Institute of Linguistics.

Hoernle, A. F. Rudolph (1880) *A Comparative Grammar of the Gaudian (Aryo-Indian) Languages with Special Reference to Eastern Hindi,* London: Trüner & Co. (Reprinted (1975), Amsterdam: Philo Press).

Jeffers, Robert J. (1976) 'The position of the Bihārī dialects in Indo-Aryan', *Indo-Iranian Journal* 18: 215–25.

Katre, S. M. (1968) *Problems of Reconstruction in Indo-Aryan,* Simla: Indian Institute of Advanced Study.

Kellog, Rev. S. H. (1875) *A Grammar of the Hindi Language,* London: Routledge & Kegan Paul, Ltd (Reprinted 1975).

Li, Charles N. and Thompson, Sandra A. (1976) 'Subject and Topic: A New Typology of Languages', in Li Charles N. (ed.) *Subject and Topic,* New York: Academic Press.

Mesthrie, Rajend (1992) *Language in Indenture: A Sociolinguistic History of Bhojpuri-Hindi in South Africa,* London: Routledge.

Moag, Rodney (1977) *Fiji Hindi: A Basic Course and Reference Grammar,* Canberra: Australian National University Press.

Mohan, Peggy R. (1978) *Trinidad Bhojpuri: A Morphological Study,* Ph.D. Dissertation, Ann Arbor: University of Michigan.

Ranjan, Rakesh (1997) *Some Morphological and Syntactic Features of Mauritian Bhojpuri,* Ph.D. Dissertation, Delhi: University of Delhi.

Saksena, Babu Ram (1937) *The Evolution of Awadhi (a branch of Hindi),* Allahabad: The Indian Press, Ltd. (Reprinted (1971), Delhi: Motilal Banarsidass).

Shukla, Shaligram (1981) *Bhojpuri Grammar,* Washington, D.C.: Georgetown University Press.

Tiwari, Udai Narain (1960) *The Origin and Development of Bhojpuri,* Calcutta: The Asiatic Society.

Upadhyay, Dr. Krishnadeva (1972) *Bhojpūrī Sāhitya kā Itihās,* Varanasi: Bharatiya Lok Sanskriti Shodh Sansthan.

Verma, Manindra K. (1971) *The Structure of the Noun Phrase in English and Hindi,* Delhi: Motilal Banarsidass.

—— (1990) 'Experiencer subjects in Bhojpuri and Magahi', in Verma, Manindra K. and Mohanan, K. P. (eds.) *Experiencer Subjects in South Asian Languages*, Stanford: CSLI, Stanford University, pp. 85–103.

—— (1991) 'Topic and Subject', in Prakasam, V. (ed.) *An Encyclopaedia of the Linguistic Sciences*, Delhi: Allied Publishers, pp. 210–18.

—— (1992) 'Non-finite Verbals in Bhojpuri', in Dimock, Edward C., Jr. et al. (eds.) *Dimensions of Sociolinguistics in South Asia*, New Delhi: Oxford and IBH Publishing Co. Pvt. Ltd., pp. 199–209.

FURTHER READING

Abbi, Anvita (1992) *Reduplication in South Asian Languages*, New Delhi: Allied Publishers Limited.

Chatterji, S. K. (1960) *Indo-Aryan & Hindi*, Calcutta: Firma K. L. Mukhopadhyay.

Grierson, Sir George A. (1903–28) *Linguistic Survey of India*. 11 volumes in 19, Calcutta: Office of the Superintendent of Government Printing. (Reprinted (1967–8), Delhi: Motilal Banarsidass).

Masica, Colin P. (1991) *The Indo-Aryan Languages*, Cambridge: Cambridge University Press.

Sinha, Dr. Lakshaman Prasad (1969) *Rūpvijñān kī Dṛṣṭi se Magahī aur Bhojpūrī, Patna: Aṁśukamal Prakashan.*

Sinha, Dr. Shukadeva (1967) *Bhojpūrī Aur Hindī*, Muzaffarpur: Bhawana Prakashan.

Tiwari, Udai Narain (1954) *Bhojpūrī Bhāṣā Aur Sāhitya*, Patna: Bihar Rashtra Bhasha Parishad.

Zograph, Georgii A. (1982) *Languages of South Asia*, London: Routledge & Kegan Paul Ltd.

CHAPTER FIFTEEN

NEPALI

Theodore Riccardi

CONTENTS

1 INTRODUCTION

Nepali is the national language of the Kingdom of Nepal. It is also employed widely in other parts of the Himalayas, both as a first language and a lingua franca, and by a small but growing Nepali diaspora throughout the world. Since 1992, it has been included in the Eighth Schedule of the Indian Constitution, making it one of the official languages of India.

Because of its history as the language of an economically and politically dominant elite, Nepali has become over the last two centuries the most widely spoken language of Nepal. It is now the language of modern communication, education and government in that country, and the main language of its growing middle and upper classes. Outside Nepal, it is a language of major importance in Sikkim, in the Darjeeling-Kalimpong area of Bengal, and in the Kingdom of Bhutan as the language of a significant and increasingly oppressed minority. Its speakers are most densely concentrated in Nepal in the central hills of the eastern Himalayas, but it is spoken and understood by some from the Kashmir border to Arunachal Pradesh and into Burma. Its inroads in the northern areas of the Himalayas, where the majority speaks Tibetan and related dialects, are fewer but increasing. In the southern flatlands that border India, such as the Nepalese Tarai, where its chief rivals are Maithili, Bhojpuri and Hindi, the number of Nepali speakers has increased dramatically due to migration from the hills to the richer agricultural lands of the south, and to increased usage of the language in schools and by the mass media.

Despite its official status and the standardization that often accompanies such a position, Nepali is subject to much variation. Its history over the last two and a half centuries is that of a language imposed at least in part through military conquest and sustained by political domination. Some form of it, therefore, is spoken by many who do not come to it as their mother tongue, but as a second language, spoken not in the intimacy of the family but in public encounters. In this sense, it remains a lingua franca, a language of communication between linguistically disparate groups, one that is often not known in any depth nor used with any great sophistication. Nepali must therefore also be understood to include a number of related dialects spoken and understood throughout the Himalayas and the areas contiguous to them. Some of these dialects are major and have a long history, particularly in western Nepal where the oldest evidence for them is found; others are the result of more recent migrations and dislocations.

In the past, Nepali has had several other designations by which it has been known, some of which are still in use. The first of these is 'Khas kura', or 'Khas bhasa', 'language of the Khas,' the Khas (Skt. *khaśa*) being a nomadic group that was presumably absorbed or transformed at some point into the Chetri caste. The term is still heard but with decreasing frequency. A second term, 'Gorkhali' or 'Gurkhali', has a long history but is rarely heard today. It means 'the language of Gorkha', Gorkha being the town from which a ruling elite and its army, initially under the king Prithivi Narayan Shah, began and sustained military conquests throughout the Himalayas from the middle of the eighteenth century through the early decades of the nineteenth. The extensive Himalayan kingdom that resulted from these conquests became the Kingdom of Gorkha, and its language was known as 'Gorkhali' until the name of the kingdom was changed officially, sometime in the early twentieth century, to the 'Kingdom of Nepal', and the designation of its language to 'Nepali'. Finally, the terms 'pərbətiya', 'pərbəte' (anglicized early on as 'purbatti'), and 'pəhaṛi' are three synonymous terms used to designate the language and are still heard in rural areas. They mean 'mountain language' or 'language of the parvat' or 'pəhaṛ', the terms used to refer to the middle altitude ranges of the Himalayas that distinguish them from the Himal, the high ranges to the north, and the Tarai, the flat plains to the south.

'Nepali', or sometimes 'Nepali Bhasa', the last and most permanent designation, is one that became generally accepted in the early decades of the twentieth century and it has had a longer history among British writers than it has had in Nepal itself. Originally, and to a limited extent locally even now, the word 'Nepal' applied only to the Kathmandu Valley. The British, however, often used the term to refer to the entire country. It was only in the early part of the twentieth century that the term 'Nepal' was taken as the name of the entire country and the name of the language derived from it. In 1930, the official government body charged with language and publication issues, the Gorkhali Bhasa Prakasini Samiti, changed its own name to 'Nepali Bhasa Prakasini Samiti', the 'Nepali Language Publication Committee', making the name 'Nepali' official. Since the word 'Nepal' has long historic associations with the Newars, the inhabitants of the Kathmandu Valley who preceded the Gorkhalis, the name 'Nepali' and the phrase 'Nepali Bhasa' are carefully distinguished from the phrase 'Nepal Bhasa', which refers to the Newari language.

1.1 Geography

Most Nepali speakers live in the central hills of the Himalayas. These hills range from roughly 2500 to 8000 feet in altitude. Living also in this area is a variety of groups whose languages belong to the Tibeto-Burman family of languages. Below these altitudes, Hindi, Maithili, and Bhojpuri are more common. Above them, in the high Himal, Tibetan and its dialects prevail.

Kathmandu and Darjeeling, both cities in the central hills, are the chief urban centres of Nepali, though more and more it is a language of increasing importance in the fast growing towns of the Nepalese Tarai, such as Nepalganj, Birganj and Biratnagar, and towns such as Gangtok in Sikkim, and Phuntsoling in southern Bhutan. Kathmandu, the capital of Nepal, is the centre of commerce and government, which conducts all of its affairs in Nepali. It is also the centre of the communications media, all of which publish and broadcast almost exclusively in Nepali. In Darjeeling, the Nepali speaking community, which has had nationalist aspirations for a separate state in north India to be called Gorkhaland, has more recently infused the language with powerful political sentiment and produced a significant literature. In neither place, however, is Nepali the only language used. In the Kathmandu Valley, Newari, a Tibeto-Burman language with a large number of native speakers and a long literary tradition, remains strong. Nepali has been in constant contact with this language for several centuries, and there are a variety of mutual influences in grammar and syntax that have yet to be explored. In addition, there are a significant number of Tibetan speakers, some from the Himal, some refugees from Tibet itself, now living permanently in Kathmandu, most of whom speak Nepali as well. In Darjeeling, Nepali is spoken alongside Bangla and Tibetan. Both Kathmandu and Darjeeling are literary centres, and the number of novels, short stories, plays, literary journals, monographs and studies published is very high. In both places, the increasing influence of English is apparent.

A large but indeterminate diaspora of Nepali speakers in South Asia has brought the language to many places with which it has no long historical association. Small pockets of speakers may be found in cities of India, Pakistan and Bangladesh. This diaspora began in the early nineteenth century and has had three causes, all of which are fundamentally economic in origin and reflect the poverty of the Nepalese countryside and its increasing population: the recruitment of young Nepali men into the British and Indian armies, a phenomenon that began in the nineteenth century and continues to this day; the migration of men and women, sometimes including their families, to the cities of the Indian subcontinent in search of largely menial work, often in road gangs; and the illegal kidnapping of young Nepali women into the cities of South Asia for prostitution. It is estimated that over 200,000 Nepali women are now enslaved in brothels in India alone.

The use of Nepali in the British and Indian armies has led to the development of what has been called 'line bat', the military dialect used by recruits and their officers. Recruits in the British army, with no regard to the caste or tribe in which they originated, were called and still are called by the term 'Gurkha', a variant of the name of the town of Gorkha. The Gurkhas were employed in many places by the British, particularly in the First and Second World Wars. They have served in Singapore, Hong Kong, and some are now regularly employed in the army of the Sultan of Brunei. Although most of these soldiers return home upon retirement, many have remained abroad forming the nucleus of small but growing Nepali communities worldwide.

Increasing numbers of Nepalis have left Nepal to study and work in the United States, England, Europe and Japan. There are no accurate figures available, but it is safe to assume that the populations are very small, the largest numbering no more than five or six thousand. The greatest number has gone to the United States, where over the last decade they have settled mostly in Boston, New York, Washington and other larger cities. There are, however, small numbers of Nepalis in towns throughout the United States. In Britain, the largest number lives in London with small numbers living in Edinburgh, Manchester and Birmingham. In Europe, because of the language difficulties, there are fewer students. In Japan, however, there is a sizable number of Nepalis now living and working.

Finally, because of the large number of foreigners who have lived in Nepal since it opened to the outside world in 1951, including participants in long-standing programmes like the United States Peace Corps, there is a foreign community that speaks the language with relative fluency.

1.2 Speakers

No accurate count of the present number of speakers exists, and any figures are no more than reasonable estimates. In Nepal, past censuses register about sixty per cent of the population as speakers of Nepali as a first language and about ten per cent as secondary speakers (Clark 1969). The population of Nepal is now estimated to be about twenty million inhabitants. Using the same percentages would yield figures of twelve million for native speakers, and two million for secondary speakers. In the present context, however, these percentages are highly conservative, for the use of the language has increased greatly in recent decades, particularly among secondary speakers, and, though unsupported, Acharya's statement (1991: 1) that 'the rest of the people of Nepal speak Nepali as their second language' may indeed be valid. There are no accurate figures available for Nepali speakers in the Himalayas west of Nepal, or in Sikkim, Bengal, in Bhutan, or the rest of South Asia, but the figure may be as high as three or four million. The total number of Nepali speakers may be, therefore, as high as twenty-three or twenty-four million people. Hutt (1997a) is far more conservative in his estimates.

The native speaker of Nepali has traditionally been a member of certain castes: the high castes of Brahmans, Thakuris and Chetris, all of whom are collectively known as *biṣṭ*, and the low castes such blacksmiths (*kāmi*), scavengers (*cāme*), itinerant musicians (*gāine*) and a few others, all collectively known as *ḍom*. This continues to be so. But because of its position as the language of a powerful ruling military elite, Nepali became, and has continued to be, the language of an increasing number of people whose native languages are weakening or dying in the face of its growing prestige and power. In Nepal, large numbers of Newars, Gurungs, Magars, Rais, Limbus, Thakalis, and some Tibetans now use Nepali with increasing fluency and in many cases it has become their first language. Since Nepali is the medium of education throughout Nepal, the younger generations of all groups are schooled almost exclusively in it. The only languages that appear to have a strong chance of long term survival are Newari and Tibetan, both of which are written languages, with their long literary traditions and strong elites. The future of the others, despite strong local sentiment that has resulted in political demonstrations and ethnic movements, is far more problematic.

1.3 Dialects

Despite its increasing standardization, Nepali still has several major dialects, most of which appear to have originated west of the Kathmandu Valley. Prominent among these is a group of dialects spoken in far western Nepal along the Indo-Nepalese frontier, in towns such as Baitadi and Doti. To the east of these, there is a second group of dialects spoken in and around Jumla. It is in this area that the inscriptions are found that may be the earliest evidence of the language. The chief dialect, however, is that which originates east of Jumla, in Gorkha and the areas contiguous to it, in central Nepal. It is the dialect on which the modern standard language is based and now has as its chief centre the city of Kathmandu. To the east of Kathmandu, there are several dialects, but they are the result of more recent migration. The chief of these is the Darjeeling-Kalimpong dialect, which is based on and differs far less from that of Gorkha, but has its own peculiarities based on local influences, and its own literary tradition. Speakers of the Gorkha and Darjeeling dialects understand each other well, but immediately recognize their respective places of origin. The Jumla dialect and the dialects to the west of it present immediate difficulties to speakers from Kathmandu and Darjeeling. The western dialects form the bridge between Nepali and Kumaoni, the nearest language to the west, and in many respects they are closer to that language.

1.4 History

The earliest linguistic evidence found until now in what is Nepalese territory are a few but important inscriptions of the third century BC. These are of the Emperor Ashoka and are written in what is usually called Ashokan Prakrit. They are limited to the Tarai in the southern part of the country. None has been found in the mountains. There is also a large group of stone inscriptions of later date found in and on the rim of the Kathmandu Valley. Written in Sanskrit and often referred to as the Licchavi inscriptions, these number well over two hundred and date from the fifth to the eighth centuries AD. Except in a most general way, none of these is a direct part of the history of the Nepali language. The Ashokan Prakrit is not related as an earlier stage of the language, and the Licchavi inscriptions contain no clear evidence of any Indo-Aryan vernacular. Most of what is not Sanskrit in these inscriptions appears to be of Tibeto-Burman origin. These elements consist mainly of proper names (places, rivers, etc.), administrative terms, and a few nouns scattered throughout the corpus that appear at least in some cases to be related to some older form of the Newari language.

Nepali has therefore no retrievable history thus far in the earliest records found in Nepal, and the first evidence available to us in a dialect related to it is of a much later period and supports the thesis that the language is an intrusion from the west or northwest into the central Himalayas. This evidence consists of inscriptions from what is now western Nepal composed during the rule of the Khaśa, a group of Indo-Aryan speakers who, if we are to accept the interpretation of the evidence usually given, slowly migrated from the northwest toward the southeast in the central Himalayas and established at some point in the eleventh or twelfth century, an empire that extended from Guge in Tibet to the north and to Sija near Jumla in present day Nepal to the south. Earlier references to the Khas or Khaśa in classical sources may indicate a much longer history for this group, but the oldest of the inscriptions discovered so far is a copper plate of the king Asokacalla, dated to 1255 AD. Nepalese and foreign scholars have well documented these inscriptions, and there is no question that they bear a close relation to Nepali. Indeed, most Nepalese scholars have considered them the earliest examples of the language. That they are Indo-Aryan and that they bear a strong relationship to the modern Nepali language is indisputable, but the exact nature of that relation, and whether they can be considered the earliest form of the language, is still undecided. In many ways, the language of these inscriptions appears to be directly related to the dialects of Jumla and western Nepal rather than a direct forerunner of the Gorkha dialect that became the Nepali language. If this turns out to be the case, then the known history of the Nepali language may be far shorter and its earliest known examples far later in time.

The earliest examples of the Nepali language that are indisputably part of its history date from the middle of the seventeenth century. One of these is the so-called Rani Pokhari inscription of King Pratap Malla. The inscription, dated to about AD 1670, has been taken to indicate the presence of a substantial number of Nepali speakers at this early date in the Kathmandu Valley itself (Clark 1957). The other documents are in manuscript form and are literary in nature. The oldest is a version of the *Svastānīvratakathā*, dated 1648. This is followed by an anonymous version of the *Khaṇḍakhādya* (1649), the *Bājaparīkṣa* (1700), and the *Jvarotpatticikitsā* of Banivilas Jyotirvid (1773) and *the Prāyaścittapradīpa* (1780) of Premnidhi Pant. By this last date, however, the documentation in the language is quite large and includes letters, stone and copper inscriptions, biographies, coins and other materials.

In the late nineteenth and early twentieth centuries, a large body of literary works began to appear in Nepali. Many of these were in the nature of translations and adaptations of Sanskrit works. Still others were original works of literature. Among the latter should be mentioned a number of unique local histories, often referred to as vamsavalis, most of which were anonymously authored. They exist in both Buddhist and Hindu versions, and are a distinctive part of Nepalese historiography. The most original and revered figure in nineteenth century Nepali literature is, however, the poet, Bhanubhakta Acharya (1872–1939), whose *Rāmāyaṇ* is still considered to be the most influential and formative work in the history of the language.

In 1853, the Nepalese government promulgated a legal code, the *Muluki Ain*, that was the first attempt to codify law and administration throughout the country. Written entirely in Nepali, it significantly increased the use of the language in the public sphere. It appeared in printed form in 1870, thus making it one of the earliest printed works in Nepali.

In the twentieth century, Western literary forms, in poetry, and in the short story, the novel, and the essay, became established in Nepal. They were brought to a high level by such writers as Jyotisvallabh Joshi, Pushkar Shamsher, Guruprasad Mainali and Bal Krishna Sama. In the judgement of many, however, the most important Nepali writer of the last century is Laksmiprasad Devkota, whose works, in both poetry and prose, have influenced the present generation of writers more than any other. Works of the major writers of the last three decades, among them Bhupi Sherchen and Parijat, have been translated and are becoming well known to an international as well as local audience.

Nepali became a print language in the nineteenth century with the publication of a few texts in Calcutta and the establishment of the first printing presses in Kathmandu and Darjeeling. Western missionary activity in Bengal led to the early translation and promulgation in printed form of the New Testament and other Christian works. In Banaras, a variety of Hindu texts were translated and printed in Nepali. In Nepal, where Christian missionary activity was banned, the government controlled all presses, and it was only with difficulty that anything that did not serve its interests was allowed to appear. Among the most important of the early printed materials were the government newspaper, the *Gorkha Patra*, and a number of literary reviews.

Since 1951, when Nepal was first opened to the outside world, the number of publications in Nepali has increased dramatically. Beginning in the early fifties, Nepali has been broadcast regularly over Radio Nepal. In the 1980s, Nepal TV began telecasts in Nepali and now reaches the entire country.

1.5 Relation to other languages

1.5.1 The Indo-Aryan languages

Sir Ralph Turner, the chief lexicographer of the Nepali language, argues in his *Nepali Dictionary* that, although Nepali is indisputably an Indo-Aryan language ultimately of Indo-European origin, its exact position within the Indo-Aryan family is less clear. Turner's observations, based almost exclusively on the phonology of Nepali, relate it closely to Panjabi, Lahnda, Hindi and Kumaoni. From the point of view of its lexicon, grammar and syntax, the situation is far more complex, however. There are features that appear to relate it to Rajasthani, Gujarati and Bangla, and to distinguish it from Hindi and Panjabi. All of these relations have yet to be studied.

Historically, Sanskrit is the most important source of Nepali vocabulary, and Nepali, like other South Asian languages, continues to borrow from it for its present needs. Like all the modern Indo-Aryan languages, however, its own grammar is far simpler in comparison to the elegant and intricate structure of the older language. There is little that remains in Nepali of the declensional system of nouns, adjectives, and pronouns, or of the complex structure of the Old Indo-Aryan verb, with its tense systems, conjugations and verbal classes. Instead, Nepali has evolved a nominal system of great simplicity, and a verbal system that relies heavily on periphrasis, something that is a relatively minor feature of the Old Indo-Aryan verbal system.

Because of India's political and economic dominance in the region, Hindi and Urdu are pervasive in the Himalayas. Hindi and Urdu speakers move freely between India and Nepal and other parts of the region. They come from all economic classes and range from rich businessmen to day labourers. Hindi and Urdu are omnipresent in the cinema, television, radio and the print media, all of which originate in India. Most educated Nepali speakers, therefore, understand and speak some Hindi, and its vocabulary, idioms and usage enter the language constantly. In Nepali writing, the continued marking of the feminine in verbal forms, and the persistence of feminine endings for some nouns and adjectives may be attributable at least in part to these strong features of Hindi grammar. In addition, the increases in the use of indirect discourse and of clausal relativization rather than phrasal relativization, may be due to some extent to Hindi influence. Beyond these points, however, it is difficult to speak with precision about the relations. Because Nepali and Hindi use Sanskrit as a common source of vocabulary, there has been a tendency to exaggerate their similarity and to describe their relationship as closer than it really is. At the most basic levels, Nepali has made choices, including lexical ones, that distinguish it greatly from Hindi.

The languages closest to Nepali in vocabulary and grammar are the Pahari dialects spoken in the Himalayas to the west of the Nepalese border. The most important of these is Kumaoni, spoken in the central hills of northern Uttar Pradesh. Nepali also shares common elements with the languages to the south of it, Maithili and Bhojpuri, and with languages like Rajasthani, Gujarati and Bangla. Some scholars have believed the relationship with the last three to be a close one, a theory that is indirectly supported by Nepalese histories that give credence to the legendary migration of Rajputs from Rajasthan and western India to the Himalayas, in particular to the town of Gorkha, after the fall of Chittor. With present knowledge, the questions regarding these relations must remain open.

1.5.2 Tibeto-Burman languages

For much of its history, Nepali has been in close contact with the Tibeto-Burman languages, a family of languages whose speakers may antedate the intrusion of Nepali into the area. In Nepal, the chief languages of this family are Tibetan and Newari, both of which have long literary traditions, and the largely unwritten languages of Magar, Gurung, Tamang, Rai, Limbu, Chepang, Sunwar, Lepcha and Hayu, among others. From the twelfth to the fifteenth centuries, the western dialects of Nepali were in close contact with Magar, Gurung and Tibetan, appearing in bilingual inscriptions with that language. From the fifteenth century onward, Nepali has also been in close contact with the Newari language, the main language of the Kathmandu Valley, and with the unwritten language known first as Murmi and then as Tamang. Later, as Nepali spread through the mountains in the eighteenth and nineteenth centuries, it came into increasing contact with Rai and Limbu, languages of eastern Nepal.

Nepali has influenced many of these languages and in some instances now threatens their survival. They are riddled with Nepali vocabulary and expressions and in many areas are falling into disuse. That these languages have influenced Nepali is not as clear, however. In vocabulary, Nepali appears to have borrowed little, and although similarities in grammar and syntax between Nepali, Newari and Tamang have been pointed out in a variety of studies, it is not clear from where these similarities derive.

1.5.3 Dravidian languages

The relationship of the Dravidian languages to Nepali is even more difficult to determine since there is little evidence that Nepali has had extensive contact with the languages of this family, or that Dravidian languages were ever commonly spoken in the Himalayas. Lexically, there are few borrowings, and these may have entered through other Indo-Aryan sources and not directly. There are studies, however, that indicate that Nepali shares with some Dravidian languages syntactic features that merit further investigation, particularly in the area of relativization, which in Nepali, parallels that of Telugu closely both in form and in the varieties of ambiguity created by such relativization (Ramarao 1982).

1.5.4 Persian and Arabic

As early as the sixteenth century and perhaps even earlier, Nepali came into contact with Hindustani, the lingua franca of northern India, and it is through it that a large number of vocabulary items entered the language. The ultimate origin of these words is Persian and Arabic. During the Mughal period in India, many legal, administrative, military and cultural terms were borrowed. The number of these is probably far fewer than those found in Hindustani, and many of them have undergone phonetic change appropriate to Nepali.

In the seventeenth and eighteenth centuries, Persian was employed extensively at the various courts in the Himalayas, and in some instances came to be employed as a language of diplomacy. In its relations between Nepal and Tibet, for instance, treaties and other official documents were rendered in Nepali and Tibetan, with Persian as the language mutually agreed upon for official texts. Persian vocabulary is also the chief source for much of the special language that is used with royalty and at the court.

1.5.5 Modern European languages

The Western language that has had the most influence on Nepali is of course English, and, with Hindi and Sanskrit, it continues to be one of the three most potent forces with which it must contend. Historically, the influence of English is far more recent than it is in the case of other languages of the Indian subcontinent. Nepal was never directly colonized, settled or ruled by the British. The influence of English was therefore indirect, and was limited to a very small elite that had monopolized local contact with the British. It was only in the early nineteenth century that English began to influence Nepali directly and this in three ways: through mercenary recruits entering the British Army and retiring after service to their homes in Nepal; through the influence on the Nepalese ruling families, Ranas and Shahs, and the other members of the aristocracy, who more and more were educated in English schools and mimicked the ruling classes of England; and through borrowings of vocabulary and idiom that had already entered Hindi and other Indian languages.

Today, the pervasive influence of English through international communication and through education in the schools has led to the phenomenon common throughout the world of a spoken language heavily laced with English vocabulary and grammar. In general, this loose form of the language is used mostly by urban classes, particularly the bureaucracy. It is rarely heard in rural areas, where television and radio are less available and where English competence is relatively low. In written forms of the language, Acharya (1990) has noted the heavy use of English in advertising, and the heavy borrowing of Sanskrit in newspaper editorials, law, and of course, religious contexts. Hybrid commercial expressions, such as 'Krishna Loph' (Krishna Loaf), 'Pashupati Biskat' (Pashupati Biscuit), and 'Saraswati Telors' (Sarasvati Tailors) abound, and the borrowing of technical terms in scientific fields, particularly in computers and computer science, far outstrips the attempts to create what are often at least as cumbersome neologisms from Sanskrit and other local sources.

Despite the increase, English plays a smaller role in Nepal than it does in the other countries of the subcontinent, particularly in the urban centres. Even now the influence it has had on Nepali is far less than it has had on Hindi. Few Nepalese are truly bilingual, and Nepali maintains its linguistic integrity despite the massive intrusion of English.

No other European language has exerted any appreciable influence on Nepali. After English, the chief source of loanwords is probably Portuguese, through which a small number have entered. Presumably most of these were borrowed from Hindustani and not from direct contact with the Portuguese.

1.6 Earlier descriptions

1.6.1 Grammars in Nepali

Through the excellent studies of Acharya and others, we now have a clearer idea of the nature of the main grammars of Nepali produced by Nepalese scholars. The tradition of Nepali grammar is not an ancient one and, as far as we know now, only a little over a century old. The first grammar to survive, that of Veerendra Kesari Aryal, entitled *Nepālī Vyākaraṇ* was written between 1891 and 1905. A manuscript of part of this work has survived and was only recently discovered, edited and published by Acharya (1980). The grammar appears to be based on a modified Paninian model. It also equates Nepali with Prakrit, 'Nepali' being the name for 'the mountain Prakrit', and pairs it with Pali, the 'Prakrit of the Tarai'. This grammar had little immediate influence, however, for the Gorkha Bhasha Prakashini Samiti, the official body founded in 1912 to deal with language and publication issues, in 1920 adopted the work of another grammarian, Pandit Hemraj Pandey, entitled *Candrikā Gorkhā Bhāṣā Vyākaraṇa*, as the official grammar of the language. Somnath Sharma then popularized this grammar in his simplified derivative work, the *Madhyacandrikā* (1932). To both grammars the word *candrikā* was added in honour of Chandra Shamshere, the Rana maharaja ruling at the time, but neither appears to have had any real influence until the Rana regime made the 'Chandrika' grammar the standard for examinations ten years later in 1942. Interestingly, Acharya has shown that Sharma's grammar was based, not on a Paninian or native model, but on the grammar of J. A. Nesfield, the English grammar that was standard in India and England at the time.

1.6.2 Grammars in English

The first attempts by foreigners to describe Nepali are limited to the vocabulary lists prepared by the early nineteenth century English writers Kirkpatrick (1811) and Buchanan Hamilton (1819). These were followed by word lists prepared by Brian Houghton Hodgson, who resided in Kathmandu from 1820 to 1843.

Much of the early grammatical work was published in India and not Nepal, and missionaries did much of it. The three cities of publication were Calcutta, Darjeeling and Bombay. The earliest grammar is that of J. A. Ayton, *A Grammar of the Nepalese Language* (Calcutta, 1820). This was followed by A. Turnbull, *Nepali Grammar and Vocabulary* (Darjeeling, 1887); M. E. Dopping-Heppenstal and Subadar Kushalsingh Burathoki, *Gurkhali Grammar and Vocabulary* (Calcutta, 1899), and G. W. P. Money, *Gurkhali Manual* (Bombay, 1918). Two later grammars, those of Meerendonk (1949) and Rogers (1950), arise out of the authors' Gurkha military experiences and are based mainly on the speech of Gurkha soldiers.

The first grammar of the modern language based on linguistic work done in Nepal is that of T. W. Clark (1963). Essentially a course for the beginning student, it contains the most accurate and complete account of the grammar to that time, and it has the rare virtue that all of the utterances and prose passages were recorded in real conversations, or were composed by Nepalese. A second edition (1977), edited by Burton-Page, attempts to include some forms associated with Darjeeling speech. Clark's grammar was followed by that of David Matthews (1984), which, while not departing substantially from Clark's analysis, is far easier to use. More recently, Michael Hutt (1988) has described the development of Nepali as a national language, and, in a second work (1997b) has produced an introductory reader of literary Nepali that contains an important description of written Nepali.

Some work has been done on the earlier stages of the language, though much remains to be investigated. Adhikary has produced a short study that includes the texts of the earliest record (1988). Clark (1957) made an important study of one of the earliest inscriptions found in the Kathmandu Valley, and Riccardi (1971) produced a monograph on the nineteenth-century language, which includes an edited text in the original, a translation, and a grammatical sketch.

The first full descriptive grammar of the language is that of J. Acharya (1991), which is at present the most complete account of Nepali in any language. Readers of this article are referred to this work for further study.

1.6.3 Lexicons

Students of Nepali are fortunate in having at their disposal a group of dictionaries superior to those of many other Indo-Aryan languages. Turner (1931) is one of the great monuments of British Oriental philology, a work rich not only in definitions but also in etymologies, cognates with other languages and cultural material. Curiously, the work was produced through the mails with the aid of scholars from both Nepal and Darjeeling and was completed long before Turner ever visited Nepal. Despite the archaic quality of some of it, it still ranks as a work without peer.

In 1960, the Royal Nepal Academy published the *Nepālī Śabda Koś*, compiled by Balchandra Sharma. It is the first major dictionary of the language in Nepali. Among English–Nepali dictionaries, one should mention the work of Pushkar Shamshere, *Āngrejī- Nepālī Śabdakoś*, which is a meticulous translation into Nepali of the *Shorter Oxford English Dictionary*, and the recent dictionary by Schmidt et al (1993).

1.7 Chief characteristics of the language

In assessing the relation of Nepali to the other languages of the Indian subcontinent, it might be useful to keep in mind some of its chief peculiarities, many of which are not shared by its relatives:

(1) with reference to nominal forms, its almost total loss of gender and plural markings;
(2) with regard to verbal morphology, its frequent use of infixation to form the negative;
(3) the full development of status/honorific registers, both in pronouns and verbs, that range from intimate/abusive usage to forms of address for royalty;
(4) the use of numerical classifiers, distinguishing human/non-human inanimate categories;
(5) the strong preference for direct as opposed to indirect discourse;
(6) the strong preference for phrasal or participial structures as opposed to clausal relativization;
(7) a distinctive vocabulary at the most basic level that represents uncommon choices from the point of view of some of its neighbours, such as Hindi;
(8) the number, variety and complexity of onomatopoeic expressions.

2 DESCRIPTIVE SKETCH

2.1 Introduction

The description that follows is of the Nepali language as spoken by an educated native speaker of Kathmandu. It attempts to present the main facts of the spoken language in concise form, and also makes reference to the differences found in the written language. Authorities include Clark (1963), Matthews (1984) and Acharya (1991). In addition, the writer was fortunate in having available during the writing of this text a native speaker from Gorkha, Ms Shanti Gurung.

2.2 Phonology and script

The phonemic structure of Nepali has been well established by Bandhu et al. (1971) and Acharya (1991). In general, it parallels that of Sanskrit and the modern Indo-Aryan languages, but the simplification and reduction of Sanskrit phonemic structure is immediately apparent. Contrastive pairs given are illustrative rather than exhaustive. The phonemic inventory follows below.

2.2.1 Vowels

The following vowel phonemes, given in the usual order, are distinguished in Nepali:

Simple:	oral	nasal
High front	i	ĩ
High back:	u	ũ
Mid front:	e	ẽ
Mid central:	a	ã
Mid back:	o	
Low central:	ə	ə̃
Diphthongs:	əi	əĩ
	əu	əũ

All vowel phonemes, with the exception of /o/, occur in both oral and nasal forms. With regard to the simple vowels, Nepali distinguishes only /i/ and /u/ phonemically, the short forms of these occurring as allophones only. Nasal /o/ occurs only as allophonic variant: /hoco/ hõco/. Mid front vowel /e/ has a common allophone ẽ that occurs commonly in such environments as /yəs-/ and /tyəs-/. It is also pronounced in some environments with palatal onset, e.g. /seto/ 'white', often pronounced [syeto].

With regard to the diphthongs, it is important to note that the initial element in both is /ə/, not /a/. In some environments /əi/ approximates /e/, and /əu/ approximates /o/. Acharya's analysis of the second element of these as the glides /y/ and /v/ should also be noted (Acharya 1991: 32).

The so-called vowels /r̥/ and /r̥̄/ occur only in Sanskrit loanwords and are often rendered in Nepali pronunciation as /ri/ or simply /i/. Sanskrit ḷ does not occur.

Minimal contrastive pairs are the following: oral: ə/a: /məl/ 'fertilizer' : /mal/ 'things', ī/i/ e: /mil/ 'meet' : /mel/ 'peace', u/o: /mul/ 'root' : /mol/ 'price', o/au: /gəryo/ 'he did' : /gərəu/ 'you did', ai/au: /məilo/ 'dirty' : /məul/ 'sacrificial post'; nasal: ə/ə̃: / tə/ 'but' : /tə̃/ 'you', a/ā: /kaṭh 'wood' : /kãṭh/ 'suburbs', i/ī: /uhi/, 'this very one' : /uhĩ/ 'right there', u/ū: /gau/ 'sing' : /gaũ/ 'let me sing', əi/əĩ: /nai/ emphatic particle : /naĩ/ 'no', əu/əũ: /gəryəu/ 'you did' : /gəryəũ/ 'we did'.

2.2.2 Consonants

The consonantal phonemes are as follows:

Occlusives: (1–5)
(1) Gutturals:	k	kh	g	gh ṅ
(2) Palatals:	c	ch	g	gh
(3) Cerebrals:	ṭ	ṭh	ḍ	ḍh
(4) Dentals:	t	th	d	dh n

(5) Labials: p ph b bh m
    Semivowels: y r l v
    Sibilant: s
    Aspirate: h

The occlusives are distinguished by place of articulation, voicing and aspiration. These features are strongest in initial position, and both aspiration and voicing tend to weaken intervocalically and in final position, or to drop altogether.

The gutturals call for no special comment except that /ṅ/ does not occur initially and therefore, as Acharya has put it, bears a light load in the language. It is phonemic only in final position. The others are preserved in parallel form to those of other Indo-Aryan languages.

With the palatals, it should be noted that in the speech of some, particularly those whose first language is Tibeto-Burman and not Nepali, the unvoiced /c/ and /ch/ often have a high degree of affrication in pronunciation, particularly in medial position, with little or no aspiration. The nasal /ñ/ does not occur phonemically but as an allophone of /n/.

The cerebral consonants show less retroflexion than in other Indian languages according to some observers, and they are variously described as alveolars or alveopalatals (Clark 1969: 267, Acharya 1991: 19). The voiced consonants /ḍ/ and /ḍh/ are often pronounced as flap /ṛ/ and /ṛh/ medially, as in Hindi. The cerebral /ṇ/ does not occur phonemically but as an allophone of /n/. Since the cerebrals do not occur in Tibeto-Burman languages, their absence or misplacement is a highly characteristic feature of certain dialects and sociolects in the Himalayas, particularly that of the Newars.

The dentals need no special comment, though it must be emphasized that the difference in pronunciation between these and the cerebral consonants is fundamental.

With the bilabials, it should be noted that /ph/ is always an aspirated bilabial /p/. This is true of words borrowed from Hindi and Urdu, e.g. Nepali /jəvaph/ 'answer', /phərsi/ 'pumpkin', /phirəngi/ 'foreigner'. /b/ tends to lose its voicing in final position and to approach /p/ in pronunciation, e.g. /kitap/ 'book', and /jərsap/ 'General Sahib'.

With regard to the semi-vowels, /y/ and /v/ are glides, /r/ is lightly trilled and is in phonemic contrast to the flap /ṛ/ as described above.

Unlike Sanskrit, Nepali possesses only /s/ among the sibilants or fricatives, though /ś/ and /ṣ/ occur as allophones, particularly in initial position.

The aspiration /h/ occurs initially, but intervocalically or finally it tends to be lost. The visarga of Sanskrit, /ḥ/, occurs only in Sanskrit loanwords and in Nepali tends to be dropped in pronunciation.

Minimally contrasting pairs are exemplified by the following:

gutturals: k/kh: /kəsnu/ 'to harness' : /khəsnu/ 'to fall', g/gh: /gan/ 'song' : /ghan/ 'blame', ṅ/n: piṅ 'swing' : /pin/ 'grind'

palatals: c/ch: /copnu/ 'to dip' : /chopnu/ 'to cover', j/jh: /jari/ 'adultery' : /jhari/ 'bush'

cerebrals: t/th: /ṭik/ 'gold necklace' : /ṭhik/ 'correct', ḍ/ ḍh: /ḍoka/ 'basket' : /ḍhoka/ 'door'

dentals: t/th: /tan/ 'loom' : /than/ 'place', d/dh: /dau/ 'turn, opportunity' : /dhau/ 'ore', n/d: /nam/ 'name': /dam/ 'money'

bilabials: p/ph: /purnu/ 'to fill' : /phurnu/ 'to throb', b/bh: /bitto/ 'pressing' : /bhitto/ 'wall', m/b: /mit/ 'friend' : /bit/ 'pass time'

glides: y/v: /yəhã/ 'here' : /vəhã 'there'
tap: r/ḍ: /ramro/ 'good' : /ḍamro/ 'blister'
lateral: l/r: /laj/ 'shame': /raj/ 'rule'
fricative: s/r: /sat/ 'seven': /rat/ 'night'
aspiration: h/s: /hat / 'hand' : /sat/ 'seven'

2.2.3 Distribution

The phonemic structure of Nepali, in comparison with that of Old Indo-Aryan, thus shows a net reduction in the number of phonemes distinguished. This reduction comes in the vowels (i, u, ṛ and ḷ are not phonemic), among nasal consonants (ṇ and ṅ are allophones of /n/), among sibilants (ś and ṣ are allophones of /s/), and the visarga (ḥ). The remaining phonemes bear an unequal workload within the language in terms of occurrence, particularly in initial position. In this position, among the consonants, the greatest frequency of occurrence is attributable to the bilabials, followed in descending order by the velars, dentals, palatals, sibilants, semivowels, aspiration (h) and the cerebral series.

Although much of the Old Indo-Aryan phonemic system is preserved in Nepali, its distribution is far simpler. Except in Sanskrit and other loanwords preserved in their original form, Nepali simplifies clusters of dissimilar consonants, permitting geminated consonants to occur regularly but other clusters to occur only rarely and as the result of suffixation to verbal roots. Clusters of dissimilar consonants in initial position are not permitted, and Nepali employs a variety of ways to avoid them, including epenthesis and metathesis (Acharya: 1991: 32).

2.2.4 The syllable and stress accent

The shape of the Nepali syllable is most often vowel (V), consonant-vowel (CV) and consonant-vowel-consonant (CVC). The largest exception to this is in finite verb forms where the combination of root and suffix may result in consonant clusters of three consonants followed by vowels: e.g. -nthy-, -nth-; -rth-, -rthy-.

Most descriptions follow the traditional analyses that divide syllables into two categories, usually termed open and closed: an open syllable is one that ends in a vowel, a closed syllable one that ends in a consonant. In addition, a distinction is made between syllables containing long or short vowels, and those ending in more than one consonant. Stress, the degree of force with which an individual syllable is uttered falls on different syllables within a word. In Nepali the following rules hold, with some exceptions (Matthews 1992:18):

(1) In disyllabic words, the stress falls on the first syllable if the final syllable is open or if the final is closed and contains a short vowel: 'baṭo 'road', 'bharət 'India'; however, it falls on the final syllable if it is closed and contains a long vowel: ne'pal 'Nepal'.

(2) In words of three or more syllables the second to the last is stressed if it has a long vowel: si'mana 'boundary'; if the final syllable is closed with a long vowel or it ends in two consonants, it is stressed: iti'has 'history', bəndo'bəst 'arrangement'; if the second to the last is short and the final is open or closed containing a short vowel followed by one consonant, the antepenultimate is stressed: sə'manəta 'resemblance'.

It should be noted that stress in Nepali is phonetic and not phonemic in regular utterance, but it may be phonemic when emphasis is introduced. For a discussion of this as well as other suprasegmental features, see Acharya (1991: 46).

2.2.5 *The Devanagari script and orthography*

Nepali has been written in the Devanagari script or local variants of it from as early as the thirteenth century. Today the form of Devanagari used is virtually indistinguishable from that used in Sanskrit, Hindi, and other languages of the subcontinent. It is used to represent the sound system of the language with a fair degree of consistency, and therefore in common parlance it is said to be highly 'phonetic'.

The inventory of graphemes in Nepali is the same as that used in the writing of Sanskrit. Nepali uses the entire corpus of conjunct characters available in the script, but it also uses some not permissible in Sanskrit: -nch, as in bhanchan 'they say', for example. The language also makes inconsistent use of the halanta or virāma, its sporadic use only sometimes indicating that an inherent vowel, medial or final, should be pronounced.

The script employs single or double vertical bars to indicate the end of a sentence. In handwritten manuscripts and other traditional documents, no other punctuation is used. In modern written Nepali, particularly printed documents, however, many of the punctuation marks of English are employed: quotation marks, the question and exclamation marks, colons, semicolons and ditto marks are widely used more or less as in English. No distinction is made in the script between capital and lower case letters.

Nepali orthography is far more conservative than pronunciation, which has changed more than spelling would indicate. In general, Nepali preserves Sanskrit orthography in all words borrowed from it. In Nepali words, it preserves the use of the Sanskrit symbols for short /i/ and /u/ even though only the long form of these appears phonemically. The graphemes for /b/ and /v/ are often written interchangeably. In words borrowed from English, the cerebral series is used to transliterate English alveolars /t /and /d/. In older manuscripts as well as in older printed books, /ṣ/ is given the value /kh/, /ch/ is written for /kṣ/, and there is confusion in the writing of /p/, /y/, and /th/, all of which bear a general similarity to each other.

2.3 Morphology

2.3.1 *General*

Most descriptions of Nepali nominal morphology, whether native or foreign, have used either Sanskritic models of case declension or the Hindi paradigm of direct and oblique cases. These are of course related systems, but neither is particularly appropriate to Nepali. The first is merely a correlation of common postpositions with case meaning arranged in the usual case order, and it disregards entirely the difference between an inflected language and one like Nepali. The second paradigm is based on the fact that Nepali has certain features that can be organized according to the direct/oblique model: in a limited vocabulary Nepali preserves gender and number-markings, and in some nominal forms, primarily in the pronouns, it preserves what may be seen as an oblique stem.

The Nepali verbal system, like that of other modern Indo-Aryan languages, is simplified in comparison to Sanskrit. The complex edifice of the Sanskrit verb, its classifications and conjugations, its tenses and participial forms, are barely in evidence. Instead, the verbal system relies far more heavily on periphrasis. It is a system of roots, affixes and auxiliary verbs, through which a highly nuanced system of meanings comes into play.

2.3.2 Nominal forms: nouns, adjectives and pronouns

In Nepali, there are no definite or indefinite articles. Nouns and adjectives have one form for singular and plural and plurality is often indicated through context. It may also be shown by an adjective or adverb of quantity, or by a number. A principle of economy rather than of agreement operates here: one indicator of plurality is sufficient and little or no attempt is made to have consistent agreement between plural markers of nouns and verbs. Modifying adjectives remain unchanged. Examples:

ekjəna manche
one cl. man
'one man'

tinjəna manche
three cl. man
'three men'

tinjəna manche aeko chə
three cl. man ppp. come be- sg. pres.
'Three men have come.'

dherəi manche aeka chən
adv. man ppp.come-pl. be-3 pl. pres.
'Many men have come.'

ṭhulo manche
adj. big n.-man
'a big man'

dherəi ṭhulo manche aeka chən
adv. adj.-sg. n. ppp.-come-pl. be-3 pl. pres.
'Many great men have come.'

The language possesses one commonly used suffix, *-haru*, which is often appended to nouns to indicate plurality, but the rules for its use are complex. It is rarely used when nouns are preceded by adjectives or adverbs of quantity, or numbers. It rarely indicates simple plurality: it often means that other objects of the same or a like class are also indicated and may be translated as 'and other things'. Thus: *kitab-həru* 'books and other things', *sudip-həru* 'Sudip and the other children'. Postpositions are regularly appended to *-həru*: *sudip-həru-lai* 'for Sudip and the others'.

In speech, Nepali distinguishes natural gender only. Grammatical gender, in the sense that every noun has a specific gender marker – masculine, feminine, and/or sometimes neuter – is not a feature of Nepali. Nouns denoting males and females are marked, but nouns denoting inanimate objects, including abstract ideas, are not. In writing, there has been a strong tendency by some to extend the use of feminine markers beyond their use in speech to include the consistent marking of certain adjectives with feminine endings. This tendency is strengthened by some Nepali grammars and may be reinforced by the influence of Hindi upon both speech and writing. Gender marking may be said to be somewhat in flux, therefore, and reflects a tension between speech and the written language.

Nouns denoting male and female beings are sometimes distinguished by suffixation, or through pairs of lexically differing terms. With nouns denoting human beings, the suffixes are *-o/ -a* (masculine) or *-i* (feminine). Masculine nouns ending in *-i* or in consonants add the feminine suffix *-ni* to the masculine form. Examples:

(1) *-o/ -a/ -i*: /*-i keta* 'boy' : *keti* 'girl', *chora* 'son' : *chori* 'daughter', *ṭhiṭo* 'boy' : *ṭhiṭi* 'girl', *jeṭho/-a*, 'oldest son': *jeṭhi* 'oldest daughter', *budho* 'old man' : *budhi* 'old lady'

(2) *-i/-ni*: *tarun* 'youth' : *taruni* 'young woman', *bahun* 'Brahman' : *bahuni* 'Brahman woman', bhai 'younger brother' : *bahini* 'younger sister', *məgər* 'Magar' : *məgərni* 'Magar woman', *chetri* 'Chetri' : *chetrini* 'Chetri woman', *kukur* 'dog' : *kukurni* 'bitch'

Words denoting male/female pairs have little consistency or similarity : *logne* 'male' : *svasni* 'female, woman', *babu* 'male child' : *nani* 'female child', *boko* 'goat' : *bakhra* 'female goat'

2.3.3 Comparison of adjectives

Since adjectives have only one form, they do not change when used in comparisons. Where there is no explicit object of comparison, the meaning depends on context. Thus in the following case, three meanings are possible:

yo ramro
this good
'This is good.' 'This is the better one.' 'This is the best one.'

When the object of comparison is explicit, the postposition *-bhənda* 'than' is used in the comparative, and the phrase *səb-bhənda* 'than all', is employed in the superlative:

tyo-bhənda yo ramro
pr.-postp.-saying pr. adj.
saying that this good
that-than this good.
'This is better than that.'

yo səb-bhənda ramro
pr. adj.-all-postp. saying good
his all-than good
'This is the best of all.'

2.3.4 Nominal compounds

Nominal compounds in Nepali are frozen expressions of usually two members that are lexically related. When the two members are nouns, they are coordinating compounds or dvandvas: a. *keṭakeṭi* 'children', b. *budhabudhi* 'old man and old woman'.

A large number of Sanskrit nominal compounds have been borrowed into Nepali in their original form. These are of the common tatpuruṣa, karmadhāraya, and dvandva varieties and call for no special comment. Bahuvrīhi compounds, however, are usually marked by the addition of the Nepali adjectival participle *bhəeko/-ka/-ki* to a Sanskrit or Nepali compound to form adjectival phrases: *cətur vərnə* 'four castes', *cətur vərnə bhəeko* 'having four castes', *ṭhulo hat* 'large hand', *ṭhulo hat bhəeko* 'large handed'.

2.3.5 Personal pronouns and adjectives

Nepali has first, second, and third person pronouns, both singular and plural. The first person pronouns are: sg. *mə* 'I', pl. *hami, hamihəru* 'we'. Second and third person pronouns are graded according to status and respect. The use of ordinary or lowest grade pronouns often indicates familial intimacy, inequality, or even abuse. The other pronouns show varying degrees of respect, from use among equals to a full set of expressions for royalty.

The ordinary pronouns are the following:

sg.	pl.
(2) *tə* 'you'	*tə-haru*
timi 'you'	*timi-haru*
(3) *u* 'he, she, it'	
uni, tini 'he, she, it'	*unihəru, tinihəru* 'they'

Among the second person pronouns, *tə* is the most intimate as well as the most abusive. *timi* is used between family members who are equals or inferiors in relationship or age. It is regularly referred to as a middle grade honorific. In the third person, the pronoun *u* shows the least respect, *uni/tini* and their plurals showing the middle grade. With the latter, plural verb forms are often used. For the second person, the pronoun *tapai*/pl. *tapaĩhəru* is commonly used as a sign of respect or remoteness among perceived equals or to a superior. The corresponding third person forms are *yəhã* or *vəhã* although these may also be used as indirect second person honorifics. In addition, the word *həjur* 'you', 'Sir', adopted from Persian, is often used as a respectful form of address and must also be used with honorific forms of the verbs as well. For royalty, forms of address are all indirect and include a variety of circumlocutory titles.

The possessive adjectives corresponding to these forms are the following:

(1) *mero* 'my'	*hamro, hami-həru-ko* 'our'
(2) *tero* 'your'	*tã-haru-ko* 'your'
timro 'your'	*timi-həru-ko* 'your'
(3) *us-ko* 'his, her, its'	*uni-həru-ko* 'their'
un-ko 'their'	*tini-həru-ko* 'their'
in-ko 'their'	*yini-həru-ko* 'their'

2.3.6 Other pronouns

The other pronouns and adjectives are interrogatives, relatives, indefinites and demonstratives. There are regularities in these forms that should be noted: interrogatives and indefinites begin with *k-*, relatives with *j-*, demonstratives with *y-* or *u-* or *ty-*. Pronominal adjectives and adverbs follow these forms in close analogy.

Interrogative	Relative	Demonstrative	
ko 'who'	*jo* 'he who'	*u/yo* 'this'	*tyo* 'that'
ko ko 'who' (pl.)	*jo* 'they who'	*yi* 'these'	*ti* 'these'
ke 'what'	*je* 'whatever'	"	"
kun 'which'	*jun* 'whichever'	"	"

Interrogative	Relative	Demonstrative	
koi 'some(one)'	*jesukəi* 'whichever'	"	
kəso 'how'	*jəso* 'how'	*yəso/uso* 'like this'	*tyəso* 'like that'
kəsto 'how'	*jəsto* 'like'	*yəsto* 'like this'	*tyəsto* 'like that'
kətro 'how big'	*jətro* 'as big'	*yətro/utro* 'so big'	*tyətro* 'that big'

The forms *ko, jo, u, yo,* and *tyo* change to *kəs-, jəs-, us-, yəs-, tyəs-* before postpositions. For *koi* the form before postpositions is *kəsəi-*.

2.3.7 *Postpositions*

Postpositions occur after nominal forms to show grammatical relations. They cannot occur in isolation and in most cases they are appended to the word that precedes them. They are of two kinds: simple and compound. Simple postpositions consist of one postposition. Compound postpositions consist of either the postposition *-ko/-ro* or *-le* followed by another postposition, adjective, or adverb. These second elements may occur separately. The most common simple postpositions are the following: *-lai* 'to, for' and marker of direct object; *-le* 'by', marker of subject; *-ko/-ro* 'of', *-ma* 'in', *-tələ* 'below', *-muni* 'under', *-dekhi* 'from', *-bəṭə* 'from', *-sə̃gə* 'with', *-sita* 'with', *-pəchi* 'after', *-səmmə* 'up to', *-bittikəi* 'as soon as'. The following are compound postpositions: *-ko lagi* 'for', *-ko nimitta* 'for', *-ko pəchaḍi* 'behind', *-ko əgaḍi* 'in front of', *-ko biruddha* 'against', *-le gərda* 'because of'.

Two of the simple postpositions call for special comment:

(1) *-ko* 'of', a postposition that is used to indicate possession, may be used with all nouns and pronouns except some of the personal possessive adjectives where it is replaced by *-ro*. In the written language, *-ko/-ro* often mark the gender and/or the number of the person possessed. The endings which they take are the usual: *-o*, masculine and neuter singular; *-i*, feminine singular; and *-a*, plural of masculine and feminine, or *i*, feminine. Examples:

> *us-ko chora* 'his son'
> *us-ko chori* 'his daughter' (spoken)
> *us-ki chori* 'his daughter' (written)
> *us-ko chorachori* 'his children' (spoken)
> *us-ka chorachori* 'his children' (written)

The plural is used with abstract nouns as well: *licchəvikal-ka abhilekh* 'the inscriptions of the Licchavi period'.

(2) The postposition *-le* marks what is often called the ergative or agentive use, a common feature of most Indo-Aryan languages. In Nepali, it marks the subject word of a sentence under certain circumstances, sometimes optionally, sometimes necessarily. With intransitive verbs, *-le* is rarely used. When the verb is transitive and in a present or future tense, the use of *-le* is optional. When the verb is past and transitive, *-le* must be used. With the pronouns *mə* and *tə̃*, the vowel of the pronoun changes to *-əi* before *-le*. Examples:

> present/future tenses: optional use
> *mə gərchu* 'I do.'
> *məi-le gərchu* 'I do.'
> *ram-le gərchə* 'Ram does it.'

past: required use
tə̃-le gəris 'You did.'
təpə̃-le gərnubhæenə 'You did not do.'

A number of postpositions originate as verbal forms: *-dekhi* 'from' (lit. 'having seen'), *-lai/-lagi* 'to, for' (lit. 'having been applied'). This is true of some subordinating conjunctions as well.

2.3.8 Conjunctions: coordinating and subordinating

Coordinating conjunctions are used to join like elements: simple sentences, the members of compound subjects and predicates, and compound modifiers. The most commonly employed are: *rə* 'and', *tərə* 'but', *va* 'or', *əthəva* 'or'. Examples:

ram rə sita bən-ma gəe
pn. conj. pn. N.-postp. in go-3pl. perf.
Ram and Sita forest-in went
'Ram and Sita went into the forest.'

Ram rə Ləchmən bahirə gəe tərə Sita ghərma bəsyo
pn. conj. pn. adv. go–3pl. perf. conj. pn. house-postp. in stayed 3sg.
Ram and Laksman out went, but Sita house-in remained
'Ram and Laksman went out, but Sita stayed home.'

Sita royo rə kehi pəni bhənenə
pn. cried–3sg. perf. conj. pr. adv. say-3sg neg.
Sita cried and something at all said not
'Sita cried and said nothing.'

Subordinating conjunctions are used to connect subordinate or dependent clauses with full sentences. Except for two, they appear at the end of the clauses. The following commonly appear at the end of a clause: *əghi* 'before', *tapəni* 'nevertheless', *pəni* 'although', *bhəne* 'if', *bhənerə* 'so that'. Examples:

kam gəros bhanera mə gə̃e
n. do-3sg. imper. having said-conj. pr. go-1sg. perf.
work he might do having said I went
'In order that he might work, I left.'

u gəyo bhəne, mə janchu
pr. go-3sg. perf. conj.-if saying, pr. go-1sg. pres.
he went if I go
'If he goes, I shall go.'

The conjunctions *ki* 'that' and *kinaki* 'since' appear at the beginning of a clause:

us-le bhənyo ki khəbər ayo
pr-postp.-erg. Say-3sg.perf. conj. n. come-3sg. perf.
he said that news came
'He said that the news arrived.'

2.3.9 Numbers and classifiers

2.3.9.1 Cardinals and ordinals

The cardinal numbers resemble those of Hindi and other Indo-Aryan languages. In Nepali, they are used in counting, computation, telling time, and other calculations. They are as follows:

1–10	11–20	21–30	31–40	41–50
ek	eghərə	ekkais	ekətis	ekəcalis
dui	barə	bais	bəttis	bəyalis
tin	tehrə	teis	tettis	tritalis
car	cəudhə	cəubis	cəũtis	cəuvalis
pãc	pəndrə	pəccis	pẽttis	pẽtalis
chə	sorə	chəbbis	chəttis	chəyalis
sat	səttrə	səttais	sətətis	sətəcalis
aṭh	əṭharə	əṭṭhais	əṭhətis	əṭhəcalis
nəu	unnais	unəntis	unəncalis	unəncas
dəs	bis	tis	calis	pəcas

51–60	61–70	71–80	81–90	91–100
ekaunnə	ekəsəṭṭhi	ekəhəttər	ekasi	ekənnəbbe
baunnə	bayasəṭṭhi	bəhəttər	bəyasi	bəyannəbbe
tripənnə	trisaṭṭhi	trihəttər	triyasi	triyannəbbe
cəuvənnə	cəusaṭṭhi	cəuhəttər	caurasi	cəurannəbbe
pəcəpənnə	paĩsəṭṭhi	pəc-həttər	pəcasi	pancannəbbe
chəpannə	chəyasəṭṭhi	chəihəttər	chəyasi	chəyannabbe
sətaunnə	satəsəṭṭhi	sət-həttər	sətasi	səntannabbe
əṭhaunnə	əṭhəssəṭṭhi	əṭhhəttər	əṭhasi	əṭhənnəbbe
unənsəṭṭhi	unansəttəri	unasi	unənnəbbe	unansəy
saṭhi	səttari	əsi	nəbbe	səy

Above one hundred, the numbers follow the following pattern: *ek səy* 'one hundred', *ek səy ek* 'one hundred one', etc.

For numbers above 999, the following are used: *həjar* or *səhəsrə* (1000); *lakh* (100,000), *kəror* (10,000,000). Note also *həjarəũ* or *səhəsrəũ* 'thousands', *lakhəũ* 'lakhs, hundreds of thousands', and *kərorəũ* 'crores, tens of millions'.

Ordinal numbers from one to three are: *pəhilo, dosro, tesro*. From four onward, the suffix *-əũ* is added to the cardinal number, usually without change: *carəũ, pācəũ,* (but *chaiṭəũ* 'sixth').

2.3.9.2 Classifiers

Nepali possesses two noun classifiers that are employed when numbers are used to enumerate objects. One of them, *-jəna*, is suffixed to numbers only when enumerating human beings; the other, *-ṭa,* or *-əuṭa,* is suffixed to numbers enumerating nouns that denote all animate beings as well as inanimate objects. Note the following: *ekjəna manche* 'one man', *dəsjəna aimai* 'ten women', *tinəuṭa manche* 'three men', *tinəuṭa kələm* 'three pens'.

The suffix *-ṭə/-auṭa* occasionally causes a change in the form of the number. Thus, *euṭa* 'one', not *ekṭa,* which does not occur in Nepali. For example, *euṭa manche* 'one man'.

The classifiers are not used if a word indicating a quantity or container of items precedes the noun: *ek bətta curot* 'a pack of cigarettes', *ek dharni masu* 'a *dharni* of meat', *ek gilas pani* 'a glass of water'. But note that the classifier is used if the container or quantity occurs alone: *euta gilas* 'one glass'.

These classifiers are also used with adverbs of quantity: *kətijəna manche* 'how many persons?', *katiəuta kitab* 'how many books?'

2.3.10 The verbal system

2.3.10.1 General

The verbal system can be analysed into a number of roots, a series of affixes, and a group of auxiliary verbs. Roots carry the fundamental meaning of the verb, while affixes define its particular use. Auxiliaries consist of a very small number of verbs 'to be', which are used in the formation of different tenses. The whole verbal system therefore consists in the combinations of roots, affixes, and auxiliaries, and the rules by which they are combined. Neither roots nor affixes occur in the language in isolation. They occur only in combination. Auxiliaries, since they are already complete verbal forms, may occur alone or in combination with other verbal forms.

2.3.10.2 Roots and affixes

Roots are most commonly monosyllabic or disyllabic, rarely trisyllabic. They may end in either consonants or vowels. Those ending in vowels often require vowel change or nasalization before affixes may be added to them. Some roots have two forms, usually designated as primary and secondary. Each of these is limited to combination with a certain group of affixes, the primary form to affixes associated with the present and future tenses, the secondary to affixes associated with the past or perfect tenses. Roots that end in vowels often undergo vowel change to form the secondary base. Two common roots form the secondary root irregularly: *ja-/gə-* 'go' and *hu-/bhə-* 'be'.

Affixes are of three kinds: a negative prefix; infixes, by which roots are extended to form verbal stems to which further suffixes may be added; and suffixes, or final affixes, which, when appended to roots, result in verbal forms or words with verbal meaning.

There is only one verbal prefix in the language: the negative particle *nə*. This is prefixed to all non-finite verb forms, to all forms of the imperative and optionally to the future non-definite, to form the negative.

Infixes are small in number and of three kinds:

(1) negative infixes, through which negative stems are made: *-nə-/ -əinə-, -oinə-, ooinə*
(2) impersonal, through which impersonal/passive stems are formed: *- ĩ/-i*
(3) infixes through which transitive, and causative stems are formed: *-au-/-a-*

The various uses of these elements are discussed below.

Suffixes are far more numerous and are either non-finite, through which non-finite forms (infinitives, participles and gerunds) are made, or finite, through which verbal forms showing tense, number, person and sometimes gender are constructed. Feminine suffixes do not appear regularly in the spoken language, and appear only inconsistently in writing. The most common are given in parentheses.

Verbal suffixes are the following:

(1) Finite:

	sg.	pl.
present:	*-u -ə*	*əũ*
	-s	*-əu*
	-a/ (-e)	*-n/ (-in)*
future:	*-ũla*	*-ə̃ula*
	-las	*-əula*
	-la	*-lan*
imperative:	*-ũ*	*-ũ, -əũ*
	ÿ, -es	*-ə/e and e-u/o*
	-os	*-un*
past:	*ẽ*	*-yəũ*
	-is	*-yəu*
	-yo	*-e*

(2) Non-finite:
  (a) infinitival: *nu, -nə, -na, -ne*
  (b) participial:
       present: *-ta/-da; -təi/-dəi; -to/-do-; -ti/-di*
       past: *-e*
       adjectival: to *-e* past above may be added: *-ko, -ki, -ka*
       gerund: to *-e* (above) may also be added: *-rə*
       gerund: *-i/-kənə*

2.3.10.3 Auxiliary verbs

Three roots, all having the meaning 'be/was', are used widely in the language on their own and as auxiliaries. They are at the base of the conjugational periphrasis of the verbal system. The first of these, *ch-* 'be' is perhaps of the most frequent occurrence. It appears conjugated only in the present tense, positive and negative, and carries with it when used alone locational and existential meaning: 'being there', 'there are/there are not'. Its full paradigm is:

Positive 'I am' etc.		Negative 'I am not' etc.	
sg.	pl.	sg.	pl.
(1) *chu*	*chəũ*	*chəinə̃*	*chəinəũ*
(2) *chəs*	*chəu*	*chəinəs*	*chəinəu*
(3) *chə*	*chən*	*chəinaə*	*chəinən*

As an auxiliary, this is attached in full conjugational form to roots to form one of the present tenses (see below), and is collocated with a number of non-finite forms to produce a number of compound tenses. It has only one non-finite form, the present participle in *-da/-dəi, chə̃da, chə̃dəi*, which is used as an emphatic verb to be: *chə̃dəichə* 'it still is'.

The second of these auxiliaries is what Clark (1963: 130) has called the paradigm *ho*. It occurs as a separate verb, where it is used in defining and descriptive contexts rather than existential or locational ones. It is formally related to the root *hu-/bhə-* 'be', but is supernumerary to it in that *hu-/bhə-* is a complete verb without it. Unlike *ch-*, it has forms in all the simple tenses:

Present

Positive			Negative	
'I am' etc.			'I am not' etc.	
sg.	pl.		sg.	pl.
(1) *hũ*	*həũ*		*hoinə̃*	*hoinəũ*
(2) *hos*	*həu*		*hoinəs*	*hoinəu*
(3) *ho*	*hun*		*hoinə*	*hoinən*

Future

Positive			Negative	
'I shall be' etc.			'I shall not be' etc.	
sg.	pl.		sg.	pl.
(1) *hũla*	*hoũla*		*hooinə̃*	*hooinəũ*
(2) *holas*	*hoəula, holau*		*hooinə*	*hooinəu*
(3) *hola*	*holan*		*hooinə*	*hooinən*

An alternative negative of this tense is made by the prefixing of *nə* to the positive forms given above. It is also in common use.

Imperative

Positive			Negative	
'Let me be'			'Let me not be'	
sg.	pl.		sg.	pl.
(1) *hũ*	*hũ, hoaũ*		*nə hũ* etc.	*nə hũ* etc.
(2) *ho, bhəes*	*hou, bhəe*			
(3) *hos, hoos*	*hun, houn*			

Perfect

Positive			Negative	
'I was' etc.			'I was not' etc.	
sg.	pl.		sg.	pl.
(1) *bhəə̃*	*bhəyəũ*		*bhəenə̃*	*bhəenəũ*
(2) *bhəis*	*bhəyəu*		*bhəenəs*	*bhəenəu*
(3) *bhəyo*	*bhəe*		*bhəenə*	*bhəenə*

The last of the auxiliary roots is *thi-/- th-* 'was'. The first form occurs as a verb with a full paradigm in the past tense used with a number of non-finite forms to form complex tenses:

Positive			Negative	
'I was' etc.			'I was not' etc	
sg.	pl.		sg.	pl.
(1) *thiẽ*	*thiyəũ*		*thienə̃*	*thienəũ*
(2) *thiis*	*thiyəu*		*thienəs*	*thienəu*
(3) *thiyo*	*thie*		*thienə*	*thienən*

The second form, *-th-*, is really an apocopated form of the preceding. In its shortened form it is suffixed to roots to form a past habitual tense. There is no negative of this form as such. Its full conjugation in the positive is as follows:

sg.	pl.
-thẽ	*-thyəũ*
-this	*-thyəu*
-thyo	*-the*

2.3.10.4 Verbal forms: finite and non-finite

Finite verb forms are those in which tense, number, and person are distinguished. With these, tenses are formed that are often given by both foreign and native grammars in the form of verbal paradigms. Tenses are either simple or complex.

Non-finite forms do not distinguish tense, number or person, and consist of what are traditionally designated as infinitives, participles and gerunds. Some of these are employed as complete verbal utterances on their own, often in place of finite forms, or may be incorporated into complex tenses. Some of them are of particular importance syntactically in that they make possible the wide use of phrasal relativization in Nepali (see section 2.4.2.1).

In addition, all verbal forms can be seen to fall either into a present system or a past system. The present system consists of the non-finite forms referred to above as infinitives and the tenses associated with the present and the future, including the imperative. The past system consists of the nonfinite forms referred to as participles and gerunds and the tenses associated with the past. The future tenses may be divided in definite and indefinite tenses, and the past into known and unknown (Acharya 1991).

2.3.10.5 Verb negation

The negation of verbs in Nepali is peculiarly complex morphologically. In the case of non-finite forms and the imperative mode, its formation of the negative is simple: the negative particle *nə* is prefixed to the verb. In the case of most finite forms, however, the negative is infixed, resulting in complex combinations in all tenses. In one tense, the negative may be prefixed or infixed. In addition, roots and stems ending in vowels have more than one negative form. In these the negative infix *-n-* is attached directly to the root or stem followed by the person endings. These forms are identical in meaning, but differ in emphasis and style. Finally, in at least one case, negative forms from one tense have been borrowed into another. Because of this complexity, negative paradigms are given with the positive wherever necessary.

2.3.10.6 Non-finite verb forms

With the non-finite suffixes listed above, a group of infinitives, participles and gerunds are formed. They may occur: (1) alone as independent verb forms in place of finite forms, (2) as part of compound tenses, (3) as verbal nouns or as adjectives. Their specific formation and uses are as follows.

Infinitives:

(1) *-nu*. The basic form of the infinitive is made with this suffix. It is used both as an infinitive and as a verbal noun, with variants in *-nə* and *-na* collocated with different verbs or with postpositions:

    gərnu 'to do'
        yo kam gərnu parchə 'One must do this work.'
    gərnə 'to do'
        yo kam gərnə səkīchə 'This work can be done.'
        yo kam gərnə thalyo 'This work began to be done.'
    gərna 'to do'
        gərna-le 'by doing'
        gərna-ma 'in doing'

(2) -*ne*. These function as verbal nouns or adjectives, often with present or future meaning:

gərne 'doing'; e.g. *gərne-ma* 'in doing', *kam gərne manche* 'a work-doing person'. They also function as parts of compound tenses: *gərnechu* 'I shall do', *gərne thiẽ* 'I would have done.'

Participles:

(1) in -*də/-dəi/-da/-do* and its allomorphs -*tə/-təi/-ta/-to*. This participle is used in a large variety of constructions:
(a) as a participle with or without postpositions: *gərda* 'doing', *gərda gərdəi* 'while doing', *gərda-kheri* 'while doing'.
(b) as constituent of tenses or other verbal expressions: *gərdəchu*' I am doing', *gərdəichu* 'I am doing', *gərdəi gərdinã* 'I will not do', *gərdo rəhechə* 'he seems to be doing'.
(c) collocated with the postposition -*le*, it is used as a subordinating conjunction to mean 'because of', or 'on account of': *us-le gərda* 'because of him'.
(2) in -*e*. This form is conditional in meaning when it is used alone, but it may be used with a variety of postpositions or conjunctions that cancel its conditional meaning: *gəre* 'if one does', *gəre pəchi* 'after one does, did', *gəre pəni* 'even if one does'. It is at the base of the past unknown tenses: *gərechə* 'he appears to have done it', *gərethyo* 'he appeared to have done it'. With the suffixation of the postposition -*ko,* it forms an adjectival participle as well as a constituent of compound tenses: *gəre-ko* 'done', *gəreko kam* 'done work, work that has been done', *gəreko chu* 'I have done', *gəreko thiẽ* 'I had done.' The form in -*ko* may take additional postpositions: *gəreko-ma* 'in having done', *gəreko-le* 'because one did.' With the suffixation of -*rə*, this forms a derivate that functions as a gerund: *gəre-ra* 'having done'.
(3) in -*i*: This functions as a gerund: *gəri* 'having done'. The postposition -*kənə* may be added without change of meaning: *gəri-kənə* 'having done'. This form is used increasingly in the negative, with the positive reserved for the form in -*rə*: *nə gərikənə* 'not having done, without having done'. The form in -*i* also functions as the first constituent of all compound verbs: *gərirəhənchu* 'I keep on doing', *gərisəkẽ* 'I have already done it.'

There is, finally, the royal register: *gəribəksinchə* 'His/Her Majesty does.'

2.3.10.7 Finite verb forms: tense

The number of tenses in Nepali is large. The charts given by Acharya (1991: 152–7) list thirty separate tenses. Some of these are used only occasionally, and others are of extremely rare occurrence. Only those in common use are given here.

The tenses of Nepali may be divided into three groups:

(1) simple tenses: these are the most common and represent the core of the verbal tense system. They are formed by the combination of roots/stems with finite suffixes or auxiliaries.
(2) complex tenses: these are collocations of non-finite forms with auxiliaries. They expand the meanings of the simple tenses.
(3) compound tenses: these are combinations of the gerund in -*i* collocated with (a) the verb *rah-* 'remain' to form continuous tenses and (b) with certain verbs to produce aspectual nuances of completed action (*sək-, hal-, ja-*).

For the simple tenses, full paradigms of the root gər- 'do' positive and negative, are given below. For the other tenses, only the first person, positive and negative, is given. Since all finite verbs show person and number, the use of personal pronouns is optional in Nepali, and the paradigms given here do not include them.

2.3.10.7.1 Simple tenses
The simple tenses are the following: (1) present indefinite; (2) perfect; (3) future indefinite; (4) imperative; and (5) pluperfect.

Present indefinite

This tense is formed by the collocation of a root or stem with the auxiliary verb ch- 'be'. Roots and stems ending in vowels are nasalized by the addition of -n- or by the nasalization of the final vowel. The tense has two basic meanings: (1) repeated action in the present: 'I do, always do', (2) action in the immediate future: 'I shall do'.

The negative of this tense is not based morphologically on the positive but is borrowed from the present continuous tense listed below. Because of its very common occurrence it is given here as well. Roots that do not end in consonants have an alternative negative paradigm which is formed by the infixation of -n- before the person endings.

gər- 'do':

sg.	pl.
(1) gərchu 'I do'	gərchəū 'we do'
(2) gərchəs 'you do'	gərchəu 'you do'
(3) gərchə 'he, she, it does'	gərchən 'they do'

Negative: 'I do not do' etc.:

(1) gərdinə̄	gərdainəū
(2) gərdəinəs	gərdəinəu
(3) gərdəinə	gərdəinə

Perfect tense

This tense is formed by the addition of the perfect suffixes directly to the root. It is used to refer to actions completed in the past. Roots that end in a vowel often change it to form this tense, and the small number of roots that has more than one root use the secondary one. Examples:

gər- 'do':

(1) gərē 'I did'	gəryəū 'we did'
(2) gəris 'you did'	gəryəu 'you did'
(3) gəryo 'he, she, it did'	gəre 'they did'

Negative 'I did not do' etc.:

(1) gərinə̄	gərenəū
(2) gərenəs	gərenəu
(3) gərenə	gərenən

Note the irregular root ja- 'go', the secondary base of which is : gə-:

(1) gəē̃ 'I went'	gəyəū 'we did not go'
(2) gəis 'you went'	gəyəu 'you did not'
(3) gəyo 'he, she, it went'	gəe 'they went'

Negative: 'I did not go' etc.:

(1) *gəenə̃*   *gəenə̃ũ*
(2) *gəenəs*   *gəenəu*
(3) *gəenə*   *gəenən*

Pluperfect

This tense refers to actions completed in the distant past or prior to another action ('I had done'), to habitual actions in the past ('I used to do, I would do'), and to conditional actions ('I would have done'). It is made by suffixation of the shortened auxiliary *-th-* to the root. Verbs that have two bases employ the primary one. The negative is formed irregularly by the suffixation of *-th-* to the negative first and third person singular of the present continuous tense:

(1) *gərthẽ* 'I had done'   *gərthyəũ* 'we had done'
(2) *gərthis* 'you had done'   *gərthyəu* 'you had done'
(3) *gərthyo* 'he, she, it, had done' *gərthe* 'they had done'

Negative: 'I had not done' etc.:

(1) *gərdinəthẽ*   *gərdəinathyəũ*
(2) *gərdainəthis*   *gərdəinathyəu*
(3) *gərdəinəthyo*   *gərdəinəthe*

Future non-definite

This tense refers to future actions, but only to those in which there is less than certainty. It is often translated as 'I shall probably do' etc. It is made by adding the future suffixes to the root.

To form the negative, the particle *nə* may be prefixed to the verb. Another negative form is made by the infixation of *-oin-* before the final suffixes:

(1) *gərũla* 'I shall do'   *gərəũla* 'we shall do'
(2) *gərlas* 'you shall do'   *gərəula* 'you will do'
(3) *gərla* 'he, she, it will do'   *gərlan* 'they will do'

Negative: 'I shall not do' etc.:

(1) *gəroinə̃*   *gəroinəũ*
(2) *gəroinəs*   *gəroinəu*
(3) *gəroinə*   *gəroinən*

Imperative

The imperative, also called the injunctive tense, is used in injunctions in the first and third person ('let me, let us', etc.) and in commands, polite or otherwise, for the second person. It is made by suffixing the imperative endings to the root. The negative is made by prefixing the negative particle *nə*:

(1) *gərũ* 'may I do'   *gərəũ* 'may we do'
(2) *gər, gares* 'do'   *gərə* 'do'
(3) *gəros* 'may he, she, it do'   *gərun* 'may they do'

Negative: 'may I not do' etc.: *nə gərũ* etc.

2.3.10.7.2 Complex tenses
Complex tenses are formed by the collocation of a non-finite verbal form and a form of one of the auxiliary verbs, *ch-*, *hu-*, or *thi-*.

Present continuous

The present continuous tense consists of the present participle in *-dəi/-təi* with the auxiliary *ch-*. It refers to actions continuing in the present and to actions that continue on into the future ('I am doing'). The negative is formed by the infix *-n-* added to the participle followed by the person endings. In the case of the first person singular the suffix is *-di-/-ti*: *gərdəichu*, *bəstəichu*; negative *gərdinə̃*, *bəstinə̃*.

Past continuous

This tense is parallel to the above and consists of the present participle in *-dəi-/-təi-* with the auxiliary *thi-*. It refers to actions continuing in the past ('I was doing'). The negative is formed by the negation of the auxiliary *thi-* in the usual way: *gərdəithiẽ* 'I was doing', *gərdəithienə* 'I was not doing'.

Future

The future tense refers to actions that will take place in the future with certainty on the part of the speaker. It is far stronger than the future indefinite. It consists of the infinitive in *-ne* with the auxiliary *ch-*. The negative is formed by the negation of the auxiliary: *gərnechu* 'I shall do', *gərne chəinə* 'I shall not do.'

Conditional

This tense is formed by the collocation of the infinitive in *-ne* with the auxiliary *thi-*. It refers to actions that might or would have taken place ('I would do, I would have done'). Its negative is formed by the negation of the auxiliary: *gərne thiẽ*, *gərne thienə*.

Present perfect

This tense refers to actions performed in the recent past ('I have done'). It consists of the past participle in *-ko* with the auxiliary *-ch-*. The negative is made by the negation of the auxiliary: *gareko chu*, *gareko chəinə*.

Past perfect

This tense refers to actions completed in the distant past or actions completed in the past prior to others ('had done'). Its negative is made by negation of the auxiliary: *gəreko thiẽ*, *gareko thienə*.

Present unknown

This tense has the participle in *-e* and the auxiliary *ch-*. It is, with the one following, among the most interesting of Nepali tenses. In it, there is (1) a sense of recent discovery or experience of the action of the verb or (2) of uncertainty with regard to the action. Note the following pairs of contrasting sentences in which the first contrasts with the second, which is placed in this tense:

birsẽ 'I forgot.'
birsechu 'I seem to have forgotten.'

In the first, the speaker expresses his forgetfulness directly. In the second, he has just realized that he has forgotten. Similarly,

ko ayo? 'Who came?'
ko aechə? 'Who came?'

In the first, the speaker is sure that someone has come even though he does not know who it is. In the second, the reader surmises that someone has come, through some indirect evidence (noise, footsteps) but is not sure. The negative is made by infixing *-nə-* before the auxiliary: *birsechu, birsenəchu.*

In addition, the verb *rəh-* 'remain' is used commonly as an alternative to the roots *ch-* 'be', *hu-/bhə-* 'be' in this tense when there is uncertainty about the existential or definitional status of an action, property or thing:

ḍhoka-ma ko rəhechə?
n-postp.-in pn. remains–3sg.pst unkn.
'Who seems to be at the door?'

koi r6əhenəchə
'Nobody seems to be there.'

Past unknown

This tense is parallel to the above, only its reference is to time further in the past. It has the past participle in *-e* with the auxiliary *-th-*: *birsethẽ, birsenəthẽ.*

2.3.10.8 Verbal compounds

Verbal compounds further extend and modify the tense system, and they may be divided into two groups: (1) progressive tenses through which the action of the verb is made progressive or continuous and (2) perfectives, through which the perfection or completion of the action is indicated.

Continuous tenses

In these, the participle in *i* of any verb occurs with forms of the root *rəh-*'remain':

gərirəhənchu 'I keep on doing.'
gərirəhẽ 'I kept on doing.'
gərirəhũ 'I may keep on doing.'
gərirəhũla 'I shall keep on doing.'
gərirəhənthẽ 'I was doing.'
gərirəhənechu 'I shall keep on doing.'
gərirəhəne thiẽ 'I had kept on doing.'
gərirəheko chu 'I have been doing.'
gərirəheko thiẽ 'I had been doing.'
gərirəhechu 'I seem to keep on doing.'
gərirəhethẽ 'I seemed to keep on doing.'

All non-finite forms also occur: *gərirəhənu* 'to continue to do' etc.

Perfectives

The perfectives consist of the participle in *-i* of any root plus a form of the verbs *hal-* 'pour', *sək-* 'be able', and less often *ja-/gə-* 'go'. With *hal-* and *sək-*, the use of the second verb emphasizes the completion of an action. *hal-* often indicates that a completed action is sufficient or more than sufficient. *sək-* indicates that an action is definitely completed or already done. It should be noted here that Nepali possesses no separate adverb meaning 'already', the verb *sək-* functioning often as an exact equivalent of that word:

bhəihalyo
ger. having been pour-3sg. perf.
having been it poured.
'It's enough.'

yo kam gərisəkyo
pron. adj. work having done able-3sg. perf.
this work done could be.
'This work has already been done.'

bhəigəyo
ger. having been go-3sg. perf.
having been it went
'It's enough.' 'It's fine.'

2.3.10.9 Causatives

For many roots attaching *-au-*, used in the present and future tenses, or *-a-*, in the past, results in causative stems: e.g. *gər-* 'do', *gərau-/gəra-* 'cause to do'. From these all verbal forms may be formed, finite and non-finite, by the addition of the appropriate suffixes:

Non-finite:	*gəraunu* 'to cause to do'
	gəraeko 'caused to be done'
Finite:	*gəraũchə* 'he, she, it causes to do'
	gərayo 'he, she, it caused to do'

With some roots, particularly those ending in vowels, there is some irregularity in the formation of the stems: *khel-* 'play', *khilau-/khila-* cause to play'; *kha-* 'eat', *khuvau-/khuva-* 'cause to eat, feed'.

As an alternate causative form, the verb *ləgau-* 'be applied' is used with the main verb in the infinitive in *nə: aunə ləgaunu* 'to cause to come'.

With *ləgau-* also, a secondary causative, 'to cause to cause someone to do something', is made. As in the case mentioned directly above, the main verb is usually in the causative of the infinitive in *-nə: gəraunə ləgaunu* 'to make someone get something done'.

2.3.10.10 Passives/impersonals

The infixes *ĩ-/-i-* may be added to the root to make stems which are passive or impersonal in meaning. These appear almost always in the third person singular among finite forms, and in all non-finite forms:

Finite forms:	*gərĩchə* 'it is done'	*gəriyo* 'it was done'
	səkĩchə 'it can be ...'	*səkiyo* 'it was finished'
	cahĩchə 'one wants'	*cahiyo* 'one wanted'
Non-finite:	*gərinu* 'to be done'	
	gərine 'to be done'	

Non-finite: *gərieko* 'done'
               gərie 'if done'
               gərierə 'having been done'

2.3.10.11 Honorific and royal registers

The honorific register

To indicate respect, equality or remoteness, special verbal forms are used with the honorific pronouns *təpaĩ, yəhã, vəhã* and *həjur*. These forms may be constructed in any tense in both positive and negative forms, but finite forms are always employed in the third person singular only. They are formed by letting the infinitive of the verb carrying the primary meaning be followed by a form of the verb *hu-/bhə-* 'be'. The latter form carries the person, number and tense. Non-finite forms are: *gərnuhunu, gərnuhune, gərnubhəe, gərnubhəeko, gərnubhəera, gərnubhəi.*

The negative of the non-finite forms is made by prefixing *nə.*

Finite forms:

Simple:
Positive	Negative
gərnuhunchə 'you do'	*gərnuhunnə* 'you do not do'
gərnubhəyo 'you did'	*gərnubhəenə* 'you did not do'
gərnuhunthyo 'you did'	*gərnuhunnəthyo* 'you did not do'
gərnuhola 'please do'	*nəgərnuhola,* 'please don't do'
gərnuhos 'please do'	*nəgərnuhos* 'please don't do'

Complex:
Positive	Negative
gərdəihunuhunchə 'you are doing'	*gərdəihunuhunnə*
gərnuhunechə 'you will be doing'	*gərnuhunechəinə*
gərnuhune thiyo 'you would have done'	*gərnuhune thiena*
gərnubhəeko chə 'you have done'	*gərnubhəeko chəinə*
gərnubhəeko thiyo 'you had done'	*gərnubhəeko thienə*
gərnubhəechə 'you appear to have done'	*gərnubhəenəchə*

The continuous and perfective forms also occur: *gərirəhənuhunchə* 'you keep on doing', *gərisəknuhunchə* 'you already do' as well as the causative: *gəraunuhunchə* 'you cause to do'.

The royal register

Nepali employs special verbal forms and vocabulary for the royal family and members of the court. This register is used by members of the royal family with each other, and by lesser mortals when addressing them or describing their activities. This form of the language appears regularly in newspapers and the other media to describe the activities of the king and members of the royal family.

No special study of this aspect of the language exists. Knowledge of it is incomplete and is based largely on newspaper usage, radio, and television. Its chief characteristics are the following:

(1) the use of forms of address and titles that derive from Sanskrit and Persian, all of which are equivalent to 'His, Her, or Your Majesty': *sri pãc* (lit. sri five times), *sri pãc sərkar, mosuph sərkar.*
(2) use of *bəksənu* or *bəksinu,* an honorific verb that means literally 'to give' but is the chief marker of the royal register. *bəksənu* is used in the third person singular only and is collocated with forms of the participle in *-i.*

The verb 'to be' in this register has a special form: it consists of the participle *hoi-*, which occurs nowhere else in the language:

> *sri pãc hoibəksinchə* 'His, Her Majesty is.'
> *sri pãc hoibəksyo* 'His, Her Majesty was.'

(3) the use of a special vocabulary, derived from Persian and considered to be honorific, to replace ordinary Nepali vocabulary: *səvari hoibəksənu* 'to go', *junar hoibəksənu* 'to eat'.

2.3.10.12 Special verbal usages: *gər-, pər-, bhən-, lag-, hu- /bhə-*

The verbs listed above carry a very heavy workload in the language, and their special usage are noted here:

gər-: When used alone this verb covers the range of meanings of the English verbs *do, make, work*. In addition it combines with a number of nouns to create what are additional verbs with special meaning. The nouns are sometimes borrowed from Sanskrit sources, sometimes from Perso-Arabic, and often there are synonymous pairs available to the speaker, sometimes three choices: *suru gərnu* 'to begin', *arəmbh gərnu*, 'to begin', *sri gənes gərnu* 'to begin'. This construction is used widely for the many borrowings from English; e.g. *chek gərnu*, 'to check'. *gər-* is also used in constructions with the present participle in which repeated action is meant: *aũdəi gərnuhos* 'please keep on coming'.

Two of the non-finite forms, *gəri* and *gərda* have special usages. *gəri*, the gerund, combines with certain adjectives to form adverbs. These occur either in combination in which the two words appear in full form, or in combination in shortened form. In the latter case, the last vowel of the adjective, usually *-o*, is dropped, and the adjective combined with *-əri*, the *g-* of *gəri* having dropped as well: *ramro* 'good', *ramro gəri* 'well', *ramrəri* 'well'.

pər-: This verb carries the general meaning of 'to fall' or 'befall', but often carries the meaning of strong obligation. It is used most often in the third person singular collocated with infinitives in *-nu*: *gərnu pərchə* 'one must do'. It also appears in a variety of idiomatic expressions: *mən pərnu* 'to like', *pani pərnu* 'to rain'.

bhən-: The meaning of this verb is 'to say' and it is used in all contexts where this meaning is indicated. More than any other verb in Nepali, however, it has taken on special functions in which its literal meaning is not evident or is indirectly registered. This is true particularly of its non-finite forms, many of which have specialized meaning. *bhəne* 'if', *bhənerə* 'so that', and *bhəndа* 'than' have been discussed above.

In addition, there are the following usages: *bhənerə*, and its synonym *bhəni*, marks off direct quotations:

> *məjanchu bhənerə bhənyo*
> pr. go-1pres. having said say-3sg. perf.
> I go having said he said.
> "I'm going" he said. 'He said he was going.'

bhənne 'saying' marks direct quotes or reports:

> *mero bhai ṭhik chəina bhənne khəbər ayo*
> pr. adj. brother adj. 3sg. is neg. part. news came-3sg. perf.
> my brother well is not saying news came.
> 'The new came that my brother is not well.'

lag-: This verb means literally 'to adhere', 'to be applied to', often 'to feel', 'to seem', and this meaning may be seen in many of the idioms with which it is associated: *ago lagnu* 'to burn', *un lagnu* 'to feel sleepy', *jaḍo lagnu* 'to feel cold', *bhok lagnu* 'to be hungry', *tirkha lagnu* 'to feel thirsty', *mən lagnu* 'to like'. Collocated with infinitives ending in *-nə* it means 'to begin':

> *kam gərnə lagyo*
> n. do-inf in. *nə* begin-3sg.perf.
> work to do began.
> 'He began to work.'

The gerund *lagi* is used as part of the common compound postposition *ko lagi* 'for', and in shortened form it appears as the postposition *-lai* 'to, for'.

hu-/bhə: This verb is the only full verb 'to be' in the language, the others being truncated paradigms. In addition to the meanings given above, it is used in the expression of general truths and carries the meaning of being in general, of 'being that is morally right', or of becoming. Note following examples:

> *dui rə dui car huncha*
> two conj two four be-3sg. pres.
> 'Two and two are four.'

> *gərib-lai pəisa dine hunchə*
> n.-postp.-to n. give-inf. be-3sg. pres.
> to poor money to give is
> 'It is good to give money to the poor.'

> *bholi mə pəni ṭhulo hunchu bhənerə chori-le bhənyo*
> adv. pr. adv. adj. is-1sg. pres said-ger. daughter-post. say-3 perf.
> tomorrow I also big will be having said daughter said.
> 'My daughter said that tomorrow she too would grow up to be big.'

In the past, it is used in the sense of 'to happen': *ke bhayo*? 'What happened?'

2.3.11 Adverbs

2.3.11.1 Adverb sets

A class of adverbs shares, with pronouns and pronominal adjectives, the characteristic series of initial sounds in 2.3.6:

kəsəri 'how'	*jəsəri* 'howsoever'	*yəsari* 'like this'	*tyəsəri* 'like that'
kəti 'how many'	*jəti* 'as much'	*yəti/uti* 'so much'	*tyəti* 'that much'
kəhã 'where?'	*jəhã* 'wherever'	*yəhã* 'here'	*tyəhã* 'there'
kəta 'where?'	*jəta* 'to wherever'	*yəta* 'here'	*tyəta* 'there'
kəhĩ 'somewhere'	*jəhĩ* 'wherever'	*yəhĩ* 'right here'	*tyəhĩ* 'right there'

2.3.11.2 Anukaran (onomatopoeia)

Nepali possesses a large number of onomatopoeic words that have been called *anukaran* 'imitative'. They are in common use, mostly as adverbs but sometimes as nouns or adjectives. Many contain double consonants, most often *-kk-*, but also *-rr-* and *-ll-*, preceded by a vowel. Some show reduplication of the initial syllable with a rhyming syllable beginning with -*m*-. Some repeat the first word or syllable but with different vowels. Still others are unchanged repetitions. The onomatopoeic nature of some is clear, but in many this origin is less apparent. Some of them can be defined in isolation, others appear almost always collocated with particular verbs. Among the most common are the following: *svīkka* 'the crack of a whip', *svãkka* 'snivelling', *balla balla* 'reluctantly, barely', *akkamakka parnu* 'to be bewildered', *ukusmukus* 'stuffy, difficult to breathe', *jilla pərnu* 'to be amazed', *kəchang kuchung* 'pieces of food', *kəcyak kucuk*, 'broken, rough'.

2.3.11.3 Interjections and nuance particles

Interjections are a class of unchanging particles that are independent syntactically (Acharya 1991: 141). The following are among the most common: *əyya* (pain), *babəi* (surprise), *dhətteri*, *dhətterika* (frustration), *aməi* (amazement, surprise), *oho* (surprise), *chih* (disgust), *dhət* (anger).

Nuance particles are far fewer in number and are used to emphasize, to assert, and to contradict. The most common are: *ta* 'but', *ni* 'mind you' (emphasis), *na* 'I tell you' (urgency), *po* 'but' (asserts contradiction).

2.4 Notes on syntax

2.4.1 General features

The syntax of Nepali bears many similarities to that of other modern Indo-Aryan languages and even many of its special features fall within the general characteristics of this language family. Some writers, in discussing Nepali, observe the distinction often made between lexical and grammatical items. This distinction, arbitrary and difficult as it is to justify theoretically, is heuristically useful. Lexical items consist of those words that have been included above under the rubrics of nouns, pronouns, adjectives, verbs and adverbs. Grammatical items, also referred to as operators, include postpositions, conjunctions, nuancers and enclitic particles. Some verbal forms may fall into either category, depending on their function within the utterance. In Nepali, whether in a phrase, clause or sentence, lexical items tend to order and combine as prefixes, and grammatical items as suffixes. That is, lexical items form linear series by preceding the words to which they relate, and grammatical items form series by following the words to which they relate. Thus, Nepali syntax may be said to recapitulate its morphology, though without the degree of rigidity of position that characterizes morphemic ordering. This distinction between lexical and grammatical order, combined with the order of the main categories in sentences and clauses, constitutes the fundamental rules of the word order of Nepali syntax.

The sentence in Nepali is a complete utterance and consists of a minimum of two categories, the subject and predicate in that order. The subject may be filled with one or more lexical items, usually a nominal form, with or without modifiers preceding. A predicate consists of a verb with or without modifiers preceding it. If the predicate consists of a finite verbal form, it is often tied to the subject by markers of number, person and sometimes gender. Modifiers may be single adjectives or adverbs, or clusters of these, which are called phrases. In addition, verbs may be preceded by complements. Complements may be predicate nouns or predicate adjectives, direct or indirect objects. All precede the verb, but not all may be present in the same sentence. If a sentence contains both indirect and direct objects, the indirect will precede the direct. Both direct and indirect objects may have any number of modifiers.

Simple sentences may be declarative, interrogative or imperative: they may declare or describe facts or situations, ask questions, or give commands. But the order of elements remains fundamentally the same. Order changes only when the speaker modifies it to add emphatic or emotional quality to the utterance. Simple sentences may be joined by coordinating conjunctions to form complex sentences. They may also be combined with clauses, utterances that contain both subject and predicate but end with a subordinating conjunction, participial form or postposition. Clauses combine with sentences as lexical items, that is, they precede simple sentences to form compound sentences.

Simple sentences may consist of one word, a verb positive or negative. In such sentences, the subject is unstated but indicated by the verb:

januhos 'Please go.'
na khau 'Don't eat (that).'

Word order in simple declarative sentences is subject (S), object (O) verb (V). Adjectival phrases precede the subject; adverbial phrases precede the verb. Adjectival phrases may consist of single adjectives:

ṭhulo ghər ho
adj. n. be-3sg pres.
big house is
'It is a big house.'

u dherəi kam gərchə
pr. adv. work do-3sg. pres.
he much work does
'He does much work.'

Questions may be marked by interrogative words. In these, the interrogative word is placed at the beginning or alternatively after the subject word:

ko ho
'Who is it?'

kəhã chə
'Where is it?'

Often the verb 'to be' as copula is omitted:

tyo ke
that what (is)?
'What is that?'

A phrase indicating location may be placed optionally before the verb or before the subject:

pani dhara-ma chə
water well-post. in be-3sg pres.
'Is there water in the well?'

dhara-ma pani chə
well-postp. in water is
'Is there water in the well?'

Complex sentences

Simple sentences may be combined to form complex sentences. These may be combined by a coordinating conjunction:

>*yo mero ghər ho, tərə ahile mə yəhã bəstinə*
>pr. poss. adj. n. be-3sg. pres. conj. adv. pr. adv. live-1sg. pres. neg.
>this my house is, but now I here live-not
>'This is my house, but I don't live here now.'

Sentences concerning two actions performed one after the other and having the same agent often have a gerund as the first element. Examples:

>*khaerə jau*
>ger. go-imper.
>having-eaten, go.
>'Go after you eat.'

>*khaerə sutẽ*
>ger. sleep-1sg. perf.
>having eaten I slept
>'I went to sleep after eating.'

Parallel to these is the use of the gerund *bhənera* 'having said':

>*dhara-ma pani chə ki bhənerə herna gəẽ*
>well-postp. in water be-3sg. pres. conj. ger. inf. go-1sg. perf.
>well-in water is ? having said to see went I.
>'I went to see if there was water in the well.'

Clauses

Clauses contain a subject and a predicate but are marked at the end by a subordinating conjunction, postposition or non-finite verbal form functioning as a conjunction. Such clauses are termed subordinate because they do not stand alone but occur in conjunction with sentences. The verb may be finite or non-finite: (1) with subordinating conjunctions/ non-finite forms: *səhər gəe* 'if he went to the city', *səhər gəe tapəni* 'although he went to the city', *səhər gəyo bhəne* 'if he goes to the city', *gəe pəchi* 'after he goes to the city'. (2) with postpositions: *pani nəpəreko-le* 'because it did not rain', *pani-le gərda* 'because of the rain', *səhər jane-bittikəi* 'as soon as he goes to the city'.

2.4.2 Special features

The most remarkable features of Nepali syntax are (1) strong preference for phrasal relativization; (2) strong preference for employing direct discourse rather than indirect; and (3) the use of non-finite verbal forms as equivalents or in place of finite forms.

2.4.2.1 Phrasal relativization

Nepali has a full inventory of relative and correlative pronouns, adjectives and adverbs, with which subordinate clauses may be constructed. Such constructions, however, occur with far less frequency than in some other Indo-Aryan languages. Rather than construct subordinate clauses, Nepali shows a marked preference for relativization through adjectival phrases. In constructing these, it employs two non-finite forms, the participle in -*ko* for past constructions, and the infinite in -*ne* for constructions in the present and future. These non-finite forms are employed essentially as adjectives through which the action of the verb is ascribed to the noun or pronoun it precedes. Thus, in English, the utterance 'the man who came yesterday' is equivalent to the Nepali utterance 'the yesterday came man' and the utterance 'the man who will come tomorrow' has 'the tomorrow coming man' as its literal counterpart. Such constructions are hardly unknown in other Indo-Aryan languages, but the extent to which they are permitted in Nepali is unusual. Note that the verbal element may be either transitive or intransitive:

> *hijo aeko manche*
> adv. adj-part. man
> yesterday come man
> 'the man who came yesterday'

> *məile hijo gəreko kam*
> pr.-postp. adv. adj.-part. work
> me by yesterday done work
> 'the work I did yesterday'

> *bholi aune manche*
> adv. come-inf. man
> tomorrow coming man
> 'the man who will come tomorrow'

> *bholi gərne kam*
> adv. inf. doing work
> tomorrow doing work
> 'the work to be done tomorrow'

In addition, the adjectival phrase is functionally equivalent to any noun phrase (adjective plus noun) and it may function in utterances in a variety of ways, including as either a subject or verbal complement:

> *hijo aeko manche-lai khanə diẽ*
> adv. adj-part. man-postp. to inf. give 1sg. perf.
> yesterday came man-to to eat gave-I
> 'I gave food to the man who came yesterday.'

> *bholi aune manche dherəi khala*
> adv. inf. man adv. eat-3sg. fut. nondef.
> tomorrow coming man much eat will
> 'The man who will come tomorrow may eat a lot.'

> *bholi aune manche-lai khanə diulã*
> adv. inf. man-postp.to eat-inf. give-3sg. fut. nondef.
> tomorrow coming man-to to eat give shall I
> 'I shall/may give food to the man who comes tomorrow.'

Note that Nepali also permits the construction in cases such as the following:

> *hijo aeko bela* 'the time at which (he) came yesterday'
> *məi-le hijo khaeko cəməc* 'the spoon with which I ate'

In these, the construction introduces a strong element of ambiguity, since the first could mean 'the time that came yesterday' and 'the spoon that I ate yesterday'. In such cases, only context determines the sense. Ramarao (1982) has remarked on this ambiguity and what appear to be exact parallels in the Dravidian languages, Telugu in particular.

2.4.2.2 Direct and indirect discourse

Nepali shows a marked preference for direct quotation of speech rather than some indirect rendering of it. This is done either (1) through the construction of subordinate clauses marked by a conjunction or (2) by the construction of adjectival phrases in which the quote is ascribed adjectivally to a nominal form. In both cases, the quote is marked only at its end, not at its beginning.

Both of these may be seen as subclasses of types of utterances already described. The first is a subclass of utterances in which the first verb is a gerund ending in -rə; the second is a subclass of the adjectival phrases using the infinitive in -ne discussed immediately above. In both cases non-finite forms of the root bhən- 'say' are used to mark the quotation.

In the first case, the direct quote of the speaker is marked by the gerund bhənerə followed by the main verb:

> mə səhər janchu bhənerə bhənyo
> pr. city go-1sg. pres. ger. say-3sg. perf.
> I city go having said he said.
> 'He said, "I am going to the city".'
> 'He said that he was going to the city.'

The quotation may be a question:

> mə səhər janchu ki bhənerə sodhyo
> pr. city go-3sg. pres. conj. ger. ask-3sg. perf.
> I city go having said asked-he
> 'He asked, "Shall I go to the city?"'
> 'He asked whether he should go to the city.'

In the next case, the quote is not of a direct utterance of the speaker, but is a reported utterance. The marker of the reported utterance is bhənne, the infinitive in -ne of the root bhən-, used to ascribe the quote to a nominal form that follows. These nominal forms are words that indicate some form of news or report (khəbər, səmacar) or mental utterance (asə 'hope', ḍər 'fear'). Thus:

> prədhan məntri nepal phərkənubhəyo bhənne səmacar ayo
> adj. n. Nepal return-3sg. hon. say-inf. news come-3sg. perf.
> prime minister Nepal returned saying news came.
> 'The news came that the Prime Minister returned to Nepal.'

> prədhan məntri nepal phərkənubhəyo bhənne khəbər sunē
> adj. n. Nepal return-3sg. hon. say-inf. news hear-1sg. perf.
> prime minister Nepal returned saying news heard I
> 'I heard the news that the Prime Minister had returned to Nepal.'

prədhan məntri nepal phərkənecha bhənne asə gərdəichu
adj. n. Nepal return-3sg. fut say-inf. hope do-1sg. pres. cont.
prime minister Nepal return will saying hope do I
'I hope that the Prime Minister will return to Nepal.'

2.4.2.3 Ellipsis

Finite verb forms, with their specificity of person, number, and sometimes gender markers, are often replaced, particularly in conversation, with non-finite forms, particularly the infinitive in *-ne*. The non-specificity of such forms often softens the utterance, but it also makes it highly dependent on context for meaning. Note the following:

əhile khanuhunchə? 'Will you eat now?'
əhile khane? 'Will you eat now?'

In the first sentence, the verb shows tense and person, and is in the honorific register. In the second, the verb merely indicates the action and gives a general reference to time. It may function as the equivalent of the first sentence, but it also has a variety of possible meanings depending on the context and may be ascribed to a wide number of actors. In principle, since the subject of the verb is not marked with regard to person or number, the verb can refer to any person or any number of persons. Note the following example and translations:

bholi jane 'Let's go tomorrow.' 'I'll go tomorrow.' 'You're going tomorrow.'

2.4.2.4 Syntactic filler words

Nepali is rich in filler words, expressions that have little meaning in themselves but are part of the general habit of utterance. They are akin to the constant use in English by some of repeated habitual expressions such as *like, you know, totally*. In Nepali, they often appear to give the speaker time to formulate thoughts, to make amendments to utterances, to change the forms of utterances as they are being constructed, and often to mark the boundaries between utterances. So widespread is their usage that no discussion of Nepali syntax can avoid them. Thus the utterance: *hamro nepalma kəsto huncha bhəndakherima caine tapaĩko ...* simply means what the first two words mean and no more: 'in our Nepal ...', the rest being filler. A full translation would be something like, 'While in speaking, right, yours, of how it is in our Nepal ...'. The rules for their insertion in a variety of utterances remain to be studied, but some of the most common are the following: *u* 'that one', *u ke re* 'that ... what do you call it?' *u tyo* 'that over there', *caine* 'right', *lə* 'well', *təpaĩko* 'yours', *bhənera* 'having said', *bhənda-kheri/ bhənda-kheri-ma* 'while saying', *bhəni-dekhin* 'having said'.

REFERENCES

Acharya, Jayaraj (1980) *Traditional Grammars: English and Nepali. A Study*, Kathmandu: Navin Press.
—— (1990) 'Lexical modernization in Nepali: a study of borrowing', *Georgetown Journal of Languages and Linguistics* 1.3: 267–89.
—— (1991) *A Descriptive Grammar of Nepali and an Analyzed Corpus*, Washington, D.C.: Georgetown University.
Adhikary, Surya Mani (1988) *The Khaśa Kingdom*, Jaipur and New Delhi: Nirala Publications.

Bandhu, Churamani, Dahal, B. M., Holzhausen, A., and Hale, Austin (1971) 'Nepali segmental phonology'. (unpublished paper).

Clark, T. W. (1957) 'The Rani Pokhari Inscription, Kathmandu', *Bulletin of the School of Oriental and African Studies* 20: 167–187.

—— (1963) *Introduction to Nepali: A first year course*, Cambridge: W. Heffer and Sons. (Revised edition (1977) by John Burton-Page, London: School of Oriental and African Studies).

—— (1969) 'Nepali and Pahari', in Sebeok, Thomas A. (ed.), *Current Trends in Linguistics*, 5: *Linguistics in South Asia*, The Hague: Mouton, pp. 249–276.

Hamilton, Francis Buchanan (1819) *An Account of the Kingdom of Nepal*, Edinburgh: Archibald Constable.

Hodgson, Brian Houghton (1874) *Essays on the Languages, Literature and Religion of Nepal and Tibet, together with papers on the Geography, Ethnology and Commerce of those Countries*, London: Trubner.

Hutt, Michael (1988) *Nepali: A National Language and its Literature*, New Delhi and London: SOAS and Sterling Publishers.

—— (1997a) 'Being Nepali without Nepal: reflections on a South Asian diaspora', in Gellner, D., Pfaff-Czarnecka, J., and Whelpton, J. (eds.), *Nationalism and Ethnicity in a Hindu Kingdom: The Politics of Culture in Contemporary Nepal*, London: Harwood Academic Publishers, pp. 101–44.

—— (1997b) *Modern Literary Nepali: An Introductory Reader*, New Delhi: Oxford University Press.

Kirkpatrick, Lt. Col. (1811) *An Account of the Kingdom of Nepaul*, London: William Miller.

Matthews, David (1984) *A Course in Nepali*, London: School of Oriental and African Studies. (second edition, 1992).

Meerendonk, M. (1949) *Basic Gurkhali Grammar*, Singapore: Sen Wah Press.

Ramarao, C. (1982) 'Phrasal Relatives in Telugu, Bengali, and Nepali', in Kansakar, R. Tej (ed.) *Occasional Papers in Nepalese Linguistics*, Kirtipur, Kathmandu: Linguistic Society of Nepal.

Rana, Puskar Samser Jang Bahadur (1936) *Agreji Nepali Koś*, Kathmandaũ: Nepali Bhasa Prakasini Samiti.

Riccardi, Theodore (1971) *A Nepali Version of the Vetālapañcaviṃśati,* New Haven: American Oriental Society.

Rogers, Lt. Col. G. G. (1950) *Colloquial Nepali*, Calcutta: Thacker Spink.

Sarma, Bal Chandra (1962) *Nepali Śabda Koś*, Kathmandu: Royal Nepal Academy.

Sarma, Somnath (1976 VS) *Madhyacandrika*. Kaṭhmandau: Nepali Bhasa Prakasini Samiti.

Turnbull, A. (1888) *Nepali Grammar and Vocabulary*, Delhi: Asian Educational Service (reprinted 1982).

Turner, Ralph Lilley (1931) *A Comparative and Etymological Dictionary of the Nepali Language*, London: Routledge and Kegan Paul.

FURTHER READING

1. Learning grammars

Clark, T. W. (1963) *Introduction to Nepali: A First Year Course,* Cambridge: W. Heffer and Sons. (Revised edition (1977) by John Burton-Page, London: School of Oriental and African Studies).

Matthews, David (1984) *A Course in Nepali*, London: School of Oriental and African Studies.

Rogers, Lt. Col. G. G. (1950) *Colloquial Nepali*, Calcutta: Thacker Spink.

2. Descriptive grammar

Acharya, Jayaraj (1991) *A Descriptive Grammar of Nepali and an Analyzed Corpus*, Washington, D.C.: Georgetown University.

3. Earlier stages of the language

Adhikary, Surya Mani (1988) *The Khaśa Kingdom*, Jaipur and New Delhi: Nirala Publications.
Clark, T. W. (1957) 'The Rani Pokhari Inscription, Kathmandu', *Bulletin of the School of Oriental and African Studies* 20: 167–187.
Riccardi, Theodore (1971) *A Nepali Version of the Vetālapañcaviṃśati*, New Haven: American Oriental Society.

4. Lexicons

Schmidt, Ruth Laila et al. (eds.) (1993) *Vyāvahārik Nepāli-Aṅgrejī Śabdakoś A Practical Dictionary of Modern Nepali*, Delhi: Ratna Sagar.
Sharma, Bal Chandra (1962) *Nepali Śabda Koś*, Kathmandu: Royal Nepal Academy.
Turner, Ralph Lilley (1931) *A Comparative and Etymological Dictionary of the Nepali Language*, London: Routledge and Kegan Paul.

5. Language and literature

Hutt, Michael (1988) *Nepali: A National Language and its Literature*, New Delhi and London: SOAS and Sterling Publishers.
—— (1997a) 'Being Nepali without Nepal: reflections on a South Asian diaspora' in Gellner, D., Pfaff-Czarnecka, J., and Whelpton, J. (eds.), *Nationalism and Ethnicity in a Hindu Kingdom: the Politics of Culture in Contemporary Nepal*, London: Harwood Academic Publishers, pp. 101–44.
—— (1997b) *Modern Literary Nepali: An Introductory Reader*, New Delhi: Oxford University Press.

PANJABI

Christopher Shackle

CONTENTS

LIST OF TABLES

1 INTRODUCTION

In dealing with language matters in the famously complex South Asian context, it is always difficult to strike an appropriate balance between doing justice to the sheer complexity of the data and undertaking the degree of simplification necessary for concise exposition, even where simplification is not imposed by intrinsic gaps in the current state of knowledge. While aiming for clarity, this chapter also attempts to survey a wider than usual range of regional and historical data from the Panjabi area in order to establish a reasoned basis for comparisons with other Indo-Aryan languages. A general context is first established in this introductory section, before the chapter proceeds to deal with phonology, script, morphology and syntax.

1.1. Preliminary definitions

Definitions of 'Panjabi' which probe beyond the straightforward etymological gloss as 'language of the five rivers (Persian *panj āb* 'five waters')', i.e. the terrritory of the five great tributaries of the Indus, are as difficult as any to establish clearly within Indo-Aryan. All the familiar complications inhibiting a simple taxonomy are certainly here present in full measure. These include often blurred linguistic frontiers; widespread diglossia and bilingualism with influential languages of high cultural prestige; a degree of internal dialectal variation sufficient to call the unicity of 'Panjabi' into serious question; historical patterns of divergent religious and cultural traditions; and the sociolinguistic consequences of the political partition of the Panjab in 1947 between India and Pakistan.

The Panjabi area in its most general sense constitutes the northwestern corner of the main Indo-Aryan territory (see Map 16.1). It is linguistically quite well defined in relation to the Dardic area to the north, to Pashto in the west and to Sindhi in the southwest. To the east, however, the linguistic boundaries are less well defined, and in the case of the Hindustani heartland to the southeast have been further blurred by long contact with the linguistically cognate and culturally prestigious Hindi-Urdu (Shackle and Snell 1990).

Internally, very considerable differences of phonology, morphology and lexis led Grierson in his still influential *Linguistic Survey of India* to make a novel distinction between the central and eastern dialects, which alone he described as 'Panjabi' and assigned to the same volume as Western Hindi (Grierson 1916: 607–24), from the western dialects for which he coined the term 'Lahnda' (<Panjabi *lẽda* 'west') and described in the same volume as Sindhi (Grierson 1919: 233–45). This term, or the feminine 'Lahndi', has achieved a certain level of later academic acceptance (Rossi 1974, Smirnov 1975, Campbell 1995: 293–7), although this has hardly extended to the elaborate superstructure of the 'Inner' Panjabi overlaying the 'Outer' Lahnda which was central both to Grierson's division of the area (Masica 1991: 447–60) and his recognition of the difficulty of any absolute distinction between the two. But it seems preferable to disregard Grierson's awkward construct, which is quite absent from popular local usage, in favour of a closer attention both to objective linguistic features (Shackle 1979) and to the locally current perceptions of linguistic identity which derive from the usual complex interface between these features and politico-cultural factors.

1.2. History and contemporary situation

Chief among the factors inhibiting linguistic standardization in the Panjabi area has been a long historical preference for the use of non-local standard languages. The cultural supremacy of Persian endured until the British conquest of the Panjab in the 1840s extended the pattern already established in northern India of Urdu as a standard language below the elite tier assigned to English. Panjabi, however defined, was by contrast largely restricted to oral discourse and used only for certain types of popular verse literature, whose earliest and most significant record is in the substantial local linguistic component of the mixed language of the hymns of the *Ādi Granth* (1604), the Sikh scriptures compiled in the Gurmukhi script.

As elsewhere in India, an increasing polarization of religious identities during the century of British rule of the Panjab had important linguistic consequences, first in establishing an ever closer link between religion and cultural language, then in effecting massive disturbance to local dialectal patterns as the result of the communal transfer of populations in 1947.

MAP 16.1: THE PANJABI AREA

For the Muslims who dominated the western districts and constituted slightly more than half the total population, the official encouragement of Urdu coincided with their own cultural preferences for the language which had come to be seen as the prime vehicle of South Asian Islam. In the larger western part of the Panjab awarded to Pakistan, the old imperial triglossia has thus been maintained since 1947, with the position of Urdu reinforced as the provincial as well as the national language by the Islamicizing programmes of successive regimes (Rahman 1996). Two local standards have nevertheless emerged against this general trend, although the status of both remains subordinate to Urdu. Some success in securing a greater recognition for Panjabi has been secured by cultural activists principally based in Lahore, the provincial capital (Shackle 1970), but only at the cost of provoking reactions from rival groups of activists from other regions, especially the Siraiki region in the southwest (Shackle 1977a) which is linguistically the most divergent from the central Lahore norm. Yet another movement has arisen in the northwest, across the Panjab frontier in NWFP, for the recognition of Hindko as a third incipient standard (Shackle 1983b).

Amongst the non-Muslim population of British Panjab, the process of increasing communal polarization naturally induced many Panjabi Hindus to follow the example of their co-religionists to the east in identifying with the new Khari Boli-based modern standard Hindi as their preferred cultural language. This in turn provoked the reformist leaders of late nineteenth century Sikhism to develop for the first time a modern standard literary Panjabi written in the Gurmukhi script (Shackle 1988). After 1947 the entire Hindu and Sikh populations of the undivided province were clustered in the smaller eastern part of the Panjab awarded to India. A concerted campaign for a Sikh-dominated state was mounted by the Sikh leadership and in 1966 eventually prevailed over strong Hindu opposition (Brass 1974: 277–400). A truncated Panjab with Panjabi in Gurmukhi script as its official language was separated from Haryana to the southeast with Hindi as its official language, as it was also in Himachal Pradesh, to which some hill districts were transferred from northeastern Panjab. Finally in Jammu, a linguistically cognate but administratively separate Hindu majority area, there has been some cultivation since 1947 of Dogri as a distinct local standard.

The result of these complex developments has been to make it virtually impossible to arrive at accurate figures for present numbers of speakers. The best available source (Breton 1997: 200–1) suggests a 1991 estimate of 24 million Panjabi speakers in India, plus another 2 million Dogri speakers, against the much larger total of 70 million speakers in Pakistan, where they would be a large absolute majority of the total population, but where many would (if given the opportunity denied to them by the most recent census) prefer to define themselves as speakers of Siraiki or Hindko. Outside South Asia, there are significant numbers of Panjabi speakers from both India and Pakistan in the diaspora, especially in the United Kingdom, Canada and the western United States.

1.3. Scope of treatment

Most accounts of 'Panjabi', including the standard reference grammars (Gill and Gleason 1969, Bhatia 1993) are based more or less exclusively upon the modern standard Panjabi (MSP) of India, where it is recognized both as a language of the constitution and as the state language of Panjab. While this practice has the merit of convenience and some degree of comprehensiveness since the same language with the usual lexical differences is also widely current in Pakistan, it risks seriously distorting any general understanding of the Panjabi linguistic area as a whole.

It would hardly be possible within the scope of a chapter of this size to do adequate justice to all varieties of language current in such a large and very diverse area. Systematic comparison is therefore restricted to parallel citations of features of Siraiki (Shackle 1976), which has the advantage of being both the variety most consistently divergent from MSP norms and the one with the best local claim to separate recognition. Features and forms from Hindko and other local varieties and dialects are cited only where they contrast particularly interestingly with MSP and Siraiki. The third main point of reference is provided by citation of forms from the older language of the *Ādi Granth*, which often help account for divergent modern developments. AG forms (Shackle 1983a) are cited in a standardized transliteration, as opposed to the transcription used for all modern varieties. Terms like 'general Panjabi feature' are here expressly intended to transcend definitions narrowly based on MSP alone.

It is hoped that this explicit triangulation between MSP, Siraiki and AG may help to give a greater depth of both synchronic and diachronic perspective than is available from other accounts. Since linguistic relationships with Hindi and Urdu are so close and so powerfully reinforced by diglossia and bilingualism, the opportunity is also regularly taken at appropriate points of the chapter to draw attention to comparisons and contrasts with Hindi-Urdu (HU), and to address the lack of a convenient account elsewhere of the more notable Panjabisms characteristic of most Panjabis' HU speech.

1.4. Dialectal and other studies

For much further detail the user must be referred to the dialectal and other studies available in addition to the often uneven and inaccurate coverage in the *Linguistic Survey* (Grierson 1916, Grierson 1919). Besides some still valuable studies of Siraiki (Jukes 1900, O'Brien 1903, Bahl 1936), western dialects described include Hindko in Kohat and Peshawar (Shackle 1980), in NWFP (Rensch et al. 1992) and in Mianwali (Shackle 1992), Awankari (Bahri 1962, Bahri 1963), Kahuni (Varma 1936), Pothohari (Language Department 1960a), Shahpuri (Wilson 1899), and Wazirabadi (Bailey 1904, Cummings and Bailey 1912, Bailey 1914). Descriptions of northern varieties are available for Dogri (Shankar 1931, Bahri 1969, Pandotra 1974, Sharma 1975), Kangri (Bailey 1908, Sharma 1974b, Bala 1983), and other hill dialects (Bailey 1908, Bailey 1915: 231–64, Ranganatha 1980) on the uncertain frontier with Himachali proper (Hendriksen 1985, Hendriksen 1987). Descriptions of eastern dialects (Singh 1970, Gill 1973) include studies of Malvai-Doabi (Jain 1934), and Puadhi (Language Department 1960b, Sandhu 1968b). Besides general comparisons with Hindi (Arun 1961, Sharma 1971), the linguistic border with Bangru in Haryana (Singh 1970) is of special interest to comparativists (Jain 1929, Varma 1964, Varma 1965), as are the remoter connections with Dakhni Urdu (Sherani 1930, Shakeel 1973, Sharma 1974a).

Sociolinguistic variation (Gupta 1983, Koul and Bala 1989, Rensch 1992) has been examined in the context of the argots of marginal groups (Bailey 1908, Bailey 1915: 265–77, Bailey 1938: 176–83, Padam 1992) and social stratification (Singh 1979). Several studies have been devoted to bilingualism with Hindi in India (Gumperz 1971, Agnihotri 1985, Rangila 1986, Dass 1987, Mizokami 1987, Mukherjee 1996), with Urdu in Pakistan (Shackle 1970, Mansoor 1993) and in the diaspora (Khan 1991), and with English in Britain (Agnihotri 1984, Linguistic Minorities Project 1985, Romaine 1986, Mahandru 1991, Rampton 1991, Moffatt and Milroy 1992, Romaine 1995).

For MSP there are several introductory teaching grammars (Bahri 1972, Shackle 1972, Mizokami 1981, Bhardwaj 1995, Kalra and Purewal 1999), also Panjabi–English dictionaries (Newton and Janvier 1854, Singh 1895, Panjabi University 1994b), besides English–Panjabi (Singh 1980, Panjabi University 1994a), Panjabi–Urdu (Bukhari 1989) and Panjabi–Panjabi dictionaries (Language Department 1955–83). Other lexical aspects are less well covered, although there are studies of historical phonology (Jain 1934, Bahl 1962) and Persian loans (Nirvair 1975, Shackle 1978), besides specialist AG dictionaries (Nabha 1960, Shackle 1995). Three bibliographies include additional Panjabi linguistic titles (Bahl 1969, Gupta 1971, Koul and Bala 1989).

2 PHONOLOGY

The following description is based primarily upon MSP (Gill and Gleason 1963: 7–36, Gupta 1972, Dulai and Koul 1980, Bhatia 1993: 330–51, Malik 1995), with systematic attention to contrasts with Siraiki (Shackle 1976: 12–41) and selective mention of distinctive features from elsewhere. Older AG forms are cited only where helpful in understanding diverse modern developments. Prominence is given to phonological features of particular interest within Indo-Aryan as a whole, especially to contrasts with HU, such as the realization of some diphthongs, the prominence of retroflex consonants (and in Siraiki of implosives), syllabic structures and word-accent, and above all the aspirate-derived tones.

2.1. Vowels

MSP has ten vowel phonemes (table 16.1). Phonetic realizations (Sandhu 1974) are similar to HU, except that the markedly lower quality of ε accounts for this being a prominent shibboleth of Panjabi speakers' pronunciation of HU. Contrasts may be established by complete sets of sub-minimal pairs (table 16.2).

Vowel-length is taken to be phonetically less significant than quality. The important systemic contrast between the historically 'short' vowels ə, I, U and the seven 'long' vowels a, i, u, e, ε, o, ɔ is therefore described as an opposition between 'centralized' and 'peripheral' vowels. The contrast is crucial to the analysis of syllabic structures and of

TABLE 16.1: VOWEL PHONEMES

	front unrounded				back rounded
			peripheral		
high	i		centralized		u
		I		U	
mid	e				o
	ε		ə		ɔ
back			a		

TABLE 16.2: VOWEL CONTRASTS

məl	'filth'	mal	'goods'
mIl	'meet'	mil	'mile'
mUl	'price'	mul	'root'
mel	'connection'	mεl	'dirt'
mol	'value'	mɔli	'ribbon'

the effects of word-accent, besides having some morphological function in the verbal system. Since the structurally important loss of the morphologically very significant AG final short vowels, only peripheral vowels may appear in word-final position.

Phonemic nasalization is confined to the peripheral vowels. Nasalized peripheral vowels may occur in all positions, with the exception of initial ĩ-, ẽ-, õ-. The phonemic contrast between simple and nasalized vowels is strongest in word-final position, where it often marks important morphological distinctions (table 16.3).

Only rising diphthongs of centralized plus peripheral vowel occur. MSP has only the eight diphthongs listed in table 16.4. The first element in types (a) and (b) with a front vowel as first or second element is fronted as a short ĕ, but it is more convenient to follow the divergent Gurmukhi orthographies than to phonemicize a separate vowel. There are no falling diphthongs. Most combinations of two peripheral vowels are possible, other than sequences of identical vowels or combinations involving ɛ and ɔ. The phonetic y-glides generated by many combinations of front vowels are not phonemically distinctive, and transcription here follows the Gurmukhi spelling of e.g. ləṛkiã 'girls' rather than HU ləṛkīyã.

All these structural features of MSP, including the set of common diphthongs with ĕ as first element, are general Panjabi characteristics, although a remarkably large number of diphthongs and vowel sequences occurs in many western varieties (Varma 1936: 61–72, Bahri 1963: 65–98), e.g. Awankari o ala ola e 'he has come'. The point of greatest structural instability is ɔ, replaced by o or əo in Siraiki and neighbouring western dialects. This somewhat unstable nine-vowel system gives way to an eight-vowel system in the southernmost varieties of Siraiki, where ɛ is replaced by e or əe. Siraiki is also distinguished by a markedly open and low back quality of ə in accented position, resulting in some loss of distinction from a in the vicinity of aspiration.

TABLE 16.3: CONTRASTIVE NASALIZATION

a/ã	pàia	'O brother'	pàiã	'brothers' (obl.)
i/ĩ	lái	'removed' (f.)	láĩ	'remove!'
u/ũ	páu	he'll put'	páũ	'I'll put'
e/ẽ	kəre	'he does'	kərẽ	'you do' (2 sg.)
ɛ/ɛ̃	hɛ	'is'	hɛ̃	'you are' (2 sg.)
o/õ	pàio	'O brothers'	pàiõ	'from the brother'
ɔ/ɔ̃	sɔ	'hundred'	sɔ̃	'sleep'

TABLE 16.4: DIPHTHONGS

(a)	Ia (= ĕa)	gIa	'he went'
	Io (= ĕo)	pIo	'father'
	Iɔ (= ĕɔ)	llɔṇa	'to bring'
(b)	əi (= ĕi)	gəi	'she went'
	əe (= ĕe)	gəe	'they went'
(c)	əu	rə́u	'he'll live'
	əo	rə́o	'live!'
(d)	Ua	gUaca	'lost'

2.2. Consonants

The tonal realization of the historical voiced aspirates *gh, jh, ḍh, ḍh, bh* has reduced the number of MSP consonant phonemes (table 16.5). Lists of minimal pairs (cf. Dulai and Koul 1980: 53–62) are here provided (table 16.6) only for the important systematic contrast in medial and final positions between retroflex and (apico-)dental nasals, flaps and liquids, and the noteworthy further three-way contrast *ḍ/ṛ/ḷ*.

The three retroflex consonants *ṇ ṛ ḷ* do not occur initially, and the nasals *ṅ* and *ñ* occur only as allophones of *n* in clusters with velars and palatals. The separate status of *š* is well established by such pairs as *šal* 'shawl' versus *sal* 'year', or its use in native echo-doublets, e.g. *roṭi šoṭi* 'stuff to eat'. The retroflex *ṣ* occurs only allophonically in learned clusters with retroflexes, e.g. *kəṣṭ* 'trouble'. The phonemic status of other fricatives varies with familiarity with Urdu norms, and is highest in educated urban Pakistani speech, with the pairs *f/ph, z/j, χ/kh* and *γ/g* being systematically distinguished in

TABLE 16.5: PANJABI CONSONANT PHONEMES

	Glottal	Velar	Palatal	Retroflex	Dental	Labial
stops:						
vcls.		*k*	*c*	*ṭ*	*t*	*p*
vcls./asp.		*kh*	*ch*	*ṭh*	*th*	*ph*
vcd.		*g*	*j*	*ḍ*	*d*	*b*
nasals				*ṇ*	*n*	*m*
flaps				*ṛ*	*r*	
laterals				*ḷ*	*l*	
vcls.fric.		*(χ)*	*š*		*s*	*(f)*
vcd.fric.	*h*	*(γ)*			*(z)*	
semivwls		*y*				*v*

TABLE 16.6: PANJABI CONSONANT CONTRASTS

Retroflex versus dental:

ṇ/n	*uṇi*	'not full' (f.)	*uni*	'woollen'
	məṇ	'maund'	*mən*	'mind'
ṛ/r	*naṛi*	'vein'	*nari*	'woman'
	moṛ	'turn'	*mor*	'peacock'
ḷ/l	*boḷi*	'deaf' (f.)	*boli*	'language'
	jəḷdi	'burning' (f.)	*jəldi*	'speed'
	teḷ	'dew'	*tel*	'oil'

Retroflex contrasts:

ḍ/ṛ	*saḍi*	'our' (f.)	*saṛi*	'burnt' (f.)
ḍ/ḷ	*goḍa*	'knee'	*goḷa*	'sphere'
ṛ/ḷ	*kòṛi*	'mare'	*kòḷi*	'dissolved' (f.)
	paṛ	'span'	*paḷ*	'row'

approximately that order of frequency. HU *q* is absent even from the Urdu of educated Panjabi speakers.

The aspirate *h* is voiced, except in pronunciations affected by HU norms. It normally occurs in initial position only, except in a few common words like *aho* 'yes' or learned loans, having been replaced elsewhere by tonal realizations. The semivowel *y* is similarly restricted to initial position by the already noted disregard of glides between vowels. The other semivowel *v* may be initial and medial, but not final. The phonemic status of the semivowels is established by such sets as *yar* 'friend', *var* 'attack', besides *jar* 'adulterer', *bar* 'upland'.

The MSP consonant inventory (Sandhu 1986) is based upon that of the central Majhi dialect, shared by the dialects spoken to its immediate west. Eastern dialects (Jain 1934) are predictably closer to HU in such features as the neutralization of the contrasts *ṇ/n* and *ḷ/l* in favour of a dental (alveolar) *n* and *l* in all positions, the retention of intervocalic *-h-*, and the replacement of initial *v-* by *b-*, e.g. *bí* 'twenty' (cf. HU *bis* versus MSP *ví*).

The number of consonant phonemes is greater in varieties of Hindko in the northwest, e.g. Kahuni (Varma 1936: 72–87) and Awankari (Bahri 1963: 101–54), since these retain voiced aspirates in at least some positions, besides having quite full sets of contrastive retroflex phonemes, and some phonemically contrastive fricatives, as is consistent with their location on the Indo-Iranian linguistic frontier.

All these features help account for the very large consonantal inventory which may be distinguished for Siraiki (table 16.7). Here the number of phonemes is increased by phonemically contrastive implosives (table 16.8), a full set of nasal phonemes (with *ñ* better established than *ṅ*) and contrastive aspirate sonants (with *lh* and *ṛh* the best established). The four Siraiki implosives are similar to the better known Sindhi set in their origins and their phonetics (Bahl 1936). All except the bilabial *ɓ* are distinguished by markedly more forward articulation than their explosive counterparts. There is no

TABLE 16.7: SIRAIKI CONSONANT PHONEMES

	Glottal	Velar	Palatal	Retroflex	Dental	Labial
stops:						
vcls.		*k*	*c*	*ṭ*	*t*	*p*
vcls./asp.		*kh*	*ch*	*ṭh*	*th*	*ph*
vcd.		*g*	*j*	*ḍ*	*d*	*b*
vcd./asp.		*gh*	*jh*	*ḍh*	*dh*	*bh*
implosives		*ɠ*	*ʄ*	*ɗ*		*ɓ*
nasals		*ṅ*	*ñ*	*ṇ*	*n*	*m*
asp.				*ṇh*	*nh*	*mh*
flaps				*ṛ*	*r*	
asp.				*ṛh*	*rh*	
lateral					*l*	
asp.					*lh*	
vcls.fric.		*χ*	*š*		*s*	*f*
vcd.fric.	*h*	*γ*			*z*	
semivwls			*y*			*v*
asp.						*vh*

TABLE 16.8: SIRAIKI CONSONANT CONTRASTS

Voiced explosives versus implosives:

g/ɠ	gol	'round'	ɠol	'search'
j/ʄ	jala	'niche'	ʄala	'cobweb'
ḍ/ɗ	ḍakṭər	'doctor'	ɗak	'mail'
d/ɗ	dər	'door'	ɗər	'fear'
b/ɓ	bəs	'bus'	ɓəs	'enough'

Nasals:

ṅ/n	cəṅa	'good'	cəna	'gram'
ñ/ṇ	thəñ	'mother's milk'	thəṇ	'udder'
ñ/n	vəñ	'go'	vən	'sort'

Sonants and aspirates:

m/mh	nImmi	'impregnated' (f.)	nImmhi	'I'm not'
r/rh	keri	'ashes'	kerhi	'who?' (f.)
l/lh	sal	'year'	salh	'reed hut'
v/vh	nIvẽ	'bow!'	nIvhẽ	'you're not'
ṛ/ṛh	rəṛ	'roar'	rəṛh	'crop'

structural room for a dental implosive, given the phonetic character of ʄ as an implosive palatalized d, and the notably lesser retroflexion of ɗ as compared with ḍ.

2.3. Word-accent and syllables

Many of the differences in the syllabic structure of words between most varieties of Panjabi and HU (Sharma 1971) are to be directly related to the highly characteristic Panjabi preservation of MIA doubled consonants in accented syllables, e.g. 'əgge 'before', 'Iṭṭā 'bricks', 'bUḍḍa 'old', where HU aligns with most eastern and southern NIA languages in having reduced the geminate to a single consonant usually with compensatory lengthening of the preceding vowel, as in the corresponding age, īṭẽ, buṛha. MSP permits all consonants other than r and the positionally restricted ṇ r ḷ h y v to occur as medial geminates after centralized vowels in accented syllables and before another vowel in the same word. Lengthened articulation marks the doubling of sonants, while delayed release marks the doubling of stops, including the structurally analogous cluster of voiceless unaspirate plus aspirate, e.g. 'cUnni 'scarf', 'mIṭṭi 'clay', 'kəttha 'catechu', versus 'cUni 'picked' (f.), 'mIṭi 'erased', 'kətha 'story'.

The prominence of the accented syllable within a word is consequently greater in Panjabi than in HU, and this is further reinforced by the coincidence of the tones with the accent. In rural speech, it is further marked phonetically by the historically unjustified doubling of consonants after peripheral vowels, e.g. pəñ'jabbi 'Panjabi', 'roṭṭi 'bread', and in all styles of speech by neutralizations and reductions of pre-tonic syllables, e.g. kə'tab 'book', s'maj 'society' versus HU kItab, səmaj.

In spite of such reductions, there is such a strong contrary tendency to break initial clusters in loans, e.g. pə'rem 'love', sə'kul 'school' (HU prem, Iskul) that all initial consonant clusters are of doubtful status. Final clusters are restricted to five types of two-consonant combinations (Gill and Gleason 1963: 13–14) with sonant or sibilant as first member, e.g. *sə'kInṭ* 'second', *pUḷs* 'police', *gərm* 'hot', *khərg* 'sword', *məst* 'intoxicated'.

Final geminates are phonetically realized only in pause or when strongly emphasized, otherwise being regularly simplified as e.g. *həth* 'hand' versus pl.obl. *hətthã*. Medial geminates are similarly often simplified by morphophonemic rules e.g. *pətthər* 'stone' but pl.obl. *pəthrã*, *ṭUṭṭa* 'broken' but *ṭUṭda* 'breaking'. Of the many possible types of medial cluster, special mention need only be made of those beginning with a homorganic nasal. These must follow a centralized vowel, but are otherwise not subject to the same positional restrictions as geminates, e.g. *əṅ'gur* 'grapes', *'pIñjra* 'cage', *ənt* 'end'. The rule that homorganic nasal clusters must follow a centralized vowel is complementary to the already stated phonemic restriction of nasalization to peripheral vowels. Phonetic realities are less neat, since there may be some regressive nasalization of pre-nasal vowels and some detectable homorganic nasal glide after nasalization. Non-phonemic nasalization is phonetically far more pronounced in Panjabi than in HU, both progressively and regressively in the vicinity of *n* e.g. *'paṇi/'pãṇĩ* 'water', progressively after *n* and *m*, e.g. *'sona/'sonã* 'gold', *'kəmmi/'kammĩ* 'labourer', and regressively through vowel sequences and across *-v-* before phonemic nasalization e.g. *'kUṛiã/kUṛĩã* 'girls', *ávãga/ãvãga* 'I shall come'.

Most words consist of one, two or three syllables. All monosyllables other than a very small class of clitics carry inherent word-accent. The position of the accent in polysyllables is largely predictable, normally occurring on the first syllable. Second syllable accent regularly occurs when the first syllable is weak, with a centralized vowel, and the second is strong, with a peripheral vowel plus consonant or a centralized vowel plus cluster, e.g. *cU'taḷi* 'forty-four', *cUr'vəñja* 'fifty-four' versus *'cədã* 'fourteen'. Attempts to establish a phonemic status for word-accent on the limited basis of causatives, e.g. *bə'ca* 'save' versus *'bəcca* 'child', must be regarded as doubtful.

Most of these MSP structural rules apply across the area. Phonetic realizations naturally differ, e.g. in the much less marked realization of geminates in Siraiki (Shackle 1976: 27). Particular mention need here be made only of the special status in Siraiki of preserved and developed clusters of dental + *r*, which occur freely in both initial and final positions, e.g. *'trUṭṭən* 'to break', *pUtr* 'son', *cəndr* 'moon' (versus MSP *'ṭUṭna*, *'pUttər*, *cənd*).

2.4. Aspiration and tone

The reduction of historical voiced aspiration to tones is generally taken to be single most distinctive feature of Panjabi within Indo-Aryan. First systematically described for Wazirabadi Bailey (Bailey 1904, Cummings and Bailey 1912, Bailey 1914), the tones receive regular attention in all subsequent general accounts of MSP, and have been the subject of several special studies (Bahl 1957, Haudricourt 1971, Sandhu 1968a, Bhatia 1975, Wells and Roach 1980). The word-accent is often described as a mid-tone, contrasting on an equal structural basis with the aspirate-derived high and low tones. But the latter occur only in accented position, and each accounts for no more than about 10% of all words. It therefore seems preferable to regard tone as an additional distinctive feature structurally similar to the contrastive nasalization of peripheral vowels, and to distinguish minimal sets accordingly (table 16.9). The tones are principally distinguished by pitch-contour, with the return to normal level from the pitch of the initial onset, whether downwards in the high-falling tone or upwards in the low-rising tone, being effected in the tone-tail which normally occurs in following syllable, or

TABLE 16.9: PANJABI TONAL CONTRASTS

Unmarked accent		Accent + high tone		Accent + low tone	
ca	'fervour'	cá	'tea'	cà	'peep'
'koṛa	'whip'	kóṛa	'leper'	kòṛa	'horse'

within a monosyllable in pause position. The low tone, additionally distinguished by some initial glottal closure and creakiness of articulation, is a particularly obvious feature of MSP pronunciation.

The relation between historical aspiration, word-accent and tone is most easily understood from schematic illustration (table 16.10). In MSP, low tone results from an historical aspirate before the accented vowel, as in *hàr* (also *har* without tone), *kàṇi*, *nàve, pəṛài, vədài.* Word-initial historical voiced aspirates also become voiceless, as in *tì* 'daughter', cf. MSP *kə̀r* 'house', *kòṛa* 'horse' versus HU *ghər, ghoṛa.* High tone normally results from an historical aspirate after the accented vowel, as in *rái, pə́ṛIa,* and in *və́d* where there is no loss of voicing. Historical aspiration does not account for quite all cases of high tone, which also occurs in exceptional items like *bə́ld* 'ox' and regularly in the imperative and future tenses of verbal stems without tone, e.g. *jáo* 'go!', *jávega* 'he will go', versus *jaṇa* 'to go'.

To the west, the two-tone MSP pattern extends beyond Wazirabadi to include Pothohari. The same pattern occurs in all eastern varieties (Jain 1934, Sandhu 1968b, Joshi 1973), with a significant set of isoglosses running through the Ambala area marking the boundary between the Panjabi tonal area and Hariyanvi Hindi to the southeast (Jain 1929, Varma 1965). The same two-tone pattern extends northwards beyond the plains to cover Dogri (Bahri 1969) and Kangri (Sharma 1974b), before giving way in the east to the rather different Himachali pattern (Hendriksen 1985: 32–8).

In the Dardic northwest, tonal systems also characterize the phonology of e.g. Kohistani (Baart 1999) and Shina (Bailey 1924). Within the neighbouring area of

TABLE 16.10: ASPIRATION AND TONE

	Siraiki		Hindko	Peshawar	MSP
(a) Historical *h*:					
h-	har	'necklace'	har	hʿár, ʿár	har, hàr
-ʾh-	kə'haṇi	'story'	kə'haṇi	kʿáṇi	kàṇi
-h	'rahi	'traveller'	rái	rái	rái
(b) Historical voiced aspirate sonants:					
nh-	nhave	'bathes'	nhave	nʿáve	nàve
-ṛh-	pə'ṛhai	'education'	pə'ṛhai	pəṛʿái	pəṛài
-ṛh	pəṛhIa	'read'	pə́ṛhIa	pə́ṛIa	pə́ṛIa
(c) Historical voiced aspirate plosives:					
dh-	dhi	'daughter'	dhi	tʿí	tì
-ḍh-	və'ḍhai	'congratulations'	və'ḍhai	vəḍʿái	vədài
-dh	vədh	'more'	və́d	və́d	və́d

NWFP and northwestern Panjabi, the high tone is also found in the Hindko dialects of Kahuni (Varma 1936), Awankari (Bahri 1963) and Kohati (Shackle 1980: 487–8). But this Hindko pattern (table 16.10) has no low tone and regularly preserves preceding voiced aspirates. Only the Hindko of Peshawar (Shackle 1980: 498–9) unusually combines the glottal constriction and devoicing of the MSP low tone with the Hindko high tone.

The need for caution in regarding the MSP tones as characteristic of the Panjabi area as a whole is further underlined by the complete absence of tone in Siraiki, where historical aspiration may be lost but is more frequently subject to quite complex patterns of phonetic realization (Shackle 1976: 30–6). These may involve both alterations of vowel-quality and transfers of aspiration across syllable-boundaries. The historical contrast of length between AG *rah-* 'live' and *cāh-* 'want', which is preserved with alterations of quality in MSP *rḗda* 'living', *cõ̃da* 'wanting', is thus neutralized in Siraiki *rə̃hda*, *cə̃hda*, in free variation with *rãdha*, *cãdha*.

3. SCRIPTS

Several different scripts have always been used in the culturally and religiously diverse Panjabi area. One of the factors distinguishing the region from the vast Hindi belt is the scant use of the Devanagari script to write any variety of Panjabi. The only significant exception has been the employment of Devanagari in post-1947 Jammu by the Hindu protagonists of Dogri as a distinctive literary medium. Much more significant local use continues to be made of the various local scripts whose principal member is Gurmukhi, and of the Persian script.

3.1. Local scripts

The indigenous regional scripts form a typologically distinct group (Grierson 1904). They are closer to Brahmi norms than to Devanagari and other modern North Indian scripts in their general avoidance of conjuncts and their minimal graphic distinction of the preserved MIA geminates which are so distinctive of Panjabi. These features appear in their simplest form in the commercial shorthands, variously known as Mahajani, Kirakki (*kIṛəkki* 'banya writing') or Lande (*ləṇḍe* 'docked letters'), which were once widespread in different regional forms (illustrated in Leitner 1883) and are still not entirely obsolete in India. These scripts are alphabetical on the restricted Semitic model of Ugaritic cuneiform, with three vowel-letters to distinguish initial *A, I, U* but without post-consonantal signs to distinguish vowels in other positions.

The Lande alphabets possess full sets of consonants, even separate letters to write the common western clusters *tr* and *dr*. But the difficulties of reading unfamiliar material written in them are formidable. During the nineteenth century, some efforts were made in the hill states to promote improved versions with vowel signs (illustrated in Grierson 1916: 637–42, 767–801), but these are all obsolete.

3.2. Gurmukhi script

The only member of the northwestern script group to have secured full modern currency is Gurmukhi (Gill 1996). Its close association with the Sikhs is indicated by its name, i.e. 'script of those guided by the Guru (*gUrmUkh*)'. It has long been recognized that the pious attribution of its invention to the second Sikh Guru Angad (d. 1552) is suspect, but its earlier history (Singh 1972) and its relationship to Lande have yet to be fully determined. Attested from the sixteenth century as the normal script of the Sikh scriptures and continuing to be the preferred script of the later Sikh literature produced in Braj Bhasha from the later seventeenth century, Gurmukhi was further standardized during the nineteenth century as the script of modern standard Panjabi, and is now recognized in India as the sole official script for Panjabi. Gurmukhi is quite similar in overall appearance to Devanagari, indeed confusingly so in the values assigned to the graphs *s, t`, ph, m* which are visually identical with Devanagari *m, p, ḍh, bh*, but it is rather different in several aspects of fundamental organization.

The number of letters (*əkkhər*) in the Gurmukhi alphabet (table 16.11) accounts for its common name *pēti* 'thirty-five'. They are arranged in seven sets of five letters each. The close relationship of Gurmukhi to Lande is apparent both from the order of letters and their distinctive names. As in Lande, the first set begins with the three vowel-letters called *uṛa, eṛa, iṛi*, followed by the single sibilant *səssa* and the aspirate *haha*. Then come the usual five sets, beginning with *kəkka, khəkkha, gəgga*, etc. (the letter *ṭ* is called *ṭēka*, avoiding the near homophony with *ṭəṭṭi* 'latrine'). The seventh set embraces the familiar Indic quartet *yəya, rara, ləlla, vəvva* plus the distinctive Gurmukhi graph for *ṛ* called *ṛaṛa*.

The nineteenth-century standardization of the script added five dotted letters, permitting the previously unmarked distinction of *š* from *s*, and the Devanagari-style distinction of the less well established loan-phonemes *χ, γ, z, f*. The desire to keep these additional letters as another set of five may help account for the absence of diacritics to mark the Urdu *q* which is absent from the Panjabi phonemic inventory, or to distinguish the retroflex *ḷ*, although this is phonemically distinct from dental *l* in many central dialects (table 16.6).

Although sporadically used for the writing of *tatsama* words in the *Ādi Granth* and later Sikh literature, conjunct consonants are not a natural or a common feature of

TABLE 16.11: GURMUKHI LETTERS

The alphabet:

ੳ	(U)	ਅ	ə	ੲ	(I)	ਸ	s	ਹ	h-, `, ´
ਕ	k	ਖ	kh	ਗ	g	ਕ਼	k`-, -g`, -´g	ਙ	ṅ
ਚ	c	ਛ	ch	ਜ	j	ਜ਼	c`-, -j`, -´j	ਞ	ñ
ਟ	ṭ	ਠ	ṭh	ਡ	ḍ	ਡ਼	ṭ`-, -ḍ`, -´ḍ	ਣ	ṇ
ਤ	t	ਥ	th	ਦ	d	ਧ	t`-, -d`, -´d	ਨ	n
ਪ	p	ਫ	ph	ਬ	b	ਭ	p`-, -b`, -´b	ਮ	m
ਯ	y	ਰ	r	ਲ	l, ḷ	ਵ	v	ੜ	ṛ

Dotted letters:

ਸ਼	š	ਖ਼	χ	ਗ਼	γ	ਜ਼	z	ਫ਼	f

Subscripts:

੍ਨ	n`, -´n	੍ਮ	m`, -´m	੍ਰ	r`, -´r	੍ਲ	l`, -´l	੍ਰ	r`, -´r
੍ਕਰ	kr	੍ਤਰ	tr	੍ਦਰ	dr	੍ਪਰ	pr		
੍ਸਵ	sv								

Gurmukhi. Here, as in the lack of a zero-vowel sign corresponding to the Devanagari *vIram*, Gurmukhi is notably different from all other modern North Indian scripts. Instead, modern Gurmukhi orthography has standardized the use of subscript letters already sporadically present in AG spellings (Shackle 1995: xxii–iii). The commonest subscript is *haha*, used with the sonants *n*, *m*, *r*, *l*, *ṛ* to indicate tonal realizations of historical voiced aspiration, just like the five letters corresponding in alphabetic position to the Devanagari *gh*, *jh*, *ḍh*, *dh*, *bh* (here transliterated as such only in writing AG words), whose Gurmukhi names are *kə̀gga*, *cə̀jja*, *ṭə̀ḍḍa*, *tə̀dda*, *pə̀bba*. The quite common subscript *rara* is used like the Devanagari subscript *-r-*, but there is no equivalent to *reph*. The subscript *vəvva* is largely confined to writing *sv-* in *tatsama* words.

Like the letters of the alphabet, the vowel signs (*ləga matrã*) have distinctive names, viz. *mUkta* (-ə, -ø), *kənna* (-a), *sIàri* (-I), *bIàri* (-i), *ɔ̃kər* (-U), *dUlɛ̃kṛe* (-u), *lã* (-e), *dUlaiã* (-ɛ), *hoṛa* (-o), *kənɔṛa* (-ɔ). These signs (table 16.12) are combined with the three vowel-letters to indicate independent or initial vowels. The unusual alphabetic order of these independent vowels is dictated by the primacy of the first vowel-letter *uṛa*, which is used to write the sacred syllable *õ* and the corresponding Sikh formula *Ik oə̃kar*. It is replaced by the usual order of other South Asian scripts when the vowel-signs are written with consonants.

The earliest records of the Gurmukhi script (illustrated in Mann 1996: 192–207) indicate some divergence from modern norms of vowel-spelling, e.g. in the frequent omission of *kənna* to denote AG *-ā* as well as the preference for digraphs in AG *-aï* and

TABLE 16.12: OTHER GURMUKHI SIGNS

Independent vowels:

ઉ	U	ઉ	u	ઓ	o				
ਅ	ə	ਅ'	a	ਐ	ɛ	ਔ	ɔ		
ਇ	I	ਈ	i	ਏ	e				

Consonants with vowel-signs:

ਸ	sə	ਸ'	sa	ਸਿ	sI	ਸੀ	si	ਸੁ	sU
ਸੁ	su	ਸੇ	se	ਸੈ	sɛ	ਸੋ	so	ਸੌ	sɔ

Nasal signs:

ਅਂ	ə̃	ਅਂi	ã	ਇਂ	Ĩ	ਈਂ	ĩ	ਉਂ	Ũ	ਊਂ	ũ
ਸਂ	sə̃	ਸਂi	sã	ਸਿਂ	sĨ	ਸੀਂ	sĩ	ਸੁਂ	sŨ	ਸੂਂ	sũ

Geminates:

ਅੱਧ	ə́ddək	ਸੱਸ'	səssa	ਹੱਥੀ	hə́tthĩ	ਤਿੰਨ	tInn	ਲੰਮ	ləmme

Numerals:

੧	੨	੩	੪	੫	੬	੭	੮	੯	੦
1	2	3	4	5	6	7	8	9	0

(especially) AG *-aü* over the simple signs *-ɛ*, *-ɔ*. More significantly, many features of AG orthography continue to be reflected in the systematic modern Gurmukhi preference for spellings with *-I-*, *-i-* where Devanagari has *-y-*, *-Iy-*, thus MSP *pIar* 'love', *kUttiã* 'bitches' (versus Hindi *pyar*, *kUttIyã*). Other apparent irregularities in modern Gurmukhi usage (Gill and Gleason 1969: 53–6) are similarly attributable to the enduring influence of AG norms.

AG usage (Shackle 1995: xxiii–iv) is typical of medieval North Indian spellings in very frequently omitting any indication of vowel nasalization. Modern Gurmukhi makes systematic use of two nasal signs, the rounded *ṭIppi* and the superscript dot *bIndi*. The distinction between these two Gurmukhi signs does not quite coincide with that between Devanagari *ǝnUsvar* and *cǝndrǝbIndU*, but is determined graphically, by the nature of the vowel to be marked. Thus the sign *ṭIppi* is reserved for use with *ǝ* and *I* in all positions, while *bIndi* is used with all other vowels, except in the particular case of *U* and *u*. Here the shape of the bearer *uṛa* with its extension above the line determines the exclusive use of *bIndi* with independent *U-* and *u-*, while *ṭIppi* is used with both the subscripts *-U* and *-u*. Nasal signs with the centralized vowels *ǝ*, *I*, *U* denote a nasal consonant of the same class as the following consonant in a nasal cluster, while nasal signs with other vowels indicate nasalization.

Doubled consonants are not indicated in AG orthography, except for the special case of the doubled nasals *-nn-*, *-mm-*, written with *ṭIppi* with following *-n-* or *-m-*. This convention continues in modern Gurmukhi spelling. Another sign was added to the script in the early nineteenth century to indicate the very numerous doublings of other consonants which are so prominent a feature of the conservative historical phonology of Panjabi. Apparently first attested in the Christian missionary literature, and perhaps based on the example of the Urdu *tǝšdid*, this is the open semi-circle called *ǝddǝk*. It is written above the line of writing just before the doubled letter, including doubled voiceless aspirates as e.g. *ǝddǝk* before *th* to indicate *-tth-*. Although it has long been in general use, the writing of *ǝddǝk* is still not fully standardized. It is not always written where required to indicate consonant doubling, but is also sometimes written to indicate not a geminate but a second-syllable accent as in e.g. *bǝ'ca*. Neither *ǝddǝk* nor the nasal signs affect the alphabetical arrangement of most dictionaries, which is determined exclusively by the basic consonants (irrespective of diacritics) and the vowel-signs.

Other Gurmukhi signs include a distinctive set of numerals, although these are increasingly displaced by the international Arabic set, and the use of the vertical stroke (*dǝṇḍi*) rather than the full stop alongside the usual English punctuation marks. Most features of the modern orthography as compared with the AG system, including the sometimes complex match of script with pronunciation, are illustrated in the following sample.

ਆਪੇ ਕਰੇ ਕਰਾਏ ਕਰਤਾ, ਕਿਸ ਨੋ ਆਖਿ ਸੁਣਾਈਐ ।
ਦੁਖ ਸੁਖ ਤੇਰੈ ਭਾਣੈ ਹੋਵੈ, ਕਿਸਥੈ ਜਾਇ ਰੁਆਈਐ ।
ਹੁਕਮੀ ਹੁਕਮਿ ਚਲਾਏ ਵਿਗਾਸੈ, ਨਾਨਕ ਲਿਖਿਆ ਪਾਈਐ ।੭।੨।

ਕਿਤਨਾ ਭਿਆਨਕ ਦ੍ਰਿਸ਼ ਹੈ ! ... ਜਿਨ੍ਹਾਂ ਪੰਜਾਬੀਆਂ ਨੇ ਸੰਨ ੧੯੪੭ ਦੀ ਦੇਸ-ਵੰਡ ਵੇਲੇ ਪੰਜਾਬ ਦੇ ਪਿੰਡਾਂ ਸ਼ਹਿਰਾਂ ਵਿਚ ਹੋਏ ਅੱਤਿਆਚਾਰ ਅੱਖੀਂ ਵੇਖੇ ਸਨ, ਇਹਨਾਂ ਅਸਹਿਪਦੀਆਂ ਵਿਚ ਬਿਆਨ ਕੀਤੀ ਦਰਦ-ਭਰੀ ਕਹਾਣੀ ਦੀ ਸਹੀ ਸੂਝ ਉਹਨਾਂ ਨੂੰ ਹੀ ਪੈ ਸਕਦੀ ਹੈ । ਮਾਪਿਆਂ ਨੇ ਜਿਗਰ ਦੇ ਟੋਟੇ ਪਿਆਰੇ ਬੱਚੇ ਨਹੀਂ ਸਨ ਸੰਭਾਲੇ, ਗੱਭਰੂ ਵੀਰ ਜੁਆਨ ਭੈਣਾਂ ਦੀ ਇੱਜ਼ਤ ਨਹੀਂ ਸਨ ਬਚਾ ਸਕੇ ।

(a) AG verses and modern prose in transliteration:

> *āpe kare karāe karatā, kisa no ākhi suṇāīai.*
> *dukhu sukhu tere bhāṇai hovai, kisathai jāi rūāīai.*
> *hukamī hukami calāe vigasai, nānaka likhiā pāīai. 7.12.*

kitnā bhiānak driśś hai! . . . jinhāṁ pañjābīāṁ ne sann 1947 dī des-vaṇḍ vele pañjāb de
piṇḍāṁ šahirāṁ vic hoe attiācār akkhīṁ vekhe san, ihnāṁ aśṭapadīāṁ vic biān kītī
dard-bharī kahāṇī dī sahī sūjh uhnāṁ nūṁ hī pai sakdī hai. māpiāṁ ne jigar de ṭoṭe
piāre bacce nahīṁ san sambhāle, gabbhrū vīr juān bhaiṇāṁ dī izzat nahīṁ san bac˘ā
sake.

(b) the prose in transcription:

> *kItna plànək d(ə)'rIš hɛ! . . . jĩnā pəñjabiã ne sən 1947 di des-vəṇḍ veḷe pəñjab de pIṇḍã*
> *śérã vIc hoe əttlacar əkkhĩ vekhe sən, énã əśṭəpədiã vIc bIan kiti dərd-pəri kàṇi di səi súj*
> *ónā nũ i pɛ səkdi hɛ. maplã ne jIgər de ṭoṭe plare bəcce nə̃ĩ sən səmbàḷe, gə́bru vir jUan*
> *pèṇã di Izzət nə̃ĩ sən bə'ca səke.*

3.3. Persian script

The religious associations of the Gurmukhi script have not commended its use to
Muslims, whose use of the Persian script for writing Panjabi is well attested from the
seventeenth century. The orthography of older manuscripts is close to Persian norms.
The influence of Urdu rules increases during the nineteenth century in such features as
the regular distinction of the three retroflex letters *ṭ*, *ḍ*, *ṛ* with special diacritics, and the
marking of word-final nasalization by use of the undotted *nun*.

Only the Perso-Urdu script is used to write Panjabi in Pakistan. Some minor
modifications have been proposed, notably the distinction of the retroflex *ṇ*, with either a
small *toe* or an additional dot written vertically above the intrinsic dot of the *nun*. The
heavy load of *nun* to indicate the two phonemes *n* and *ṇ* plus both phonemic and non-
phonemic nasalization is certainly one of the most confusing features of Persian-script
Panjabi orthography. But neither this proposal nor others for specially modified forms of
the letter *he* to indicate the tones have achieved anything like universal acceptance.

TABLE 16.13: SIRAIKI DIACRITICS

	Urdu	Urdu with diacritics				Sindhi
ɓ	ب	ـ ب	ب °	ب ؚ	ب ⋮	ب
ʄ	ج	ج	ج	ج		ج
ɗ	ڈ		ڌ	ڎ	ڌ	ڎ
ɠ	گ	گ	گ	گ	گ	گ
ñ	ڃ		ڃ	ڃ	ڃ	ج
ṅ	نگ		نگ	نگ	نگ	گ
ṇ	ن		نڙ	ڻ		ٹ

Further systematic modifications to the Persian script have been introduced in recent decades for writing Siraiki. These which notably include the distinction of the four implosives as well as the nasals *ṅ*, *ñ*, *ṇ* (table 16.13). The prior existence of separate graphs for all these sounds in the Sindhi alphabet has certainly been a factor encouraging the development of this conscious graphic distinction of Siraiki from Panjabi spellings.

4. MORPHOLOGY

MSP morphology is similar in organization to HU. The main formal distinction is between nouns, including adjectives, pronouns and other word-classes, and verbs. Inflections of both nouns and verbs are marked by the addition or alternation of word-final morphemes. MSP is somewhat more complex in detail than the highly regularized norms of HU. Differences between MSP and Siraiki morphology are often most easily understood by reference to the older language of the AG, which differs significantly from both in marking many morphological distinctions with final short vowels which have subsequently been lost. Maximum use is here made of outline summaries and paradigms in figures, leaving the reader to consult the sources noted for details.

4.1. Nouns

Nouns (Gill and Gleason 1969: 4–11, Shackle 1976: 42–9, 1983a: 88–95) inflect for number and for case. There are two numbers, singular and plural, and five cases, including besides the familiar direct, oblique and vocative, also an ablative and a locative/instrumental. The vocative is logically restricted to the names of animates. The ablative occurs only in the singular, in free variation with oblique case plus ablative postposition. The locative/instrumental, although fully productive in AG, is now confined to set adverbial expressions.

Different patterns of inflection characterize the MSP declensions, with assignment being determined by grammatical gender. Names of males and most nouns with singular direct in unaccented *-a* are masculine, while names of females and most nouns in unaccented *-i* are feminine. The gender of other nouns is historically determined, with only a few differences from HU, whether in core IA vocabulary, e.g. MSP *nək* m. 'nose', or in Persian loans, e.g. *fīkər*, m. 'worry', *mez* m. 'table', *mərəz* f. 'disease'.

There are two masculine declensions, as in HU. The MSP unextended declension is considerably simplified by the loss of final short vowels from the AG paradigm (table 16.14). It includes all masculines ending in a consonant, e.g. *kər* (AG *gharu*) 'house', or vowels other than unaccented *-a*, e.g. *nã* 'name', *pài* 'brother', pl.obl. *navã*, *pàiã*. The extended AG sg.obl. *-ai* accounts for the regular marking of this case as *ghare*, *kəre* in most northern varieties, including Hindko, Dogri and Kangri. Siraiki follows MSP, apart from having sg.abl. in all declensions with *-ū* versus MSP *-õ*, and southern Siraiki dialects also have pl.obl. *-ẽ* throughout for the usual Panjabi *-ã*. An interesting small subclass of Siraiki disyllables inflects through stem alternation as the result of regressive vowel-harmony, e.g. *kUkkUṛ* 'cock', sg.obl., pl.dir. *kUkkəṛ* (AG *kukkaṛu*, *kukkaṛa*).

All masculines ending in unaccented *-a* (< OIA *-aka-*) are assigned to the extended declension (table 16.15), including nouns of the type *raja* 'king', pl. *raje*. Here MSP and the identical Siraiki declension show fewer differences from the AG paradigm. The case-morphemes, very similar to those of the unextended declension, are added to the

TABLE 16.14: UNEXTENDED MASCULINE DECLENSION

	AG		MSP	
sg.dir.	-u	gharu	-ø	kə̀r
sg.obl.	-a	ghara	-ø	kə̀r
	-ai	gharai		
sg.voc.	-ā	gharā	-a	kə̀ra
sg.abl.	-aṁhu	gharaṁhu	-õ	kə̀rõ
sg.loc./instr.	-i	ghari		
	-e	ghare	-e	kə̀re
pl.dir.	-a	ghara	-ø	kə̀r
pl.obl.	-āṁ	gharāṁ	-ã	kə̀rã
pl.voc.	-aho	gharaho	-o	kə̀ro
pl.loc./instr.	-īṁ	gharīṁ	-ĩ	kə̀rĩ

TABLE 16.15: EXTENDED MASCULINE DECLENSION

	AG		MSP	
sg.dir.	-ā	ghoṛā	-a	kòṛa
sg.obl.	-e	ghoṛe	-e	kòṛe
sg.voc.	-iā	ghoṛiā	-Ia	kòṛIa
sg.abl.	-iaṁhu	ghoṛiaṁhu	-Iõ	kòṛIõ
sg.loc./instr.	-ai	ghoṛai	(-e	kòṛe)
pl.dir.	-e	ghoṛe	-e	kòṛe
pl.obl.	-iāṁ	ghoṛiāṁ	-Iã	kòṛIã
pl.voc.	-iho	ghoṛiho	-Io	kòṛIo
pl.loc./instr.	-īṁ	ghoṛīṁ		

obl. base -e-, which is shortened to -I- (phonetic -ĕ-, cf. table 16.4) before back vowels, and is lost before front vowels.

Unlike HU, MSP has only one feminine declension, with pl. -ã. There is no distinction between dir. and obl. in either number, and sg.voc. -e contrasts with the corresponding m. -a. This declension includes both feminines ending in a consonant corresponding to the main AG unextended declension, exemplified by gəll (AG galla) 'thing' (table 16.16) and those in -i corresponding to the AG extended declension, exemplified by səkhi (AG sakhī) 'girlfriend' (table 16.17.). Northern varieties mark the sg.obl. of unextended feminines with -a or -e, e.g. gəlla, gəlle.

Siraiki shares this MSP feminine declension, with sg.abl. -ŭ, sg.voc. -a, southern pl.obl. -ẽ. But it also continues to distinguish the separate AG feminine -i declension which is obsolete in MSP, thus Siraiki ratĩ 'night', pl. ratĩ (AG rāti, rātīṁ), versus MSP rat, ratã. Disyllabic feminines corresponding to the masculine subclass with stem alternants are assigned to this Siraiki declension, e.g. kUkkIṛ 'hen', pl. kUkṛĩ (AG kukkaṛi, kukkaṛīṁ). The poorly represented AG class of feminines in -u results in a vestigial third feminine declension in Siraiki, e.g. həñj 'tear', pl. həñjŭ.

TABLE 16.16: UNEXTENDED FEMININE DECLENSION

	AG		MSP	
sg.dir./obl.	-a	galla	-ø	gəll
sg.voc.	-e	(galle)	-e	(gəlle)
sg.abl.	-aṁhu	gallaṁhu	-õ	gəllõ
sg.loc./instr.	-i	galli	-e	galle
	-e	(gəlle)		
pl.dir/obl.	-āṁ	gallāṁ	-ã	gəllã
pl.voc.	-aho	(gallaho)	-o	(gəllo)
pl.loc./instr.	-īṁ	gallīṁ	-ĩ	gəllĩ

TABLE 16.17: EXTENDED FEMININE DECLENSION

	AG		MSP	
sg.(all cases)	-ī	sakhī	-i	səkhi
sg.voc.	-īe	sakhīe	-ie	səkhie
pl.dir/obl.	-īāṁ	sakhīāṁ	-iã	səkhiã
pl.voc.	-īho	sakhīho	-io	səkhio
pl.loc./instr.	-ūīṁ	sakhīīṁ		

4.2. Adjectives and numerals

As in most NIA languages, the word-class of adjectives (Gill and Gleason 1969: 11–16, Shackle 1976: 49–55) overlaps quite closely with that of nouns proper. When adjectives are used as modifiers, only extended adjectives with m.sg.dir. -a inflect. This MSP adjectival declension (table 16.18) is similar in Siraiki. It is simpler than the corresponding declensions of extended masculine and feminine nouns in -a and feminines in -i, although additional inflections are often marked in colloquial speech, e.g. f.sg.voc. *ni sohṇie kUṛie* 'hey pretty girl!'

TABLE 16.18: ADJECTIVAL DECLENSION

	Masculine		Feminine	
sg.dir.	-a	cəṅga	-i	cəṅgi
sg.obl.	-e	cəṅge	-i	cəṅgi
pl.dir.	-e	cəṅge	-iã	cəṅgiã
pl.obl.	-e	cəṅge	-iã	cəṅgiã
	-Iã	cəṅgIã		

Numerals are a special subclass of adjectives. MSP cardinals (table 16.19) can inflect to distinguish obl. -ã. The lower numerals have the corresponding emphatics *dovẽ* 'both', *tInne* 'all three', *care* 'all four'. The lower ordinals *péla* 'first', *duja* 'second', *tija* 'third', *cɔtha* 'fourth' inflect as adjectives in -a, while the higher ordinals in -vã (*pəñjvã*

TABLE 16.19: CARDINAL NUMERALS 1–100

1	Ik	26	chəbbi	51	Ikvəñja	76	chlə̀ttər
2	do	27	sətai	52	bəvəñja	77	sətə̀ttər
3	tIn	28	əthai	53	tərvəñja	78	əthə̀ttər
4	car	29	Unətti	54	cUrvəñja	79	Unasi
5	pəñj	30	tí	55	pəcvəñja	80	əssi
6	che	31	Ikətti	56	chlvəñja	81	Ikasi
7	sətt	32	bətti	57	sətvəñja	82	blasi
8	əṭṭh	33	tēti	58	əthvəñja	83	tlrasi
9	nɔ̃	34	cɔ̃ti	59	Unáth	84	cUrasi
10	dəs	35	pẽti	60	səṭṭh	85	pəñjasi
11	glarã	36	chətti	61	Ikáth	86	chlasi
12	barã	37	sẽti	62	báth	87	sətasi
13	terã	38	əthətti	63	təréth	88	əthasi
14	cɔdã	39	Untali	64	cɔ̃́th	89	Unanvẽ
15	pəndrã	40	cali	65	pếth	90	nəbbe
16	solã	41	Iktali	66	chláth	91	Ikanvẽ
17	sətarã	42	bətali	67	sətáth	92	banvẽ
18	ətharã	43	tərtali	68	əthath	93	tlranvẽ
19	Unni	44	cUtali	69	Unə̀ttər	94	cUranvẽ
20	ví	45	pəñjtali	70	səttər	95	pəcanvẽ
21	Ikki	46	chlali	71	Ikə̀ttər	96	chlanvẽ
22	bai	47	səntali	72	bə̀ttər	97	sətanvẽ
23	tei	48	əthtali	73	tlə̀ttər	98	əthanvẽ
24	cóvvi	49	Unəñja	74	cUə̀ttər	99	nərInvẽ
25	pə́ñji	50	pəñjá	75	pəñjə̀ttər	100	sɔ

'fifth', *chevã* 'sixth', etc.) inflect m. as *-vẽ*, f.sg. *-vĩ*. Ordinals formed from cardinals ending in *-ã* have high tone, thus *bárvã* 'twelfth' from *barã* 'twelve'. The systems of AG (Shackle 1983a: 152–3) and Siraiki numerals are similar.

4.3. Postpositions

Postpositions normally follow a noun in the oblique case. The commonest adjectival postposition (corresponding to HU *ka*) is the possessive *da*, universal across the Panjabi area except for Pothohari *na*. Other core postpositions vary from one part of the region to another, thus the objective/dative marker (HU *ko*) is MSP *nũ* but Pothohari *ki*, Hindko *ã*, Siraiki *kũ*.

Many common postpositions are locatives in origin, as shown by their AG forms, e.g. MSP and Siraiki *vIc* (colloquially *c*) 'in', MSP *əndər*, Siraiki *əndIr* 'inside', MSP *əgge*, Siraiki *əɠɠe* 'before' (AG *vicci, andari, aggai*). All such postpositions also have corresponding ablative forms, thus MSP *vIccõ, cõ*, Siraiki *vIccũ, cũ* 'from in, among', *əndrõ*, Siraiki *əndrũ* 'from inside', *əggõ*, Siraiki *əɠɠũ* 'from before' (AG *viccaṁhu, andaraṁhu, aggaṁhu*). All such postpositions may either follow a noun in obl. case directly or with the inflected linker *de*, e.g. *pài naḷ* or *pài de naḷ* 'with (my) brother' (HU *bhai ke sath*). Both simple and ablative postpositions may also function independently as adverbs.

4.4. Pronouns

True personal pronouns are restricted to the first and second persons, with the plural bases *əs-* and *tUs-* being universal Panjabi features. The 2pl. *tUsĩ* also functions as a polite pronoun to the exclusion of HU 3pl. *ap*. The MSP declension (table 16.20) reveals systematic differences from HU. The only common use of the oblique is as agentive (not marked by *ne*) in the ergative construction. The objective/dative and ablative cases, correspond to HU forms with *-e/ko* or *se*. Other varieties have similar patterns, with many distinctive forms. Some reflect older distinctions subsequently levelled in MSP, e.g. Dogri 1sg.dir. *əũ* 'I' (AG *haũṁ*), Shahpuri 2sg.dir. *tŪd* 'you' (AG *tuddhu*), while others are dictated by local choices of postposition, e.g. for the 1sg.obj. Pothohari *mIki*, *mIγi*, Hindko *mā̃*, *mḙ̃ḍe ã̃*, Siraiki *mɛkũ* 'me'. The MSP reflexive pronoun *ap* has poss.adj. *apṇa*.

All other pronouns (Gill and Gleason 1969: 7–9, Shackle 1976: 59–61) follow a common declension, much reduced from the complex AG paradigms (Shackle 1983a: 102–5). The demonstratives have replaced the normal AG third person pronoun *so* (f. *sā*, obl. base *t-*). The declension of the near demonstrative 'this' (table 16.21), with MSP one word sg. obj. *énũ*, poss. *éda* versus pl. *énã nu*, *énã da*, is exactly parallel to that of

TABLE 16.20: PERSONAL PRONOUNS

	1 sg.	2 sg.	1 pl.	2 pl.
dir.	*mɛ̃*	*tũ*	*əsĩ*	*tUsĩ*
obl.(ag.)	*mɛ̃*	*tũ*	*əsã*	*tUsã*
obj.	*mɛnũ*	*tɛnũ*	*sanũ*	*tUànũ*
abl.	*mɛthõ*	*tɛthõ*	*sathõ*	*tUàthõ*
poss. adj.	*mera*	*tera*	*saḍa*	*tUàḍa*

TABLE 16.21: NEAR DEMONSTRATIVE PRONOUNS

	AG base *i-*	base *e-*	MSP	Siraiki
(a) Simple:				
sg.dir.	*ihu* (f. *iha*)	*ehu* (f. *eha)*	*é*	*e*
sg.obl.	*isu, isa*	*esu, esa*	*é, ɛs*	*ĩ, hĩ*
sg.ag.	*ini*	*eni*	*én, éne*	*(ĩ)*
sg.loc.	*itu*	*etu, aitu*	*(ɛt)*	
pl.dir.	*ihi*	*ehi, e*	*é*	*e*
pl.obl.	*inhāṁ*	*enhāṁ*	*énã*	*Inhã, Inhɛ̃*
pl.loc.(ag.)	*inhīṁ*	*enhīṁ*		
(b) Emphatic:				
sg.dir.		*eho* (f. *ehā*)	*éi*	*iho* (f. *iha*)
sg.obl.		*ese, ɛse*		*Ihĩ*
pl.dir.			*éi*	*ihe*
pl.obl.			*énã i*	*Inhã i, Inhɛ̃ i*

the remote demonstrative *ó* (Siraiki *o*) 'that, he, she, it'. The relative *jo* (obl.sg. *jĺ-*, *jIs*, pl. *jĺnã*, Siraiki *jẽ*, pl. *jInhã*, *jInhẽ*) 'who, which' and the interrogative *kɔṇ* (obl.sg. *kĺ-*, *kIs*, pl. *kĺnã*, Siraiki *kẽ*, pl. *kInhã*, *kInhẽ*) 'who?, which?' are often replaced in speech by MSP *jéṛa*, Siraiki *jeṛha*, *jeṛha* 'which' and MSP *kéṛa*, Siraiki *keṛha*, *keṛha* 'which?'. The indefinite pronoun is historically an extension of the interrogative, so *koi* (obl. *kIse*) 'someone', with the AG distinction of gender in the direct case preserved in Siraiki m. *koi*, f. *kai* (common obl. *kəhĩ*). Separate neuter pronouns are MSP *kí*, Siraiki *kIa* 'what?', MSP *kŪj*, Siraiki *kUjh* 'something'. The pronominal pl.obl. *-nã* also occurs in *Ik*, *Iknã* 'some', *hor*, *hornã* 'others', *sə́b*, *sə́bnã* 'all' (Siraiki *hIk*, *hIkṇã*; *ɓIa*, *ɓInhã*; *səbh*, *səbhṇã*).

Further symmetrical sets of adjectives and adverbs formed from the pronominal bases *e-*, *o-*, *j-*, *k-* are illustrated for MSP (table 16.22), with indefinites being extended forms of the interrogative *k-* set, e.g. *kĺdre* 'somewhere', *kəde* 'sometimes'. There is considerable regional variation in the similar sets present in Siraiki (Shackle 1976: 62–3) and all other dialects. Many compound sets are also in use, e.g. MSP *jéṛe veḷe* 'at which time, i.e. when', *kéṛe veḷe* 'when?', often with colloquial contractions (Jaggi 1975).

TABLE 16.22: PRONOMINAL SETS

Adjectives:

				jéṛa	'who'	*kéṛa*	'who?'
éo jĺa	'like this'	*óo jĺa*	'like that'	*jĺa*	'like which'	*kĺo jĺa*	'like which?'
Inna	'this much'	*Unna*	'that much'	*jInna*	'as much'	*kInna*	'how much?'
eḍa	'this big'	*oḍa*	'that big'	*jIḍḍa*	'as big'	*kIḍḍa*	'how big?'

Adverbs:

ethe	'here'	*othe*	'there'	*jItthe*	'where'	*kItthe*	'where?'
ethõ	'hence'	*othõ*	'thence'	*jItthõ*	'whence'	*kItthõ*	'whence?'
édər	'hither'	*ódər*	'thither'	*jĺddər*	'whither'	*kĺddər*	'whither?'
[*hUṇ*	'now']	*odõ*	'then'	*jədõ*	'when'	*kədõ*	'when?'
evẽ	'thus'	*ovẽ*	'thus'	*jIvẽ*	'as'	*kIvẽ*	'how?'

4.5. Verbs

Verbs (Joshi 1981, 1989, Puar 1990) are the most complex Panjabi word-class. Their morphology includes stem-alternation, inflection by morphemic addition or alternation to produce verbal nouns and adjectives besides purely verbal tense-forms, and periphrastic combinations which may involve elisions. Apart from the present and past substantive verb, there is only one system of conjugation for all verbs, but both MSP (Gill and Gleason 1969: 18–41) and Siraiki (Shackle 1976: 71–100) have many more irregular and unpredictable forms than the structurally similar but more highly regularized HU paradigms.

4.5.1. Verbal stems

Apart from the closed class of paired stems of intransitives and transitives distinguished by vowel-quality, e.g. *mər-* 'die', *mar-* 'kill, strike', there are many parallel sets of simple stems and of causatives formed by the addition of accented -'a- or -'va- and weakening of the stem-vowel, e.g. *mar-* 'strike', *mə'rva-* 'cause to be struck', *kheḍ-* 'play', *khI'ḍ(v)a-* 'amuse', *bol-* 'speak', *bU'la-* 'call'. MSP stems with high tone have causatives with low tone in the second syllable (table 16.23).

TABLE 16.23: DERIVED VERBAL STEMS

(a) MSP and Siraiki causatives + -'a-, -'va-:

suṇ-		'hear'
sU'ṇa-		'tell'
sU'ṇva-		'cause to be told'
MSP	Siraiki	
póṛ-	*pəṛh-*	'study'
pəṛà-	*pə'ṛha-*	'teach'
pəṛvà-	*pə'ṛhva-*	'cause to be taught'

(b) Siraiki passives + -'ij-:

kər-	'do'
kə'rij-	'be done'

(c) Siraiki present-future + -'e-:

kər-	*kə're-*	'do'
sU'ṇa-	*sU'ṇe-*	'tell'

Siraiki also has passive stems formed with accented -'ij- and the same weakenings of stem-vowels, e.g. *mar-* 'kill', *mə'rij-* 'be killed'. In the Siraiki conjugation of many transitive verbs and all causatives, a secondary present-future stem with accented -'e- is used in the formation of the present participle and the future, e.g. *mə'rēda* 'killing', *sU'ṇesi* 'he will tell'.

The absolutive is normally equivalent to the bare stem. It is uninflected, like the conjunctive participle marked by the addition of *ke* to the absolutives of all verbs, e.g. *kərke* 'having done', *bolke* 'having spoken'.

4.5.2. Infinitive and participles

The infinitive, gerundive, present participle and past participle (table 16.24) inflect as nouns or adjectives. The standard citation-form of verbs is the infinitive, a verbal noun originally following the unextended masculine declension (AG *likhaṇu*, obl. *likhaṇa*, loc./instr. *likhaṇi*). In MSP it coincides in the direct case with the gerundive, an adjective following the extended declension (AG m.sg.dir. *likhaṇā*, f. *likhaṇī*). Stems ending in -*r*- or a retroflex sonant have -*n*-, e.g. *kərna* 'to do', obl. *kərən*, *sUṇna* 'to hear', obl. *sUṇən*. The infinitive participle, which often has a future sense, is formed from the oblique infinitive, as *lIkhəṇvaḷa* 'about to write'. Siraiki is similar but distinguishes infinitive dir. and obl. *lIkhəṇ* 'to write, writing' from gerundive *lIkhṇa* 'having to be written'.

The present participle is an adjective in -*da* added directly to stems ending in consonant, e.g. *lIkhda* 'writing', but with nasalization of vowel-stems, e.g. *ro-* 'weep', *rõda* 'weeping'. Siraiki present-future stems in -'e- are similarly nasalized, e.g. *sU'ṇa-* 'tell', *sU'ṇēda* 'telling' versus *sUṇda* 'hearing'. Adverbial forms are marked by either of the masculine pl.obl. morphemes, and often have similarly inflected perfective

TABLE 16.24: INFINITIVE AND PARTICIPLES

		lIkh- 'write'	*ro-* 'weep'	*a-* 'come'
(a) Infinitive:				
dir.	*-ṇa*	*lIkhṇa*	*roṇa*	*ɔṇa*
obl.	*-(ə)ṇ*	*lIkhəṇ*	*roṇ*	*ɔṇ*
abl.	*-ṇõ*	*lIkhṇõ*	*roṇõ*	*ɔṇõ*
infinitive ptc. (future ptc.):				
	-(ə)ṇvaḷa	*lIkhəṇvaḷa*	*roṇvaḷa*	*ɔṇvaḷa*
gerundive:				
	-ṇa	*lIkhṇa*	*roṇa*	*ɔṇa*
(b) Present ptc.:				
dir.	*-(~)da*	*lIkhda*	*rõda*	*ɔ̃da*
adv.	*-(~)dIã/e*	*lIkhdIã, lIkhde*	*rõdIã, rõde*	*ɔ̃dIã, ɔ̃de*
present ptc. II:				
dir.	*-na*	*lIkhna*	*rona*	*ɔna*
(c) Past ptc.:				
dir.	*-Ia*	*lIkhIa*	*roIa*	*aIa*
adv.	*-Iã/e*	*lIkhIã, lIkhe*	*roIã, roe*	*aIã, ae*

extension, e.g. *lIkhdIã hoIã* 'while writing'. Pothohari has *-na* for *-da* throughout. Elsewhere the present participle in *-na*, versus infinitive *-ṇa*, is used only in the periphrastic present indicative (table 16.29, section 4.5.4.).

A number of morphophonemic rules govern the formation of the infinitive and present participle, notably the MSP change of all *-a-* stems (except *kha-* 'eat', *ja-* 'go'), including all causatives, to *-ɔ-*, e.g. *a-* 'come', versus *ɔṇa* 'to come', *ɔ̃da* 'coming' (AG *āvaṇu, āvaṁdā*), while *ho-* 'be' has pres.ptc. *hUnda*. Siraiki keeps *avəṇ* 'to come', *āda* 'coming', etc., but the distinctive *vəññəṇ* 'to go' has pres.ptc. *vẽda* 'going'. Siraiki stems with *-h-* have nasalization, with possible displacement of aspiration, e.g. *rə̃hda, rãdha* 'living'.

The past participle is an adjective in *-Ia* added directly to all stems, e.g. *lIkhIa* 'written', m.pl. *lIkhe*, f.sg. *lIkhi*, f.pl. *lIkhiã*. Perfective forms with the past participle of *ho-* 'be' are very common, e.g. *lIkhIa hoIa*, f. *lIkhi hoi*, etc. '(in a state of having been) written'. Many irregular past participles are commonly used in MSP (table 16.25). The first element of the diphthongs in the inflected forms of set (b), e.g. *gIa* 'gone', m.pl. *gəe*, f.sg. *gəi*, f.pl. *gəiã*, is *-ĕ-* throughout (cf. table 16.4). The greater conservatism of Siraiki accounts for its retention of still more irregular past participles, e.g. *ghInnəṇ* 'to take' *ghIdda* 'taken', *thivəṇ* 'become' *thIa* 'become', *dekhəṇ* 'to see' *dIṭṭha* 'seen', *vəññəṇ* 'to go' *gIa* 'gone', *vəssəṇ* 'to rain' *vUṭṭha* 'rained', *vəhəṇ* 'to flow' *vUṛha* 'flowed'.

4.5.3. *Inflected tenses*

Only four tenses are inflected by direct addition of personal morphemes to the stem. While the old AG general present has become a present subjunctive in all modern varieties (table 16.26), the terminations have largely remained constant. In contrast to

TABLE 16.25: IRREGULAR PAST PARTICIPLES

(a) -a	ṭUṭṭ-	'break'	ṭUṭṭa	'broken'
	ləgg-	'begin'	ləgga	'begun'
	lə́bb-	'find'	lə́bba	'found'
(b) -Ia	ja-	'go'	gIa	'gone'
	pɛ-	'lie'	pIa	'lain'
	ré-	'remain'	rĭa	'remained'
	lɛ-	'take'	lIa	'taken'
(c) -Ia	mər-	'die'	moIa	'died'
(d) -ṭṭha	nəss-	'run'	nəṭṭha	'ran'
(e) -ṭha	pí-	'grind'	piṭha	'ground'
	bé-	'sit'	bɛṭha	'sat'
(e) -tta	sɔ̃-	'sleep'	sUtta	'slept'
	de-	'give'	dItta	'given'
(f) -ta	kər-	'do'	kita	'did'
	khəlo-	'stand'	khəlota	'stood'
	tò-	'wash'	tòta	'washed'
	nà-	'bathe'	nàta	'bathed'
	pi-	'drink'	pita	'drunk'
(g) -dda	bɔ́nn-	'tie'	bɔ́dda	'tied'
(h) -da	kha-	'eat'	kháda	'eaten'
	lIa-	'bring'	lIáda	'brought'

HU, there is a full set of six distinctive personal endings. The only unmodified survival of the AG 1 pl. *-aṁha* is in Shahpuri *lIkhã̂*. This awkward tonal shift (Shackle 1979: 208) is elsewhere avoided, as in Pothohari *lIkhã* identical with the 1 sg., or by the use of different contrastive endings, like the Siraiki *-ũ*, or the MSP *-ie*. The last is transferred from the old passive third singular present, i.e. *lIkhie* 'let us write' (AG *likhīai* 'it is to be written'). The origin of the HU polite imperative *lIkhIye* 'please write' is of course identical, and it is doubtless the need to keep the different modern meanings of the termination separate which accounts for the preference in the Panjabi-influenced Urdu of Pakistan for the 3 pl. *(ap) lIkhẽ* 'please write'. The termination of the MSP 3 pl. *-ən* is now identical with the oblique infinitive, with the same substitution of *-ən* after *-r-* and retroflexes, e.g. *sUṇən* 'let them hear', while Siraiki *-In* results from regressive vowel harmony, e.g. *sUṇln* (< **suṇinhi*, AG *suṇanhi*). Vowel-stems usually add *-v-* before all personal endings other than 1 pl. and 3 pl., e.g. 1 sg. *avã* 'let me come', 2 sg. *avẽ*, 3 sg. *ave*, 1 pl. *aie*, 2 pl. *a(v)o*, 3 pl. *ən*. Stems in *-ɛ-* follow the pattern of 1 sg. *rə́vã* 'let me remain', 2 sg. *rə́vẽ*, 3 sg. *rə́ve*, 1 pl. *rə́ie*, 2 pl. *rə́o*, 3 pl. *rə́ṇ*.

There are two imperatives, with second person only. The aorist implies greater politeness. All stems other than those with low tone have high tone in the MSP simple imperative, although this is not always written (with *h*) in the Gurmukhi or Persian scripts. There is a shift of accent in the Siraiki second plural aorist imperative with weakening of the stem-vowel, as in *avẽ* 'please come', pl. *ə'vahe*.

All three modern formations of the future (table 16.27) are attested in the AG variants *likhaigā*, *likhagu*, *likhasī* (Shackle 1983a: 83–4). The standard MSP future closely resembles the HU pattern, distinguishing genders by adding inflected *-ga* to the

TABLE 16.26: PRESENT AND IMPERATIVES

	AG		MSP		Siraiki	
Present:						
1 sg.	-āṁ	likhāṁ	-ã	líkhã	-ã	líkhã
2 sg.	-aṁhi	likhaṁhi	-ẽ	líkhẽ	-ẽ	líkhẽ
3 sg.	-ai	likhai	-e	líkhe	-e	líkhe
1 pl.	-aṁha	likhaṁha	-ie	líkhie	-ũ	líkhũ
2 pl.	-ahu	likhahu	-o	líkho	-o	líkho
3 pl.	-anhi	likhanhi	-əṇ	líkhəṇ	-In	líkhIn
Present imperative:						
2 sg.	-u	likhu	-ø	líkh	-ø	líkh
2 pl.	-ahu	likhahu	-o	líkho	-o	líkho
Aorist imperative:						
2 sg.			-ĩ	líkhĩ	-ẽ	líkhẽ
2 pl.	-iho	likhiho	-io	líkhio	-'ahe	lí'khahe

TABLE 16.27: FUTURE

	MSP + -ga			MSP short		Siraiki + -s-	
		masc.	fem.				
1 sg.	-ã-	líkhãga	líkhãgi	-ũ	líkhũ	-sã	líkhsã
2 sg.	-ẽ-	líkhẽga	líkhẽgi			-sẽ	líkhsẽ
3 sg.	-e-	líkhega	líkhegi	-u	líkhu	-si	líkhsi
1 pl.	-ã-	líkhãge	líkhãgiã			-sũ	líkhsũ
2 pl.	-o-	líkhoge	líkhogiã			-so	líkhso
3 pl.	-əṇ-	líkhəṇge	líkhəṇgiã			-sIn	líkhsIn

present subjunctive. The 1 sg. forms *-ãga/-ũga* are in free variation, with *-ãge* regular in the 1 pl. All stems other than those with low tone have high tone in the MSP futures, although this is seldom written in the Gurmukhi or Persian scripts. The colloquial MSP short future with 1 sg. *-ũ*, 3 sg. *-u* is to be connected with the northern short *g*-forms of e.g. Dogri 3 sg. *líkhəg*, Kangri *líkhga*. The sigmatic future without gender distinctions is characteristic of all western dialects, most of which have personal endings identical with those of the present subjunctive, but 3 sg. *-si*. The future of many Siraiki transitive verbs is formed from the present-future stem in *-'e-*, e.g. *kə'resi* 'he will do', *sU'ṇesi* 'he will tell' versus *sUṇsi* 'he will hear'. The negative *na* 'not' is used with all stem tenses except MSP future *nə̃ĩ ávega* 'he will not come' (Siraiki *na asi*).

4.5.4. Substantive verb

The substantive verb stands outside the regular conjugational system. Its inflection is restricted to present and past (table 16.28), with other forms being supplied from *ho-* 'be'. Three sets of inflected forms for the present are characteristic of Panjabi as a whole. Weak

TABLE 16.28: SUBSTANTIVE VERB

	Present:					Past:	
	MSP		Siraiki			MSP	Siraiki
1 sg.	*hã*	*ã*	*hã*	*ã*		*sã*	*həm*
2 sg.	*hɛ̃*	*ɛ̃*	*hɛ̃*	*ɛ̃*		*sɛ*	*havẽ*
3 sg.	*hɛ*	*ɛ*	*he*	*e*		*si*	*ha*, f. *həi*
1 pl.	*hã*	*ã*	*hɛ̃*	*se*	*ũ*	*sã*	*hase*
2 pl.	*ho*	*o*	*ho*	*o*		*sɔ*	*have*
3 pl.	*hən*	*ne*	*hIn*	*In*		*sən*	*hən*

forms without *h-*, before which preceding vowels are often elided, are normal when the verb occurs as copula or as auxiliary with participle to form periphrastic tenses. Forms with *h-* are more marked and more formal, with MSP 3 pl. *hən* (AG *hanhi*) restricted to the most formal Indian registers only. Stronger emphasis still is indicated by reinforcements, in MSP as e.g. *hɛve* or *hɛga* (f. *hɛgi*) '(there) *is*', past *hɛsi* or *siga* (f. *sigi*) '(there) *was*'. Inflections of the past vary notably, with *tha* or *sa* inflected on the HU pattern in the east, and personal endings added to the base *á-* or *é-* in Hindko (Shackle 1980: 494, 505). Negatives are formed with *nə̃̄ı̃* (Siraiki *nhı̃*, *koInhı̃*). Siraiki has an inflected negative present (Shackle 1976: 107) and the negative past is *(koI)nəha*.

Combinations of weak forms of the present with participles to form periphrastic tenses involve numerous vowel elisions. The informal MSP present indicative (table 16.29) also uses the second present participle in *-na* in first singular, second singular and first-plural. Otherwise the MSP periphrastic tenses (table 16.30) are of the familiar HU type, with the addition of the habituals using the present indicative and imperfect of *ho-*. Apart from the conditional *na ɔ̃da* 'would not come', negatives are formed with *nə̃̄ı̃*, with the preferred MSP word order *nə̃̄ı̃ si kərda* 'used not to do', *nə̃̄ı̃ si ai* 'she didn't come'.

4.5.5. Conjunct and compound verbs

As in HU, nouns and adjectives are very freely converted to verbs by conjunction with one of a few common verbs, e.g. from *šUru* 'beginning' the transitive *šUru kər-* 'begin (something)' and the MSP intransitive *šUru ho-* '(something) to begin'. Previously used to naturalize many Persian nouns and adjectives, the formation of conjuncts is actively applied to English components, with the speech of bilinguals (Romaine 1995: 131–42) producing such examples as *lUk ḍɔn əpən kər-* 'look down upon'. For the typical intransitive marker *ho-*, Siraiki uses *thi-* 'become', e.g. *šUru thi-* 'begin'.

Compound verbs in which the signifying element is a verb followed by a conjugated verb with a modal sense are also generally similar to the HU types, including perfectives or 'intensives' (Gill and Gleason 1969: 77–82, Shackle 1976: 123–5) formed from the absolutive with the reinforcers MSP *ja-* 'go', *de-*, 'give', *pɛ-* 'fall', *lɛ-* 'take' (Siraiki *vəññ-*, *ɗe-*, *po- ghInn-*). The commonest types of true modal compound verbs (table 16.31) are also very similar to HU, except for the continuous with present participle and *pIa* which is strongly preferred in Siraiki, e.g. *o pIa kəm kəˈrɛ̃da ha* 'he was working' for MSP *ó kəm kər rIa si*. Besides the MSP passive (Puar 1985) formed from the past participle + *ja-* (*vəññ-*), Siraiki freely uses forms conjugated from the passive stem, e.g.

TABLE 16.29: PRESENT INDICATIVE

MSP masculine paradigms:

	formal	informal
1 sg.	*lIkhda hã*	*lIkhnã*
2 sg.	*lIkhda hẽ*	*lIkhnẽ*
3 sg.	*lIkhda hɔ*	*lIkhdɛ*
1 pl.	*lIkhde hã*	*lIkhnIã*
2 pl.	*lIkhde ho*	*lIkhdIo*
3 pl.	*lIkhde hən*	*lIkhde ne*

TABLE 16.30: PERIPHRASTIC TENSES

(a) Present participle:

–	conditional	*lIkhda*	'would write'
+ pres. aux.:	present indicative	*lIkhda hɛ*	'writes'
+ past aux.:	imperfect	*lIkhda si*	'used to write'
+ *hovega*:	future II	*lIkhda hovega*	'will be writing'
+ *hove:*	pres. subjunctive II	*lIkhda hove*	'may be writing'
+ *hUnda hɛ*:	present habitual	*lIkhda hUnda hɛ*	'writes habitually'
+ *hUnda si*:	past habitual	*lIkhda hUnda si*	'wrote habitually'

(b) Past participle:

–	past	*lIkhIa*	'wrote'
+ pres. aux.:	present perfect	*lIkhIa hɛ*	'has written'
+ past aux.:	past perfect	*lIkhIa si*	'had written, did write'
+ *hovega*:	future perfect	*lIkhIa hovega*	'will have written'
+ *hove:*	subjunctive perfect	*lIkhIa hove*	'may have written'

TABLE 16.31: MODAL COMPOUND VERBS

(a) Absolutive:

+ *cUkk-*	completion	*lIkh cUka hɛ*	'has finished writing'
+ *bé-*	completion	*lIkh beṭha hɛ*	'has finished writing'
+ *rÍa*	continuous I	*lIkh rÍa hɛ*	'is writing'
+ *sək-*	ability	*lIkh səkda hɛ*	'can write'

(b) Oblique infinitive:

+ *de-*	allowing	*lIkhəṇ devega*	'will let write'
+ *ləgg-*	starting	*lIkhəṇ ləgga*	'started writing'

(c) Present participle:

+ *pIa*	continuous II	*lIkhda pIa hɛ*	'is writing'
+ *ré-*	continuity	*lIkhda rÍa*	'went on writing'

(d) Past participle:

+ *kər-*	regularity	*lIkhIa kə́ro*	'keep writing'
+ *ja-*	passive	*lIkhIa jãda hɛ*	'is written'

present subjunctive (usually with a gerundive sense) *ll'khije* 'may be written, is to be written', future *ll'khisi* 'will be written', present indicative *ll'khĩda he* 'is written'. MSP has only a vestigial passive present participle in *-ida*, usually with a gerundive sense, as in *'llkhida hɛ* 'is to be written'.

5. SYNTAX

The syntax of all varieties of Panjabi (Gill and Gleason 1969: 42–154, Shackle 1976: 109–73, Bhatia 1993: 1–163) is characterized by SOV order (with a considerable degree of freedom in the ordering of adverbial phrases), in which the head nouns in nominal phrases are normally preceded by any adjectives (including pre-modifiers linked by the possessive *da*) and followed by any postpositions, and in which the head verb in verbal phrases is normally preceded by any nominal signifier and followed by verbal modifiers, ending with auxiliaries. These fundamentals are illustrated in the following sentence:

> *heṭhã   rəsoi   vlc ónã̲   diã̲   dovẽ tiã̲*
> below   kitchen   -in that-pl.obl. -poss.f.pl. both daughter-pl.
> (adverb) (adverb)   (subject)
> down in the kitchen   both their daughters

> *kə̀r   di   roṭi   χUši χUši   tlar kər rə́iã̲   sən*
> house -poss.f.sg. food   happy-happy ready -do-continuous-f.pl. were-3pl.
> (object)   (adverb)   (verb)
> the family meal   happily   were preparing.
> 'Downstairs in the kitchen their two daughters were happily preparing the family meal.'

The sentence also illustrates the characteristically full pattern of Panjabi grammatical concord of both modifier (*ónã̲ diã̲*) and verb (*tlar kər rə́iã̲ sən*) with a feminine plural subject (*tiã̲*). Given the generally close structural similarities with HU syntax, the next paragraphs concentrate at the expense of such intrinsically interesting features as intonation (Sethi 1971, Joshi 1973) or the related use of clitics (Gill and Gleason 1969: 113–27, Shackle 1976: 156–60) upon a few other distinctive contrasts which are of most interest from a comparativist perspective. These syntactic contrasts are also important in helping account for the Panjabisms frequent in the HU speech of bilinguals (marked below as PHU), and may be noted as such together with the passing references already made to Panjabisms resulting from phonological and morphological interferences.

5.1. Dative subjects

As in other NIA languages, marked direct objects have the same marker MSP *nũ* 'to' (Siraiki *kũ*) as indirect objects, as in the polite formula:

> *énã̲ nũ   mÍḷo*
> this-pl.obl.-dat. meet-imper.-2pl.
> (direct object)   (verb)
> 'Please meet him/them' (= 'May I introduce ...').

This marking of the direct object of *mIḷ-* 'meet' (similarly of *pUcch-* 'ask') is liable to be reflected in PHU *In ko mIllye*, where standard Urdu marks the direct object with the ablative postposition as *In se mIllye*.

Many types of sentences imply the use of logical 'dative subjects' marked by oblique case plus the dative postposition MSP *nũ* (Siraiki *kũ*), contrasting with the grammatical subject in direct case which determines verbal concord, here based on *səza* f. 'punishment':

raje nũ	*mɔt di*	*səza*	*ho cUki*	*si*
king-sg.obl.-dat.	death -poss.f.sg.	punishment	be- -finished-f.sg.	was
(dative subject)	(grammatical subject)		(verb)	

'The king had already been punished by death.'

Dative subjects are also implied in constructions of obligation involving the gerundive with forms of the specialized passive present *cáida hɛ* 'is necessary'. As always in sentences with logical dative or ergative subjects but no grammatical subject, the verb is masculine singular in the following example:

tUànũ	*kə́l*	*ɔṇa*	*cáida*	*si*
you-pl.dat.	yesterday	having-to-come	necessary-m.sg.	was
(dative subject)	(adverb)	(gerundive)	(verb)	

'You ought to have come yesterday.'

Constructions of the gerundive with *pɛ-* 'fall to' similarly imply a dative subject:

bəndenũ	*kItab*	*pə́ṛni*	*pə̀vegi*
man-sg.obl.-dat.	book (f.)	having-to-be-read-f.sg.	fall to-fut.f.3sg.
(dative subject)	(grammatical subject)	(gerundive)	(verb)

'The man will have to read the book.'

Some verbs which have direct subjects in HU have dative subjects in Panjabi, e.g. HU *bhul-* 'forget' versus MSP *pÙll-* (Siraiki *vIsIr-*) 'be forgotten'. The confusion is illustrated in a Panjabi songwriter's well known Urdu verse:

PHU *zIndəgi bhər*	*nəhĩ*	*bhulegi*	*vo bərsat ki rat*
life-long	not	be forgotten-fut.3sg.	that-rainy season's night
(adverb)	(adverb)	(verb)	(grammatical subject)

'All my life I'll not forget that rainy season's night.'

Here *bhulegi* for the expected future masculine 1 sg., i.e. standard HU *(mɛ̃) nəhĩ bhulũga* is influenced by the dative subject of MSP *(mɛnũ) nə́ĩ pÙllegi ó bərsat di rat*.

5.2. Ergative subjects

Panjabi shares the common NIA ergative construction of tenses formed from the past participle of most transitive verbs, in which verbal concord is determined by the logical object as grammatical subject. The ergative subject was marked in AG by use of the then fully functional locative/instrumental case:

AG *guri*	*dānu*		*dittā*
guru-sg.loc./instr.	gift-sg.dir.		given-m.sg.
(ergative subject)	(grammatical subject)		(verb)

'The Guru gave the gift.'

With the subsequent restriction of the locative/instrumental to set adverbial expressions (e.g. *pIchli dInĩ* 'in recent days', *hətthĩ* 'with the hands'), the ergative subject is marked in Siraiki by the oblique case without postposition:

ũ	sakũ	trε	botlā	dĭttiã	hən
he-obl.sg.	us-to	three bottles		given-f.pl.	were
(ergative subject)	(indirect object)	(logical subject)		(verb)	

'He did give us three bottles.'

But in MSP most ergative subjects other than the four personal pronouns (table 16.20, section 4.4) are marked by the agentive postposition *ne*, so the MSP equivalent of the above is:

óne	sanū	tĭn	botlā	dĭttiã	sən

The frequent use of perfective past participles plus *hoIa* as main verbs is a notable MSP feature often transferred to Panjabi speakers' HU, e.g.

PHU *Unhõ ne*	*ye kam*	*kIya hUa*	*hε*
them-erg.	this work	done-perfective	is
(ergative subject)	(logical subject)	(verb)	

'They have done this job.'

Here the interference with standard HU *Unhõ ne ye kam kIya hε* is due to the underlying MSP *ónã ne é kəm kita hoIa hε*.

The best known of all Panjabisms in HU arises from the regular Panjabi use of an ergative subject with the gerundive and substantive verb (as opposed to the constructions of the gerundive with dative subjects described in section 5.1 above) where HU regularly has a dative subject, hence the usual contrast:

PHU *Unhõ ne*	*jana*	*hε*
them-erg.	having-to-go	is
(ergative subject)	(gerundive)	(verb)

HU	*Unko (Unhẽ)*	*jana*	*hε*
	them-dat.		
	(dative subject)		

'They have to go.'

Here the interference is from the ergative subject of MSP *ónã ne jana hε* (Siraiki *Unhã vəñña he*). A similar interference operates with a personal pronoun as subject, as in PHU *mẽ ne jana hε* 'I must go', although there is no agentive marker in the corresponding MSP *mẽ jaṇa hε*.

5.3. Pronominal suffixes

All varieties of Panjabi to the west of Majhi possess pronominal suffixes which may be attached to inflected verbal forms to express various syntactic relationships of the pronoun to the verb. Use of pronominal suffixes normally presupposes suppression of the full pronominal forms capable of expressing the same syntactic functions. Sharply distinctive from MSP and HU, the pronominal suffixes are an areal feature common also to Sindhi, and across the Indo-Iranian linguistic frontier to Pashto and Persian. The full accounts available for Wazirabadi (Cummings and Bailey 1914: 349–60) and Siraiki (Shackle 1976: 101–8, 150–3, 181–2) may be used to supplement the following brief account of the Siraiki pronominal suffixes (table 16.32).

The incomplete set of direct suffixes is commonly used only as an optional way of distinguishing person at the expense of gender in the simple past tense. The table

TABLE 16.32: SIRAIKI PRONOMINAL SUFFIXES

	dir.suff.	*ɠla* 'went'	obl.suff.	*kita* 'did'
1 sg.	-s	ɠlos	-m	kitUm
2 sg.	-õ	ɠlõ	-o	kito
			-i	kItoi
3 sg.			-s	kitUs
1 pl.	-se	ɠlose	-se	kItose
2 pl.	-he	ɠlohe	-he	kItohe
3 pl.			-ne	kItone

indicates the equivalence of the direct suffixes to a suppressed direct pronominal subject, e.g. *ɠlom* 'I went' versus m. *mẽ ɠla*, f. *mẽ ɠəi*.

The much more frequent oblique suffixes are used with many more inflected verbal forms to express a variety of syntactic functions. These include suppressed possessive pronouns connected with the subject (or object), e.g.:

> *nã   kIa   Is*
> name   what   is+suff.3sg.
> (subject) (complement) (verb + suffix)
> 'What is her name?'

The equivalent with unsuppressed possessive pronoun in the subject is:

> *ŭda nã   kIa   he*
> her name what   is

The oblique pronominal suffixes are often equivalent to a dative pronoun with the marker *kŭ*, whether this is syntactically (a) an indirect object, (b) a direct object, or (c) a dative subject, e.g.

(a) *bəχši   hUi   thivi*
    grant-past ptc.-f.sg. perfective-f.sg. become-pres.subj.3sg.+suff.2sg.
    (adjective)   (verb + suffix)
    'May she be granted to you!'

(b) *mẽ   d̲ekhsəĩ*
    I   see-fut.1sg.+suff.2sg.
    (subject) (verb + suffix)
    'I shall see you.'

(c) *ma te bhen̲ vi   yad   a ɠlonIs*
    mother-and-sister-too   to-mind -come-reinforcer-past 3pl.+suff.3sg.
    (grammatical subject)   (conjunct verb + suffix)
    'He remembered his mother and sister too.'

The equivalents with dative pronouns marked with *kŭ* would be (a) *tɛkŭ bəχši hUi thive*, (b) *mẽ tɛkŭ d̲ekhsã*, (c) *ŭkŭ ma te bhen̲ vi yad a ɠlã*.

The commonest use of the oblique suffixes is to indicate a suppressed ergative subject (cf. table 16.32), e.g.

sarlã   *kũ*   *catUs*
all-m.pl.obl.   -obj.   raised-m.sg.+3sg.
(object)   (verb + suffix)
'He lifted them all up.'

This is equivalent to an ergative subject in the unmarked oblique case:

ũ   *sarlã*   *kũ*   *cata*
he-sg.obl.   all-m.pl.obl.   -obj.   raised-m.sg.
(ergative subject) (object)   (verb)

An oblique suffix may similarly be used to indicate the ergative in the gerundive construction:

kId̯ahĩ   *vəñna*   *həs*
somewhere   having-to-go   was+suff.3sg.
(adverb)   (gerundive)   (verb + suffix)
'He had to go somewhere.'

The unsuppressed equivalent is *ũ kId̯ahĩ vəñna ha*.

Double suffixes are also possible in the special case of 1 sg. *-m* as ergative plus 3 sg. *-s* as object-related, e.g. as direct object in the example most commonly cited by Siraiki speakers proud of this special device of their language:

əkhIomIs
(verb + suffix + suffix)
'I said to him.'

Here the equivalent is *mẽ ũkũ akhIa*. Another example shows the 3 sg. suffix expressing a suppressed possessive modifier of the object:

khir   *pitɛmIs*
milk   drunk-pres.perfect m.3sg.+suff.1sg.+suff.3sg.
(object)   (verb + suffix + suffix)
'I have drunk his milk.'

The equivalent with unsuppressed pronouns would be:

mẽ   *ũda*   *khir pitɛ*
me-erg.   his   milk drunk-pres.perfect m.3sg.
(ergative subject) (object)   (verb)

The MSP equivalent would be *mẽ óda dÚd pitɛ*, HU *mẽ ne Uska dudh pIya hɛ*.

5.4. Illustrative styles

More elaborate features may be most economically illustrated by analysis of two brief samples. The first is a complex sentence composed in literary MSP (Gurmukhi text in section 3.2, sample on p. 597). It consists of two paratactic clauses, the introductory relative *jĩnã* being resumed by the demonstrative *ónã* in the second clause. The first clause has an ergative subject (*jĩnã pəñjabiã ne . . . əttIacar. . . vekhe sən*), while the second has a dative-subject (*súj . . . ónã nũ i . . . pɛ səkdi hɛ*), with emphasis of the subject marked by deferral from the usual initial position and by the clitic *i*. Within the simple paratactic frame which is seldom exceeded in any style of Panjabi, the long pre-modifiers and adverbial phrases are characteristic of most formal styles:

jĩnã   pəñjabiã ne sən 1947 di   des-vənḍ
which-pl.obl. -pl.obl.-erg. year-   -poss.f.sg. country-division
(ergative subject)   (adverb)

veḷe   pəñjab de pĩnḍã   šérã   vIc hoe
time-obl.   -poss.m.obl. village-pl.obl. city-pl.obl. -in occurring-m.pl.
(object)

əttIacar əkkhĩ   vekhe   sən,
atrocity eye-pl.instr. see-past-m.pl. was-3pl.
           (adverb)   (verb)

énã   əšṭəpədiã   vIc bIan kiti   dərd-pəri
this-pl.obl. verse-pl.obl. -in description-done-fsg. pain-filled-f.sg.
(grammatical subject)

kàṇi di   sə́i súj ónã   nũ i
story-poss.f.sg. true sense that-pl.obl. to (clitic)-only
                                  (dative subject)

pɛ səkdi   hɛ.
fall can-pres.ptc.f.sg. is.
(verb)

'Only those Panjabis who saw with their own eyes the atrocities taking place in the villages and cities of the Panjab at the time of the Partition of 1947 can get the true sense of the painful story described in these verses.'

The second sample is taken from a Siraiki novel (Shackle 1976: 169). Although of equivalent length to the first, it is quite different in its syntactic organization. The loosely linked series of many short sentences of a basic SV or SOV type is typical of all Panjabi informal styles, although the pronominal suffixes (*ləɗɡ́Is, thivi, ghInnIs*) are distinctively Siraiki syntactic markers:

šala   nəzər   na ləɗɡ́Is.   eɗa
O-that   evil-eye not strike-pr.subj.3sg.+suff.3sg. so-m.sg.dir.
(interjection) (subject) (verb + suffix)   (subject)
'May she not be struck by the evil eye!'   'Such a

sohṇa   ɓal vəsti vIc kəhĩ da   vi   kɛnhĩ.
lovely-m.sg. child village -in any-obl.-poss.m.sg. (clitic)-even there-is-not.
           (adverb) (adjective)   (verb)
lovely child   in the village anyone at all's   there isn't.'

əllah   kəre   bəχši hUi
God   do-pr.subj.-3sg. grant-past ptc.-f.sg. -perfective-f.sg.
(subject) (verb)   (adjective)
'May God ensure   she be granted to you.'

thivi.   vəsai   nazu kũ   pIar
become-pr.subj.3sg.+suff.2sg.   -to   kiss
(verb + suffix)   (ergative subject) (indirect object) (direct object)
                         Vasai   giving Nazu a kiss

dẽdĩa   *hoĩa*   *akhĩa.*
give-pres.ptc.-adv.   -perfective-adv.   say-past ptc.-m.sg.
(adverbial participle)   (verb)
                                          said.

mərĩəm   sUrme da   *ṭIkka zərur*
            eye-black-sg.obl.-poss.m.sg.   mark surely
(vocative) (object)   (adverb)
'Maryam, be sure always to mark her with eye-black.'

laĩa   *kər.*   *koi*   *nəzər*   *na*
fix-past ptc.-m.sg. -do-imper.2sg.   any-m.sg.   evil-eye   not
(verb)   (subject)   (object)   (adverb)
                                  'Let no one with the evil eye

mar   ghInnIs.
strike- -take-pr.subj.3sg.+suff.3sg.
(verb)
strike her!'

REFERENCES

AG Ādi Granth

Addleton, J. S. (1986) 'The importance of regional languages in Pakistan', in M. Geijbels and J. S. Addleton (eds.) *The Rise and Development of Urdu and the Importance of Regional Languages in Pakistan*, Rawalpindi: Christian Study Centre.

Agnihotri, R. K. (1984) *Processes of Assimilation: a Sociolinguistic Study of Sikh Children in Leeds*, University of York Ph.D. thesis.

Agnihotri, V. B. (1985) 'Assimilation of Punjabi speech sounds by migrant Hindi speakers in Punjab', *Pàkha Sanjam* 18: 33–44.

Arun, V. B. (1961) *A Comparative Phonology of Hindi and Punjabi*, Ludhiana: Punjabi Sahitya Akademi.

Baart, J. L. G. (1999) 'Tone rules in Kalam Kohistani', *Bulletin of the School of Oriental and African Studies* 62: 88–104.

Bahl, K. C. (1957) 'Tones in Panjabi', *Indian Linguistics* 17: 139–47.

—— (1962) 'A problem in Punjabi substantive inflections', *Indian Linguistics* 23: 26–30.

—— (1969) 'Panjabi', in Sebeok, T. A. (ed.) *Current Trends in Linguistics* 5, The Hague: Mouton.

Bahl, P. (1936) *Étude de phonétique historique et expérimentale des consonnes injectives du Multani*, Paris: Adrien-Maisonneuve.

Bahri, H. (1962) *Lahndi Phonology, with Special Reference to Awáṇkárí*, Allahabad: Bharati Press.

—— (1963) *Lahndi Phonetics, with Special Reference to Awáṇkárí*, Allahabad: Bharati Press.

Bahri, U. S. (1969) 'Phonology of Dogri', *Pàkha Sanjam* 1, 2: 75–107.

—— (1972) *An Introductory Course in Spoken Punjabi*, Chandigarh and New Delhi: Bahri Publications.

Bailey, T. G. (1904) *Panjabi Grammar: a Brief Grammar of Panjabi as Spoken in Wazirabad District*, Lahore: Punjab Government Press.

—— (1908) *The Languages of the Northern Himalayas*, London: Royal Asiatic Society.

—— (1914) *A Punjabi Phonetic Reader*, London: Trübner.

—— (1915) *Linguistic Studies from the Himalayas*, London: Royal Asiatic Society.

—— (1924) *Grammar of the Shina (Ṣiṇā) Language*, London: Royal Asiatic Society.

—— (1938) *Studies in North Indian Languages*, London: Lund Humphries.

Bala, M. (1983) 'A comparative study of Kāṅgaṛī and Pañjābī linguistics', *Vishveshvaranand Indological Journal* 21: 191–200.

Bhardwaj, M. R. (1995) *Colloquial Panjabi: a Complete Language Course*, London and New York: Routledge.

Bhatia, T. K. (1975) 'The evolution of tones in Punjabi', *Studies in Linguistic Sciences* 5, 2: 12–24.

—— (1993) *Punjabi: a Cognitive-Descriptive Grammar*, London and New York: Routledge.

Brass, P. R. (1974) *Language, Religion and Politics in North India*, Cambridge: Cambridge University Press.

Breton, R. J.-L. (1997) *Atlas of the Languages and Ethnic Communities of South Asia*, New Delhi: Sage Publications.

Bukhari, T. (1989) *Panjābī-Urdū Lughat*, Lahore: Urdu Science Board.

Campbell, G. L. (1995) *Concise Compendium of the World's Languages*, London and New York: Routledge.

Cummings, T. F. and Bailey, T. G. (1912) *Panjabi Manual and Grammar*, Calcutta: Baptist Mission Press.

Dass, T. (1987) 'Problems of language maintenance and language shift in Lahnda speech community', *Indian Linguistics* 48: 33–43.

Dulai, N. K. and Koul, O. N. (1980) *Punjabi Phonetic Reader*, Mysore: Central Institute of Indian Languages.

Emeneau, M. B. (1980) 'India and linguistic areas', in Dil, A. S. (ed.) *Language and Linguistic Area: Essays by Murray B. Emeneau*, Stanford: Stanford University Press.

Gill, H. S. (1996) 'The Gurmukhi script', in Daniels, P. T. and Bright, W. (eds.), *The World's Writing systems*, New York and Oxford: Oxford University Press, pp. 395–8.

Gill, H. S. and Gleason, H. A. (1969) *A Reference Grammar of Panjabi*, 2nd ed., Patiala: Punjabi University.

Gill, H. S. et al. (eds.) (1973) *Linguistic Atlas of the Punjab*, Patiala: Department of Anthropological Linguistics, Punjabi University.

Grierson, G. A. (1904) 'On the modern Indo-Aryan alphabets of North-Western India', *Journal of the Royal Asiatic Society*: 67–75.

—— (1916) 'Western Hindī and Pañjābī', *Linguistic Survey of India* 9:1, Calcutta: Superintendent of Government Printing, India.

—— (1919) 'Sindhī and Lahndā', *Linguistic Survey of India* 8:1, Calcutta: Superintendent of Government Printing, India.

Gumperz, J. J. (1971) 'Hindi-Punjabi code switching in Delhi', in Dil, A. S. (ed.) *Language in Social Groups: Essays by John J. Gumperz*, Stanford: Stanford University Press, pp. 205–19.

Gupta, B. R. (1971) 'Annotated bibliography of Punjabi language', *Parkh* 1: 1–22.

—— (1972) 'Phonology and morphology of Punjabi', *Parkh* 2: 19–56.

—— (1983) *Research in Indian Linguistics*, New Delhi: Ariana Publishing House.

Haudricourt, A. G. (1971) 'On tones in Punjabi', *Pàkha Sanjam* 4: 1–3.

Hendriksen, H. (1985) *Himachali Studies: 3. Grammar*, København: Det Kongelige Danske Videnskabernes Selskab.

—— (1987) 'A language group and its position: thoughts of linguistic relationship', *Acta Linguistica Hafniensia* 20: 29–53.

Jaggi, V. (1975) 'Some observations on reduced forms in Hindi and Punjabi', *Indian Linguistics* 36: 276–84.

Jain, B. D. (1929) 'Isophones of the orthographic *gh-, bh-, dh-*, etc., and of *h-* in the Ambala District', *Bulletin of the School of Oriental Studies* 7: 329–33.

—— (1934) *A Phonology of Punjabi and a Ludhiani Phonetic Reader*, Lahore: Punjab University.

Joshi, S. S. (1971) '[l], [ḷ], [r] and [ṛ] Sounds in Panjabi: a study in retroflexion', *Pàkha Sanjam* 4: 185–90.

—— (1973) 'Pitch and related phenomena in Panjabi', *Pàkha Sanjam* 6: 1–62.

—— (1981) 'Some aspects of phonology of Punjabi verbs', *Pàkha Sanjam* 14: 21–46.

—— (1989) *The Phonology of the Panjabi Verb: a Polysystemic Analysis*, New Delhi: Classical.
Jukes, A. (1900) *Dictionary of the Jatki or Western Punjábi Language*, Lahore: Religious Book Trust Society.
Kalra, S. S. and Purewal, N. K. (1999) *Teach Yourself Panjabi*, London: Teach Yourself Books.
Khan, F. (1991) 'The Urdu speech community', in Alladina, S. and Edwards, V. (eds.) *Multilingualism in the British Isles*, 2, London and New York: Longman.
Khubchandani, L. M. (1979) 'A demographic typology for Hindi, Urdu, Punjabi speakers in South Asia', in Wurm, S. A. (ed.) *Language and Society*, The Hague: Mouton, pp. 183–94
Koul, O. N. and Bala, M. (1989) *Modes of Address and Pronominal Usage in Punjabi: a Sociolinguistic Study*, Mysore: Central Institute of Indian Languages.
—— (1992) *Punjabi Language and Linguistics: an Annotated Bibliography*, Patiala: Indian Institute of Language Studies.
Language Department (1955–83) *Pañjābī Koš*, 6 vols, Patiala: Language Department, Panjab.
—— (1960a) *Poṭhohārī Šabad-Koš*, Patiala: Language Department, Panjab.
—— (1960b) *Puādhī Šabad-Koš*, Patiala: Language Department, Panjab.
Leitner, G. W. (1883) *A Collection of Specimens of Commercial and Other Alphabets and Handwritings, as also of Multiplication Tables Current in Various Parts of the Punjab, Sind and the North West Provinces*, Lahore: Punjab Government Press.
Linguistic Minorities Project (1985) *The Other Languages of England*, London: Routledge and Kegan Paul.
Mahandru, V. K. (1991) 'The Panjabi speech community', in Alladina, S. and Edwards, V. (eds.) *Multilingualism in the British Isles*, 2, London and New York: Longman, pp. 115–27.
Malik, A. N. (1995) *The Phonology and Morphology of Panjabi*, New Delhi: Munshiram Manoharlal.
Mann, G. S. (1996) *The Goindval Pothis: the Earliest Extant Source of the Sikh Canon* Cambridge Mass.: Department of Sanskrit and Indian Studies, Harvard University.
Mansoor, S. (1993) *Punjabi, Urdu and English in Pakistan: a Sociolinguistic Study*, Lahore: Vanguard.
Masica, C. P. (1991) *The Indo-Aryan Languages*, Cambridge: Cambridge University Press.
Mizokami, T. (1981) *Panjabi*, Tokyo: University of Foreign Studies.
—— (1987) *Language Contact in Panjab*, New Delhi: Bahri Publications.
Moffatt, S. and Milroy, L. (1992) 'Panjabi/English language alternation in the early school years', *Multilingua* 11: 355–85.
Mukherjee, A. (1996) *Language Maintenance and Language Shift: Panjabis and Bengalis in Delhi*, New Delhi: Bahri Publications.
Nabha, K. S. (1960) *Gurušabd Ratnākar Mahān Koš [Encyclopaedia of Sikh Literature]*, 2nd ed., Patiala: Language Department, Panjab.
Newton, J. and Janvier, L. (1854) *A Dictionary of the Punjábi Language, Prepared by a Committee of the Lodiana Mission*, Ludhiana: Baptist Mission Press.
Nirvair, D. S. (1975) 'Persian words in Pañjābī: a semantic overview', *Vishveshvaranand Indological Journal* 13: 151–7.
O'Brien, E. (1903) *Glossary of the Multani Language*, 2nd ed. rev. J. Wilson, Lahore: Punjab Government Press.
Padam, P. S. (1992) *Khālsaī Bolle*, Patiala: Kalam Mandir.
Pandotra, H. R. (1974) *Ḍogrī-Hindī Šabdakoš*, Jammu: Jammu Kashmir Akademi.
Puar, J. S. (1985) 'Passivization in Punjabi', *Pàkha Sanjam* 18: 45–52.
—— (1990) *The Panjabi verb: Form and Function*, Patiala: Punjabi University.
Punjabi University (1994a) *English–Punjabi Dictionary*, 4th ed., Patiala: Punjabi University.
—— (1994b) *Punjabi–English Dictionary*, Patiala: Punjabi University.
Rahman, T. (1996) *Language and Politics in Pakistan*, Karachi: Oxford University Press.
Rampton, M.B.H. (1991) 'Interracial Panjabi in a British adolescent peer group', *Language in Society* 20: 391–422.

Ranganatha, M. R. (1980) *Survey of Mandeali and Kului in Himachal Pradesh*, New Delhi: Office of the Registrar General, India.

Rangila, R. S. (1986) *Maintenance of Panjabi Language in Delhi: a Sociolinguistic Study*, Manasagangotri: Central Institute of Indian Languages.

Rensch, C. R., et al. (1992) *Hindko and Gujari*, Islamabad: National Institute of Pakistan Studies and Summer Institute of Linguistics.

Romaine, S. (1986) 'The Syntax and Semantics of the Code-Mixed Compound Verb in Panjabi/English Bilingual Discourse', in Tannenn, D. and Alatis, J. E. (eds.) *Language and Linguistics: the Interdependence of Theory, Data and Application (GURT 1985)*, Washington D.C.: Georgetown University Press.

—— (1995) *Bilingualism*, 2nd ed., Oxford: Blackwell.

Rossi, A. V. (1974) 'La posizione del "Lahndi" e la situazione linguistica nel Panjab Pakistano', *Annali dell'Insituto Orientale di Napoli*, N.S. 24: 347–65.

Sandhu, B. S. (1968a) 'The Tonal System of the Panjabi Language', *Parkh* 2 (special issue).

—— (1968b) 'A Descriptive Grammar of Puadi', *Parkh* 2 (special issue).

—— (1974) 'The Articulatory and Acoustic Structure of the Panjabi Vowels', *Parkh* 4 (special issue).

—— (1986) *The Articulatory and Acoustic Structure of the Punjabi Consonants*, Patiala: Punjabi University.

Sethi, J. (1971) *Intonation of Statements and Questions in Punjabi*, Hyderabad: Central Institute of English.

Shackle, C. (1970) 'Punjabi in Lahore', *Modern Asian Studies* 4: 239–67.

—— (1972) *Punjabi*, London: Teach Yourself Books.

—— (1976) *The Siraiki Language of Central Pakistan: a Reference Grammar*, London: School of Oriental and African Studies.

—— (1977a) 'Siraiki: a language movement in Pakistan', *Modern Asian Studies* 11: 379–403.

—— (1977b) '"South-Western" elements in the language of the *Ādi Granth*', *Bulletin of the School of Oriental and African Studies* 40: 36–50.

—— (1978) 'Approaches to the Persian loans in the *Ādi Granth*', *Bulletin of the School of Oriental and African Studies* 41: 73–96.

—— (1979) 'Problems of classification in Pakistan Panjab', *Transactions of the Philological Society*.

—— (1980) 'Hindko in Kohat and Peshawar', *Bulletin of the School of Oriental and African Studies* 43: 482–510.

—— (1983a) *An Introduction to the Sacred Language of the Sikhs*, London: School of Oriental and African Studies.

—— (1983b) 'Language, dialect and local identity in Northern Pakistan', in Zingel, W. P. and Lallémant, S. (eds.) *Pakistan in its Fourth Decade*, Hamburg: Deutsches Orient-Institut, pp. 175–87.

—— (1988) 'Some observations on the evolution of Modern Standard Punjabi', in O'Connell, J. T. et al. (eds.) *Sikh Religion and History in the Twentieth Century*, Toronto: Centre for South Asia Studies, pp. 101–10.

—— (1992) 'Micro and macro from Mianwali', *SOAS Centre of South Asian Studies Newsletter* 21: 9–12.

—— (1995) *A Gurū Nānak Glossary*, 2nd ed., New Delhi: Heritage.

Shackle, C. and Snell, R. (1990) *Hindi and Urdu Since 1800: a Common Reader*, London: School of Oriental and African Studies.

Shakeel, A. G. (1973) 'Certain linguistic features of the Dakhni Urdu of Mysore and the Panjabi', *Pàkha Sanjam* 6: 129–34.

Shankar, G. (1931) 'A short account of Dogri dialect', *Indian Linguistics* 1, 2: 1–83.

Sharma, D. D. (1971) *Syllabic Structure of Hindi and Punjabi*, Chandigarh: Punjab University.

—— (1974a) 'Striking similarities in Dakhinī Hindī and Pañjābī', *Vishveshvaranand Indological Journal* 12: 336–50.

Sharma, S. (1974b) *Kāgaṛī: a Descriptive Study of the Kangra Valley Dialect of Himachal Pradesh*, Hoshiarpur, Vishveshvaranand Vishva Bandhu Institute.
—— (1975) 'Some Phonological Characteristics of Ḍogarī Language', *Vishveshvaranand Indological Journal* 13: 311–7.
Sherani, H. M. (1930) *Panjāb meṁ Urdū*, Lahore: Islamia College.
Singh, A. (1970) 'An introduction to the dialects of Punjabi', *Pàkha Sanjam*, 1, 2: 120–52.
—— (1979) 'Linguistic interaction and social differentiation in a Punjab village', *Indian Linguistics* 40: 294–300.
—— (1981) 'Problems of systematic linguistic differences among different social status: a case study of a Punjabi village', *Pàkha Sanjam* 14: 95–104.
Singh, G. B. (1972) *Gurmukhī Lipī dā Janam te Vikās*, 2nd ed., Chandigarh: Punjab University.
Singh, I. (1981) *A Critical Assessment of the Teaching of Punjabi in the Punjab State at the School Stage*, Ludhiana: Lahore Book Shop.
Singh, J. D. (1970) *A Descriptive Grammar of Bangru*, Kurukshetra: Kurukshetra University.
Singh, M. (1895) *The Panjábí Dictionary*, Lahore: Munshi Gulab Singh.
Singh, T. (1980) *English–Panjabi Dictionary*, 4th ed., Ludhiana: Lahore Book Shop.
Smirnov, Y. A. (1975) *The Lahndi Language*, Moscow: Nauka.
Tolstaya, N. I. (1981) *The Punjabi Language: a Descriptive Grammar*, tr. G. L. Campbell, London: Routledge and Kegan Paul.
Varma, S. (1936) 'The phonetics of Lahnda', *Journal of the Royal Asiatic Society of Bengal*, N.S. 2: 47–118.
—— (1964) 'The role of consonants in the stress and syllabification of the Ambalvi dialect', *Indian Linguistics* 25: 61–6.
—— (1965) 'Aspiration in North-West sub-Himalayan Indo-Aryan dialects', *Indian Linguistics* 26: 175–88.
Vatuk, V. P. (1964) *Panjabi Reader*, 2 vols, Fort Collins: Colorado State University.
Wells, C. and Roach, P. (1980) 'An experimental investigation of some aspects of tone in Punjabi', *Journal of Phonetics* 8: 85–9.
Wilson, J. (1899) *Grammar and Dictionary of Western Panjabi, as Spoken in the Shahpur District*, Lahore: Punjab Government Press.

FURTHER READING

Bahri, H. (1963) *Lahndi Phonetics, with Special Reference to Awáṇkárí*, Allahabad: Bharati Press.
Bhardwaj, M. R. (1995) *Colloquial Panjabi: a Complete Language Course*, London and New York: Routledge.
Bhatia, T. K. (1993) *Punjabi: a Cognitive-Descriptive Grammar*, London and New York: Routledge.
Gill, H. S. and Gleason, H. A. (1969) *A Reference Grammar of Panjabi*, 2nd ed., Patiala: Punjabi University.
Koul, O. N. and Bala, M. (1992) *Punjabi Language and Linguistics: an Annotated Bibliography*, Patiala: Indian Institute of Language Studies.
Punjabi University (1994) *Punjabi–English Dictionary*, Patiala: Punjabi University.
Shackle, C. (1970) 'Punjabi in Lahore', *Modern Asian Studies* 4: 239–67.
—— (1976) *The Siraiki Language of Central Pakistan: a Reference Grammar*, London: School of Oriental and African Studies.
—— (1979) 'Problems of Classification in Pakistan Panjab', *Transactions of the Philological Society*.
—— (1980) 'Hindko in Kohat and Peshawar', *Bulletin of the School of Oriental and African Studies* 43: 482–510.
—— (1983) *An Introduction to the Sacred Language of the Sikhs*, London: School of Oriental and African Studies.
—— (1995) *A Gurū Nānak Glossary*, 2nd ed., New Delhi: Heritage.

SINDHI

Lachman M. Khubchandani

CONTENTS

LIST OF TABLES

1 BACKGROUND

1.1 Current state of Sindhi and Sindhi studies

Sindhi occupies a prominent place among the languages of South Asia. According to the 1991 estimates, Sindhi is spoken by approximately 18 million people in the Indian subcontinent. Over eighty percent of them are in the Sindh and Lasa B'elo (Baluchistan) regions of Pakistan. Nearly three million Sindhi speakers are in India; about one third of them are from the Kutch-Saurashtra region in Gujarat and the Jaisalmer district in Rajasthan. The rest are associated with the post-partition migration from Sindh; they are now spread throughout the urban and semi-urban centres in the country with concentrations in the states of Maharashtra, Gujarat, Rajasthan, Madhya Pradesh and the National Capital Territory of Delhi. Many Sindhi speakers, engaged in overseas trade called 'Sindhwork', are also scattered in important trade centres throughout the Southeast Asia region (Singapore, Jakarta, Manila), Hongkong, Japan, the Gulf, the African west coast, Spain and Gibraltar.

Different varieties of Sindhi speech are generally classified into six major dialects:

(1) Siraiki, spoken in Siro, i.e. Upper Sindh;
(2) Vicholi, in Vicholo, i.e. Central Sindh;
(3) Lari, in Laru, i.e. Lower Sindh;

(4) Lasi, in Lasa B'elo, a part of Kohistan in Baluchistan on the western side of Sindh;
(5) Thari or Thareli, in Tharu, the desert region on the southeast border of Sindh and a part of the Jaisalmer district in Rajasthan;
(6) Kachhi, in the Kutch region and in a part of Kathiawar in Gujarat, on the southern side of Sindh.

Vicholi is considered as the standard dialect by all Sindhi speakers, except those speaking Kachhi. It is commonly used among the educated class and is accepted as the language of literature and education (also for administration in Sindh). Although Kachhi is very close to Sindhi and the standard dialect Vicholi is quite intelligible to a Kachhi speaker, he does not feel drawn to imitate the prestige dialect, since the Sindh and Kutch regions have grown as separate political and social units during the past six centuries. Kachhi speakers generally show a closer sociocultural affinity with the Gujarati-speaking community or aspire to maintain a separate identity of their own. Since 1947, with the partition of the Indian subcontinent, the Sindh-Kutch border forms the international boundary demarcating Pakistan and India on the western side.

Kachhi has many characteristics in common with Lari and Vicholi. It has also imbibed certain features of Gujarati and Marwari. A northern sub-variety adjoining the Sindh border, called B'ani, is closer to the standard Vicholi.

The partition of the Indian subcontinent into two sovereign states – India and Pakistan – in 1947 hit the Sindhi language quite hard. It witnessed a great ordeal of mass migration of the Hindu population. A migration on such a scale has led to the scattering and reassembling of speakers of different dialects from one part of the region to another. With these disruptions, communication patterns in the region have gone through a considerable change. Many rural speakers in Sindh, previously living in an unidialectal environment have now reassembled in different urban and semi-urban settlements in India, and the Sindhi language has got moulded in multidialectal and multilingual environments.

1.1.1 Influences

The Sindhi region is surrounded by Dravidian, Iranian and Indo-Aryan languages: Balochi (an Iranian language) and Brahui (a North Dravidian language) in the west, Pashto (another Iranian language) in the north, Multani and Bahawalpuri (Lahnda dialects, northwest Indo-Aryan) in the north and northeast, Marwari (a Rajasthani dialect, central Indo-Aryan) in the east, and Gujarati (central Indo-Aryan) in the south.

Sindh, situated astride some of the major approaches to northwestern South Asia, had been a much frequented invasion route and it has been known as a 'gateway' to immigrants from the northwest: Aryans, Greeks, Scythians, Arabs, Turks, and so on. It has been a meeting ground of different cultures; hence Sindhi shows great susceptibility towards borrowings from different languages. Since the eighth century AD after the first invasion of Sindh by the Arabs, the vocabulary and grammar of the Sindhi language have been saturated with Arabic and Persian elements in roughly similar proportions as English is with French. Besides, with the persistent influence of Hinduism, the Bhakti movement and the spread of the Sikh faith (during fifteenth to eighteenth centuries), along with the cultural impact of British rule during the one hundred years before 1947 and the influence of modern technological advancement in the South Asian subcontinent, Sindhi includes a large stock of borrowings and re-borrowings from

Sanskrit, Hindi-Urdu, Persian–Arabic, and English, as a pan-Indian characteristic (Khubchandani 1963).

During the five decades since partition in 1947, the Sindhi language in Pakistan and in India has drifted in two different directions. The language of post-partition Sindh continues to lean heavily towards Perso–Arabic and Urdu styles to identify itself with the Islamic culture, whereas in the Sindhi of Indian migrants the use of unassimilated Perso-Arabic elements has been considerably reduced, in favour of tatsamization under the influences of Sanskrit and Hindi, in order to conform to the general Indian milieu. Another prominent feature affecting modern Sindhi is the drift towards Englishization under cosmopolitan and modern influences in both countries (Khubchandani 1963: 72–5).

1.1.2 Sindhi studies

Linguistic studies of Sindhi can be traced back to the middle of the nineteenth century, which produced great scholars like Stack and Trumpp in the fields of lexicography and grammar.

Descriptions of the language written by Princep (1835), Ramos (1836), and Wathen (1836) are first attempts. Grammars prepared by Capt. Stack (1853), Moonshi Oodharam (1857), and Meean Mohamed and Moonshi Pribhdas (1860) are authentic and meritorious works, primarily meant for teaching Sindhi to European officers and missionaries. The first detailed grammar based on philological comparisons with Sanskrit and Prakrit was written by Trumpp (1872). At the same time, Beames (1872–9) also wrote a comparative grammar of modern Indo-Aryan languages, covering Hindi, Bengali, Oriya and Sindhi, among others. Capt. Stack (1849, 1855) and Rev. Shirt and Mirza (1879) did pioneering work in the preparation of Sindhi dictionaries.

During the twentieth century, linguistic studies on Sindhi have developed along more or less the same lines as Indian linguistics in general. Grierson's *Linguistic Survey of India* (1903–28) is an achievement unparalleled in this century. In Volume VIII (1919), he surveys all dialects of Sindhi and presents a brief account of standard Sindhi. Parmanand Mewaram's *Sindhi–English Dictionary* (1910) and *English–Sindhi Dictionary* (1933) are leading contributions in the field of lexicography. German scholars including Trumpp (1866), Sorley (1940) and Schimmel (1981) have particularly concentrated on the language of the Sufi poet Shah Abdul Latif (1689–1752), popularly known as 'Shah Bhitai'. In writing the history of Sindhi language and literature, Memon (1937), Sehwani (1940), Bherumal Advani (1941), Pandit Jetley (1957), Baloch (1962), Siraj-ul-Haq (1964), Yegorova (1966), Jotwani (1966), and Jatoi's (1968) attempts are significant.

After the turmoil of the partition subsided, Sindhi immigrants, through their sustained endeavours in education and literature, have transplanted firm roots on Indian soil and Sindhi studies have made a steady progress parallel to the studies in other major Indian languages. In Pakistan also, during the past five decades, the vacuum in Sindhi studies created by the migration of Sindhi Hindus has been filled to a considerable extent, and language studies are making steady progress.

In the post-Independence era, there has been considerable increase in research on the Sindhi language in both Pakistan and India, to introduce modern techniques for describing the language. In this respect, the phonological and morphophonemic accounts of Bordie (1958), and Khubchandani (1961, 1963), and the application of the transformation-generative model on phonology by Ruplin and Steinmetz (1967), instrumental phonetics by Nihalani (1972, 1974), and Mukherjee (1998), morphosyntactic description by M. K. Jetley (1965) and by Tolani-Parchani (1973) and on historical phonology by Wadhwani (1997) are noteworthy. In the field of lexicography, Baloch's *Comprehensive Sindhi Dictionary* in five volumes (1961–81) and Kishnani's *Sindhi* proverbs and idioms (1993) are regarded as monumental works. Linguistic characteristics of Sindhi dialects have been extensively covered under the folklore studies by Baloch (1965), Sandeelo (1973), Allana (1979), Jonejo and Hidayat Prem (1994) in Pakistan, and Bharati (1991), Gidwani (1971), Rohra (1968), and Lalwani (1998) in India. Sociolinguistic accounts of the transplantation of Sindhi in India by Khubchandani (1963, 1997), Barnouw (1954, 1966), Daswani and Parchani (1978), and of the stratificational networks of Sindhi in Pakistan by Bughio (1992) also have made a significant contribution to Sindhi studies. In addition, the phenomenon of language contact in a historical perspective is highlighted in monographs on Arabic elements in Sindhi by Allana (1964), similarities with Dravidian (through the influence of Brahui) by Gidwani (1996), on writing system by Allana (1967), and by M. K. Jetley (1999).

1.2 Historical background

Sindh was the seat of the ancient Indus Valley civilization during the third millennium BC, as discovered from the Mohen-jo-daro excavations. The pictographic seals and clay tablets obtained from these excavations still await proper decipherment by epigraphists. 'It is one of the unsolved puzzles regarding the peoples of the ancient cities of the Indus; the script remains as unknown as Goethe's "she"' (Possehl 1996: 1), (for a comprehensive review of the contending claims in the field, see Possehl 1996, 1999).

Attempts to read the Indus Valley inscriptions are marked by a wide range of hypotheses claiming language affiliations from Dravidian, Indo-Aryan, Sumerian, Egyptian, even Malayo-Polynesian. Though there is very little agreement among the scholars concerning the nature of the writing system and its history, most scholars hold the common ground that the script is to be read from right to left (Zvelebil 1970, 1990).

On the basis of cultural connections with Mesopotamia, early archaeologists believed these seals have correspondence with Sumerian or Proto-Elamite writing (cf. findings of Gad 1931, Petrie 1932, Hunter 1934, cited in Possehl 1996). Later, some attempts were made to see a close relation with Indo-Iranian (Hrozny 1939), as the progenitor of Brahmi writing; Rao (1992) assumes that the Harappans invented the alphabet and the seals excavated from Lothal and other sites in Kathiawar show resemblances with a kind of Proto-Sanskrit. By and large, many epigraphists including the Soviet team (Knorozov, Gurov and others 1968) and the Finnish team (Asko Parpola and others 1969, 1994), Mahadevan (1979), using computer techniques, support the reading of Dravidian in these inscriptions.

On linguistic grounds, Grierson (1919) has classified Sindhi as a member of the northwestern group of the Indo-Aryan family. Another member of the group is Lahnda (also known as Siraiki/Multani) in Western Punjab in Pakistan. Sindhi shares the antiquity of Primary Prākrits with its sister modern Indo-Aryan languages, and has been reconstructed through the stages of Old Indo-Aryan (OIA) and Middle Indo-Aryan (MIA).

Trumpp initiated studies on historical phonology of Sindhi to Sanskrit and Prakrit. Later, in the introduction to *Sindhi Grammar* (1872), Trumpp proclaims: 'The Sindhi is a pure Sanskritical language, more free from foreign elements than any other of the North Indian vernaculars ... It is much more closely related to the Old Prakrit than the

Marathi, Hindi, Panjabi and Bengali of our days and it has preserved an exuberance of grammatical forms, for which all its sisters may well envy it' (p. I). Beames' *Comparative Grammar* (Vol. 1 1872, Vol. 2 1875, and Vol. 3 1880), and Hoernle's *A Comparative Grammar of the Gaudian Languages* (1880), comparing seven Indo-Aryan languages – Hindi, Punjabi, Sindhi, Gujarati, Marathi, Oriya and Bengali – are also significant contributions to New Indo-Aryan (NIA) studies.

Pischel, in *Grammatik der Prākrit-Sprachen* (1900), has claimed it to be directly derived from the Vracada Apabhraṁśa, on the basis of Markandeya's statement in *Prakṛtasarvasva* that 'the Vracada Apabhraṁśa form of Prakrit has its origin in Sindhu Desa'. Very little is known about the Vracada itself, except nine peculiarities noted by Markandeya. Grierson (1902) has supported Markandeya's statement by illustrating certain Vracada characteristics in Sindhi – cerebralization of MIA dental stops, implosive [ĵ], representing Vracada [yj], etc. In support of his theory of Inner and Outer Indo-Aryan languages, he claimed that the modern languages of northwest India (including Sindhi) are intimately connected with those of the East (from Bihar to Assam).

Turner (1924) discusses the development of cerebrals in Sindhi from Primitive Indian dentals, suggesting that Dravidian speech habits may have affected the final direction of a tendency already existing in the language: Sanskrit. *putraḥ*, Sindhi *pUṭU* 'son'; Skt. *dīrgha*-, Sd. *ḍIgho* 'long'; Skt. *devaraḥ*, Sd. *ḍerU* 'brother-in-law'; Skt. *janaḥ*, Sd. *ĵəṇo* 'person'. Turner (1924) claims the development of recursives in Sindhi, termed 'implosives' by Bailey (1922), from geminated voiced plosives: Skt. *agra*, Pali *agga*, Sindhi *əĝU* 'before'.

During the present century, various Indo-Aryan scholars have modified the myth that all NIA languages could be traced directly from early 'primary' Prakrits spoken during the Vedic period and that classical Sanskrit depicts a standardized variety of one of the later 'secondary' Prākrits. In this light, Jairamdas (1957) raises doubts concerning Pischel's and Grierson's view that the Sindhi language was derived from Vracada, and suggests that an ancient variant of the pre-Vedic period, spoken by the people of the Lower Indus Valley, has probably continued to evolve, acquiring the form of Old Sindhi in the phase of the Secondary Prakrits.

A few earlier accounts written in the Sindhi language have supported Pischel and Grierson's treatment in this regard (Sehwani 1940, Advani 1941). On the other hand, a few scholars in post-partition Sindh have been painfully striving to demonstrate the ancestry of Sindhi as being different from the Indo-Aryan languages (Baloch 1962, Jatoi 1968, Allana 1974, Panwhar 1988). Baloch (1962) goes to the extent of speculating on its close relation with Semitic languages and claims that 'the Sanskrit–Prākrit languages have only insignificant influence on Sindhi' (p. 12).

Another line of investigation, based on the debate over the decipherment of the Indus Valley seals and clay tablets, referred to above, has led to many speculative inferences of claiming a unique character of the language, its antiquity and its supposed superiority over its sister languages. Under the spell of language chauvinism, Ruchandani (1963) and Siraj-ul-Haq (1964) biased to claim the heritage of the Indus Valley civilization, identify the supposed pre-Indo-Aryan stage anterior to Sanskrit with the proto-stage of the Sindhi language. Ruchandani tries to show the correspondences of modern Sindhi vocables with Phoenician and Sumerian sources; etymologizing 'Phoenician' as *paṇi* or *ponir* mentioned in Ṛgveda and then correlating it with Sindhi *vāṇyo*, Sanskrit *vaṇij*- 'trader'; it has been claimed that the Indus Valley civilization had spread to the Babylonian and Sumerian people. Taking the cue from Kramer's remarks on Dilmun, a

Sumerian site near the Gulf, Siraj surmises that the Phoenician script is derived from Proto-Sindhian of the Mohen-jo-daro times. Pandit Jetley (1985) has attempted to read *haṭavāṇika* letters (a traders' script, without vowel markers) in these inscriptions.

Structural evidence of the language, however, establishes beyond any doubt its affinity with the Indo-Aryan language family. Various works of Indian philologists – Bhandarkar (1914), Gune (1918), Chatterji (1942), Vale (1948) and Katre (1961) – include Sindhi among their comparative studies of NIA languages. Turner's *Comparative Etymological Dictionary of the Nepali Language* (1931) and his magnum opus *A Comparative and Etymological Dictionary of the Indo-Aryan Languages* (1966), compares Sindhi data in a comprehensive manner. Samtani (1957) attests the phonological correspondences of Sindhi and Sanskrit, and extends them to Pali. Khubchandani (1961) presents phonological material on Sindhi when correlating its development with other Indo-Aryan languages. Yelizarenkova's (1964) typological observations about new Indo-Aryan phonology based on Sindhi, and Khubchandani's (1966) reconstruction of different stages of borrowings from Sanskrit provide finer shades of relating Sindhi to Indo-Aryan.

1.2.1 Written records

At present, there is no earlier record of or reference to the features of the Sindhi language than Bharatamuni's *Nāṭyaśāstra* of the second century AD, which makes mention of the language of the people of Sindhu-Sauvira, and refers to some of its features. The language of the Saindhavas figured among the important *deśabhāṣās* of the country in Uddyotana's *Kuvalayamālā* written in AD 779 (Upadhye 1959). It includes short specimens of early NIA dialect variations, including the variety spoken by Saindhavas. In this work, the author speaks of the poetry of the people of Sindh as 'graceful, sweet, soft-toned and inspired by patriotic sentiment' (Jairamdas 1958). Hemchandra's *Deśīnāmamālā* also includes a specimen of Sindhi (Pischel 1938).

Chatterji (1958) referred to a Persian version of the *Mahābhārata* translated by Abu-ul-Hassan in AD 1026 from Arabic, which itself was translated from an Indian language by Abu Salih. On the basis of the phonological study of the forms of the Indian names, as they can be reconstructed from the Arabic transcription, Chatterji claims that the language of the original composition may be called Old Sindhi – the Sindhi language at the time of its emergence as NIA speech from MIA, prior to or around AD 1000. The initial portion of the Persian version covers the early history of Sindh prior to Sindh's connection with the *Mahābhārata* heroes. Jairamdas (1958) refers to the same version, summarized at a later date, in *Mujamil-al-Tārikh* and on the strength of certain historical references, infers that the original Sindhi composition must be around 300 BC, written by a minister of the court named Sapar. Khubchandani (1959), on the basis of the phonological reconstruction of the proper names, supports Chatterji's conservative claim for the original composition being around AD 1000.

Through certain oblique references in the historical records of Al-Biruni (eleventh century) and other Arab writers, it can be deduced that Sindhi was available in written form during the eighth century AD. The *Quran* was first translated into Sindhi in AD 883. A Persian history of ancient Sindh, written around AD 1216 called *Chachanama*, also refers to varieties of writing prevalent in Sindh during the eighth and ninth centuries.

The folklore attributed to Mamui *fakirs*, Qazi Qadan and Rajput poets is traced back to fourteenth and fifteenth centuries AD (cf. Thakur 1997). From the sixteenth century onwards till the beginning of prose in Sindhi in the nineteenth century, writings in

Sindhi are available mainly in the form of devotional poetry, attributed to Sufi *derveshes* such as Shah Latif, and Sachal Sarmast, and Hindu Vedantis Pran Nath, Sami and others.

2 PHONOLOGY

2.1 Introduction

The phonological system of Sindhi in most respects resembles that of other Indo–Aryan languages. Sindhi has 53 distinct sound-units, called segmental phonemes: 39 consonants, 3 semivowels, 10 vowels, and a unit of nasalization. These sounds can be tabulated as shown in table 17.1.

2.2 Consonants

2.2.1 General

The Sindhi consonant system consists of 25 stops (including 4 palatal affricates), 5 nasals, 6 fricatives and 3 liquids. Consonantal sounds show five-fold contrast in the place of articulation: labial, dental, retroflex, palatal and velar. Uvular voiceless consonant *q* occurs only in the formal speech of Persian-oriented speakers.

TABLE 17.1: SEGMENTAL PHONEMES

	Labials	Dentals	Retroflex	Palatals	Velars	Uvular
Consonants						
Stops						
vl. unasp.	*p*	*t*	*ṭ*	*c*	*k*	*(q)*
vl. asp.	*ph*	*th*	*ṭh*	*ch*	*kh*	
vd. unasp.	*b*	*d*	*ḍ*	*j*	*g*	
vd. asp.	*bh*	*dh*	*ḍh*	*jh*	*gh*	
implosives	*ɓ*		*ɗ*	*ʄ*	*ĝ*	
Nasals: vd.	*m*	*n*	*ṇ*	*ñ*	*ṅ*	
Fricatives						
vl.	*f*	*s*		*ś*	*x*	
vd.		*z*			*ɣ*	
Liquids						
Lateral vd.		*l*				
trill vd.		*r*				
flap vd.			*ṛ*			
Semivowels	*v*			*y*		*h* (glottal)
Vowels						
	Front	Central	Back			
High	*i*		*u*			
Lower high	*I*		*U*			
Mid	*e*	*ə*	*o*			
Lower mid	*ɛ*		*ɔ*			
Low		*a*				
Nasalization	*ṽ* (accompanying vowels)					

Note: vl.: voiceless, vd.: voiced, unasp.: unaspirated, asp.: aspirated.

2.2.2 Stops

Sindhi has the fullest stop system of any of the Indo-Aryan languages. The stop series shows contrast between voicing and unvoicing – *b p*, aspiration – *ph p*, and pressure and suction – *b ɓ*. The palatal series consists of affricate sounds, but it functions like other stop series, maintaining the contrast of voicing, aspiration and suction. Fricatives also show contrast between voicing and unvoicing. Nasals and liquids are only voiced.

A series of four implosive stops – *ɓ ɗ ʄ ɠ* (in sounding them the breath is drawn in instead of being expelled as in *b ḍ j g*) is a striking characteristic of Sindhi phonology. There is a conspicuous gap of dental implosive in the system:

> *barU* 'load', *ɓarU* 'child'
> *ḍohU* 'treachery', *ɗohU* 'fault'
> *jaro* 'shelf', *ʄaro* 'web'
> *gano* 'song', *ɠano* 'reed'.

Sindhi is the only Indo-Aryan language which has six distinct nasal sound-units: five nasal consonants and one nasalization (accompanying vowels):

> *kəmU* 'work', *kənU* 'ear', *kəṇU* 'particle'
> *thəñU* 'breast-milk', *səṅU* 'relation', *kə̃vəlU* 'lotus'.

It is interesting to note that the sub-varieties of the Kachhi dialect which are closer to Gujarati retain a lesser number of implosives and nasal phonemes than other dialects of Sindhi. The Bani variety includes all the four implosives and six nasal phonemes as in standard Sindhi. But the Mandvi variety has only two implosives *ɓ ɗ* and five nasal contrasts (with the gap of palatal *ñ*) and the Vagdi variety has only one implosive – *ɓ* – and four nasal contrasts (with the gap of *ñ* and *ṅ*).

Fricatives *f z* occur only in Perso-Arabic and English borrowed items, and *q x ɣ* occur only in Perso-Arabic words.

Many consonant-ending items borrowed from Perso-Arabic, English and Sanskrit-Hindi sources generally add final *-U* if assigned to masculine gender, or *-a*, *-i* if assigned to feminine gender:

> masculine: *mərzU* 'disease', *ṭvalU* 'towel', *pUstəkU* 'book'
> feminine: *relə* 'railway train', *ləkirə* 'line', *jəngI* 'war',
>   *nərsI* 'nurse', *bəratI* 'marriage-procession'.

Certain borrowed items, occurring indeclinable in the source language, do not add any vocalic ending in Sindhi and retain their consonantal ending even when these occur in isolation or in slow speech:

> *beśək* 'undoubtedly', *fasṭ* 'quick, fast', *hasṭIl* 'hostel',
> *om* 'the sacred letter (in Hindu rituals)', *dUkhədayk* 'sorrowful'.

In rapid and informal speech, word-final *I* or *U* is often not pronounced, and thus the consonant preceding the potential vowel occurs in final position:

> *chokərU, chokər* 'boy', *chokərI, chokər* 'girl', *xərabU, xərab* 'bad',
> *cəyãĩsI, cəyãĩs* 'He (she) told him/her'.

In contrast to other Indo-Aryan languages, doubling of consonants is not significant in Sindhi. Very few consonant clusters occur in the items of native stock, and these too only in medial position, always across a syllable boundary:

surmo 'hero', *chIṛbə* 'rebuff', *səmḍU* 'ocean',
ḍəndU 'tooth', *vəɲjU* 'trade'.

In slow speech, two segments of a non-homorganic cluster are often separated by *-I-*:
kUṛmi or *kUṛImi* 'farmer', *ənbho* or *əṇIbho* 'dry' (through want of oil).

Extensive borrowings from Perso–Arabic, Sanskrit–Hindi and European (mainly English and, to some extent, Portuguese) sources have brought considerable changes to the cluster pattern of the language. Many new clusters have been added, quite frequently in medial position. Initial and final clusters are non-existent in the native stock. But occasional examples of such clusters do occur in borrowed items, especially in the speech of bilinguals. These borrowings have also introduced a few three-member clusters in the speech of the elite:

IśqU 'love', *gasleṭU* 'gaslight (kerosene oil)',
ekta 'unity', *sənbandhU* 'relationship',
ḍrama 'drama', *snehU* 'affection', *bUlənd* 'high',
ṭɛks 'tax' *eksre* 'X-ray', *raśṭriy* 'national'.

2.3 Semivowels

In Sindhi *v y h* function similarly to consonants in initial and certain medial positions. But in final position and also medially when preceding or following a consonant, these occur as vocalic glides; thus forming diphthongs with preceding or following vowels. Hence these are classified as semivowels.

Consonantal sounds:

yUdhI 'battle', *cəyo* 'said', *ãhyā* '(I) am',
vəlI 'creeper', *sava* 'green (m. pl.)', *təhvarU* 'festival',
heṭhI 'below', *səho* 'rabbit', *təvhĩ* 'you (pl.)', *ekĨhĩ* 'twenty-first (f.)'.

Vocalic glides:

poy 'afterwards', *bhayṭi* 'niece', *b̂yõ* 'second (m. sg.)',
jiv 'soul, person', *Utavlo* 'impatient', *kvãri* 'bride', *kə̃h* 'who',
sahmi 'weighing balance', *əhnsa* 'non-violence'.

A few triphthongs, in which one semivowel occurs as an on-glide and other as an off-glide to a vowel, also occur in non-initial position:

cəryaypə 'madness', *vIdhvavnI* 'widows (pl. obl.)', *hyãv* 'heart',
dhvũy 'We wash (it) for you'.

2.4 Vowels

Sindhi has a ten-vowel system, showing three-fold contrast in the tongue-position: front, central and back; and five-fold contrast in the tongue-height: high, lower-high, lower-mid and low. These vowels are phonetically and structurally divided into two classes:

(1)   *I U ə* are phonetically short, and
(2)   *i e ɛ a ɔ o u* are phonetically long.

Short vowels in final position are pronounced very lightly and when occurring unstressed, they are not easily perceptible to a non-native listener:

chokərI 'girl', *chokərU* 'boy', *chokərə* 'boys'.

In Sindhi *ε ɔ* are noticeably less frequent, occurring in borrowed items. These are often replaced by *e o*, respectively:

εśU or *eśU* 'luxury', *nɔdU* or *nodU* 'stubborn, blockhead'.

All vowels occur in initial, medial and final positions, and sequences of two vowels also occur in all these positions. A few sequences of diphthong plus vowel, and of three vowels, also occur in final position:

oi 'small waterbag', *juərI* 'millet', *kə̃ẽ* 'several', *aino* 'mirror', *poay* 'get (beads etc.) threaded!', *myãũ* 'mewing (of a cat)', *hũə̃ĩ* 'nevertheless', *maiə* 'woman (obl.)'.

2.5 Nasalization

Every vowel has a nasalized counterpart in the language:

əsi 'eighty',	*əsĩ* 'we';
dehI 'body',	*mēhĨ* 'buffalo';
me 'May (month)',	*mẽ* 'in, into';
mɛdo 'fine flour',	*mɛ̃s* 'within';
huə 'she',	*hũə̃* 'otherwise';
ĝay 'Sing!',	*gãy* 'cow';
kɔri 'bitter (f.)',	*tɔ̃ri* 'mat';
həthyo 'handle',	*məthyõ* 'upper (m. sg.)';
mohU 'attachment',	*mŨh̃Ũ* 'face';
khau 'glutton, bribe-taker',	*khãũ* 'Let's eat'.

The feature of nasalization runs through the sequence of vowels, and often when two vowels are intercepted by semivowels. It is also extended to the preceding and following semivowels:

hĩə̃rə 'now', *nãĩ* 'ninth (f.)', *kə̃və̃lU* 'lotus', *ĝãyũ* 'we sing', *ãhyã* '(I) am', *ə̃hvĩ* 'you (pl.)'.

2.6 Syllables

Syllable division in a word is predictable in Sindhi. Word-stress is also predicated on the strength of the syllable structure. Sindhi is primarily an open-syllable language, i.e. syllables mostly end with a vowel or semivowels. Words in Sindhi mostly have vocalic ending and the occurrence of consonant cluster is also sporadic in the language. Close syllables are very infrequent in the language.

A syllable in Sindhi consists of at least one vowel or at most five sound-units, in which one is a vowel and others are non-vocalic sounds (consonants or semivowels preceding or following the vowel). Open syllables with a single consonant (CV) are most frequent in the language:

ɛ̃ 'and', *jay* 'place', *hyãv* 'heart', *ṭe* 'three', *dhvo* 'Wash! (pl.)', *nə-ve* 'ninety', *ə-ke-lo* 'lonely'.

A word in Sindhi consists of one or more syllables. It can have a maximum of eight syllables. Words with two or three syllables predominate in the language:

ɗəh-kav 'terror', *kha-in-do* 'he will eat', *pəñ-jvəñ-ja-hU* 'fifty-five', *ve-sa-hə-gha-ti* 'faithlessness', *və-ɗə-maṇ-hI-pa-i* 'a high notion of one's dignity, snobbery', *ə-ṇə-vI-kam-jən-də-ṛU* 'unsalable', *mo-kI-la-ra-in-do-sã-sI* 'I (m.) shall get (it) sent to him/her'.

2.7 Stress

In Sindhi, stress has only a limited use for demarcating words and putting emphasis on a particular word in an utterance. There are three distinct stresses: word stress, emphatic stress and drawled stress.

At the word-level, difference in relative loudness or prominence of syllables is not a distinctive feature. A phonologic word has only one prominent syllable, that is, syllable with primary stress, and other syllables in a word have secondary or weak stresses. The position of these stresses is predicted in a word on the basis of syllable division:

phə-ṭa-ko 'fire-cracker', *kha-in-də-ṛU* 'one who eats'.

Sindhi allows placing an emphatic stress on any word in an utterance. The stress is normally used in an emphatic statement and its position in an utterance shifts according to the object of emphasis:

mã	pəñjə	həfta	tərsyUsI	'I waited for five weeks.'
mã	pəñjə	həfta	tərsyUsI	'I (not any one else) waited for five weeks.'
mã	**pəñjə**	həfta	tərsyUsI	*'I waited for full five (not one or two) weeks.'*
mã	pəñjə	**həfta**	tərsyUsI	'I waited for a stretch of five weeks (not days).'

In Sindhi conversation often length and syllables preceding and following a syllable are stretched four to five times their normal length, and syllables preceding and following the drawled syllable are very much shortened. The drawling of the initial syllable usually denotes confirmation or encouragement and is often used in baby-talk or in patronizing speech, whereas the drawling of the final syllable denotes persuasion or irritation: *ahIste, aste* 'slowly', *aaaste* '(yes) still slower', *asteee* '(I again remind you) be slow'.

2.8 Intonation

Most of the Indian languages have identical intonational systems. In Sindhi, there are four pitch-levels: low, mid, high and extra-high. The common intonation of an ordinary utterance is mid-high-low, the mid pitch-level occurring at the beginning, high at the centre, and low at the end. A large sentence usually has the intonation pattern of mid-high-extra high-low. At the clause boundary, the final pitch is generally at the mid level. These four pitch-levels can be transcribed as 1, 2, 3, 4 respectively:

2 cəṅo	*2 haṇe +*	*bhəlI*	*3 nə + 1 əcU*
alright	now	as you desire	no come

'Alright, (you) needn't come now.'

2 əjU +	*3 tũ +*	*4 zərurU +*	*mũsã +*	*3 gəɗU +*	*1 həlU*
today	you	certainly	me-with	together	come

'You must accompany me today.'

2.9 Juncture

Every word is normally separated by a slight pause between sound-units and certain rhythmical features of overall intensity and pitch pattern. The pause characterizing a word boundary is known as internal open juncture (+). A sharp shift (without any pause) from one sound-unit to another marks the syllable boundary (-):

və-ḍa-i 'pride, arrogance', *və-ḍa* + *i* 'even elders'.
cho-kI-ri 'girl', *cho* + *kI-ri* 'Why did (she) fall?'.

A longer pause and slowed-up articulation marks the clause boundary, and somewhat longer pause and gradual cut-off of voicing plus other intonational features mark the completion of an utterance. Terminal juncture with falling pitch marks the declarative utterance, whereas terminal juncture accompanied by rise in pitch characterizes the exclamatory or interrogative utterance:

pUṭU + *nə* + *dhiə*   'Neither son nor daughter.'
pUṭU | *nə* + *dhiə*   'Son, not daughter.'
pUṭU + *nə* | *dhiə*   'Not son, (only) daughter.'

khirU + *cãhĨ* | 'Milk, tea '(Let me see, what else. ....?).'
khirU + *cãhĨ* ↓   'Milk (and) tea (complete list).'
khirU + *cãhĨ* ↑   '(Did you say) milk (and) tea?'

3 WRITING SYSTEM

3.1 Introduction

Sindhi has used various scripts during the course of its history. Stack, in his *Grammar of the Sindhi Language* (1853), referred to various forms of Devanagari and Lunda scripts prevalent at that time in Sindhi among Hindu traders and Ismaili Muslims: Khudawadi, Shikarpuri, Sakhru, Thattai, Larai, Wangai, Rajai, Khwajiko, Memanko, Sewhani Bhambhira. Modified Perso-Arabic characters, called Ab-ul-Hassan Sindhi, and the Gurmukhi script, which is an improved form of Lunda with borrowed features from the Devanagari script, were also in use for literary and religious writings.

3.2 Script reforms

The policy of British rulers to run their administration at the lower level in the native language was instrumental in evolving one script for Sindhi in the midst of diverse usage. Initially some efforts were made to devise an improved Lunda script, mainly based on Khudawadi and Shikarpuri forms of writing. Many scholars, like Stack and Trumpp, prepared a modified version of the Devanagari script to suit the needs of the Sindhi language. But ultimately due to the pressures from Muslims and Persian-oriented Hindus, later a modified Perso-Arabic alphabet was adopted for the language, extending the twenty-nine Arabic letters to fifty-two, to express Sindhi sounds. The revised script was mainly used for the purposes of administration and education. But the use of other scripts continued, in a limited way, for commercial, religious and personal purposes. A few rural schools and *rātripāṭhaśālās* (night classes) in urban areas continued to teach Sindhi in Devanagari or Gurmukhi characters.

After the migration of Sindhi Hindus to India, the movement of reviving the Devanagari script for educational and literary purposes has gained ground. The Union Government recognizes both Perso-Arabic and Devanagari scripts for the language. Hence, some schools and colleges in India have introduced the teaching of Sindhi in the Devanagari script. Recently, certain literary works have also been transliterated into Devanagari characters. In post-Independent India, a few literary writings in Kachhi Sindhi have introduced Gujarati characters (a variety of the Devanagari script).

3.3 Sindhi–Arabic script

The Sindhi–Arabic script is adapted from the Persian system of writing, which itself is an adaptation of the Arabic system. Arabic characters are written from right to left. The script comprises fifty-two characters and seven diacritic signs:

(i) twenty-nine characters of the Arabic script.

(ii) three modified characters adopted from the Persian script: پ   چ   گ
       p   c   g

(iii) twenty modified characters to represent Sindhi sounds:

Retroflex sounds:	ٽ	ٺ	ڊ	ڍ	ڌ	ڻ	ڙ
	ṭ	ṭh	ḍ	ḍh	ḍ	ṇ	ṛ
Rest: vl. aspirates:	ڦ	ٿ	ڇ	ک			
	ph	th	ch	kh			
vd. aspirates:	ڀ	ڌ	جھ	گھ	(palatal and velar aspirate		
	bh	dh	jh	gh	digraphs are taken from Urdu)		
implosives:	ٻ	ڃ	ڳ				
	ɓ	ʄ	ɠ				
nasals:	ڃ	ڱ					
	ñ	ṅ					

TABLE 17.2: SINDHI–ARABIC ALPHABET

th ٺ	t ت	bh ڀ	ɓ ٻ	b ب	ə,I,U, ا
ĵ ڄ	j ج	p پ	s ث	th ٿ	ṭ ٽ
x خ	h ح	ch ڇ	c چ	ñ ڃ	jh جھ
z ذ	ḍh ڍ	ḍ ڊ	ḍ ڏ	dh ڌ	d د
s ص	ś ش	s س	z ژ	ṛ ڙ	r ر
f ف	ɣ غ	ə,I,U ع	z ظ	t ط	z ض
ɠ ڳ	g گ	kh ک	k ك	q ق	ph ڦ
ṇ ڻ	n ن	m م	l ل	ṅ ڱ	gh گھ
	(hamza – base for the succession of another vowel) ء	y ي	h هـ	v و	

Note: The lexical order is given from right to left.

Generally, short vowels remain unindicated in a Sindhi-Arabic text. In a careful text, these are hinted at by the following diacritic signs placed on the top or bottom of the letter:

(1) zabara ◌َ *bə* بَ *ə* أ

(2) zera ◌ِ *bI* بِ *I* إ

(3) peshu ◌ُ *bU* بُ *U* أُ

Long vowels are indicated by the diacritic signs with the base: *ə* ا , *y* ي, *v* و.

(4) alaf-madd ا *ba* با *a* آ

　 ye ي *be* بِي *e* اي

　 ye-zera ۍ *bi* بِّي *i* ائِي

　 ye-hamza ئ *bɛ* بِّي *ɛ* ائي

　 vaav و *bo* بو *o* او

　 vaav-peshu ُو *bu* بُو *u* اُو

　 vaav-hamza ُؤ *bɔ* بُؤ *ɔ* اؤ

Other diacritic signs used for modifying consonant characters are as follows:

(5) jazma (halant): ◌ْ : بْ indicates that the consonant is not followed by a vowel: *səxti* سَمْخْتِي

(6) tashdida: ◌ّ : بّ indicates gemination of the consonant character: *Izzət* عِزّت

(7) tanvin (nunation): ◌ً, ◌ٍ : بً indicates final nasalization of a vowel following the consonant with alaf, or a final nasal: *jəḍəIhĪ* جَدّ هِنْ　 *āv* آءً　 *ItIfaqən* اِتِفاقَنْ اِتِفاقاً

3.4 Sindhi–Devanagari script

The Sindhi–Devanagari script is adapted from the Sanskrit system of writing. Each character in the Devanagari system represents a syllable. It consists of either a vowel, or a consonant followed by the vowel अ *ə* : क *kə*. Devanagari characters are written from left to right.

The Sindhi–Devanagari script consists of forty-four consonant characters, eleven vowel characters, and one vowel modifier, called *anusvara*. Thirty-three consonant characters of the Sanskrit-Devanagari script have been extended to forty-four to represent Sindhi sounds. Modified characters are as follows:

(i) four implosives: ॿ *ɓ* ॾ *ɗ* ॼ *ʄ* ॻ *ɠ*

(ii) two retroflex flaps: ड़ *ɾ* ढ़ *ɾh*

(iii) five sounds acquired through Perso-Arabic borrowings: क़ *q* फ़ *f* ज़ *z* ख़ *x* ग़ *ɣ*

Sindhi–Devanagari characters are arranged in the traditional order on the basis of the Sanskrit phonological system. Modified characters follow respective unmodified characters in the successive order–implosive, flap, Perso-Arabic characters:

TABLE 17.3: SINDHI–DEVANAGARI CHARACTERS

Vowels

अ	आ	इ	ई	उ	ऊ	ऋ	ए	ऐ	ओ	औ	अं	अः
ə	a	I	i	U	u	r̥	e	ɛ	o	ɔ	ə̂	əh

Consonants

velars	क	क़	ख	ख़	ग	ग	ग़	घ	ङ			
	kə	qə	khə	xə	gə	g̱ə	ɤə	ghə	ṅə			

palatals	च	छ	ज	ज	ज	झ	ञ					
	cə	chə	jə	ĵə	zə	jhə	ñə					

dentals	त	थ	द	ध	न							
	tə	thə	də	dhə	nə							

retroflex	ट	ठ	ड	ड	ड	ढ	ढ़	ण				
	ṭə	ṭhə	ḍə	ḑ̣ə	ṛə	ḍhə	ṛhə	ṇə				

labials	प	फ	फ़	ब	ब	भ	म					
	pə	phə	fə	bə	ḇə	bhə	mə					

semivowels and liquids	य	र	ल	व	श	ष	स	ह				
	yə	rə	lə	və	śə	ṣə	sə	hə				

क क़, ख ख़, ग ग ग़, घ . . . .
ज ज ज़, झ . . . .
ड ड ड़, ढ ढ़, ण . . . .
फ फ़, ब ब, भ . . . .

The lexical order of the Sindhi–Devanagari characters is given in table 17.3.

Each of the vowel characters, except ə, has a corresponding vowel-sign, called *matra*, which is added to a consonant character to represent a syllable consisting of an initial consonant or consonant-cluster followed by one of the vowels: *a* to *ɔ*. There is no separate *matra* for vowel ə ; it is realized with every consonant character unless this is marked with the *halant* sign, or is without the upright stroke called *pai*: क *kə* क् *k*.

क (क्)	का	कि	की	कु	कू	कृ	के	कै	को	कौ	कं	कः
k	*ka*	*kI*	*ki*	*kU*	*ku*	*kr̥*	*ke*	*kɛ*	*ko*	*kɔ*	*kə̂*	*kəh*

Devanagari letters denoting consonant ष *ṣ*, vowel ऋ *r̥*, and *visarga* अः *əh* are confined to *tatsama* borrowings and these have consonantal values in Sindhi:

ऋषि *r̥ṣi*, कृष्ण *kr̥ṣṇə* (*tatsama*), किशिनु *kIśInU* (*tadbhava*)
स्वाः *svaha*, दुःखु *dUkhU* (*tatsama*), डुखु *ḑUkhU* (*tadbhava*)

Sindhi has only four implosives, with a gap of dental implosive in the fivefold stop series. Hence many Sindhi writers, in the process of unplanned switch-over from the Sindhi–Arabic to the Sindhi–Devanagari system of writing, have been erroneously representing the retroflex implosive with the modified dental character, instead of the correct representation. Captain Stack, in the *Sindhi–English Dictionary* (1849) has also indicated the retroflex implosive by modifying the character ड *ḍ* to ड *ḑ*. Trumpp has also supported Stack's modification in his *Sindhi Grammar* (1872). Here, the character ड *ḑ* is recommended for the retroflex implosive in Sindhi.

4 MORPHOLOGY

4.1 Word structure

The Sindhi lexicon consists of two types of words: simple and complex. Simple words consist of one meaningful unit, called 'morpheme': *paṭU* 'floor', *bə* 'two'. Complex words can be segmented into more than one meaningful unit: *khaṭ-U* 'Win!', *ənə-vən-ənd-əṛ-U* 'unpleasant (m. sg.)'. Words with more than one morpheme predominate in the language.

Complex words have one unit as a root, which constitutes the core of the word, and one or more other units as modifiers, called 'affixes'. Roots are of two types:

(1) potentially free, a unit which can be spoken by itself in normal speech: *kəmU* 'work', *kəm-a-yt-o* 'useful (m.sg.)', *nI-kəm-i* 'useless (f.)'; *jay* 'place', *sə-jay-o* 'purposeful' (m. sg.)'
(2) bound, a unit which never appears by itself: *kər-əṇU* 'to do', *kər-I* 'Do!', *səj-ə dhəj-ə* 'pomp and show', *səj-a-y-o* 'got dressed, decorated (m. sg.)'.

An affix is added to the stem, which is composed of either a root alone, or of a root plus one or more affixes.

lIkh-əṇU 'to write', *lIkh-a-yṇU* 'to make one write', *lIkh-a-ra-yṇU* 'to get (something) written (through some one)', *lIkh-a-ra-ṇi* 'writing fees'; *be-vəfa* 'faithless', *be-vəfa-i* 'faithlessness, infidelity'.

Affixes are of two types:

(1) Derivatives, which modify the scope of a stem: *vəḏ̂-o* 'big (m. sg.)', *vəḏ̂-Iṛ-o* 'somewhat big (m. sg.)', *vəḏ̂-ai* 'arrogance'; *mav* 'mother', *ma-si* 'mother's sister', *ma-sə-ṛU* 'mother's sister's husband', *ma-sa-t-U* 'mother's sister's son', *ma-sa-t-I* 'mother's sister's daughter'. Most of the derivatives occur after the stem: *chokIr-o* 'boy', *chokIr-i* 'girl', but a few do precede the stem; these are called 'prefixes': *ənə-b̂Udh-o* 'unheard (m. sg.)', *Uṇə-ṭi-hə* 'twenty-nine (one less–thirty)'.
(2) Inflectional, which express grammatical function (number, case, person, etc.) of the stem – simple or derived. Inflection affixes always follow the stem, hence are called 'inflectional suffixes': *əc-U* 'Come! (imp. sg.)', *nəndy-ũ* 'rivers (f. pl.)', *pəṛh-ənd-o* 'He will read', *pəṛh-ənd-i* 'She will read', *pəṛh-yəl-U* 'literate (m. sg.)', *pəṛh-yəl-ə* 'literate (f. sg., also m./f. pl.)'.

Sindhi has two classes of words:

(1) Declinable words, which express their grammatical function through inflectional suffixes. Parts of speech known as nouns, pronouns, verbs, certain adjectives and cardinal numbers, and a few postpositions belong to this class.
(2) Indeclinable words, which do not get modified in speech and whose grammatical function is denoted by the pattern of occurrence in the sentence. The remaining parts of speech such as adverbs, conjunctions, vocatives, most of the postpositions, certain adjectives and cardinal numbers, and also a few nouns and pronouns belong to this class.

4.2 Grammatical categories

All declinable words except the verb take 'case inflections', whereas verbs are declined according to 'person inflections'. Words declined according to case inflections are called 'nominals' or 'substantives'. Case inflection denotes grammatical categories of case-number-gender, or of case-number. Person inflection denotes grammatical categories of person-number-gender-mood, or of person-number-mood. The inventory of Sindhi inflectional categories is as follows:

Cases – 4 (+2): nominative (nom.), vocative (voc.), oblique (obl.), locative (loc.).

This category has two optional cases: instrumental (instr.), ablative (abl.), marked by certain nouns as a remnant of the past.

Persons – 3: first (1p.), second (2p.), third (3p.).
Moods – 3: indicative (ind.), imperative (imp.), subjunctive (subj.).
Numbers – 3: singular (sg.), plural (pl.), indefinite plural (indef. pl.), marked only for certain numeral nouns.
Genders – 2: masculine (m.), feminine (f.).

4.3 Nominals

4.3.1 Introduction

On the basis of gender inflection, nominals can be further divided into two sub-classes:

(1) Nouns, pronouns, and cardinals which are marked as such by the inflection for case and number. Most of the noun stems have inherent gender. In the case of certain nouns and pronouns, the stem is modified according to the gender before it is inflected. The cardinals 2 to 58 are inflected for case in plural number only. Gender is irrelevant for them.
(2) Declinable adjectives and a few postpositions are marked as such by the inflection for case, number, and gender.

4.3.2 Nouns

Sindhi nouns generally show distinction of three cases – nominative, vocative, and oblique – and two numbers – singular and plural. Nouns denoting place, time and currency, and cardinal numbers 2 to 58 are inflected for locative case as well. Numeral nouns denoting units 'hundred' *sɔ* and above distinguish three numbers – singular, plural, and indefinite plural. Certain noun stems belonging to the basic vocabulary are optionally inflected for additional cases – locative, ablative and instrumental, which in the normal course are denoted by oblique case plus appropriate postposition. Infinitives are considered as masculine nouns and they are declined only in oblique singular. A few borrowed nouns are not marked by any declension: *eksre* 'X-ray', *marśɔlla* 'martial law'.

A bare stem indicates nominative singular for all nouns: *ghɔrU* 'house', *nɔndi* 'river'; for certain nouns, singular in three regular cases – nominative, vocative, oblique – and nominative plural are indicated by the bare stem. Different sets of inflections are conditioned by gender and stem-endings. Feminine nouns have identical inflection in nominative and vocative case.

The bulk of masculine nouns have stems ending in *-o* or *-U*: *mɔtho* 'head', *pUṭU* 'son'. A few masculine stems end in *-i*, *-u*, *-ɔ* and *-v* : *pani* 'water', *taru* 'swimmer', *tɔ* 'heat', *piv* 'father'. Borrowings have added a few masculine stems ending in -*a* and -*ɛ* : *xUda* 'God', *vIdyalɛ* 'school'.

The bulk of feminine nouns have stems ending in -*I*, -*i*, and -*ə* : *chati* 'chest', *bhItI* 'wall', *khəṭə* 'cot'. A few feminine stems end in -*a*, -*ũ*, -*U*, -*ɛ* and -*y* as well: *pUcha* 'enquiry', *kəchũ* 'tortoise', *səsU* 'mother-in-law', *śɛ* 'thing, *jay* 'building, place'. A few nouns borrowed from English have consonant-ending stems: *moṭər* 'motor car'. Sindhi nominal forms are given in table 17.4.

4.3.3 Pronouns

Most of the pronouns are marked as such by the inflection of two cases – nominative and oblique, and two numbers – singular and plural. The first and second person pronouns do not show distinction of gender: *mã* 'I (m./f.)', *təvhĩ* 'you (pl., m./f.)'. All third person pronouns are derived from neutral stems by adding a masculine or feminine pronoun suffix. Neutral stems are identified as simple, demonstrative, unspecified, relative, correlative and interrogative: *h- i-v* 'he', *I-h-o* 'this (m.)', *k-o* 'some one (m.)',

TABLE 17.4: NOMINAL FORMS

	Masculine		Feminine	
	singular	plural	singular	plural
nom.	*ghoṛo* 'horse'	*ghoṛ-a*	*gaḍi* 'carriage'	*gaḍy-ũ*
voc.	*ghoṛ-a*	*ghoṛ-ɔ*		
obl.	*ghoṛ-e*	*ghoṛ-ənI*	*gaḍi-ə*	*gaḍy-UnI*

	Nominative case	Oblique and other cases
ghərU	'house, home', m. sg.	*ghər-ə* m. sg.
		Additional cases
		ghər-ɪ / ghər-ə mẽ
		'at home' loc. m. sg.
ĝoṭhU	'village' m. sg.	*ĝoṭh-ã / ĝoṭh-ə mã*
		'from the village' abl. m. sg.
pəñjə kəlak-ə	'five hours' m. pl.	*pəñj-ẽ kəlak-ẽ / pəñj-ənI*
		kəlak-ənI mẽ
		'in five hours' loc. pl.
carI pãy-ũ	'four pies' f. pl.	*cə̃-ĩ pã-ẽ / cə-InI pay-UnI mẽ*
		'in four pies' loc. f. pl
sahUr-a	'in-laws' m. pl.	*sahUr-ẽ / sahUr-ənI mã*
		'from in-laws', abl. m. pl.
ɓar-ə ɓɔc-a	'children' m. pl.	*ɓar-ẽ ɓɔc-ẽ / ɓar-ənI ɓɔc-ənI sudho*
		'along with children' instr. m. pl.
sɔ	'hundred' m. sg.	
sɔv-ə	'hundreds' pl.	*sə̃v-ẽ* 'various hundreds'
		nom. indef. pl.
həzarU	'thousand' m. sg.	
həzar-ə	'thousands' m. pl.	*həzar-ẽ* 'various thousands'
		nom. m. indef. pl.

j-o 'who (m. relative)', *s-o* 'that one (m.)', *ker-U* 'who? (m.)'. Simple and demonstrative roots are distinguished by proximity or remoteness: *h-i-ə* 'she (prox.)', *h-u-ə* 'she (remote)', *I-h-a* 'this (f.)', *U-h-a* 'that (f.)'. Demonstrative roots are further modified by 'specific' or 'present' derivation, before adding the gender derivative: *I-h-o* 'this (m.)', *I-jh-o* 'existing one (m.)'. Relative and correlative roots can further be identified by 'inclusive' derivation before adding gender: *j-o* 'who (m.)', *je-k-o* 'whoever (m.)', *s-o* 'that one (m.)', *te-k-o* 'whosoever (m.)'. Syntactically all three person pronouns function as adjectivals as well.

Bare stem indicates nominative singular for all pronouns. The inventory of Sindhi pronouns is given in table 17.5.

Present demonstrative and inclusive (relative and correlative) pronouns are declined only in the nominative case. Unspecific compound pronouns *hər-ko* 'every one (m.)' and *səbh-ko* 'every one amongst all (m.)' are declined only in singular number.

A few pronouns, such as *paṇə*, *xUdI* 'self', *kUjhU* 'something', *cha* 'what?', are indeclinable.

4.3.4 Number words

Cardinal numbers from 2 to 58 show distinction of three cases in plural only: nominative, oblique and locative. These are not marked for vocative case:

(1) Numbers 2–48 distinguish all three cases:
   b̂ə 'two (nom.)' *b̂-InI* '(obl.)' *b̂-i bəj-e* (loc.) 'at two o'clock'
   ḍəhə 'ten (nom.)', *ḍəh-ənI* '(obl.)', *ḍə̃h-ẽ ḍə̃h-ẽ sal-ẽ* (loc.) 'every ten years'.
(2) Numbers 49–58 have identical inflection in nominative and oblique cases:
   pəñjahU 'fifty (nom./obl.)', *pəñjāh-ẽ* '(loc.)', *pəñjahU rUpəy-ənI mẽ* 'in fifty rupees',
   Uṇ-vəñjāh-ẽ rUpə-e 'at (the rate of) forty-nine rupees'.

The singular number *hIkU* 'one' and certain fractional numbers *ḍeḍhU* 'one-and-a-half', *mUno* 'three-quarters (of a unit)', take adjective declension. Numbers from 59 to 99 and the fractional numbers *səva* 'one-and-a-quarter' and *əḍhai* 'two-and-a-half' are indeclinable: *ədhU* 'half' is declined as a regular noun.

Syntactically, all cardinals function as adjectival phrases.

4.3.5 Adjectives

Sindhi has two classes of adjectives: declinable and indeclinable. Declinable adjectives are inflected for two genders – masculine and feminine, two numbers – singular and plural, and three cases – nominative, vocative and oblique. These are declined according to two inflectional sets, conditioned by stem endings:

(1) Stems adding -*o* suffix in masculine nominative singular and -*I* suffix in feminine nominative singular. The inflectional sets of these adjectives are similar to masculine -*o* stem nouns, and feminine -*I* stem nouns: *poṛh-o* 'aged (m.)', *poṛh-i* 'aged (f.)'
(2) Stems formed with (a) past participle verb-base plus agent suffix *əl*- and (b) present participle verb-base plus agent suffix -*əṛ*-. Their inflectional sets are similar to masculine -*U* stem nouns and feminine -*ə* stem nouns: *pəṛh-yəl-U* '(one who is) read, learned (m.)' *pəṛh-ənd-əṛ-ə* 'reader, learner (f.)'. Numeral adjectives *hIkU* 'one', *ḍeḍhU* 'one-and-a-half', declined only in singular, also belong to this class.

TABLE 17.5: PRONOUNS

Person		Singular nom.	obl.	Plural nom.	obl.
First		*mã*	*m-ũ, mU-khe* 'to me' *mŨhĨ-jo* 'my (m.)'	*əsĩ*	*əs-ã*
Second		*tũ*	*t-o* *tŨhĨ-jo* 'yours (m.)'	*tə̃vhĩ* *ə̃vhĩ*	*tə̃vh-ã* *ə̃vh-ã*
Third					
proximate:	m.	*hi-U, hi*	*h-I-nə*	*hi*	*h-In-ənI*
	f.	*hi-ə*			
remote:	m.	*hu*	*h-U-nə*	*hu*	*h-Un-ənI*
	f.	*hu-ə*			
Demonstrative, specific					
proximate:	m.	*I-h-o*	*I-nh-ẽ*	*I-h-e*	*I-nh-ənI*
	f.	*I-h-a*			
remote:	m.	*U-h-o*	*U-nh-e*	*U-h-e*	*U-nh-ənI*
	f.	*U-h-a*			
Demonstrative, present					
proximate:	m.	*I-jh-o*	–	*I-jh-e*	–
	f.	*I-jh-a*			
remote:	m.	*o-jh-o*	–	*o-jh-e*	–
	f.	*o-jh-a*			
unspecified:	m.	*k-o*	*k-ə̃h*	*k-e*	*k-InI*
	f.	*k-a*			
		'some one'			
	m.	*hər-k-o*	*hər-k-ə̃h*	–	–
	f.	*hər-k-a*			
		'every one'			
	m.	*səbh-k-o*	*səbhə-k-ə̃h*	–	–
	f.	*səbh-k-a*			
		'every one amongst all'			
Relative:	m.	*j-o*	*j-ə̃h*	*j-e*	*j-InI*
	f.	*j-a*			
Relative, inclusive:	m.	*je-k-o*	–	*je-k-e*	–
	f.	*je-k-a*			
Correlative:	m.	*s-o*	*t-ə̃h*	*s-e*	*t-InI*
	f.	*s-a*			
Correlative, inclusive:	m.	*te-k-o*	–	*te-k-e*	–
	f.	*te-k-a*			
Interrogative:	m.	*ker-U*	*k-ə̃h*	*ker-ə*	*k-InI*
	f.	*ker-ə*			

All ordinal numerals and those denoting multiplication, fold, units, etc. derived from cardinals, are inflected as declinable adjectives of set 1: *ṭe* 'three', *ṭy-õ* 'third (m.)', *ṭi-ṇ-õ* 'triple (m.)', *ṭI-ṭ-o* 'three-fold (m.)', *ṭI-k-o* 'the figure three (in playing cards, etc.) (m.)'.

A few postpositions denoting possession or quality are also inflected on the pattern of these adjectives, with slight modification in the oblique case: *j-o* 'of', *sənd-o* 'belonging to', *sudh-o* 'along with', *j-əhṛ-o* 'similar', *j-eḍ̂-o* 'equal to'. An oblique noun or pronoun, plus one of such postpositions, functions as an adjectival phrase in concordance with the following governing noun:

kItab-ə   sudh-o   chokIr-o
book-obl   inclusive-m. child-m.
'boy along with a book'

ĝoth-ə   j-e   chokIr-y-UnI   lay
village-obl of-obl   child-f.-pl. obl   for
'for girls of the village'

Indeclinable adjectives are defined on the basis of their syntactic position in an utterance. Indeclinable forms which occupy the identical position of declinable adjectives in an utterance are called indeclinable adjectives. These adjectives generally have vocalic endings, except for a few borrowings which end in consonants: *vədhikə* 'more', *ghətI* 'less', *ədhai* 'two-and-a-half, *sUstU* 'lazy', *jUda* 'separate', *xas* 'special', *ənek* 'several', *fasṭ* 'quick'.

4.4 Verbs

4.4.1 Stem types

A verb stem in Sindhi may be simple, i.e. consisting of a verb root only, or may be derived, i.e. consisting of a root along with one or more derivational suffixes. A root is either inherently transitive (tr.) or intransitive (intr.) or is neutral (nt.). Stems derived from these verbal or neutral roots are as follows:

(1) Intransitive stem can be derived from a transitive or neutral root:
   dhv-ənU 'to wash (tr.)', *dho-p-ənU* 'to be washed (intr.)', *vIk-am-ənU* 'to be sold (intr.)'.

(2) Transitive stem can be derived from an intransitive or neutral root:
   ɓUḍ-ənU 'to be drowned (intr.)', *ɓor-ənU* 'to drown (tr.)'; *sIr-ənU* 'to be moved (intr.)', *ser-ənU* 'to move (tr.)', *vIk-In-ənU* 'to sell (tr.)'

(3) First causative (1st c.) stem can be derived from a transitive stem (root or derived):

   dhv-ar-ənU   *vIk-In-a-ynU*
   wash-1st c.-inf   sell (nt)- tr.-1st c.- inf
   'to get washed'   'to get sold'

(4) Second causative (2nd c.) stem can be derived only from a stem having first causative:

   dhv-a-ra-ynU   *kha-ra-ra-ynU*
   wash-1st c.-2nd c.-inf   eat-1st c.- 2nd c.-inf
   'to arrange to get (something) washed'   'to get (one) to feed'.

(5) Passive (pass) stem can be derived from a transitive, intransitive or causative stem:

   hIr-j-e
   be accustomed (intr.)-pass-subj 3p sg.
   'Let one be accustomed to.'

   her-j-ũ
   make accustomed (tr.)-pass-subj 1p pl.
   'Let us be made accustomed to.'

likh-Ij-I
write (tr.)-pass-subj 2p sg.
'Let you (sg.) write (it).'

lIkh-a-yj-o
write (tr.)- 1st c.-pass-subj 2p pl.
'Let you (pl.) get (it) written.'

lIkh-a-ra-yj-e
write (tr.)-1st c.- 2nd c.-pass-subj 3p sg.
'Let (it) be arranged (by some one) to be written.'

(6) Participial stems: Present and past participial stems can be derived from any non-participial stem (root or derived), whereas impersonal and indirect participial stems can be derived from only non-passive non-participial stems (root or derived) by adding a participial infix:

(a) Present participle

hIr-ənd-o
be accustomed (intr.)-pres ptcpl-3p m. sg.
'He'll be accustomed to.'

her-ind-ẽ
make accustomed (tr.)-pres ptcpl-2p m.sg.
'You (sg.) will make (one) accustomed to.'

lIkh-a-ind-i
write (tr.)-1st c.- pres ptcpl-3p f. sg.
'She'll get (it) written.'

(cIṭhi) lIkh-a-ra-yj-ənd-i
(letter f.) write(tr.)-1st c.- 2nd c.- pass-pres ptcpl-3p f. sg.
'(Letter) will be arranged to be written.'

(b) Past participle

a-y-UsI	*ve-ṭh-ĩ-ə̃*
come (intr.)-pst ptcpl-1p m. sg.	sit (intr.)-pst ptcpl-2p f. sg.
'I (m.) came.'	'You (f. sg.) sat.'

(ghoṛo) vIk-am-j-y-o / vIk-am-y-o
(horse m. sg.) sell (nt.)-intr.-(pass)-pst ptcpl. -m. sg.
'Horse was sold.'

(ghoṛo) vIk-Iṇ-a-ra-y-o
(horse m.) sell (nt.)-tr.-1st c.- 2nd c.-past ptcpl- m. sg.
'It was arranged to get (the horse) sold.'

khə̃-y-ə̃-mI
lift (tr.)-pst ptcpl- f. sg./pl.-bp: 1p
'I lifted (obj f./ pl.).'

(c) Impersonal participle

(jəvabU) ghUr-b-UsI
(answer m. sg.) ask (tr.)-impers ptcpl-1p m. sg.
'(Answer) will be asked.'

piṛ-b-asĩ
torture-(intr.) -impers ptcpl-1p m. pl.
'We'll be tortured.'

(xətU) lIkh-a-ra-yb-o
(letter m. sg.) write (tr.)-1st c.- 2nd c.-impers ptcpl-m. sg. 3p
'One will get (the letter) written.'

vəñ-Ib-o
go (intr.)-impers ptcpl- m. sg. 3p
'One will go.'

(d) Indirect participle

cəv-ən-o
say (tr.) indir ptcpl- m. sg.
'It (m.) is to be said.'

pəṛh-In-i
read (tr.)- indir ptcpl- f. sg.
'It (f.) is to be read, a reading (of a manuscript).'

sUmh-In-o
sleep (intr.) -indir ptcpl- m. sg.
'One is to sleep.'

sUmh-ar-In-o
sleep (intr.) -1st c.-indir ptcpl- m. sg.
'One is to be put to sleep.'

4.4.2 Tense and mood forms

On the basis of gender-inflection, verb stems can be divided into two main classes: (1) non-participial stems (roots and derived stems), (2) participial stems (derived stems). Non-participial stems are marked by two moods: imperative and subjunctive; two numbers: singular and plural; and three persons: first, second and third. Participial derived stems are marked by two genders: masculine and feminine; two numbers: singular and plural; and three persons: first, second and third. Participial stems signify indicative mood.

4.4.2.1 Imperative mood

Verbs in imperative mood denote command or request. These are conjugated only in second person, singular and plural. Gender is not distinguished in the imperative mood. Stems in imperative mood form three sets of conjugation:

(i) All intransitive stems (roots and derived), and a limited number of transitive stems (roots and derived) add singular -*U* and plural -*o* suffixes. Such verbs are identified as Class 1 verbs:

əc-U	*kha-o*
come (intr.)-imp. sg.	eat (tr.)-imp. pl.
'Come! (sg.)'	'Eat! (pl.)'

> *ghət-Ij-o*   *vIk-Iṇ-U*
> reduce (nt.)-pass-imp. pl.   sell (nt.)-tr.-imp. sg.
> 'Be reduced! (pl.).'   'Sell! (sg.)'

(ii) Most other transitive stems (roots and derived stems), called Class 2 verbs, and all causal stems add singular -*I* and plural -*yo*:

> *tər-I*   *dIgh-eṛ-yo*
> fry (tr.)-imp sg.   length (nt.)-1st. c. -imp. pl.
> 'Fry! (sg.)'   'Lengthen (it)! (pl.)'
>
> *ḍekh-ar-I*   *lIkh-a-ra-y*
> show (tr.)-1st c.-imp. sg.   write (tr.)-1st c- 2nd c.-imp. sg.
> 'Show (it)!'   'Arrange to get it written!'

(iii) All passive stems add singular -*I*, or -*ãy* and plural -*o*, and they denote polite suggestion (courteous imperative):

> *ə c-Ij-I* / *ə c-Ij-ãy*   *kha-ra-Ij-o*
> come (intr.)-pass-imp. sg.   eat (tr.)-1st c.- pass-imp. pl.
> Let you (sg.) come!'   'Let you (pl.) feed!'

4.4.2.2 Subjunctive mood

Verbs in the subjunctive mood refer to the possibility or virtuality of action. These are inflected in three persons and two numbers; subjunctive suffixes, denoting person and number, are added to the verb stem in concordance with the subject. Gender is not distinguished in the subjunctive mood. There are two sets of conjugation covering (1) stems belonging to the first and third sets of imperative mood, (2) stems belonging to the second set of imperative mood as shown in table 17.6.

TABLE 17.6: VERBS IN SUBJUNCTIVE MOOD

Set one			Set two	
	chIk-Ij-əṇU	'to be pulled'	*chIk-əṇU*	'to pull'
	chIk-Ij-U	'Let you be pulled'	*chIk-I*	'Pull! (sg.)'
Person	singular	plural	singular	plural
First	*chIk-Ij-ã*	*chIk-Ij-ŭ*	*chIk-yã*	*chIk-yŭ*
	'Let me be pulled'	'Let us be pulled'	'Let I pull'	'Let we pull'
Second	*chIk-Ij-ĩ*	*chIk-Ij-o*	*chIk-ĩ*	*chIk-yo*
Third	*chIk-Ij-e*	*chIk-Ij-ənI*	*chIk-e*	*chIk-inI*

4.4.2.3 Indicative mood

A set of indicative suffixes denoting gender, number and person of the governing subject or object is added to different participial stems.

(1) The present participial stem, followed by an indicative suffix in accordance with the subject, forms a verb in future indicative mood as shown in table 17.7.

TABLE 17.7: VERB IN INDICATIVE MOOD

Person	Masculine singular	plural	Feminine singular	plural
First	*lIkh-ənd-UsI* 'I'll write'	*lIkh-ənd-asĩ* 'We'll write'	*lIkh-ənd-əsI*	*lIkh-ənd-yũsĩ*
Second	*lIkh-ənd-ē*	*lIkh-ənd-ɔ*	*lIkh-ənd-ĩɔ̃*	*lIkh-ənd-yũ*
Third	*lIkh-ənd-o*	*lIkh-ənd-a*	*lIkh-ənd-i*	*lIkh-ənd-yũ*

(2) The past participial stem followed by an indicative suffix denotes past indicative mood. The conjugation of intransitive stems and all passive stems is governed by the gender, number and person of the subject, whereas the conjugation of transitive stems and all causal stems is governed by the gender and number of the direct object (only third person). In this environment, the subject functions as agent of the verbal phrase, and occurs in the oblique case. But when the object is followed by the postposition *khe,* the verb is invariably conjugated in the third person masculine singular, without any concordance with the subject or the direct object.

> *pəṛh-əṇU* (intr.) 'to study, to get education'
> *pəṛh-əṇU* (tr.) 'to read (something)'.

> *mã   kəraci-ə   mẽ   pəṛh-y-UsI*
> I   Karachi-obl. in   study-pst-1p m. sg.
> 'I (m.) studied in Karachi.'

> *mũ   kItab-ə   pəṛh-y-a*
> I-obl. book-m. pl. read-pst-m. pl.
> 'I read (past) books.'

> *əs-ã   akhaṇi   pəṛh-i*
> we-obl. story(f.) read-pst.-f. sg.
> 'We read (past) a story (f. sg.).'

> *chokIr-y-UnI   h-U-nə   mai-ə   khe   ḍi-ṭh-o*
> child-f.-pl.(obl.) 3p-remote-obl. woman-obl. to   see-pst-m. sg.
> 'Girls looked at that woman.'

(3) The impersonal participial stem followed by an indicative suffix denotes passive future mood. The conjugation of transitive stems and all causal stems is governed by the gender, number and person of the subject, whereas intransitive stems are invariably conjugated in third person masculine singular and they always occur in the impersonal voice.

> *dUśmən-ənI vəṭ-ã   əsĩ tə   p-ya   loy-b-asĩ*
> enemies-obl. to-loc. we however lie (aux.)-pst malign (tr.)-impers.
>   ptcpl pl.   ptcpl–1p m. pl.
> 'We will, however, be maligned by the enemies.'

> *əc-Ib-o*
> come-impers ptcpl-m. sg.
> 'One will come (intr. m.).'

(4) The indirect participial stem, followed by an indicative suffix (in the third person only), denotes passive present mood. When the subject is in the nominative case, the conjugation of intransitive stem is governed by its gender and number. But when the subject is in the oblique case, the verb is invariably conjugated in the third person masculine singular. At the same time, the conjugation of transitive stems and all casual stems is governed by the gender and number of the direct object:

> *əsĩ   əʄU   vəñ-Iṇ-ã*   *hU-asĩ*
> we   today   go-indir ptcpl-m. pl.   be (pst)-1p m. pl.
> 'We (m.) were to go today.'

> *cIṭhy-ũ   ḑy-ən-yũ*   *hŨ-yũ*
> letter-f. pl.   give-indir ptcpl-f. pl.   be (pst)-3p f. pl.
> 'Letters (f.) were to be delivered.'

> *to-khe   hI-te*   *sUmh-Iṇ-o*   *ah-e*
> you (sg. pl.)-to   proximate-place   sleep-indir ptcpl-m. sg.   be (pres)-m. sg.
> 'You are (supposed) to sleep here.'

Most of the participial verbs denoting third person singular masculine or feminine occur as nouns or adjectives, and are declined in the pattern of masculine *-o* stem and feminine *-i* stem nouns or adjectives: *həl-ənd-i* 'approach, influence (f.)', *kha-dh-o* 'edible thing, food (m.)', *mɔla-ḑIn-o* 'God-given, proper name (m.)', *a-y-o v-y-o* 'come-gone (m. sg.), passer-by, guest', *mər-Iṇ-o* 'event of death (m.)', *cəv-əṇ-i* 'saying, proverb (f.)', *khIl-Iṇ-o ḃarU* 'smiling child', *nəc-ənd-i niṅgər-I* 'dancing girl', *lIkhy-o lekhU* 'written-writing, fate'.

4.4.3 Compound verbs

Sindhi has a large number of compound verbs. These are formed by combining two, sometimes three or more verbs. The first verb of the compound is usually the main one and the remaining verbs are subsidiary, serving to modify the aspect of the main verb. Various aspects of subjunctive and indicative moods are denoted by combining an auxiliary verb to the main verb formation:

> *khã-ĩnd-o*   *rəh-ənd-o*   *ãh-yã*
> eat-pres ptcpl-m. sg.   stay (aux.)-pres ptcpl-m. sg.   be-subj -1p sg.
> 'I keep on eating.'

The main verb has either subjunctive or indicative formation, or the stem gets modified with three indeclinable verbal modifiers. There are three verbal modifiers with a high frequency:

(1) the verb stem of Class 1 is attached with 'absolutive' suffix *-i* and of Class 2 is attached with suffix *-e*:

> *sUmh-ĩ*   'having slept',   *sUmh-ar-e*   'having put one to sleep',

> *jay   ḑis-i*   *vər-t-i*   *hU-i-sĩ/h-i-sĩ*
> place (f.)   see-abs.   take-pst-f. sg.   be-3p f.(obj)-bp: 2ppl.(subj)
> 'We had looked up the place.'

(2) 'repetitive' suffix -*yo* (-*yõ* when the stem is nasalized) is added to the verb stem:

> *vəñ-ənU* 'to go' : *vəñ-yõ* 'having gone repeatedly'
> *kha-InU* 'to eat' : *kha-yo* 'having eaten persistently'
> *khəṇ-əṇU* 'to lift' : *khə̃-yõ* 'having lifted continuously'

> *rozU kha-yo vəñ-ã*
> daily eat-rept go-subj 1p sg.
> 'I habitually eat away every day.'

(3) 'conditional' modifier *hã* (often written as a separate word) follows the verbal stem:

> *kha-i vəñ-ã hã*
> eat-pst ptcpl go (aux.) subj 1p. sg. cond
> 'I would have eaten (it) away.'

4.5 Indeclinables

4.5.1 Postpositions

A postposition occurs after an oblique noun, pronoun or noun phrase, to denote its position in relation to other words or phrases in the utterance. Most of the postpositions are indeclinable, but a few, denoting possession or quality of the following noun, are declined on the pattern of adjectives. Indeclinable postpositions can be either simple (i.e. monomorphemic) or derived.

> simple: *khe* 'to', *sã* 'with' *mẽ* 'in', *vəṭI* 'near to'
> derived: *m-ã* 'from inside', *t-ã* 'from above', *vəṭ-ã* 'from near',
> *kh-ã poy* 'after', *məñ-jhI* 'within', *məñ-jh-ã* 'from within'

In a few cases, a postposition consists of two units. The first unit -*je* is optional: *hUnə je parã, hUnə parã* 'on behalf of him/her'.

A few postpositions, such as *bIna, kh-ã səvay* 'without', can optionally be shifted to the position preceding the noun phrase. The noun phrase is added with another postposition -*je*.

kh-ã səvay occurring as a preposition is reduced to *səvay*:

> *to-kh-ã səvay / səvay tŨhĨ-je*
> *to bIna / bIna tŨhĨ-je* 'without you'.

4.5.2 Adverbs

Adverbs are indeclinable in Sindhi. These indicate manner as well as situation in time and space. These can be either simple or derived.

> simple: *haṇe* 'now', poy 'afterwards', *heṭhI* 'below', *təmam* 'very much',
> *ahIste / aste* 'slow', *vəri* 'again', *ȷaṇU* 'soon', *nə̃* 'no'.
> derived: *h-I-te* 'here (lit. this place)', *h-U-te* 'there (lit. that place)', *h-ĩ-ərə* 'at this
> moment', *səc-i* 'really', *məth-e* 'above', *əĝ-e* 'before', *əĝ-yã* 'in front',
> *bhəl-e / bhəl-i* 'well, agreed', *sUbh-ã* 'tomorrow, lit. on the morning',
> *paṇə̃-hĩ / paṇə̃-ĩ* 'on one's own accord', *pə-rĩhə̃* 'day after tomorrow',
> *ə-rĩhə̃* 'two days after tomorrow'.

Certain adjectives inflected only in nominative singular and certain noun-stems representing nominative singular (masculine or feminine), as well as a few reduplicated phrases having one or both elements from other form-classes, function as adverbs:

təkIr̥-o 'quick (adj. m.), quickly', *sUṭh-o* 'good (adj. m.), nicely',
pəkə 'surety (nom. f.), surely', *zərurU* 'necessity (nom. m.), necessarily',
ɲaṇi vaṇi 'knowingly', *jĩə̃ tĩə̃* 'any how', *hərubəru / hərubhəru*
'unnecessarily', *həkũnakũ* 'without any reason or rhyme' (Arabic *həq na-həq*).

4.5.3 Conjunctions

Conjunctions are also indeclinable in Sindhi. These function as the connecting link between two words, phrases or sentences. They can be divided into two classes on the basis of their function in a phrase, clause or sentence:

(1) coordinating conjunctions: those joining two mutually independent words, phrases or clauses: *ɛ̃* 'and', *yã* 'or', *toṛe* 'as well as', *pərə* 'but'.

hU-nə-j-o   *pUṭU toṛe*   *dhiə*   *b̂ə-i*
3p remote sg.-obl.-pass-m. sg. son   as well as daughter two-empht
hUśyarU ah-InI
intelligent be (pres)-3p pl.
'Both, his/her son as well as daughter, are intelligent.'

(2) subordinating conjunctions: those joining one or more subordinate phrases or clauses:

je 'if', *tə* 'then', *cahe* 'let', *mətã* 'lest', *bI* 'also'.

je tũ yadI   *d̂y-ar-ind-ẽ*   *tə*   *mã to-sã*
if you memory give-1st c.-pres ptcpl-2p m. sg. then I   you-obl.-with
həl-ənd-U-sI
come-pres ptcpl–1p m. sg.
'If you remind me, I'll come with you.'

4.5.4 Interjections

Interjections are expressions for addressing the listener and also of response or strong feelings of the speaker. These can occur independently, or can be accompanied by a noun phrase in vocative case. Such interjectional phrases can be treated as minor sentences, having independent stress pattern and intonation. Sindhi interjections are of two types:

(1) basic: *əṛe* 'Hey!', *ha* 'Yes', *hã* 'Is it so?', *vah vah* 'Bravo!', *hay hay* 'Alas!'
(2) words which also function as other parts of speech, occur as interjection:

cəṅo 'O.K.', *hed̂ã* 'Oh, here!', *nə* 'No', *jiv / ji* 'Long life, Yes (polite)!', *ghoṛa ṛe ghoṛa* 'Help! (lit. Horse, hey, horse!; Attention, horses are slipping away!)', *əla, əla-ṛe* 'Oh, my God! (expressing shock)', *mar* 'What a sight! (lit. Got hit!, expressing surprise)'.

5 SYNTAX

5.1 Introduction

Preliminary observations pertaining to the syntactic structure in Sindhi reveal that to a large extent these resemble those of other Indo-Aryan languages. Prominent features of Sindhi syntax are briefly described below.

5.2 Sentence structures

The nuclear structure of sentences in Sindhi is as follows:

(1) Verb phrase (in impersonal voice):

> *vəñIbo* 'One will be going', *əcIbo ahe* 'One keeps coming'.

(2) Subject + Verb phrase (intransitive other than in impersonal voice):

> *g̃othə   jo mUkhi vəñi   rəhyo   ahe*
> village-obl. of chief   go-pst ptcpl stay (aux.)-pst ptcpl-m. sg. be (pres) 3p sg.
> 'The village-chief is going away/passing by.'

(3) Subject + Object + Verb phrase (transitive):

> *hu   chokIra əmbə   khainI   tha*
> 3p remote-pl. boy-pl.   mango-pl. eat-subj 3p pl. be (pres)-m. pl.
> 'Those boys are eating mangoes.'

These sentence types can further be expanded by indirect object, and location, and time and manner strings:

> *hastIllI mẽ rozU səvelə UthIbo   ho*
> hostel in   daily early   rise-impers ptcpl-m. sg. be (pst)-m. sg.
> 'Daily one used to get up early in the hostel.'

> *ramU tŨhĨje   ghərI   zərur   i-nd-o*
> Ram   you-of-obl home-loc certainly come-pres ptcpl-m. sg.
> 'Ram shall certainly come to your place.'

> *mũ   ramə   khe ketIrai   kItabə   d̃Ina*
> I-obl. Ram-obl. to much-pl.-sort of   book-pl.   give-pst-ptcpl-m.pl.
> *hunda*
> be-pres ptcpl-m. pl.
> 'I must have given several books to Ram.'

5.3 Phrase order

The order of phrases in a sentence is quite flexible. In colloquial speech various phrases can occur in different positions in an utterance. In a sentence with usual word-stress, the initial phrase normally indicates prominence:

> *ramU naṭIkU d̃ise   tho*
> Ram play   see-subj- sg. be(pres)-m. sg.
> 'Ram is seeing a play, Ram sees a play.'

Variations indicate prominence to the initial phrase (with emphatic word-stress):

> *naṭIkU   ɗise tho   ramU,* or
> *ɗIse tho   ramU   naṭIkU*

5.4 Optional deletions

The conjugation of a verb in Sindhi is usually governed by the number and the person, also by the gender in certain cases, of the subject. However, a transitive verb in past indicative, and in future and present passive moods, is governed by the gender and the number of the direct object. Hence in colloquial speech one can optionally drop the subject or direct object (pronoun or otherwise) predicted from the context, and which can be identified from the conjugation of the verb:

> *sUbhaṇe   indasĩ*
> morning-on   come-pres ptcpl-1p m. pl.
> 'We (m.) shall come tomorrow.'

> *chokIriə   ĝayo / ĝato*
> child-f.-obl.   sing-pst ptcpl-m. sg.
> 'The girl sang (a song, etc., dir obj m. sg.).'

5.5 Bound-pronouns

Sindhi optionally adds pronominal suffixes to verbs, all declinable and certain indeclinable postpositions, and certain nouns denoting relationship and some parts of body, substituting regular pronouns. Lahnda, another Indo-Aryan language of the northwest group, also uses pronominal suffixes with certain verbs and nouns. Most of the Dardic and Iranian languages also share this feature (for details, cf. Khubchandani 1962b, Yegorova 1964).

There are two sets of pronominal suffixes, called bound-pronouns (bp), added to the inflected verbs: (1) agent bound-pronouns (2) indirect object bound-pronouns.

An agent bound-pronoun, when added to a transitive verb in the past indicative mood, optionally substitutes for the pronominal subject functioning as agent of the verb phrase: *mũ raĝU ĝayo, raĝU gayU + mI / ĝatU + mI,* 'I sang a song.'

The indirect object bound-pronoun, when added to any verb phrase (except in the present passive mood), optionally substitutes for the pronominal indirect object:

> *hInə   mẽ paṇi vIjh-U   paṇi vIjh-i + sI*
> this-obl. in water pour-imp sg. water pour-imp sg. + bp: 3p sg.(loc)
> 'Pour water in it.'

> *mã tə̃vhã   vəṭI ind-əsI*
> I   you-obl near come-pres-ptcpl-f. sg.-1p
> *mã ind-isã + və*
> I come-pres ptcpl–1p f. sg. + bp: 2p pl. (loc)
> 'I (f.) shall come to you (pl.).'

A transitive verb in the past indicative mood can add both bound-pronoun suffixes, or agent pronominal suffix followed by indirect object pronominal suffix:

> *mũ   tokhe   əmbU ɗIno*
> I-obl. you-obl.-to mango give-past ptcpl-m. sg.

tokhe əmbU ɖInU + mI
-        -   -   + bp: 1p sg. (agent)
əmbU ɖIn-o + mã   *+ y*
-        + bp: 1p sg. (agent) + 2p sg. (obj).
'I gave you a mango'.

to   mUkhã   ĝalhI   pUch-i
you-obl. me-to-loc incidence ask-pst ptcpl f. sg.
mU-kh-ã ĝalhI pUch-yə + y
-        -   + bp: 2p sg. (agent)
ĝalhI pUch-yə + y   *+ mI*
-        -   +bp: 2p sg. (agent) + 1p sg. (abl)
'You (sg.) asked me the incidence (f. sg.)'.

The pronouns and their substitute agents and indirect object bound-pronouns are listed in table 17.8.

tũ   mũsã ĝəɖU   hələnd-ẽ
you I-obl. along with come-pres ptcpl- 2p m. sg.
(tũ) hələnd-ẽ + mI / hələnd-ẽ + mI
                  + bp: 1p sg. (instr)
'You (m. sg.) will come with me.'

hUnə   əsã   lay kItabə   and-a
3p-remote-obl we-obl. for book-pl. bring-pst ptcpl -m. pl.
əsã lay kItab-ə a-nd-ã + ĩ
-   -   -   -   + bp: 3p sg. (agent)
kItab-ə a-nd-ã + ĩ   *+ ũ*
-        -   + bp:3p sg. (agent) +1p pl.(obl)
'He (she) brought books for us.'

Bound-pronouns optionally added to postpositions and nouns are less frequent in the language. Certain postpositions add bound-pronouns representing the set of indirect object suffixes for substituting all singular and only third person plural pronouns in an oblique case. Suffixes denoting first and second plural have become obsolete in modern Sindhi. The usage of bound-pronouns for first and second singular is also on the decline:

TABLE 17.8: BOUND-PRONOUNS

Persons	Singular				Plural			
	pronouns		bound forms		pronouns		bound forms	
	nom	obl	agent	indir obj	nom	obl	agent	indir obj
First	*mã*	*mũ*	+ *mĨ*	+ *mĨ*	*əsĩ*	*əsã*	+ *sĩ/-sũ*	+ *ũ*
Second	*tũ*	*to*	+ *I*	+ *I*	*tͻ̃vhĩ*	*tͻ̃vhã*	+ *və*	+ *və*
Third proximate	*hi-U* (m.) *hi-ə* (f.)	*hInə*	+ *ĩ*	+ *sI*	*hi*	*hInənI*	–	–
remote	*hu* (m.) *hu-ə* (f.)	*hUnə*	+ *ĩ*	+ *sI*	*hu*	*hUnənI*	–	–

hUnə khe / khe + sI 'to him/her (remote)', *mũ vəṭã / vəṭãU + mI* 'from me';
hInənI jo, hInənI səndo/səndU + nI, 'theirs (prox m.)',
hUnə jeḍ̂i / jeḍ̂yə + sI 'equal to her'.

Certain nouns, denoting relationship and some parts of body, also add bound-pronouns representing the set of indirect object suffixes, for substituting possessive nouns in all singular and only third person plural formations. Bound-pronouns denoting first and second person plural are found in nineteenth century Sindhi, but have become obsolete in modern language.

tŨhĨjo caco / cacə̃ + hĨ	'your uncle (paternal)'
hInəjo mUṛsU / mUṛsU + sI, mUṛsə̃h + sI	'her husband'
hUnənji dhiv / dhiṇ + ənI	'their daughter'
mŨhĨja neṇə / neṇə + mI	'my eyes'.

In the present work, statements regarding syntax have been restricted to only preliminary observations, since a detailed study of the syntactic structure of Sindhi, based on modern linguistic techniques, is yet to be made.

REFERENCES

Advani, Bherumal Mehrchand (1941) *Sindhi B'olia ji Tarikha* (A History of the Sindhi Language), Karachi. (Reprinted (1956), Hyderabad Sindh: Sindhi Adabi Board).

Allana, Gulam Ali (1964) *The Arabic Elements in Sindhi*, M.A. Thesis, London: University of London.

—— (1967) *Sindhi Suratkhati* (Sindhi Writing System), Hyderabad Sindh (Reprinted (1993) Sindhi Language Authority).

—— (1974) *Sindhi B'olia jo Buṇu Bunyadu* (Origins of Sindhi Language), Hyderabad Sindh: Zaib Adabi Markaz.

—— (1979) *Sindhi B'olia ji Lisani Jagrafi* (Linguistic Geography of Sindhi Language), Jamshoro: University of Sindh, Institute of Sindhology. (Revised edition 1995).

Bailey, T. E. (1922) 'The Sindhi implosives – a note', *Bulletin of The School of Oriental and African Studies* 2. pp. 835–6.

Baloch, Nabi Bux Khan (1962) *Sindhi B'olia ji Mukhtasir Tarikha* (A Short History of the Sindhi Language), Hyderabad Sindh: Sindhi Adabi Board.

—— (1961–81) *Jamia Lughat Sindhi* (A Comprehensive Sindhi Dictionary), 5 vols., Hyderabad Sindh: Sindhi Adabi Board.

—— (1965) *Sindhi Loka Geeta* (Sindhi Folk Songs), Hyderabad Sindh: Sindhi Adabi Board.

Barnouw, Victor (1954) 'The social structure of a Sindhi refugee camp', *Social Forces*, 33. 151ff.

—— (1966) 'The Sindhis: merchantile refugees in India: problems of their assimilation', *Phylon: Review of Race and Culture*, Atlanta University 27. 1: 40–9.

Beames, John (1872–9) *A Comparative Grammar of the Modern Aryan Languages of India – Hindi, Punjabi, Sindhi, Gujarati, Marathi, Oriya, Bengali*, 3 vols, London. (Reprinted (1966), Delhi: Munshiram Manoharlal).

Bhandarkar, R. G. (1914) *Wilson Philological Lectures on Sanskrit and the Derived Languages*, delivered in 1877 Bombay. (Reprinted (1974) from the *Collected Works of Sir R. G. Bhandarkar*, Vol. IV Poona: Bhandarkar Oriental Research Institute).

Bharati, Narayan (1991) *Sindhi Loka Geetan mein Samajik Pasmanzar* (A Social Perspective of Sindhi Folk Songs), Ph.D. dissertation, Bombay: Bombay University.

Bordie, John (1958) *A Descriptive Sindhi Phonology*, Ph.D. dissertation, Austin: University of Texas; Ann Arbor, MI: University Microfilms.

Bughio, Qasim (1992) *A Comparative Study of Rural and Urban Sindhi: Social Networks*, Ph.D. dissertation, Colchester: University of Essex.

Chatterji, Suniti Kumar (1942) *Indo-Aryan and Hindi*, Calcutta: Firma K. L. Mukhopadhyay. (Revised edition 1960).

—— (1958) 'An early Arabic version of the Mahabharata story from Sindhi', *Indo-Asian Culture*, 7. 1: 50–71.

Daswani, Chander J. and Parchani, Sundri (1978) *Sociolinguistic Survey of Indian Sindhi*, Mysore: Central Institute of Indian Languages.

Gidwani, Parso J. (1971) *A Phonology of Lari*, M.A. Thesis, Poona: Poona University and Deccan College Postgraduate Research Institute.

—— (1996) *Similarities in Sindhi and Dravidian Languages*, Delhi: Sindhi Academy.

Grierson, Sir George A. (1902) 'Vracada and Sindhi', *Journal of the Royal Asiatic Society of Great Britain and Ireland*, pp. 47–8.

—— (1919) *Linguistic Survey of India*, Vol. VIII : 1, *Indo-Aryan Family, North Western Group: Sindhi and Lahnda*, Calcutta: Government Printing Press.

Gune, P. D. (1918) *Introduction to Comparative Philology*, Bombay. (Reprinted (1970) Poona: Oriental Book House).

Gurov, N. V. (1968) 'Prospects for the linguistic interpretation of the Proto-Indian texts (on the basis of the Dravidian languages)', in Knorozov, Yu. V., Volchok, B. Ya. and Gurov, N. V. (eds.). *Proto-Indica: 1968 Brief Report on the Investigations of the Proto-Indian Texts*, Moscow: Academy of Sciences of the U.S.S.R., Institute of Ethnography.

Hoernle, A. F. R. (1880) *A Comparative Grammar of the Gaudian Languages with Special Reference to Eastern Hindi*, London: Trübner & Co.

Hrozny, Bedrich (1939) *Über die älteste Völkerwanderung über das Problem der Proto-Indischen Zivilisation: Ein Versuch die Proto-Indischen von Mohenjo-daro*, Prague: Monographie Archivu Orientalniho 3. 1–24.

Jairamdas Doulatram (1957) 'The ancestry of Sindhi', *Bharatiya Vidya*, 17.3–4: 41–59.

—— (1958) 'Sindhi', in Narasimhan, V. K. et al. (eds.) *The Languages of India: A Kaleidoscopic Survey*, Madras, pp. 63–6.

Jatoi, Ali Nawaz H. (1968) *Ilm Lisan ain Sindhi Zabaana* (Linguistics and Sindhi Language), Hyderabad Sindh; 2nd ed. 1983, Institute of Sindhology.

Jetley, Kishinchand T. (1957) *Sindhi Bhaṣa ka Sankṣipt Parichay* (A Short Introduction to Sindhi Language), Poona.

—— (1985) 'Mohan-je-dare ji lipi ain hatavaṇikaa akhara' (The Script of Mohenjo-daro and Hatavanikaa letters). *Sindhi Suhon*, issues 1 and 2, Pune: Akhil Bharatiya Sindhi Sahitya Vidvat Parishad (cited in Possehl 1996).

Jetley, Murlidhar K. (1965) *A Descriptive Analysis of Vicholi: The Standard Sindhi Dialect*, Ph.D. dissertation, Poona: Poona University and Deccan College Postgraduate Research Institute.

—— (1999) *B'olia jo Sirishto ain Likhaavata: Sindhi B'olia jun Lipyun* (Language Structure and Writing: Scripts of Sindhi Language), Delhi: Akhil Bharatiya Sindhi Sahitya Vidvat Parishad.

Jonejo, Abdul Jabbar and Prem, Hidayat (1994) *Thara ji B'oli* (Thari Dialect), Hyderabad Sindh: Sindhi Language Authority.

Jotwani, Motilal W. (1966) *Sindhi Bhaṣa, Lipi aur Sahitya* (Sindhi Language, Script and Literature). Delhi: Raj Jotwani.

Katre, S. M. (1961) *Introduction to Modern Indian Linguistics*, Gauhati: University of Gauhati.

Khubchandani, Lachman M. (1959) 'D'ahin sadia mein Sindhi Mahabharat jo Arbi naqulu (An Arabic version of the 10th century Sindhi Mahabharat), Sindhi tr. *Kahani*, Bombay, pp. 49–66.

—— (1961) *The Phonology and Morphophonemics of Sindhi*, M.A. Thesis, Philadelphia: University of Pennsylvania.

—— (1962a) 'Sindhi linguistics', in Ghatage, A. M. and Kalelkar, N. G. (eds.) *Workbook in Modern Linguistics*, Poona: Linguistic Society of India.

—— (1962b) 'Pronominal suffixes in Sindhi', *Indian Linguistics* 23. 72–81.

—— (1963) *The Acculturation of Indian Sindhi to Hindi: A Study of Language in Contact*, Ph.D. dissertation, Philadelphia: University of Pennsylvania; Ann Arbor, MI: Univ.

Microfilms; 1964 'Abstract' *Dissertation Abstracts* 25: 1. (Reprinted (1965) *Linguistics: An International Review*, Vol. 12).

—— (1966) 'Sound structure of Sindhi and Hindi: a contrastive study', Poona: Deccan College Postgraduate Research Institute (mimeograph).

—— (1983) 'Arabic script for non-Semitic languages', Proceedings of the CALTIS Conference, Poona.

—— (1997) *Sindhi Heritage: The Dynamics of Dispersal*, Delhi: Sindhi Academy.

Kishnani, Santdas P. (1993) *Sindhi Pahaaka ain Muhavara* (A Dictionary of Sindhi Proverbs and Idioms), Poona: P. V. Kishnani Trust.

Lalwani, Jetho (1998) *Sindhi Folklore*, Ahmedabad: Stage Publication.

Mahadevan, Iravatham (1979) 'Study of the Indus script through bilingual parallels', in Possehl, G. L. (ed.) *Ancient Cities of the Indus*, Delhi: Vikas, pp. 261–7.

Memon, Mohd. Siddique (1937) *Sindhu ji Adabi Tarikha* (A Literary History of Sindh), Karachi.

Mohamed, Meean and Pribhdas, Moonshi (1860) *Sindhi Sarf-o-nahv* (Sindhi Grammar), Karachi. (Reprinted (1960) Hyderabad Sindh: Sindhi Adabi Board).

Mukherjee, Subasis (1998) 'Statistical measurements in speech analysis: a study on Sindhi vowels', International Conference on Computational Linguistics, Indian Statistical Institute, Calcutta.

Nihalani, Paru (1972) *The Aerodynamic Investigation of Stops in Sindhi*, Ph.D. dissertation, Edinburgh: University of Edinburgh.

—— (1974) 'Lingual articulation of stops in Sindhi', *Phonetica* 30. pp. 197–212.

Oodharam, Thanwardas Moonshi (1857) *Elementary Grammar of the Sindhi Language*, Kotree. (Revised edition 1879, Karachi).

Panwhar, M. H. (1988) 'Language of Sind between Rise of Amri and fall of Mansura i.e. 5000 Years Ago to 1025 AD', in Jonejo, A. J. and Bughio, M. Q. (eds.) *Cultural Heritage of Sind*, Hyderabad Sindh: Sindhi Adabi Board.

Parmanand Mewaram, (1910) *A Sindhi–English Dictionary*, Hyderabad Sindh: The Sind Juvenile Cooperative Society.

—— (1933) *A New English–Sindhi Dictionary*, Hyderabad Sindh: Jote Publication.

Parpola, Asko (1994) *Deciphering the Indus Script*, Cambridge: Cambridge University Press.

—— (1997) 'Deciphering the Indus script: methods and interpretations', *Occasional Paper* series, Vol. 2, Wisconsin: University of Wisconsin-Madison, Center for South Asia.

Parpola, Asko, Koskenniemi, S. Parpola, S. and Aalto, P. (1969) *Decipherment of the Proto-Dravidian Indus Script: A First Announcement*, Copenhagen: Scandinavian Institute of Asian Studies.

Pischel, Richard (1900) *Grammatik der Prākrit–Sprachen, Series: (Encyclopedia of Indo-Aryan Research), Grundriss der indo-arischen Philologie und Altertumskunde*, Strassburg: Karl J. Trübner (English tr., Jha, Subhadra (1957) *A Comparative Grammar of the Prakrit Languages*, Delhi: Motilal Banarsidass, 2nd ed. 1965, Reprinted 1981).

—— (1938), *The Deśīnāmamālā of Hemachandra* edited with Critical Notes, 2nd ed. by Paravesta Venkata Ramanujaswami, Poona: Bhandarkar Oriental Research Institute.

Possehl, Gregory L. (1996) *Indus Age: The Writing System*, New Delhi: Oxford and IBH.

—— (1999) *Indus Age: The Beginnings*, New Delhi: Oxford and IBH.

Princep, J. (1835) *A Grammar of the Scindee Language*, Bombay.

Ramos, F. D. (1836) *A Grammar of the Sindhi Language*.

Rao, S. R. (1992) 'Decipherment of the Indus script throws new light on the religion and polity of the Harappans', in Possehl, G. L. (ed.) *South Asian Archaeology Studies*, Delhi: Oxford and IBH, pp. 57–80.

Rohra, Satish Kumar (1968) *Descriptive Analysis of Kacchi*, Ph.D. dissertation, Poona: Poona University and Deccan College Postgraduate Research Institute.

Ruchandani, Lilo (1963) *Sindhua ji Jhalaka* (Glimpses of Sindhu Culture), Ahmedabad.

Ruplin, F. and Steinmetz, D. (1967) 'A transformational-generative phonology of Sindhi', X International Congress of Linguistics, Bucharest.

Samtani, Narain H. (1957) 'Sindhia jo Sanskrit ain Palia saan samb'andhu' (Relationship of Sindhi with Sanskrit and Pali), *Hindvasi*, Bombay (June issue).

Sandeelo, Abdul Karim M. (1973) *Lok Adaba jo Tahqeeqee Jaizo* (A Critical Assessment of Sindhi Folk Literature). Ph.D. dissertation, Hyderabad Sindh: University of Sindh.

Schimmel, Annemarie (1981) 'The German contribution to the study of Sindhi and Panjabi' in *German Contributions to the Study of Indo-Pakistani Linguistics*, Hamburg: German– Pakistan Forum, pp. 95–137.

Sehwani, Fateh Mohd, (1940) *Aftab-e-Adab* (An Account of Sindhi Language and Literature), Karachi. (Reprinted 1956).

Shirt, Rev. G., Thanvurdas Udharam and Mirza, S. F. (1879) *A Sindhi–English Dictionary*, Kurrachee: The Commissioner's Printing Press.

Siraj-ul-Haq (1964) *Sindhi B'oli* (Sindhi Language), Hyderabad Sindh.

Sorley, H. T. (1940) *Shah Abdul Latif of Bhit: His Poetry, Life and Times*, London: Oxford University Press. (Reprinted 1966).

Stack, Capt. George (1849) *A Dictionary–English and Sindhi*, Bombay. (Reprinted (1986) New Delhi: Asian Educational Services).

—— (1853) *A Grammar of the Sindhi Language*, Bombay: American Mission Press.

—— (1855) *A Dictionary–Sindhi and English*, Bombay. (Reprinted (1986) New Delhi: Asian Educational Services).

Thakur, Hiro (1997) 'Puraanan datstakhatan ji parhniia ja masaila (Issues of reading old manuscripts)' *Tahqeeqa ain Tanqeeda* (Literary Essays), Delhi.

Tolani-Parchani, Sundri (1973) *A Transformational Grammar of Sindhi*, Ph.D. dissertation, Poona: Poona University and Deccan College Postgraduate Research Institute.

Trumpp, E. (1866) *Sindhi Literature – The Divan of Abd-ul-Latif Shah known by the name of Shaha jo Risalo* (Poetry Collection of Shah Abdul Latif), Leipzig: F.A. Brockhaus.

—— (1872) *Grammar of the Sindhi Language Compared with the Sanskrit, Prakrit, and the Cognate Indian Vernaculars*, London and Leipzig: Trubner & Co.

Turner, Ralph L. (1924) 'The Sindhi recursives or voiced stops preceded by glottal enclosure', *BSOAS* 3. pp. 301–15.

—— (1931) *A Comparative Etymological Dictionary of the Nepali Language*, London: Oxford University Press.

—— (1966) *A Comparative Dictionary of the Indo-Aryan Languages*, Vol. 1; Indexes (1969) by Dorothy R. Turner, London: Oxford University Press.

Upadhye, A. N. (1959) *Uddyotana-sūri's Kuvalayamālā (A Unique Campū in Prākrit) and Ratnaprabha-sūri's Kuvalayamālā-Kathā* (A stylistic digest of the above in Sanskrit), *part I: Kuvalayamālā Prākrit-Text & Various Readings* (Singhi Jain series 45), Bombay: Bharatiya Vidya Bhavan.

Vale, Ramachandra (1948) *Verbal Composition in Indo-Aryan*, Poona: Deccan College Postgraduate Research Institute.

Wadhwani, Yashodhara (1997) *Sindhi and Sanskrit: Linguistic and Literary Connection*, Delhi: Sindhi Academy.

Wathen, W. H. (1836) 'A Grammar and Vocabulary of the Sindhi Language', *Journal of the Royal Society of Bengal*, Calcutta.

Yegorova, Raya P (1964) 'Pronominal enclitics for verb in Sindhi' (in Russian), *Indo-Iranian Philology*, Moscow; pp. 125–41.

—— (1966) *Yazik Sindxi* (Sindhi Language), Moscow: Nauka Publishing House.

Yelizarenkova, T. Y. (1964) 'Concerning the philological typology of some Indo-Aryan languages', XXVI International Congress of Orientalists, New Delhi.

Zvelebil, Kamil (1970) 'The so called "Dravidian" of the Indus inscriptions', *Proceedings of the Third International Conference – Seminar of Tamil Studies*, Paris, pp. 32–41.

—— (1990) *Dravidian Linguistics: An Introduction*, Pondicherry: Pondicherry Institute of Linguistics and Culture.

FURTHER READING

Haskell, Charles W. (1942) *A Grammar of Sindhi Language*, Karachi.

Khubchandani, Lachman M. (1969) 'Sindhi' in Sebeok, Thomas A. (ed.) *Current Trends in Linguistics*, vol. 5: *Linguistics in South Asia*, The Hague: Mouton, pp. 201–34. (Revised ed. (2000) *Sindhi Studies 1947–1967: A Review of Sindhi Language and Society*, Pune: Centre for Communication Studies).

Mirchandani, Dayaram V. (1965) *Sindhi Vyakaraṇu* (Sindhi Grammar in Devanagari Script), Bombay.

Prem, Hidayat (1994) *Sindhi B'olia ja Muhaqeeqa* (Research Scholars of Sindhi Language), Hyderabad Sindh: Sindh Tahqeeqi Board.

Qaleech Beg, Mirza (1916–21) *Sindhi Vyakaraṇu* (Sindhi Grammar), 4 vols., Hyderabad Sindh. (Reprinted 1960–1).

CHAPTER EIGHTEEN

GUJARATI

George Cardona and Babu Suthar

CONTENTS

LIST OF TABLES

1 INTRODUCTION

1.1 Gujarati is the official language of Gujarat state, on the west coast of India, with an area of 196,024 square kilometres. Within the Republic of India, Gujarat borders Rajasthan, Madhya Pradesh and Maharashtra; it also borders Pakistan to the northwest. The languages spoken in the areas contiguous to the Gujarat within India are Marwari, Hindi and Marathi. The 1991 Census of India reports 40,673,814 speakers, accounting for approximately five per cent (4.85%) of the population. This includes Gujaratis living outside Gujarat state, in Maharashtra (Mumbai has a substantial Gujarati population), Rajasthan, Madhya Pradesh and Karnataka, as well as dialects for which separate figures are given (Vijayanunni 1997: 11); e.g. Saurashtri is listed with 220,116 speakers. Gujarati speakers also reside in many other countries, principally Pakistan, Singapore, Fiji, South Africa, the United Kingdom, the United States and Canada. Although the first generation of immigrants in these areas maintained Gujarati as a family language, one can see a gradual diminution in its use in successive generations.

The accepted standard dialect is the speech of the area from Vadodara (formerly Baroda) to Amdavad (formerly Ahmedabad) and north. There are other major dialect areas, principally those of the south and Saurashtra. See Vyas 1974: 131–74, Acharya 1985, Mistry 1997: 670–1, as well as Učida 1990, 1991.

1.2 The history of Gujarati is traditionally divided into three major stages: Old Gujarati (twelfth to fifteenth centuries), Middle Gujarati (fifteenth to eighteenth centuries), and Modern Gujarati. From the beginning, there were major works in various genres, for the most part in verse form, such as: *rāsa*, predominantly didactic narrative; *phāgu*, in which spring time is celebrated; *bārmāsī*, describing natural beauty during each of the twelve months; and *ākhyāna*, in which different sections are each in a single metre. The earliest rāsa known is Śālibhadrasūri's *Bharateśvara-bāhubali* (1185). The earliest phāgu is Jinapadmasūri's *Sirithūlibadda* (ca. 1335), but the most famous such work is the *Vasantavilāsa*, of unknown authorship, a work whose precise date – somewhere in the fourteenth or fifteenth century, though some scholars think it is earlier – has not been determined. Traditionally, Narasimha Mehta (*c.* 1414–80) is viewed as the father of modern Gujarati poetry. Another major poet of this period is Bhalan (1405–89), best known for his translation of Bāṇa's *Kādambarī*. Not all early Gujarati literature was in poetical form however. An important prose work by virtue of its early age and because it has been very well edited (Pandit 1976) is the fourteenth-century commentary of Taruṇaprabha, the *Ṣaḍāvaśyakabālabodhavṛtti*. Bhayani (1988: 45–9) gives a summary list of major works in Gujarati of different stages from the twelfth to the sixteenth centuries and (1988: 73–105, 108–84, 193–214, 217–44, 254–318, 327–56) and summarizes the major grammatical features of the language in each era.

1.3 The stages noted in section 1.2 are characterized by certain sound changes (see Pandit 1961, 1966, 1976: 33–8). Major changes characteristic of the transition between Old and Middle Gujarati are: *i, u* develop to *a* in open syllables; diphthongs *ai* and *au* change to *ε* and *ɔ* in initial syllables, to *e* and *o* elsewhere; *aü* develops to *ɔ̃* in initial syllables, to *ũ* in final syllable. For example (citing in transliteration except for *ε* and *ɔ*): *milaï* 'meets' > *maḷe*, *rāti* 'night' > *rāt*, *viḍhaï* 'quarrels' > *vaḍhe*; *mānusa* 'man' > *mānasa*, *āju* 'today' > *āja*; *païsaï* 'enters' > *pεse*, *baïsaï* 'sits' > *bεse*, *kaüḍaü* 'cowrie' > *kɔḍo*, *maüḍaü* 'late' > *mɔḍo*; *saüghũ* 'cheap' > *sɔ̃ghũ*. Phonological developments had grammatical consequences; for example, the contrast between nominative-accusative singular in *-a* (e.g. *hātha* 'hand') and instrumental-locative singular in *-i* (e.g. instr. sg. *hāthi*) of Old Gujarati was eliminated, both forms now ending in *-a*. One of the major changes in the transition from Middle Gujarati to Modern Gujarati involves final syllables, where *-a* is deleted, so that the modern language has consonant-final words, unlike the earlier language; e.g. *rāta* 'night' > *rāt*. In addition, a new plural marker, *-o* is characteristic of Modern Gujarati.

2 PHONOLOGY

2.1 Vowels

Gujarati is generally considered to have an eight vowel system (table 18.1), including ε and σ (see Turner 1925, Pandit 1955, 1966: 105, 108–115, Firth 1957, Cardona 1965: 20–3, Vyas 1977: 67–76, Mistry 1997: 656–657): high, high-mid, mean-mid, and low, front and back; back vowels are rounded. There are also murmured and nasalized vowels (see sections 2.2.3, 5). *e*, *o* and *ε*, *ɔ* contrast in limited contexts, essentially between consonants. Moreover, *e* and *o* do not have nasalized or murmured counterparts, and in absolute word-final position the higher and lower vowels of these sets vary. Examples of contrasts, in accordance with the generally accepted system, are shown in table 18.2.

TABLE 18.1: GUJARATI VOWELS

i		*u*
e		*o*
ε	*ə*	*ɔ*
	a	

TABLE 18.2: VOWEL CONTRASTS

ji 'particle of respect'		*ju* 'louse'
ši 'which?' (f)		*šũ* 'what?' (nt)
taḷi 'clapping'		*taḷũ* 'padlock'
vəhi 'account book'		*vəhu* 'bride'
mir 'nobleman'		*mur* 'a caste'
mil 'mill'		*mul* 'price'
ĩṭ 'brick'		*ūṭ* 'camel'
		curi 'crushed' (f)
che 'is, are'	*chə* 'six'	*cho* 'you are'
je 'who'		*jo* 'if'
še 'what?'		*šo* 'which?' (m)
kərše 'will do' (3sgfut)		*kəršo* 'will do' (2pl)
	cəri 'grazed' (f)	*cori* 'theft'
bɛ 'two'		*mɛ̃* 'I' (agn)
mer 'side, a caste'		*mor* 'peacock'
mɛr (an exclamation)	*mər* 'die' (imp)	*mɔr* 'mango blossom'
		mɔ̃h 'face'
kɛm 'how?'	*kəm* 'less'	*kom* 'a caste'
mɛl 'dirt'		*mɔl* 'a crop'
bhɛ̃s 'buffalo'		*sɔ̃p* 'entrust' (imp)
		cɔri 'altar'
		sɔ̃pi 'handed over' (f)
	məḷi 'was met with' (f)	
	ja 'go' (imp)	
	ša 'what?'	
	mar 'beat' (imp)	
	mal 'goods, luggage'	
	cari 'was grazed' (f)	
	maḷi 'gardener'	

Modi (1994) has taken up the issue of which dialects have eight vowel systems and which do not have contrastive ɛ and ɔ.

Although vowel length is not contrastive in Gujarati, vowels have longer and shorter varieties according to phonological contexts. Thus, in monosyllables and in word-final position, vowels are longer than elsewhere, and nasalized vowels are relatively longer than oral vowels. For example, *i*, *u* and *ə* in *ghi* 'clarified butter, ghee', *lu* 'a hot wind, sunstroke' and *sə̃yəm* 'restraint, control' are phonetically longer that the *i*, in *divəs* 'day', and the first *u* and *ə* of *lukhũ* 'dry (nt)', *səkhət* 'strong, strict'. See Pandit 1958: 213–14, Desai 1992: 102.

2.2 Consonants

2.2.1 Introduction

Consonants (table 18.3) are: glottal, velar, palatal, postalveolar (commonly called retroflex), dental and labial according to places of articulation; stops, nasal continuants, fricatives, laterals, flap, and semivowels according to mode of production. Examples of contrasts are shown in table 18.4.

TABLE 18.3: GUJARATI CONSONANTS

		Glottal	Velar	Palatal	Postalveolar (retroflex)	Alveolar	Dental	Labial
Stops								
voiceless	unaspirated		*k*	*c*	*ṭ*		*t*	*p*
	aspirated		*kh*	*ch*	*ṭh*		*th*	*ph*
voiced	unaspirated		*g*	*j*	*ḍ*		*d*	*b*
	aspirated		*gh*	*jh*	*ḍh*		*dh*	*bh*
Nasals					*ṇ*		*n*	*m*
Spirants								
voiceless					*š*		*s*	
voiced		*h*					(*z*)	
Lateral					*ḷ*	*l*		
Tap					*r*			
Semivowels (Glides)				*y*			*v*	

TABLE 18.4: CONSONANT CONTRASTS

Stops			
Voiceless		Voiced	
Unaspirated	Aspirated	Unaspirated	Aspirated
kam 'work'		*gam* 'village'	
kərvũ 'to do'	*khərvũ* 'to fall'	*gər* 'pulp'	*ghər* 'home'
	khəṭ 'six'		*ghəṭ* 'body'
nak 'nose'	*lakh* '100,000'	*nag* 'mythical snake'	*vagh* 'tiger'
baki 'remaining'	*makhi* 'a fly'		
	rakho 'keep' (imp)	*nago* 'naked' (m)	*agho* 'distant'
		səgi 'cognate' (f)	*mərghi* 'hen'

Voiceless		Voiced	
Unaspirated	Aspirated	Unaspirated	Aspirated
cuni 'nose ring'		*juni* 'old' (f)	
cəḷ 'itching'	*chəḷ* 'cheating'		
	chal 'bark of a tree'		*jhal* 'catch!' (2sg imp)
		jɔmvũ 'to eat'	*jhəmvũ* 'to leak'
nac 'dance'		*naj* 'pride'	
	pucho 'ask' (imp)	*pujo* 'venerate' (imp)	
sacũ 'true (nt.)'		*sajũ* 'whole, healthy' (nt)	
ṭok 'goading'		*ḍok* 'neck'	
	ṭhɔg 'thief'		*ḍhɔg* 'much'
paṭ 'bench'	*paṭh* 'lesson'		
		ḍal 'tree branch'	*ḍhal* 'slope'
vaṭ 'road'		*vaḍ* 'hedge'	*ašaḍh* 'name of a month'
moṭi 'big, older' (f)		*mɔḍi* 'late' (f)	*pɔḍhi* 'slept' (f)
		vaḍi 'small garden'	*vaḍhi* 'cut' (pftv f)
toḍvũ 'to break'		*dɔḍvũ* 'to run'	
tɔḍ 'crack'	*thɔḍ* 'tree trunk'		*dhɔḍ* 'torso'
		dan 'gift'	*dhan* 'grain'
vat 'matter, story'	*sath* 'company'	*vad* 'discussion'	*sadh* 'accomplish, consult' (2sg imp)
səti 'virtuous woman'		*sədi* 'century'	*vədhi* 'remained over' (pftv f)
suto 'sleeping (m)'		*judo* 'different (m)'	
pap 'sin'		*bap* 'father'	
pəḷ 'moment'	*phəḷ* 'fruit'	*bar* 'twelve'	*bhar* 'weight'
	phal 'crop'		*bhal* 'name of an area'
cup 'quiet'		*khub* 'much'	
təpas 'inquiry'		*kəbaṭ* 'closet'	
	bəpharo 'sultriness, sweat'		*əbhagi* 'luckless'

Nasals
nəgər 'city' *məgər* 'crocodile' *kaṇ* 'a particular rite' *kan* 'ear' *kam* 'work' *paṇi* 'water' *pani* 'heel' *kami* 'sexual'

Spirants
šap 'curse' *sap* 'serpent' *šal* 'shawl' *sal* 'year'
kəš 'rope, whip' *kəs* 'essence' *koš* 'dictionary' *kos* 'a measure of distance'
vaši 'stale' *vasi* 'inhabitant'
həkikət 'circumstance, fact' *hath* 'hand' *himmət* 'courage' *hĩcko* 'a swing' *hũ* 'I'
səlah 'advice' *suleh* 'compromise'
vəhu 'wife' *kəhyũ* 'said'

Laterals
maḷ 'storey of a building' *mal* 'goods' *laḷ* 'saliva' *lal* 'red'
puḷo 'bundle of grass' *culo* 'stove'
gəḷni 'tea strainer' *cəḷni* 'current'
kaḷe 'black' (loc) *kale* 'yesterday, tomorrow'

Flap (see section 2.3)
rat 'night'
car 'four' *cal* 'go!' (imp)
vər 'bridegroom' *vəḷ* 'a twist'
sari 'good' (f) *saḍi* 'saree'
məryo 'he died' *məḷyo* '(was) encountered' (m)

Semivowels
yad 'remembrance' *vad* 'doctrine, -ism' *dəya* 'mercy' *dəva* 'medicine'

2.2.2 Stops

Stops are voiced or voiceless, each either aspirated or unaspirated. A notable exception concerns /ph/, which is usually realized as a spirant [f] in the standard language (Vyas 1977: 31). Palatal stops have affricated release. Stops occurring as first members of clusters followed by consonants other than *r*, *y*, *v* are unreleased and are optionally unreleased in final position (Vyas 1977: 50, Mistry 1997: 660). The absence of release entails deaspiration of voiceless stops (Cardona 1965: 29). Intervocalically, *gh*, *dh* and *bh* have variant realizations, as aspirated stops and as voiced spirants [ɣ], [ð], [β], with murmur of vowels, and spirantalization of non-palatal voiceless aspirates has been reported (Cardona 1965: 23, Vyas 1977: 31–50, Mistry 1997: 657). Intervocalically and in final position, voiced retroflex stops are realized as flapped [ɽ], [ɽʰ].

2.2.3 Nasals

n and *m* occur initially, finally, and intervocalically, but *ṇ* does not occur initially. Moreover, intervocalically *ṇ* is realized as a flap (Cardona 1965: 26, Mistry 1997: 659). An abstract nasal *N* is recognized (Pandit 1957: 165–9, Cardona 1965: 26, Mistry 1997: 659) to account for certain nasal segments in particular environments: (a) velar [ŋ] between *ə* and velar stops (e.g. *pəNkho* [pəŋkʰo] 'fan', *əNguli* [əŋguli] 'finger'), (b) palatal [ɲ] between *ə* and palatal stops (e.g. *səNco* [səɲtʃo] 'machine', *əNjən* [əɲdʒən] 'collyrium'), (c) nasalized varieties of other vowels and of *ə* in other contexts (e.g. *aNkh* [ãkʰ] 'eye', *tyaN* [tyã] 'there'). Before velar and palatal stops, nasalized vowels vary with sequences of such vowels and homorganic nasals; e.g. *maNgvuN* ([mãgvũ, mãŋgvũ]) 'ask for', *hiNcko* ([hĩcko, hĩɲcko]) 'a swing'.

2.2.4 Sibilants

There are different systems of sibilants, depending not only on the regions in question but also on whether speakers are conservative or innovating and use educated standard or substandard registers of speech. The largest number of sibilants is three: *š*, *s*, and *z*. The last occurs in borrowings from Arabic, Persian, Urdu, and English; e.g. *zor* 'strength', *zukam* 'catarrh', *azad* 'free', *myuziəm* 'museum'. In conservative educated speech, this is replaced by *j*: *jor*, *jukam*, *ajad*, *myujiəm*. There is also a reduced system, in which *š* and *s* do not contrast and the former occurs contiguous to palatal segments; e.g. *sũ* 'what (nt.)?', *stesən* 'railway station', *ši* 'which (f.)?', *šivay* 'besides' versus standard *šũ*, *stešən*, *šũ*, *sivay*. There are also social dialects that prefer *š* instead of *s* (Vyas 1977: 58). Further, in a register that may be characterized as substandard or supercolloquial (Cardona 1965: 25, Mistry 1997: 658), voiceless *h* replaces *š* and *s*: *hũ* 'what (nt.)?', *hat* 'seven', *harũ* 'good (nt.)', *hɔ* 'hundred', *dəh* 'ten', *kərhũ* 'we will do', *hahri* 'in-laws' village' instead of *šũ*, *sat*, *sarũ*, *sɔ*, *dəs*, *kəršũ*, *sasri*. In accordance with the conditions associated with these systems, the replacement by *h* does not apply to learned borrowings from Sanskrit used by educated speakers using supercolloquial forms. Moreover, in some areas, *h* replaces only *s* and not *š*.

2.2.5 h and murmur

Voiced *h* occurs in word initial, medial and final position, as illustrated in table 18.4. A sequence *əhV₂* of formal speech such that V_2 is not a high vowel alternates in more casual speech with a murmured vowel V_2^h. For example: *bəhɛn/bɛ^{h}n* 'sister', *kəhe/kɛ^h* 'say (imp.)', *vəhɛlo/vɛhlo* 'early (m.)', *kəho/kɔ^h* 'say (imp.)', *bəhar/ba^{h}r* 'outside'. In similar sequences where V_2 is a high vowel, the alternative is a sequence in which murmuring extends over the whole: *məhino/mə^{h}ino* 'month', *əhĩ/ə^{h}ĩ* 'here', *šahukar/ša^{h}ukar* 'banker', *kəhũ/kə^{h}ũ* 'I may say'. The high vowel is susceptible of replacement by a corresponding glide, with nasalization also extending over the whole: *mə^{h}yno*, *ə^{h}yN*, *ša^{h}vkar*, *kə^{h}vN*.

Sequences of initial *hV-* also alternate with murmured vowels; e.g. *hisab/i^{h}sab* 'account', *humlo/u^{h}mlo* 'attack', *hũ/ũ^h* 'I', *hath/a^{h}th* 'hand'. In addition, murmuring applies to vowels preceding voiced aspirated stops, with deaspiration of the stop; e.g *vagh/va^{h}g* 'tiger', *vaghən/va^{h}ɣən* 'female tiger', *dudh/du^{h}d* 'milk', *labh/la^{h}bh* 'profit'.

Such murmured vowels can lose their murmured quality: *bɛn, isab* etc.. In addition, there are items in which murmured and unmurmured vowels alternate and which differ from those considered above in that they do not have a distinct element *h*. For example, *nanũ/na^{h}nũ* 'small', *təme/tə^{h}me* 'you'.

Vowel murmuring, considered from the viewpoints of phonology, phonetics, and its historical sources, has been the object of several studies and discussions; see Pandit 1957, 1966: 121–5, Cardona 1965: 29–30, 50, R. Dave 1967, Fischer-Jørgensen 1967, Vyas 1977: 74–6, Modi 1987, Mistry 1997: 666–9.

2.2.6 Laterals

ḷ and *l* contrast in word-interior and final position, but *ḷ* does not occur as a word-initial consonant. Moreover, in many cases intervocalic *-ḷ-* can be replaced optionally by *-l-*, as in *kəḷa/kəla* 'art', *taḷi/tali* 'a clap'.

2.2.7 Tap and semivowels

Contrasts of *r* and semivowels with other consonants are illustrated in table 18.4. *v* has two variants: labio-dental fricative [v] and bilabial approximant [w], the former in word-initial position (e.g. *vat* 'matter, story', *vrət* 'vow', *vyəkti* 'individual'), the latter elsewhere, and either – in free variation – intervocalically. A group of words has final *-i* and *-u* following a vowel in lento variants of synonymous terms with *-y* and *-v*: *rai/ray* 'mustard', *koi/koy* 'someone', *hau/hav* 'a cry', *beu/bev* 'both'.

2.3 Consonant clusters

Clusters of dissimilar consonants occur in all positions, and geminate consonants occur medially. Biconsonantal initial clusters beginning with stops have *y*, *v*, *r* and *l* as second members; for example: *kyare* 'when?', *kvath* 'decoction', *krupa* 'kindness', *kleš* 'distress, affliction, quarrel'. *gn-* occurs in Sanskrit loans for *jñ-*; e.g. *gnan* 'knowledge'. *m-, n-, l-* and *w-* cluster with *y*, *-r-* can form a cluster with *m-* or *w-*, and *-l-* can cluster with *m-*; for example: *myan* 'sheath', *nyay* 'justice', *lyanət* 'disgrace', *vyəNjən* 'consonant', *mrutyu* 'death', *vrət* 'oath', *mlan* 'withered'. Initial *s* forms biconsonantal clusters with *y*, *v*, *r* as well as non-palatal voiceless stops and *n*, *m*, as in *syəndən* 'chariot', *svikar* 'accepting', *srušṭi* 'the universe', *skhələn* 'deviation', *skul* 'school', *sṭešən* 'railway station', *stuti* 'praise', *sneh* 'affection', *smarək* 'memorial'. *š-* clusters with *y*, *v*, *r*, *l* and *m*: *šyam* 'dark', *švas* 'breath', *šruti* 'sacred literature, the Vedas', *šlok* 'a metre', *šməšan* 'cremation ground'. Triconsonantal initial clusters involve *s-* followed by *-tr-*, *-pr-*, or *-mr-*: *stri* 'lady', *spruha* 'desire', *smruti* 'remembrance'. Most such clusters occur in borrowings, from Sanskrit, Arabic, Persian, and English. For details see Cardona 1965: 37–9, Pandit 1966: 136–42, Vyas 1977: 80–2, Desai 1992: 106–32, Mistry 1997: 665–6.

2.4 Syllable structure and tonic placement

2.4.1 Syllable structure

Syllables can be of the following types (Vyas 1977: 79–80): V (*a* 'this', *e* 'that'), VC (*un* 'wool', *ek* 'one', *ãkh* 'eye'), VCC (*ənt* 'end'), CV (*te* 'that one', *ke* 'or', *mẽ* 'I (agn)'), CVC (*kɛm* 'how?', *bap* 'father'), CVCC (*dost* 'friend'), CCV (*kyã* 'where?', *tyã* 'there', *šri* 'sir, Mr'), CCVC (*kvath* 'decoction', *kleš* 'distress, quarrel'), CCVCC (*prant* 'area').

In general, syllable division follows the pattern (C)V-CV-, (C)VC-CV (see Cardona 1965: 31–2): *a-po* 'give (imp)', *khə-mis* 'shirt'; *ʈəp-kũ* 'a drop', *aj-kal* 'nowadays', *sər-kar* 'government'.

2.4.2 Tonic placement

Stress is not contrastive, but particular syllables of items with more than one syllable have greater prominence. Tonic placement depends on the particular vowels of syllables and whether the syllables are open or closed. In general, the first syllable of disyllables is tonic unless the second syllable contains *a* and the first contains a vowel other than *a*. In trisyllables, the second syllable is tonic unless the first contains *a*, in which case there is variation between initial and penultimate stress:

> *bíjũ, bíjo, bíji* 'other (nt, m, f)', *píũ* 'I drink', *dívəs* 'day', *júləm* 'tyranny', *khéḍut* 'farmer', *ʈébəl* 'table', *óphis* 'office', *mótər* 'car', *cális* '40', *ápũ* 'I give', *sáme* 'in front', *jə́ldi* 'quickly', *və́stu* 'matter', *pə́Nkho* 'fan'
>
> *siváy* 'besides, in addition to', *dukán* 'store', *dekháy* 'appear(s)', *boláy* 'is (are) spoken', *kəlák* 'hour'
>
> *nəmúno* 'sample', *cummóter* '74', *utáru* 'passenger', *betáḷis* '42'

There is some disagreement concerning tonic placement rules even among Gujarati linguists; see Cardona 1965: 31–5, Modi 1979: 224–6, Mistry 1997: 660.

2.5 Phonological adjustments

Phonological adjustments take effect in contexts which involve boundaries and can be conditioned by properties which are either phonological or specifically grammatical. For example, *ə* in a final open syllable is deleted before a vocalic affix: *mokəl* (*mokəlvũ* 'to send'): *mokle* 'sends', *mitrə* 'friend': *mitr-o* 'friends'. There is also a process of inserting *ə*; e.g. *ek* 'one': *ekəj* 'only one', with *ə* inserted with the particle *j* (section 6.2), which appears after vowels that have not been inserted, as in *e-j* 'only this', *məne-j* 'only me'. Causatives and passives involve alternations in verb bases (see section 5.1). See also Cardona 1965: 50–2, Mistry 1997: 660–3.

3 WRITING SYSTEM

The Gujarati writing system is comparable to other scripts used in Indo-Aryan languages, such as the Devanāgarī and Bangla scripts. It is a combination syllabary and alphabet, in which a consonantal symbol lacking diacritics designates a consonant followed by *a*. The traditional sound list begins with independent symbols for vowels, followed by consonantal symbols with the default vowel, in the order stops, *y r l v*, voiceless spirants, *h*, and *ḷ*. These symbols are shown in table 18.5.

In addition, a superscript dot called *ənusvar* represents vowel nasality and nasal stops homorganic with following stops, in the way that *N* does (see section 2.2.3): આંખ (*aNkh*), ત્યાં (*tyaN*), પંખો (*pəNkho*), અંગુલિ/અંગુલી (*əNguli*), સંચો (*səNco*), અંજન (*əNjən*). Separate status is also given to three symbols which appear only in Sanskrit loans: the conjunct symbols ક્ષ (<kṣ> = /kš/), જ્ઞ (<jñ> = /gn/, /gny/) and : (called *visərgə*), as in અક્ષર (*əkšər*) 'syllable', જ્ઞાન (*gnan*) 'knowledge', દુઃખ (*dukh*) 'pain, suffering'.

Symbols have independent and conjunct forms. Conjunct forms for vowel symbols are shown in table 18.6. There are special symbols for some conjoined vowels: ઝ = અ + ઈ, ઝ = અ + ઉ, રૂ = ર + ઉ, રૂ = ર + ઊ. The conjoined symbol corresponding to the independent symbol ઋ is ૃ as in ઽ. Conjunct forms of consonant symbols are of two general types, depending on whether or not the symbol for the first consonant of the sequence has a vertical right stroke (*kaṇo*) or not. If the independent symbol has this stroke, the conjunct form lacks it: ખ : ખ , ગ : ગ , લ : લ and so on. If an independent symbols does not contain a kaṇo, it is conjoined to a following consonant symbol through closer spacing; e.g. ક ય : ક્ય. Certain consonant symbols have special conjunct counterparts. Corresponding to independent ર there are three conjoined symbols. If *r* is the second consonant, there are two symbols, depending on whether: the second consonant has a kaṇo or is rounded and open to the left or is rounded and open to the right; a third symbol is used if *r* is the first consonant. For example: ત્ર = ત + ર , ક્ર = ક + ર , ડ્ર = ડ + ર , ર્ક = ર + ક. For additional details, see Cardona 1965: 53–60, Mistry 1996.

TABLE 18.5: GUJARATI SCRIPT SYMBOLS WITH TRANSLITERATION AND TRANSCRIPTION

Vowels										
અ	આ	ઇ	ઈ	ઉ	ઊ	ઋ	એ	ઐ	ઓ	ઔ
a	*ā*	*i*	*ī*	*u*	*ū*	*ṛ*	*e*	*ai*	*o*	*au*
ə	*a*	*i*	*ī*	*u*	*ū*	*ru*	*e,ɛ*	*əi*	*o,ɔ*	*əu*

Consonants										
ક	ખ	ગ	ઘ	ઙ			હ	ક્ષ		
k	*kh*	*g*	*gh*	*ṅ*			*h*	*kṣ*		
ચ	છ	જ	ઝ	ઞ	ય	શ		જ્ઞ		
c	*ch*	*j*	*jh*	*ñ*	*y*	*ś*		*jñ*		
ટ	ઠ	ડ	ઢ	ણ	ર	ષ			ળ	
ṭ	*ṭh*	*ḍ*	*ḍh*	*ṇ*	*r*	*ṣ*			*ḷ*	
ત	થ	દ	ધ	ન	લ	સ				
t	*th*	*d*	*dh*	*n*	*l*	*s*				
પ	ફ	બ	ભ	મ	વ					
p	*ph*	*b*	*bh*	*m*	*v*					

Numerals									
0	૧	૨	૩	૪	૫	૬	૭	૮	૯
0	1	2	3	4	5	6	7	8	9

Note: The default vowel is omitted in transliteration/transcription; in the traditional order, read stops in groups of five, then *y r l v, ś ṣ s h*.

TABLE 18.6: SYMBOLS FOR VOWELS AND DIPHTHONGS IN DIFFERENT POSITIONS

Segments	Transliteration	Independent form	Conjoined form	Example (with k)
ə	u	અ		ક
a	ā	આ	ા	કા
i	i	ઇ	િ	કિ
i	ī	ઈ	ી	કી
u	u	ઉ	ુ	કુ
u	ū	ઊ	ૂ	કૂ
e, ɛ	e	એ	ે	કે
əi	ai	એ	ૈ	કૈ
o, ɔ	o	ઓ	ો	કો
əu	au	ઔ	ૌ	કૌ

Note: Independent forms also occur after vowel symbols.

4 NOMINAL SYSTEM

4.1. Introduction

The nominal system comprises substantives, adjectives and pronominals (pronouns and pronominal adjectives). Substantives and adjectives take part in a system of three genders and two numbers: masculine, feminine, neuter; and singular, plural. Bases and stems are distinguished, as are variable and invariable stems. Nominal stems are followed by postposed elements which signal syntactic roles (see section 4.6).

Gender distinctions are marked for variable stems through contrasting stems with direct singular forms in -o (m), -ũ (nt), -i (f) (see sections 4.2–3). A derivational suffix can also serve to form a feminine (see section 4.7). Formal gender distinctions can be associated with several semantic correlations. There are pairs such as rəNgaro 'a dyer': rəNgari 'dyer's wife', in which related male and female counterparts are involved. Similarly, chokro and chokri refer respectively to a boy and a girl. In addition, the neuter chokrũ designates a child in general.

The neuter is similarly used neutrally with indeterminate reference, as in

(1) kɔṇ   av-y-ũ
     who? come-pftv-nt sg
     'Who has come?'

(2) bədh-ã lok-o   sathe   jə-š-e
     all-nt pl people-pl together go-fut-3p
     'Everybody will go together.'

The person asking (1) does not know whether the one who has arrived is a man or a woman, and (2) refers to a group of both men and women. In addition, the neuter plural is used as an honorific with reference to a woman, e.g.

(3) təmar-ã   ma   kɛm   ch-e
     your-nt pl mother how? be-3p
     'How is your mother?'

There are also sets, involving inanimates, which involve contrasts of the type large versus small and coarse versus fine. For example:

> *oṭlo* 'large verandah' : *oṭli* 'small veranda' *kothḷo* 'large bag, sack' : *kothḷi* 'small bag',
> *cəmco* 'large spoon' : *cəmci* 'teaspoon' *cɔpḍo* 'ledger' : *cɔpḍi* 'book'
> *roṭlo* 'thick bread' : *roṭli* 'roṭī' : *roṭlũ* 'coarse bread (pejorative)'
> *nɔkri* 'job, service' : *nɔkrũ* 'job that is looked down upon'.

As can be seen from (3), number distinctions can be associated not only with actual counting but also with differences in how a person is treated, a plural being used as an honorific. The plural marker is *-o*, which can be omitted if plurality is signalled otherwise in an utterance. For example, in

(4) *rəmeš-e   cɔpḍ-i-o   khərid-i*
     Ramesh-ag book-f-pl   buy-pftv-f
     'Ramesh bought some books.'

the overtly plural *cɔpḍi-o* is used, with plurality not signalled by the verb *khərid-i* (←
khərid-y-i) or any other item, but in

(5) *rəmeš-e   keṭl-i   cɔpḍ-i khərid-i*
     Ramesh-ag how many-f   book-f buy-pftv-f
     'How many books did Ramesh buy?'

(6) *rəmeš-e   trəṇ cɔpḍ-i khərid-i*
     Ramesh-ag three book-f buy-pftv-f
     'Ramesh bought three books.'

plurality is signalled by the quantitative *keṭli* in construction with the count noun *cɔpḍi* and by the number word *trəṇ*. Similarly,

(7) *urmila-e təmara   dikra-ne jo-y-o*
     Urmila-ag your-m obl son-obj saw-pftv-msg
     'Urmila saw your son.'

(8) *urmila-e təmara   dikra-ne jo-y-a*
     Urmila-ag your-m.obl son-obj saw-pftv-mpl
     'Urmila saw your son(s).'

contrast in that the first has the singular verb form *joyo* and the second has the corresponding plural *joya*, which can be used honorifically; if true plural number is unambiguously intended, *dikra-o-ne* is required.

4.2 Substantives

Substantives are either variable or invariable. Variable substantives distinguish a base and stem forms: direct and oblique. They are also associated with a system of gender distinctions. Direct masculine and neuter forms end in *-o* and *-ũ* respectively. Corresponding oblique forms have *-a*. Neuters have *-ã* in plural forms. In general, oblique forms are followed by postposed elements; the plural marker *-o*, however, is subject to omission (see section 4.1), so that *-a* and *-ã* alone can signal plurality. There is also a vocative singular in *-a*. Base forms occur before postposed *-e* designating an agent or a locus. Corresponding to the above, there are feminine stems in *-i*, which show no variation. Examples are shown in table 18.7, with the variable substantives *chokr-o* 'boy, child', *chokr-ũ* 'child', *chokr-i* 'girl', *dikr-o* 'son', *dikr-i* 'daughter', *ɔrḍ-o* 'room', *əthvaḍi-ũ* 'week', the postposed elements *-e* (agentive, locative), *thi* ('from, by'), *mã* ('in'), *-o* (plural marker), and *-ni sathe* ('together with').

Invariable substantives do not have distinct stem forms that depend on whether a postposed element occurs, although substantives in *-ə* drop this vowel before vocalic clitics (see section 2.5). Invariable substantive can end in any permissible final consonant and any vowel other than *e* or *ɛ*. Examples are given in table 18.8.

The noun *ghər* 'home, house' occupies a special status in one respect: in addition to *ghər-e* 'at home, in the house', with postposed locatival *-e*, there is a synonymous frozen form *ghɛr*.

4.3 Adjectives

Adjectives also are either variable or invariable. The former are similar to variable substantives, as shown in table 18.9. They do not, however, take the plural marker *-o*.

Invariable adjectives may end in any admissible final consonant and any vowel except *-o*, *-ɛ*, *-ɔ*. For example: *khərab* 'bad' *sundər* 'beautiful' *sərəs* 'good' *videši* 'foreign' *calu* 'functioning' *bənne* 'both' *bhartiyə* 'Indian' *səva* 'plus one fourth' (see section 4.4).

Both attributive and predicative adjectives show number and gender agreement with substantives with which they are construed. Attributive adjectives, moreover, form phrases with following substantives such that postposed elements regularly follow the phrase alone. See section 4.6.

Comparison involves particular syntactic constructions. *-thi* or *-kərtã* – usually but not always alternative – is postposed to a substantive with respect to which something is compared:

TABLE 18.7: VARIABLE SUBSTANTIVES

	Singular			Plural		
	M	Nt	F	M	Nt	F
Base						
+ -eag	*chokr-e*					
	dikr-e					
+ -eloc	*ɔrḍ-e*	*əthvaḍi-e*				
Dir						
	chokr-o	*chokr-ũ*	*chokr-i*	*chokr-a-(o)*	*chokr-ã-(o)*	*chokr-i-(o)*
	dikr-o		*dikr-i*	*dikr-a-(o)*		*dikr-i-(o)*
Voc						
	chokr-a	*chokr-a*	*chokr-i*	*chokr-a-o*	*chokr-ã-o*	*chokr-i-o*
Obl						
+ -eag	*chokra-e*	*chokra-e*		*chokra-(o)-e*	*chokr-i-(o)-e*	*chokr-i-(o)-e*
	dikra-e			*dikra-e*		
+ -thi	*chokra-thi*	*chokra-thi*	*chokri-thi*	*chokr-a-(o)-thi*	*chokr-ã-(o)-thi*	*chokr-i-(o)-thi*
	dikra-thi	*dikra-thi*	*dikri-thi*			*dikri-(o)-thi*
+ -mã	*ɔrḍa-mã*			*ɔrḍa-(o)-mã*		
+ -ni sathe	*chokra-ni-sathe*	*chokra-ni-sathe*	*chokri-ni-sathe*	*chokra-(o)-ni-sathe*	*chokr-ã-(o)-ni-sathe*	*chokr-i-(o)-ni-sathe*

TABLE 18.8: EXAMPLES OF INVARIABLE SUBSTANTIVES

M	F	Nt
pak 'crop'	*chalɔk* 'a wave'	*nak* 'nose'
lekh 'written article'	*ākh* 'eye'	*vakh* 'poison'
pɔg 'foot'	*vɔg* 'influence'	*jɔg* 'world'
vagh 'tiger'		
kac 'glass'	*cõc* 'peak'	*sac* 'truth'
choch 'fastidiousness'	*pɔṇɔch* 'bow string'	*mũch* 'moustache'
ɔvaj 'sound'	*laj* 'shame'	*mɔgɔj* 'brain'
koṭ 'coat'	*vaṭ* 'road'	*ghɔṭ* 'body'
hoṭh 'lip'	*poṭh* 'lot, multitude'	*juṭh* 'a lie'
pɔhaḍ 'mountain'	*vaḍ* 'hedge'	*jhaḍ* 'tree'
sāḍh 'bull'	*sũḍh* 'elephant's trunk'	
kɔṇ 'a grain'	*maṇ* 'kind of pot'	*daṇ* 'toll'
mɔt 'opinion, vote'	*vat* 'matter, story'	*vrɔt* 'vow'
rɔth 'chariot'	*nath* 'an ornament'	*juth* 'group'
vad 'dispute'	*lad* 'manure'	*kɔd* 'weight'
vɔdh 'killing'	*šodh* 'search'	*mɔdh* 'honey'
kan 'ear'	*jan* 'marriage party'	*mɔn* 'mind, intellect'
sap 'snake'	*lɔp* 'trouble, obstacle'	*map* 'measure'
bɔrɔph 'ice'		
dɔb 'pressure'	*chab* 'a type of basket'	*šɔb* 'corpse'
labh 'gain, profit'	*jibh* 'tongue'	*nɔbh* 'sky, cloud'
jam 'bowl'	*kɔlɔm* 'pen'	*kam* 'work'
mɔgɔr 'crocodile'	*dhar* 'edge'	*šɔhɛr* 'city'
tɔl 'skin mole'	*šal* 'shawl'	*kul* 'river bank'
jiv 'life'	*rav* 'complaint'	*taḷav* 'tank, pool'
naš 'destruction'	*chaš* 'buttermilk'	*vɔrš* 'year'
manɔs 'man'	*vas* 'scent'	*khɔmis* 'shirt'
maḷ 'storey'	*dhuḷ* 'dust'	*muḷ* 'root'
raja 'king'	*rɔja* 'vacation'	
dhobi 'washerman'	*saḍi* 'saree'	*paṇi* 'water'
hau 'bugbear'	*vɔstu* 'matter, affair'	*kaju* 'cashew'
ghɔũ 'wheat'		
	gho 'a reptile'	

TABLE 18.9: VARIABLE ADJECTIVES

	M		Nt		F
	Sg	Pl	Sg	Pl	Sg/Pl
Dir	*-o*		*ũ*		
		-a		*-ã*	*-i*
Obl	*-a*		*-a*		
	saro 'good'		*sarũ*		
		sara		*sarã*	*sari*
	sara		*sara*		

(1)   *e   mara bhai-thi/kərtã   moṭo   ch-e*
      he my   brother-*thi/kərtã* big, old (m sg) be–3sg
      'He is older than my brother.'

Superlative degree is designated by *səv-thi* 'than all' in construction with an adjective or by means of an adjective with postposed *-mã* 'in, among' following a stem of the same adjective:

(2)   *səv-thi uNcũ* (nt sg) 'tallest, highest'

(3)   *uNca-mã uNcũ* 'tallest, highest'.

4.4 Number words

There are terms for cardinals, ordinals and fractions. The set of cardinal number words from one to ninety-nine consists of ten base terms ('1'–'10'), eight intermediate terms ('11'–'18'), eight terms for decades ('20'–'90'), and compound terms. The last are additive terms of the type *ek-vis* (1 plus 20) except for numerals preceding decades thirty through eighty, which are subtractive terms of the type *ogəṇ-is* (20 minus 1), *ogəṇ-tris* (30 minus 1). The number words from one to one hundred are shown in table 18.10. Multiples of one hundred are designated by *sɔ* preceded by base number words, with a

TABLE 18.10: GUJARATI NUMBER WORDS

1–10	11–20	21–30	31–40	41–50	51–60
ek	*əgyar/əgiyar*	*ekvis*	*ekətris*	*ektaḷis*	*ekavən*
bɛ	*bar*	*bavis*	*bətris*	*betaḷis*	*bavən*
trəṇ	*ter*	*trevis*	*tetris/tẽtris*	*tetaḷis*	*tepən/trepən*
car	*cɔud*	*cɔvis*	*cɔtris/cɔ̃tris*	*cummaḷis*	*cɔpən*
pãc	*pəndər*	*pəccis*	*pãtris*	*pistaḷis*	*pəNcavən*
chə	*soḷ*	*chəvvis*	*chətris*	*chetaḷis*	*chəppən*
sat	*səttər*	*sattavis*	*saḍtris*	*suḍtaḷis*	*səttavən*
aṭh	*əḍhar*	*əṭṭhavis*	*aḍtris*	*əḍtaḷis*	*əṭṭhavən*
nəv	*ogəṇis*	*ogəntris*	*ogəncaḷis*	*ogəṇpəcas*	*ogəṇsayth*
dəs	*vis*[1]	*tris*	*caḷis*[2]	*pəcas*	*sayth/sath*

61–70	71–80	81–90	91–100
eksəth	*ikoter*	*ekyaši*	*ekanũ*
basəth	*boter/bɔ̃ter*	*byaši*	*baṇũ*
tesəth/tresəth	*toter/tɔ̃ter*	*tyaši*	*traṇũ*
cɔsəth//cɔ̃səth	*cummoter*	*cɔraši/cɔryaši*	*cɔraṇũ*
pãsəth	*pəNcoter/piNcoter*	*pəNcaši*	*pəNcaṇũ*
chasəth/chãsəth	*choter/chɔ̃ter*	*chyaši*	*chənnũ*
səḍsəth	*sətyoter/sittoter/sityoter*	*sətyaši/sityaši*	*səttaṇũ*
əḍsəth	*əṭṭhyoter/iṭṭhyoter/əṭṭhoter*	*əṭṭhyaši/iṭṭhyaši əṭṭhaši*	*əṭṭhaṇũ*
ogəṇsitter/	*ogəṇyasi*	*nevyaši/nevaši*	*nəvvaṇũ*
ogəṇsiter/ogəṇoter			
sitter	*ẽ̄ši*	*nevũ*	*sɔ*

Notes:
1 *vis*, *tris* and related number words have variants with *-š* instead of *s* (Desai 1992: 224).
2 *caḷis*, *ektaḷis* and so on have variants with *-l-* (*calis*, *ektalis*) instead of *-ḷ-*; see section 2.2.6 and Desai 1992: 224.

variant *bə* instead of *bɛ* : *bə sɔ, trən sɔ, car sɔ, ek sɔ ek* ('101'), *ek sɔ dəs* ('110'), and so on. Designations for numbers above 999 are substantives; the most common are: *həjar* '1000', *lakh* '100,000 (1,00,000), a lakh', *kərod* 'ten million', *əbəj* 'thousand million'.

Ordinals are variable adjectives (see section 4.3) generally composed of cardinal terms followed by *-m-* and gender markers. For example, using the neuter *-ũ* as a citation form: *pãcmũ* 'fifth', *satmũ* 'seventh', *aṭhmũ* 'eighth', *nəvmũ* 'ninth', *dəsmũ* 'tenth', *əgyarmũ* 'eleventh', *ogənismũ* 'nineteenth', *vismũ* 'twentieth', *sɔmũ* 'hundredth'. Exceptions to this are: *pəhɛlũ* 'first', *bijũ* 'second', *trijũ* 'third', *cɔthũ* 'fourth', *chəthũ* 'sixth'.

Terms for fractions are: *pa* 'one fourth' *əddhũ/ərdhũ* 'one half' *səva* 'one and one-fourth, plus a fourth' *saḍa* 'plus one half' *pɔṇũ* 'three fourths, minus a fourth' *dɔḍh* 'one and one-half, half again'. *pa* and *əddhũ/ərdhũ* are used in construction with substantives, *saḍa* only in construction with cardinals; the rest are construed with either. For example:

(1) *pa roṭlo* 'a fourth of a bread'
(2) *əddho/ərdho kəlak* 'half an hour'
(3) *saḍa sat* 'seven and a half'
(4) *səva rupyo* 'a Rupee and a fourth'
(5) *səva trən* 'three and a quarter'
(6) *pɔṇo vagyo* 'twelve forty-five'
(7) *pɔṇo sɔ* 'seventy-five'
(8) *dɔḍh rupyo* 'one and one-half Rupees'
(9) *dɔḍh sɔ* 'one hundred fifty'
(10) *ədhi kəlak* 'two and a half hours'
(11) *ədhi sɔ* 'two hundred fifty'

Indefinite numbers are designated by derivates with *-ek: trən-ek* 'around three', *dəs-ek* 'around ten'. *ek*, on the other hand, is followed by *-ad: ek-ad* 'around one'.

4.5 Pronominals

Pronouns are personal, demonstrative (deictic), relative, interrogative, indefinite, and reflexive.

Personal pronouns (see table 18.11) have distinct singular and plural forms and distinguish between inclusive and exclusive first person plural. Second person forms take part in a tripartite contrast of familar, polite and extremely formal usage. The singular pronoun is used with inferiors, children or someone treated as intimate. *ap* is used to address a high superior or when affecting such a situation. Polite *təme* and so on are used in other circumstances.

Personal pronouns with *m-*, *əm-* and *t-* have forms *mar-*, *əmar-*, *tar-*, and *təmar-* corresponding to nominal forms with *-n-* (see section 4.6): *mar-ũ, tar-ũ, əmar-ũ, təmar-ũ*. These also connect with postposed elements in the way that *-n-*forms do: *marũ pustək* 'my book', *maro dikro* 'my son', *mari dikri* 'my daughter', *mari sathe* 'with me', *mara kərtã* 'than me', *mare maṭe* 'for me'.

Demonstratives show three degrees of deixis: proximate *a* 'this', distal *pelũ/o/i* (nt, m, f) 'that', and neutral *e/te*. These terms function both as pronominal adjectives and independent pronouns:

(1) *a   maṇəs-ne   puch-o*
     this man-obj   ask-2pl
     'Ask this man.'

TABLE 18.11: PERSONAL PRONOUNS

	First person		Second person	
Singular				
Subject	*hũ*		*tũ*	
Object	*mə-ne*		*tə-ne*	
Agent	*mɛ̃*		*tɛ̃*	

	Inclusive	Exclusive	Polite	Extremely Formal
Plural				
Subject	*apṇ-e*	*əm-e*[1]	*təm-e*	*ap*
Object	*apṇ-ne*	*əm-ne*	*təm-ne*	*ap-ne*
Agent	*apṇ-e*	*am-e*	*təm-e*	*ap-e*

Note:
1 *əme, əmne* and *təme, təmne* also occur with murmured vowels: *əʰme, əʰmne* and *təʰme, təʰmne*.

(2) *a   lekh   e   lekhək-e   ləkh-y-o*
this article that writer-ag write-pftv-m sg
'That writer wrote this article.'

(3) *a-ne   pucho*
this-obj ask–2pl
'Ask this one.'

(4) *a   lekh   ɛ-ṇe   ləkh-y-o*
this article that-ag write-pftv-msg
'He/she wrote this article.'

in which *a* and *e* are parts of the phrases *a maṇəs-ne* and *e lekhək-e* and separate pronouns.

pelũ is formally like a variable adjective (section 4.3). The others have a pronominal agentive *-ṇe*. See table 18.12. Plural pronoun forms with the plural marker *o* and with *-m-* are regularly used in referring to humans.

The relative pronoun is *je*, which is syntactically linked with *e/te* as correlative:

(5) *jɛ-ne   təm-e   bolav-y-o   e   av-i   gə-y-o*
who-obj you-agtv invite-pftv-msg he come go-pftv-m sg
'The man you invited has arrived.'

The interrogative pronouns are *kɔṇ, kɔ* 'who?' and *šũ* 'what?'. *kɔṇ* occurs as a subject form and followed by agentive *-e*; *kɔ* occurs with the object marker *-ne* and in pronominal adjectives with *-n-* and gender markers. *šũ* occurs as a direct form, and *šɛ/ša* is followed by *-n-* and gender markers in pronominal adjectives and by postpositions. There is also an interrogative *kəy-ũ/o/i* used to inquire about a particular entity of a known group.

koi is an indefinite pronominal. In addition, *kəĩ, kəšũ* are used with reference to inanimates:

(6) *koi   cɔḍ-i lav-y-ũ   hə-t-ũ*
someone book-f bring-pftv-ntsg aux-impfctv-ntsg
'Someone brought a book.'

TABLE 18.12: DEMONSTRATIVE AND RELATIVE PRONOUNS

	Singular	Plural
Subject	*a*	*a*
	(t)e	*(t)e (t)eo*
	je	*je(o)*
Object	*a-ne*	*a-ne am-ne*
	(t)ɛ-ne[1]	*(t)e-ne te-o-ne tɛm-ne*
	jɛ-ne	*jɛ-ne je-o-ne jɛm-ne*
Agent	*a-ṇe*	*a-ṇe am-ṇe*
	(t)ɛ-ṇe	*(t)ɛm-ṇe*
	jɛ-ṇe	*je(o)-ṇe jɛm-ṇe*

Note:
1 *(t)ɛne*, *(t)ɛṇe*, *(t)ɛmne*, *(t)ɛmṇe*, and *jɛ-ne*, *jɛne*, *jɛmṇe* also occur with murmured vowels: *(t)ɛʰne* and so on.

(7) *təme koi-ne   cɔpḍ-i ap-i   ch-e*
     you   someone-obj book-f give-pftv-fsg be-3p
     'Have you given a book to somebody?'

(8) *kəĩ kam   che*
     any work be–3p
     'Is there anything I can do?'

(9) *mara-maṭe kəšũ   lav-y-a   ch-o*
     me-for   something bring-pftv-mpl aux-2ppl
     'Have you brought anything for me?'

Although *koi* can be followed directly by postpositions of the type *-mã*, *-thi* (see section 4.6), it also shares with other non-personal pronouns being connected with such postpositions by *-n-* with a gender marker:

(10) *a   kam koi-na-thi   kəra-y-ũ   nəhi*
     this work someone-*na*-by do-pass-pftv-nt sg not
     'No one was able to do this.'

with *koi-na-thi* comparable to *ɛ-na-thi*, *je-na-thi*, *kɔ-na-thi*. The demonstratives *a* and *e/te* share this feature, with an additional specification: they do not occur directly followed by postposed items such as *-mã*, *-thi* when they refer to animates:

(11) *ɛ-na-thi   nəhi jəw-a-y*
     he-na-by   not   go-pass-3p
     'He will not be able to go.'

(12) *e-mã-thi   pəysa kaḍh-o*
     that-in-from money take out-2pl
     'Take the money out of that.'

pot is the base of the reflexive pronoun, as in *pot-e* (subject, agent):

(13) *pote kər-j-o*
     self do-pol-imp
     'Please do it yourself.'

Before other postposed elements, *pot-a-* occurs, as in *pota-ne* (obj), *pota-n-ū* 'of one's own'; *pot-pota-* occurs in the distributive *pot-pota-nū* 'each one's own'.

Such distributive sequences are formed from other pronouns also; e.g. *je je* 'who all', *kɔṇ kɔṇ* 'who all?', *šū šū* 'what all?'. Non-personal pronouns also have in common that they take part in sets of derivates of the types *jɛm* 'in which manner', *jyare* 'at which time', *jyā* 'where', *jevū* 'or which sort', *jeṭlū* 'of which amount'. These are shown in table 18.13.

4.6 Postposed adnominal elements

The syntactic function of nominals is signalled by postposed elements, including what are commonly called postpositions.

The plural marker *-o* follows nominal stems and is itself followed by other postposed elements. For example, *chokra-o-e* (agn), *chokra-o-ne* (obj) 'boys', *orḍa-o-mā-thi* 'from inside the rooms, from the rooms'. As shown, the object marker *-ne* is one of the clitic elements which can follow a nominal. This is used for both direct and indirect objects. The group of postpositions that directly follow nominals includes this and: *-e* (agn), *-e* (loc.), *-mā* 'in', *-thi* 'from, by (agn)', *-pər* 'upon', *-sər* 'according to'. As shown, a combination of these is possible, as in *ɔphis-e-thi* 'from the office', *orḍa-(o)-mā-thi* 'from the room(s)'.

-n- is a relational element that has to be followed by a gender marker and which serves to connect nominals and phrases. For example:

(1) *bhai-n-ū ghər* 'brother's house'
(2) *bhai-n-a dikra* 'brother's sons'
(3) *bhai-n-i dikri* 'brother's daughter'

in which *-n-* is followed by the neuter, masculine, and feminine gender markers, according with the genders of the substantives with which *bhai* 'brother' is connected. *-n-* also serves to connect with following elements giving complex postpositional items of the types *-n-i- sathe* 'together with', *-n-i-pase* 'near, at, by (also agentive)', *-n-a-kərtā* 'than', *-n-a-sivay* 'besides, in addition to', *-n-e-bədle* 'instead of', *-n-e-maṭe* 'for the sake of'. For additional details, see Cardona 1965: 143–8, Desai 1992: 176–88.

In general, postposed elements follow phrases, as in

TABLE 18.13: PRONOMINAL DERIVATES

	Demonstrative	Relative	Interrogative
Manner	*am*		
	(t) ɛm	*jɛm*	*kɛm*
Place	*tyā*	*jyā*	*kyā*
Time	*tyare*[1]	*jyare*	*kyare*
Quality	*avū*		
	(t)evū	*jevū*	*kevū*
Quantity	*aṭlū*		
	(t)eṭlū	*jeṭlū*	*keṭlū*
Size	*avḍū*		
	(t)evḍū	*jevḍū*	*kevḍū*

Note:
1 *tyare, jyare, kyare* also occur with murmured *a*: *tyaʰre* and so on.

(4) *lãba   səməy-thi*
    long$_{obl}$ time-from
    'for a long time'

(5) *juda   juda   deš-o-mã*
    different different country-pl-in
    'in various different countries'

Postposed agentive and locative *-e*, however, behave like case endings in that they may occur both with substantives and adjectives preceding these, though this is not obligatory. For example:

(6) *avt-e   əthvaḍi-e*
    coming-*e*$_{loc}$ week-*e*$_{loc}$
    'in the coming week, next week'

(7) *gə-i   kal-e*
    go-pftv fem yesterday/tomorrow-*e*$_{loc}$
    'yesterday'

(8) *mar-e   tyã*
    my-*e*$_{loc}$ there
    'my place'

Nevertheless, none of the postposed elements behaves in precisely the manner of Old and Middle Indo-Aryan case markers, which signal both syntactic functions and numbers; even *-e* marks only syntactic functions and not also number.

4.7 Nominal derivation

There are affixes which serve to derive nominals (Cardona 1965: 155–63, Desai 1992: 331–69). These include suffixes that follow verb bases to supply nominal forms in the verbal system (section 5.12). Others form derivates from both verbal and nominal bases; for example:

ləḍ-ai 'war' : *ləḍ* 'fight', *ləmb-ai* 'length' : *lãb-ũ* 'long'
gulam-i 'slavery' : *gulam* 'slave', *vis-i* 'group of twenty' : *vis* 'twenty'
ek-ta 'unanimity' : *ek* 'one'
tel-i 'oil seller' : *tel* 'oil'

The following examples illustrate feminine derivates corresponding to masculine counterparts:

tel-i 'oil seller' : *tel-əṇ* 'wife of an oil seller, female oil seller'
dhobi 'washerman' : *dhob-əṇ* 'wife of a washerman, female clothes washer'
vagh 'tiger' : *vagh-əṇ* 'tigress'

In addition, some suffixes serve to form adjectives; for example:

gujrat-i 'Gujarati' : *gujrat* 'Gujarat'
varš-ik 'yearly' : *vərš* 'year'.

There are also prefixes; for example:

əṇ-səmju 'ignorant' : *səmju* 'knowing'
ger-hajər 'absent' : *hajər* 'present'
be-nəmun 'unprecedented' : *nəmuno* 'sample'.

Suffixes and affixes are drawn from Sanskrit and Perso-Arabic, but not from English, although Gujarati has many English borrowings.

4.8 Compounds

Gujarati has several types of compounds (Cardona 1965: 164–5, J. C. Dave 1972: 59–135, Vyas 1977: 280–90, Desai 1992: 370–85), corresponding to different kinds of syntactic strings. Examples of the different types are:

> *prəkruti-nirupəṇ* 'description of nature', *nəgər-pati* (city-master) 'mayor', *həkikət-doš* (information-fault) 'faulty information', *kəpəṭ-koṭ* (fraud-fort) 'sham wall (set up to deceive)'
> *suk-ləkḍi* 'dry wood', *ədh-ghəḍi* 'half a moment', *ədh-khulũ* 'half closed'
> *ghər-rəkhu* (adj.) '… who manages a house well', *haḷ-kheḍyũ* 'tilled [*kheḍelũ*]) with a plough'
> *papəḍ-puri* (papad-puri) 'a puri that is thin as a papad', *kajəḷ-kaḷũ* (collyrium-black) 'black as collyrium, pitch black', *ũṭ-vaidya* (camel-doctor) 'quack'
> *bhai-behɛn* 'brother and sister', *ma-bap* 'mother and father', *nɔkəri-dhəndho* 'work and similar', *khaṭũ-miṭhũ* 'sour and sweet', *ũcũ-nicũ* 'high and low', *av-ja* 'coming and going',
> *kaḷ-jibhũ* (black-tongue) 'foul tongued'.

Gujarati is comparable to other modern Indo-Aryan languages in forming compound-like sequences, meaning 'x and such things', which consist of a term followed by an echo word, formed by replacing the initial consonant of a term with *b* or *ph* or supplying such a consonant in the case of vowel-initial terms: *chətri-bətri* 'umbrellas and such', *orḍo-borḍo* 'rooms and such'.

5 VERB SYSTEM

5.1 Introduction

The verb system has temporal, aspectual and modal contrasts as well as distinctions of person and number: first, second, and third persons, singular and plural. Singular and plural second person forms are also associated with degrees of familiarity and formality, singular forms used for persons considered intimates or inferiors and plural forms used for persons treated as equals (pronoun *təme*) or superior (pronoun *ap*, section 4.5).

There is a sigmatic future suffix (section 5.5). Temporal auxiliaries *ch*, *ho/hə* (sections 5.2–3) occur in complex forms such as *kəre che* 'does, makes, is doing, is making'; *kərto həto* (msg), *kərti həti* (f), *kərta həta* (mpl) 'used to do, used to make, was doing, was making'. Forms such as *avyo* (msg), *avi* (f), *avyũ* (ntsg), *avya* (mpl), *avyã* (ntpl) 'came', *kəryo*, *kəri*, *kəryũ*, *kərya*, *kəryã* 'made' have a perfective suffix *-y-*, and an imperfective suffix *-t-* occurs in forms of the type *kərto*, *kərti*, *kərta* 'used to do, would do, used to make, would make' and complex forms such as *kərto həto*, *kərti həti* 'was doing, making', *kərta həta*, *kərti həti* (sections 5.3–4). The person-number endings which occur with bases in neutral forms (section 5.2) are shown in table 18.14.

Verb bases are transitive and intransitive, as reflected in different patterns of agreement in perfective forms (section 5.4). In addition to primitive bases, there are causative and passive derivates formed with affixes (sections 5.8–9). Certain verb forms

TABLE 18.14: PERSON-NUMBER VERB ENDINGS

	Singular		Plural
1st person	-ũ/ø[1]		-ie/ũ[2]
2nd person	-e/ø[3]		-o
3rd person		-e[4]	

Notes:
1 ø in future forms (see section 5.5).
2 -ũ in future forms (see section 5.5).
3 ø in future forms (see section 5.5).
4 -y after bases in -a or -o.

also show suppletion: *ja* : pftv *gə* 'go' *kər*: *ki* (pftv in some dialects) 'do, make' *jo/ju* : *diṭh* (pftv in some dialects) 'see, look'.

All verbs, whether primitive or derived, occur both in simple and complex forms, the latter with temporal auxiliaries, and enter into construction with auxiliary verbs such as *šək* 'be able' as well as forming complexes called compound verbs (section 5.12).

Some bases show vowel alternation (see Cardona 1965: 110–11):

a/ə : *ja/jə* 'go' *tha/thə* 'become, occur'
e/ɛ/ə/ø : *le/lɛ/lə/l* 'take' *de/dɛ/də/d* 'give (aux)'
o/u : *jo/ju* 'see, look' *dho/dhu* 'wash'
o/ə : *ho/hə* 'be'

Further, in northern and central Gujarat, bases in -*a* regularly have -*ə* before -*iš*- of future forms (see section 5.5); e.g. *kha* 'eat': *khə-iš*, *khə-išũ* (Desai 1992: 256). Vowel alternation is also a characteristic of causative and passive derivates (sections 5.8–9).

5.2 Neutral and present forms

Neutral forms consist of a verb base with person-number endings. In combination with non-negative *ch* used as a temporal auxiliary, these supply a present indicative, used with reference to current acts – both continuous and non-continuous – as well general truths. Simple and combined forms of *av* 'come', *kər* 'do, make', *pi* 'drink', *ja* 'go', *le* 'take', *jo* 'see', *ho* 'be' are given in table 18.15. Examples:

(1)   *kyare av-ũ*
      when come–1sg
      'When shall I come?'

(2)   *hũ pəys-a   ap-ũ*
      I   money-mpl give-1sg
      'I'll pay (i.e. let me pay).'

(3)   *rəmeš šũ   kam kər-e ch-e*
      Ramesh what work do-3p aux-3p
      'What does Ramesh do?'

(4)   *rəmeš vəkil ch-e*
      Ramesh lawyer be-3p
      'Ramesh is a lawyer.'

(5) *sũ   vãc-o   ch-o*
what read–2pl aux-2pl
'What are you reading?'

(6) *subodh-n-i   nəv-i   kəvita vãc-ũ   ch-ũ*
Subodh-*n*-f new-f poem read-1sg aux-1sg
'I'm reading a new poem of Subodh's.'

(7) *moṭ-e   bhag-e   a   vəkhət-e e ɔphis-mã ho-y   ch-e*
great-loc part-loc this time-loc he office-in be-3p aux-3p
'He is generally at the office at this time.'

(8) *ətyar-e   e   ɔphis-mã   ch-e*
now-loc he office-in be-3sg
'Right now he is in the office.'

(9) *moṭ-a   bhai   aj-e   pach-a   nəhi av-e*
big-mpl brother today-loc back-mpl not come-3p
'My older brother won't come back today.'

(10) *marə-thi a   kam   nəhi kər-a-y*
I-ag this work not do-pass-3p
'I won't be able to do this job.'

TABLE 18.15: NEUTRAL AND PRESENT VERB FORMS

	Singular				Plural	
1p	*avũ*	*avũ chũ*			*avie*	*avie chie*
	kərũ	*kərũ chũ*			*kərie*	*kərie chie*
	piũ	*piũ chũ*			*pie*	*pie chie*
	jaũ	*jaũ chũ*			*jɔie*	*jɔie chie*
	lɔũ	*lɔũ chũ*			*lɔie*	*lɔie chie*
	joũ	*joũ chũ*			*joie*	*joie chie*
	hoũ	*hoũ chũ*			*hoie*	*hoie chie*
2p	*ave*	*ave che*			*avo*	*avo cho*
	kəre	*kəre che*			*kəro*	*kəro cho*
	pie	*pie che*			*pio*	*pio cho*
	jay	*jay che*			*jao*	*jao cho*
	lɛ	*lɛ che*			*lɔ*	*lɔ cho*
	jue	*jue che*			*juo*	*juo cho*
	hoy	*hoy che*			*ho*	*ho cho*
3p			*ave*	*ave che*		
			kəre	*kəre che*		
			pie	*pie che*		
			jay	*jay che*		
			lɛ	*lɛ che*		
			jue	*jue che*		
			hoy	*hoy che*		

5.3 Imperfective *t*

Imperfective forms have the imperfective suffix *-t-* followed by the gender markers *-ũ* and so on (see sections 4.2–3). Of themselves, these forms are used to speak of acts that regularly took place in the past:

(1) *te   jəman-e hũ dər   əṭhwaḍi-e vəḍodra   jə-t-o*
    that time-loc I every week-loc Vadodara go-impfctv-msg
    'At that time, I would go to Vadodara every week.'

The imperfective auxiliary corresponding to *ch* in present forms (see section 5.2) is *hə-t-*:

(2) *təme sũ   vãc-t-a   hə-t-a*
    you   what read-impfctv-mpl aux-impfctv-mpl
    'What were you reading?'

5.4 Perfective

The general perfective affix is *-y-*, as in *av-y-* (*av* 'come'), *kər-y-* (*kər* 'do, make'), but certain bases take others:

> *dh*: *kha-dh-* (*kha* 'eat') *di-dh-* (*de/dɛ* 'give') *pi-dh-* (*pi* 'drink') *li-dh-* (*le/lɛ* 'take')
> *ki-dh-* (*kər* 'do, make' [in addition to *kər-y-*])
> *ṭh*: *na-ṭh-* (*nas* 'flee') *pɛ-ṭh-* (*pɛs* 'enter') *bɛ-ṭh-* (*bɛs* 'sit') *dī-ṭh* (*jo* 'see, look' [in addition to *jo-y-*])

In addition, some bases show suppletive variants in the perfective, as in *jə/ja* 'go': *gə-y-* (see section 5.1).

   Perfective suffixes are followed by gender-number markers whose choice is determined by an agreement system that depends on the kind of verb involved. Intransitive and transitive verbs respectively show subject and object agreement. An agent of a transitive verb is signified by a nominal with the agentive element *-e* and by special pronominal forms (see section 4.5 with table 18.11). Examples:

(1) *kɔṇ av-y-ũ* (4.1 ex. 1)
(2) *a lekh e lekhək-e ləkh-y-o* (4.5. ex. 2)
(3) *jɛ-ne təm-e bolav-y-o e av-i gə-y-o* (4.5. ex. 5)
(4) *urmila-e təmara dikra-ne jo-y-o* (4.1. ex. 7)
(5) *urmila-e təmara dikra-o-ne jo-y-a* (4.1. ex. 8)
(6) *rəmeš-e cɔpḍi-o khərid-i* (4.1. ex. 4)
(7) *rəmeš-e keṭl-i cɔpḍi khərid-i* (4.1. ex. 5)
(8) *rəmeš-e trəṇ cɔpḍi khərid-i* (4.1. ex. 6)
(9) *təm-e koi-ne cɔpḍi ap-i ch-e* (4.5. ex. 7)

Derivate of the types *ləkh-v-ũ*, *ləkh-v-a-n-ũ* (see section 5.12) from transitive verb such as *ləkh* occurs also in a construction of the type

(10) *mar-e ek lekh   ləkh-v-o   ch-e*
     I-ag one article write-*v*-msg be-3p
     'I want to write an article.'

(11) *mar-e ek lekh   ləkh-v-a-n-o   ch-e*
     I-ag one article write-*v-a*-msg be-3p
     'I have to write an article.'

There is a small group of verbs – *cuk* 'miss', *bol* 'speak', *bhən* 'study', *šikh* 'learn', *səməj* 'understand', *kud* 'jump', *oḷəNg* 'cross', *tər* 'swim, cross' – perfective forms of which show the agreement usual for intransitives but which in the constructions illustrated by (10)–(11) behave like transitive verbs:

(12) *kišor   dhime   bol-y-o*
      Kishor low   speak-pftv-msg
      'Kishor spoke softly.'

(13) *mar-e gujrati bhaša bol-v-i   ch-e*
      I-ag   Gujarati language speak-*v*-f be-3p
      'I want to speak Gujarati.'

(14) *koi   cɔpḍ-i   lav-y-ũ   hə-t-ũ* (4.5 ex. 6)
      someone book-f bring-pftv-ntsg aux-impfctv-ntsg

(15) *mara-maṭe kəšũ   lav-y-a   ch-o* (4.5 ex. 9)
      me-for   something bring-pftv-mpl aux-2ppl

(16) *mar-e bhai-maṭe keṭl-i-k   cɔpḍ-i-o   lav-v-a-n-i   ch-e*
      I-ag   brother-for some-f-indef book-f-pl bring-*v*-a-n-f be-3p
      'I have to bring some books for my brother.'

As shown in (9), clauses with perfective forms can include the temporal auxiliary. Similarly,

(17) *gə-i   kal-e   rəmeš   təmar-e tyã   av-y-o   hə-t-o*
      go-pftv-f yesterday-loc Ramesh your-loc there come-pftv-msg aux-impfctv-msg
      'Yesterday Ramesh went to your place.'

(18) *e bəhar gə-y-o   hə-š-e*
      he out   go-pftv-msg aux-fut-3p
      'He's probably gone out.'

5.5 Future

The future is characterized by the future suffix *-iš-/-š-* followed by personal endings (see table 18.14). Future forms of the verbs given in table 18.15 are shown in table 18.16. The formal future is used not only with reference to future time but also to signal probability or possibility:

(1)   *rəmeš   av-t-o   hə-š-e*
      Ramesh come-impfctv-msg aux-fut-3p
      'Ramesh is probably/doubtless on his way.'

Moreover, future forms such as *kəršo – kəršo ji*, with the honorific particle *ji* – are used in polite commands.

5.6 Imperative

Neutral imperative forms are available for second and third persons. Informal second person imperatives consist of the verb base alone; e.g. *av* 'come', *pəkəḍ* 'take, catch', *lɛ* 'take'. Polite second person imperatives have *-o* following a base; e.g. *av-o, pəkḍ-o, l-o*. A homophonous form supplies third person forms also. In addition, there is a future

TABLE 18.16: FUTURE FORMS

	Singular	Plural
1p	*aviš*	*aviš̃ũ/avš̃ũ*[1]
	kəriš	*kəriš̃ũ/kərš̃ũ*
	piiš	*piiš̃ũ/piš̃ũ*
	jəiš	*jəiš̃ũ/jəš̃ũ*
	ləiš	*ləiš̃ũ/lɛš̃ũ*
	joiš	*joiš̃ũ/još̃ũ*
	hoiš	*hoiš̃ũ/həš̃ũ*
2p	*avis/avse*[2]	*avšo*
	kəriš/kərše	*kəršo*
	piiš/piše	*pišo*
	jəiš/jəše	*jəšo*
	ləiš/lɛse	*lɛšo*
	joiš/joše	*jošo*
	hoiš/həše	*həšo*
3p	*avše*	
	kərše	
	piše	
	jəše	
	lɛše	
	joše	
	həše	

Notes:
1 The type *avš̃ũ* is considered more colloquial than the type *aviš̃ũ*.
2 The types *aviš* and *avše* vary (Cardona 1965: 99, Desai 1992: 256).

imperative, used in attenuated commands, characterized by *-j-* followed by endings; e.g. *av-j-e*, *av-j-o* 'please come, goodbye', *ap-j-e*, *ap-j-o* 'please give'. As noted in section 5.5, future forms too can be used in expressing polite commands.

5.7 Conditional

The conditional is marked by the ending *-t* – with a variant *-te* – which follows a base and is common to all endings. This is used in speaking of contrafactual conditions:

(1)   *mar-e kam   kərva-n-ũ na   hɔ-t   to   hũ təmar-i-sathe   av-ət*
      I-agn work do_{vbn}-n-nt neg be-cond ptcle I   you-f-together come-cond
      'If I did not have work to do, I would come with you.'

5.8 Impersonal verbs

There is a small group of verbs used impersonally, that is, which do not regularly occur with subject forms of personal pronouns. The principal verbs in question are *avəḍ* 'be known', *gəm* 'be pleasing', *dukh* 'pain', *phav* 'be suitable', *bhav* 'be suitable', *joi* 'be necessary'. For example,

(1) *təm-ne gujrati ləkh-tã avḍ-e   ch-e*
    you-obj Gujarati write   be known-3p aux-3p
    'Do you know how to write Gujarati?' (see section 5.12)

(2) *rəma-ne chokr-o   gəm-y-o*
    Rama   child-msg be pleasing-pftv-msg
    'Rama liked the boy.'

(3) *mar-e/mə-ne   ghɛr jə-v-ũ   joi-e*
    me-ag/me-obj home go-v-nt be necessary-3p
    'I should go home.'

5.9 Causative

Causatives are derived from primitive verb bases through affixation and vowel and consonant alternation (see Cardona 1965: 112–13, Desai 1992: 237–42). The causative affixes are *-av-, -ḍav-, -v-, -aḍ-, -eḍ-*; and *-v-* is inserted after bases in final vowels and *-h*. There are also second causatives derived from first causatives. For example:

> *kər*'do, make' : *kər-av-* 'have ... do, make' *səməj* 'understand' : *səmj-av-* 'explain, convince'
> *jan* 'know' : *jən-av-* 'inform'
> *kha* 'eat' : *khəv-ḍāv* 'feed' *pi* 'drink' : *piv-ḍav* 'give to drink' *nah* 'bathe' : *nəhv-ḍav* 'bathe (tr)'
> *phər* 'turn, go around' : *pher-əv-* 'turn (tr)' *məl* 'meet, encounter' : *meḷ-əv-* 'mix'
> *šikh* 'learn' : *šikh-əv-* 'teach'
> *jag* 'wake' : *jəg-aḍ-* 'awaken' *dekh* 'see' : *dekh-aḍ-* 'show' *bɛs* 'sit' : *bɛs-aḍ-* 'seat'
> *ughəḍ* 'open (intr) : *ughaḍ* 'open (tr) *utər* 'descend' : *utar* 'get down' *pəḍ* 'fall' : *paḍ* 'cause to fall' *mər* 'die' : *mar* 'beat, kill'
> *chuṭ* 'get loose' : *choḍ* 'let loose, quit' *tuṭ* 'break (intr)' : *toḍ* 'break (tr)'
> *phuṭ* 'crack (intr)' : *phoḍ* 'crack (tr)'
> *kər-av-* : *kər-av-ḍav* *bɛs-aḍ-* : *bɛs-aḍ-av-*

Whether a base is intransitive or transitive and the semantics of a base determine the functions of causatives and their syntax. For example:

(1) *ɛ-ni-pase kam kər-av-j-o*
    he-by   work do-caus-imp-2pl
    'Please have him do the work.'

(2) *mẽ ɛ-ni-pase kam kər-av-ḍav-y-ũ*
    Iag he-by   work do-caus-caus-pftv-nt sg
    'I had him get the work done.'

(3) *ɛ-ne   bɛs-aḍ-o*
    he-obj sit-caus-2pl
    'Please seat him.'

(4) *ɛṇe   bəhɛn-ne sundər kəṇṭhi   dekh-aḍ-i*
    heag sister-obj beautiful necklace see-caus-pftv-f
    'He showed his sister a beautiful necklace.'

In (1), the agent of the non-causative *kər* is signified by *ɛ-ni-pase*, with the agentive postposition *pase*, and in (2) the agent of the causative *kər-av-* is signified by *ɛ-ni-pase*, but in (3)–(4) the agent of the intransitive is the object of the causative, referred to by *ε-ne* and *bəhɛn-ne*, with the object marker *-ne*. For additional details, see section 7.2 and Cardona 1965: 113–114, Desai 1992–242–243.

5.10 Passive

Gujarati has both a morphological and a periphrastic passive formation (see Cardona 1965: 116–18, Desai 1992: 244–5). The morphological passive is formed by affixing *-a-* to a base verb or a causative, with replacement of *a* by *ə* in primitive bases (*ap* 'take' : *əp-a kha* 'eat' : *khə-v-a vapər* 'use' : *vəpr-a vãc* : *vəNc-a* 'read' *av* 'come' : *əv-a*) and base suppletion (*jo/ju* 'see, look': *dekh* : pass *dekh-a-* 'appear'); vowel-final bases have *-v-* before the passive affix (*le* 'take' : *lev-a-*). As in other New Indo-Aryan languages, formation of passives is not restricted to transitive verbs and has a restricted domain of usage except in special registers. Passive sentences with overtly expressed agents regularly concern accidental performance, permissibility or ability, as in

(1) *mara-thi a kam nəhi kər-a-y* (5.2 ex. 10)

The construction type

(2) *kər-v-a-mã av-e*
 do-*v*-g-in come-3p

supplies a periphrastic equivalent to morphologic passives of the type *kər-a-y*. For additional details see Cardona 1965: 116–18, Desai 1992: 247–8.

5.11 Summary of forms

As shown in preceding sections, neutral, imperfective and perfective forms can occur independently or in combination with forms of temporal auxiliaries. The array of such possible forms with imperfectives and perfectives is summarized in table 18.17, using *av* 'come' and *kər* 'do' to illustrate intransitive and transitive bases. See also Desai 1992: 271–7.

5.12 Nominal forms of the verb system

Nominal forms in the verb system are derivates (traditionally called *krudənt* [Skt. *kṛdanta*]) formed from bases with derivational affixes (Cardona 1965: 133–7, Desai 1992: 300–7).

TABLE 18.17: SUMMARY OF VERB FORMS

Imperfective	Auxiliary	Perfective
avtũ, kərtũ	*che* *hɔy* *həše* *hətũ* *hɔt*	*avyũ, kəryũ*

Note: 3sg and nt sg in *-ũ* represents all gender-number forms

-v- followed by number-gender markers appears in derivates of the type *av-v-ũ, kər-v-ũ*. Such derivates are followed by postpositions in constructions of the type *kər-v-a mate* 'in order to do', *kərva-mã* (section 5.10, ex. 2). They also supply verbal adjectives, as in

(1) *mar-e   a   cɔpḍi vãc-v-i   ch-e*
     I-ag   this book read-*v*-fem be-3p
     'I want to read this book.'

(2) *təm-ne   kyã   jə-v-ũ   ch-e*
     you-obj where go-*v*-nt be–3p
     'Where do you want to go?'

In addition, with relational *-n-* (section 4.6), *-v-* supplies adjectives of the type *-v-a-n-ũ*, as in

(3) *mar-e   a   cɔpḍi vãc-v-a-n-i   ch-e*
     'I have to read this book.'

(4) *təm-ne   kyã   jə-v-a-n-ũ   ch-e*
     'Where do you have to go?'

See section 5.4.

Imperfective *-t-* (section 5.3) also occurs in adjectival forms, as in *av-t-e əthvaḍi-e* 'next week' (section 4.6 ex. 6), *joi-t-a pəysa* 'required money', *pur-t-a pəysa* 'sufficient money', *bola-t-i bhaša* 'spoken language'. In addition, verb bases are followed by *-tã* in constructions of the type *ləkhtã avḍe* (section 5.8 ex. 1) as well as in adverbs of the type in *caltã avyo* 'came on foot'.

Perfective *-y-* (section 5.4) appears in the form *-y-a* in the construction type *kam kər-y-a pəchi* 'after doing the work'. *-y-* also parallels imperfective *-t-* in adjectival forms, as in *gə-e* (← *gə-y-e*) *əthvaḍi-e* 'last week', *gə-i kal-e* 'yesterday'.

-el- (+ gender-number markers) forms perfective verbal adjectives; e.g. *av-el-o mənəs* 'the man who has come', *ləkh-el-o kagəḷ* 'the letter written'. Such derivates are also used as alternatives to perfect forms with *-y-*:

(5) *ɔphis-e-thi   av-el-o   ch-ũ*
     office-loc-from come-el-msg aux-1sg
     'I've come from the office.'

-i- follows bases to form verb stems, used with modal auxiliaries (section 5.13) and followed by *-ne*, as in *kər-i-ne* 'after making, doing', in constructions of the type

(6) *nasto   kər-i-ne   av-y-o   ch-ũ*
     breakfast make-*i*-ne come-pftv-msg aux-1sg
     'I had breakfast before coming.'

-nar can follow any verb base to form an agentive of the type *ganar* 'singer'. Such derivates are also used as future forms.

5.13 Non-temporal auxiliaries

Certain verbs are used as auxiliaries with particular verbal derivates (see Cardona 1965: 118–33, Desai 1992: 284–96). Different auxiliaries occur with particular verb forms. Some have very general scopes, others are more restricted in their occurrence. Thus *šək* 'can, be able' can be used with any verb stem in *-i* (section 5.12), as in *avi šəkšo* 'Will you be able to come?', *kəri šəkay* 'can be done'. The following occur in construction with derivates in *-v-* (section 5.12) in the meanings shown:

-v-ũ joi : 'ought to': *jə-v-ũ joi-e* (section 5.8 ex. 3)
-v-ũ pəḍ ('fall'): obligation over which one has no control: *jə-v-ũ pəḍ-e ch-e* '... must go'
-v-a dɛ ('give'): 'permit': *jə-v-a dɛ* 'allow to go'
-v-a lag: 'begin': *ləkh-v-a lag* 'begin to write'

Subject to conditions of semantics, *ja* 'go', *av* 'come', *rəh* 'remain' can be used with any imperfective (section 5.3), the first two when speaking of acts viewed as progressively going on (e.g. *vəpratũ thətũ jay che* 'gets more and more used', *thətũ ave che* 'is coming along in getting done'), the last when speaking of acts that may continue (e.g. *calta rəho* 'go on walking').

Perfective *-y-* occurs with *kar* marking an emphasis on an act continuing despite circumstances or wishes (e.g. *thəya kəre che* 'happen').

In addition, stems in *-i* occur with auxiliaries to constitute semantic units – commonly called compound verbs – with shadings of meanings that are not always predictable; for example:

av-i ja 'come' (*avi-i gə-y-o* 'has come', section 4.5 ex. 5) *jan-i ja* 'learn, find out'
pəhɔ̃c-i ja 'arrive' *bhagi ja* 'flee'
jo-i lɛ 'have a look' *paḍi lɛ* 'get down' *su-i lɛ* 'get some sleep'
jo-i dɛ 'take a look (for someone else)' *choḍi dɛ* 'let loose'
utri pəḍ 'descend quickly' *həsi pəḍ* 'burst out laughing'
sũghi jo 'take a whiff'.

5.14 Nominal-verb complexes

There are complexes in which a nominal item with a verb functions in the manner of a verbal base. For example, in *mɛ̃ nədi par kəri* 'I crossed the river', *par kər* functions as a unit in a transitive construction such that *kər-i* agrees in gender and number with *nədi* 'river'. *par kər* differs from a complex like *rah jo* 'wait', as in *mɛ̃ təmari rah joi* 'I waited for you', where *joi* agrees with *rah* 'way (f)', construed in turn with *təmari* (your-fem).

6 ADVERBS AND OTHER ADJUNCTS

6.1 Adverbs

In addition to lexical items such as *əhĩ* 'here', *əndər* 'inside', *bəhar* 'outside', *agəḷ* 'in front', *pachəḷ* 'in back', *pəchi* 'afterwards', there are derived adverbs formed through affixation. Of this type are pronominal derivates like *am, ɛm, jɛm, kɛm* (see section 4.5 with table 18.13) and the relative-correlative pairs *jo ... to* 'if ... then' (see section 7.4.1). Moreover, there are adverbial derivates with *-ā* that are related to items with the gender-number affix: *pəhɛlā* 'first' (*pəhɛlũ* 'first') and derivates with the imperfective affix *-t-* (*cal-t-ā* 'walking, on foot'). For additional details, see Desai 1992: 308–20.

6.2 Particles

A small group of clitic elements is traditionally classed as particles (Cardona 1965: 148–9, Desai 1992: 321 3). The major particles are: exclusive *-j*; inclusive *-pəṇ, -y*; indefinite *-k, -ek, -ad*; honorific *-ji*; interrogative *-ke, -ne*.

-j follows an item to exclude anything other than what that item signifies: *šureš-əj* 'only Suresh (and no one else)', *ek-əj* 'only one', *tyã-j* 'only there, right there', *rəmeš-ne-j pucho* 'ask Ramesh (and no one else)'. Conversely, *-pəṇ* and *-y* serve to include the significands of items they follow in larger groups: *šila-pəṇ, šila-y* 'also Sheila', *hũ-pəṇ, hũ-y* 'I too', *həju-pəṇ, həju-y* 'even now', *chətã-pəṇ, chətã-y* '(it being thus also, that is) nevertheless'.

Indefinite *-k* has a wider distribution that *-ek* and *-ad*, which occur with number words (section 4.4): *thoḍũ-k* 'a bit', *thoḍa-k* 'a few', *keṭla-k* 'some'.

-ji occurs not only with nominals whose semantics allows for honorificity (e.g. *pita-ji* 'father', *mata-ji* 'mother', *bhau-ji* 'brother', *sasũ-ji* 'mother-in-law', *səsra-ji* 'father-in-law') but also in expressions such as *ha-ji* 'yes', *na-ji* 'no' and in polite commands (*kəršo-ji*, section 5.5).

-ke and *-ne* function as sentence tags, as in

(1) əndər av-ũ   ke
    in   come-1sg
    'Shall I come in?' 'May I come in?'

(2) keri   kha-š-o   ke
    mango eat-fut-2pl
    'Wouldn't you like to have a mango?'

(3) mar-e gher   av-j-e   ne
    my-loc house$_{loc}$ come-fut imp-2sg
    'Come to my house, won't you?

(4) kha-o ne
    eat-2pl
    'Eat something, won't you?'

(5) məhɛman-o av-y-a   ch-e   ne
    guest-pl   come-pftv-mpl aux-3p
    'The guests have come, haven't they?'

6.3 Connectives

Connectives (Cardona 1965: 150–2, Desai 1992: 324–7) link both sentences and smaller units. They can be classed into six groups, as described below.

Conjunctive *əne/ne* link sentences as well as smaller elements; their more formal equivalent is *tətha*:

(1) rəmeš   əne gita ga-š-e
    Ramesh and Gita sing-fut-3p
    'Ramesh and Gita will sing.'

(2) rəmeš   vajũ   vəg-aḍ-š-e   (ə)ne gita git   ga-š-e
    Ramesh harmonium sound-caus-fut-3p and Gita song sing-fut-3p
    'Ramesh will play the harmonium and Gita will sing a song.'

The major disjunctives are *ke*, its formal equivalent *əthva*, and the sentence disjunctive combination *əthva to*: *dipək ke sureš* 'Deepak or Suresh', *pustək ke pensil* 'a book or a pencil', *bhegi cah ke chuṭi cah* 'blended tea (with milk and sugar brewed in) or loose tea (with milk and sugar separate)',

(3)   *prəbodh av-š-e   əthva to sureš   av-š-e*
      Prabodh come-fut-3p or   Suresh
      'Prabodh will come or else Suresh will come.'

ke 'that' and *eṭle* (formal equivalent *ərthat*) 'that is' function as explicatives:

(4)   *kal-e   eṭl-i   bədh-i gərmi hə-t-i   ke   hũ   akh-o*
      yesterday-loc that much-f all-f   heat   be-impfctv-f that I   entire-m
      divəs ghɛr   rəh-y-o
      day   house_loc remain-pftv-msg
      'Yesterday it was so hot that I stayed home all day.'

(5)   *kal-e   eṭl-o   bədh-o vərsad pəd-t-o   hə-t-o*
      yesterday-loc that much-m all-m   rain   fall-impfctv-msg aux-impfctv-msg
      ke   na puch-o   vat
      that not ask-2pl imp story
      'It was raining so much yesterday, you shouldn't even ask about it.'

(6)   *jhiroks eṭle š-ũ*
      Xerox   what-nt sg
      'What is meant by "xerox"?'

(7)   *paṇini eṭle paṇini*
      Pāṇini   Pāṇini
      'Pāṇini is unique.'

ke functions also as a quotative:

(8)   *kišor-e   kəh-y-ũ   ke   mar-i rah   jo-jo*
      Kishore-ag say-pftv-nt sg my-f way look-2pl   imp
      'Kishore told me to wait for him.'

Correlatives, adversatives and causal connectives are considered in section 7.4.

7 SYNTAX

7.1 Introduction

The general, unmarked word order is noun phrase followed by verb phrase, with final verb. Adjectives, both attributive and predicative, exhibit gender and number agreement with substantives with which they are construed. Attributive modifiers precede substantives. Adjectival agreement applies also in constructions of the type *ghəṇi sundər* 'very beautiful' (ex. 5 below) and *pacha ave* (ex. 6 below, cf. Mistry 1997: 663). Adverbs usually occur preceding a noun phrase or a verb. There is also considerable freedom of movement, depending on emphasis and related meaning factors. Syntactic-semantic roles of participants in actions are conveyed by verbal affixes and elements postposed to nominals (section 4.1) and case forms of personal pronouns (section 4.5). Verb forms with person-number affixes (sections 5.1–5.2 with tables 18.14–15) show agreement with subject forms of nominals; verb forms with gender-number-marking –

imperfectives and perfectives (sections 5.3–5.4) – agree in gender and number with subject forms of nominals except for perfectives of transitive verbs, which show agreement with objective nominals. The neuter is also used neutrally, with indeterminate reference (section 4.1). Forms of *ch* are omissible in non-negative sentences, as shown in examples (4)–(5) below. Personal pronouns can be omitted if there use is not intended for contrastive emphasis. For example:

(1) *(hũ) kyare av-ũ*
     (I) when come-1sg
     'When shall I come?' (cf. 5.2 ex. 1)

(2) *hũ pəys-a   ap-ũ* (5.2. ex. 2)
     I   money-mpl give–1sg

(3) *subodh-n-i nəv-i   kavita vãc-ũ   ch-ũ*(5.2 ex. 6)
     Subodh-n-f new-f poem   read-1sg aux-1sg

(4) *subodh-n-i nəv-i   kavita sar-i   (ch-e)*
     Subodh-n-f new-f poem   good-f (be-3p)
     'Subodh's new poem is good.'

(5) *subodh-n-i nəv-i   kavita ghəṇ-i   sundər   (ch-e)*
     Subodh-n-f new-f poem   much-f   beautiful (be-3p)
     'Subodh's new poem is very beautiful.'

(6) *moṭa   bhai   aj-e   pach-a   nəhi av-e* (5.2 ex. 9)
     big-mpl brother today-loc back-mpl not come-3p

(7) *ətyare   e   ɔphis-mã ch-e* (5.2 ex. 8)
     now   he office-in be-3p

(8) *moṭ-e   bhag-e   a   vəkhət-e e   ɔphis-mã hɔ-y ch-e* (5.2 ex. 7)
     great-loc part-loc this   time-loc he office-in be-3p aux-3p

(9) *gə-i   kal-e   rəmeš   təmar-e tyã   av-y-o* (5.4 ex. 17)
     go-pftv-f yesterday-loc Ramesh your-loc there come-pftv-msg
     hə-t-o
     aux-impfctv-msg

(10) *urmila-e   təmara   dikra-ne jo-y-o* (4.1 ex. 7)
     Urmila-ag your-m obl son-obj saw-pftv-msg

(11) *urmila-e təmara   dikra-o-ne jo-y-a* (4.1 ex. 8)
     Urmila-ag your-m.obl son-pl-obj saw-pftv-mpl

(12) *rəmes-e   trəṇ cɔpḍ-i khərid-i* (4.1 ex. 6)
     Ramesh-ag three book-f buy-pftv-f

7.2 Causatives (section 5.9)

A distinction has been observed (see Mistry 1969: 152, Desai 1992: 242–3) between causative constructions in which the agent of a non-causative is designated by a nominal with *-pase* and with *-ne*. The former construction is used to speak of having one do or causing one to do something, the latter to speak of someone helping or assisting another:

(1) *hũ rəma-pase vasəṇ məNj-av-ũ   ch-ũ*
     I   Rama-ag vessels clean-caus-1sg aux-1sg
     'I am having Rama clean the vessels.'

(2) *hũ rəma-ne vasəṇ məNj-av-ũ   ch-ũ*
     I   Rama-obj vessels clean-caus-1sg aux-1sg
     'I'm helping Rama clean the vessels.'

7.3 Passive (section 5.10)

A noteworthy feature concerning the passives is that it involves passivizing a verb while maintaining the syntactic marking of an object relative to the act in question. For example, in

(1) *əNgreji-mã maṇəs-ne   šũ   kəhv-a-y*
     English-in man-obj   what say-pass-3p
     'How does one say "man" in English?'

(2) *ɛ-ne   nəhi pəkḍ-a-y*
     him-obj not   catch-pass-3p
     'He won't be able to get caught.'

maṇəs-ne and *ɛ-ne* have the object marker *-ne* just as they would in a corresponding active sentences. Similarly, in

(3) *keṭl-a-k   polis-ne paḍ-i de-v-a-mã av-y-a*
     how many-mpl-indef police-obj fell-i give-*v-a*-in come-pftv-mpl
     hə-t-a
     aux-impfct-m pl
     'Several policemen were killed.'

polis-ne, with the object marker, is in construction with a periphrastic perfect including the masculine plural in the perfective verb phrase, determined by the passive object.
     In addition, the auxiliary *šək* is made passive, as in

(4) *am   kər-i šək-a-y*
     this way do-i be able-pass-3p
     'It can be done this way.'

7.4 Relative, correlative, adversative and causal clauses

7.4.1 Relative and correlative clauses

In relative sentences (Cardona 1965: 80–1, 96, 142, 150 [§§ 4.2.10, 4.3.6, 6.1.2.1, 6.4.3], Vyas 1977: 270–3, Desai 1992: 465–6, 486–7), relative pronominals (section 4.5) and *jo* 'if' are linked with correlatives, that is, corresponding forms of demonstratives as well as *to* 'then'. Relative phrases precede correlative phrases and are characterized by *j-*; such clauses with *j-*forms other than non-adjectival pronouns are omissible:

(1) *je   nəvəlkətha mẽ ləkh-i   te   tɛmṇe chap-i*
     rel novel   I$_{ag}$ write-pftv-f corr he$_{ag}$ print-pftv-f
     'He published the novel I wrote.'

(2) (*jɛm*) *təm-ne   gəm-e   tɛm kər-o*
     (as)   you-obj please-3p thus do-2p
     'Do as you please.'

(3) (*jyã*) *təme jə-š-o   tyã   əme-pəṇ   jə-iš-ũ*
     (where)   you_subj go-fut-2pl. we_subj-also go-fut-1pl
     'We'll also go where you go.'

(4) (*jyare*) *ɛ-ne mə-ne səval   puch-y-o   tyare-j*
     (when) he-ag I-obj   question ask-pftv-msg then-excl
     mẽ jəvab ap-y-o
     I_agn answer give-pftv-msg
     'I answered as soon as he asked me.'

(5) *jev-o   bap   ev-o   chokr-o*
     such-msg father such-msg child-msg
     'like father like son'

(6) *jeṭl-a   joi-e   teṭl-a   l-ɔ*
     as much-mpl need-3p that much-m pl take-2pl
     'Take as many as you need.'

(7) *jevḍ-o   ṭukḍ-o   joi-e   tevḍ-o   phaḍ-i l-ɛ*
     as large-msg piece-msg need-3p so large-msg tear-*i* take-2p
     'Tear off as big a piece as you need.'

(8) (*jo*) *təme   phon   kər-š-o   to   anənd   thə-š-e*
     (if) you_subj phonecall do-fut-2pl then happiness come about-fut-3p
     'I'd be happy if you give me a call.'

(9) *mar-e kam kərva-n-ũ na hɔ-t   to   təmar-i-sathe av-ət*
     I-agn work do_vbn-*n*-nt neg be-cond ptcle you-f-together go-cond
     (5.7 ex. 1)

On *jo ke* 'although', see section 7.4.2, ex. 12.

7.4.2 Adversative clauses

The most common adversative particles, which introduce clauses, are *pəṇ* (also *to pəṇ*) 'but', *chətã* (*chətã pəṇ*), *bəlke* 'nevertheless', and formal *kintu, pərəntu* 'but'. For example:

(10) *lila rəmeš-n-e   tyã gə-i   pəṇ ɛ-n-a   ghɛr   taḷũ*
      Lila Ramesh-*n*-loc there go-pftv-f but he-*n*-nt_obl home_loc padlock
      hə-t-ũ
      be-impftv-ntsg
      'Lila went to Ramesh's place, but his house was locked.'

(11) *ɛ-ne vərtən   sar-ũ nə rakh-y-ũ   chətã   kam sar-ũ kər-y-ũ*
      he-ag behaviour good not keep-pftv-ntsg nevertheless work good do-pftv-ntsg
      'He did not behave well, but nevertheless he did good work.'

(12) *jo-ke ɛ-ne kam sar-ũ kər-y-ũ to-pəṇ vərtən sarũ nə rakh-y-ũ*
      'Although he did good work, still he did not behave well.'

7.4.3 Causal clauses

Causal clauses are introduced by *kɛm-ke* or the slightly more formal *karəɳ ke*:

(13) *hũ parti-mã nə   gə-y-o   kɛm-ke mə-ne tav   hə-t-o*
     I party-in not go-pftv-msg because I-obj fever be-impftv-msg
     'I didn't go to the party because I had a fever.'

7.5 Serial verbs

Verbal derivates of the type *kər-i-(ne)* – consisting of a base with *-i* and optional *-ne* –
are used with reference to an action performed prior to the performance of another act.
For example:

(1) *te   kha-i-ne   hath dhu-e   ch-e*
     he/she after eating hands wash-3p aux-3p
     'He/she washes his/her hands after eating.'

(2) *vãc-i-ne   rəmeš su-i   gə-y-o*
     after reading Ramesh sleep-*i* go-pftv-msg
     'Ramesh went to bed after reading.'

7.6 Negation

The negative particles are *nə*, *nəhi*, *na* and *ma* (Cardona 1965: 137–40, Pancholi 1965).
na – polite *na ji* – and *nəthi* can stand alone as negations of sentences and the
appropriate verb (see below):

(1)a *subodh-bhai   ghɛr   ch-e*   b *na nəthi*
     Subodh-brother home$_{loc}$ be-3p   'No, he is not.'
     'Is Subodh at home? No.'

Accordingly, *na* is used with *kəh* 'say' *pad* ('make fall'), as in

(2) *ɛ-ɳe   na pad-i*
     he/she-ag no make fall-pftv-f
     'He/she said no.'

The positive counterpart has *ha: ɛ-ɳe ha pad-i* '... said yes.'
   nə is the negative for imperfective forms with *hə*:

(3)a *te   vəkhət-e e šũ   kər-t-o   hə-t-o*
     that time-loc he what do-impftv-msg aux-impftv-msg
     'What was he doing at that time?'

   b *te   vəkhət-e e kəšũ-j kər-t-o nə hə-t-o*
     'He was not doing anything at all at that time.'

With perfectives, *nə(hi)/na* are used:

(4) *kal-e   aruɳa-bɛn gam   nə gə-y-ã*
     yesterday-loc Aruna-hon village not go-pftv-ntpl
     'Aruna did not go to the village yesterday.'

(5) *a   kam   koi-na-thi   kəra-y-ũ   nəhi* (4.5 ex. 10)
     this work someone-*na*-by do-pass-pftv-ntsg not

nəhi is also used with other verb forms, as in

(6) *moṭa   bhai   aj-e   pach-a   nəhi av-e* (5.2 ex. 9)
     big-mpl brother today-loc back-mpl not come-3p
     'My older brother won't come back today.'

(7) *mara-thi a   kam   nəhi kər-a-y* (5.2 ex. 10)
     I-ag   this work not do-pass-3p
     'I won't be able to do this job.'

However, in such contexts, it can alternate with *nə*. Moreover, *na* is preferable to some speakers.

Reflecting a pattern that was already established in earliest Middle Indic, *nəthi* occurs as the invariant negative corresponding to all forms of *ch* and is construed with an imperfective form:

(8)a *rəmeš   šikšək   ch-e*   b *rəmeš šikšək nəthi*
      Ramesh teacher be-3p
      'Ramesh is a teacher.'   'Ramesh is not a teacher.'

(9)a *mar-ã   mabap   vəḍodra-mã   rəh-e   ch-e*
      my-npl mother-father Vadodara-in stay-3p aux-3pl
      'My parents are living/live in Vadodara.'

   b *mumbəi-mã nəthi rəh-t-ã*
      Mumbai-in not   stay-impftv-npl
      'They are not living in Mumbai.'

Imperatives are negatable with *nə*, *nəhi*, and *ma*, the last either preceding or following the verb form:

(10)a *cinta   nə/nəhi kər-o*
       worry not   do-2pl imp
    b *cinta   ma   kər-o*
    c *cinta   kər-o   ma*
       'Don't worry.'

REFERENCES

[Titles of works in Gujarati are given in transliteration, and English equivalents are given in brackets.]

Acharya, Shantibhai (1985) *Halari Dialect* (*A Linguistic-Geographical Study*), Ahmedabad: Gujarat Vidyapith. [Revised English version of *Hālārī Bolī* (*Eka Bhāṣāvaijñānika Adhyayana*) (1978), Ahmedabad: Gujarat Vidyapith.]

Bhayani, Harivallabh C. (1988) *Gujarati Bhāṣānuṁ Aitihāsika Vyākaraṇa* [A Historical Grammar of Gujarati], Gandhinagar: Gujarāt Sāhitya Akādamī.

Cardona, George (1965) *A Gujarati Reference Grammar*, Philadelphia: University of Pennsylvania Press.

Dave, J. C. (1972) *Gujarātī* (*nāmika*) *samāso* (*eka varṇanātmaka adhyayana* [Gujarati (Nominal) Compounds (A descriptive study)], Ahmedabad: Gurjar Grantharatna.

Dave, Radhekant (1967) 'A formant analysis of the clear, nasalized, and murmured vowels in Gujarati', *Indian Linguistics* 28: 1–30.

Desai, Urmi G. (1992) *Vyākaraṇa vimarśa* [A Grammatical Treatise], Ahmedabad: University Grantha Nirmāṇa Board.

Firth, J. R. (1957) 'Phonetic observations on Gujarati', *Bulletin of the School of Oriental and African Studies* 20: 231–41.

Fischer-Jørgensen, Eli (1967) 'Phonetic analysis of breathy (murmured) vowels', *Indian Linguistics* 28: 71–139.

Mistry, Purushottam J. (1969) *Gujarati Verbal Constructions*, UCLA doctoral dissertation, unpublished. [University Microfilms, 1971.]

—— (1996) 'Gujarati writing', in Daniels, Peter T. and Bright, William (eds.) *The World's Writing Systems*, New York: Oxford University Press, pp. 391–4.

—— (1997) 'Gujarati phonology', in Kaye, Alan S. (ed.) *Phonologies of Asia and Africa*, Winona Lake, IN: Eisenbrauns, pp. 653–73.

Modi, Bharti (1979) *Paścimamaṁ vyākaraṇa mīmāṁsā comskīan yuga* [The Beginning of Generative Grammar–Chomskian Period (1955–70)], Ahmedabad: Gujarat University.

—— (1987) 'Rethinking of "murmur in Gujarati"', *Indian Linguistics* 47: 39–55.

—— (1994) 'The phonetics and phonology of mid-vowels in Gujarati', *Indian Linguistics* 55: 51–76.

Pancholi, R. M. (1965) 'The negative particles in Gujarati', *Indian Linguistics* 26 (*Sukumar Sen Felicitation Volume*): 137–8.

Pandit, Prabodh B. (1955) '*E* and *O* in Gujarati', *Indian Linguistics* 14: 36–44.

—— (1957) 'Nasalization, aspiration and murmur in Gujarati', *Indian Linguistics* 17: 165–222.

—— (1958) 'Duration, syllable and juncture in Gujarati', *Indian Linguistics* 1 (*Turner Jubilee Volume II*): 212–19.

—— (1961) 'Historical phonology of Gujarati vowels', *Language* 37: 54–66.

—— (1966) *Gujuratī bhāṣā nuṁ dhvanisvarūpa ane dhvaniparivartana* [Phonological Structure and Change in Gujarati], Ahmedabad: Gujarat University. [Reprinted 1974]

—— (1973) 'Gujarātī bhāṣānāṁ vidhāyako paribaḷo' [Formative factors of the Gujarati language], in Jośī, Umāśaṁkara, Rāvaḷ, Anaṁtarāya, and Śukla, Yaśavanta (eds.) *Gujarātī Sāhityano Itihāsa, Graṁtha 1* [*Ī. S. 1150–1450*] [History of Gujarati Literature, Volume I (A.D. 1150–1450)], Ahmedabad: Gujarātī Sāhitya Pariṣad, pp. 50–76.

—— (1976) *A Study of the Gujarati Language in the 14th Century with Special Reference to a Critical Edition of Ṣaḍāvaśyaka-bālāvabodhavṛtti of Taruṇaprabha*, Bombay: Bharatiya Vidya Bhavan.

Patel, Gokalbhai D. (1981) *Samāsa: eka adhyayana* [Compounds: A Study], Ahmedabad: Adarsh Prakashan.

Turner, Ralph L. (1925) 'The *e* and *o* vowels in Gujarati', in *Ashutosh Mukherji Silver Jubilee Volume*, *Orientalia II*.2, pp. 337–47. [Reprinted in Turner (1985), pp. 229–38.]

—— (1985) *R. L. Turner, Indo-Aryan Linguistics – Collected Papers 1912–1973*, edited by J. Brough, Delhi: Disha Publications. [Originally published 1973, London: School of Oriental and African Studies.]

Učida, Norihiko (1990) *A Saurashtra-English Dictionary, with appendices by Muddan Nagabhushana and Obulan S. Subramanian* (Neuindische Studien 11), Wiesbaden: Harrassowitz.

—— (1991) *The Language of the Saurashtrans in Tirupati* (Intercultural Research Institute Monography Series 14), Bangalore: Mahalaxmi Enterprises.

Vijayanunni, M. (1997) *Census of India 1991, Series 1-India, Paper 1 of 1997: Language, India and States*, New Delhi: Government of India Press.

Vyas, Yogendra. D. (1974) *Bolīvijñāna ane Gujarātnī bolīo* [Dialectology and Dialects of Gujarat], Ahmedabad: University Grantha Nirmāṇa Board.

—— (1977) *Gujarātī bhāṣānuṁ vyākaraṇa* [A Grammar of the Gujarati Language], Ahmedabad: Sāhitya Mudraṇālaya for the Gujarat University.

FURTHER READING

Acharya, Shantibhai (1966) *Kacchī Śabdāvali* [Kacchi Vocabulary], Ahmedabad: Gujarat Vidyapith.

Bhandari, Aravind (1951) *Gujarātī Vibhakti Vicāra Thoughts on Gujarati Case*, Ahmedabad: Gujarat University.

—— (1990) *Gujarātī Vākyaracanā* [Gujarati Syntax], Ahmedabad: University Grantha Nirmāṇa Board.

Bhayani, Harivallabh C. (1978) *Thoḍok vyākaraṇa vicāra* [Some Grammatical Thoughts], Ahmedabad: Vora.

Buch, Hasit H. (1979) *An Introduction to Gujarati Language Gujarātī bhāṣā-paricaya*, Gandhinagar: Directorate of Languages, Gujarat State. [Hasit H. Buch is not listed as author, but appears as the signatory of the Preface in his capacity of Director of Languages.]

Dave, T. N. (1930–2) 'Notes on Gujarati phonology', *Bulletin of the School of Oriental and African Studies* 6: 673–8.

Divatia, N. B. (1921–32) *Gujarâtî Language and Literature, being the Wilson Philological Lectures*. 2 volumes, Bombay, Calcutta, Madras and London: Macmillan and Company, Limited for the University of Bombay.

Dwyer, Rachel (1995) *Teach Yourself Gujarati: A Complete Course for Beginners*, London: Hodder Headline Plc., Lincolnwood (Chicago): NTC Publishing Group.

Grierson, George A. (1908) 'Gujarati', in *Linguistic Survey of India, Volume IX: Indo-Aryan Family, Part II: Specimens of Rājasthānī and Gujarātī*, Calcutta: Office of the Superintendent of Government Printing, pp. 323–477. (Reprinted (1968), Delhi: Motilal Banarsidass).

Joshi, Dayashankar M. (1975) 'Gujarati verb forms reconsidered', *Indian Linguistics* 36: 285–9.

—— (1978) See Pandit, Prabodh B. (1978).

Kothari, Jayant (1973) *Bhāṣāparicaya ane Gujarāti bhāṣānuṁ svarūpa* [Introduction to Language and Structure of Gujarati Language], Ahmedabad: University Grantha Nirmāṇa Board.

Lambert, H. M. (1971) *Gujarati Language Course*, Cambridge: Cambridge University Press.

Pandit, Prabodh B. (1962) 'Gujarātī dhvanitantra', *Saṁskṛti* October 1962: 374–84, November 1962: 420–8.

—— (1969) 'Gujarati', in Sebeok, Thomas A. (ed.) *Current Trends in Linguistics, volume 5: Linguistics in South Asia*, The Hague, Paris: Mouton, pp. 105–21.

—— (1978) *Vākyanā artha ane ākāra – vyākhānakāra Prabodha Paṁḍiat sampādaka Dayāśaṁkara Jośī* [Sentence Meaning and Form – Lecturer Prabodh Pandit, editor Dayashankar Joshi], Ahmedabad: University Grantha Nirmāṇa Board.

Taylor, G. P. (1908) *The Student's Gujarati Grammar, with Exercises and Vocabulary*, Bombay: Thacker & Co. Ltd. (Reprinted (1985), New Delhi: Asian Educational Services).

Tisdall, W. St. Clair Towers (1892) *A Simplified Grammar of the Gujarati Language, together with a short reading book and vocabulary*, London: K. Paul Trench, Trübner & Co. Ltd. (Reprinted (1961), New York: Frederick Ungar Publishers (1986), New Delhi: Asian Educational Services.)

Turner, Ralph L. (1921) 'Gujarati phonology', *Journal of the Royal Asiatic Society* 1921: 329–65, 505–44. (Reprinted in Turner (1985), pp. 88–145).

CHAPTER NINETEEN

MARATHI

Rajeshwari Pandharipande

CONTENTS

1 INTRODUCTION

Marathi, a major modern Indo-Aryan language and the language of the Maharashtra state, is one of the eighteen official languages in India. The name Marathi is etymologically derived from Mahārāṣṭrī '(the language) of the great (*mahā*) land/nation (*rāṣṭra*)'. The state covers a large area of 118,758 square miles which includes thirty districts grouped in six sociolinguistic regions in Maharashtra where the following six major dialects are spoken:

(i) *Konkaṇī* (see note 1, p. 726),
(ii) *Konkaṇī Desī* in Konkan (the coastal area in the west),
(iii) *Kkāndesī* in Khandesh (the northwestern region),
(iv) *Desī* in Desh (Puṇe and the southwestern region next to Konkan), and in Marathwada (the eastcentral region),
(v) *Varhāḍī* in Varhad (the north-central region),
(vi) *Nāgpurī* in Vidarbha (the northeastern region; Varhad, and Vidarbha are generally viewed as two divisions of Mahavidarbha).

In spite of certain differences, the dialects of Marathi show a remarkably high level of mutual intelligibility as has been already noted by Grierson (1905). Additionally, there are several local/caste dialects of Marathi. (For details see Grierson (1905), Ghatage (1963) and Agnihotri (1983).)

There are approximately sixty-two million speakers of Marathi, including speakers outside the native state of Maharashtra. Marathi occupies a geographically unique position since it is spoken in the area which links two major language families – Indo-Aryan in the north and Dravidian in the south. Marathi belongs to the 'outer circle' of Indo-Aryan languages (Grierson 1905).

Maharashtra, traditionally called *dakṣiṇāpath* 'the avenue to the south', clearly has been viewed as a geographic, cultural and linguistic link between the north and the south. Marathi is surrounded by Indo-Aryan languages such as Gujarati and Hindi in the north, and Dravidian languages such as Kannada and Telugu in the south. Marathi shares features of both Indo-Aryan and Dravidian languages. Additionally, within Maharashtra, Marathi has had sustained contact with politically dominant languages such as Telugu and Kannada (during the Yadav period AD 1000–1300), Persian (Mughal period AD 1300–1700), and English (British period AD 1700–1947). This contact has resulted in large scale borrowings from these languages into Marathi.

The genetic roots of Marathi (i.e., Mahārāṣṭrī Prākṛta > Mahārāṣṭrī Apabhraṁśa) are well known. The major stages of the development of Marathi are Old Marathi (AD 1000–1300), Middle Marathi (AD 1300–1800), and Modern Marathi (1800–). The first Marathi sentence, dated AD 1117, appears in the inscription on the statue of Gomateshwar at Shrāvana Belagola in Mysore state. The earliest grammars of Konkaṇī (which was viewed as a variety of Marathi) were written in Portuguese by Christian missionaries in Goa in the seventeenth century (see Arjunwadkar 1987: 2).

The Marathi grammatical tradition has been rich and shows three major influences on its development:

(a) the European tradition (primarily of the Latin grammars, e.g. Carey (1805) and Burgess (1854) among others),
(b) the native Sanskrit grammatical tradition (Damle (1965 [1911]) and others), and
(c) the current western linguistic tradition, e.g. Kelkar (1958) and Apte's (1962).

While the European tradition inspired by the Bible translation described Marathi grammar on the model of Latin-based languages, the Sanskrit tradition, explained it on the model of Sanskrit grammar. The current tradition analyzes Marathi grammar within the framework of universal linguistic patterns and allows cross-linguistic comparisons.

The two comprehensive studies on the historical grammar of Marathi are Bloch (1920, 1970 (translated into English from French by Chanana)), and Master (1967). The two notable studies on Marathi dialects are Ghatage (1963) and Grierson (1905).

The early Marathi linguistic and literary traditions were dictated by the Sanskrit tradition. Jñāneśwar's thirteenth-century monumental contribution to Marathi, *Jñāneś-warī*, established and authenticated a strong literary and 'socially realistic' linguistic tradition in Marathi.

Marathi has consistently maintained a very rich literary tradition from its earliest beginning to the present. Throughout the turbulent history of Mughal and then British rule, Marathi struggled to survive under the influence of Persian and English, the official languages during the Mughal and the British rule respectively. The dictionary, named *Rājyawyawahār koś*, prepared under the rule of Shivaji, a seventeenth-century king, marked the first attempt in the history of India to preserve the linguistic identity of a language. Sanskrit was used extensively as a source from which to borrow or derive new vocabulary to replace Persian, which had reduced the native Marathi vocabulary to 14.4 per cent in the lexicon (Gramopadhye 1941: 11). A similar situation recurred after the end of the British rule in 1947 when the government of India, the newspapers and the education department of Maharashtra worked toward developing a Marathi lexicon to replace English words in the language. Sanskrit was once again used as the reservoir from which the appropriate vocabulary was borrowed and derived. The influence of Persian and English has not completely disappeared from Marathi; but it has become restricted to certain registers and/or styles of Marathi (cf. section 5).

Marathi uses the Devanagari script, locally known as *bāḷbodh* (understood by children, i.e., simple), with additional characters for /ḷ/ and /r-/ in /r/- conjuncts. This chapter primarily describes Standard Marathi (SM). However, important dialectal variation is also discussed.

Though the transcription used in this chapter follows most of the conventional practices in the linguistic literature on Marathi and other Indo-Aryan languages, there are a few notable exceptions to make the pattern (of transcription) fairly transparent. Thus, the distinction between the alveolar and alveo-palatal affricates is represented by the symbols /ts/, /dz/, and /dzh/ (alveolar affricates) and /tS/, /tSh/, /dʒ/, and /dʒh/ (alveo-palatal affricates) respectively. (For details see table 19.4.) Since Marathi does not have the labio-dental fricative /v/, the labial glide /w/ is used instead. In transcribing proper names, /v/ is retained in the English glosses and translations.

TABLE 19.1: THE MARATHI ALPHABET

Independent vowels:

a	ā	i	ī	u	ū	e	ai
अ	आ	इ	ई	उ	ऊ	ए	ऐ

o	au
ओ	औ

Independent consonants:

k	kh	g	gh	ŋ
क	ख	ग	घ	ङ

ts	tSh	dz	dzh	ñ
tS		dʒ	dʒh	
च	छ	ज	झ	ञ

ṭ	ṭh	ḍ	ḍh	ṇ
ट	ठ	ड	ढ	ण

t	th	d	dh	n
त	थ	द	ध	न

p	ph	b	bh	m
प	फ	ब	भ	म

y	r	l	w	ś
य	र	ल	व	श

ṣ	s	h	ḷ	kṣ	dñy	ṛ
ष	स	ह	ळ	क्ष	ज्ञ	ऋ

Dependent vowels (following consonants):

a	ā	i	ī	u	ū	e	ai
none	ा	ि	ी	ु	ू	े	ै

o	au
ो	ौ

Homorganic nasal or nasalized vowel:

ं

Consonants (first) in a consonant cluster:

k	kh	g	gh	ŋ
क्	ख्	ग्	घ्	ङ्

ts	tSh	dz	dzh	ñ
tS		dʒ	dʒh	
च्	छ्	ज्	झ्	ञ्

ṭ	ṭh	ḍ	ḍh	ṇ
ट्	ठ्	ड्	ढ्	ण्

t	th	d	dh	n
त्	थ्	द्	ध्	न्

p	ph	b	bh	m
प्	फ्	ब्	भ्	म्

y	l	w	ś	r
य्	ल्	व्	श्	र्

ṣ	s	h	ḷ	kṣ	dñy
ष्	स्	ह्	ळ्	क्ष्	ज्ञ्

r (variants: after consonant): ╱ and ╮

ṛ (after consonant): ╷

2 MORPHOLOGY

Marathi has three genders (masculine, feminine and neuter) and two numbers (singular and plural). It expresses the syntactic and semantic functions of noun phrases primarily by case-suffixes and postpositions. A brief description of morphology follows (for a detailed description, see Kelkar (1958), and Pandharipande (1997)).

2.1 Nouns

Nouns are divided into different classes according to gender and the phonological shape of their base-forms and they are declined differently for number and cases according to their respective classes. Only the -ā-final masculine nouns undergo change in their plural forms (*ghoḍā* > *ghoḍe*).

Feminine nouns except for those ending in -ā *and* -ū, undergo change in their plural forms as in (1)–(7).

(1)	consonant -final	wāṭ 'path'	wāṭā 'paths'
(2)	cosonant-final	bahīṇ 'sister'	bahiṇī 'sisters'
(3)	-ā-final	śāḷā 'school'	—
(4)	-ī-final	nadī 'river'	nadyā 'rivers'
(5)	-ū-final	wāḷū 'sand'	wāḷū 'different types of sand'
(6)	-a-final	bhinta 'wall'	bhintī 'walls'
(7)	-o-final	bāyko 'wife'	bāykā 'wives'

Except for those ending in -ī, all neuter nouns undergo changes in (8)–(11) below.

(8)	consonant-final	ghar 'home'	ghara 'homes'
(9)	-ū-final	pillū 'baby animal'	pilla 'baby animals'
(10)	-a-final	taḷa 'lake'	taḷī 'lakes'
(11)	-ī-final	pāṇī 'water'	—

Example (12) illustrates the various case markers following the masculine noun *palang* 'bed/cot'.

(12)	Case	Marker	Example
	Nominative	ø	palang
	Accusative	-lā	palangālā
	Instrumental	-ne	palangãne
	Dative	-lā	palangālā
	Ablative	-(h)ūn	palangāhūn
	Possessive-genitive	-tsā/tSī/tse	palangātsā
	Locative	-t	palangāt
	Vocative	-ā	palangā

The following remarks on variation in these case markers are in order:

(i)   The accusative/dative markers -s and -te are variants of the accusative/dative markers -lā (sg) and -nā (pl). The use of -lā (sg) and -nā (pl) is most frequent in SM, while the use of -s was more widespread in Old Marathi (for further discussions on -s, see Bloch (1970)). In SM, the use of -s is restricted to the formal written register, specifically, to official memos, while in Nagpuri Marathi (NM), it marks the speech of the 'uneducated.'

(ii) -*te*, the variant of the dative suffix in Old Marathi (especially, in Marathi poetry), is lost in modern Marathi.

(iii) The instrumental suffix -*śī*, a variant of -*ne* (sg) and -*nī* (pl), is (alternatively) used only in the variety of Marathi spoken near Madhya Pradesh.

(iv) The locative suffix -*ī*, a variant of -*t*, is used for some consonant-final stems, e.g. *sakāḷ* 'morning', *sakāḷī* 'in the morning'/*sakāḷt, *ghar* 'house' (i.e., *gharāt/gharī* 'in the house'), etc.

(v) An oblique form of a noun-stem functions as its vocative form with the plural vocative suffix -*no* affixed to the plural oblique forms, as in (13)–(13a).

	Stem	Oblique	Vocative
pelā 'glass'			
(13) Singular	pelā 'glass'	pelyā	pelyā 'o, glass!'
(13a) Plural	pele 'glasses'	pelyā	pelyãnno 'o, glasses!'

Noun stems are augmented before case-suffixes/postpositions. Those augments vary according to the gender, number and the morphological class of the nouns. The distribution of the augments is as follows:

(a) -*ā* is used for all masculine nouns (vowel - as well as consonant-final singular as well as plural) The noun-stems undergo additional changes before the augment (cf. section 4.6).

(b) -*e* is used for the -*ā* ending and consonant-final feminine singular stems (*śāḷā* : *śāḷe*, *wāṭ* : *wāṭe*).

(c) Consonant-final feminine nouns such as *bahīṇ* 'sister', which have an -*ī* ending plural form, use the plural form (*bahiṇī*) as the oblique form of the stem.

(d) All feminine noun-stems use their corresponding plural forms as oblique plural forms.

(e) All neuter noun-stems take the augment -*ā* before the case-suffixes (*dzāḍ* > *dzāḍā*, *taḷe* > *taḷyā*).

(f) Plural oblique forms of all nouns, regardless of their gender and morphological class, take the augment -*n*, which occurs between the augment -*ā* and the instrumental, dative, possessive and vocative case-suffixes. In these cases, -*ā* is nasalized (*ghoḍyãn* (m), *śāḷãn* (f), *pillãn* (n)).

(g) As opposed to SM, in the South-Konkan dialect of Marathi, ablative, possessive and locative plural forms are pronounced with a nasalized vowel (-*ã*) without a dental nasal -*n* before the suffixes, e.g. *ghoḍyã-hūn* (ablative), *ghoḍyã-tsā* (possessive) and *ghoḍyã-t* (locative).

(h) In the locative plural, the nasalization of the vowel (-*ã*) is lost and is only optionally retained in orthography in SM.

As mentioned earlier, case-relations are expressed by the postpositions following nouns, infinitives and gerunds. For example, dative: (*tSā*) *kartā* 'for', instrumental: (*tSā*) *muḷe* 'because of', ablative: (*tSā*) *pāsūn* 'from', locative: (*tSā*) *madhe* 'in', etc. Complex postpositions are derived by adding case-markers to postpositions: (*tSā*) *bādzū-ne* (inst) 'from the side', (*tSā*) *war-ūn* (abl) 'from the top', etc. Postpositions govern the possessive case marked by (*tSyā*) and require nouns, infinitives, etc. to change to their oblique forms.

Postpositions are not as inalienable from the (noun) stem as case-suffixes. Clitic particles can optionally intervene between the noun and a postposition (e.g. *dewātSyā*-

ts-sāṭhi 'for the sake of the god alone') but not before the case-suffix (e.g. **dewā-ts-lā* 'for god alone'). Clitics *-ts* and *-hī* are used to express emphatic/exclusive and inclusive meanings respectively. However, they do not express the grammatical relation of a noun phrase with other constituents in the sentence.

Nouns borrowed from English which are perceived as native Marathi vocabulary (e.g. *tikiṭ* 'ticket', *ṣṭeśan* 'station'), are included in the class of the nouns of the same endings and are declined accordingly. However, those borrowings which are perceived as non-native, are not declined for number and do not take the augment before the case-suffixes (e.g. *ḍɔkṭar* > *ḍɔkṭar-lā* 'to the doctor', *ɔfis* > *ɔfis-lā* 'to the office', etc.)

2.2 Pronouns

Personal pronouns are illustrated in table 19.2. Note that gender distinction is maintained only in the third person and the third person pronouns are separated by the parameter of proximity and remoteness. Demonstrative pronouns are the same as the third person pronouns. Plural forms of the pronouns are used to express politeness or respect. Reflexive pronouns (both emphatic and anaphoric) occur with all pronouns in all persons.

Between the second person plural pronouns, *āpaṇ* (compared to *tumhī*) has been traditionally used to express a higher degree of respect towards the addressee. However, in contemporary India, the use of *tumhī* is becoming more prevalent for expressing deference than *āpaṇ*.

Similar to nouns, pronouns are declined for cases and they have their corresponding oblique forms. The following paradigms are representative of the basic and the oblique forms of the pronouns in the three persons.

(14) 1st person:

cases	singular forms	plural forms
nom	mī	āmhī/āpaṇ
obl	ma	āmhā-/āpyā

2nd person:

nom	tū	tumhī/āpaṇ
obl	tu	tumhā/āplyā

TABLE 19.2: PERSONAL PRONOUNS (see note 2, p. 726)

Person	Prox/Rem	Gender	Number			
			S	Pl	Incl	Excl
First	–	–	mī	āmhī	āpaṇ (you+I)	
Second	–	–	tū	tumhī/		āpaṇ
Third	Proximate	mas	hā	he		
		fem	hī	hyā		
		neut	he	hī		
	Remote	mas	to	te		
		fem	tī	tyā		
		neut	te	tī		
Reflexive	emphatic		swatāhā/āpaṇswatāhā			
	anaphoric		āpaṇ (with the case endings)			

3rd person (proximate):

cases	singular forms			plural forms		
	mas	fem	neut	mas	fem	neut
nom	hā	hī	he	hc	hyā	hī
obl	hyā	hi	hyā	hyãn	hyãn	hyãn

The possessive pronouns agree in gender and number with the noun of possession, i.e., *mādzha* 'my (sn)', *mādzhā* 'my (sm)', *madʒhī* 'my (sf)', *madʒhī* 'my (pl.n)', *mādzhe* 'my (pl.m)', *mādʒhyā* 'my (pl.f)'. All pronouns take postpositions to express various semantic relations (e.g. *mādʒhyā-barobar* 'with me', *tudʒhyā-war* 'on you', *tyātSyā-sārkhā* 'like him', etc.). The ergative postposition is added only to the third person pronouns and the resulting forms are given below:

(15)

singular forms			plural forms		
mas	fem	neut	mas	fem	neut
to	tī	te	te	tyā	te
tyāne	tine	tyāne	tyãnnī	tyãnnī	tyãnnī

Reflexive pronouns – emphatic (*swatāhā*/*āpaṇswatāhā*) and possessive (*āpaṇ* (*āplyā* - obl.) take the full range of case-forms. The proximate and remoteness distinction is based on the spatial, temporal as well as psychological distance of the referent of the pronoun from the speaker, and not from the hearer.

There are two types of interrogative pronouns: general (*koṇ* 'who', and *kāy* 'what') and specific (*koṇtā* 'which-he (i.e., 'who' sm)', *koṇtī* 'which she (i.e., 'who' sf)', *koṇta* 'which-it' (i.e., sn), and its variant). The general interrogative pronouns are used in unmarked contexts to get basic information about the referent and the specific interrogative pronouns are used to get more information about the presupposed referent(s) with which they agree in person, gender and number.

2.3 Adjectives

Marathi has three major types of adjectives: (i) Simple adjectives such as *sundar* 'beautiful', *niḷā* 'blue', *moṭhā* 'big', etc. (ii) Adjectives derived from nouns and adverbs, as in (16).

(16)
Nouns	Adjectives
(a) puruṣ 'man'	puruṣ-ī 'masculine'
(b) himmat 'courage'	himmat-wālā 'courageous'

Adverbs	
(c) dzawaḷ 'near'	dzawaḷ-tsā 'close'

(iii) Participal adjectives. Participial adjectives are derived by adding suffixes to verbs (cf. examples (53)–(57)).

Adjectives can be vowel or consonant-ending. Except for the *-ā*-ending adjectives, all adjectives remain in their invariable form, as in (17).

(17)
(a)	moṭhā 'big'	moṭhe parvat 'big mountains'
(b)	sundar 'beautiful'	sundar parvat 'beautiful mountains'

Deletion of a noun or the position of a noun influences the agreement of adjectives with nouns.

There are no native Marathi suffixes which mark comparative adjectives. The Sanskrit comparative suffixes -*tara* (comparative), and -*tama* (superlative) are added to Sanskrit adjectives which are retained in Marathi. Consider the examples in (18).

(18) sundar   'beautiful'
       sundar-tar(a)   'more beautiful'
       sundar-tam(a)   'most beautiful'

Adverbs of degree such as *khūp* 'very', *thoḍa* 'little' are used to indicate the degree of the adjectives such as *lahān* 'small', *lãmb* 'long', etc. Reduplication of adjectives expresses intensification or distributive meanings, e.g. *lāl lāl* 'dark red', *ghar ghar* 'every house'. Additionally, Marathi uses the device of word-compounding to indicate intensity:

(19) lāl-tsuṭuk 'very red'
       piwḷā-dhamak 'very yellow'

The first member of the compound is an adjective; the second member does not express any independent meaning and functions exclusively as an intensifier.

2.4 Verbs

The verb is the obligatory constituent in a sentence. In the imperative and in affirmative sentences, it can be the only constituent. Verbs occur in finite and non-finite forms (participials and infinitives), and both are declined for tense, aspect, gender and number.

Marathi shares the following major features of Indo-Aryan languages: (a) the Old Indo-Aryan feature of a morphologically related set of verbs (causatives), (b) the Modern Indo-Aryan feature of compound verbs, and (c) homophonous suffixes for expressing aspect and tense. However, like Dravidian languages, it has a much larger range and use of participles (Bloch (1920)), and finite negative verbs.

(20) Morphologically related verbs:

Intransitive	Transitive	Causative
mar 'die'	mār 'kill'	māraw 'cause to kill'
bas 'sit'	basaw 'seat'	
——	kar 'do'	karaw 'cause to do'

2.4.1 Tense

Tense is marked by a suffix, which immediately follows the verb stem and precedes all other suffixes. The agreement markers for person, number and gender are different in different tenses. The tense, aspect and mood system of Marathi is complex: (a) tense and aspect markers often merge, (b) several explicator verbs carry the function of aspect/tense markers, and (c) time reference is not always determined by tense markers on a verb within the same clause.

Three tenses – present, past, and future – are formally distinguished as in (21).

(21)

Tense	Marker	Example	Gloss
Present	-t	basto	'he sits'
Past	-l+vowel	baslā	'he sat'
Future	vowel + l/n	basel	'he will sit'

The present tense verb forms are shown in (22).

(22) *karṇe* 'to do':

	Singular		Plural	
	mas	fem	mas	fem
1p	karto	karte	karto	karto
2p	kartos	kartes	kartā	kartā
3p	karto	karte	kartāt	kartāt

The past tense suffix *-l* is homophonous with the perfective aspectual suffix. Past habitual and past progressive are the only non-perfective aspects in Marathi. There is no independent past imperfective in Marathi. The pattern of verb agreement in the past tense differs from that in the present tense. In the past tense, an intransitive verb agrees with the subject, while a transitive verb agrees with the direct object. Marathi shares this 'ergative' pattern with other Indo-Aryan languages. The agent of transitive verb is marked with *-ne* only in the third person (see examples (44)–(47)). (For further discussion, see Pandharipande (1991).)

The paradigm of the transitive verb in the past tense is illustrated by

(23) Transitive verb *karṇe* 'to do'

	Singular	Plural
Masculine	kelā	kele
Feminine	kelī	kelyā
Neuter	kela	kelī

In the above example, the agreement is with the direct object and the subject is either in the first or in the third person, and the verb does not have any agent marking. With a second person subject, the verb takes additional second person (agent) markers (*-s* for singular, and *-t* for plural): *kelā-s /kele-t* (masculine), *kelī-s/kelī-t* (feminine) and *kela-s/ kelī-t* (neuter).

Although *-l* is described as the future tense marker (in the traditional grammars), there is variation in the marking of the future tense in different persons as in:

(24) *pāhṇe* 'to see':

	Singular		Plural	
	mas	fem	mas	fem
1p	pāhīn	pāhīn	pāhū	pāhū
2p	pāhśīl	pāhśīl	pahāl/pāhāl	pahāl/pāhāl
3p	pahīl	pāhīl	pāhtīl	pāhtīl

2.4.2 Aspect

In Marathi, as in Hindi, imperfective and perfective aspect markers are homophonous with the present and past tense markers *-t* and *-l* respectively. When a verb is not followed by any auxiliary verb, it expresses present and past tense, and when it is followed by the auxiliary *as* 'to be', it expresses the perfect aspect. Various tense-forms of *as* 'to be' express the imperfect and perfect aspect in different tenses – present, past, and future.

The following examples illustrate these three types of perfect aspect.

(25) *present perfect*:

gītā   śāḷet   gelī   āhe
Geeta   school-loc   go-perf-3sf   be-pres-3s
'Geeta has gone to school.'

(26) *past perfect*:
 sohan kāl   dewḷāt gelā   hotā
 Sohan yesterday temple-loc go-perf-3sm be-pst-3sm
 'Sohan had gone to the temple yesterday.'

(27) *future perfect*:
 tū yesīl   to paryãnta mī Nāgpūrlā gelī/e   asen
 you come-fut-2s then by   I Nagpur-dat go-perf-1sf be-fut-1sf
 'By the time you come (lit: 'you will come'), I will have gone to Nagpur.'

The perfect aspect is also expressed in Marathi by using the past/perfective participial form of the verb followed by the auxiliary verb (which indicates the tense). Marathi shares this feature of perfect aspect with the Dravidian language Kannada (see Sridhar (1990: 228–9)). The perfective participles *gelelī*, *gelelā* and *gelele* replace their corresponding perfective forms in (25), (26) and (27) respectively.

The progressive aspect is expressed by using the existential form of the copula *as* 'to be', which immediately follows the imperfective form of the verb (marked with *-t*) as in (28).

(28) *present progressive*:
 madhū āŋghoḷ karīt/karat/karte āhe
 Madhu bath-sf do-prog   is
 'Madhu is taking a bath.'

Unlike the above pattern in SM, Nagpuri Marathi, like Hindi, has the progressive marker – the auxiliary verb *rāh* 'to live' (in its perfective form, as in (29)) which bears the agreement markers. The main verb is in the conjunctive participial form. (For details see Pandharipande (1986).)

(29) mula   kheḷūn   rāhilī   āhet
 children-pl.n play-conj.part prog-perf-3pl.n be-pres-3pl
 'The children are playing.'

There is no separate marker for the habitual aspect. Present imperfect expresses habitual aspect as well. The present imperfect verb form followed by the copula *as* 'be', with appropriate tense and agreement markers, expresses past and future habitual aspect.

Marathi expresses moods by suffixes, auxiliaries, or by the combination of both. Marathi maintains the Old Indo-Aryan moods namely, indicative, imperative, optative and conditional. Indicative is the unmarked mood expressed in a statement in any tense. The second person, singular imperative form of the verb is the same as the stem. However, the rising intonation of the imperative distinguishes it from the stem. The plural/polite forms are marked by the suffix *-ā*, as in (30).

(30) | | verb stem/
imperative singular | | plural/polite
imperative plural |
|---|---|---|---|
| (a) | kar | 'do' | karā |
| (b) | ho | 'be' | whā |

The optative suffix *-wa* (and its variants) when added to the verb stem expresses suggestion, demand and obligation (for further discussion, see Pandharipande (1990)). The subject/agent of the intransitive (31) as well as the transitive verb (32) takes the suffix *-ne* (same as the ergative) and the verb does not agree with the subject/agent in both cases.

(31) tine   ātā   gharī   dzāwe
she-ag now home-loc go-opt-3sn
'She may go home now.'

(32) tyāne   kame   karāwīt
he-ag jobs-pl.n do-opt-3pl.n
'He should do the jobs.'

Conditional is expressed by (a) the present tense form of the verb *-asṇe* 'to be'; and (b) *-asṇe* 'to be' marked with *-lā* (and its variants). While the form in (a) refers to the condition in the past, the form in (b) refers to the condition in the future. In both cases the main verb precedes the auxiliary *-as ṇe* and can occur in the perfect, imperfect, progressive, perfective participle, and potential aspect. The following examples of the verb *dzāṇe* 'to go' illustrate those forms.

(33) Past conditional perfect   gelā astā
     Past conditional imperfect progressive   dzāt astā
     Past conditional perfect participle   gelelā astā
     Past conditional potential   dzāṇār astā

(34) Conditional perfect   gelā aslā
     Conditional imperfect progressive   dzāt aslā
     Conditional perfect participle   gelelā aslā
     Conditional potential   dzāṇār aslā

It should be noted here that the form *-aslā* in (34) may be replaced by the future tense form *asel* of the verb *asṇe* 'to be'.

2.4.3 Conjunct verbs

Marathi has a highly productive process of deriving verbs from nouns, e.g. *pasanta* 'choice' : *pasanta karṇe* 'to do choice', 'to choose'. This process is used to assimilate borrowings from English, Persian and Sanskrit. Adjectives and adverbs also occur in the place of nouns.

Noun	Marathi verb	Conjunct verb
(35) śɔk 'shock' (E)	bas-ṇe 'to sit'	śɔk basṇe 'to get a shock'
(36) nirṇay 'decision' (Skt)	ghe-ṇe 'to take'	nirṇay gheṇe 'to decide'
(37) tārīf 'praise' (P)	kar-ṇe 'to do'	tārīf karṇe 'to praise'

2.4.4 Serial verbs

Marathi uses verb-serialization as one of the most productive processes to express aspectual, and other meanings. The major types are discussed below.

(a) Compound verbs:
    Compound verbs involve a sequence of a main verb and an explicator (auxiliary). The primary meaning of this compound is determined by the lexical meaning of the main verb. The explicator verb adds an additional meaning to the meaning of the main verb (in conjunctive participial form) and receives the tense and aspectual marking, as in (38).

(38) tyāne   patra   lihūn   ṭākla
he-ag letter-sn write-conj.part drop-pst-3sn
'He wrote off the letter' (to get rid of the responsibility of writing it!).

Some commonly used explicators and their meanings are given below:

(i)   *deṇe* 'to give': expresses action performed for the beneficiary other than the
      agent: *mī tyālā ghar* **gheūn deīn** 'I will buy a house for him.'
(ii) *yeṇe* 'to come': indicates action toward the subject or the focal point: *ti-tse
      ḍoḷe* **bharūn āle** 'Her eyes got filled up with tears.'
(iii) *dzāṇe* 'to go': indicates action away from the subject or the focal point or
      action performed inadvertently: *tī he* **bolūn gelī** 'She said this inadvertently.'
(iv) *gheṇe* 'to take': expresses action beneficial to the agent: *te kapḍe* **dhuūn ghetīl**
      'They will get the clothes washed for themselves.'
(v)   *dākhawṇe* 'to show': indicates determination of the subject to complete the
      action: *mī ḍɔkṭar* **houn dākhwīn** 'I will certainly become a doctor.'
(vi) *soḍṇe* 'to leave': indicates determination of the subject to pursue the action
      until its completion: *tyāne tilā weḍa* **karūn soḍla**: 'He drove her crazy.'

(b) Modal verbs:
Marathi uses various auxiliary/modal verbs, such as *pāhidʒe* 'should', *deṇe* 'to
allow', *lāw* 'to force to do', *lāg* 'have to', etc., which modify the meaning of the
main verb (see section 3.2).

(c) Reduplication:
Reduplication of verbs expresses various meanings:

(i) intensification of the meaning of the verb:

     (39) present progressive:
          kām karat karat ...
          'while continuously doing the work'

     (40) conjunctive participle:
          kām karūn karūn thaklā
          'He got tired of continuously doing the work.'

     (41) verb stem:
          tī raḍ raḍ raḍlī
          'She cried a lot.'

(ii) a sequence of gerunds to express the meaning 'as soon as':

     (42) *anū gharī ālyā ālyā dzhopte*
          'Anu goes to sleep as soon as she comes home.'

(d) Negation by verb serialization: (cf. section 3.8).

3 SYNTAX

The word order in a Marathi sentence is subject, object, verb. Adjectives or other
nominal complements precede or follow the noun depending upon their attributive or
predicative function. Adverbs generally immediately precede the verb. The position of
the verb is relatively fixed. Since the grammatical functions of nouns are expressed by

the case-suffixes/postpositions and verb agreement, their position is flexible. A change in focus affects the word order.

3.1 Verb agreement

Generally, the verb agrees with the unmarked noun. When the subject is not followed by a suffix/postposition, the verb agrees with it:

(43) tī āmbe khāte
she mango-pl.m eat-pres-3sf
'She eats mangoes.'

If the subject is followed by a suffix, the verb agrees with the unmarked object:

(44) mulī-ne gāṇī mhaṭlī
girl-ag song-pl.n sing-pst-3pl.n
'The girl sang songs.'

When both the subject and the object are marked with a suffix, the verb remains in its unmarked form (3rd person, singular, masculine):

(45) rām-ne pakṣānnā uḍawla
rām-ag bird-pl.m fly-caus-sn
'Rām made the birds fly (away).'

The following are the exceptions: (a) the transitive verb in a perfective ergative sentence agrees with the object even when the subject (in the first and the second person) is unmarked:

(46) mī/āmhī/tū/tumhī gāṇī mhaṭlī
I,we, you (sg), you (pl) song-3pl.n sing-pst-3pl.n
'I/we/you (sg)/you (pl) sang songs.'

(b) Similarly, the verb agrees with the object in optative sentences, although the subject is unmarked (cf. (32)). (c) In the ergative constructions, it bears double (second person object-subject) agreement. Also, the verb optionally agrees with the object followed by a suffix as in (47).

(47) mī tilā pāhilī/pāhila
I she-acc see-pst–3sf/3sn
'I saw her.'

(For details on the ergative construction see Pandharipande (1991).)

3.2 Volitionality

Marathi makes a distinction between volitional and non-volitional verbs. Typical transitive volitional verbs are: *karṇe* 'to do', *mārṇe* 'to beat', *toḍṇe* 'to break'. Intransitive volitional verbs are *basṇe* 'to sit', *dzāṇe* 'to go', etc. The subject of these verbs is agent/actor and is in the nominative case (except in non-ergative constructions). However, a large number of intransitive verbs express non-volitional actions, e.g. *hoṇe* 'to happen', *tuṭṇe* 'to be broken', *paḍṇe* 'to fall'. Here the actor is either absent or it is indicated by an instrumental suffix *-ne/-kaḍūn* 'by' as in:

(48) (mādȝhyāne) baśī   phuṭlī
     (I-inst)   plate-sf break-pst-3sf
     'The plate broke (by me).'

A class of non-volitional verbs expressing psychological states require their subject
(who is the experiencer of these states) to take the dative suffix *-lā*, e.g. *rāg* (anger)*yeṇe*
(come) 'to be angry', *dukkha* (sorrow) *hoṇe* (happen) 'to be sorry', *ānanda* (joy) *hoṇe*
(happen) 'to be happy', *wāṭne* 'to feel', *āwaḍne* 'to like', etc. For example:

(49) āīlā   rāg   ālā
     mother-dat anger come-pst-ms
     'Mother became angry.'

Marathi has pairs of verbs which differ from each other in terms of volitionality: *disṇe*
'to happen to see' versus *pāhṇe* 'to deliberately look', *āṭhwaṇ yeṇe* 'to remember (lit:
for memory to come)' versus *āṭhwaṇ karṇe* 'to remember deliberately', etc. Volitionality
can be cancelled by using the explicator verb *dzāṇe* 'to go' following the main volitional
verb: *to he bolūn* (said) *gelā* (went) 'He said this inadvertently.' Where it is implied that
the action is performed without the performer's volition, the subject takes the dative
suffix *-lā*, e.g. (a) the obligational construction: *tyālā* (he-dat) *dzāwa lāgel* (will have to
go) 'He will have to go', and (b) the causative construction: *mī* (I) *tilā* (she-dat) *khāylā*
(to eat) *lāwte* (force) 'I force her to eat.'

3.3 Passive

While the passive is not used frequently in the spoken and informal registers of Marathi,
its use in the written and formal registers of newspapers and official correspondence is
quite common. The passive sentences with the agent express the agent's capability to
carry out the action expressed by the verb. This usage of the passive construction is
commonly shared by other Indo-Aryan languages such as Hindi, Kashmiri, Nepali and
Panjabi but not by the Dravidian languages. (For a detailed discussion, see
Pandharipande (1981).) Only the volitional transitive verbs form passives. The passive
verb expresses the capability determined by agent-internal factors as in (50). Unlike the
passive, the modal *śakṇe* 'can' is neutral with regard to the capability of the agent.

(50) mādȝhyā   kaḍūn   kām   kela gela nāhī
     I-obl   by   work   do-pst-3sn go-pst-3sn neg
     (passive)
     'The work was not done by me.' (I was unable to do the work due to a headache,
     pain, bad mood, etc.)

An agentless/impersonal passive sentence also expresses a volitional act (51) and
therefore, it is semantically different from the other agentless construction (which
expresses a non-volitional act) (52).

(51) ghara   dzāḷḷī   gelī
     houses–3pl.n burn-pst-3pl.n   go-pst-3pl.n (passive)
     'Houses were burnt (intentionally).

(52) ghara   dzaḷḷī
     houses-pl.n burn(intr)-3pl.n
     'Houses got burnt.'

3.4 Participles, gerunds and infinitives

In Marathi, participles are preferred over finite clauses for modifying nouns and for conjoining clauses. However, in contrast to other Indo-Aryan languages, participles in Marathi encode a full range of tense, aspect, voice, mood and polarity (positive/ negative) distinctions. In this respect, Marathi is similar to Dravidian languages. The adjectival (relative) participles are shown in (53)–(57).

(53) Present/habitual participle: *yeṇārā* (mas-sg)
come-pres.part
'The one who comes'

(54) Past / perfective: *ālelā* (mas-sg)
come-perf.part
'The one who has come'

(55) Future: *yeṇār aslelā* (mas-sg)
come-fut be-perf.part
'The one who is going to come'

(56) Progressive: *yet aslelā* (mas-sg)
come-prog be-perf.part
'The one who is (in the process) of coming'

(57) Passive: *kelā gelelā* (mas-sg)
do-perf go-perf.part
'That which is done'

All of the above participles have their respective negative counterparts formed by adding the negative particle *na*; e.g. *na yeṇārā* 'the one who does not come', *na ālelā* 'the one who has not come', etc. Additionally, adverbial participles ((58)–(61)) and (b) gerundive constructions ((62)–(63)) express various meanings.

Adverbial participles:

(58) Simultaneity of actions:
tī   kām   kartānā   gāte
she work do-pres.part   sing-pres-3sf
         (while doing)
'While doing (her) work, she talks.'

(59) The period of time:
tyālā tiha dzāūn   khūp diwas dzhāle
he-dat here go-conj.part many   day   happen-pst–3pl.m
'It has been many days since he has gone.'

(60) A conjunctive participle indicating a temporal sequence of actions:
raghū ne pustaka   utslūn   kapāṭāt   ṭhewlī
Raghu-ag book-pl.n pick up-conj.part cupboard-loc put-pst-3pl.n
'Having picked up the books, Raghu put (them) in the cupboard.' (i.e., Raghu first picked up the books and then he put them in the cupboard.)

(61) The past (perfective) participle is used to indicate time of the occurrence of the action in the matrix clause.

    rām   mumbaĩlā   gelā   astānā   tyātSyā   gharī   tsorī
    Ram   Bombay-dat   go-pst–3sm   be-part   he-poss   home-loc   theft-sf
    dzhālī
    happen-pst-3sf
    'When Ram had gone to Bombay his house was robbed.' (lit: 'When Ram had
    gone to Bombay, a theft occurred (at his house).')

The combinations gerund+*lā* (dative), and gerund+postposition in Marathi serve as gerundival constructions:

(62) gerund + dative suffix:
      tyālā   itha   ālyālā   ek   mahinā   dzhālā
      he-dat   here   come-ger-dat   one   month   happen-pst-3sm
      'It has been a month since he came.' (lit: 'A month has happened since he came.')

(63) gerund + postposition/suffix *pāsūn* 'since':
      itha   ālyāpāsūn   to   agdī   khūṣ   āhe
      here   come-ger-abl-since   he   absolutely   happy   is
      'He is absolutely happy since he came here.'

The coreferentiality of the subject in the matrix and the embedded clause is generally required in the case of conjunctive participles but not in other adverbial participles.

    The following adverbial construction is interesting because it involves the invariant form of the verb followed by the suffix-*ī* and a postposition or a noun (indicating time).

(64) anū   parat   yeīparyãnta   mī   dʒewṇār   nāhī
      Anu   back   come-till   I   eat-fut   neg
      'I will not eat till Anu returns.'

Infinitives are formed by adding the suffix -*ṇe* to the verb stem, e.g. *ye* 'come' : *yeṇe* 'to come'. These derived infinitives behave like (neuter) nouns and take case-suffixes/postpositions, e.g. *yeṇyā-lā* (dat.) 'for coming', *yeṇyā-muḷe* 'because of'. They lack subject-verb agreement and tense.

3.5 Relative clauses

Although participles are preferred, full relative and other subordinate clauses are used in linguistically determined environments (written langauge, emphasis, etc.). The relative marker is *dzo* and the correlative marker is *to*, homophonous with the remote demonstrative/third person pronoun. Both of these have their corresponding direct and oblique forms. The relative clause can precede or follow the main clause; it is not the constituent of the noun phrase as in (65). The relative and correlative pronouns agree with the head noun in gender and number. The deletion of the coreferential/identical Np in the main or the subordinate clause is optional.

(65) dzo mānūs itha rāhto   to   ø   madzhā   mitra   āhe
      rel   man   here   live-pres-3sm   cor   (man)   I-poss-sm   friend   is
      'The man who lives here is my friend.'

Variants of (65) are shown in (65a)–(65f) which differ from one another in terms of the deletion of the head noun phrase, copying and deletion of relative/correlative markers, and the sequential order of the relative and the main clause. The symbol ø indicates the site of the head noun phrase prior to its deletion.

Deletion of the identical NP in the relative clause:

(65a) dzo ø itha rāhto   to māṇūs mādzhā   mitra āhe
      rel ø here live-pres–3sm cor man   I-poss-sm friend is
      'The man who lives here is my friend.'

Deletion of the relative marker:

(65b) ø itha rāhto   to māṇūs mādzhā   mitra āhe
      ø here livepres-3sm cor man   I-poss-sm friend is
      'The man who lives here is my friend.'

Main clause precedes the relative clause:

(65c) to māṇūs mādzhā   mitra āhe dzo ø itha rāhto
      cor man   I-poss-sm friend is rel ø here lives
      'The man who lives here is my friend.'

Copying the correlative marker and insertion of the relative clause after the head noun:

(65d) to māṇūs dzo itha rāhto   to mādzhā mitra āhe
      cor man   rel here live-pres-3sm cor poss-ms friend is
      'The man who lives here is my friend.'

Deletion of the head noun phrase in the relative clause and copying the correlative:

(65e) to ø dzo itha rāhto   to māṇūs mādzhā   mitra āhe
      cor ø rel here live-pres–3sm cor man   I-poss-sm friend is
      'The man who lives here is my friend.'

Placement of the head NP after the correlative and relative markers followed by a copy of the correlative:

(65f) to dzo māṇūs itha rāhto   to mādzhā   mitra āhe
      cor rel man   here live-pres-3sm cor I-poss-sm friend is
      'The man who lives here is my friend.'

The head noun is moved to the sentence-initial position to indicate emphasis. Any constituent of the main and the subordinate clause except the verb can be relativized in a finite relative clause. While the participle can readily relativize any element in the main clause its use in relativizing the elements in the subordinate clause is rare. The restricted and non-restricted interpretation of the relative clauses is determined by the degree to which the head noun phrase is identifiable through various (including) non-linguistic clues. For discussion see Pandharipande 1997: 82–4.

3.6 Quotatives

In a manner comparable to what Dravidian languages do, Marathi uses the quotatives *mhaṇūn* 'having said', and *asa* 'thus' which occur elsewhere in the language as the conjunctive participle form of the verb *mhaṇ* 'say' and an adverbial relative particle respectively. Quotatives mark direct speech and follow the quoted material.

(66) anū udyā   yeīl   asa/mhanūn rām bollā
     Anu tomorrow come-fut-3sm quot   Ram say-pst-3sm
     '"Anu will come tomorrow," thus Ram said.'

Marathi uses the complimentizer *kī* (which it shares with other Indo-Aryan languages) to mark indirect speech; the quotative markers optionally occur after the subordinate clause as in (67).

(67) rām mhaṇto   kī   to/mī sindhī śikel/śiken   (asa/mhaṇūn)
     Ram say-pres-3sm comp he/I Sindhi learn-fut-3s/1s (quot)
     'Ram says that he will learn Sindhi.'

One of the most interesting features of the quotative markers *asa* and *mhaṇūn* is that these two can be used to introduce indirect speech as well. Consider example (68).

(68) tyātSī badlī   dzhālī   asa/mhaṇūn to bollā
     his   transfer happen-pst quot   he say-pst-3sm
     'He said (that) he had been transferred.' (lit: 'He said his transfer happened.')

3.7 Topic and emphasis

The sentence-initial position and the particles *tar* and *mhaṇdʒe* mark the topic.

(69) tudzha dzaṇa tar/mhaṇdʒe āwaśyak hota
     your   going emph   necessary was
     'It was indeed necessary for you to go.'
     (lit: 'Your going indeed was necessary.')

Additionally, emphasis is expressed by (rising) intonation, stress, particles (*-ts* 'only', *hī/suddhā* 'also'), movement of the emphasized element (to the postverbal position) (70), and repetition (cf. section 2.4.4). The particles which mark the topic also express emphasis.

(70) kāl   bādzārāt   gelā   hotā   to
     yesterday market-loc go-pst-3sm be-pst-3sm he
     'He had gone to the market yesterday (as opposed to anyone else).'

3.8 Negation

Marathi negation is expressed by the following: negative particles *na* and *nāhī* and the negative verbs *nāhī* 'does not exist' and *nako* 'do not want'; by prohibitive negative verbs *nako* 'do not do X' and *naye* 'should not do X'; and the verb used to negate identity *nawhe* 'X is not Y'. The negative particles precede, while the verbs follow, the negated element. Constituent negation can also be expressed by placing extra stress on the constituent.

Negative verbs:

(71) te   yethe nāhīt
     they here are not (neg-pl)
     'They are not here.'

nako 'do not want':

(72) tilā   ãmbe   nakot
     she-dat mangoes do not want (pl)
     'She does not want mangoes.'

nako 'do not do':

(73) tumhī   gharī   dzāū   nakā
you (pl) home-loc go   do not (pl)
'You (pl) do not go home.'

naye 'should not':

(74) mulãnnī   ase   sineme baghū nayet
children-ag like these movies see   should not (pl)
'The children should not see movies like this.'

nawhe 'X is not Y':

(75) mī tudʒhī   maitrīṇ   (Sudhā) nawhe
I   your-sf   friend-sf (Sudha) neg-s
'I am not your friend (Sudha).' (i.e., 'Do not mistake me for your friend Sudha, I am somebody else.')

When negative verbs are not in the sentence-final position, they negate the immediately preceding constituent.

(76) tyā   nāhīt   yethe
they are not (neg-pl) here
'They are not here (somebody else is (here)).'

The negative particle *na* is used to negate a participle (*na kartānā* 'while not doing'), infinitive (*na bolṇa* 'not talking'), and gerund (*na ālyāne* 'because of not coming').
    The other negative particle *nāhī* is used for constituent negation.

Negation of adverb:

(77) te   kāl   nāhī bādzārāt   gele
they yesterday neg   market-loc go-pst-3pl.m
'They did not go to the market yesterday (i.e., they went to market some other day).'

The negative particle *nāhī* lacks agreement marking and, therefore, differs from the homophonous verb *nāhī*.

4 PHONOLOGY

The distinctive segments of Standard spoken Marathi are given in tables 19.3 and 19.4.

TABLE 19.3: VOWELS AND DIPHTHONGS

		Front	Central	Back
High:	tense/long	i		u
	lax/short	I		U
Mid		e		o
Mid Low		əi, *æ	ə	əu, *ɔ
Low			a	

Note: * occurs only in words borrowed from English.

TABLE 19.4: CONSONANTS

		Labial	Dental	Alveolar	Retroflex	Alveopalatal	Velar	Glottal
Stop	vl. unasp.	p	t		ṭ		k	
	vl. asp.	ph	th		ṭh		kh	
	vd. unasp.	b	d		ḍ		g	
	vd. asp.	bh	dh		ḍh		gh	
Nasal		m	n		ṇ			
Flap					r			
Lateral					ḷ		l	
Affricate	vl. unasp.			ts		tS		
	vl. asp.			–		tSh		
	vd. unasp.			dz		dʒ		
	vd. asp.			dzh		dʒh		
Fricative	vl.	*f	s		ṣ	ś		h
	vd.	*v						
Semivowels		w					y	

Note: * occurs only in words borrowed from English or Persian/Arabic.

The vowel segments /i/, /I/, /e/, /əi/, /æ/, /ə/, /a/, /u/, /U/, /o/, /əu/ and /ɔ/ are transcribed as /ī/, /i/, /e/, /ai/, /æ/, /a/, /ā/, /ū/, /u/, /o/, /au/ and /ɔ/, respectively. Also, it is important to mention here that the precise difference between ə and a is not very clear at this point. Therefore, although in table 19.3 I have characterized these two vowels as qualitatively different, more research is needed to resolve this ambiguity.

Marathi has retained the old Indo-Aryan contrasts between voiced aspirated and unaspirated stops (*ghār* 'kite' versus *gār* 'cold') and between voiceless aspirated and unaspirated stops (*phār* 'a lot' versus *pār* 'shore'). Similarly, another Indo-Aryan feature, retroflexion, is retained. Unlike Hindi, Marathi does not have retroflex flaps /r̥/ and /r̥h/. It does have a retroflex liquid /ḷ/ which contrasts with the voiced dental lateral liquid /l/ (*pāḷ* 'raise' versus *pāl* 'lizard'). Affricates are a salient feature of Marathi. It distinguishes the alveolar affricates from their palatal counterparts (*-tsal* 'come along' versus *tSal* 'moving element'), voiceless from voiced (*dʒap* 'repetition of God's name' versus *dzap* 'take care!'), as well as aspirated and unaspirated affricates (*dzarā* 'a little' versus *dzharā* 'a small spring'). Alveolar affricates are palatized, obligatorily before /y/ and /i/ and optionally before /e/. This palatalization is not reflected in the orthography. The voiceless retroflex (apico-post-alveolar) sibilant /ṣ/ is largely restricted to Sanskrit vocabulary. The voiceless labio-dental fricative is used only loanwords from English and Perso-Arabic sources; e.g. *fī* 'fee' (English), *tārīf* 'praise' (Perso-Arabic). Similarly, a voiced labio-dental fricative /v/ is restricted to vocabulary borrowed from English, e.g. *VCR, vote*, etc. However, a large number of Marathi speakers replace it with the voiced bilabial glide /w/.

Marathi maintains the contrast between /a/ and /ā/ (*dzaḍ* 'heavy', and *dzāḍ* 'thick') /i/ and /ī/ (*tSir* 'cut!', and *tSīr* 'a cut'), and /u/ and /ū/ (*pur* 'bury!', *and pūr* 'flood'). This distinction is neutralized in word-final position where vowels are generally long. The vowels /ɔ/ and /æ/ are restricted to English borrowings such as *dɔktar* 'doctor', and *hæt* 'hat'. Also, the morphophonemic alternation of vowels of *guṇa* and *vṛddhi* is maintained in a large number of verb roots and nominal compounds (e.g. *phuṭ-ṇe* 'to be broken' and *phoḍne* 'to break', and *parama* + *īśwar* = *parameśwar*.).

There are no inherently nasal vowels in contemporary Standard Marathi. Vowels are nasalized before a nasal consonant, e.g. *ā̃mbā* 'mango', *tõṇd* 'month'. Kelkar (1958: 12) claims that vowels are semi-nasalized before a nasal. An in-depth analysis of the nasalization of vowels is necessary. The question of the phonemic contrast between oral and nasal vowels is controversial in Marathi and in other Indo-Aryan languages (see Masica 1991: 117 for further details). In contemporary Standard Marathi, the nasal vowels of Old Marathi are realized either as a sequence of a nasalized vowel and a nasal consonant homorganic with the following consonant (*mulā̃-nā* > *mulā̃nnā* 'to the children') or simply as an oral vowel (*gharā̃-t* > *gharāt'in* 'many houses') although the orthography may show nasalization (i.e., *gharā̃t*). However, South-Konkani and some other dialects of Marathi do maintain this phonemic contrast. The adverbs *kẽwhā̃* 'when', *tẽwhā̃* 'then', *dʒẽwhā̃* 'when' (rel) of Old Marathi have lost the nasalization on the final vowel. In these examples there is alternation between /ẽ/ and /e/ in contemporary Marathi. It should be noted here that those speakers who pronounce a nasal /ẽ/ in *kẽwhā*, *tẽwhā*, and *dʒẽwhā* add a nasal consonant /m/ after it and also tend to retain the nasality on the final vowel. Thus the pronunciation of these words in this case is *kẽmwhā̃*, *tẽmwhā̃* and *dʒẽmwhā̃* or alternatively, *kẽw̃whā̃*, *tẽw̃whā̃* and *dʒẽw̃whā̃* where /m/ is replaced by a nasalized glide /w/. Although in orthography there is a free alternation between /ẽ/ and /e/, the word final /ā̃/ of Old Marathi words is always represented as /ā/.

Marathi has a nasal diphthong /ā̃ũ/ which is restricted to loanwords from Sanskrit. Historically, this nasal diphthong is a result of *aṁ* changing to *ā̃ũ*. This change is restricted to Sanskrit loans. The deletion of /ṁ/ takes place only before sibilants and liquids. Examples are given below.

Sibilant:

(78) haṁs   →   hā̃ũs   'swan'

Liquid:

(79) saṁrakṣaṇ   →   sā̃ũrakṣaṇ 'protection'

Glides /y/ and /w/ are nasalized when preceded or followed by a nasalized vowel.

(80) (i) tyā-tsa   'his'
          he-poss-3sn
     (ii) tyā̃-tsa   'their'
          they-poss-3pl.m

4.1 Canonical syllable

A canonical syllable in Marathi consists minimally of a single vowel, which may be short or long, preceded by up to three consonants, and which may be followed by a single consonant:

(C) (C) (C) V (V) (C)

Syllable boundaries in Marathi fall as follows: between successive vowels (*ā-ī* 'mother'), between a vowel and the following consonant (*ḍo-ḷā* 'eye'), and between two consonants (*kap-ḍā* 'cloth'). If there is a triple cluster in the medial position, in a bisyllabic word, the first consonant is assigned to the first syllable, while the other two consonants are assigned to the second syllable, e.g. *tan + tra – > tantra* 'technique'.

4.2 Stress

Stress is not distinctive in Marathi. It is perhaps one of the least investigated areas of Marathi phonology. Therefore any statement about the role of stress is tentative at this point. Syllable stress is determined by the weight of the syllable. The distinction between light and heavy syllables is based on the length of the vowel and the coda consonant, if any. Thus, CV is a light syllable and CVV and CVC are heavy and CVV(C) is super heavy. *[ī]*, *[ū]*, *[ā]*, *[e]* and *[o]* are treated as VV and *[a]*, *[i]* and *[u]* are treated as V.

Stress rules:

(i) In a word, if there is only one heavy or a super heavy syllable, it is always stressed regardless of its position. In the following examples, bold and underlined letters show the locus of the main/primary stress in a word.

(81) i**t̲h̲e̲**   'there'
      d**ā̲**ra   'doors'
      u̲ṣṭa   'polluted'
      sam**a̲**sta   'entire'
      mhāt**ā̲**rpaṇa 'old ages'

(ii) In bisyllabic words, if both syllables are heavy, then the initial syllable gets stressed.

(82a) w**ā̲**rā   'wind'

If both syllables are light, then the first is stressed.

(82b) ph**a̲**ḷa   'fruit (pl)'

(iii) There are no trisyllabic words in which all syllables are light. In trisyllabic words, when the first two syllables are heavy, the first syllable is stressed.

(83a) dh**ī̲**rāna   'courageously'
       bh**ā̲**wātsa   'brother's'

If all syllables are heavy, the stress falls on the first syllable.

(83b) p**ā̲**wsāḷā   'rainy season'

If the second and the third syllables are heavy, the stress is on the second syllable.

(83c) puḍh**ā̲**rī   'leader'

If only the last syllable is heavy, the stress is on that syllable.

(83d) garib**ī̲**   'poverty'

If the middle syllable is heavy, the stress is on that syllable.

(83e) duk**ā̲**na   'shops'

The stress rules are equally applicable to nouns and verbs. Stress on a word is used for emphasis (cf. section 3.7).

4.3 Intonation

There is no systematic study of the patterns of intonation in Marathi. However, the most commonly observed patterns are given below.

(i)   Yes-no, tag, reconfirmation and echo questions have a final rising intonation.
(ii)   Reconfirmation questions (in which the focused constituent is fronted) have a final rising intonation.
(iii) Echo questions have a final rising intonation.
(iv)   Statements, information questions, imperatives and blessings, curses and doubt have a final falling intonation.
(v)   Similarly, repeated affirmative responses (*ho, ho* 'yes, yes') or negative responses (*nāhī, nāhī* 'no, no') have a level intonation.
(vi)   The process of extra vowel lengthening is used to express emphatic intonation. In the example (84) below, the underlined vowel is extra long. The extra length of a vowel in orthography is generally indicated by the use of the symbol *s* (which Marathi has retained from Sanskrit *avagraha*) after the vowel. This symbol is repeated to express increased emphasis.
(vii) Contrastive stress may be used to shift the peak of intonation to the stressed syllable or to create an additional intonation peak, as in (84).

    (84) to   tSalākh   mulgā   āhe
         he   clever   boy   is
         'He is a clever boy. (as opposed to naive)'

Change in the intonational pattern affects the syntactic/semantic function of the sentence. For example, the final rising intonation in a statement transforms the statement into a question without an overt question word.

4.4 Morphophonological processes

(a) Nasal assimilation

    Stops become homorganic nasals before nasals (+ denotes a morpheme boundary in the following example):

    (85) bhagawat + nām   →   bhagawannām 'god's name'
         god   + name

(b) Retroflexion

    (i)   /l/ becomes /ḷ / after /ḷ/ .

         (86) kaḷ-l-a   →   kaḷḷa   '(it was) found out'
              find out-pst-3sn

    (ii) /t/ becomes /ṭ / after /ṭ /

         (87) ghoṭ-tānā   →   ghoṭṭānā   'while stirring'
              stir-adv.part

(c) Palatalization

   (i) Alveolar affricates are palatalized before the high front vowel and the palatal glide.

    (88) sudhā–ts-ī   →   sudhātSī   'Sudha's (3sf)
          Sudha-poss-sf

    (89) dzo-ā   →   dʒyā   'who' (obl)
          who-obl

   (ii) The dental stop /t / is palatalized before a palatal affricate.

    (90) sat   + dʒan   →   sadʒdʒan   'good people/person'
          good + people/person

   (iii) A dental sibilant is palatalized before a palatal sibilant.

    (91) has   + śīl   →   haśśīl   'you will laugh'
          be   + fut-2s

4.5 High vowel shortening

High vowels /ī/, /ū/ are shortened to /i/ and /u/ respectively, when followed by either a vowel-initial or consonant-initial suffix.

(92) pī 'drink'   →   pi-īn   'I will drink'
               drink-fut-1s

(93) dhū 'wash'   →   dhu-to   'he washes'
               wash-pres–3sm

4.6 Glide formation

Stem final /ī/ and /ū/ change to /y/ and /w/ respectively before /ā/.

(94) telī-āt   →   telyāt   'in the oilman'
    oilman-loc

(95) lāḍū-ā-lā   →   lāḍwālā   'to the desert (lāḍū)'
    lāḍū-incr-dat

4.7 Vowel raising

There is no vowel raising in SM (except in fast speech, cf. example (110)). However, in the Nagpuri variety of Marathi, the first person singular feminine agreement suffix /e/ (used for the subject of intransitive verbs in past tense) as well as the agentive marker -*ne* (in perfective) have a morphological variant /ī/, as in the following example.

(96) āle   →   ālī   'I came'
    come-pst-1sf

4.8 Vowel lowering

Vowel lowering is absent in Standard Marathi. However, in the Nagpuri variety of Marathi, the neuter plural (past tense) suffix /ī/ has a morphological variant /e/ as in the following example.

(97) ghare paḍlī   →   ghara   paḍle
                          houses   fall-pst-3pl.n
                          'houses fell'

However, the marker /e/ in *ghare* is optionally lowered to /a/ (pronounced as a lengthened schwa) in all varieties of Marathi. Historically, the /e/ marker was nasalized. In the variety of Marathi spoken in Konkan and Goa the nasalized /ẽ/ is still maintained. In other varieties (i.e., Puṇe, Bombay, Nagpurī and Khāndeśī), the nasalization is maintained only in the speech of people over 60 years old. This loss of nasalization (except in the speech of the people in Konkan and Goa) is a widespread phenomenon in Marathi. In orthography, the marker of nasalization (i.e., *anusvāra* indicated by the dot above the horizontal line on the consonant) is still maintained on the final consonant, although it functions as the phonetically lengthened vowel /a/ in contemporary Marathi. Examples (98)–(103) illustrate the process.

Neuter third person plural:

(98) mulẽ   →   mula/mule   'children'

Neuter third person singular:

(99) khelṇẽ   →   khelna/khelṇe   'toy'

Infinitive:

(100) bolṇẽ–3sn   →   bolna/bolṇe   'talk'

Neuter third person singular verb suffix:

(101) dilẽ   →   dila/dile   'gave (3sn)'

Pronouns/adverb:

(102) kasẽ   →   kasa/kase   'how'

(103) ithẽ (adv) →   itha/ithe   'here'

4.9 Vowel lengthening

Word-final short vowel /i/ is lengthened in words inherited or borrowed from Sanskrit

(104) mati   →   matī   'intellect'

4.10 Metathesis

When *ho* and *hū* are followed or preceded by the vowel /a/ or /ā/, the /o/ and /u/ change to /w/, and /h/ and /w/ are metathesized to yield the /wh/ sequence. Examples:

(105) ho-ā   →   whā   'be!'
      be-imp-2pl

(106) gahū-ā-tsa   →   gawhātsa   'of the wheat'
      wheat-incr-poss-3sm

4.11 Deletion and insertion

4.11.1 Deletion processes

The following types of deletion processes are observed:

(a) Intervocalic degemination:

    gãmmat-ī-ne   →   gamtīne   'jokingly'

(b) Word-final schwa deletion
     A large number of noun/adjective-stems borrowed from Sanskrit lose their word-final schwa.

    (107) vidʒaya(Skt) → vidʒay   'victory'

    (108) rakṣaka(Skt) → rakṣak   'protector'

However, Marathi retains the word-final schwa of Sanskrit stems if deletion would result in a consonant cluster word-finally. Also, schwa deletion may fail to apply in a few *tatsama* words (i.e., words inherited from Sanskrit e.g. *sama* 'similar to', *tSala* 'moving', etc.). In fact, this word-final schwa is a marker of the Sanskritized register of modern Marathi.

    (109) hasta (Skt)   →   hasta   'hand'

(c) The stem final vowel /e/ is optionally deleted before /ī/ (in the fast speech).

    (110) de-īn   →   deīn/dīn   'I will give'
         give-fut-is

(d) A long vowel in a final syllable is deleted when a suffix with a long vowel is added.

    (111) parīṭ-ā-lā   →   parṭālā   'to a washerman'
         washerman-incr-dat

(e) When a suffix/postposition is added, deletion of the short vowels /a/, /i/, and /u/ in open (including the stem final) but non-initial syllable is a common process in Marathi

    (112) gavat-ā-var   →   gavtāvar   'on the grass'
         grass-incr-on

4.11.2 Insertion processes

(a) An increment vowel is inserted between nominal, infinitival, adjectival and participial stems and the case-suffixes or postpositions (cf. section 2.1).
(b) The environments for glide insertion are described below.
    (i) /y/ is inserted between /ī/ and /ā/ and /w/ is inserted between /ū/ and /ā/.

        (113) bī-ā   →   bi-y-ā   'seeds'
           seed-pl

(114) dhū - ā → dhu-w-ā 'wash (imp-pl)'
wash-conj.part

(ii) /w/ is optionally inserted when /e/ and /o/ are followed by /ū/.

(115) ho-ūn → howūn 'having become'
be-conj.part

(116) ghe-ūn → ghewūn/ gheūn 'having taken'

(c) Vowel insertion for cluster simplification
Word-initial consonant clusters are simplified by the insertion of a vowel between the two consonants. The strategy of inserting a vowel before or after the cluster is also frequently used to move the cluster to the medial position. This process is restricted to the speech of uneducated Marathi speakers.

(i) Vowel-insertion between consonants:

(117) bhyālā → bhiyālā 'he feared'
fear-pst-3sm

(ii) Vowel-insertion in initial position:
This insertion is observed in borrowings from English and Sanskrit.

(118) steśan(E) → iṣṭeśan 'station'
station
strī (Skt) → istrī 'woman'

(iii) Word-final vowel-insertion:
A vowel is inserted word-finally to move the consonant cluster to the medial position in all varieties of Marathi.

(119) durust → durusta 'repaired'
repaired

In order to avoid word-final consonant clusters, final vowels in borrowed Sanskrit vocabulary are retained in Marathi (e.g. *mukta* 'free', *aṣṭa* 'eight', *puṣpa* 'flower', etc.)

(iv) In order to avoid consonant clusters word-finally, -*a* vowel is inserted between the two consonants.

(120) tsālat - ts → tsālatats 'walking, indeed!'
walk - emph

4.12 Gemination

/ū/ and /ī/ followed by /w/ and /y/ respectively are subject to a process that results in glide gemination, as shown in the following examples.

(121) naū - wādztā → nawwādztā 'at nine o'clock'
nine - at

(122) nāhī - yet → nāhyyet 'does not come'
neg - come-pres

5 CONCLUSION

To sum up, Marathi grammar maintains a combination of the salient features of Modern Indo-Aryan such as the SOV word order, compound verbs, ergativity, volitional verbs and experiencer subjects, and of the Dravidian features such as the quotatives, participles and negative verbs. Also, the above discussion shows the impact of Marathi's contact with Sanskrit, Persian and English on its structure. A few remarks on the functional impact of the contact are in order. The two major Marathi styles are *grānthik* 'written/literary' (marked by Sanskrit borrowings) and *bolbhāṣā* 'spoken/colloquial' (with Perso-Arabic and English borrowings). The presence of the English lexicon as well as syntax has increased in the last 100 years in the spoken language. However, the use of the Sanskrit lexicon distinguishes formal Marathi speech from its colloquial counterpart.

At present, the style/registral repertoire of the Marathi speech community includes three well-defined styles/registers: Sanskritized, Persianized and Englishized. These are used in mutually exclusive domains. The Sanskritized style/register (which is marked by the extensive use of Sanskrit vocabulary and syntax) is used in the religious domain and the formal speech. The Persianized style/register is used in courts of law, police stations, etc. The Englishized style/register marks the colloquial educated speech and is used at social gatherings, in business transactions, etc. (For further discussion on style repertoire, see Pandharipande (forthcoming).)

The Marathi speech community in Maharashtra is largely bi/multilingual and diglossic. Its linguisitc repertoire is large, generally including a local dialect, the Standard dialect and Hindi. The functional distribution of these codes is given below:

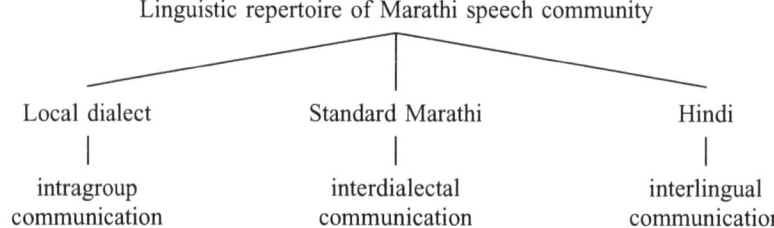

Linguistic repertoire of Marathi speech community

Local dialect	Standard Marathi	Hindi
intragroup communication	interdialectal communication	interlingual communication

In addition to the above three codes, the languages of other states (such as Gujarati, Kannada, Telugu) are included in the repertoire of Marathi speakers in the areas which intersect with other states.

NOTES

1 It must be noted that the term *konkaṇī* used here refers to the regional dialect of Marathi spoken in the coastal area of Konkan in the Maharashtra state and not to the separate language *Konkaṇī* which is primarily spoken in Goa, and by the people who migrated from Goa to Maharashtra, Karnataka and Kerala (for further discussion on *Konkaṇī* as a separate language, see Miranda 1992: 213–21).
2 Tables 19.2–4 are taken from Pandharipande, R. V. (1997) *Marathi*, London, New York: Routledge (1997).

REFERENCES

Agnihotri, D. H. (1983) *Abhinav Marathi-Marathi Śabdakoś*, Poona: Venus Publishing House.
Apte, M. L. (1962) *A Sketch of Marathi Transformational Grammar,* Ph.D. Dissertation, Madison: University of Wisconsin.
Arjunwadkar, K. S. (1987) *Marathi Vyākaraṇ: Vād āṇi Pravād*, Pune: Sulekha Prakashan.
Bloch, J. (1920) *La Formation de la Langue Marathe*, (English translation (1970) *The Formation of the Marathi Language,* by D. R. Chanana), Delhi: Motilal Banarsidass.
Burgess, E. (1854) *A Grammar of the Marathi Language*, Bombay: American Mission Press.
Carey, W. (1805) *A Grammar of the Mahratta Language*, Serampur: The Mission Press.
Damle, M. K. (1911) *Śāstrīya Marathi Vyākaraṇ*, Pune: Damodar Sawalaram ani Company. (1965 edition).
Ghatage, A. M. (1963) *A Survey of Marathi Dialects*, Bombay: Maharashtra State Literature and Culture Board.
Gramopadhye, G. B. (1941) *Peśwe Daptarātīl Marāṭhī Bhāṣetse Swarūp*, Pune: Nerlekar.
Grierson, G. A. (1905) *Linguistic Survey of India, Vol. VII*, Calcutta: Office of the Superintendent of Government Printing (Reprint (1967), Delhi: Motilal Banarsidass).
Kelkar, A. R. (1958) *The Phonology and Morphology of Marathi*, Ph.D. Dissertation, Ithaca: Cornell University.
Masica, C. P. (1991) *The Indo-Aryan Languages*, New York: Cambridge University Press.
Master, A. (1967) *A Grammar of Old Marathi*, Oxford: Clarendon Press.
Miranda, R. V. (1992) 'Language standardization in progress: the case of Konkani', in Dimock, Jr., E. C., Kachru, B. and Krishnamurty, Bh., *Dimensions of Sociolinguistics in South Asia*, New Delhi: Oxford & IBH Publishing Company. Pvt. Ltd., pp. 213–21.
Pandharipande, R. (1981) *Syntax and Semantics of the Passive Construction in Selected South Asian Languages*, Ph.D. Dissertation, Urbana: University of Illinois at Urbana–Champaign.
—— (1986) 'Language contact and language variation: Nagpuri Marathi' in Krishnamurti, Bh., Masica, C. and Sinha, A. (eds) *South Asian Languages: Structure, Convergence, and Diglossia,* Delhi: Motilal Banarsidass, pp. 219–31.
—— (1990) 'Experiencer (dative) NPs in Marathi', in Verma, M. K., and Mohanan, K. P. (eds.) *Experiencer Subjects in South Asian Languages*, Palo Alto: Center for The Study of Language and Information, Stanford University, pp. 161–80.
—— (1991) 'Some issues related to ergativity in Marathi'. Presented at the 20th Annual Conference on South Asia in Verma, M. K. (ed.) *Verb Agreement in South Asian Languages* (Conference Proceedings of 20th Annual Conference on South Asia), (in press) Madison: University of Wisconsin.
—— (1997) *Marathi*. London, New York: Routledge.
—— (forthcoming) Sociolinguistic Dimensions of Marathi: Multilingualism in Central India, Delhi: Manohar.
Sridhar, S. N. (1990) *Kannada*, London: Routledge.

FURTHER READING

Cardona, G. (1974) 'Indo-Aryan Languages', *Encyclopedia Britannica*, 15th edition, Vol. 9: 439–50.
Dhongde, R. V. (1974) *Tense, Aspect, and Mood in English and Marathi*. Ph.D. Dissertation, Poona: University of Poona.
Gumperz, J. (1971) 'Convergence and Creolization: A Case from the Indo-Aryan/Dravidian Border in India', in Dil, A. (ed.) *Language in Social Groups: Essays by John J. Gumperz*, Stanford: Stanford University Press, pp. 251–73.
Gupte, S. M. (1975) *Relative Constructions in Marathi*, Ph.D. Dissertation, Ann Arbor: Michigan State University.
Hook, P. E. (1990) 'Experiencers in South Asian languages: A gallery', in Verma, M. K., and Mohanan, K. P. (eds.) *Experiencer Subjects in South Asian Languages*, Stanford: The Center for the Study of Languages and Information, Stanford University, pp. 319–34.

Junghare, I. (1973) 'Restrictive Relative Clauses in Marathi', *Indian Linguistics*, pp. 34.4: 251–62.

Khokle, V. (1969) Two Models of Phonological Distinctive Features: An Evaluation as Applied to Marathi, Ph.D. Dissertation, University of Minnesota, Minneapolis.

Laddu, T. K. (1911) 'Genitive accusative in Marathi', *Journal of the Royal Asiatic Society*, London: 819–21.

Miranda, R. V. (1978) 'Caste, Religion, and Dialect Differentiation in the Konkani Area', in Kachru, B. B. and Sridhar, S. N. (eds.) *International Journal of the Sociology of Language* 16 (*Aspects of Sociolinguistics in South Asia*.), pp. 77–9.

Pandharipande, R. (1981) 'Nativization of Lexicon: The Case of Marathi', *Linguistics* 19: 987–1001.

Tulpule, S. G., (ed.) (1960) *An Old Marathi Reader*, Pune: Venus Prakashan.

Wali, K. (1976) *Two Marathi Reflexives and Their Implication for Causative Structure*, Ph.D. Dissertation, Syracuse: Syracuse University.

KONKANI

Rocky V. Miranda

CONTENTS

LIST OF TABLES

1 INTRODUCTION

1.1 General

Konkani is spoken in Goa as well as in parts of the neighbouring states of Maharashtra, Karnataka and Kerala where Konkani speakers from Goa migrated mostly after the Portuguese arrived. The Portuguese conquered the central portion of Goa in the first half of the sixteenth century. This consists of the talukas of Bardes and Tiswadi to the north of the river Zuari and the talukas of Saxtti and Mormugao to the south. They called this area Velhas Conquistas (Old Conquests). The peripheral portions of Goa consisting of all the other talukas were conquered in the latter half of the eighteenth century. So, these were called Novas Conquistas (New Conquests).

According to the Census of India 1991 (1991: 34), the number of Konkani speakers was 1,760,607. Of these, 602,626 (34.2%) were from Goa, 312,618 (17.8%) from Maharashtra, 706,397 (40.1%) from Karnataka and 64,008 (3.6%) from Kerala. Over 80% of the Konkani speakers in Maharashtra are from metropolitan Bombay. In Karnataka, over 80% of the Konkani speakers are from the coastal districts of North and South Kanara. At the time of the 1991 census, the (undivided) South Kanara district consisted of the present South Kanara and Udupi districts. Nearly half the Konkani speakers in Kerala are from the Ernakulam district.

Konkani speakers are mostly multilingual (68.4%, as calculated from data reported in the Census of India 1981a: 150) since they must learn other languages used in educational and other official spheres in various regions: Kannada and Malayalam in the southern states; Marathi in Maharashtra and, to some extent, in Goa; English in all the areas. Formerly, in Goa, many found it necessary to learn Portuguese as well. Konkani speakers need to communicate with their non-Konkani neighbours in a different language where the majority of the people speak other languages: e.g. Marathi or Bazaar Hindi in metropolitan Bombay, Kannada or Tulu in the coastal districts of Karnataka, and Malayalam in Kerala. The literacy level in the Konkani areas is higher than the national average. For instance, in Goa, Daman and Diu, where the majority of the population is Konkani-speaking, 57% of the people were literate according to the Census of India 1981 (1981b: 49). The medium of instruction in schools, however, is normally a different language.

Konkani is fragmented into numerous dialects according to region, religion and caste. Of these, the following five are the major dialects:

(i)   Goa Hindu Konkani, which is spoken all over Goa with minor variations.
(ii) Southern Saraswat Konkani, which is spoken by the Saraswat Brahmans of the coastal districts of Karnataka, and of Kerala. There are minor variations in the speech of these areas.
(iii) Bardes Christian Konkani, which is spoken in Bardes and Tiswadi, the northern part of the Old Conquests.
(iv) Saxtti Christian Konkani, which is spoken in Saxtti and Mormugao, the southern part of the Old Conquests.
(v)   Karnataka Christian Konkani, which is spoken in the coastal districts of Karnataka with minor variations.

There are minor differences between the speech of the Brahmans and the non-Brahmans. The differences between the speech of the Hindu Brahmans and non-Brahmans are the same as those between the speech of the Christian Brahmans and non-Brahmans. It is interesting that the Christians have retained these differences centuries after their conversion to Christianity. Both among the Hindus and the Christians in various regions, it is normally the Brahman dialects that are used in writing. For more information on Konkani dialects, see sections 3.2 and 3.3.

1.2 Konkani scripts

The Goan Hindus use the Nagari script in their writings but the Goan Christians use the Roman script. The Saraswats of Karnataka use the Nagari script in the North Kanara district but the Kannada script in Udupi and South Kanara. The Malayalam script was used in Kerala but now there is a move to use the Nagari script. The Karnataka Christians use the Kannada script.

The Nagari script has been adopted as the official script for Konkani in Goa. It has some practical advantages. It is the script of some of the major Indian languages with rich literature: Sanskrit, Marathi and Hindi. Because of the introduction of Hindi on a national basis, the Nagari script is likely to be readily learned by new generations of literate Konkani speakers in all the regions.

According to the statements of the Portuguese and other European missionaries who arrived in Goa in the sixteenth and seventeenth centuries, the usual script for Konkani at that time was Kannada and not Nagari. However, the European missionaries introduced the Roman script as they found it easier in writing as well as in printing. In the Roman script as used in Konkani writings some characters have special phonetic values: **tt, dd, nn,** and **ll** indicate the retroflex consonants [ṭ], [ḍ], [ṇ] and [ḷ] respectively. **nh** stands for [ñ]. Word-finally, **m** usually indicates that the preceding vowel is nasalized. In Old Konkani, the tilde is commonly used to indicate nasalization. In the manuscripts, a variant of the tilde that looks like ' is also used to indicate nasalization. Also in Old Konkani, [ə] and [a] are represented respectively by *a* and **a** in print and by **a** and **â** in manuscripts. In modern Goan Christian Konkani, [ə] has changed into [o] and, therefore, **a** now represents [a] alone. **ch** is pronounced as [č] before front vowels, but as [ts] elsewhere. Similarly, **z** is pronounced as [ǰ] before front vowels, but elsewhere it is [dz] or [z] ([dz] word-initially and [z] in other environments). **s** is [š] before front vowels. [š] is sometimes also written **x**, as in Portuguese. Also as in Portuguese, **c** is [k] in Konkani before back vowels and in final position, **qu** and **gu** represent just [k] and [g] respectively before front vowels, and **ç** stands for [s].

Some conventions have been proposed in the use of Nagari script for Konkani by various Konkani institutions. For the most part, they are arbitrary. According to these, the same sound *əy* must be written differently in different words. On the other hand, different Konkani phonemes such as *e* and *ɛ* or *o* and *ɔ* must be written the same way. Use of diacritics to indicate the difference between *e* and *ɛ* or *o* and *ɔ* is forbidden! There is no phonemic contrast either between short and long *i* or between short and long *u* in Konkani. However, short *i* and *u* are distinguished from long *i* and *u* in the Nagari script. In Konkani, long letters are to be used in the final syllable provided that it ends in a vowel or a single consonant or a two-consonant cluster beginning with *r*. The short letters are to be used elsewhere. For the most part, the use of short and long vowel letters in this fashion does not reflect any actual phonetic variation in Konkani. Only in monosyllables, vowels are predictably long in Konkani except when they end in a consonant cluster other than *r* followed by another consonant. In proper nouns and some unassimilated Sanskrit borrowings, etymological spellings are to be used.

1.3 Konkani during the Portuguese rule in Goa

When they first arrived in the sixteenth century, the Portuguese were quite zealous in imposing their creed and culture on the native population. They used coercion to spread Christianity among the Hindus. At the outset, the Portuguese missionaries made considerable effort to study the local language, Konkani, as they considered it essential in their proselytizing activities. Thanks to the Portuguese missionaries, Konkani happens to have the earliest grammars and dictionaries of any modern Indo-Aryan language. The earliest available grammar of Konkani, *Arte da Lingoa Canarim*, was probably written circa 1600 by Thomas Stephens, an English Jesuit who came to Goa as a Portuguese missionary. Stephens, known to the Portuguese as Thomaz Estevão, was the first Englishman to set foot in India. He arrived in Goa in 1579 (thirteen years after St. Francis Xavier) and died there in 1619 at the age of seventy. The grammar that he wrote was published twenty-one years after his death in 1640. The Konkani language was then called Canarim by the Portuguese. Since Konkani was written in Kannada characters when the Portuguese came, they might have initially mistaken it for Kannada. They must have soon realized that it was not Kannada but the name Canarim continued to be used for a long time. Other Konkani grammars written during this period are available only in manuscripts (see S. Miguel [no date] and de Jesus 1635). Among the Konkani lexicographical works of this period, the best-known is *Vocabulario da Lingoa Canarim*, a Konkani–Portuguese and Portuguese–Konkani dictionary compiled by Diogo Ribeiro in Saxtti, Goa, in 1626. In addition to copious information on Konkani vocabulary and usage, it also contains valuable commentary on the religious beliefs and customs of the seventeenth-century Konkani people. The author, Diogo Ribeiro, was a Portuguese Jesuit who came to Goa in 1580. In addition to Ribeiro's dictionary, several other Konkani dictionaries compiled during this period are available in manuscript form. Ribeiro is also known for his revision of Stephens' *Arte da Lingoa Canarim* and for a work on Christian doctrine in Konkani entitled *Declaraçam da Doutrina Christam*, which was published in 1632. Another work on Christian doctrine in Konkani by Thomas Stephens called *Doutrina Christam* had already appeared in 1622. In addition to these works on the Christian doctrine, the Portuguese missionaries wrote several other religious treatises in Konkani during the seventeenth century.

In spite of their noteworthy initial contributions, the Portuguese did great disservice to Konkani when they later attempted to suppress this language. The Viceroy, Francis de Tavora, issued the first decree for this purpose in 1684:

In order to put an end to all inconveniences, it would be suitable to set aside the use of the vernacular idiom ... The people of the place shall try to learn the Portuguese language. The parish priests and the school teachers shall impart instruction in that language so that in course of time the Portuguese idiom will be common to one and all, to the exclusion of the mother tongue. (Cunha Rivara 1857: 183)

The Viceroy was persuaded by the Portuguese clergy that the Konkani Christians should be compelled to give up Konkani in favour of Portuguese for the welfare of their souls. It was argued that if the Christians used only the Portuguese language they would then be cut off from the Konkani-speaking Hindus and their Hindu religious influence. Cunha Rivara (1857: 184) points out that the clergy was also motivated to take a stand against Konkani by the prospect of not having to learn a difficult exotic tongue in order to preach to the Konkani Christians.

The Portuguese Inquisition in Goa suppressed many native customs of the Christian converts which it regarded as pagan. Among the many such usages and customs that the 1736 edict of the Goa Inquisition forbids, we find the following:

The same natives of India are hereby ordered that on the occasions of their marriages and all other functions which they might order or direct to take place for solemnizing marriages, either in the house of the bridegroom or of the bride, songs, which are customarily sung in the language of the land, commonly known as vovios [= songs in the vhovi meter], should not be sung either publicly or in private; and when they desire to hold celebrations in demonstration of their joy, this should not be done with songs which may have a resemblance with the said vovios; and female relatives or Daijis of the bridegroom should never sing in such functions. The same natives of India are hereby ordered that in their houses should not be sung on any occasion and under any pretext, songs called vovios, either in public or in private so that the use of these songs among the faithful Christians would thereby effectively cease. (Priolkar 1961: 99)

The literary and historical value of these wedding songs makes them a precious heritage of the Konkani language. They are still sung by the Konkani Christians who left Goa at the time of the Goa Inquisition, but the Inquisition did succeed in stamping out the custom of singing these Konkani songs among the Goa Christians.

In 1745, Archbishop de Santa Maria issued orders that native Christians who do not know or speak Portuguese should not be allowed to marry:

For sound reasons regarding the common and individual good ... after mature consideration, believing it to be for the service of God and good of our flock, we institute, create, and place anew for this Island of Goa, and its two Provinces, Bardes and Salcete, the impediment that no person contract any marriage, whether it be a man or woman, who does not know or speak the Portuguese language. (Cunha Rivara 1857: 212–13)

The Archbishop also decreed in his pastoral that

we shall not admit any person, of whatever position he may be, to the Orders [to be ordained for priesthood] ... unless he knows and speaks Portuguese only ... This pertains not only to the candidate himself but also to his close relatives of both sexes. (Cunha Rivara 1857: 212)

Archbishop de S. Galdino ordered in 1812 that children should be forbidden to speak the vernacular in the school once they learnt Portuguese (Cunha Rivara 1857: 214). The civil authorities cooperated with the ecclesiastical authorities. The Viceroy, D. Manuel de Portugal e Castro, issued the following circular in 1831:

> It is recommended to the primary teachers and specifically to the Professors who teach Latin grammar that they first apply themselves with every possible diligence to the teaching of this same language (Portuguese) to their students, forbidding them the use of their vernacular in the schools. (Cunha Rivara 1857: 216)

The use of Konkani was forbidden in the seminaries as well. Archbishop da Silva Torres, in his Regulations to the Seminaries, dated 15 June 1847, states: 'It is absolutely forbidden both to the students and any ecclesiastic residing in the seminary, to converse with one another in the language of Goa (Cunha Rivara 1857: 215).'

During the subsequent years of Portuguese rule, Konkani remained a neglected language in Goa. Cunha Rivara tried to revive interest in Konkani when he came to Goa as Chief Secretary in 1855. He wrote a 'Historical Essay on the Konkani Language' which has been greatly relied on here for the documentation of the plight of the Konkani language under the Portuguese. The 'Essay' appeared as an introductory article in the second edition of Thomas Stephens' Konkani grammar edited and published by Cunha Rivara in 1857 under the title *Grammatica da Lingua Concani*. He published, in addition, a Konkani grammar and a Portuguese–Konkani dictionary written by an Italian missionary. Cunha Rivara wanted Konkani to be introduced into the primary schools but his efforts did not succeed.

In the nineteenth and twentieth centuries, while other modern Indian languages made significant progress in their literature, Konkani lagged behind. Yet, books and periodicals started appearing in several Konkani dialects. The first Konkani periodicals appeared in the Bardes Christian dialect in the last decade of the nineteenth century. A substantial number of writings are available only in three of the dialects: Goa Hindu, Bardes Christian and Karnataka Christian. A few writings are also available in the Karnataka Saraswat dialect.

In 1939, the first All India Konkani Conference was held in Karwar, North Kanara. The objectives of the Conference were to (i) bring together Konkani speakers from different regions, (ii) instill into the Konkani people the love of their mother tongue, (iii) make Konkani a more uniform language, (iv) encourage the use of a single script (Nagari) for Konkani, and (v) raise the status of Konkani literature and culture (Martyres 1974). In the resolutions passed at the Conference, the [British] Government was urged to (i) use Konkani as a medium of instruction in areas where Konkani speakers lived in significant numbers, (ii) appoint Konkani representatives to textbook committees and prepare Konkani textbooks, (iii) approve the inclusion of Konkani books in public libraries, and (iv) continue to show the Konkani population figures in the Census of India under a separate category (and not merge them with the figures for the Marathi language). The Conference advocated the use of the Nagari script and suggested that illiterate Konkani speakers be introduced to literacy through the Nagari script. Konkani institutions were asked to support the publication of Konkani books and periodicals. Konkani speakers were urged to use Konkani in their personal correspondence and record-keeping. At the next conference, the All India Radio was requested to introduce Konkani programmes. A Konkani Language Association was founded when the third conference met in Bombay in 1942.

1.4 Konkani after the departure of the Portuguese from Goa

At the end of 1961, when India expelled the Portuguese from Goa, the future of Konkani seemed rather uncertain. Even in Goa, the only area where Konkani was the majority language, it had no political patronage. Konkani writings were scattered among several dialects which employed three different scripts. Language loyalty among Konkani speakers was rather weak. Except for a few settlers in Maharashtra who switched to Marathi, the Konkani Hindus continued to speak their language wherever they went but there was a serious lack of enthusiasm among them with respect to the use of Konkani as a literary language. The paucity of writings in the Hindu Konkani dialects reflected this situation. They have made some noteworthy contributions to Marathi and Kannada literature which indicate their potential for making a valuable contribution to the literature of their own language as well. In Goa, a substantial number of Konkani Hindus regarded Marathi as their literary language and Konkani merely a local colloquial dialect. The Konkani Christians lacked language loyalty to a still greater degree in spite of showing greater political support for Konkani. The urban educated Christians, particularly in Bombay and Goa, had in large numbers abandoned the use of Konkani at home in favour of English or Portuguese. The elite segment of the Christian community which could have contributed something worthwhile to Konkani literature showed complete apathy to it.

The Portuguese language enjoyed a dominant status in Goa for centuries, but when the Portuguese left, it declined rapidly and faced extinction (Wheritt 1985). When India took over Goa, Portuguese was abruptly discontinued from schools and government offices. It was an unfamiliar language to the Indian bureaucracy and was viewed as an imperialist tongue. However, Konkani did not benefit from this situation. The Indian bureaucracy simply replaced Portuguese with English, an imperialist tongue that it was conversant with. The people who once sent their children to Portuguese schools now send them to English schools. The westernized Konkani families that once used to speak Portuguese at home have now largely switched over to English.

After the first elections in post-Portuguese Goa, Konkani faced a serious crisis. Goa, the only area where Konkani had the potential of achieving a dominant status and of flourishing as a literary language, was expected to merge with Maharashtra. Not only Maharashtrians, but even the majority of Goans seemed to favour the merger, since the pro-merger Maharashtravadi Gomantak party had just won the election in Goa. Those who were in favour of the merger asserted that Konkani was only a dialect of Marathi and used this claim as a justification for merger with Maharashtra since states in India were for the most part organized on a linguistic basis. If Goa had merged with Maharashtra, the future of Konkani would have been seriously jeopardized. However, in 1967, when a referendum was held on the issue of merger, it went against the merger proposal.

Once the status of Goa as a separate political unit became secure, there was considerable improvement in the status of Konkani despite the lukewarm attitude towards it of the local Maharashtravadi Gomantak party government which remained in power until 1980. The recognition of Konkani as one of India's literary languages by the Sahitya Akademi (Academy of Letters) in 1976 must be considered a significant landmark in its history. In the seventies, Konkani came to be taught as an elective language in Goan schools all the way up to the twelfth grade, that is, the pre-university level. In 1980, the University of Bombay approved the introduction of Konkani at the university level. After the establishment of the Goa University, a chair for Konkani was instituted there and a postgraduate programme in Konkani was introduced. A number of institutions have also come into existence in Goa in recent years that are concerned with the development of the Konkani language. Konkani gained some recognition in the neighbouring states of Karnataka and Kerala as well. In Kerala, Konkani has been introduced in primary schools.

Konkani had no official status in government offices for a long time. However, in 1985, there was a movement for the acceptance of Konkani as the official language of Goa. Some political leaders wanted to accord such a status to both Konkani and Marathi. The Konkani activists insisted that Konkani should be the sole official language. This controversy led to serious political disturbances in Goa at the end of 1986. Finally, in 1987, Konkani came to be accepted as the sole official language of Goa. In 1992, Konkani was included in the Eighth Schedule of the Indian Constitution as one of India's national languages along with Manipuri and Nepali.

In 1963, Ravindra Kelekar, a prominent Konkani writer and publisher in Goa, published a bibliography of Konkani literature (Kelekar 1963). The writings from the Goa Christian dialect listed in Kelekar 1963 number over a thousand. Some of these go back to the nineteenth century. About four hundred items listed in the bibliography are from the South Kanara Christian dialect. The number of writings in the Goa Hindu dialect included in the bibliography is only about eighty. All except a dozen of these items had appeared after 1940. Over a quarter of them were produced by one man, Vaman Varde Valaulikar (popularly known as Xennoi Goembab), the founder of the literary tradition in the Goa Hindu dialect. Only about a dozen items in the bibliography are from the Southern Saraswat dialect. Kelekar does not claim it to be an exhaustive bibliography of Konkani publications, but it seems to contain almost everything published in the Goa Hindu and the Goa Christian dialects, and most of what had been published in the other dialects by that date. As for literary merit, the small body of writings in the Goa Hindu dialect clearly stands out. The dominant genre there is poetry. B. B. Borkar, Manohar Sardesai, and R. V. Pandit, all renowned Konkani poets, published their first collections of poems about that time. Altogether, nine collections of their poems appeared between 1961 and 1963. There was much less material of literary merit in the far more numerous writings available in the Goa Christian and the Karnataka Christian dialects at that time. A large number of these writings were produced for the propagation of religion by the Catholic clergy. Popular fiction was also quite abundant.

Some Konkani activists are of the opinion that Konkani need not have a single standard literary dialect. They contend that if all groups adopt a single script and avoid excessive borrowing from Portuguese and other languages, the remaining differences should be no serious problem. Chandrakant Keni, a well-known Konkani writer, in his presidential address to the eleventh All India Konkani Conference, remarked,

> There will be a place of honor in Konkani writing to each and every (dialect) form. There is no need to give up any. Everyone may write in his own dialect. However, he could ascertain that the regional form has its roots in the region and try to free it from the undesirable influences of Portuguese, English, Marathi, Kannada, Malayalam, and Sanskrit. (Keni 1976: 27)

Multiple standard dialects are not always detrimental to the development of a language. Languages such as English and Hindi–Urdu have flourished in spite of multiple standard dialects. However, English and Hindi–Urdu have a large number of speakers (over four hundred million each). Konkani, with its two million speakers, cannot afford such fragmentation. The number of readers for the writings in each literary dialect of Konkani is so small that the publishers often find it difficult to recover the cost of publishing these writings. Also, since Konkani is a minor language, Konkani schoolchildren have relatively greater need of learning some of the major Indian languages. If they need to master several literary dialects of their mother tongue in addition, it will be an undue burden on them.

If a single standard dialect is to be adopted, which one should it be? José Pereira, who has contributed a great deal to the study of Konkani, has advocated the creation of a new standard dialect based on the written Konkani of the seventeenth century (Pereira 1973). However, most advocates of a single literary standard are of the opinion that one of the prevailing dialects of Konkani would be a more practical choice.

Among the Konkani dialects, the Goa Hindu dialect has already emerged as the de facto standard dialect in Goa. It has several points in its favour. It is spoken by the majority of the Konkani speakers in Goa. It has the best literature if not the most abundant. It has already established itself as the school dialect in Goa. The textbooks all the way up to the university level are in this dialect. Moreover, it does not show as much regional diversity as the Goa Christian speech. It also occupies a middle position among the Konkani dialects without too many archaisms, innovations, or non-Sanskrit loans that might hamper cross-dialectal communication. Sanskrit loans do not in general pose such a problem as they are very much a pan-Indian phenomenon. However, the archaisms in the Southern Saraswat speech, the innovations in the Goa Christian dialects, and the non-Sanskrit loans in several dialects (Portuguese loans in the Goa Christian dialects and Dravidian loans in the Southern dialects) can be legitimately regarded as a disadvantage in the context of cross-dialectal communication.

The fact that the Goa Hindu dialect already uses the Nagari script is also a point in its favour, since the Nagari script has the best prospects of becoming the common script. (See section 1.2 on the advantages of the Nagari script.) It is much more important that the various Konkani groups adopt a single script than a single literary dialect. There is, after all, a good degree of mutual intelligibility among the dialects whereas the diversity of scripts is a more serious barrier.

Good literary works continue to be produced in the Goa Hindu dialect. The writers of the literature in this dialect are no longer exclusively the Goa Hindu Brahmans. Some Hindus of other castes and some Christians have also come to accept it and use it as a literary dialect.

The Goa Christian literary dialect based on the Bardes Christian dialect is converging towards the Goa Hindu dialect. The form of the dialect employed in writing used to show a much greater influence of Portuguese vocabulary and syntax than the colloquial speech of Goa Christians. The Christian phonological variants, quasi-Portuguese syntax, and Portuguese lexical items that characterized the Goa Christian literary dialect are now coming to be regarded as corruptions in many Christian circles. These are now being replaced by the Hindu phonological variants, Indic syntax, and Sanskritic vocabulary. The Goa Christian readers often find the recently introduced Sanskritic vocabulary difficult and unfamiliar, but they have not revolted. The Catholic church, which is very influential in the Konkani area, has also adopted the Sanskritization policy. The Goa Christian writers, however, continue to use the Roman script since there is still considerable resistance to the use of the Nagari script among the Christian readers.

Southern Saraswat Konkani has many archaic characteristics which sets it apart from the other Konkani dialects. The influence of Kannada is conspicuous in the dialects spoken by the Hindus as well as Christians in Karnataka. As Kannada has undergone profound Sanskritization in its history, the majority of Kannada loans in the Konkani dialects of Karnataka are ultimately not of Dravidian but of Sanskrit origin. This is not an undesirable situation, since these Kannada loans of Sanskrit origin largely overlap with the loans of Sanskrit origin that are found in the Goan dialects. Some Indo-Aryan loans in Kannada have undergone considerable phonological or semantic alteration, but the number of such items that have come into Konkani is small. Some Karnataka Konkani writers have shown an interest in eliminating Kannada loans – not those that are of Sanskrit origin, but those that have wholly or partially Dravidian elements.

Although the Konkani-speaking Hindus and Christians use the same script (Kannada) in Karnataka, they normally read only the writings from their own dialect as there are striking phonological, morphological and lexical differences between their dialects. There has been no effort to bring these two dialects closer to each other. The Goa Hindu dialect has not established itself in Karnataka. Its literature is not much known in the other areas. However, in recent years, there have been some attempts to disseminate the literature written in one script among the readers of other scripts through transliteration.

The status of Konkani continues to be precarious, however. Language loyalty among the Konkani speakers is still weak. Konkani has only a shaky foothold in the schools. Probably the greatest problem for Konkani is that it has several different literary dialects each of which has a woefully small number of readers.

2 DESCRIPTION OF THE LANGUAGE

The information in section 2 is based on the standard dialect unless specified otherwise.

2.1 Phonology

The phonemes of Konkani are given in table 20.1.

The alveolar and palatal stops are affricates. The palatal glides are truly palatal but the other consonants in the palatal column are alveopalatal. ['] indicates palatalization. The voiced/voiceless contrast is found only in the stops and affricates. The fricatives are all voiceless and the sonorants are all voiced. The aspirate/non-aspirate contrast is found in all stops and affricates (except the voiceless labial stop as the old voiceless aspirated stop has changed into the fricative [f] in the standard dialect), in the non-retroflex nasals and laterals, and in the glides. The initial-syllable vowel is shortened after the aspirates and also after the fricatives. Many speakers substitute unaspirated consonants for aspirates. The contrast is still maintained by retaining the shorter vowel in the initial syllable when the aspirate occurs in the initial position. Aspirates in a non-initial position are rare and occur usually only in careful speech. Also, there is a palatalized/ non-palatalized contrast which is found in all obstruents except for the alveolars and the palatals. Where a palatalized alveolar is expected according to the phonological pattern, a palatal is found instead. In the case of sonorants, this contrast is found only among the unaspirated consonants. Among the glides, only the labio-velar glide shows this contrast. As for the vowels, there is a contrast between oral and nasal vowels.

According to what the phoneticians call the principle of temporal compensation, units of speech such as words tend to undergo quantitative adjustment so as to approach equal duration in a given environment although they might vary in terms of number of syllables as well as number of segments. The relatively short units stretch and the

TABLE 20.1: KONKANI PHONEMES

Consonants

	Labial	Dental	Alveolar	Palatal	Retroflex	Velar	Glottal
Stops							
voiceless							
unaspirated	p, p'	t, t'	c	č	ṭ, ṭ'	k, k'	
aspirated		tʰ, tʰ'	cʰ	čʰ	ṭʰ, ṭʰ'	kʰ, kʰ'	
voiced							
unaspirated	b, b'	d, d'	j	ǰ	ḍ, ḍ'	g, g'	
aspirated	bʰ, bʰ'	dʰ dʰ'	jʰ	ǰʰ	ḍʰ, ḍʰ'	gʰ, gʰ'	
Fricatives	f, f'		s	š			h, h'
Nasals							
unaspirated	m, m'		n, n'		ṇ, ṇ'		
aspirated	mʰ		nʰ				
Flaps			r, r'				
Laterals							
unaspirated			l, l'		ḷ, ḷ'		
aspirated			lʰ				
Glides							
unaspirated	w, w'			y			
aspirated	wʰ			yʰ			

Vowels

	Front	Central	Back
High	i, ī		u, ũ
High-mid	e, ẽ	ɔ, ɔ̃	o, õ
Low-mid	ɛ, ɛ̃	ʌ, ʌ̃	ɔ, ɔ̃
Low		a, ã	

relatively long units contract in this process. Konkani is a good example of this principle. Note the lengthening of monosyllabic words and the contraction of polysyllabic words in Konkani in table 20.2.

The morpheme *uṭ* is perceptibly longer in the monosyllabic second person singular imperative form and perceptibly shorter in the trisyllabic third person singular future indicative form than in the disyllabic second person plural imperative and third person singular present indicative forms. There is evidence from comparative data that this is a reflection of actual sound changes. The cognates of Konkani monosyllabic words like *uṭ*

TABLE 20.2: MONOSYLLABIC LENGTHENING AND POLYSYLLABIC SHORTENING IN KONKANI

Item in phonemic form	*uṭ-* 'get up' Item in phonetic form	Gloss
uṭ	[ūṭ]	2sg imperative
uṭa	[uṭa]	2pl imperative
uṭṭa	[uṭṭa]	3sg present
uṭṭʌlɔ	[ũṭṭʌlɔ]	3sg future

do not show any perceptible lengthening in related languages such as Hindi. The perceptible polysyllabic shortening characteristic of the Goan dialects of Konkani is absent even in the Karnataka Christian dialect of Konkani.

The fact that such quantitative adjustment is not limited to the initial syllable can be seen from the examples relating to Konkani plural formation in table 20.3.

Note the modification of the feminine -*i* nouns in the plural (table 20.3, item 1). When the plural suffix -*o* is added, the stem-final -*i* remains a vowel in the case of the monosyllabic stems, but is reduced to a glide in the case of the disyllabic stems which have a single intervocalic consonant and to mere palatalization of the preceding consonant in the case of longer stems (i.e. disyllabic stems which have more than one consonant in the medial position and stems containing more than two syllables). The stem-final -*ũ* behaves similarly in the neuter nouns (table 20.3, item 2). When the plural suffix -*ã* is added, it remains a vowel in the case of the monosyllabic stems and is reduced to a glide in the case of the disyllabic stems which have a single intervocalic consonant. However, it is reduced to zero in the case of longer stems.

Some of the major phonological alternations of Konkani are described in the following paragraphs.

Lower mid vowels alternate with higher mid vowels when a high or higher mid vowel occurs in the next syllable; e.g. (intr) verb stem *pʌḍ-ʌ-*, 3 sg subj *pəḍ-ši* 'fall'; (intr) verb stem *moḍʌ-*, infinitive *moḍ-ũ-k* 'break'. The stem vowel is deleted where the conditions for syncope (stated in the next paragraph) are met.

Vowels alternate with Ø in a medial syllable provided that there is no cluster of non-homorganic consonants next to them; e.g. dir sg *fator*, obl sg *fatr-a* 'stone'; (tr) verb stem *dəwər-i-*, 3sg subj *dəwr-i-t*, 3sg pres imperf *dəwər-t-a* 'place'. Note that such syncope is involved in the alternations described below as well. It gives rise to new consonant clusters which are then subject to various assimilatory processes.

Voiced stops alternate with voiceless ones before voiceless consonants; e.g. verb stem *cab-ʌ-*, 2sg subj *cap-ši* (< *cab-ʌ-ši*), 3sg pres imperf *cap-t-a* (< *cab-ʌ-t-a*) 'bite'.

Non-palatal sibilants alternate with palatal ones before front vowels and palatal consonants; e.g. dir sg *was-ɔ*, dir pl *waš-ɛ* 'bamboo'; dir sg *bhac-ɔ*, dir pl *bhač-ɛ* 'nephew'; dir sg *aj-ɔ*, dir pl *aǰ-ɛ* 'grandfather'; intr verb stem *las-ʌ-*, tr verb stem *laš-i-* 'burn', 2 sg subj of both *laš-ši* (< *las-ʌ-ši* and *laš-i-ši*), participle nt sg of both *laš-čɛ̃* (< *las-ũ-č-ɛ̃*).

Dental consonants alternate with retroflex ones after retroflex consonants; e.g. verb stem *kər-i-*, 3 sg pres imperf *kər-t-a* (< *kər-i-t-a*) 'do', but (intr) verb stem *moḍ-ʌ-*, 3 sg pres imperf *moṭ-ṭ-a* (< *moḍ-ʌ-t-a*) 'break'.

TABLE 20.3: TEMPORAL COMPENSATION AS REFLECTED IN KONKANI PLURAL FORMATION

1.	Feminine singular	Feminine plural	Gloss
	bi	*bi(y)-o*	seed
	dori	*dory-o*	rope
	ãkri	*ãkr'-o*	sprout
	mhatari	*mhatar'-o*	old woman
2.	Neuter singular	Neuter plural	Gloss
	jũ	*jũ(w̃)-ã*	yoke
	tarũ	*tarw̃-ã*	ship
	wasrũ	*wasr-ã*	calf

The flap *r* alternates with *l* before *l*; e.g. verb stem *mar-i-*, 3nt sg perf *mal-l-ɛ̃* (< *mar-i-l-ɛ̃*) 'hit'.

Some of the synchronic statements made above do not faithfully reflect the sound changes which brought about the alternations. For instance, historically, the original mid vowels were *e, ə, o* which developed lower mid variants (*ɛ, ʌ, ɔ*) in final position and when a low vowel followed in the next syllable. However, this development became opaque due to later developments such as syncope and apocope; e.g. 'god': dir sg *dew-ŭ* > *dew*, dir pl *dɛw-ʌ̃* > *dɛw* 'god'; 3 sg pres imperf *moḍ-i-t-a* > *moṭ-ṭ-a* 'break' (tr), 3sg pres imperf *mɔḍ-ʌ-t-a* > *mɔ-ṭ-ṭ-a* 'break' (intr). In the case of sibilants, Konkani had *s, č* and *ǰ* at the earlier stage. Historically, *s* alone became palatalized in the circumstances mentioned above whereas, in the case of the affricates *č* and *ǰ*, what occurred was depalatalization except before y and front vowels.

2.2 Nouns and pronouns

Nouns in Konkani show a three-gender system (masculine, neuter and feminine) and most of them belong to one of two declensional classes. They show special singular and plural oblique forms except in the case of the unassimilated loans ending in a vowel which form a separate declensional class. The oblique form of the noun is normally used when a postposition follows it. Occasionally, the oblique form of a noun appears without an overt postposition where a specific postposition can be considered to have been deleted.

Except for certain feminine nouns, class 1 nouns have diagnostic endings in the direct singular that indicate their gender: *ɔ* (m), *ɛ̃* (nt), *i* (f). Some feminine nouns ending in a consonant or *-u*, such as *ǰib* 'tongue' and *taḷu* 'roof of the mouth', can also be accommodated in class 1 although they do not have the diagnostic ending *-i* in the direct singular form, since they show the same declensional pattern as nouns in *-i*. The declensional pattern of class 1 nouns can be seen in table 20.4.

Class 2 nouns mostly end in a consonant, but this class also includes some masculine nouns ending in *-i* and *-u* and neuter nouns ending in *-ĩ* and *-ũ*. Several class 2 masculine nouns ending in a consonant and containing a mid vowel in the final syllable (such as *dew* 'god', *cor* 'thief', and *fator* 'stone') show stem-vowel alternation. The declensional pattern of class 2 nouns is given in table 20.5.

As mentioned earlier, unassimilated loans form a separate declensional class which is illustrated in table 20.6.

TABLE 20.4: CLASS 1 NOUNS

	'worm' (m)	'roof' (nt)	'wrinkle' (f)
Direct singular	kiḍ-ɔ	pak-ɛ̃	mir-i
Direct plural	kiḍ-ɛ	pak-ĩ	mir-y-o
Oblique singular	kiḍ-'a	pak-'a	mir-y-e
Oblique plural	kiḍ-'ã	pak-'ã	mir-y-ã

	'tongue' (f)	'roof of the mouth' (f)
Direct singular	ǰib	taḷu
Direct plural	ǰib-o	taḷw-o
Oblique singular	ǰib-e	taḷw-e
Oblique plural	ǰib-ã	taḷw-ã

TABLE 20.5: CLASS 2 NOUNS

	'parrot' (m)	'flower' (nt)	'granddaughter' (f)
Direct singular	kir	phul	nat
Direct plural	kir	phul-ã	nat-i
Oblique singular	kir-a	phul-a	nat-i
Oblique plural	kir-ã	phul-ã	nat-ĩ

	'laundryman' (m)	'pearl' (nt)
Direct singular	dhobi	motĩ
Direct plural	dhobi	moty-ã
Oblique singular	dhoby-a	moty-a
Oblique plural	dhoby-ã	moty-ã

	'grandson' (m)	'girl' (nt)
Direct singular	natu	čeḍũ
Direct plural	natu	čeḍw-ã
Oblique singular	natw-a	čeḍw-a
Oblique plural	natw-ã	čeḍw-ã

	'god' (m)	'thief' (m)	'stone' (m)
Direct singular	dew	cor	fator
Direct plural	dɛw	cɔr	fatʌr
Oblique singular	dɛw-a	cɔr-a	fatr-a
Oblique plural	dɛw-ã	cɔr-ã	fatr-ã

TABLE 20.6: CLASS 3 NOUNS

	'priest' (m)
Direct singular	padri
Direct plural	padri
Oblique singular	padri
Oblique plural	padrĩ

Konkani pronouns show several cases at the morphological level, unlike nouns. The genitive ending consists of an element *c-* (with the variant *j-* occurring after certain pronouns and the variant *l-* occurring when the preceding pronoun or noun denotes a human) plus a class 1 adjective ending (which indicates gender and number of the following noun and must be in the oblique form if the following noun is in the oblique form). Table 20.7 shows the declensional pattern of Konkani personal pronouns, and table 20.8 shows the declensional pattern of some other pronouns.

2.3 Adjectives and adverbs

Only class 1 adjectives are declined. They follow the pattern of the class 1 nouns in general. However, when the adjectives are used attributively, the same oblique form is used in the singular as well as the plural in the case of the masculine and the neuter forms. The oblique form of an adjective is used when a postposition follows it or follows the noun it qualifies. The declensional pattern of class 1 adjectives is given in table 20.9. Class 2 adjectives (such as *lãb* 'tall', *həṭhi* 'stubborn') are indeclinable.

As shown in table 20.10, the pattern of class 1 adverbs is like that of class 1 adjectives except that they have no oblique forms. Class 2 adverbs, such as *sʌwkas* 'slowly', *wegĩ* 'fast', are indeclinable.

TABLE 20.7: PERSONAL PRONOUNS

	Singular	Plural
First Person		
Nominative	*haw̃*	*am-i*
Accusative/Dative	*mha-ka*	*am-kã*
Agentive/Instrumental	*haw-ɛ̃*	*am-i*
Genitive	*mhʌ-j-ɔ*	*am-c-ɔ*
Superessive	*mhə-ǰer*	*am-čer*
Second Person		
Nominative	*tũ*	*tum-i*
Accusative/Dative	*tu-ka*	*tum-kã*
Agentive/Instrumental	*tu-(w)-ɛ̃*	*tum-i*
Genitive	*tu-j-ɔ*	*tum-c-ɔ*
Superessive	*tu-ǰer*	*tum-čer*

	Masculine/Neuter Singular	Feminine Singular	Masculine/Neuter/ Feminine Plural
Third Person/Demonstrative (obviative)			
Nominative	*t-ɔ* (m)	*t-i*	*t-ɛ* (m)
	t-ɛ̃ (nt)		*t-ĩ* (nt)
			t-'-o (f)
Accusative/Dative	*ta-ka*	*ti-ka*	*tã-kã*
Agentive/Instrumental	*ta-ɲɛ*	*ti-ɲɛ*	*tã-ɲi*
Genitive	*ta-j-ɔ*	*ti-j-ɔ*	*tã-c-ɔ*
	~ *ta-c-ɔ*	~ *ti-c-ɔ*	
Superessive	*ta-ǰ-er*	*ti-ǰ-er*	*tã-č-er*
	~ *ta-č-er*	~ *ti-č-er*	

TABLE 20.8: OTHER PRONOUNS

	Interrogative		Reflexive
	'who?'	'what?'	
Nominative	*kɔṇ*	*kit-ɛ̃*	*apuṇ*
Accusative/Dative	*kɔṇ-a-k*	*kit-'a-k*	*apṇ-a-k*
Agent	*kɔṇ-ɛ*	*kit-'a-n*	*apṇ-ɛ̃*
Genitive	*kɔṇ-a-l-ɔ*	*kit-'a-c-ɔ*	*ap-l-ɔ*
Superessive	*kɔṇ-a-čer*	*kit-'a-čer*	*apṇ-a-čer*

Note: Some speakers substitute *kidɛ̃* (oblique *kid'a-*) for *kitɛ̃* (oblique *kit'a-*).

TABLE 20.9: CLASS 1 ADJECTIVES USED ATTRIBUTIVELY

	Masculine	*kaḷɔ* 'black' Neuter	Feminine
Direct singular	*kaḷ-ɔ*	*kaḷ-ɛ̃*	*kaḷ-i*
Direct plural	*kaḷ-ɛ*	*kaḷ-ĩ*	*kaḷ-'-o*
Oblique singular	*kaḷ-'a*	*kaḷ-'a*	*kaḷ-e*
Oblique plural	*kaḷ-'a*	*kaḷ-'a*	*kaḷ-'-a*

TABLE 20.10: CLASS 1 ADVERBS

	Masculine	pʌrtɔ 'again' Neuter	Feminine
Singular	pʌrt-ɔ	pʌrt-ɛ̃	pərt-i
Plural	pʌrt-ɛ	pərt-ĩ	pərt-'-o

2.4 Postpositions

There are two kinds of postpositions in Konkani, clitic postpositions and secondary postpositions. Clitic postpositions such as (accusative/dative) *k*, (agentive/instrumental) *n*, (genitive) *c-ɔ* (see remarks on the structure of the genitive ending in section 2.2 under pronouns), (superessive) *r*, and (subessive) *ĩ* are considered to be case suffixes in traditional Konkani grammars. However, they function like true suffixes with pronominal stems, but are not strictly bound to nominal stems. For instance,

kaḷ-ɛ̃   mɛj
black -nt sg dir   table
'black table'

kaḷ'a   mɛj-a-r
black -nt sg obl   table -nt sg obl-on
'on the black table'

*kaḷ'a-r   mɛj-a-r
black-nt sg obl-on   table-nt sg obl-on
'on the black table'

With the exception of the superessive, clitic postpositions occur after the oblique form of a noun or pronoun. Secondary postpositions can occur after the oblique form of a noun or non-personal pronoun or after the genitive oblique singular form of the same (oblique form of the noun or pronoun plus oblique singular of the genitive marker), but they must occur only after the genitive oblique singular form of a personal pronoun (oblique form of the personal pronoun plus oblique singular form of the genitive marker). They also occur independently as adverbs. Many of them are transparently oblique forms or case forms of nouns. For example,

ghʌr-a-(ča)   pɔ̃da
house -m sg obl (-gen m sg obl) under
'under the house'

The postposition *pɔ̃da* can occur also as an adverb. *pɔ̃da* is the oblique form of the neuter noun *pɔ̃d* 'bottom'.

2.5 Verbs

Konkani verb roots mostly end in a consonant, but a few end in a vowel. For example, *uṭ-* 'get up', *pʌrt-* 'change', *mɔḍ-* 'break', *kha-* 'eat', *dhu-* 'wash'. Verb stems consist of the verb root and a suffix such as *-ʌ*, *-i*, *-əy* or *-ay*. As a result of the phonetic form of the suffix, verb stems always end in a vowel or glide. Usually, verb stems with the suffix *-ʌ* are intransitive, those with the suffix *-i* are transitive, and those with the suffix *-əy* or *-ay* causative. For example, *uṭ-ʌ-* 'get up', *mɔḍ-ʌ-* 'break' (intr), *kirl-ʌ-* 'sprout', *moḍ-i-* 'break' (tr), *pərt-i-* 'change' (tr), *moḍəy-* 'make (someone) break (something)', *khawəy-* 'make (someone) eat', *kirl-ay-* 'make (something) sprout'. There are also a good number of verb stems with the suffix *-ɛ* which are usually intransitive. For example, *aš-ɛ-* 'desire', *bhuk-ɛ-* 'be hungry'. There are a few monosyllabic verb roots ending in a vowel; e.g. *di-* 'give', *yɛ-* 'come', *ghɛ-* 'take', *dhu-* 'wash', *ja-* 'become', *nha-* 'bathe', *kha-* 'eat'. Among these stems, those ending in a front vowel appear to take no suffix at all in the formation of the verb stems whereas those ending in a back vowel have an added suffix *-y* in their stems, but only in some contexts (in the first and third person singular of the subjunctive forms and in negative forms containing the verb stem).

Some verb stems have special unpredictable allomorphs used in the perfect tenses (perfect, present perfect, past perfect) as shown in table 20.11.

Verb stems have oblique forms which occur in certain verb forms: the first plural of the subjunctive verb forms, optative verb forms, and in certain non-finite verb forms such as infinitives and participles. These vary according to stem type as can be seen in table 20.12.

The imperfect base of the verb is formed by adding the imperfect marker *t* to the verb stem and the perfect base by adding the perfect marker *l* to the verb stem. The tense aspect markers which are given below are added to the imperfect or perfect base:

Non-past marker: *-(ʌ) l*. The vowel in this marker may be dropped in syncope.
Past imperfect marker: *-al*. The vowel in this marker does not undergo syncope.
Past Perfect marker: *-l*

There are several sets of verb endings that indicate person and number: present, non-present, subjunctive, optative and imperative. The non-present endings show gender distinction as well. In general, these endings show the person, number and gender of the subject. However, in perfect verb forms, if there is an agentive marker after the subject (see description of the ergative construction in section 2.6 for conditions under which the

TABLE 20.11: VERB STEMS WITH IRREGULAR PERFECT ALLOMORPHS

Verb stem	Perfect allomorph	Gloss
yɛ-	*ay-*	come
wʌc-ʌ	*gɛ-*	go
mʌr-ʌ	*mɛ-*	die
whʌr-ʌ	*whɛ-*	take away
kər-i	*kɛ-*	do, make

TABLE 20.12: VERB STEMS AND THEIR OBLIQUE FORMS

Stem type	Example	Oblique	Gloss
-ʌ stems:	*mɔḍ-ʌ-*	*moḍ-ũ-*	break (intransitive)
-i stems:	*moḍ-i-*	*moḍ-ũ-*	break (transitive)
-əy stems:	*moḍ-əy-*	*moḍ-ɔw̃-*	make (someone) break (something)
-ay stems:	*kirl-ay-*	*kirl-aw̃-*	make (something) sprout
-ɛ stems:	*bhuk-ɛ-*	*bhuk-ew̃-*	be hungry
CV stems:	*kha-*	*kha-w̃-*	eat

TABLE 20.13: VERB ENDINGS

	Singular	Plural
1. Present endings		
1st person	-$\tilde{a}$	-at
2nd and 3rd person	-a	-at
2. Non-present endings[1]		
1st person	-$\tilde{\jmath}$ (m), -$\tilde{\varepsilon}$ (nt), -$\tilde{\imath}$ (f)	-ε (m), -$\tilde{\imath}$ (non-m)
2nd and 3rd person	-$\jmath$ (m), -$\tilde{\varepsilon}$ (nt), -i (f)	-ε (m), -$\tilde{\imath}$ (nt) -'o (f)
3. Subjunctive endings		
1st person	-n	-$\varnothing$[2]
2nd person	-ši	-šat
3rd person	-t	-tit
4. Optative endings[3]		
1st person	-$\varnothing$	-$\varnothing$; (inclusive) -ya
3rd person	-di	-dit
5. Imperative endings[4]		
2nd person	-$\varnothing$	-a(t)

Notes:

1 The non-present endings are identical with the class 1 adjective endings except in the first person, where the first person singular marker [˜] is added to the singular forms and the distinction between the feminine and the neuter gender is not maintained in the plural forms.

2 In the first plural, the oblique form of the verb stem is used.

3 The optative endings are added to the oblique form of the verb stem.

4 In polysyllabic verb stems ending in ʌ and i, the final vowel is deleted in the imperative second singular except when it is preceded by a consonant cluster.

subject takes the agentive marker), third person endings are used that show the number and gender of the object. Such agreement is not blocked even if there is an accusative marker after the object. If there is no object to agree with, the neuter singular form is used.

The present and non-present endings are added to the imperfect or perfect base after the tense-aspect marker, if any. The subjunctive, optative, and imperative endings are added directly to the verb stems. The different sets of endings are given in table 20.13. In illustrating the various verb forms in the rest of this section, the verb pʌrt-ʌ- 'change' (transitive) is used.

There are several non-finite verb forms such as participles, gerunds, infinitives, and others. The declensional pattern of the participles is shown in table 20.14.

The gerund is formed by adding the suffix -ʌp to the oblique form of the verb stem. The neuter singular form of the simple participle is also used as a gerund. It is far more common in some dialects. Gerund formation according to stem types is shown in table 20.15. The examples given in this table show some phonological modification due to syncope, denasalization before an oral vowel, etc.

There are two types of infinitives: simple infinitive and gerundial infinitive. The simple infinitive is far more frequent than the gerundial infinitive. However, in Southern Saraswat and Saxtti Christian dialects, the gerundial infinitive is the norm. They are formed as follows:

Simple infinitive: verb stem oblique + dative case marker; e.g. pərt-ū-k 'to change'
Gerundial infinitive: gerund formed from simple participle (neuter singular oblique) + dative case marker; e.g. pər-t-ū-č-a-k 'to change'.

TABLE 20.14: PARTICIPLES

	Masculine	Neuter	Feminine
1. Simple participle: verb stem (oblique) + genitive marker[1]			
Direct singular	pərt-ū-cɔ	pərt-ū-čɛ̃	pərt-ū-či
Direct plural	pərt-ū-čɛ	pərt-ū-čɨ̃	pərt-ū-čo
Oblique singular	pərt-ū-ča	pərt-ū-ča	pərt-ū-če
Oblique plural	pərt-ū-ča	pərt-ū-ča	pərt-ū-ča
2. Imperfect participle: imperfect base + non-past marker + class 1 adjective endings			
Direct singular	pʌrt-ʌ-t-l-ɔ	pʌrt-ʌ-t-l-ɛ̃	pərt-ə-t-l-i
Direct plural	pʌrt-ʌ-t-l-ɛ	pərt-ə-t-l-ɨ̃	pərt-ə-t-l-'o
Oblique singular	pʌrt-ʌ-t-l-'a	pʌrt-ʌ-t-l-'a	pərt-ə-t-l-e
Oblique plural	pʌrt-ʌ-t-l-'a	pʌrt-ʌ-t-l-'a	pʌrt-ʌ-t-l-'a
3. Perfect participle: perfect base + class 1 adjective endings[2]			
Direct singular	pʌrt-ʌ-l-ɔ	pʌrt-ʌ-l-ɛ̃	pərt-ə-l-i
Direct plural	pʌrt-ʌ-l-ɛ	pərt-ə-l-ɨ̃	pərt-ə-l-'o
Oblique singular	pʌrt-ʌ-l-'a	pʌrt-ʌ-l-'a	pərt-ə-l-e
Oblique plural	pʌrt-ʌ-l-'a	pʌrt-ʌ-l-'a	pʌrt-ʌ-l-'a
4. Past perfect participle: perfect base + past perfect marker + class 1 adjective endings			
Direct singular	pʌrt-ʌ-l-l-ɔ	pʌrt-ʌ-l-l-ɛ̃	pərt-ə-l-l-i
Direct plural	pʌrt-ʌ-l-l-ɛ	pərt-ə-l-l-ɨ̃	pərt-ə-l-l-'o
Oblique singular	pʌrt-ʌ-l-l-'a	pʌrt-ʌ-l-l-'a	pərt-ə-l-l-e
Oblique plural	pʌrt-ʌ-l-l-'a	pʌrt-ʌ-l-l-'a	pʌrt-ʌ-l-l-'a

Notes:

1 The simple participle and the imperfect participle are both semantically equivalent to the present principle in English and are used interchangeably.

2 This participle does not occur as a regular participle, i.e. as a noun modifier. However, the neuter singular oblique form of it occurs before certain postpositions (for example, pʌrt-ʌ-l-'a nəntər 'after changing'. Also, the perfect forms of the verb are based on this participle.

TABLE 20.15: GERUNDS

Stem type	Example	Gerund 1	Gerund 2	Gloss
-ʌ stems:	mɔḍ-ʌ-	mɔḍ-ʌp	moḍ-č-ɛ̃	break (intransitive)
-i stems:	moḍ-i-	moḍ-ʌp	moḍ-č-ɛ̃	break (transitive)
-əy stems:	moḍ-əy-	moḍ-w-ʌp	moḍ-əw̃-č-ɛ̃	make (someone) break (something)
-ay stems	kirl-ay-	kirl-aw-ʌp	kirl-aw̃-č-ɛ̃	make (something) sprout
-ɛ stems:	bhuk-ɛ-	bhuk-ew-ʌp	bhuk-ew̃-č-ɛ̃	be hungry
CV stems:	kha-	kha-w-ʌp	kha-w̃-č-ɛ̃	eat

There are several other non-finite forms; e.g. pərt-ū-n 'having changed', pʌrt-ʌ-l'ar 'if one changes, on changing', pʌrt-ʌ-t 'changing' (iterative), pʌrt-ʌ-t-ã, or pʌrt-ʌ-t-ã-pʌrt-ʌ-t-ã 'changing' (iterative), pʌrt-ʌ-t-ana 'while changing', pʌrt-ʌ-t-ʌc 'on changing'. pərt-ū-n consists of the oblique form of the stem + -n, pʌrt-ʌ-l-'a-r of the perfect participle oblique + -r (superessive). The other forms are built on the imperfect base.

Finite verb forms may be divided into three broad classes on the basis of formation: (i) forms built on the imperfect base, (ii) forms built on the perfect base, and (iii) forms built on the verb stem. Table 20.16 illustrates verb forms built on the imperfect base, and table 20.17 illustrates verb forms built on the perfect base. Table 20.18 has verb forms built on the verb stem.

TABLE 20.16: VERB FORMS BUILT ON THE IMPERFECT BASE

	Singular	Plural
(a) Present Imperfect: imperfect base + present endings		
1st person	pʌrt-ʌ-t-ã	pʌrt-ʌ-t-at
2nd and 3rd person	pʌrt-ʌ-t-a	pʌrt-ʌ-t-at
(b) Future: imperfect base + non-past marker + non-present endings[1]		
1st person	pʌrt-ʌ-t-l-ɔ̃ (m)	pʌrt-ʌ-t-l-ɛ (m)
	pʌrt-ʌ-t-l-ɛ̃ (nt)	pərt-ə-t-l-ĩ (non-m)
	pərt-ə-t-l-ĩ (f)	
2nd and 3rd person	pʌrt-ʌ-t-l-ɔ (m)	pʌrt-ʌ-t-l-ɛ (m)
	pʌrt-ʌ-t-l-ɛ̃ (nt)	pərt-ə-t-l-ĩ (nt)
	pərt-ə-t-l-i (f)	pərt-ə-t-l-'o (f)
(c) Past Imperfect: imperfect base + past imperfect marker + non-present endings		
1st person	pʌrt-ʌ-t-al-ɔ̃ (m)	pʌrt-ʌ-t-al-ɛ (m)
	pʌrt-ʌ-t-al-ɛ̃ (nt)	pʌrt-ʌ-t-al-ĩ (non-m)
	pʌrt-ʌ-t-al-ĩ (f)	
2nd and 3rd person	pʌrt-ʌ-t-al-ɔ (m)	pʌrt-ʌ-t-al-ɛ (m)
	pʌrt-ʌ-t-al-ɛ̃ (nt)	pʌrt-ʌ-t-al-ĩ (nt)
	pʌrt-ʌ-t-al-i (f)	pʌrt-ʌ-t-al-'o (f)

Note:
1 The future forms are based on the imperfect participle (imperfect base + non-past marker + class 1 adjective endings) where the class 1 adjective endings are replaced by non-present endings.

TABLE 20.17: VERB FORMS BUILT ON THE PERFECT BASE

	Singular	Plural
(a) Perfect: perfect base + non-present endings[1]		
1st person	pʌrt-ʌ-l-ɔ̃ (m)	pʌrt-ʌ-l-ɛ (m)
	pʌrt-ʌ-l-ɛ̃ (nt)	pərt-ə-l-ĩ (non-m)
	pərt-ə-l-ĩ (f)	
2nd and 3rd person	pʌrt-ʌ-l-ɔ (m)	pʌrt-ʌ-l-ɛ (m)
	pʌrt-ʌ-l-ɛ̃ (nt)	pərt-ə-l-ĩ (nt)
	pərt-ə-l-i (f)	pərt-ə-l-'o (f)
(b) Present perfect: perfect participle (perfect base + class 1 adjective endings) + present endings[2]		
1st person	pʌrt-ʌ-l-ã (m)	pʌrt-ʌ-l-'at (m)
	(pʌrt-ʌ-l-ɔ- ã)	(pʌrt-ʌ-l-ɛ -at)
	pʌrt-ʌ-l-ã (nt)	pʌrt-ʌ-l-'ãt (non-m)
	(pʌrt-ʌ-l-ɛ̃ -ã)	(pʌrt-ʌ-l-ĩ -at)
	pʌrt-ʌ-l-'ã (f)	
	(pʌrt-ʌ-l-i -ã)	
2nd and 3rd person	pʌrt-ʌ-l-a (m)	pʌrt-ʌ-l-'at (m)
	(pʌrt-ʌ-l-ɔ -a)	(pʌrt-ʌ-l-ɛ -at)
	pʌrt-ʌ-l-ã (nt)	pʌrt-ʌ-l-'ãt (nt)
	(pʌrt-ʌ-l-ɛ̃ -ã)	(pʌrt-ʌ-l-ĩ -at)
	pʌrt-ʌ-l-'a (f)	pʌrt-ʌ-l-'at (f)
	(pʌrt-ʌ-l-i -a)	(pʌrt-ʌ-l-'o -at)
(c) Past perfect: perfect base + past perfect marker + non-present endings[3]		
1st person	pʌrt-ʌ-l-l-ɔ̃ (m)	pʌrt-ʌ-l-l-ɛ (m)
	pʌrt-ʌ-l-l-ɛ̃ (nt)	pərt-ə-l-l-ĩ (non-m)
	pərt-ə-l-l-ĩ (f)	
2nd and 3rd person	pʌrt-ʌ-l-l-ɔ (m)	pʌrt-ʌ-l-l-ɛ (m)
	pʌrt-ʌ-l-l-ɛ̃ (nt)	pərt-ə-l-l-ĩ (nt)
	pərt-ə-l-l-i (f)	pərt-ə-l-l-'o (f)

Notes on table 20.17:

1 The perfect forms are based on the perfect participle (perfect base + class 1 adjective endings) where the class 1 adjective endings are replaced by non-present endings.

2 Present perfect forms are also based on the perfect participle. Here, however, the present endings do not replace the class 1 adjective endings but are just added on. Certain phonological modifications take place in this process: the final vowel of the participle is deleted before the following vowel of the ending. However, prior to its loss, its nasality affects the ending if it is nasal. Also, if it is palatal, it leaves behind palatalization on the preceding consonant. According to regular phonetic development, the neuter singular form should have been *pʌrt-ʌ-l'ã* in all persons, but it has lost the palatalization due to the influence of the masculine singular forms. Alternatively, the present perfect forms can be derived from the perfect forms of the verb in the same fashion.

3 The past perfect forms are based on the past perfect participle (perfect base + past perfect marker + class 1 adjective endings) where the class 1 adjective endings are replaced by non-present endings.

TABLE 20.18: VERB FORMS BUILT ON THE VERB STEM

	Singular	Plural
(a) Present: verb stem + present endings (as-a 'be')[1]		
1st person	*as-ã*	*as-at*
2nd and 3rd person	*as-a*	*as-at*
(b) Subjunctive: verb stem + subjunctive endings		
1st person	*pʌrt-ʌ-n*	*pərt-ũ*
2nd person	*pərt-ə-ši*	*pʌrt-ʌ-šat*
3rd person	*pʌrt-ʌ-t*	*pərt-ə-tit*
(c) Optative: verb stem oblique + optative endings		
1st person	*pərt-ũ*	*pərt-ũ; (inclusive) pərt-ũ-ya*
3rd person	*pərt-ũ-di*	*pərt-ũ-dit*
(d) Imperative: verb stem + imperative endings		
2nd person	*pʌrt-ʌ*	*pʌrt-a(t)*

Note:

1 Only the copula and a couple of defective verbs (*na-* 'not be', *jaṇ- ʌ-* 'know', etc.) show the present forms.

2.6 Word order and agreement

As for word order, Konkani shows the SOV pattern which is usual in the South Asian linguistic area: object–verb, adverb–verb, main verb–auxiliary, indirect object–direct object, adjective–noun, genitive–noun, standard marker–adjective, etc. Because of the influence of Kannada, it shows many features that are characteristic of the strict SOV languages. For more information on the phonological and syntactic characteristics Konkani shares with Kannada, see section 3.4.

When the subject is in the nominative case, the verb agrees with the subject in person, and number. If the verb has non-present endings, it can show gender agreement as well. In addition to verbs, genitive markers, certain adjectives, adverbs and pronouns show agreement for number and gender. The following sentences illustrate such agreement.

(1) *t-ɔ   rama-l-ɔ   dhakl-ɔ   put hanga kʌs-ɔ   paw-l-ɔ*
     that -M SG Rama's-M SG little-M SG son here   how-M SG reached M SG
     'How did that younger son of Ram get here?'

(2) *t-i   ghʌra-č-i   adl-i   caw-i   hanga kəš-i   paw-l-i*
   it F SG   house-'s-F SG old-F SG key-F SG here how-F SG reached-F SG
   'How did that old key of the house get here?'

(3) *t-'o   ghʌra-č-o   adl-'o   caw-y-o   hanga kəš-o   paw-l-'o*
   it-F PL house-'s-F PL old-F PL1 key-F PL here how-F PL1 reached-F PL1
   'How did those old keys of the house get here?'

(4) *t-ɛ̃   tu-ǰ-ɛ̃   dhakl-ɛ̃   mɛj   hanga kʌš-ɛ̃*
   that-NT SG   your-NT SG   little-NT SG table here how-NT SG
   paw-l-ɛ̃
   reached-NT SG
   'How did that small table of yours get here?'

In the above sentences various parts of speech agree with a noun in number and gender: *put*, a masculine singular noun in (1); *cawi*, a feminine singular noun in (2); *cawyo*, feminine plural in (3); and *mɛj*, a neuter singular noun in (4). *tɔ, ti, tɛ̃* are pronominal adjectives in the above sentences but they can also function as pronouns.

Konkani has an ergative construction which is found only in the perfects. As a rule, transitive verbs take an ergative construction in the perfects and intransitive verbs do not. Exceptions include a few transitive verbs that do not take an ergative construction (such as *uləy-* 'speak', *wisʌr-ʌ-* 'forget', *piye-* 'drink'). In the ergative construction, the subject takes the agentive marker and the third person form of the verb which agrees with the object in number and gender is used. The third person neuter singular form of the verb is used when there is no explicit object. For example,

(5) *čɛḍ-ɔ   kɛḷ-ɛ̃   kha-t-al-ɔ*
   boy-M SG   banana-NT SG eat-IMPERF-PST IMPERF-M SG
   'The boy was eating a banana.'

(6) *čɛḍ-'a-n   kɛḷ-ɛ̃   kha-l-ɛ̃*
   boy-OBL SG AGN   banana-NT SG eat-PERF-NT SG
   'The boy ate a banana.'

(7) *čɛ̌ḍ-'a-n   kha-l-ɛ̃*
   boy-OBL SG AGN   eat-PERF-NT SG
   'The boy ate.'

2.7 Innovations in the gender system

At an earlier stage in Konkani, nouns denoting males were masculine, nouns denoting females feminine, and nouns denoting both – i.e. 'common gender' nouns – like *baḷ* 'infant' were neuter. Nouns denoting some animals also were assigned gender in the same fashion. The gender of other nouns was not ordinarily predictable from their meaning. Then, one 'common gender' noun *čeḍũ* (from earlier **čeḍrũ*) underwent a semantic change from 'child' to 'girl' except in a couple of dialects but still continued as a neuter noun. On the analogy of this noun, some pronouns and nouns denoting women came to be used in the neuter gender in these dialects in accordance with certain social considerations. This had already happened when the Portuguese missionaries were composing texts in Old Konkani in the seventeenth century. Ribeiro 1626 has the lexical item *čeḍũ* with the gloss 'menina, filha' (i.e. 'girl, daughter') and there are sentences in the same work where a woman is referred to in the neuter. For example, under *akully* 'low lineage', one of the Ribeiro manuscripts has the adage

akullieche'	*hâddilale'*	*kullâ*	*nâssu*
low lineage-of	brought	lineage-of	destruction

'One [a woman] brought from a low lineage is the [cause of] destruction of the lineage.'

In the standard dialect, a woman uses the pronoun *haw̃* (1sg) in neuter agreement when she is speaking to someone who is of the same age group or older. In several dialects including the standard dialect, a speaker uses the pronoun *tũ* (2sg) in neuter agreement while addressing (a) a girl or (b) a woman who is of the same age group or younger whom he has known since her girlhood. Also, a speaker uses the pronoun *tẽ* (3 nt sg) instead of *ti* (3 f sg) in referring to (a) a girl or (b) to a woman who is of the same age group or younger whom he has known since her girlhood. For example, one will address and refer to his daughters and older or younger sisters in the neuter gender but, he will not thus address or refer to women of an older generation such as his mother or grandmother. Since it is relative age that matters, even an old woman who is a grandmother can be addressed or referred to in the neuter by someone who is of the same age group or older and who has known her since her girlhood. If a romantic novel or movie with a young heroine were to have the title *She*, its appropriate translation in Konkani would be *tẽ*, not *ti*. In a formal situation or when a woman has a special status, however, she might be addressed in the feminine gender even though the usual conditions for the use of the neuter gender are met. In the Karnataka Christian dialect, all nouns denoting women can be used in neuter agreement in accordance with social considerations described above. In these dialects, the old neuter gender can be said to have evolved into a second feminine gender. In the Southern Saraswat dialect, the noun *čerḍũ* 'child' (from earlier **čeḍrũ*), which corresponds to *čeḍũ* in the other dialects, has not undergone the semantic change mentioned above and so the gender system also has not changed in the above fashion. Southern Saraswats address and refer to girls of any age in the feminine gender. Saxtti Christians of Saraswat (Brahman) origin address and refer to girls of any age in their own community in the feminine gender but address or refer to non-Brahman girls in the neuter gender. Also, they use a feminine noun *cəli* to refer to a Brahman girl but the neuter noun *čeḍũ* to refer to a non-Brahman girl. In the standard dialect, however, the noun *cəli* is now a neuter noun.

In the Karnataka Christian dialect, this development has given rise to an interesting anomaly in agreement: in the case of most nouns that can be feminine or neuter according to social considerations, even when the non-attributive elements going with the nouns show neuter agreement, the attributive elements continue to show feminine agreement.

(1)	*t-i*	*ǰɔni-č-i*	*dhakṭ -i*	*bhəyṇ*
	pr-3 F SG	John's-F SG	little-F SG	sister
or	*t-ẽ*	*ǰɔni-č-i*	*dhakṭ-i*	*bhəyṇ*
	pr-3 NT SG	John's-F SG	little-F SG	sister

'She is John's little/younger sister.'

(2) | *ǰɔni-č-i* | *bhəyṇ* | *dhakṭ-i* |
|---|---|---|
| | John's-F SG | sister | little-F SG |
| or | *ǰɔni-č-i* | *bhəyṇ* | *dhakṭ-ẽ* |
| | John's-F SG | sister | little-NT SG |

'John's sister is little/younger.'

(3) *jɔni-c-i*   *dhakṭ-i*   *bhəyn*   *ay-l-i*
     John's-F SG little-F SG sister   come-F SG
or   *jɔni-c-i*   *dhakṭ-i*   *bhəyn*   *ay-l-ẽ.*
     John's-F SG little-F SG sister   came-NT SG
     'John's little/younger sister came.'

(4) *jɔni-č-o*   *dhakṭ-'-o*   *bhəyn-i*   *ay-l-'-o*
     John's-F PL little-F PL sister-F PL came-F PL
or   *jɔni-č-o*   *dhak -'-o*   *bhəyn-i*   *ay-l-ĩ*
     John's-F PL little-F PL sister-F PL came-NT PL
     'John's little/younger sisters came.'

However, the attributive as well as the non-attributive elements must all show the same
gender agreement. The following sentences are, therefore, ungrammatical:

(5) **t-ẽ*   *jɔni-č-i*   *dhakṭ-ẽ*   *bhəyn*
     pr-3 NT SG John's F SG little NT SG sister
     'She is John's younger sister.'

(6) **t-ẽ*   *hanga* *kəš-i*   *ay-l-ẽ*
     pr-3 NT SG here   howF SG came-NT SG
     'How did she come here?'

And, if the non-attributive elements show feminine agreement, the attributive elements
must show feminine agreement as well. Therefore, the following sentences are
ungrammatical:

(7) **t-i*   *jɔni-č-ẽ*   *dhakṭ-ẽ*   *bhəyn*
     pr-3 F SG John's-NT SG little-NT SG sister
     'She is John's younger sister.'

(8) **jɔni-č-ẽ*   *bhəyn* *dhakṭ-i.*
     John's-NT SG sister   little-F SG
     'John's sister is younger.'

Further, in the plural, a noun denoting a female can take only the feminine allomorph of
the plural suffix and then its attributive elements also must have feminine plural
agreement, too. The following sentences, therefore, are ungrammatical:

(9) **jɔni-č-ĩ*   *dhakṭ-ĩ*   *bhəyn-ã*   *ay-l-ĩ*
     John's-NT PL little-NT PL sister-NT PL came NT PL
     'John's little/younger sisters came.'

(10) **jɔni-č-ĩ*   *dhakṭ-ĩ*   *bhəyn-i*   *ay-l-ĩ*
     John's-NT PL little-NT PL sisters-F PL came NT PL
     'John's little/younger sisters came.'

2.8 Negation

Konkani has a negative particle *nhəỹ* and also a negative verb *na* (with its past variant
nas-), which has evolved from the agglutination of the older negative particle *nə* with
the verb *as-a* 'be' (reduced to *ah-a* or *a-a* in casual speech in some dialects). An
examination of copula deletion in Konkani makes it clear that the negative verb is
equivalent to the negative particle + copula synchronically as well. The negative verb is

TABLE 20.19: THE NEGATIVE VERB

	Singular	Plural
Present		
All persons	*na*	*nãt*
Past		
1st person	*nasl-ɔ̃* (m)	*nasl-ɛ* (m)
	nasl-ɛ̃ (nt)	*nasl-ĩ* (non-m)
	nasl-ĩ (f)	
2nd and 3rd person	*nasl-ɔ* (m)	*nasl-ɛ* (m)
	nasl-ɛ̃ (nt)	*nasl-ĩ* (nt)
	nasl-i (f)	*nasl-'o* (f)

TABLE 20.20: NEGATIVE FORMS OF VERBS

	Singular	Plural
1. Present imperfect negative: verb stem+ negative verb present		
All persons	*pʌrt-ʌ na*	*pʌrt-ʌ nãt*
2. Future negative: simple participle + negative verb present		
1st person	*pərt-ŭ-c-ɔ na* (m)	*pərt-ŭ-č-ɛ nãt* (m)
	pərt-ŭ-č-ɛ̃ na (nt)	*pərt-ŭ-č-ĩ nãt* (non-m)
	pərt-ŭ-č-i na (f)	
2nd and 3rd persons	*pərt-ŭ-c-ɔ na* (m)	*pərt-ŭ-č-ɛ nãt* (m)
	pərt-ŭ-č-ɛ̃ na (nt)	*pərt-ŭ-č-ĩ nãt* (nt)
	pərt-ŭ-č-i na (f)	*pərt-ŭ-č-o nãt* (f)
3. Past imperfect negative: verb stem + negative verb past		
1st person	*pʌrt-ʌ naslɔ̃* (m)	*pʌrt-ʌ naslɛ* (m)
	pʌrt-ʌ naslɛ̃ (nt)	*pʌrt-ʌ naslĩ (non-m)*
	pʌrt-ʌ naslĩ (f)	
2nd and 3rd person	*pʌrt-ʌ naslɔ* (m)	*pʌrt-ʌ naslɛ* (m)
	pʌrt-ʌ naslɛ̃ (nt)	*pʌrt-ʌ naslĩ* (nt)
	pʌrt-ʌ nasli (f)	*pʌrt-ʌ nasl'o* (f)
4. Perfect negative: perfect + negative verb present		
1st person	*pʌrt-ʌ-l-ɔ̃ na* (m)	*pʌrt-ʌ-l-ɛ nãt* (m)
	pʌrt-ʌ-l-ɛ̃ na (nt)	*pərt-ə-l-ĩ nãt* (non-m)
	pərt-ə-l-ĩ na (f)	
2nd and 3rd person	*pʌrt-ʌ-l-ɔ na* (m)	*pʌrt-ʌ-l-ɛ nãt* (m)
	pʌrt-ʌ-l-ɛ̃ na (nt)	*pərt-ə-l-ĩ nãt* (nt)
	pərt-ə-l-i na (f)	*pərt-ə-l-'o nãt* (f)
5. Present perfect negative: Infinitive + negative verb present		
All persons	*pərt-ŭ-(k) na*	*pərt-ŭ-(k) nãt*
6. Past perfect negative: infinitive + negative verb past		
1st person	*pərt-ŭ-(k) naslɔ̃* (m)	*pərt-ŭ-(k) naslɛ* (m)
	pərt-ŭ-(k) naslɛ̃ (nt)	*pərt-ŭ-(k) naslĩ* (non-m)
	pərt-ŭ-(k) naslĩ (f)	
2nd and 3rd person	*pərt-ŭ-(k) naslɔ* (m)	*pərt-ŭ-(k) naslɛ* (m)
	pərt-ŭ-(k) naslɛ̃ (nt)	*pərt-ŭ-(k) naslĩ* (nt)
	pərt-ŭ-(k) nasli (f)	*pərt-ŭ-(k) nasl'o* (f)
7. Imperative negative: verb stem + verb naka 'not want' (without person marking)		
2nd person	*pʌrt-ʌ naka*	*pʌrt-ʌ nakat*

conjugated as shown in table 20.19. The negative forms of verbs in Konkani are formed with the negative verb occurring as an auxiliary verb after the main verb. These are shown in table 20.20.

2.9 Copula deletion in Konkani

It was claimed in section 2.8 that the negative verb is equivalent to the negative particle + copula. In the following sentences, it can be seen that in equative sentences where copula deletion is obligatory in the affirmative sentences, the corresponding negative sentences must have the negative particle and not the negative verb (see (1), (2) and (3) below). In attributive sentences where copula deletion is optional in the affirmative sentences, the corresponding sentences can have either the negative verb or the negative particle. However, such sentences with the copula deleted do not have the same meaning as the same sentences with the copula not deleted (see (4)–(7) below). In locative sentences where the affirmative sentences cannot have copula deletion, the corresponding negative sentences must have the negative verb and not the negative particle (see(8)–(12) below). Sentences (11) and (12) are locative but the location is not specified.

(1) *t-ɔ   mhʌj-ɔ   isṭ*
     pr-3 M SG my-M SG friend
     'He is my friend.'

(2) *t-ɔ   mhʌj-ɔ   isṭ   nhəy̆*
     pr-3 M SG my-M SG friend neg ptcle
     'He is not my friend.'

(3) **t-ɔ   mhʌj-ɔ   isṭ   na*
     pr-3 M SG my-M SG friend neg vb 3 SG PRES
     'He is not my friend.'

(4) *tẽ   mow*
     pr 3 NT SG   soft
     'It is soft (by nature).'

(5) *tẽ   mow nhəy̆*
     pr 3 NT SG   soft   neg ptcle
     'It is not soft (by nature).

(6) *tẽ   mow as-a*
     pr 3 NT SG   soft   be 3 SG PRES
     'It is soft (at the moment).'

(7) *tẽ   mow na*
     pr 3 NT SG   soft   neg vb 3 SG PRES
     'It is not soft (at the moment).'

(8) *tɔ   iskɔlãt   asa*
     pr-3 M SG   school-at be 3 SG PRES
     'He is at school.'

(9) *tɔ   iskɔlãt   na*
     pr-3 M SG   school-at neg vb SG PRES
     'He is not at school.'

(10) *tɔ   iskɔlãt   nhəỹ
pr-3 M SG school-at neg ptcle
'He is not at school.'

(11) tẽ   asa.
pr 3 NT SG   be 3 SG PRES
'It/ that is there.'

(12) tẽ   na.
pr 3 NT SG   neg vb 3 SG PRES
'It/ that is not there.'

In 'dative subject' constructions such as the following (abstract qualities, enumeration of relatives or parts of the body), copula deletion is optional:

(13) taka   dubaw (asa)
pr 3 M/N SG DAT doubt   be 3 SG PRES
'He has doubt.'

(14) taka   dɔg bhaw   (asat)
pr 3 M/N SG DAT two brothers be 3 PL PRES
'He has two brothers.'

(15) taka   don-ũc pay (asat)
pr 3 M/N SG DAT two-only legs be 3 PL PRES
'He/it has only two legs.'

Note, however, that the copula cannot be deleted in the following sentences which indicate that someone has brothers, legs, etc. but do not enumerate them.

(16) taka   bhaw   asat
pr 3 M/N SG DAT brothers be 3 PL PRES
'He has brothers.'

(17) taka   pay asat
pr 3 M/N SG DAT legs be 3 PL PRES
'He/It has legs.'

3 HISTORICAL PERSPECTIVES

3.1 The place of Konkani among Indo-Aryan languages

Konkani is a member of the southern group of Indo-Aryan languages and is most closely related to Marathi within this group. Like Marathi and Gujarati, the other members of this group, and like Pahadi languages such as Bhadrawahi, it has preserved the Old Indo-European arbitrary three-gender system. However, the old neuter gender has undergone significant innovation in Konkani as described in 2.7. Konkani and the other languages in the southern group have retained the ergative construction like the western Indo-Aryan languages. However, they have more significant ties with the eastern Indo-Aryan languages with which they share certain innovations: for instance, they have all lost the length distinction in the high vowels and all except Gujarati use the -l suffix to indicate the perfect aspect. (Even Gujarati has the -l suffix in its past active participle.)

3.2 Old Konkani

Adequate documentation is available for Old Konkani from only around 1600. Some documents available for the study of Old Konkani, such as grammars, dictionaries and religious treatises prepared by the Portuguese missionaries, have been mentioned in section 1.3. Some indigenous Old Konkani literature (stories from the Rāmāyaṇa and the Mahābhārata) transcribed in the Roman script by the Portuguese has also been preserved.

Old Konkani words show medial syllable vowels and final short vowels which are lost in modern standard Konkani though they are mostly intact in the Southern Saraswat dialect and are retained in special contexts in the Christian Saxtti dialect. In Old Konkani, class 2 adjectives have a full declensional pattern which resembles the declensional pattern of class 2 nouns as can be seen in table 20.21. In Old Konkani adjectives, the oblique singular is distinguished from the oblique plural as shown in table 20.22 just as in the case of nouns. In most modern dialects including the standard dialect, class 2 adjectives have become indeclinable. In addition to the negative forms of verbs found now in which mostly non-finite forms of verbs are followed by a negative verb, Old Konkani also has the older negative forms of verbs in which just the negative particle *nə* preceded the usual affirmative verb form. For instance,

(1) *tẽ ghəḍə   na*
    it happen (stem) neg vb SG PRES
    'It does not happen.'

(2) *tẽ nə   ghəḍə*
    It neg ptcle happen SG PRES

The ergative construction in Old Konkani operates somewhat differently in complex sentences where one clause is attached to another by means of the so-called conjunctive participle. In Old Konkani, whether the subject takes the agentive marker or not depends on the verb which is in the same clause as the subject. It does not matter whether it is finite or not. If it is transitive and underlyingly perfect, the subject takes the agentive marker even though the finite verb in the sentence may be intransitive:

TABLE 20.21: CLASS 2 ADJECTIVES IN OLD KONKANI

| | *wayṭ* 'evil', class 2 | | | |
	Direct singular	Direct plural	Oblique singular	Oblique plural
Masculine	*wayṭŭ*	*wayṭ˜*	*wayṭa*	*wayṭã*
Neuter	*wayṭ˜*	*wayṭã*	*wayṭa*	*wayṭã*
Feminine	*wayṭĩ*	*wayṭi*	*wayṭi*	*wayṭĩ*

TABLE 20.22: OBLIQUE FORMS OF ADJECTIVES IN OLD KONKANI

| | *kaḷɔ* 'black', class 1 | | *wayṭ* 'evil', class 2 | |
	Oblique singular	Oblique plural	Oblique singular	Oblique plural
Masculine	*kaḷ'a*	*kaḷ'ā*	*wayṭa*	*wayṭã*
Neuter	*kaḷ'a*	*kaḷ'ā*	*wayṭa*	*wayṭã*
Feminine	*kaḷe*	*kaḷ'ā*	*wayṭi*	*wayṭĩ*

(3) ta-ṇẽ   hatī   maḷa gheunu   ǰəpə   kərūkə bəysəlo
     he-AGN hand-LOC beads take-CONJ meditation do-to   sat 3 M SG
     'He took the beads in his hand and sat down to meditate.'

In modern Konkani, whether the subject takes the agentive marker or not depends on the finite verb in such a sentence. It does not matter whether that verb is in the same clause as the subject or not:

(4) tɔ   hatãt   maḷa ghewn   ǰəp   kərūk bʌslɔ
     he hand LOC beads take CONJ meditation do-to sat 3 M SG
     'He took the beads in his hand and sat down to meditate.'

The old negative constructions and the old ergative constructions are not found in any of the modern dialects.

Unfortunately, Old Konkani grammars and dictionaries do not explicitly describe regional dialect differentiation. The grammars, dictionaries and the other works were composed mostly in Saxtti. However, the Konkani described by the grammars cannot be said to be in agreement with the Saxtti dialect in all respects. The dictionaries include most lexical items that are now associated with the Bardes dialect as well as those that are now associated with the Saxtti dialect. The fact that Hindus and Christians who belonged to Bardes or Saxtti originally but have lived for centuries outside Goa have yet retained in their dialects characteristic features associated with Bardes or Saxtti makes it clear that dialect differences associated with Bardes and Saxtti are quite old and must have already existed in Old Konkani times. The Hindus of Goa, for instance, had already left Goa because of the coercive proselytization policy of the Portuguese when the Old Konkani grammars and dictionaries were being prepared.

The Brahman–non-Brahman differences in speech must have already existed when Konkani speakers were converted to Christianity by the Portuguese since the Brahman variants found among Hindu Brahmans are also shared by Christians of Brahman origin. The grammars, dictionaries and other Konkani works of the Old Konkani period often make it quite explicit in the title itself that they are using the Brahman dialect: witness titles like *Sintaxis Copiozissima na Lingoa Bramana* (S. Miguel, no date) and *Doutrina Christam em Lingoa Bramana* (Stephens 1622). Given this policy, it is not surprising that non-Brahman variants are not recorded in these works. Even until recently, only Brahman variants were used in writing by Hindus and Christians of all castes.

The peculiarities of the Brahman dialects are restricted to a few lexical items: certain forms of the third person/demonstrative pronouns and the verbs 'come' and 'go' as can be seen from table 20.23. However, these are high frequency items.

3.3 The evolution of the modern Konkani dialects

There is considerable difference between the Konkani spoken by the Hindus and Christians in Bardes, Saxtti and Karnataka. This is because the Hindus and Christians who live in the same area now did not always live together and they came from different areas and at different times. The ancestors of the Karnataka Hindus came from Saxtti and mostly in the sixteenth century. The Christians of Karnataka came from Bardes and about two centuries later. In Goa, because of religious persecution the Hindus had mostly left the Old Conquests and migrated to Maharashtra and Karnataka. Since Marathi is close to Konkani, they must have generally switched to Marathi in Maharashtra. For instance, Saraswat Brahmans in Maharashtra are not originally

TABLE 20.23: BRAHMAN AND NON-BRAHMAN FORMS IN KONKANI

	Brahman	Non-Brahman
Third person or demonstrative pronoun, obviative (oblique stem)		
Masculine/Neuter Singular	*ta-*	*tɛ-*
Feminine Singular	*ti-*	*tie-*
Masculine/Neuter/Feminine Plural	*tã-*	*tẽ-*
Demonstrative pronoun, proximate (oblique stem)		
Masculine/Neuter Singular	*ha-*	*hɛ-*
Feminine Singular	*hi-*	*hie-*
Masculine/ Neuter/Feminine Plural	*hã-*	*hẽ-*
'go' present stem[1]	*wʌ-, wɛ-*	*(w)oy-*
'come' past stem[1]	*ay-*	*(y)ey-*

Note:
1 The initial *y* and *w* glides are automatic in certain dialects before palatal and rounded vowels respectively.

Maharashtrian but are from the Konkani area but they now speak Marathi. The Hindus that moved south to Karnataka and Kerala must have been from the southern Old Conquests, i.e. Saxtti. They continued to speak Konkani where they went and although their dialect differs a great deal from the dialect of the Karnataka Christians, it is remarkably close to the dialect of the Saxtti Christians. After about two centuries of ruling the Old Conquests the Portuguese conquered the peripheral areas of Goa known as the New Conquests. By this time, the Portuguese had given up their old policy of compelling Hindus to become Christians or leave Goa. The Hindu temples in the Old Conquests were all destroyed by the Portuguese in the sixteenth century but they did not destroy the temples in the New Conquests when they came there two centuries later. So the Hindus in the New Conquests did not flee the Portuguese territory. However, they moved in large numbers to the Old Conquests where there were better economic opportunities. The conspicuous difference between Hindu and Christian Konkani in Bardes and Saxtti is due to the fact that the Hindu Konkani speakers who now live there are mostly from the New Conquests. They are not originally from Bardes and Saxtti. For this reason, the Konkani spoken by Hindus in Bardes and Saxtti today is not much different from the Konkani spoken in the New Conquests where there is hardly any difference between the speech of Hindus and Christians.

In the Southern Saraswat dialect, the final short vowels from the Middle Indo-Aryan stage are intact and consonant gemination is also almost intact. The old geminate consonants are degeminated in all the other dialects. The Saxtti Christian dialect retains the Old Konkani final short vowels under certain conditions. These are lost in the Bardes Christian and the Karnataka Christian dialects and also in the Goa Hindu dialect. In Saxtti Christian and Southern Saraswat dialects, the final vowel (short or long) is elided when another word follows without a pause. There is no such elision in the other dialects. Class 2 adjectives are inflected in the Saxtti Christian and the Southern Saraswat dialects. In the other dialects, class 2 adjectives have become indeclinable. As shown in table 20.24, the Saxtti Christian dialect and the Southern Saraswat dialect have certain inflectional endings that are different from those of the other dialects. In these two dialects, several lexical items show different derivational suffixes that are not found elsewhere. Table 20.25 illustrates these differences. Occasionally, the Goa Hindu dialect in Saxtti agrees with the Saxtti Christian dialect as it has come under its influence to some extent.

TABLE 20.24: DIFFERENCES IN INFLECTIONAL ENDINGS AMONG KONKANI DIALECTS

	Southern Saraswat (SS) and Saxtti Christian (SC)	Other dialects
Infinitive ending	-ŭčakã́ (SS) -ŭčak(ɔ) (SC)	-ŭk
Genitive ending in personal pronouns	-gɛl-ɔ, -gɛl-ɛ̃, gɛl-i	-c-ɔ, -čɛ̃, -č-i or -j-ɔ, -ǰ-ɛ̃, -ǰ-i
Plural ending in class 2 nouns	-o	-i

TABLE 20.25: DIFFERENCES IN DERIVATIONAL ENDINGS AMONG KONKANI DIALECTS

	Southern Saraswat (SS) and Saxtti Christian (SC)	Other dialects: Goa Hindu (GH), Bardes Christian (BC), Karnataka Christian (KC)
(1)	'armpit' (n) khakk-ɛ̃ (nt) (SS) xãk-ɛ̃ (nt) (SC) khak-ɛ̃ (nt), khãk (f) (GH-Saxtti)	khãk (f) (GH-Bardes, BC) kak (f) (KC)
(2)	'banana plant' (n) kɛḷ-ĭ (f) (SS) kɛḷ-(i) (f) (SC)	kɛḷ-m-ɔ (m) (GH) kɛḷ-mb-ɔ (m) (KC) key-mb-ɔ (m) (BC)
(3)	'itch' (vb) khorj-ʌ- (SS) xɔrj-ɔ- (SC)	khorju- (GH-Bardes, KC, BC) khʌrjʌ- (GH-Saxtti)
(4)	'limp' (vb) kuṇṭ-w-i- (SS) kŭṭ-i- (SC)	kuṇṭ -ʌ- (GH, KC)
(5)	'mid' (adj) mʌddɛ-č-ɛ̃ (SS) mɔdɛ̃-č-ɛ̃ (SC)	mʌd-l-ɛ̃ (GH) mɔd-l-ɛ̃ (BC, KC)
(6)	'mosquito' (n) jʌḷar-ã́ (nt) (SS) jɔḷar-(ɔ) (nt) (SC) jʌḷar (nt) (GH-Saxtti)	jʌḷar (f) (GH-Bardes, KC) juar (f) (BC)
(7)	'needle' (n) suw-ã́ (nt) (SS) suw-(ɔ) (nt) (SC)	suw-i (f) (GH, KC, BC)
(8)	'relative' (n) dayj-ɔ (SS, SC)	dayǰ-i (GH, KC, BC)
(9)	'rice water' (n) nišš-ɛ̃ (nt) (SS) niš-ɛ̃ (nt) (SC)	niwɔḷ (m) (GH) nis (m) (KC, BC)
(10)	'rind' (n) car-ĭ (f) (SS) car-(i) (f) (SC) car (GH-Saxtti)	car-kʌṇ (nt) (GH-Bardes, KC) car-kɔṇ (nt) (BC)
(11)	'rope' (n) dɔr-ã́ (nt) (SS) dɔr-(ɔ) (nt) (SC)	dor (m) (GH, KC)
(12)	'stem of areca palm leaf' (n) pɔȳ-ã́ (nt) (SS) pɔȳ-(ɔ) (nt) (SC)	pow̃-l-i (f) (GH) pow-l-i (f) (KC, BC)

There are also numerous sporadic differences that serve to distinguish the Southern Saraswat and the Saxtti Christian dialects from the other dialects. There are many lexical items that are shared by these two dialects which are not found elsewhere (see table 20.26). In a few cases, the Goa Hindu dialect in Saxtti has come to agree with the Saxtti Christian dialect as it has come under its influence.

Bardes Christian and Saxtti Christian dialects have undergone one common change that is rather conspicuous: the merger of the mid central vowels with the mid back vowels (ə and ʌ merging with o and ɔ, respectively). It should also be noted that the Christian dialects of Goa are far more influenced by Portuguese than the Hindu dialect since the Christians have lived under the Portuguese for a much longer period and also because they were more susceptible to Portuguese influence because of the religious ties.

3.4 Influence of other languages on Konkani

Being on the Indo-Aryan-Dravidian border, Konkani has been profoundly influenced by Kannada. Goa, the Konkani homeland, was under Kannada rule for several centuries before the advent of the Portuguese. Consequently, Old Konkani documents from the sixteenth and seventeenth centuries already show considerable Kannada influence in grammar as well as vocabulary. Like the Dravidian languages in the south, Konkani has the prothetic glides y- (in words beginning with front vowels) and w- (in words beginning with rounded vowels). These were always written with the glide in Old Konkani. So, in seventeenth-century Konkani dictionary manuscripts, there are no words under E and O. The reader is instead instructed to look for these under I (equivalent to modern I and Y) and U (equivalent to modern U and W), respectively. In modern Konkani, these glides are even more pronounced in the southern dialects than in the Goan dialects of Konkani. The convergence towards Kannada is more evident in Konkani syntactic structure. The question marker in yes/no questions and the negative marker are sentence final. Non-finite forms of the verb are used in the various tense-aspect forms of negative sentences. The subordinate clauses (such as the relative clause, the conditional clause, the purpose clause, and adverbial clauses of manner, place, and time) are placed before the main clause with the 'subordinator' appearing at the end of the subordinate clause. Although subordinate clauses with finite forms of verbs still occur, subordinate clauses with various non-finite forms of verbs have also developed. The old correlative structures are seldom used. The old relative pronouns are still used in Goa but are almost obsolete in the dialects spoken in Karnataka and Kerala. The copula deletion rules in Konkani are remarkably similar to those in Kannada. In the complement construction, the complementizer is a non-finite form of the verb 'to say' and is placed at the end of the complement. Many of the Kannada loanwords found in Old Konkani, however, are no longer found in the Konkani spoken in Goa.

It should be noted that the syntactic convergence of Konkani towards Kannada is by no means total. Conspicuous Indo-Aryan traits like the ergative construction and the arbitrary three-gender system are still there even in the southern dialects. These Indo-Aryan traits, on the other hand, have disintegrated in some of the southern dialects of Marathi and Hindi–Urdu.

Another language that has conspicuously influenced Konkani is Portuguese. But, such influence is limited to the Goan Christian dialects. Dalgado (1913) has a list of Portuguese words borrowed into Goan Christian Konkani. The number of Portuguese words included in his list is about 1800. The literary dialect of the Goan Christians

TABLE 20.26: LEXICAL DIFFERENCES AMONG KONKANI DIALECTS

	Southern Saraswat (SS) and Saxtti Christian (SC)	Other dialects: Goa Hindu (GH), Bardes Christian (BC), Karnataka Christian (KC)
(1)	'cold' (n)	
	thəṇḍi (SS)	*šeḷ* (GH, KC)
	thõḍi (SC)	*šew* (BC)
(2)	'comb' (vb)	
	wəḷəy- (SS)	*ugəy-* (GH-Bardes, KC)
	wɔḷɛ- (SC)	*ugoy-* (BC)
	wʌḷɛ- (GH-Saxtti)	
(3)	'custard apple' (n)	
	ʌṇṇʌṇʌ (SS)	*ātɛr* (GH, BC)
	anɔn(ɔ) (SC)	*at* (KC)
(4)	'drip' (vb)	
	nistʌ- (SS)	*pagʌḷʌ-* (GH, KC)
	nisnɔwɔ- (SC)	*pagɔwɔ-* (BC)
(5)	'fly' (n)	
	kimusã (SS)	*musʌk* (GH, KC)
	kimus(ɔ) (SC)	
(6)	'grinding stone' (n)	
	rʌgḍ ɔ (SS, GH-Saxtti)	*wan* (GH-Bardes, KC, BC)
	rɔgḍɔ (SC)	
(7)	'groan' (vb)	
	pʌrw̃ʌ- (SS)	*pirŋgʌ-* (GH, KC)
	pɔrwɔ- (SC)	*pirŋgɔ-* (BC)
(8)	'groaning' (n)	
	pərwəṇi (SS)	*pirŋgoṇi* (GH-Bardes, KC, BC)
	pɔrwɔṇ(ɔ) (SC)	*pirŋgʌp* (GH-Saxtti)
(9)	'kick' (n)	
	latã (SS)	*khə̃ṭ* (GH)
	lat(i) (SC)	*khɔṭ* (KC, BC)
(10)	'a variety of jackfruit' (n)	
	bʌrkɔ (SS)	*kapɔ pəṇos* (GH, KC)
	borkoy (SC)	*kapɔ poṇos* (BC)
(11)	'pestle' (n)	
	kaṇḍʌṇã (SS)	*musʌḷ* (GH, KC)
	kãḍɔṇ(ɔ) (SC)	*musɔw* (BC)
(12)	'press' (vb)	
	čirḍi- (SS)	*dami-* (GH, BC)
	čiḍḍi- (SC)	*dābi-* (KC)
(13)	'prickly heat' (n)	
	ukrãbɔ (SS)	*ghamɔḷẽ* (GH)
	ukrũbɔ (SC)	*ghamaḷẽ* (KC)
		ghamayẽ (BC)
(14)	'see' (vb)	
	coy- (SS, SC)	*pʌḷɛ-* (GH)
		pəḷəy- (KC)
		powoy- (BC)
(15)	'sweat' (vb)	
	humɛ- (SS, SC)	*ghamɛ-* (GH, KC, BC)
(16)	'sweat' (n)	
	humã (SS)	*gham* (GH, KC, BC)
	hum(ɔ) (SC)	
(17)	'walk' (vb)	
	cʌmkʌ- (SS)	*cʌlʌ-* (GH, KC)
	cɔmkɔ- (SC)	*cɔlɔ-* (BC)

(based on the Bardes Christian dialect) shows widespread syntactic modification due to the influence of Portuguese but such modification is confined to writing and formal speech (such as sermons). The Portuguese patterns have only an optional status in this dialect. Old Konkani does not show any conspicuous influence of Portuguese. The earliest specimens of conspicuous Portuguese syntactic influence go back only to the later decades of the nineteenth century. This phenomenon appears to have been noticed first by Chavan (1924) who complained that, in this dialect of Konkani, 'the construction of sentences awkwardly follows the Portuguese style of sentences'. He selected a few sentences of such modified Konkani from a couple of Goan Christian Konkani periodicals. Two of the sentences from Chavan's specimens were reproduced by Katre (1942) in *The Formation of Konkani*. These sentences, which are from *The Goa Mail*, 8 July 1923, are given below along with comments on their syntactic structure.

(1) *Vortouta tumcho chodd gorgecho anim bari   caido   diuncheak*
     is   your   very essential and important obligation to-give
     bori dek   tumcheam burgueanc astanam tim   lanam
     good example your   children-to being they little.
     'It is your very essential and important obligation to give a good example to your children while they are little.'

The above sentence shows the Portuguese sentence structure NP-Copula-NP, with the sentential subject noun phrase extraposed also as in Portuguese. In normal Konkani, its structure should be NP-NP-Copula where the copula is deleted and the sentential subject noun phrase is not extraposed. In the main clause of the sentence contained in the subject NP *diuncheak bori dek tumcheam burgueanc*, the direct object *bori dek* and the indirect object *tumcheam burgueanc* follow the verb *di*, as in Portuguese, and the verb is in the infinitive form *diuncheak*, also as in Portuguese. According to normal Konkani structure, the direct and the indirect objects should precede the verb and the verb should be in the participle/gerund form *diuncho, diunchi* or *diunchem*. The dependent clause of the sentence contained in the subject NP *astanam tim lanam* follows the main clause as in Portuguese and also shows the word order Copula-NP-Adjective which is compatible with Portuguese. According to normal Konkani structure, this dependent clause should have the word order NP Adjective Copula and it should also precede the main clause.

(2) *Avoi bapui sabar pauttim   khens cortat aplim   burguim aiconant*
     many   times complain parents   one's own kids   listen-not
     vo bexearmi cortat munn aplea   sangnneanc
     and ignore   thus one's own instructions-to
     'Parents often complain that their children disregard and ignore their instructions.'

In this second sentence, the complement clause occurs after the main clause as in Portuguese. In the complement clause, the direct object *aplea sangnneanc* occurs after the verbs *aiconant vo bexearmi cortat* and even after the complementizer *munn*. In normal Konkani structure, the complement occurs usually before the main clause with the complementizer placed at the end of the complement. Also, the object precedes the verb.

In the above two sentences, we have seen instances of the direct object and the indirect object occurring after the verb, the predicate adjective or noun phrase occurring after the copula, and the dependent clause occurring after the main clause. There are also instances of extraposition of a sentential subject noun phrase, the infinitivization of the verb in the sentential noun phrase, and non-deletion of the copula where it is normally deleted. Goan Christian literature also shows other instances of Portuguese syntactic influence such as the occurrence of the adjective, the genitive noun phrase, and the relative clause after the head noun and the occurrence of adverbial phrases after the verb. In the comparative construction, the standard appears after the adjective although the comparison marker still occurs after the standard. There is, however, not a single instance of the occurrence of an adposition before the noun. In the case of the comparative construction, since an adposition is used as the comparison marker in the comparative construction, its occurrence after the standard is in keeping with the general behaviour of the adpositions in this dialect.

Portuguese syntactic influence can be seen not only in the Christian religious literature but also in the secular literature of this dialect. Among the approximately one thousand Goan Christian Konkani works listed in Kelekar (1963), about 175 (about 17%!) show influence of Portuguese word order in their very titles! In most of these cases, the title consists of a head noun followed by a relative clause or reduced relative clause. The most common Portuguese syntactic pattern in these titles is the placement of the genitive noun phrase after the head noun (about 125 cases out of 175). Here are a few examples:

(3)   *Noven   Perpet   Socor   Saibinnichem*
      Novena Perpetual Succour Lady-'s
      'Novena to Our Lady of Perpetual Succour'

(4)   *Preparaçâo   comunhavachem*
      preparation   communion-of
      'Preparation for communion'

(5)   *Educassaum   amchea   ostreanchem*
      education   our   women-of
      'The education of our women'

(6)   *Icravo   mandament   povachea upegacho*
      eleventh commandment people-of use-of
      'The eleventh commandment of use to the people'

(7)   *Porzoll   Goa   xaracho*
      brilliance Goa   city-of
      'The brilliance of the city of Goa'

(8)   *Contha   Concani   bhaxechi*
      story   Konkani   language-of
      'The story of the Konkani language'

After the departure of the Portuguese, there has been an attempt to purge this dialect of excessive Portuguese influence as a result of which the practice of using Portuguese syntactic patterns in Goan Christian Konkani is being gradually abandoned.

REFERENCES

Census of India (1981a) *Population by Bilingualism*, Series 1, Part IVB(ii), Delhi: Office of the Registrar General, Census of India.
—— (1981b) *A Portrait of Population: Goa, Daman and Diu*, Goa: Directorate of Census Operations, Goa, Daman and Diu.
—— (1991) *Language: India and States*, Series 1 (India), Paper 1 of 1997: see Vijayanunni, M.

Chavan, V. P. (1924) 'The Konkan and the Konkani Language', *Journal of the Anthropological Society of Bombay* XII, No. 7: 853–917, New Delhi: Asian Educational Services (Reprinted as booklet (1995) New Delhi: Asian Educational Services).

Cunha Rivara, J. H. da (1857) 'O Ensaio Historico da Lingua Concani', in J. H. da Cunha Rivara (ed.) *Grammatica da Lingua Concani pelo Padre Thomaz Estevão*, Nova Goa: Imprensa Nacional. English translation by Theophilus Lobo entitled 'An Historical Essay on the Konkani Language', in Priolkar, A. K. (1958) *The Printing Press in India*, Bombay: Marathi Samshodhan Mandal, pp. 141–236. [All quotations from Cunha Rivara in this paper are from Theophilus Lobo's translation and the page references also relate to the same work.]

Dalgado, S. R. (1913) *Influéncia do Vocabulário Portugués em Línguas Asiáticas*, Coimbra: University Press.

de Jesus, Christovão (1635) *Gramatica da Bramana*, MS, London: School of Oriental and African Studies, London University.

Katre, S. M. (1942) *The Formation of Konkani*, Poona: Deccan College (Reprinted 1966).

Kelekar, Ravindra (1963) *A Bibliography of Konkani Literature in Devanagari, Roman, and Kannada Characters*, Goa: Gomant Bharati Publications.

Keni, Chandrakant (1976) 'Novea porvachea humbravelean' (On the threshold of a new era), Presidential Address to the Eleventh All India Konkani Conference, Mangalore: V. J. P. Saldanha. (In Konkani).

Martyres, F. J. (1974) 'Porishodechim postis vorsam: fattlea nnov porishodancho itihas' (Thirty-five years of the conference: an account of the last nine conferences), in *Okhil Bharotiya Konkani Porishod, Dhavi Boska* (All India Konkani Literature Conference, Tenth Meeting), Panaji, Goa: U. Bhembro. (In Konkani).

Pereira, José (1973) *Literary Konkani: A Brief History*, Dharwar, India: Konkani Sahitya Prakashan.

Priolkar, A. K. (1961) *The Goa Inquisition*, Bombay: Bombay University Press.

Ribeiro, Diogo (1626) *Vocabulario da Lingoa Canarim*, MS 1 entitled Vocabulario da Lingoa Canarim, Panaji, Goa: Central Library; MS 2 entitled *Vocabulario da Lingoa da Terra*, Lisbon: Biblioteca Nacional da Ajuda; MS 3 entitled *Vocabulario da Lingoa Canarina com Versa Portugueza* containing only the Konkani–Portuguese part and not bearing the name of the author, Lisbon: Arquivo Histórico Ultramarino. (Facsimile edition of MS 3 (1973), Lisbon: Junta de Investigações do Ultramar.) [The 3 manuscripts contain different versions of the same work.]

—— (1632) *Declaraçam da Doutrina Christam*, Rachol, Goa: Collegio de S. Ignacio.

S. Miguel, Gaspar de (no date) *Sintaxis Copiozissima na Lingoa Bramana e Pollida*, MS, London: School of Oriental and African Studies, University of London.

Stephens, Thomas (1622) *Doutrina Christam em Lingoa Bramana Canarim*, Rachol, Goa: Collegio de Rachol da Cõpanhia de Jesus. Facsimile edition, Mariano Saldanha (ed.) (1945) *Doutrina Cristã em Lingua Concani por Tomás Estévão*, Lisbon: Agencia Geral das Colonias.

—— (1640) *Arte da Lingoa Canarim*, Rachol, Goa: Collegio de S. Ignacio. Second edition, J. H. da Cunha Rivara (ed.) (1857) *Grammatica da Lingua Concani pelo Padre Thomaz Estevão*, Nova Goa: Imprensa Nacional.

Vijayanunni, M. (1997) *Census of India 1991, Series 1-India, Paper 1 of 1997: Language, India and States*, New Delhi: Government of India Press.

Wheritt, Irene (1985) 'Portuguese language use in Goa, India', *Anthropological Linguistics* 27: 437–51.

FURTHER READING

Almeida, Mathew (1989) *A Description of Konkani*, Miramar, Goa: Thomas Stephens Konkani Center.

Konow, S. (1905) 'Konkani', in Sir George A. Grierson (ed.) *Linguistic Survey of India* Vol. 7, Calcutta: Office of the Superintendent of Government Printing (Reprinted (1968) Delhi: Motilal Banarsidass).

Maffei, A. F. X. (1882) *A Konkani grammar*, Mangalore, India: Basel Mission Press.

Miranda, Rocky V. (1978) 'Caste, religion, and dialect differentiation in the Konkani area', in Kachru, Braj B. and Sridhar, S. N. (eds.) *Aspects of Sociolinguistics in South Asia*, *International Journal of the Sociology of Language* 16: 77–91.

—— (1982) 'The status of Konkani during the Portuguese era', *South Asian Review* 6.3: 204–13.

—— (1992) 'Language standardization in progress: the case of Konkani', in Dimock, Edward C. Jr., Kachru, Braj B. and Krishnamurti, Bh. (eds.) *Dimensions of Sociolinguistics in South Asia: Papers in Memory of Gerald B. Kelley*, New Delhi: Oxford and India Book House Publishing, pp. 213–21.

Pereira, José (1971) *Konkani, a Language*, Dharwar: Karnataka University.

CHAPTER TWENTY–ONE

SINHALA

James W. Gair

CONTENTS

LIST OF TABLES

1 GENERAL BACKGROUND

Sinhala (also known as Sinhalese) is the native language of approximately 74 per cent of the population of Sri Lanka (estimated 18.5 million in 1998) or approximately thirteen and a half million speakers. It was made the official language of the country in 1956, a status extended to Tamil in 1987, with English given official recognition as a link language. Sinhala-speaking areas cover the major proportion of the island, including the southwest, the south-central highland, and most of the north-central dry zone. The northern part of the island and much of the east coast are predominantly Tamil-speaking, and there is a significant Tamil population in the highland regions as a result of imported labour for the tea (and earlier coffee) plantations.

According to Sinhala tradition, the language reached there with a band of North Indian wanderers led by a Prince Vijaya, synchronically with the final passing (Pali *parinibbāna*) of Gotama (Gautama) Buddha, traditionally dated 543 BC. Inscriptions in the earliest attested form of the language, Sinhala Prakrit, date from the third to second centuries BC, following the arrival of Buddhism in the third century. By that time, the language had already taken on a special character, suggesting a sufficient interval for the relevant changes to occur (Geiger 1938). Given that the only clear close relative is Dhivehi (= Maldivian, and on Minicoy as Mahl), with none on the mainland, a sixth to fourth centuries BC date for the language to have reached the island, and perhaps the Maldives and Minicoy as well, does not seem unreasonable. References in Pali texts and in later commentaries point to an apparently extensive early Buddhist literature, which was unfortunately lost, and the earliest available literary works date from about the tenth century on to the present day (Karunatillake 1969, Paranavitana 1956, Wijeratne 1945–57). Fortunately, the epigraphical records continued up to and past that time, yielding a continuous record of examples of the language from third to second centuries BC to the present (an unusual and probably unique feature among Indo-Aryan languages).

There is a considerable literature, most of it until fairly recently Buddhist in nature, encompassing both prose and poetry as well as commentarial works (see Geiger 1935, Godakumbura 1955, Reynolds 1970, 1987). Although earlier works were often renditions of Pali works, they generally took on a local character of their own in content and style, and many of them are still read today with affection. In the nineteenth century the novel was introduced followed by the short story and the drama, and these genres are flourishing today. The Sinhala stage in particular exhibits tremendous vitality, and often addresses contemporary problems and themes.

The rate of literacy is high (over 85 per cent), resulting from a long tradition of vernacular education in the Buddhist temple and later in state schools under the British. The implementation of the 1956 Official Language Act, whatever its other results, extended Sinhala into new domains where English had predominated, and added new flexibility to the language. (Fernando 1977, Gair 1983a)

1.1 The position of Sinhala within Indo-Aryan

Though geographically isolated from all of the mainland Indo-Aryan languages, Sinhala is without doubt an Indo-Aryan language. Some earlier scholars, such as Rask, had held it to be Dravidian, but the resemblances are clearly the result of structural influence and lexical borrowing at different times over two millennia. Consideration of the basic vocabulary, as well as a number of fundamental grammatical properties leave no doubt as to its membership in the IA family (see Geiger 1937, Hettiaratchi 1959 for an account).

Sinhala has been variously placed as eastern, western, southern and southwestern IA (see Karunatillake 1974, Masica 1991: Appendix II, 446–63, and De Silva 1979: 13–20). There are few if any common changes that can be adduced to connect it with any specific mainland language or group of languages, and some of the proposed evidence for classification consists of retentions, and is thus not conclusive, such as initial /v/-, shared by Marathi and other western languages. In this context, we may note that Sinhala also retained initial /y/, as opposed to the general change of /y-/ to /j-/ in the rest of Middle-Indo Aryan, which gives evidence of early isolation rather than subgroup affiliation. As Geiger stated in 1935 (xxiii)

> Summarizing the discussion, we may say that owing to the geographical isolation and peculiar development of the Sinhalese language, it is extremely difficult and perhaps impossible to assign it to a definite place among the modern Indo-Aryan Dialects.

One reason for this indeterminacy, as Geiger noted, is that more than one dialect appears to have entered into the formation of the language. Another important reason is that the language was established on the island before most of the changes generally adduced in the classification of its northern relatives occurred. Thus, those changes from OIA into the earliest inscriptional Sinhala Prakrit that were shared with mainland languages applied to Prakrits generally or are problematic in India as well. The epigraphical history, with the work of scholars such as Wijeratne and Karunatillake, makes it clear that some changes that might appear to be shared with mainland Indo-Aryan in fact occurred independently (or were shared with Dhivehi) after separation from other Indo-Aryan. For example, the simplification of geminates, with compensatory vowel lengthening (VCC > VVC) dates from the second to fourth centuries AD. A particularly striking example is the coalescence of /ṇ/ and /n/ into /n/, since, in contrast with what occurred in the mainland languages, the distinction was maintained until the eighth century AD. (Karunatillake 1969: 112–14).

Although proposed affiliations have been more often with western, southern or southwestern Indo-Aryan, perhaps the strongest evidence links it with the east. A number of the inscriptions have nominative singular in -*e*, as in Magadhi, prose Ardhamagadhi and eastern inscriptions. This was noted by Geiger (1935: xx), but there is strong indirect evidence as well. 'Umlaut' of long vowels was triggered by a following /i/ (fourth century), but there are also many forms in Sinhala that show the results of umlaut (vowel fronting) in which their OIA or MIA etymons lacked an /i/. A plausible explanation for many if not most of these instances is that fronting was indeed triggered by a following /i/, but one that resulted from an otherwise attested merger of final /e/ with /i/. Thus /bæt-a/ 'paddy; from */bāti/ < */batte/ (OIA /bhaktam/, Pali /bhattam/). For a fuller account see Karunatillake 1969: 81–93. This in turn indicates the presence of more final -*e* forms than directly attested in the lithic record.

On the other hand, evidence for classification with Dhivehi (Maldivian) is strong. The most obvious of these is the complete loss of aspiration in both languages; e.g. Sinh. /dunna/ 'bow', Dhiv. /duni/ 'arrow', Sanskrit /dhanus/; Sinh. /aṅdura/, Dhiv. /aṅdiri/ 'dark'. Sanskrit /andhakāra/. Given the persistence of the feature in Indo-Aryan generally, it is perhaps the single most distinguishing feature of Sinhala-Dhivehi phonology vis-à-vis the others. Note also the development of prenasalized stops in Sinhala and Dhivehi (see section 4.2).

There are no examples of early inscriptions for Dhivehi, and the relative order or simultaneity of settlement with Sinhala is disputed, as is the date of their separation (Geiger 1919, De Silva 1970, Maloney 1978, Wijesundera et al. 1988, Cain and Gair 2000, Cain 2000, and Fritz 2002). However, the phonological evidence so far, based on common and independent changes, suggests that a tenth century AD split as proposed by Geiger is too late, while a split prior to the third or fourth century is too early. Further work, including morphological and syntactic evidence, is proceeding.

1.2 Influence of Dravidian and the South–South Asia linguistic area

Not unexpectedly, given its long isolation from other Indo-Aryan, Sinhala exhibits considerable influence from the neighboring Dravidian languages. Although Tamil is usually cited, 'South Dravidian' or 'Tamil-Malayalam' would be more appropriate, since much of the influence precedes the split of the latter. Sinhala has thus become a member of a South-South Asia linguistic area (Gair 1994). The influence is not uniform across levels of structure, however. In lexicon, there is considerable Dravidian borrowing, and it extends to much ordinary vocabulary. In phonology, although claims have been made for heavy Dravidian influence at a very early date (Elizarenkova 1972), the situation is not that clear when carefully examined (Gair 1985). Simply put, aside from the loss of aspiration dating from the earliest records, the Sinhala phonological system is not at any period what one would expect if it were filtered in some way through South Dravidian.

In syntax, the Dravidian influence is indeed considerable, appearing in numerous features by which Sinhala differs from its northern kin, and only a few of the most striking can be mentioned here (see Gair 1985, 1986a, Ratanajoti 1975 for a fuller account).

The most striking evidence for influence is the thoroughgoing left-branching nature of Sinhala, comparable to that of South Dravidian. For example, the relative clause structure is of the verbal adjective (sometimes called 'participial') type in which the modifying clause precedes the head (see section 6.7), and this has been virtually exclusive from the earliest records (Paranavitana 1956). Geiger noted in his grammar that 'the relative pronoun does not exist in Sinhalese' and that 'This remarkable fact may partly be attributed to the influence of the Dravidian languages which do not possess a relative pronoun' (1937: 130).

In fact, the correlative structure does exist in literary Sinhala, and makes use of a reflex of MIA *ya* (probably locative *yamhi* and possibly a reborrowing), unlike the Dravidian languages that use an interrogative (Wh) form. However, the construction is no more visible than in Dravidian languages, and it is not even a standard equivalent for correlatives in works that adapt Pali originals (Wijemanne 1984). Moreover, it is generally limited to indefinite or conditional use, as in Dravidian, and it includes a clause final question particle *da* or a conditional form, another similarity to Dravidian.

The use of the postposed question particle is in itself another feature shared with Dravidian. Another notable feature is the existence of a focused or cleft sentence construction (see section 6.4.3) lacking in mainland Indo-Aryan, and apparently originating in a Dravidian model, though much elaborated and increased in frequency in Sinhala (Gair 1986a, Paolillo 1994).

It is important to note, however, the degree to which Sinhala maintains its Indo-Aryan character or has innovated independently. In the structures mentioned, the morphological correlates are characteristically Indo-Aryan. The question particle *da*, for example, while patterning much (though by no means completely) like the corresponding South Dravidian forms, has an apparent IA etymon in OIA/ Early MIA *ca* 'and' (Geiger 1941: 68), and the cleft construction makes use of IA morphological material (Gair 1986a). Thus despite a sizable element of Dravidian lexicon, the functional categories of Sinhala are characteristically IA (Geiger 1937), and it is important not to overlook this and the extent to which Sinhala has innovated. For example, case endings have IA sources, such as the general dative ending *-ṭa* (cf. Early MIA *aṭṭhāya*), and the animate genitive *-gē* (cf. Pali *gēhē* [Geiger 1938: 110]). Also the complex derivational system of active, involitive and causative in Sinhala verbs is built on IA morphological material but differs from both Dravidian and mainland IA.

Furthermore, in individual instances where Dravidian influence could be adduced, it is not always possible to rule out typological pressure (Gair 1994), such as increasing conformity to a right-branching model as evidenced in such languages as Japanese as well as in Dravidian. Taking all of the features together, however, the case for influence, particularly in syntax, becomes clear.

2 VARIETIES AND DIGLOSSIA

2.1 Regional varieties

There has been little work done on regional dialects so far, though it is clear that there are at least some general regional dialects including a southern one, an upcountry (Kandyan) one, and a southwestern one that includes the region of the capital Colombo. In so far as there is an emerging spoken standard, it appears to be based on the southwestern one, with some admixture of the southern. There are lexical differences, extending to such items as kin terms, and some differences in grammatical forms. Among the latter are forms of the infinitive, ending in *-ṇḍə* in the Colombo area, *-nṭə* in the upcountry, and *-nnə* in the south. The *-nṭə* variant in particular is markedly regional, but whether *-nnə* or *ṇḍə* is the dominant standard form is not clear. Disanayaka 1991 ascribes that status to the latter, but *-nnə* is the one most commonly taken as basic in texts for foreigners such as Fairbanks, Gair and De Silva 1968, Macdougall 1979, Karunatillake 1992, and Reynolds 1995. It appears that all dialects are mutually intelligible once some relatively minor adjustments are made, and in any event the importance of a standard spoken variety is diminished by the strongly diglossic nature of Sinhala (section 2.2).

2.2 Sinhala diglossia

One variety of Sinhala is generally referred to as Literary Sinhala, though it is by no means restricted to literature *per se*. It is the vehicle of virtually all written materials or materials expressed orally but written in advance or formulaic, including news broadcasts, government documents and forms, newspaper editorials and airline announcements. It differs in grammar and lexicon from all spoken varieties, collectively referred to as Spoken Sinhala. There are sub-varieties of Literary Sinhala, but all of them share a set of properties, of which the most notable is the presence of verb agreement, in contradistinction to all spoken varieties, which lack it. This along with some accompanying features has been taken as the fundamental defining feature of the distinction between the (hyper-)varieties (Gair 1968, 1986b, 1992, 1998, but see De Silva 1974, 1976 and Paolillo 1992 and especially 1997).

There are several varieties within Spoken Sinhala, ranging from the colloquial one that is the usual vehicle of informal face-to-face interaction to formal varieties used in lectures, sermons, media interviews and other oral presentations not written in advance. Table 21.1 (adapted by Paolillo 1997 from Gair 1986b) gives the distribution of functions of the varieties and a comparison with the values that would be predicted for 'standard' diglossia as in Ferguson 1959. Most notable is the use of a formal spoken variety for several functions for which H would be predicted.

TABLE 21.1: FUNCTIONS OF H AND L VARIETIES: SINHALA AND OTHERS

	Sinhala variety used	Predicted variety
Instructions to servants, waiters workmen, clerks	Spoken	L
Conversation with family, friends, colleagues	Spoken	L
Radio 'soap opera'	Spoken	L
Caption on political cartoon	Spoken	L
Folk literature	Spoken	L
Sermon in church or mosque	Spoken (Formal)	H
University lecture	Spoken (Formal)	H
Speech in parliament, political speech	Spoken (Formal)(or Literary)[1]	H
Personal letter	Spoken (Formal)(or Literary)[1]	H
Novels (Conversational parts)	Spoken	L^2
(non-conversational parts)	Literary	H^2
News broadcast	Literary	H
Newspaper editorial, news story, picture caption	Literary	H
Poetry	Literary	H
Government documents, forms	Literary	H^2
Airline announcements	Literary	H^2

Notes:
1 Depending on circumstances such as degree of spontaneity and formality.
2 Not in Ferguson 1959.

Formal spoken Sinhala has been defined (Gair 1986b [1998: 226]) as a variety that '… makes use of one, and usually more, grammatical features of Literary (other than verb agreement) with relative consistency. It characteristically makes considerable use of a formal lexicon shared with Literary.'

One factor in the use of this sub-variety appears to be the difficulty for users in coping with the grammatical features of the literary variety, and especially with agreement and its structural ramifications in 'on the spot' production. The use of such a formal spoken variety for debates and presumably sermons, etc. goes back to at least the nineteenth century, and its use is increasing as Sinhala is called upon to fill an increasingly wide range of public functions, partly as a result of language policy (Fernando 1977, Gair 1983a). For further discussion and examples, see especially Paolillo 1992, 1997.

Literary Sinhala differs from spoken, and especially from colloquial Sinhala, at all levels of structure, except for phonology. There the difference is minimal since oral production of written materials makes use of the spoken inventory and differences extend largely to performance factors such as a reading pronunciation adhering to the written form.

Not unexpectedly, there are differences in lexicon, but for many items there is a continuum from colloquial to literary (De Silva 1974, Paolillo 1992, 1997). This is partly if not largely a result of the use of formal vocabulary shared with literary in formal spoken, so that one often cannot assign a form exclusively to one hyper-variety or the other, though some forms would be used in colloquial but not formal presentations.

One notable feature of Sinhala diglossia is that lexical differences between varieties extend to function words, so that in progressing from colloquial to literary different sets of prepositions, conjunctions, etc. are employed. Thus *handa*, *hinda*, *nisaa*, all mean 'because' and exhibit a progression from colloquial to literary with the first form characteristic of colloquial, and the last one generally used in literary, though it could also be used in formal spoken situations. The set *gaawə*, *laṅgə*, *asala* 'near' represent a similar progression. Current literary Sinhala, especially in technical usage, makes heavy use of a Sanskritic vocabulary, which may appear in adapted or inherited form in spoken varieties. Thus *varšā* 'rain', with a Sinhala ending *(v)ə*, appears in literary and can be used in formal Sinhala, but spoken Sinhala has *warusaawə* and *wæssə* (stem *wæhi*), the latter an inherited form. [Here and throughout, literary forms are given in transliteration and spoken forms appear in phonemic transcription, thus avoiding some problems in reconciling the forms (see Gair 1968).]

Interestingly, inherited forms (tadbhavas), especially in the form that they would have in approximately the thirteenth century, may have even more formal or prestigious overtones from a 'truly Sinhala' perspective than their Sanskritic counterparts and thus appear in advertisements and the names of government or 'national' organizations. Thus, Laksala (*laṇkā śālā*) and Osusala (*auṣadha śālā*) for the names of the government handicrafts shops and medicine outlets respectively.

The pronominal systems and inventories differ across the varieties. Thus, the third person pronouns *hē* or *hetema* 'he', *ō*, *ōtomō* 'she', *eya* 'it' are literary forms; Spoken has *eyaa* '(s)he' and *eekə* 'it' as the nearest equivalents.

In morphology, the difference is considerable and encompasses differences in categories as well as items. For example, literary Sinhala has an oblique form that functions as a free-standing accusative as well as a base for further case affixes. In colloquial Sinhala this survives in attenuated form only as a stem for case affixes. Instead, there is an accusative affix -*wə* that applies only to animate nouns (and is then not found in all dialects) and has a quite different syntactic distribution (see section 6.4.1.1). Table 21.2 gives forms in colloquial and literary Sinhala for three cases of the animate noun *minihā* and the inanimate noun *potə* 'book' (for full spoken paradigms, see section 5.1).

The difference in verb forms is even greater than in nominals. The major, but by no means only, difference is that spoken Sinhala lacks verbal agreement, while literary Sinhala has a strong system of agreement, involving person, number and gender. Table 21.3 presents limited paradigms for comparison.

There are other verbal forms that exist in only one or the other of the varieties, or which have different uses in the two. For example, the volitive and involitive optative forms, such as *balannaŋ* 'I/we will look', *balaavi/balayi* '(someone) might look' are limited to the spoken variety (see section 5.4), although the second of these may now be finding some literary use (W. S. Karunatillake, personal communication). In contrast, the concurrent, absolute and passive participles *balamin*, *balat*, and *balanu* belong to the Literary variety; see Gair and Karunatilaka 1974, 1976 for the literary forms and contrastive information.

There are also differences in idiom between the varieties. Thus literary example (1a) would have its nearest morphologically direct spoken translation in (1)b:

(1)a *yakšaniya duṭu kumarā esēma pævasīya*
     demoness-ACC see-PAST-REL prince thus speak-PAST-3SG
     'The prince who saw the demoness spoke thus.'

 b *yakšini (wə) dækkə kumaarəya ehemə kiwwa*
     demoness (ACC) see-PAST-REL prince thus speak-PAST
     'The prince who saw the demoness spoke thus.'

TABLE 21.2: SPOKEN AND LITERARY NOUNS

Case	Singular		Plural
	Definite	Indefinite	
Animate			
Direct			
Coll	*miniha* 'the man'	*minihek*	*minissu*
Lit	*minisā*	*minisek*	*minissu*
Accusative			
Coll	*minihawə*	*minihekwə*	*minissunwə*
Lit	*minisā*	*minisaku(-eku)*	*minisun*
Dative			
Coll	*minihaṭə*	*minihekuṭə*	*minissunṭə*
Lit	*minisāṭa*	*minisakuṭa*	*minisunṭa*
Inanimate			
Direct[1]			
Coll and Lit[2]	*potə/pota* 'the book'	*potak*	*pot*
Dative			
Coll and Lit	*potəṭə/potaṭa*	*potəkəṭə/potakaṭa*	*potwələṭə/potvalaṭa*

Notes:
1 Nouns of this type have no separate accusative in either variety but only a direct case in both functions.
2 Colloquial forms are represented phonemically, Literary forms in transliteration. Read aloud, the Literary and Colloquial Inanimate nouns would not differ.

TABLE 21.3: SPOKEN AND LITERARY VERBS

	Singular	Plural
Verb balanawā/balənəwa 'look, observe'		
Present tense		
Literary		
First person	*balami*	*balamu*
Third person	*balayi*	*balati*
Spoken		
All persons and numbers	*balənəwa*	
Past tense		
Literary		
First person	*bæluvemi,*	*bæluvemu*
Third person		
Masculine	*bæluvēya*	
Feminine	*bæluvāya*	*bæluvōya*
Neuter	*bæluvēya*	
Spoken		
All persons, numbers, and genders	*bæluwa*	

However, in discourse, (1a) can mean 'Having seen the demoness, the prince spoke thus'. The use of a relative clause in discourse linking of this kind is essentially a literary device, and in Colloquial Sinhala (1b) would more likely be interpreted in the literal sense given, with the 'having seen' sense more likely to be be expressed there as (2) with a conjunctive participle. (Thanks are owed to W. S. Karunatillake for this example.)

(2) *yakšini (wə) dækəla kumaarəya ehemə kiwwa.*
     demoness (ACC) see-PAST -PPL prince thus speak-PAST
     'The prince who saw the demoness spoke thus.'

Thus the native speaking Sinhala student, in learning the literary language, is essentially faced with a second, albeit closely related, language. Not surprisingly, full competence is often lacking (see De Silva 1967, 1974, 1976), and this may account at least in part for the wide use of a formal spoken variety in live, spontaneous production situations.

2.3 Previous descriptive work on the varieties

Prior to World War II, most published grammars of Sinhala, including the classic ones of A. Mendis Gunasekara (1891) and Wilhelm Geiger (1938) dealt almost exclusively with the Literary language, with essentially side glances at the spoken varieties, and Geiger's work was primarily directed at the historical dimension. There was also a local tradition, based largely on the classical thirteenth century grammar *Sidatsañgarā*, and a descriptive/prescriptive school represented by the works of Munidasa Kumaranatunga, which included a critical study of the *Sidatsañgarā* (1934). Both of these local traditions continue. Beginning in the 1950s, however, with the flourishing of structural-descriptive linguistics and its attention to spoken languages, and notably with the pioneering work of M. W. S. De Silva, attention turned to the colloquial language, and since that time descriptive work expanded and focused on that variety. This included the production of texts for teaching the language, such as Fairbanks, Gair and De Silva 1968, Macdougall 1979, Reynolds 1980/1995, Gair, Karunatillake and Paolillo 1987, and Karunatillake

1992. In the absence of prior description, these works necessitated considerable groundwork and they still contain much of the available descriptive information.

However, since the 1960s there there has been a considerable amount of work on the language, especially in phonology and syntax, reflecting the changes in linguistic theory to the present. Most work of this kind is to be found in dissertations and in papers scattered in various journals and collections. Aside from the teaching texts referred to earlier, books and monographs devoted to description and analysis of the language have been largely absent since Gair 1970, which was based largely on work from the early 1960s. Recently, a brief descriptive sketch has appeared (Gair and Paolillo 1997). De Silva 1979 devotes a chapter to the history of descriptive studies up to the late 1970s.

Though dialect studies are few, there has been considerable work on Sinhala diglossia and the relations, both in structure and usage, between the varieties. An account of that work up to the late 1970s can be found in De Silva 1979, extended in Paolillo 1992.

2.4 The varietal scope of this chapter

From the foregoing, it will be clear that, given the number of differences between the spoken and literary varieties, with categories not matching on a one-to-one basis, it would be necessary to virtually double the length of this chapter if both were to be described. A sense of the magnitude of the difference may be gained simply by scanning the considerable amount of grammatical description in a basic text for the literary language that assumes a knowledge of the spoken variety. The amount of such description that proved necessary there provides a tangible measure of the degree and nature of the distance between the varieties (Gair and Karunatillake 1974). This chapter thus describes the spoken variety only, except for the few examples cited above in section 2.2.

For the literary language, except for the textbook just referred to, which requires a knowledge of the Sinhala script, there is little available in English except for such older works mentioned earlier as those by Mendis Gunasekara (also requiring the script) and Geiger, which still retain their value. A descriptive study in Sinhala of the literary variety has recently appeared (Karunatillake 1995), and efforts are underway to produce an English version.

3 ORTHOGRAPHY

The Sinhala writing system is unique to Sinhala, except for its use in Sri Lanka to write Pali, and sometimes Sanskrit. It is of the Brahmi-derived 'alphasyllabic' type common in South Asia, in which vowels are written as modifications of the consonants, except word-initially, where independent vowel symbols are used. There are actually two recognized forms of the script, one a subset of the other. The full set is known as the *miśra siṇhala hōḍiya*, or 'mixed alphabet', and includes the symbols necessary for writing loanwords or texts from Sanskrit and Pali, most notably the aspirated consonants, which do not occur in spoken Sinhala (see section 4.2). A subset of this inventory is called the *eḷu hōḍiya*, from the classical language Eḷu, as described in the classical grammar *Sidatsaṅgarā* (*c.* AD 1300; see De Alwis 1852, De Silva 1986b). That smaller alphabet is still regarded by many as the authoritative, truly Sinhala one, and it appears in current school charts and grammars even today. The character for /c/ is commonly omitted, since it is not listed in the *Sidatsaṅgarā*. Interestingly, the classical alphabet, with <c> added, suffices as a good representation of current Colloquial Sinhala. The 'inherent ' vowel, <a> associated with unmarked consonant symbols is pronounced [a] or [ɔ] depending on position, and if one allows for this together with some other positionally determined vowel alternations such as vowel shortening (see section 4) and adds a few symbols for loanwords (notably for /f/ and /š/), the *eḷu hōḍiyə* can serve as a phonemically adequate representation of current spoken Sinhala. The alphabet is displayed in table 21.4 with letters included in the classical alphabet having their transcriptions in italics. For a fuller description of the Sinhala writing system, see Gair 1995, Gair and Karunatillake 1976.

4 PHONOLOGY

4.1 Vowels

Sinhala has seven basic vowel qualities, indicated in table 21.5. Each vowel occurs long and short, but the long schwa, /əə/, has a marginal status, occurring only in English loanwords such as /šəət/ 'shirt', /səəwis/ 'service'.

The vowel pairs [ə] and [a], on the one hand, and and [a] and [aa] on the other, are in a complex relationship involving both complementation and overlap. Essentially, the situation is as follows (for a fuller account see Karunatillake 1987b, Letterman 1997, Gair and Paolillo 1997).

TABLE 21.4: THE SINHALA ALPHABET

Vowels

අ	ආ	ඇ	ඈ	ඉ	ඊ
a	*ā*	*æ*	*ǣ*	*i*	*ī*
උ	ඌ	ඍ	ඎ	ඏ	ඐ
u	*ū*	ṛ	r̥̄	ḷ	ḹ
එ	ඒ	ඓ	ඔ	ඕ	ඖ
e	*ē*	ai	*o*	*ō*	au

Consonants

ක	බ	ග	ඝ	ඞ	ඟ
ka	kha	*ga*	gha	ṅa	ṅ̆ga
ච	ඡ	ජ	ඣ	ඤ	ඦ
ca	cha	*ja*	jha	ña	ñja
ට	ඨ	ඩ	ඪ	ණ	ඬ
ṭa	ṭha	*ḍa*	ḍha	ṇa	ṇ̆ḍa
ත	ථ	ද	ධ	න	ඳ
ta	tha	*da*	dha	na	ñda
ප	ඵ	බ	භ	ම	ඹ
pa	pha	*ba*	bha	*ma*	m̆ba
ය	ර	ල	ව		
ya	ra	la	va		
ශ	ෂ	ස	හ	ළ	
śa	ṣa	*sa*	ha	ḷa	

TABLE 21.5: SINHALA VOWELS

	Front		Central		Back	
	short	long	short	long	short	long
High	*i*	*ii*			*u*	*uu*
Mid	*e*	*ee*	*ə*	(*əə*)	*o*	*oo*
Low	*æ*	*ææ*			*a*	*aa*

(1) In initial syllables, [ə], [a] and [aa] contrast, but [ə] occurs in only a few forms, essentially forms of the verb /kərə/ 'do', and following certain consonant clusters, primarily consonant + /r /; e.g. /prəsiddə/ 'famous', /krəmee/ 'method'.
(2) In medial open syllables, [ə] and [aa] contrast, but with [a] rather than [ə] occurring following an /h/ that is immediately preceded by [ə], [a] or [aa].
(3) In medial syllables followed by a geminate consonant or cluster, [a] and [aa] contrast, and [ə] does not occur.
(4) In final syllables preceding a final consonant, [a] and [aa] contrast, and [ə] does not occur, but there are some exceptions to this, for more "sophisticated" speakers in English loans such as /ṭikəṭ/ 'ticket'.
(5) [ə], [a] and [aa] occur as final vowels, but [a] and [aa] are in complementation, depending on the canonical shape of the word. The conditions here are complex, but can be summarized as:
   (a) If the penultimate syllable is long (VV or V(V)CC), [a] occurs.
   (b) If the penultimate syllable (including the first syllable of disyllables) is short: in disyllables [aa] will occur; in longer forms, the distribution is more complex, modulated by specific consonants and syllable sequences.

Thus it is possible, setting aside the invariant occurrences of [ə] in the initial syllables in some forms, to postulate two underlying vowels /a/ and /aa/ (for one attempt of this kind see De Silva 1963). In this chapter, however, the three-way contrast will be written, in part because it gives a better idea of the relative frequencies of [ə] and the other two, and especially the pervasiveness of /ə/, which is a noteworthy characteristic of Sinhala.

4.2 Consonants

Sinhala consonants are shown in table 21.6.

The existence of a series of prenasalized stops, sometimes referred to as 'half-nasals', is noteworthy. They contrast with nasal+ (voiced) stop clusters; e.g. *kambee*

TABLE 21.6: SINHALA CONSONANTS

	Labial	Dental	Retroflex-alveolar	Palatal	Velar	Glottal
Voiceless	*p*	*t*	*ṭ*	*c*	*k*	
Voiced	*b*	*d*	*ḍ*	*j*	*g*	
Nasal	*m*	*n*		*ñ*	*ŋ*	
Prenasalized	*m̃b*	*ñd*	*ñḍ*	*ñj*	*ŋ̃g*	
Fricatives	(*f*)	*s*		(*š*)		*h*
Sonorants	*w*	*l*	*r*	*y*		

'rope' versus *kambe* 'book cover', *aṅgə* 'horn' versus *angə* 'features, components', *kaṅdə* 'tree trunk' versus *kandə* 'hill'. The prenasalized stops behave like single consonants in relation to such phenomena as syllable weight and gemination (see below), but attempts have been made to account for them in different terms, such as syllabification (Coates and De Silva 1960, Feinstein 1979 among others; see Letterman 1997 for an account). /ñj/ is rare, and sometimes not listed.

The two segments in parentheses in the table 21.6 represent phonemes introduced through loanwords. Earlier Sinhala had retroflex /ṇ/ and /ḷ/ (and indeed they are still written distinctly), but they have merged with /n/ and /l/ respectively in modern Sinhala. Similarly, retroflex <ṣ> is written but is not distinct from palatal /š/ in pronunciation.

4.3 Phonological processes

There are a number of phonological processes, including vowel reduction to /ə/, final vowel shortening, *-y-* and *-w-* glide insertion, and *-s/h* alternation. Two particularly important ones that interact with morphology are vowel fronting ('umlaut') and gemination. These are illustrated briefly below (for a fuller account, see Letterman 1997, Gair and Paollilo 1997 and references therein).

Non-high short vowels in medial syllables commonly undergo reduction to [ə]. The [a] and [ə] alternation described earlier reflects this: [balənə] 'seeing (REL), versus [balannə] 'see-INFIN'. Similarly, alternations such as [wærədi] 'fault-PL' versus [wæræddə] 'fault-DEF', [penəli] 'firebrand-PL' versus [penella] 'firebrand-DEF'.

The insertion of *-w-* and *-y-* occurs largely in connection with noun and other endings (see section 5.1). For example *senaa* 'army-STEM', *senaawə* 'army-DEF'; *santoosə* 'joy, pleasure-STEM', *santoosəyə* 'joy, pleasure-DEF' (commonly pronounced as /santoose/). *-w-* occurs after back vowels (other than ə) and æ/ææ: *hændææ* 'evening-STEM', *hændææwə* 'evening-DEF'; *amaaru* 'difficult', *amaaruwə* 'difficulty-DEF'. *-y-* occurs after front vowels other than æ/ææ: *ṭæksi* 'taxi-STEM', *ṭæksiyə* -'taxi-DEF'.

-s- and *-h-* alternate in some specific lexical items: *rasə/raha* 'tasty'; but also medial *-h-* regularly occurs as *-s-* where it would be final or geminated: *gaha* 'tree', *gas* 'trees'; *wæhi* 'rain-STEM', *wæssə* 'rain-DEF'.

A number of morphological processes trigger vowel fronting (sometimes referred to as 'umlaut', particularly in historical contexts). These include past tense formation and the perfect participle forms of Class II verbs (see section 5.4.1), the involitivization of active verbs (see section 5.4.3), and feminine forms of animate nouns (see section 5.1). In vowel fronting, back vowels alternate with front ones of the same height. Some examples are: *koṭənəwa* 'dig-PRES', *keṭuwa* 'dig-PAST'; *badinəwa* 'fry-PRES', *bædəla* 'fry-PPL', and *hapənəwa* 'bite-PRES', *hæpenəwa* 'bite-INVOL-PRES'.

Gemination of consonants is involved in the formation of singular definite nouns from stems ending in *-i* or *-u*, the past tense of Class II verbs, and the formation of causatives of some verbs. Some examples are: *potu* 'bark-STEM', *pottə* 'bark-DEF'; *adinəwa* 'draw, pull-PRES'. *ædda* 'draw, pull-PAST', *addənəwa* 'draw, pull-CAUS-PRES'; *kapənəwa* 'cut-PRES', *kappənəwa* 'cut-CAUS-PRES' (besides *kapəwənəwa*). *-h-* geminates as *-ss-*: *bahinəwa* 'descend-PRES', *bæssa* 'descend-PAST'. The prenasalized stops geminate as full nasal+stop clusters: *baṅdinəwa* 'tie-PRES', *bænda* 'tie-PAST'.

In colloquial speech, all nasals are commonly neutralized to *-ŋ* word-finally: *gamə* 'village-DEF', *gaŋ* 'village-PL'; *kanə* 'ear-DEF', *kaŋ* 'ear-PL'. If an alternation places a prenasalized stop in final position, it also neutralizes: *aṅgə* 'horn-DEF', *aŋ* 'horn-PL'; *liṅdə* 'well-DEF', *liŋ* 'well-PL'. However, the introduction of loanwords, along with increasing urbanization and the use of more formal and technical words appears to be weakening this neutralization.

5 WORD CLASSES AND MORPHOLOGY

5.1 Nouns

The basic division of nouns in Sinhala is between animate and inanimate. Virtually all nouns of all classes inflect for two numbers: singular and plural. Singular nouns also inflect for definiteness. Inanimate nouns inflect for four cases: nominative (or direct) dative, genitive (also serves as locative) and instrumental (also serves as ablative). Paradigms of two classes of inanimates are given in table 21.7. Another class, consisting largely of place or location nouns, resembles that of *potə*, except that the genitive is the same as the nominative, ending in -*ə*, and the instrumental is generally -*iŋ*. These three classes account for the vast majority of inanimate nouns in Sinhala. Note that nouns of the *potə* class are typologically unusual in that the plural is the unmarked form. It is also the compounding stem; thus *pot saappuwə* 'book shop'.

Nouns of the *daane* class often have a formal variant in -*əyə*. This reflects an earlier sound change /əyə/ > /e/ or /ē/ but it is also a live process in that this class is the one into which Sanskrit masculine/neuter nouns of the -*a* class are borrowed by the addition of -*ə* (written -*a*), with -*y*- insertion. *daane* (Literary *dānaya*) is an example. Similarly Sanskrit feminine nouns in *ā* are borrowed by adding -*ə* (written -*a*) with -*w*- (literary -*v*-) insertion; e.g. *senaawə* 'army' (literary *senāva*).

With some borrowed inanimate nouns, primarily those from English, the numeral -*ekə* 'one' functions as the adapting affix. The inflection is like the *potə* class, and the bare noun serves as plural and stem; e.g. *bas-ekə* 'the bus', *bas-ekətə* 'to the bus', *bas* 'busses', etc.

Animate nouns inflect for the same cases as inanimates, plus a distinct accusative and vocative. The accusative affix -*wə* has an optional character, (see section 6.4.1.1). There are several classes of animate nouns. Two common ones are represented in Table VIII. The *miniha* class has a geminated plural; the *balla* class has a plural in -*o*, becoming -*a*- in the non-nominative plural. Otherwise the case and definite forms are the same for these and for animate nouns of other classes. The -*n*- preceding the plural case affixes

TABLE 21.7: INFLECTED FORMS OF INANIMATE NOUNS

	Singular		Plural
	Definite	Indefinite	
potə 'the book' (stem *pot*)			
Direct	*potə*	*potak*	*pot*
Dative	*potətə*	*potəkətə*	*potwələtə*
Genitive-Locative	*potee*	*potəkə*	*potwələ*
Instrumental-Ablative	*poteŋ*	*potəkiŋ*	*potwəliŋ*
daane 'meal for monks' (stem *daanə*)			
Direct	*daane*	*daaneak/-əyak*	*daanə*
Dative	*daanetə*	*daanekətə/-əyəkət ə*	*daanəwələtə*
Genitive-Locative	*daane*	*daanekə/-əyakə*	*daanəwələ*
Instrumental-Ablative	*daaneŋ*	*daanekiŋ/-əyəkiŋ*	*daanəwəliŋ*

represents an earlier oblique form that was free-standing as an accusative/ oblique form, and that remains the case in the literary language (see section 2.2).

Although there is no masculine-feminine gender distinction, there are some correlations of noun forms with male/female reference (De Silva 1958, Karunatillake 1987a). Nouns ending in -*a/aa*, may be masculine, feminine or sex-neutral in reference, and usually animate. Thus, *putaa* 'son', *taatta* 'father' are masculine; *amma*, 'mother', *akka*, 'elder sister' are feminine; but *laməya* 'child', *maalawa* 'fish' and *aliya* 'elephant' are sex neutral. However, there are derivational processes that produce specifically masculine and feminine forms, such as *balla* 'dog', *bælli* 'bitch' (stem *balu*); *kukula* 'rooster', *kikili* 'hen' (stem *kukul*); *manamaaləya* 'bridegroom', *manəmaali* 'bride' (stem *manəmaalə*); *šišyəya* 'male student', *šišyəyaawə* 'female student' (stem *šišyə*). As the last example shows, some of these processes occur in borrowed forms and directly reflect Sanskrit ones, while others involve Sinhala phonological processes such as fronting (see section 4.3).

The vocative endings are sensitive to both sex and kinship. The general affix for animate nouns is -*o*, as shown in table 21.7, but with feminine and kinship nouns, the usual affix is -*e/ee*: *kolla* 'lad' vocative *kollo*, *yakaa* 'devil', vocative *yakoo*; *ayya* 'elder brother', vocative *ayye*; *putaa* 'son', vocative *putee*; *kellə* 'lass', vocative *kelle*; *gææni* 'woman', vocative *gææniye*.

5.2 Pronouns and deictic forms

5.2.1 Deictic categories

There are four deictic/anaphoric categories in Sinhala, generally represented by *m*-, *o*-, *a*-, and *e*- (in some forms *u*- or Ø) that are reflected in demonstratives, third person pronouns, and deictic adverbials. This distinction seems to be unique among the languages of South Asia. These categories, along with their core meanings and the designations given to them in Gair 1970: 31ff. and subsequent work (see Gair 1991 for

TABLE 21.8: INFLECTED FORMS OF ANIMATE NOUNS

	Singular		Plural
	Definite	Indefinite	
miniha 'the man' (stem *minis*)			
Nominative	*miniha*	*minihek*	*minissu*
Accusative	*minihawə*	*minihekwə*	*minissunwə*
Dative	*minihaṭə*	*minihekuṭə*	*minissunṭə*
Genitive	*minihage*	*minihekuge*	*minissunge*
Instrumental-Ablative	*minihageŋ*	*minihekugen*	*minissungeŋ*
Vocative	*miniho*	—	*minissune*
balla 'the dog' (stem *balu*)			
Nominative	*balla*	*ballek*	*ballo*
Accusative	*ballawə*	*ballekwə*	*ballanwə*
Dative	*ballaṭə*	*ballekuṭə*	*ballanṭə*
Genitive	*ballage*	*ballekuge*	*ballange*
Instrumental	*ballageŋ*	*ballekugeŋ*	*ballangeŋ*
Vocative	*ballo*	—	*ballane*

details), are illustrated by their representations in the demonstrative adjectives in table 21.9 (adapted from Gair and Paolillo 1997). The existence of the fourth APH category is of special interest from a typological standpoint. Though all of the categories are used in discourse/pragmatic function, only the first three are used in situational deixis, and APH is specialized for discourse reference (see Gair 1991, Gair and Karunatillake 1998 and 2000). That is, APH is anaphoric in the wider sense, including both intra-sentential and discourse referential dependency (see section 7).

To these four categories, we may usefully add an interrogative one, generally represented by *k-* or *m-*, occurring in interrogative ('Wh equivalent') forms in Sinhala, since there is generally an interrogative counterpart to deictic forms that resembles them in formation. This category has thus been included in table 21.9.

5.2.2 Non-interrogative pronouns

Pronouns inflect for the same cases as nouns, except for the vocative, and for singular and plural.

5.2.3 First and second person pronouns

The first person pronouns are *mamə* 'I' and *api* 'we'.

There are several second person pronouns, which vary with dialect as well as respect and intimacy (see De Silva 1960, Karunatillake and Suseendirarajah 1975, Karunatillake 1992 and Paolillo 1992 for examples). Very commonly, second person pronouns are avoided and left unexpressed, or names (often initials, such as 'A. J.', 'J. B.', 'C. R.', pronounced as in English) or titles such as *mahattəya* 'gentleman', *noona* 'lady', or *baas unnæhee* 'craftsman, mechanic' are used. Currently, with urbanization, the form *oyaa* (literally 'that one by you' – see section 5.2.4) appears to be coming into use as a general second person pronoun.

5.2.4 Third person pronouns

Third person pronouns are generally morphologically complex and transparent, composed of one of the four deictic/demonstrative elements (section 5.21) and a nominal element. The basic gender distinction is animate/ inanimate, as with nouns.

TABLE 21.9: DEICTIC AND INTERROGATIVE CATEGORIES

Form	Gloss	Category	Deictic sense
mee	'this, these'	First Proximal (1PROX)	proximal to speaker, or to both speaker and hearer
oyə	'that, those (by you)'	Second Proximal (2PROX)	proximal to hearer
arə	'that, those (over there)'	Distal (DIST)	distal from both speaker and hearer, generally in sight
ee	'that, those (in question)'	Anaphoric (APH)	reference to something in the code or message, usually preceding in the discourse
monə/koyi	'what/which'	Interrogative	questioning a sentence or constituent

However, there is also a further distinction within animate pronouns into animal and human. Both of the latter also include specifically feminine forms. Nevertheless, this does not constitute a true masculine/feminine distinction, since there are no specifically masculine forms, and the non-feminine forms are the ones generally used to refer to either feminine or masculine beings. Feminine forms are used where specifically feminine reference is called for, and constitute a marked category in spoken Sinhala. The feminine human forms are restricted to certain dialects, and where used, may be generally non-respectful. In literary Sinhala, however, this is not the case, and there is a true masculine/feminine distinction in which *æ* serves as a non-impolite oblique for the feminine pronoun *ō* (see Gair and Karunatillake 1974, 1976). The animal pronouns, especially in their shorter forms, are also used for derogatory human reference (for a fuller listing, see Gair 1970, 1991). Table 21.10 shows a representative subset of the third person pronouns (from Gair and Paolillo 1997).

Pronominal function in Sinhala is commonly expressed by ellipsis, that is, a phonologically unrealized (null) form (see section 7.2).

5.2.5 Interrogative pronouns

Interrogative pronouns are formed with an interrogative element *k-* or *m-* and generally parallel the deictic pronouns in formation: *kawuru/kawu* 'who', *kooka* 'which animal', *mokaa* 'what animal'; *kookə* 'which one (inanimate)'; *mokə* 'what one (inanimate)'.

kawuru does not inflect for definiteness or plural; the remainder generally inflect for those categories like the deictic pronouns in table 21.10.

5.2.6 Reflexive pronouns

There is a reflexive pronoun *taman*, with an alternate form *tamun*, and a somewhat more formal nominative form *tamaa*. The pronoun *taman/tamun* is human, may be either masculine or feminine, singular or plural, and is generally third person in reference. In colloquial Sinhala its case forms are plural in form, regardless of reference, though the more formal *tamaa* is only singular in reference (see section 7.1).

5.2.7 Deictic and anaphoric adverbials

Deictic and interrogative adverbials contain the same deictic or interrogative categories as the pronouns. Thus, *mehee* 'here', *ohee, arəhe, ehee* 'there'; *kohee* 'where', etc.

TABLE 21.10: THIRD PERSON PRONOUNS

Category	1PROX	2PROX	DIST	APH
Human	*meyaa*	*oyaa*	*areya*	*eyaa*
Feminine	*mææ*	—	—	*ææ*
Plural	*meyaala*	*oyaala*	*areyala*	*eyaala*
Animal	*meeka/muu*	*ooka*	*arəka/aruu*	*eeka/uu*
Feminine	*meeki*	*ooki*	*arəki*	*eeki*
Plural	*meekuŋ/muŋ*	*ookuŋ*	*arəkuŋ/aruŋ*	*eekuŋ/uŋ*
Inanimate	*meekə*	*ookə*	*arəkə*	*eekə*
Plural	*meewa*	*oowa*	*arəwa*	*eewa*

5.3 Numerals

Sinhala numerals operate on a decade system, and from 20 up are quite transparent. Numerals inflect for case and definiteness, and have animate and inanimate gender forms. The first ten numerals are given in table 21.11. There are also honorific forms for Buddhist monks, formed with the numeral stem and *namə* 'name': *haamuduruwəru tunnamak* 'three monks-INDEF', etc.

5.4 Verbal morphology

5.4.1 Inflected verb forms

Inflected verb forms are built on three bases: present, past and perfect (sometimes referred to as non-past, past and participial). Spoken Sinhala verb forms do not show inflectional agreement for any category, in contradistinction to the literary verb, which shows agreement for person, number and gender.

There are three major classes of regular verbs, and a relatively small number of irregular verbs. The forms of the three regular classes, defined by the ending of the present base in *-ə*, *-i*, or *-e*, are shown in table 21.12, with three representative verbs. Category names are for the most part self-explanatory; notes on others are in 5.4.2. Verbs are generally cited in their simple present form.

5.4.2 Functions of the inflected forms

The uses of a number of these forms will be treated in the syntax section, but some require mention here.

The volitive optative is generally confined to the first person, and indicates that the speaker is proposing to do something. It invites assent or disagreement on the part of the speaker.

The involitive optative indicates that something may occur, generally not under the control of the speaker. It thus commonly occurs with subjects other than first person.

TABLE 21.11: NUMERAL FORMS

		Inanimate		Animate	
Number	Stem	Definite	Indefinite	Definite	Indefinite
1	*ek*	*ekə*	*ekak*	*ekkennaa*	*ekkenek*
2	*de*	*dekə*	*dekak*	*denna*	*dennek*
3	*tun*	*tunə*	*tunak*	*tundenaa*	*tundenek*
4	*hatərə*	*hatərə*	*hatərak*	*hatərədenaa*	*hatərədenek*
5	*pas*	*paha*	*pahak*	*pasdenaa*	*pasdenek*
6	*hayə*	*hayə*	*hayak*	*hayədenaa*	*hayədenek*
7	*hat*	*hatə*	*hatak*	*hatdenaa*	*hatdenek*
8	*aṭə*	*aṭə*	*aṭak*	*aṭədenaa*	*aṭədenek*
9	*namə*	*namee*	*naməyak*	*namədenaa*	*namədenek*
10	*daha*	*dahayə*	*dahayak*	*dahadenaa*	*dahadenek*

TABLE 21.12: INFLECTED VERB FORMS

	Class I	Class II	Class III
Present base	*balə* look	*adi*-pull, draw	*wæṭenə*
Simple present	*balənəwa*	*adinawa*	*wæṭenəwa*
Verbal adjective (relativizing)	*balənə*	*adinə*	*wæṭenə*
Focusing (emphatic)	*balanne*	*adinne*	*wæṭenne*
Infinitive/neutral imperative	*balannə/ṇḍə/nṭə*	*adinnə/ṇḍə/nṭə*	*wæṭennə/ṇḍə/nṭə*
Volitive optative	*balannaŋ*	*adinnaŋ*	*wæṭennaŋ*
Hortative	*baləmu*	*adimu*	*wæṭemu*
Involitive optative	*balaawi/balayi*	*adiiwi/adiyi*	*wæṭeewi/wæṭeyi*
Contemporaneous	*baladdi*	*adiddi*	*wæṭeddi*
Past base	*bælu-*	*ædd-*	*wæṭun-*
Simple past	*bæluwa*	*ædda*	*wæṭuna*
Relativizing (verbal adjective)	*bæluwə*	*æddə*	*wæṭunə*
Focusing (emphatic)	*bæluwe*	*ædde*	*wæṭune*
Prior temporal	*bæluaamə*	*æddaamə*	*wæṭunaamə*
Conditional	*bæluwot*	*æddot*	*wæṭunot*
Concessive	*bæluwat*	*æddat*	*wæṭunat*
Permissive	*bæluwaawe*	*æddaawe*	*wæṭunaawe*
Perfect base	*balə-*	*ædə*	*wæṭi*
Perfect (conjunctive ppl.)	*baləla*	*ædəla*	*wæṭila*
Relativizing (verbal adjective)	*baləpu*	*ædəpu*	*wæṭiccə*
Reduplicated	*baləbalə*	*ædəædə*	*wæṭi wæṭi*
Prior temporal	*baləpuaamə*	*ædəpuaamə*	*wæṭiccaamə*
Concessive	*baləlat*	*ædəlat*	*wæṭilat*
Permissive	*baləpuwaawe*	*ædəpuwaawe*	*wæṭiccaawe*
Surprise	*baləpi*	*ædəpi*	*wæṭicci*

The perfect participle, sometimes referred to as the simple perfect, serves as the conjunctive participle but in Sinhala it also appears as the verb of main clauses (see section 6.8.2).

The past and perfect relativizing forms (verbal adjectives) appear not to differ in meaning. The same holds for the past and perfect prior temporal forms. The latter are derived from the verbal adjective plus a form *hamə*, and these full forms are sometimes encountered: *bæluwə hamə/ baləpu hamə*.

The concessive forms can also be analysed as the simple past or simple perfect forms plus the clitic *-t* 'also'.

The surprise form indicates that the speaker was surprised at, and usually not happy about, a completed action: *laməya gaha kapəpi* (child tree cut-SURP) 'Oh!, the child has gone and cut the tree.'

There are additional verb forms not shown here, in particular a number of imperatives of different grades of respect, for which see De Silva 1960.

5.4.3 Stem morphology: active, causative and involitive forms

There is an interaction of the inflectional class of verbs with their internal morphological composition, interacting in turn with their syntactic function. Class I verbs with simple stems, such as *balə-* are active verbs. Class I as an inflectional class also includes causative verbs, which include a causative (CAUS) morpheme, appearing on the present stem as *-wə* or gemination. The causative may relate to class I, II or some Class III verbs. Thus active *hədə-nəwa* (Class I) 'make', past *hæduwa*, causative *hadəwə-nəwa* 'cause to make, have repaired', past *hædewwa*; *ari-nəwa* (Class II) 'open (trans) past *æriya*, *arəwə-nəwa* 'cause (someone) to open', past *ærewwa*; *wæṭe-nəwa* (Class III) 'fall', past *wæṭuna*, *waṭṭə-nawa* 'drop', past *wæṭṭuwa*. The formation of causative verbs from Class I active verbs and Class II verbs is thoroughgoing. Class III verbs are involitive verbs, including an involitive morpheme (INVOL). They commonly have active counterparts of Class I or II. Thus, *balənəwa* (Class I)'look', *bælenəwa* (Class III), 'look involuntarily'; *arinəwa* (Class II) 'open (transitive)', *ærenəwa* (Class III) 'open involuntarily (or intransitive)'. There are thus numerous three-member sets such as in table 21.13.

There are some defective sets, however. Commonly, they include a causative-involitive pair with no active counterpart, as in table 21.14.

Class II verbs, although active, include a subset that has a past tense formation like that of Class III. Thus, *nawatinəwa* 'stop, halt, stay', past *næwətuna*; *warədinəwa* 'go wrong, mistake', past *wærəduna* . These are commonly intransitive verbs with a stative or involitive sense.

While the terms active, involitive and causative do generally characterize the semantic and syntactic nature of the verbs within them, the correspondence is by no means complete. For example, there are morphologically involitive verbs such as *hærenəwa* 'turn' and *igilenəwa* 'fly' that are usually used in a non-involitive sense, and there is a considerable amount of semantic specialization. Thus *teerenəwa* can be considered the involitive of *toorənəwa* 'explain', but is the general verb for 'understand', and *kiyəwənəwa*, the causative of *kiyənəwa* 'say' is virtually always used in its sense 'read'. See further section 6.4.1.2.

5.5 Quasi-verbs and modal adjectives

There are a number of forms in Sinhala that do not inflect for tense, but which have verbal properties, including inflection for some of the categories pertinent to verbs, such as focusing, relativizing and conjunctive participle forms. They characteristically occur alone as predicators of sentences, or with a dependent verb form, usually an infinitive, in

TABLE 21.13: BASIC VERB, INVOLITIVE AND CAUSATIVE SETS

Basic verb	Gloss	Involitive	Gloss	Causative	Gloss
hadənəwa	'make'	*hædenəwa*	'have made'	*hadəwənəwa*	'cause to make'
kapənəwa	'cut'	*kæpenəwa*	'be/get cut'	*kapəwənəwa*	'cause to cut'
arinəwa	'open'	*ærenəwa*	'open(invol)'	*arəwənəwa*	'cause to open'

TABLE 21.14: INVOLITIVE AND CAUSATIVE SETS

hærenəwa	turn (intrans)	*harəwənəwaa*	'cause to turn'
peenəwa	'see, be visible'	*pennənəwa*	'show'
wæṭenəwa	'fall'	*waṭṭənəwa*	'drop'

a semantically modal function. They have thus been designated as quasi-verbs (Gair 1967 and 1971) and the term has become the usual one. They include *æti* 'might (be)', the negator *næ̂æ̂*, *kæmɘti* 'like', and, *bæ̂æ̂* 'cannot'; there are other dialectal forms.

There are a few forms, including *puluwaŋ* and *hæki* 'can, possible' and *oonɘ* 'want, need', that share syntactic properties with the quasi-verbs but lack their inflectional properties. They have thus been referred to as modal adjectives. Unlike consonant final adjectives, *puluwaŋ* has an alternate *puluwɘni* with the assertion marker (see section 5.6) when it appears in a main predicate. *oonɘ* and *hæki* are invariant in form (though *hæki* occurs in literary Sinhala, where it does inflect). The forms of both quasi-verbs and modal adjectives are shown in table 21.15 (adapted from Gair and Paolillo 1997).

5.6 Clitics

Sinhala has a number of clitics that follow the forms to which they pertain. A number of these have 'syntactically transparent' functions in that they perform discourse or semantic functions without having an effect on sentence structure. These include *mɘ* 'emphasis, only, itself', *-(u)t* 'also', and *hemɘ* 'et cetera', as in (3) and (4).

(3) *adɘ mamɘmɘ nuwɘrɘṭɘ yanɘwa*
today I-EMPH Kandy-DAT go-PRES
'Today I myself am going to Kandy.'

(4) *ehenaŋ mamat ennaŋ*
in-that-case I also come-VOLOPT
'In that case, I'll come too.'

The emphatic *-mɘ* also obligatorily co-occurs discontinuous with the quantifiers *mulu* '(the) whole' and *hæmɘ* 'all', as in *hæmɘ potakmɘ* (every book -INDEF EMPH) 'every book'; *mulu gameemɘ* (whole-village-LOC-EMPH) 'in the whole village'.

The clitic *-(u)t* may be used in discourse linking, but it also enters into a kind of coordination, and there is also a conjunctive clitic *-yi*, (below, and see 6.6).

Other clitics interact with and have an effect on sentence or phrase structure. One that figures strongly in Sinhala syntax is the assertion marker *-yi*. It surfaces as -/y/ following vowels other than /i/, and as lengthening of /i/ (which may be lost in rapid speech). Following consonants, it appears as /i/. It is glossed as ASSM here (see sections 6.4.2.4, 6.4.2.5 and 6.4.3). Another is the question marker *dɘ* glossed as QUES here (see section 6.4.5). These two clitics and several others have the special property that when they do not follow the main predicator of a sentence, they require the item on which they

TABLE 21.15: QUASI-VERB AND MODAL ADJECTIVE FORMS

Form	'might be'	'not'	'like'	'can'	'can'	'can't'	'want'
Simple	*æti*	*næ̂æ̂*	*kæmɘtii*	*puluwaŋ* *puluwɘni*	*hæki*	*bæ̂æ̂*	*oonɘ*
Focusing	*ætte*	*nætte*	*kæmætte*	*puluwaŋ*	*hæki*	*bæri*	*oonɘ*
Conditional	*ættot*	*nættot*	*kæmættot*	—	—	—	—
Concessive	*ættat*	*nættat*	*kæmættat*	—	—	—	—
Relativizing	*æti*	*næti*	*kæmɘti*	*puluwaŋ*	*hæki*	*bæri*	*oonɘ*
Perfect Ppl.	*ætuwɘ*	*nætuwɘ*	—	—	—	*bæruwɘ*	—

occur to become the focus of a focused (cleft) sentence. They have thus been called 'focus marking forms' (see sections 6.4 and especially 6.4.3).

Other clitics include the conjunction -*yi*, homonymous with the assertion marker, (see section 6.6) and the comparative *wagee* 'like', which also occurs as a sentence clitic.

6 SYNTAX

6.1 Word order

The basic order in Sinhala is S(ubject)-O(bject)-V(erb). However, other orders are both possible and common. Thus, for a simple SOV sentence like (5), all orders of the major constituents are possible, as in (6). Not surprisingly, there will be differences in topic, emphasis, afterthought, etc., accompanied with intonation (as yet insufficiently studied).

(5) *siri loku aliyekwə dækka*
    Siri big elephant-ACC see-PAST
    'Siri saw a big elephant.'

(6) *siri loku aliyekwə dækka*
    loku aliyekwə siri dækka
    loku aliyekwə dækka siri
    siri dækka loku aliyekwə
    dækka siri loku aliyekwə
    dækka loku aliyekwə siri

Rightward dislocation is common in discourse, and is responsible for several of the examples in (6). It can apply to large constituents as in (7) and be recursive, as in (8) (see section 6.4.3).

(7) *sæliiṭə matəkə də arə maŋ laṅgə tiyenə alutmə šəərṭ-ekə*
    Sally-DAT remember QUES that I near be-REL new-EMPH shirt-INDEF
    'Sally, do you remember that brand new shirt that I have (with me)?

(8) *yamu də ehenaŋ ee hooṭəleeṭə tee-ekak bonnə*
    go-HORT QUES then that hotel-DAT tea-INDEF drink
    'In that case, should we go to that hotel to have a tea?'

6.2 Noun phrases

Demonstratives, genitives and adjectives precede the head noun (9)–(11):

(9) *mee bohomə alut sinhələ potə*
    this very new Sinhala book
    'this very new Sinhala book'

(10) *hoňdə alut sinhələ potak*
    good new Sinhala book-INDEF
    'a good new Sinhala book'

(11) *gunəpaaləge alutmə iŋgriisi nawəkataa potə*
    Gunapala-GEN new-EMPH novel book
    'Gunapala's newest English novel'

Numerals generally follow the head noun, and bear the definiteness and case inflection, as in (12)–(14):

(12) *mee hoňdə pot tunə*
      good book-PL three-DEF
      'these three good books'

(13) *hoňdə pot tunak*
      good book-PL three-INDEF
      '(a) three good books'

(14) *hoňdə lamay tundenekuṭə (tæægi dennə)*
      good child-PL three-ANIM-INDEF-DAT (presents give)
      '(Give presents) to three good children.'

Relative clauses are dealt with in section 6.7.

6.3 Postpositional phrases

Sinhala lacks prepositions, but has postpositions, which may require specific cases on their complements as in (15)–(17):

(15) *maamage wattə laňgə (tiyenəwa)*
      uncle-GEN estate-NOM near (exist-PRES)
      '(It is) near (maternal) uncle's estate.'

(16) *(mamə) geyiŋ piṭə (bæluwa)*
      I house-INSTR outside (look-PAST)
      '(I looked) outside the house.'

(17) *maamage watte iňdəla (aawa)*
      uncle-GEN estate-GEN from
      '(came) from (maternal) uncle's estate.'

Some postpositions (nominal postpositions) may themselves take case. Compare (18) and (19) with (15):

(18) *maamage wattə laňgəṭə (yannə)*
      uncle-GEN estate near-DAT (go)
      '(Go) to near (maternal) uncle's estate'

(19) *maamage wattə laňgiŋ (yannə)*
      uncle-GEN estate near-INST (go)
      '(go) by way of (maternal) uncle's estate'

6.4 Simple sentences: verbal and non-verbal predicators

In addition to predicates headed by verbs, Sinhala has a wide range of non-verbal forms that head predicates to form predicator phrases. There are also numerous generalizations that cross these types, and within the non-verbal set there are several subtypes (Gair 1970, Gair and Paolillo 1988). It is thus useful to use the cover term 'predicator' for predicate heads in general, subsuming all types, even while treating the verbal and non-verbal types separately, as in the following sections.

6.4.1 Verbal sentences

6.4.1.1 Subject and object case

Sinhala subjects may be found in any case except the genitive (Gair 1990). Nominative and dative appear to be the most common and least semantically specialized, though there is a connection of dative with absence of volition or control (Gair 1970, 1971 and especially Inman 1993).

There is one postpositional phrase in *atiŋ* with subject properties (see section 6.4.1.2).

Direct objects are generally in the nominative case, or, if animate, may be in the accusative in *-wə*. Considered cross-dialectally, the *-wə* form must be considered optional, since the extent of its use varies with speaker and dialect. Thus it is rare or lacking in some, notably southern, dialects, and for those who use *-wə*, it may be more common on pronouns than nouns, though this remains to be investigated on an extensive natural corpus. Some verbs require a dative case direct object. Examples (20) through (35) with associated comments will illustrate the general range of possibilities. It should also be emphasized here, that this relates only to spoken Sinhala, and that as stated in section 2.2, the case system for the literary language, not illustrated here, is quite different (see the references in that section and Gair and Karunatilaka 1974, 1976 for details).

Examples (20)–(25) have nominative case subjects; (20)–(21) are intransitive; (23)–(25) are transitive; (25) illustrates a dative case direct object. Indirect objects are in the dative, as in (24). Note that there are distinct existential 'be' verbs for animate and inanimate subjects, as shown in (20) (21) and (22).

(20) *poolimee hiṭapu senəgə bas-ekəṭə nægga*
     queue-LOC be-ANIM crowd bus-DAT climb-PAST
     'The crowd that was waiting in the queue climbed into the bus.'

(21) *laŋkaawe rilaw huñgak innəwa*
     Sri Lanka monkey-PL many be-ANIM-PRES
     'There are many (macaque) monkeys in Sri Lanka.'

(22) *mee iskoole sinhələ panti tunak tiyenəwa*
     this school-LOC Sinhala class-PL three-INDEF be-INAN-PRES
     'There are three Sinhala classes in this school.'

(23) *loku mahattəya laməya(wə) tæpæl kantooruwəṭə yæwwa*
     big gentleman child(-ACC) post office-DAT go-CAUS-PAST
     'The boss sent the child to the post office.'

(24) *ee noona salli næti ayəṭə nitərəmə æñduŋ denəwa*
     that lady money not-REL people-DAT always clothes give-PRES
     'That lady always gives clothes to people without money.'

(25) *taatta apee gedərəṭə aapu laməyaṭə bænna*
     father our house come-PAST-REL scold-DAT
     'Father scolded the child who came to our house.'

Examples (26)–(29) illustrate dative subjects. (26) is intransitive; (27)–(29) are transitive. Note that animate direct objects in dative subject sentences may occur with the marked accusative, as in (28) and (29).

(26) *minihaṭə diwenəwa*
man-DAT run-INVOL-PRES
'The man runs (involuntarily).'

(27) *maṭə koləṁbə bas-ekə hæmədaamə warədinəwa*
I-DAT Colombo bus every-day miss.
'I miss the Colombo bus every day.'

(28) *apiṭə ee mahattəyawə tissemə matak-wenəwa*
we-DAT gentleman-ACC throughout memory-become-PRES
'We always remember that gentleman.'

(29) *məṭə kæleedi aliyekwə penuna*
I-DAT jungle-in elephant-ACC see-PAST
'I saw the elephant (while) in the jungle.'

In (30) and (31), the subject is in the accusative case. Accusative subjects occur only with intransitive verbs, and the sense is generally involitive with the implication that some external force is responsible.

(30) *iṅdəlahiṭəla gas madinə minissuwə kaṁbeŋ wæṭenəwa*
occasionally, tree tap-PRES-REL man-PL-ACC rope-DEF-INST fall-PRES
'Now and then, the tree tapping men fall from the ropes.'

(31) *maawə yantaŋ beeruna*
I-ACC barely escape-PAST
'I barely escaped.'

Instrumental subjects refer to 'corporate' entities, such as governments, committees or organizations, and verbs with which they occur also allow nominative subjects. Compare (32) with (33), which has the same verb but a nominative subject. Example (34) shows clearly that there is not a partitive explanation, and again compare (35).

(32) *nidahas utsəweeṭə aaṇḍuwen hungak wiyədaŋ kərənəwa*
independence festival-DAT government-INST much expense do-PRES
'The government spends a lot on the Independence Celebration.'

(33) *pereera magul kææməṭə huṅgak wiyədaŋ keruwa*
Perera-NOM wedding food-DAT much expense do-PAST
'Perera spent a lot on the wedding.'

(34) *poliisiyeŋ gunəpaaləṭə hariyəṭə gæhuwa lu*
police-INST Gunapala-DAT really hit-PAST REPORT
'The police really beat Gunapala, they say.'

(35) *siriseenə gunəpaaləṭə hariyəṭa gæhuwa*
Sirisena-NOM Gunapaala-DAT really hit-PAST
'Sirisena really beat Gunapaala.'

6.4.1.2 Case marking and verbal morphology

There is an interaction between subject case marking and the morphological composition of verbs (Gair 1970, 1971, Inman 1993). Non-nominative subjects commonly occur with morphologically involitive verbs, and thus there are possible sets such as (36) and (37) (non-causative active verbs are taken as unmarked – see section 5.4.3).

(36)a *mamə yannə hitənəwa*
       I go-INFIN think-PRES
       'I am thinking of going.'

   b   *matə yannə hitenəwa*
       I -DAT go-INF feel-INVOL-PRES
       'I feel like going.'

(37)a *mamə natənəwa*
       I-NOM dance-PRES
       'I dance.'

   b   *mata næṭuna*
       I-DAT dance-INVOL-PAST
       'I danced (by impulse).'

   c   *maawə næṭuna (nætəwunaa)*
       I-ACC dance-INVOL-PAST (CAUS-INVOL-PAST)
       'I danced (for some external reason).'

However, as noted in section 5.4.3. the correlation is far from complete, since there are morphologically involitive verbs such as *igilenəwa* 'fly' and *hærenəwa* 'turn' that are commonly used with a volitive sense. Such verbs commonly lack an active form, though they are likely to have a corresponding causative. Thus, *hærenəwa* is used freely in volitive contexts as in (38), but may also be used with a non-nominative subject and involitive sense as in (39). It has a causative *harəwənəwa* 'turn (transitive), cause to turn', as in (40).

(38) *handiyəṭə gihiŋ mamə vaməṭə hæruna*
      corner-DAT go-PPL I left-DAT turn-PAST
      'I went to the corner and turned left.'

(39) *(saddəyak æhila) maawə/matə hæruna*
      (sound-INDEF hear-PPL) I-ACC/ I-DAT turn-PAST
      '(Hearing a sound) I turned (involuntarily).'

(40) *dæmmə kaar-ekə harəwannə*
      now-EMPH car turn-INFIN
      'Turn the car right now.'

Colloquial Sinhala lacks a true passive construction (Gunasinghe 1985). However, there is a construction with an instrumental nominal with subject properties, an involitive verb, and commonly a capabilitive implication of some kind, as in (41) and (42).

(41) *ammageŋ sinhələ kææmə hoñdəṭə hædenəwa*
      mother-INST Sinhala food well make-INVOL-PRES
      'Mother (always) makes Sinhala food well.'

(42) *mageŋ ewwage wædə kerenne nææ*
      I-INST that-kind work do-INVOL-PRES NEG
      'I don't do that kind of work.'

A postpositional phrase noun + *atiŋ* has subject properties and appears almost exclusively with involitive verbs (Gair 1970, Inman 1993). It commonly has a sense of involuntary, accidental participation. Compare (43a) with (43b).

(43)a *laməya wiiduruwə binda*
    child- NOM glass break-PAST
    'The child broke the glass (purposefully).'

   b *laməya atiŋ wiiduruwə biňduna*
    child-atiŋ glass break-INVOL-PAST
    'The child broke the glass (accidentally).'

A volitive/involitive distinction, with different subject case, can also be implemented by the use of different sets of lexical verbs rather than with verb morphology. One set is *wenəwa* 'become' (past *unaa*) versus *yanəwa* 'go' (past *giyaa*), as in (44) and (45), and there are other sets as well (Gair 1971, Inman 1993). Some verbal predicators can be either volitive or involitive, with case alone signalling the distinction, as in (46) and (47).

(44) *mamə eekəţə hinəha unaa*
    I that-DAT laugh become-PAST
    'I laughed at that (voluntarily, or controllably).'

(45) *maţə eekəţə hinəha giyaa*
    I that-DAT laugh go-PAST
    'I laughed at that (involuntarily).'

(46) *ee gaman gihilla, maţə mahansi unaa*
    that trip take-PPL I-DAT tired become-PAST
    'Having taken that trip, I got tired.'

(47) *apee palaate minissu kuṁburu wæḍə kərannə bohomə mahansi wenəwa*
    our region-LOC man-PL-NOM paddy-field work do-INF much tired become-PRES
    'People in our region take a great deal of effort in paddy cultivation.'

6.4.2 Non-verbal sentences

Non verbal predicators include adjectives, nouns (case-marked or non-case marked), quasi-verbs. and postpositional phrases, as well as forms of other categories. Only a limited set of the most common types (nominals, adjectives and quasi-verbs) can be given here. The case-linked volitive/involitive type of distinction applies to non-verbal sentences as well, with subjects in the nominative or accusative. See Gair 1970, Gair and Paolillo 1988 for further examples and discussion.

6.4.2.1 Nominal equational sentences

Equational sentences with nouns as predicators have both nouns in the nominative case, as in (48)–(49). There is no copula in any tense. The verb *wenəwa* 'become' may form predicative phrases with nouns (or adjectives), as in (50), but the 'become' sense is present. See Gair and Paolillo 1988 for discussion.

(48) *gunəsiri mahattəya apee iskoole mul guruwərəya*
    Gunasiri gentleman our school-LOC head teacher
    'Mr Gunasiri is the head teacher of/in our school.'

(49) *ookə parənə bohomə durləbə puskolə potak*
that-one old much rare ola-leaf book-INDEF
'That one (by you) is an old, very rare ola-leaf book.'

(50) *gunəsiri mahattəya apee iskoole mul guruwəreya unaa*
Gunasiri gentleman our school-LOC head teacher become-PAST
'Mr Gunasiri became the head teacher of our school.'

6.4.2.2 Dative subject nominal sentences

There are nominal dative subject sentences, as in (51)–(52), characteristically with an experiencer or patient sense.

(51) *maṭə mæleeriyaawə*
I-DAT malaria.
'I have malaria.'

(52) *maṭə niwaaḍu.*
I-DAT leave-PL
'I'm on vacation.'

6.4.2.3 Action nominal sentences

Action nominal sentences constitute an especially interesting type of nominal predicator sentence. They resemble nominal equational sentences in that both nouns are in the nominative, but the predicative noun is one referring to an action, and the sense is that the action is underway at the time of occurrence, as in (53) and (54). There is no verb, and one cannot be inserted and retain the sense, so that they are an independent type not derived by verb deletion. See Gair and Paolillo 1988 for discussion.

(53) *mamə gedərə aawaamə lamay paaḍəmə*
I home come-when children lesson
'When I came home the children were/are busily doing their lessons.'

(54) *ee særee andəree hitə ætuleŋ hinaha*
that time Andare mind inside-INSTR laughter
'Then Andare was really laughing to himself.'

6.4.2.4 Adjectival predicator sentences

As predicates of main clauses, adjectives ending in a vowel are marked with the assertion marker clitic -*yi*, e.g. (55)–(56) (see 5.6). Consonant ending adjectives do not take any marking, as in (57)–(58). As with nominal predicates, some adjectives take a dative subject, as in (59).

(55) *mee amu miris hari særayi*
these raw chilli-PL really strong-ASSM
'These green chillies are really strong.'

(56) *api dæŋ innə gee ṭikak poḍii*
we now exist (ANIM)-REL house somewhat small-ASSM
'The house we are in now is rather small.'

(57) *arə yaapənee aṁbə alut*
     those Jaffna-LOC mango-PL new
     Those (over there) Jaffna mangoes are fresh.'

(58) *mee dawaswələ haal bohomə ganaŋ*
     these days-PL-LOC rice much expensive
     'These days (uncooked) rice is very expensive.'

(59) *apee babaatə tikak asəniipayi*
     our child–DAT somewhat sick-ASSM
     'Our child is a bit sick.'

An adjectival predicator sentence with an infinitive expression as subject is illustrated in (60):

(60) *ee ræswiimwələtə enə minissu kataakərənə widiyə ahagənə innə lassənayi*
     those meeting-PL-DAT come-PRES-REL talk-PRES-REL manner listen-PERF
     be-INFIN beautiful-ASSM
     'To be listening to the way the people who come to those meetings talk is great'.

6.4.2.5 Quasi-verb and modal adjective predicator sentences

The syntax of quasi-verbs and modal adjectives is complex, with individual forms differing in their syntactic properties. The negative quasi-verb *nææ* will be treated later (section 6.4.4), and only a sample of the others will be given here to indicate the range of properties (for a table of syntactic properties and further examples, see Gair and Pailolillo 1997: 27)

The case of subjects and objects of quasi-verbs without dependent verbs depends on the specific form. Thus, *puluwaŋ* 'can, might' and *oonə* 'want/need' take dative subjects and nominative (or accusative for animates) objects, as in (61) and (62), whereas *kæməti* 'like' takes a nominative subject and accusative object, as in (63). *kæməti* takes the assertion marker and *puluwaŋ* does so optionally.

(61) *matə gedərə wædə kərannə hoňdə kenekwə oonə*
     I-DAT house work do-INF good person-INDEF-ACC want
     'I want/need a good person to work in the house.'

(62) *ee laməyatə demələ hoňdətə puluwaŋ / puluwəni*
     that child Tamil good-DAT can / can-ASSM
     'That child can speak Tamil well.'

(63) *mamə ingriisi nawakataawələtə kæmətii*
     I English novel-PL-DAT like-ASSM
     'I like English novels.'

However, quasi-verbs and modal adjectives characteristically occur with a dependent verb in a specific form that they require. In this usage, they thus have modal force, expressing such notions as potentiality, desirability, evidentiality, etc. Thus, *oonə, puluwaŋ* and *kæməti* occur with dependent infinitives, as in (64)–(66). Subject case is the same as with nominal objects (for relational properties between main and infinitive subject, i.e. 'control', see Gair 1997).

(64) *maṭə ee wæḍə kərannə puluwəni*
I-DAT that work do-INFIN can-ASSM
'I can do that work.'

(65) *maṭə heṭə koləṁbə yannə oonə*
I-DAT tomorrow Colombo go-INFIN oonə
'I want to go to Colombo tomorrow.'

(66) *gunəpaalə eteṇṭə hæmədaamə yannə kæmətii*
Gunapala-NOM there-DATevery-day go-INFIN like-ASSM
'Gunapala likes to go there every day.'

If the subjects of *kæməti* and the infinitive are different, however, the verb of the dependent clause is in the same basic tensed form that occurs in finite clauses, but parallel to nominal objects, the verb itself is marked with the dative, as in (67). This case marking of finite verbs is a typologically rare property of Sinhala, and it also occurs in other structures.

(67) *mamə gunəpaalə yanəwaṭə kæmətii*
I Gunapala go-PRES-DAT like-ASSM
'I like for Gunapala to go there.'

puluwaŋ 'can, might' and *oonə* 'want/need' also occur with infinitival sentences as subjects, as in (68) and (69). Sentences such as these have commonly been analysed so as to have *puluwaŋ* and *oonə* occurring with nominative subjects, but they are better analysed as having the relevant nominal as subject of the infinitive. One clear indication of this is sentences such as (68), in which the dative nominal is governed by the infinitive (*puluwaŋ* in the 'might, possibly' sense does not take a dative subject or a nominal object; compare (69)). There are also sentences like (70) with *oonə* with both subjects present, and overt subjects of infinitives are possible in other constructions in Sinhala (for relevant constraints and argumentation, see Gair 1997).

(68) *ee laməyaṭə eekə æhennə puluwani*
that child-DAT that hear-INF might
'That child might hear that.'

(69) *mamə heṭə koləṁbə yannə puluwani*
I-NOM tomorrow Colombo go-INF might
'I might go to Colombo tomorrow.'

(70) *ammaṭə laməya wibaage paas-wennə oonə*
mother-DAT child-NOM examination pass-INF oonə
'Mother wants the child to pass the examination.'

The quasi-verb *æti* 'might (be)' can occur as a main predicator with a nominative subject and an existential sense, as in (71). It may also occur with a tensed verb in the simple present form and the sense 'might be the case that' as in (72).

(71) *ee gamee parənə pansəlak æti*
that village-LOC old temple-INDEF might-be
'There might be an old temple in that village.'

(72) *siri dæŋ koləṁbə wišwawidyaale ugannənəwa æti*
Siri now Colombo university teach-PRES might
'Siri might be teaching in Colombo University now.'

æti may also occur with an infinitive, and the sense is then always 'conjectural perfect', i.e., 'must have', as in (73).

(73) *amma gedərə yannə æti*
mother home go-INF must
'Mother must have gone home.'

6.4.3 Focused (cleft) sentences

Sinhala has a focused construction, also called a cleft construction, with both verbal and non-verbal types, that usually involves different, often special, forms of the predicator. In Indo-Aryan languages they appear to occur only in Sinhala and in Dhivehi (Cain and Gair 1995). A Dravidian model has been proposed for them, but with considerable elaboration and extension in Sinhala (Gair 1986a, Wijemanne 1984, Paolillo 1994). Sentences of this kind may indicate either focused information (as in focus of contrast) or new information (as in presentational sentences). They are extremely common in discourse, and one study found that in one corpus they accounted for 10.5% of the sentences in a given narrative (Herring and Paolillo 1995). Their prominence may be at least in part accounted for by the high sensitivity of Sinhala to presupposition and focus, and their consequent intersection with other grammatical processes, particularly questions and negation (see sections 6.4.4 and 6.4.5). The English translation as a cleft ('It is X that ...') is thus commonly too strongly emphatic in discourse. For the syntax of Sinhala focused sentences, see Gair 1970, 1983b, 1986a, Gair and Sumangala 1991, and Sumangala 1992. Little has been published on their discourse properties beyond Herring and Paolillo 1995.

6.4.3.1 Focus marking forms

A number of forms, primarily clitics with a sentence function, require that when they occur on a form other than the main predicator, the constituent with which they occur must be the focus of a cleft sentence, with the predicator taking the appropriate form. They have accordingly been termed 'focus-marking forms' in the literature. However, that term maybe somewhat misleading, since, though they require clefting, the reverse is not the case. That is, clefting requires the predicator to occur in the form appropriate to cleft sentences, but it does not require one of those focus-marking forms to occur with the focused element. Clefting can be indicated by the form of the predicator with the focused constituent unmarked except by position and/or intonation. (74) provides an example. Focus-marking forms include the assertion marker *-yi* (which may function as an emphatic), the question marker *də*, the reportative *lu* 'it seems, it is said', the negative form *nemey/newi*; the conjunction *naŋ* 'if', the dubitative marker *yæ* 'as if', and the emphasizing particle *tamaa/tamay* 'indeed', as well as some phrasal forms like *wennə æti* 'might be (that)' and *wennə bææ* 'can't be (that)'. These forms thus occur in only two positions: they immediately follow the predicate (whether nominal or verbal) in a non-focused sentence, or the focused form in a focused sentence. One can thus regard the predicator of a non-focused sentence as a kind of focus, and in fact as the unmarked case of sentence/predicator focus (see Gair 1970: 49–50).

6.4.3.2 Verbal predicator focused sentences

Verbal focused sentences utilize a special tensed form of the verb, (FOC) ending in *-e* or *-ee* (see section 5.4). Examples are given in (74)–(82) and others will appear in sections 6.4.4 and 6.4.5. The focused form may be right-shifted as in (74) and (75), or may occur in its position in a non-focused counterpart, as in (76) and (77). If one of the focus-marking forms does not appear on the form, right-shifting is common, but the focus may also be marked by intonation. Not only subjects and objects, but other constituents such as adverbs and subordinate clauses are eligible for clefting (80)–(81). COMP in (81) is the sentence complementizer (see 6.5.4.2).

(74) *dæŋ api padiñci welaa inne æmerikaawe*
      now we settled become-PERF be(anim)-PRES-FOC America-LOC
      'We are now settled down in America.' ('It's in America that . . .'

(75) *apee gedərə wæḍə okkomə kəranne mamə tamayi*
      our house-LOC work all do-PRES-FOC I EMPH
      'It is I who do all the work in our house.'

(76) *mamə tamayi apee gedərə wæḍə okkomə kəranne*
      I EMPH our house-LOC work all do-PRES-FOC
      'It is I who do all the work in our house.'

(77) *Siri waḍuwæḍə tamayi kəranne*
      Siri woodworking EMPH do-PRES-FOC
      'It is certainly woodworking that Siri does.'

(78) *mamə ee salli dunne siriṭayi*
      I that money give-PAST-FOC Siri-DAT ASSM
      'It was to Siri that I gave that money.'

(79) *mee eloolu nuwərə iñdəla genaawe dæn tamayi*
      these vegetables-PL Kandy-LOC from bring-PAST-FOC now EMPH
      'These vegetables were brought from Kandy just now.'

(80) *ee dostərə leḍḍu balanne hawəsə hayee iñdəla namee wenəkaŋ witərayi*
      That doctor patient-PL see-PRES-FOC evening six-LOC from nine become-until
      only ASSM
      'The doctor sees patients only from six in the evening until nine.'

(81) *meekəṭə api kiyanne kænal kərənəwa kiyəla*
      this-DAT we say-PRES-FOC channel do-PRES COMP
      'This we call "channeling (of doctors)".'

6.4.3.3 Long distance focus

Focusing is not limited to occurrence within a single clause, but may reach from a matrix into an included clause, as in (82a and b), in which the verb of the higher clause bears the focusing affix, but the focused element is located in the lower clause. In (82a) it is in its position in the included clause, but it has been right-shifted in (82b). For further details and constraints on the process see Gair 1970, 1976b, 1986a, Gair and Sumangala 1991, and Sumangala 1992.

(82)a *siripaalə eekə gunəpaaləṭə də dunna kiyəla oyaa kiwwe*
　　'Siripala that Gunapala-DAT-QUES give-PAST COMP you say-PAST-FOC
　　'Was it to Gunapala that you said that Siripala gave that.'

　b *siripaalə eekə dunna kiyəla oyaa kiwwe gunəpaaləṭə də*
　　Siripala that give-PAST COMP you say-PAST-FOC Gunapala-DAT-QUES
　　'Was it to Gunapala that you said that Siripala gave that?'

6.4.3.4 Non-verbal focused sentences

Adjectival predicators lose the assertion marker when some constituent within the sentence is focused, as in (83). Consonant final adjectival predicators and nominal predicators are unchanged in form, with focusing indicated by the presence of a focus-marking form and/or position and intonation, e.g. (84) and (85). Quasi-verbs that have a FOC-equivalent form will occur in that form, as in (86)–(87).

(83) *sinhala igənagannə hoñdə mee potayi*
　　Sinhala learn-INFIN good this book-EMPH
　　'It is this book that is good for learning Sinhala.'

(84) *mee potə tamayi alut*
　　this book indeed new
　　'It is indeed this book which is new.'

(85) *alut potə meekə tamayi.*
　　new book this-one indeed
　　'This is indeed (the one that is) the new book.'

(86) *adə apee guruwərəya ætte gedərə*
　　today our teacher must-be-FOC home
　　'Our teacher must be at home today.'

(87) *laməyaṭə kiyəwannə bæri mee potə də*
　　child-DAT read-INFIN cannot-FOC this book QUES
　　'Is it this book that the child cannot read?'

Negated sentences may also be focused – see exx. (95), (96) and (99) below.

6.4.4 Negation

Verbal and adjectival sentences are negated with the quasi-verb *næ̃æ*. Tensed verbs with *næ̃æ* appear in the focusing (FOC) form, as in (88)–(89). Adjectives that take the assertion marker lose it before *næ̃æ*, as in (90).

(88) *mee dawaswələ apee daruwo iskoole yanne næ̃æ*
　　these days-LOC our children school go-FOC næ̃æ
　　'These days our children don't go to school.'

(89) *taatta giyə sumaane kantooruwəṭə giyee næ̃æ*
　　Father last week office-DAT go-PAST-FOC not
　　'Father didn't go to the office last week.'

(90) *mamə iiye gattə pot sinhələ kiyəwannə igənagannə hoñdə næ̃æ*
　　I yesterday get-PAST-INSTR book-PLSinhala read-INF learn-INF good not
　　'The books that I bought yesterday are not good for learning to read Sinhala.'

Existential sentences with either the animate existential verb *innəwa* or the inanimate one *tiyenəwa* negate with *nææ*, which replaces them, as in (91)–(94).

(91) *ee raṭee ali innəwa*
      that country-LOC elephant-PL exist(anim)-PRES
      'There are elephants in that country.'

(92) *ee raṭee ali nææ*
      that country-LOC elephant-PL exist not
      'There are not elephants in that country.'

(93) *mee kaḍee hoňdə eloolu tiyenəwa*
      this shop-LOC good fruit exist(inanim)-PRES
      'There is good fruit in this shop.'

(94) *mee kaḍee hoňdə eloolu nææ*
      this shop-LOC good fruit not.
      'There is not good fruit in this shop.'

nææ is a quasi-verb, with a focusing form *nætte*, and sentences with it can be clefted. Compare (95) and (96) with (88) and (93).

(95) *mee dawaswələ iskoole yanne nætte apee daruwo*
      these days-LOC school go-FOC nææ-FOC our children
      'These days it is our children who don't go to school.'

(96) *mee kaḍee nætte hoňdə eloolu*
      this shop-LOC nææ-FOC good fruit.
      'What there is not in this shop is good fruit.'

Nominal Predicator sentences and focused sentences negate with a form *nemeyi* (dialectally also *neweyi, newi*), as in (97)–(98).

(97) *gunəsiri mahattəya apee iskoole mul guruwarəya nemeyi*
      Gunasiri gentleman our school head teacher *nemeyi*
      'Mr Gunasiri is not the head teacher of/in our school.'

(98) *mamə dække gunəpaaləwə nemeyi*
      I saw-FOC Gunəpalə-ACC *nemeyi*
      'It wasn't Gunapala that I saw.'

There is a third negator: a verbal prefix *no-*. It is limited in distribution primarily to verbs with the focusing affix, as in (99), and verbs of subordinate clauses such as (100), with an infinitive, or (101), with a perfect (conjunctive) participle, but the precise range is not yet clear. For some speakers, at least, it may occur with some main but untensed verbs, as in (102) (De Abrew 1981, Foley and Gair 1993).

(99) *miniha noyanne ee gaməṭə*
      man not-go-FOC that village-DAT
      'It's to that village that the man does not go.'

(100) *malliṭə nopenennə almaariyə uḍin araṇ tiyannə*
       brother-DAT no-see-DAT cupboard above take-PPL place-DAT
       'Put (it) on top of the cupboard so that (younger) brother won't see it.'

(101) *mehe wæḍə nokərə innə bææ.*
here work no-do-PERF be(Anim)-DAT can't
'You can't stay here without working.'

(102) *miniha gaməṭə noyaawi*
man to-the-village no-go-INVOLOPT
'The man might not go to the village.'

The modal adjective *puluwaŋ* 'can' negates with a suppletive quasi-verb *bææ*, as in (103). The modal adjective *oonə* with a nominal object and 'want' sense has alternate negations *oonə nææ* and suppletive *epaa*, as illustrated in (104).

(103) *maṭə ee wæḍə kərannə bææ*
I-DAT that work do-INFIN cannot
'I cannot do that work.' (cf. (63))

(104) *maṭə oyə parənə luunu oonə nææ/ epaa*
I-DAT tomorrow those old onion-PL want not/ don't-want
'I don't want those old (by you) onions.' Compare (61).

6.4.5 Question formation

6.4.5.1 Yes-no questions

Yes-no questions, whether verbal or non-verbal, are formed with the question marker *də* (QUES) following the predicator, as in (105)–(108). Forms that take the assertion marker lose it, as in (106); compare (55).

(105) *siri waḍuwæḍə kərənəwa də*
Siri woodworking do-PAST- QUES
'Does Siri do woodworking?'

(106) *mee amu miris hari særə də*
these raw chilli-PL really strong QUES
'Are these green chillies really strong?'

(107) *arə yaapənee aṁbə alut də*
those Jaffna-LOC mango-PL new QUES
'Are those (over there) Jaffna mangoes fresh?'

(108) *mee dawaswələ haal bohomə ganaŋ də*
these days-PL-LOC rice much expensive QUES
'Is (uncooked) rice very expensive these days?'

6.4.5.2 Constituent questions

Constituent questions, which focus on and question a specific form within the sentence, add *də* to the relevant item. As stated earlier, *də* is a focus-marking form. Thus the sentence must be clefted, as in (109)–(111). As with focusing in general, right-shifting may occur, as in (111).

(109) *Siri waḍuwæḍə də kəranne*
Siri woodworking QUES do-PAST-FOC
'Is it woodworking that Siri does?'

(110) *Siri də waḍuwæḍə kəranne*
       Siri QUES woodworking do-PAST-FOC
       'Is it Siri who does woodworking?'

(111) *hari særə mee amu miris də*
       really strong these raw chilli-PL QUES
       'Is it these green chillies that are really strong?'

6.4.5.3 Interrogative word (Wh) questions

In Sinhala, interrogative ('Wh') forms virtually always co-occur with the question marker *də*, a way in which it differs from other languages such as the South Dravidian ones and current Japanese, in which they are in complementation. The question marker virtually always immediately follows the interrogative word or phrase, and since the question marker is a focus-marking form, focusing of interrogative word questions is then obligatory, e.g. (112)–(114). Note that, as in (113), the focus-marking form follows the entire focused phrase, and may thus be discontinuous from the interrogative (Wh) word itself.

(112) *mee koocciyə yanne kohaaṭə də*
       this train go-PRES-FOC where-DAT QUES
       'Where is this train going?'

(113) *adə kiyəwannə koyi nawəkətaa potə də gatte*
       today read-INFIN which novel book QUES take-PAST-FOC
       'Which novel did you bring to read today?'

(114) *ammat ekkə wenə kawudə yanne*
       mother-also with other who QUES go-PRES-FOC
       'Who else is going with mother?'

As with focusing in general, focusing of interrogative+*də* is not sentence bound, but may reach into subordinate clauses, as in (115):

(115) *Siri keruwa kiyəla oyaa kalpənaa-kəranne mokak də*
       Siri do-PAST COMP] you think-PRES-FOC what QUES
       'What do you think that Siri does?'

Exceptions to the adjacency of the question marker and interrogative words or phrases are primarily in questions with quantifier interrogative words, in which it is optional with a difference in sense and may be either a question or exclamation, as in (116). Non-quantifier question words without an adjacent question marker generally occur in 'general doubt' questions, especially when embedded under an expression of doubt, as in (117). In these instances, *də* follows the predicator, as in simple interrogative sentences. Interrogative word focusing may thus be considered a subcase of constituent focusing in questions.

(116) *mee laməya bat koccarə kanəwa də*
       this child rice how-much eat-PRES QUES
       'How much rice does this child eat?', or 'How much rice this child eats!'

(117) *nimal dæŋ mokak kərənəwa də danne næ*
       Nimal now what do-PRES QUES know not
       '(I) don't know what Nimal is doing now.'

6.4.6 Comparison

Comparatives can be expressed with the dative case of the standard, and the form *wædiye* 'much, more', as in (118).

(118)   *mee potə ee potəṭə wædiye hoňdayi*
        this book that book-DAT more-than good-ASSM
        'This book is better than that book'.

'As (much as)' may be expressed with *taraŋ*. The standard precedes, but is in the case parallel to the one compared, as in (119)–(120).

(119)   *mee potə taraŋ oyə potə amaaru næ̈æ*
        this book as that book difficult not
        'This book (by me) is not as difficult as that one (by you)'

(120)   *maṭə taraŋ malliṭə sinhəla kiyəwannə puluwaŋ*
        I-DAT as brother-DAT Sinhala read-INF can
        '(Younger) brother can read Sinhala as well as I can.'

6.5 Complex sentences

The elements signalling subordinate clauses in Sinhala always follow the subordinate clause. In general, there are three types of subordinators: (1) verbal affixes such as the infinitive, perfect participle, conditional, concessive, and prior temporal forms (see section 5.4); (2) complementizers that require a specific verb form to precede them, such as *koṭə* 'when' or *nisaa* 'because'; and (3) independent complementizers such as *kiyəla* 'quotative'. This classification of forms cross-cuts their functions. The examples that follow will be organized primarily on the basis of function, but will also take into account the formal nature of the forms in terms of the categorization above.

6.5.1 Sentential complements and subjects

Sentential complements may be either finite or non finite, and may occur with verbal or non-verbal higher (matrix) predicators. Sentential subjects are generally non-finite, but finite ones may occur with specific verbal or non-verbal predicators (see section 6.5.3).

6.5.2 Non-finite complements and subjects

6.5.2.1 Infinitives

In (121) and (122) the infinitive expressions are complements to verbal predicators that have nominative and dative subjects respectively. Examples (123) and (124) are parallel to them, but with related active and involitive verbs, showing that it is the verb base that determines the type of complement. Examples (125) and (126) illustrate infinitives dependent on non-verbal predicators with nominative and dative subjects.

(121)   *mamə nowærədiimə oyaage gedərəṭə ennə balannaŋ*
        I without-fail your home-DAT come-INF look-VOLOPT
        'I will try to come without fail to your home.'

(122) *oyaaʈə sinhələ kææmə kannə hambə-unaa də*
you-DAT Sinhala food eat-INF meet QUES
'Have you had a chance to eat Sinhala food?'

(123) *mamə lankaawəʈə yannə hitənəwa*
I Sri-Lanka-DAT go-INF think-PRES
'I am thinking of going to Sri Lanka.'

(124) *maʈə lankaawəʈə yannə hituna*
I-DAT Sri-Lanka-DAT go-INF think-INVOL-PAST
'I felt like going to Sri Lanka.'

(125) *mamə nawəkataa pot kiyəwannə kæmətii*
I novel book-PL read like-ASSM
'I like to read novels.'

(126) *maʈə mee dawaswələ ee pætte ennat bææ*
I-DAT these day-PL-LOC that area-LOC come-INF-also can't
'I can't come that way these days, either.'

6.5.2.2 Nominalizations with *ekə*

Sinhala has a range of nominalizing devices by which entire sentences may be nominalized and serve as subjects, objects or adverbials and be case-marked as appropriate. One common device is to employ the relativizing form of the verb, either present, or past or perfect, preceding *ekə* 'one', which here has no numerical function. Examples are (127)–(132)

(127) *miniha hæmədaamə nuwərə yanə-ekə mamə dannəwa*
man every-day Kandy go-PRES-INSTR-*ekə* I know-PRES
'I know that the fellow goes to Kandy.'

(128) *gunəpaalə wæɖə iwərə kərəpu-ekə mahattəyaʈə kiwwa*
Gunapala work finish do-PERF-REL-*ekə* one gentleman-DAT say-PAST
'Gunapala told the boss that he finished the work.'

In (129) and (130) the nominalizations are the subjects of non-verbal predicators. Note that the nominalization in (130) includes a non-verbal (*puluwaŋ*) sentential object of *kiwwə* 'said' and that *puluwaŋ* in turn has an infinitival object:

(129) *dawəsəgaane šišyəyot ekkə kataabaha kərənə-ekə loku satuʈak*
daily students-also with conversation do-PRES one big joy
'Talking with students daily is a great joy.'

(130) *banɖaʈə ee deməla potə kiyəwannə puluwaŋ (kiyəla) kiwwə-ekə pudumayi*
Banda that Tamil book read-INF can (COMP) say-PAST-REL-*ekə* one surprising-ASSM
'It is surprising that Banda said that he can read that Tamil book.'

For the optional complementizer see section 6.5.4.2.1.

In (131) the nominalization is case-marked dative as complement of *kæməti*; compare (67), in which the finite verb is directly case marked.

(131) *putaa rasaaweŋ rasaawəṭə yanə ekəṭə amma kæməti næə*
son job-INST job-DAT go-PRES-REL mother like not
'Mother doesn't like her son going from job to job.'

6.5.2.3 *bawə* and *wagə* nominalizations

There are also nominalizations with the relativizing form plus *bawə* or *wagə*, roughly '(the fact) that'. These occur as complementizers not only with relativizing forms, as in (132), but also with the perfect participle, as in (133), with non-verbal predicator sentences, and even with cleft sentences, as in (134). They thus cross the line between nominalizations and complement structures (cf. *kiyəla*, section 6.5.4.2.1). *bawə* and *wagə* are generally restricted to factual and/or knowledge contexts, as illustrated in (132)–(134).

(132) *meekə kanə bawə mamə dannəwa*
this-one eat-PRES-REL-fact I know-PRES
'I know that one eats this. (i.e., 'It is edible.')'

(133) *eyaa nuwərə gihilla bawə/wagə maṭə aaranciyi*
he Kandy go-PPL-fact I-DAT news-ASSM
'I heard that he has gone to Kandy.'

(134) *amma kossak gatte gee pihidannə bawə mamə dannəwa*
mother broom-INDEF buy-PRES-FOC house sweep-INFIN fact I know-PRES
'I know that it was in order to sweep the house that mother bought a broom.'
(Weerakoon 1988: 169)

6.5.2.4 Gerunds

There are also inflected nominalized verb forms, i.e., gerunds, in *-iimə* and *-illə*: *kæpiimə/ kæpillə* 'cutting', *bæliimə/ bælillə* 'looking', etc. These are characteristic of the literary variety, but also occur in spoken. They differ from the sentence nominalizations above in the important respect that they do not retain the subject in its case in finite clauses, but if the subject appears it is in the genitive, as with gerunds in English and other languages:

(135) *minihage gas kæpiimə hoňdə næə*
man-GEN tree-PL cutting good not.'
'His cutting trees is not good.'

(136) *ee ammage lamayi hædillə hoňdə næə*
that mother child-PL making good not
'The way that mother raises her children is not good.'

6.5.3 Finite sentential subjects

Finite sentential subjects occur with a few verbal predicates, generally verbs of perception or expression, as in (137):

(137) *ṭikak innə! koocciyə enəwa peenəwa*
little-INDEF be-INF train come-PRES appear-PRES
'Wait a bit! It looks like the train is coming.'

They also occur with some non-verbal predicators, as in (138).

(138) *gunəpaala mee dawaswələ gedərə innəwa hoñdayi*
       Gunapala these days-GEN home be(anim) -PRES good-ASSM
       'It's good that Gunapala is staying at home these days.'

The quasi-verb *æti* 'might be' when it occurs with a finite sentence may be an example of this construction:

(139) *mahattəya adə gedərədi wæɖə karənəwa æti*
       gentleman today home-while work-do-PRES might-be
       'The gentleman might be working at home today.'

6.5.4 Finite sentential complements

6.5.4.1 Finite complements without a complementizer

Some verbs, generally of experience, perception, or expression, may allow finite clause complements without any complementizing form, as in (140)–(141):

(140) *siri horaa paare duwənəwa dækka*
       Siri thief road-LOC see-PAST
       'Siri saw the thief running on the road.'

(141) *ammaṭə maalini sindu kiyənəwa æhuna*
       mother-DAT Malini song-PL say-PRES hear-PAST
       'Mother heard Malini singing songs.'

Indirect questions are also formed in this way, by simply placing the question, unchanged in form, as the complement of the verb of asking or saying, illustrated in (142):

(142) *mehee ṭæksiyak ganne kohomə də kiyannə*
       here taxi take-PRES-FOC how QUES say-INF
       'Tell me how to get a taxi here.'

6.5.4.2 Finite complements with a complementizer

6.5.4.2.1 The complementizer (COMP) *kiyəla*
The most general complementizer for finite clauses is *kiyəla* (glossed as COMP). Though this is etymologically the perfect participle of *kiyənəwa* 'say', it has become an independent form with a wide range of functions. Examples (143) and (144) show it in its role as a marker of indirect and direct quotation. As the translation indicates, (144) is actually ambiguous, and can be interpreted as either a direct or indirect quotation with different meanings. As (145) shows, *kiyəla* has been extended beyond saying into perception, and it has an even more distant relation to saying in functions such as motivation or cause, as in (146) and (147). The assertion marker may optionally precede *kiyəla* as in (147). In some structures, *kiyəla* is optional (see (130)).

(143) *Gunəpaalə maṭə ee salli dennə mehee enne nææ kiyəla kiwwa*
       Gunapala I-DAT that money give-INF here come not COMP say-PAST
       'Gunapala said that he is not coming here to give me the money.'

(144) *maṭə waḍuwǣdə kərannə bǣæ kiyəla nimal kiwwa*
I-DAT carpentry do-INF can't COMP Nimal say-PAST
Nimal said 'I can't do carpentry.', or 'Nimal said that I (speaker) can't do carpentry.'

(145) *gihiŋ malli tamange kaaməree innəwa də kiyəla balannə*
go-PPL brother self-GEN room-LOC be(anim) QUES COMP look-INF
'Go and see if (younger) brother is in his (own) room.'

(146) *taattage upandinə kiyəla api keek hǣduwa*
father-GEN birthday COMP we cake make-PAST
'We made a cake on father's birthday.' (Weerakoon 1988: 49)
(i.e., 'since it was his birthday', or 'realizing it was his birthday'.

(147) *somə wibaage kərənəwayi kiyəla paaḍaŋ kərənəwa*
Soma examination do-pres-ASSM COMP study do-PRES
'Soma is studying because she is taking the examination.' (Weerakoon 1988: 48)

6.5.4.2.2 The complementizer *naŋ* 'if'
The complementizer *naŋ* forms conditional clauses, and like *kiyəla* is clause-final. The embedded sentence is unchanged in form, except for the loss of the assertion marker on forms that require it, as in (149):

(148) *sinhələ pot huñgak kiyəwənəwa naŋ sinhələ ikmənəṭə igənəgannə puluwəni*
Sinhala book-PL read-PRES if Sinhala quickly learn-INF can
'If you read a lot of Sinhala books, you can learn Sinhala quickly.'

(149) *mee potə hoñdə naŋ mamə putaaṭə dennə gannəwa*
this book good if I son-DAT give-INF buy-PRES
If this book is good, I'll buy it to give our son.

naŋ can form past counter-to-fact clauses, as in (150). Note the sequence of tenses.

(150) *tawə ṭikak parakku unaa naŋ, eyaawə allagannə hambəwenne nǣæ*
still -a-little late become-PAST if he-ACC catch-INF meet-PRES–FOC not
'If I had been a bit later, I wouldn't have had a chance to catch him.'

naŋ is a focus-marking form (section 6.4.3.1), and thus it can follow the focused item in a clefted clause (151):

(151) *oyaa yanne nuwərəṭə naŋ udee koocciyeŋ yannə*
you go-PRES-FOC morning train go-INF
'If it is to Kandy that you are going, go by the morning train.'

6.6 Coordination

Sentences and constituents may be coordinated without a conjunction, employing only intonation, (indicated here by commas) (152)–(154):

(152) *mamə, taatta, maama, koləm̃bəṭə giyaa*
I father uncle Colombo-DAT go-PAST
'I, father and (maternal) uncle went to Colombo.'

(153) *api bat kanəwa, paaŋ kanəwa*
we rice eat bread eat
'We eat rice and we (also) eat bread.'

(154) *gunəpaala ehee wǣdə kərənəwa, siri mehee wǣdə kərənəwa*
Gunapala there work do-PRES Siri here work do-PRES
'Gunapala works there and Siri works here.'

Coordination of constituents can also employ the conjunction clitic *-yi* , generally repeated on each item, as in (155). Many speakers resist coordinating full sentences in this way, so that sentences like (156) are doubtful.

(155) *mamayi, taattayi, maamayi, koləm̌bəṭə giyaa*
I-CONJ father-CONJ uncle-CONJ Colombo-DAT go-PAST
'I, father, and (maternal) uncle went to Colombo.'

(156) *api bat kanəway paan kanəway*
we rice eat-PRES-CONJ bread- eat-PRES-CONJ
??'We eat rice and we (also) eat bread.'

Constituents can also be coordinated with the clitic *-(u)t*, as in (157)–(158). This allows serial coordination ('and also') and thus has a different sense from the *yi … yi* coordination, which implies a group. It is commonly accompanied by a resumptive numeral or other quantifier:

(157) *ammat taattat ayyat naŋgit hatərədenaamə adə pansələṭə giyaa*
mother-also father-also brother-also sister-also four(ANIM)-EMPH today
temple-DAT go-PAST
'Mother, father, (older) brother, and (younger) sister, all four went to the temple today.'

(158) *kaḍeeṭə yandat baḍu geenḍat redi hoodanḍat oyə okkoṭoomə inne mamə witərayi*
shop-DAT go-INF-also goods bring-INF-also clothes wash-INF-also that all-DAT
be(anim)-PRES-FOC I only
'To go to the shop, fetch goods, and wash clothes, there is only me here.'
(Karunatillake 1992: 163)

6.7 Relative clauses

Relative clauses always precede the noun head. The verb of the clause is marked with one of the three relativizing (verbal adjective) affixes: present, past or perfect. As stated in section 5.4.2, the latter two are alternates that do not differ in meaning. As (159)–(164) show, all major constituents within the relative clause are eligible for relativization. As (165)–(168) demonstrate, relative clauses may be formed with adjectival and quasi-verbal predicators.

(159) *siri gunəpaalaṭə dunnə potə*
Siri Gunapala-DAT give-PAST-REL book
'the book that Siri gave Gunapala'

(160) *gunəpaaləṭə potə dunnə siri*
Gunapala-DAT book give-PAST-REL Siri
'(the) Siri who gave the book to Gunapala'

(161) *siri potə dunnə gunəpaalə*
Siri book give-PAST-REL Gunapala
'(the) Gunapala to whom Siri gave the book'

(162) *arə atənə ratu šərṭ-ekak æñdəla hiṭəgenə innə miniha*
that there red shirt-INDEF wear-PPL stand-PRES-REL man
'the man wearing the red shirt standing over there'

(163) *iiye wattedi parənə rabər gas kæpuwə baṇḍa*
yesterday estate-LOC-in old rubber tree-PL cut-PAST-REL Banda
'the Banda who cut the old rubber trees in the estate yesterday'

(164) *baṇḍa iiye wattedi kapəpu parənə rabər gas*
Banda yesterday estate-LOC-in cut-PERF-REL old rubber tree-PL
'the old rubber trees that Banda cut in the estate yesterday'

(165) *apee daruwo dæŋ yanə hoňdə iskoole*
our children now go-PRES REL good school
'the good school that our children go to now'

(166) *sinhələ igəgannə hoňdə pot (tiyenəwa də)*
Sinhala learn-INFIN good book-PL be-INANIM-PRES QUES
'(Are there) books that are good for learning Sinhala?'

(167) *gunəpaaləṭə dæŋ oonə salli (maṭə adə dennə bææ)*
Gunapala-DAT now want money I-DAT today give can't
'The money that Gunapala wants now (I can't give today).'

(168) *iskoole yanne næti lamayinṭə (rassaawak hoyaagannə amaaruyi)*
school go-PRES not-REL child-PL-DAT job seek-take-INF difficult-ASSM
'(For) children who don't go to school (it is hard to find a job).'

6.8 Adverbial clauses

There are several types of adverbial clauses. All of them have the subordinating element on the right margin, consistent with the left-branching character of Sinhala. In general, these elements are of two types: (a) a verbal inflection, such as the conjunctive (perfect) participle, conditional, concessive, or prior temporal forms, or (b) a relativizing (verbal adjective) form followed by a lexical form such as *koṭə* 'when' or *kaŋ* 'until'. These are illustrated below (for a fuller list, see especially Gair 1970).

6.8.1 Adverbial clauses with verbal inflection

6.8.1.1 The conjunctive (perfect) participle

The existence of a conjunctive participle (sometimes called 'absolutive') has frequently been remarked on as a feature of the South Asian linguistic area. Characteristically, this is a non-finite form linking actions sequentially, or sometimes in terms of cause or manner, within the sentence. In Sinhala, this function is fulfilled by the perfect participle, as in (169)–(171):

(169) *ehenaŋ putaaṭə kæ̈æmə diila, apit kæ̈æmə kaala iiṭə passe tee-ekak bomu*
in-that-case son-DAT food give-PPL we-also food eat-PPL that-DAT after tea -
INDEF drink-VOLOPT
'In that case, let's feed the child (son), eat dinner ourselves and then drink tea.'

(170) *mahattəya kæ̈məti naŋ mamə miris daala kariyak hadannaŋ*
gentleman like if I chillies put-PPL curry-INDEF make-VOLOPT
'If you (sir) like, I will make a curry putting in chillies.'

(171) *paaredi minissu dennek pərs-ekə uduraagenə diwwa*
road-on man-PL two (ANIM)- INDEF) purse snatch-PPL run-PAST
'While on the road, two people snatched my purse and ran.'

In (169)–(171), the subjects of the main clause and the participial clauses are identical,
and the participial structure can be considered as internal to the main clause; that is, as
within its verb phrase. However, Sinhala can also form sentential adverbs with the
perfect participle, and then different subjects are allowed, as in (172). For discussion and
evidence from acquisition, see Gair, Lust, Sumangala and Rodrigo 1989.

(172) *amma leḍə welaa gedərə seerəmə wæḍə kəranne api*
mother sick become-PPL house all work do-FOC we
'With mother sick, it is we that (have to) do all the housework!'

Also, in Sinhala the perfect participle is not confined to subordinate structures, but can
serve as a finite main verb – e.g. (173)–(174) an unusual if not unique feature among
South Asian languages. It is in fact the usual form in Sinhala when one asserts that the
action is completed, or when one infers its completion without direct knowledge. It
contrasts with the simple past, which generally implies more direct knowledge on the
part of the speaker.

(173) *koləm̆bə bas sṭænḍ-ekə dæŋ hun̆gak wenas kərəla*
Colombo bus stand now much different make-PPL
'The Colombo bus stand has been changed a lot now.'

(174) *noona koləm̆baṭə enəkoṭə mamə nuwərə gihilla.*
lady Colombo-DAT come-when I Kandy go-PPL
'When my wife came to Colombo, I had gone to Kandy.'

The perfect participle, with the clitic *-(u)t* 'also', can form a concessive clause (175):

(175) *eccərə kərəlat, oyaaṭə salli hambəwenne næ̈æ*
that-much do-PPL-also you-DAT money meet-PRES-FOC not
'Even having done that much, you won't get money.'

6.8.1.2 The reduplicated perfect participle

The stem of the perfect participle can be reduplicated to express continuous action,
generally simultaneous with the main verb, as in (176)–(178). Here the matrix and
embedded subjects are virtually always coreferential.

(176) *laməya an̆də-an̆də gedərə duwəla aawa*
child cry-PPL cry-PPL home run-PPL came
'The child came home crying.'

(177) *eyaa baḍu vikunə-vikunə innəwa*
he goods sell-PPL sell-PPL be(anim)-PRES
'He is (continuously) selling goods.'

(178) *oyaa kataa kərə-kərə pot kiyəwanne kohomə də*
you speech do-PPL do-PPL book-PL read-PRES-FOC how QUES
'How do you read books while talking?'

6.8.1.3 Conditional and concessive forms

The conditional and concessive forms of the verb, illustrated in (179)–(181), form sentence adverbials with the meaning suggested by their names. As (181) illustrates, post main clause positioning is possible, as it is generally with adverbial clauses. These forms refer to actions that have not yet occurred; past conditional and counterfactual senses are expressed with the conjunction *naŋ* (see section 6.5.4.2.2).

(179) *oyaa ehemə keruwot okkomə hari yayi*
you that-way do-CONDIT correct go-VOLOPT
'If you do it that way, everything might go OK.'

(180) *ehemə keruwat wæḍak nææ*
that-way do-CONCESS use-INDEF NEG
'Even if you do it that way, it's no use.'

(181) *mahattəyaṭə narəkə də mee paarə paarlimeentuwəṭə idiripat unot*
sir-DAT bad QUES this time parliament-DAT forward become-CONDIT
'Would it be bad for you if you came forward (to run) for parliament, sir?'

6.8.1.4 The prior temporal (-aamə) form

The prior temporal (*-aamə*) form indicates action prior to the main clause, as in (182)–(183):

(182) *gunəpaalə gaməṭə giyaamə eyaa gangee nææwa*
Gunapala village-DAT go-after he/she river-LOC bathe-PAST
'When (after) Gunapala went to the village, he (or someone else) bathed in the river.'

(183) *amma aawaamə mamə wæḍə kərannaŋ*
mother come-after I work do-VOLOPT
'I will work when (after) mother comes.'

The *-aamə* affix is historically derived from a lexical form *hamə*, and the latter still occurs, with either the past or perfect relativizing form, as in (184)–(185), which are alternates to (183). Thus the line between inflected forms and the next type (relativizing form plus complementizing form) is not always clear.

(184) *amma aawə hamə mamə wæḍə kərannaŋ*
mother come-PAST-REL-after I work do-VOLOPT
'I will work when (after) mother comes.'

(185) *amma aapu hamə mamə wæḍə kərannaŋ*
mother come-PERF-REL-after I work do-VOLOPT
' I will work when (after) mother comes.'

6.8.2 Adverbial clauses with relativizing form plus complementizing form

koʈə and *kaŋ* forms will serve to illustrate the formation of adverbial clauses with a complementizing form preceded by a relativizing form, as in (186)–(187). There are several other complementizing forms that occur in this way, such as *gamaŋ* 'while, during' and *handa, hinda* or *nisaa* 'because' (Gair 1970).

(186)   *oyaa koləṁbəʈə yanə-koʈə api oyat-ekkə yannaŋ*
        you Colombo-DAT go-PRES- REL-when we you-with go-VOLOPT
        'When you go to Colombo, we'll go with you.'

(187)   *maama enə-kaŋ putaa isʈeesəmeemə innə*
        uncle come-PRES -until son station-EMPH be(anim)-INFIN
        'You (son) stay right in the station until (maternal) uncle comes.'

Recall also that the nominalizing forms *bawə* and *wagə* can also occur in such structures (section 6.5.2.3).

7 ANAPHORA

7.1 Reflexive usages of pronominal forms

There is a reflexive pronoun *taman*, with an alternate form *tamun*, and a somewhat more formal nominative form *tamaa* (see section 5.2.6). The pronoun *taman/tamun* is human, may be either masculine or feminine, singular or plural, and is generally third person in reference. In colloquial Sinhala its case forms are plural in form, regardless of reference, though there is a singular form *tamaa* found in literary and formal spoken Sinhala. The distribution of *taman/tamun* is complex, but in general, it is most commonly used within the same sentence as its antecedent, as in (188)–(190). It characteristically refers back to the subject of the sentence, but that includes subjects in non-nominative cases, as illustrated by (190), where the subject is in the accusative (see section 6.4.1.1).

The pronominal APH form *eyaa* (see section 5.2.4 and Table 21.9) may also be used similarly, but it is normally strengthened by the emphatic clitic *mə* when it is coreferential with the subject and not possessive. *taman/tamun* emphasizes the coreferentiality (cf. English 'one's own'), and *eyaa (+mə)* allows a discourse antecedent. For details see Gair and Karunatillake 1998 and 2000. Compare (191)–(192) with (188) and (189).

(188)   *gunəpaalə tamanwə kannaaḍiyen dækka*
        Gunapalai self-ACC mirror-INSTR see-PAST
        'Gunapala saw himself in the mirror.'

(189)   *gunəpaalə tamunge kaar-ekə vikka*
        Gunapala his/self's car-DEF sell-PAST
        'Gunapala sold his (own) car.'

(190)   *minihawə tamaŋge pokune wæʈuna*
        man-ACC self-GEN pond-GEN(LOC) fall-PAST
        'The fellow fell in his own pond.'

(191) *gunəpaalə eyaawəmə kannaaḍiyen dækka*
       Gunapalai (s)he-ACC-EMPH mirror-INSTR see-PAST
       'Gunapala saw himself (or someone else) in the mirror.'

(192) *gunəpaalə eyaage(mə) kaar-ekə vikka*
       Gunapala (s)he-GEN-EMPH car-DEF sell-PAST
       'Gunapala sold his(own) (or someone else's) car.'

7.2 Null pronouns and 'pro-drop'

It was mentioned earlier (section 5.2.4) that Sinhala commonly made use of elided (or 'null') pronouns in all positions and indeed the most common 'pronoun' in Sinhala discourse may be null. Though this may resemble 'pro-drop', in more familiar European languages such as Spanish and Italian, it is more thoroughgoing and not limited to subjects, but extends to objects and other positions. It is interesting to note that it is much more characteristic of the colloquial rather than the literary variety, even though the former but not the latter lacks verbal agreement.

The brief exchange in (193) will illustrate (adapted from Fairbanks et al. 1968: Lesson 10). The *eyaa* pronouns in parentheses were not in the original, but were added here to indicate the 'missing' unexpressed pronouns. Expressing them all, though grammatical, would lead to intolerable redundancy in natural Sinhala discourse. 'A' and 'B' represent the discourse participants.

(193)A *siri dæŋ gedərə innəwa də*
        Siri now home be(ANIM) QUES
        'Is Siri at home now?'

     B *nææ. (eyaa) taamə kantooruwe*
        no (he) still office-LOC
        'No. He is still at the office.'

     A *(eyaa) kiiyəṭə də gedərə enne*
        (he) when QUES home come-FOC
        'What time does he come home?'

     B *kantooruwə wahanne hatərəṭə*
        office close-FOC four-DAT
        'They close the office at four.'

        pahaṭə witərə (eyaa) gedərə eewi
        five about (he) home come-might
        'He is likely to come home at about five.'

ACKNOWLEDGEMENTS

Thanks are due, as they so often are, to Professor W. S. Karunatillake, who kindly checked the manuscript at short notice for errors in examples and corrected or supplied a number of them. Any errors that may remain or that I failed to correct are of course my responsibility. I also thank Bruce Cain for serving as e-mail conduit to Sri Lanka, as well as for his own suggestions.

REFERENCES

Cain, Bruce D. (2000) *Dhivehi (Maldivian): A Synchronic and Diachronic Study*. Ph.D. dissertation, Cornell University.

Cain, Bruce D. and Gair, James W. (2000) *Dhivehi (Maldivian)*, Languages of the World/Materials 63, Munich: Lincom Europa.

Coates, William, and De Silva, M. W. S. (1960) 'The segmental phonemes of Sinhalese', *University of Ceylon Review* 18. 3–4: 163–75.

De Abrew, Kamal K. (1981) *The Syntax and Semantics of Negation in Sinhala*, Ph.D. dissertation, Cornell University.

De Alwis, James (1852) *The Sidath Sangarawa, A Grammar of the Sinhalese Language Translated Into English*, Colombo, Sri Lanka: Government Printer.

De Silva, M. W. S (1958) 'Gender in colloquial Sinhalese', *University of Ceylon Review* 16. 3–4: 119–24.

—— (1960) 'Verbal categories in spoken Sinhalese', *University of Ceylon Review* 18.1: 96–112.

—— (1963) 'A phonemic statement of the Sinhalese vowels [a] [a] and [aa]', University of Ceylon Review 21: 71–5.

—— (1967) 'Effects of purism on the evolution of written language', *Linguistics* 36: 5–17.

—— (1970) 'Some observations on the history of Maldivian', *Transactions of the Philological Society of London*, 1970: 137–62.

—— (1974) 'Convergence in diglossia: the Sinhalese situation', *International Journal of Dravidian Linguistics* 3.1: 60–91.

—— (1976) *Diglossia and Literacy*, Mysore: Central Institute of Indian Languages.

—— (1979) *Sinhalese and Other Island Languages in South Asia*. Tubingen: Gunther Narr Verlag.

—— (1986a) 'Typology of diglossia and its implications for literacy', in Krishnamurti et al. (eds), pp. 304–11.

—— (1986b) 'The Sidat Sangara as a contrastive grammar of poetry and prose', *Journal of the Royal Asiatic Society (Sri Lanka)* 31: 1–39.

Disanayake, J. B. (1986) 'Maldivian and Sinhala: some phonological observations', *Journal of the Royal Asiatic Society (Sri Lanka)* 30: 81–100.

—— (1991) *The Structure of Spoken Sinhala: 1: Sounds and Their Patterns*, Maharagama, Sri Lanka: National Institute of Education.

Elizarenkova, T. (1972) 'Influence of Dravidian phonological system on Sinhalese', *International Journal of Dravidian Linguistics* 1.2: 127–37.

Fairbanks, Gordon W., Gair, James W. and De Silva, M. W. S. (1968) *Colloquial Sinhalese (Sinhala)*, books 1 and 2, Ithaca NY: Cornell University South Asia Program (second reprinting 1981 and 2001).

Feinstein, Mark (1979) 'Prenasalized stops and syllable structure', *Linguistic Inquiry* 10.2: 245–78.

Ferguson, Charles A. (1959) 'Diglossia', *Word* 15: 325–40.

Fernando, Chitra (1977) 'English and Sinhala Bilingualism in Sri Lanka', *Language in Society* 5: 341–60

Foley, Claire and Gair, James W. (1993) 'The distribution of *no-* in Sinhala', Paper given at SALA (South Asian Language Analysis) conference, University of Iowa, June 1993. Manuscript, Cornell University.

Gair, James W. (1967) 'Colloquial Sinhala inflectional categories and parts of speech', *Indian Linguistics* 27: 31–45 (Reprinted in Gair 1998).

—— (1968) 'Sinhalese diglossia', *Anthropological Linguistics* 10.8: 1–15 (Reprinted in Gair 1998).

—— (1970) *Colloquial Sinhalese Clause Structures*, The Hague: Mouton.

—— (1971) 'Action involvement categories in Colloquial Sinhalese', in Zamora M. D., Maher, J.M. and Orenstein, H. (eds.) *Themes in Culture, Essays in Honor of Morris E. Opler,* Quezon City: Kayamanggi, pp. 238–56 (Reprinted in Gair 1998).

—— (1976a) 'The verb in Sinhala, with some preliminary remarks on Dravidianization', *International Journal of Dravidian Linguistics* 5: 259–73 (Reprinted in Gair 1998).

—— (1983a) 'Sinhala and English: the effects of a language act', *Language Problems and Language Planning* 7.1: 43–59.

—— (1983b). 'Non-configurationality, movement, and Sinhala focus', Paper presented to the Linguistics Association of Great Britain, Newcastle (Reprinted in Gair 1998).

—— (1985) 'How Dravidianized was Sinhala phonology: Some conclusions and cautions', in Acson, Veneeta Z. and Leed, Richard L. (eds.) *Festschrift for Gordon H. Fairbanks,* (Oceanic Linguistics Special Publication 20), University of Hawaii Press, pp. 37–55.

—— (1986a) 'Sinhala focused sentences: naturalization of a calque', in Krishnamurti, Bh. et al. (eds.), pp. 147–64 (Reprinted in Gair 1998).

—— (1986b) 'Sinhala diglossia revisited, or diglossia dies hard', in Krishnamurti, Bh. et al. (eds.), pp. 322–36 (Reprinted in Gair 1998).

—— (1990) 'Subjects, Case and INFL in Sinhala', in Verma, M. and Mohanan, K. P. (eds.) *Experiencer Subjects in South Asian Languages,* Stanford: Center for the Study of Language and Information, pp. 13–41 (Reprinted in Gair 1998).

—— (1991) 'Discourse and situational deixis in Sinhala', in Lakshmi Bai, B. and Reddy, R. Ramakrishnan (eds.) *Studies in Dravidian and General Linguistics,* pp. 448–467. Hyderabad, India: Centre of Advanced Study in Linguistics, Osmania University (Reprinted in Gair 1998).

—— (1992) 'AGR, INFL, Case and Sinhala diglossia, or, can linguistic theory find a home in variety?', in Kachru Braj, Dimock, Edward C. and Krishnamurti, Bh. (eds.) *Dimensions of South Asia as a Sociolinguistic Area: Papers in Memory of Gerald B. Kelley,* New Delhi: Oxford and IBH, pp. 179–97.

—— (1994.) 'Universals and the South-South Asian language area', Paper presented at SALA (South Asian Language Analysis) conference, University of Pennsylvania, June 1994.

—— (1995) 'The Sinhala writing system', in Bright, William and Daniels, Peter (eds.) *The World's Writing Systems,* Oxford, Oxford University Press, pp. 408–12.

—— (1997) 'Some problems of control in Sinhala', Paper presented at the Workshop on Nulls in South Asian Languages, University of Delhi, January 1997, Manuscript, Cornell University.

—— (1998) *Studies in South Asian Linguistics: Sinhala and Other South Asian Languages,* Oxford: Oxford University Press.

Gair, James W. and Karunatilaka (Karunatillake) (1974) *Literary Sinhala,* Ithaca NY: Cornell University South Asia Program.

—— (1976) *Literary Sinhala Inflected Forms: A Synopsis with a Transliteration Guide to Sinhala Script,* Ithaca NY: Cornell University South Asia Program.

—— (1998) 'Pronouns, reflexives and anti-anaphora in Sinhala,' in Gair 1998: 126–39.

—— (2000) 'Lexical pronouns and anaphors in Sinhala', in Lust, Barbara, Wali, Kashi, Subbarao, K. and Gair, J. W. (eds.) *Lexical Anaphors and Pronouns in Selected South Asian Languages: a Principled Typology,* Mouton-De Gruyter, Berlin, pp. 715–73.

Gair, James W., Karunatillake, W. S. and Paolillo, John C. (1987) *Readings in Colloquial Sinhala,* Ithaca NY: Cornell University South Asia Program.

Gair, James W., Lust, Barbara, Sumangala, Lelwala and Rodrigo, Milan (1989) 'Acquisition of empty categories in Sinhala adverbial clauses', *Papers and Reports on Child Language Development* 28, pp. 97–106, Stanford University.

Gair, James W. and Paolillo, John C. (1988) 'Sinhala non-verbal sentences and argument structure', *Cornell Working Papers in Linguistics* 8: 39–78.

—— (1997) *Sinhala (Languages of the World/Materials* 34), München: Lincom.

Gair, James W. and Sumangala, Lelwala (1991) 'What to focus in Sinhala', in Germán F. Westphal et al. (eds.) *Ohio State Working Papers, Escol 91*: 93–108.

Geiger, Wilhelm (1919) *Maldivian Linguistic Studies*, Journal of the Ceylon Branch of the Royal Asiatic Society 27 (extra number), edited by H. C. P. Bell. (Reprinted (1986), Male', Maldives: National Centre for Linguistic and Historical Research).

—— (1935) 'Sinhalese language and literature', in Jaytilaka, D. B. et al. (eds.) *Dictionary of the Sinhalese Language Volume 1*, Colombo: Royal Asiatic Society, pp. xvii–xxxviii.

—— (1937) 'The linguistic character of Sinhalese', *Journal of the Royal Asiatic Society, Ceylon Branch* Vol. 34, No. 90, 16–43.

—— (1938) *A Grammar of the Sinhalese Language*, Colombo: Royal Asiatic Society.

—— (1941) *An Etymological Glossary of the Sinhalese Language*, Colombo: Royal Asiatic Society.

Godakumbura, C. E. (1955) *Sinhalese Literature*, Colombo, Colombo Apothecaries Ltd.

Gunasekara. A. Mendis (1891) *A Grammar of the Sinhalese Language. Adapted for the Use of English Readers and Prescribed for the Civil Service Examination*, Colombo: Government Press. (Reprinted (1962), Sri Lanka Sahitya Mandalaya, Colombo).

Gunasinghe, C. Khema Hemamala Himaransi (1985) *Passive Voice, a New Perspective: Some Evidence for a Re-analysis from Sinhala*, Ph.D. thesis, University of Victoria.

Gurulugomi, ?. (1959) *Amāwatura* (ed. by Pandita Kodaagoda Nyaanaaloka Sthawira), Colombo: M.D. Gunasena.

Herring, Susan C. and Paolillo, John C. (1995) 'Focus position in SOV languages', in Noonan, M., and Downing, P. (eds.) *Word Order and Discourse*, Amsterdam: Benjamins, pp. 163–98.

Hettiaratchi, D. E. (1959) 'The languages of Ceylon', in Senarat Paranavitana (ed.) *The History of Ceylon Volume I, part 1*, Colombo: Ceylon University Press Board, pp. 33–45.

Inman, Michael V. (1993) *Semantics and Pragmatics of Colloquial Sinhala Non-volitional Verbs*, Ph.D. dissertation, Stanford University.

Karunatillake, W. S. (1969) *Historical Phonology of Sinhalese: From Old Indo-Aryan to the 14th Century AD*, Ph.D. dissertation, Cornell University.

—— (1974). 'The position of Sinhala among the I-A languages', *Indian Journal of Linguistics*, 4: 1–6.

—— (1987a) 'Category of gender in Sinhala', in Hiran, M. and Jayasuriya, F. (eds.) *Gate Mudaliyar W. F. Gunawardhana Commemoration Volume*, Colombo: Sri Lanka, pp. 85–97.

—— (1987b) 'Some observations on the phonetics of the word in Sinhala', Manuscript, Kelaniya University: Sri Lanka.

—— (1992) *An Introduction to Spoken Sinhala*, Colombo: Gunasena.

—— (1995) *Siṁhala Bhāṣā Vyākaraṇaya*, Colombo: Gunasena.

Karunatillake, W. S. and Suseendirarajah, S. (1975) 'Pronouns of address in Tamil and Sinhalese – A sociolinguistic study', *International Journal of Dravidian Linguistics* 4.1: 83–96.

Krishnamurti, Bh., Masica, Colin P. and Sinha, Anjani K. (eds.) (1986) *South Asian Languages: Structure, Convergence and Diglossia*, Delhi: Motilal Banarsidass.

Kumaranatungoa, Munidasa (1934) *Sidat Saṅgarā Vivaraṇaya*, Colombo: K. D. Perera and Son. [date given in Buddhist era as 2478]

Letterman, Rebecca S. (1997) *The Effects of Word-Internal Prosody in Sinhala: A Constraint-Based Analysis*, Ph.D. dissertation, Cornell University.

Macdougall, Bonnie G. (1979) *Sinhala: Basic Course*, Washington D.C. Foreign Service Institute, Department of State.

Maloney, Clarence (1978) *People of the Maldive Islands*, Madras: Orient Longman.

Masica, Colin P. (1991) *The Indo-Aryan Languages*, Cambridge UK: Cambridge University Press.

Paolillo, John C. (1991) 'Sinhala diglossia and the theory of Government and Binding', *Southwest Journal of Linguistics* 10.1: 41–59.

—— (1992) *Functional Articulation in Diglossia: a Case Study of Grammatical and Social Correspondences in Sinhala*, Ph.D. dissertation, Stanford University.

—— (1994) 'The co-development of finiteness and focus in Sinhala', in Pagliuca, William (ed.) *Perspectives on Grammaticalization*, Amsterdam: Benjamins, pp. 151–70.

—— (1997) 'Sinhala diglossic variation: continuous or discrete?', *Language in Society* 26.2: 269–96.

Paranavitana, Senaviratna (1956) *Sigiri Graffiti, Sinhalese Verses of the Eighth, Ninth and Tenth Centuries*, London: Oxford University Press.

Ratanajoti, Hundirapola. (1975) *The Syntactic Structure of Sinhalese and its Relation to that of the Other Indo-Aryan Dialects*, Ph.D. dissertation, University of Texas.

Reynolds, C. H. B. (ed.) (1970) An Anthology of Sinhalese Literature up to 1815, London: George Allen and Unwin.

—— (ed.) (1987) An Anthology of Sinhalese Literature of the Twentieth *Century*, Woodchurch, Kent, Paul Norbury/Unesco.

—— (1995) Sinhalese: An Introductory Course, Second Edition, London: School of Oriental and African Studies (First edition 1980).

Sumangala, Lelwala (1992) *Long Distance Dependencies in Sinhala: the Syntax of Focus and WH Questions*, Ph.D. dissertation, Cornell University.

Weerakoon, Hema (1988) *Nominalization in Sinhala*, Ph.D. dissertation, University of Kelaniya.

Wijemanne, Piyaseeli (1984) *Amavatura, A Syntactical Study*, Colombo: Ministry of Higher Education.

Wijeratne, P. B. F. (1945–57) 'Phonology of the Sinhalese Inscriptions up to the end of the 10th Century A.D.', *Bulletin of the School of Oriental and African Studies:* 11.3 (1945): 580–94, 11.4 (1946): 823–36, 12.1 (1947): 163–83, 13.1 (1949): 166–81, 14.2 (1952): 263–98, 193 (1957): 479–514.

Wijesundera, S., Wiyayawardhana, G. D., Disayanaka, J. B., Manik, H. A. and Luthfie, M. (1988) Historical and Linguistic Survey of Dhivehi: Final Report, Colombo: University of Colombo.

FURTHER READINGS

De Silva, M. W. S. (1979) *Sinhalese and Other Island Languages in South Asia*, Tübingen: Gunther Narr Verlag.

Dharmadasa, K. N. O. (1992) *Language, Religion, and Ethnic Assertiveness: The Growth of Sinhalese Nationalism in Sri Lanka*, Ann Arbor: University of Michigan Press.

Fairbanks, Gordon W., Gair, James W. and M. W. S. De Silva. (1968) *Colloquial Sinhalese(Sinhala),* books 1 and 2, Ithaca NY: Cornell University South Asia Program.

Gair, James W. (1970) *Colloquial Sinhalese Clause Structures*, The Hague: Mouton.

—— (1998) *Studies in South Asian Linguistics: Sinhala and Other South Asian Languages*, Oxford: Oxford University Press.

Gair, James W. and Karunatillake, W. S. (1974) *Literary Sinhala*, Ithaca NY: Cornell University South Asia Program.

—— (1976) *Literary Sinhala Inflected Forms: A Synopsis with a Transliteration Guide to Sinhala Script,* Ithaca NY: Cornell University South Asia Program.

Gair, James W. and Paolillo, John C. (1997) *Sinhala (Languages of the World/Materials 34)*, München: Lincom.

Geiger, Wilhelm (1938) *A Grammar of the Sinhalese Language*, Colombo: Royal Asiatic Society.

Gunasekara, A. Mendis (1891) *A Grammar of the Sinhalese Language. Adapted for the Use of English Readers and Prescribed for the Civil Service Examination*, Colombo: Government Press. Reprinted 1962, Sri Lanka Sahitya Mandalaya, Colombo.

Reynolds, C. H. B. (ed.) (1970) *An Anthology of Sinhalese Literature up to 1815*, London: George Allen and Unwin.

Reynolds, C. H. B. (ed.) (1987) *An Anthology of Sinhalese Literature of the Twentieth Century*, Woodchurch, Kent, Paul Norbury/Unesco.

CHAPTER TWENTY–TWO

DARDIC

Elena Bashir

CONTENTS

1 INTRODUCTION

1.1 Overview

'Dardic' is a geographical cover term for those Northwest Indo-Aryan languages which, because of their isolation in the mountains of the Hindu Kush, Swat and Indus Kohistan, the Karakorams and the Western Himalayas, have retained ancient and developed new characteristics different from the IA languages of the Indo-Gangetic plain. Although the Dardic and the Nuristani (previously 'Kafiri') languages were formerly grouped together, Morgenstierne (1965) has established that the Dardic languages are Indo-Aryan, and that the Nuristani languages constitute a separate subgroup of Indo-Iranian. The meaning of the umbrella term 'Dardic' thus includes both 'genetic' and geographic components. The designation 'Dardic' implies neither ethnic unity among the speakers of these languages nor that they can all be traced to a single stammbaum-model node. The task of subgrouping and clarifying the historical relationships among these languages is complicated by the fact that throughout their history they have been and continue to be influenced by mutual contact. The similarities of the Dardic languages today are due to differentially shared retentions, innovations affecting various subsets of these languages, and contact (areal) developments.

Dardic languages on the whole underwent fewer of the major MIA phonological and morphological developments than plains IA. Important MIA phonological developments are the reduction of the OIA three-sibilant system to one- or two-member systems and reduction of consonant clusters to geminates or single consonants. A central MIA morphological development is the loss of OIA finite preterite tenses with development of participial tenses and the accompanying split-ergative systems of NIA.

Dardic languages were formerly spoken over a wider area than they are today, and each language (cluster) has been affected differentially by these changes. Specific phonological changes occurred in some languages but not others; for example, OIA *tr* remained in Kalasha, Khowar, Dameli, Palula, some dialects of Pashai, and Tirahi, but > λ in Gawarbati and Dir Kohistani, *ṣl* in Ningalami, θ in some Pashai dialects, *ç* in Torwali and Shina, and *c* in Indus Kohistani (Morgenstierne 1934: 174). Although almost all of the Dardic languages lost the OIA finite preterital tenses, Khowar and Kalasha did not, with the result that only they have purely nominative-accusative case marking (Morgenstierne 1947a: 8).

Retained OIA phonological characteristics present in most Dardic languages include: contrasting dental, palatal and retroflex sibilants; and more consonant clusters than plains IA (Morgenstierne 1934, 1947b, Grierson 1931, Turner 1927).

Most Dardic languages show (partial) loss of aspiration, especially of voiced aspirates. This loss is recent and in some languages voiced aspirates remain (Torwali, Indus Kohistani, Palula, Kalasha). In others, traces remain as tonal differences (Khowar *buúm* 'earth', Pashai *dū^um* 'smoke'). This process can be observed today in Kalam Kohistani, where the aspiration contrast is evolving into a tonal system (Baart 1997). In some languages, secondary aspiration has developed (Khowar *khabáab* 'kabab').

A widespread innovation in the phonological inventories of Dardic languages is retroflex affricates *ç*, *çh*, *ǰ*, *ẓ*, which have developed from OIA clusters and been maintained and reinforced under areal influences (Tikkanen 1995). Local developments include the velarized *l* found in Kalasha, Khowar and Palula and the voiceless lateral λ found in Gawarbati, Kalam Kohistani, Wotapuri-Katarqalai, Shumashti and Grangali.

Morphological innovations include the differential development of split ergative systems, found in most of the Dardic languages but with considerable variety and notable exceptions. Kalasha and Khowar are nominative-accusative, while Shina is fully ergative. In Dameli, Gawarbati, Grangali, Shumashti, Pashai and Kalam Kohistani, case marking is split ergative, but the verb always agrees with the subject. Systems of pronominal affixes have developed, most elaborately in Pashai but also in Wotapuri, Shumashti, Grangali, Tirahi, Kalasha and possibly Dameli.

Inherited gender has been partially lost in some languages (Brokskat), fully in others (Kalasha, Khowar). In many, vowel fronting or raising (Dameli, Shumashti, Kalam and Indus Kohistani, Torwali, Kanyawali, Wotapuri) or palatalization of consonants (Pashai, Shumashti) marks feminines. Animacy has become grammaticized in the nominal morphology of Khowar, Kalasha, Torwali and Sawi; in the verb systems of Kalasha, Khowar, Shumashti and Pashai; and in the deictic system of Torwali and Kalam Kohistani.

In the Kalasha and Khowar verb systems the semantic parameter of evidentiality has become centrally grammaticized. One set of forms encodes actions or events witnessed by the speaker or part of his established knowledge, while another reports hearsay information or new knowledge (Bashir 1988a, 1988b: 31–8).

The Dardic languages exist in the borderlands between South and Central Asia. They have developed under influences from both directions and constitute a transitional subarea, which includes the Nuristani languages, Northwest Indo-Aryan, eastern Iranian, Turkic, Tibeto-Burman and Burushaski. More localized contact zones also exist within the Dardic region. Some phonological characteristics which can be attributed to areal influences, either wide or localized are: oppositions between dental, palatal and retroflex sibilants and affricates (see Tikkanen 1995), the development of tonal systems in Dameli, Kalam Kohistani, Kohistani Shina and Torwali; and a pitch accent system in Gilgit Shina, the Jijālī dialect of Indus Kohistani (Zoller, p.c.) and probably Khowar.

Areally clustered morphological features include the vigesimal counting system; the (10 + n) structure for teen numerals as opposed to the inherited (n + 10), infinitives in -k (Gawarbati, Kalasha, Khowar, Gilgit Shina), and use of the conjunctive participle of the verb meaning 'to adhere to' as the postposition marking the causative agent (Kalasha, Khowar, Palula, Gilgit Shina) (see Bashir 1988b, Edelman 1980 and Tikkanen 1988, 1995).

An important characteristic of several Dardic languages is a three- (or greater) term deictic system, in which the distinctions visible-not visible, or known-not known are grammaticized. Languages with three-term systems are Pashai, Shumashti, Khowar, Kalasha, Torwali, Indus Kohistani, Shina and Palula. Grangali may have more than three terms. Tileli Shina has a four-term system (Schmidt 1998a: 2); Radloff (Radloff and Shakil 1998) analyses Gilgit Shina as four-termed; and Baart (2001) analyses Kalam Kohistani as having five values in the demonstrative adjective system.

Some syntactic characteristics show a distribution which suggests substratal and areal influences. Several languages have almost exclusively left-branching structures: complementizers developed from the verb 'say' (Kalasha, Khowar, Shina, Palula, Torwali, Kalam Kohistani); and prenominal relative clauses which employ no relative or indefinite pronominal element and have a fully finite verb, with or without a resumptive pronoun in the matrix clause. These structures are important in Khowar, Kalasha and Shina, and are shared with neighbouring non-Dardic languages.

1.2 Writing systems

Of the languages discussed here, Shina (Pakistan) and Khowar have developed a written tradition, and a significant body of written material exists. Both languages are written in a modified Perso-Arabic script, and in both language communities work toward standardization of script and orthography is in progress. Recently Kohistani and Schmidt (1996) have developed a system for writing Kohistani Shina phonemically using Perso-Arabic script. Rajapurohit (1983) gives Perso-Arabic and Devanagari schemes for Drasi

Shina in India. Work on a script for Kalam Kohistani is under way (Baart 1997). Lexicographic work on Torwali using a Perso-Arabic based script is in progress (Inamullah p.c.). Various persons are also working on devising scripts for Kalasha (Heegaard and Mørch 1998). The other languages are not (yet) written.

1.3 Languages and dialects

The following list is arranged according to two principles: historical subgrouping approximations and geographical distribution. The major groups are arranged roughly from west to east, but within them the subgroupings do not always correspond with present geographical proximities. The headword for each language is the conventional English spelling of the most commonly used name; other names appearing in the literature are in parentheses. Phonetic representations appear in square brackets, and names by which the speakers of the language themselves refer to it are italicized.

I   Pashai (*Laghmānī, Deganó*, Dehgānī)
    Eastern dialects
        Northeastern group (Strand 1973)
            Chugani dialect
            Chalās-KuRangal dialect
        Southeastern group (Strand 1973)
            Sum dialect (Sali, Sāri)
            Damench dialect
            Upper Darra-i-Nur dialect
            Lower Darra-i Nur dialect
            miscellaneous dialects
    Western dialects
        Southwestern group (5 dialects), (Morgenstierne 1973: 14)
        Northwestern group (17 dialects) (Morgenstierne 1973: 16, 333)
II   Kunar Group
    Gawarbati type
        Gawarbati (Gawar Bati, Narisāṭī, Narsāṭī, Gabari)
        Shumashti [*šumāštī*]
        Grangali [*graŋgali*]-*Ningalami* (Ningalama)
        Dameli [(*dâmiabâṣa, damēḍī, gaḍojo/ī*)]
III   Chitral Group
    Khowar (Kohwar, Chitrālī, Chetrārī, Arniya, Qashqari, Kivi)
    Kalasha [(*kalāṣamon(d)(r)*)]
        Northern
            Rumbur-Bumburet
            Birir-Jinjiret
        Southern
        Eastern
IV   Kohistan Group
    Tirahi
    Dir-Swat
        Dir Kohistani (Rensch 1992)
            Kalkoti

   Rajkot/Patrak
  Kalam *Kohistani* (*Kohistana*, *Garwa*, *Gārwī* (LSI), Gowri, Diri, Bashkarik)
   Dashwa
  Torwali
  Wotapuri-Katarqalai [woṭapūrī-kaṭārqalāi] (*Degano*)
  Indus Kohistan
   Indus *Kohistani* (Maiyã̄, *Kohistẽ*)
    Inner varieties (Zoller p.c.)
     Seo-Patan-Jijal (villages)
     Kanyawālī
     Bankhari [bankhaṛī]
     Kayali
    Outer varieties (Zoller p.c.)
     Duber-Kandia (valleys)
     Chiliso [*čilīso*](Chilisso, *čiliseo*, Chilis)
     Bhatise [*bhaṭīse*, bhayṭōz, Zoller p.c.], *bhaṭésa* Strand p.c.] (Baterawal,
      Bateri)
     Gabar (*zīb*) [gabār] (*gabrāl*, Gowro, [ghã̄vār zib])
     Shatoti [šāṭoṭī]
V *Shina* [*ṣiṇā*] (Schmidt 1998a, b)
  Kohistan group (Radloff's Diamer and Kohistan clusters [1992: 201])
   Kohistyõ (dialects of Palas, Jalkot, Koli)
   Ushojo
   Tangir-Darel (valleys)
   Chilasi
  Astor group (Radloff's eastern cluster)
   Astori
   Drasi
   Guresi
   Gultari
  Gilgit group (Radloff's northern cluster)
   Gilgiti
   Hunza-Nagari
   Punyali
   Brokskat (*Dōkskat*, *kyango*)
   Palula [*paḷūḷa*] (Dangarik(wār), Phaluṛa, Palola)
   Sawi [sāvī], *Sauji*
VI *Kashmiri* (see Kashmiri chapter in this volume)

Short sketches of individual languages follow. For Shina and Khowar, tone and pitch are represented using the notation developed for Burushaski by Berger (1960), which has been found appropriate for Gilgit Shina also (Buddruss 1996, Radloff and Shakil 1998). Long vowels are analysed as bimoraic, and represented by doubling the vowel symbol. Stress on the first or the second mora produces high falling tone/pitch or low rising tone/ pitch, respectively. High falling pitch is represented by marking the mora stress on the first vowel, and low rising pitch by placing the stress on the second. This notation is now also being used by Hook, Radloff and Bashir in descriptions of languages with similar phenomena. For Kalam Kohistani, Baart's phonemic representation is maintained in examples from his materials. Morgenstierne's and Buddruss' original notation is maintained, unless more recent work justifies normalization. Other examples are in phonetic representation.

To list consonants, I use standard but unlabelled arrays: horizontal axis = place of articulation (left > right = front > back); vertical axis (top > bottom) stops (voiceless, voiced; plain, aspirated), affricates, sibilants, nasals, flaps, liquids, glides.

2 PASHAI

2.1 Introduction

Pashai is spoken in northeast Afghanistan north of the Kabul River and south of Nuristan (Morgenstierne 1973a: 1, Ovesen 1982: 132). The number of speakers is difficult to estimate: the latest reported figure of 108,000 (Ethnologue 1996) repeats a 1982 estimate. Pashai-speaking communities have been differentially affected by the recent war, those in the eastern regions more than the western, and many of them are/ have been in refugee camps in Pakistan (Ovesen, Strand, Lincoln Keiser p.c.).

Morgenstierne considered Pashai to be descended from the languages of Hindu and Buddhist civilization in eastern Afghanistan (1965: 138). Ovesen (p.c.) and Keiser (1974), however, argue that the Pashai tribes are culturally close to the Nuristani peoples to the north and are indigenous to the Hindu Kush. The present linguistic neighbours of Pashai are Pashto and Persian, Shumashti (enclave), and Nuristani languages (north). Of these, Pashto and Persian are influencing Pashai, while it has influenced Shumashti. Pashai has a rich oral literature, some of which is recorded in Morgenstierne's (1944) volume of texts and in Buddruss (1959b).

Subgrouping of the Pashai dialects is a vexed question. Morgenstierne (1973a: 6) says that 'Pashai is split up into a large number of in many cases mutually incomprehensible dialects.' Scholarly opinion differs about the extent to which specific dialects are mutually intelligible. Keiser (p.c.) considers that many of the dialects are, indeed, mutually unintelligible. Ovesen (1982: 133), however, reports that speakers from Alingar, Darra-i-Nur, and Darra-i-Mazar – locations spanning Morgenstierne's northeastern and southeastern groups – understand each other despite differences of pronunciation, and stresses the linguistic unity of the Darra-i-Nur region. Morgenstierne (1973a: 8–11) and Ovesen (1982: 138) see a major dialectal divide between eastern and western dialects. The northeastern and southeastern subgrouping approximations in this chapter follow Strand (1973), and rectify the printing error in that article which included Pashai under the Kunar group. Strand's groupings of Morgenstierne's sampled dialects represent either geographic clusters or ethnonyms, on the assumption that dialect boundaries will coincide with ethnic boundaries.

Pashai dialects share the following morphological features: (1) feminines in -c from masculines in -k; (2) genitive in -s(t); (3) oblique cases before pronominal affixes; (4) intransitive perfect in -tek; (5) formation of present in consonant (k, g, t, r) (Morgenstierne 1973a: 7–8).

Given the complexity of the Pashai situation, a skeleton sketch of a Darra-i-Nur dialect (SE) is assembled here, based on information in Morgenstierne (1973a), hereafter (M: page). Morgenstierne (1944: 290–9) gives a skeleton grammar of the Laurowan dialect (SW).

2.2 Phonology

Vowels. a/ä, i/e, u/o, ā, ǟ, ī, ū, ǖ, ō, ē (M: 251–3)

Vowels are represented phonetically; although length is clearly contrastive (for *a* and *e*): *šal* 'lame', *šāl* 'rice', *tiste* 'stand! 2s IMP', *tistē* 'stand! 2p IMP' (M: 251–2). Tones correlated with historical aspiration are present: *bás* (low-rising tone, overlong vowel) 'steam' (M: 252).

Consonants (M: 253).

p	t	ṭ		k	q	
b	d	ḍ		g		
			c			
			j			
	s	ṣ	š			
	z					
f				x		h
				ɣ		
	r	ṛ				
	λ					
	l					
m	n	ṇ		ŋ		
w			y			

2.3 Morphology

2.3.1 Nominal

2.3.1.1 Nouns and adjectives

Gender and number are usually marked on adjective and verb forms rather than on nouns: marked ms/fs/p adjectives end in *-ā/-ī/-ī* or *-k/-c/-c* respectively (M: 263):

(1)   *dāar/pan   ōbarā/ī   šē*
      hill(m)/road(f) steep(m/f) be(INAN)PRES3s
      'The hill/road is steep.' (M: 263)

Most nouns do not have a marked nominative plural; some loanwords for animates have nominative plural in *-ān*: *nōkarān* 'servants'. Other case endings include: oblique *-ē, ū*; locative *-a/ā*, ablative *-ai/āi*, genitive *-{a/e}s*, illative *-na*.

Case marking is tense-aspectually split ergative: subjects of past tenses of transitives are oblique, others nominative. Direct objects are nominative (indefinite) or oblique (definite).

2.3.1.2 Pronouns

Personal pronouns (M: 266)

1.	Sg.	Pl.	2.	Sg.	Pl.
NOM	*ā, mam* (dial. diff.)	*(h)amā*		*tu*	*(h)ēma, ima*
OBL	*ā, mam* (dial. diff.)	*(h)amā*		*tō*	*(h)ēma, ima*
DAT	*mēnē*	*amānē*		*tēnē*	*emānē*

The first and second singular genitive forms *mēnā/tēnā* are adjectival, agreeing with the 'possessed' noun:

(2)   *mēnā   lāy-ām*   *mēnī   sāy-ām*
      my(ms)   brother-PS1s   my(fs)   sister-PS1s
      'my brother'   'my sister' (M: 266)

One of the most salient features of Pashai morphology is the complex system of pronominal affixes, the defining elements for which are given below (M: 267).

	1.	2.	3.
Sg.	-*m*	-*ē*, -*ai*	-*e/a*
Pl.	-{*e/a*}*n*	-*ū*, -*ō*	-*e/a*

With nouns, the pronominal affixes indicate possession; they follow the case endings and are sometimes modified by them. With verbs in all tenses they index direct and indirect objects.

Pashai has a threefold demonstrative system. Nominative forms for one Darra-i-Nur dialect are (M: 269–70): proximate 'this' *yo*, distal 'this' *e-lo*, remote 'that' (*e*)*-sē*. The difference between *elo* and (*e*)*se* is probably between visible and not visible (M: 270), as in other Dardic languages. The Pashai system seems to include an emphatic element (*e-*), as do Kalasha, Khowar and Palula.

2.3.2   Verbal

2.3.2.1   Non-finite forms

(1) A static participle in -*wā* (m)/-*wī* (f/p), formed for intransitives, denotes a state resulting from an action/event (M: 292).
(2) passive participle (root + -{*e/i*}*n*) (M: 296)
(3) past participle in -(*i*)*k/c* (m/f) (M: 297)
(4) agent noun in -*kālā* (M: 297)
(5) conjunctive participle in -*ta*, -*t*{*a/ā*}*n* (M: 297):

(3)   *mam   λām   kata   gik-em*
      I(NOM/OBL)   work(NOM)   do(CP)   go(PST)-PS1s
      'Having done the work, I went.' (M: 297)

2.3.2.2   Tense-aspect forms

The Pashai verbal system is constructed on three stems: root, present (root + -*k/g*) and past (root + {*k/g*}/*c*). Transitive past stems have a characteristic vowel which distinguishes them from present, perfect and past perfect (M: 287).

The present tense of the auxiliary distinguishes for animacy in the third person (M: 274):

	1.	2.	3. animate	3. inanimate
Sg.	*āem* 'I am'	*āī*	*ās*	*š*{*ī/ē*}
Pl.	*āis*	*āī*	*ā(e)n*	*šen*

Subjunctive-future (aorist M: 278–9): root + personal endings. Pronominal affixes indexing direct object or indirect object can attach to each form. One illustrative paradigm without pronominal affixes is (M: 278 D.q. dialect):

	1.	2.	3.
Sg.	*ka-m* 'I (will) do' *ka-ī*	*k-ē*	
Pl.	*ka-s*	*ka-da*	*ka-n*

(4) *nan λām na kā-gā-m   sabá   λām ka(y)é̄-m*
    today work not do-PRES-1s tomorrow work do(FUT)-1s
    'Today I am not working; tomorrow I shall work.' (M: 279)

With pronominal affixes:

(5) *unj-im-ī*
    wash-1s-PS3s
    'I wash it.' (M: 279)

Present: present stem + personal endings. When pronominal affixes are employed with the present, the formula is: root + object (PS) + present marker + subject (PS) (M: 283), giving SOV[os] order. For example, for a second person plural subject acting on a first singular object, the verbal morpheme string would be Verb-PS1s-g-PS2p, as in:

(6) *emā   mam   tar-īm-k-o*
    you(NOM/OBL) I(OBL)   see-PS1s-PRES-PS2p
    'You(pl.) see me.' (M: 284)

Imperfect: present stem + (abraded) past of auxiliary, *payā-k/c-em* 'I(m/f) was going' (M: 285). In this tense, with prononimal affixes, the verb-string order is VSO:

(7) *pac-al-éā-ci-m-i*
    cook-CS-IMPERF-f-1s-PS3s
    'I(f) cooked it.' (M: 286)

Past. Intransitives: past stem + personal endings. Gender agreement with the subject is effected by *-k/c* alternation of the preterite marker; e.g. *gi-k/c-em* 'I(m/f) went.' Transitives: root + V + *k/c* + personal endings or pronominal suffixes; *k/c* alternation marks object agreement. Example:

(8) *ar-ē-c-am*
    hear-PST(V)-f-1s
    'I heard it(f)' (M: 288)

With pronominal affixes, the verb-string order is: root + *-k/c* + personal endings + pronominal suffix, giving overall SOV[so] order:

(9) *mam   tō   läy-ek-am-ī*
    I(NOM/OBL) you(OBL) see-PSTms-1s-PS2s
    'I saw you(m).' (M: 289)

Past perfect. Intransitive: root + V + -{*k/c*} + personal endings: *e-á̄ {k/c}-em* 'I(m/f) had come', *k/c* alternation marking subject agreement (M: 290). Transitive: root + V + {*k/c*} + personal endings (+ PS). *k/c* alternation marks agreement with the direct object, and a pronominal suffix sometimes indexes it:

(10) *pac-al-eā-c-am*
     cook-CS-PST(V)-f-1s
     'I had cooked (f DO).' (M: 291)

(11) *kaṭ-eá̃-k-em*
   sting-PST(V)-m-PS1s
   'had stung me(m)' (M: 291)

Perfect. This tense is sparsely attested. Example: *pat-ek^y-em* 'I have gone' (M: 291). Static perfect. Static participle + present auxiliary. A static pluperfect is formed similarly with the past auxiliary:

(12) *dūr*   *wiy-awā*   *šē*
   door(NOM)   shut-STAT PPL   be(INAN)3s
   'The door is shut.' (M: 293)

3 GAWARBATI

3.1 Introduction

Gawarbati (GB) is spoken in villages Nishagam (Palazgór), Nari, Birkot, and Dokalam in the Kunar valley (Afghanistan), and in Arandu (Pakistan) (Cacòpardo, A. S. 2001). The number of speakers is estimated at 8000–10,000, of whom 6500–8500 were in Afghanistan before the recent war (Decker, K. D. 1992: 156); most were displaced during the war, but many have now returned to their homes (Akhtarjan Kohistani, p.c.).

GB shows historical affinities with Pashai and Dir-Swat Kohistani, and with Nuristani languages. Shumashti, Ningalami and Grangali are closely related to GB and point to an earlier wider extent of GB-type languages. Before the advance of Khowar southward and Pashto northward, GB was contiguous with Dir-Swat Kohistani, Tregami and southern Kalasha (Morgenstierne 1950: 6–7). Its present linguistic neighbours are Dameli, Kati, Khowar and Pashto, with most bilingualism obtaining with Pashto and Khowar (Decker, K.D. 1992: 164). Increasingly, Urdu is being used as contact language.

The sketch of GB below is based on a 1993 unpaginated manuscript by Akhtarjan Kohistani, hereafter (K), and on data in Morgenstierne (1950), hereafter (M: page). In some cases Kohistani's forms differ from Morgenstierne's, particularly with regard to aspiration.

3.2 Phonology

Vowels. i, e(?), a, o(?), u; ī, ē, ā, ō, ū
   Length is contrastive for *a*, *dar* 'door', *dār* 'wood'. Tone was not observed; stress is unpredictable, and appears to be contrastive, *búṛa* 'grandfather', *buṛá* 'dear' (M: 9).
   Consonants.

p	t	ṭ		k
ph	th	ṭh		kh
b	d	ḍ		g
(bh)	(dh)			(gh)
	ts	ç	c	
	tsh	çh	(ch)	
	(dz)		j	

	s	ṣ	š	x	h
	z		ž	ɣ	
m	n	ṇ		(ŋ)	
	r	ṛ			
	λ				
	l				
w			y		

Voiced aspirates are probably extinct in GB; and even the status of voiceless aspirates is unclear. Gemination is present: *baṭṭawār* 'Thursday', *giḍḍa* 'carpet', *mullācirga* 'sp. of goose', *phaṭṭa* 'feather' (M: 8).

3.3 Morphology

3.3.1 Nominal

3.3.1.1 Nouns and adjectives

Some nouns have characteristic gender suffixes: *ānda* 'meat (m)', *āṇḍa* 'egg (m)', *tekora* 'boy (m)'; *tekori* 'girl (f)', *ētsī* 'cow (f)'; others are unmarked, *bluz* 'birch (m)' or *māl* 'property (f)'. Plural forms exist for some nouns, *-gila* (kinship terms) and *-nam*, *tekora* 'boy', *tekora-nam* 'boys'; *baɣ* 'garden', *baɣ-nam* 'gardens' (K).

There are four basic case forms: nominative, agentive, oblique and dative. Other case relations are indicated with postpositions following the oblique form. Subjects of transitive verbs in past tenses are agentive. The genitive suffix is *-nā/nī* (m/f) which agrees in gender with the noun possessed. Forms for *bab* 'father' illustrate the paradigm (K):

	Sg.	Pl.
NOM	*bab*	*babgila, babnam*
OBL	*bab-a*	*babgila, babnam*
AG	*bab-e*	*babgila-e, babnam-e*
DAT	*bab-ã, bab-ānke*	*babgil-ānke, babnam-anke*

Adjectives have marked and unmarked classes: *subana/i* 'beautiful' (m/f) (K); *ḍal* 'big' (m/f). Comparison is expressed with the ablative postposition *perena* 'from': *mō-na āma perene tō-na āma ḍal thana* 'From my house your house is big(ger).' (M: 17)

3.3.1.2 Pronouns

Personal pronouns (K).

1.	Sg.	Pl.	2.	Sg.	Pl.
NOM	*a*	*ama*		*tu*	*me*
OBL	*mo*	*ama*		*tu*	*me*
AG	*mui*	*amai*		*tui*	*me*
DAT	*man-ke*	*aman-ke*		*tan-ke*	*mean-ke*

Two terms are attested in the demonstrative system (K):

	Proximal		Distal	
	Sg.	Pl.	Sg.	Pl.
NOM	*woi*	*emi/ame*	*se, ase*	*themi*
OBL	*asa*	*asu*	*tasa*	*tasu*
AG	*en*	*asui*	*ten*	*tasui*
DAT	*asan-ke*	*asuan-ke*	*tasan-ke*	*tasuan-ke*
ACC	*asa*	*asa*	*tasa*	*tasu*

Pronominal suffixes indicate possession; examples attested involve kinship terms. Forms are: 1s *-e*, 2s *-es* (?), 3s *-(i)(e)s*. The pronominal suffix precedes the case ending, whereas in Shumashti it follows: *tasa (mānuṣa-na) puλ-ies-ana āma* 'the house of that man's son' (M: 18).

3.3.2 Verbal

3.3.2.1 Non-finite forms

A gerund in -{*a/e*}wa, and a gerundive in invariable *-andiman* are formed. The following example illustrates their use.

(1) *zaka   ui   har   bati ci   moma-i   keros-i*
    because of this each word that uncle-AG do(PST3s)-PS2s?
    asa saṣi qalam gow-andiman wozela kayaz gow-andiman
    this after pen   take-GNDV   white   paper take-GNDV
    kayaz kaṇṣ ker-ewa   koṣ-andiman
    paper black make-GND   need-GNDV
    'For the sake of every word that Uncle uttered you now have to take a pen, you have to take some white paper and you need to turn the paper black.'(K)

Infinitive. Stem + *-ik*: *tsasik* 'to cough'. The infinitive is declined, and functions in various constructions: *dār kērik-e buo* 'he was (in) fetching wood.' (M: 23)

Agent noun. Stem + *-λa*: *λam-keriλa* 'servant' (work-doer).

Conjunctive participle. Stem + *-i*: *nis-i* 'having gone out'. It forms the base of the perfect tenses.

Transitivity relations. Transitives/causatives are formed by *-a* infixation: *nišimim* 'I sit down', *nišamim* 'I seat someone'.

3.3.2.2 Tense-aspect forms

Forms of *th-* and *b-* function as auxiliaries.

Present of *th-* 'be' (K).

	Sg.	Pl.
1.	*t(h)-anaim* 'I am'	*th-enaik/thenek*
2.	*t(h)-anais*	*th-enaw*
3.	*t(h)-ana* (m) *th-eni* (f) *t(h)-enait(h)*	

Future of *th-* 'be' (K).

	Sg.	Pl.
1.	*t(h)i-ma*	*t(h)i-ka*
2.	*t(h)i-sa*	*t(h)i-wa*
3.	*t(h)i-ba*	*t(h)i-ta*

Future Perfect of *th-* 'be' (K).

1.	*t(h)i-tema*	*t(h)i-tika*
2.	*t(h)i-tisan*	*t(h)i-tewa*
3.	*t(h)i-tian*	*t(h)i-teta*

Past of *b-* 'be' (K).

1.	*boi-m* 'I was'	*boi/e-k*
2.	*boi-s*	*boi-w*
3.	*bow-a* (m) *bo-(w)i* (f)	*boe-th*

Future of *b-* 'become'.

	1.	2.	3.
Sg.	*bim-a (LSI)*	*bam-is* (K)	*bem-an* (K)
Pl.	NA	NA	NA

Imperative. For singular intransitives, imperative = stem: *nis* 'sit down!'; for transitives, stem + *-a: lik-a* 'write!'; for plural, stem + *-au: ants-au* 'dress!' (tr.) (M: 20).

Present. Present stem + personal endings, as in the present of *lik-* 'write' (K):

	1.	2.	3.
Sg.	*lik-im-im* 'I write, am writing'	*lik-im-is*	*lik-im-an*
Pl.	*lik-im-ik*	*lik-im-anew*	*lik-im-ith*

Future: root + thematic vowel + personal endings for both intransitives and transitives. Future of *λe-* 'give, beat' (K).

	1.	2.	3.
Sg.	*λe-ma*	*λe-sa*	*λe-ba*
Pl.	*λi-ka*	*λi-wa*	*λi-ta*

Past imperfective: present stem + *-an* + past of *b-: λimān boet* 'they were giving' (M: 21); *lariman boit* 'they used to have', *a keriman boim* 'I used to do' (K).

Subjunctive. *bo*, an invariant form of *b-* 'become', gives subjunctive meanings: *thana bo* 'may be' (M: 21 from LSI); *likimim bo* 'If I were writing' (K).

Optative. The following forms are noted:

	1.	2.	3.
Sg.		*ja* 'come'	*ker-eau* 'do', *keret-eau* 'do (Cs.)'
Pl.	*λešaika* 'send'		*ped-eau* 'reach', *jeth-eau* 'come'

(2) *ama-ni   sumi watan   naši-thena*
we-GEN   all   country   be ruined(PRES PERF3s)
xodai   ama   manzi ithefaq ker-eau
God   we-GEN   among unity   make-OPT
'All our country has been destroyed. (May) God bring unity among us.' (K)

Past. Intransitive: past stem + intransitive personal endings.
Past of *a-* 'come' (K):

	1.	2.	3.
Sg.	*a aye-m*	*tu aye-s*	*se ay-a* (m) *se ay-e* (f)
Pl.	*ama aye-k*	*me aye-w*	*themi aye-t(h)* (m/f)

Transitive: past stem + transitive personal endings.
Past of *ker-* 'do' (K).

	1.	2.	3.
Sg.	*ker-um*	*ker-u*	*ker-us*
Pl.	*ker-owa*	*ker-ow*	*ker-on*

Gender is distinguished only in the third singular of intransitives.

Verb agreement. The verb in transitive past tenses agrees with the agentive subject:

(3) *dos   hela moi   mo-na dost-a   tav-um*
yesterday night I(AG) I-GEN friend-OBL   see(PST)-1s
'Last night I saw my friend.' (K)

Perfect: conjunctive participle + present of *th-* 'be': *niši than-ek* 'we have sat down (i.e., are sitting)' (M: 22), *mui tōni tāti šuni-than-aim* 'I have heard your word' (M: 22–3). But we have also the following paradigm from Kohistani (perfect of *lik-* 'write' [K]):

	1.	2.	3.
Sg.	*mui likit-um* 'I have written'	*tui likit-u*	*then likit-us*
Pl.	*amai likit-ua*	*me likit-uw*	*tasui likit-un*

Past perfect: conjunctive participle + past of *b-* 'be': *mī bua* 'he (had) died' (M: 23 from *LSI*). A second past perfect consists of conjunctive participle + the past of *dar-* 'remain'.
Past Perfect 2 of *ga-* 'take' (K).

	1.	2.	3.
Sg.	*(mui) goi-darum* 'I had taken' *goi-daru*		*goi-darus*
Pl.	*goi-darua*	*goi-daru*	*goi-darun*

This form functions in both the remote past and the past perfect senses. Examples:

(4) *tene waxt-a   nuristan-na   xalek jehalat-a   boi-t*
     that time-OBL Nuristan-GEN people ignorance-OBL be(PST)-3p
     au ama-na lama-na   sumi xalek-a   mari-dar-un
     and we-GEN village-GEN all   people-OBL kill-PST PERF-3p
     'At that time the people of Nuristan were infidels and they killed all the people of our village.'(K)

(5) *a   kabul-ini   ji-tanim   karia   kitab-una*
     I(NOM) Kabul-ABL go-PRES PERF1s whatever book-p
     ci   mui   riki-dar-um   ya   yadaš goi-dar-um
     that I(AG) write-PST PERF–1s or   notes take-PST PERF–1s
     timē mõ   perena kabul-a   däyi-tenit
     they I(GEN) behind Kabul-OBL   leave-PRES PERF-3p
     'I have gone from Kabul and whatever books I had written or notes I had taken – they have been left behind me in Kabul.'(K)

Future perfect. Conjunctive participle + future of *th-*.
     Future perfect of *ga-* 'take' (transitive) (K)

	1.	2.	3.
Sg.	*gai-tima* 'I will have taken'	*gai-tisan*	*gai-dari-then*
Pl.	*gai-thekan*	*gai-thewa*	*gai-thetan*

Note the element *-dari-* in the third singular, apparently the conjunctive participle of *dar-* 'remain', the past tense of which appears throughout the paradigm of the past perfect 2.

4 SHUMASHTI

4.1 Introduction

Shumashti is a Gawarbati type language spoken (1929) in a few households in the village of Upper Shumasht (Afghanistan). All its speakers were bilingual in Pashai, and the language is heavily influenced by Pashai (Morgenstierne 1945: 245). The data in this sketch are from Morganstierne (1945), hereafter (M: page).

4.2 Phonology

Vowels. i, e, a, o, u; ā, ū, ī

Length is contrastive: *kam* 'little', *kām* 'tribe'; *muλ* 'urine', *mūλe* 'understand'; *nim* 'half', *nīl* 'blue' (M: 248).

Consonants.

p	t	ṭ		k	
ph	th	ṭh			
b	d	ḍ		g	
	ts	ç	c		
		çh			
			(j)		
	s	ṣ	š	x	(h)
	z		ž		
m	n	ṇ		ŋ	
	r	ṛ			
	λ				
	l				
w ṷ			y		

4.3 Morphology

4.3.1 Nominal

4.3.1.1 Nouns and adjectives

Masculine/feminine pairs are indicated by vowel fronting/raising and/or suffixing -*ik* for feminine: *kyēta* 'boy', *kyēṭi* 'girl'; *kukuṛ* 'cock', *kukuṛik* 'hen'. No nominative plural ending is recorded. Nouns have three case forms: nominative, oblique -*a*, and genitive -(*a*)*s*. No distinct agentive form is recorded.

Most adjectives end in -*a*, *xuṭa* 'lame'; some in -*ik*, *dunik* 'far'. M:251).

4.3.1.2 Pronouns

Personal pronouns (M: 251)

1.	Sg.	Pl.	2.	Sg.	Pl.
NOM	*ā*	*ābə*		*tu*	*wī*
OBL	*mō*	*ama*		*tō*	*ima*
AG	*mū̃i* (*mē̃*)	*amai*		*tūi*	*imai*
GEN	*mo-no*	*ama-na*		*to-no*	*ima-na*

For pronouns, the genitive is adjectival, with -*no*/-*na* (s/p) suffixed to the oblique.

The demonstrative system has three values, as in Pashai (two in GB). Demonstrative adjectival-pronominal forms recorded are (M: 253):

	Proximate		Distal		Remote	
	Sg.	Pl.	Sg.	Pl.	Sg.	Pl.
DIR	*ṵoi* 'this/(s)he'	NA	*aloi* 'that/(s)he'	NA	*ase* 'that/(s)he'	(*a*)*te*
OBL	*ame*	NA	*aləmə*	NA	*atese*	NA
AG	NA	NA	NA	NA	*aten*	NA

The following pronominal suffixes are recorded (M: 254): Sg. 1. *-(V)m*, 2. *-u*, 3. *-(V)s*; Pl. 1. *-ani/e*, 2. *-i*, 3. *-at*. With nouns they indicate possession; with verbs in both past and non-past tenses they reference direct object or beneficiary. More than one pronominal suffix can attach to a word, and a pronominal suffix can appear together with a full pronoun or genitive. Examples:

(1) *ima-ne kām-as   nām-as-i*
     you-of   tribe-GEN name-PS3s-PS2p
     'the name of your tribe' (M: 255)

(2) *mo-no bā-m*
     I-GEN father-PS1s
     'my father' (M: 252)

(3) *gai-m-u*
     see(PST)-1s-PS2s
     'I saw you.' (M: 257)

4.3.2 Verbal

Material available is not sufficient to describe the system fully, but the following tense-aspect paradigms are suggestive.

'be' - Present (auxiliary) (M: 255)

	1.	2.	3.
Sg.	*in-a-m* (m) *in-i-m* (f) 'I am'	*inas*	*in-e* (m) *in-i* (f) *šū-e* (INAN) 'it is'
Pl.	*in-am-as*	*inoũ*	*inat*

Present. Intransitive and transitive presents are conjugated differently: *utth-in-am* 'I rise' and *phoṭṭ-ayā-m* 'I break(tr)' (M: 256). *pi-* 'drink' illustrates the transitive case (M: 256).

	1.	2.	3.
Sg.	*pī-iam*	*pī-ieu*	*pī-ico*
Pl.	*pī-{i/ē}ni*	*pī-i, pi-ēy*	NA

Past tenses (transitive). Two types are attested: (1) past stem in *-t*; (2) stem in *-i*. Personal endings differ in second singular and third plural (M: 257).

	Type 1		Type 2	
	Sg.	Pl.	Sg.	Pl.
1.	*zōet-im* 'I ate'	*zōet-ini/e*	*gāi-m* 'I saw, was seeing'	NA
2.	*zōet-iu(e)*	*zōet-i(y)e*	*gäi-u̯*	*läy-e* 'you beat'
3.	*zōet-is*	*zōet-ian*(?)	*gai-t*	*lay-at* 'they beat'

Preterital forms with *-ara* probably are perfects, *λam-a di bam ara* 'I (m) have gone to work' (M: 258). A form in *-dār-* seems parallel to the GB past perfect:

(4) *tō   gai-dār-im-o   yek piāl*
     you(OBL) see(PST PERF?)-1s-PS2s one day
     'I had seen you(s) one day.' (M: 258)

Case marking is split ergative. Nominal and pronominal subjects of transitive past tenses are nominative and agentive, respectively. The verb always agrees with the subject, and pronominal suffixes reference the direct object or beneficiary.

(5) *ā   piēn-iām-as   atese*
     I(DIR) know-PRES1s-PS3s him(OBL)
     'I know him.' (M: 251)

(6) *mūi   bō   maĩse   gäyet-im-at*
     I(AG) many men(OBL) see(PST1)-1s-PS3p
     'I saw many men.' (M: 257)

5 GRANGALI

5.1 Introduction

Grangali and Ningalami are two closely related dialects of the GB type (Buddruss 1979: 21). Grangali was still spoken in 1970 by about 50 households in village Grangal on a tributary of the Pech (Grjunberg 1971, Buddruss 1979); Ningalami was already (almost) extinct by 1949 (Morgenstierne 1950: 58). A few paradigms and salient points about Grangali are given for comparison with Shumashti and Gawarbati. The information below is based on Grjunberg (1971), hereafter (G: page).

5.2 Phonology

Vowels. i, e, a, o, u, ü, ə
 Consonants.

p	t	ṭ		k	
b	d	ḍ		g	
	ts		c		
	dz		j		
	s		š	x	h
	z		ž		
m	n	ṇ		ŋ	
	r	ṛ			
			λ		
			l		
w			y		

j occurs in borrowings. Grangali has only two sibilants. Aspiration is completely absent.

5.3 Morphology

5.3.1 Nominal

5.3.1.1 Nouns and adjectives

Most nouns do not mark nominative plural; a few have exceptional plurals: *gulə* 'tree', *gule-tə* 'trees'. Case forms for nouns include *-a* (locative), *-e* (agentive), *-(ə)m* (genitive) (G: 8).

Most adjectives are marked for gender: masculine forms end in -*a*/-*ə*, feminines in -*ī*: *picala*/*picalī* 'old(m/f)'.

5.3.1.2 Pronouns

Personal pronouns (G: 9)

1.	Sg.	Pl.		2.	Sg.	Pl.
NOM	*abə*	*abə (šukə* 'all')			*tu*	*mī*
ACC	*mei*	*aba*			*tei*	*me*
AG	*me*	*abe*			*tē*	*mi*
GEN	*mam*	*abəm*			*tam*	*mem*

The demonstrative system may have as many as four terms. Primary nominative forms attested are (G: 9):

	Sg.	Pl.		Sg.	Pl.
Near	*wu*	NA	Far	*atə*	NA
	alə	NA		*atsə*	NA

Pronominal suffixes. Forms are recorded for: 2s -*u*, 3s -*as*/-*əs*, 3p -*ən*. They appear with nouns and verbs; e.g. *le-u* 'your brother'. A pronominal suffix can co-occur with a coreferential full pronoun:

(1)   *te*   *atsío*   *pásdau-ən*
       you(AG)   them(ACC)   see(PST2s)-PS3p
       'You saw them.' (G: 10)

5.3.2 *Verbal*

Auxiliary forms are:

as- 'be' - Present

	1.	2.	3.
Sg.	*asīm, ahīm*	*asīs, ahīs*	*as(i), ahi*
Pl.	*asīk, ahīk*	*asīu, ahīu*	*asīn, ahīn*

The following tense-aspect forms are attested: imperative, present, past–1, past–2, past–3, past perfect, future–1 and future–2. The meaning differences between the three past and the two future forms are not clear. These forms are constructed with two sets of personal endings (G: 11).

	Type 1		Type 2	
	Sg.	Pl.	Sg.	Pl.
1.	-*im*	-*ik*	-*m*	-*ei*
2.	-*is*	-*iu*	-*u*	-*ei*
3.	-*i*	-*in*	-*s*	-*n*

The distribution of these endings is complex, and not fully understood. As examples, the past-1 of *gi*- 'take' (transitive) and *dza*- 'come' (intransitive) are given.

Past-1 of *gi-* 'take' (G: 12).   Past-1 of *dza-* 'come' (G: 13).

	Sg.	Pl.		Sg.	Pl.
1.	*gi-m*	*g-ī*		*a-ím*	*a-í*
2.	*gi-u*	*g-ī*		*a-ís*	*a-iu*
3.	*gi-s*	*gī-n*		*a-í*	*a-ín*

Verb agreement in transitive past tenses is with the subject; however with second singular and third singular objects the direct object is indexed on the verb with pronominal suffixes:

(2) *me*   *tei*   *pas-ím-u*
     I(AG) you(s)(ACC) see(PST)-1s-PS2s
     'I saw you (s).' (G: 15)

6 DAMELI

6.1 Introduction

Dameli is spoken in the Damel valley on the left bank of the Chitral River, by about 5000 people (Decker, K. D. 1992: 118) in three dialectal variants (Cacòpardo, Al. and Au. 1995: 246).

Dameli shows both Dardic and Nuristani characteristics, and on the basis of phonological developments it is not yet possible to decide whether it is a Dardic language heavily influenced by Nuristani or a Nuristani language influenced by Dardic. It reflects ancient contact with a now extinct Nuristani language, later with Dir-Swat Kohistani and Kalasha (M: 144–7). Present interactions are with Palula, Khowar, Pashto and Urdu. Synchronic lexical similarity percentages with neighbouring languages are: Byori Palula-44, Arandu Gawarbati-44, Urtsun Kalasha-42, Langorbat Shekhani-33, Bargromatal Eastern Kativiri-29 (Decker, K. D. 1992: 120). Morgenstierne's (1942: 146) counts of Dameli words shared with other languages show the highest counts with Nuristani languages and Kalasha, and lowest with Gawarbati, Khowar and Kohistani.

The following sketch is based on Morgenstierne (1942), hereafter (M: page).

6.2 Phonology

Vowels (M: 123).

Short			Long	
Front	Back		Flat	Rounded
i [I]	u		ī	ū
e [ɛ]	o [ɔ]		ē	ō
ä	a		ā	â

The status of length is not clear; stress is strong, affecting vowel quality. Contrastive tones are identified: low rising and high (falling): *žăn* (LR) 'snake', *žàn* (H) 'mill'; *sán* (LR) 'hole', *sàn* (H) 'hill'. However, their distribution does not correlate straightforwardly with historical aspiration (M: 125). Tone distinguishes present and past tenses: *bánnúm* 'I dress', *bánùm* 'I dressed'. Phonetic nasalization is common (M: 121).

Consonants (x and ɣ in loanwords):

p	t			ṭ	k
ph	th			ṭh	kh
b	d			ḍ	g
	ts	c		ç	
	tsh	ch		çh	
	s	š		ṣ	(x)	h
	z	ž		(ẓ?)	(ɣ)
m	n			ṇ	(ŋ?)
	r	ř			
		l			
w		y			

ř represents a weakly sounded palatal fricative: *kuřãk* 'puppy' (M: 122). Morgenstierne also represented the Kalasha sounds now analysed as retroflexed vowels with *Vř*, which may indicate that Dameli also has retroflex vowels. Geminates occur: *khuṭṭa* a 'knee'(M: 123).

6.3 Morphology

6.3.1 Nominal

6.3.1.1 Nouns and adjectives

Most nouns do not mark number in the nominative, but a few special plurals appear: *brâ/brâdī* 'brother/brothers'. Gender is marked on many nouns and adjectives: *tsuna/ tsuni* 'dog (m/f)', *drīga/drīgi* 'long (m/f)'.

Non-nominative singular case endings attested are *-e* (oblique), *-a* (locative), and *-sã̃* (genitive). Most postpositions follow the nominative, which also denotes the goal of motion. The oblique functions as subject of perfective tenses of transitives: *īç-é daš culãi* 'the bear stretched out its paw' (M: 133).

6.3.1.2 Pronouns

Personal pronouns (M: 134)

1.	Sg.	Pl.	2.	Sg.	Pl.
NOM	*ai*	*ai*		*tu*	*bi*
OBL	*mū*	*amâ*		*tō*	*mya*
GEN	*mâ/mâi* (m/f)	*amuna/amuni* (m/f)		*tã̃/tã̃i* (m/f)	*mina*

Genitives of personal pronouns are adjectival, agreeing in gender with the noun modified. A possible second singular pronominal suffix occurs in *gannum-ī* 'I say to you'(M: 135).

Demonstrative pronouns. Two degrees of distance are attested. (M:136).

	Proximal		Distal	
	Sg.	Pl.	Sg.	Pl.
NOM	*yē, (yeg), ī*	*im^yē*	*(i)se(g)*	*(i)t^yē*
AG	*manī*	*masū̊*	*tani*	*tasū*
OBL	*mas*	*masū̊*	*tas*	
DAT	*masa ki*		*tasa ki*	
GEN	*masã*	*masúna*	*(i)tas(s)ã̄*	*(i)tasuna*

Genitives of demonstratives are not adjectival. The facultative *i-* element seems parallel to the (emphatic) *ša-*, *h-* and *e-* of Kalasha, Khowar and Pashai, respectively. This element plays a role in differentiating demonstrative-anaphoric meanings.

6.3.2 Verbal

6.3.2.1 Non-finite forms

The conjunctive participle ends in *-i* or *-ai/-e* and forms the base of the perfect tenses. The infinitive has not been identified.

6.3.2.2 Tense-aspect forms

Auxiliary forms include:

th- 'be' Present (M:138).

	1.	2.	3.
Sg.	*thum*	*thōp*	*tha/thui (thü) (m/f)*
			daro/daroi (m/f)
Pl.	*th{ū/ǔ}ma*	*thōba*	*thun*

The distinction between *tha* and *daro* involves the parameters of alienable versus inalienable possession, existence in a particular place, assertion of identity and ascription of qualities.

There are two conjugational classes, the first mostly intransitives and the second transitives and causatives. The main tense-aspect forms are illustrated for *kur-* 'do' (M: 139).

	Present/future (non-specific) (aorist-future)		Present (specific)	
	Sg.	Pl.	Sg.	Pl.
1.	*kur-ím*	*kur-íma*	*kur-in-um, ku-n-úm*	*kur-in-uma, ku-n-úma*
2.	*kur-és*	*kur-íba*	*kur-in-op, ku-n-óp*	*kur-in-oba, ku-n-óba*
3.	*kur-ó*	*kur-in*	*kur-in-a, kun-á (m)*	*kur-in-un, ku-n-ún*
			kur-in-i (f)	

Past imperfective: present + *tha*: *kunum tha* 'I was doing'. It is marked for person and number, and gender in third singular.

Past. Transitives and intransitives differ: (a) in personal endings; (b) with intransitives, the third singular distinguishes gender. The forms for *â-* 'come' (M: 142) and *kur-* 'do' (M: 139) are:

	Sg.	Pl.	Sg.	Pl.
1.	*âgʸ-em*	*âgʸ-ema*	*kur-úm*	*kur-ǔ́ma*
2.	*âgʸ-ep*	*âgʸ-eba*	*kur-ṓp*	*kur-ṓba*
3.	*âg-{a/o}/âg-ei* (m/f)	*âgy-en*	*kur-ẽ́*	*kur-ẽ́n*

Present perfect: conjunctive participle + present of *th-* 'be': *niši-thum* (> *niš-thum*) 'I have sat down', *tō kuri thōp* 'you have done'. Gender is marked in the third singular. Example:

(1) *se   ḍũ   zuān-sã̃   mukh-a   niší   thui*
  that fly(f) young man-GEN face-LOC sit(CP) be(PRES)3s.f
  'The fly was seated on the young man's face.' (M: 151)

Stative/resultative meaning can be specified by adding *-san*: *niši-san thum* 'I am sitting down' (H-Ur. *baiṭhā huā hũ̃*). *-san* also appears with participles and other adjectives: *biläi-san giř* 'melted ghee', *ṣâ nitoi-san* 'the head is bald' (M: 143).

Past perfect: present perfect plus *tha*: *žoi-thum tha* 'I had eaten' (M: 143).

6.4 Syntax

Case marking is split ergative; however, perfective tenses of transitives agree with the subject: *mū kurú-m* 'I did'. In non-perfective transitive tenses both noun-phrase and pronominal subjects are nominative; pronominal direct objects are oblique, while noun-phrase direct objects are nominative. Examples:

(2) *bi   ku   amâ   yaṇḍ̂ây-uba*
  you(NOM) why us(OBL) beat(PRES-2p)
  'Why do you beat us?' (M: 135)

(3) *ai   yē̃   mac   yaṇḍā-im*
  I(NOM) this man(NOM) beat(PRES-1s)
  'I beat this man.' (M: 136)

In perfective tenses, first and second person subjects are oblique, and third person subjects are agentive:

(4) *mya   kram   kur-ṓba*
  you(OBL) work(NOM) do(PST-2p)
  'You(p) worked.' (M: 135)

A second person direct object of a first person subject is nominative:

(5) *mō   tu   bʸin-um*
  I(OBL) you(NOM) see(PST-1s)
  'I saw you.' (M: 134)

However, a third person direct object of a first person subject is oblique.

(6) *mū   tas   yaṇḍ-ám*
  I(OBL) him(OBL) beat(PST-1s)
  'I beat him.' (M: 137)

A first person direct object of a third person subject is oblique.

(7) *manī̃   mū   biny-ế*
  he(AG) me(OBL) see(PST-3s)
  'This one saw me.' (M: 136)

7 KHOWAR

7.1 Introduction

Khowar, the lingua franca of Chitral, is spoken by about 300,000 people, mainly in District Chitral. There are also Khowar-speaking villages in Ishkoman and Yasin (Northern Areas), and upper Swat; and Khowar-speaking communities in Peshawar and Karachi. An isolated Khowar dialect (Kivi) has also been identified in the village of Vrang in Wakhan (Buddruss 1989). Many Khowar speakers also know Urdu and Pashto. Although there is relatively little dialectal variation in Khowar, the speech of the Lutkoh Valley and of Ishkoman differs noticeably from the majority variety.

Considered to be the most archaic of the Dardic languages, Khowar preserves many OIA words and phonological and grammatical characteristics. For example, *ašrú* 'tear' is identical to the Sanskrit word. Its lexicon consists of its OIA base, with accretions of Iranian vocabulary at different time depths (Morgenstierne 1936, 1957; Bashir 2001b), Burushaski loans – e.g. *tácing* 'leather foot wrappings' – and some yet unidentified words.

This sketch is based on the author's ongoing fieldwork.

7.2 Phonology

Vowels.

i		u
e		o
	a	

Stress is contrastive: *bélu* '20 seer weight, type of basket': *belú* 'flute, blowpipe'. Three degrees of length appear: short (*dón* 'tooth'), medium-long (*tóonj* 'destroyed, lost'); and long (*doón* 'ghee'). Length and tone/pitch interact in phonemic contrasts. Medium-long vowels are associated with high-falling tone and long vowels with low-rising tone: *dii* 'yes', *di* 'also'; *baás* 'flame', *bás* 'bus' (Eng.), 'enough' (< Ur.); *doón* 'ghee', *dón* 'tooth'. Contrasts between short and long vowels can arise from suffixing a vocalic suffix to an identical word-final vowel, as in *hayá* 'this' versus *hayaá* 'here' (< *hayá+a*). It appears that length alone is not contrastive and that Khowar may be characterizable as a pitch accent system like that of Gilgit Shina (Radloff and Shakil 1998: 9).

Consonants.

p	t		ṭ			k	q		
ph	th		ṭh			kh			
b	d		ḍ			g			
	ts		ç	c					
	tsh		çh	ch					
	(dz)		j̣	j					
f	s		ṣ	š		x			h
	z		ẓ	ž			γ		
m		n							
		l					ł		
		r							
w				y					

In Khowar, /q/, /x/, /ɣ/, and /f/, often restricted in other IA languages to Perso-Arabic loans, occur frequently in native words: *ḍaq* 'boy', *qaf* 'claw', *šax* 'vegetable', *ṣadáɣ* 'third month in Khowar calendar', *yáaɫ* 'polo, hockey'. Although /ɫ/ has been called 'retroflex', and the Khowar writing system represents it with the character used for Urdu /ṛ/ (absent in Khowar), /ɫ/ is a velarized lateral, similar to Kalasha and Palula /ɫ/.

7.3 Morphology

7.3.1 Nominal

7.3.1.1 Nouns and adjectives

Khowar has lost OIA gender, but, like Kalasha, has grammaticized animacy in the verb system. All nouns distinguish singular and plural in the oblique; only a few have distinct nominative plurals, e.g. *žau* 'son', *ži-žáu* 'sons', *nan* 'mother' *nangíni* 'mothers', *buzúrg* 'elder' *buzurgán* 'elders'.

Nouns have two basic case forms, nominative and oblique. In addition, inanimate nouns take several locative case endings as well as instrumental and ablative endings:

	NOM	OBL	LOC-1	LOC-2	LOC-3	LOC-4	INST	ABL
Sg.	Ø	*-ó/-o*	*-a*	*-i*	*-tu*	*-o*	*-éen*	*-áar*
Pl.	*-án, -gíni,* REDUPLICATION	*-án*	*-éen*	*-éen*	*-éen*	*-éen*	*-an sóra*	*-an sáar*

The distribution of the four locative cases is based on the parameters of verticality and horizontality. Locative–2 encodes horizontal motion or location; locative–3 encodes motion or location upward; locative–4 motion or location downward with respect to vertically oriented objects; and locative–1, the most general, encodes point location and is subject to much semantic and grammatical generalization, to the extent that it acts like a second oblique (Bashir 2001a). Examples:

(1)   *awá   buní-tu   bíman*
      I(NOM) Booni-LOC3 go(PF-S)1p
      'I am going up to Booni.' (if travel up valley is required)

(2)   *tóq-o   yeértai*
      mud-LOC4 fall (PST-A) 3s
      'S/he fell (down) in the mud.'

(3)   *çhétr-i   joṣ   šéni*
      field-LOC2 weeds be(INAN)(P)3p
      'There are weeds (horizontally extended) in the field.'

(4)   *tseq   keɫ-ik-a   prai*
      child(NOM) cry-INF-LOC1 beat-give(PST-A)3s
      'The child began to cry.'

(5)   *zom-éen   bayátam*
      mountain-INST go(PST-A)1s
      'I went by way of the mountains.'

A set of preverbal adverbs encodes the parameters of verticality and direction toward or away from the speaker.

	toward speaker	away from speaker
upward/horizontally	*yíi*	*aih*
downward	*yúu*	*af*

Example:

(6)   *yíi*   *tar-áw-e*   *bohrt-ó*
    up here   reach-Cs-IMPs   stone-OBL
    'Hand (me) the stone up here.'

Adjectives are normally invariant; however, plurality can be indicated by reduplication: *ju jamjám žižáw* 'two good(pl) sons'.

7.3.1.2 Pronouns

Personal pronouns

1.	Sg.	Pl.	2.	Sg.	Pl.
NOM	*awá*	*ispá*		*tu*	*pisá*
OBL	*ma*	*ispá*		*ta*	*pisá*

Postpositions indicating specific case relations follow the oblique: *má-t(e)(n)* 'to me (DAT)'.

Khowar has a three-term deictic system. The prefixal element *h(a)*- plays a role in distinguishing demonstrative and anaphoric uses. Adjectival forms are slightly different. Demonstrative pronouns.

	Proximal		Distal		Remote (not visible)	
	Sg.	Pl.	Sg.	Pl.	Sg.	Pl.
NOM	*(ha)yá*	*(ha)mít*	*(h)es*	*(h)et*	*(ha)sé*	*(ha)tét*
OBL	*(ha)mó*	*(ha)mítan*	*(h)oró*	*(h)étan*	*(ha)toyó*	*(ha)tétan*

7.3.2 Verbal

For regular verbs, the infinitive stem = root + -*i* for intransitives, and root + -*eéi* for transitives and causatives: *pošík* 'to see', *pašeéik* 'to show; have shown'. The past stem of some verbs includes a surviving OIA *a*- augment: *ar*- < *kor*- 'do', *oš*- < *š*- 'be', *obrit*- < *br*- 'die', *oyó*- < *žib*- 'eat'.

7.3.2.1 Non-finite forms

Perfective participle: root + -*i*: *kor-i* 'having done'. Functions: (a) base for perfect tenses; (b) in construction with 'go', 'let go' and 'sit', it forms a compound verb in the usual South Asian sense; (c) conjunctive participle, linking two clauses or imparting adverbial meanings.

Imperfective participle: root + -*áu*: *kor-áu* 'doing'. Functions: (a) base of imperfective tenses; (b) used adverbially: *ḍaq keɫáu bayái* 'The boy went (away) crying'.

Oblique imperfective participle: root + -*áw-a*, *kor-áwa* 'while doing'. Functions: (a) forms a second past imperfective-inferential tense; (b) adverbial: *boyáw-a ta-t paysá doóm* 'As (i.e. when) you/I are/am going, I will give you some money.'

Past participle: root + -*íru* or -*rdu*: *ganíru* 'taken' < *gan*-; *raa-rdu* 'said' < *re*-. Functions: (a) base of past tenses; (b) substantively: e.g. *birdú* 'dead person'; (c) attributively: *hayá chírdu išnyári* 'This is a broken thing'; (d) in participial relative clauses: *tu fuṭú pašeéiru ḍaq* 'the boy to whom you showed the photograph'.

Passive participle: root + *-ónu*: *korónu* 'done'. Forms passive construction: *boxt-ó hayaá lakhónu biti šeér* 'The stone has been placed here.'

Second passive participle: root + *-ín*. This functions as an 'abilitative' passive: *nivešín* 'be written' < *nivéš-* 'write', *boxt-ó hayaá lakhín boy-án* 'The stone can be placed here.'

Infinitive: root + *-ík, korík* 'to do'. Functions: (a) substantive; (b) in complement structures, e.g. infinitive-oblique + *bik* 'be able': *hes hayá korm-ó kor-ík-o boói* 'He can do this work.'

Agent noun: root + *-ák, kor-ák* 'a doer'. Functions: (a) in tense-aspect forms; (b) forms relative clauses.

Desiderative nominal: root + *-áaru*: *piyáaru* 'desire to drink', *ma žibáaru góy-an* 'I feel like eating'; parallel with Kalasha *-álak*.

Necessitative: (a) infinitive-oblique + *baṣ*, (2) root + *-éli(k)*: *ma pešáur-o-te boyélik* 'I have to go to Peshawar', *hayá no korík-o baṣ kórum* 'This is something that shouldn't be done.' These two forms also have parallels in Kalasha.

7.3.2.2 Tense-aspect forms

The Khowar verb system can be described in terms of the following oppositions: tense (past and non-past), aspect (durative and non-durative), evidentiality (actual and inferential), specificity (specific and non-specific). Inferential verbs encode those actions or events which are either not witnessed directly, or are newly acquired knowledge (Bashir 1988a).

as-, *š-*, and *b-* function as auxiliaries.

as- 'be (animate)'

	Present Actual		Past	
	Sg.	Pl.	Sg.	Pl.
1.	*asúm*	*asúsi*	*asítam*	*asítam*
2.	*asús*	*asúmi*	*asítau*	*asítami*
3.	*asuúr*	*asúni*	*asítai*	*asítani*

š- 'be' (inanimate)

	Present Actual		Present Inferential	
3.	*šeér*	*šéni*	*širái*	*širáni*

	Past Actual	
1.	*ošótam*	*ošótam*
2.	*ošóu*	*ošótami*
3.	*ošói*	*ošóni*

The past of *š-* retains the OIA augment. It is not restricted to inanimate subjects and has first and second person forms.

b- 'become'

	Present-Future (non-specific) Actual		Past Inferential		Past Actual	
	Sg.	Pl.	Sg.	Pl.	Sg.	Pl.
1.	*boóm*	*bósi*	*birétam*	*birétam*	*hótam*	*hótam*
2.	*bos*	*bómi*	*biráu* (*birétau*)	*birétami* (*birámi*)	*hou*	*hótami*
3.	*boói*	*bóni*	*birái*	*biráni*	*hoói (hor)*	*hóni*

The following tense-aspect forms are illustrated for *kor-* 'do'.

(a) Present/future, non-specific (actual) (P/F-NS-A): stem + person-number suffixes: *koróm/koóm* 'I do, will do.'

Sg.	1.	2.	3.	Pl.	1.	2.	3.
	-m	-s	-r		-si	-mi	-ni

Present/future, non-specific forms are used with future meaning and as a generic-habitual present: *púši no wax-ír*, 'A cat doesn't bark'.

(b) Present/future, specific (actual) (P/F-S-A): present/future, non-specific-actual + *-an*, parallel to Kalasha present/future, specific forms in *-dai*: *kóman* 'I am doing.'

(c) Present/future (inferential) (P/F-I): agent noun + past-I of *bik* 'become'; functions as inferential counterpart of present/future, non-specific (actual) and the present/future, specific: *korak birétam* 'Apparently I (can) do it.' Example:

(7) *hasé khowár korák birái*
he Khowar do(PF-I)-3s
'Apparently s/he can speak Khowar.'

(d) Past-Actual (PST-A): past stem + *-ist-* + past personal endings. Today, *-ist-* is reduced, becoming *-st, -t-*, or Ø: *arétam* 'I did'.

	1.	2.	3.
Sg.	-am	-au	-ai
Pl.	-am	-ami	-ani

Example:

(8) *hasé lahúr-o-te bay-ái*
s/he Lahore-OBL-DAT go(PST-A)-3s
'S/he went to Lahore.'

(e) Present Perfect-Actual (P PERF-A): perfective participle + present of *asík/šik* 'be': (ANIM/INAN) *korí asúm* 'I have done'.

(f) Past Perfect-Actual (PST PERF-A): perfective participle + past of *as-* 'be': *korí asítam* 'I had done'.

(g) Perfect-Inferential (PERF-I): perfective participle + agent noun of *asik/šik* 'be' + past-I of *bik* 'become'. Function: inferential counterpart of present perfect-actual and past perfect-actual: *korí asák birétam* 'Apparently I did (unwittingly)'.

(h) Imperfective Habitual-Actual (IMPFV HAB-A): imperfective participle + present of *as-*: *koráu asúm* 'I have been doing'.

(i) Imperfective Habitual-Inferential (IMPFV HAB-I): imperfective participle + agent noun of *as-* 'be' (animate) +past-I of *b-* 'become': *koráu asák birétam* '(It turns out that) I was/have been doing (it) (unwittingly)'.

(j) Past Habitual$_1$ (PST HAB$_1$): imperfective participle + *-t-* + past person-number suffixes: *koráutam* 'I used to do'. Example:

(9) *hasé noyór-a payrá koráu-tai*
he(NOM) fort-LOC watch do(PSTHAB1)-3s
'He used to do sentry duty at the fort (but no longer does).'

(k) Past Habitual$_2$: (PST HAB$_2$): *koráur/koráuni* 'He/they used to do'. This form has the same meaning as Past Habitual$_1$ and appears to exist only for the third person.

(l)   Past Imperfective-Actual (PST IMPFV-A): imperfective participle + past of *š*- 'be': *koráu ošótam* 'I was doing'.

(m) Inferential Past Imperfective₁ (PST IMPFV-I₁): imperfective participle + past of *as*- 'be': *koráu asítam* 'I was doing(reportedly); would have done'.

(n)   Inferential Past Imperfective₂ (PST IMPFV-I₂): imperfective participle(OBL) + past-inferential of *b*- 'become': *koráwa birétam* 'I was doing; was about to do (mistakenly)'. Example:

(10) *awá   plakh-ó   nuroyí   çakeáwa birétam*
      I   spark plug-OBL upside down put in(PST IMPFV-I₂)-1s
      jam bélut   misrí   paydá hoói
      fortunately mechanic appear(PST-A)-3s
      'I was about to put the spark plug in upside down; fortunately a mechanic turned up.'

Forms built with the past participle are:

(o)   Past-Inferential (PST-I): past participle: *se bóydu* 's/he went'.

(p)   Past Perfective-Actual (PST PFV-A): past participle + past-actual of *š*- 'be': *kardu ošótam* 'I had done; would have done'. Example:

(11) *awá   hatoyó   dirú ošótam*
      I   him(OBL) beat(PST PFV/CTF)-1s
      'I was about to beat him (but I didn't).'

(q)   Past Perfective-Inferential (PST PFV-I): past participle + past-inferential of *b*- 'become': *kardu birétam* 'Apparently I did (unwittingly)'. Example:

(12) *ohóo tonjeéiru birétam*
      oh   ruin(PST PFV-I)1s
      'Oh, I have (unwittingly) ruined it.'

(r)   Perfective-Inferential (PFV-I): past participle + agent noun of *as*- 'be' + past-inferential of *b*- 'become': *kardu asák birétam* '(It turns out that) I have done it (unwittingly)'.

(s)   Subjunctive (SUBJN): stem + *-es-* + subjunctive personal endings, illustrated for *kor*- 'do':

	1.	2.	3.
Sg.	*kor-es-ám*	*kor-es-ú*	*kor-es-ír*
Pl.	*kor-es-ám*	*kor-es-ími*	*kor-es-íni*

(t)   Irrealis (IRR): past participle + *-a*: *awá kardú-a* 'If/would that I had done it.'

(u)   Imperative-optative meanings are expressed by a suppletive paradigm. Personal endings used with imperative-optatives are:

	1.	2.	3.
Sg.		*-é(h)*	*-ár (-uúr)*
Pl.	*-si*	*-úr/-or/-awér*	*-áni*

Compound verb (CV). Compound verbs are formed with the vectors *b*- 'go', *laák*- 'release', and *niš*- 'sit' (Bashir 1988b). Examples:

(13) *tu   puluí-bis*
      you burn(CP)-go(PF-NS)-2s
      'You will get burned.'

(14) *thúu palóy-an   bezemí-laákit-am*
alas   apples-OBL   sell(CP)-release(PST-A)-1s
'Alas, I sold the apples (mistakenly).'

(15) *hasé   boók-o   lakhí-nišái*
he(NOM) wife-OBL put(CP)-sit(PST-A)-3s
'He divorced his wife (the action has been completed).'

7.4 Syntax

Case marking is nominative-accusative. Non-specific and specific direct objects are nominative and oblique, respectively:

(16) *awá   dzoóy   nó   poší asúm*
I(NOM) yak(NOM) NEG   see(P PERF-A)-1s
'I have not seen a yak.'

(17) *awá   ta   puši-ó pošítam*
I(NOM) your cat-OBL see(PST-A)1s
'I saw your cat.'

Indigenous subordinate clause structures are left branching; in addition, right branching structures (< Persian and Urdu) are increasingly used, especially in writing. The two main complementation structures are: (1) clause-final *reé* (conjunctive participle of *reék* 'to say') and (2) clause-initial *ki* (Persian). The 'say' complementizer has a wide range of functions (Bashir 1996); (18) illustrates *reé* and *ki* clauses.

(18) *ispá tat **ki**   haái ispá báan doói **reé**   tsetséq buhtuítani*
our father **when** came us stick beat(PF-NS3s) **COMP** children fear(PST-A)3p
'Thinking "When our father comes he will beat us," the children were afraid.'

Relative clause strategies combine left and right branching elements. The purely left branching structures are represented by:
(a) sentence-initial finite relative clause with demonstrative in the matrix clause (MC):

(19) *páyp-a   góy-an   hes jam wa*
pipe-LOC1 come(PF-S)3s it   good EMPH
'The (water which) is coming in the pipe is good.'

(b) participial relative clause:

(20) *ţelivížan širú-an   dur-éen*
television be(INAN)(PST PPL)OBLp house-LOCp
'in the houses where there is television'

(c) agent noun:

(21) *rah-éen   boyák   moóš*
road-LOCp go-AG NOUN man
'a man who walks on the roads'

The second type combines an overall left branching structure in the sentence with a right branching relative clause. The relative clause is introduced with *kya* NP *ki*; the invariant *kya* is homophonous with the indefinite adjective *kya* 'some'. In the matrix clause the demonstrative is coreferential with the relative noun, which bears the case dictated by its role in the relative clause; in the matrix clause the correlative pronominal is marked for its matrix clause role.

(22) [*kya   ḍaq-ó   ki* tu   tang arú]   [*hasé   thanedár-o   žau*]
     [**REL** boy-OBL **ki** you tease(PST-A)-2s] [**he**(NOM) thanedar-OBL son]
     'The boy you teased is the son of the head of the police station.'

This is an incipient relative-correlative strategy because, although it utilizes an indefinite element rather than a true relative like the IA *j*- forms, it regularly preposes the RC, employs the same case-marking strategy, and represents the head NP in the MC with a demonstrative pronominal element.

8 KALASHA

8.1 Introduction

Kalasha is spoken by about 4000–5000 people in southern Chitral, in three dialect areas: northern (Rumbur, Bumburet, Birir and Jinjiret valleys); southern (Urtsun valley) (Morgenstierne 1973b: 188); and eastern (Shishi Kuh except village Birga, which has northern dialect) (Cacòpardo 1991). New research indicates that Kalasha is (1990) understood, though seldom spoken, in Shishi Kuh by perhaps 500–800 people (Cacòpardo 1991). Mørch and Heegaard (1997: Chapter 7) find that Rumbur-Bumburet and Birir-Jinjiret constitute two subgroups of the northern dialect; Urtsun is separate; and the eastern villages form another separate but heterogeneous area.

Formerly spoken over much of southern Chitral, Kalasha is now contiguous with Kativiri (Nuristani) on the west, and Khowar on the north, east, and south. Most Kalasha speakers know Khowar; many, especially high in the valleys, also speak Kativiri.

Kalasha's closest relationship is with Khowar. Some unique similarities seem to result from a period of uniquely shared development:

(1) nominative-accusative case marking and retention of the OIA augment;
(2) common Kalasha-Khowar forms: **jhū* > N. Kal. *chū(ḷ)*, S. Kal. *jhūr*, Kho. *žuúr* 'daughter';
(3) past participle formation: **karitaka* > **kardau* > Kho. *kardu*, Kal. *káda* (Morgenstierne 1973b: 188);
(4) morphologization of inferentiality;
(5) loss of inherited gender and grammaticization of animacy;
(6) close morphological parallelisms (Bashir 1998b).

The following sketch is based on Bashir (1988b).

8.2 Phonology

Vowels (northern).

i		u
e		o
	a	

Each of these has contrastive nasalized and/or retroflexed versions, yielding 20 contrastive vowel phonemes. Except for one syllable type, length is not contrastive (Mørch and Heegaard 1997: Ch. 7). (Northern) Kalasha has salient pitch/tone contours, which nccd investigation.

Consonants.

p	t		ṭ	k
ph	th		ṭh	kh
b	d		ḍ	g
bh	dh		ḍh	gh
	ts	c	ç	
	tsh	ch	çh	
	dz	j	ẓ	
	jh			
	s	š	ṣ	h
	z	ž	j̣	
m	n	(ñ)	(ṇ)	(ŋ)
	l			ł
	r			
w		y		

Bashir (1988b) has *ñ*; Mørch and Heegaard (1997) have *ṇ* and *ŋ*.

In Kalasha, /ž/ and /j/, often free variants in other Dardic languages, contrast: *juk* 'louse', *žuk* 'to eat'. /ł/ is a velarized lateral; and /l/ is strongly palatalized. The status of *ñ* is uncertain.

8.3 Morphology

8.3.1 Nominal

8.3.1.1 Nouns and adjectives

Kalasha has lost OIA gender, but has grammaticized animacy. Most nouns distinguish plurals only in non-nominative cases. However, a few nouns referring to specific categories of humans take nominative plural in *-an*: *gaḍerak-an* 'elders'. A small class of kinship terms has a specialized plural form in *-áutr*: *bayáutr* 'mutual brothers'.

Case suffixes for inanimates, animate common nouns, and proper names are:

	Inanimate			Animate		Proper names		
	NOM	OBL	INST	NOM	OBL	NOM	OBL	DAT
Sg.	Ø	*-as*	-an	Ø	*-as*	Ø	-as	-a
Pl.	Ø	*-an/-in*	?	*-an, -áutr*	*-an/-in/-ón*	Ø		

Various locative cases are also recorded. The particular case ending assigned to express a particular local relation depends both on the semantics of the temporal or spatial relation involved, and on the declension class of the noun. These case desinences include: ablative *-a, -ani, -ei*; locative (spatial) *-a, -ai, -una*; locative (temporal)-*asa, -ano*.

Adjectives are invariant. Comparison is expressed with a postpositional phrase with *pi* 'from':

(1) *a tása   móc-as   pi   tagalá*
     I   that(OBL) man-OBL   from strong
     'I am stronger than that man.'

8.3.1.2 Pronouns

1.	Sg.	Pl.		2.	Sg.	Pl.
NOM	*a*	*ábi*			*tu*	*ábi*
OBL	*mai*	*hóma*			*tai*	*mími*

Kalasha has a three-term demonstrative system, with a facultative (emphatic) element *š(a)-* throughout.

	Present-near		Present-far		Absent	
	Sg.	Pl.	Sg.	Pl.	Sg.	Pl.
NOM	*(š)íya*	*émi*	*(š)ása*	*éli*	*(ša)sé*	*te*
ACC	*áma*	*émi*	*áła*	*éli*	*to*	*te*
OBL	*ísa*	*ísi*	*ása*	*ási*	*tása*	*tási*

Pronominal suffixes are used with kinship terms to indicate possession; they agree in person with the possessor and in number with the possessed (kin term). This is their only function; they are not used with verbs to index core arguments. They are:

Sg.	1.	2.	3.		Pl.	1.	2.	3.
	-a	*-au*	*-as*			*-a-i*	*-ał-i*	*-as-i*

                                        ($u > l$ word-medially)

Example:

(2) *te   mai   pútr-a-i (*putr, *putr-a, *putr-as) roksát   pron*
     they I(OBL)   son-PS1p (*NOMØ*PS1s/*OBL) departure give(PST-A-3p)
     'They sent off my sons.' (Bashir 1988b: 43)

The pronominal suffix *-a-i* agrees in person (1st) with the possessor 'I' but in number (plural) with the possessed 'sons'.

Subjects of all verbs in all tenses are nominative. Direct objects are either nominative or OBL, depending on specificity, animacy and position in the person hierarchy:

(3) *ghrast   pai   udrus-éł*
     wolf(NOM) goat(NOM)   scatter-Cs(P/F-NS)-3s
     'A wolf scatters goats.'

(4) *sud-ón   istorí   kar-ék*
     child-OBLp horseback do-Cs(P/F-NS)-1p
     'We make the children ride horseback.'

Third person pronominal direct objects are accusative; first and second person are oblique:

(5) *a   áła   tupék gri   bih-é-s*
     I(NOM) him(ACC)   gun   with fear-Cs(PST-A)-1s
     'I frightened him with a gun.'

8.3.2 *Verbal*

Kalasha verbs fall into two classes: (a) all forms formed on a single stem, consisting of root I -*i/-e*; (b) past stem consists of *a*- augment + root + stem formant vowel.

8.3.2.1 Non-finite forms

Perfective participle: root + -*i*: *žú-i* 'having eaten'. Functions: (a) base for perfect tenses; (b) forms compound verbs; (c) conjunctive participle, conveying meanings of anteriority, manner, circumstance, and cause; (d) followed by *pişţau* 'after', it forms subordinate temporal clauses; (e) complement of the phrasal verb *khulék* 'to finish': *nivéši khul-ém* 'I will finish writing'. It is not used attributively or to form participial relative clauses.

Imperfective participle: root + -*íman*: *kar-íman* 'doing'. Functions: (a) forms imperfective tenses in construction with *as*- 'be(ANIM)' and *š*- 'be(INAN)'; (b) adverbially: *tro-íman par-áu* 's/he went, crying', but not attributively: *tro-íman súda 'crying child(ren)'.

Past participle: (a) in -*ta/-da*: *dí-ta* 'given', *ká-da* 'done'; (b) in -*(i)ła*: *hú-ła* 'became'; (c) in -*ála*: *nis-ála* 'seated'; (d) in -*úna*: *nis-úna* 'sat'. Functions: (a) base for past inferential tense; (b) attributive adjective: *nígiła pyalá* 'washed cup'; (c) forms participial relative clauses: *tai káda krom bo pruşţ* 'the work you did is very good'.

Infinitive: root + -*ik*: *par-ik* 'to go'. Functions: Declined like other inanimates, it forms many complement structures, e.g. *ík-as páti* 'for the sake of coming'. Also (a) abilitative construction: infinitive + *bhá*- 'be able': *áma krom kár-ik bhá-am* 'I can do this work'; (b) necessitative: infinitive(-*as*) *baş*; (c) infinitival relative clauses; (d) with -*wéw* 'time' it forms temporal subordinate clauses.

Passive/middle participle: stem + -*un*: *sapráun* 'found'; parallels Khowar forms in -*ín*. In construction with *par*- 'go' it forms an abilitative passive: *íya darwazá ne umrá-un par-iú* 'this door can't be opened'.

Necessitative: stem + -*éli*. Expresses necessity: *kar-éli* 'must be done, must do'.

Agent noun: stem + -*áw*: *jan chaławáw* 'one who takes lives'.

Desiderative: stem + -*álak* meaning 'desire to V': *žuálak* 'desire to eat'.

Transitivity-causativity relations. (a) intransitive or transitive root + -*á*- yields a transitive or causative: *piík* 'to drink' > *piék* (< *pi-á-ik) 'to cause to drink'; (b) root + -*aw*- + -*á* yields a second causative: *karawáik* 'to have done (by someone)'. Causees in -*awá*- causatives are indicated in three ways: simple oblique, with the postposition *şatawái*, or *kai maĩ* 'saying to':

(6) *mai   šamónd   aú   pac-aw-á-i*
     I(OBL) so much   bread cook-Cs(PST-A)-2s
     'You got me to cook so much bread.'

(7) *darzí-as   şaţawái   ek   pirán sawz-aw-á-am*
     tailor-OBL   by   one   shirt make-Cs(P/F-NS)1s
     'I will get a shirt made by the tailor.'

(8) *kas   kai maĩ   kar-aw-á-ik*
     who-OBL   to speak(CP)   do-Cs(P/F-NS)-1p
     'Who shall we get to do it?'

Compound verbs are formed with the vectors *par-* 'go', and *tha-* 'put':

(9) *baabá-a   cei   uzuk-í   par-áu*
    sister-OBL tea   spill(CP) go(PST-A)-3s
    'Sister's tea spilled.'

(10) *šúda   šuru-á-i   athá-i*
     baby   fall-Cs-CP   put(PST-A)-2s
     'You let the baby fall.'

8.3.2.2 Tense-aspect forms

The Kalasha verb system can be described with reference to parameters of aspect (durative or non-durative; perfective or non-perfective), tense (past or non-past), specificity (specific or non-specific), inferentiality (inferential or actual) and modality. The nominal category of animacy intersects each of these dimensions.

The verb agrees with the subject in person, number and animacy. The auxiliary has separate forms for animate and inanimate entities, and since five of the basic tense-aspect forms consist of a participle + auxiliary, the animacy distinction is central to the verb system (Bashir 1988b).

Forms of the auxiliary *ásik*, *šik* 'be' (animate, inanimate).

	Present		Past-actual	
	Sg.	Pl.	Sg.	Pl.
1.	*á-am* (*ás-am*)	*á-ik* (*á-sik*)	*áy-is* (*ás-is*)	*áy-imi* (*ás-imi*)
2.	*á-as* (*ás-as*)	*á-a* (*á-sa*)	*áy-i* (*ás-i*)	*áy-ili* (*ás-ili*)
3. ANIM	*á-au* (*ás-au*)	*á-an* (*ásan*)	*áy-is* (*ás-is*)	*áy-ini* (*ás-ini*)
INAN	*ší-u*	*ší-an*	*aš-ís*	*aš-íni*

Tense-aspect forms are illustrated for *par-* 'go' in the first singular:

Present/future-non-specific (P/F-NS): stem + present personal endings, *par-ím* 'I go, will go.'

Present/future-specific (P/F-S): P/F-NS + *-dai*, *par-ím-dai* 'I am/will be going.'

Present perfect (P PERF): perfective participle + present of AUX, *pai á-am* 'I have gone.'

Past-actual (PST-A): stem + past personal endings, *par-á* 'I went.'

Past-inferential (PST-I): past participle + P/F-NS of *h-* 'become'; *gála him* 'Apparently I went.'

Past imperfective-actual (PST IMPFV-A): imperf. participle + past-actual of 'be' *paríman áyis* 'I was going.'

Past imperfective-inferential (PST IMPFV-I): imperf. participle + past-inferential of 'be' + P/F-NS of *h-* 'become' *paríman ásta him* 'Apparently I was going.'

Past perfect-actual (PST PERF-A): perfective participle + past-actual of 'be' *pai áy-is* 'I had gone.'

Past perfect-inferential (PST PERF-I): perfective participle + past-inferential of 'be' + P/F-NS of *h-* 'become'; *pai ásta him* 'Apparently I had gone.'

In the first and second persons of the past inferential tenses, person and number of the agent are specified by the present/future-non-specific forms of *h-* 'become'.

Non-indicative forms are:

Imperative: singular = (a) verb root: *žu* 'eat!'; (b) root + formant vowel: *kár-i* 'do!';
(c) verb root + -Vs: *upáç-as* 'open (your) eyes!' (< *upáç-*); (d) *h-* 'become' is irregular:
ha 'become!'. The second plural and first plural imperatives are identical respectively
with the second plural and first plural of the present/future-non-specific.

Hortative/optative: finite verb + -*óri*: *se par-iú-óri* 'Let him go/he should go.'
Subjunctive: finite verb + *háw-au* (> *háu*) 'became' (past-actual 3s of *h-* 'become').
This serves to report situations which are uncertain in some way:

(11) *a*   *ne   jhón-im*   *se kawá   apáu deł*   *háu*
     I(NOM) not know(P/F-NS)-1s he where   stay(P/F-NS-3s) become(PST-A)-3s
     'I don't know where he lives.'

Necessitative. Like Khowar, Kalasha has doublet necessitative constructions: (a)
stem + -*éli*: *kar-éli* (<*kar-* 'do') 'one must do'. This form is invariant; an auxiliary is
always third singular inanimate, and an expressed agent is oblique. (b) nominative or
oblique infinitive + *baṣ*:

(12) *tai*   *bo   paysa   tása*   *di-éli*
     you(OBL) much money he(OBL) give-NEC
     'You have to give him a lot of money.'

(13) *mai   par-ik(as)-báṣ*
     I(OBL) go-INF(OBL)-NEC
     'I have to/should go.'

8.4 Syntax

Kalasha is a left-branching language which is assimilating some right-branching
structures. Complement structures include (a) sentential, with complementizers *ghõi* or
ki; (b) infinitival; and (c) nominalized. The sentential type with *ghõi*, conjunctive
participle of *ghõ-*'say', is most common. *ghõi* has developed a wide range of semantic
functions (Bashir 1988b, 1996).

(14) *šurú-am*   *ghõi   bih-iú-dai*
     fall(P/F-NS)-1s COMP fear(P/F-S)-3s
     'She is afraid of falling.'

(15) *doṣ   ṣułá   ón-im*   *ghõi   ne   abhá-is*
     yesterday firewood bring(P/F-NS)-1s COMP not be able(PST-A)-1s
     'Yesterday I wasn't able to bring firewood.'

(16) *a salím-a   kai ayá   ík-as*   *báti mãi áy-is*
     I Salim-OBL to here come(INF-OBL) for speak(PST PERF-A)-1s
     'I told Salim to come here.'

Some predicates, such as *lasék* 'to let go, allow', take nominalized complements:

(17) *phao žú-una   sudáyak-as mo lasái*
     soil eat-LOC   baby-OBL   not let(IMP2s)
     'Don't let the baby eat soil.'

Kalasha has several indigenous and two borrowed relativization strategies. The indigenous strategies are left-branching.

(a)   In the most common structure, a prenominal finite relative clause precedes the main clause, and a resumptive pronoun sometimes appears in the main clause. The case of the resumptive pronoun coreferential with the head noun is determined by its role in the main clause. Examples:

> (18) *khur trupél-lai   š-asé   moc kúra*
>   foot hurt(P/F-S)-3s EMPH-that man who
>   'Who is that man whose foot is hurting?'

> (19) *tai   dukán-una šiála   to/*se   guum a a-grí-s*
>   your shop-LOC be(PST-I)3s that(ACC/*NOM) wheat I   take(PST-A)-1s
>   'I bought the wheat which was in your shop.'

(b)   Participial relative clause:

> (20) *tai   káda   krom mai   bo   khoš*
>   you(OBL) do(PST-PPL) work I(OBL) very   pleasing
>   'I like the work you did very much.'

(c)   The morpheme *-lei* can be added to participles, postpositional phrases, adjectives, nouns or finite verbs to form relative clauses, much as *-wālā* in Urdu:

> (21) *káda   darwáza-ta umrái   aghő-au*
>   do(PST PPL)   door-TOP open(IMP2s) say(PST-A)-3s
>   *umrála-lei-o   kári   aghő-au*
>   open(PST PPL)-one-CONTRAST do(IMP2s)   say(PST-A)-3s
>   '"Open the door which is closed", he said. "Close the one which is open".'

(d)   Infinitival:

> (22) *a sabák mấik-as   ṭém-una ábi çatráu par-ómi*
>   I lesson read(INF)-OBL time-LOC we   Chitral go(PST-A)-1p
>   'While I was studying we went to Chitral.'

Nominalization:

> (23) *íya mai ṣ̃ŏa našawáw-as   pútr-as*
>   this my dog kill(AG N)-OBL son-PS3s
>   'This is the son of the one who killed my dog.'

Borrowed structures.

(a)   an indefinite element *k- + ki* is employed in the function of relative marker, and a demonstrative serves as correlative element in the matrix clause. This structure is probably borrowed from Khowar. It can be considered an incipient relative-correlative strategy. Example:

> (24) *kíya cakú gri   ki krom karíman áyis   se   ḍhābá*
>   what knife with ki work do(PST-IMPFV-A)-1s that dull
>   *húla*
>   become(PST-I)-3s
>   'The knife with which I was working was dull.'

(b) *-wālā*, from Urdu:

> (25) *ása udulúna pirán-wála moc kúra*
> that torn   shirt REL   man who
> 'Who is that man with the torn shirt?'

9 TIRAHI

9.1 Introduction

At the time (1929) when Morgenstierne worked on Tirahi, it was spoken in a few villages southeast of Jalalabad in Afghanistan (Morgenstierne 1934: 161–2). Tirahi-speakers had been expelled from Tirah by Pathans a few centuries earlier. It showed much superstratal influence from Pashto in phonology, lexicon and even morphology. With respect to phonology and morphology, Tirahi appears to occupy an intermediate position between Pashai and the Kohistani group; however, vocabulary points to a closer connection with the Kohistani dialects (Morgenstierne 1934: 171). Morgenstierne (1965: 138–9) concludes that Tirahi is 'probably the remnant of a dialect group extending from Tirah through the Peshawar district into Swat and Dir . . . connected with Kalam Kohistani and Torwali, but retaining forms of a Lahnda type'.

9.2 Phonology

Vowels. a, ā, ə, i, ī, e, ē, u, ū, o, ō (Edelman 1983: 192).
  Consonants (Edelman 1983: 192).

p	t	ṭ		k	
ph	th			kh	
b	d	ḍ		g	
	ts		c		
			ch		
			j		
	s		š	x	h
	z			ɣ	
m	n				
	r				
	l				
w			y		

x and *ɣ*, respectively, derive from *ṣ* and *ẓ*: *āxt* 'eight', *kəɣən* 'black' [< *kṛẓṇa*]). Length and aspiration (voiceless stops) are contrastive; only *ṭ* and *ḍ* contrast for retroflexion.

9.3 Morphology

9.3.1 Nominal

9.3.1.1 Nouns and adjectives

Some marked feminines end in *-e/-ē* (*strē* 'woman'), but gender is usually observed in adjective and verb agreement. For vowel-final nouns, nominative and oblique singular are identical. Consonant-final nouns add *-a* or *-e* in the oblique; however, the use of the marked oblique is not consistent. Oblique singular and nominative plural usually have the same form. Oblique plurals often end in *-an*. Dative and genitive suffixes attach to the oblique. Grierson (1927: 269, 273–4) gives the following forms:

	Sg.	Pl.		Sg.	Pl.
NOM	*mala* 'father'	*mala*	NOM/ACC	*adam* 'man'	*adam-a*
OBL	*mala*	*mal-an*	OBL/AG	*adam-a*	*adam-an* [Grierson 1925: 410]
GEN	*mala-s*	*mála*	GEN	*adam-a-s*	*adam-an*
DAT	*mala-si*	*mála-si*	DAT	*adam-a-si*	*adam-an*
ABL	*mala-ma*	*mala-si*	ABL	*adam-a-ma*	*adam-an-si*

Some adjectives have characteristic terminations: *sura/surē* 'small (ms/fs)'; but the pattern is not clear.

9.3.1.2 Pronouns

Personal pronouns (Grierson 1927; Morgenstierne 1934, Grierson 1925).

1.	Sg.	Pl.
NOM	*au, ao*	*mā* (M: 162), *ao*? (G1927: 282)
OBL	*mē*	*mēn* (G1927: 282)
DAT	*ma-si*	*ma-si*
GEN	*myāna* (ms)	NA
	myānī (fs [M: 162])	NA
	myāna (m/f p? [M: 162, G1927: 279])	NA
2.		
NOM	*tu, to*	*tao*
OBL	*tē, te*	*tā*
DAT	*ta-si* (M: 188)	NA
GEN	*cā-na* (m)	*tāma, tema* (G1927: 281)
	cā-nī (p? [M: 178])	
	cā-nī (f)	
	cā-nā (mfp?)	

The genitive ending, *-na/-nī*, may agree with the noun modified in gender (and number?).

There appear to be (at least) two values in the deictic system: *lē* 'this' and *la* 'that' (Morgenstierne 1934: 163). These forms do not distinguish gender. Various oblique forms are recorded (Grierson 1927: 283), but their functional distribution is not clear. The pronouns *ase* and *esa* 'it' may be specifically anaphoric: *au esa acūm ī* 'I take it' (Morgenstierne 1934: 176).

Pronominal suffixes.

Sg.	1.	2.	3.	Pl.	1.	2.	3.
	-m	*-e*	*-(V)s; -n*		NA	NA	NA

These suffixes attach to nouns, showing possession, and to verbs, indexing direct or indirect objects:

(1)   *abō-e*   *kata*   *dūr thī*
village-PS2s how much far is(ms)
'How far is your village?' (Morgenstierne 1934: 163)

(2) *malə-s   malə-m   thī*
     father-PS3s father-PS1s is(ms)
     'He is my father's father.' (Morgenstierne 1934: 163)

(3) *lema-manzum sŭrĕ   putər mala   dita-n-as*
     them-of   young   son   father said-PS3s-PS3s
     'Of them, the younger son said to to his father.' (Grierson 1927: 294, 296)

9.3.2 Verbal

9.3.2.1 Non-finite forms

Infinitive: stem + *-an*: *karan* 'to do, make', *diyan* 'to beat' (Grierson 1927: 289). Past participle: *dita* 'gave'. The present participle ends in *-ū*, *car-ū* 'grazing'.

9.3.2.2 Tense-aspect forms

Imperative: singular = stem; plural = stem + V (Grierson 1927: 289).

Grierson (1925: 413) gives the following auxiliary forms (Morgenstierne 1934 has *th-* consistently):

	Present of *t(h)-* 'be'		Past of *b-* 'become'	
	Sg.	Pl.	Sg.	Pl.
1.	*tim*	*tima*	*wāma (wām?)*	*wāma*
2.	*tis*	*tiza*	*wāz, wē*	*wāma* (? *wāza*)
3.	*ti* (m), *tē* (f)	*tīna* (m/f)	*wā* (m), *wē* (f)	*wāna* (m/f)
				(Grierson 1927: 288)

Tense-aspect forms observed are:

Present-future: root + the following personal endings 1s *-m*, 2s *-s*, 3s *-e*, 3p *-en* (Morgenstierne 1934: 165)

Definite present: *da/de/də* + present-future (Morgenstierne 1934: 165):

(4) *pali   de   kham*
     bread DEF   eat (P/F)1s
     'I am eating bread.' (Morgenstierne 1934: 165)

Definite future: *ba-* (< Pashto) + present-future: *au ba-dēm* 'I shall give' (Grierson 1925: 414).

Past: past participle (+ pronominal suffix):

(5) *lā brōk odasta gā*
     he very hungry become/go (PST3s-m)
     'He became/is very hungry.' (Grierson 1927:293)

(6) *ao   marā ga-m*
     I (NOM)   die   become/go (PST)-PS-1s
     'I died/am dead.' (Grierson 1925:416)

Perfect: past participle + present of *th-* 'be', *chāna brā ŭ ti* 'Your (sg) brother has come' (Grierson 1927: 294).

Past perfect: past participle + past of *b-* 'become':

(7) *mē   dita   wa*
     I(OBL) hit(PST PPL)   become(PST)ms
     'I (had) hit (ms DO).'

9.3.2.3 Case marking and verb agreement

Subjects of transitive past tenses are oblique or nominative/oblique if no oblique is distinguished, and the verb agrees with the direct object. Nominal direct objects are nominative. Examples:

(8) *mala   gaṇa putr-asi   jawāb   dita*
     father(NOM/OBL) elder son-DAT reply   give(PST)
     'The father gave a reply to the elder son.' (Grierson 1927: 298)

(9) *sure   putar   tānu māl   jama kere*
     young son(NOM/OBL) self's property(NOM) collect(PST)-3s
     'The younger son collected his property.' (Grierson 1925: 410)

10 SWAT-DIR KOHISTANI

10.1 Introduction

Swat-Dir Kohistani is spoken in the upper reaches of Swat Kohistan (villages Kalam, Utror, Ushu, Matiltan) and in Dir Kohistan (villages Thal, Lamuti, Biar, Barikot), by 60,000–70,000 (1995) people (Baart 1997: 4). Aside from Kalam Kohistani, important varieties are those of Rajkot/Patrak in Dir (most different from Kalami), Kalkot (Dir), and Dashwa (Kalam). There is more linguistic diversity in Dir than in Swat Kohistan (Rensch 1992: 6–8). Most people in Dir and Swat also speak Pashto.

The sketch below of Kalam Kohistani is based on Baart (1995, 1997) and the author's field notes.

10.2 Phonology

Vowels (Baart 1997: 31).

	Front	Back
Close	*i, ī*	*u, ū*
Mid	*e, ē*	*o, ō*
Open	*ä, ǟ*	*a, ā*

Length is contrastive for each vowel quality: *kan* 'ear', *kān* 'arrow' (Baart 1997: 32). It is also functional in the morphological distinctions in causative formation. Except for *o*, oral vowels have nasalized counterparts, and nasalization is phonemic: *mā* 'from', *mã* 'my(ms)' (Baart 1997: 33).

Baart (1995: 11) documents five contrastive tones: high level (H); high-to-low falling (HL); delayed high-to-low falling (H(L)); low level (L); low-to-high rising (LH). These are illustrated here (Baart 1997: 41): *bōr* 'lion' (H), *bōr* 'lions' (HL), *bōr* 'Pathan' (L), *bōr* 'deaf' (H(L)), *gōr* 'horse' (LH). The distributions of tones and aspiration are correlated: aspiration almost always co-occurs with L or LH melody, while lack of aspiration often co-occurs with H, HL or H(L) melody (Baart 1995: 13–4). Stress is also predictable from tone (Baart 1997: 48).

Consonants (Baart 1997: 19).

p	t	ṭ		k	q
ph	th	ṭh		kh	
b	d	ḍ		g	
	ts	c̣	c		
	tsh	c̣h	ch		
			j		
f	s	ṣ	š	x	h
	z		ɣ		
m	n	ṇ		ŋ	
	λ				
	l				
	r	ṛ (?)			
w			y		

f, *q*, *ɣ*, *z*, and *x* occur mainly in loanwords (Baart 1995: 5).

Aspiration is losing its contrastiveness in Kalam Kohistani; Baart notes that it is difficult to find minimal pairs for aspiration, since aspiration is almost always predictable from tone (1997: 20).

10.3 Morphology

10.3.1 Nominal

10.3.1.1 Nouns and adjectives

Nouns form plurals by: (a) suffixation: *miž* 'man', *miž-āl* 'men'; *īz* 'woman', *is-āl* 'women' (Bashir: notes); (b) stem vowel changes: *šāk* 'a piece of wood', *šə̄k* 'pieces of wood' (Baart 1995: 15); (c) tone differences: *bōr* (H) 'lion', *bōr* (HL) 'lions' (Baart 1995: 15). Feminine counterparts of masculine nouns are also related by fronting: *kukur* 'rooster', *kikir* 'hen'.

Many nouns have two basic case forms: nominative and an inflected form used for plural as well as general oblique (Baart 1995: 15). A locative in *-a* attaches to the nominative: *ma bābas-a* 'in my arm'. The genitive ending is adjectival: *ã̄/-ä ̃/-ẽ̄* (ms/mp/ f); e.g. *mīš-ã̄ bob* 'the man's father', *mīš-ẽ̄ yey* 'the man's mother' (Baart 1997: 33).

Adjectives agree for number and gender. Fronting and raising distinguish masculine singular from masculine plural and feminine: *raan/rään/reen* 'good(ms/mp/f)' (Baart 1995: 4).

10.3.1.2 Pronouns

Personal pronouns (Baart 2001).

1.	Sg.	Pl.	2.	Sg.	Pl.
NOM	*ya*	*mä*		*tu*	*thä*
OBL	*mäy* (L)	*mā*		*thäy*	*thā*
ACC	*mäy* (L)	*mä*		*thäy*	*thä*
AG	*mäy* (H)	*mä*		*täy*	*thä*
GEN	*mã̄* 'my' (ms)	*mũ* 'our' (ms)		*chã̄* 'your (s)' (ms)	*thũ̄* 'your' (p) (ms)

Genitive forms are adjectival, showing masculine singular, masculine plural and feminine forms: *mã/mā̃/mɛ̃* 'my (ms/mp/f)'.

Demonstratives. Kalam Kohistani has a complex deictic system. In Baart's analysis (2001), there are two demonstrative pronouns, indicating visible or not-visible entities, and distinguishing animacy in the oblique singular. The nominative and oblique forms are:

	Visible		Non-visible	
	Sg.	Pl.	Sg.	Pl.
NOM	*äy*	*am*	*sā*	*tam*
OBL	*äs* (anim), *än* (inanimate)	*am*	*tā̃* (animate), *tän* (inanimate)	*tam*

Demonstrative adjectives, however, according to Baart (2001), have five distinct forms:

		Sg.	Pl.
Visible			
	near, unmarked	*ĩ*	*ami*
	near, marked	*äthã̃* (m), *äthɛ̃* (f)	*äthã̃* (m), *äthɛ̃* (f)
	far, unmarked	*ṣĩ*	*amṣĩ*
	far, marked	*äṣĩ*	
Not visible		*täthĩ*	*tamthĩ*

10.3.2 Verbal

10.3.2.1 Non-finite forms

Infinitive: stem (= root + long vowel) + *-g*. Causative stems are formed by changing the stem-final thematic vowel and/or stem-vowel change: *kʸerūg* 'to do', *kʸerōg* 'to cause to be done'; *phuṭūg* 'to break (intr.)', *phoṭāg* 'to break (tr.)'. Passive/middle stems insert *j-* between root and thematic vowel: *λārūg* 'to sell' *λærjúg* 'to be sold' (Bashir: notes).

Conjunctive participle = stem: *dā* 'having given' (< *dāg*), *diā* 'having caused to be given' (< *diāg*). Some common verbs are irregular: *gī* (< *ginūg* 'to take').

Past participle: consonant-final stem + *-āl*(m)/*-īl*(f): *ləŋ-āl/ləŋ-īl* 'passed (m/f)'; or vowel-final stem + *-gʸāl/-gʸīl (m/f)*.

10.3.2.2 Tense-aspect forms

The non-specific present/future and the specific present mark number and gender, distinguishing ms, mp and f, but not person. The paradigms are illustrated for *yāg* 'to come' (Bashir: notes).

Present/Future (non-specific)		Present (specific)	
Sg.	Pl.	Sg.	Pl.
yɔ̃/yɛ̃ (m/f)	*yā/yɛ̃* (m/f)	*yɔn/yɛn* (m/f)	*yan/yɛn* (m/f)

This present ending is underlyingly *-Vnt*, but today the final *-t* is usually lost in ordinary speech. Baart has *ho-änt* 'are(mp)', while the (phonetic) forms in my notes consistently lack *-t*, which only surfaces before a vowel-initial complementizer or interrogative particle *-ā*. Thus the (audible) difference between these two tense forms is now the contrast between a nasal consonant and a nasalized vowel. Morgenstierne (1940) noted forms with *-t* consistently.

The specific future agrees with its subject in person (first or non-first), and number in first person.

Future (specific)

	1.	2–3.
Sg.	*yəm* (m/f)	*yɛg* (m/f)
Pl.	*yī* (m/f)	*yɛg* (m/f)

Past imperfective: stem + vowel (modified to mark gender and number agreement with subject) + *-š*: *täl-āš* 'send (IMPFVms)', *jän-ä-š* 'know(IMPFVmp)' (Baart 1997), *kʸer-eš* 'were doing(f)' (Bashir: notes). This form appears to be an abraded imperfective participle + the abraded past tense of 'be': *yãs* 'I(m) was coming' < **yānt ašū* (Morgenstierne 1940: 221).

Contrafactual. Distinct from the imperfective, this form consists of stem + *m* + *š*: *khāmš* 'would have eaten' (Baart 1999: ms. 13).

Simple Past. Several formations occur: (a) forms in *-t*: *yāt* 'came(ms)'; (b) root + thematic vowel: *læŋ-u* 'passed(m)'; (c) irregular forms: *kīr* 'made'. Vowel modification marks gender agreement with the direct object or subject for transitives and intransitives, respectively: *gas* '(s/he) caught him'; *gis* '(s/he) caught her' (*LSI*: 510–11); *si na jɔla byēg* 'she was not able to speak' (Bashir: notes).

Present Perfect: past + *-t*: *āj ága muc-u-t* 'today it has rained' (Bashir: notes).

Past perfect: past + *-š*: *täl-u-š* 'had sent (msDO)' (Baart 1997: 70).

Optative. A 3rd person form is recorded that consists of root + *da*: *yāda* (< *yā-* 'come' 's/he should come'.

10.4 Syntax

Relative clause. Several relative clause structures are attested.

(a) Participial:

(1) *athã   jel-mɔ   ḍawāl   miš   thū*
     this   jail-from run(PST PPL) man   be(ms)
     'This is a man who has run away from jail.' (Bashir: notes)

(b) Some relative clauses consist of a prenominal finite clause with no relative marker, and a demonstrative pronoun in the matrix clause:

(2) *tan   seɭʸīm marūš   tətĩ   chūr məi   lə̄d*
     he(AG)   Salim   kill(PST PERFms)   that   knife I(AG) find(PSTms)
     'I found the knife with which he killed Salim.' (Bashir: notes)

(c) There is also an incipient relative-correlative structure, employing an interrogative element in the relative clause and a demonstrative in the matrix clause:

(3) *kän   nä   män-uš   tam   änpaḍ   där-u*
     who-AG not   say-PST PERF(m)   those illiterate remain-PST(m)
     'Those that did not study remained illiterate.' (Baart 1997: 69)

There is some development of complementizers from 'say' as in other Dardic languages:

(4)   *zōr zumää mäy äro   kōn   kam   is-pōjā   ya jäätäk*
      old time in QUOT when who   women-folk   or menfolk
      gänäär h-uš   tē   tam   gī   cō
      aged   become(PST PERFm) then they take(CP) go(CP)
      ṭhōk-ä   tā̃l-ā̃-š   äro   äy gänäär h-ut
      cliff-LOC send(PST IMPFVmp) QUOT this aged   become(PRES
      PERFms)

      'It is said that in the old times, when a women or a man had become old, they
      would take them and push them off a cliff, saying, "This one has become
      old".' (Baart 1997: 69)

The form *äro*, glossed 'QUOT' here, is a tense form of a verb meaning 'say'. This verb has only
two past tense forms: *maro* 'I/we said', and *aro* 'you(s/p)/he/she/they said' (Bashir: notes).

    Subject marking and verb agreement are split ergative: subjects are nominative with
intransitives and non-perfective transitives, agentive with perfective transitives. Nominal
direct objects are usually nominative, and perfective tenses of transitives agree with the
direct object. Case assignment to the subjects of conjunctive participles when the
transitivity status of the conjunctive participle and finite verb differs depends not on the
transitivity status of the conjunctive participle or the matrix verb, but on the tense-aspect
of the matrix verb. If the finite verb is perfective (either transitive or intransitive), the
subject is agentive or oblique. If the finite verb is non-perfective the subject is
nominative. For example (Bashir: notes):

(5)   *mǝi   gyel khā   nīn   gā*
      I(AG) bread eat(CP) sleep go(PSTms)
      'I went to sleep after eating.'

(6)   *mǝi   ithī   kɔ́car camákū*
      I(AG) rise(CP) clothes wash(PSTm)
      'I got up and washed clothes.'

(7)   *tan   tā́nī koṭ na ṣɔ́ (HF)   yāg*
      he(OBL) self's coat not put on(CP) come(PSTms)
      'He came without putting on his coat.'

(8)   *yɨ   gyel khā   nīn   bacɔ̃*
      I(NOM) bread eat(CP) sleep go(P/F-NS1s)
      'I will eat bread and go to sleep.'

(10) *yɨ   ithī   kɔ́car camákɔ̃*
      I(NOM) rise(CP) clothes wash(P/F-NS1s)
      'I will get up and wash clothes.'

11 TORWALI

11.1 Introduction

Torwali is spoken in the Swat valley north of Madyan and in the Chail side valley by
approximately 60,000 people (Rensch 1992: 33). There is extensive bilingualism in
Pashto and increasing bilingualism in Urdu. The following description depends mostly
on the author's field notes (1989) and transcription is broad phonetic; materials from
other sources are so noted.

11.2 Phonology

Vowels: a, ā, u, ū, o, ɔ, I, ī, ɛ, ē, æ, [ə], [ɨ]

/ē/, /ɛ/, and /æ/ are distinct phonemes: *šēn* 'leafy vegetables', *šɛn* 'Ur. *cārpāī*', *šæn* 'low stool (Ur. *caukī*)'. The status of length is not certain. Tonal contrasts are salient; e.g. *bhái* (HF) 'bundle of grass', *bhaái* (LR) 'sat'; *çhií* (LR) 'milk', *çhí* (HF) 'woman', and occur with short vowels also: *dar* (HL) 'valley near Madyan', *dar* (L) 'door'. Informants characterized the low(-rising) and the high(-falling) tones as spoken 'softly' or 'strongly', respectively.

Consonants.

p	t	ṭ		k	
ph	th	ṭh		kh	
b	d	ḍ		g	
bh	dh	ḍh		gh	
		ç	c		
		çh	ch		
		j̣	j		
			jh		
(f)	s	ṣ	š	x	h
	z	ẓ	ž	ɣ	
m	n	ṇ			
mh	nh	ṇh		ŋ	
	r	ṛ			
	l				
	lh				
w			y		

Voiced aspirates are robustly present: *ghō* 'horse', *mhes̩* 'buffalo', *ghəm* 'wheat', *ḍhak* 'old', *dho* 'distance', *lhado* 'finished', *jhēl* 'woollen blanket', *bhun* 'plain, lowlands'. Zoller (p.c.) attests *ṇh*.

11.3 Morphology

11.3.1 Nominal

11.3.1.1 Nouns and adjectives

Only a few nouns have distinct plural forms: *dhū* 'daughter', *dhī* 'daughters'; *gā* 'cow', *gai* 'cows' (Grierson 1929: 11). Gender is marked by vowel alternation for masculine/ feminine, as in *ghō* 'male horse' *ghē* 'mare', or, more usually, reflected in adjectival and verbal forms: *pešæt* 'showed (fsDO)', *pašāt* 'showed (msDO)'; *nútu* 'is not (ms), *níši* 'is not (fs). Case endings are illustrated for *šir* 'house' (after Grierson 1929: 26):

	DIR	OBL	ABL	GEN
Sg.	šir	šir-ē	šir-ā	šir-sī
Pl.	šir	šir-ā	šir-ā-mā	NA

Other case relations are indicated with postpositions: *šir-ke* (DAT), *šir-{ma/kejā}* (ABL).

Adjectives are marked for gender by stem vowel fronting: *lohūr/lehīr* 'red (m/f)'. This occurs even with loans: *kamzōr/kemzer* 'weak (m/f)'. Comparison is expressed with the postposition *kejā* and nominative of the standard: *šū kejā ucat* 'taller than the sister'. The superlative is expressed by *buḍ* 'all' with the postposition *mē* 'among', *buḍā mē ucat* 'high among all' (Grierson 1929: 35–9).

11.3.1.2 Pronouns

Personal pronouns (Bashir: notes).

1.	Sg.	Pl.	2.	Sg.	Pl.
NOM	*ā*	*mho*		*tu*	*tho*
AG	*mæ*	*mho-é*		*tæ*	*tho-é*
ACC	*mhæ*	*mhō*		*thæ*	*thō*
DAT	*mhæ-yé*			*t(h)æ-yé*	*tho* (?)
ABL	*mhe*	*mho*		*the*	*thō*
GEN	*mhī*	*mhūn*		*chī*	*thun*

Genitive forms of pronouns are not adjectival. The reflexive pronoun is *tunú*. Pronominal suffixes do not occur.

Three values are recorded for the demonstrative system: proximal, distal-visible, and remote-not visible. Nominative singular forms are:

	Pronominal	Adjectival
Proximal (visible)	*æ*	*æ*
Distal (visible)	*hɛ*	*pʷɛ*
	pāe (Grierson 1929: 54)	*paiyē* (Grierson 1929: 54) *pāe* (Inamullah)
Remote (not visible)	*se*	*se* (animate), *te* (inanimate)

Animacy is distinguished in the remote, non-visible category.

11.3.2 Verbal

11.3.2.1 Non-finite forms

Infinitive: root + *-ú/û̃*: *baj-ú* 'to go'. Declined as a noun, it forms various complement structures:

(1) *ā   sabzī-sī   gin-û̃-e   bɔyə́dū*
    I(NOM) vegetables-GEN take-INF-OBL go(PRES)-ms
    'I am going to get vegetables.'

(2) *tī   pexɔr-kye   boy-ū-ma   inkār   kī*
    he(AG) Peshawar-to   go-INF-from   refusal do(PST)
    'He refused to go to Peshawar.'

An inceptive construction consists of infinitive + *sæt*: *pīš/pūš čhií pū-sæt* 'the cat (f/m) began to drink milk (m)'.

The Torwali infinitive resembles the infinitive of Wotapuri-Katarqalai in *-u/-û̃/-û̃n* (Buddruss 1960: 64), and Kanyawali (Buddruss 1959a), which terminates in various nasalized vowels, rather than that of its synchronic neighbour Kalam Kohistani (in -*g*). Like Wotapuri-Katarqalai, Torwali appears not to have an inherited conjunctive participle, but it constructs a form analogous in function by adding -*te*/-*de* to a verbal noun resembling the present stem (cf. the W-K 'second infinitive' in -*i* Buddruss 1960: 65):

(3) *mæ   gyel   khyæ-de   hūd/hīt*
    I(AG) bread   eat-*de*   sleep(PST)ms/fs
    'I ate bread and slept.'

The case of the subject here is determined by the non-finite transitive verb 'ate', not by the matrix verb 'slept'.

Morphological causative formation is productive: *xuṛugū* 'to boil (intr.), *xuṛugā* 'to boil (tr.)'. Examples:

(4) *ū   xuṛugú-dū*
    water(m)(NOM) boil(PST)-be(PRESms)
    'The water has boiled.'

(5) *mæ   cei-sī   kye   ū   xuṛugāt*
    I(AG) tea-GEN to   water(m)(NOM) boil(CS-PSTms)
    'I boiled water for tea.'

The past participle ends in -*él*/-*il* (tr./intr.): *xuṛug-él* 'boiled' (*xuṛugā* 'boil' [tr.]).

11.3.2.2 Tense-aspect forms

Imperative: singular = stem: *baš* 'go!' (< *baž* < *baj*); plural = stem + -*ā̌*: *bayā̌* 'go(p)!' (< *bažā̌* < *bajā̌*).

Auxiliary forms distinguish number and gender but not person. They are:

	Present of *th*- 'be'.		Past of *aš*- 'be'.	
	Sg.	Pl.	Sg.	Pl.
m	*thu*	*thī*	*ašú̃*	*āšî*
f	*chī*	*thī*	*æšî*	*āšî*

	Present of *h*- 'become'.		Past of *h*- 'become'.	
m	*hodu*	*hodī*	*hū*	*huí*
f	*hoyī* (< *hojī*)	*hodī*	*hī*	*huí*

Subjunctive: stem + personal endings. This is the only Torwali verb form marked for person:

	1.	2.	3.
Sg.	-*i*	-Ø (= stem = IMP)	-*é*
Pl.	-*i*	-*ā* (= IMP)	-*én*

Present: stem + V + -*du*(ms)/-*ji*(fs)/-*di*(mfp) (present of *th*- 'be', where intervocalically *th*- > *d*- and *c* > *j* (> *ž*: *gina-žī* 'she takes'). The present is marked for number, and for gender in the singular. Intransitive: *a/tu/se šir kye bajédu* (ms)/*bajéji* (fs) '... go(es)/is going home'. Transitive: *a/tu/se gyel khādú/khāji* '... (m/fs) eat(s) bread'. *mo/tho/se gyel khādí* 'We/you(p)/they eat bread.' Transitives and intransitives agree with a nominative subject.

Future. Torwali has a unique development to express future time: stem + invariant *-nín*: *baj-* 'go' > *baj-nín* 'I/you/he/she/it/we/they will go'. Pronominal subjects in the future are oblique/agentive for both intransitives and transitives: *tæ bajnín* 'you(AG) will go', *mhoɛ gyel khanín* 'We(AG) will eat bread.' Full noun phrase subjects, however, can be nominative or oblique, probably depending on animacy:

(6) *tī   banū   tonɔ́l loló   awo-nín*
    he(AG) say(PSTms) rice tomorrow come-FUT
    'He said that the rice would come tomorrow.'

Past imperfective: root + *-u-* + *-dút*. Invariant form for both intransitives and transitives. *ā/tu/se/mho/tho/se bɔjudút* 'I/you(s)/(s)he/we/you(p)/they used to go' (Ur. *jātā thā*), *ā/tu/se/mho/tho/se gyel khōwdút* 'I etc. used to eat bread'.

Past. Past stems end in (a) vowel, (b) consonant, as in past stems of derived transitives and causatives in *-t*; e.g. *læṭ phirī* 'the stick (f) broke (f)', *læṭ phærǽt* '...broke (f) the stick (f)'. This tense is marked for number, and for gender only in the singular. Gender-number agreement markers involve stem and/or suffix vowel alteration. Intransitive: verb agrees in number and gender with subject: *kužū́/kižī́ dɛɔ́u/deī́* 'the dog (m/f) ran away', *kužū́/kižī́ duéi* 'the dogs (m/f) ran away'. Transitive: verb agrees in gender with the direct object: *mæ/tæ/tī gyel/ān khyeéy/khōw* 'I/you/(s)he ate bread (f)/an egg (m).'

Present Perfect: past stem + *-du* (ms)/*-di* (fs)/*-dī* (p). Transitive: subject is oblique/agentive and verb agrees with direct object in gender and number: *mæ gyel/ān khɔ̄īdi/khōwdu/khóidī* 'I have eaten a bread/an egg/{breads/eggs}.'

Past Perfect: past stem (with vowel alternation for number and gender) + *-š* + *ū* (ms)/*-ī* (fs)/*-i* (p). Intransitive: *a gíšū́/géšī́* 'I (m/f) had gone', *se gɨyšī́* 'they (mf) had gone'. Transitive: *mæ gyel* (fs)/*ān* (ms)/*gyel* (fp) *khɔ́išī̄/khōwšū́/khoíši* 'I had eaten bread/an egg/breads.'

11.4 Syntax

Pronominal subjects of perfective tenses of transitive verbs are oblique/agentive; noun phrase subjects, however, are sometimes nominative. For certain nouns the nominative and oblique may be identical; e.g *bɔb* 'father'. Grierson (1929: 28) noted that the oblique is rarely used for subjects of transitive past tenses, and the subject is often in the nominative form. Examples:

(7) *mho-ē̆   thæ-ɛ́   tonú klsén   chæl   pešæt*
    we(AG) them-DAT self's black(f) nanny goat show(PSTfs)
    'We showed them our black goat.'

(8) *māš   mē xān-ma   tapōs   kī*
    man(NOM) this Khan-from question do(PSTms)
    'The man(NOM) made inquiry from this khan.'(Grierson 1929: 28)

(9) *mhī po-e   šir-sī   kām ni kī*
    my son-OBL house-GEN work not do(PSTms)
    'My son did not do his house chores.'

Nominal direct objects are nominative; pronominal direct objects are accusative:

(10) *tæ   tes   mhī   kyæš-kye pɛ́ɔ́w*
    you(AG)   him(ACC) I(GEN) to   send(PSTms)
    'You sent him to me.'

(11) *tī   thæ   mhī   kyæš-kye pɛ́ɔ́w*
    he(AG)   you(ACC) I(GEN) to   send(PSTms)
    'He sent you to me.'

Relative clause. Participial and hybrid relative-correlative types are attested. For example,

(12) *thin   banél   bāt   sæz   hoyī*
    they(GEN) say(PST PPL) word(f) truthful(fs) is(fs)
    'Words which they say are truthful.'

In the hybrid relative-correlative construction, *ya* functions as a relative pronoun:

(13) *pʷɛ mās*   [*ya hɛ roḍ-te   rawān thū*] *hɛ mī mam*   *thū*
    that man(NOM) who he road-by going   is he my maternal uncle is
    'The man walking on the road is my maternal uncle.'

12 WOTAPURI-KATARQALAI

12.1 Introduction

In 1935, this language was spoken in about 60 households in village Katarqala, and only a few old people in Wotapur (Buddruss 1960: 1), having been replaced by Pashto. In 1955–6, Buddruss found only one informant in Katarqala. By now this language is probably extinct. The language as recorded shows much recent influence from Pashai and Pashto. Its linguistic neighbours were Gawarbati type languages, Pashai and Nuristani languages; however, it is genetically closer to the Kohistani languages (Buddruss 1960: 71–2). This sketch is based on Buddruss (1960), hereafter (Bd: page).

12.2 Phonology

Vowels.

ī   ū   i   u
    ē   ō   e   o
        ā   a

Length is phonemic: *nam* 'new', *nām* 'name' (Bd: 14). Tonal contours were observed in some words, but phonemic oppositions not attested. All vowels can be nasalized. Stress is strong and falls on the final syllable of nominal and verbal stems regardless of length; unstressed vowels are reduced (Bd: 15).

Consonants.

p   t   ṭ   k   q
ph   th   ṭh   kh
b   d   ḍ   g

	ts	c	ç		
	tsh	ch	çh		
	dz				
		j			
(f)	s	š	(ṣ)	x	h
	z				
m	n		ṇ		
	r		ṛ		
			λ (rare)		
	l				
	w		y		

No voiced aspirates were noted; aspiration is phonemic for voiceless consonants but wavers. The following alternations were observed: *x~ kh, dz~ z, f~ ph, ts~ s, ṛ~ [l]*. *š* and *c* are pronounced farther back than in other Dardic languages and seemed not to contrast with *ṣ* and *ç* (Bd: 26).

12.3 Morphology

12.3.1 Nominal

12.3.1.1 Nouns and adjectives

Most nouns with stem vowels *a* or *u* are masculine, while most with *e* or *i* are feminine. Some m/f pairs are related by fronting: *gōṛ* '(male) horse', *gēṛ* 'mare'; *kukuṛ* 'cock', *kikiṛ* 'hen'. Case endings do not differentiate gender. Endings observed in various functions are (Bd: 37):

	Sg.	Pl.
NOM	—	-ẽ̃,-ẽ, -ē
GEN	-an, (-en)	-an, (-en)
ACC	NA	-ã, -an, -a, -ẽ, -ē
ABL 1.	-ã, -an, -a	-a
2.	-gesa	-an-gesa, -ã-gesa
INST	-ĩ̃, -ĩ, -ĭ, -īn	ũ
AG	-ĩ̃, -ĩ, -ê, -īn	ũ, aũ, aõ
LOC	-ĩ̃, -ĭ, -ĭn, -ẽ	-ũ, õ, -aũ

These appear to fall into three distinct groups: nominative, oblique 1 (genitive/ accusative/ablative) and oblique 2 (instrumental/agentive/locative). The dative post-position is -{g/k}e, added to oblique 1.

   Both unmarked and marked adjectives are found. Feminine is marked by raising: *tat/ tyet* 'warm(m/f)'; present participle *karan/karen/karanē/karenē* 'doing' (ms/fs/mp/fp); future participle *pašun/pašin/pašunē/pašinē* 'one who sees'(ms/fs/mp/fp); *zwān* 'young (common)'. Ordinary adjectives do not change for case, but used substantively they are declined as nouns.

12.3.1.2 Pronouns

Personal pronominal forms attested are (Bd: 44–5):

1.	Sg.	Pl.	2.	Sg.	Pl.
NOM	au	mũ/mun/man		tu (thu?), tũ	thũ/thõ
GEN	men	mũ/mun		then	thum
DAT	makḗ	maŋke		takḗ	NA
ACC	mai/maĩ	mā		thaĩ/thain/thai	tā, yiman
AG	mai/maĩ	mũ		thaĩ	NA
ABL	mayā́	mū́na		tayā́	táŋ-gesa

Demonstratives show two values: proximal and distal. Pronominal case endings are similar to nominal endings (Bd: 48). Demonstrative adjectives agree in case with the nouns they modify, distinguishing three (proximal) or four (distal) forms, but do not mark number (Bd: 47–8).

	Proximal			Distal		
	Adjectival	Pronominal		Adjectival	Pronominal	
	Sg./pl.	Sg.	Pl.	Sg./pl.	Sg.	Pl.
NOM	ai	ai	NA	sē	sē	t(h)eũ
OBL/ACC	ma	mas	NA	ta	tas	NA
GEN	ma	mas-an	NA	ta	tas-án	thaún
DAT	ma	mas-aŋ-gē	NA	ta	tas-áŋ-gē	taŋ-kē
ABL	ma	məs-á	NA	ta	tas-á, t(h)i	táŋ-gesa
AG	mē	NA	NA	thē	tē, t(h)ī́	NA
LOC	mē	NA	NA	tē	NA	NA

Examples:

(1) mē   maníš-i   alā́   ni   kaṛū́
    this(AG) man(AG) word(m) not do(PSTms)
    'This man did not speak.' (Bd: 47).

(2) ai   nyāṛ ma   zū́y-en   dū   thī
    this(NOM) girl this(GEN) woman-GEN daughter is(fs)
    'This girl is the daughter of this woman.' (Bd: 47)

Pronominal suffixes. Fragmentary information indicates a third singular form *-es*, observed with nouns: *máth-es* 'his head' (cf. GB). A first singular form *-a/-ā/-an* and a third plural form *-wa* occurring with transitive aorist forms may be pronominal suffixes (Bd: 46, 54). There is much less use of pronominal suffixes than in GB or Shumashti.

12.3.2 Verbal

12.3.2.1 Non-finite forms

Two verbal nouns have infinitive functions: (1) in *-ú/-ū́/-ûn*: *khā-ûn* 'to eat'; (2) stem + *-ī́*: *as-ī́* 'to speak'. Infinitive 1 appears with the postposition *dəpā́ra* 'for': *khāûn dəpā́ra* 'for eating'. Infinitive 2 appears (a) as complement of *bā-* 'be able': *ni bấn-aũ asī́* 'he couldn't speak'; (b) in forming the periphrastic irrealis conditional: *au ni tsuī́ thimánaũ* 'if I had not gone' (Bd: 65). An agent noun is formed from Infinitive 1 + *-kai*: *khāûnkai* 'eater'. No unique conjunctive participle is identified.

Perfective participle: stem + -(y)el for both genders. It can be used both attributively, *dazyél girḗṛ* 'burned bread' (Bd: 63), or predicatively, *au pyēl thū* 'I am lying down' (Bd: 122) (H-U *maĩ leṭā huā hū̃*).

12.3.2.2 Tense-aspect forms

Imperative: singular = stem; plural = stem + -*ā̃*.

Subjunctive (aorist). This is the only tense conjugated for person. It conveys meanings of potentiality. Endings are (Bd: 54):

	1.	2.	3.
Sg.	*-m, -am*	NA	*-ē*
Pl.	*-ĩ, ī̃,-īn*	NA	*-ē*

Future. In most Dardic languages the subjunctive (= aorist) has the function of an indefinite present-future. W-K, however, has separate future forms, varying according to verb class. (a) deverbal nominal (root + -*un*/-*wun*) that agrees with its subject in number and gender: *au/tu/sē pašún/pašín* 'I/you/[s]he/it (ms/fs) will see' and *mũ/thũ/téũ pašúnē/ pašínē* 'we/you/they will see (mp/fp)'. (b) root + -*mán*/-*m(y)én*/-*mánē*/-*m(y)énē* (ms/fs/ mp/fp). In this form, root vowels *ē* and *ō* shorten to *i* and *u* respectively: *dē-* 'give', *dimán* 'he will give' (Bd: 57–8).

Future forms denote future time and modal senses:

(3) *mũ*   *sabā́r*   *tsu-mánē*
   we(NOM)   morning   go-(FUTmp)
   'We will go in the morning.' (Bd: 59)

(4) *maĩ*   *tasá*   *šid*   *kir*   *zī*   *au*   *tsu-mán*
   I(AG)   him   question   do(PSTms CONJ   I(NOM)   come(FUTms)
   'I asked him whether I should come.' (Bd: 59)

A periphrastic future consisting of present + *thimán* 'will be' appears in conditional sentences:

(5) *kə tu*   *maĩ*   *dēn thimán*
   if you(NOM)   I(ACC)   beat will be
   'If you beat me.' (Bd: 59)

Present: present participle (root + -V(˜)*n*). The present marks gender and number agreement with the subject: *au/tu/sē karán*(ms)/*karén*(fs) 'I, you(s), (s)he/it does'; *mũ/ thũ/téũ karánẽ/karénẽ* (mp/fp) 'we/you/they do'. The present of *th-* 'be', used as present auxiliary, follows this pattern: *au/tu/sē thū/thī* (ms/fs) 'I/you/[s]he/it is', *mũ/thũ/téũ thē* 'We/you/they are.' (Bd: 56)

Past imperfective: present + unstressed invariant -*aũ* (< *išáũ* 'was'); however, the plural termination -*ẽ* of the participle is lost so that singular and plural fall together:

(6) *au*   *kam*   *karán-aũ*
   I(NOM)   work   do(IMPFVm)
   'I(m) was working.' (Bd: 57)

(7) *sē*   *pyā́nī*   *pṓn-aũ/pyḗn-aũ*
   he/she(NOM)   water   drink(IMPFVm/f)
   'He/she was drinking water.' (Bd: 57)

Past. Two types are found: strong: *bud/bid* (ms/fs) 'heard'; weak in -*ú/-ūī/-ú̃(y)ē* (ms/fs/pl): *zūī phidū̃ī* 'the woman arrived'. Most verbs have the weak formation. The past tense of *š-* 'be', functioning as past auxiliary, has only one form for both numbers and genders: *išáũ* 'was/were' (Bd: 56).

Perfect: past + *thū/thī/thē* (ms/fs/p): *tu kéjeī paidā́ wú̃ thū* 'where were you (s) (m/f) born? (Bd: 63)

Past perfect: past + -*aũ*: *au bayíṭ-aũ* 'I had sat'. (Bd: 63–4)

Conditional: future + -*aũ*. This form signifies past or present irrealis: *tsumán-aũ* 'if he were going/if he had gone'. Periphrastic forms distinguish between present and past time. For present irrealis, present + *thimánaũ*: *au tsōn thimánaũ* '(if) I were going'; for past irrealis, infinitive 2 + *thimánaũ*: *au ni tsuī́ thimánaũ* 'if I had not gone'. In this form, transitive past tense subjects can be nominative or agentive: *kə au* (or *maī̃*) *girēṛ khāī́ thimánaũ* 'if I had eaten bread' (Bd: 59–60).

12.4 Syntax

Case marking is split ergative: nominal subjects of transitive perfective tenses are agentive.

(8) *manís-aũ   kam   kir*
    man-AGp   work do(PST)
    'The men worked.' (Bd: 41)

Singular pronominal subjects distinguish nominative and agentive and show agentive subjects in transitive past tenses:

(9) *tē   ma-kḗ isú̃*
    he(AG) I-DAT say(PSTms)
    'He said to me.' (Bd: 48)

However with plural pronouns, distinct forms for nominative and agentive are not attested; plural subjects appear to be nominative for all tenses of both intransitive and transitive verbs:

(10) *mū   májaī thē*
     we(NOM) here   are
     'We are here.' (Bd: 45)

(11) *mū   kam   kír-thū*
     we(NOM) work do(PST)-AUXms
     'We have worked.' (Bd: 45)

Direct objects are accusative in both non-past and past tenses:

(12) *ta   maníš-a   au   ni   pirānán*
     those man-ACCp I(NOM) not know(PRES)ms
     'I(m) don't know those men.' (Bd: 39)

In transitive perfective tenses the verb agrees with the object, which if plural is accusative and if singular is identical with the nominative:

(13) *maī̃   ta   maníš/zūī   paš-ū/pašū̃ī*
     I(AG)   that man(NOM)/woman(NOM) see(PST)-ms/fs
     'I saw that man/woman.' (Bd: 62)

(14) *maĩ   ma   maníš-ã   ne   paš-ū̃ē   thē*
    I(AG)   these man-ACCp   not   see(PST)-mp AUX(mp)
    'I have not seen these men.' (Bd: 40)

Relative clauses. Relative clauses can be formed with the conjunction *zī*, which also functions to introduce many other types of subordinate clauses.

(15) *yek maníš diṭ zī   girẹ̃r   khằn-aũ*
    one man   saw who   bread   eat(IMPFV-m)
    '... saw a man who was eating bread' (Bd: 57)

13 INDUS KOHISTANI

13.1 Introduction

Indus Kohistani is the main language of District Kohistan, spoken by a total of more than 200,000 people (Hallberg 1992: 89). Claus Peter Zoller (p.c.) finds that the dialects fall into 'core' and 'outer' regions, the outer dialects somewhat more conservative than the core. Zoller's core and outer classification corresponds closely to the division between the dialects of Seo-Patan-Jijal and Duber-Khandia (Hallberg 1992: 93). Indus Kohistani is in local contact with Kohistani Shina, Pashto and Urdu. Hallberg (1992) gives language similarity data for the varieties of Indus Kohistani and its local neighbours.

Chiliso, an outer variety (treated as a separate language in Hallberg 1992), is spoken by several thousand people on the east bank of the Indus in District Kohistan. It displays 69–71% and 48–56% lexical similarity with other varieties of Indus Kohistani and with Kohistani Shina, respectively (Hallberg 1992: 118).

Gabar (Gowro, Hallberg 1992) is spoken by perhaps 200 people in village Mahrin on the east bank of the Indus. It has 68%, 61–3%, and 41–3% lexical similarity with Mahrin Chiliso, other Kohistani varieties, and Kohistani Shina dialects, respectively. Gabar speakers are all bilingual in Shina (Hallberg 1992: 125–9).

New research by Zoller (in preparation) indicates that Jijālī (cf. Kanyawali) has a pitch accent system with two accents. Zoller (p.c.) thinks that this system is probably shared by all Indus Kohistani dialects, with the possible exception of Bhatise. Now see Zoller (2005).

13.2 Bhatise

Bhatise is the most divergent of the Indus Kohistan dialects (Zoller p.c.); Hallberg 1992 treats it as a separate language. It is spoken by twenty to thirty thousand people in Batera, on the east bank of the Indus opposite Besham (Hallberg 1992: 133–41).

Work in progress by Zoller (p.c.) indicates that Bhatise has a complex phonology involving a 15-vowel system and interacting tonal/pitch and stress accents.

Vowels

i i-			u⁺ u	
I	e e-	o⁺ o	U	
	ɛ æ	ɔ		
	a⁺ a			

i and *e* have both backed (*i-*, *e-*) and lowered (*I*, *ɛ*) counterparts; *u* and *o* have both fronted (*u+*, *o+*) and lowered counterparts (*U*, *ɔ*); *a* has a fronted counterpart (*a+*); *æ*, each of these vowels has a long counterpart. The p is always long. Except for the lowered versions and *æ*, each of these vowels has a long counterpart. The pairs *ku+l* 'flesh of fruit, kernel of nut', *kUl* 'corn particle'; *zīg* 'long (m)', *zīg* 'long (f)' illustrate two of the vowel contrasts involved.

Consonants. Zoller (p.c.) provides the following consonant inventory for Bhatise, and considers that – with the exception that *ṇ* probably occurs only in Gabar – it applies to all the Indus Kohistani dialects.

p	t		ṭ	k	q
ph	th		ṭh	kh	
b	d		ḍ	g	
bh	dh		ḍh	gh	
	ts	c	ç		
	tsh	ch	çh		
	dz	j	j̣		
	dzh	jh	j̣h		
(f)	s	š	ṣ	x	h
	z	ž	z̧	ɣ	
			z̧h		
m	n		(ṇ)		
mh	nh				
	r		ṛ		
	rh		ṛh		
		l			
		lh			
v		y			

13.3 Kanyawali

13.3.1 Introduction

The best known variety to date (2000) is Kanyawali, spoken in about 30 households in the village of Bangkari, a linguistic island in the Shina-speaking Tangir Valley (Buddruss 1959a). According to Buddruss (1959a: 8), Hallberg (1992: 99–100), and Zoller (p.c.), Kanyawali is close to the Seo-Patan-Jijal dialects. The following sketch of Kanyawali is based on Buddruss (1959a), hereafter (Bd: page).

13.3.2 Phonology

Vowels. *ī*, *ē*, *ā*, and *a* are distinct phonemes: *pašágil* 'saw', *pašā́gil* 'showed'. The status of length for *ī*, *ē* and of *o/ō/u/ū* is unclear (Bd: 9).

Consonants occurring in Buddruss' materials are (Bd: 9-11):

p	t	ṭ		k

ph	th		kh		
b	d	ḍ	g		
bh	dh		gh		
	ts	ç	c		
	tsh		ch		
			j		
f	s	ṣ	š	x	h
v	z	ẓ	ž	ɣ	
m	n	ṇ			
	r	ṛ			
		ṛh			
	l				
w			y		

f, x and *ɣ* occur in loans.

Aspiration of both voiced and voiceless consonants is clear: *ghin-* 'take', *khor* 'foot'. Vowel nasalization has replaced postvocalic *m, n* and *ṇ*: *gã* 'village', *bhĩ* 'sister', *lũ* 'salt'.

13.3.3 Morphology

13.3.3.1 Nominal

13.3.3.1.1 Nouns
Consonant-final nouns are masculine or feminine. Masculines can be extended by *-k*, e.g. *mā́š(uk)* 'man'. Feminines are formed with *-i* and/or stem-vowel change; e.g. *ghō/ghuí* 'horse(m/f)'. A few plurals are formed by vowel fronting: *bāl* 'word', *b{a/e}il* 'words'.

Case suffixes (Bd: 13-16).

	NOM/ACC	OBL-1	OBL-2
Sg.	Ø	-e	-a
Pl.	-a, Ø	-õ̃	-õ̃

In the singular, oblique–1 has dative, directional and agentive functions; oblique–2 is used before postpositions. In the plural, oblique functions as genitive, dative, agentive, postpositional and vocative, e.g. *ghõ̃ baspūr* 'the feet of the horses'.

The singular genitive ending *-ã̃* (m), *-eĩ/-aĩ* (f) is adjectival, agreeing in gender with the noun modified: *maṭ-ã̃ mahā́la* 'the boy's father', *maṭ-eĩ mahā́lī* 'the boy's mother'.

Nominal subjects of all verbs in non-perfective tenses, and of transitives in perfective tenses are nominative and oblique, respectively. Singular pronominal subjects of perfective transitives have a distinct agentive form.

13.3.3.1.2 Pronouns

Personal pronouns (after Bd: 16)

1.	Sg.	Pl.	2.	Sg.	Pl.
NOM	ma	bẽ		tu	tus
AG	mẽ	zaũ̃		tẽ	tsaũ̃
OBL	mī	zaũ̃		tī	tsaũ̃
GEN	mĩ	zã̃		tĩ, tĩ	tsã̃ (f. tsaĩ)

Four distinct forms are attested: nominative, agentive, oblique – which has accusative, and postpositional functions – and genitive, which appears to be adjectival. Clitic pronouns are not attested.

The demonstrative system has three values; nominative singular forms are: proximal *ṣu*, half remote (anaphoric?) *u/ū*, remote (not visible?) *so* (Bd: 17–19).

13.3.3.2 Verbal

13.3.3.2.1 Non-finite forms

Perfective participle: stem + *-l(ă)/-él(a)*. This forms the base of the past perfect tense, and is used both attributively and predicatively: *du tsiz-élă zuṛa* 'two torn clothes', *zanzēr ghanélă thū* 'the chain is fastened' (Bd: 27) .

Infinitive. This has been attested ending in various back or front nasalized vowels. The front vowel versions are grammatically feminine: *huĩ bẽ thī* 'Now someone has to go' (Ur. *abhī jānā hai*) (Bd: 29). The infinitive is declined: *utheyã* (GEN) *waxa mā* 'at the time of getting up' (Bd: 28–9).

Conjunctive participle. Conjunctive participles of intransitives and transitives end in *-í* and *-é*, respectively: *bazí* 'having gone', *karé* 'having done'. A functionally similar form ends in *-gil-e* (= past + *e*); (cf. *LSI*-Maiyã *kuṭa-galai* 'having beaten'): *kará-gil-e* 'having done' (Bd: 28).

Agent noun: present (without aspiration) + *-uk*: *dẽtuw-uk* 'a giver' (Bd: 29); cf. the Gilgit Shina use of *-k*.

13.3.3.2.2 Tense-aspect forms

Imperative: singular = stem (+ {*-a/-e*}); plural not attested.

Subjunctive (aorist). This is the only form marked for person; it is illustrated for *khā-* 'eat' (Bd: 21): sg. 1. *khām*, 2–3. *khā*; pl. 1. *khež*, 2–3. *khei*.

Present: present of *th-* 'be': *thū/thē/thī* [ms/mp/f] 'is/are'. The present of other verbs agrees with the subject in number and gender: *karã-th(ă)/karã-thẽ/karã-thi* (ms/mp/f) 'does' (Bd: 22).

Past imperfective: stem +*-ãs* (past of *as-* 'be'): *karãsă/karãse* 'he was/they (m) were doing', *khãsă/khãẽs/khãse/khãsi* (ms/fs/mp/fp) 'was/were eating' (Bd: 22).

Future: stem *-šat/*{*-ša(i)ti/-šet*}*/-šat(h)e* (ms/fs/mfp): *bā-šati* 'she will go', *kará-šat* 'he will do' (Bd: 22–3).

Past. Intransitive regular forms are the past stem (+ *-gā* (ms)/*-gī* (fs)/*-gē* (mfp)). Thus, *bhéṭă* 'sat (ms)', *bheṭ-gī/bheṭ-gē* 'she/they sat down'. Transitives consist of the past stem + *-l* or *-il*; there are alternate invariant forms ending in *-gil* (also in *LSI* 'Maiyã'): *pašíl* and *pašá-gil* 'saw'; *pašã́-gil* 'showed'; *kará-gil* 'did'; *ne-ril* 'did not do' (Bd: 23–5). The past tense forms in *-gā/gī/gē* and *-gil* may be functionally parallel to compound verbs with *jā-* 'go' of NIA languages.

Present perfect. Intransitive: past + auxiliary *-thū* (ms)/*-thī* (fs)/*-thē* (mfp): *bheṭă-thū* 'he has sat', etc. Transitive: past stem + auxiliary *-thū*: *kará-thū* 'has done', as in *LSI* 'Maiyã' (Bd: 23, 26).

Past perfect. Intransitive: past + auxiliary *ãs-* 'be' (*-ãs* [ms]/*-ẽs* [fs]/*-ãse* [mfp]): *bhẽṭ-ẽs* 'she had sat'. Transitive: perfective participle in *-l* or *-él* + auxiliary: *pašél-ãs* 'had seen', *karél-ãs* 'had done' (Bd: 23, 27).

14 SHINA

14.1 Introduction

Shina is spoken in Gilgit, Hunza, the Astor valley, the Tangir-Darel valleys, Chilas, Indus Kohistan, and also in the upper Neelam valley and isolated communities in Ladakh. There are three major dialect groups, plus synchronically outlying Ushojo, Palula, Sawi and Brokskat.

Ushojo is spoken in the Bishigram side valley of the Swat River, by about 2000 people whose ancestors are said to have migrated from the Kolai area in Indus Kohistan several hundred years ago. Now many Ushojo speakers also speak Torwali and Pashto (Decker, S. 1992: 66). Lexical similarity comparisons indicate that Ushojo is most closely related to Kohistani Shina. The following example shows the Shina character of Ushojo: *ana ase goṭ hani* 'this house is ours' (Decker, S. 1992: 72). Palula, Sawi and Brokskat are described separately.

Estimates of the total number of Shina speakers in Pakistan vary widely, from over three million (Schmidt 1988c: 107–8) to about half a million (Radloff 1992: 93). Radloff (1992: 93) estimates 20,000 in India. Present linguistic interactions in Pakistan involve Balti and Kashmiri with the eastern dialects, Burushaski and Khowar with the Gilgit dialect, and Pashto and Indus Kohistani with the Kohistan dialects, all in addition to Urdu.

Features common to all Shina dialects are: three contrasting sibilants; retroflex fricatives; contrastive tones or pitch accent – attested in Gilgiti, Kohistani, Astori, Gultari (Hook 1996: 131), and Guresi dialects (possibly also in Drasi), only Brokskat showing no trace of this tonal system (Schmidt 1998b: 4) – and deictic systems of three or more terms. The synchronic groupings possibly reflect an earlier split between Gilgit Shina and other varieties (Schmidt 1998a: 1–2). The past tense suffix in *-eégas*, and the infinitive suffix *-oóik^y* distinguish Gilgiti from other dialects, which have infinitives in *-n* (Lorimer 1927, Schmidt 1998b: 2).

The following sketch is of Gilgit Shina, the variety best described so far, and possibly the older and more basic dialect (Schmidt 1998b: 4–5).

14.2 Phonology

Vowels: *a, aa, e, ee, i, ii, o, oo, u, uu*. All vowels except *e* have nasalized counterparts (Radloff 1999: 17).

Gilgit Shina has a pitch accent system, in which long vowels are analysed as consisting of two moras, with the intonation peak falling either on the first or the second mora. Stress on the first mora results in a high falling pitch, while stress on the second produces a low rising pitch (Radloff and Shakil 1998, henceforth R&S: page). The Shina pitch accent system is similar to that of Burushaski (Buddruss p.c.) and probably of Khowar (Bashir: notes).

Consonants (R&S: 8–9).

p	t	ṭ		k
ph	th	ṭh		kh
b	d	ḍ		g
	ts	c̣	c	

	tsh	ch	ch		
			j		
	s	ṣ	š		h
	z	ẓ			
m	n	ṇ		ŋ	
	r	ṛ			
	l				
w			y		

14.3 Morphology

14.3.1 Nominal

14.3.1.1 Nouns and adjectives

Nouns have three basic cases: nominative, oblique and agentive:

	NOM	OBL	AG
Sg.	Ø	-e	-se, -s
Pl.	-e, -i	-o	-se, -s

Nominative plurals are variously formed; agentive singular -se, -s occur respectively with consonant-final and vowel-final stems; the agentive plural attaches to the nominative plural. Further case distinctions are made by secondary case markers and postpositions following the oblique. Direct objects are nominative.

Adjectives with the masculine singular ending -ŭ form feminines in -i or by stem vowel changes: *miṣṭŭ/miṣṭi/miṣṭe/miṣṭye* 'good(ms/fs/mp/fp)', *jaru/jeri/jere/jerye* 'old(ms/fs/mp/fp)' (Bailey 1924: 25). Unmarked adjectives are invariant.

14.3.1.2 Pronouns

Personal pronouns (R&S: 191)

1.	Sg.	Pl.	2.	Sg.	Pl.
NOM	*ma*	*be*		*tu*	*tsho*
AG	*mas*	*bes*		*tus*	*tshos*
GEN	*mey*	*aséy*		*they*	*tshey*

Demonstrative pronouns/adjectives (R&S: 192).

	Sg.		Pl.
	m	f	
Near	*anú*	*ané*	*aní*
Not-near (visible)	*oó*	*eé*	*eé*
[Distant (visible)	*paar oó*	*paár eé*	*paár eé*]
Remote (not visible)	*ro*	*re*	*ri*

The clitic -(e)k (< 'one') functions as an indefinite marker and also as a multifunctional nominalizer. It attaches to nouns, pronouns, adjectives and verbs. The future + -ak/-ek forms an 'agent noun' used nominally and functioning in tense-aspect forms and relative clauses: *manuẓa-k-e* 'to a man', *tu ko-k hano* 'who are you', *miṣṭu-k theé prayé* 'mend it well', *thay ẓas bechītu-k koyni hanu* 'where is the thing your brother asked for' (Bailey 1924: 82–3).

14.3.2 Verbal

14.3.2.1 Non-finite forms

Infinitive. The infinitive in *-oik^y* is declined as a singular noun, functioning in a variety of structures: *vayoĭkyĕi khăbar* 'the news of his coming' (Bailey 1924: 69).

Agent noun–1: infinitive + -{*i/e*}*k*: *ṣĭdŏíkīk* 'striker' (Bailey 1924: 84).

'Agent noun'–2: future + -(*a*)*k* (Bailey 1924: 84)

Conjunctive participle: stem + *-eé/-ií*: *theé* 'having done/said'.

Imperfective participle: stem + *-óoje* (Bailey's [1924: 70] *ōža*): *róoje álu* 'he came crying'.

Past participle (= stative participle): stem + *-tu*: *zakhmi bītu* 'wounded' (Bailey 1924: 69).

Transitive-causative and passive stems are formed with *-ar-* and *-ij-* (Bailey: *-iž-*), respectively: *zamóik^y* 'to beat', *zam-ar-óik^y* 'to cause to be beaten', *zam-iž-óik^y* 'to be beaten'.

14.3.2.2 Finite forms

The future is the base for the present and the past imperfective. Person-number suffixes for the future are (R&S: 186):

	1.	2.	3.
Sg.	*-am*	*-ee*	*-ey*
Pl.	*-on*	*-at*	*-an*

Tense forms which incorporate forms of *as-* 'be' as auxiliary are marked for person and gender in the singular; and person in the plural.

Present: future + abraded forms of present auxiliary.

Past imperfective: future + past auxiliary.

The simple past is the base for the present perfect and the past perfect. The simple past person-number endings are (R&S: 184–6):

	1.	2.	3.
Sg.	*-us/-as** (m); *-is* (f)	*-oo/-aa** (m); *-iee* (f.)	*-u* (m); *-i* (f)
Pl.	*-es*	*-et*	*-e*

*-as and *-aa* occur with transitives.

Present perfect: past + present auxiliary.

Past perfect: past + past auxiliary. The specific shapes of the resulting forms result from varying degrees of reduction/change in the incorporated auxiliary forms, fronting and/or raising for feminines, conjugation type, and the basic person-number marker forms. The stress pattern varies with conjugation class.

Additional tense forms are:

Past conditional: future + *-sik^(y)*, used in irrealis sentences with past or non-past time reference: *dem-sik* 'I would have given', *mas jēk them-sik* 'what could I do?' (Bailey 1924: 77, 71).

'Dubitative' constructions: finite tense + *-daṣ*: *rēgun-daṣ* 'he will no doubt have said' (Bailey 1924: 28–33, 71). These forms are similar in sense to the 'presumptive' use of the future of 'be' in Hindi-Urdu.

14.4 Syntax

Subject marking. All verbs in all tenses agree with the subject. Intransitive subjects are nominative, while those of transitives in all finite and non-finite forms are agentive. Examples involving imperative, infinitive, present participle, and conjunctive participle follow:

(1) *tu-s   hĩṣ   neé   the*
     you-AG word not do(IMP2s)
     'Don't say a word!' (R&S: 81)

(2) *rinéy dádo-s   ga tu   khoók   dubéy*
     their grandfather-AG also you(NOM) eat(INF) be unable(FUT3s)
     'Even their grandfather will not be able to eat you.' (R&S 1998: 81)

(3) *re-s   khóoro baš-óoje   aály   beé-iš*
     she-AG tin can strike-PRS PART there sit(PST IMPFV3sf)
     'She used to sit there beating on the tin can.' (R&S: 145)

(4) *deéw-se   daruú   deé   way-oósang*
     giant-AG hunting give(CP) coming-until
     'until the giant came (back) after hunting ...' (R&S: 152)

When the transitivity status of a conjunctive participle and matrix verb differ, and the subject precedes the former, the case of the subject is usually determined by the conjunctive participle, not by the matrix verb:

(5) *phaṛáko šuúo-s   búj-am   theé   garás bugú*
     bald   small one-AG go-FUT(1s) say(CP) ready become(PST)-3sm
     'The bald son agreed to go and got ready.' (R&S: 63)

(6) *šáal   taṣ beé   ikhaií   ḍaḍang-é-jo   khuj-eég-u*
     wolf(NOM) slip out(CP) come out(CP) drum-OBL-from ask(PST)-3sm
     'The wolf slipped out and asked the drum.' (R&S: 89)

If the subject follows the conjunctive participle clause, however, its case is determined by the matrix verb:

(7) *ĩç   phaṛáko šúu-e-kac   phat theé ri   sábe*
     bear(NOM) bald   son-OBL-near leave(CP) they(NOM) utensils
     waloók   šor   bigé
     bring(INF) dispersed become(PST)3p
     'Leaving the bear near the bald son, they dispersed to bring the dishes.' (R&S: 97)

Subordinate clauses. In Gilgit Shina left-branching structures predominate: the interrogative morpheme *-aa*, the conjunction *to* 'if, then', and the multifunctional complementizer *theé* (conjunctive participle of *thoóik*[y] 'do', 'say', see Bashir 1996) are clause final. The nominalizer *-k* which forms relative structures is enclitic. In reported speech the complement clause precedes the main verb. Examples:

(8) *ma-s rés-eṭ   wa   th-eég-as*
     I-AG him-DAT come(IMP) do(PST)-1s
     'I told him to come.' (Bashir: notes)

(9) *aṣ   juma han theé   ma góṭ-ar   beéṭ-us*
     today Friday is COMP I   home-LOC am sitting
     'Since today is Friday I am sitting at home.' (Bashir: notes)

Infinitival complements include an inceptive construction 'to begin to' consisting of infinitive + *ṣaáç-* 'to attach to':

(10) *ṭíki   khoók   ṣaát-u*
     bread(NOM) eat(INF) begin-PST3s
     'He began to eat.' (R&S: 82)

Infinitive + *baṣ* yields a construction meaning 'about to' or 'fit to':

(11) *ro wayoóik   baṣ   han*
     he come(INF) about to is(3sm)
     'He is about to come.' (Bashir: notes)

Shina does not use a relative-correlative structure for relative clauses. The (headless) relative clause illustrated below employs *k-* nominalization:

(12) *akó-ṭ   rak   áalo-k   kha*
     self-DAT desire come(PST3sm)-nominalizer eat(IMPs)
     'Eat what(ever) you wish.' (R&S: 81)

The most common strategy employs a finite verb in the prenominal relative clause without any pronominal element:

(13) *ráloo   ẓiík chin-eé ĩç beéyey   jéel-e-waar   géi*
     from there boldly   bear stay(FUT3s) jungle-OBL-toward go(PST3sf)
     'From there she went boldly to the jungle where the bear lived.' (R&S: 132–3)

The main clause may also include a demonstrative pronoun:

(14) *muçhoo vat-u   oó mušaá*
     before come(PST3sm) that man
     'The man who came before' (Bailey 1924: 62)

15 PALULA

15.1 Introduction

Palula has developed from an archaic variety of Shina transplanted about two hundred years ago (Morgenstierne 1941: 8; Cacòpardo, Al. and Au. 1995) from the Chilas area into Lower Chitral and the village of Sau in Afghanistan (Buddruss 1967). It is spoken by about 7000–9000 people in the villages of Ashret, Kalkatak, Byori, Ghos and Purigal in southern Chitral, a complex multilingual region (Decker, K. D. 1992: 75–6). Today contiguous languages are Khowar, Kalasha, Dameli, Gujari, Shekhani, Dir Kohistani, and increasingly Pashto (Decker, K. D. 1992: 67–8).

The following sketch of Palula is based on Morgenstierne (1941), hereafter (M: page), and the author's field notes; unmarked examples are from these notes, with original (non-normalized) transcription.

15.2 Phonology

Vowels. *i, e, a, o [ɔ], u [U]; ī, ē, ā, ō, ū*

The phonological status of length is not clear. Morgenstierne (1941: 11) did not identify lexically or morphologically relevant tone; however, one of the most salient features of Palula is its pitch contours. I have indicated them in my own materials (when noted) using the same notation as for Shina and Khowar. Morgenstierne's examples remain in his transcription. Nasalization is phonetically salient in Palula: its phonemic status is not known.

Consonants

p	t		ṭ	k	
(ph)	(th)		(ṭh)	(kh)	
b	d		ḍ	g	
(bh)	(dh)		(ḍh)	(gh)	
		c	ç		
		(ch)	(çh)		
		j	ĵ		
		(jh)			
	s	š	ṣ	x	h
	z	ž		ɣ	
	ts				
	(tsh)				
	dz				
m	n		ṇ	(ŋ)	
	r	l	ṛ	(ł)	
w [v]		y			

Velarized *l* is phonetically salient, but may be conditioned, usually appearing in my materials before back vowels. There is also some alternation between *l* and *r̥*. Aspiration is phonetically salient, notably for voiced stops but probably not phonological (M: 11). Secondary aspiration has also developed (M: 14). Morgenstierne considered voiced aspirates to be consonant clusters, a slight vowel sound appearing between the stop and h: [d^{u}humī] 'smoke' (M: 12); however in my notes they are clearly aspirates.

15.3 Morphology

15.3.1 Nominal

15.3.1.1 Nouns and adjectives

Feminine gender is marked in some nouns by *-i* and/or root vowel alternation: *inç* 'he-bear' *inçi* 'she-bear' (M: 15). Consonant or *-a* final stems are either masculine or feminine.

There are three basic case forms: nominative, oblique/agentive and genitive/ablative. Feminines in *-i/-ī* are unchanged in the singular, while masculines have three distinct forms, illustrated here for *mīš* 'man' and *kuṛī* 'woman' (Edelman 1983: 265).

	Sg.	Pl.	Sg.	Pl.
NOM	mīš	mīš-a, moš-a	kuṛī	kuṛī-na
OBL	mīš-a	moš-am	kuṛī	kuṛī-nam
GEN	mīš-i	moš-amī	kuṛī	kuṛī-namī

The nominative functions as subject, except for transitive past tenses, and direct object. The genitive indicates possession, source, partitivity, place and direction. The oblique is used for subjects of transitive verbs in past tenses, beneficiaries, and some locative expressions.

Adjectives are marked for gender and number: ghāṇu/ghēṇi/ghāṇa/ghēṇim 'big (ms/fs/mp/fp)' (M: 17).

15.3.1.2 Pronouns

Personal pronouns (M: 18)

1.	Sg.	Pl.	2.	Sg.	Pl.
NOM	ma	be		tu	tus
OBL/ACC/DAT	ma	asām		tu	tusām
AG	mī	asim		thī	tusim
GEN	mī	asī		thī	tusī

Demonstrative pronouns. Palula appears to have a three-term deictic system. The following nominative forms are from Morgenstierne (M) and Bashir's notes (B).

	m sg.	f sg.	m/f pl.
near, visible	nu (B)		
	a-nu (M, B)	a-ni (M, B)	a-ni (M, B)
distal-visiblel	l{o/U} (B)	le (B)	le (B)
	á-ṛo (M, B)	á-ṛɛ (M)	á-ṛɛ (M, B)
	ha-ro (B)	ha-ṛe (B)	
distant, not visible	s{o/u} (B)	se (M, B)	se (B)
	ha-so (B)	(hɛ)-se (M)	(hɛ)-se (M)
	(hɛ)-so (M)		

The Palula deictic system resembles Khowar's. Palula too (obligatorily?) marks vertical and horizontal direction and position of individuals and events; viz. the fused forms phar-aṛo 'that in front, distant', huṇḍ-aṛŏ 'that above', bhun-aṛó 'that below': bhunære ghōṣṭa bhunaṛænĭe 'Those houses down there belong to those men down there' (M: 20). Also, there is an element (h)a- parallel to that in Kalasha and Khowar, which must play a role distinguishing the deictic/anaphoric functions of these forms.

15.3.2 Verbal

15.3.2.1 Non-finite forms

Verbal nouns. 1. stem + í: thení 'to do'. 2. stem + -a: nivéša 'to write'. These function as conjunctive participle and infinitive:

(1) *tu*   *xat   na niveša   bahṛ*
     you(NOM) letter not write(VN–2) be able(FUT2s)
     'You won't be able to write the letter.'

(2) *bidrag-í   mūṛu/mUṛī*
     sicken-VN-1 die(PSTms/fs)
     'He/she got sick and died.'

(3) *kuṇāk buchēl-i-ba   rū-ḷ-u*
     child   hunger-VN-1-*ba* cry(PSTms)
     'The child became hungry and cried.'

Reinforcement with *ba* also allows the verbal noun to be used to connect clauses with different subjects/agents, e.g.

(4) *žandur-á   tes   cuk-i-ba   su   múṛu*
     snake-OBL him(OBL) bite-VN-1-*ba* he(NOM) die(PST)ms
     'A snake bit him and he died.'

Past participle: stem + *-ōḷu, -iḷu* or irregularly in *-ṭ/du, -ṭ/ṛu*. This forms the past tense, and is used adjectivally.

Necessitative participle: stem + (*V*)*n* + *-ḍeo*:

(5) *chúpan-ḍeo dúbaḷa kursí žúli chóre*
     wash-NEC clothes chair on put(IMPs)
     'Put the clothes that need to be washed on the chair.'

15.3.2.2 Tense-aspect forms

Imperative. Second singular: stem (+ *-a* (M)/*-e* (B)): *ye* 'come!'; second plural: stem + *-o/-wa*.

Future-subjunctive (aorist). Three conjugation classes depend on stem shape, transitivity status, and thematic vowel preceding the personal endings (M: 21). This form agrees for person and number, but not gender. Unlike the present-future of Khowar and Kalasha, it appears not to be used for present time reference. The endings are:

	1.	2.	3.
Sg.	*-m*	*-ṛ*	*-a, -ī, -ō -ei*
Pl.	*-ya, -ōn*	*-t*	*-an, -īn, -ōn, -ēn*

Imperfective: future + *de* 'was'. Like the future, this form does not mark gender. E.g.

(6) *dhoṛ   bihāḷa ma   gúḷⁱi tham-de*
     yesterday night   I(NOM) bread make(1s-IMPERF)
     'Last night I(m/f) was cooking bread.'

Present: present stem (= root + *-n-*) + number-gender agreement markers *-ānu, -ēni, -āna, -ēnim*, respectively for masculine singular, feminine singular, masculine plural and feminine plural subjects:

(7) *ma gúḷⁱi th-eenᵛi/thaanu*
     I   bread am cooking(fs/ms)
     'I (m/f) am cooking bread.'

Past: past participle + number-gender agreement marker: *yōłu/yēłi/yōła/yēłim* '*came* (ms/fs/mp/fp)'

Perfect: past + *hinu*(ms)/*hinī* (fs): *mī so krām thīłu hinu* 'I(AG) have done(ms) that work (ms)' (M: 23).

Past perfect: past + *de* 'was'. Example:

(8) *thi   ma-the xat   dení-di   muṣṭú so*
     you(AG)   I-DAT letter give(VN-1)-from before he(NOM)
     yūłu-de
     come(PST PERF)ms
     'Before you gave me the letter he had come.'

Transitivity relations. Transitivity sets are regularly formed by addition of *-a-/-e-* to the stem for transitives/causatives and *-ij-* for passive/middle:

(9) *mi góṣṭ-a   ãgár ṣaá-ṭu*
     my house-OBL fire attach-PST(ms)
     'My house caught on fire.'

(10) *mi góṣṭ-a   ãgár ṣaauúłu*
     my house-OBL fire attach-CS-PST(ms)
     '(Someone) set my house on fire.'

Causees are marked by the postposition *ṣaáwa*, verbal noun-2 of the causative of *ṣaa-* 'adhere to'. Examples:

(11) *thi   nawkár-a   ṣaáwa kram thauú-łu*
     you(AG)   servant-OBL by   work do-CS-PST(ms)
     'You got the servant to do the work.'

(12) *dúbala   chup-ij-iła*
     clothes(NOM)   wash-PASS-PSTmp
     'The clothes are/have been washed.'

(13) *raziyá   dúbala   chup-iła*
     Razia-OBL clothes(NOM) wash-PSTmp
     'Razia washed the clothes.'

15.4 Syntax

Subjects of intransitive verbs in all tenses and of non-past transitive tenses are nominative; nominal and pronominal subjects of past tenses of transitive verbs are oblique, and the verb agrees with the direct object. Direct objects are nominative. Examples:

(14) *salím-a   gubá   nivéśiłu*
     Salim-OBL what(m) wrote (PSTms)
     'What did Salim write?'

(15) *aṛi   guḷⁱi   kheḷⁱi*
     s/he(AG) bread (f)(NOM) eat(PSTfs)
     'S/he ate bread.'

Subordinate clauses. Like other languages in the region, Palula uses complementi-zers from SAY in many functions:

(16) *ma   salím-a   sãngi milaau bhaam thaní   yuułu*
I(NOM) Salim-OBL with will meet   say-VN-1 came(ms)
'I(m) came to meet Salim.'

Participial relative clauses are common:

(17) *saṛak-i   phara   bayaamu haro mi   mamaa*
road-GEN over there   going   he I(GEN) uncle
'The man walking over there on the road is my uncle.'

16 SAWI

16.1 Introduction

Sawi is a dialect of Palula, spoken in the village of Sau south of Arandu on the middle Kunar, an enclave in the Gawarbati area. By now, influenced by Gawarbati, it is a distinct dialect, although it is partially mutually intelligible with Palula. K. D. Decker (1992: 80) finds 56–8% lexical similarity between Sawi and Palula. In 1956 there were 100 homes in Sau (approx. 2000 speakers). Since the war in Afghanistan, Sawi speakers have been dispersed in refugee camps in Chitral and Dir, and their present number is not known. In 1992 the number of speakers was estimated at 2000 households (8000–12,000 people) (Decker, K. D. 1992: 77–8).

The sketch below is based on Buddruss (1967), hereafter (Bd: page).

16.2 Phonology

Vowels (Bd: 12–14)

i					u
	e			o	
		ɛ		ɔ	
			a	ā	

In some cases, length is contrastive: *gaḍ* 'pull', *gāḍ thē-* 'mix'. Stress is not salient, and tonal distinctions are not attested.

Consonants (Bd: 15–16)

p	t	ṭ	k	q	
ph	th	ṭh	kh		
b	d	ḍ	g		
bh	dh		gh		
	ts	ç	c		
		çh	ch		
			j		
f	s	ṣ	š	x	h
	z		(ž)	γ	
m	n	ṇ	(ŋ)		
	r	ṛ			
	l	λ			
w			y		

q, *ts*, *f*, *x*, *z* and *y* occur in loanwords; *ž* alternates with *j*. Sawi differs from Palula in that Sawi has *λ*, but lacks *tsh*, *jh*, *ḍh* and *j*. Aspiration is clear for *kh*, *ṭh*, *th*, *ph*; less clear for *ch*, *çh*; and uncertain for voiced aspirates.

16.3 Morphology

16.3.1 Nominal

16.3.1.1 Nouns and adjectives

Unmarked nouns are masculine or feminine: *ṣiṣ* 'head (m)', *him* 'snow (f)'. Marked nouns end in -*o/u* (m) and -*i* (f), *bắtso/byētsi* 'calf (m/f)'. In the singular there are three distinctive case endings: nominative (Ø, -*a*, -*i*), oblique (-*e*), and -*ã/(õ)* (genitive/ablative, with inanimates only). Oblique has agentive, accusative, dative, locative, and general oblique functions. There may also be a locative in -*i*. In the plural there are distinctive nominative endings (-*a*, -*e*, -*ɛ*) and a general oblique (-*õ/-ũ* (-*un*)) for all nouns in all non-nominative functions.

All Sawi adjectives end in -*u/o* (m) and -*i* (f), *lawu/léwī* 'small (m/f)'. This pattern is also extended to Persian loanwords. Adjectives are not declined for case; used substantively, they are declined as nouns.

16.3.1.2 Pronouns

Two forms, nominative/oblique/accusative and agentive/genitive, are distinguished in the first singular and second singular; in the first plural and second plural there are three distinct forms: nominative, oblique/accusative and agentive/genitive.

1.	Sg.	Pl.	2.	Sg.	Pl.
NOM	*ma*	*b{e/ē}*		*tu*	*tu* (Bd: 39)
OBL/ACC	*ma*	*asã(n)*		*tu*	*tusã(n)*
AG/GEN	*m{i/ī}*	*as{i/ī}*		*t(h)i*	*tus{i/ī}*

In the demonstrative system only two degrees are attested: *la* 'this' and *se* 'that' (Bd: 41).

16.3.2 Verbal

16.3.2.1 Non-finite forms

Verbal nouns. (1) A form in -*í* appears in construction with *b(u)(w)-* 'be able': *ma ni parují bwāno* 'I cannot understand' (Bd: 56). (2) A form in -*élu/o* functions as inceptive: *se ḍaḍak-ēlu théni* 'he began to shiver' (Bd: 55). (3) A functional equivalent to the passive is constructed from a verbal noun in -*ã/-õ* + *ba-* 'go': *goš žup-ã bãnu* 'the house will be built', *xat likn-õ geinī* 'The letter has been written' (Bd: 56). This construction is suggestive of both the NIA *jānā* passive and the compound verb in *jānā*.

A conjunctive participle in -*iwó* is found (< OIA -*tvā*?); a few common verbs are irregular: *be* 'having become' (< *b(h)o-*), *thewá/ó* 'having made' (< *thē-*) (Bd: 57).

Past participle: (a) stem + -*ilo/-ili/-ile* (ms/fs/p), (b) stem + -*to/-ti/-te*, (ms/fs/p) (Bd: 51).

Passive/middle participle: stem + -*ij-ilo/ili/ile*: *picijili meṇḍili* 'baked bread' (Bd: 56).

16.3.2.2 Tense-aspect forms

The subjunctive (= aorist) is sparsely attested. Personal endings -*Vm* (1s), and -*e* (3s/p, 1p) are noted. Second person forms are identical to the imperative (Bd: 55).

Sawi builds a future form by adding the particle -*mnó*/-*mnî̃*/-*mnễ*/-*mnɛ* (ms/fs/mp/fp) to the subjunctive: *se maru-mnó* 'he will die' (Bd: 54).

The present is similar to that of Palula: *ma*/*tu*/*se thä́nu*/*thé̃ni* 'I/you(sg)/(s)he does(m/ f)', *bē*/*tu*/*sē thä́ne*/*thé̃ni* 'we/you/they do(m/f)' (Bd: 48). The imperfect is formed from the present followed by the past of *as-* 'be' (*alo*/*eli*/*ale*/*elɛ* [ms/fs/mp/fp]): *thä́n-alo*/*thé̃n-eli*/*thä́n-ale*/*thé̃n-elɛ* 'did(ms/fs/mp/fp DO)' (Bd: 49). A form parallel to this imperfect has not been recorded for Palula.

Past: (a) in -*ilo*/-*elo*: *chinilo* 'cut (ms)'; (b) in -*älo*; (c) in -*lo*; (d) in -*to*: *uthito*/*uthiti* 'stood up (ms/fs)'; (e) irregularly (Bd: 50–2)

Perfect: past + -*no*/-*ni*/-*ne*/-*nɛ* (ms/fs/mp/fp), deriving from *hino* 'is': *mi aŋguṛi chinilinī* 'I have cut (fs) my finger (fs)' (Bd: 52).

Past perfect: past stem + -*alo*/-*eli*/-*ale*/-*elɛ* (ms/fs/mp/fp): *mi pilálo* 'I had drunk (ms DO)' (Bd: 52).

Case marking is tense-aspectually split ergative. Direct objects are usually nominative, but sometimes oblique; oblique direct objects appear to be specific/definite.

(1) *bä̃b-e   monuṣ   dēṣálo*
     father-OBL man(NOM) send(PST PERFms)
     'The father sent a man.' (Bd: 33)

(2) *mi   la monuṣ-e dərṣó̃no*
     I(AG) that man-OBL see(PERF)(ms)
     'I have seen that man.' (Bd: 52)

The subject of a conjunctive participle can be oblique even when the finite verb is intransitive:

(3) *monuṣ-e meṇḍili   gin-iwó kha-wó go*
     man-OBL bread(NOM) take-CP eat-CP go(PSTms)
     'The man took the bread, ate, and left.' (Bd: 57)

17 BROKSKAT

17.1 Introduction

Brokskat is spoken around the village of Garkhon in Ladakh by approximately 3000 people (Ethnologue 1996). Though historically it belongs with the Gilgit group, Brokskat has converged with Tibeto-Burman languages and is not mutually intelligible with other Shina dialects (Schmidt 1998a, b, Radloff 1992: 99).

17.2 Phonology

Vowels (Ramaswami 1975: 64, 1982: 7)

i,ī		u,ū
e,ē		o,ō
	a,ā	

Length is contrastive (Ramaswami 1975: 64–66).
    Consonants (Ramaswami 1975: 67)

p	t	t̠			k	q	h
ph	th	t̠h			kh		
b	d	d̠			g		
		t̠s	c				
			ch				
			j				
f		s̠	ṣ	š	x	x̣	
v		z̠	ẓ	ž	ɣ	ɣ̣	
m		n̠			ŋ		
		l̠					
		r̠					
			y				

Consonants in the third column are alveolar.

17.3 Morphology

17.3.1 Nominal

17.3.1.1 Nouns and adjectives

The Shina gender distinction is maintained in Brokskat, but it is not consistently marked on nouns. Brokskat marks singular, dual and plural numbers with the suffixes -k, -hoyo and -i/-yo/-da respectively. Adjectives are marked for gender and number: bōno/bōne/bōni bāyo/bāyoda/sās 'elder brother/brothers/sister(s)' (Ramaswami 1982: 39–41). Case is indicated by agentive, dative/accusative, locative and genitive case suffixes and by postpositions.

Subjects of transitives in all tenses take an agentive marker: -sa and -ya/-i in present and past respectively. The verb always agrees with the subject (Ramaswami 1982: 4, 50).

17.3.1.2 Pronouns (Ramaswami 1982: 5).

1.	Sg.	Pl.	2.	Sg.	Pl.	3.	Sg.	Pl.
NOM	ma, mo	ba		ti, tu	tsi, tso		so (m), sa (f)	te
AG	mas(a)	bas(a)		tis(a)	tsis(a)			

There are two demonstratives: proximate and remote.

17.3.2 Verbal

17.3.2.1 Non-finite forms

A verbal noun is formed by suffixing -po to a verb: zāzis-po 'walking'. The infinitive consists of verb stem + -ta. An adjectival participle consists of verb + -i + auxiliary: baži hani mole 'sitting girl' (Ramaswami 1982: 64). Causative stems are formed from root + aṛa.

17.3.2.2 Tense-aspect forms

Person/number endings distinguish between first and other persons (Ramaswami 1982: 70):

	1.	2.	3.
Sg.	-s	-e	-e (m) -i (f)
Pl.	-es	-en	-en (m/f)

There are two tenses: past and non-past, and three aspects: perfective, progressive and habitual.

Forms of *baɳd* 'run' illustrate tense/aspect formations (Ramaswami 1982: 84–5): *sosa baɳdisūɳ* 'he runs', *sosa baɳdyūɳ* 'runs', *sosa baɳdyāle* 'is running', *soya baɳdet* 'ran', *soya baɳdaɳ* 'has run', *soya baɳdāv* 'had run', *soya baɳdisšunisula* 'may run', *soya baɳdābāsu* 'would have run', *soya baɳdetopa* 'might have run', 'the one who ran'.

ADDENDUM

Since the writing of Sections 10 on Swat-Dir Kohistani and 13 on Indus Kohistani, Baart (1999b) and Hallberg, D.G. and C.E. (1999) have appeared. These works should be consulted for the most recent published findings.

REFERENCES

Baart, Joan L. G. (1995) 'The Tones of Kalam Kohistani (Garwi, Bashkarik)', paper presented at the Third International Hindukush Cultural Conference held in Chitral, Pakistan, September 1995.
—— (1997) *The Sounds and Tones of Kalam Kohistani*, Islamabad: National Institute of Pakistan Studies, Quaid-i-Azam University and Summer Institute of Linguistics.
—— (1999a) 'Tone rules in Kalam Kohistani (Garwi, Bashkarik)', *Bulletin of the School of Oriental and African Studies*, Feb. 1999.
—— (1999b) *A Sketch of Kalam Kohistani Grammar*, Islamabad: National Institute of Pakistan Studies, Quaid-i-Azam University and Summer Institute of Linguistics.
Bailey, T. Grahame (1924) *Grammar of the Shina Language*, London: The Royal Asiatic Society.
Bashir, Elena (1988a) 'Inferentiality in Kalasha and Khowar', *Papers from the 24th Regional Meeting of the Chicago Linguistic Society, Part I: The General Session*, Chicago: Chicago Linguistic Society, pp. 47–59.
—— (1988b) *Topics in Kalasha Syntax: An Areal and Typological Perspective*, Ph.D. dissertation, The University of Michigan-Ann Arbor. Ann Arbor: University Microfilms.
—— (1996) 'Mosaic of Tongues: Quotatives and Complementizers in Northwest Indo-Aryan, Burushaski, and Balti', in Hanaway, William L. and Heston, Wilma (eds.), *Studies in Pakistani Popular Culture*, Lahore: Sang-e-Meel Publishers and Lok Virsa Publishing House, pp. 187–286.
—— (2001a) 'Spatial Expressions in Khowar', in Okrent, A. and Boyle, J. P. (eds.), *Papers from the 36th Regional Meeting of the Chicago Linguistic Society (CLS 36), Part I: The General Session*, Chicago: Chicago Linguistic Society, pp. 15-30.
—— (2001b) 'Khowar-Wakhi Contact Relationships', in Loenne, D. (ed.) *Festschrift Helmut Nespital*, Reinbeck: Wezler.
Berger, Hermann (1960) 'Bericht über sprachliche und volkskundliche Forschungen im Hunzatal', *Anthropos* 55: 657–64.
Buddruss, Georg (1959a) *Kanyawali. Proben eines Maiyã Dialektes aus Tangir (Hindukusch)*, Munich: J. Kitzinger.
—— (1959b) *Beiträge zur Kenntnis der Pasai-Dialekte* (Abhandlungen für die Kunde des Morgenlandes, Deutsche Morgenländische Gesellschaft), Wiesbaden: Franz Steiner Verlag.

—— (1960) *Die Sprache von Woṭapur and Kaṭārqalā* (Linguistische Studien im afghanischen Hindukusch), Bonn: Orientalischen Seminar der Universität Bonn.

—— (1967) 'Die Sprache von Sau in Ostafghanistan: Beiträge zur Kenntnis des Dardischen Phalūra', *Münchener Studien zur Sprachwissenschaft*, Beiheft M, Munich: J. Kitzinger.

—— (1979) 'Gṛangali. Ein Nachtrag zum Atlas der Dardsprachen', *Münchener Studien zur Sprachwissenschaft* 38: 21–39

—— (1989) 'Kommentar zu einem Kivi-vokabular aus dem sowjetischen Pamir', *Studien zur Indologie und Iranistik* 15: 197–205.

—— (1996) 'Shina Rätsel' in Dieter B. Kapp (ed.) *Nānāvidhaikatā: Festschrift für Hermann Berger*, Weisbaden: Harrassowitz, pp. 29–54.

Cacòpardo, Alberto (1991) 'The Other Kalasha. Part I: The Eastern Area', *East and West* 41: 273–310.

Cacòpardo, Alberto and Cacòpardo, Augusto (1995) 'Peoples of Southern Chitral: A survey of some so-far unstudied ethnic groups of Northern Pakistan, Part I: The Damel, Part II: The Palulo', paper presented at the Third International Hindukush Cultural Conference, held in Chitral, September 1995.

Cacòpardo, A. S. (2001) 'The Gawar', in Cacòpardo, A. M. and Cacòpardo, A. S., (2001), pp. 227–246

Cacòpardo, A. M. and Cacòpardo, A. S. (2001) *Gates of Peristan: History, religion and society in the Hindu Kush*, Rome: Istituto Italiano per l'Africa e l'Oriente.

Decker, Kendall D. (1992) *Languages of Chitral, Sociolinguistic Survey of Northern Pakistan*, *Volume 5*, Islamabad: National Institute of Pakistan Studies, Quaid-i-Azam University and Summer Institute of Linguistics.

Decker, Sandra J. (1992) 'Ushojo', in Rensch et al. (1992), pp. 66–80.

Edelman, Dzhoi (1980) 'K substratnomu naslediju tsentralno asiatskogo jazykogo sojuza', *Voprosy jazykoznanija* 5: 21–32.

—— (1983) *The Dardic and Nuristani Languages*, Moscow: Nauka.

Grierson, George Abraham (1919) *Linguistic Survey of India, Vol. VIII, Part 2* (*Specimens of the Piśacha Languages, including Kashmiri*), Calcutta: Superintendent Government Printing, India.

—— (1925) 'On the Tirahi Language', *Journal of the Royal Asiatic Society* 1925 3: 405–16.

—— (1927) *Linguistic Survey of India, Vol. I, Part 1, Introduction and Addenda Majora*, Calcutta: Office of the Superintendent of Government Printing (Reprinted (1967), Delhi: Motilal Banarsidass), pp. 265–327.

—— (1929) *Torwali: An Account of a Dardic Language of the Swat Kohistan*, London: Royal Asiatic Society.

—— (1931) 'Conjunct Consonants in Dardic', *Bulletin of the School of Oriental Studies* 6(2): 349–68.

Grjunberg, A. L. (1971) 'K dialektologii dardskikh jazykov (glangali i zemiaki)', *Indijskaja i iranskaja filologija. Voprosy dialektologii*, Moscow: Nauka, pp. 3–29.

Hallberg, Daniel G. (1992) 'The Languages of Indus Kohistan', in Rensch et al. (1992), pp. 83–141.

Hallberg, Daniel G. and Hallberg, Calinda E. (1999) *Indus Kohistani: A Preliminary Phonological and Morphological Analysis*, Islamabad: National Institute of Pakistan Studies, Quaid-i-Azam University and Summer Institute of Linguistics.

Heegaard, Jan, and Mørch, Ida E. (1998) 'Linguistic and political aspects of alphabet-making for a threatened language', Paper presented at the 17th Nordic Conference of Linguists, Nyborg(DK) 20–2 August 1998. [To appear in *Odense Working Papers in Language and Communication (OWPLC)*.]

Hook, Peter Edwin (1996) 'Kesar of Layul: A Central Asian Epic in the Shina of Gultari', in Hanaway, William L. and Heston, Wilma (eds.), *Studies in Pakistani Popular Culture*, Lahore: Sang-e-Meel Publishers and Lok Virsa Publishing House, pp. 121–83.

Keiser, R. Lincoln (1974) 'Social structure in the Southeastern Hindu-Kush: Some implications for Pashai ethno-history', *Anthropos* 69: 445–56.

Kohistani, Akhtarjan (1993) 'Gawarbati', unpublished manuscript.

Kohistani, Razwal with Schmidt, Ruth Laila (1996) *Shina Environmental Primer*, Islamabad: Himalayan Jungle Project.

Lorimer, D. L. R. (1927) 'The Conjugation of the Transitive Verb in the Principal Dialects of Shina', *Journal of the Royal Asiatic Society*, 717–64.

Mørch, Ida E. and Heegaard, Jan (1997) 'Retroflekse vokalers oprindelse i kalashamon i historisk og areallingvistisk perspektiv. Variation i sprogbeskrivelsen: vokallængde i kalashamon. To emner i kalashamon-fonologien', University of Copenhagen. [MA thesis.]

Morgenstierne, Georg (1934) 'Notes on Tirahi', *Acta Orientalia* 7: 161–89.

—— (1936) 'Iranian Elements in Khowar', *Bulletin of the School of Oriental and African Studies* 8: 657–71 (Reprinted (1973), in *Irano-Dardica*, Wiesbaden: Dr. Ludwig Reichert Verlag, pp. 241–55).

—— (1940) 'Notes on Bashkarik', *Acta Orientalia* 18: 206–57.

—— (1941) 'Notes on Phalūṛa: an Unknown Dardic Language of Chitral', *Skrifter Utgitt av det Norske Videnskaps Adademi i Oslo*, II. Hist.-Filos. Klasse No. 5, Oslo: Jacob Dybwad.

—— (1942) 'Notes on Dameli', *Norsk Tidsskrift for Sprogvidenskap* 12: 115–98.

—— (1944) *Indo-Iranian Frontier Languages, Vol. III, the Pashai Language, Part 2, Texts and Translations*, Oslo: H. Aschehoug & Co. (W. Nygaard).

—— (1945) 'Notes on Shumashti', *Norsk Tidsskrift for Sprogvidenskap* 13: 240–81.

—— (1947a) 'Some Features of Khowar Morphology', *Norsk Tidsskrift for Sprogvidenskap* 14: 5–28.

—— (1947b) 'Metathesis of Liquids in Dardic', in *Festskrift til Prof. Olaf Broch, Norske Videnskaps Akademi i Oslo, Skrifter, Hist-Fil. Klasse*, 2: 145–54.

—— (1950) 'Notes on Gawar Bati', *Videnskaps Akademi Skrifter* 2 (1).

—— (1957) 'Sanskritic Words in Khowar', in S. Radhakrishnan et al. (eds.), *Felicitation Volume Presented to Professor Sripad Krishna Belvalkar*, Varanasi: Motilal Banarsidass, pp. 84–98 (Reprinted (1973) in *Irano-Dardica*, Wiesbaden: Dr. Ludwig Reichert Verlag, pp. 256–72).

—— (1965) 'Dardic and Kafir languages', in *Encyclopedia of Islam*, new edition, Leiden: E. J. Brill, volume 2, pp. 138–9.

—— (1973a) *Indo-Iranian Frontier Languages, Vol. III, the Pashai Language, Part 1, Grammar* (2nd edition), Oslo: Universitetsforlaget.

—— (1973b) *Indo-Iranian Frontier Languages, Vol. IV, The Kalasha Language*, Instittutet for Sammenlignende Kulturforskning, Serie B: Skrifter, Oslo, Bergen-Tronso: Universitetsforlaget.

—— (1974) 'Languages of Nuristan and Surrounding Regions', in Karl Jettmar and Lennart Edelberg (eds.) *Cultures of the Hindu Kush: Selected Papers from the Hindu-Kush Cultural Conference held at Moesgard 1970*, Weisbaden: Franz Steiner Verlag, pp. 1–10.

Ovesen, Jan (1982) 'A note on the relation between language and culture: the Pashai case', in *Acta Iranica: Monumentum Georg Morgenstierne, II*, Deuxième Serie, Hommages et Opera Minora, Volume 8 (*Acta Iranica* 22), Leiden: E. J. Brill, pp. 131–40.

—— (1986) 'The construction of ethnic identities: the Nurestani and the Pashai (eastern Afghanistan)', in Erwin Orywal (ed.) *Die ethnischen Gruppen Afghanistans*, Wiesbaden: Reichert Verlag, pp. 239–53.

Radloff, Carla F. (1992) 'Dialects of Shina', in Peter C. Backstrom and Carla C. Radloff (eds.) *Languages of Northern Areas, Sociolinguistic Survey of Northern Pakistan, Volume 2*, Islamabad: National Institute of Pakistan Studies, Quaid-i-Azam University and Summer Institute of Linguistics, pp. 89–203.

—— (1999) *Aspects of the Sound System of Gilgiti Shina*, Islamabad: National Institute of Pakistani Studies, Quaid-i-Azam University and Summer Institute of Linguistics.

Radloff, Carla F. with Shakil, Ahmad Shakil (1998) *Folktales in the Shina of Gilgit (Text, Grammatical Analysis and Commentary)*, Islamabad: National Institute of Pakistan Studies and Summer Institute of Linguistics.

Rajapurohit, B. B. (1983) *Shina Phonetic Reader*, Mysore: Central Institute of Indian Languages.
Ramaswami, N. (1975) *Brokskat Phonetic Reader* Mysore: Central Institute of Indian Languages.
—— (1982) *Brokskat Grammar*, Mysore: Central Institute of Indian Languages.
Rensch, Calvin R. (1992) 'Patterns of language use among the Kohistanis of the Swat Valley', in Rensch et al., pp. 3–62.
Rensch, Calvin R., Decker, Sandra J., and Hallberg, Daniel G. (1992) *Languages of Kohistan, Sociolinguistic Survey of Northern Pakistan, Volume I*, Islamabad: National Institute of Pakistan Studies, Quaid-i-Azam University and Summer Institute of Linguistics.
Schmidt, Ruth Laila (1998a) 'Typology of Shina Pronouns', paper presented at the 15th European Conference on Modern South Asian Studies, Prague, 8–12 September 1998.
—— (1998b) 'Where have the Shina Speakers Come From: Some Linguistic Clues.' Revised ms.
—— and Kohistani, Razwal (1998) 'Páalus /kostyõ/ Shina revisited', *Acta Orientalia* 59:106–49.
Strand, Richard F. (1973) 'Notes on the Nuristani and Dardic Languages', *Journal of the American Oriental Society* 93: 297–305.
Summer Institute of Linguistics (1996) 'Ethnologue' http://www.sil.org/ethnologue/countries/ Afghanistan.
Tikkanen, Bertil (1988) 'On Burushaski and other ancient substrata in northwestern South Asia', *Studia Orientalia* 64: 303–25.
—— (1995) 'Some areal linguistic isoglosses in the transitional zone between Central and South Asia', Paper presented at the Third International Hindukush Cultural Conference, 26–30 September, 1995, Chitral.
Turner, Ralph L. (1927) 'Notes on Dardic', *Bulletin of the School of Oriental Studies* 4: 533–41.
Zoller, Claus Peter, (in preparation) *A Grammar of Indus Kohistani*, to appear in Neuindischen Studien (Heidelberg).

FURTHER READING

Biddulph, J. (1880) *Tribes of the Hindoo Koosh*, Calcutta: Office of the Superintendent of Government Printing (Reprinted (1971) (ed. K. Gratzl), Graz: Akademische Druck u. Verlagsanstatt).
Endresen, R. T. and Kristiansen, Knut (1981) 'Khowar Studies', *Acta Iranica* 21: 210–43.
Fussman, Gerard (1972) *Atlas linguistique des parlers dardes et kafires, Vol. I. Cartes, Vol. II. Commentaire*, Paris: Ecole Française d'Extrême Orient.
Grierson, George Abraham (1906) *The Piśāca Languages of North-Western India*, London: The Royal Asiatic Society.
Jettmar, Karl and Edelberg, Lennart (eds.) (1974) *Cultures of the Hindu Kush* (selected papers from the Hindu-Kush Cultural Conference held at Moesgard 1970), Wiesbaden: Franz Steiner Verlag.
Morgenstierne, Georg (1926) *Report on a Linguistic Mission to Afghanistan*, Oslo: Instittutet for Sammenlignende Kulturforskning, Serie CI-2.
—— (1932) *Report on a Linguistic Mission to Northwestern India*, Oslo: Instituttet for Sammenlignende Kulturforskning.
—— (1975) *Irano-Dardica*, Beiträge zur Iranistik, Band 5, Wiesbaden: Reichert Verlag.
Schmidt, Ruth Laila (1983) 'Shina Speakers of Pakistan and India', in Weekes, Richard V. (ed.) *Muslim Peoples: A World Ethnographic Survey*, Westport: Greenwood Press, pp. 678–84.
Schmidt, Ruth Laila and Koul, Omkar N. with Vijay Kumar Kaul (1983) *Kohistani to Kashmiri: An Annotated Bibliography of Dardic Languages*, Patiala, India: Indian Institute of Language Studies.
Turner, R. L. (1966) *A Comparative Dictionary of the Indo-Aryan Languages*, London: Oxford University Press.

KASHMIRI

Omkar N. Koul

CONTENTS

LIST OF TABLES

1 INTRODUCTION

1.1 Area and speakers

The Kashmiri language is called *kãšur* or *kãšir zabān* by its native speakers. It is primarily spoken in the Kashmir Valley of the state of Jammu and Kashmir in India. According to the 1981 census there are 30,76,398 speakers of the language. The census was not conducted in the year 1991. Keeping in view the rise of the population over subsequent years, the current number of its speakers will be around four million. Kashmiri is also spoken by Kashmiris settled in other parts of India, and other countries. The language spoken in and around Srinagar is regarded as the standard variety. It is used in literature, mass media and education.

1.2 Classification and dialects

There is a general consensus amongst historical linguists that Kashmiri belongs to the Dardic branch of the Indo-Aryan family. Grierson (1919), Morgenstierne (1961) and Fussman (1972) classify Kashmiri under the Dardic group of Indo-Aryan languages. The term Dardic is stated to be only a geographical convention and not a linguistic expression. The classification of Kashmiri and other Dardic languages has been reviewed in some works (Kachru 1969b, Strand 1973, Koul and Schmidt 1984) with different purposes in mind. Kachru points out linguistic characteristics of Kashmiri. Strand presents his observations on Kafir languages. Koul and Schmidt have reviewed the literature on the classification of Dardic languages and have investigated the linguistic characteristics or features of these languages with special reference of Kashmiri and Shina.

Kashmiri is closely related to Shina and some other languages of the Northwest frontier. It also shares some morphological features such as pronominal suffixes with Sindhi and Lahnda. However, Kashmiri is different from all other Indo-Aryan languages in certain phonological, morphological and syntactic features. For example, Kashmiri has a set of central vowels /ɨ, ɨ̄, ə, ə̄/ which are not found in other Indo-Aryan languages. In a similar way, in Kashmiri the finite verb always occurs in the second position except in relative clause constructions. The word order in Kashmiri thus resembles that of German, Dutch, Icelandic, Yiddish and a few other languages. These languages form a distinct set and are currently known as Verb Second (V-2) languages. Note that the word order generated by V-2 languages is quite different from Verb middle languages such as English. In a V-2 language, any constituent of a sentence can precede the verb. It is worth mentioning here that Kashmiri shows several unique features which are different from the abovementioned other V-2 languages.

Kashmiri has two types of dialects: (a) regional dialects and (b) social dialects. Regional dialects are further of two types: (i) those regional dialects or variations which are spoken in the regions inside the valley of Kashmir and (ii) those which are spoken in the regions outside the valley of Kashmir. The Kashmiri speaking area in the valley is ethno-semantically divided into three regions: (1) Maraz (southern and southeastern region), (2) Kamraz (northern and northwestern region) and (3) Srinagar and its neighbouring areas. There are some minor linguistic variations, mainly at the phonological and lexical levels.

Kashmiri spoken in the three regions is not only mutually intelligible but quite homogeneous. These dialectical variations can be termed as different styles of the same speech. Since the Kashmiri, spoken in and around Srinagar, has gained some social prestige, very frequent 'style switching' takes place from Marazi or Kamrazi styles to that of the style of speech spoken in Srinagar and its neighbouring areas. This phenomenon of style switching is very common among the educated speakers of Kashmiri. The Kashmiri spoken in Srinagar and surrounding areas continues to hold the prestige of being the standard variety which is used in mass media and literature.

There are two main regional dialects, namely Poguli and Kashtawari spoken outside the valley of Kashmir (Koul and Schmidt 1984). Poguli is spoken in the Pogul and Paristan valleys bordered on the east by Rambani and Siraji, and on the west by mixed dialects of Lahnda and Pahari. The speakers of Poguli are found mainly to the south, southeast and southwest of Banihal.

Poguli shares many linguistic features including 70% vocabulary with Kashmiri (Koul and Schmidt 1984). Literate Poguli speakers of Pogul and Paristan valleys speak standard Kashmiri as well. Kashtawari is spoken in the Kashtawar valley, lying to the southeast of Kashmir. It is bordered on the south by Bhadarwahi, on the west by Chibbali and Punchi, and on the east by Tibetan speaking region of Zanskar. Kashtawari shares most of the linguistic features of standard Kashmiri, but retains some archaic features which have disappeared from the latter. It shares about 80% vocabulary with Kashmiri (Koul and Schmidt 1984).

No detailed sociolinguistic research work has been conducted to study speech variations of Kashmiri spoken by different communities and speakers who belong to different areas, professions and occupations. In some earlier works beginning with Grierson (1919: 234) distinction has been pointed out in two speech variations of Hindus and Muslims, two major communities who speak Kashmiri natively. Kachru (1969) has used the terms Sanskritized Kashmiri and Persianized Kashmiri to denote the two style differences on the grounds of some variations in pronunciation, morphology and vocabulary common among Hindus and Muslims. It is true that most of the distinct vocabulary used by Hindus is derived from Sanskrit and that used by Muslims is derived from Perso-Arabic sources. The dichotomy of these social dialects is not always clear-cut. One can notice a process of style switching between the speakers of these two dialects in terms of different situations and participants. The frequency of this style switching process between the speakers of these two communities mainly depends on different situations and periods of contact between the participants of the two communities at various social, educational and professional levels. Koul (1986) and Dhar (1984) have presented correlation between certain linguistic and social variations of Kashmiri at different social and regional levels. The sociolinguistic variations of the language deserve a detailed study.

1.3 Script

Various scripts have been used for Kashmiri. The main scripts are Sharda, Devanagari, Roman and Perso-Arabic. The Sharda script, developed around the tenth century, is the oldest script used for Kashmiri. The script was used for writing Sanskrit by the local scholars at that time. It does not represent all the phonetic characteristics of the Kashmiri language. It is now being used for very restricted purposes (for writing horoscopes) by the priestly class of the Kashmiri Pandit community. The Devanagari script with additional diacritical marks has also been used for Kashmiri and continues to be used by writers and researchers in representing the data from Kashmiri texts in their writings in Hindi related to language, literature and culture. It is being used by two journals namely *Koshur Samachar* and *Kshir Bhawani Times* on a regular basis.

A certain amount of inconsistency prevails in the use of diacritic signs. There is scope for its standardization. The Roman script has also been used for Kashmiri but could not become popular. The Perso-Arabic script with additional diacritical marks now known as Kashmiri script has been recognized as the official script for Kashmiri by the Jammu and Kashmir Government and is now widely used in publications in the language. It still lacks standardization (Koul 1996).

2 PHONOLOGY

2.1 Segmentals

The inventory of the distinctive segments of Kashmiri is given in table 23.1. Note that Kashmiri has two short and two long central vowels /ɨ/, /ɨ̄/, /ə/ and /ə̄/ which are not found in other South Asian languages.

TABLE 23.1: KASHMIRI PHONEMES

	Bilabial	Dental	Retroflex	Palatal	Velar	Glottal
Consonants						
Stops						
vl.unasp	*p*	*t*	*ṭ*		*k*	
vl.asp	*ph*	*th*	*ṭh*		*kh*	
vd.unasp	*b*	*d*	*ḍ*		*g*	
Affricates						
vl.unasp		*ts*		*č*		
vl.asp		*tsh*		*čh*		
vd.unasp				*j*		
Nasal	*m*	*n*				
Trill			*r*			
Lateral		*l*				
Fricatives						
vl.		*s*		*š*		*h*
vd.		*z*				
Semi-vowels	*v*		*y*			

Vowels

	Front	Central	Back
High	*i*	*ɨ*	*u*
Lower High	*ī*	*ī̵*	*ū*
Mid	*e, ē*	*ə, ə̄*	*o, ō*
Lower Mid	*a*	*ɔ*	
Low		*ā*	

2.1.1 Vowels

There is a contrast of the position of tongue, height of the tongue and the rounding of lips in the articulation of vowels:

/i/: *(y)imtihān* 'examination', *sir* 'secret', *beni* 'sister'
/ī/: *(y)īd* 'Eid (a Muslim festival)', *sīr* 'brick', *jaldī* 'quickly'
/e/: *reh* 'flame', *tre* 'three'
/ē/: *tsēr* 'late'
/ɨ/: *akɨ̄l* 'wisdom', *gandɨ* 'dirty'
/ī̵/: *ī̵ṭhim* 'eighth', *tī̵r* 'cold'
/ə/: *əčh* 'eye', *gər* 'watch'
/ə̄/: *ə̄s* 'mouth', *phə̄ydɨ* 'profit'
/a/: *az* 'today', *par* 'read', *na* 'no'
/ā/: *ār* 'pity', *gām* 'village', *saphā* 'clean'
/u/: *panun* 'own', *su* 'that/he'
/ū/: *ūtrɨ* 'day before yesterday', *sūd* 'interest'
/o/: *on* 'blind', *son* 'deep'
/ō/: *ōl* 'nest', *sōn* 'our', *valō* 'come (imp)'
/ɔ/: *dɔd* 'milk', *sɔ* 'she'

Nasalization is phonemic in Kashmiri. All the vowels can be nasalized: *p̃tsh* 'a little (fsg)', *kẽh* 'some', *šẽkh* 'conch', *kĩtsh* 'youngest (fsg)', *ə̃z* 'goose', *ə̃ṭ* 'stone of a fruit', *ãgrēz* 'an Englishman', *ãgun* 'compound', *kũz* 'key', *vũ̃ṭh* 'camel', *gõd* 'bouquet', *gõd* 'gum'.

/ə/, /o/, /ē/ do not occur in word-final position, and /i/, /e/, /u/, and /ɔ/ do not occur in word-initial position. Usually /y/ is added in the initial position of the words beginning with /i/, /ī/, /e/ and /ē/. Similarly, /v/ is added to words beginning with /u/, and /ū/. The following are pairs of words in free variation: *irādi/yirādi* 'determination', *ehsān/ yehsān* 'kindness', *ēlān/yēlān* 'announcement', *ujāḍi/vujāḍi* 'deserted', *ũ̃ṭh/vũ̃ṭh* 'camel'. Only some educated persons who are conscious about the original pronunciation of the Hindi-Urdu borrowed words make efforts to pronounce some such words without the semivowel in the word-initial position.

Sequences of vowels do not occur in Kashmiri. Combinations of some segments such as /ui/, /ūi/, and /ōə/ can be treated as diphthongs. Their occurrence is restricted to word-initial and medial positions: *šuir* 'child (fsg)', *gūir* 'milkmaid', *ōəl* 'nest', *gōəl* 'round'.

2.1.2 Consonants

2.1.2.1 Inventory and contrasts

Consonants are classified into different groups on the basis of their manner and place of articulation, as shown in table 23.1. Examples are presented below in phonetic transcription.

Stops
/p/: *pakh* 'walk', *kapur* 'cloth', *pop* 'ripe'
/ph/: *phal* 'fruit', *saphēd* 'white', *pāph* 'sin'
/b/: *bar* 'door', *akhbār* 'newspaper', *nab* 'sky'
/t/: *tarun* 'to cross', *katun* 'to spin', *tot* 'hot'
/th/: *thod* 'tall', *mathun* 'to rub', *sath* 'seven'
/d/: *dər* 'window', *l'odur* 'yellow', *band* 'close'
/ṭ/: *ṭūkir* 'basket', *raṭun* 'to catch', *hoṭ* 'throat'
/ṭh/: *ṭhūl* 'egg', *miṭhāy* 'sweets', *z'ūṭh* 'tall'
/ḍ/: *ḍūn* 'walnut', *ganḍun* 'to tie', *yaḍ* 'belly'
/k/: *kan* 'ear', *kɔkir* 'hen', *tsok* 'sour'
/kh/: *khanun* 'to dig', *khɔkhur* 'hollow', *krakh* 'cry'
/g/: *gardan* 'neck', *gagur* 'rat', *rag* 'vein'

Affricates
/ts/: *tsās* 'cough', *natsun* 'to dance', *sits* 'tailor'
/tsh/: *tshor* 'empty', *gatshun* 'to go', *latsh* 'dust'
/č/: *čōn* 'your', *nečuv* 'son', *koč* 'unripe, raw'
/čh/: *čhān* 'carpenter', *račhun* 'to save', *məčh* 'fly'
/j/: *jān* 'good', *paji* 'baskets', *tāj* 'crown'

Fricatives
/s/: *sath* 'seven', *sasti* 'cheap', *nas* 'nose'
/z/: *zālun* 'to burn', *pazar* 'truth', *az* 'today'
/š/: *šakh* 'suspicion', *kəšīr* 'Kashmir', *paš* 'roof'
/h/: *hos* 'elephant', *bahār* 'spring', *reh* 'flame'

Nasals

/m/: *mas* 'hair', *tsāman* 'cheese', *kam* 'less'
/n/: *nam* 'nail', *anun* 'to bring', *son* 'deep'

Trill

/r/: *raz* 'rope', *narɨm* 'soft', *tār* 'wire'

Lateral

/l/: *lūkh* 'people', *kalam* 'pen', *zāl* 'net'

Semi-vowels

/v/: *van* 'forest', *davun* 'to run', *nāv* 'boat, name'
/y/: *yaḍ* 'belly', *yakhtiyār* 'right', *jāy* 'place'

Palatalization is phonemic in Kashmiri. All non-palatal consonants have palatal counterparts:

pan 'thread' : *p'an* '(they) will fall', *phal* 'fruit': *ph'al* 'boil'
bon 'heap' : *b'on* 'separate'
tal 'under' : *t'al* 'a piece', *thakun* 'to be tired': *th'akun* 'to exaggerate'
dal 'group' : *d'al* 'bark'
həṭ 'piece of wood' : *həṭ'* 'throats', *ṭə̄ṭh* 'dear one (f)' *ṭə̄ṭh'* 'dear ones (mpl)'
bəḍ 'big (fsg)' : *bəḍ'* 'big ones (mpl)'
kath 'story' : *k'ath* 'in (something)', *khav* 'a ditch' : *kh'av* 'ate'
bāgvān 'gardener' : *bāg'vān* 'lucky'
tsal 'run away (imp)' : *ts'al* 'pressure', *tshoṭ* 'short' : *tsh'oṭ* 'polluted'
ə̄m 'unbaked (fsg)' : *ə̄m'* 'unbaked (mpl)'
nūl 'mongoose' : *n'ūl* 'blue'
gə̄s 'gas' : *gə̄s'* 'slothful', *zal* 'urine' : *z'al* 'cream layer'
han 'a piece' : *h'an* 'to be afraid'
mə̄l 'appetite' : *mə̄l'* 'father (erg)'
parun 'to read' : *par'un* 'sieve'
vath 'road' : *v'ath* 'river Vitasta'

2.1.2.2 Phonological changes in loanwords

Voiced aspirated /bh/, /dh/, /ḍh/, /jh/, and /gh/ in Perso-Arabic and Hindi-Urdu borrowed words are deaspirated to /b/, /d/, /ḍ/, /j/, and /g/ respectively in Kashmiri. Similarly, the Perso-Arabic uvular stop /q/ is replaced by /k/, and fricatives /f/, /x/, and /ɣ/ are replaced by /ph/, /kh/, and /g/ respectively. Voiceless unaspirated stops /p/, /t/, /ṭ/, and /k/ in borrowed words are aspirated in word-final position in Kashmiri: Hindi-Urdu *pāp* 'sin', *rāt* 'night', *kōṭ* 'coat', *pāk* 'pure': Kashmiri *pāph*, *rāth*, *kōṭh*, *pākh*.

2.1.2.3 Consonant clusters

Word-initial consonant clusters are not as frequent as word-medial clusters. The second member of an initial cluster is always /r/, and the first consonant is a stop, affricate or fricative. Examples: *prasun* 'to give birth', *phras* 'poplar tree', *bram* 'illusion', *tre* 'three', *drog* 'expensive', *ṭrak* 'truck', *ḍram* 'drum', *krakh* 'cry', *grākh* 'a customer', *tshraṭh* 'mischief', *srod* 'joint', *šrān* 'bath'.

There is a very frequent occurrence of consonant clusters in medial position. Most of these clusters are formed across syllable or morpheme boundaries. Some of them are broken optionally by the insertion of the vowel /i/. There are some restrictions in the formation of consonant clusters, as follows: (i) two aspirated consonants do not combine to form a consonant cluster, (ii) /čh/ is not combined to form a consonant cluster, (iii) /ḍ/ does not occur as the second member of a consonant cluster. Examples of medial clusters are: *kaptān* 'captain', *šabnam* 'dew', *kithkin'* 'how', *adphar* 'fragrance', *taḍpun* 'to suffer in pain', *maktab* 'school', *rangrēz* 'dyer', *ačkan* 'a long button up coat', *khəjlī* 'insult', *tsamṭhun* 'to shrink', *zanti* 'as if', *dušman* 'enemy', *albən'* 'plough', *gurbath* 'poverty', *azmāvun* 'to try', *rəhbar* 'guide'.

There are only a limited number of medial clusters of three consonants possible in Kashmiri. In all such instances the first consonant is /n/: *əndrim* 'internal', *andkār* 'darkness', *bandgī* 'worship', *gənzrun* 'to count'.

There is less frequency of consonant clusters in word-final position. The first member of the consonant cluster is any of the nasals /m, n/ or fricatives /s, š/. The second consonant is any of the stops: *lamp* 'lamp', *amb* 'mango', *dand* 'teeth', *khaṇḍ* 'sugar', *bank* 'bank', *šankh* 'conch', *rang* 'colour', *mast* 'carefree', *gašt* 'round', *kašṭ* 'trouble'.

2.1.2.4 Syllable structure

Kashmiri has a (C)(C)V(C)(C) syllable structure. Vowel-initial syllables are found only in the initial position of the words. The first consonant of a medial cluster is assigned to the preceding syllable and the remaining elements of the unit to the following syllable. In the following examples the syllable boundary is marked with a [+] sign: *nak + ši* 'map', *mən + zil* 'destination', *kis + mat* 'fate'. The assignment of the medial units to syllables does not depend on morphological structure.

2.2 Suprasegmentals

2.2.1 Length

There are seven pairs of short and long vowels. The following minimal pairs illustrate the contrast in the length of these vowels: *sir* 'secret' : *sīr* 'brick', *zen* 'mud' : *zēn* 'win (imp)', *tir* 'a piece of cloth' : *tīr* 'cold', *lər* 'house' : *lə̄r* 'cucumber', *nar* 'male' : *nār* 'fire', *kun* 'alone' : *kūn* 'corner', *son* 'deep' : *sōn* 'our'.

2.2.2 Stress

Stress is not a distinctive feature of Kashmiri. Stress is not in phonemic contrast. Kashmiri being a syllable-timed language, sometimes individual words may be stressed for emphasis only.

2.2.3 Intonation

There are four major types of intonational patterns: (1) high–fall, (2) high–rise, (3) rise-and-fall, (4) mid–level. Intonations have syntactic rather than emotional content.

Statements have high–fall intonation pattern. Intonation peaks are generally positioned on the penultimate word or on the negative particle, if any.

(1) *su čhu kitāb parān*
he is book read-pres
'He is reading a book.'

(2) *palav čhini mēzas peṭh*
clothes are not table-dat on
'The clothes are not on the table.'

Yes-no questions and tag questions have a high–rise intonation.

(3) *su āvā rāth?*
he came-ques ptcle yesterday
'Did he come yesterday?'

(4) *su gav dili, gav nā?*
he went Delhi-abl went neg ques ptcle
'He went to Delhi, didn't he?'

Information questions have rise-and-fall intonation. The rise in intonation is registered on the question word and fall is attained gradually.

(5) *toh' kar gəyivi bāzar?*
you when went market
'When did you go to the market?'

Commands generally follow the mid-level intonational pattern.

(6) *darvāzi kar band*
door do close
'Close the door.'

The contrastive and emphatic intonations are same, as they employ more than the average stress on the constituents of a sentence. The element to be contrasted carries slightly higher stress than the emphasized segment. For example, any of the elements in (7) can be emphasized, depending on the degree of emphasis (emphasis is represented by bold italic).

(7)a ***toh'*** *gətshiv dili*
you go-fut–2p Delhi
'You will go to Delhi.'
 b *toh'* ***gətshiv*** *dili*
 c *toh'* *gətshiv* ***dili***

2.3 Morphophonology

2.3.1 Alternations

There are two types of alternations: (i) alternations between vowel segments, and (ii) alternations between consonant segments. In (i), the vowel of a monosyllabic stem and the second vowel of disyllabic stems undergo changes when inflectional suffixes are added to them. There are three types of vowel changes: (i) lowering of a vowel, (ii) raising of a vowel, and (iii) centralization of a vowel.

/ə/, /ə̄/ and /ū/ of monosyllabic stems are lowered to /a/, /ā/ and /ō/ respectively when a plural forming suffix *-i* or *-i* is added to them: *gər* 'watch'+ *i* : *gari* 'watches', *nər* 'arm' + *i* : *nari* 'arms', *gə̄ḍ* 'fish' + *i* : *gāḍi* 'fish (pl)', *kūr* 'girl' + *i* : *kōri* 'girls'.

/a/ and /ā/ in CVC stems are raised to /ə/ and /ə̄/ respectively when a suffix beginning with -*i* is added to a stem: *kar* 'do' + *iv* : *kəriv* 'do (imp pl)', *nāg* 'spring' + *in* : *nə̄gin* 'small spring'.

The back vowels /u/, /ū/, /o/, and /ō/ change to central vowels /ɨ/, /ɨ̄/, /ə/, and /ə̄'/ respectively when suffixes beginning with -*i*, or -*y* are added to their stems. The addition of *y* results in the palatalization of the final consonant. Examples: *gāṭul* 'wise' + *y* : *gāṭil'* 'wise (pl)', *krūr* 'well' + *y* : *krɨ̄r'* 'wells', *rūn* 'husband' + *y* : *rɨ̄n'* 'husbands', *koṭ* 'boy' + *is* : *kəṭis* 'to the boy', *on* 'blind' + *is* : *ənis* 'to the blind', *mōl* 'father' + *y* : *mə̄l'* 'the father (erg)'

A second vowel /u/ of disyllabic words with the structure CVCVC is changed to the central vowel /a/ when the plural forming suffix -Ø is added: *batukh* 'duck' + Ø : *batakh* 'ducks', *gagur* 'rat' + Ø : *gagar* 'rats', *kɔkur* 'cock' + Ø : *kɔkar* 'ducks', *vātul* 'cobbler' + Ø : *vātal* 'cobblers'.

As a result of adding suffixes to stems, different types of consonant changes as well as some vowel changes take place. Retroflex /ṭ /, /ṭh/ and /ḍ/ occurring in feminine singular stems change to affricates /č/, /čh/ and /j/ respectively, when the plural forming suffix is added to them: *zəṭ* 'rag' + *i* : *zači* 'rags', *mɔṭh* 'handful' + *i* : *mɔčhi* 'handfuls', *bəḍ* 'big (f)' + *i* : *baji* 'big ones'. Word-final dental stops /t/, /th/, /d/ change to affricates /ts/, /tsh/ and fricative /z/ respectively when the feminine forming suffix -Ø is added: masculine *mot* 'mad', *yuth* 'this type', *thod* 'tall' : feminine *məts*, *yitsh*, *thəz*. Velar stops /k/, /kh/ and /g/ change to affricates /č/, /čh/ and retroflex /ḍ/ respectively when the feminine forming suffix Ø is added: masculine *tsok* 'sour', *hokh* 'dry', *lang* 'branch' : feminine *tsoč*, *hoǎh*, *ləṇḍ*. Final /l/ changes to the affricate /j/ as a result of adding the feminine suffix: masculine *kol* 'dumb', *hol* 'twisted': feminine *kəj*, *həj*. Stem-final aspirated voiceless stops are deaspirated when suffixes beginning with vowels are added: *tāph* 'sunny' + *as* : *tāpas* 'in the sun', *sath* 'seven' + *im* : *sətim* 'seventh', *raṭh* 'hold' + *un* : *raṭun* 'to hold'.

2.3.2 Deletion and insertion

2.3.2.1 Deletion

Final /ɨ/ of a CVCV stem is deleted when a vowel-initial suffix is added: *kalɨ* 'head' + *as* : *kalas* 'to the head', *rāmɨ* 'Ram' + *un* : *rāmun* 'Ram's'. /u/, or /ɨ/ in the second syllable of a CVCVC stem is deleted when a vowel-initial suffix is added: *gobur* 'son' + *is* : *gobris* 'to the son', *gɔgɨj* 'turnip' + *i* : *gɔgji* 'to the turnip', *nəgɨr* 'town' + as : *nəgras* 'to the town'.

2.3.2.2 Insertion

/y/ is inserted between a final front vowel of a stem and a suffix beginning with /i/: *khe* 'eat' + *iv* : *kheyiv* 'eat (imp pl)', *di* 'give' + *iv* : *diyiv* 'give (imp pl)'. /v/ is inserted between a stem-final front vowel and a suffix beginning with /a/ : *če* 'drink' + *ān* : *čevān* 'drinking', *di* 'give' + *ān* : *divān* 'giving'. /m/ is inserted between a final front vowel of a verb stem and the suffixes /ɨ/ or /a/ for deriving first person future forms: *ni* 'take' + *ɨ* : *nimɨ* 'I'll take', *khe* 'eat' + *av* : *khemav* 'we'll eat'. In the derivation of compounds, /ɨ/ is added as a linking morpheme between a consonant-final stem and a consonant-initial stem: *nūn* 'salt' + *dən'* 'pot' : *nūnɨdən'* 'salt pot', *čāy* 'tea' + *dən'* 'pot' : *čāyɨdən'* 'tea pot'.

3 NOMINAL MORPHOLOGY

3.1 Introduction

Nouns in Kashmiri follow the traditional classification scheme of (i) proper nouns (human animate, non-human animate and inanimate), and (ii) common nouns (count, mass). Nouns are not formally distinguished for being definite or indefinite. The demonstrative adjectives may optionally be used as a means to indicate definiteness. The forms of *vōl* and genitive phrases modifying a noun also express definiteness. Indefiniteness is expressed either by the use of indefinite numerals or qualifiers or markers. The marking of definiteness or indefiniteness in a noun phrase is not obligatory and can be inferred from the context also. Nouns are inflected for gender, number and case.

3.2 Noun inflection

3.2.1 Gender

Nouns are divided into two classes: masculine and feminine. Animates follow the natural gender system. The gender of a large number of inanimate nouns can be predicted by their endings. Gender formation processes from masculine to feminine or vice versa are irregular. The main gender formation processes involve (i) suffixation, (ii) changes in vowels and consonants, and (iii) suppletion. Most of the phonological and morphological changes are regular.

Derivates with the suffixes *-dār, -dar, -vōl, -ul,* and *-ur* are masculine. As a result of adding of these suffixes certain morphophonemic changes take place. Examples: *dukān* 'shop' : *dukāndār* 'shopkeeper', *ṭhēki* 'contract' : *ṭhēkidar* 'contractor', *dɔd* 'milk' : *dɔdivōl* 'milkman', *gāṭi* 'wisdom' : *gāṭul* 'wise man', *sāl* 'feast' : *sālur* 'guest'.

The following suffixes are added to nouns to form corresponding feminines: *-en', -in', -ɔ̄n', -bāy, -ir.* Examples: masculine *dãdur* 'vegetable seller', *khar* 'an ass', *gujur* 'Gujar', *māstar* 'teacher', *votsh* 'calf': feminine *dãdren', khərin', gujrɔ̄n', māstarbāy, vatshir.* Feminine forms are also derived by palatalization of final consonants, e.g. *on :* ɔn' 'blind', *zon : zən'* 'person'.

Feminine formations involve additional vowel and consonant changes.

(i) /u, ū, o, ō/ in masculine nouns with the structure CVC are diphthongized or replaced by the central vowels at the same height: masculine *šur* 'child', *gūr* 'milkman', *gob* 'heavy', *koṭ* 'boy': feminine *šuir* 'child', *gūər* 'milkwoman', *goəb* 'heavy', *kəṭ* 'girl'.
(ii) Penultimate /u/ of masculine nouns with the structure CVCVC is replaced by /ɨ/: *kōtur* 'pigeon', *kɔkur* 'cock': feminine *kōətɨr, kɔkɨr* 'hen'.
(iii) Word-final consonants /l, k, kh, t, g/ are replaced by /j, č, čh, ts, ḍ/ respectively: *mōl* 'father' : *məj* 'mother', *gāṭul : gāṭij* 'wise', *tsok : tsoč* 'sour', *hokh : hoč h* 'dry', *tot :* *təts* 'hot', *long* 'lame man': *lənḍ* 'lame woman'.

Some feminine nouns present examples of suppletion, as follows: *dãd* 'bull' : *gāv* 'cow', *marɨd* 'man' : *zanān* 'woman', *nečuv* 'son' : *kūr* 'daughter'.

Kashmiri borrows words from Perso-Arabic, Sanskrit, Hindi-Urdu and English. Nativized loans from these languages fall in two genders: masculine and feminine. It is interesting to note that a large number of words borrowed from Hindi-Urdu have different genders from their sources (see for details Koul 1983). A few examples are:

Hindi-Urdu *ādat* (f) 'habit', *kīmat* (f) 'price', *davā* (f) 'medicine', *kismat* (f) 'luck', *tār* (m) 'telegram', *rupayā* (m) 'rupee', *rumāl* (m) 'handkerchief': Kashmiri *ādath* (m), *kīmath* (m), *davā* (m), *kismath* (m), *tār* (f), *rɔpay* (f), *rumāl* (f).

A number of other nouns also have different genders in Hindi-Urdu and Kashmiri. For example, days of a week (except *jumāh* 'Friday') are masculine in Hindi-Urdu, but are feminine in Kashmiri.

3.2.2 Number

There are two numbers: singular and plural. Most count nouns form their plurals from singular form. Some count nouns have the same form for both numbers. Mass nouns do not show number distinction.

Plurals are formed from singulars by suffixation, palatalization and vowel changes. The main rules for the formation of masculine plural forms are as follows:

(i) The mid back vowel /o/ in nouns with the structure CVC changes to a central vowel and the final consonant is palatalized; the high back vowel /u/ and /ū/ remain unchanged: singular *mōl* 'father', *koṭ* 'boy', *kul* 'tree', *gur* 'horse', *ḍūn* 'walnut': plural *məl'*, *kə'*, *kul'*, *gur'*, *ḍūn'*.

(ii) The second vowel of nouns with the structure CVCVC changes to a central vowel and the final consonant is palatalized: singular *gāṭul* 'wise', *latshul* 'broom': plural *gāṭil'*, *latshil'*.

(iii) Penultimate /u/ of nouns with the structure (C)VCVC changes to /a/: singular *gagur* 'mouse', *kōtur* 'pigeon', *ōluv* 'potato': plural *gagar*, *kōtar*, *ōlav*.

(iv) Masculine nouns ending in /i/ do not change in their plural form: *gilāsi* 'glass', *makāni* 'house', *bāni* 'utensil', *nalki* 'tap', *kamri* 'room', *darvāzi* 'door', etc.

(v) Nouns of the shape CVC with a central vowel do not change in their plural form: *khar* 'donkey', *vāl* 'hair', *mām* 'maternal uncle', *sih* 'lion', etc.

(vi) Consonant-final masculine nouns borrowed from Hindi-Urdu and English do not change in their plural form: *bemār* 'sick', *gərīb* 'poor', *mozūr* 'labourer', *hōṭal* 'hotel', *saykal* 'cycle', etc. (They do, however, undergo phonological changes.)

The main rules for the formation of feminine plural forms are as follows:

(vii) The vowel of nouns with the structure CVC(C) is lowered and /i/ is added at the end: singular *nər* 'arm', *dər* 'window', *vəj* 'ring', *kūr* 'girl' : plural *nari*, *dāri*, *vāji*, *kōri*.

(viii) Retroflex /ṭ/, /ṭh/, /ḍ/ change to palatal /č/, /čh/ and /j/ respectively: singular *ləṭ* 'tail', *kuṭh* 'grain store', *lənḍ* 'branch' : plural *lači*, *kučhi*, *lanji*.

(ix) Penultimate /i/ of a CVCVC structure is dropped, with the plural suffix /i/ added (see section 2.3.2.1): singular *gagir* 'rat', *gɔgij* 'turnip' : plural *gagri*, *gɔgji*.

(x) The plural marker /i/ is added to feminine nouns of the form CVC with a low vowel: singular *kath* 'story', *nāv* 'boat', *dɔs* 'wall': plural *kathi*, *nāvi*, *dɔsi*.

(xi) Final /th/ changes to /ts/ and the preceding vowel is raised: singular *rāth* 'night', *zāth* 'caste' : plural *rəts*, *zəts*.

(xii) A few feminine nouns do not change in their plural form, e.g. *əčh* 'eye'.

3.2.3 Case

Case suffixes added to nouns and noun phrases occur as bound morphemes. The case suffixes added to nouns are given in table 23.2. Notice that dative and locative case suffixes are the same. Similarly, the case suffixes of ablative and instrumental are identical. Since they take different postpositions, they have been listed separately. Note that there is a complexity in the masculine singular forms in both ergative and dative cases. Masculine nouns that form their plurals by palatalization (e.g. *mōl* 'father', *māl'* 'fathers') have nominative plural forms homophonous with ergative singular forms. Thus the form *māl'* is used both as a nominative plural and as an ergative singular. Palatalized masculine plural forms also act as a base for forming their corresponding masculine singular dative forms. They use the dative suffix *-is* in place of the regular *-as*. Similarly, the feminine proper nouns that end in *i* take the masculine singular ergative and dative suffix in place of the prescribed *i*. Genitive case suffixes are of two types. The first is identical with the dative form and the second with the ablative. Vocative case suffixes as given above are added to the nouns, which are preceded by various informal vocative markers, given in table 23.3.

3.2.4 Postpositions

There are two major types of postpositions: (a) those which govern the dative case, and (b) those which govern the ablative. There are a few postpositions which govern both. Examples of these postpositions are given below:

(a) postpositions governing the dative case: *peṭh* 'on, upon', *andar* 'in/inside', *manz* 'in', *keth* 'in', *k'uth* 'for', *niši* 'near', *hund/sund* 'of' *sān, sīth'/ sīt'an* 'with, together with'.

(b) postpositions governing the ablative case: *peṭhi* 'from', *əndri* 'from within, from among', *kin'* 'by, owing to', *niši* 'from near', *uk* 'of', un 'of', *sān* 'with', *sīth'/ sīt'in* 'with, by means of'.

TABLE 23.2: CASE SUFFIXES

	Masculine		Feminine	
	sg	pl	sg	pl
Case				
Nominative	-Ø	-Ø	-Ø	-Ø
Dative	-as/-is	-an	-i	-an
Ergative	-an	-av	-i	-av
Locative	-as/is	-an	-i	-an
Ablative	- i	-av	-i	-av
Instrumental	- i	-av	-i	-av
Genitive I	-as	-an	-i	-an
II	- i	-av	-i	-av
Vocative	-ā	-av	-iy	-av

TABLE 23.3: INFORMAL VOCATIVE MARKERS

Masculine		Feminine	
sg	pl	sg	pl
hayā	*hayō*	*hayē*	*hayē*
hatā	*hatō*	*hatay*	*hatay*
hayō	*hayō*	*hɔ̄y*	*hɔ̄y*

The postpositions *sān, niši, sīth'/sīt'an* govern both cases. The meaning of the postposition *sān* in both cases remains unchanged, but the other postpositions change their meanings according to the case they govern.

The role of case suffixes and postpositions is explained in the paradigms of *lədki* 'boy' and *kūr* 'girl', given in table 23.4

Genitive postpositions are like adjectives and they agree with the governing noun in gender, number and case. There are three types of these postpositions. The forms of all the three types are as shown in table 23.5. Type I and II postpositions are governed by the ablative case, and Type III by the dative case. Type I postpositions are used with inanimate nouns: *dukānuk darvāzi* 'the door of the shop', *dukānik'darvāzi* 'the doors of the shop', *dukānič dər* 'the window of the shop', *dukāniči dāri* 'the windows of the shop'. Type II postpositions are used with animate human proper nouns: *mohnun bōy* 'Mohan's brother', *mohnin' bəy* 'Mohan's brothers', *mohnin' beni* 'Mohan's sister', *mohnini beni* 'Mohan's sisters'. Type III postpositions are used with the rest. Notice that /s/ or /h/ is added in the initial position of these postpositions depending on the structure of the subject nouns along with their case suffixes. /h/ is added to the postpositions of all the plurals and feminine singular subject nouns. /s/ is added to the postpositions following singular masculine nouns ending with dative case suffixes. Adding of case suffixes results in certain morphophonemic changes in the stem nouns. Case relations are expressed by the use of case suffixes as well as postpositions which undergo certain changes. Examples of the use of these postpositions are:

kūr + i + und/ind'/inz/inzi = kōri hund/hind'/hinz/hinzi
lədki + as + und/ind'/inz/inzi = lədki sund/sind'/sinz/sinzi

TABLE 23.4: SAMPLE PARADIGMS

	Noun + Marker				
Case	sg	pl	sg	pl	Postposition
Nominative	*lədki*	*lədki*	*kūr*	*kōri*	Ø
Dative	*lədkas*	*lədkan*	*kōri*	*kōren*	(*k'uth*)
Ergative	*lədkan*	*lədkav*	*kōri*	*kōrev*	Ø
Locative	*lədkas*	*lədkan*	*kōri*	*kōren*	*peṭh/niš/tal*
Ablative	*lədki*	*lədkav*	*kōri*	*kōrev*	*peṭhi*
Instrumental	*lədki*	*lədkav*	*kōri*	*kōrev*	*sīth'*
Genitive	*lədki*	*lədkan*	*kōri*	*kōren*	*und/ind'/inz/inzi*
Vocative	*hayā lədkā*	*hayō lədkav*	*hayē kūrī*	*hayē kōrev*	
	'O boy!'	'O boys!'	'O girl!'	'O girls!'	

TABLE 23.5: GENITIVE POSTPOSITIONS

	Masculine		Feminine	
	sg	pl	sg	pl
Type I	*-uk*	*--ik'*	*--ič*	*--iči*
Type II	*-un*	*--in'*	*--in'*	*--ini*
Type III	*-und*	*--ind'*	*--inz*	*--inzi*

bōy + is + und/ind'/inz/inzi = bǝy sund/sind'/sinz/sinzi
kōri + an + und/ind'/inz/inzi = kōren hund/hind'/hinz/hinzi
lǝḍki + an + und/ind'/inz/inzi = lǝḍkan hund/hind'/hinz/hinzi

as in:

(1) a.   *kōri hund bōy* 'girl's brother'   b.   *kōri hind' bǝy* 'girl's brothers'
(2) a.   *kōri hinz kitāb* 'girl's book'   b.   *kōri hinzi kitābi* 'girl's books'
(3) a.   *lǝḍki sund kalam* 'boy's pen'   b.   *lǝḍki sind' kalam* 'boy's pens'
(4) a.   *lǝḍki sinz kursī* 'boy's chair'   b.   *lǝḍki sinzi kursiyi* 'boy's chairs'
(5) a.   *lǝḍkan/kōren hund māṣṭar* 'boys'/girls' teacher'
     b.   *lǝḍkan/kōren hind' māṣṭar* 'boys'/girls' teachers'
(6) a.   *lǝḍkan/kōren hinz māj* 'boys'/girls' mother'
     b.   *lǝḍkan/kōren hinzi māji* 'boys'/girls' mothers'

3.2.5 Pronouns

3.2.5.1 Introduction

Pronouns are inflected for gender, number and case. Pronominals in Kashmiri do not make a distinction between inclusion and exclusion. There is a three-term set of pronouns in Kashmiri. Third person pronouns exhibit a three-term distinction of the participants in speech acts: proximate, remote (within sight) and remote (out of sight). Although the case system of pronouns is essentially the same as that of nouns, pronouns have more case forms than nouns. There are no special indefinite pronouns. Indefiniteness is expressed in different ways: (i) by using the second person pronoun, (ii) by omitting third person pronouns, (iii) by using generic nouns such as *yinsān, manuš* 'man/human', and (iv) by using indefinite quantifiers such as *kãh* 'someone'.

All pronouns are free. They occur in all positions. They can be dropped if they are recoverable from the verb or from the context. Kashmiri has a system of pronominal suffixes/clitics, which are added to the verbs to refer to the subject, object, and indirect object. See Koul and Hook 1984: 123–35, Wali and Koul 1994, Wali and Koul 1997.

Status distinction is indicated by using the plural pronominal forms instead of singular forms. Occasionally, honorific titles *māhrā, haz* and *jināb* 'sir' may also be used after the second person plural form used for honorific singular subjects. The honorific *māhrā* is used with Hindus, *haz* with Muslims and *jināb* is a neutral term used for any person.

3.2.5.2 First, second and third person pronouns

Case forms of first, second and third person pronouns are shown in table 23.6. Notice that there is no gender distinction in the first and second person personal pronouns. Second and third person plural forms are used for honorific singulars as well. There is a two-way distinction in the third person pronouns: within sight and out of sight. The forms of pronouns in the genitive case, agreeing with a modifier in person and number, are shown in table 23.7.

TABLE 23.6: FIRST, SECOND AND THIRD PERSON PRONOUNS

Case	Person	Deixis	Gender and number			
			Masculine		Feminine	
			sg	pl	sg	pl
Nom.						
	First		bɨ	əs'	bɨ	əs'
	Second		tsɨ	toh'	tsɨ	toh'
	Third	Proximate	yi	yim	yi	yimɨ
		Remote 1	hu	hum	hɔ	humɨ
		Remote 2	su	tim	sɔ	timɨ
Dat.						
	First		me	asi	me	asi
	Second		tse	tɔhi	tse	tɔhi
	Third	Proximate	yemis	yiman	yemis	yiman
		Remote 1	homis	human	homis	human
		Remote 2	təmis	timan	təmis	timan
Abl.						
	First		me	asi	me	asi
	Second		tse	tɔhi	tse	tɔhi
	Third	Proximate	yemi	yimav	yemi	yimav
		Remote 1	homi	humav	homi	humav
		Remote 2	tami	timav	tami	timav
Erg.						
	First		me	asi	me	asi
	Second		tse	tɔhi	tse	tɔhi
	Third	Proximate	yem'	yimav	yemi	yimav
		Remote 1	hom'	humav	homi	humav
		Remote 2	təm'	timav	tami	timav

TABLE 23.7: GENITIVE–POSSESSIVE PRONOUN FORMS

Modifier Person	Deixis	Complement Gender and number			
		Masculine		Feminine	
		sg	pl	sg	pl
1sg		m'ōn	mēn'	mēn'	m'āni
1pl		sōn	sə̄n'	sə̄n'	sāni
2sg		čōn	čə̄n'	čə̄n'	čāni
2pl		tuhund	tuhɨnd'	tuhɨnz	tuhɨnzɨ
3sg	Proximate	yem'sund	yem'sɨnd'	yem'sɨnz	yem'sɨnzɨ
3pl	Proximate	yihund	yihɨnd'	yihɨnz	yihanzɨ
3sg	Remote 1	hom'sund	hom'sɨnd'	hom'sɨnz	hom'sɨnzɨ
3pl	Remote 1	huhund	huhɨnd'	huhɨnz	huhɨnzɨ
3sg	Remote 2	təm'sund	təm'sɨnd'	təm'sɨnz	təm'sɨnzɨ
3pl	Remote 2	tihund	tihɨnd'	tihɨnz	tihɨnzɨ

3.2.5.3 Emphatic pronouns

Emphatic forms of pronouns are formed by adding emphatic particle *-iy* to pronouns in all cases. When this particle is added as a suffix to the pronoun, certain phonological changes take place. The emphatic forms in nominative are shown in table 23.8.

3.2.5.4 Demonstrative pronouns

Demonstrative pronouns have the same forms as the personal third person pronouns. There are, however, some additional demonstrative pronouns such as *ti* 'that (out of sight)', which is used with inanimate nouns. Its dative form is *tath*. The demonstrative pronouns are used also as demonstrative adjectives.

3.2.5.5 Relative pronoun

The relative pronoun *yus* 'who, which, that' is inflected for number, gender and case. Forms are shown in table 23.9.

3.2.5.6 Reflexive and reciprocal pronouns

The main reflexive in Kashmiri is *pān* 'self'. The compound form *panun pān'* is comparable to Hindi *apne āp*. The case forms of *pān* are: *pān* (nom), *pānas* (dat), *pāni̇* (abl), *pānan* (erg). In possessive structures, the reflexive form *panun* 'self' is used in place of personal possessive pronouns. The possessive *panun* agrees with the following noun in number and gender as shown in table 23.10. Examples: *panun kul* 'own tree', *pani̇n' kul'* 'own trees', *pani̇n' kəmīz* 'own shirt', *pani̇ni kəmīzi̇* 'own shirts'. Genitive

TABLE 23.8: EMPHATIC PRONOUN FORMS

Person	Deixis	Masculine		Feminine	
		sg	pl	sg	pl
First		*bi̇y*	*əsiy*	*bi̇y*	*əsiy*
Second		*tsi̇y*	*tohiy*	*tsi̇y*	*tohiy*
Third	Proximate	*yihoy*	*yimay*	*yihɔ̄y*	*yimay*
	Remote 1	*hohay*	*humay*	*hɔhɔ̄y*	*humay*
	Remote 2	*suy*	*timay*	*sɔy*	*timay*

TABLE 23.9: RELATIVE PRONOUN FORMS

	Masculine		Feminine	
	sg	pl	sg	pl
Nominative	*yus*	*yim*	*yɔs*	*yimi̇*
Dative	*yemis*	*yiman*	*yemis*	*yiman*
Ablative	*yemi*	*yimav*	*yemi*	*yimav*
Ergative	*yem'*	*yimav*	*yemi*	*yimav*
Genitive	*yem'sund*	*yihund*	*yem'sinz*	*yehnzi̇*

TABLE 23.10: CASE FORMS OF *PANUN*

	Masculine		Feminine	
	sg	pl	sg	pl
Nominative	*panun*	*panɨn'*	*panɨn'*	*panɨni*
Dative	*panɨnis*	*panɨn'an*	*panɨni*	*panɨn'an*
Ablative	*panɨni*	*panɨn'av*	*panɨni*	*panɨn'av*
Ergative	*panɨn'*	*panɨn'av*	*panɨni*	*panɨn'av*
Genitive	*panɨn'sund*	*panɨn'sɨnd'*	*panɨn'sɨnz*	*panɨn'sɨnzɨ*

forms are used in idiomatic contexts only. The emphatic forms are: *pə̄n' pānɨ* 'only by self' and *pānay* 'self'.

The reciprocal form is *akh əkis* 'to one another'. It is a compound of the cardinal *akh* 'one' and its dative case form *əkis*. The distributive form is *pānɨvə̄n'* 'mutual'. The case forms of the reciprocal are as follows: dative *akh əkis*; genitive *akh ək'sund* (msg), *akh ək'sɨnd'* (mpl), *akh ək'sɨnz* (fsg), *akh ək'sɨnzɨ* (fpl). There is no nominative/absolutive form of the reciprocal and the dative form is used where nominative/absolutive is required. Examples:

(1) *lədkav lōy akh əkis*
      boys-erg beat-pst one another
      'The boys beat each other.'

(2) *əs' chi akh ək'sund garɨ gatshān*
      we are each other home go-pres
      'We visit each other's homes.'

3.2.5.7 Interrogative pronouns

There are two main interrogative forms: *kus* 'who' and *k'ā* 'what', the case forms of which are as shown in table 23.11.

TABLE 23.11: INTERROGATIVE PRONOUNS *KUS* 'WHO', *K'Ā* 'WHAT'

	Masculine		Feminine	
	sg	pl	sg	pl
Nominative	*kus*	*kam*	*kɔs*	*kamɨ*
Dative	*kəmis/kas*	*kɨman*	*kəmis/kas*	*kɨman*
Ablative	*kami*	*kɨmav*	*kami*	*kɨmav*
Ergative	*kəm'*	*kɨmav*	*kami*	*kɨmav*
Genitive	*kəm'sund*	*kəm'sɨnd'*	*kəm'sɨnz*	*kəm'sɨnzɨ*
	kɨman hund	*kɨmanhɨnd'*	*kɨman hɨnz*	*kɨman hɨnzɨ*
	kuhund	*kɨhɨnd'*	*kɨhɨnz*	*kɨhɨnzɨ*
Nominative	*k'ā*	*k'ā*	*k'ā*	*k'ā*
Dative	*kath*	*kɨman*	*kath*	*kɨman*
Ablative	*kami*	*kɨmav*	*kami*	*kɨmav*
Genitive	*kam'uk*	*kamik'*	*kamič*	*kamiči*

Other question words also begin with the question element *k*. These include adverbs, qualifiers and interrogative adjectives. The question words are: *kus h'uv* 'which one', *kar* 'when', *k'āzi* 'why', *kati* 'where', *kapər'* 'which direction', *kithɨ kɨn'* 'how, which manner', *kōtāh* 'how much', etc. Some of these have alternative forms as well. Their forms along with related demonstrative forms are as given in table 23.12.

(1) *yeten čha rab*
     here(prox) is mud
     'There is mud over here.'

(2) *hoten čhanɨ rab*
     there(remote-I) is-neg mud
     'There is no mud over there.'

(3) *taten čhunɨ pōn'*
     there(remote-II) is-neg water
     'There is no water over there.'

3.3 Adjectives

There are two types of adjectives: base adjectives and derived adjectives. Derived adjectives are those formed from nominal, verbal and other bases by adding certain suffixes. Examples are shown in table 23.13.

Adjectives can be further divided into two classes: those which are inflected for number, gender and case of the noun they modify and those which are not. To illustrate

TABLE 23.12: PRONOMINAL DERIVATES

	Interrogative	Proximate	Remote (within sight)	Remote (out of sight)
			Demonstrative	
Place	*kati*	*yeti*	*hoti*	*tati*
	katen	*yeten*	*hoten*	*taten*
	katinas	*yetinas*	*hotinas*	*tatinas*
	kateth	*yeteth*	*hoteth*	*tateth*
Direction	*kapər'*	*yapər'*	*hɔpər'*	*tapər'*
Manner	*kithɨ kɨn'*	*yithɨ kɨn'*	*huthɨ kɨn'*	*tithɨ kɨn'*
Quantity	*kūtāh*	*yūtāh*	*hūtāh*	*t'ūtāh*

TABLE 23.13: EXAMPLES OF DERIVED ADJECTIVES

Base	Suffix	Derived form
mal 'dirt'	*ɨ*	*mālɨ* 'dirty'
gulāb 'rose'	*C'*	*gulɔb'* 'pink'
dɔ̄r 'beard'	*al*	*dār'al* 'bearded'
mazi 'taste'	*dār*	*mazidār* 'tasty'
madad 'help'	*gār*	*madadgār* 'helpful'
kɨmat 'price'	*ī*	*kɨmtī* 'expensive'

the first category of adjectives, forms of *n'ūl* 'blue' are given in table 23.14. For example: *n'ūl kōṭh* 'blue coat', *nīl' kōṭh* 'blue coats'; *nīj kəmīz* 'blue shirt', *nīji kəmīzɨ* 'blue shirts'. Other adjectives in this category are: *vɔzul* 'red', *kruhun* 'black', *gāṭul* 'wise', *tshoṭ* 'short, dwarf', *z'ūṭh* 'tall'. Adjectives like *sāph* 'clean', *məlɨ* 'dirty', *jān* 'good', *dānā* 'wise', *sabɨz* 'green', *saphēd* 'white' belong to the second category. For example: *sāph kamrɨ* 'clean room', *sāph palav* 'clean clothes', *sāph dəj* 'clean handkerchief', *sāph daji* 'clean handkerchiefs'.

Adjectives can be either qualitative or quantitative. The former constitutes a large class. All modifiers of quality like different colours (*vɔzul* 'red', *n'ūl* 'blue', *saphēd* 'white', etc.), personal qualities (*čālākh* 'clever', *dānā* 'wise', *buzdil* 'coward', etc.), physical qualities (*thod* 'tall', *tshoṭ* 'short', *v'oṭh* 'fat', *zɔ̄v'ul* 'slim', etc.), qualities of taste (*modur* 'sweet', *tsok* 'sour', *ṭ'oṭh* 'bitter', etc.) fall under this category. The category of quantitative adjectives includes the numerals (cardinals, ordinals, fractions, multiplicatives), intensifiers (*kēh* 'some', *sɔ̄rī* 'all', *seṭhā* 'many, very', *kam* 'little'), demonstrative adjectives (*yūt* 'this much', *t'ūt* 'that much'), and so on. Cardinals from one to five and their corresponding ordinals are given in table 23.15.

Fraction terms are: *oḍ* 'half', *svād* 'one and a quarter', *ḍoḍ* 'one and a half', *ḍāyi* 'two and a half', *sāḍɨ tre* 'three and a half'. Multiplicatives are derivates of the type *dogun* 'two-fold', *trogun* 'three-fold', *tsogun* 'four-fold', and so forth.

4 VERB MORPHOLOGY

4.1 Introduction

Verbs are classified as intransitives, transitives and causatives, with further subclassification such as statives and actives. There is also a special group of verbs that require their subject to be in the dative. Some of these dative verbs have a thematic argument, which is marked nominative.

TABLE 23.14: INFLECTED ADJECTIVE FORMS

	Masculine		Feminine	
	sg	pl	sg	pl
Nominative	*n'ul̀*	*nīl'*	*nīj*	*nīji*
Dative	*nīlis*	*nīlen*	*nīji*	*nījan*
Ablative	*nīli*	*nīl'av*	*nīji*	*nījav*
Ergative	*nīl'*	*nīl'av*	*nīji*	*nījav*

TABLE 23.15: CARDINALS AND ORDINALS

Cardinals	Ordinals
akh 'one'	*əkim* 'first'
zɨ 'two'	*doyim* 'second'
tre 'three'	*treyim* 'third'
tsōr 'four'	*tsūrim* 'fourth'
pā̃tsh 'five'	*pī̃tsim* 'fifth'

4.2 Intransitive verbs

Intransitive verbs, stative or active, have only one argument, namely the subject. The subject of most intransitives is marked with the nominative case across all tenses. A few exceptional intransitives like *natsun* 'to dance', *vadun* 'to cry' take ergative subjects in the past tense:

(1)a *bɨ notsus*　　　　　b *me nots*
　　 I-nom danced-1　　　　 I-erg danced
　　 'I danced.'

(2)　 *təm' vod*
　　 he-erg wept
　　 'He wept.'

4.3 Transitive verbs

Transitive verbs may have two or three arguments. The arguments may be subject, direct object, and indirect object. In the past tense these verbs take ergative case invariably. The verbs which take only a direct object are known as monotransitives, and the verbs which take direct as well as indirect objects are called double or ditransitives. Examples are:

(1)　 *aslaman khev batɨ*
　　 Aslam-erg ate food
　　 'Aslam ate food.'

(2)　 *aslaman d'ut mohnas akhbār*
　　 Aslam-erg gave Mohan-dat newspaper
　　 'Aslam gave a newspaper to Mohan.'

Certain transitive verbs may be derived from intransitive verbs by vowel changes:

intransitive: *tar* 'cross', *mar* 'die', *gal* 'melt', *ḍal* 'move'
transitive: *tār* 'take across', *mār* 'kill', *gāl* 'melt', *ḍāl* 'move'.

4.4 Dative verbs

Dative verbs form a special class, involving what are known as psychological predicates. The subject of these predicates is marked dative in all tenses and aspects. Some of these verbs may also take a second argument, and a so called thematic object. This object is marked nominative. The class mostly comprises verbs of perception, knowledge, belief, mental and physical state, and verbs of desire, etc. Examples are:

(1)　 *təmis ōsnɨ bōznɨ yivān*
　　 he-dat was-neg see-inf-abl come-pres
　　 'He was not able to see.'

(2)　 *mohnas čhu nɨ urdū tagān*
　　 Mohan-dat is neg Urdu know-pres
　　 'Mohan does not know Urdu.'

(3)　 *mohnas čhu bāsān bɨ čhus apuz vanān*
　　 Mohan-dat is believe-pres I-nom am lie tell-pres
　　 'Mohan believes that I am telling a lie.'

(4) *kōri ləj treš*
     girl-dat struck thirst
     'The girl was thirsty.'

4.5 Causative verbs

Causative verbs are formed from intransitive, transitive and ditransitive verbs by a productive process of suffixation. Two causative suffixes, *-āv/-ināv* (called the first causative suffix) and *-ināvināv* (called the second causative suffix) are added before the infinitive marker *-un*. All vowel-final roots and a few consonant-final verb stems take *-āv* as a first causal suffix, while all others take *-ināv*. Some vowel ending stems take either of the two suffixes. The second causative suffix *-ināvināv* is added to all consonant-final verb stems directly; it is added after the first causal suffixes in vowel-final stems. Examples are given in table 23.16. The process of causativization results in certain morphophonemic changes.

There are some verbs which have dual valency. They can be used either transitively or intransitively. Sometimes, the direct object can be dropped to render their corresponding intransitive usage. These verbs are: *parun* 'read, study (in school etc.)', *sõčun* 'to think', *zānun* 'to understand'.

4.6 Inflection of verbs

Verbs are inflected for voice, tense, aspect, mood and person-number-gender. These are briefly discussed below.

4.6.1 Voice

Traditionally there are two voices: active and passive. The passive formation involves changes not only in the verb form, but also in the subject case and addition of explicator/ auxiliary verb. The passive involves the following changes:

(i)   The subject of the active sentence is followed by the compound postposition *-ini/ indi zəriyi* 'by' (*-ini/indi* are the forms of a genitive postposition followed by ablative case),
(ii) The auxiliary/ explicator verb *yun* 'come' is employed, and the passive marker *-ni* is added to the main verb root. The explicator receives the tense-aspect agreement endings. The former object is in the nominative and controls the agreement on *yun*.

TABLE 23.16: CAUSATIVE DERIVATION

Stem	Causative I	Causative II
khe 'eat'	*kh'āv*	*kh'āvināv/kh'āvināvināv*
he 'buy'	*h'āv*	*h'āvināv/h'āvināvināv*
di 'give'	*d'āv*	*d'āvināv/d'āvināvināv*
ni 'take'	*n'āv*	*n'āvināv/d'āvināvināv*
mitsar 'open'	*mitsirāv*	*mitsirāvināv*
āpar 'feed'	*āprāv*	*āpirāvināv*
par 'read'	*parināv*	*parināvināv*

Passive transitive sentences express both the personal passive as well as the capability meaning. The intransitive passive conveys only the capability meaning. Though agents can be dropped in both the constructions, it is more frequently done in the case of personal passive:

(1) *kitāb āyi nɨ parnɨ*
     book came-fsg neg read-pass
     'The book was not read.' or 'The book couldn't be read.'

(2) *tōr āv nɨ gatshnɨ*
     there came neg go-pass
     'No one could go there.'

Only the direct object is sensitive to passivization and indirect objects cannot be passivized.

4.6.2 Tense

4.6.2.1 Present tense

The present indicative tense is formed by using the present form of the auxiliary verb 'be' and the imperfective aspectual marker *-ān*, added to the main verb stem. The auxiliary is placed in the second position and is inflected for number, gender, person and case as shown in table 23.17.

Masculine plural forms of second and third person subjects are used for honorific singulars as well:

(1) *toh' čhiv vakīl*
     you-hon sg are lawyer
     'You are a lawyer.'

(2) *tim čhi dānā*
     he-hon sg is wise
     'He is wise.'

In case the subject noun is in dative case, particular forms of the auxiliary verb 'be' are used (see table 23.17). Note that if the dative verb has a theme, then the verb shows agreement with the theme.

TABLE 23.17: PRESENT AUXILIARY 'BE'

Case	Person	Masculine		Feminine	
		sg	pl	sg	pl
Nominative					
	1	čhus	čhi	čhas	čha
	2	čhukh	čhiv	čhakh	čhavɨ
	3	čhu	čhi	čha	čha
Dative					
	1/3	čhu	čhi	čha	čha
	2sg	čhuy	čhiy	čhay	čhay
	2pl/hon	čhuvɨ	čhivɨ	čhavɨ	čhavɨ

4.6.2.2 Past tense

Morphologically, the past tense has three forms: proximate/simple, indefinite and remote. Proximate past forms are derived by means of the infix -*v/y*. The indefinite and remote past are formed by adding the suffixes to the verb stem, noted in the second and third lines respectively of table 23.18. The addition incurs certain morphophonemic changes in the verb stem.

Note that in the past, the subject of transitives and a few exceptional intransitives is marked ergative and the direct object, which may be animate or inanimate, takes nominative case. Transitive verbs agree with the absolutive object in gender and number. In case the subject is first or third person, forms of the verbs agreeing with the object in gender and number as illustrated by the examples in table 23.19.

In Kashmiri the second person is a highly marked category. The verb obligatorily inflects for second person pronominal suffixes. In the past tense the second person ergative subject marks the verb with -*th/ov* (sg/pl), in contrast to first and third person. These second person suffixes of the subject follow the gender number suffixes of the absolutive object. The personal suffixes given in table 23.20 are added to the inflected forms given above for first and third person forms to derive the second person singular forms shown. The suffixes in (i) are added to consonant-final verb forms, those in (ii) to vowel-final verb forms. The suffix -*vɨ* is added to the inflected forms given above for first and third person forms to derive the second person plural subject forms as shown. These forms are used for honorific singulars as well.

Most intransitive verbs, with the few exceptions noted below, agree in person, gender and number with the subject, which is in the nominative case. Some intransitives

TABLE 23.18: PAST TENSE AFFIXES

Person	Masculine		Feminine	
	sg	pl	sg	pl
1/3	-*v*	-*yi*	-*yi*	-*yi*
	-*yōv*	-*ēyi*	-*ēyi*	-*ēyi*
	-*ēyōv-*	-*ēyēyi*	-*ēyēyi*	-*ēyēyi*
2sg	-*yōth*	-*ēyath*	-*ēyath*	-*ēyath*
	-*yēyōth*	-*ēyath*	-*ēyath*	-*ēyath*
2pl	-*yōvɨ*	-*ēyvɨ*	-*ēyvɨ*	-*ēyvɨ*
	-*ēyōvɨ*	-*ēyēyvɨ*	-*ēyēyvɨ*	-*ēyēyvɨ*

TABLE 23.19: FIRST AND THIRD PERSON VERB–OBJECT AGREEMENT

Verb	Masculine		Feminine	
	sg	pl	sg	pl
par 'read'	*por*	*pər'*	*pər*	*pari*
čhal 'wash'	*čhol*	*čhəl'*	*čhəj*	*čhaji*
an 'bring'	*on*	*ən'*	*ən'*	*ani*
khe 'eat'	*khev*	*kheyi*	*kheyi*	*kheyi*
ni 'take'	*n'uv*	*niyi*	*niyi*	*niyi*

TABLE 23.20: SECOND PERSON SUFFIXES AND FORMS

	Masculine		Feminine	
	sg	pl	sg	pl
(i)	*-uth*	*-ith*	*- ɨth*	*-ath*
(ii)	*-ōth*	*-yath*	*-yath*	*-yath*
Singular subject				
	poruth	*pərith*	*pərith*	*par'ath*
	čholuth	*čhəlith*	*čhəjith*	*čhajath*
	onuth	*ənith*	*ənith*	*an'ath*
	kh'ōth	*kheyath*	*kheyath*	*kheyath*
	n'ūth	*niyath*	*niyath*	*niyath*
Plural subject				
	porvɨ	*pərivɨ*	*pərivɨ*	*parivɨ*
	čholvɨ	*čhəlivɨ*	*čhəjivɨ*	*čhajivɨ*
	onvɨ	*ənivɨ*	*ənivɨ*	*anivɨ*
	kh'ōvɨ	*kheyvɨ*	*kheyivɨ*	*kheyɨvɨ*
	n'uvɨ	*niyivɨ*	*niyivɨ*	*niyivɨ*

undergo transitive type morphophonemic changes, others do not change. The forms of the intransitive verbs used with the first person subject are illustrated in table 23.21. In case the subject is second person non-honorific singular, the suffixes *kh* (msg), *ivɨ* (mpl), *akh* (fsg), *ivɨ* (fpl) are added to verb stems to derive forms examples of which are also given in table 23.21.

Exceptional intransitives like *asun* 'to laugh', *natsun* 'to dance' and *vadun* 'weep', mark their subject in ergative case and show neutral agreement. The forms are given in table 23.22.

Morphologically, past tense is subclassified according to the degree of remoteness also. There are two degrees of remoteness: Remote I and Remote II. These are indicated

TABLE 23.21: INTRANSITIVE PAST FORMS

Subject Verb	Masculine		Feminine	
	sg	pl	sg	pl
First person				
gatsh 'go'	*gōs*	*gəyi*	*gəyas*	*gəyi*
yi 'come'	*ās*	*āyi*	*āyas*	*āyi*
pak 'walk'	*pokus*	*pək'*	*pəčis*	*pači*
vas 'descend'	*vothus*	*vəth'*	*vətshɨs*	*vatshɨ*
khas 'climb'	*khotus*	*khət'*	*khətsɨs*	*khət'*
Second person non-honorific				
	gōkh	*gəyivɨ*	*gəyakh*	*gəyivɨ*
	ākh	*āyivɨ*	*āyakh*	*āyivɨ*
	pokukh	*pəkivɨ*	*pəčikh*	*pačivɨ*
	vothukh	*vəthivɨ*	*vətshɨkh*	*vatshɨvɨ*
	khotukh	*khətivɨ*	*khətsɨkh*	*khatsɨvɨ*

TABLE 23.22: EXCEPTIONAL INTRANSITIVES

Subject	Verb	Masculine		Feminine	
		sg	pl	sg	pl
	asun				
1/3		*os*	*os*	*os*	*os*
2		*osuth*	*osɨvɨ*	*osuth*	*osɨvɨ*
	vadun				
1/3		*vod*	*vod*	*vod*	*vod*
2		*voduth*	*voduvɨ*	*voduth*	*voduvɨ*
	natsun				
1/3		*nots*	*nots*	*nots*	*nots*
2		*notsuth*	*notsɨvɨ*	*notsuth*	*notsɨvɨ*

by adding suffixes to the verb roots agreeing with the object in gender and number, and with the subject in the second person as shown in table 23.23. Adding of the above suffixes result in different morphophonemic changes. Examples of their use are:

(1) *me par'ōv/parēyōv akhbār*
     I-erg read-Remote-I/Remote-II newspaper
     'I had read the newspaper.'

(2) *tse par'ōth/parēyōth mazmūn*
     you-erg read-Remote-I/Remote-II essay
     'You had read an essay.'

Notice that Remote II forms are different for masculine singulars only in the case of certain verbs.

The suffixes given in table 23.24 are added to intransitive verbs in the simple past for deriving their remote forms.

TABLE 23.23: REMOTE PAST

	Masculine		Feminine	
	sg	pl	sg	pl
1/3	*par'ōv*	*parēyi*	*parēyi*	*parēyi*
	parēyōv	*parēyāyi*	*parēyāyi*	*parēyāyi*
	niyōv	*niyēyi*	*niyēyi*	*niyēyi*
	niyēyōv	*niyēyāyi*	*niyēyāyi*	*niyēyāyi*
2sg	*par'ōth*	*parēyath*	*parēyath*	*parēyath*
	parēyōth	*parēyath*	*parēyath*	*parēyath*
	niyōth	*niyēyath*	*niyēyath*	*niyēyath*
	niyēyōth	*niyēyath*	*niyēyath*	*niyēyath*
2pl	*par'ōvɨ*	*parēyvɨ*	*parēyvɨ*	*parēyvɨ*
	parēyōvɨ	*parēyēyvɨ*	*parēyēyvɨ*	*parēyēyvɨ*
	niyōvɨ	*niyēyvɨ*	*niyēyvɨ*	*niyēyvɨ*
	niyēyōvɨ	*niyēyvɨ*	*niyēyvɨ*	*niyēyvɨ*

TABLE 23.24: INTRANSITIVE REMOTE PAST SUFFIXES

	Masculine		Feminine	
Person	sg	pl	sg	pl
1	-yōs	-ēyi	-ēyas	-ēyi
	-ēyōs	-ēyēyi	-ēyēyas	-ēyēyi
2	-yōkh	-ēyvi	-ēyakh	-ēyvi
	-yēyōkh	-ēyvi	-ēyakh	-ēyvi
3	-yōv	-ēyi	-ēyi	-ēyi
	-ēyōv	-ēyēyi	-ēyēyi	-ēyēyi

4.6.2.3 Future tense

The future tense is formed by adding two types of suffixes: (i) agreeing with the subject in person and number, and (ii) agreeing with the subject in person and number and with the object in number. Gender distinctions are absent in both types. Suffixes of type (1) differ according to whether the consonant ending verb stem ends in a consonant or a vowel. The future suffixes are shown in table 23.25. Since the subject noun can be indicated by the suffixes, it can be optionally dropped. In that case the word order of the sentence undergoes a change as exemplified below.

(1) *tsi parakh dəh kitābi > dəh kitābi parakh*
     you read-fut ten books
     'You will read ten books.'

     tsi vučhakh philim > philim vučhakh
     you see-fut film
     'You will watch a film.'

Future tense is used to indicate not only future time but also probability. Morphologically, future is neither subdivided according to degree of remoteness nor

TABLE 23.25: FUTURE SUFFIXES

	Person	Singular	Plural
Type (i)			
Consonant-final stem			
	1	-i	-av
	2	-akh	-iv
	3	-i	-an
Vowel-final stem			
	1	-mi	-mav
	2	-kh	-yiv
	3	-yi	-n
Type (ii)			
	1sg	-an	-akh
	1pl	-ihōn	-ihōkh
	2sg	-ihɔn	-ihɔkh
	2pl	-ihūn	-ihūkh
	3sg	-yas	-yakh
	3pl	-inas	-inakh

does it have any modal or aspectual value. The future perfect is formed by using the past participial form of the main verb and the future form of the auxiliary verb 'be'.

4.6.3 Aspect

4.6.3.1 Perfective

The perfective is formed by the use of auxiliary verbs and by adding the following suffixes to the past inflected forms of the main verb stems agreeing with the object in gender and number in case of transitive verbs, and with the subject in case of intransitive verbs: *-mut* (msg), *-mit'* (mpl), *-mits* (fsg), *-matsi* (fpl). The perfective occurs in three tenses: present perfect, past perfect and future perfect, marked by present, past and future copular forms respectively. The present, past and future forms of the copular verb in the ergative case are as shown in table 23.26. The subject noun/pronoun is used in ergative case. The perfective can be used with present, past and future reference. It can be used to indicate a situation which has taken place previously leading to the present and to indicate the result of a past situation.

4.6.3.2 Imperfective

The imperfective aspect marker *-ān* is added to the main verb stems and the auxiliary verb is inflected for tense, gender, number, person and case. The imperfective aspect reflects progressive present, universal habitual act. Stative verbs can also be used in the imperfective.

4.6.3.3 Progressive

The progressive aspect is expressed by the aspect marker *-ān* added to the main verb stem. The auxiliary verb is inflected for the tense, gender, number, person and case markers. Notice that the aspect markers for progressive and imperfect aspect are identical.

TABLE 23.26: COPULAR VERB IN THE ERGATIVE CASE

Tense	Person	Masculine		Feminine	
		sg	pl	sg	pl
Present					
	1/3	čhu	čhi	čha	čha
	2sg	čhuth	čhith	čhath	čhath
	2pl	čhuvɨ	čhivɨ	čhavɨ	čhavɨ
Past					
	1/3	ōs	ɔ̄s'	ɔ̄s	āsɨ
	2sg	ōsuth	ɔ̄sith	ɔ̄sith	āsath
	2pl	ōsivɨ	ɔ̄sivɨ	ɔ̄sɨv	āsivɨ
Future					
	1/3	āsi	āsan	āsi	āsan
	2sg	āseth	āsnath	āseth	āsnath
	2pl	āsivɨ	āsɨnav	āsivɨ	āsɨnav

(1)   *aslam čhu kitāb parān*
      Aslam is book read-prog
      'Aslam is reading a book.'

The progressive is used for active verbs alone. Stative verbs are not used in the progressive.

Kashmiri makes a distinction between regular and intermittent habituality (frequentatives). Frequentatives are expressed by compound verb constructions involving perfective or imperfective aspect:

main verb: stem + imperfect *-ān*   explicator: *ās* 'be' + imperfect *-ān*

For example,

(2)   *sɔ čha asān āsān*
      she is laugh-imperf be-imperf
      'She laughs frequently.'

There are no special aspect markers to express simultaneous aspect. This is expressed by using participial forms as adverbs of the matrix verb. The participial forms are duplicated:

(3)   *aslam čhu asān asān kathɨ karān*
      Aslam is laugh-prog laugh-prog talk do-prog
      'Aslam talks smilingly.'

The aspectual system is subject to certain formal and grammatical constraints. The aspectual imperfective/progressive markers are suffixed to the verb stems. The copular verb 'be' is inflected for tense, person, gender and number. The inflected forms of perfective are derived as a result of adding a perfective $\emptyset$ marker to the verb stems. Wherever main verbs and explicators are used, there are co-restrictions on their use. There are other restrictions on grammatical and semantic grounds on the combinations of various aspectual combinations. For example, the following combinations will result in ungrammatical sentences: habitual + completive, completive + iterative, progressive + stative verbs, durative + iterative.

4.6.4 Mood

Mood is associated with the manner of action indicated by the verb. Moods can be expressed by means of modal verbs and/or auxiliaries. There is no special marking for the indicative mood. It is obligatorily present in simple declarative sentences. It contrasts with other moods such as imperative, and conditional, which are overtly marked.

The conditional markers are added to the auxiliary stem *ās* 'be'. In the absence of the auxiliary they are added to the main verb. The markers are used along with the aspectual forms of main verbs. The conditional markers are as shown in table 23.27, agreeing with the subject in person and number in case of subjectival constructions using intransitive verbs, and also with the object in objectival constructions using transitive verbs (Koul 1987: 37). Examples (1) and (2) respectively illustrate the conditional with and without the auxiliary *ās* 'be'.

(1)   *bɨ āsɨhə gōmut*
      I be-cond go-past ptcpl
      'I would have gone'

TABLE 23.27: CONDITIONAL MARKERS

Person	Masculine		Feminine	
	sg	pl	sg	pl
1	*-ihɔ̄*	*-ihɔ̄v*	*-ihē*	*-ihɔ̄n*
2	*-ihɔ̄kh*	*-ihīv*	*-ihēth*	*-ihēvi*
3	*-ihē*	*-ihɔ̄n*	*-ihē*	*-ihēn*

(2) *bi parihɔ̄ kitāb magar . . .*
    I read-cond book but
    'I would have read the book but . . .'

Notice that conditional imperfect/perfect/progressive sentences can be formed without adding the conditional markers to the copular verb, but the sentences become ambiguous between the conditional and the future meaning:

(3) *su āsi kitāb lēkhān*
    he be-cond book write-imperf
    'He may /will be writing a book.'

4.7 Non-finite verb forms

Non-finite verb forms are of two types: infinitives and participles. It should be noted here that the non-finite verbal forms are not sensitive to tense, voice, aspect and mood. The past and present participial forms maintain their aspectual reference.

4.7.1 Infinitives

Infinitives are derived by means of the marker *-un* added to the verb stem. Stems ending in vowels undergo certain morphophonemic changes. The infinitive marker agrees with the gender and number of intransitive subjects and transitive objects just in case they are in the nominative case. The infinitive does not agree with the oblique arguments. The forms of the marker are shown in table 23.28.

TABLE 23.28: INFINITIVES

	Masculine		Feminine	
	sg	pl	sg	pl
Marker	*-un*	*-in'*	*-in'*	*-ini*
Verb				
par-	*parun*	*parin'*	*parin'*	*parini*
vuch-	*vuchun*	*vuchin'*	*vuchin'*	*vuchini*
di-	*d'un*	*din'*	*din'*	*dini*
pe-	*p'on*	*pen'*	*pen'*	*peni*

4.7.2 Participles

4.7.2.1 Present participle

The present participle is marked by the suffix *-ān* added to the verb stem. A glide *v* is inserted if the stem ends in a vowel. The participle does not inflect for gender and number. These markers are carried by the auxiliary, which always accompanies the participle in the root clause: *lēkh + ān = lēkhān, če + vān = čevān*.

4.7.2.2 Perfect participle

The perfect participle is marked by the various forms of the suffix *-mut*. It is used to form present, past and future perfect forms of the verb. The marker agrees with the intransitive nominative subject, and with the nominative transitive direct object. Examples are given in table 23.29.

4.7.2.3 Conjunctive participle

The conjunctive takes the suffix *-ith*. The suffix stays invariant, unlike the past participle and the infinitive. The negative conjunctive participle is formed with the negative *nay* 'not/without'. The conjunctive participle functions as an adverbial clause and is used to express an act that precedes the main clause act:

> *təm' čeyi čāy akhbār pərith*
> he-erg drank tea newspaper read-cp
> 'He drank tea after reading the newspaper.'

5 ADVERBS

Adverbs may be classified into the following groups: (a) basic adverbs, (b) derived adverbs, (c) phrasal adverbs, (d) reduplicated adverbs, (d) particles. Basic adverbs are either lexical items like *az* 'today', *hamēši* 'always' or noun/adjective adverbs. Derived adverbs, such as locatives and directional, are formed by adding certain adverbial suffixes to the base form of the demonstrative, relative, correlative and interrogative pronouns.

Locative adverbs are marked by suffixes such as *-ti/-ten/-tinas*: *yeti/yeten/yetinas* 'here', *hoti/hoten/hotinas* 'there', *tati/taten/tatinas* 'there', *kati/katen/katinas* 'where (inter)'. Directional adverbs are marked by the suffix *-pər'*: *yepər'* 'in this direction', *hopər'* 'in that direction' (Remote I), *tapər'* 'in that direction' (Remote II), *kapər'* 'in which direction

TABLE 23.29: PERFECT PARTICIPLE

Masculine		Feminine	
sg	pl	sg	pl
pormut	*pər'mit'*	*pərmits*	*parimatsi*
l'ūkhmut	*līkh'mit'*	*līčhmits*	*lēčhimatsi*
du'tmut	*dit'mit'*	*ditsmits*	*ditsimatsi*
čōmut	*čemit'*	*čemits*	*čemitsi*

(inter)'. Manner adverbs are formed by adding the suffixes *-thikin'/-pǝth'*: *yithikin'/ yithipǝth'* 'in this manner', *huthikin'/huthipǝth'* 'in that manner' (Remote I), *tithikin'/ tithipǝth'* 'in that manner' (Remote II), *kithikin'/kithipǝth'* 'in which manner (inter)'.

Phrasal adverbs are formed by adding a simple or a compound postposition to a noun. For example:

(1)   *treyi reti pati*
      three-obl month-obl after
      'after three months'

(2)   *parni brõh*
      read-inf-obl before
      'before reading'

(3)   *dukānas pati kani*
      shop-dat back side
      'in the back of the shop'

Adverbs are reduplicated for showing intensity and distribution; for example, *tēz tēz* 'fast', *vāri vāri* 'slow', *kot kot* 'where', *kar kar* 'when', *kuni kuni* 'sometimes'. Reduplicated adverbs may be separated by the negative particles *nati* as in the phrases *kuni nati kuni vizi* 'sometime or other'. This type of adverbial expresses indefiniteness.

The emphatic particle *-iy* (*yōt*) can co-occur with an adverb or a noun to render adverbial reading: *vakhitiy yōt* 'only/merely time', *aslamiy yōt* 'only Aslam', etc.

Various overt cases and postpositions such as dative, locative, ablative and instrumental are employed with a noun to render adverbial reading. For example, *subihas* 'in the morning', *dēvāras peth* 'on the wall', *gari pethi* 'from the house', *šrāpiči sīt'* 'with the knife'.

Adverbs may also be grouped by their functional use:

(a)   time/duration: *az* 'today', *rāth* 'yesterday', *subihan* 'in the morning'
(b)   place or direction: *andar* 'in/inside', *nebar* 'out/outside'
(c)   manner: *āsǝnī sān* 'easily', *vāri vāri* 'slowly'
(d)   reason: *gǝrībī kin'* 'because of poverty', *kamzūrī kin'* 'because of weakness'
(e)   instrument: *kalmi sīt'* 'with a pen', *šrāpči sīt'* 'with a knife'
(f)   purpose: *parni khǝtri* 'for reading', *kāmi khǝtri* 'for work'
(g)   comitative adverbs: *X -as sit'* 'with/in the company of X'
(h)   degree/intensity: *sethā* 'very', *kǝphī* 'enough', *khāl kǝ̃h* 'hardly any', *lagbag* 'approximately'.

Note that adverbs may be placed in preverbal or postverbal position in a simple clause:

(4)a *su čhu pakān vāri vāri*
      he is walk-pres slowly
   b *su čhu vāri vāri pakān*
      he is slowly walk-pres
      'He walks slowly.'

6 SYNTAX

In this section various phrases and sentence types are described. Phrases are described as constituents of different sentences.

6.1 Phrases

There are four major types of phrases in Kashmiri: (a) noun phrase, (b) adjective phrase, (c) adverb phrase, and (d) postpositional phrase. The structure of these phrases is described below.

6.1.1 Noun phrases

A simple noun phrase may consist of a noun, pronoun or a non-finite sentential clause. A complex noun phrase may consist of relative clauses or adverbial clauses. A noun phrase may function as subject, object or indirect object. It also occurs as a complement of a postposition or as a predicate nominal of a copula.

There are no articles in Kashmiri. However, a demonstrative pronoun does at times function as a definite article. There is also an indefinite article suffix -āl/-āh. A noun phrase is modified by an adjective, or a relative clause. Some examples are:.

(1) Definite: *hu ləḍki* 'that boy'
(2) Indefinite: *akh ləḍkāh* (one boy-indef) 'some boy'
(3) Adjective + Noun: *nəv kitāb* 'new book'
(4) Relative clause + Noun: *yus kōṭh tse h'otuth su ...*
                              rel coat you-erg bought that
                              'the coat which you bought that...'

6.1.2 Adjective phrases

An adjective phrase is part of a noun phrase. The adjective phrase may consist of an adjective itself or may expand as a relative clause:

(1) *yi bəḍ kitāb*
    'this big book'

(2) *hum tre bəḍ' mez*
    'those three big tables'

(3) *yɔs kitāb tami ən' sɔ ...*
    rel book she-erg me-dat brought-fsg that-fsg
    'The book which she brought that ...'

Adjectives may be modified by adverbs:

(4) *yi čhu seṭhā boḍ kul*
    this is very big tree
    'This is a very big tree.'

6.1.3 Adverbial phrases

Adverbial phrases may consist of simple or derived adverbs, postpositional phrases, or a string of adverbs as exemplified below:

(1) *šur čhu tēz dōrān*
    child is fast run-pres ptcpl
    'The child runs very fast.'

(2) *su čhu seṭhā zōri zōri kathi karān*
he is very loud loud talk make-pres ptcpl
'He talks very loudly.'

6.1.4 Postpositional phrases

A postpositional phrase consists of a noun phrase followed by a postposition. Postpositions can be divided into three types: postpositions that require a dative case in their noun phrase, postpositions that require an ablative case, and those that require no case. Postpositional phrases usually function as adverbs. Examples:

(1) *kitāb čha mēzas peṭh*
book is table-dat on
'The book is on the table.'

(2) *tavliyā čha bālṭīnas manz*
towel is bucket-dat in
'The towel is in the bucket.'

(3) *me ən' nəv' palav šuren kith'*
I brought new clothes children-dat for
'I brought new clothes for children.'

(4) *su āv gari peṭhi*
he came home-abl from
'He came from his home.'

It is worth noting here that certain postpositions such as *-nay, varəy, badli* 'without/instead' modify verbs and infinitives:

(5) *su čhu srān karinay daphtar gatshān*
he is bath do-without office go-pres ptcpl
'He goes to the office without taking his bath.'

(6) *su āv vāpas čiṭh' hāvinay*
he came back letter show-without
'He came back without showing the letter.'

6.2 Sentence types

This section describes simple, complex and compound sentence types. Major simple sentence types are: copular, declarative, imperative and interrogative. Complex constructions involve subordinate clause(s). The formation of compound sentence is only through coordination.

6.2.1 Simple constructions

6.2.1.1 Copular sentences

The verb *āsun* 'to be' is employed in copular sentences. The copula may take a predicate noun, predicate adjective, or a predicate adverb as a complement. Examples:

(1)   *su čhu ḍākṭar*
       he is doctor
       'He is a doctor.'

(2)   *sɔ čha zīṭh*
       she is tall
       'She is tall.'

(3)   *təm'sɨnz āvāz čha mədɨr*
       his/her voice is sweet
       'His/Her voice is sweet.'

The copula verb is obligatorily retained in both affirmative and negative sentences. In the case of coordinate structures, it is optionally deleted under identity. Examples:

(4)   *mohnɨ čhu vakīl /* mohnɨ vakīl*
       Mohan is lawyer
       'Mohan is a lawyer.'

(5)   *aslam čhu nɨ ḍākṭar /* aslam nɨ ḍākṭar*
       Aslam is not doctor
       'Aslam is not a doctor.'

(6)a   *aslam tɨ mohnɨ čhi ḍākṭar*
       'Aslam and Mohan are doctors.'
   b   *aslam čhu ḍākṭar tɨ mohnɨ ti*
       Aslam is doctor and Mohan also
       'Aslam is a doctor and so is Mohan.'
   c   *na čhu aslam vəkīl tɨ na mohnɨ*
       not is Aslam lawyer and not Mohan
       'Neither Aslam nor Mohan is a lawyer.'

The copula is used for universal truths, existence, definition, identity, etc.:

(7)   *khɔdā čhu*
       God is
       'God exists.'

(8)   *nəsīb čhu panun panun*
       luck is self self
       'One is born with his/her own luck.'

(9)   *poz čhu pazān*
       truth is revealed
       'The truth (eventually) comes out.' or 'The truth cannot be hidden.'

The copula verb always takes a complement. Sentence (7) can be interpreted as:

(10)   *khɔdā čhu poz/mūjūd/prath jāyi*
       'God is true/present/everywhere.'

In (7) the complement does not appear at the surface and is understood as *poz* 'true', *mūjūd* 'present', *prath jāyi* 'everywhere'.

The copula is also used as a member in the compound verb sequence *ās* 'be' + *khasun/gatshun/sapdun* 'climb/go/become' which renders the meaning of 'to become':

(11) *azkal čhu siriyi jalɨd khasān*
nowadays is sun quick climb-pres ptcpl
'The sun rises early in the morning these days.'

(12) *dɔh khɔtɨ dɔh čhu gatshān vakhɨt krūṭh*
day more day is go-pres ptcpl time difficult
'The time is becoming difficult day by day.'

(13) *azkal čha sapdān sulī anigaṭɨ*
nowadays is becoming early dark
'It becomes dark early (in the evening) these days.'

6.2.1.2 Declarative sentences

In declaratives the finite predicate (auxiliary or a verb) occupies the second position. The first position is usually occupied by a subject, but it may also be occupied by other constituents of the sentence best known as topic in a V-2 language.

(1)a *aslaman dits kitāb mohnas rāmɨni khɘtrɨ rāth gari*
Aslam-erg gave-fsg book Mohan-dat Ram-dat for yesterday home-abl
'Aslam gave Mohan a book for Ram yesterday at home.'
b *mohnas dits aslaman kitāb rāmɨni khɘtrɨ rāth gari*
c *rāth dits aslaman gari kitāb mohnas rāmɨni khɘtrɨ*
d *gari dits aslaman rāth mohnas kitāb rāmɨni khɘtrɨ*

As shown, the constituents following the predicate show a considerable freedom of movement.

Declarative sentences can be grouped into three categories on the basis of the classification of verbs: intransitive, transitive and dative. The subjects may be realized as agents, experiencers (i.e., dative subjects), themes (i.e., passive subjects) or expletive forms. The subjects of most transitives and a few intransitives are marked ergative in the past tense. The subjects are marked dative in the context of a dative predicate. All other subjects are marked nominative.

(2) *mohnɨ āv rāth*
Mohan came yesterday
'Mohan came yesterday.'

(3) *mohnan d'ut nɘsīmas kalam*
Mohan-erg gave Nasim-dat pen
'Mohan gave a pen to Nasim.'

(4) *me ākh tsɨ pasand*
I-dat came you-nom like
'I liked you.'

(5) *palav āyi nɨ mīnɨni zɘriyi čhalnɨ*
clothers came-pass neg Meena by wash-inf
'The clothes were not washed by Meena.'

(6) *kitāb pɘrɨm*
book read-sg
'I read a book.'

(7)   *kitāb ditsnas*
      book gave-3sg
      'He gave her/him a book.'

Note that a few intransitives such as *asun* 'to laugh', *vadun* 'to weep', *laḍun* 'to quarrel' take ergative subjects in the past tense (for details of their forms see Koul 1987: 43–4):

(8)   *me/asi/təm'/tami/timav os/vod/loḍ*
      I/we/he/she/they-erg laughed/wept/quarrelled
      'I/we/he/she/they laughed/wept/quarrelled.'

(9)   *tse osuth/voduth/loḍuth*
      you-sg-erg laughed/wept/quarrelled

(10) *tɔhi osuvi/vodivi /loḍivi*
      you-pl-erg laughed/wept/quarrelled

The intransitive verb natsun 'to dance' takes an ergative as well as a nominative subject:

(11)a *bi notsus*
       I-nom danced-1sg
    b *əs' nəts'*
       we-nom danced
    c *me/asi/təm'/tami nots*
       I/we/he/she-erg danced
       'I/we/he/she danced.'

A transitive direct object may also be overt or 'pro' form. In the perfective the direct object is marked with nominative case. In the non-perfective the case of the pronominal direct object is decided by person hierarchy.

(12) *səlīman roṭus bi*
      Salim-erg caught me-abl sg
      'Salim caught me.'

Perfective 'pro' object:

(13) *səlīman roṭus*
      Salim-erg caught-1sg
      'Salim caught me.'

Direct object in the nominative:

(14)a *bi čhusath tsi parināvān*
       I am you teach-pres ptcpl
       'I am teaching you.'
    b *parināvān čhusath*

(15)a *bi čhusan su parināvān*
       I am he teach-pres ptcpl
       'I am teaching him.'
    b *parināvān čhusan*

(16)a *tsi čhuhan su parināvān*
       you are he teach-pres ptcpl
       'You are teaching him.'
    b *parināvān čhuhan*

Direct object in the dative:

(17)a *su čhu me parināvān*
     he is me teach-pres ptcpl
     'He is teaching me.'
  b *parināvān čhum*

(18)a *su čhu təmis parināvān*
     he is him-dat teach-pres ptcpl
     'He is teaching him/her.'
  b *parināvān čhus*

The indirect object is always marked dative. The verb inflects for first and third person only if pronouns are not overtly present. The verb obligatorily inflects for the second person pronoun, which may be optionally deleted.

(19) *təm' d'ut me/təmis akhbār*
    he-erg gave me-dat/him-dat newspaper
    'He gave me/him a newspaper.'

(20) *akhbār d'utnam/d'utnas*
    newspaper gave-1sg psfx-1sg psfx/gave-3sg psfx-3sg psfx
    'He gave me/him a newspaper.'

It is worth mentioning here that weather expressions in Kashmiri fall into two categories. The first type does not have any expletive subject as in:

(21) *rūd p'av*
    rain fell
    'It rained.'

The second type carries the third person singular pronominal suffix *-n* on the verb.

(22) Regular weather expression   Alternative form
     obur khot   *obur khoru-n*
     clouds rose   clouds rose-3sg
     'It has clouded over.'   'X has raised the clouds.'

Note that the third singular suffix *-n* is also found in some other expressions such as natural processes, natural forces, expressions of health etc.

6.2.1.3 Imperative sentences

The basic imperative is expressed in the unmarked form. There is also a polite form known as precative. Both forms inflect for number. The plural forms are used to express honorific status. The unmarked form is expressed by the verb stem itself. Imperative forms are given in table 23.30. For example:

(1) *čiṭh' par/pəriv*
    letter read/read
    'Read the letter.'

(2) *šuris di/diyiv miṭhəy*
    child-dat give sweets
    'Give sweets to the child.'

TABLE 23.30: IMPERATIVES

Verb stem	Addressee	
	Singular	Plural/honorific
par 'read'	*par*	*pəriv*
an 'bring'	*an*	*əniv*
di 'give'	*di*	*diyiv*
khe 'eat'	*khe*	*kheyiv*

TABLE 23.31: PRONOMINAL SUFFIXES

Subject 2nd person	Object (dative) 1st person		3rd person	
	sg	pl	sg	pl
sg	*-um*	—	*-us*	*-ukh*
pl	*-v'ūm*	—	*-v'ūs*	*-hūkh*

In the above examples the imperative is preceded by a topic element. The verb may stand alone if it is flanked by pronominal objects. The presence of the pronominal objects is indicated by the pronominal suffixes shown in table 23.31. Examples:

(4)a *hāvum*
    show-1sg psfx
    'Show me.'
  b *həv'ūm*
    show-1sg psfx
    'Please show me.'

The polite imperative is expressed by the precative suffix *-ti/-tav* (sg/pl) as in

(5)a *čiṭh' parti*
    letter read
    'Read the letter.'
  b *čiṭh' pər'tav*
    letter read
    'Please read the letter.'

The obligative imperative, which expresses moral obligation, and duties, is formed by means of the suffix *-izi/-izev* (sg/pl) as in

(6) *čiṭh' līkhizi/līkhizev*
     letter write/please write
     'You should write a letter.'

(7) *poz vən'zi/vən'zev*
     truth say
     'You should tell the truth.'

The imperative may be negated by means of the particles *mi* and *mati*. The particle precedes the verb and may be inflected by the precative marker *t* as in

(8) *pōš mɨ tsaṭh*
flowers not pluck
'Don't pluck the flowers.'

(9) *tsēr matɨ kartɨ*
delay not do
'Don't be late.'

6.2.1.4 Interrogative sentences

Two types of interrogative sentences will be discussed: (a) yes-no questions, and (b) question word questions.

Yes-no questions fall into three major categories: (i) neutral, (ii) leading and (iii) alternative questions depending on the answer sought by the interrogator. Neutral yes-no questions are generally marked by the question marker *ā*, added to the finite predicate at the end of all inflections.

(1) *mohnan līčhā čiṭh'?*
Mohan-erg wrote-ques letter
'Did Mohan write a letter?'

An optional question marker *k'ā* may also be added to these constructions. *k'ā* usually occurs in sentence-initial position and throws the verb into third position:

(2) *(k'ā) tsɨ lēkhɨkhā az čiṭh'?*
you write-fut today letter
'Will you write the letter today?'

Kashmiri maintains its verb second order in yes-no questions, provided *k'ā* is not counted as the first element. Most V-2 languages do not allow verb second order in such constructions.

The negative marker precedes the question marker:

(3) *tsɨ yikh nā pagāh daphtar?*
you come-fut neg-ques tomorrow office
'Won't you come to office tomorrow?'

The prohibitive imperative marker *mɨ* is placed in the preverbal position and is attached to the question marker *ā*.

(4)a *tsɨ mɨ gatsh pagāh bāzar*
you neg-ques go-fut tomorrow market
'Don't go to the market tomorrow.'

  b *tsɨ mā gatshakh pagāh bāzar?*
you neg-ques go-fut tomorrow market
'Are you going to go to the market tomorrow?'

(5)a *tsɨ nērakh nɨ az*
you leave-fut not today
'You will not leave today.'

  b *(k'ā) tsɨ nērakh nā az?*
ques you leave-fut not-ques today
'Won't you leave today?'

(6)a *tsɨ mɨ nēr az*
  you not leave-fut today
  'Don't leave today.'
 b *(k'ā) tsɨ mā nērakh az?*
  (ques) you neg-ques leave-fut today
  'Aren't you leaving today?'

Leading questions are followed by a negative tag if the expected answer is positive. If the expected answer is negative, the main statement is expressed in the negative form and the tag takes the positive shape.

(7)a *az čha garmī, čha nā?*
  today is hot is neg-ques
  'It is hot today, isn't it?'
 b *ā az čha garmī*
  yes today is hot
  'Yes, it is hot today.'

(8)a *az čha nɨ garmī, čhā?*
  today is neg hot is-ques
  'It is not hot today, is it?'
 b *na az čha nɨ (garmī)*
  no today is not
  'No it is not (hot).'

In alternative questions, a special marker *kinɨ* is placed between the alternative elements, and the verb is suffixed with *-ā*:

(9) *tsɨ yikhā az kinɨ pagāh?*
  you come-fut-ques today or tomorrow
  'Will you come today or tomorrow?'

(10) *tsɨ gatshkhā daphtar kinɨ nɨ?*
  you go-fut-ques office or neg
  'Will you go to the office or not?'

Alternative questions can be used in finite subordinate clauses, which results in the placement of the verb at the end of the clause:

(11) *me čhu nɨ patā (zi/ki) su čeyā dɔd yā na*
  I be not know that he drink-fut-ques milk or not
  'I don't know whether he will take milk (or not).'

In question word questions, question words such as *kus* 'who', *k'ā* 'what', *k'āzi* 'why' are placed immediately before the finite predicate. Question words may be immediately preceded by a subject or other sentence constituents. Note that no constituent can be placed between a question word and the predicate/verb. The question word may be preceded by one constituent only. All the constituents of a sentence may be questioned:

(12)a *mohnan kəmis līčh čiṭh' rāth daphtaras manz?*
  Mohan-erg who-dat wrote letter yesterday office-dat in
  'Who did mohan write a letter to in the office yesterday?'
 b *kəm' līčh čiṭh' rāth daphtaras manz?*
  who-erg wrote letter yesterday office in
  'Who wrote a letter yesterday in the office?'

In order to question more than one constituent two types of strategies are employed. In the first type all the question words are moved before the finite predicate:

(13)a *mohnan kəmis k'ā d'ut bāgas manz?*
Mohan-erg who-dat what gave garden-dat in
  b *kəm' kəmis k'ā d'ut bāgas manz?*
who-erg who-dat what gave garden-dat in

In the second type the question words may be left *in situ*. However, it is obligatory to move at least one question word before the finite predicate:

(14) *kəm' kəmis k'ā dits bāgas manz?*
who-erg who-dat what gave garden-dat in
'Who gave what to whom in the garden?'

Multiple reduplicated question words are used in a distributive sense. These follow the single word question word question pattern. The paired elements are always treated as a single unit.

(15) *doyimi vəriyi kus kus yiyi yōr?*
next year-abl who who come-fut here
'Next year who will come here?'

(16) *mohnan k'ā k'ā h'ot šuren hindi khə̄tri?*
Mohan-erg what what bought children for
'What are the items Mohan bought for his children?'

(17) *dili kɔs kɔs jāy vučhivi tɔhi?*
Delhi-abl which which place saw you-erg
'Which places did you see in Delhi?'

6.2.1.5 Minor sentence types

Apart from the above-mentioned four types of simple sentences, some minor sentence constructions may be of exclamatory, vocative and interjection types. Exclamatory sentences are marked by strong intonation or are preceded by exclamatory question words as exemplified below.

(1) *az kōtāh jān dɔh čhu!*
today how good day is
'What a pleasant day it is!'

(2) *kə̄tsāh šərīph kūr!*
how-fsg gentle girl
'What a gentle girl!'

(3) *vāh k'ā bə̄th!*
oh what song
'What a song it is!'

Vocative expressions consist of address terms as follows:

(4) *hayō nazīrā!*
oh-msg Nazir-voc
'O Nazir!'

(5) *hayē kūrī!*
     oh-fsg girl-voc
     'O girl!'

(6) *hē dōstā/bāyā/bəy səbā/ṭāṭh'ā*
     oh-msg friend/brother/brother-hon/ dear one
     'O friend/brother/dear one!'

Interjections are usually one-word emotive utterences which express surprise, delight, etc. The expressions are: *ah, ahā, oh, šābāš, vāh vāh,* etc.

6.2.2 Complex and compound constructions

6.2.2.1 Complex sentences

Complex sentences are formed with the help of one or more subordinate clauses, which may be either finite or non-finite. Finite and non-finite subordinate clauses are described below. Some of the complex constructions involving relative and adverbial clauses are also discussed.

Finite subordinate clauses are linked to the main clause by the subordinator *zi/ki*, which follows the main verb. The word order in a finite subordinate clause follows the root clause V-2 pattern.

(1)a *me čhu patā ki/zi təm' h'ot nov kōṭh bāzri*
       I-dat is knowledge that he-erg bought new coat market
    b *me čhu patā ki/zi bāzri h'ot təm' nov kōṭh*
       I-dat is knowledge that market-dat bought he new coat
       'I know that he bought a new coat in the market.'

The elements of the subordinate may not be moved to the main clause:

(1)c * *me čhu patā təm' ki/zi h'ot bāzri nov kōṭh*
    d * *me čhu patā təm' ki/zi bāzri h'ot nov kōṭh*

Finite subordinate clauses may be subjects, objects, or complements of predicates.
   Non-finite subordinate clauses in the infinitive also function as subjects and objects. The infinitive is inflected for gender, number and case and is placed in final position. Infinitival object complements omit the subject of the embedded clause, which is the same as the matrix subject.

(2) *bi čhus yatshān mohnas samkhun*
     I am want-pres Mohan-dat meet-inf
     'I want to see Mohan.'

The subject is marked possessive just in case the infinitive is nominalized:

(3) *təm'sund dili gatshun čhu mumkin*
     his Delhi go-inf is possible
     'His going to Delhi is possible.'

Question words with the infinitive, and non-finites in general, have a scope over the entire sentence and form a direct question. All overt elements of the infinitival clause may be questioned.

(4)a *kəmis gəyi səlīmas kitāb din' məšith?*
who-dat did Salim-dat book give-inf forgot-past ptcpl
 b *səlīmas kəmis gəyi kitāb din' məšith?*
Salim-dat who-dat was book give-inf forget-past ptcpl
'Who did Salim forget to give the book to?'

6.2.2.2 Relative sentences

Relative clauses may be finite or non-finite; finite clauses may be correlative or headed type. Relative sentences with finite clauses are marked by the relative pronoun *yus* and the correlative *su*, which decline for gender, number and case and show different forms for animate and inanimate nouns.

(1) *yɔs kūr dili čha rōzān sɔ čha zǝvij*
rel girl Delhi-abl is live-pres cor is slim
'The girl who lives in Delhi is slim.'

(2) *dili (manz) rōzan vājen' kūr čha zǝvij*
Delhi-dat in live-inf agn girl is very slim
'The girl who lives in Delhi is very slim.'

In the correlative type, the matrix clause follows the relative clause. The head noun usually follows the relative clause but it may also occupy other positions, as shown below.

(3)a *yɔs kūr tse pasand čhay sɔ kūr čha me ti pasand*
rel girl you-dat like is cor girl is me too like
 b *[yɔs kūr tse pasand čhay] me ti čha sɔ kūr pasand*
rel girl you like is me also is she girl like
'The girl who you like, I like her too.'

In the headed relative the head noun immediately precedes the relative clause. In both the correlative and the headed clause, pronouns may be followed by a full lexical noun, as exemplified below.

(4)a *sɔ kūr [yɔs tse pasand čhay] čha me ti pasand*
cor girl rel you-to like is is me-to also like
'The girl who you like, I like her too.'
 b *[yɔs kūr tse pasand čhay] sɔ čha me ti pasand*
rel girl you-dat like is cor girl is me too like

All the constituents of a sentence can be relativized in both headed and correlative type relative clauses.

In a non-finite relative clause, the verb is marked with the present participle *vun* or the past participle *mut*; see table 23.32. Both the participles inflect for gender and number. The non-finite form can be used only for subjects. Examples:

(5) *vuphɨvun kāv*
fly-pres ptcpl crow
'the crow which is flying'

(6) *pašas peṭh khotmut naphar*
roof-dat on climb-past ptcpl person
'the person who climbed the roof'

TABLE 23.32: RELATIVE CLAUSE PARTICIPLES

	[Present participle]		[Past participle]	
	Masculine	Feminine	Masculine	Feminine
Singular	*-vun*	*-vɨn'*	*-mut*	*-mɨts*
Plural	*-vɨn'*	*-vɨni'*	*-mɨt'*	*-mɨtsɨ*

TABLE 23.33: ADVERBIAL TIME CLAUSE RELATIVE AND CORRELATIVE TERMS

yeli	*teli*	'when ... then'
yeli yeli	*teli teli*	'whenever'
yanɨ peṭhɨ	*tanɨ peṭhɨ*	'since'
yān'	*tān'*	'as soon as'
yuthuy	*tithuy*	'as soon as ... that very time'
yotām	*totām*	'as long as'
yami sātɨ	*tami sātɨ*	'the moment'

An agentive suffix *vōl* is used to form nouns of agency. The suffix varies with gender and number: *vōl* (msg), *vəl'* (mpl), *vājen* (fsg), *vājini* (fpl). For example,

(7) [*jemi rōzan vōl*] *l ədkɨ čhu m'ōn dōst*
Jammu-abl live-agn-msg boy is my friend
'The boy who lives in Jammu is my friend.'

6.2.2.3 Adverbial clauses

Adverbial clauses may be either finite or non-finite. Finite adverbial clauses may be placed before or after a main clause. An adverbial clause places the verb in the final position. Main clauses maintain verb second order.

Finite adverbial clauses of time are marked with relative clause time markers, as shown in table 23.33. For example,

(1) *yeli bɨ čhus gatshān teli čhu su ti gatshān*
when I am go-pres then is he too go-pres
'When I go, (then) he goes too.'

(2) *yanɨ su yōr āv tanɨ čhi əs' yikɨvaṭɨ kə̄m karān*
since he here came from are we together work doing
'Since he came here, (from that period) we work together.'

It is important to note that the time markers *yeli* or *yenɨ* do not undergo deletion though the correlative markers *teli*, *tanɨ* may do so optionally.

Participial constructions also act as time adverbials:

(3) *su āv dōrān*
he came run-pres ptcpl
'He came running.'

(4) *təm' prutsh kursii peṭh bihith*
he-erg asked chair-obl on sit-past ptcpl
'He asked (while) sitting on the chair.'

(5) *gari vətith kor tami ṭelīphōn*
home reach-past ptcpl did she-erg telephone
'She telephoned after reaching home.'

A present participle expresses an ongoing action or a process. It takes progressive aspect in the subordinate clause.

(6)a *su āv tami sāti yemi sāti su dōrān ōs*
he came at that time when he run-pres ptcpl was
'He came at that time when he was running.'

　b *su āv dōrān dōrān*
'He came (while) running.'

A verbal noun followed by *brōh* 'before', *pati* 'after', *peṭh* 'on' results in the reading of a time adverbial.

(7) *təm' sindi yini brōh yiyi ni kāh*
he-gen-obl come-inf-obl before come-fut-neg none
'No one will come before he comes.'

(8) *təm' si ndi nērni pati gatshi bi*
he-gen-obl departure after go-fut I
'I'll go after his departure.'

Manner adverbial clauses usually employ relative-like participial constructions. The finite manner markers are *yithikin'*, *yithipəṭh'* 'as/which way':

(9)a *yithikin' bi vanay tithikin' kar*
as-rel I tell-you the same way-cor do
'Do as I tell you.'

The word order of the relative manner clause and correlative manner clause can be altered:

(9)b *tithikin' kar yithikin' bi vanay*

Participial constructions express a manner:

(10) *su āv vadān vadān*
he came weep-pres ptcpl weep-pres ptcpl
'He came (while) crying.'

(11) *təm' vod kursī peṭh bihith*
he-erg wept chair-obl on sit-past ptcpl
'He cried (while) sitting on the cot.'

The negativized participial form is formed by adding *ni* + *varəy* :

(12) *təm' von asni varəy*
he-erg said laugh-pm. without
'He said without smiling.'

Sentences of infinitival/gerundive construction also express manner:.

(13) *təm' sund natsun čhu me pasand*
(s)he-gen dance-inf is I-dat like
'I like his/her dance.'

Purpose may be expressed in two ways: (a) infinitival form followed by the ablative marker *i* or the oblique form plus the postposition *khətri/bapath* 'for' and (b) the particles *tik'āzi* 'because' and *amikin* 'therefore'. Consider the following examples:

(14)a *su gav nāṭak vuchini*
    he went play see-inf-abl for
  b *su gav nāṭak vuchni khətri /bāpath*
    he went play see-inf-abl for
    'He went to see a play.'

Notice that in (14a) the ablative marker *i* is added to the infinitive form of the verb which expresses the meaning of 'for'. In (14b) the ablative marker *-i* is added before the postposition *khətri/bāpath* 'for'. In the above construction, there is an option between the two. In case the verb is not a motion verb, the use of ablative marker and the postposition is obligatory:

(15)a *me von təmis kitāb parni khətri /bāpath*
    I-erg said him book read-inf-abl for
    'I told him to read the book.'
  b **me von təmis kitāb parni*

The coreferential phrases *tik'āzi* 'because' and *amikin'* 'therefore' can also be used. Cause is expressed by means of finite clauses marked by *tik'āzi* 'because':

(16) *tik'āzi az ōs garim amikin' gōs ni bi bāzar*
    because today was hot therefore went not market
    'Because it was hot, I couldn't go to the market.'

The cause and effect clauses can be used in interchangeable order:

(17)a *su heki ni pərith tik'āzi su chu muḍi*
    he able not read-past ptcpl because he is illiterate
    'He cannot read, because he is illiterate.'
  b *tik'āzi su chu muḍi su heki ni pərith*
    'Because he is illiterate, he cannot read.'

A cause can be expressed by reduplicated present, past and conjunctive participles:

(18') *pakān pakān thok su ti b'ūth pathar*
    walk-pres ptcpl walk-pres ptcpl tired he and sat down
    'Because of walking (constantly), he was tired and sat down.'

(19) *bi ās prōr' prōr' tang*
    I came wait-past ptcpl wait-past ptcpl sick
    'I got sick of waiting.'

(20) *davā khethiy gav su ṭhīkh*
    medicine eat-conjt ptcpl-empht went he alright
    'Immediately on taking medicine, he recovered (from illness).'

Cause can be expressed by means of an infinitive followed by the postposition *sīt'* 'with':

(21) *šur' sindi yini sīt' gəyi sərī khəš*
    child-obl gen come-inf-obl with went all happy
    'Because of the arrival of the child, all were happy.'

Conditional clauses are marked by the conjunction *agar* 'if':

(22)a *agar rūd peyi, teli bani jān phasɨl*
    if rain fall-fut then get good crop
    'If it rains, then the crops will be good.'

The sequence of 'if–then' clause can be reversed:

(22)b *teli bani jān phasal agar rūd peyi*
    'The crop will be good if it rains.'

The conjunction marker *natɨ* 'otherwise' also is used in conditional clauses:

(23) *pagāh yizi jalɨd natɨ gatshɨ bɨ kunuy zon*
    tomorrow come-modal-imp soon otherwise go-fut I alone
    'Come early tomorrow, otherwise I will go alone.'

A concession clause is marked by subordinate conjunction markers such as *agarči/ yodvay* 'although', *hargāh ... tōti* 'even if', *k'āzi ... nɨ* 'why not':

(24) *agarči/hargāh sɔ seṭhā əmīr čha, tōti čha kanjūs*
    although she very rich is still is miser
    'Although she is very rich, she is a miser.'

(25) *su k'āzi kari nɨ me zārɨpārɨ, bɨ gatshɨ nɨ tōr*
    he why do not me beg I go-fut not there
    'Even if he begs me, I'll not go to his home.'

A result clause is marked by an oblique infinitive followed by the postposition *ki vajāh*. In a sentence sequence, the cause is usually given in the first sentence which is followed by another giving the result of it. The second sentence is marked by a phrase *ami kin'* 'therefore'.

(26) *rūd penɨ ki vajāh h'ōkus nɨ bɨ bāzar gətshith*
    rain fall-inf-obl reasonable-1sg not I market go-past ptcpl
    'I could not go to market because of the rain.'

(27) *rāth ōs jān mūsim, ami kin' gōs bɨ čakras*
    yesterday was good weather therefore went-1sg I walk-dat
    'It was a fine weather yesterday, therefore I went for a walk.'

6.2.2.4 Coordination

Sentence coordination is marked mainly by the morphemes *tɨ* 'and', and *magar* 'but':

(1) *bɨ gōs dili tɨ m'ōn dōs gav jom*
    I went Delhi and my friend went Jammu
    'I went to Delhi and my friend went to Jammu.'

(2) *sohnɨ gav tuhund gari magar toh' əsivɨ nɨ gari*
    Sohan went your home but you were not home-abl
    'Sohan went to your home but you were not at home.'

The conjunction marker *tɨ* 'and' can optionally be followed by another morpheme, *ti* 'also':

(3) *aslam gatshi pagāh dili ti mohni ti gatshi*
     Aslam go-fut tomorrow Delhi and Mohan also go-fut
     'Aslam will go to Delhi tomorrow and Mohan will also go.'

The alternative conjunction morphemes *yā ... yā* 'either ... or' are used as in:

(4) *yā peyī az rūd yā peyi az šīn*
     or fall-fut today rain or fall-fut today snow
     'Either it rains today or it will snow.'

Note that the word order of the constituent sentences undergoes a change. The verb is placed immediately after the coordinators. Compare (4) with the source sentences

(4)a *az peyi rūd*   (4)b *az peyi šīn*
     'It will rain today.'   'It will snow today.'

ti 'and' is used to conjoin two or more sentences or phrases. The conjunction morpheme occurs before the last conjunct.

(5) *aslam čhu kitāb parān ti nazīr čhu čith' lēkhān*
     Aslam is book reading and Nazir is letter writing
     'Aslam is reading a book and Nazir is writing a letter.'

(6) *rāji čha g'avān, umā čha natsān ti ušā čha asān*
     Raja is singing Uma is dancing and Usha is laughing
     'Raja is singing, Uma is dancing, and Usha is laughing.'

The misplacement of coordination conjunction morpheme *ti* results in ungrammatical sentences:

(5)a * *ti aslam čhu kitāb parān nazīr čhu čith' lēkhān*

(6)a * *rāji čha g'avān ti umā čha natsān ušā čha asān*

Coordination does not merely involve juxtaposition of two or more independent sentences. There are various syntactic and semantic constraints on the construction of coordinate structures. In general, coordinate sentences express contrast, cumulative effect, cause and effect, sequential action, etc. The order of the conjuncts is interchangeable if a coordinate sentence expresses contrast or cumulative effect. Consider the following examples of various types of coordinate structures.

(7)a *yi ləḍki čhu dānā ti hu ləḍki čhu bēkil*
      this boy is intelligent and that boy is stupid
      'This boy is intelligent and that boy is stupid.'
   b *hu ləḍki čhu bēkil ti yi ləḍki čhu dānā*
      'That boy is stupid and this boy is intelligent.'

(8)a *su čhu varziš karān ti sāras gatshān*
      he is exercise do-pres and walk-dat go-pres
      'He exercises and goes for a walk.'
   b *su čhu sāras gatshān ti varziš karān*

(9)a *tsūras ləj gūl' ti su gave zakhmī*
      thief struck bullet and he was injured
      'The thief was hit by a bullet and he was injured.'

b *tsūr gav zakhmī tɨ təmis ləj gūl'
'The thief was injured and he was hit by a bullet.'

(10)a toh' vučhiv jān kūr ti kəriv nēthɨr'
you see-fut good girl and do marriage
'You find a good girl and get married.'
   b * toh' kəriv nēthɨr tɨ vučhiv jān kūr
'You get married and find a good girl.'

Notice that (7) and (8) permit the reverse order, but (9) and (10) do not. The coordinate sentences (9a) and (10a) can be paraphrased to indicate that they are related with the subordination process as well.

(9)b tsūr gav gūl' lagnɨ sɨt' zakhmī
thief was bullet hit-inf-abl with injured
'The thief was injured by a bullet.'

(10)b jān kūr vučhith kəriv toh' nēthɨr
good girl find-past ptcpl do you marriage
'Please find a good girl and get married.'

In the above sentences the cause and effect, sequential action and contingency are expressed without using the conjunction morphemes. The paraphrases indicate that the first conjuncts of sentences represent adverbial complements of the second conjuncts.
   The conjunction morpheme tɨ sometimes fulfils the function of a disjunction as well. (7) can be paraphrased by using the conjunction morpheme magar 'but' as in:

(7c) yi ləḍkɨ čhu gāṭul magar hu ləḍkɨ čhu bēkɨl
'This boy is intelligent but that boy is stupid.'

Besides conjoining sentences, the coordinating conjunction marker tɨ can be used to coordinate nouns (subjects, direct and indirect objects), verbs, adjectives and adverbs. The coordination of two noun phrases yields a plural noun phrase and therefore the verb agreement is affected. In case of coordinate subjects, the verb takes a masculine plural concord, whereas in the case of coordinate objects, the verb agrees with the nearest object.

(11)a me het' tsū̃ṭh' tɨ tsērɨ
I-erg bought-mpl apples-m and apricots-f
'I bought apples and apricots.'
   b me hetsɨ tsērɨ tɨ tsū̃ṭh'
I-erg bought-fpl apricots and apples
'I bought apricots and apples.'

The coordinator magar 'but' is placed in the beginning of the second conjunct:

(12) rājɨ čha muḍɨ magar sɔ čha seṭhā dānā
Raja is illiterate, but she is very wise
'Raja is illiterate, but she is very wise.'

'But' coordination usually is used with adjectives and adverbials:

(13) šīlɨ čha muḍɨ magar gāṭɨj kūr
Shiela is illiterate but wise girl
'Shiela is an illiterate but wise girl.'

(14) *tami kər kath magar vāri vāri*
she did talk but slowly
'She talked, but in a low voice.'

'But' coordination of nouns and verbs may involve a negative particle preceding or following the adversative conjuncts:

(15) *rāmi čhu jān šur magar sohni čhuni (jān)*
Ram is good boy but Sohan is not (good)
'Ram is a good boy but Sohan is not.'

(16) *aslam nay yiyi magar bi yimi zarūr*
Aslam neg-empht come-fut but I come-fut definitely
'Aslam may not come, but I'll come definitely.'

The disjunctive marker *yā* 'or' can precede the first as well as subsequent disjuncts:

(17) *yā gatshi su dili, yā gatshi su āgrā*
either go-fut he Delhi or go-fut he Agra
'Either he will go to Delhi or he will go to Agra.'

The disjunctive markers *yā* 'or', *kini* 'or' are used to conjoin nouns, adjectives, adverbs and verbs:

(18) *majid yā aslam gatshi jom*
Majid or Aslam go-fut Jammu
'Majid or Aslam will go to Jammu.'

yā can precede any disjoined element or category but *kini* cannot:

(19) *yā gatshi šīli yā rāmi pōš tsatini*
either go-fut Shiela or Ram flower pluck-inf-abl
'Either Shiela or Ram will go to pluck flowers.'

(20) **kini gur tēz pakān kini vāri vāri*
or horse fast walk or slow

Negative disjunction is expressed by substituting a negative particle *na* for *yā*:

(21) *na kheyi su pāni na diyi me kheni*
neither eat-fut he himself nor give-fut me eat-inf-abl
'Neither will he eat himself nor will he let me eat.'

There are various structural constraints on coordination. In general members of the same class can be conjoined and not those belonging to different classes:

(22)a **sɔ čha khūbsūrath ti kūr*
she is beautiful and girl
   b *sɔ čha khūbsūrath ti gātij kūr*
she is beautiful and intelligent girl
'She is a beautiful and intelligent girl.'

6.3 Other syntactic constructions

6.3.1 Passivization

There are two categories of passive constructions: (i) personal passive, and (ii) capabilitive passive. The personal passive is marked by the auxiliary *yun* and the ablative form of the infinitive of the main verb. The passive subject of the simple transitive is marked nominative. Certain exceptional verbs such as *lāyun* 'to beat', *prārun* 'to wait' that inherently mark their objects in the dative in the active version, retain the dative case on the passive subjects. The passive nominative subject, but not the dative one, agrees with *yun*. The former subject is marked genitive followed by the ablative suffix and the postposition *zəriyi/dəs'* 'by'. The postpositional phrase is often deleted. For example:

(1)a *su chu/ōs/āsi səlīmas parināvān*
   he is/was/will be Salim-dat teaching
   'He is/was/will be teaching Salim.'

 b *səlīm čhu yivān parināvni*
   Salim is come-pass teach
   'Salim is being taught.'

(2)a *mohnan lōy səlīmas lōri sīt'*
   Mohan-erg beat Salim-dat stick-abl with
   'Mohan beat Salim with a stick.'

 b *səlīmas āv lāyni lōri sīt' səlīmni zəriyi*
   Salim-dat come-pass beat stick-abl with
   'Salim was beaten by Mohan with a stick.'

In the double transitive construction, the indirect object retains its dative case and the nominative noun phrase (i.e., the former direct object) controls the agreement:

(3)a *mohnan līčh rādāyi čiṭh'*
   Mohan-erg wrote Radha-dat letter
   'Mohan wrote a letter to Radha.'

 b *rādāyi āyi čiṭh' lēkhni*
   Radha-dat pass letter write
   'A letter was written to Radha.'

The capabilitive passive, impersonal in nature, usually requires a negative or an interrogative context. The capabilitive passive usually retains the postpositional agent. The agent is absent in certain constructions as noted below.

(4) *təm' heč ni kath kərith*
   he-erg could neg talk do-past ptcpl
   'He could not talk.'

(5) *su h'ok ni pəkith*
   he could neg walk-past ptcpl
   'He was not able to walk.'

6.3.2 Negation

Declarative sentences are negated by means of the particle *ni*, which is added to the finite verb after the agreement and pronominal suffixes:

(1)   *bi čhus ni akhbār parān*
      I am neg newspaper read-pres
      'I don't read the newspaper.'

Constituents are also negated by means of suffixes such as *nay, ros, bagǝr, varǝy*, all meaning 'without'. The suffix *nay* follows the verb stem, while the others require the ablative infinitive form of the verb. Alternatively, they may be added directly to the nominal.

(2)   *mohni gav sokūl kitābav ros/bagǝr/varǝy*
      Mohan went school books-abl without
      'Mohan went to school without his books.'

Indefinite quantifiers such as *kãh* 'someone', *kẽh* 'something', *zãh* 'ever', *kun* 'somewhere' are negated by the normal sentential negation. The indefinite quantifiers in this context are usually marked by emphatic particles.

(3)   *təmis sīth' kari ni kãh kath*
      he-dat with do-fut neg someone talk
      'No one will talk to him.'

(4)   *su kari ni dōstan hindi khǝtri kẽh*
      he do-fut neg friends-dat gen for something
      'He will do nothing for his friends.'

(5)   *təm' čha ni zãh zindgī manz čiṭh' līčhmits*
      he-erg is neg ever life-dat in letter write-past ptcpl
      'He has never written a letter in his life.'

(6)   *šīli gǝyi ni kun rāth*
      Shiela went neg anywhere yesterday
      'Shiela went nowhere yesterday.'

6.3.3 Pronominalization

Pronominalization includes reflexive, reciprocal, pronominal and deletion strategies.

6.3.3.1 Reflexivization

The main reflexive pronoun is *pān*. When followed by a postposition, this takes the oblique form *pǝn'*. The emphatic pronoun is *pāni*. The emphatic suffix *-ay-* may be added to it for extra emphasis. The result is *pānay*. The reduplicated form *pǝn' pāni* also occurs as an emphatic reflexive. The possessive reflexive form is *panun*. The reflexive *pān* is usually anteceded by a subject. The reflexive itself may be a direct, indirect object or a postpositional phrase. Examples:

(1)   *mohnan vuch panun pān ǝnas manz*
      Mohan-erg saw self's body mirror-dat in
      'Mohan saw himself in the mirror.'

(2) *mohnan von aslamas pānas mutalakh*
Mohan-erg told Aslam-dat self-dat about
'Mohan told Aslam about himself.'

(3) *vəkīlas čhu pānas peṭh' barōsɨ*
advocate has refl-dat on confidence
'The advocate has confidence in himself.'

(4) *pānas kor aslaman ārām*
refl-dat did Aslam-erg rest
'Aslam rested himself.'

Reflexivization may also be controlled by dative subjects:

(5) *aslamas čhu panun pān pasand*
Aslam-dat has self like
'Aslam likes himself.'

The scope of reflexivity is usually restricted to the clause in which it is used:

(6) *mohnan von zi su/*pānɨ vāti vakhtas peṭh*
Mohan said that he/*refl reach-fut time-dat at
'Mohan$_i$ said that he$_i$ would reach in time.'

(7) *mohnan prutsh ki təm'sɨnz/*panɨn' zanān kar yiyi*
Mohan-erg asked that his*refl wife when come-fut
'Mohan$_i$ asked when his$_i$ wife would come.'

Examples (6) and (7) show that reflexivization does not go down into subordinate clauses. Notice that reflexivization is possible within a non-finite and a small clause:

(8) *aslaman von səlīmas pānas kitsh čāy anini khətri*
Aslam-erg told Salim-dat self-dat for tea bring-abl for
'Aslam told Salim to bring tea for himself.'

(9) *aslam čhu [mohnas panun dušman] mānān*
Aslam is Mohan-dat refl enemy considering
'Aslam$_i$ considers Mohan$_j$ his$_{i,j}$ enemy.'

Example (8) is ambiguous because the reflexive pronoun is coreferential with the subject of the main as well as with the subject of the subordinate clause.

In possessive structures, the reflexive form *panun* 'self' is used in place of possessive pronouns. It agrees with the following head noun phrase in number and gender. Following are its forms in nominative case: *panun* (msg), *panɨn'* (mpl), *panɨn'* (fsg), *panɨni* (fpl). For example,

(10) *bɨ čhus panun/*m'ōn kamrɨ sāph karān*
I-m am refl/*my room clean do-pres
'I am cleaning my room.'

6.3.3.2 Reciprocals

The primary way of expressing the reciprocal relationship is by means of an expression *akh əkis* 'to one another', which is a combination of cardinal *akh* 'one' and its dative case form (*akh + is = əkis*). There is no nominative form of the reciprocal and the dative form is used in its place. The reciprocal forms can occur only within a clause, which may be simple or non-finite.

(1) *timav kor akh əkis seṭhā madath*
     they-erg did one another-dat very help
     'They helped each other very much.'

Reciprocals may be used as a direct object, indirect object, postpositional or possessive phrases:

(2) *tim samɨkh' akh əkis vāriyāhi kə̄l'*
     they-erg met one another-dat lot-abl period of time
     'They met each other after a lot of time.'

(3) *timav dit' akh əkis čōb*
     they-erg gave one another beating
     'They thrashed each other.'

(4) *tim či akh əkis peṭh takhsīr khārān*
     they are one another-dat on blame placing
     'They accuse/blame each other.'

(5) *əs' čhinɨ akh ək'sund gari gatshān*
     we are not one another-poss home go-pres
     'We don't visit each other's house.'

Mutual reciprocity is expressed by the use of *pānɨvən'* 'mutual':

(6) *tim čhinɨ pānɨvən' kath karān*
     they are not each other talk do-pres
     'They do not talk to each other.'

Personal pronouns may not have their antecedents within the same clause. They occur in all sorts of structures. For example, they occur across finite subordinate clauses, adverbial clauses, coordinate structures, discourse structures, etc. In adverbial clauses the pronoun may be optionally deleted:

(7)a [*yeli su$_i$ bāzar gav*] *sohnan$_i$ hets pānas kitsh ṭūp'*
      rel/he market went Sohan bought-fsg refl-dat for cap
      'When he$_i$ went to the market, Sohan$_i$ bought a cap for himself.'
   b [*yeli sohan bāzar gav*] Ø *pānas kitsh hetsɨn ṭūp'*
                                               bought-3sg
      'When Sohan went to the market, (he) bought a cap for himself.'
   c [*yeli sohanɨ bāzar gav*] *təm' hets pānas kitsh ṭūp'*
                                he-erg
      'When Sohan went to the market, he bought a cap for himself.'

In a narrative text or natural discourse, deletion is used very frequently to refer to a previous coreferent.

ACKNOWLEDGEMENTS

I would like to thank George Cardona, Dhanesh Jain, Kashi Wali and P. Umarani for their comments and suggestions.

REFERENCES

Census of India (1981) *Households and household population by language mainly spoken in the household*, Series 1, Paper 1 of 1987, Delhi: Office of the Registrar General, Census of India.

Dhar, Nazir A. (1984) 'A Sociolinguistic Study of Kamraz Dialect of Kashmiri'. Ph.D. dissertation, University of Poona.

Fussman, Gérard (1972) *Atlas linguistique des parlers dardes et kafirs*, Paris: École Française d'Extrême-Orient'.

Grierson, G. A. (1906) *The Pisacha Languages of North Western India*, London: Royal Asiatic Society (Reprinted (1969), Delhi: Munshiram Manoharlal).

—— (1911) *Standard Manual of the Kashmiri Language*, 2 Vols. Oxford (Reprinted 1973, Rohtak: Light and Life Publishers).

—— (1919) *The Linguistic Survey of India*, Vol. VIII, Part II, Calcutta: Royal Asiatic Society (Reprinted (1968), Delhi: Motilal Banarasidass).

Hook, Peter Edwin and Koul, Omkar N. (1984a) 'On the grammar of derived transitives and causatives in Kashmiri', in Koul and Hook (eds.), pp. 90–122.

—— (1984b) 'Pronominal suffixes and split ergativity in Kashmiri', in Koul and Hook (eds.), pp. 123–35.

—— (1985) 'Modal verbs of obligation in Kashmiri', *International Journal of Dravidian Linguistics* 14.2: 263–73.

—— (forthcoming) *Kashmiri: A study in comparative Indo-Aryan*, Tokyo: Institute for the Study of Languages and Cultures of Asia and Africa, Tokyo University of Foreign Studies.

Kachru, Braj B. (1969a) *A Reference Grammar of Kashmiri*, Urbana: University of Illinois.

—— (1969b) 'Kashmiri and other Dardic languages', in Sebeok, Thomas A. (ed.) *Current Trends in Linguistics*, Vol. V, The Hague: Mouton, pp. 284–306.

—— (1973) *An Introduction to Spoken Kashmiri*, Urbana: University of Illinois.

Koul, Ashok K. (1986) 'A Linguistic Study of Loanwords in Kashmiri', Ph.D. dissertation, Kurukshetra University.

Koul, Maharaj K. (1986) *A Sociolinguistic Study of Kashmiri*, Patiala: Indian Institute of Language Studies.

Koul, Omkar N. (1983) 'Kashmiri Hindi-Urdu: A Study in Bilingualism', in *Towards Greater Heights*, Vol. II, Mysore: CIIL.

—— (1985) *An Intensive Course in Kashmiri*, Mysore: Central Institute of Indian Languages.

—— (1987) *Spoken Kashmiri: A Language Course*, Patiala: Indian Institute of Language Studies.

—— (1996) 'On the standardisation of Kashmiri Script', in Hasnain, Imtiaz (ed.) *Standardisation and Modernisation: Dynamics of Language Planning*, New Delhi: Bahri Publications.

—— (1998) 'On Development of Kashmiri', in Jayaram, B. D. and Rajyashree, K. S. (eds.) *Goals and Strategies of Development of Indian Languages*, Mysore: Central Institute of Indian Languages.

Koul, Omkar N. and Hook, Peter Edwin (eds.) (1984) *Aspects of Kashmiri Linguistics*, New Delhi: Bahri Publications.

Koul, Omkar N. and Schmidt, Ruth Laila (1983) *Kashmiri: A Sociolinguistic Survey*, Patiala: Indian Institute of Language Studies.

—— (1984) 'Dardistan revisited: An examination of relationship between Kashmiri and Shina', in Koul and Hook (eds.) *Aspects of Kashmiri Linguistics*, New Delhi: Bahri Publications, pp. 1–26.

Morgenstierne, George (1961) 'Dardic and Kafir Languages', *The Encyclopedia of Islam*, Vol. 2, Fasc. 25, Leiden: E. J. Brill.

Strand, R. T. (1973) 'Notes on the Nuristani and Dardic Language', *Journal of the American Oriental Society* 93: 297–305.

Wali, Kashi and Koul, Ashok (1994) 'Kashmiri clitics: The role of case in CASE', *Linguistics* 32: 969–94.

Wali, Kashi and Koul, Omkar N. (1997) *Kashmiri: A Cognitive-descriptive Grammar*, London: Routledge.

GENERAL INDEX

LANGUAGE INDEX

A boldface page number indicates that the word(s) occur(s) in figures or maps.
*A page number followed by a boldface **t** indicates that the word(s) occur(s) in a table.*

INDEX OF CITED PASSAGES

(Chapters 1, 4, 5, 6, 16)

Only passages which are fully cited are included in this index, not individual words. For editions used, see the references in the chapters noted.

Text	Passage	Page
Ādi Granth (AG)		
	7.12	597
Aitareyāraṇyaka (AiĀr)		
	3.1.5	29
	3.2.1	29
	3.2.6	29
Aitareyabrāhmaṇa (AiBr)		
	1.18	137
	6.33	133, 138
	7.14	137
Apadāna (Ap)		
	75.10	181
Aṣṭādhyāyī (A)		
	1.3.1	8
	2.4.56	26
	3.2.115	20
	4.2.74	106
	6.2.70	8
	6.4.36	10
	7.1.95-97	8
	8.4.20	119
	8.4.27-28	29
	8.4.54	10
Atharvaveda (AV)		
	18.2.27cd	137
Ausgewählte Erzählungen in Mâhârâshtrî (Erz)		
	1.10-11	17
	4.23	15
	9.6-7	17
	12.8	16
	12.9-10	17
	12.12	16
	14.4-5	17
	14.5-6	17
	65.24	232
	66.l9	240

·

Lightning Source UK Ltd.
Milton Keynes UK
UKHW02f0620100718
325484UK00002B/14/P